Street by Stree

MANCHESTER

BOLTON, BURY, OLDHAM, ROCHDALE, SALFORD, STOCKPORT

Altrincham, Ashton-under-Lyne, Bramhall, Hazel Grove, Hyde, Littleborough, Middleton, Prestwich, Ramsbottom, Sale, Stalybridge, Stretford, Wilmslow

3rd edition October 2007
© Automobile Association Developments Limited 2007

Original edition printed May 2001

 This product includes map data licensed from Ordnance Survey® with the permission of the Controller of Her Majesty's Stationery Office. © Crown copyright 2007. All rights reserved. Licence number 100021153.

The copyright in all PAF is owned by Royal Mail Group plc.

Published by AA Publishing (a trading name of Automobile Association Developments Limited, whose registered office is Fanum House, Basing View, Basingstoke, Hampshire RG21 4EA. Registered number 1878835).

Produced by the Mapping Services Department of The Automobile Association. (A03490)

A CIP Catalogue record for this book is available from the British Library.

Printed by Oriental Press in Dubai

The contents of this atlas are believed to be correct at the time of the latest revision. However, the publishers cannot be held responsible or liable for any loss or damage occasioned to any person acting or refraining from action as a result of any use or reliance on any material in this atlas, nor for any errors, omissions or changes in such material. This does not affect your statutory rights. The publishers would welcome information to correct any errors or omissions and to keep this atlas up to date. Please write to Publishing, The Automobile Association, Fanum House (FH12), Basing View, Basingstoke, Hampshire, RG21 4EA. E-mail: streetbystreet@theaa.com

Ref: ML43y

Key to map pages	ii-iii
Key to map symbols	iv-1
Enlarged map pages	2-13
Main map pages	14-201
Index – towns & villages	202
Index – streets	203-261
Index – featured places	261-268
Acknowledgements	268

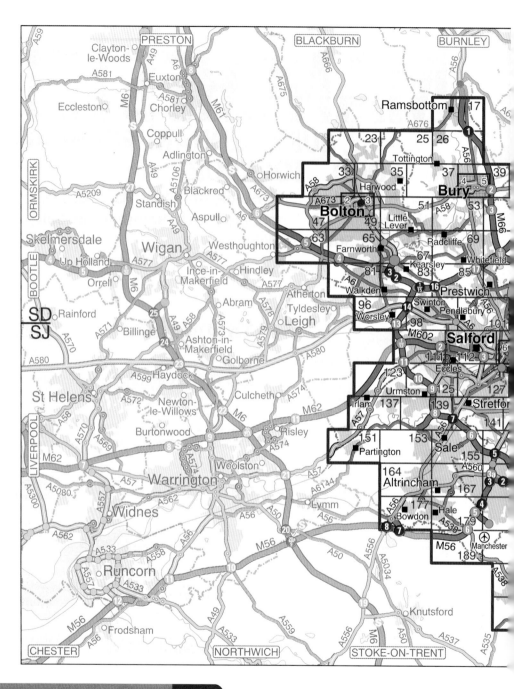

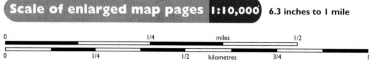

Scale of enlarged map pages 1:10,000 6.3 inches to 1 mile

| 0 | 1/4 | miles | 1/2 |
| 0 | 1/4 | 1/2 | kilometres | 3/4 | 1 |

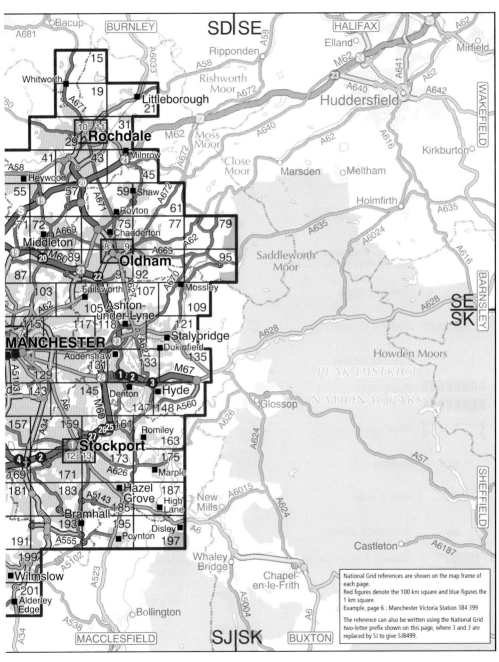

National Grid references are shown on the map frame of each page.
Red figures denote the 100 km square and blue figures the 1 km square.
Example, page 6 : Manchester Victoria Station 384 399

The reference can also be written using the National Grid two-letter prefix shown on this page, where 3 and 3 are replaced by SJ to give SJ8499.

4.2 inches to 1 mile   Scale of main map pages   1:15,000

| 0 | 1/4 | miles | 1/2 | 3/4 | 1 |

| 0 | 1/4 | 1/2 | kilometres 3/4 | 1 | 1 1/4 | 1 1/2 |

iv

Junction 9 — Motorway & junction	LC — Level crossing
Services — Motorway service area	Tramway
Primary road single/dual carriageway	Ferry route
Services — Primary road service area	Airport runway
A road single/dual carriageway	County, administrative boundary
B road single/dual carriageway	Mounds
Other road single/dual carriageway	17 — Page continuation 1:15,000
Minor/private road, access may be restricted	3 — Page continuation to enlarged scale 1:10,000
One-way street	River/canal, lake, pier
Pedestrian area	Aqueduct, lock, weir
Track or footpath	465 Winter Hill — Peak (with height in metres)
Road under construction	Beach
Road tunnel	Woodland
P — Parking	Park
P+ — Park & Ride	Cemetery
Bus/coach station	Built-up area
Railway & main railway station	Industrial/business building
Railway & minor railway station	Leisure building
Underground station	Retail building
Light railway & station	Other building
Preserved private railway	IKEA — IKEA store

City wall		Castle	
Hospital with 24-hour A&E department		Historic house or building	
Post Office		National Trust property (Wakehurst Place NT)	
Public library		Museum or art gallery	
Tourist Information Centre		Roman antiquity	
Seasonal Tourist Information Centre		Ancient site, battlefield or monument	
Petrol station, 24 hour Major suppliers only		Industrial interest	
Church/chapel		Garden	
Public toilets		Garden Centre Garden Centre Association Member	
Toilet with disabled facilities		Garden Centre Wyevale Garden Centre	
Public house AA recommended		Arboretum	
Restaurant AA inspected		Farm or animal centre	
Hotel AA inspected (Madeira Hotel)		Zoological or wildlife collection	
Theatre or performing arts centre		Bird collection	
Cinema		Nature reserve	
Golf course		Aquarium	
Camping AA inspected		Visitor or heritage centre	
Caravan site AA inspected		Country park	
Camping & caravan site AA inspected		Cave	
Theme park		Windmill	
Abbey, cathedral or priory		Distillery, brewery or vineyard	

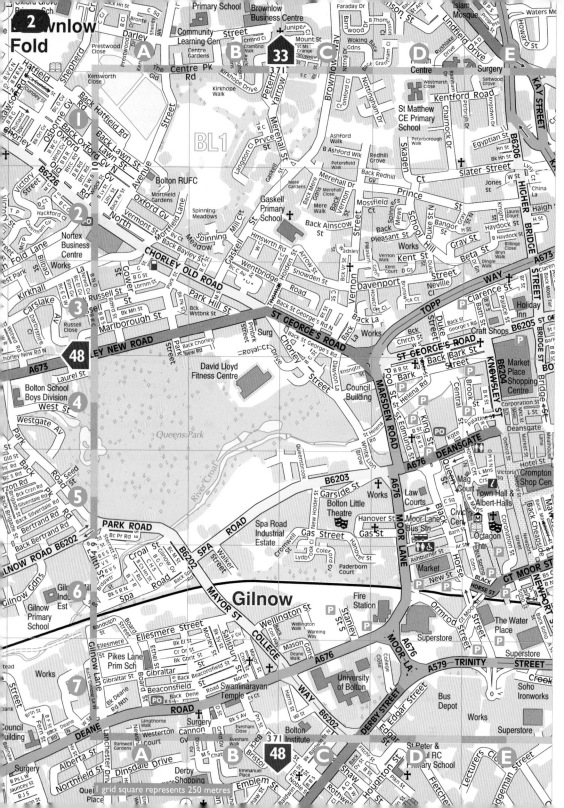

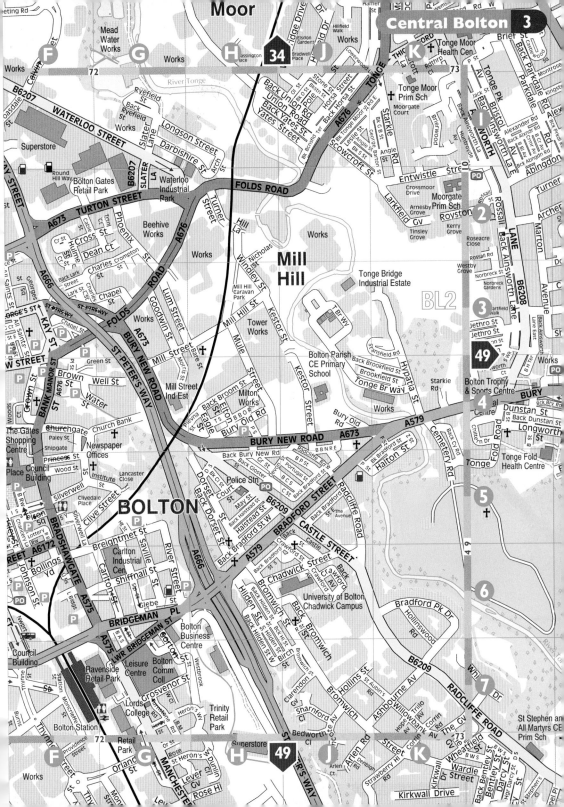

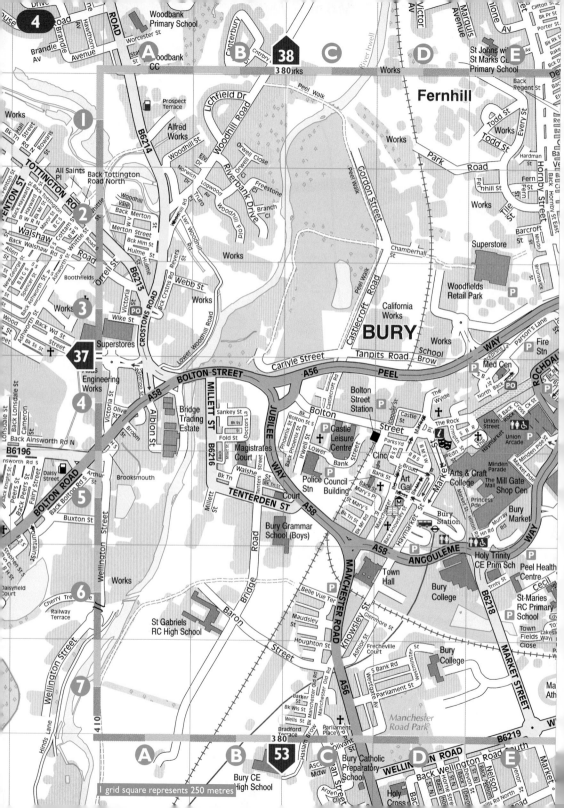

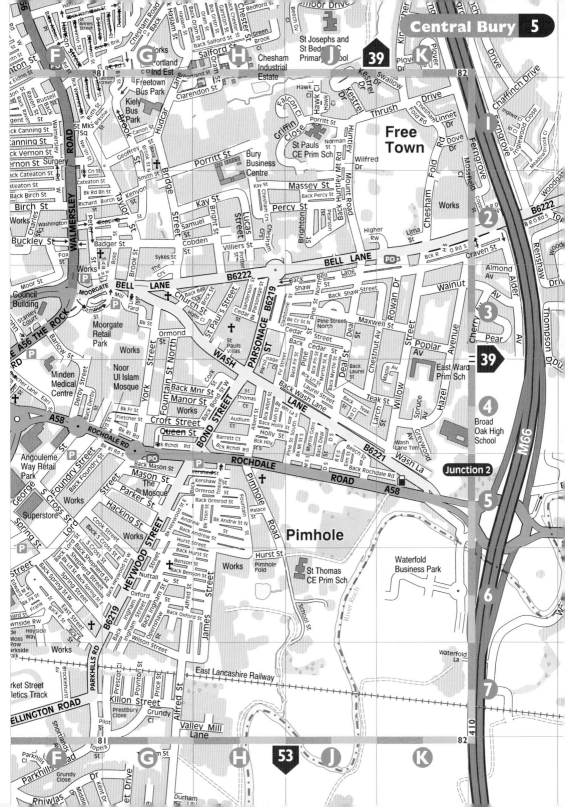

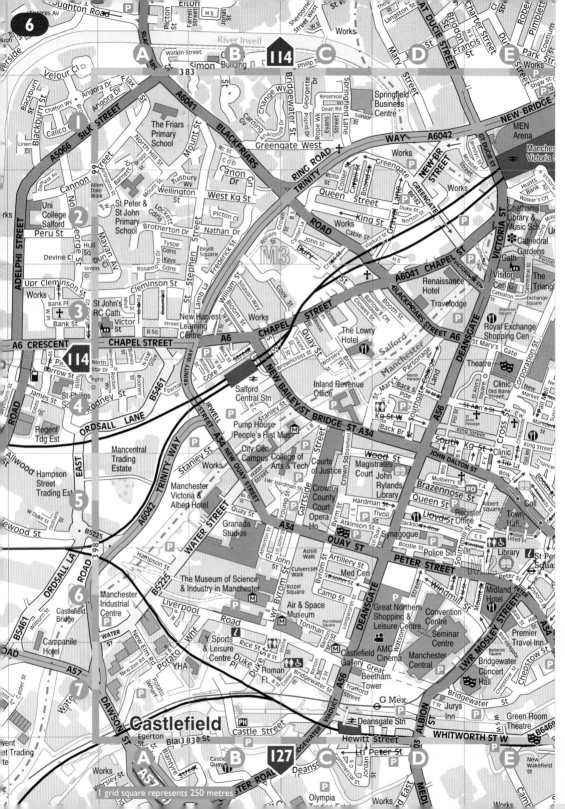

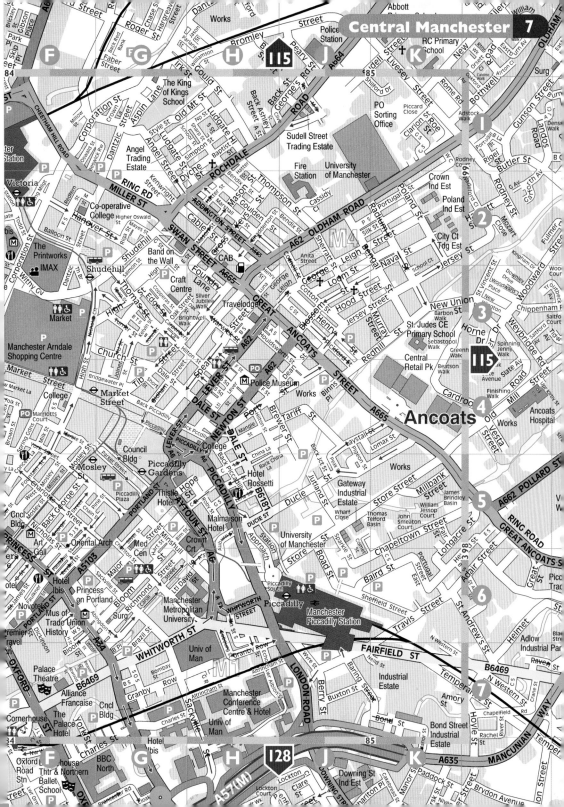

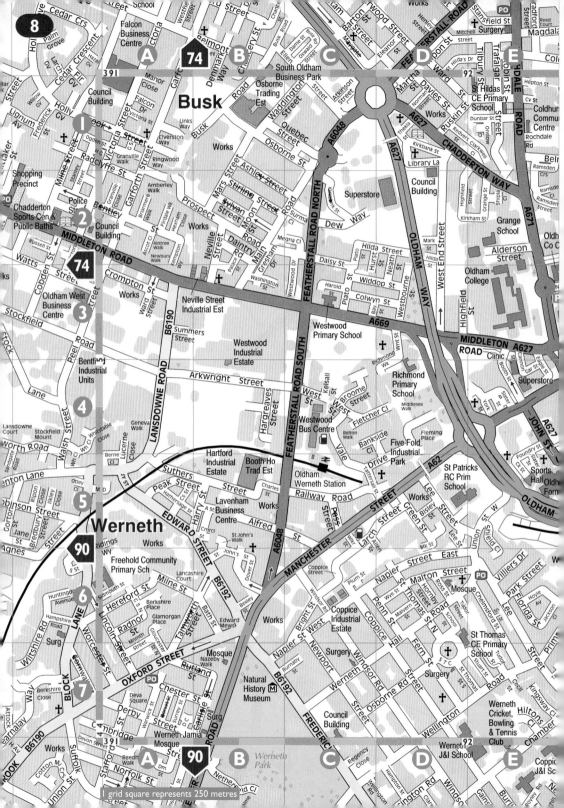

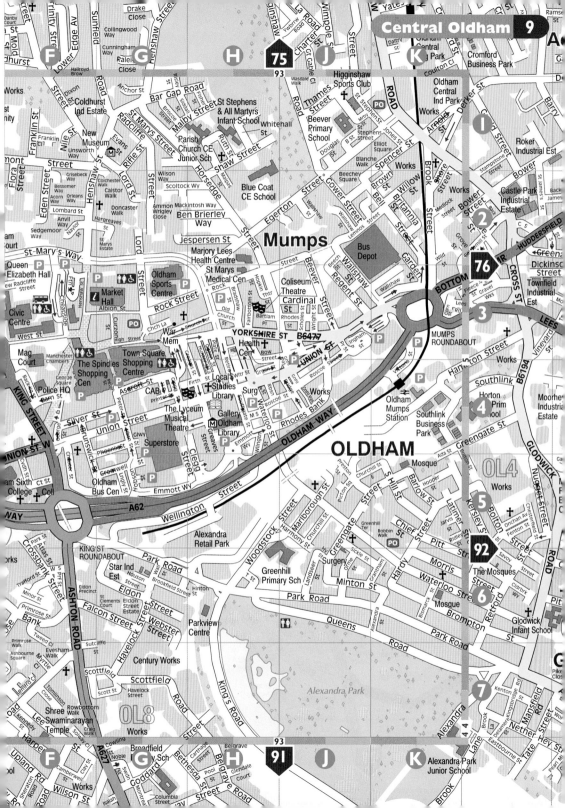

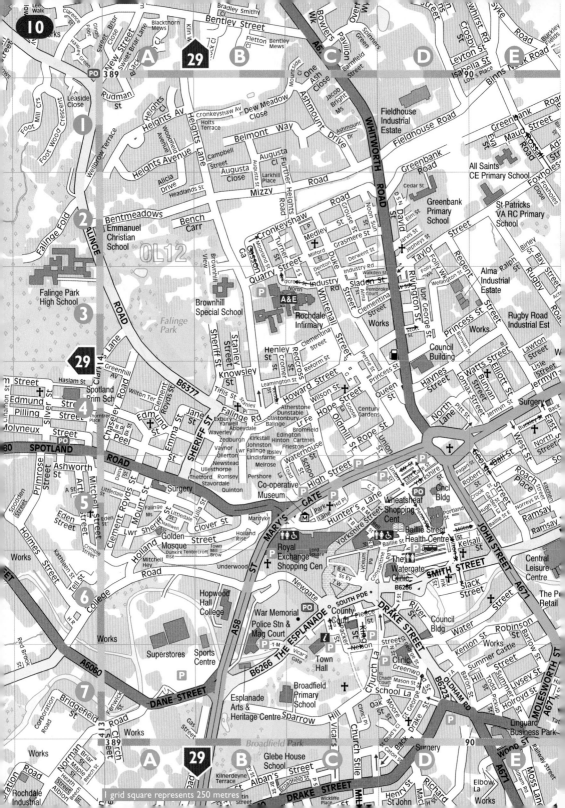

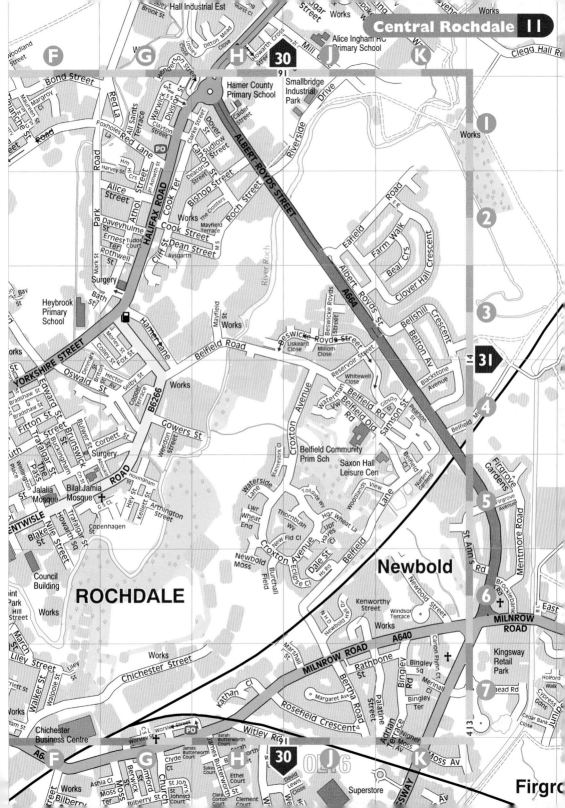

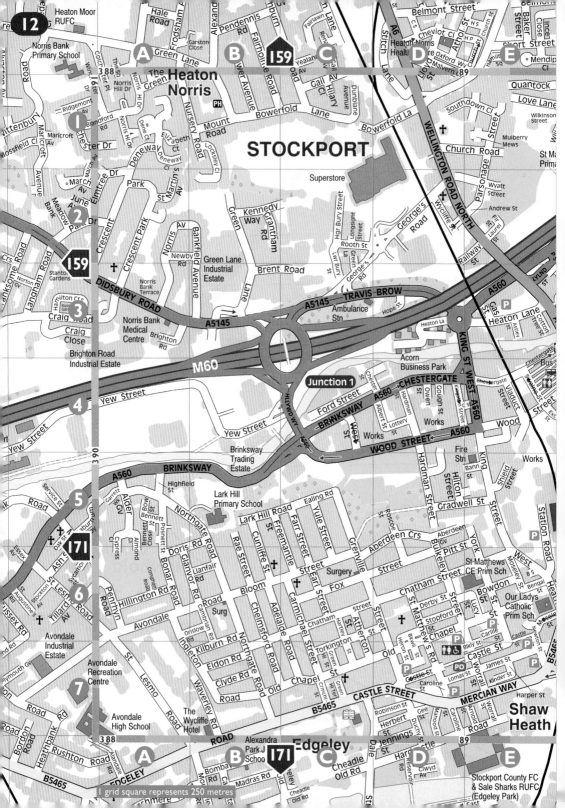

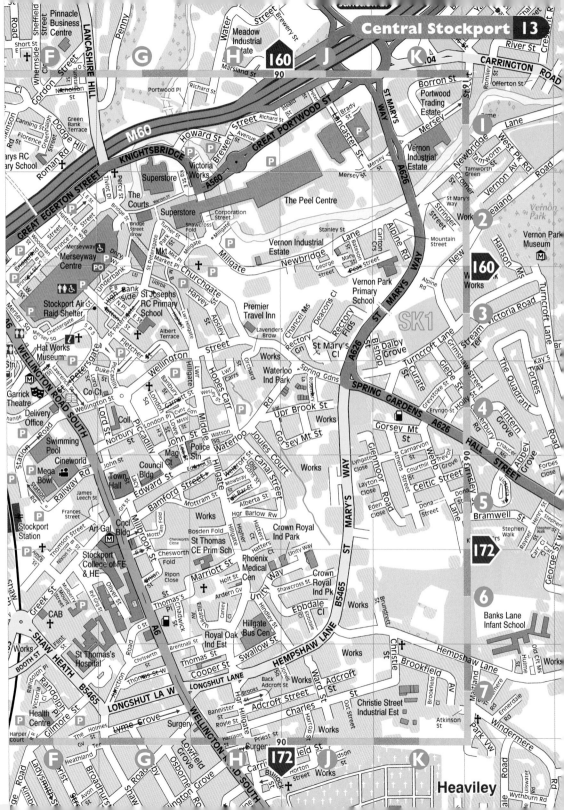

Heaviley

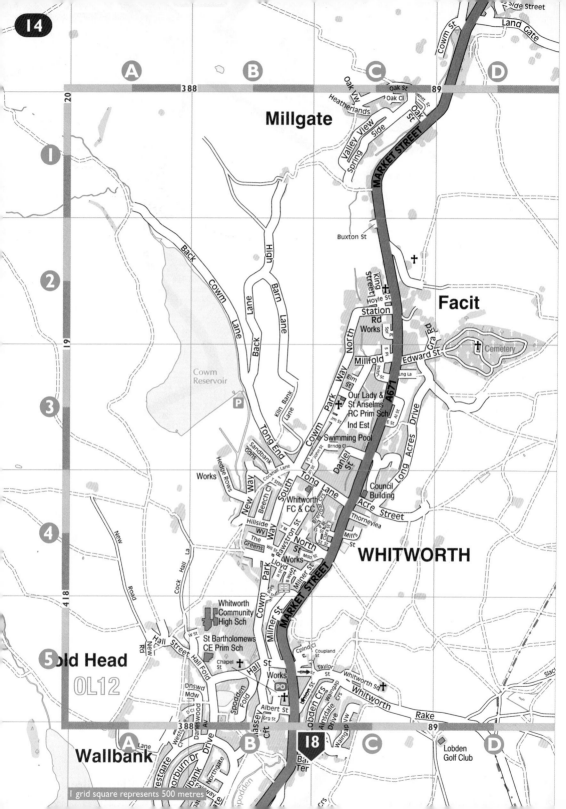

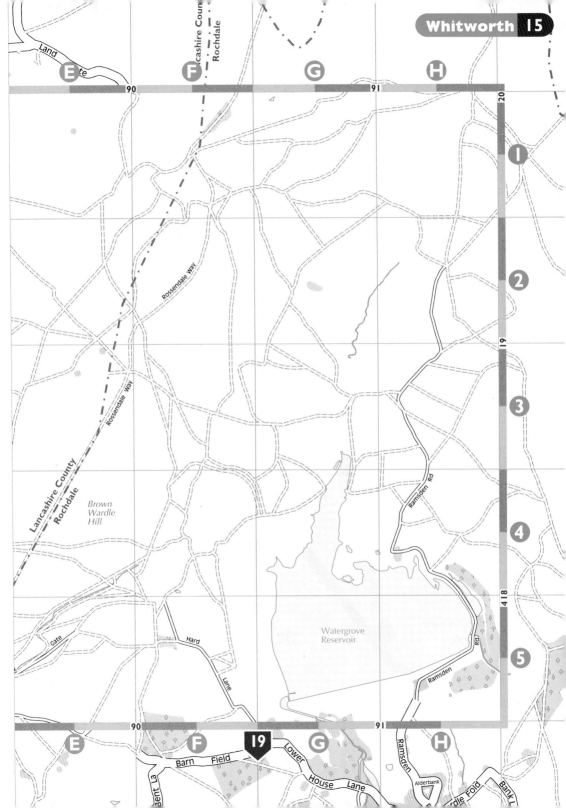

E F G H

90 91 20

1

2

19

3

Rossendale way

Rossendale Way

Lancashire County
Rochdale

Brown
Wardle
Hill

Ramsden Rd

4

418

Gate

Hard

Lane

Watergrove
Reservoir

Ramsden Rd

Ramsden

5

90 91

E F **19** G H

Barn Field

Lower

House Lane

Ramsden

Alderbank

rdle Fold

Balk L

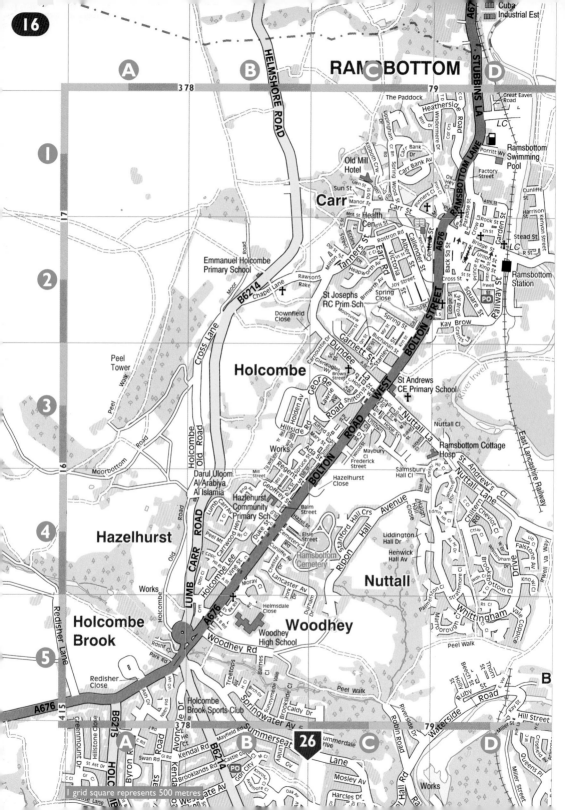

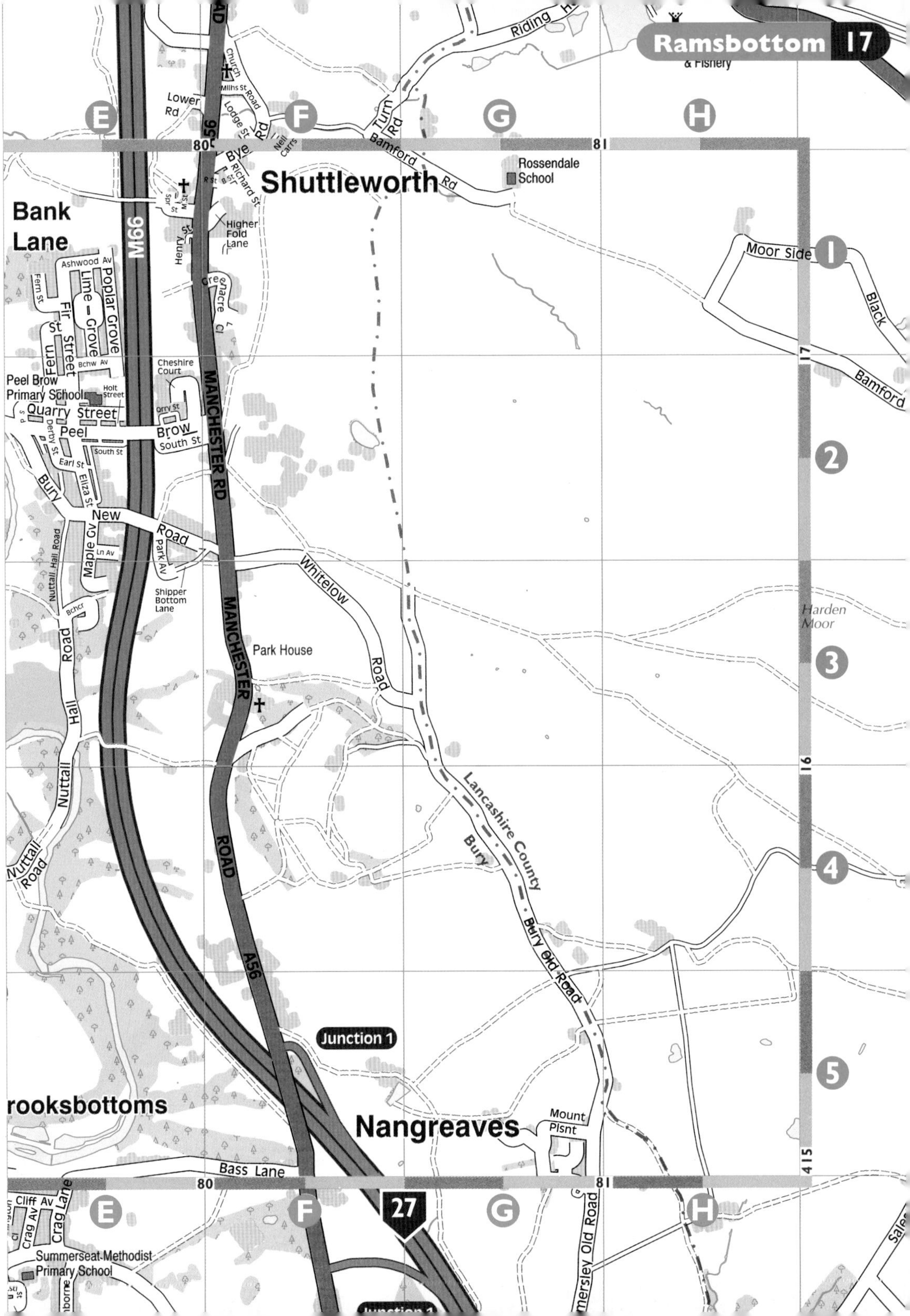

& Fishery

Riding H

E

95

80

81

F

G

H

Lower Rd

Church

Millns St

Lodge St

Turn Rd

Bamford Rd

Rossendale School

Byr

Richard St

Nell Carrs

Shuttleworth

Bank Lane

St W

Str

Henry

Higher Fold Lane

Moor Side

1

Black

Bamford

Ashwood Av

Poplar Grove

Lime Grove

Greenacre Cl

Cheshire Court

Holt Street

17

Fern St

Fir St

Elm Street

Peel Brow Primary School

Bchw Av

Orry St

Quarry Street

Derby St

Peel

Brow

South St

South St

16

2

Earl St

Eliza St

Bury

New

Road

Maple Gv

Ln Av

Park Av

Bchr

Whitelow

Road

Nuttall Hall Road

Shipper Bottom Lane

Park House

Harden Moor

3

Nuttall

Hall

Road

Lancashire County

Bury

16

MANCHESTER ROAD

MANCHESTER ROAD

Nuttall Road

A56

Bury Old Road

4

Junction 1

5

415

rooksbottoms

Bass Lane

Nangreaves

Mount Plsnt

Cliff Av

Crag Lane

Crag Lane

80

E

F

81

27

G

mersley Old Road

H

Saler

Summerseat Methodist Primary School

borne

Junction 1

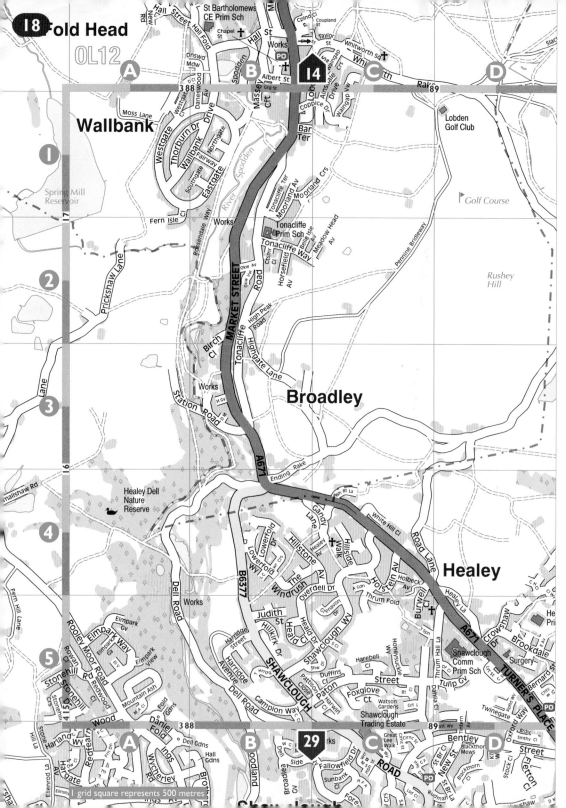

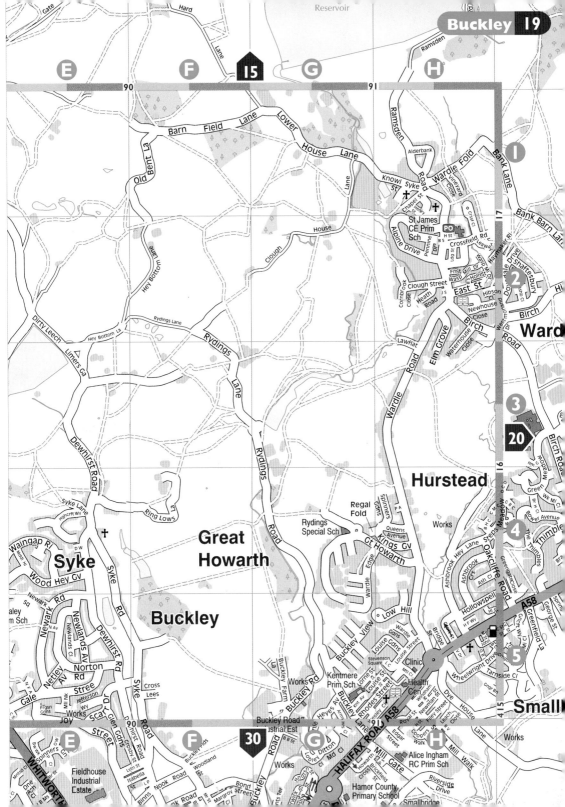

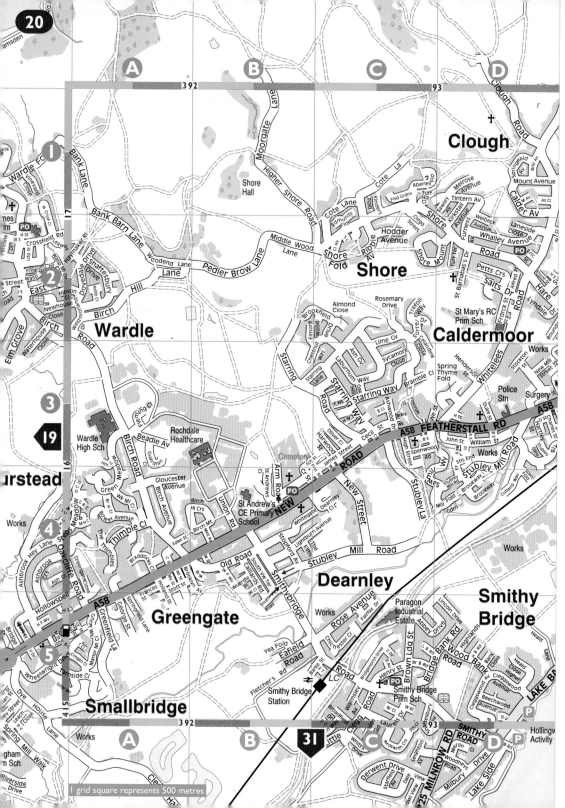

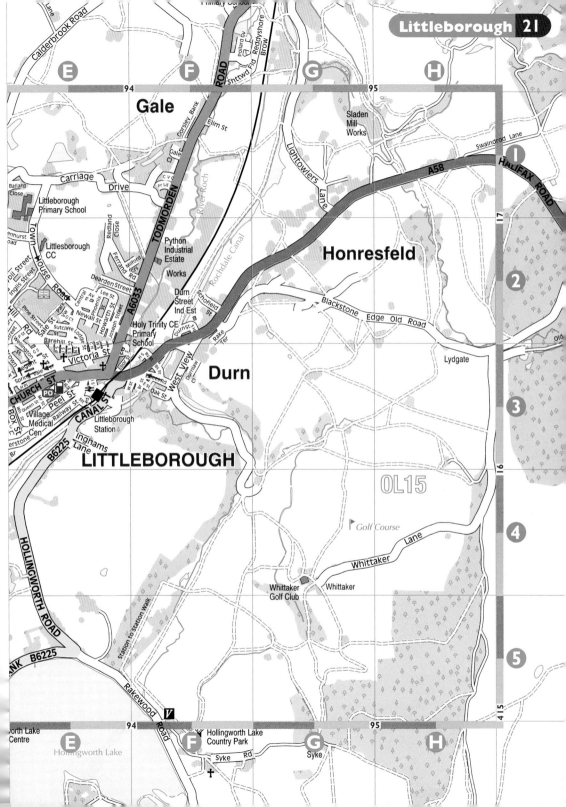

E   F   G   H

94   95

Gale

Calderbrook Road

Primary School

Pollard Gv
Shttwd Fld
Reddyshore Brow

ROAD

Elim St
Corsley Bank

Gale Cl

C V Ct
Fr La

Carriage

Drive

Ballard
Close

Littleborough
Primary School

Littlesborough
CC

TODMORDEN

Redland Close

Ferrand Rd

Milford St

Dearden Street

Lee St

Central

Phoenix St
Howarth St
Joseph Street

Newall St

A6033

River Roch

Rochdale Canal

Python
Industrial
Estate

Works

Durn
Street
Ind Est

Schofield St

Sladen
Mill
Works

Swaindrod Lane

Lightowlers Lane

A58

HALIFAX ROAD

I

17

2

Honresfeld

Blackstone Edge Old Road

Lydgate

Holy Trinity CE
Primary
School

Durn

West View

Rake Ter

Dunmaw

Oak St

WEST ST

LITTLEBOROUGH

CHURCH ST

Peel St

Victoria St

PO

Village
Medical
Cen

B6225

Inghams Lane

Railway St

CANAL ST

Littleborough
Station

HOLLINGWORTH ROAD

BANK B6225

Station to Station Walk

OL15

Golf Course

Whittaker Lane

Whittaker
Golf Club

Whittaker

3

16

4

5

415

Rakewood Road

94   95

E   F   G   H

orth Lake
Centre

Hollingworth Lake

Hollingworth Lake
Country Park

Syke Rd

Syke

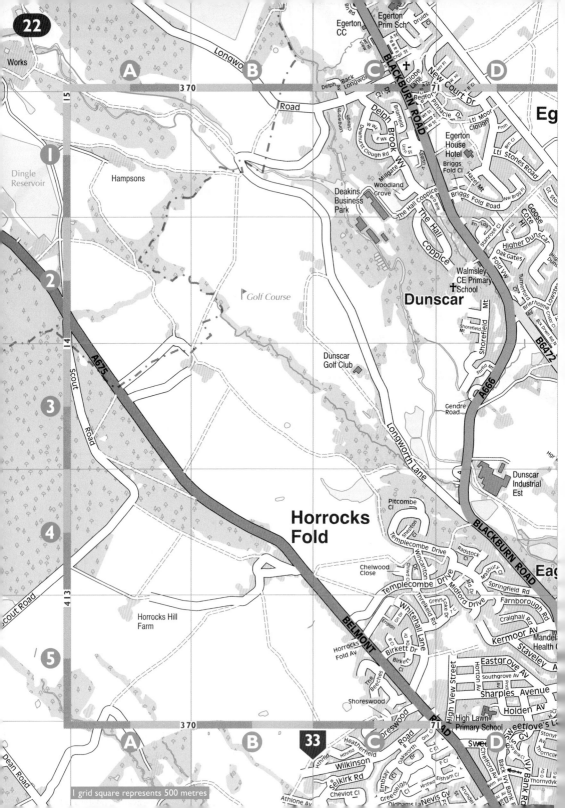

22

Works

A 370 **B** Longwo **C** BLACKBURN ROAD 71 New Court Dr **D**

Delph Back Longwor

Road

Globe

Egd

Bedford

Pinnacle

1

Dingle
Reservoir

Hampsons

Delph Brook Wy

Dewhurst Clough Rd

Egerton
House
Hotel

Briggs
Fold Cl

Hazel Mt

Ltl Stones Road

Goose Cote

15

Deakins
Business
Park

Woodland
Grove

The Hall Coppice

Briggs Fold Road

Higher Dunscar

Oak Gates

Fold Vw

2

Golf Course

The Hall Coppice

Walmsley
CE Primary
School

Dunscar

Shorefield Mt

Shorefield
Mt

14

Scout

A675

Road

Dunscar
Golf Club

Longworth Lane

Gendre
Road

A666

B6472

3

Dunscar
Industrial
Est

Eg

4

**Horrocks
Fold**

Pitcombe
Cl

Shepton

Templecombe Drive

Chelwood
Close

Templecombe Drive

Wincanton

Radstock
Cl

Mitford Drive

BLACKBURN ROAD

Eag

413

Scout Road

Horrocks Hill
Farm

Whitehall Lane

Birkett Dr

Horrocks
Fold Av

Threlkeld Rd

Springfield Rd

Farnborough Rd

Craighall Rd

Kermoor Av

Staveley

Mande
Health C

5

BELMONT

Birkett

The Beeches

Shoreswood

Eastgrove Av

Southgrove Av

Sharples Avenue

Holden Av

High View Street

A 370 **B** **33** Doreswood **C** Road ROAD 71 **D**

Heatherfield

High Lawn
Primary School

Sweetlove's L

Dean Road

Wilkinson

Selkirk Rd

Oakworth

Embsay

Greenlegh

Athlone Av

Cheviot Cl

Elsham Cl

Oldhams La

Nevis Gv

Back Chelford G

Ivy Bank Rd

Thornydyk

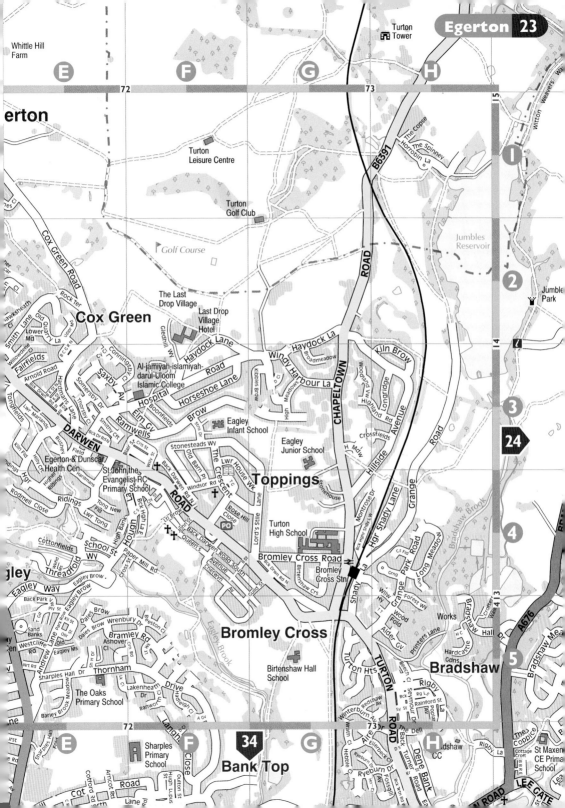

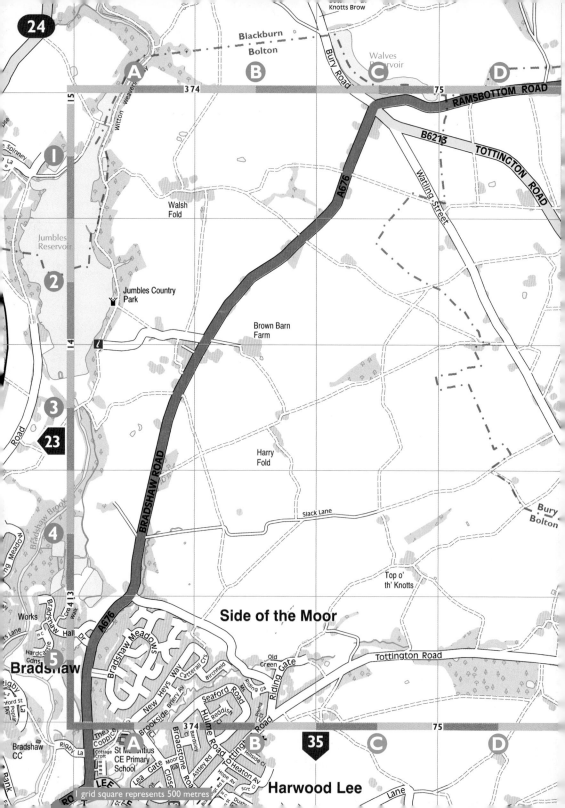

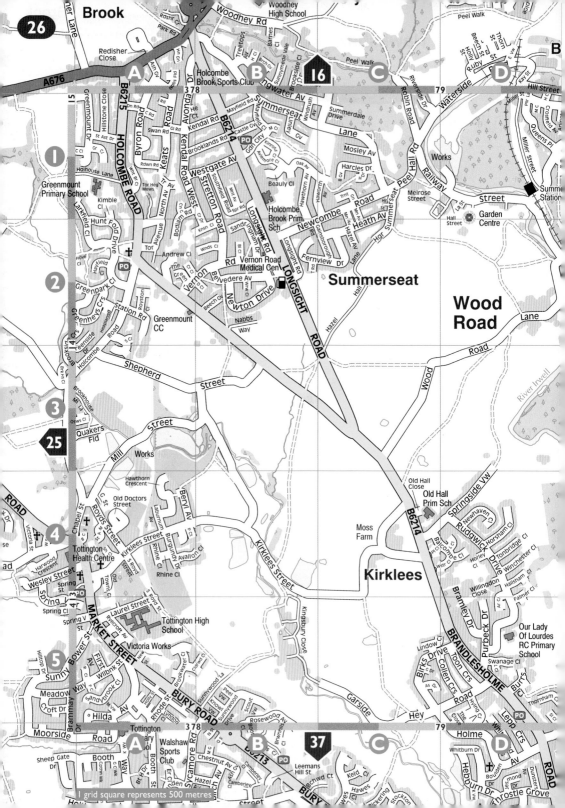

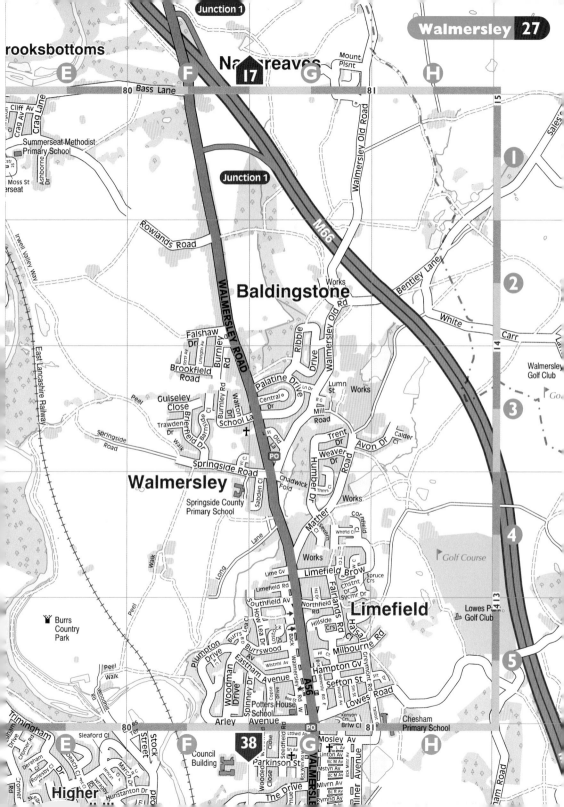

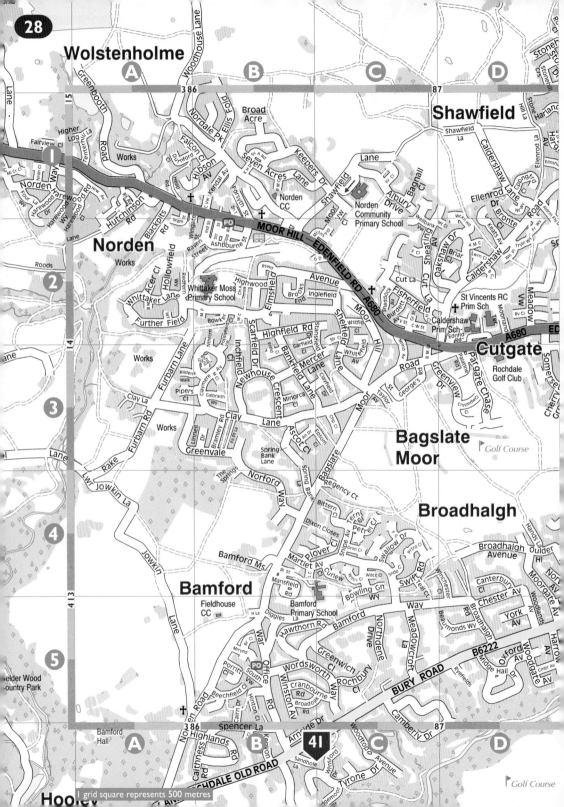

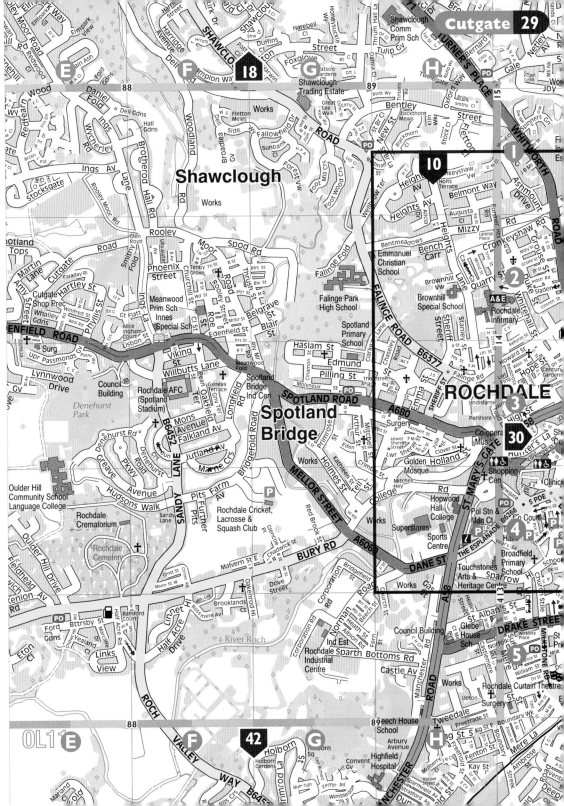

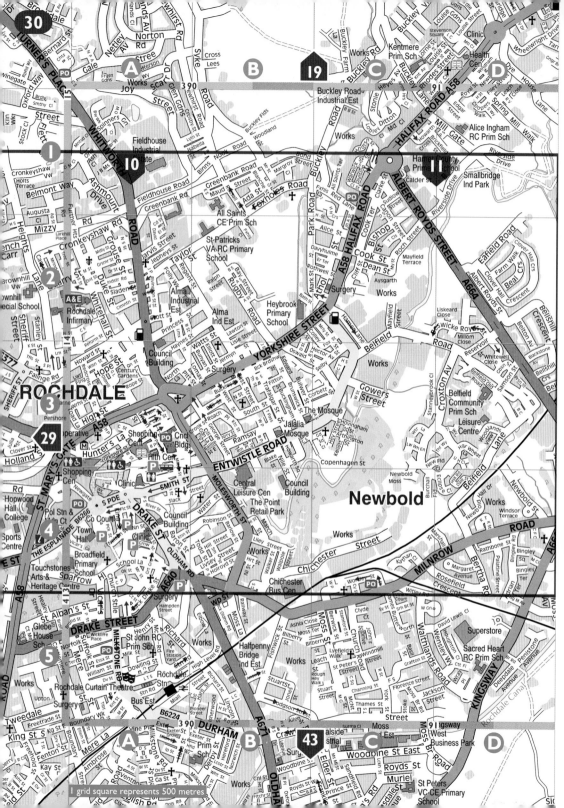

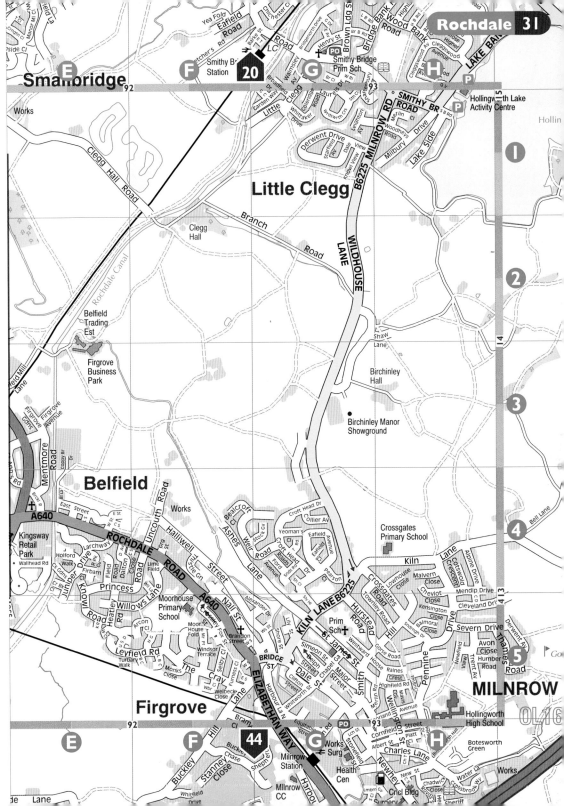

Smallbridge 92

Works

Clegg Hall Road

Rochdale Canal

Clegg Hall

Branch Road

Little Clegg

Belfield Trading Est

Firgrove Business Park

Belfield

Works

Birchinley Hall

Shaw Lane

Birchinley Manor Showground

WILDHOUSE LANE

B6225 MILNROW RD

SMITHY ROAD

SMITHY BR

Smithy-Bridge Prim Sch

Smithy B Station

Eafield Road

LC

Garden Way

Coleridge

Little Clegg Road

Whitraker Drive

Derwent Drive

Starfield Cl

Dale View

Knowl View

Woodhey Road

Melin Cl

Milbury Drive

Lake Side

Hollingworth Lake Activity Centre

LAKE BANK

Hollin

E F 20 G H P
I

2

14 15

3

4

Bell Lane

A640

Kingsway Retail Park

Wallhead Rd

East Street

Mentmore Road

ROCHDALE ROAD A640

Uncouth Road

Halliwell Street

Ashes Lane

Weir Road

Bealcroft Cl

Croft Head Dr

Ollier Av

Yeoman's Cl

Eafield Avenue

Croft Head Road

Ford Avenue

Pearson

KILN LANE B6225

Crossgates Road

Lowhouse Close

Townley Road

Kiln Lane

Crossgates Primary School

Malvern Close

Cheviot Close

Kensington Close

Mendip Drive

Alpine Drive

Cotswold Close

Cleveland Drive

Balmoral Close

Severn Drive

Avon Close

Humber Road

Thames Road

13

5

MILNROW

OL16

Moorhouse Primary School

Moor House Fold

Brandon Street

Windsor Terrace

Leyfield Rd

Turbary Walk

Monks Close

The Cray

Welbeck Close

Furness Cl

Selby St

Dalton Close

Lime Field

Firbarn Cl

Larchway

Holford Walk

Knowl Road

Heatley Cl

Willows Lane

Princess

BRIDGE ST

Clifton Street

Belph

Simeon St

Dale St

Whitworth St

Shore St

Lin St

Alexander Dr

St James St

Prim Sch

Westward Ho

Gorse Road

Chapel St

Major Street

Smith St

Highfield Rd

Raines Crest

Pennine Drive

Wellington Street

Mavis Avenue

Newfield

Trent Av

Hollingworth High School

Botesworth Green

Firgrove 92

ELIZABETH WAY

Buckley Hill

Stanney Close

Chase Cl

Shepard

Bram Cl

Harbour La N

Equitable Street

Milnrow Station

Milnrow CC

Health Cen

Works Surg

PO

Cornfield Street

Albert St

Stonefield

Platt St

Charles Lane

Newhey

Water La

Cricl Bldg

Sheriff

E F 44 G H

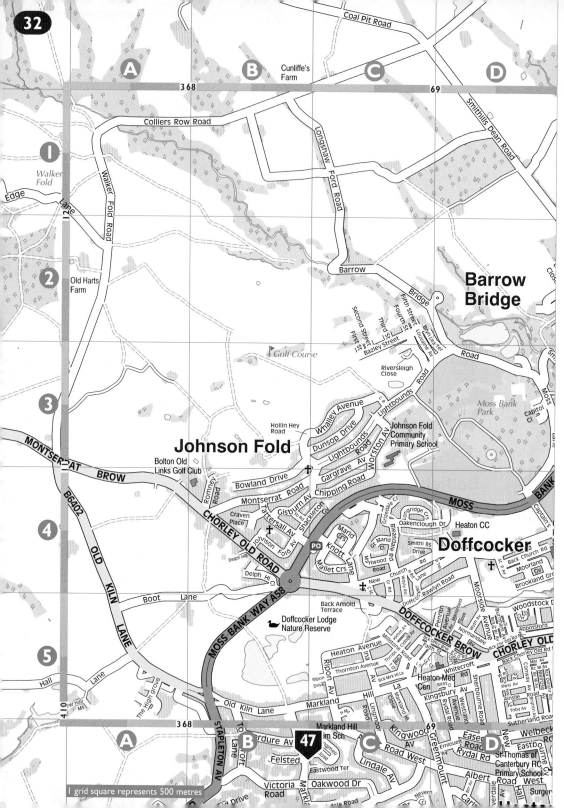

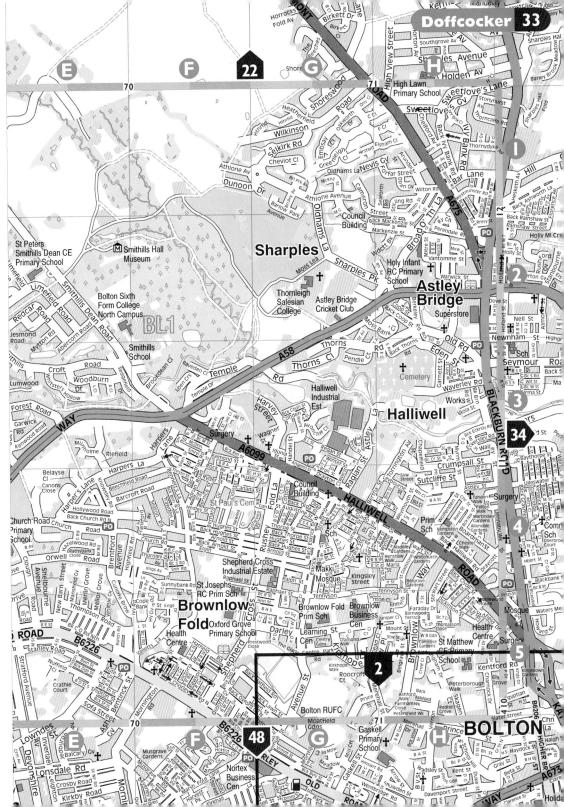

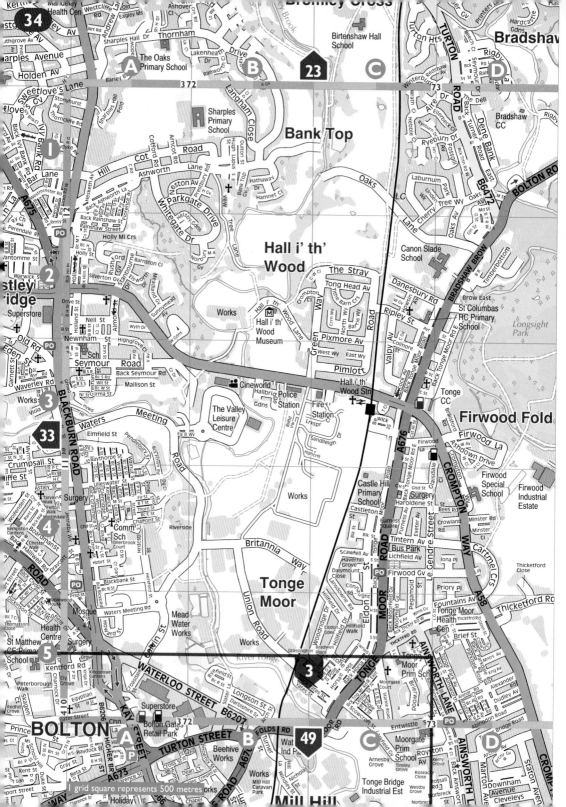

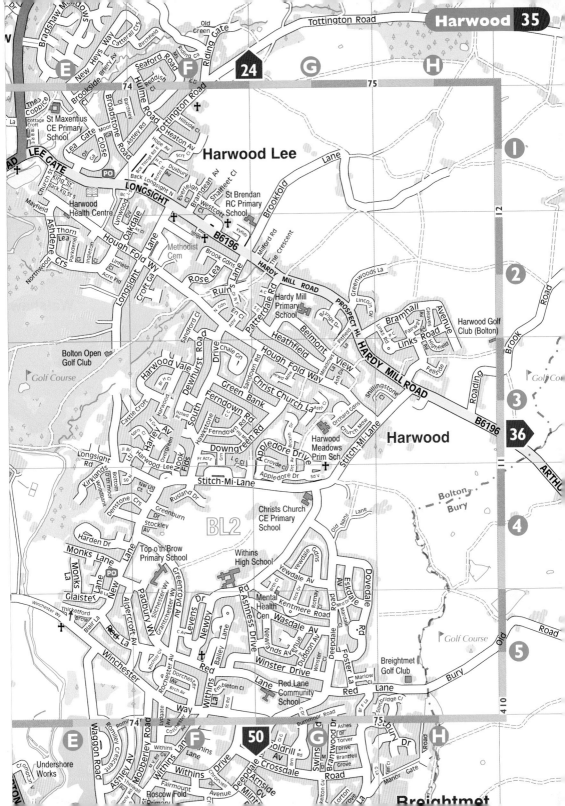

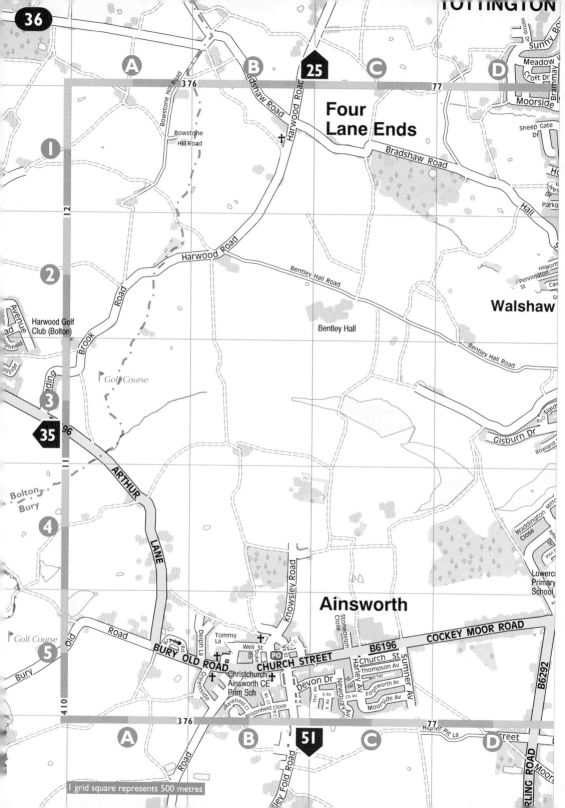

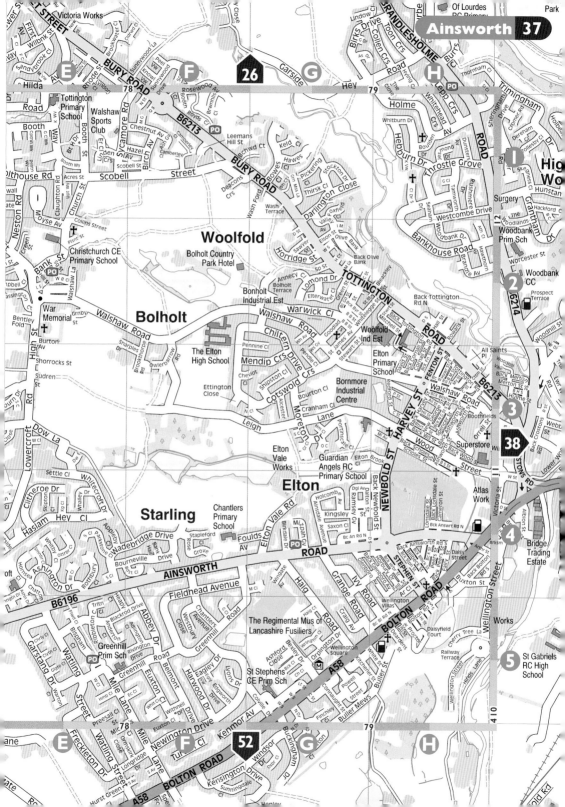

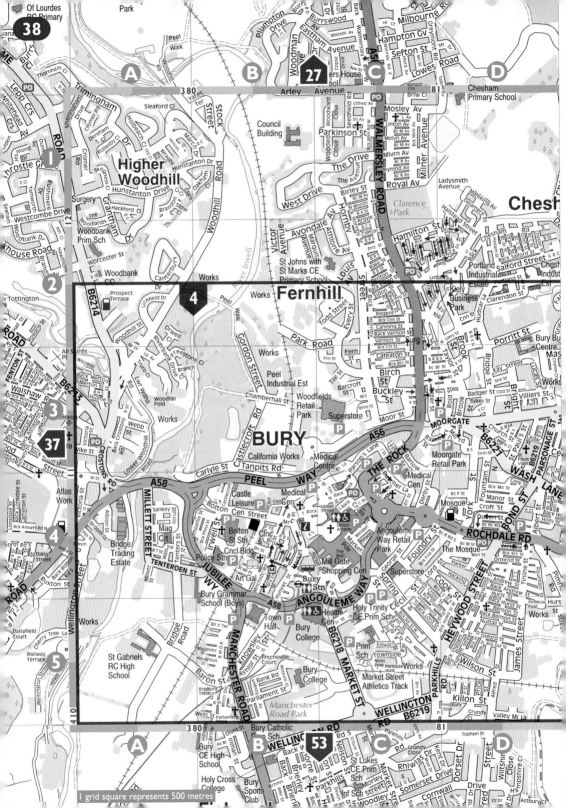

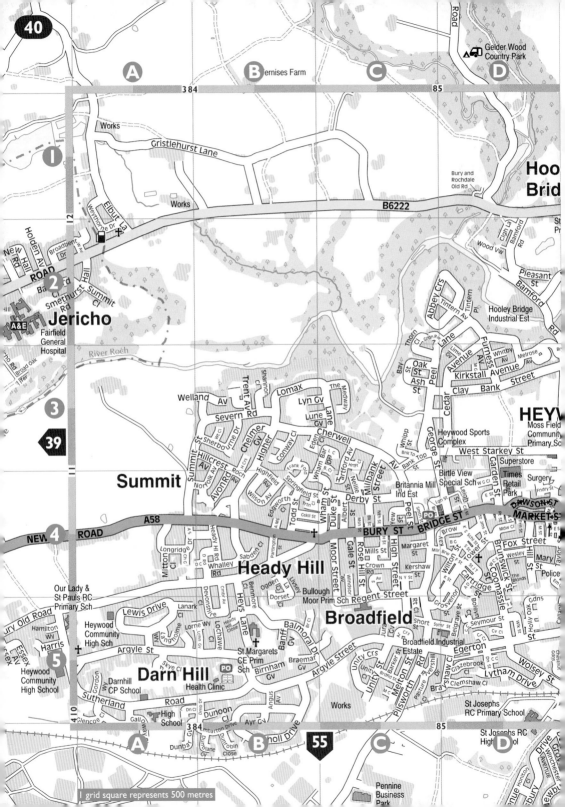

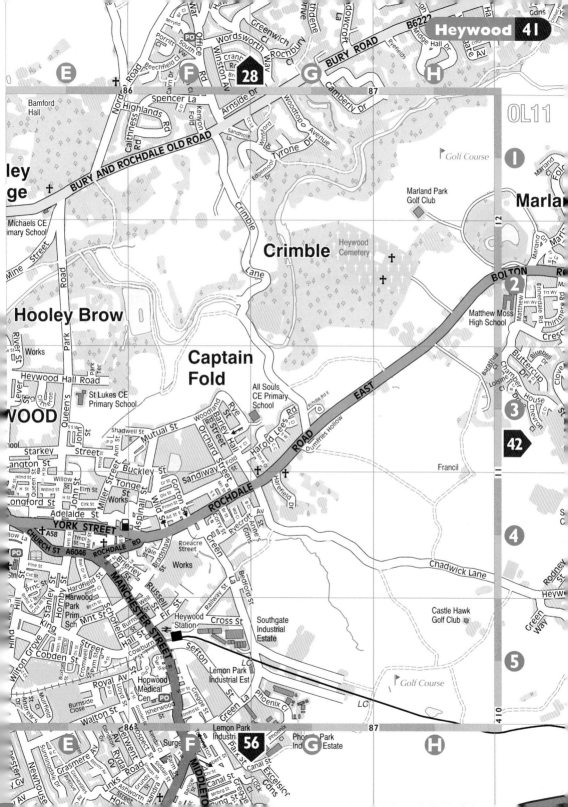

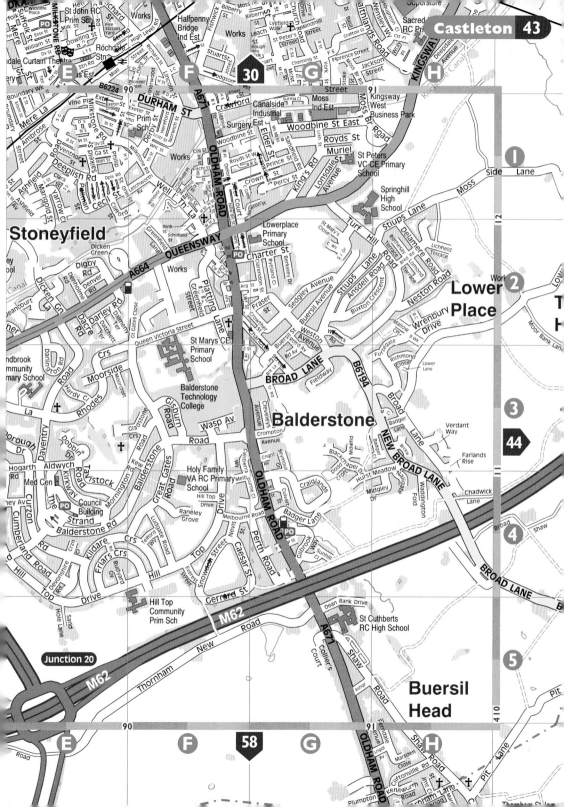

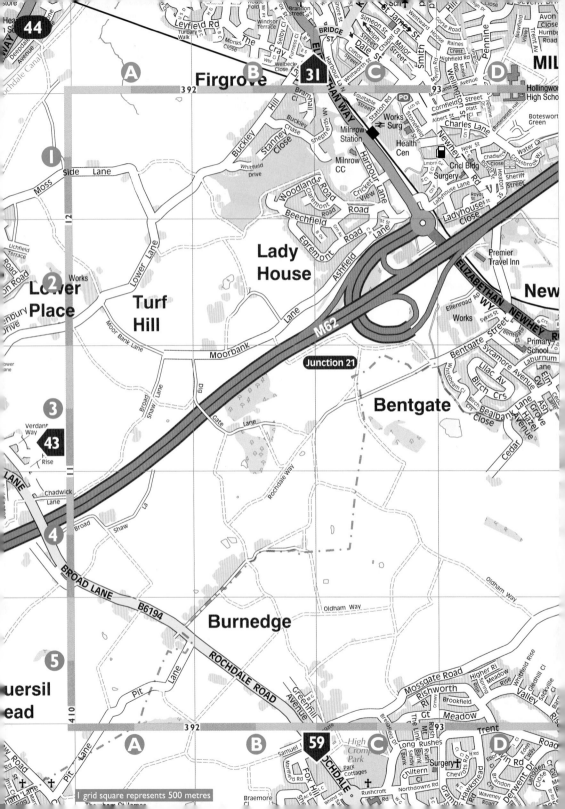

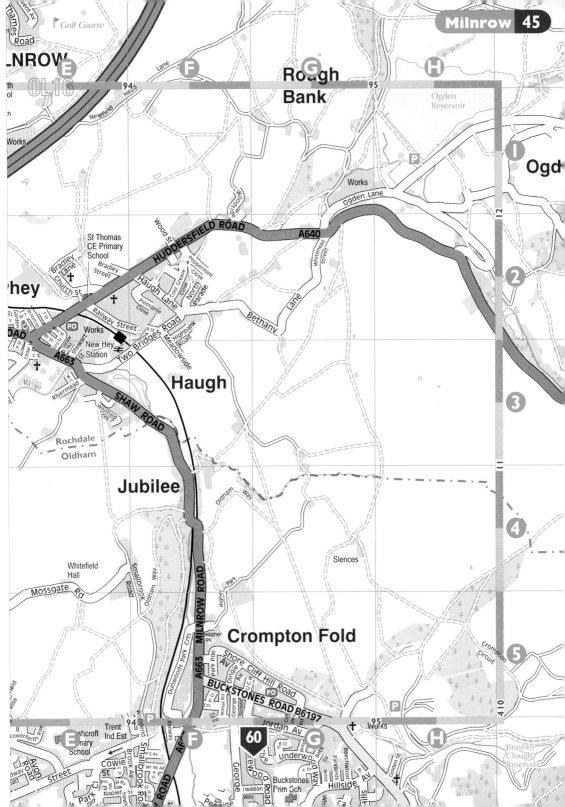

Golf Course

Thames Rd

NROW

OL16

E

F

Lane

Head

Newfield

Works

Rough Bank

G

94

95

Ogden Reservoir

H

P

I

Ogd

12

Works

Ogden Lane

Wood St

HUDDERSFIELD ROAD

A640

St Thomas CE Primary School

Bradley Lane

Church St

Bradley Street

Wood St

Peppermint Close

Cold Greave Close

North Parade

Whitehead Street

hey

Haugh Lane

Pietnorne Close

Bethany Lane

2

Railway Street

PO

Works

New Hey Station

A663

Beal

River

Rivermead

Haugh

Highbank Road

Meadowside

Two Bridges Road

SHAW ROAD

Whitfield Crs

Rochdale

Oldham

3

Jubilee

Oldham Way

11

4

Whitefield Hall

Smallbrook Way

Oldham Way

MILNROW ROAD

Park Rd

Higher Pk

Slences

Mossgate Rd

Dunwoods Park Crts

A663

Park Pde

Shore Cliff Hill Road

Crompton Circuit

5

Higher Pk

Crompton Fold

Dingle Av

George Street

BUCKSTONES ROAD B6197

PO

P

95

410

Trent Ind Est

shcroft nary School

E

94

P

F

A6

Jordan Av

Works

Brushes Clough Reservoir

H

60

G

Cowie St

Brook Av

Smallbrook Rd

ROAD

George Road

Underwood Way

Buckstones Prim Sch

Hillside

Golden St

Avon Road

Napier

Park Cl

Haddon Way

Hillside Av

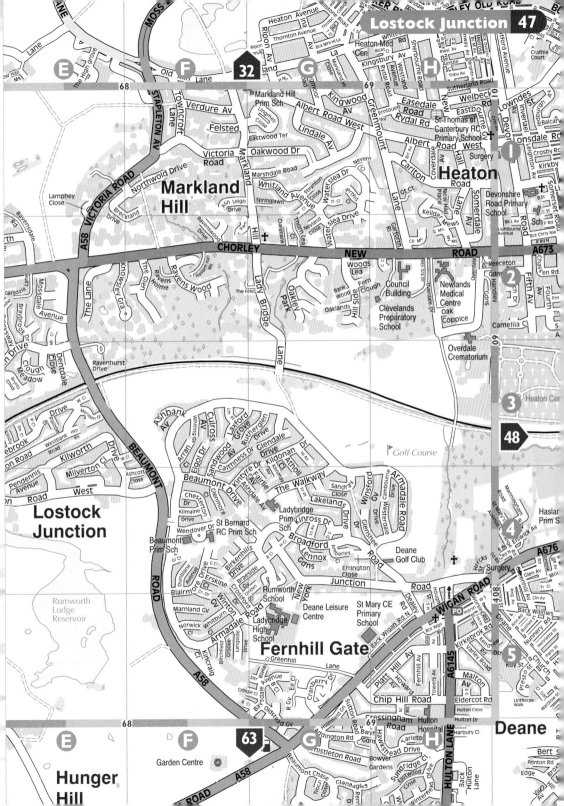

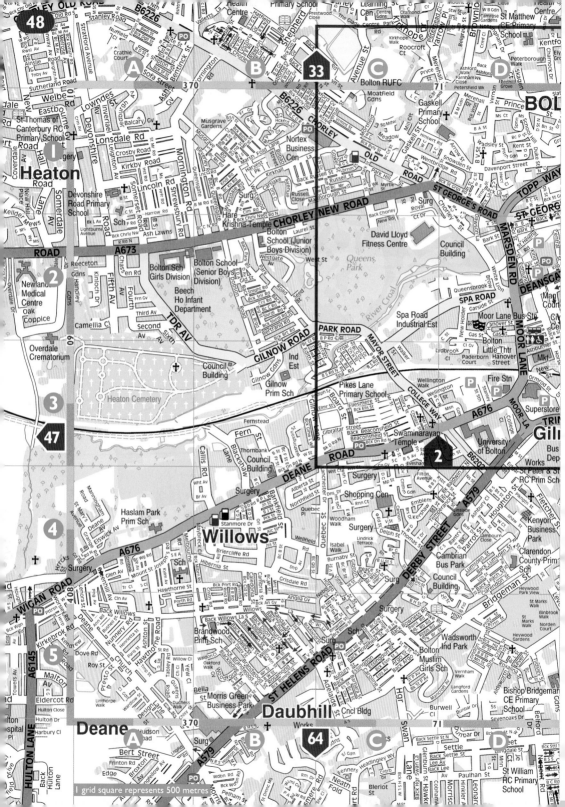

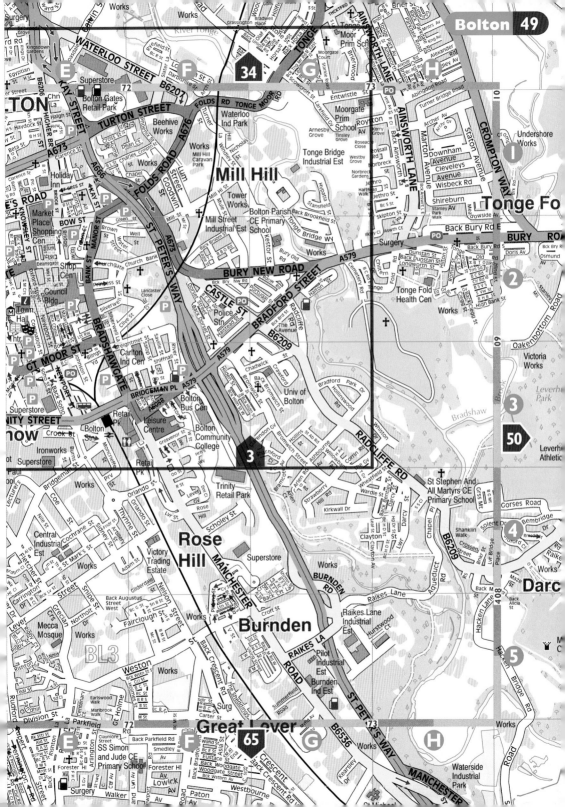

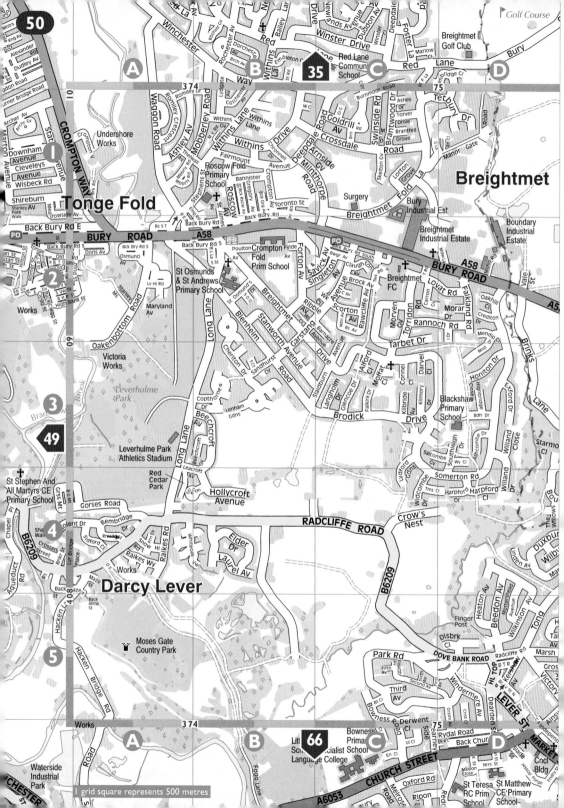

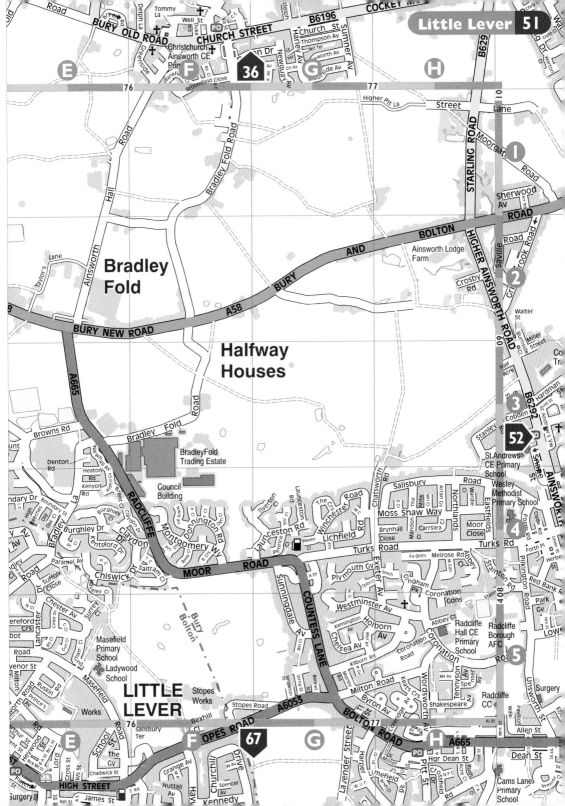

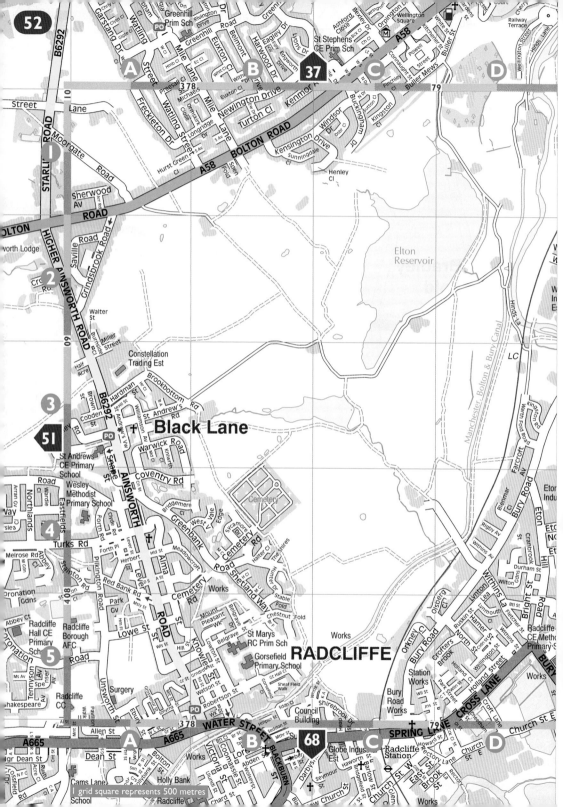

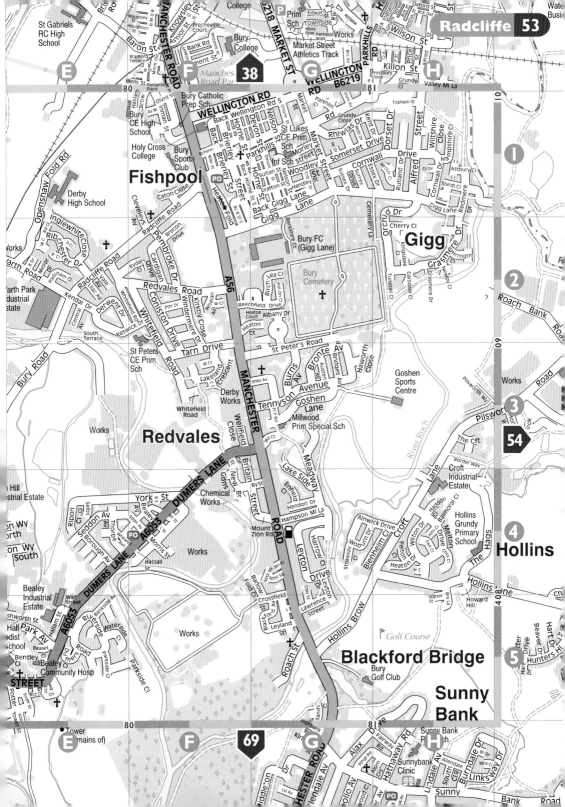

St Gabriels
RC High
School

E

Maudsley St
Houghton St
Knowsley St

MANCHESTER ROAD

Ashlor St
Frecheville
Court

Bradford
Terrace

Wells St

Parliament
Place

Haslam St

F

Bury
CE High
School

Bury Catholic
Prep Sch

Manches
Road Par

38

College

MARKET ST

S Bank Rd

Cnent St

Bury
College

Market Street
Athletics Track

WELLINGTON
RD B6219

Moss

G

WELLINGTON RD

Back Wellington Rd
Nelson St
Brierley St

Parkhills
Rd

Edward
Townside
Row

Prestbury
Close

Grundy
Cl

PARKHILLS RD

Killon St

Price St

Wilson St

Alfred

H

Valley Ml La

10

Oxford St
Bck Oxf St

Wate
Busi

I

Holy Cross
College

Bury
Sports
Club

PO

Fishpool

Caton Close

Radcliffe Road

Cleveleys
Av

Brecon
Drive

Rydal St

Cardigan
Drive

Pembroke Dr

Back Brierley St

Heaton Fold

Sultan St
Horn St

Back Gigg Lane

Inf Sch street
Woodley St

Morley St
Market

St Lukes
CE Prim
Sch

Rhiwlas
Dr

Somerset Drive

Cornwall St

Grafton St

Back Gigg
Lane

Gigg Lane

Cemetery La

Topham St

Wiltshire
Close

Hmpshire Cl

Dorset Dr

Kent Dr

Essex Cl

Alfred
Drive

Astbury Cl

Cornwall Dr

Slvrdl Cl

Redmere

Gigg Lane

Gigg

I

2

Derby High School

Openshaw Fold Rd

Inglewhite Close

Ribchester Dr

Rib Close

WC

Vale

Padiham Cl

Radcliffe Road

Derwent Dr

Kendal Dr

Central

Whitefield Road

Coniston Drive

South Terrace

Keswick Dr

Windermere dr Cl

Kirkby Close

Wrbn

Pttr Dr

Redvales Road

Beechfield Drive

Bury FC
(Gigg Lane)

Berkshire Av

Birch

Lea Cl

Bury Cemetery

Orchd Dr

Cherry Cl

Kingsdale

Grasmere Dr

Grasmere Cl

Newby Cl

Tunstall St

Carsdale Dr

Roach Bank Road

Roa

Works

2

Worth Road

Worth Park
Industrial
Estate

Bury Road

Whitefield
Road

St Peters
CE Prim
Sch

Tarn Drive

Lakeland
Crescent

WCl

Derby Works

Manchester Road

Tennyson

Wellfield Close

Shnks Av

Heaton
Ct

Albany Dr

Heaton
Court

St Peter's Road

Burns
Av

Bronte
Av

Austen

Avenue

Goshen
Lane

Haworth
Close

Bridges Av

Goshen
Sports
Centre

River Roach

Pilsworth Wy

Works

Pilsworth Road

3

54

Redvales

Whitefield
Road

Lakeland
Crescent

Millwood
Prim Special Sch

Meadway

Lake Side

Lane

The Cft

Border Way

Croft
Industrial
Estate

Haddon

Balmoral Cl

Hollins
Grundy
Primary
School

The Hags

4

Hollins

n Hill
strial
Estate

n Wy
orth
Wy
South

Ripon
Av

Seddon
Av

York St

Bealey

Selby

Thorpe Av

Borough Av

Morris St

DUMERS LANE

A6053

PO

A6053

Chemical
Works

Britain
Street

New
Gdns

New
Br
St

By St

Enfield

Hendon Dr

Hampson Ml La

Leyton Street

Mount
Zion Rd

Works

Harrow St

Leyton
Drive

Barlow
Fold

Crossfield
St

Leyland St

Lawrence
Street

Hollins Brow

Alnwick Drive

Wobn Dr

Stokesay

Blenheim Cl

Heaton Dr

Wilton Dr

Felton Dr

Haddon Cl

Melton Drive

Hollins
ne

408

Statter

Howard
Hill

Hare
tter

Hunters Dr

Beaver Dr

Hart Dr

5

Bealey
Industrial
Estate

Wild
Street

Hallam St

Bentley
Cl

Bealey
Community Hosp

STREET

Hall
Park Av

ashworth St

Riverside

Waterside

Parkside Ct

Parkside Ct

DUMERS LANE

Hassall

Works

Roach St

Blackford St

Works

Golf Course

Blackford Bridge

Bury
Golf Club

Sunny
Bank

Tower
(remains of)

E

F

69

MANCHESTER ROAD

Highbank

G

Kirk

Ajax

Fairway

Hathaway Rd

Ayton

Sthmgh Rd

PO

Apollo Av

Fairway Av

Allendale Av

Linksway

Sunnybank
Clinic

Sunny Bank
h Prim Sch

H

Lindale Av

Burndale Dr

Allendale Av

Wns Cl

Sunny
Bank Rd

80

81

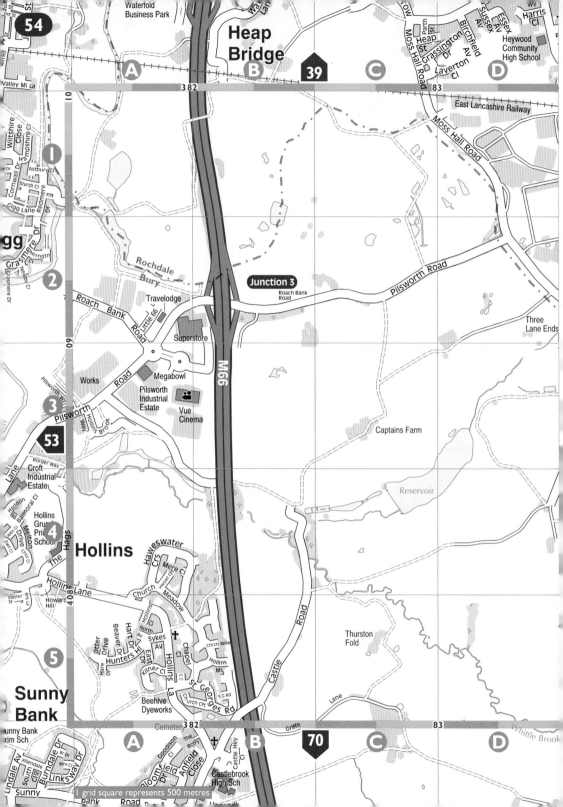

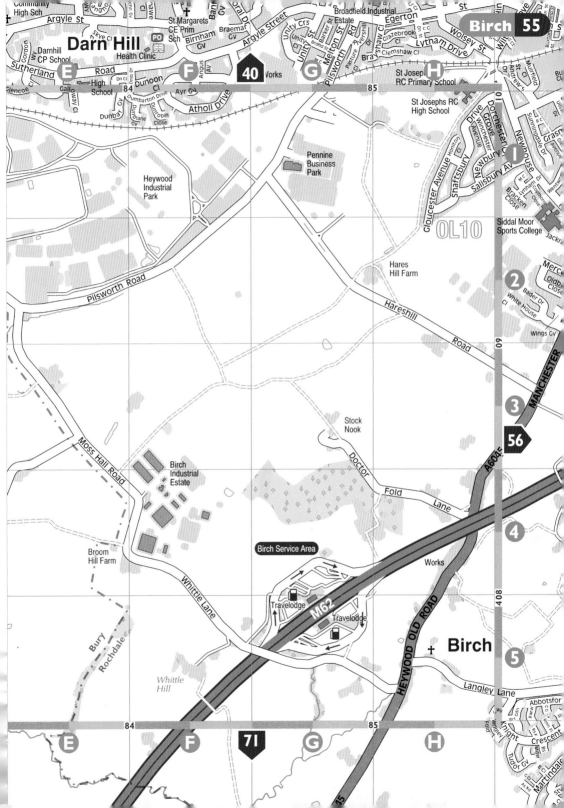

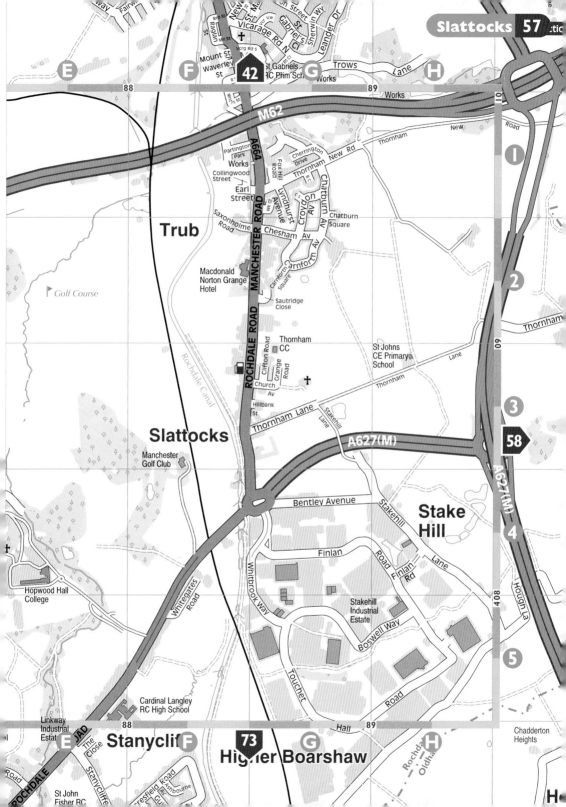

E · F · G · H

42

88 89

Works

M62

A664

Trub

Golf Course

Partington Park

Works

Collingwood Street

Earl Street

Saxonhoime Road

New St
Vicarage Rd N
St Gabriels RC Prim Sch
Raglan St
Gabriel's Cl
Sherwin Wy
Leander Dr
Mount St
Waverley St
Trows Lane
Works

New Rd
Thornham New Rd
Cherrington Drive
Fox Hill Road
Lyndhurst Avenue
Croydon Av
Chatburn Av
Chatburn Square
Chesham Av
Carnforth Av
Carnforth Square

Thornham
New Road

I

2

Thornham

MANCHESTER ROAD
ROCHDALE ROAD

Macdonald Norton Grange Hotel

Sautridge Close

Thornham CC

Clifton Road
Grange Road
Church Av
Hillbank St

St Johns CE Primary School

Thornham Lane

Thornham Lane
Stakehill Lane

Rochdale Canal

Slattocks

Manchester Golf Club

A627(M)

3

58

4

A627(M)

60

Bentley Avenue

Finlan

Stakehill Road

Finlan Rd

Stake Hill

Whitbrook Way

Stakehill Industrial Estate

Boswell Way

Houghl La

408

5

Hopwood Hall College

Whitegates Road

Touchet Road

Cardinal Langley RC High School

Linkway Industrial Estat

E

ROAD
The Close
Stanycliff
Stanycliffe
Cresfield Road
Renbourne

F

73

Higher Boarshaw

88 89

Hall

G

H

Rochdale Oldham

Chadderton Heights

ROCHDALE ROAD

St John Fisher RC

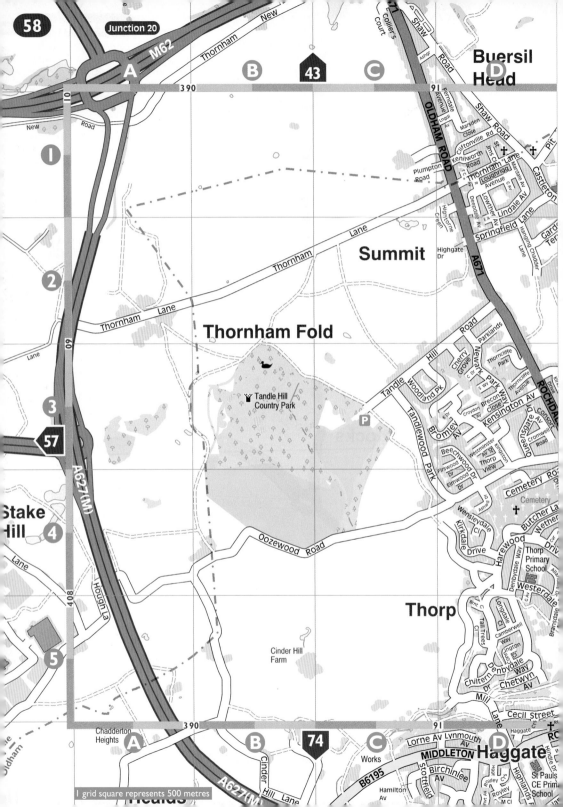

58

Junction 20

M62

Thornham New

Colliers Court

Shaw Road

Buersil Head

3 90

A

B

43

C

91

D

New

Road

Oldham Road

Ashgr

Ferndale Avenue

Lingdi Av

Marsden Close

Cliftonville Rd

Ken/worth Road

St

Jms Cl

Thornham Lane

Loughrigg Avenue

Lowther Av

Marsdale Av

Deepdale Av

Lindale AV

Castleton

Pit

10

I

Springfield Lane

Hanging Chadder

Garde Terr

Plumpton Road

Highthorne Green

A671

2

60

Thornham Lane

Thornham Lane

Summit

Highgate Dr

Highgate Dr

Thornham Lane

Thornham Lane

Thornham Fold

Road

Hill

Cherry Grove

Parklands

Newark Park

Thorncliffe Park

Rochdale

Kirk

3

Tandle Hill Country Park

Tandle

Woodland Pk

C Dr

Croydon Av

Brecon Cl

S WY

Thorncliffe Avenue

Drive

Cromwell

57

P

Bromley Av

Tandlewood Park

K Dr

Westminster AV

Kingston

Thorp

Kensington Av

Queensgate Av

Consort

4

Beechwood Dr

Firswood Dr

Elmwood Dr

Av Cl

View

Cromwell Cl

Stake Hill

408

Wensleydale Cl

Cemetery Ro

Cemetery

Butcher La

Wether

5

Kirkdale Drive

Harewood

Denbydale Way

Thorp Primary School

Westerdale

Drive

Allerdale CI

Lane

Thorp

Hough La

Longdale

Tall Trees CI

Camberwell Way

Jington CI

Birnt C

Denbydale Way

Chiltern Dr

Chetwyn Av

Cinder Hill Farm

Cecil Street

Chadderton Heights

3 90

A

Cinder Hill Lane

B

74

Works

C

B6195

Lorne Av

Stotfield Av

Birchinlee Av

Hamilton Av

91

Lynmouth Av

Haggate

Mill Lane

MIDDLETON

Haggate

St Pauls CE Prima School

Oldham

A627(M)

Heads

Oozewood Road

1 grid square represents 500 metres

Crompton
Moor

E F G H

96 97 110

Wham Lane

Lane

Corbett
Way

OLDHAM ROAD

Old
Tame

A672

DELPH ROAD

A6052

I

Lane

2

Tame

Horest Lane

Slackcote Lane

Works

Slackcote

Mantley Lane

OLDHAM ROAD

ROAD

ES

09

A6052

3

Slack

DENSHAW

Grains Bar

SHIP LANE

Ship

Lane

P

Bishop
Park

P

GRAINS ROAD

4

L

408

B6197

Medlock Valley Way

Besom
Hill

NW ROAD

cil
ng

P

5

Hill Top Lane

Spinners Way

Spring Hey

Peak
Cl

Ipsley Crs

Way

Erica Av

Juniper Cl

Ertshere Cl

Moorside Av

Arncliffe Rl

Lee Lane

**Hill Top
Community
Special School**

Whitehall La

Hayfield Cl

Broadstone Av

Oakworth Cft

Pit Lane

Medlock Valley Way

High

Edge Lane

Bl

E F **77** G H

96 97

Cabin La

Roebuck

Strine
Dale

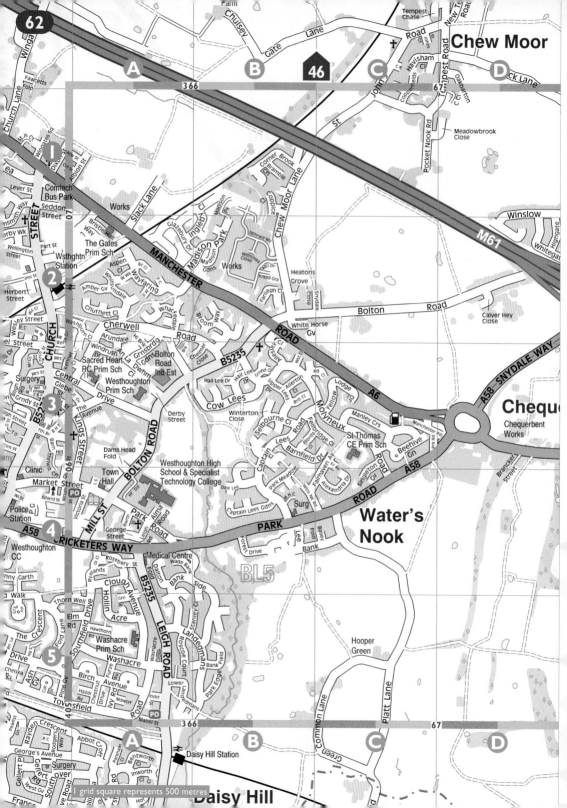

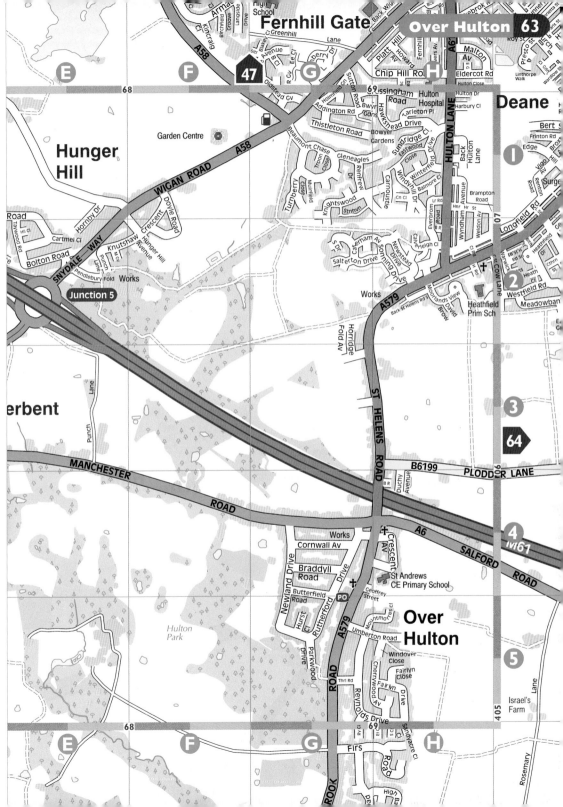

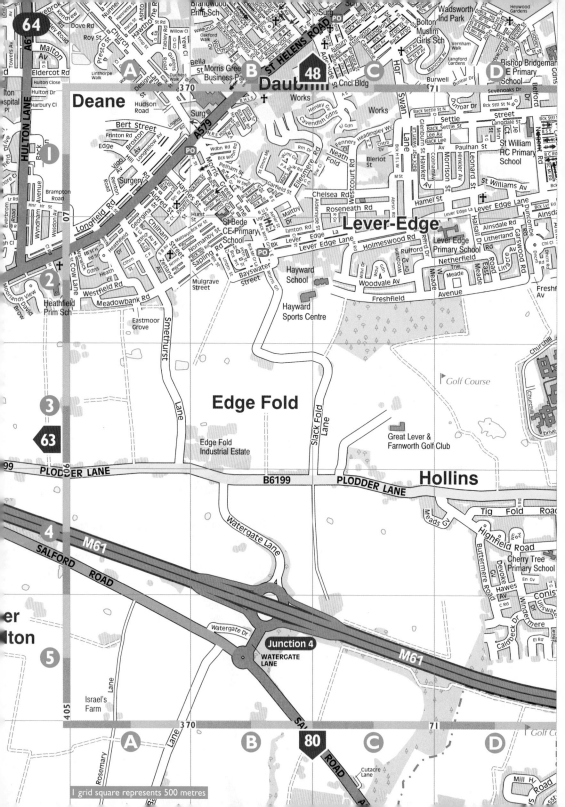

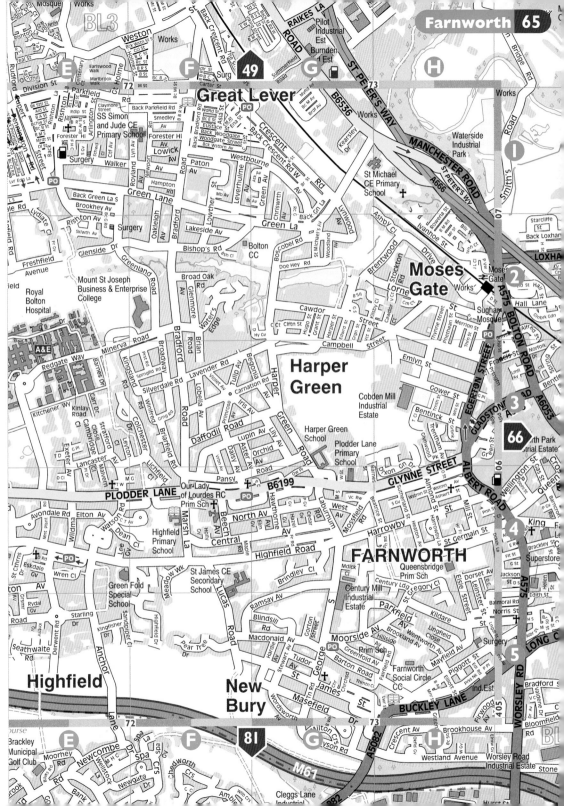

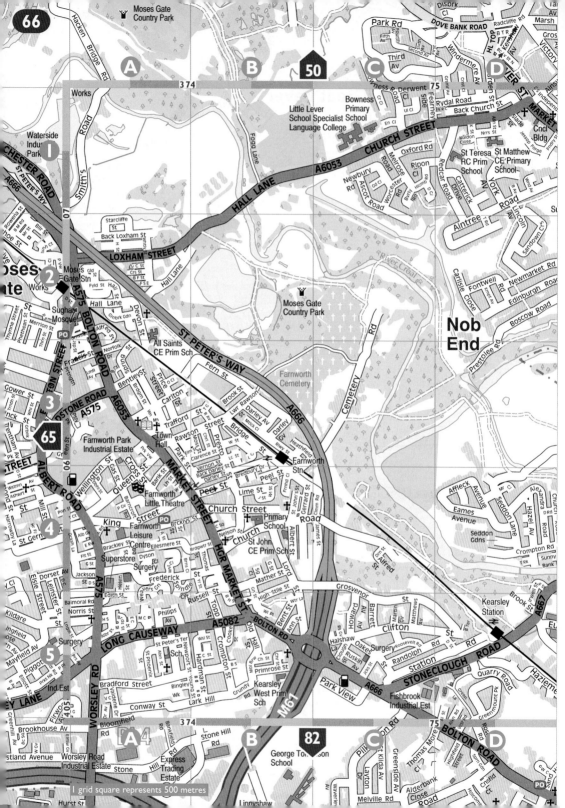

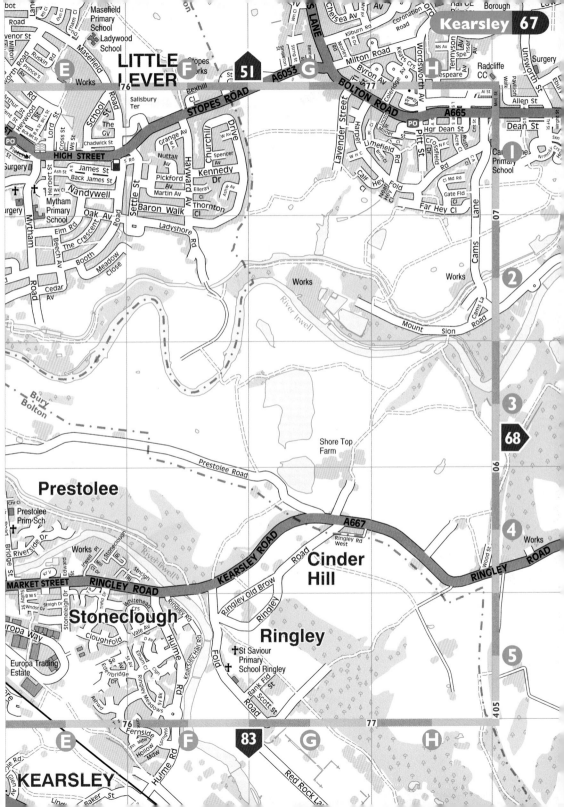

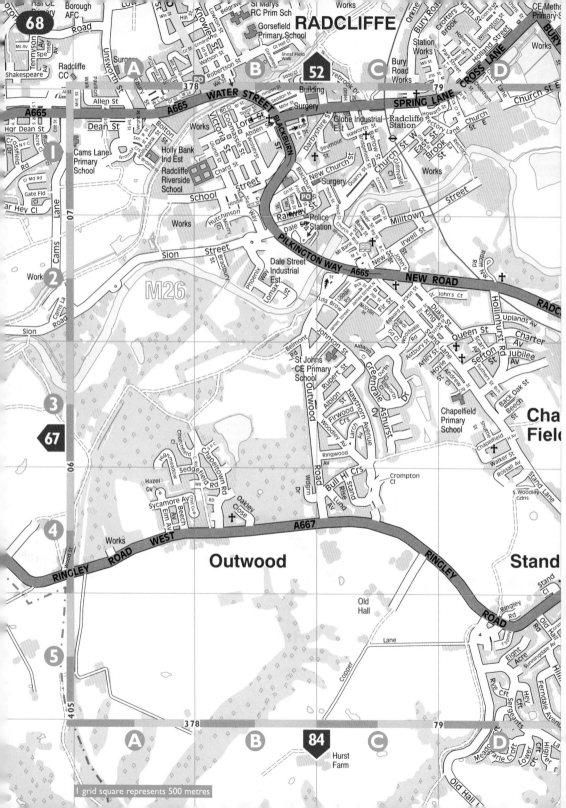

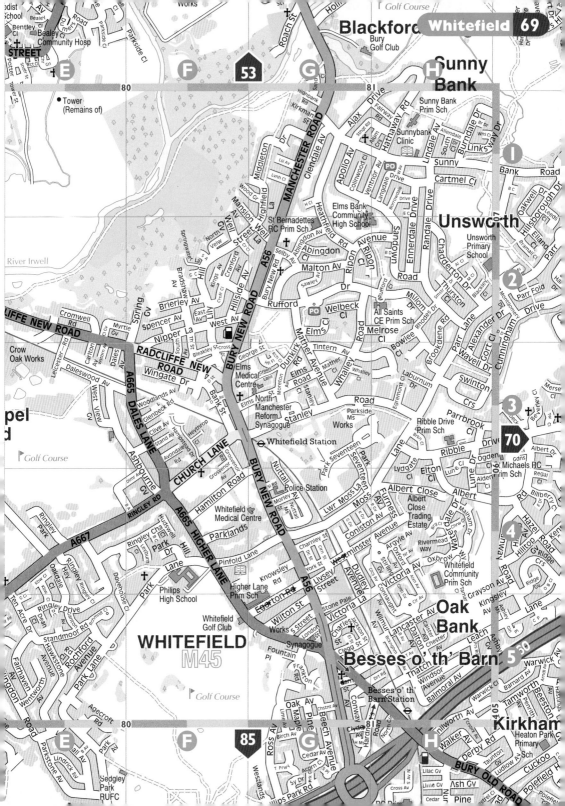

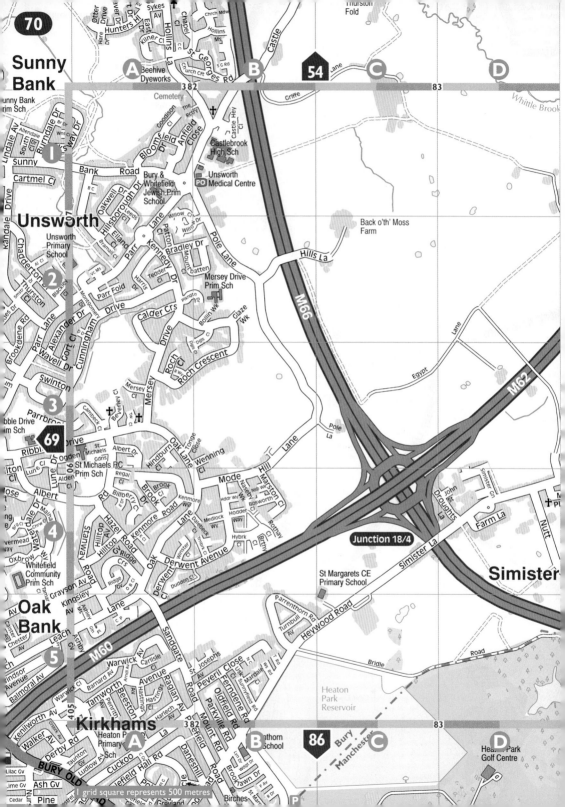

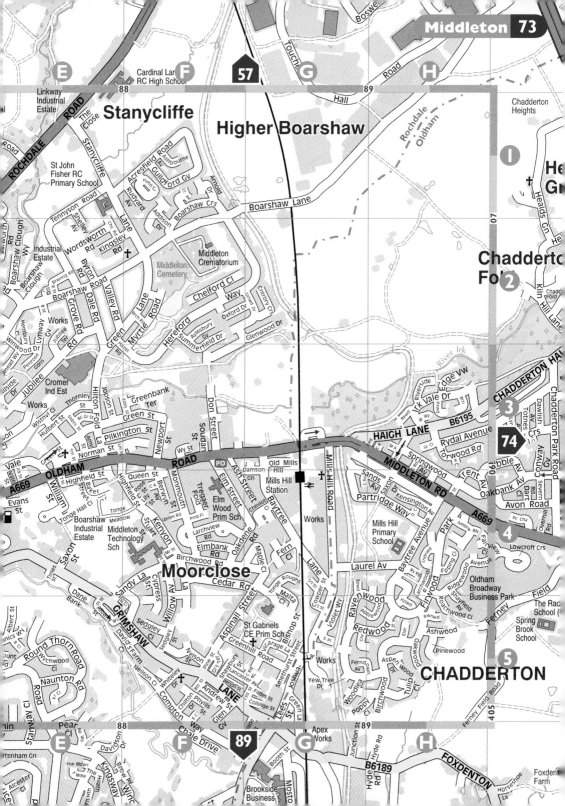

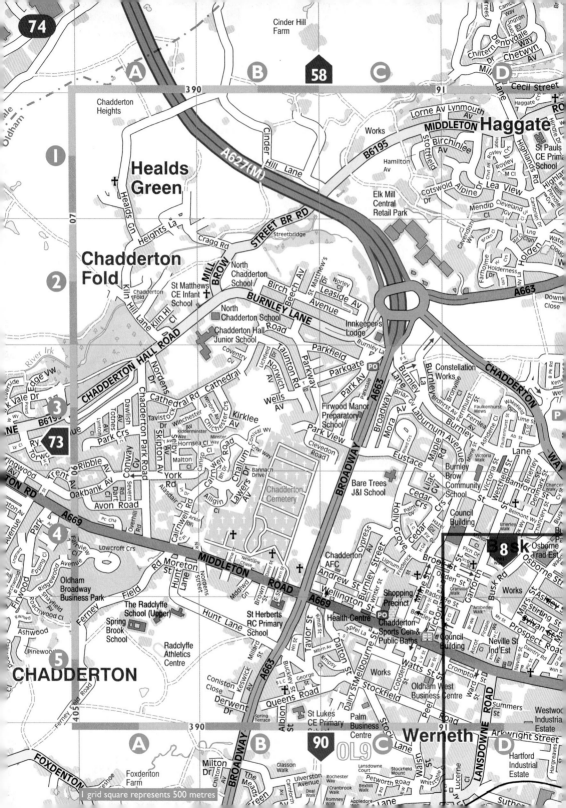

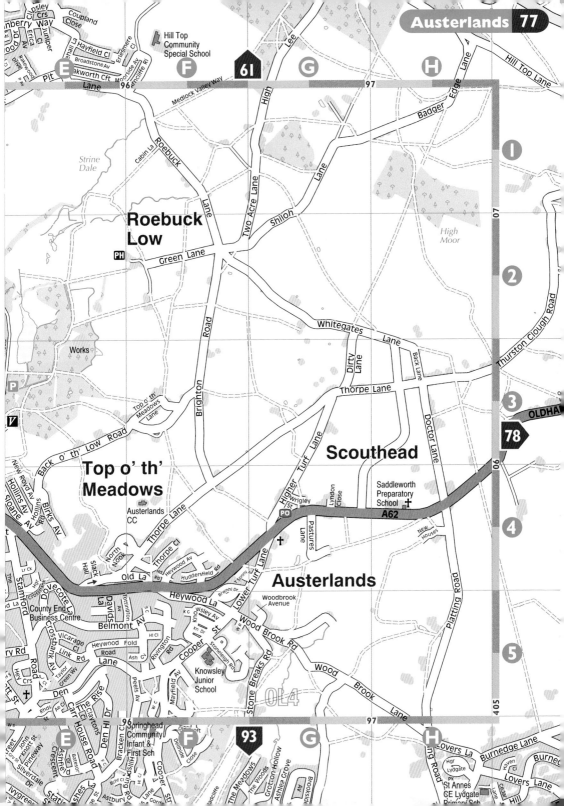

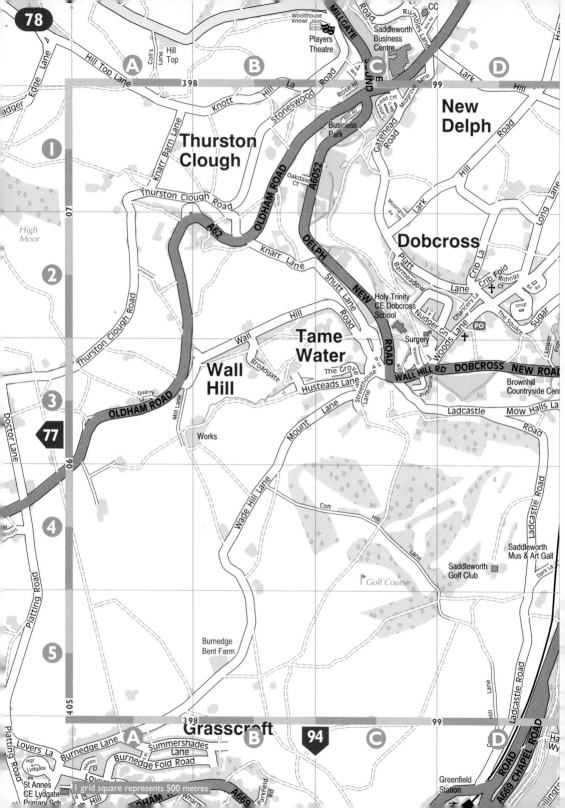

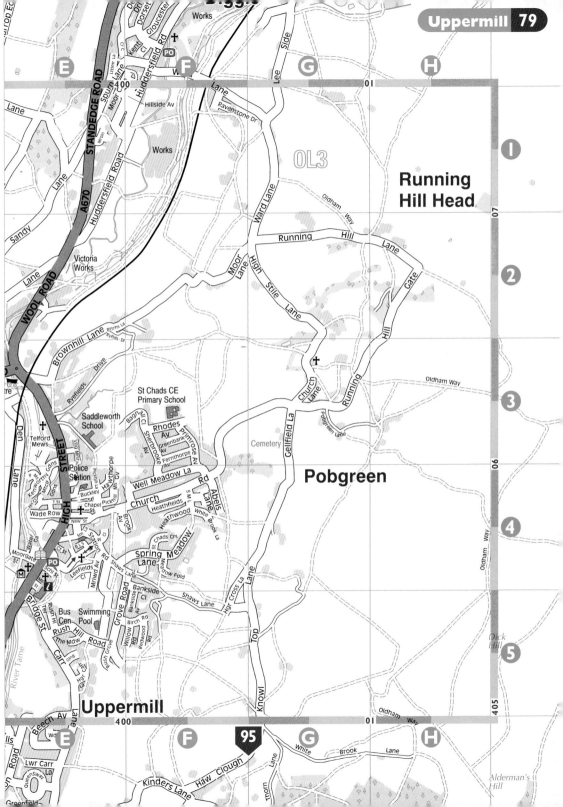

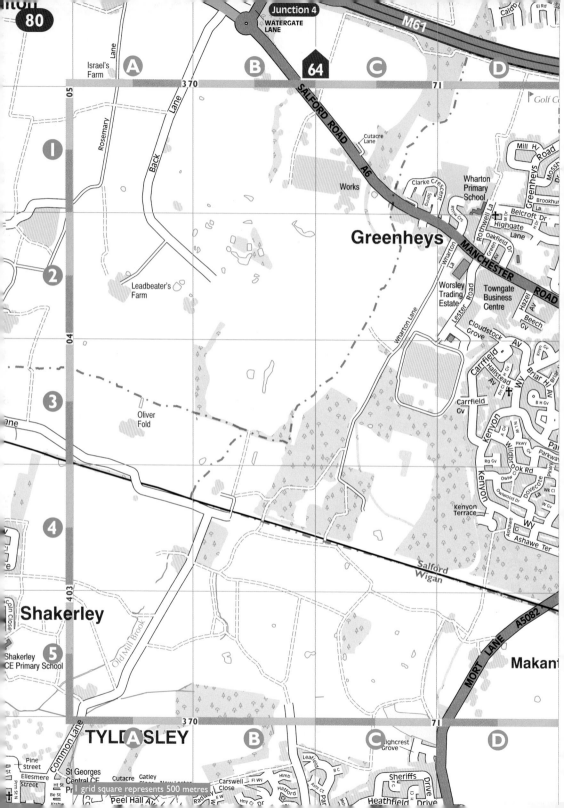

80

Junction 4
WATERGATE
LANE

M61

Caldb

El Rd

A

B

64

C

D

Israel's
Farm

Rosemary Lane

Back Lane

370

05

71

Golf C

Mill H

Greenheys Road

Mossn

I

SALFORD ROAD

A6

Cutacre
Lane

Works

Clarke Crescent

Wharton
Primary
School

Brookhu

Belcroft Dr

La

Rothwell La

Highgate
Lane

Greenheys

Wharton La

2

04

Leadbeater's
Farm

Worsley
Trading
Estate

Lester Road

Towngate
Business
Centre

Hazel
AV

Beech
Gv

Wharton Lane

Cloudstock
Grove

Carrfield AV

Halstead
AV

Briar H AV

B H Gv

3

Oliver
Fold

Carrfield
Gv

Kenyon WY

Wildbrook Rd

Parkway

Rg Gv

Lane

Salford
Wigan

Dovecote

Owlwood Dr

Kenyon WY

4

403

Old Mill Brook

Kenyon
Terrace

Ashawe

Ashawe Ter

Col'n Close

Shakerley

Shakerley
CE Primary School

5

MORT LANE

A5082

Makant

Ellesmere
Street

Common Lane

TYLDESLEY

A

B

C

Highcrest
Grove

D

370

71

Pine
Street

St Georges
Central CE
Pri

Cutacre

Gatley

New Lester

Carswell
Close

Fl WY

Hatford

Sheriffs

Heathfield Drive

Drive

Peel Hall Av

Radwy

Hny

grid square represents 500 metres

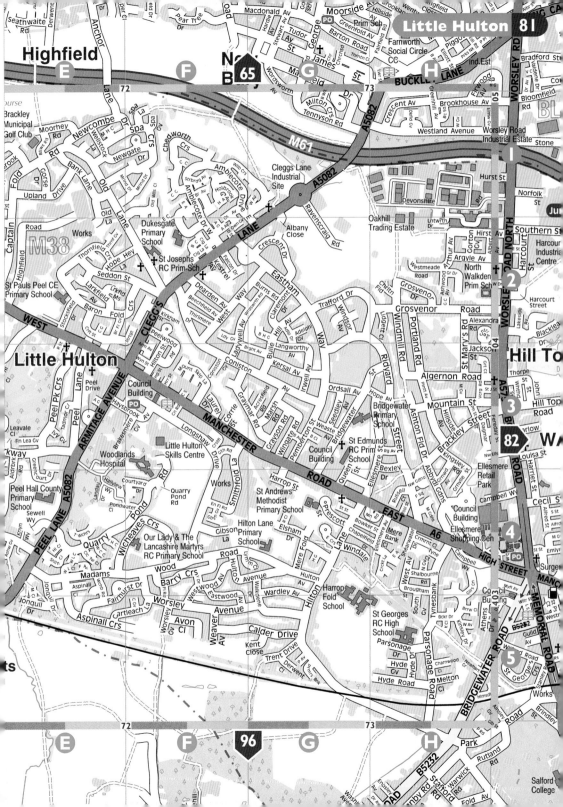

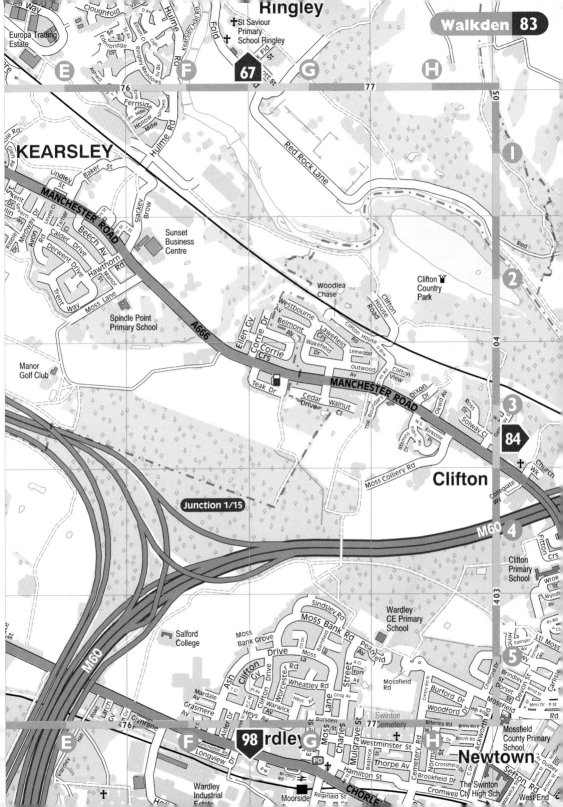

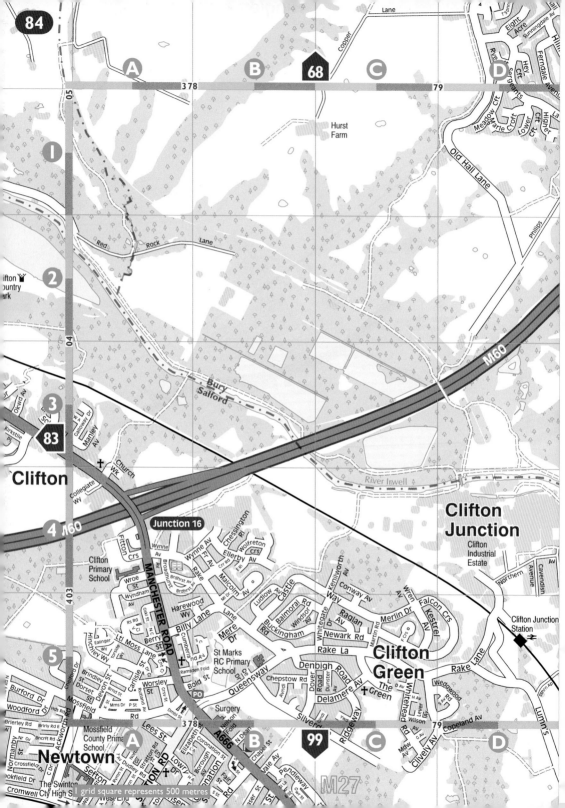

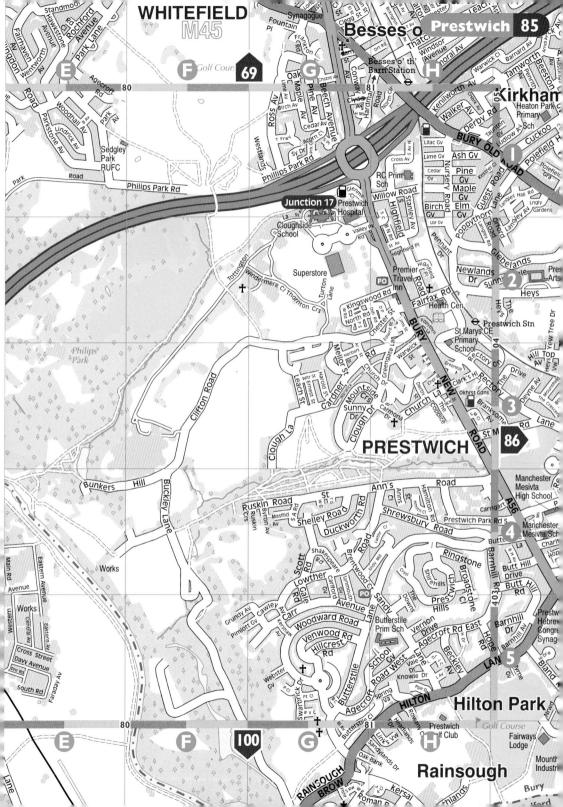

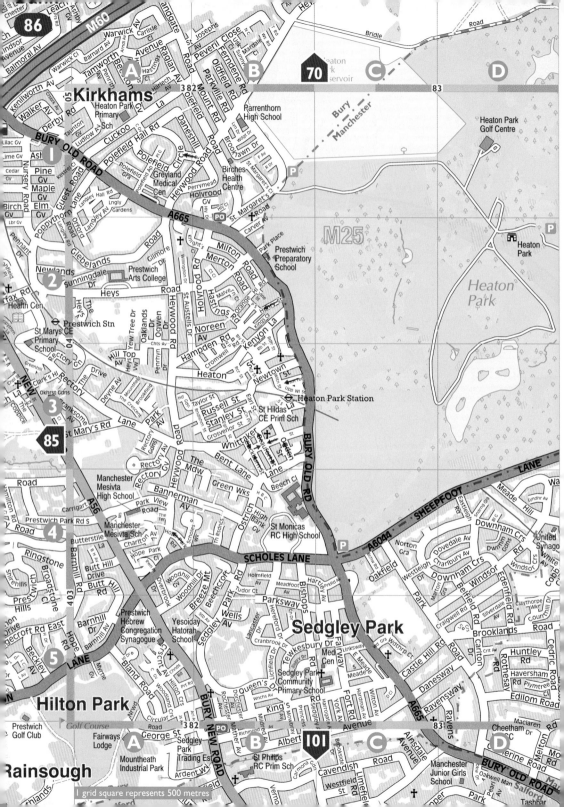

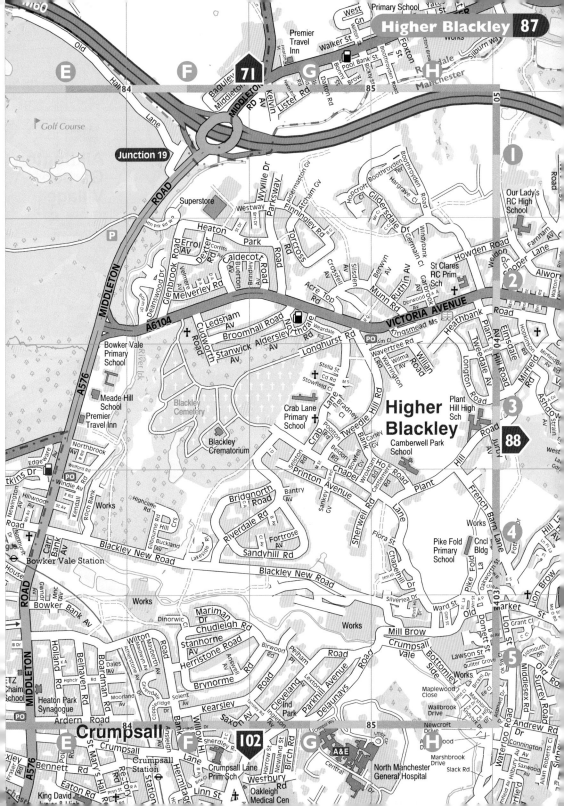

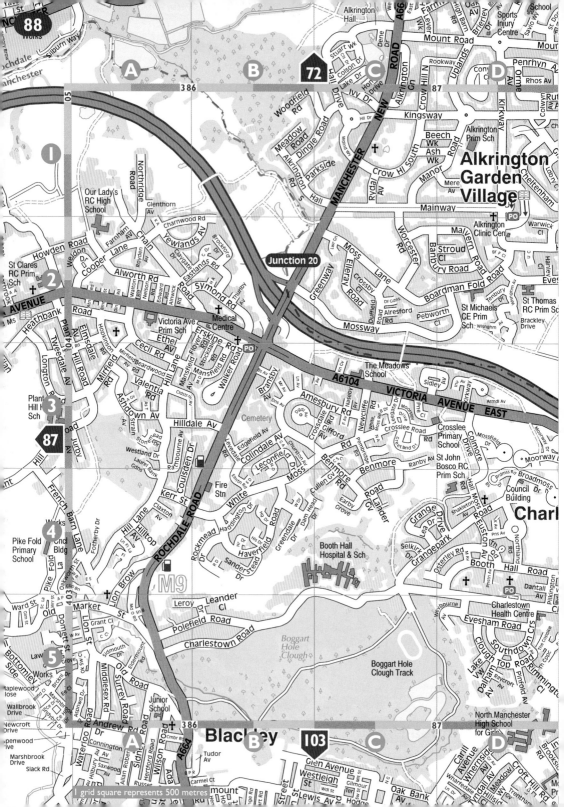

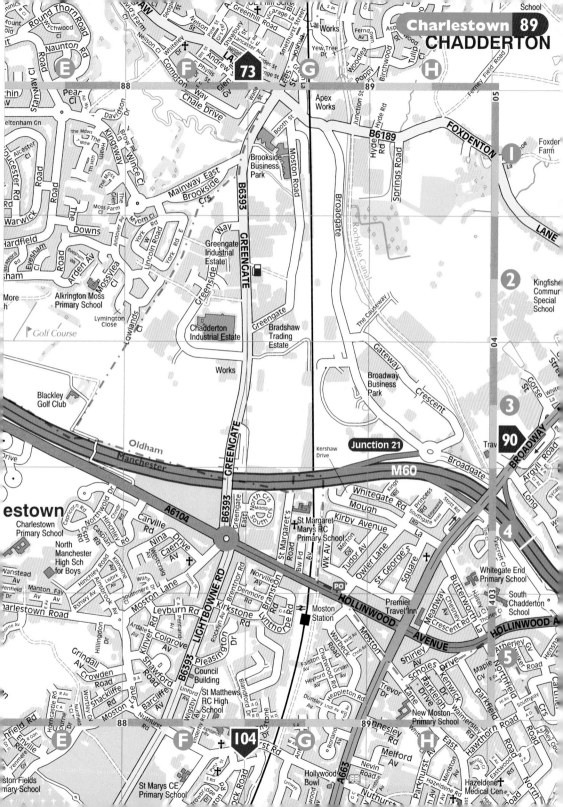

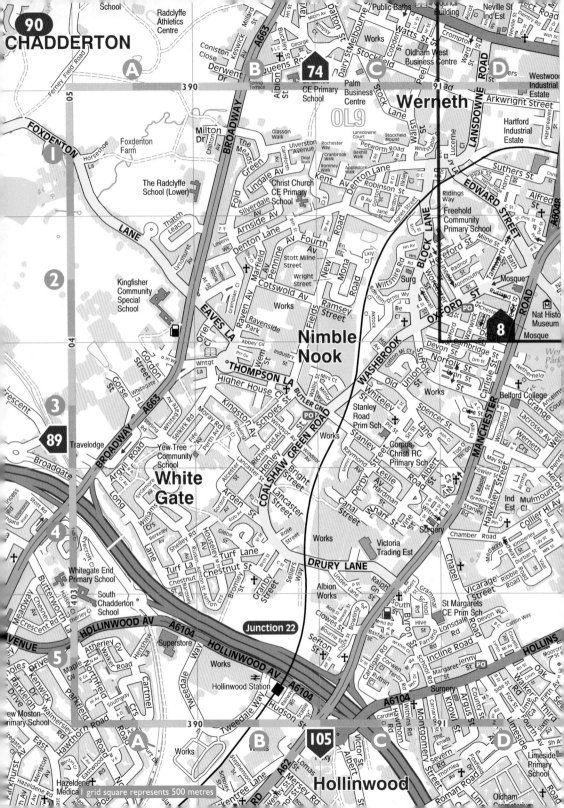

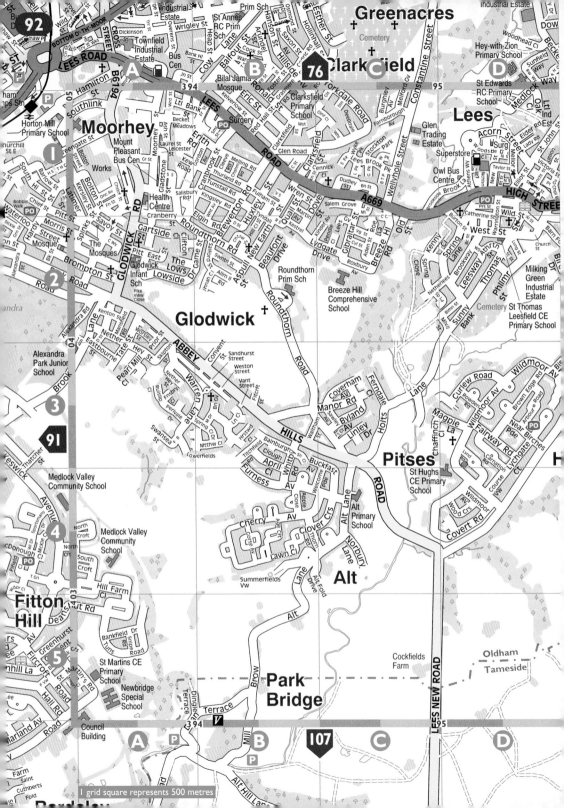

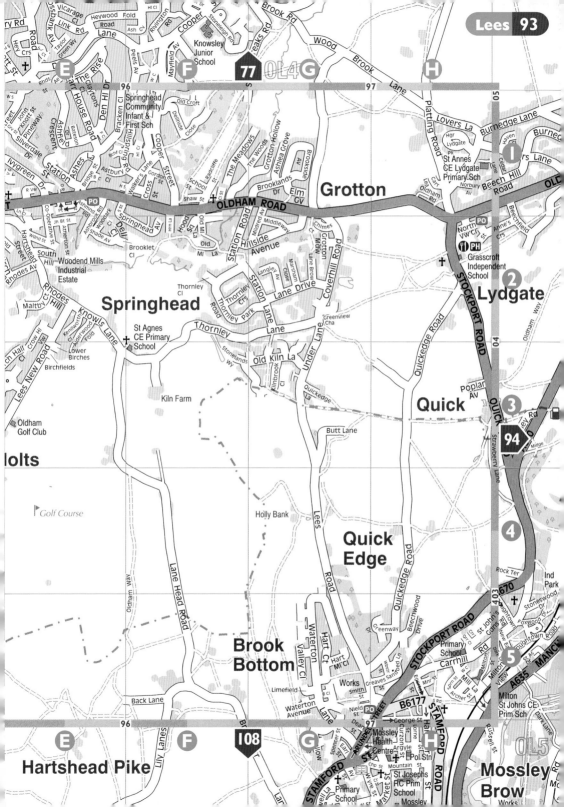

E F **77** OL4 G H

I

Grotton

Lydgate **2**

Springhead

Quick **3**

94

Quick Edge **4**

Brook Bottom

Quick

Oldham Golf Club

Golf Course

Holly Bank

5

OL5

E F **108** G H

Hartshead Pike

Mossley Brow

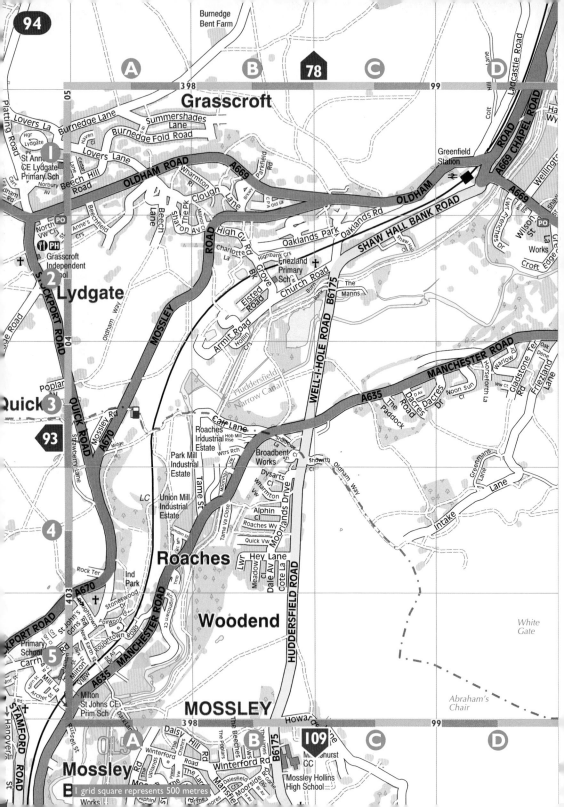

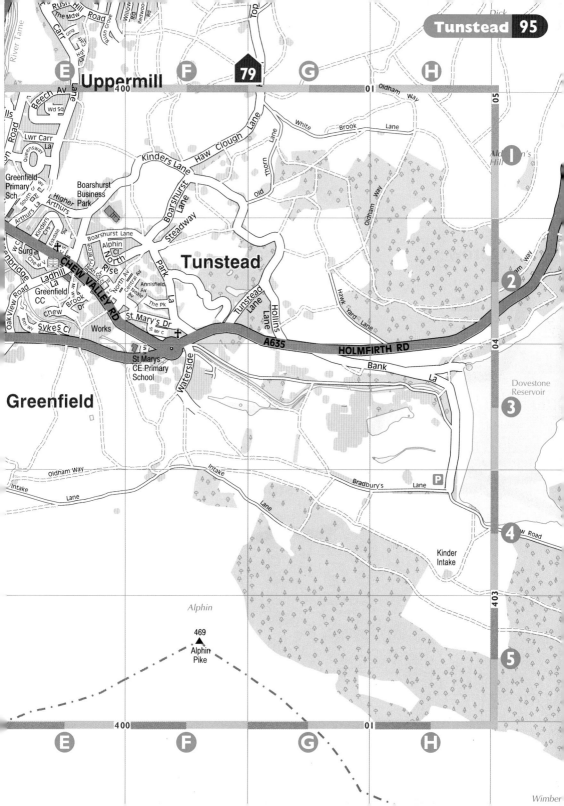

E **Uppermill** F 79 G H

Tunstead

Greenfield

River Tame

Rush Hill Road
The Mdw
Carr Long
Hat La
Willow
Redwood

Top

Dick

Aldoron's Hill I

Oldham Way

White Brook Lane

Haw Clough Lane

Kinders Lane

Thorn Lane

Old Lane

Beech Av
Wd Sq
Lwr Carr La
Queensway
Road

Greenfield Primary Sch
South
Arthurs La

Boarshurst Business Park

Boarshurst Lane

Boarshurst Lane

Steadway

Alphin North
Park

Oldham Way

2

Hawk Yard Lane

Kinders Cft
Esxdale
Surg
Ladhill La
Greenfield CC
Brook Dr
Chew W
Works
Sykes Cl

Arthurs
Rise
North Av
Central Av
The Pk
Annisfield Av Neale
St Mary's Dr
St Mr C

Tunstead Lane

Hollins Lane

CHEW VALLEY RD

Oakbridge
OakView Road
Bttr Wy

A635 HOLMFIRTH RD

04

St Marys CE Primary School

Waterside

Bank

La

Dovestone Reservoir

3

Oldham Way

Intake Lane

Intake Lane

Bradbury's Lane

P

4 w Road

403

Kinder Intake

Alphin

▲ 469
Alphin Pike

5

E 400 F G 01 H

Wimber

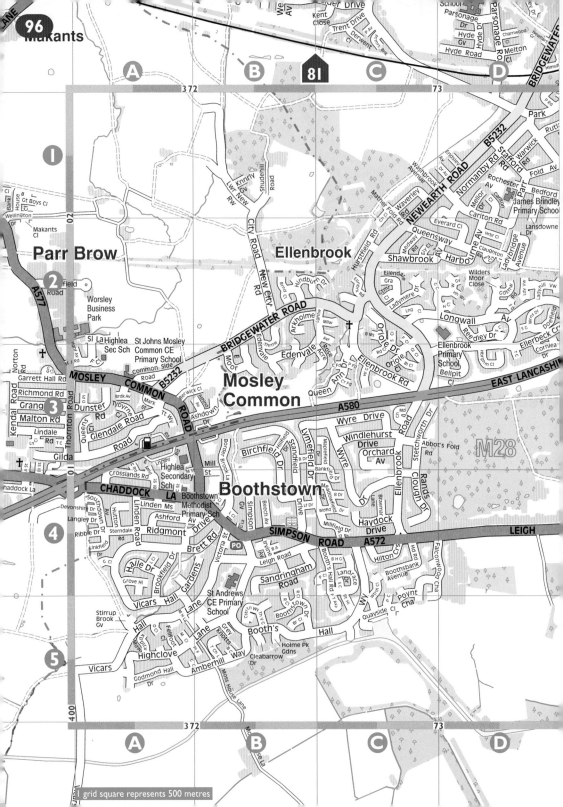

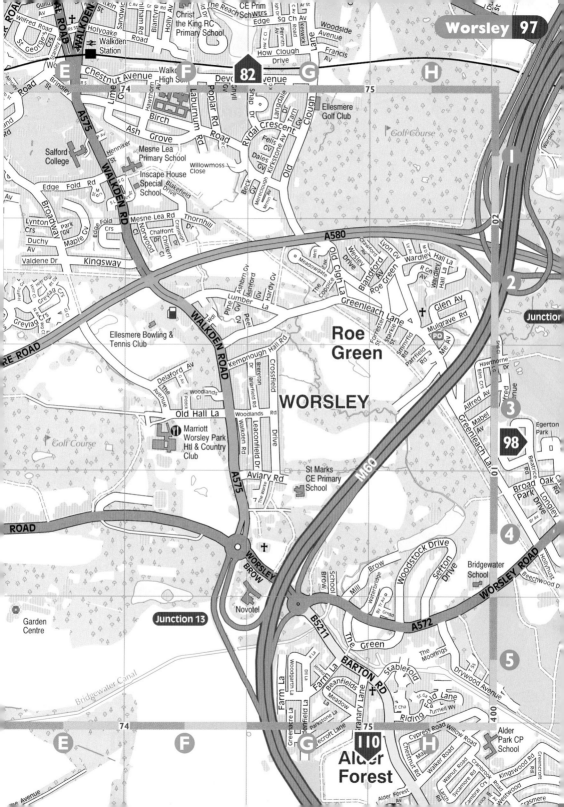

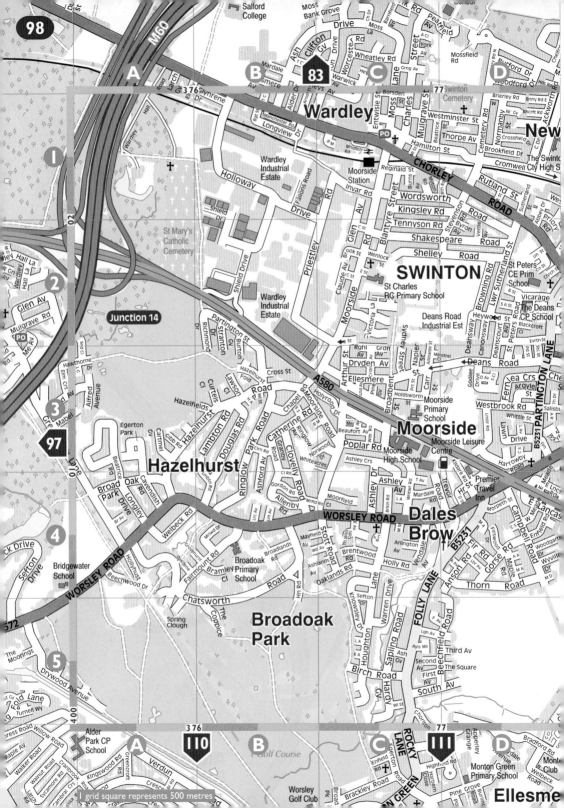

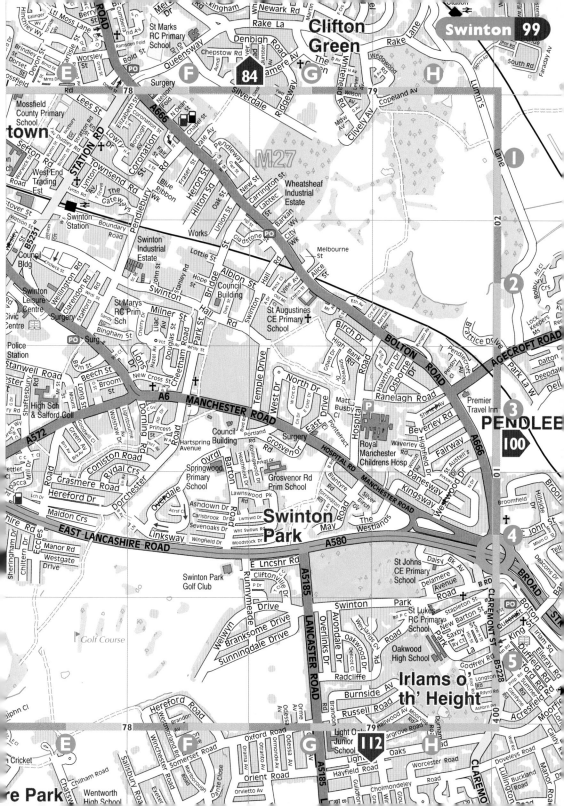

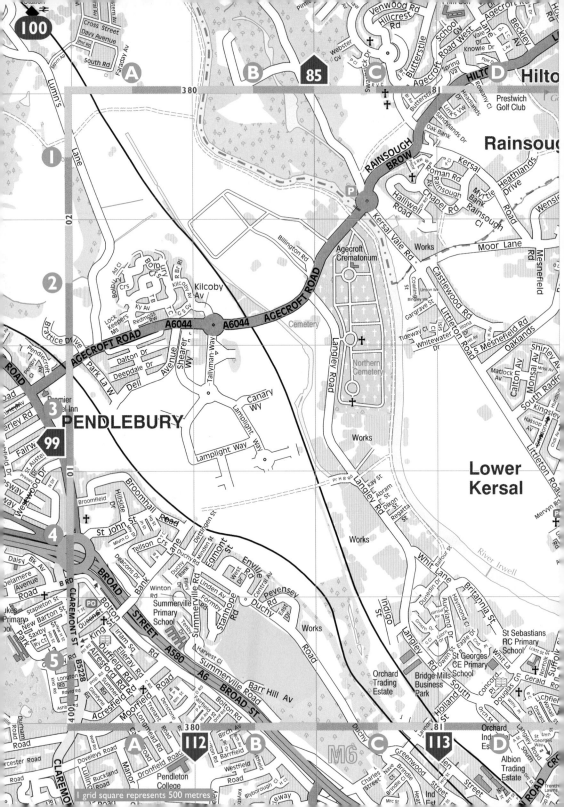

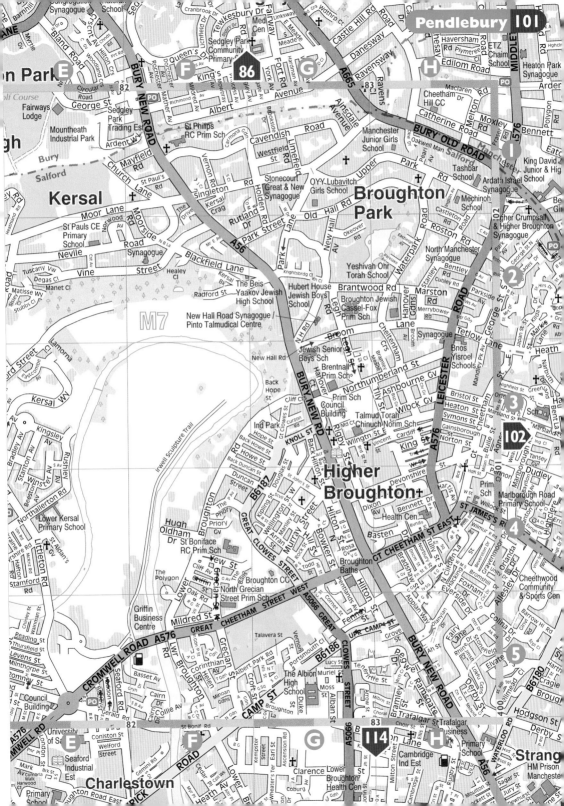

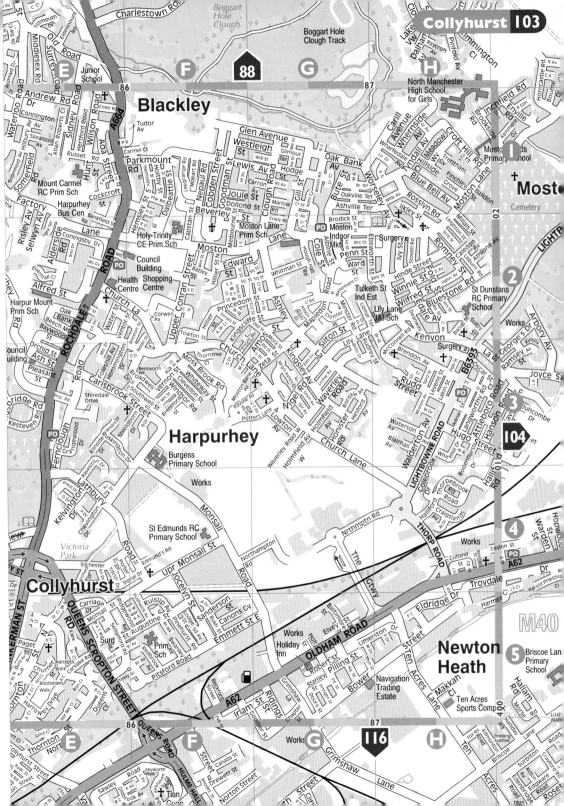

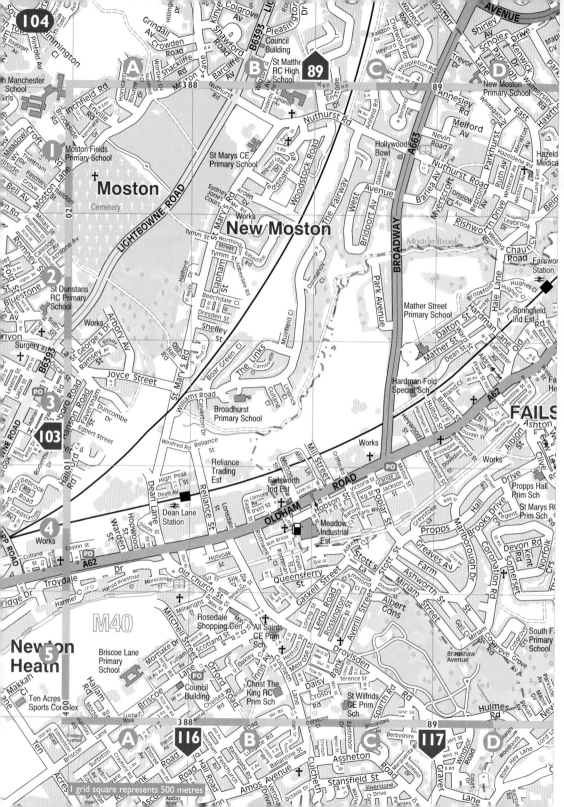

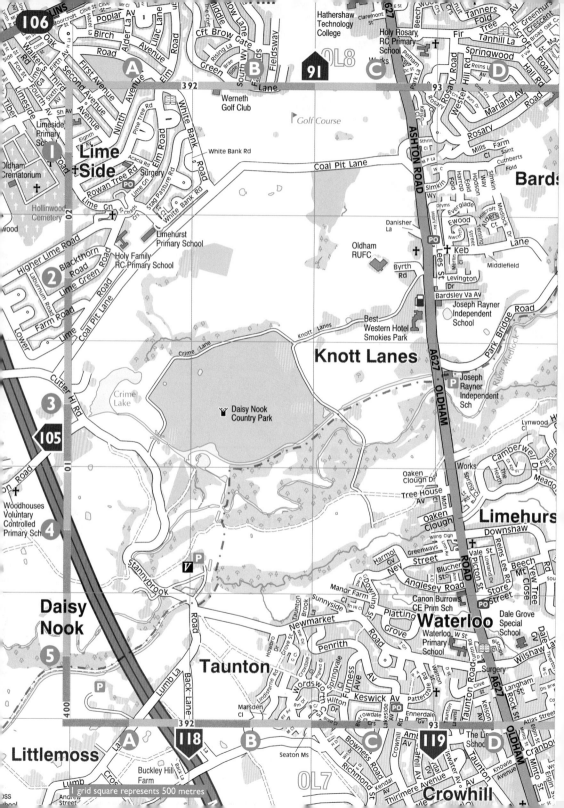

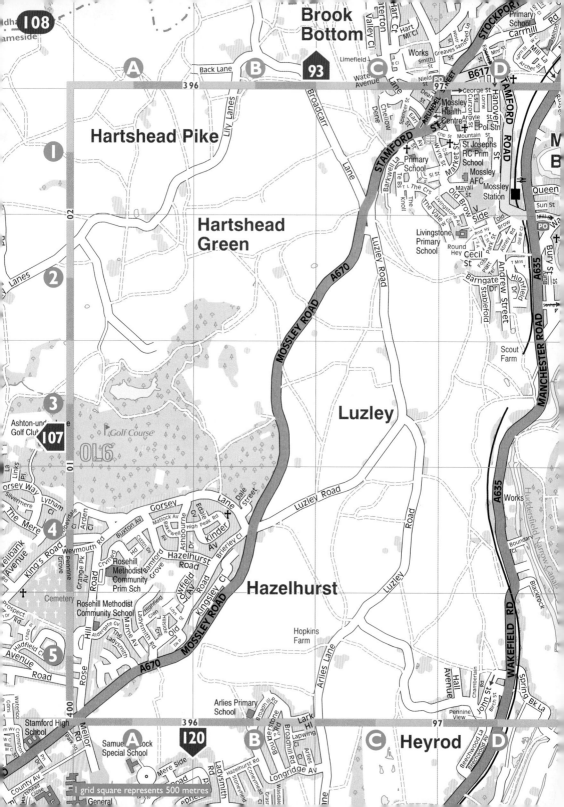

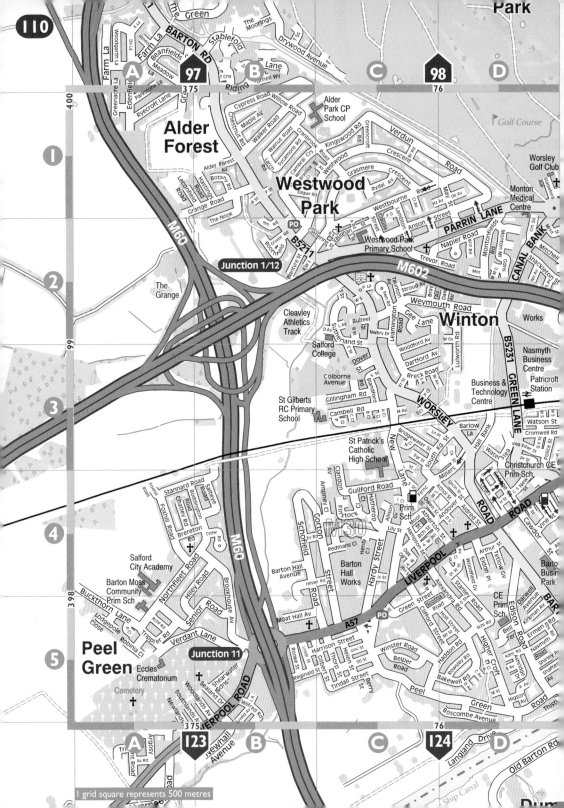

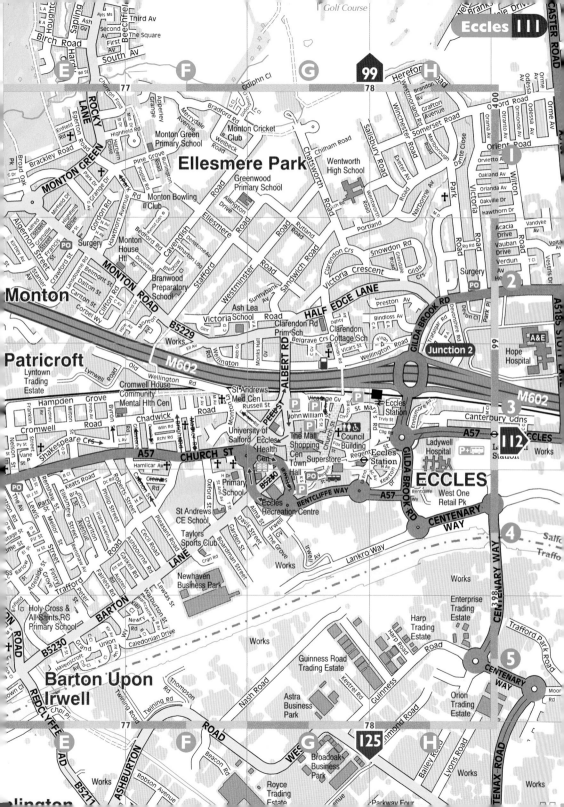

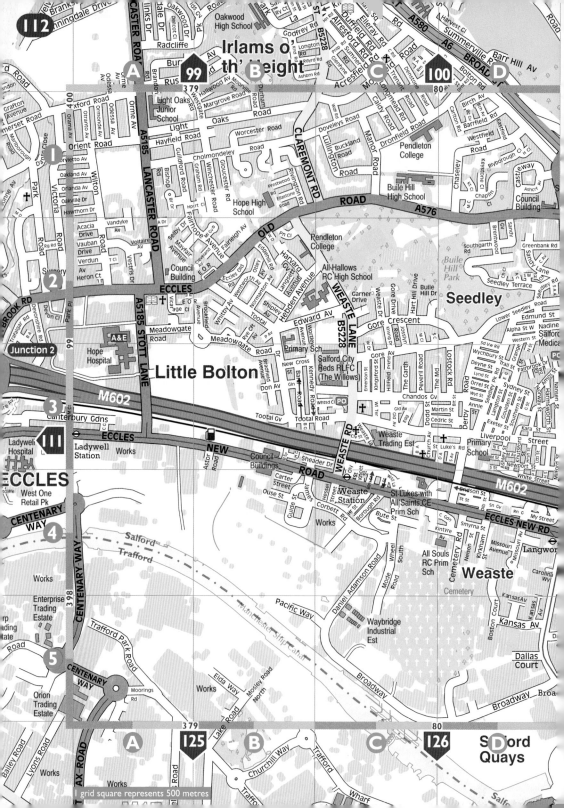

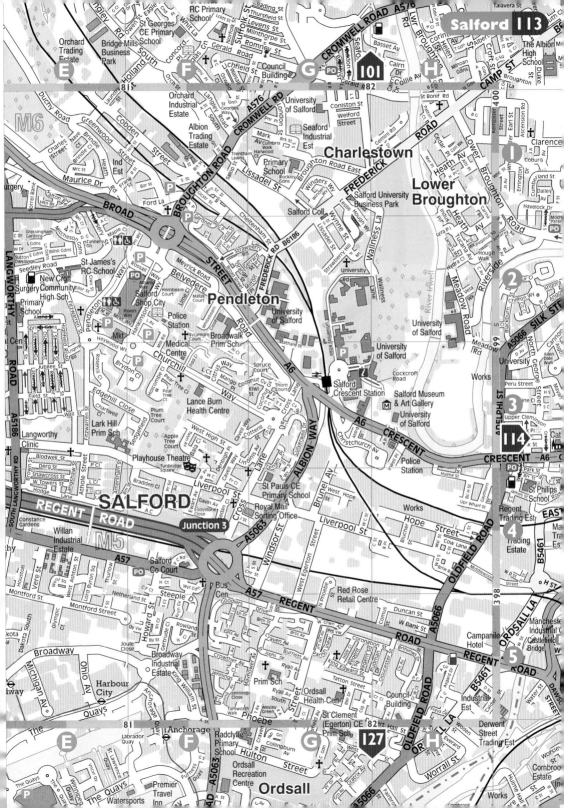

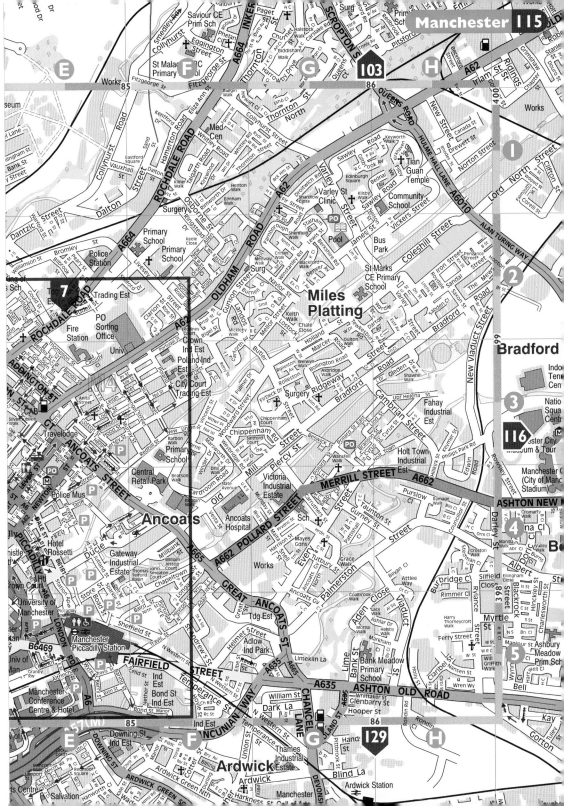

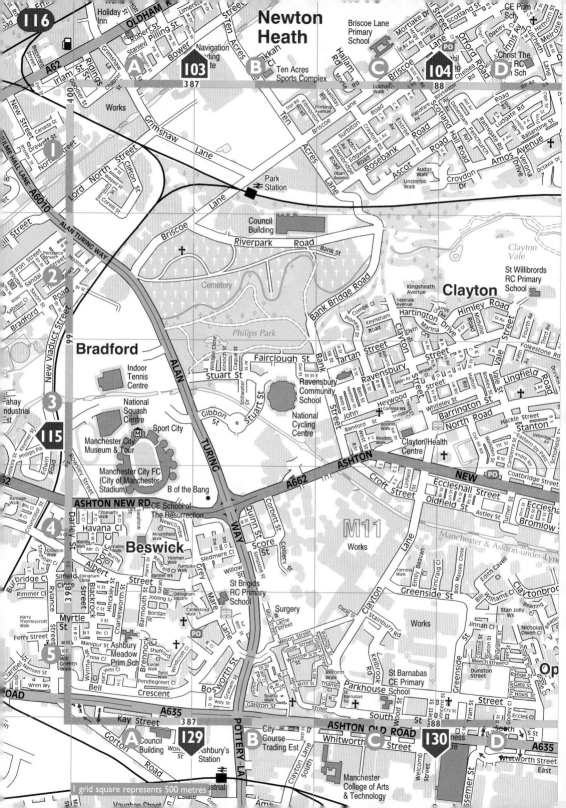

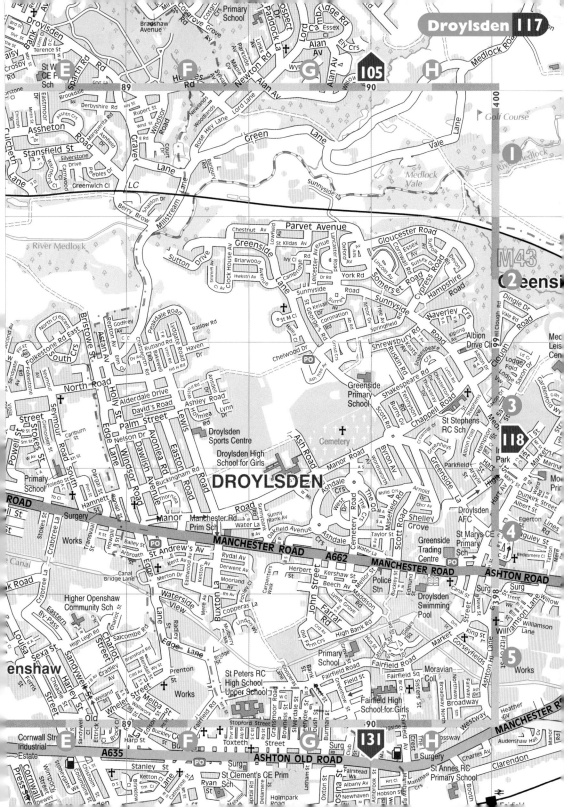

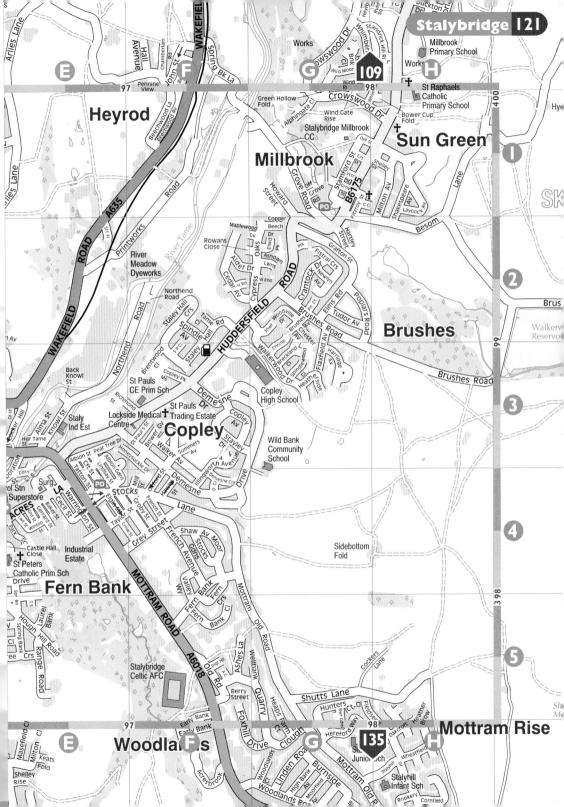

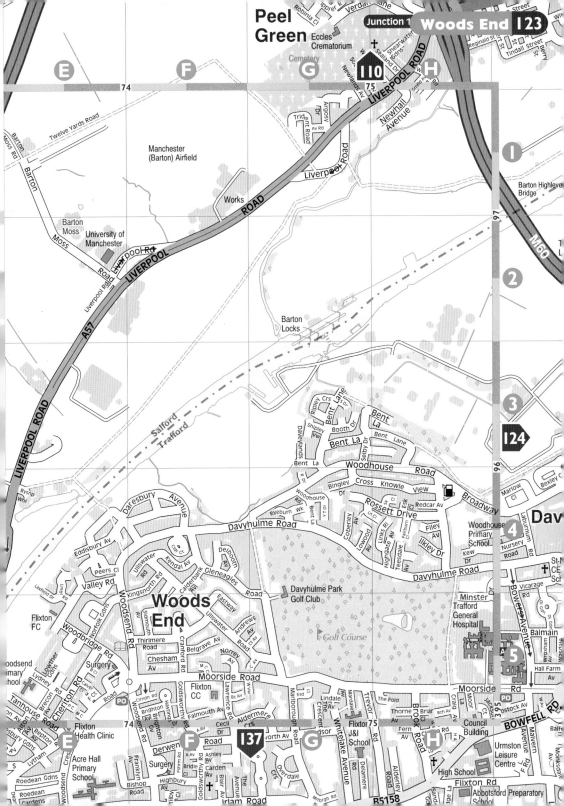

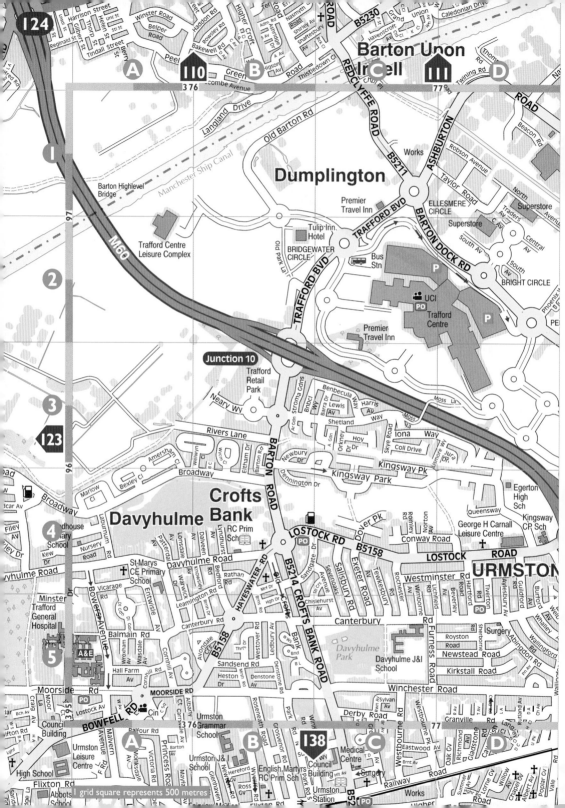

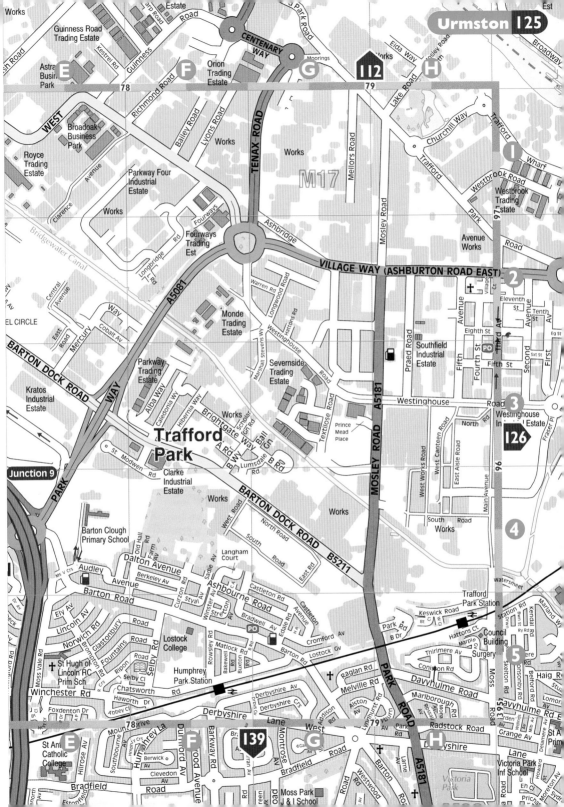

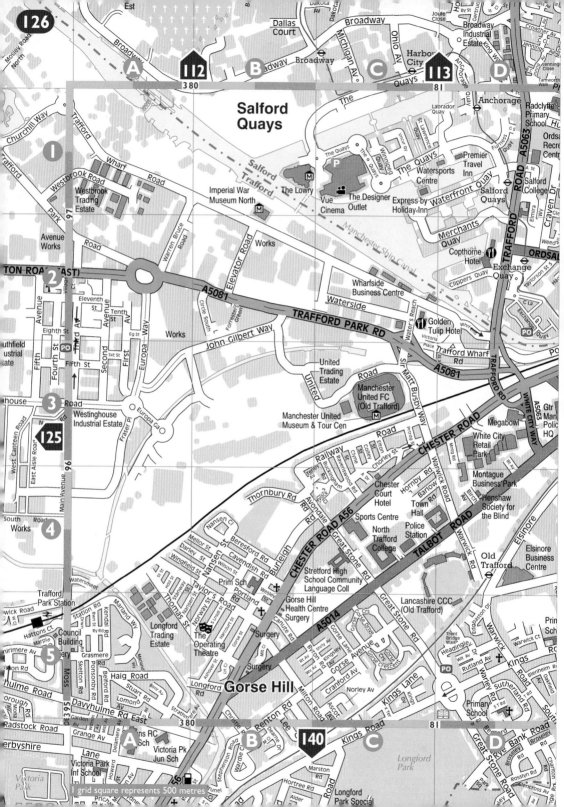

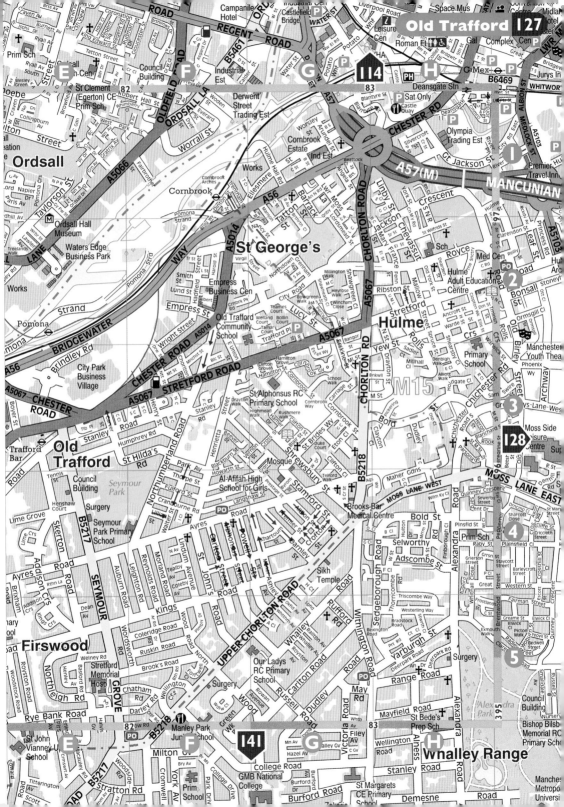

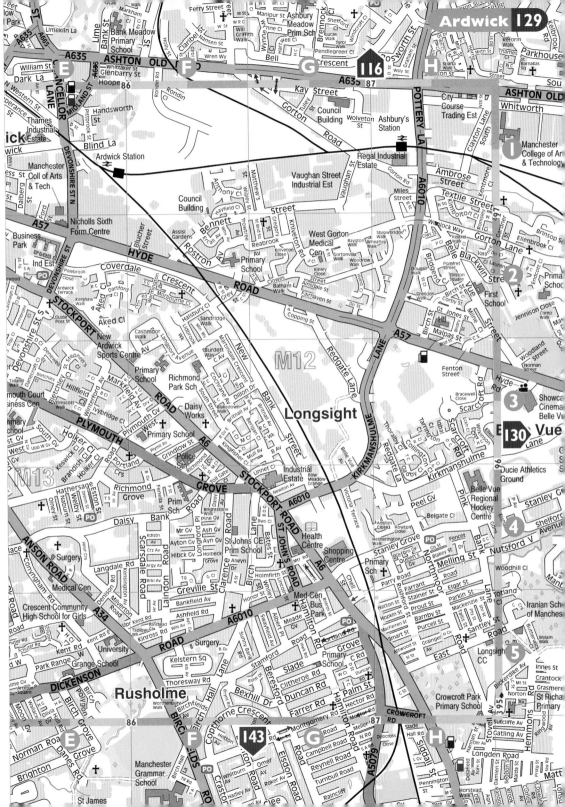

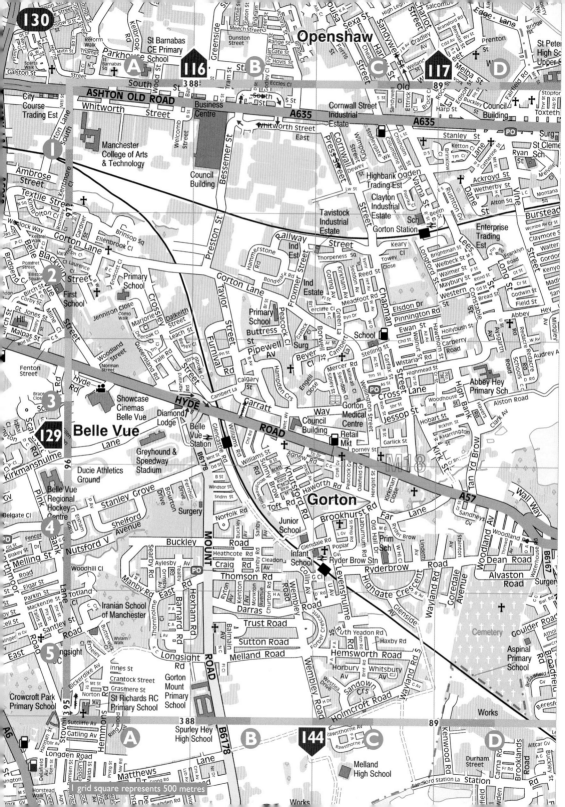

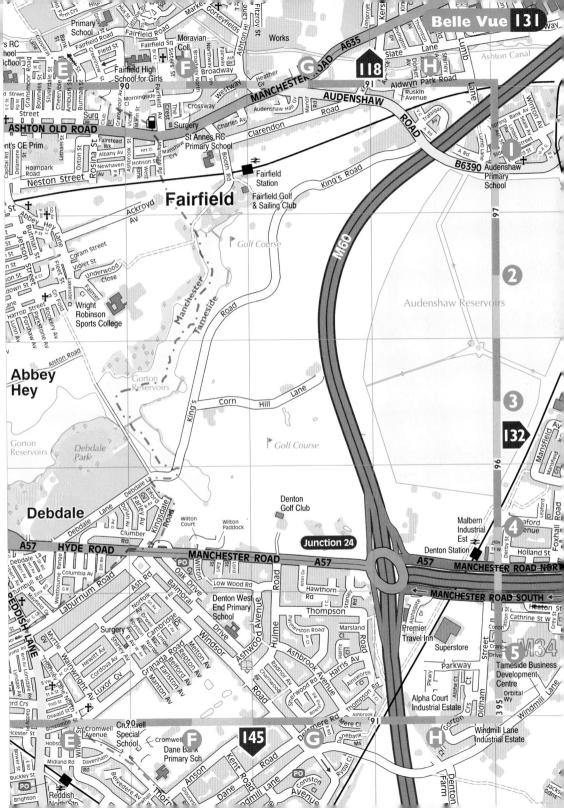

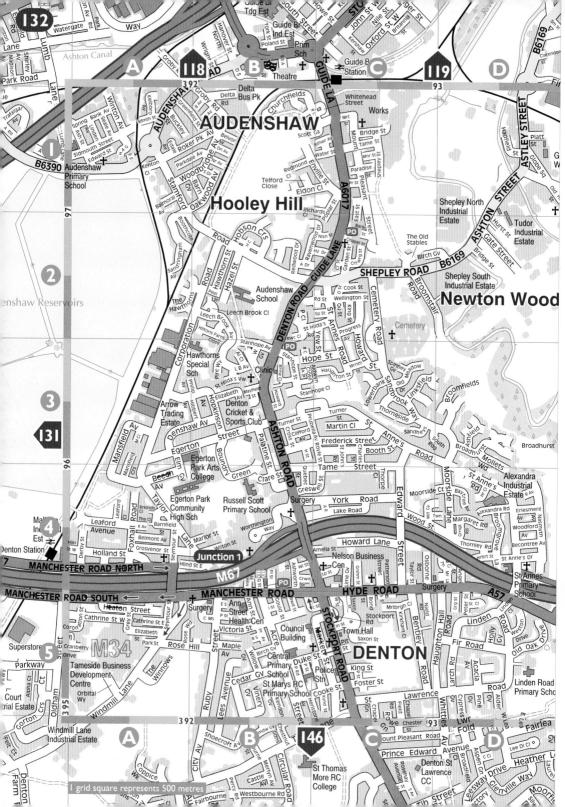

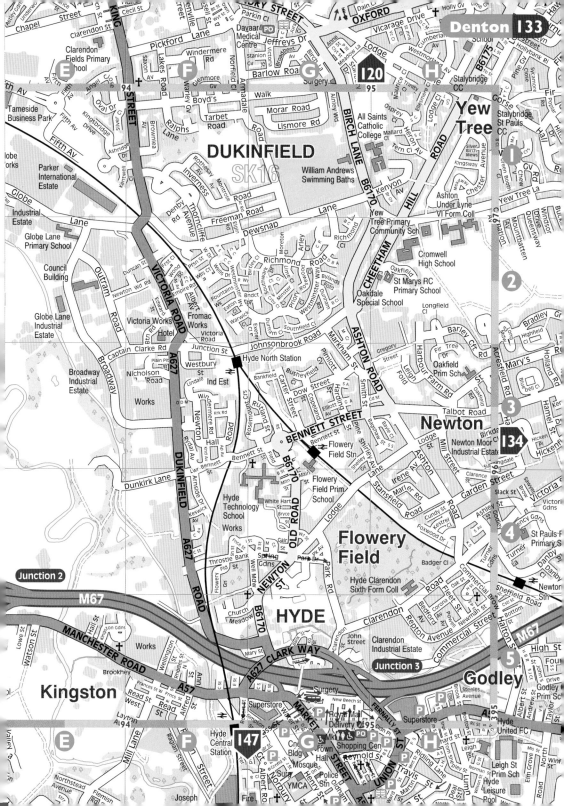

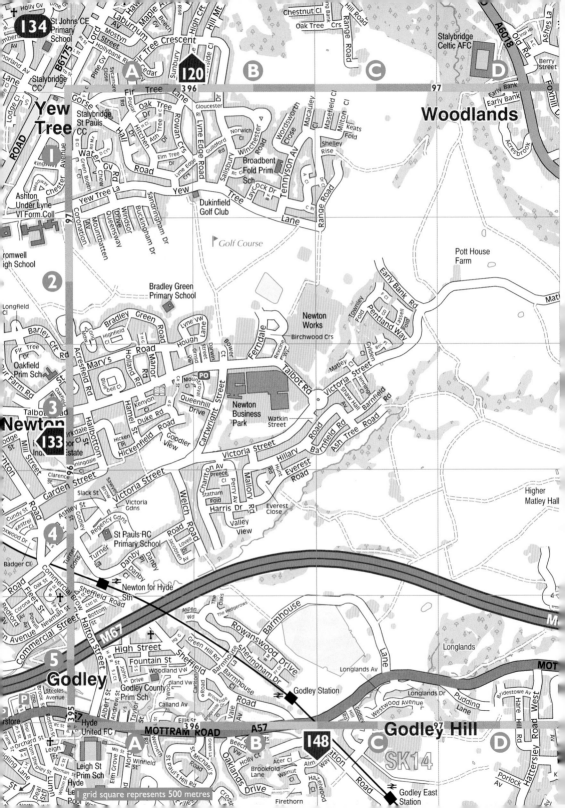

121

Mottram Rise

Mallbank Road

Heaps Farm Ct

Quarry

Woodlands Clough

Drive

Linden Road

High Bank

Burnside

Moorfield Av

Burnside Dr

Cockers Lane

Hunters Lane

Hereford Way

HVC CI

Oakcroft

Stalyhill Junior Sch

Stalyhill Infant Sch

Wheatfield

Stalyhill Av

Thistle CI

Rookery CI

Cornfield

Wildbank Chase

Fawns Keep

Heather Brow

Woodlands Road

Woodend Lane

MOTTRAM OLD ROAD

Broadacre

Meadway

Lwr Broadacre

Callowclough Rd

Matley

The Crescent

MOTTRAM ROAD

Blundering Lane

Bardsley Gate Av

Hill Vw

K F

The Mall

ey Lane

Woodend Dr

Harrop Edge

Roe Cross Green

ROE CROSS ROAD

Old Road

Hobson Moor Road

Dewsnap Lane

Rabbit Lane

Moorside Farm

Lan Gree

Hobson Mo Road

Hall Drive

Hall

Tollemache Rd

Mottram Old Hall

Hall Lane

Old Hall

Roe Cross

A6018

Ind Park

Four CI

Elm CI

Ash

Oak

Lodge Ct

BACK MOOR

B6174

STALYBRIDGE RD

Edge Road

Harrop

Edge Lane

Harrop Edge Road

Mottram in Longdendale

Meadowcroft

Rushycroft

Littlefields

T Crt

PO

Surgery

MOTTRAM MOO

HYDE ROAD

A57

Longdendale Recreation Centre

Longdale Road

ASHWORTH LANE

Atherton

Ford

Back La

Chambers Ct

Council Building

Market Street

Church Brow

Cemetery

Warhill

7

RAM ROAD

A57

Wardle Brook

Sundial Av

Wardle Brook Av

Padstow CI

Camborne Road

Further Lane

Dawlish

Colbourne Gv

Garnett Road

Arundale Primary School

Arundale Close

Arundale Grove

Vannes Gv

Lowry Grove

Kennedy Sq

Kennedy

Kenedy

Abbey Gdns

Cst CI

Mottram CE Primary School

Windlow Av

Stringe

ladbottom

littlemoor

St Ja Catholic Primary School

Doniton Av

Chrtn CI

Silverton Road

Torrington Drive

Hattersley Health Clinic

East

Melandra Cres

Kenworthy CI

Callington

149

A560

Chain

wnt CI

Br CI

B6174

Mill Grove

Bar Lane

Stringer Avenue

M

Waterside

Alder Community

Hattersley

sbrdg

E

F

G

H

I

E

F

G

H

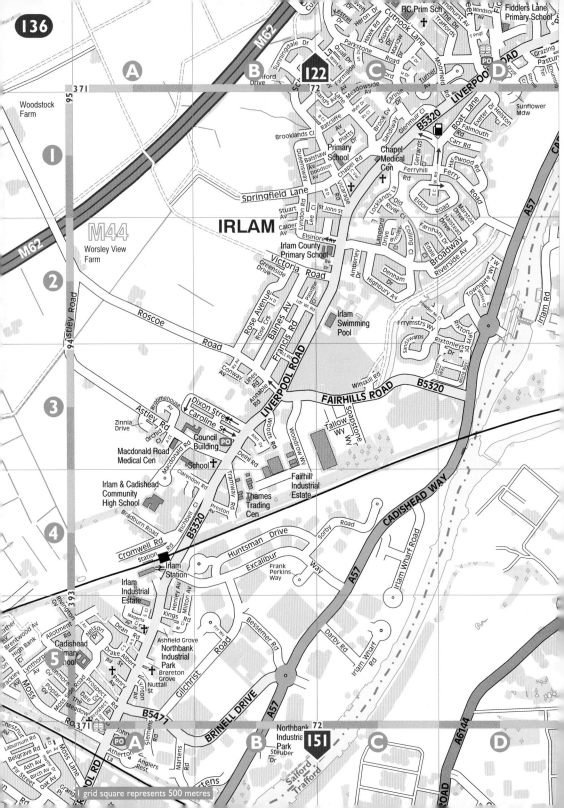

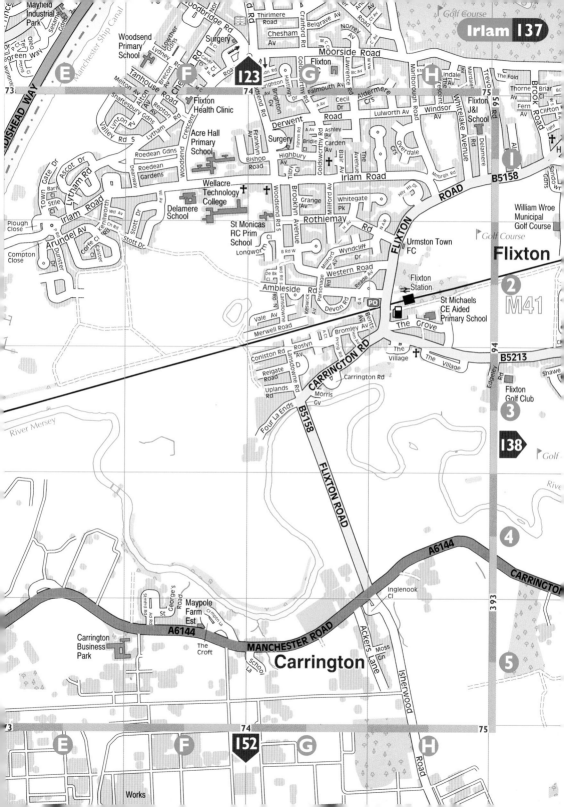

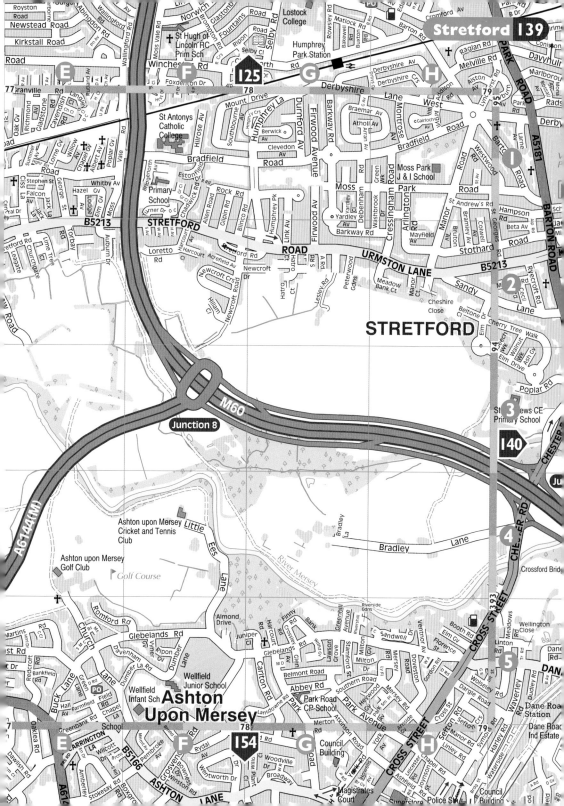

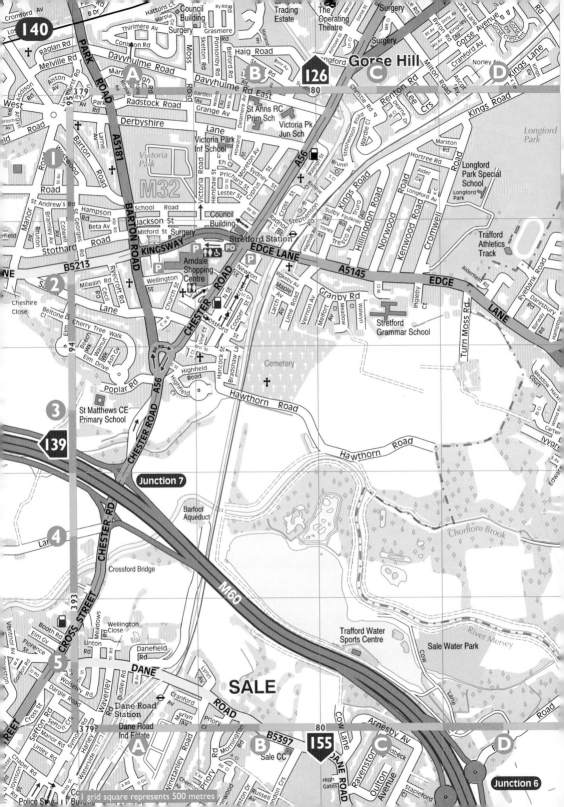

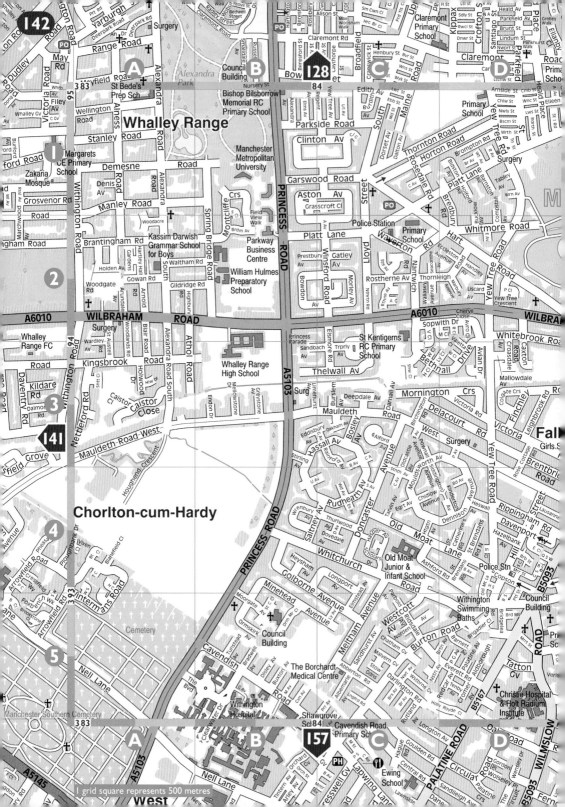

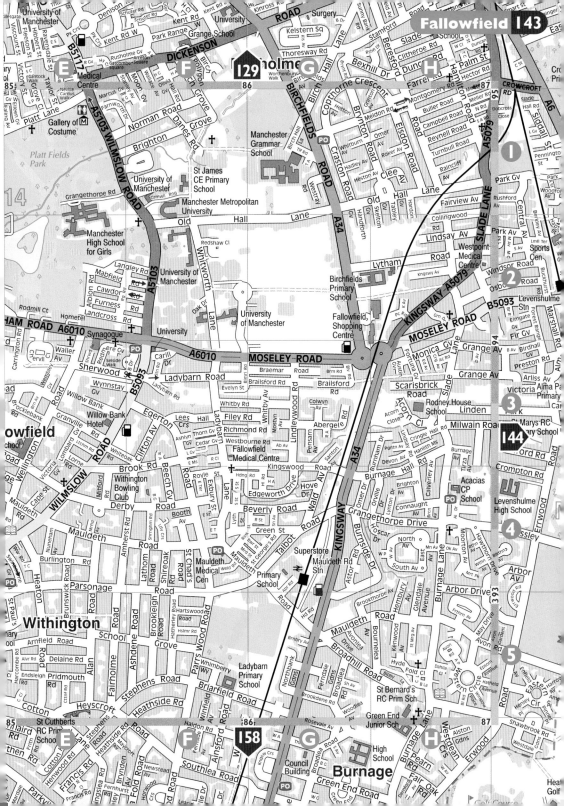

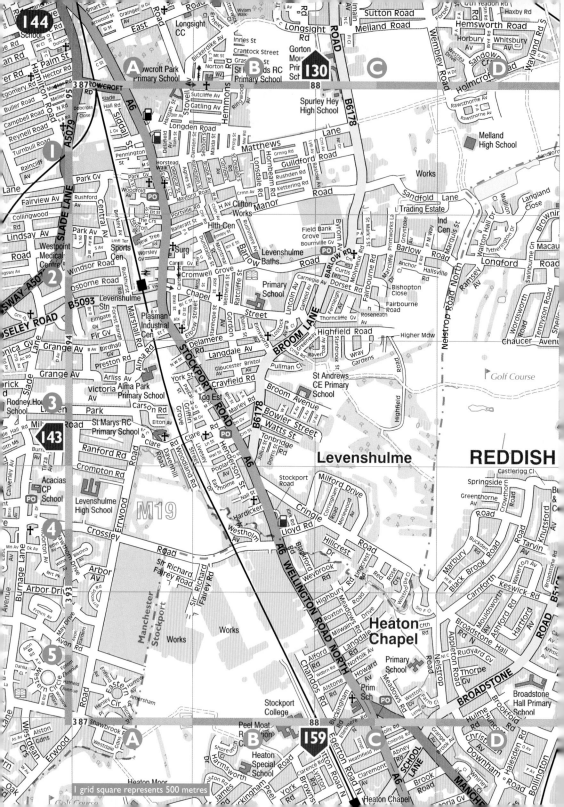

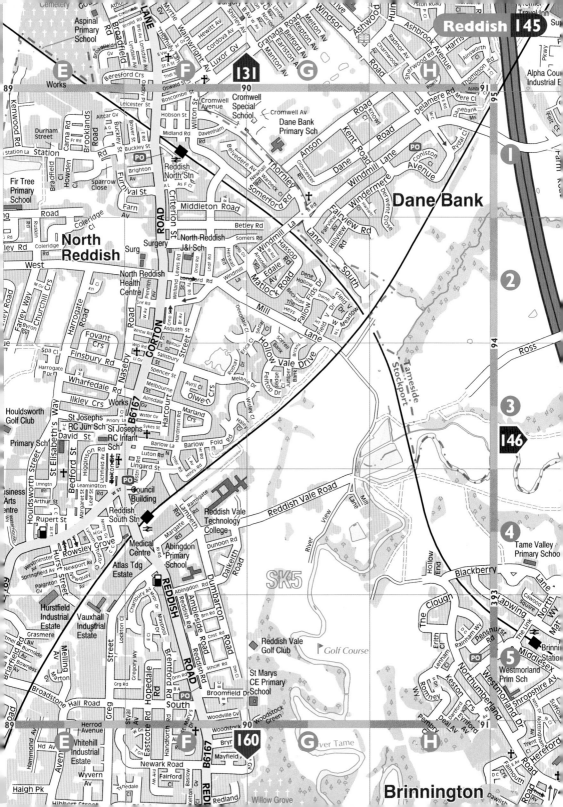

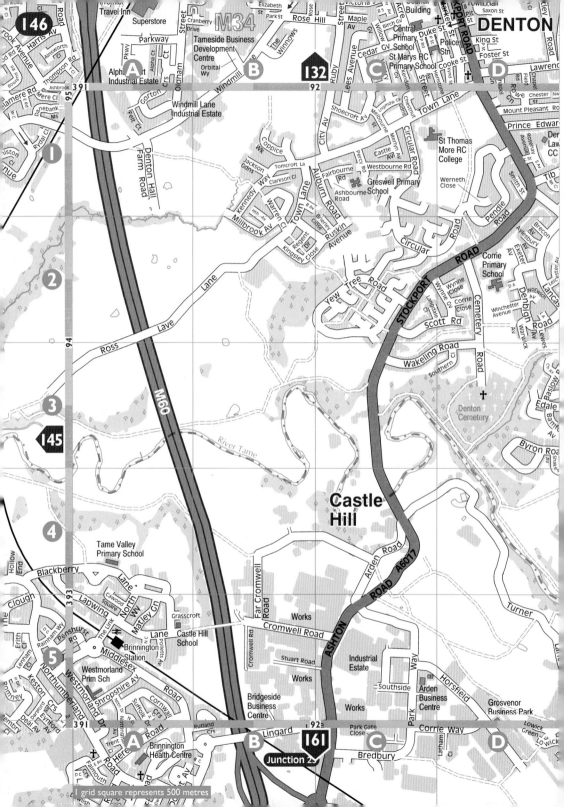

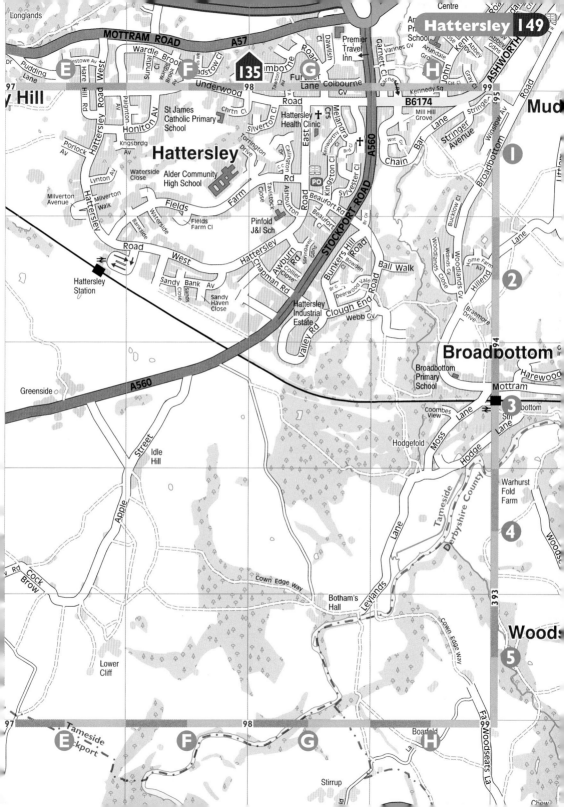

Glazebrook

Glazebrook Station

The Rhinewood Country House Hotel 370

St Mary's CE Primary School

Cadishead

Cadishead Primary School

Northbank Industrial Park

Cadishead Recreation Centre

Council Building

Dudley Road

LIVERPOOL ROAD B5320

Our Lady of Lourdes Catholic Prim Sch

Lock Lane

Forest Gate Community Prim Sch

St Helens CE Prim Sch

Manchester Ship Canal

Allinfare

Collins Green

Holly Bank Caravan Park

Warburton Park

Heathlands Farm

Jack Hey Gate Farm

1 grid square represents 500 metres

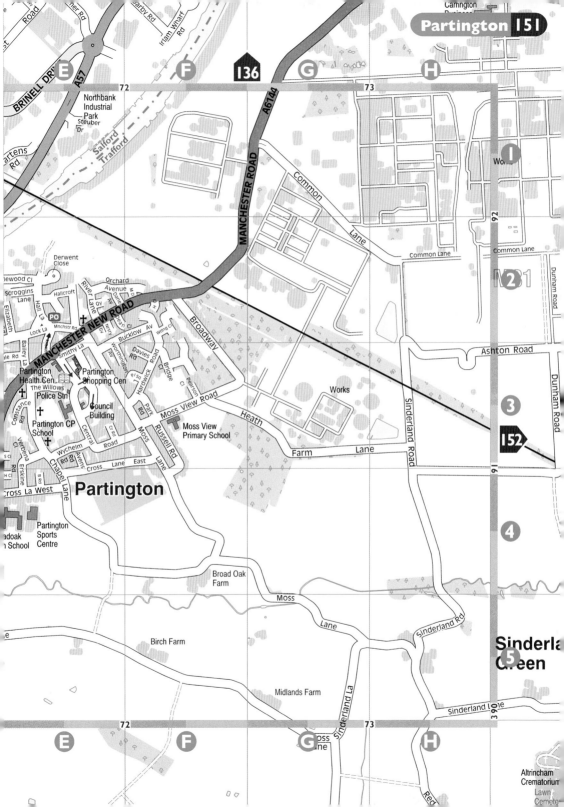

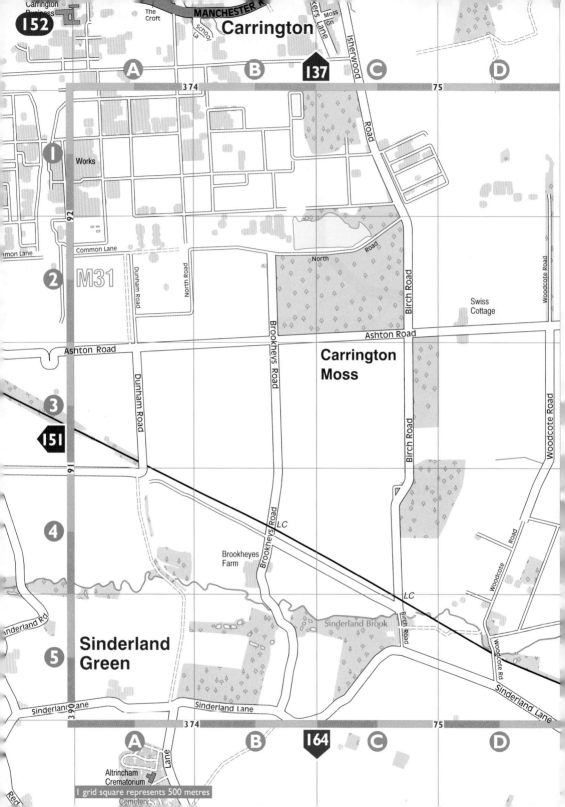

Carrington

152

The Croft

Carrington Business

152

MANCHESTER R

Carrington

A   374   B   137   C   75   D

1   Works

92

Common Lane

Common Lane

North Road

2   M31

Dunham Road

North Road

North   Road

Birch Road

Swiss Cottage

Woodcote Road

Ashton Road

Ashton Road

Brookheys Road

Carrington Moss

3   151

91

Birch Road

Woodcote Road

4

Brookheys Road

LC

Brookheys Farm

LC

Woodcote Road

Woodcote Rd

inderland Rd

Sinderland Green

5

Sinderland Brook

Birch Road

Woodcote Rd

Sinderland Lane

Sinderland Lane

Sinderland Lane

Sinderland Lane

Lane

90

374   A   75

A   B   164   C   D

Altrincham Crematorium

Red

I grid square represents 500 metres

Cemetery

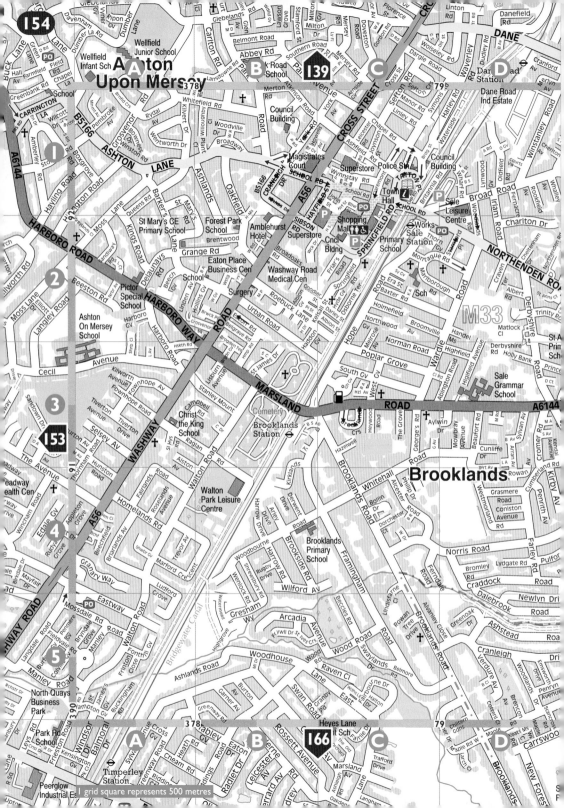

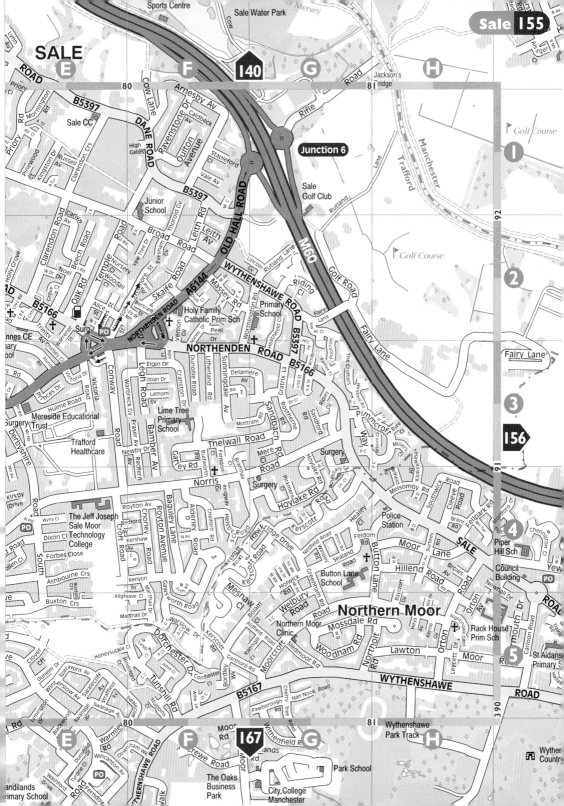

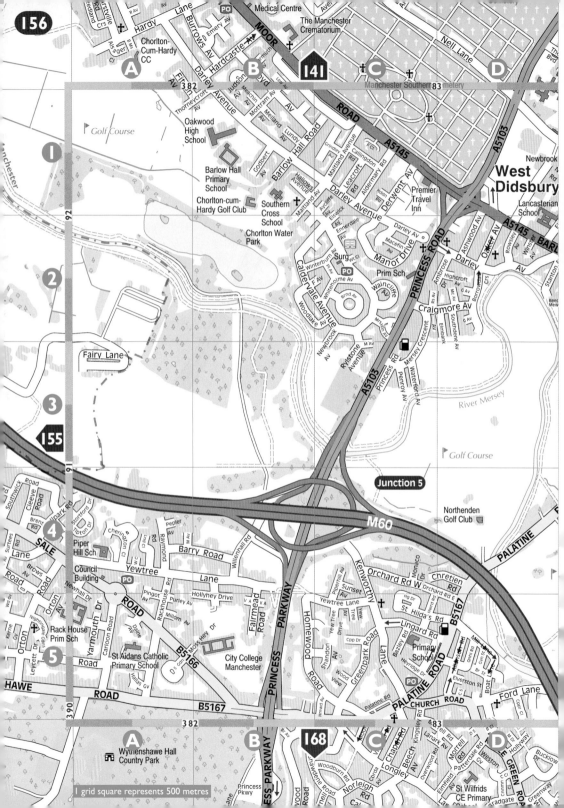

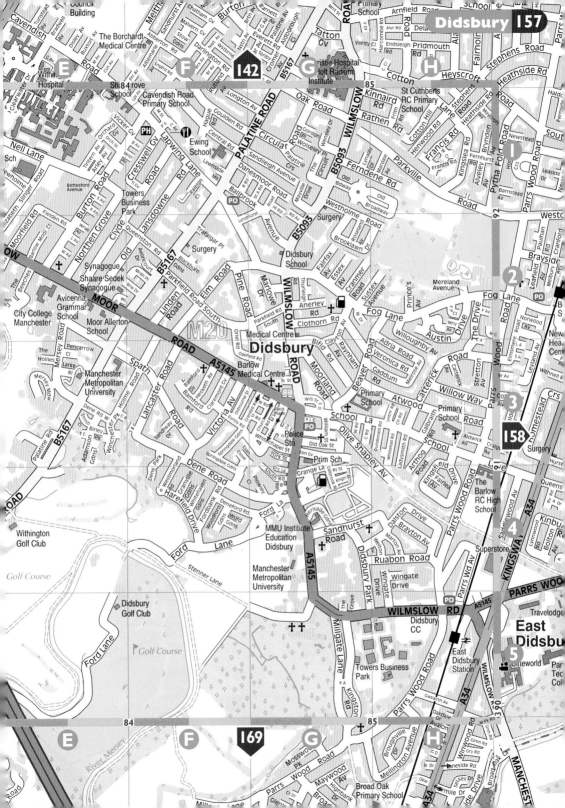

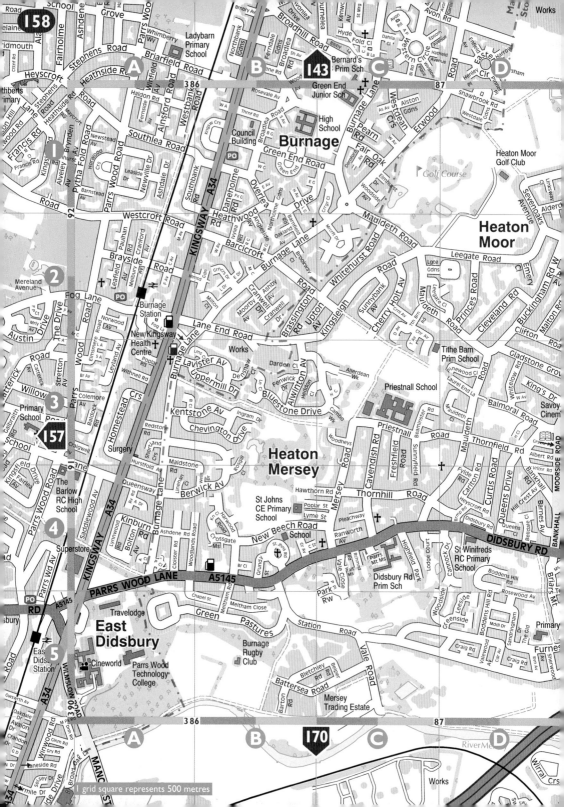

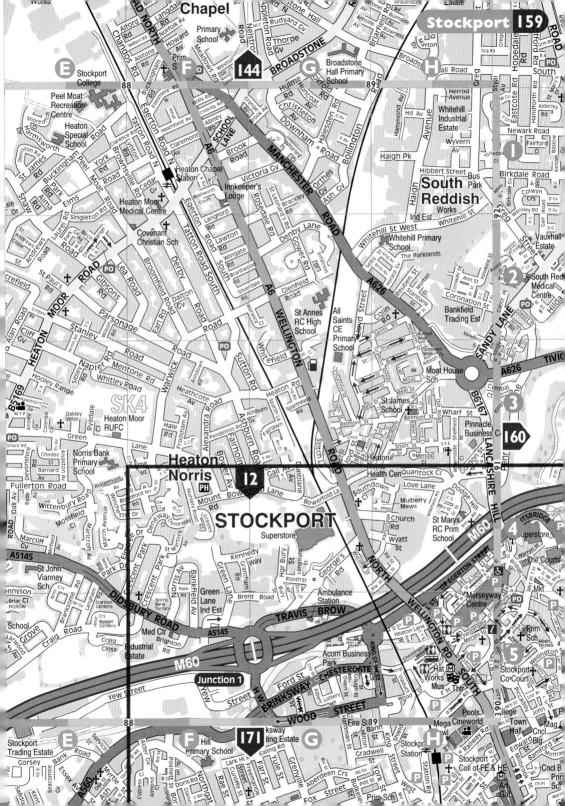

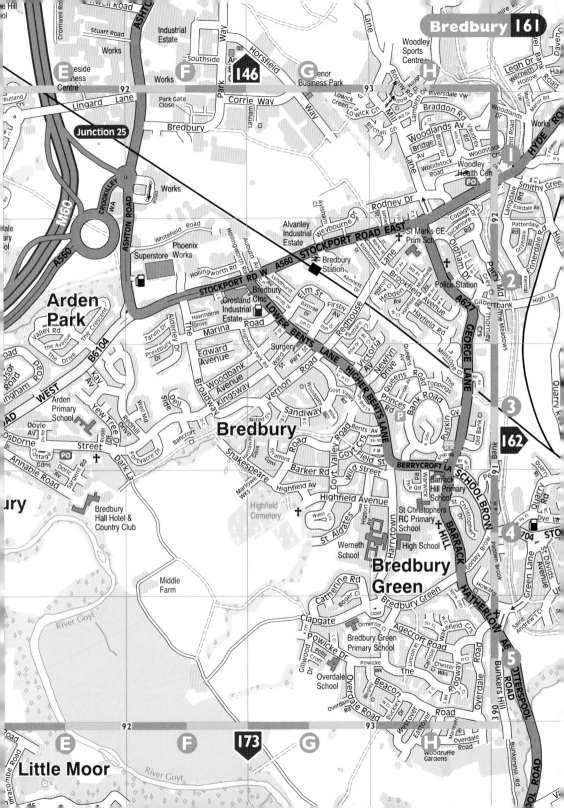

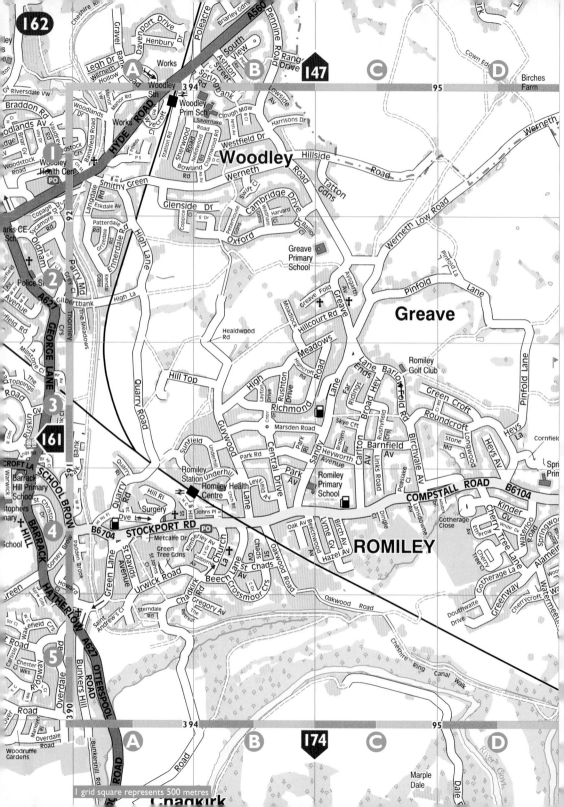

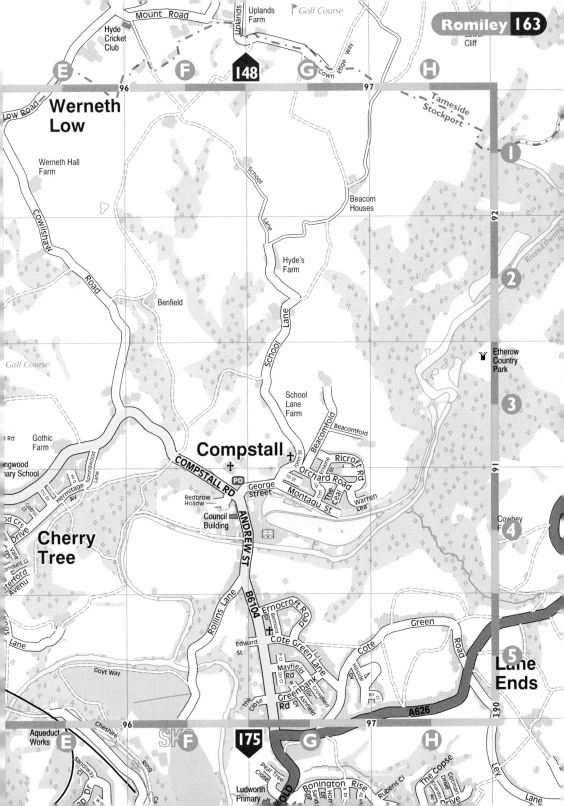

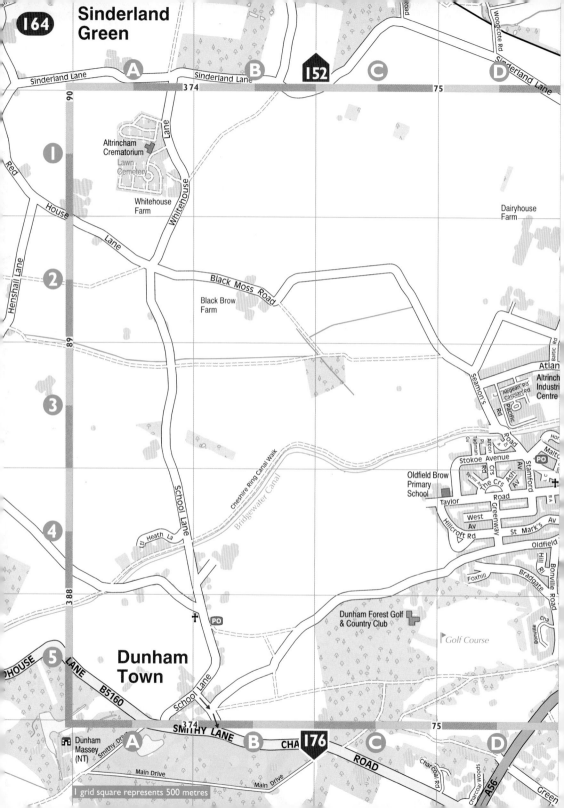

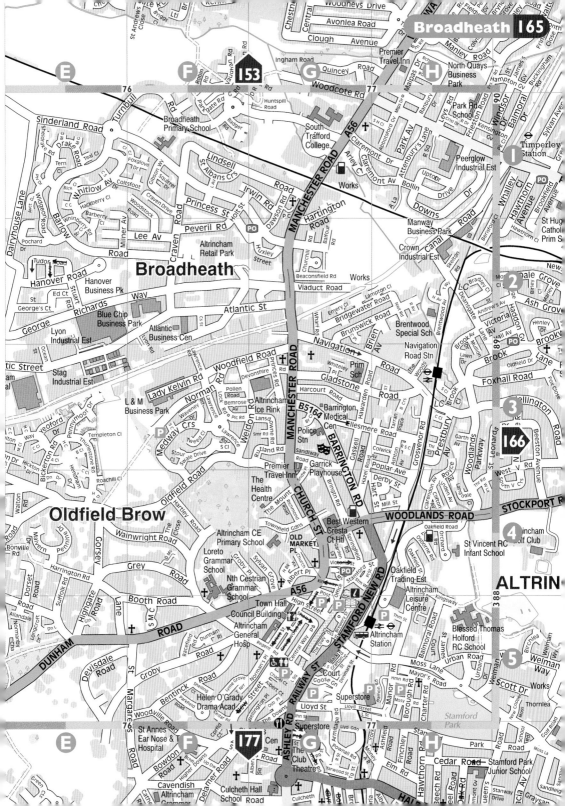

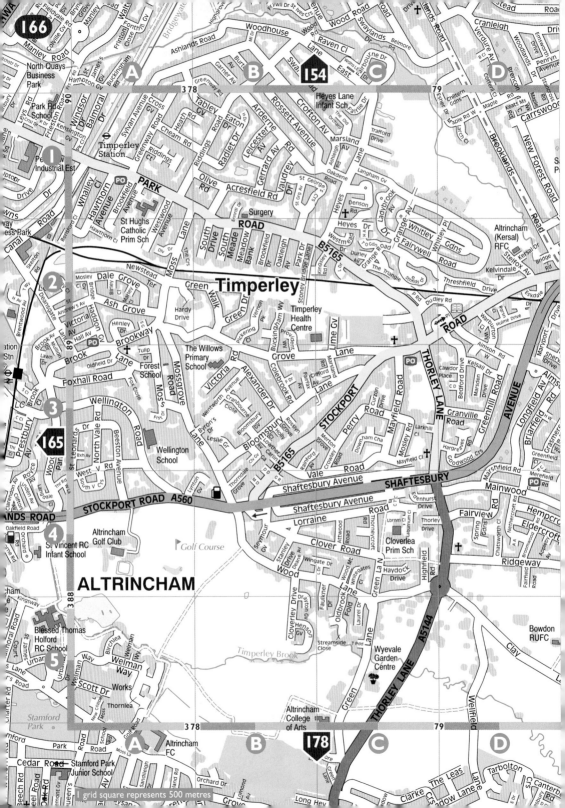

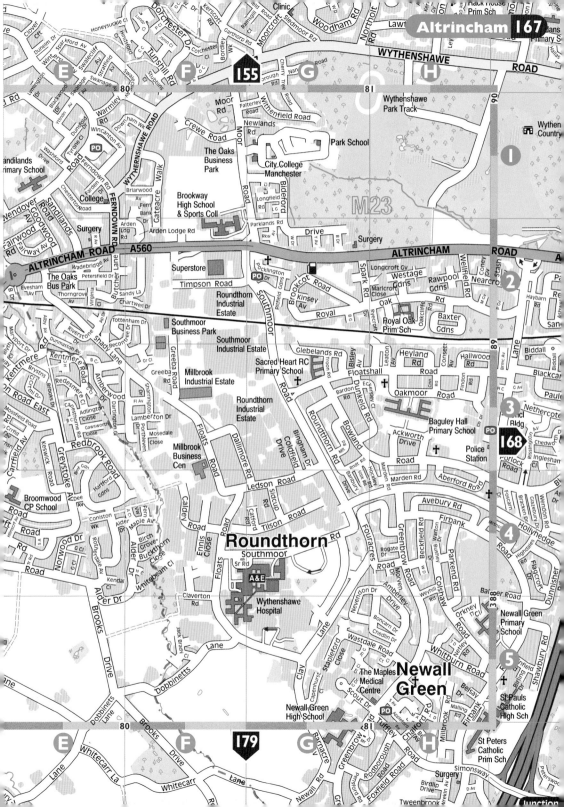

WYTHENSHAWE ROAD

Clinic

Woodham Rd

Dorchester Dr

Kerscott

Carthord Rd

Honeysuckle Cl

Ramsgill Rd

Sledmoor Rd

Moorcroft

Northolt

Lawton

Northolt

Hack House

Prim Sch

E

F

155

G

H

I

Moor Rd

Falterley Road

Wythenfield Road

Newlands Rd

Park School

Wythenshawe
Park Track

Wythen
Country

Crewe Road

Moor Road

The Oaks
Business
Park

City College
Manchester

M23

Brookway
High School
& Sports Coll

Bideford Rd

Longfield Rd

Surgery

Parklands Rd

Arden
Lodge
Dr

Arden Lodge Rd

Drive

Surgery

ALTRINCHAM ROAD A560

ALTRINCHAM ROAD A

Superstore

Pocklington

Brookcot Road

Spark Rd

Longcroft Gv

Westage
Gdns

Rawpool
Gdns

Wellfield Rd

Coney
Gv

Nearcro

2

The Oaks
Bus Park

Timpson Road

Roundthorn
Industrial
Estate

Kinsey
Av

Royal

Oak

Marlcroft
Close

Ryecroft

Oakcliffe
Rd

Baxter
Gdns

Haybarn
Dr

San

Southmoor
Business Park

Southmoor
Industrial Estate

Southmoor
Road

Glebelands Rd

Bisley

Floatshall

Heyland
Rd

Hallwood
Rd

Consett

Biddall
Dr

Blackcar

Sacred Heart RC
Primary School

Bardon
Rd

Dunkeld Rd

Troon Rd

Oakmoor

Findon
Rd

Paul

Millbrook
Industrial Estate

Roundthorn
Industrial
Estate

Greeba Road

Lamberton Dr

Mosedale
Close

Coldfield
Drive

Roundthorn
Road

Bowland

Baguley Hall
Primary School

Ackworth
Drive

Road

Police
Station

Nethercote

Bldg

Chedwo

Ingleshan

3

168

Millbrook
Business
Cen

Dallimore Road

Ledson Road

Sidcup
Rd

Marden Rd

Aberford Road

Porlock
Road

Broomwood
CP School

Caldey
Road

Ennis
Close

Catford
Rd

Tilson Road

Avebury Rd

Firbank

Hollyhedge

Road

4

Roundthorn

Southmoor
Sr Rd

A&E

Four acres

Greenbrow Rd

Beckfield Rd

Parkend Rd

Colshaw

Orkney

Newall Green
Primary
School

5

Wythenshawe
Hospital

Claverton
Rd

Clay

Lane

Stapleford
Close

Wastdale Road

Whitburn Road

Netley

St Pauls
Catholic
High Sch

Dobbinetts

Dobbinets
Lane

**Newall
Green**

The Maples
Medical
Centre

Newall Green
High School

Tuffley

Chalford Rd

Millbrook Rd

St Peters
Catholic
Prim Sch

Surgery

Simonsway

E

F

179

G

H

Whitecarr Lane

Whitecarr La

Brooks Drive

Whitecarr Lane

Greenbrow

Rodborough
Road

Newall

Foxfield Road

Birdlip
Rd

Tweenbrook

Junction

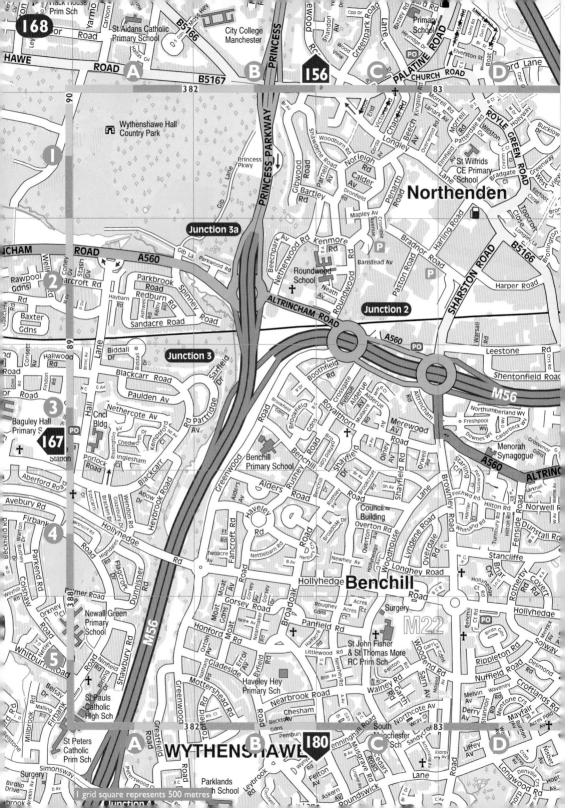

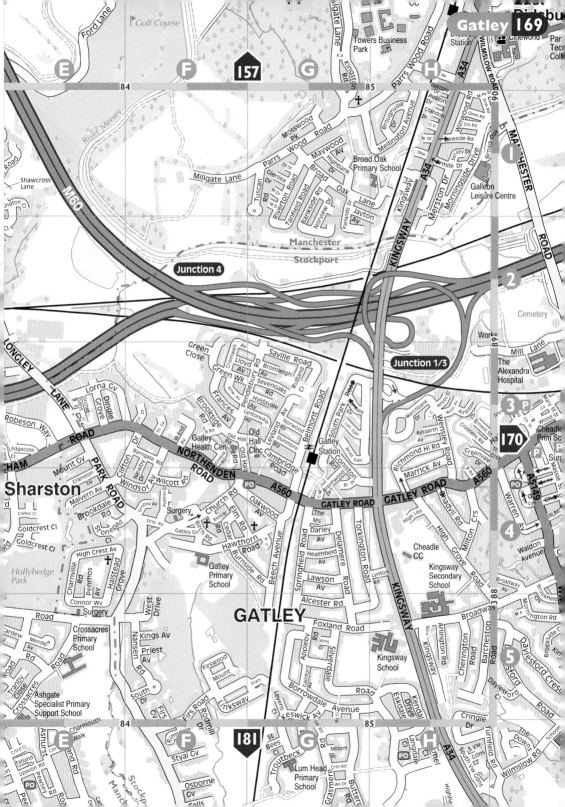

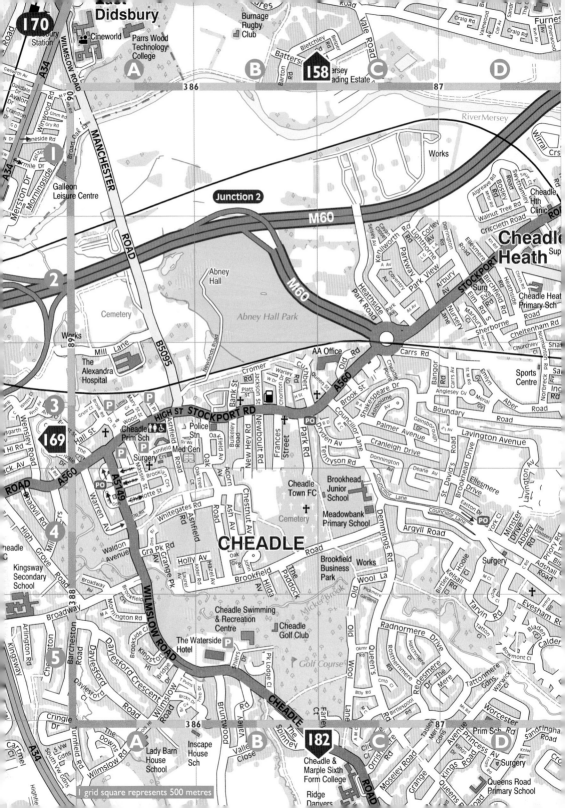

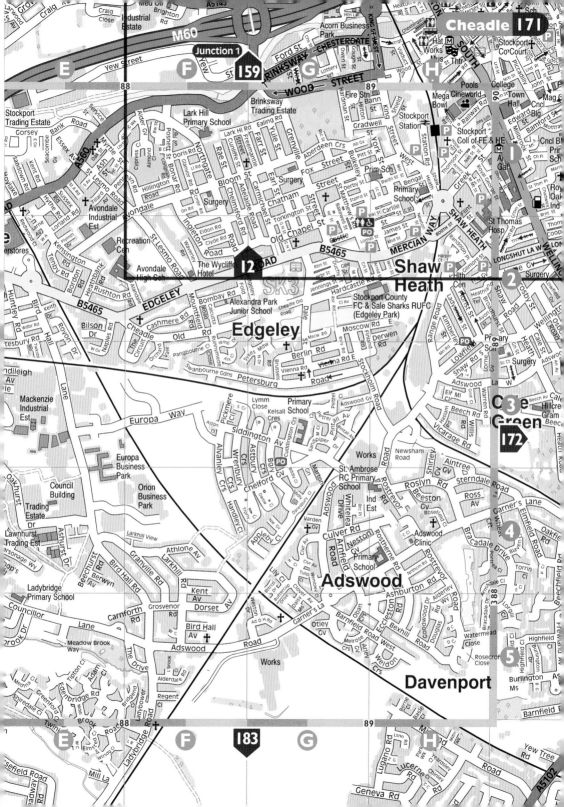

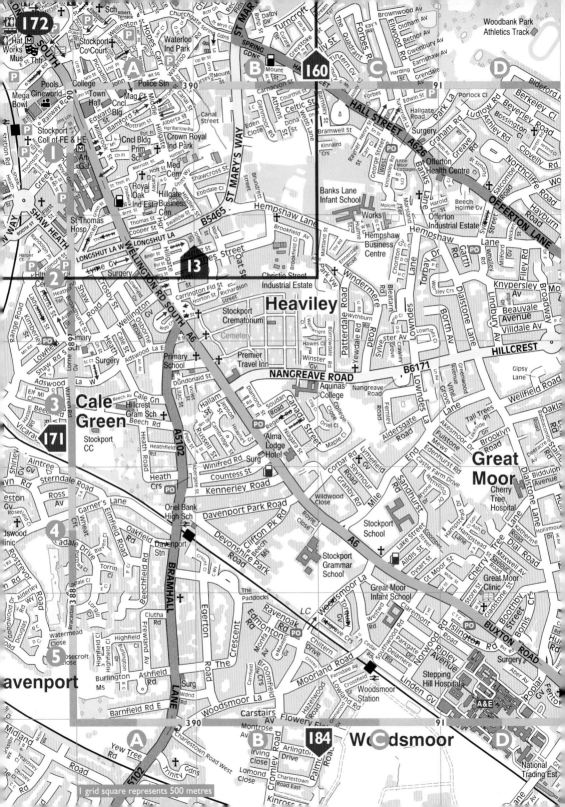

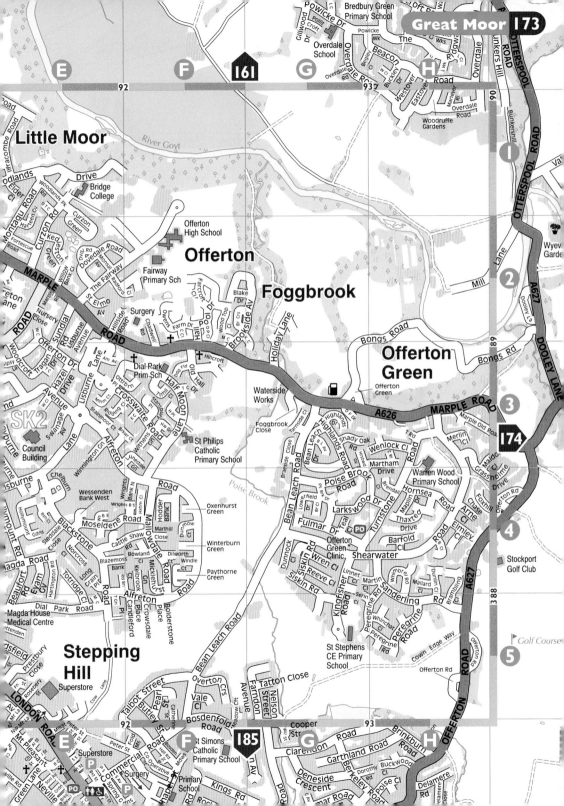

Bredbury Green
Primary School

Powicke Dr

Overdale
School

The

Beacon

Woodruffe
Gardens

Overdale
Road

Little Moor

River Goyt

Bridge
College

Drive

Curzon
Green

Offerton
High School

Offerton

Fairway
Primary Sch

Foggbrook

Surgery

MARPLE

Bongs Road

**Offerton
Green**

Offerton
Green

Bongs Rd

ROAD

Dial Park
Prim Sch

Hillcroft

Waterside
Works

A626 **MARPLE ROAD**

Marple Old Road

SK2

Council
Building

St Philips
Catholic
Primary School

Foggbrook
Close

174

Bean Leach Road

Wenlock Cl

Merlin
Cl

Warren Wood
Primary School

Crasshelme
Drive

Wessenden
Bank West

Oxenhurst
Green

Poise Brook

Poise Brook
Road

Martham
Drive

Hornsea

Thaxted

Chase

Arne

Elmley

Foxhill

Moseldene
Road

Larkswood Dr

Turnstone

Drive

Winterburn
Green

Fulmar Dr

PO

Offerton
Green
Clinic

Barfold

Shearwater

Stockport
Golf Club

Paythorne
Green

Blackstone

Alfreton
Place

Dunnock

Wren Cl

Reeve Cl

Siskin Rd

Kingfisher

Linnet

Martin

Serin

Peregrine

Whinchat

Sanderling

Mallard

Brambling

Golf Course

Magda House
Medical Centre

Dial
Park Road

Crowsdale
Place

Bolderstone
Place

Peregrine
Rd

A627

**Stepping
Hill**

Superstore

St Stephens
CE Primary
School

Cown Edge Way

Offerton Rd

5

Talbot Street

Overton Crs

Vale
Cl

Tatton Close

Farndon
Avenue

Nelson
Street

Bosdenfold
Road

Cooper
Str

LONDON ROAD

Mt Pleasant

Superstore

Green Lane

Neville

PO

Commercial

Surgery

185

St Simons
Catholic
Primary School

Primary
School

Kings Rd

Clarendon
Road

Garthland Road

Brinkburn
Road

Berkeley
Rd

Deneside
Crescent

OFFERTON ROAD

E   F   161   G   H

92   932

I

Mill   Lane

Bunkers Hill

OTTERSPOOL   **ROAD**

Wyev
Garde

A627

Dooley Ln

DOOLEY LANE

2

89

3

388

4

E   F   185   G   H

92   93

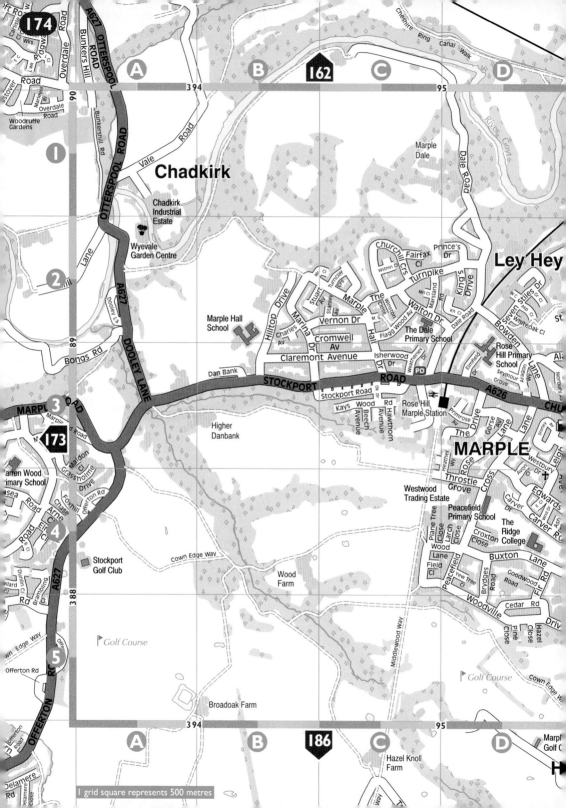

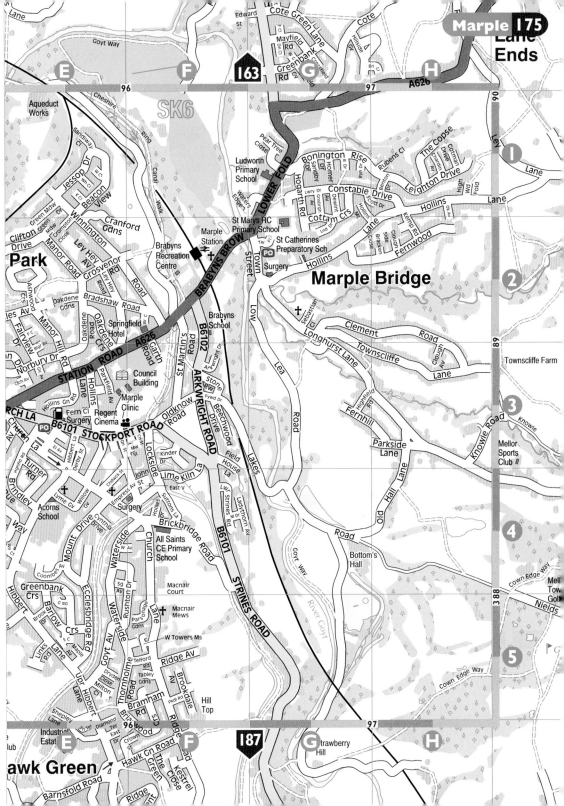

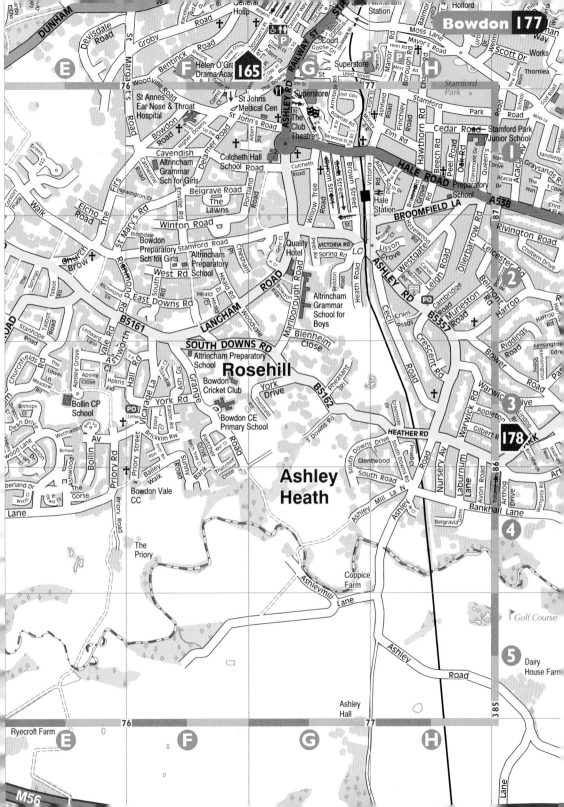

DUNHAM

Devisdale Road

Groby Road

Bentinck Road

St Margaret's Rd

Woodville Road

Helen O'Gra Drama Aca

165

RAILWAY ST

ASHLEY RD

G

Central Way

General Hosp

Regent

Court

Goose Gn

Superstore

Superstore

HALE ROAD

Manor Rd

Borough Rd

Chan

Mayor's Road

Stamford Park

Moss Lane

Balmo

Holford

Scott Dr

Works

Thornlea

E

F

H

St Annes Ear Nose & Throat Hospital

Bowdon Road

Higher Downs

St Johns Medical Cen

St John's Road

Albert Rd

Cedar Road

The Club Theatre

Cavendish

Altrincham Grammar Sch for Girls

Culcheth Hall School

Culcheth Road

Delamer Road

Enville Rd

Portland Road

Belgrave Road

The Lawns

Willow Tree Road

Brown Street

Bold Street

Hawthorn Rd

Beech Rd

Peel Road

Finchley Rd

Stamford Park Junior School

Stamford Park

I

Graysands Rd

Acacia Av

The Hvn

Winton Road

Church Brow

Elcho Road

The Firs

Catherine Road

Newington Ct

St Mary's Rd

Bowdon Preparatory Sch for Girls

Richmond Gn

West Rd

Richmond East Downs Rd

Altrincham Preparatory School

Stamford Road

Chesham

Quality Hotel

Spring Rd

VICTORIA RD

Heath Road

Hale Station

BROOMFIELD LA

A538

Lisson Grove

Westgate

Hazelwood Rd

Leigh Road

Ollerbarrow Rd

Belmont Rd

Leicester Rd

Rivington Road

Chiltern drive

2

Harrop

Riddings Rd

Kensington Gdns

Kensington Pk

B5161

Talbot Road

Stanhope Road

Ledward Lane

Vale Rd

Ashworth

Heald Rd

LANGHAM ROAD

Woodvale

Marlborough Road

Bowdon St

Altrincham Grammar School for Boys

Blenheim Close

B5162

PO

Cambridge Rd

Murieston Road

B5357

Crescent Rd

Bower Rd

Harrop Rd

3

SOUTH DOWNS RD

Rosehill

Altrincham Preparatory School

Bowdon Cricket Club

York Drive

Pheasant

Theobald

Greenside

HEATHER RD

Warwick Rd

Appleton Dr

Gilbert Rd

Lindop

178

Bishops Cl

Bollin CP School

Dean Drive

The Lowes

Apsley Grove

Apsley Close

Hpkns Fld

PO

Grange Road

York Road

Eaton Rd

Vicarage La

Brickkiln Rw

Bailey Walk

Fletcher Drive

Thatcher Close

Bowdon CE Primary School

Ashley Heath

South Downs Drive

Glentwood

South Road

Nursery Av

Laburnum Lane

Avon Road

Arthog Drive

Bankhall Lane

4

Bollin Lane

Sunny Road

Bank

Priory Street

Priory Rd

Bowdon Vale CC

The Gorse

The Priory

Ashleymill Lane

Ashley Mill La

Belgravia

Tollington Rd

Golf Course

5

Dairy House Farm

Coppice Farm

Ashley Road

Ryecroft Farm

Ashley Hall

Ashley Road

Lane

E

F

G

H

M56

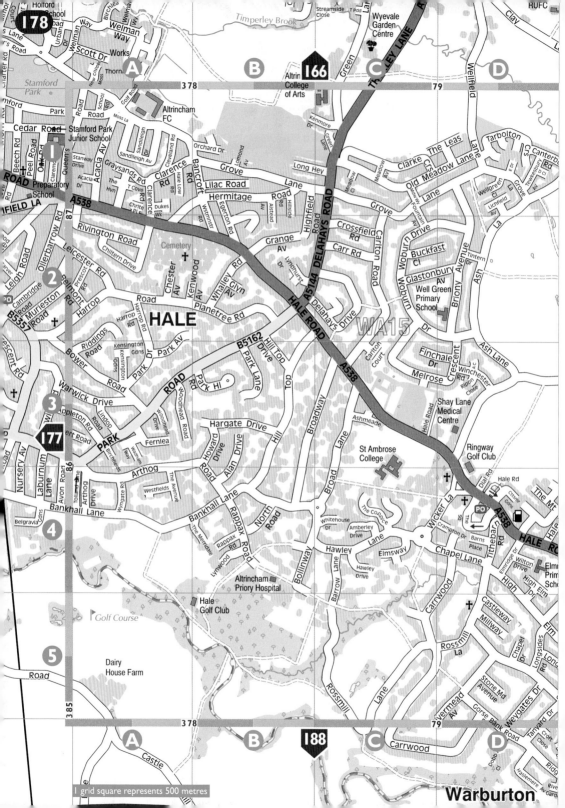

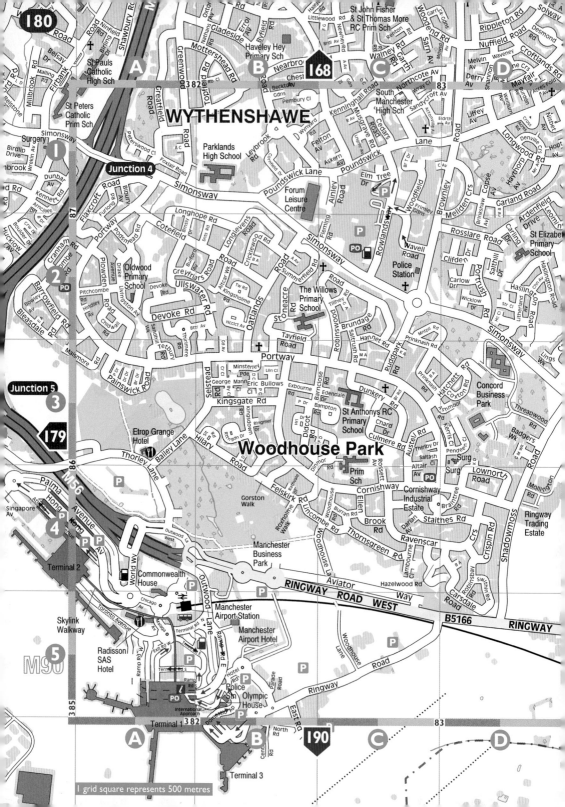

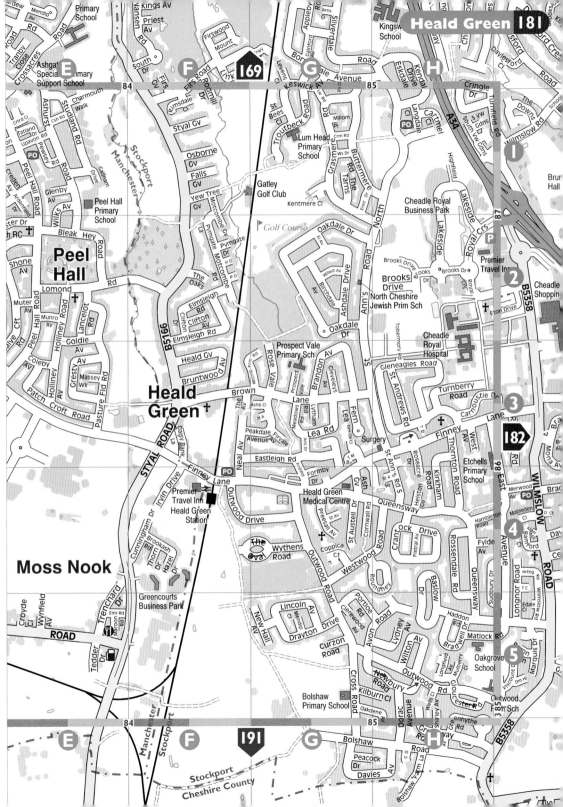

Peel Hall

Heald Green ✝

Moss Nook

Ashgate Special Primary Support School

Primary School

Peel Hall Primary School

Lum Head Primary School

Gatley Golf Club

Golf Course

Cheadle Royal Business Park

Premier Travel Inn

Brooks Drive

North Cheshire Jewish Prim Sch

Cheadle Royal Hospital

Prospect Vale Primary Sch

Heald Green Medical Centre

Etchells Primary School

Premier Travel Inn

Heald Green Station

Greencourts Business Park

Kingsway School

Oakgrove School

Outwood Prim Sch

Bolshaw Primary School

Surgery

Gleneagles Road

Turnberry Road

Stockport County

Cheshire County

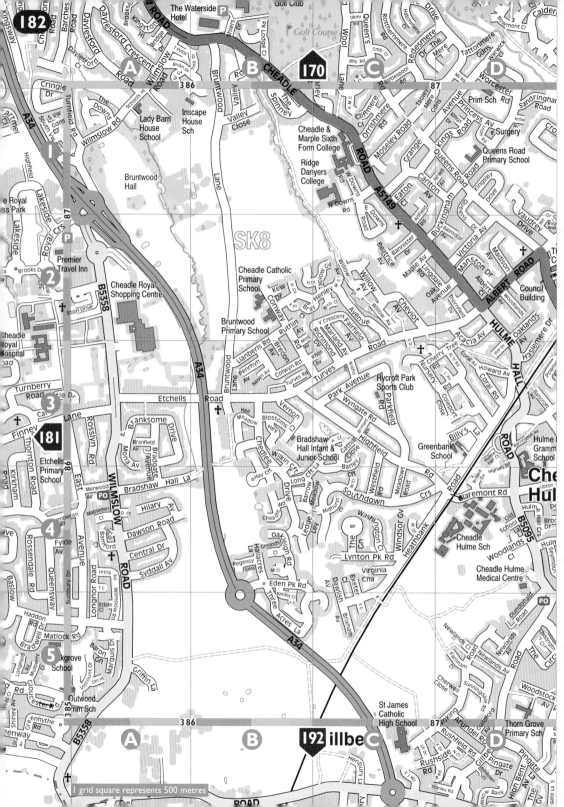

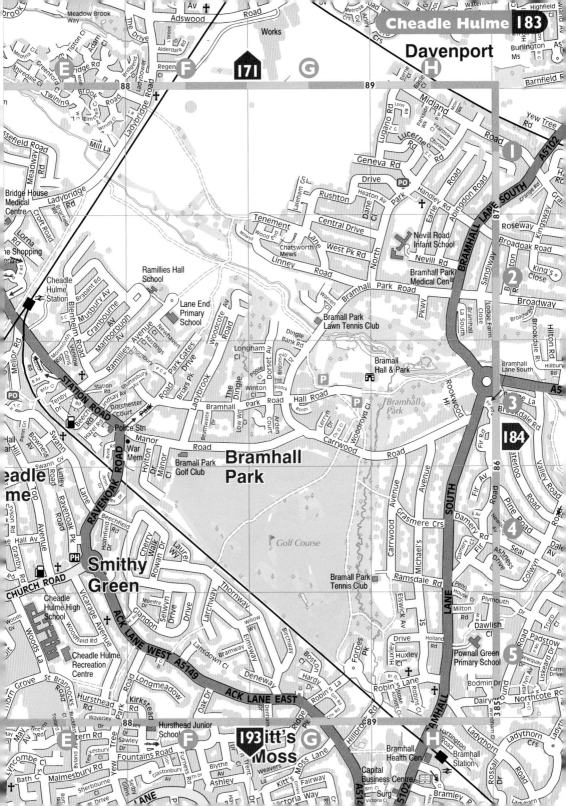

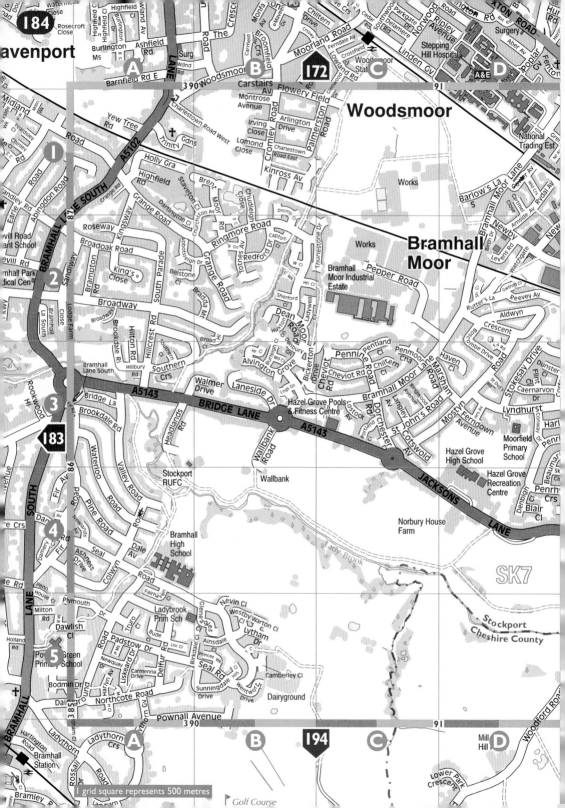

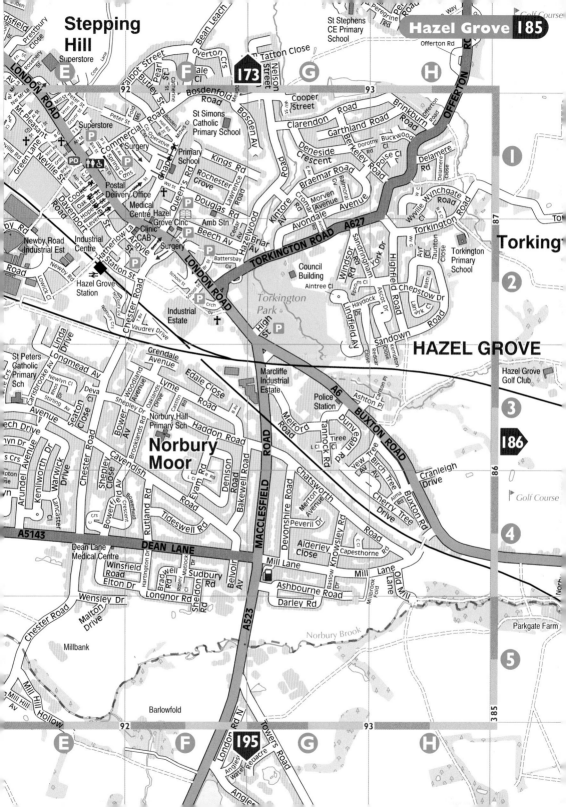

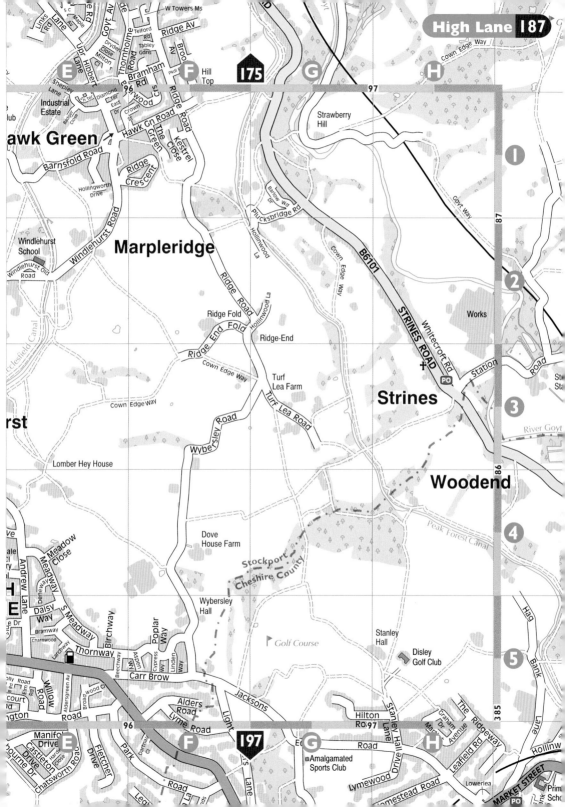

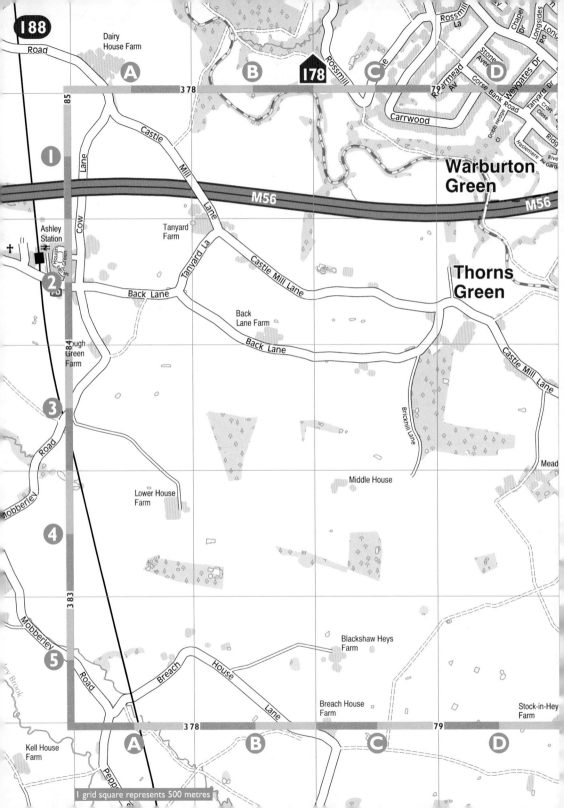

188
Road

Dairy
House Farm

A

B

178

C

Rossmill
La

Chapel

Longsides

Longs

D

85

378

Castle

79

Rossmill

Stone
Aven

Corse
Bank

Weygates Dr

Tanyard Dr

Tanyard
Croft

Dobb Hedge
Cl

Rivermead
Av

Corse Bank Road

Carrwood

Tanyard
Close

Ridg

Hasemere Av
Gardens

River

I

Cow Lane

Lane

Mill

M56

M56

**Warburton
Green**

Ashley
Station

Hough
Green

Tanyard
Farm

Lane

Castle Mill Lane

**Thorns
Green**

2

P5

Back Lane

Tanyard La

Back
Lane Farm

3

384
ough
Green
Farm

Back Lane

Back Lane

Brickhill Lane

Castle Mill Lane

Mead

Road

Mobberley

Lower House
Farm

Middle House

4

383

5

Mobberley

Road

Breach

House

Lane

Blackshaw Heys
Farm

Breach House
Farm

Stock-in-Hey
Farm

Kell House
Farm

Pepp

A

378

B

C

79

D

ay Brook

I grid square represents 500 metres

M90

Hotel

E   **F**   **179**   **G**   **H**

Warren Drive

Burnside

Road

The Copse

Bushey

Marlfield

Burnside

Road

acres Road

Greenga

Chapel Lane

Crabtree A

Cl

Warburton Cr

Sandown

Bankside

Warburton drive

Buttermer

rshill

Av

Argosy

Avro

York Drive

E81

Way

Pinfold La

Junction 6

Oak Farm

Wilmslow

Sunbank La

Old Road

Sunbank Lane

WILMSLOW ROAD

Sunbank Lane

Manchester Airport
World Freight Terminal

I

Sunbank

Lane

Halebank Farm

River Bollin

Aviation Viewing Park

Manc
Intern
Airpor

Cloughbank Farm

2

84

Castle Mill Farm

A538

3

Castle Mill Lane

Mill Lane

190

owlands

4

Altrincham
Road

E83

Holiday Inn

5

Bollin House Farm

Wood Lane

E   **F**   **G**   **H**

Wood Farm

80   81

190
M90

Radisson
SAS
Hotel

Airport Hotel

Ramp Rd W
Exit Rd W
Terminal Rd S
Ramp Rd E
Twin Rd E

Manchester Airport

Woodhouse Lane

P

P

Road

382

A

PO

Hotel
Rd
Police
Stn
Houses

Parade Road

Domestic Rd

Ramp

B

C

180

East Rd

83

C

D

Terminal 1

North Rd

P

Central Rd

P

Terminal 3

Mos

Manchester
International
Airport

Wilkins Lane

Moss

Lane

Holly

Lane

riation
ewing
ark

2

84

Manchester
Cheshire County

Lane

Norcliffe
Hall

Styal Primary
School

3

189

Oversley
Farm

River Bollin

Styal Country
Park NT

4

Altrincham Road 383

Holiday
Inn

ALTRINCHAM ROAD

A538

Road

M

5

Green

Dooley's La

Road

Nansmoss Lane

83

Wood Farm

382

A

B

Morley

C

198

D

1 grid square represents 500 metres

Morley

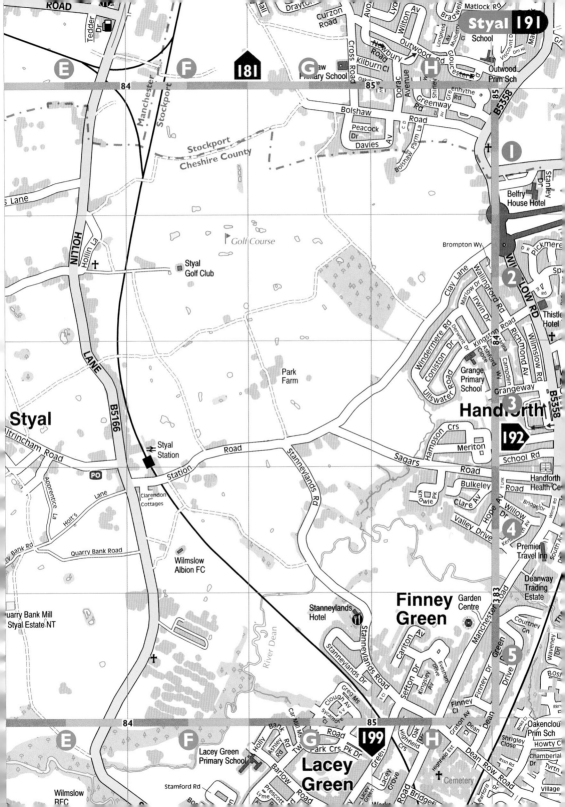

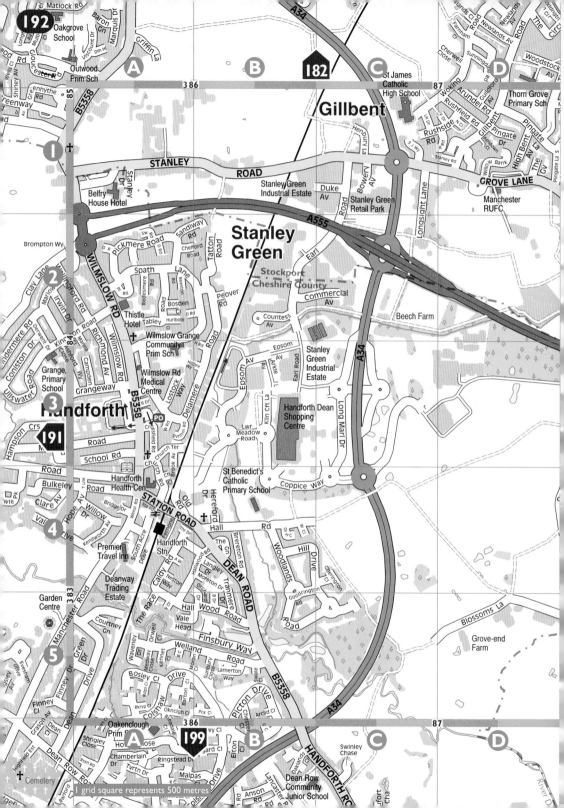

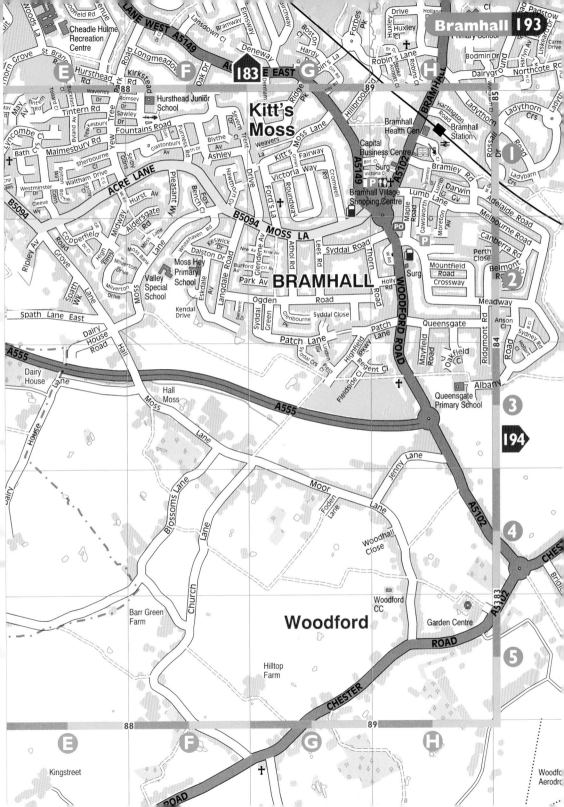

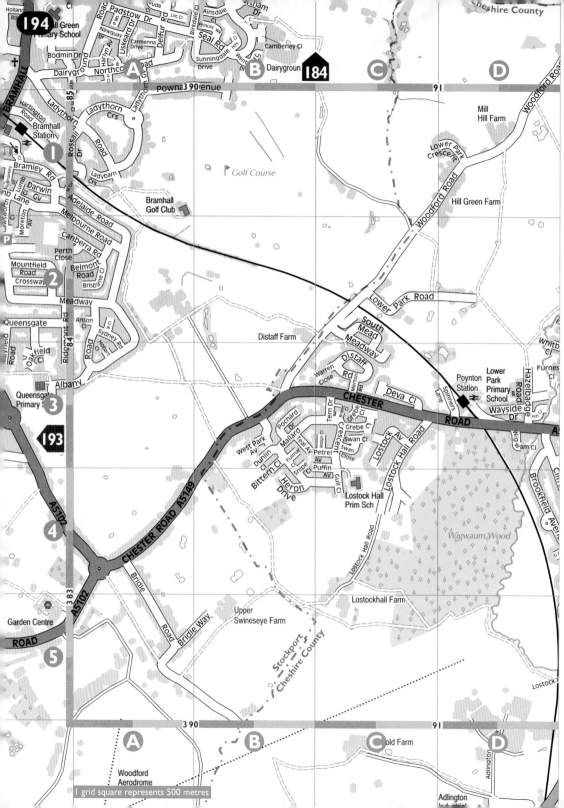

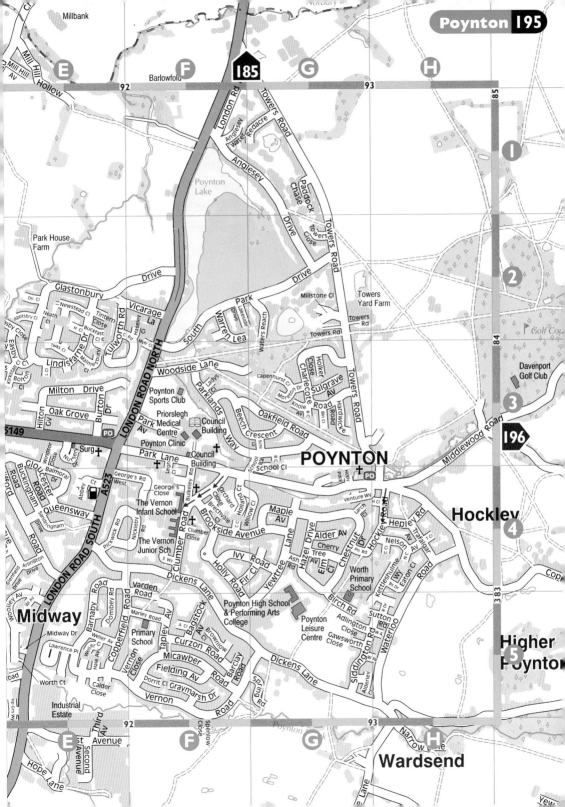

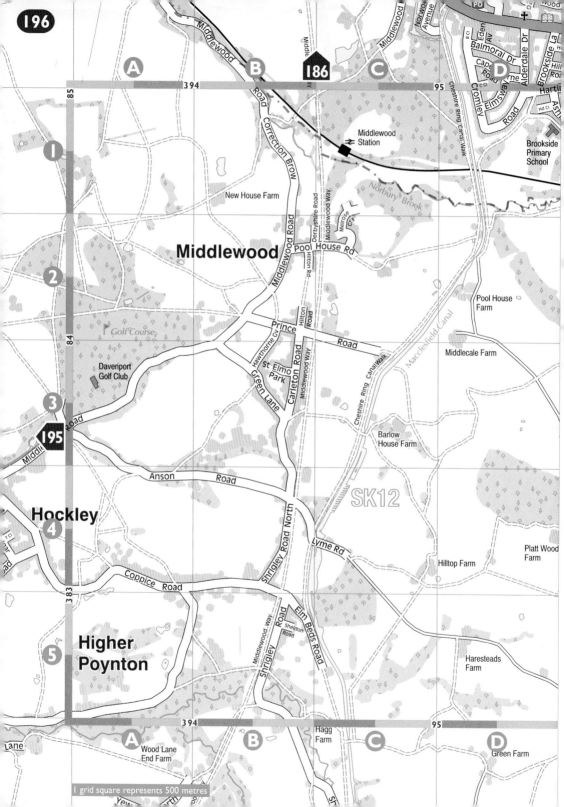

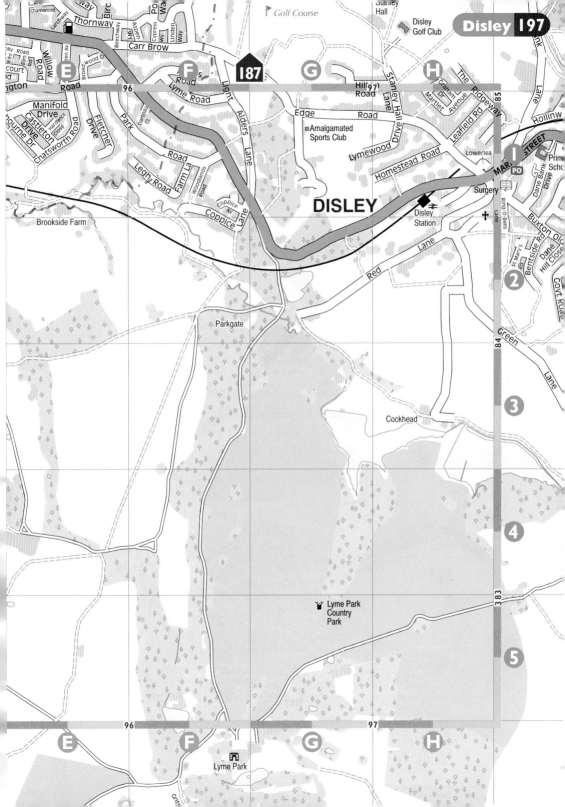

DISLEY

Golf Course

Stanley Hall

Disley Golf Club

Charnwood
Thornway
Birch Way
Larchway
Willow Road
Holly Road
Green Av
Broadwood Cl
Carr Brow
Aspen
Cypress Av
Linden Way
Beechway

E

F
Road
Lyme Road
Light Alders Lane

187

G
Hill Road
97

H
Graham Cl
Martlet
Avenue
The Ridgeway
Hollinw
Lane

96
Manifold Drive
Castleton Drive
Chatsworth Road
Hardwick
Fletcher Drive
Park Road
Legh Road
Farm La
Woodlands Road
Coppice Av
Coppice Lane

Stanley Hall Drive
Edge Road
Amalgamated Sports Club
Lymewood Drive
Homestead Road
Lowerlea
Leafield Rd

Lowerlea

MAR.
PO
STREET
Prim Sch
Dane Bank Drive
Buxton Old Road
Bentside Rd
Dane Hill Close
Govt Road

I
2

Brookside Farm

Surgery
Disley Station
Ring-O-Bells Lane
St Mary's Rd

Red Lane

Parkgate

Green Lane

84

3

Cockhead

4

83

Lyme Park Country Park

5

96
97

E
F
G
H

Lyme Park

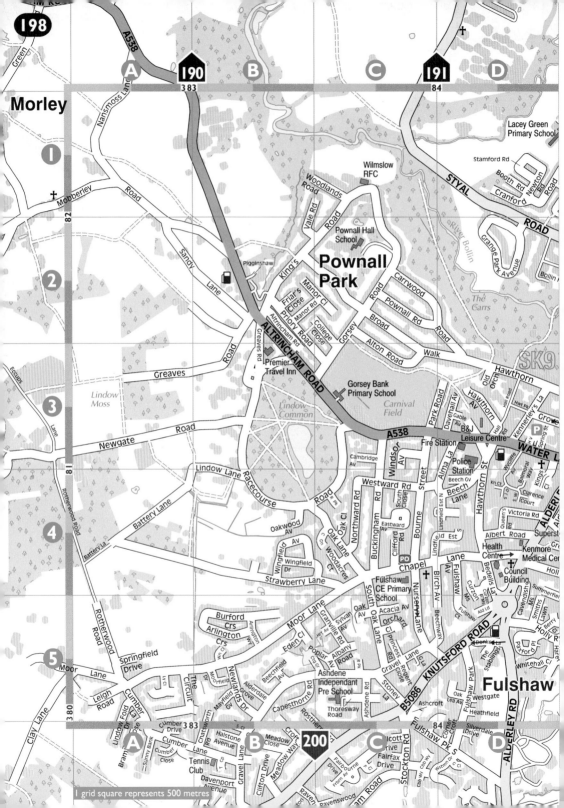

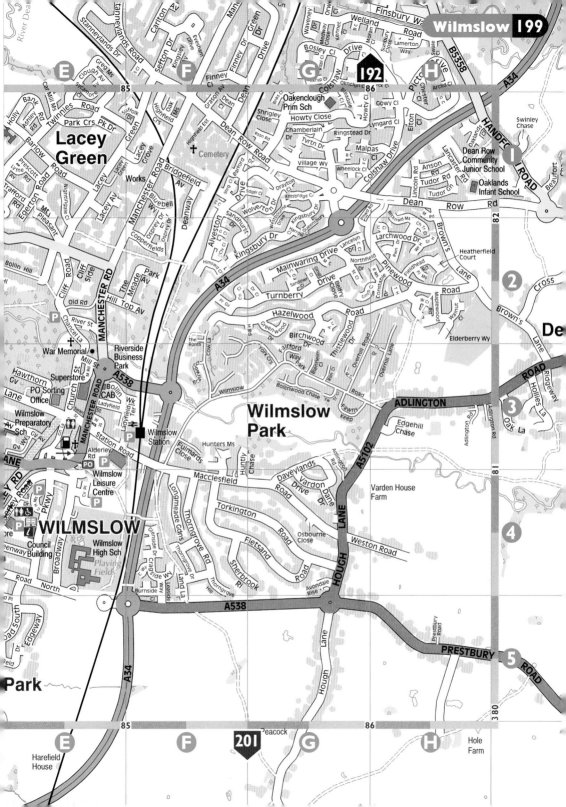

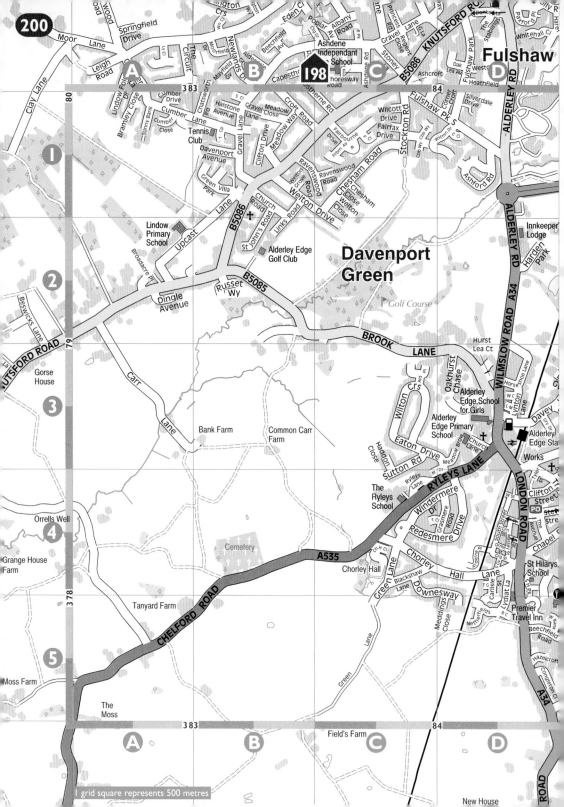

Park

E   F   **199**   G   H

85   86   80

Harefield
House

Peacock

Hole
Farm

I

Chonar Farm

Harden
Park

Heyes Lane

Hough Green
Farm

2

Fairbourne
Av

Beech
Close

Beech
Road

The
Circuit

Brook Farm

79

Elm Crescent

Maple

Heywood
Rd

Oakfield
Close

Oakfield Rd

Annis

Heywood
Crescent
Rd

Elm
Lane

Elmfield Rd

3

Hough Lane

Lower Ho

Duke Street

Moss   Road

Davey Lane

Heyes Lane

Beaufort Close

Marlborough Avenue

**ALDERLEY
EDGE**

Mottram Road

Hough

Devonshire
Drive

Moss
Lane

Lower Ho

Orchard
Green

Alderley Edge
CC

Mottram Road

Squirrel's
Jump

Findlow
Farm

4

Bramford
Road

Talbot
Road

Swiss Hill

Woodbrook

Underwood
Road

Tempest
Road

Croston Cl

378

B5087

Alderley
Edge Hotel

MACCLESFIELD ROAD

*Alderley
Edge*

Cl
Fa

Oatlands

Roan   Way

Beechfield Road

Beechfield

5

Whitebarn Road

85   86

E   F   G   The
Wizard   H

Edge House
Farm

Artists Lane

Abbey Hey 131 E3
Acre 76 A3
Adswood 171 G4
Affetside 25 E3
Ainsworth 36 C5
Alder Forest 110 A1
Alderley Edge 201 F3
Alkrington Garden Village 88 D1
Alt 32 C4
Alt Hill 107 F2
Altrincham 166 A4
Ancoats 7 K4
Arden Park 161 E2
Ardwick 128 D1
Ashley Heath 177 G4
Ashton-under-Lyne 118 D2
Ashton Upon Mersey 139 F5
Astley Bridge 33 H2
Audenshaw 132 B1
Austerlands 77 G4
Backbower 148 A3
Bagslate Moor 28 C3
Balderstone 43 G5
Baldingstone 27 F2
Bamford 28 A4
Bank Lane 17 E1
Bank Top 34 B1
Bardsley 106 D1
Barrow Bridge 32 D2
Barton Upon Irwell 111 E5
Belfield 31 E4
Belle Vue 130 A3
Benchill 168 C4
Bentgate 44 C3
Besses o' th' Barn 69 G5
Beswick 116 A4
Birch 55 H5
Blackford Bridge 53 G5
Black Lane 52 A3
Blackley 103 F1
Bolholt 37 F2
Bolton 3 G5
Boothstown 96 B4
Bowdon 176 C3
Bowgreen 176 D3
Bowlee 71 F3
Bradford 116 A3
Bradley Fold 51 E2
Bradshaw 23 H5
Bramhall 193 G2
Bramhall Moor 184 C2
Bramhall Park 183 F3
Bredbury 161 F3
Bredbury Green 161 H4
Breightmet 50 D1
Brinnington 160 C1
Broadbottom 149 H3
Broadfield 40 C5
Broadhalgh 28 C4
Broadheath 165 F2
Broadley 18 B1
Broadoak Park 98 B5
Bromley Cross 23 F5
Brook Bottom 93 F5
Brooklands 154 C4
Brooksbottoms 16 D5
Broughton Park 101 G1
Brownlow Fold 33 F5
Brunswick 128 C2
Brushes 121 H2
Buckley 19 F5
Buckton Vale 109 F5
Buersil Head 43 H5
Burnage 158 B1
Burnden 49 F5
Burnedge 44 B5
Bury 4 C3
Busk 8 A1
Cadishead 150 B2
Caldermoor 20 C2
Cale Green 172 A3
Captain Fold 41 F5
Carr 16 C1
Carrbrook 109 H3
Carrington 137 G5
Carrington Moss 152 C3
Castlefield 6 A7
Castle Hill 146 C4
Castleton 42 B4
Chadderton 73 H5
Chadderton Fold 74 A2
Chadkirk 174 A1
Chapel Field 68 D3
Charlestown 88 D4
Charlestown 113 G1
Cheadle 170 B4
Cheadle Heath 170 D2
Cheadle Hulme 182 D4
Cheetham Hill 102 C4
Chequerbent 62 D3
Cherry Tree 165 E4
Chesham 38 D1
Chew Moor 46 D5
Chorlton-cum-Hardy 141 H4
Cinder Hill 67 G4
Clarksfield 76 C5
Clayton 116 D2

Clifton 83 H4
Clifton Green 84 C5
Clifton Junction 84 D4
Clough 20 D1
Clough 60 C3
Collyhurst 103 E4
Compstall 163 F3
Copley 121 F3
Copster Hill 91 F5
Cox Green 23 E2
Crimble 41 G2
Crofts Bank 124 B4
Crompton Fold 45 F5
Crowhill 119 E1
Crumpsall 102 A1
Cutgate 28 D3
Daisy Nook 105 H5
Dales Brow 98 C4
Dane Bank 145 H1
Darcy Lever 50 A4
Dam Hill 40 A5
Daubhill 48 B5
Davenport 171 H5
Davenport Green 179 G2
Davenport Green 200 C2
Davyhulme 124 A4
Deane 64 A1
Dearnley 20 C4
Debdale 131 E4
Denton 132 C5
Didsbury 157 G5
Disley 197 G1
Dobcross 78 C2
Doffcocker 32 D4
Dog Hill 60 D2
Droylsden 117 F4
Dukinfield 133 F1
Dumplington 124 B1
Dunham Town 164 A5
Dunscar 22 C2
Durn 21 F5
Eagley 22 D4
East Didsbury 158 A5
Eccles 111 H4
Edge Fold 64 B3
Edgeley 171 F2
Egerton 22 D1
Ellenbrook 96 B2
Ellesmere Park 111 F1
Elton 37 G4
Facit 14 D2
Failsworth 104 D3
Fairfield 39 G3
Fairfield 131 F1
Fallowfield 142 D3
Farnworth 65 G4
Fern Bank 121 E4
Fernhill 4 D1
Fernhill Gate 47 G5
Finney Green 191 H5
Firgrove 31 F5
Firswood 127 E5
Firwood Fold 34 C3
Fishpool 53 F1
Fitton Hill 91 H5
Flixton 138 A2
Flowery Field 133 G4
Foggbrook 173 G2
Four Lane Ends 36 C1
Free Town 5 K1
Fullwood 60 C4
Fulshaw Park 198 D5
Gale 21 F1
Gatley 169 F5
Gee Cross 148 A4
Gigg 53 H2
Gilbent 192 C1
Gilnow 2 B6
Glodwick 92 A2
Godley 133 H5
Godley Hill 148 D1
Gorse Hill 126 B5
Gorton 130 B4
Grains Bar 61 F3
Grasscroft 94 A1
Gravel Hole 59 E2
Great Howarth 19 F4
Great Lever 65 F1
Great Moor 172 D3
Greave 162 C2
Greenacres 76 C5
Greenfield 95 E3
Greengate 20 A5
Greenheys 80 C2
Greenmount 25 H1
Greenside 118 A2
Grotton 93 G1
Guide Bridge 118 D4
Haggate 74 D1
Hale 178 A2
Halebarns 179 E4
Halfway Houses 51 F3
Hall i' th' Wood 34 B2
Halliwell 33 H5
Handforth 191 H3
Harden Park 201 E2
Harper Green 65 G3

Harpurhey 103 F3
Hartshead Green 108 B2
Hartshead Pike 108 A1
Harwood 35 H3
Harwood Lee 35 F1
Hathershaw 91 G4
Hattersley 149 F1
Haugh 45 F5
Haughton Green 147 E3
Hawk Green 186 D1
Hazel Grove 185 H5
Hazelhurst 16 A4
Hazelhurst 98 A4
Hazelhurst 108 B5
Heady Hill 40 B4
Heald Green 181 F3
Healds Green 74 A1
Healey 18 D4
Heap Bridge 39 F5
Heaton 47 H1
Heaton Chapel 144 C5
Heaton Mersey 158 B3
Heaton Moor 158 D2
Heaton Norris 12 A1
Heaviley 172 B2
Heyheads 109 E3
Heyrod 121 E1
Heyside 59 H5
Heywood 40 D3
Higginshaw 75 G2
High Crompton 59 H1
Higher Blackley 87 H3
Higher Boarshaw 73 F1
Higher Broughton 101 G4
Higher Poynton 196 A5
Higher Woodhill 38 A1
Highfield 65 E5
High Lane 186 D5
Hill Top 82 A3
Hilton Park 85 H5
Hockley 195 H4
Holcombe 16 B3
Holcombe Brook 16 A5
Holden Fold 75 E1
Hollins 54 A4
Hollins 64 C4
Hollins 72 C1
Hollinwood 105 F1
Holts 92 D3
Honresfeld 21 G2
Hooley Bridge 40 D1
Hooley Brow 41 E2
Hooley Hill 132 B1
Horrocks Fold 22 B4
Hough 201 G4
Hulme 127 H2
Hunger Hill 63 E1
Hurst 107 G5
Hurstead 19 H4
Hyde 133 G5
Irlam 136 B2
Irlams o' th' Height 99 H5
Jericho 39 H2
Johnson Fold 32 A3
Jubilee 45 E4
Kearsley 83 E1
Kersal 101 E1
Kingston 133 E5
Kirkhams 86 A1
Kirkholt 42 D3
Kirklees 26 C4
Kitt's Moss 193 C1
Knott Lanes 106 C5
Lacey Green 199 E1
Lady House 44 B2
Langley 71 H1
Lees 92 C1
Levenshulme 144 C3
Lever-Edge 64 C2
Ley Hey Park 174 D2
Limefield 27 G5
Limehurst 106 A1
Lime Side 106 A1
Limyshaw 82 B4
Little Bolton 112 A3
Littleborough 21 E5
Little Clegg 31 F1
Little Hulton 81 E3
Little Lever 51 E5
Little Moor 173 E1
Littlemoss 118 B1
Long Sight 75 F2
Longsight 129 G3
Lostock Junction 47 E4
Low Compton 59 F5
Lower Bredbury 160 D4
Lower Kersal 100 D4
Lower Place 43 H2
Luzley 108 C3
Luzley Brook 59 G4
Lydgate 93 H2
Makants 80 D5
Manchester 6 E3
Markland Hill 47 F1
Marland 42 A1
Marple 174 D3

Marple Bridge 175 G2
Marpleridge 187 E2
Matley 135 G2
Micklehurst 109 F1
Middleton 72 A3
Middlewood 196 A2
Midway 195 E5
Miles Platting 115 G2
Millbrook 121 G1
Millgate 14 B1
Mill Hill 3 H3
Milnrow 31 H5
Monton 111 E2
Moorclose 73 F4
Moorhey 92 A1
Mooriside 76 D1
Mooriside 98 C3
Moses Gate 65 H2
Mosley Common 96 B3
Mossley 94 A5
Mossley Brow 108 D1
Moss Nook 181 E4
Moss Side 128 A4
Mossley 100 A1
Mottram in Longdendale 135 G4
Mottram Rise 135 F1
Mumps 9 H2
Nangreaves 17 F5
Newall Green 167 H5
Newbold 30 D2
New Bury 65 F5
New Delph 78 D1
Newhey 44 D2
New Moston 104 B2
Newton 133 H3
Newton Heath 103 H5
Newton Wood 132 D2
Newtown 98 D1
Nimble Nook 90 B3
Nob End 66 D2
Norbury Moor 185 F3
Norden 28 A2
Northenden 168 C1
Northern Moor 155 G5
North Reddish 145 E2
Nuttall 16 C4
Oak Bank 69 H5
Offerton 173 F2
Offerton Green 173 H3
Oldfield Brow 165 E4
Oldham 9 J5
Oldham Edge 75 G3
Old Tame 61 G1
Old Trafford 127 E3
Openshaw 116 D5
Ordsall 127 E1
Outwood 68 D4
Over Hulton 63 H5
Park Bridge 92 B5
Partington 151 E4
Patricroft 110 D3
Peel Green 110 A5
Peel Hall 181 E2
Pendlebury 99 H3
Pendleton 113 F2
Pimhole 5 J5
Pitses 92 C3
Pogreen 79 G4
Portwood 160 B3
Pownall Park 198 C2
Poynton 195 G3
Prestolee 67 E4
Prestwich 85 G3
Quick 93 H3
Quick Edge 93 G4
Radcliffe 52 B5
Rainsough 100 D1
Ramsbottom 16 C1
Reddish 144 D3
Redvales 53 F3
Rhodes 71 G5
Ridge Hill 120 C1
Ringley 83 E2
Roaches 94 A4
Rochdale 11 F6
Roebuck Low 77 F2
Roe Cross 135 G3
Roe Green 97 G2
Romiley 162 C4
Rose Hill 49 F4
Rosehill 177 F3
Roundthorn 167 F4
Royton 59 G5
Running Hill Head 79 G1
Rusholme 129 E5
St George's 127 F2
Sale 140 B5
Salford 113 E4
Salford Quays 126 E1
Scouthead 77 G3
Sedgley Park 86 B5
Seedley 112 D2
Sharples 33 G2
Sharston 169 E4
Shaw 59 H3
Shawclough 29 F1
Shawfield 28 C1

Shaw Heath 12 E7
Shaw Side 60 A4
Sholver 60 C5
Shore 20 C2
Shuttleworth 17 F1
Side of the Moor 24 B5
Simister 70 D4
Sinderland Green 152 A5
Slackcote 61 G2
Slattocks 57 F3
Smallbridge 20 A5
Smallshaw 107 E4
Smithy Bridge 20 D5
Smithy Green 183 E4
South Reddish 159 H1
Spotland Bridge 29 G5
Springhead 93 E2
Spring Hill 76 C4
Stake Hill 57 H4
Stalybridge 120 C4
Stand 68 D4
Stanley Green 192 B2
Stancyliffe 73 E1
Starling 37 F4
Stepping Hill 173 E5
Stockport 12 B1
Stoneclough 67 E5
Stoneyfield 43 E2
Strangeways 114 C1
Stretford 139 H3
Strines 187 H3
Stryal 191 E3
Sudden 42 B2
Summerseat 26 C2
Summit 60 A4
Summit 50 C2
Sun Green 121 H1
Sunny Bank 53 H5
Swinton 98 C2
Swinton Park 99 G4
Syke 19 E4
Tame Water 78 B3
Taunton 106 B5
Thornham Fold 58 B2
Thorns Green 188 D2
Thorp 58 C5
Thurston Clough 78 A1
Timperley 166 B2
Tonge Fold 49 H1
Tonge Moor 34 B4
Top o' Hebers 56 B5
Top o' th' Meadows 77 E4
Toppings 23 G4
Torkington 186 A2
Tottington 25 H5
Trafford Park 125 F3
Trub 57 F2
Tunstead 95 F2
Turf Hill 44 A2
Unsworth 69 H2
Uppermill 79 E5
Urmston 124 D4
Walkden 82 A3
Wallbank 18 A1
Wall Hill 78 B3
Walmersley 27 F4
Walshaw 26 C2
Warburton Green 188 D1
Wardle 20 A2
Wardley 98 B1
Wardour 106 C5
Watersheddings 76 C3
Water's Nook 62 D1
Weaste 112 D4
Well Green 179 E1
Werneth 90 C1
Werneth Low 163 E1
West Didsbury 157 H4
Westwood Park 110 B1
Whalley Range 142 A1
Whitefield 69 F5
White Gate 90 A4
Whitworth 14 C4
Willows 48 B4
Wilmslow 199 E4
Wilmslow Park 199 F3
Windlehurst 186 D3
Winton 110 D2
Withington 143 E5
Woodend 94 B5
Woodend 187 H4
Woodford 193 G5
Woodhouse Green 16 B5
Woodhey 180 B3
Woodhouse Park 105 F4
Woodhouses 153 E4
Woodlands 134 C1
Woodley 162 B2
Wood Road 26 D2
Woods End 123 F5
Woodsmoor 184 C1
Woolfold 37 F2
Worsley 97 H2
Wythenshawe 180 A1
Yew Tree 133 H1

USING THE STREET INDEX

Street names are listed alphabetically. Each street name is followed by its postal town or area locality, the Postcode District, the page number, and the reference to the square in which the name is found.

Standard index entries are shown as follows:

Abberley Dr *NEWH/MOS* M40 ...... **89** G5

Street names and selected addresses not shown on the map due to scale restrictions are shown in the index with an asterisk:

Abbeyfield Sq *OP/CLY* M11 * **116** C5

GENERAL ABBREVIATIONS

ACC	ACCESS	CTYD	COURTYARD	HLS	HILLS	MWY	MOTORWAY	SE	SOUTH EAST

ACC.......ACCESS
ALY.......ALLEY
AP.......APPROACH
AR.......ARCADE
ASS.......ASSOCIATION
AV.......AVENUE
BCH.......BEACH
BLDS.......BUILDINGS
BND.......BEND
BNK.......BANK
BR.......BRIDGE
BRK.......BROOK
BTM.......BOTTOM
BUS.......BUSINESS
BVD.......BOULEVARD
BY.......BYPASS
CATH.......CATHEDRAL
CEM.......CEMETERY
CEN.......CENTRE
CFT.......CROFT
CH.......CHURCH
CHA.......CHASE
CHYD.......CHURCHYARD
CIR.......CIRCLE
CIRC.......CIRCUS
CL.......CLOSE
CLFS.......CLIFFS
CMP.......CAMP
CNR.......CORNER
CO.......COUNTY
COLL.......COLLEGE
COM.......COMMON
COMM.......COMMISSION
CON.......CONVENT
COT.......COTTAGE
COTS.......COTTAGES
CP.......CAPE
CPS.......COPSE
CR.......CREEK
CREM.......CREMATORIUM
CRS.......CRESCENT
CSWY.......CAUSEWAY
CT.......COURT
CTRL.......CENTRAL
CTS.......COURTS

CTYD.......COURTYARD
CUTT.......CUTTINGS
CV.......COVE
CYN.......CANYON
DEPT.......DEPARTMENT
DL.......DALE
DM.......DAM
DR.......DRIVE
DRO.......DROVE
DRY.......DRIVEWAY
DWGS.......DWELLINGS
E.......EAST
EMB.......EMBANKMENT
EMBY.......EMBASSY
ESP.......ESPLANADE
EST.......ESTATE
EX.......EXCHANGE
EXPY.......EXPRESSWAY
EXT.......EXTENSION
F/O.......FLYOVER
FC.......FOOTBALL CLUB
FK.......FORK
FLD.......FIELD
FLDS.......FIELDS
FLS.......FALLS
FM.......FARM
FT.......FORT
FTS.......FLATS
FWY.......FREEWAY
FY.......FERRY
GA.......GATE
GAL.......GALLERY
GDN.......GARDEN
GDNS.......GARDENS
GLD.......GLADE
GLN.......GLEN
GN.......GREEN
GND.......GROUND
GRA.......GRANGE
GRG.......GARAGE
GT.......GREAT
GTWY.......GATEWAY
GV.......GROVE
HGR.......HIGHER
HL.......HILL

HLS.......HILLS
HO.......HOUSE
HOL.......HOLLOW
HOSP.......HOSPITAL
HRB.......HARBOUR
HTH.......HEATH
HTS.......HEIGHTS
HVN.......HAVEN
HWY.......HIGHWAY
IMP.......IMPERIAL
IN.......INLET
IND EST.......INDUSTRIAL ESTATE
INF.......INFIRMARY
INFO.......INFORMATION
INT.......INTERCHANGE
IS.......ISLAND
JCT.......JUNCTION
JTY.......JETTY
KG.......KING
KNL.......KNOLL
L.......LAKE
LA.......LANE
LDG.......LODGE
LGT.......LIGHT
LK.......LOCK
LNDG.......LANDING
LTL.......LITTLE
LWR.......LOWER
MAG.......MAGISTRATE
MAN.......MANSIONS
MD.......MEAD
MDW.......MEADOWS
MEM.......MEMORIAL
MI.......MILL
MKT.......MARKET
MKTS.......MARKETS
ML.......MALL
MNR.......MANOR
MS.......MEWS
MSN.......MISSION
MT.......MOUNT
MTN.......MOUNTAIN
MTS.......MOUNTAINS
MUS.......MUSEUM

MWY.......MOTORWAY
N.......NORTH
NE.......NORTH EAST
NW.......NORTH WEST
O/P.......OVERPASS
OFF.......OFFICE
ORCH.......ORCHARD
OV.......OVAL
PAL.......PALACE
PAS.......PASSAGE
PAV.......PAVILION
PDE.......PARADE
PH.......PUBLIC HOUSE
PK.......PARK
PKWY.......PARKWAY
PL.......PLACE
PLN.......PLAIN
PLNS.......PLAINS
PLZ.......PLAZA
POL.......POLICE STATION
PR.......PRINCE
PREC.......PRECINCT
PREP.......PREPARATORY
PRIM.......PRIMARY
PROM.......PROMENADE
PRS.......PRINCESS
PRT.......PORT
PT.......POINT
PTH.......PATH
PZ.......PIAZZA
QD.......QUADRANT
QU.......QUEEN
QY.......QUAY
R.......RIVER
RBT.......ROUNDABOUT
RD.......ROAD
RDG.......RIDGE
REP.......REPUBLIC
RES.......RESERVOIR
RFC.......RUGBY FOOTBALL CLUB
RI.......RISE
RP.......RAMP
RW.......ROW
S.......SOUTH
SCH.......SCHOOL

SE.......SOUTH EAST
SER.......SERVICE AREA
SH.......SHORE
SHOP.......SHOPPING
SKWY.......SKYWAY
SMT.......SUMMIT
SOC.......SOCIETY
SP.......SPUR
SPR.......SPRING
SQ.......SQUARE
ST.......STREET
STN.......STATION
STR.......STREAM
STRD.......STRAND
SW.......SOUTH WEST
TDG.......TRADING
TER.......TERRACE
THWY.......THROUGHWAY
TNL.......TUNNEL
TOLL.......TOLLWAY
TPK.......TURNPIKE
TR.......TRACK
TRL.......TRAIL
TWR.......TOWER
U/P.......UNDERPASS
UNI.......UNIVERSITY
UPR.......UPPER
V.......VALE
VA.......VALLEY
VIAD.......VIADUCT
VIL.......VILLA
VIS.......VISTA
VLG.......VILLAGE
VLS.......VILLAS
VW.......VIEW
W.......WEST
WD.......WOOD
WHF.......WHARF
WK.......WALK
WKS.......WALKS
WLS.......WELLS
WY.......WAY
YD.......YARD
YHA.......YOUTH HOSTEL

POSTCODE TOWNS AND AREA ABBREVIATIONS

ALT.......Altrincham
ANC.......Ancoats
AUL.......Ashton-under-Lyne
AULW.......Ashton-under-Lyne west
ATH.......Atherton
BKLY.......Blackley
BOL.......Bolton
BOLE.......Bolton east
BOLS/LL.......Bolton south/Little Lever
BRAM/HZG.......Bramhall/Hazel Grove
BRO.......Broughton
BRUN/LGST.......Brunswick/Longsight
BNG/LEV.......Burnage/Levenshulme
BURY.......Bury
CMANE.......Central Manchester east
CMANW.......Central Manchester west
CSLFD.......Central Salford
CHAD.......Chadderton

CHD/CHDH.......Cheadle (Gtr. Man)/Cheadle Hulme
CHH.......Cheetham Hill
CCHDY.......Chorlton-cum-Hardy
DTN/ASHW.......Denton/Audenshaw
DID/WITH.......Didsbury/Withington
DROY.......Droylsden
DUK.......Dukinfield
ECC.......Eccles
EDGY/DAV.......Edgeley/Davenport
EDGW/EG.......Edgworth/Egerton
FAIL.......Failsworth
FWTH.......Farnworth
GLSP.......Glossop
GOL/RIS/CUL.......Golborne/Risley/Culcheth
GTN.......Gorton
HALE/TIMP.......Hale/Timperley
HTNM.......Heaton Moor
HEY.......Heywood

HOR/BR.......Horwich/Blackrod
HULME.......Hulme
HYDE.......Hyde
IRL.......Irlam
KNUT.......Knutsford
LHULT.......Little Hulton
LIT.......Littleborough
LYMM.......Lymm
MCFLDN.......Macclesfield north
MANAIR.......Manchester Airport
MPL/ROM.......Marple/Romiley
MDTN.......Middleton (Gtr. Man)
MILN.......Milnrow
MOSL.......Mossley
NM/HAY.......New Mills/Hayfield
NEWH/MOS.......Newton Heath/Moston
NTHM/RTH.......Northern Moor/Roundthorn
OFTN.......Offerton
OLDTF/WHR.......Old Trafford/Whalley Range
OLD.......Oldham

OLDE.......Oldham east
OLDS.......Oldham south
OP/CLY.......Openshaw/Clayton
ORD.......Ordsall
PART.......Partington
POY/DIS.......Poynton/Disley
PWCH.......Prestwich
RAD.......Radcliffe
RAMS.......Ramsbottom
RDSH.......Reddish
ROCH.......Rochdale
ROY/SHW.......Royton/Shaw
RUSH/FAL.......Rusholme/Failsworth
SALE.......Sale
SLFD.......Salford
SALQ.......Salford Quays
STLY.......Stalybridge
STKP.......Stockport
STRET.......Stretford
SWIN.......Swinton
TOT/BURYW.......Tottington/

TRPK.......Trafford Park
TRPK.......Trafford Park
TYLD.......Tyldesley
UPML.......Uppermill
URM.......Urmston
WALK.......Walkden
WGTN/LGST.......West Gorton/Longsight
WHTN.......Westhoughton
WHTF.......Whitefield
WHIT.......Whitworth
WILM/AE.......Alderley Edge
WYTH/NTH.......Wythenshawe/Northenden

Index - streets   Abb - Adr

A

Abberley Dr NEWH/MOS M40.......89 G5
Abberton Rd DID/WITH M20.......142 C5
Abbey Cl ALT WA14.......176 D3
 BOLS/LL BL3.......48 A4
 RAD M26.......51 H4
 STRET M32.......125 E5
Abbey Crs HEY OL10.......40 C2
Abbeydale WHIT OL12.......10 G4
Abbeydale Cl AUL OL6.......107 H4
Abbeydale Gdns WALK M28.......81 H5
Abbeydale Rd
 NEWH/MOS M40.......104 D2
Abbey Dr LIT OL15.......20 C5
 SWIN M27.......98 D2
 TOT/BURYW BL8.......37 F5
Abbeyfield Sq OP/CLY M11 *.......116 C5
Abbey Gdns HYDE SK14.......135 G5
Abbey Gv CHAD OL9.......90 B3
 ECC M30.......111 F3
 HYDE SK14.......135 G5
 STKP SK1.......172 C1
Abbey Hey La GTN M18.......130 D2
Abbey Hills Rd OLDS OL8.......92 A3
Abbey Lawn
 OLDTF/WHR M16.......127 E5
Abbeylea Dr WHTN BL5.......62 B2
Abbey Rd CHD/CHDH SK8.......170 D4
 DROY M43.......117 G2
 FAIL M35.......105 G2
 MDTN M24.......56 C5
 SALE M33.......139 G5
Abbeyville Wk HULME M15 *.......127 H5
Abbeywood Av GTN M18 *.......130 D4
Abbotsbury Cl POY/DIS SK12.......195 E2
Abbots Cl SALE M33.......155 E1
Abbots Fold Rd WALK M28.......96 B1
Abbot's Fold Rd WALK M28.......56 A5
Abbotsfield Dr MDTN M24.......56 A5
Abbotsford Gv ALT WA14.......165 H1

Abbotsford Rd BOL BL1.......32 D5
 CCHDY M21.......141 F2
 CHAD OL9 *.......73 H4
 OLD OL1 *.......76 A3
Abbotside Cl
 OLDTF/WHR M16.......127 G5
Abbotsleigh Dr
 BRAM/HZG SK7.......184 A2
Abbott St BOLS/LL BL3.......48 D4
 ROCH OL11.......42 A3
Abden St RAD M26.......68 B1
Abels La UPML OL3.......79 F4
Abercarn Cl OFTN SK2.......172 D5
Abercorn Rd BOL BL1.......33 E3
Abercorn St OLDE OL4 *.......92 C1
Abercrombie Ct SALE M33.......155 E1
Aberdaron Wk
 BRUN/LGST M13 *.......128 C1
Aberdeen Crs EDGY/DAV SK3.......12 C6
Aberdeen Gdns WHIT OL12.......18 C4
Aberdeen Gv EDGY/DAV SK3.......12 D5
Aberdeen St BRUN/LGST M13.......128 C3
Aberford Rd NTHM/RTH M23.......167 H4
Abergele Rd RUSH/FAL M14.......143 G3
Abergele St OFTN SK2.......172 A3
Aberley Fold LIT OL15.......20 C1
Abernant Cl OP/CLY M11.......116 A4
Aber Rd CHD/CHDH SK8.......170 D3
Abersoch Av RUSH/FAL M14.......143 G3
Abingdon Av WHTF M45.......69 G2
Abingdon Cl CHAD OL9 *.......90 C3
 ROCH OL11.......42 D2
 WHTF M45.......69 G2
Abingdon Rd BOLE BL2.......49 H1
 BRAM/HZG SK7.......183 H2
 RDSH SK5.......145 F4
 SWIN M27.......98 C5
Abingdon St AUL OL6.......120 A5
 CMANE M1.......7 F6
Abington Rd SALE M33.......154 D3
Abney Gra MOSL OL5.......109 F2
Abney Rd HTNM SK4.......159 F1
 MOSL OL5.......108 D2
Aboukir St MILN OL16.......11 F5

Abram Cl RUSH/FAL M14.......142 C2
Abram St SLFD M6.......100 C4
Absalom Dr CHH M8.......102 A3
Abson St OLD OL1.......74 D3
Acacia Av CHD/CHDH SK8.......182 D2
 DTN/ASHW M34.......132 D5
 HALE/TIMP WA15.......178 A1
 SWIN M27.......98 D4
 WILM/AE SK9.......198 C5
Acacia Dr HALE/TIMP WA15.......178 A1
 SLFD M6.......112 A2
Acacia Gv RDSH SK5.......160 A2
Acacia Rd OLDS OL8.......106 A1
The Acacias URM M41 *.......139 E1
Academy Wk HULME M15 *.......127 H3
Ace MI CHAD OL9 *.......90 A3
Acer Cl HYDE SK14.......148 C1
 ROCH OL11.......42 A4
Acer Gv BRO M7.......101 C3
Acheson St GTN M18.......130 C5
Ackers La PART M31.......137 G5
Ackers St BRUN/LGST M13.......128 C3
Acker St MILN OL16 *.......10 D5
Ack La East BRAM/HZG SK7.......183 F5
Ack La West CHD/CHDH SK8.......185 E5
Ackroyd Av GTN M18.......131 F2
Ackroyd St OP/CLY M11.......130 D1
Ackworth Dr NTHM/RTH M23.......167 H5
Ackworth Rd SWIN M27.......98 D1
Acme Dr SWIN M27.......99 C2
Acomb St HULME M15.......128 C5
 RUSH/FAL M14.......128 C5
Acorn Av CHD/CHDH SK8.......170 B4
 HYDE SK14.......148 A3
Acorn Cl BNG/LEV M19.......143 H5
 WHTF M45.......85 C1
Acorn St OLDE OL4.......92 D1
Acorn Wy OLD OL1.......9 F2
Acre Barn ROY/SHW OL2.......59 F1
Acre Fld BOLE BL2.......35 E2
Acrefield SALE M33.......154 B3
Acrefield Av HTNM SK4.......158 D2
 URM M41.......139 F2
Acre La CHD/CHDH SK8.......193 E1
 OLD OL1.......75 H3

Acresbrook STLY SK15.......134 D1
Acres Ct WYTH/NTH M22.......168 C5
Acresdale HOR/BR BL6.......46 D3
Acresfield Av
 DTN/ASHW M34.......118 A4
Acresfield Cl SWIN M27.......99 F4
Acresfield Rd
 HALE/TIMP WA15.......166 B1
 HYDE SK14.......134 A3
 LHULT M38.......81 G3
 MDTN M24.......73 F1
 SLFD M6.......100 A5
Acres Fold Av
 WYTH/NTH M22.......180 C1
Acres La STLY SK15.......121 E4
Acres Rd CCHDY M21.......141 E3
 CHD/CHDH SK8.......169 F4
Acres St TOT/BURYW BL8.......37 E1
Acre St CHAD OL9.......90 C5
 DTN/ASHW M34.......132 B5
 RAD M26.......67 H1
 WHIT OL12.......14 C4
Acre Top Rd BKLY M9.......87 G2
Acton Av NEWH/MOS M40.......116 C1
Acton St OLD OL1.......75 H4
 WHIT OL12.......10 E3
Actonville Av
 WYTH/NTH M22.......180 C1
Acton St CMANE M1.......115 F5
 ROCH OL11.......42 A4
Adam Cl CHD/CHDH SK8.......171 E5
Adams Av CCHDY M21.......141 E3
Adams Cl POY/DIS SK12.......195 F5
Adamson Gdns
 DID/WITH M20.......157 E3
Adamson Rd ECC M30.......110 D5
Adamson Wk
 RUSH/FAL M14 *.......128 C5
Adam St AUL OL6.......119 H2
 BOLS/LL BL3.......48 D3
 OLDE OL4.......91 G5
Ada St BKLY M9.......103 E1
 OLDE OL4.......9 K5
 RAMS BL0.......16 B3
 WHIT OL12.......10 E1

Adbaston Rd STRET M32.......125 F3
Adcroft St STKP SK1.......13 J7
Addenbrook Rd CHH M8.......101 H5
Addingham Dr BKLY M9.......87 H3
Addington Rd BOLS/LL BL3.......63 G1
Addington St ANC M4.......7 H2
Addison Av AUL OL6.......120 A2
Addison Cl BRUN/LGST M13.......128 D2
Addison Crs OLDTF/WHR M16.......127 E5
Addison Dr MDTN M24.......73 F2
Addison Rd HALE/TIMP WA15.......177 H2
 IRL M44.......122 D4
 PART M51.......137 F5
 STRET M32.......139 H1
 URM M41.......138 D2
Adelaide Rd BRAM/HZG SK7.......193 H1
 EDGY/DAV SK5.......12 B6
Adelaide St BOLS/LL BL3.......48 C5
 CHH M8.......102 A5
 ECC M30.......111 E4
 HEY OL10.......41 E4
 MDTN M24.......72 D4
 RAMS BL0.......16 B4
 SWIN M27.......98 C3
Adelaide St East HEY OL10.......41 F4
Adelphi Dr LHULT M38.......81 G2
Adelphi Gv LHULT M38.......81 G2
Adelphi St CSLFD M3.......114 A3
 RAD M26.......52 A4
Aden Cl WGTN/LGST M12.......115 G5
Aden St OLDE OL4.......92 C2
 WHIT OL12.......10 E2
Adisham Dr BOL BL1.......34 A5
Adlington
 HALE/TIMP WA15.......167 E3
 POY/DIS SK12.......195 G5
 TOT/BURYW BL8.......37 F5
Adlington Cl BRAM/HZG SK7.......193 H1
Adlington Dr WILM/AE SK9.......199 H3
Adlington St BOLS/LL BL3.......64 C1
 OLDE OL4.......76 C3
 WGTN/LGST M12.......115 G5
Adrian Rd BOL BL1.......33 F3
Adrian St NEWH/MOS M40.......103 H3
Adrian Ter MILN OL16.......30 D5

Adria Rd *DID/WITH* M20 157 H3
Adscombe St
OLDTF/WHR M16 127 H4
Adshall Rd *CHD/CHDH* SK8 170 D4
Adshead Cl *WYTH/NTH* M22 180 A1
Adstock Wk *NEWH/MOS* M40 7 K1
Adstone Cl *ANC* M4 115 G4
Adswood Cl *OLDE* OL4 76 C3
Adswood Gv *EDGY/DAV* SK3 171 G3
Adswood La East *OFTN* SK2 172 A3
Adswood La West
EDGY/DAV SK3 171 H3
Adswood Old Hall Rd
CHD/CHDH SK8 171 G5
Adswood Rd *CHD/CHDH* SK8 171 F5
Adswood St *NEWH/MOS* M40 115 H3
Adswood Ter *EDGY/DAV* SK3 171 H3
Aegean Cl *BRO* M7 101 F5
Aegean Rd *ALT* WA14 164 D3
Affetside Dr *TOT/BURYW* BL8 36 D4
Affleck Av *RAD* M26 66 D4
Afghan St *OLD* OL1 76 A4
Age Cft *OLDS* OL8 92 B4
Agecroft Enterprise Pk
SWIN M27 100 B3
Agecroft Rd *MPL/ROM* SK6 161 H5
SWIN M27 100 B2
WHTF M45 85 E1
Agecroft Rd East *PWCH* M25 85 H5
Agecroft Rd West *PWCH* M25 85 H5
Agincourt St *HEY* OL10 * 40 C4
Agnes Cl *CHAD* OL9 90 D3
Agnes St *BNG/LEV* M19 144 A1
BRO M7 102 A3
CHAD OL9 90 C2
Agnew Pl *SLFD* M6 113 F1
Agnew Rd *GTN* M18 130 B3
Aigburth Gv *RDSH* SK5 145 E1
Ailsa Cl *NEWH/MOS* M40 103 E5
Aimson Rd East
HALE/TIMP WA15 166 D3
Aimson Rd West
HALE/TIMP WA15 166 D3
Ainley Rd *WYTH/NTH* M22 180 C1
Ainley Wd *DUK* SK16 133 G1
Ainsbrook Av *BKLY* M9 89 E4
Ainscow Av *HOR/BR* BL6 46 A1
Ainsdale Av *BRO* M7 101 G1
TOT/BURYW BL8 37 G4
Ainsdale Cl *BRAM/HZG* SK7 184 B5
OLDS OL8 91 E3
Ainsdale Crs *ROY/SHW* OL2 75 F2
Ainsdale Dr *CHD/CHDH* SK8 181 G3
SALE M33 153 H4
WHIT OL12 18 C1
Ainsdale Gv *RDSH* SK5 145 F3
Ainsdale Rd *BOLS/LL* BL3 64 D2
Ainsdale St *WGTN/LGST* M12 129 G2
Ainsford Rd *DID/WITH* M20 158 A1
Ainsley Gv *WALK* M28 82 A5
Ainslie Rd *BOL* BL1 32 D5
Ainsty Rd *RUSH/FAL* M14 128 B4
Ainsworth Cl *DTN/ASHW* M34 131 G5
Ainsworth Ct *BOLE* BL2 49 H2
Ainsworth Hall Rd *BOLE* BL2 51 E2
Ainsworth La *BOLE* BL2 49 H1
Ainsworth Rd *BOLS/LL* BL3 66 D1
RAD M26 52 A4
TOT/BURYW BL8 37 F4
Ainsworth St *BOL* BL1 33 F4
MILN OL16 30 B5
Aintree Av *SALE* M33 153 F3
Aintree Cl *BRAM/HZG* SK7 185 G2
Aintree Dr *ROCH* OL11 28 B3
Aintree Gv *EDGY/DAV* SK3 171 H4
Aintree Rd *BOLS/LL* BL3 66 D2
Aintree St *OP/CLY* M11 116 C4
Aintree Wk *CHAD* OL9 8 A2
Airedale Cl *CHD/CHDH* SK8 169 H3
Airedale Ct *ALT* WA14 * 165 H4
Aire Dr *BOLE* BL2 34 C1
Air Hill Ter *WHIT* OL12 * 29 F2
Airton Cl *NEWH/MOS* M40 115 F2
Aitken Cl *RAMS* BL0 16 C3
Aitken St *BNG/LEV* M19 * 144 C2
Ajax Dr *BURY* BL9 69 G1
Ajax St *RAMS* BL0 16 C3
ROCH OL11 42 A3
Aked Cl *WGTN/LGST* M12 129 E2
Akesmoor Dr *OFTN* SK2 172 C3
Alamein Dr *MPL/ROM* SK6 162 D4
Alan Av *FAIL* M35 105 E5
Alanbrooke Wk *HULME* M15 * 127 H3
Alandale Av *DTN/ASHW* M34 132 B1
Alandale Rd *EDGY/DAV* SK3 171 F2
Alan Dr *HALE/TIMP* WA15 178 B4
MPL/ROM SK6 174 D3
Alan Rd *DID/WITH* M20 143 E5
HTNM SK4 159 E3
Alan St *BOL* BL1 33 G3
Alan Turing Wy
NEWH/MOS M40 115 H2
Alasdair Cl *CHAD* OL9 74 A4
Alba Cl *ECC* M30 111 E4
Alban St *BRO* M7 101 G5
Albany Av *OP/CLY* M11 131 E1
Albany Cl *LHULT* M38 81 G2
Albany Ct *URM* M41 124 A5
Albany Dr *BURY* BL9 53 G2
Albany Rd *BRAM/HZG* SK7 193 H3
CCHDY M21 141 F2
ECC M30 110 C2
WILM/AE SK9 198 C5
Albany St *MDTN* M24 73 E5
OLDE OL4 76 C3
ROCH OL11 43 F1
Albany Wy *SLFD* M6 113 F2
Alba Wy *STRET* M32 125 F3
Albemarle Av *DID/WITH* M20 142 C5
Albemarle Rd *CCHDY* M21 141 E3
Albemarle St *AUL* OL6 119 H2
RUSH/FAL M14 128 B4
Albemarle Ter *AUL* OL6 * 119 H2
Alberbury Av
HALE/TIMP WA15 167 E2
Albermarle Rd *SWIN* M27 98 D3
Alberta St *BOLS/LL* BL3 48 B4
STKP SK1 13 H5
Albert Av *DUK* SK16 133 F2
GTN M18 130 D4
PWCH M25 101 F1
ROY/SHW OL2 59 H4
URM M41 139 E1
WALK M28 82 A2
Albert Cl *CHD/CHDH* SK8 182 D2
WHTF M45 69 H4
Albert Ct *ALT* WA14 165 G5
Albert Dr *WHTF* M45 70 A3
Albert Gdns *NEWH/MOS* M40 104 C5
Albert Gv *FWTH* BL4 66 A4
WGTN/LGST M12 129 H4
Albert Hill St *DID/WITH* M20 * 157 G3
Albert Park Rd *BRO* M7 101 F5
Albert Pl *ALT* WA14 165 G4
BRUN/LGST M13 129 G5
Albert Rd *CHD/CHDH* SK8 182 D2
ECC M30 111 G3
FWTH BL4 66 A4
HALE/TIMP WA15 177 H1
HTNM SK4 158 D3
HYDE SK14 147 H1
SALE M33 154 D2
WHTF M45 69 H4
WILM/AE SK9 198 D4
Albert Rd East
HALE/TIMP WA15 177 H1
Albert Rd West *BOL* BL1 47 H1
Albert Royds St *MILN* OL16 11 H1
Albert Sq *ALT* WA14 177 G1
CMANW M2 6 E5
STLY SK15 120 C4
Albert St *BOLS/LL* BL3 * 67 E1
BRAM/HZG SK7 185 E1
BURY BL9 5 H4
CHAD OL9 90 C4
DROY M43 118 A4
DTN/ASHW M34 * 132 C5
EDGY/DAV SK3 12 D4
FWTH BL4 66 B4
HEY OL10 40 C4
HYDE SK14 134 A5
IRL M44 136 A5
LIT OL15 20 D3
MDTN M24 73 E5
MILN OL16 44 C1
OLDE OL4 92 D2
OLDS OL8 105 G1
OLDTF/WHR M16 127 F2
OP/CLY M11 116 A4
PWCH M25 * 86 B2
RAMS BL0 16 C2
ROY/SHW OL2 59 E5
ROY/SHW OL2 59 H2
WHIT OL12 14 B5
Albert St West *FAIL* M35 104 C4
Albert Ter *STKP* SK1 13 G3
Albine St *NEWH/MOS* M40 103 G2
Albion Cl *HTNM* SK4 159 H3
Albion Dr *DROY* M43 117 H3
Albion Fold *DROY* M43 117 H3
Albion Gdns *STLY* SK15 121 E3
Albion Gardens Cl
ROY/SHW OL2 59 G5
Albion Gv *SALE* M33 154 B2
Albion Pl *BRAM/HZG* SK7 * 185 E1
BRO M7 * 101 F5
ORD M5 113 H3
PWCH M25 85 H3
Albion Rd *ROCH* OL11 29 G5
RUSH/FAL M14 143 E2
Albion St *AUL* OL6 119 H2
BOLS/LL BL3 49 E4
CHAD OL9 90 B1
CMANE M1 6 D7
FAIL M35 104 D3
FWTH BL4 82 D1
HULME M15 128 A1
LIT OL15 20 D3
OLD OL1 9 G3
OLDTF/WHR M16 127 G4
RAD M26 68 C3
ROCH OL11 42 C5
SALE M33 154 C2
STLY SK15 121 E3
SWIN M27 99 F2
TOT/BURYW BL8 4 A4
Albion Wy *ORD* M5 113 G4
Albury Dr *BNG/LEV* M19 158 A4
WHIT OL12 28 C1
Albyns Av *CHH* M8 102 B3
Alcester Av *EDGY/DAV* SK3 170 C2
Alcester Cl *MDTN* M24 89 E1
TOT/BURYW BL8 37 G3
Alcester Rd *CHD/CHDH* SK8 169 G5
SALE M33 154 C4
Alcester St *CHAD* OL9 90 B4
Aldborough Cl *DID/WITH* M20 142 D5
Aldbourne Cl
NEWH/MOS M40 103 E5
Aldbury Ter *BOL* BL1 * 33 G5
Aldcroft St *GTN* M18 * 131 E2
Alden Cl *WHTF* M45 69 H4
Alder Av *BURY* BL9 39 F3
POY/DIS SK12 195 G4
Alderbank *WHIT* OL12 19 H1
Alderbank Cl *FWTH* BL4 82 C1
Alderbrook Rd *LHULT* M38 81 E4
Alder Cl *AUL* OL6 107 E3
CHD/CHDH SK8 182 A4
TOT/BURYW BL8 37 H4
Alder Ct *CHH* M8 * 102 A1
Aldercroft Av *BOLE* BL2 35 E5
WYTH/NTH M22 180 B2
Alderdale Dr *DROY* M43 117 E3
HTNM SK4 158 D1
MPL/ROM SK6 186 D5
Alderdale Gv *WILM/AE* SK9 198 B5
Alderdale Rd *CHD/CHDH* SK8 171 F5
Alder Dr *HALE/TIMP* WA15 167 F4
STLY SK15 121 F2
SWIN M27 98 B1
Alderfield Rd *STRET* M32 140 D2
Alder Forest Av *ECC* M30 110 B1
Aldergate Gv *AUL* OL6 108 A5
Alderglen Rd *CHH* M8 102 A4
Alder Gv *DTN/ASHW* M34 132 D5
EDGW/EG BL7 23 H5
EDGY/DAV SK3 12 A5
STRET M32 140 C1
Alder La *OLDS* OL8 91 E5
Alderley Av *BOL* BL1 33 H1
Alderley Cl *BRAM/HZG* SK7 185 G4
POY/DIS SK12 195 G5
Alderley Dr *MPL/ROM* SK6 161 F2
Alderley Ldg *WILM/AE* SK9 198 D5
Alderley Rd *RDSH* SK5 160 A1
SALE M33 155 F4
URM M41 138 A1
WILM/AE SK9 198 D4
Alderley St *AUL* OL6 107 G5
Alderley Wy *EDGY/DAV* SK3 171 H5
Alderman Foley Dr *WHIT* OL12 28 D1
Alderman Sq
WGTN/LGST M12 115 H5
Aldermary Rd *CCHDY* M21 156 C1
Aldermaston Gv *BKLY* M9 87 G1
Alder Meadow Cl *WHIT* OL12 28 D2
Aldermere Crs *URM* M41 137 G1
Alderminster Av *LHULT* M38 81 F2
Aldermoor Cl *OP/CLY* M11 116 D5
Alder Rd *CHD/CHDH* SK8 170 A4
FAIL M35 105 F4
MDTN M24 * 73 F2
ROCH OL11 42 C4
Alders Av *WYTH/NTH* M22 168 B4
Alders Ct *OLDS* OL8 106 D2
Aldersgate Rd
CHD/CHDH SK8 193 F2
OFTN SK2 172 C3
Aldersgreen Av
MPL/ROM SK6 187 E5
Alderside Rd *BKLY* M9 103 E2
Aldersley Av *BKLY* M9 87 G3
Alderson St *CHAD* OL9 8 E2
SLFD M6 113 F1
Alders Rd *POY/DIS* SK12 187 F5
WYTH/NTH M22 168 B4
Alder St *BOLS/LL* BL3 65 E1
ECC M30 110 B1
SLFD M6 113 E3
Aldersyde St *BOLS/LL* BL3 64 C1
Alderue Av *WYTH/NTH* M22 168 C3
Alderwood Fold *OLDE* OL4 93 E3
Aldfield Rd *NTHM/RTH* M23 155 G5
Aldford Cl *DID/WITH* M20 * 157 H3
Aldford Gv *BOLE* BL2 51 E4
Aldford Pl *WILM/AE* SK9 200 C3
Aldham Av *NEWH/MOS* M40 116 D1
Aldon St *AUL* OL6 119 H1
Aldred Cl *CHH* M8 102 C4
Aldred St *BOLS/LL* BL3 64 A1
ECC M30 110 D4
FAIL M35 104 D3
ORD M5 113 G3
Aldsworth Dr *BOLS/LL* BL3 48 D5
NEWH/MOS M40 103 F5
Aldwick Av *DID/WITH* M20 157 H3
Aldwinians Cl *DTN/ASHW* M34 132 B3
Aldworth Gv *SALE* M33 153 G2
Aldwych *ROCH* OL11 43 E3
Aldwych Av *RUSH/FAL* M14 128 C5
Aldwyn Cl *DTN/ASHW* M34 132 B3
RAD M26 68 C3
Aldwyn Crs *BRAM/HZG* SK7 184 D2
Aldwyn Park Rd
DTN/ASHW M34 131 H1
Alexander Av *FAIL* M35 105 F2
Alexander Briant Ct
FWTH BL4 * 65 H5
Alexander Dr *BURY* BL9 69 H3
HALE/TIMP WA15 166 B3
MILN OL16 31 G5
Alexander Gdns *BRO* M7 114 A1
Alexander Rd *BOLE* BL2 34 D5
Alexander St *ROCH* OL11 42 A4
SLFD M6 * 112 D3
Alexandra Av *HYDE* SK14 147 G1
RUSH/FAL M14 142 B1
WHTF M45 69 H4
Alexandra Cl *EDGY/DAV* SK3 171 F3
Alexandra Ct *URM* M41 137 G2
Alexandra Crs *OLD* OL1 76 A4
Alexandra Dr *BNG/LEV* M19 143 H4
Alexandra Gv *IRL* M44 136 B3
Alexandra Ms *OLDS* OL8 * 9 K7
Alexandra Rd *AUL* OL6 119 H1
DTN/ASHW M34 132 D4
ECC M30 110 C4
FWTH BL4 82 D1
HTNM SK4 159 F3
OLDTF/WHR M16 127 H4
RAD M26 66 D4
SALE M33 155 E3
WALK M28 81 H2
Alexandra Rd South
OLDTF/WHR M16 127 H5
Alexandra St *AUL* OL6 120 A1
BOLS/LL BL3 * 48 C5
BRO M7 * 114 A2
FWTH BL4 66 A5
HEY OL10 56 B1
HYDE SK14 147 G2
OLDS OL8 9 K6
Alexandra Ter *BNG/LEV* M19 144 A2
OLDE OL4 76 D1
Alexandria Dr *AULW* OL7 118 D4
AULW OL7 119 F4
WHTN BL5 62 C4
Alford Av *DID/WITH* M20 142 C3
Alford Cl *BOLE* BL2 50 C3
Alford Rd *HTNM* SK4 144 B5
Alford St *CHAD* OL9 90 C5
Alfred Av *WALK* M28 98 A3
Alfred James Cl
NEWH/MOS M40 115 G2
Alfred St *AUL* OL6 * 120 A1
BKLY M9 103 E2
BOLS/LL BL3 49 G4
BURY BL9 53 H1
CHAD OL9 8 B5
ECC M30 111 E2
FWTH BL4 66 A2
FWTH BL4 66 C4
HYDE SK14 133 F5
IRL M44 136 A5
LIT OL15 20 D2
RAMS BL0 16 C3
ROY/SHW OL2 59 H2
WALK M28 82 A4
WHIT OL12 14 C3
Alfreton Av *DTN/ASHW* M34 147 E3
Alfreton Rd *OFTN* SK2 173 E3
Alfriston Dr *NTHM/RTH* M23 155 H4
Alger Ms *AUL* OL6 120 A1
Algernon Rd *WALK* M28 81 H3
Algernon St *ECC* M30 111 E2
SWIN M27 98 C2
Alger St *AUL* OL6 120 A1
Algreave Rd *EDGY/DAV* SK3 170 D1
Alice Ingham Ct *ROCH* OL11 29 E2
Alice St *BOLS/LL* BL3 48 B4
HYDE SK14 148 A4
SALE M33 155 E2
SWIN M27 99 G2
WHIT OL12 11 G2
Alicia Dr *WHIT* OL12 10 A2
Alison Kelly Cl *BKLY* M9 103 G2
Alison St *ROY/SHW* OL2 59 H1
RUSH/FAL M14 128 A5
Alker Rd *NEWH/MOS* M40 * 115 G2
Alkrington Cl *BURY* BL9 69 H2
Alkrington Gn *MDTN* M24 88 C1
Alkrington Hall Rd North
MDTN M24 72 C5
Alkrington Hall Rd South
MDTN M24 88 B1
Alkrington Park Rd *MDTN* M24 72 B5
Allama Iqbal Rd *OLDE* OL4 92 B2
Allandale *ALT* WA14 165 E5
Allandale Dr *ROY/SHW* OL2 58 D4
Allandale Rd *BNG/LEV* M19 * 143 H2
Allan Roberts Cl *BKLY* M9 103 E1
Allanson Rd *WYTH/NTH* M22 156 D5
Alldis Cl *WGTN/LGST* M12 129 F3
Alldis St *OFTN* SK2 172 C4
Allen Av *HYDE* SK14 148 B3
Allenby Rd *IRL* M44 150 C2
SWIN M27 98 B4
Allenby St *ROY/SHW* OL2 60 A2
Allen Cl *ROY/SHW* OL2 59 H3
Allendale Dr *BURY* BL9 69 H1
Allendale Gdns *BOL* BL1 33 H4
Allen Dale Wk *CSLFD* M3 114 A3
Allen Rd *URM* M41 139 F2
Allen St *BOLS/LL* BL3 66 D1
MILN OL16 43 F1
OLDS OL8 8 C5
RAD M26 68 A1
TOT/BURYW BL8 37 H3
Allerdean Wk *HTNM* SK4 158 C3
Allerford St *OLDTF/WHR* M16 127 H4
Allerton Cl *WHTN* BL5 62 B3
Allerton Wk
BRUN/LGST M13 * 128 C2
Allesley Cl *WHTN* BL5 62 B3
Allesley Dr *BRO* M7 102 A5
Allgreave Cl *SALE* M33 155 F5
Alligin Cl *CHAD* OL9 74 B4
Allingham St *BRUN/LGST* M13 129 F4
Allington *ROCH* OL11 * 29 H5
Allington Dr *ECC* M30 111 F1
Alliott Wk *HULME* M15 127 H3
Allison Gv *ECC* M30 110 C4
Allison St *CHH* M8 102 A5
All Saint's Cl *ROY/SHW* OL2 59 E4
All Saints Ct *STRET* M32 * 139 H1
All Saints Pl *TOT/BURYW* BL8 37 H3
All Saints' Rd *HTNM* SK4 159 G3
All Saints' St *BOL* BL1 2 E3
NEWH/MOS M40 104 B5
All Saints Ter *WHIT* OL12 11 G1
Allsopp St *BOLS/LL* BL3 2 E7
Alma La *WILM/AE* SK9 198 D4
Alma Rd *BNG/LEV* M19 144 A3
BRAM/HZG SK7 185 H4
HTNM SK4 159 E1
SALE M33 153 H4
WHTN BL5 62 A4
Alma St *BOLS/LL* BL3 48 B5
BOLS/LL BL3 67 E1
ECC M30 111 G4
FWTH BL4 * 83 E2
RAD M26 52 A4
STLY SK15 121 E3
WHIT OL12 10 C3
Alminstone Cl
NEWH/MOS M40 117 E1
Almond Av *BURY* BL9 39 F3
Almond Cl *EDGY/DAV* SK3 12 A5
FAIL M35 105 E4
LIT OL15 20 C2
SLFD M6 113 F3
Almond Dr *SALE* M33 139 F5
Almond Gv *BOL* BL1 * 34 A3
Almond Rd *OLDE* OL4 76 C3
Almond St *BOL* BL1 34 A2
FWTH BL4 65 H4
NEWH/MOS M40 * 115 E1
Almond Tree Rd
CHD/CHDH SK8 182 D3
Almond Wy *HYDE* SK14 148 D1
Alms Hill Rd *CHH* M8 102 B3
Alness Rd *OLDTF/WHR* M16 142 A1
Alnwick Dr *BURY* BL9 53 H4
Alnwick Rd *BKLY* M9 88 A2
Alpha Ct *DTN/ASHW* M34 131 H5
Alphagate Dr *DTN/ASHW* M34 131 H5
Alpha Pl *HULME* M15 127 H1
Alpha Rd *STRET* M32 140 A1
Alpha St *OP/CLY* M11 130 D1
SLFD M6 113 E2
Alpha St West *SLFD* M6 112 D2
Alphin Cl *MOSL* OL5 94 B4
UPML OL3 95 E2
Alphingate Cl *STLY* SK15 121 G1
Alphin Sq *MOSL* OL5 109 E1
Alphonsus St
OLDTF/WHR M16 127 F4
Alpine Dr *MILN* OL16 31 H4
ROY/SHW OL2 74 D1
WHIT OL12 19 H2
Alpine Rd *STKP* SK1 13 K3
Alpine St *OP/CLY* M11 116 C3
Alport Av *OLDTF/WHR* M16 * 141 G1
Alresford Rd *MDTN* M24 88 C2
SLFD M6 100 A5
Alsager Cl *CCHDY* M21 141 F5
Alsop Av *BRO* M7 * 101 E3
Alstead Av *HALE/TIMP* WA15 178 B1
Alston Av *ROY/SHW* OL2 60 A2
SALE M33 154 A3
STRET M32 125 G5
Alston Cl *BRAM/HZG* SK7 * 184 B3
Alstone Dr *ALT* WA14 164 D3
Alstone Rd *HTNM* SK4 144 C5
Alston Gdns *BNG/LEV* M19 158 C1
Alston Rd *GTN* M18 130 D3
Alston St *BOLS/LL* BL3 * 64 D1
TOT/BURYW BL8 * 37 H2
Altair Av *WYTH/NTH* M22 180 C4
Altair Pl *BRO* M7 113 H1
Altcar Gv *RDSH* SK5 145 E1
Altcar Wk *WYTH/NTH* M22 180 B2
Alt Fold Dr *OLDS* OL8 92 B4
Alt Gv *AUL* OL6 107 E4
Altham Cl *BURY* BL9 53 E2
Alt Hill La *AUL* OL6 107 F2
Alt La *OLDS* OL8 92 C4
Alton Av *URM* M41 137 F1
Alton Cl *AUL* OL6 107 F3
BURY BL9 53 H4
Alton Rd *WILM/AE* SK9 198 C2
Alton Sq *OP/CLY* M11 130 D1
Alton St *OLDS* OL8 91 G4
Altrincham Rd
NTHM/RTH M23 167 E2
WILM/AE SK9 189 H4
WYTH/NTH M22 168 C2
Altrincham St *CMANE* M1 7 H7
Alum Crs *BURY* BL9 69 H1
Alvanley Cl *SALE* M33 154 C5
Alvanley Crs *EDGY/DAV* SK3 171 F3
Alvan Sq *OP/CLY* M11 * 130 D1
Alva Rd *OLDE* OL4 76 C2
Alvaston Av *HTNM* SK4 159 E3
Alvaston Rd *GTN* M18 130 D4
Alveley Av *DID/WITH* M20 157 H1
Alverstone Rd *DID/WITH* M20 143 E5
Alveston Dr *WILM/AE* SK9 199 F2
Alvington Gv *BRAM/HZG* SK7 184 B3
Alwin Rd *ROY/SHW* OL2 59 H1
Alwinton Av *HTNM* SK4 158 B3
Alworth Rd *BKLY* M9 88 A2
Alwyn Dr *BRUN/LGST* M13 129 F4
Ambassador Pl
HALE/TIMP WA15 * 165 H4
Amber Gdns *DUK* SK16 * 119 G5
Amber Gv *WHTN* BL5 62 A2
Amberhill Wy *WALK* M28 96 B5
Amberley Cl *BOLS/LL* BL3 47 G4
Amberley Dr
HALE/TIMP WA15 178 C4
IRL M44 136 C2
NTHM/RTH M23 167 H5
Amberley Rd *SALE* M33 153 H1
Amberley Wk *CHAD* OL9 8 A2
Amberwood *CHAD* OL9 73 H4
Amberwood Dr
NTHM/RTH M23 167 E3
Amblecote Dr East *LHULT* M38 81 F1
Amblecote Dr West
LHULT M38 81 F1
Ambleside *STLY* SK15 120 D2
Ambleside Av *AULW* OL7 119 E1
HALE/TIMP WA15 166 D4
Ambleside Cl *BOLE* BL2 35 G2
MDTN M24 72 B3
Ambleside Rd *RDSH* SK5 145 F5
URM M41 137 G2
Ambrose Ct *WYTH/NTH* M22 * 156 C5
Ambrose Dr *DID/WITH* M20 156 D2
Ambrose St *ROCH* OL11 43 E1
WGTN/LGST M12 129 H1
Ambush St *OP/CLY* M11 131 E1
Amelia St *DTN/ASHW* M34 132 C4
HYDE SK14 148 A1
Amersham Cl *URM* M41 124 A3
Amersham Pl *BNG/LEV* M19 144 A5
Amersham St *ORD* M5 113 E4
Amesbury Gv *RDSH* SK5 160 A1
Amesbury Rd *BKLY* M9 88 B3
Amherst Rd *DID/WITH* M20 143 E4
Amlwch Av *OFTN* SK2 173 E3
Ammon Wrigley Cl *OLD* OL1 9 G2
Amory St *WGTN/LGST* M12 7 K7
Amos Av *NEWH/MOS* M40 116 D1
Amos St *BKLY* M9 103 G3
SLFD M6 112 D3
Ampney Cl *ECC* M30 110 C4
Amwell St *CHH* M8 102 C3
Amy St *MDTN* M24 73 E3
WHIT OL12 29 E2
Anaconda Dr *CSLFD* M3 6 B1
Anchorage Quay *SALQ* M50 113 F5
Anchorage Rd *URM* M41 139 G2
Anchor Cl *BNG/LEV* M19 144 C2
Anchor Ct *CHH* M8 * 102 A1
Anchor La *FWTH* BL4 65 E5
Anchorside Cl *CCHDY* M21 141 F4
Anchor St *OLD* OL1 9 G1
Ancoats Gv *ANC* M4 115 G4
Ancoats Gv North *ANC* M4 115 G4
Ancoats St *OLDE* OL4 92 D1
Ancroft St *HULME* M15 127 H2
Anderton Cl *TOT/BURYW* BL8 37 E5
Anderton Gv *AUL* OL6 107 H5
Anderton Wy *WILM/AE* SK9 192 A4
Andoc Av *ECC* M30 111 G4
Andover Av *MDTN* M24 89 E2
Andover St *ECC* M30 110 D4
Andre St *OP/CLY* M11 * 116 D3
Andrew Cl *RAD* M26 68 D3
TOT/BURYW BL8 26 A2
Andrew La *BOL* BL1 23 E5
MPL/ROM SK6 186 D3
Andrew Rd *BKLY* M9 103 E1
Andrews Av *URM* M41 123 F5
Andrew St *AUL* OL6 * 107 G5
BURY BL9 5 G5
CHAD OL9 74 B4
DROY M43 118 B1
FAIL M35 104 D2
HTNM SK4 12 E2
HYDE SK14 134 A5
MDTN M24 73 F5
MOSL OL5 108 D2
MPL/ROM SK6 163 F4
Anerley Rd *DID/WITH* M20 157 G2
Anfield Cl *BURY* BL9 70 A1
Anfield Rd *BOLS/LL* BL3 64 D2

CHD/CHDH SK8...................182 C2
NEWH/MOS M40................104 C1
SALE M33............................154 D1
Angela Av *ROY/SHW* OL2.......75 F2
Angel Cl *DUK* SK16...............127 C1
Angeli Cl *BOL* BL1...................33 C3
Angelko Ri *OLD* OL1................76 C1
Angelo St *ANC* M4....................7 G1
BRAM/HZG SK7..................185 E1
DTN/ASHW M34.................132 D4
Anglers Rest *IRL* M44............150 D1
Anglesea Av *OFTN* SK2.........172 A3
Anglesey Cl *AULW* OL7..........106 C4
Anglesey Dr *POY/DIS* SK12...195 F1
Anglesey Gv *CHD/CHDH* SK8...170 C3
Anglesey Rd *AULW* OL7.........106 C4
Anglesey Water
POY/DIS SK12......................195 F1
Angleside Av *BNG/LEV* M19...158 B2
Angle St *BOLE* BL2....................3 K1
Anglia Gv *BOLS/LL* BL3...........48 B5
Angora Dr *CSLFD* M3.............114 A2
Angouleme Wy *BURY* BL9..........4 D6
Angus Av *HEY* OL10.................40 B5
Anita St *ANC* M4........................7 J2
Annable Rd *DROY* M43...........118 A4
GTN M18.............................130 D2
IRL M44...............................136 B3
MPL/ROM SK6....................161 E3
Annald Sq *DROY* M43.............117 H5
Annan St *DTN/ASHW* M34 *...132 C4
Anne Cl *AULW* OL7.................106 D4
Annecy Cl *TOT/BURYW* BL8.....37 G2
Annersley Av *ROY/SHW* OL2.....59 H5
Annesley Rd *NEWH/MOS* M40...103 E5
Anne St *DUK* SK16..................120 A5
Annie St *ORD* M5.....................112 D3
RAMS BL0.............................16 B4
Annis Cl *WILM/AE* SK9............201 E3
Annisdale Cl *ECC* M30............110 C3
Annisfield Av *UPML* OL3.............3 J5
Annis Rd *BOLS/LL* BL3.............48 A5
WILM/AE SK9.......................201 E3
Annis St *BKLY* M9...................103 F3
Ann Sq *OLDE* OL4...................119 E5
Ann St *AULW* OL7...................119 E5
DTN/ASHW M34..................132 B5
FWTH BL4..............................66 B5
HEY OL10...............................41 E3
HYDE SK14..........................133 F5
RDSH SK5............................159 H2
ROCH OL11 *........................30 A5
Anscombe Cl
NEWH/MOS M40................115 G2
Ansdell Av *CCHDY* M21..........141 F4
Ansdell Dr *DROY* M43............117 F3
Ansdell Rd *MILN* OL16.............43 G2
RDSH SK5............................145 G2
Ansdell St *CHH* M8.................102 B3
Ansell Cl *GTN* M18.................130 C2
Anselms Ct *OLDS* OL8..............90 D5
Ansleigh Av *CHH* M8...............102 B1
Ansley Gv *HTNM* SK4..............159 E3
Anslow Cl *NEWH/MOS* M40....103 E5
Anson Av *SWIN* M27..................98 D4
Anson Ct *BRAM/HZG* SK7 *....194 C1
Anson Rd *DTN/ASHW* M34......145 C1
POY/DIS SK12......................196 A4
RUSH/FAL M14....................129 E4
SWIN M27..............................98 D4
Anson St *BOL* BL1...................34 C4
ECC M30..............................110 C2
Answell Av *CHH* M8..................87 F5
Antares Av *BRO* M7................114 A2
Anthony Cl *WGTN/LGST* M12...129 F1
Anthony St *MOSL* OL5............108 C1
Antilles Cl *WGTN/LGST* M12...129 H4
Antrim Cl *BNG/LEV* M19.........158 A4
Anvil Wy *OLD* OL1......................9 F2
Apethorn La *HYDE* SK14.........147 G3
Apfel La *CHAD* OL9...................8 A2
Apollo Av *BURY* BL9..................69 G1
Apperley Gra *ECC* M30............111 F1
Appian Wy *BRO* M7.................101 H5
Appleby Av *HALE/TIMP* WA15...166 D4
HYDE SK14...........................133 F3
Appleby Gdns *BOLE* BL2 *.........3 H1
Appleby Rd *CHD/CHDH* SK8...169 G5
Apple Cl *OLDS* OL8...................92 B4
Appledore Dr *BOLE* BL2.............23 G4
NTHM/RTH M23...................167 E2
Appleford Av *NTHM/RTH* M23...167 H5
Appleford Dr *CHH* M8..............102 C4
Apple St *HYDE* SK14................148 A4
Appleton Gv *SALE* M33............153 H4
Appleton La *WHTN* BL5..............62 A3
Appleton Rd
HALE/TIMP WA15................177 H5
HTNM SK4...........................144 D5
Apple Tree Ct *ORD* M5............113 F3
Appleton Rd *MDTN* M24............89 E1
Applewood *CHAD* OL9...............73 C5
Appleyard Cl *SWIN* M27..........100 A2
Appleyard La *WILM/AE* SK9.....191 E4
April Cl *OLDS* OL8......................92 B3
Apsley Cl *ALT* WA14................177 E3
Apsley Gv *ALT* WA14...............177 E3
Apsley Rd *DTN/ASHW* M34......132 C4
Apsley St *STKP* SK1.................13 H5
Aquarius La *SLFD* M6 *............113 H1
Aquarius St *HULME* M15..........128 B3
Aqueduct Rd *BOLS/LL* BL3.......49 H5
Aragon Dr *HEY* OL10.................40 D3
Aragon Wy *MPL/ROM* SK6.......174 D3
Arbor Av *BNG/LEV* M19...........144 A4
Arbor Dr *BNG/LEV* M19............143 H4
LHULT M38.............................80 D3
Arbory Av *NEWH/MOS* M40....104 A2
Arbour Cl *BURY* BL9..................27 H1
SLFD M6..............................113 E2
Arbour Rd *OLDE* OL4................92 D3
Arbroath St *DROY* M43............117 F4

Arbury Av *EDGY/DAV* SK3.......170 C2
ROCH OL11............................42 D1
The Arcades *AUL* OL6 *..........119 G2
Arcadia Av *SALE* M33.............154 B5
Archer Av *BOLE* BL2..................49 H1
Archer Gv *BOLE* BL2.................49 H1
Archer Pk *MDTN* M24................72 B4
Archer Pl *STRET* M32..............139 F1
Archer St *MOSL* OL5.................93 H5
OFTN SK2............................172 D4
OP/CLY M11........................116 B3
Archie St *ORD* M5...................126 D1
Arch St *BOL* BL1........................3 H2
Archway *HULME* M15..............128 A3
Arclid Cl *WGTN/LGST* M12 *....48 A9
Arcon Cl *MILN* OL16...................31 F5
Arcon Dr *OLDTF/WHR* M16.....127 H5
Arcon Pl *ALT* WA14.................164 D3
Ardale Av *NEWH/MOS* M40......89 F5
Ardcombe Av *BKLY* M9............87 H2
Arden Av *MDTN* M24.................89 E2
Arden Cl *AUL* OL6...................108 A4
BURY BL9..............................53 F1
Arden Ct *BRAM/HZG* SK7......183 G3
Ardenfield Dr *NTHM/RTH* M23...147 E4
Ardenfield Dr
WYTH/NTH M22...................180 D2
Arden Gv *NEWH/MOS* M40.....104 B1
Arden Lodge Rd
NTHM/RTH M23...................167 F2
Arden Rd *MPL/ROM* SK6.........146 C4
Ardens Cl *SWIN* M27.................85 C5
Arden St *CHAD* OL9...................91 E4
Ardent Wy *PWCH* M25.............101 F1
Arderne Pl *WILM/AE* SK9........200 D4
Arderne Rd *HALE/TIMP* WA15...166 B1
Ardern Gv *STKP* SK1................13 H6
Ardern Rd *BKLY* M9.................102 A1
Ardfield Dr
WGTN/LGST M12.................128 D1
Ardwick Gn North
BRUN/LGST M13.................129 E2
Ardwick Ter *WGTN/LGST* M12...129 E2
Argo St *BOLS/LL* BL3................48 C5
Argosy Dr *ECC* M30.................123 C4
MANAIR M90.......................179 G5
Argus St *OLDS* OL8...................90 D5
Argyle Av *RUSH/FAL* M14.......129 F4
WALK M28.............................81 H2
Argyle Crs *HEY* OL10................40 C5
Argyle St *BRAM/HZG* SK7......185 F2
BURY BL9..............................38 C2
DROY M43...........................117 H4
GTN M18.............................130 C2
HEY OL10..............................40 A5
MILN OL16.............................43 F2
MOS OL5.............................108 D1
OLD OL1................................76 A4
SWIN M27..............................98 D3
Argyll Av *STRET* M32..............139 H1
Argyll Cl *FAIL* M35..................105 G3
Argyll Park Rd *FAIL* M35.........105 G3
Argyll Rd *CHAD* OL9.................90 A4
CHD/CHDH SK8...................170 C4
Argyll St *AUL* OL6...................120 B2
Arkendale Cl *FAIL* M35 *.........105 H5
Arkholme *WALK* M28.................96 B2
Arkle Av *WILM/AE* SK9............192 B3
Arkle Dr *CHAD* OL9...................74 A4
Arkley Wk *BRUN/LGST* M13...128 C2
Ark St *BNG/LEV* M19..............144 A1
Arkwright Cl *BOL* BL1................33 F5
Arkwright Dr *MPL/ROM* SK6...175 F3
Arkwright Rd *MPL/ROM* SK6...175 F3
Arkwright St *CHAD* OL9..............8 A4
Arlen Ct *BOLE* BL2....................49 G4
Arlen Rd *BOLE* BL2....................49 G4
Arlen Wy *HEY* OL10 *................40 C4
Arley Av *BURY* BL9....................38 B1
DID/WITH M20....................157 E1
Arley Cl *ALT* WA14..................165 C1
DUK SK16............................133 C2
Arley Dr *ROY/SHW* OL2.............60 B1
SALE M33............................153 H2
Arley Gv *EDGY/DAV* SK3.........171 C5
Arley Mere Cl *CHD/CHDH* SK8...182 C1
Arley Moss Wk
BRUN/LGST M13 *...............128 C1
Arley St *RAD* M26.......................68 C3
Arlies Cl *STLY* SK15................120 D1
Arlies La *STLY* SK15...............120 D1
Arlies St *AUL* OL6....................120 A1
Arlington Av *DTN/ASHW* M34...147 E1
PWCH M25............................86 A5
SWIN M27..............................98 C4
Arlington Cl *BURY* BL9...............26 D1
ROY/SHW OL2.......................75 F2
Arlington Crs *WILM/AE* SK9....198 B5
Arlington Dr *OFTN* SK2...........184 B1
POY/DIS SK12......................195 E4
Arlington Rd *CHD/CHDH* SK8...182 C1
STRET M32...........................139 H2
Arlington St *AUL* OL6...............119 H1
BOLS/LL BL3.........................65 E1
CHH M8...............................102 A1
CSLFD M3...............................6 A1
Arlington Wy *WILM/AE* SK9....198 B5
Arliss Av *BNG/LEV* M19..........143 H4
Armadale Av *BKLY* M9.............88 D3
Armadale Cl *EDGY/DAV* SK3...171 H5
Armadale Rd *BOLS/LL* BL3.......47 F5
DUK SK16............................119 H5
Armdale Ri *OLDE* OL4..............76 B5
Armentieres *STLY* SK15..........120 D4
Armitage Av *LHULT* M38...........81 E3
Armitage Cl *LHULT* M38............81 E3
MDTN M24.............................72 A5
OLDS OL8..............................90 B5
Armitage Gv *LHULT* M38...........81 E3
Armitage Rd *ALT* WA14...........177 C1
Armitage St *ECC* M30..............110 D4
Armit Rd *UPML* OL3...................94 B3
Armour Pl *BKLY* M9...................87 H5
Armoury St *EDGY/DAV* SK3......13 F6
Arm Rd *LIT* OL15.......................20 C2
Armstrong Hurst Cl
WHIT OL12............................30 C1
Arncliffe Dr *NTHM/RTH* M23...179 H1

Arncliffe Ri *OLDE* OL4...............61 F5
Arncot Rd *BOL* BL1....................34 A1
Arncott Cl *ROY/SHW* OL2.........59 H5
Arne Cl *OFTN* SK2...................173 H4
Arnesby Av *SALE* M33............140 C5
Arnesby Gv *BOLE* BL2................3 K2
Arne St *CHAD* OL9 *..................90 B2
Arnfield Dr *WALK* M28...............96 C4
Arnfield Rd *DID/WITH* M20......143 E5
EDGY/DAV SK3...................171 C4
Arnold Av *HEY* OL10..................40 B5
HYDE SK14..........................148 B4
Arnold Cl *DUK* SK16................134 B1
Arnold Dr *DROY* M43...............117 H4
MDTN M24..............................73 F1
Arnold Rd *EDGW/EG* BL7..........23 E3
HYDE SK14..........................148 B4
OLDTF/WHR M16.................142 A2
Arnold St *BOL* BL1.....................33 G4
EDGY/DAV SK3.....................12 E7
OLD OL1.................................9 K1
Arnott Crs *HULME* M15............128 A3
Arnside Av *BRAM/HZG* SK7....184 D2
CHAD OL9..............................90 B2
HTNM SK4...........................144 D5
Arnside Cl *CHD/CHDH* SK8......169 G5
MPL/ROM SK6....................146 D4
ROY/SHW OL2.......................60 C2
Arnside Dr *HYDE* SK14............133 F4
ROCH OL11............................41 F1
SLFD M6..............................112 A2
Arnside Gv *BOLE* BL2................50 B1
SALE M33............................154 C1
Arnside St *RUSH/FAL* M14......142 D1
Arran Av *OLDS* OL8...................91 C4
SALE M33............................154 D3
STRET M32...........................139 C1
Arran Cl *BOLS/LL* BL3...............47 F4
Arrandale Ct *URM* M41 *.........124 C5
Arran Gdns *URM* M41..............124 C3
Arran Gv *RAD* M26.....................51 H4
Arran Rd *DUK* SK16.................101 C4
Arran St *BRO* M7.....................101 G2
NEWH/MOS M40.................103 C2
Arras Gv *RDSH* SK5................131 E5
Arreton Sq *RUSH/FAL* M14.....129 E4
Arrowfield Rd *CCHDY* M21......141 H5
Arrowhill Rd *RAD* M26................52 A1
Arrow St *BOL* BL1.......................2 A1
BRO M7...............................101 C5
Arthington St *MILN* OL16...........11 C5
Arthog Dr *HALE/TIMP* WA15....178 A4
Arthog Rd *DID/WITH* M20.......157 H4
HALE/TIMP WA15................178 A4
Arthur Av *WALK* M28.................81 H2
Arthur La *BOLE* BL2....................36 A4
Arthur Rd *OLDTF/WHR* M16....127 F5
Arthurs La *UPML* OL3.................95 E2
Arthur St *BOLS/LL* BL3.............66 C1
ECC M30..............................110 C4
FWTH BL4..............................66 A4
HEY OL10 *............................41 E4
OFTN SK2............................172 D4
SWIN M27..............................99 F4
WALK M28.............................96 A3
Ashdown Av *BKLY* M9...............88 B3
MPL/ROM SK6....................162 B1
Ashdown Cl *CHD/CHDH* SK8...192 D1
Ashdown Dr *BOLE* BL2..............34 D3
SWIN M27..............................99 F4
WALK M28.............................96 A3
Ashdowne Lawns *STLY* SK15...121 C2
Ashdown Gv *BKLY* M9...............88 A3
Ashdown Rd *HTNM* SK4..........159 F3
Ashdown Ter *BKLY* M9...............88 A3
Ashdown Wy *ROY/SHW* OL2.....59 F1
Ashenhurst Rd *WALK* M28.........96 A3
Asher St *BOLS/LL* BL3...............64 B1
Ashes Cl *STLY* SK15................121 F5
Ashes Dr *BOLE* BL2....................50 C1
Ashes La *MILN* OL16..................31 H4
OLDE OL4..............................76 C4
STLY SK15...........................121 F5
Ashfield *DTN/ASHW* M34.........132 D5
Ashfield Av *ROCH* OL11............43 E1
Ashfield Cl *SLFD* M6................112 D2
Ashfield Crs *CHD/CHDH* SK8...170 A3
OLDE OL4..............................93 C1
Ashfield Dr *NEWH/MOS* M40...117 E1
EDGY/DAV SK3 *.................172 A5
GTN M18..............................131 E4
SALE M33............................154 C1
MPL/ROM SK6....................165 G5
Ashfield La *MILN* OL16..............44 C2
Ashfield Rd *BRUN/LGST* M13...129 F5
CHD/CHDH SK8...................170 A4
HALE/TIMP WA15................177 H1
ROCH OL11............................42 D2
SALE M33............................154 C1
URM M41.............................138 D1
Ashfield Sq *DROY* M43............117 H4
Ashford *SALE* M33...................153 F2
Ashford Av *ECC* M30...............110 D5
RDSH SK5 *.........................145 F1
SWIN M27..............................98 B4
WALK M28.............................96 A4
Ashford Cl *BOLE* BL2.................35 C5
TOT/BURYW BL8....................37 C5
WILM/AE SK9.......................191 H5
Ashford Ct *OLDE* OL4................76 C4
Ashford Gv *WALK* M28..............97 C2
Ashford Rd *DID/WITH* M20......142 C5
HTNM SK4...........................144 D5
WILM/AE SK9.......................200 D1
Ashford St *HEY* OL10.................40 A4
Ashford Wk *BOL* BL1...................2 C1
CHAD OL9..............................90 D4
CHD/CHDH SK8...................170 D4
IRL M44...............................150 C1
Ashawe Cl *LHULT* M38.............80 D4
Ashawe Gv *LHULT* M38.............81 E4
Ashawe Ter *LHULT* M38............80 D4
Ashbank Av *BOLS/LL* BL3.........33 H5
Ashbee St *BOL* BL1....................33 H3
Ashberry Cl *WILM/AE* SK9.......199 C2
Ashborne Dr *BURY* BL9.............27 E1
Ashbourne Av *BOLE* BL2............3 K3
CHD/CHDH SK8.....................73 F1
MDTN M24.............................73 E3
URM M41.............................138 C3
Ashbourne Cl *WHIT* OL12.........20 A2
Ashbourne Crs *SALE* M33.......155 E4
Ashbourne Dr *AUL* OL6...........108 B4
MPL/ROM SK6....................196 D1
Ashbourne Gv *BRO* M7...........101 H3
WALK M28.............................97 F2
WHTF M45.............................69 F4

Ashbourne Rd
BRAM/HZG SK7...................185 C4
DTN/ASHW M34...................146 C1
ECC M30..............................111 F4
SLFD M6..............................154 F4
STRET M32..........................125 F4
Ashbourne Sq *ROCH* OL11.......28 B2
Ashbourne St *ROCH* OL11.........9 F7
Ashbridge *ROCH* OL11...............28 B2
Ashbridge Rd *FAIL* M35...........105 C2
Ashbrook Av *DTN/ASHW* M34...131 C5
Ashbrook Cl *CHD/CHDH* SK8...181 C5
DTN/ASHW M34...................131 C5
Ashbrook Crs *WHIT* OL12..........19 H4
Ashbrook Farm Cl *RDSH* SK5...145 F1
Ashbrook Hey La *WHIT* OL12....19 H4
Ashbrook La *RDSH* SK5...........145 F1
Ashbrook Rd *OLDE* OL4............93 E2
Ashbrook St *OP/CLY* M11........131 F1
Ashburn Av *BNG/LEV* M19......158 C1
Ashburner St *BOL* BL1................2 D5
Ashburn Gv *HTNM* SK4...........159 F5
Ashburn Rd *HTNM* SK4...........159 F3
Ashburton Cl *HYDE* SK14........149 C1
Ashburton Rd *EDGY/DAV* SK3...171 H5
Ashburton Rd West
TRPK M17.............................124 D1
Ashbury Cl *BOLS/LL* BL3...........48 C4
Ashbury Pl *NEWH/MOS* M40 *...115 H1
Ashby Av *BNG/LEV* M19..........158 B2
Ashby Cl *FWTH* BL4...................65 C1
Ashby Gv *WHTF* M45.................69 H5
Ash Cl *AUL* OL6.......................107 C5
HYDE SK14..........................135 H4
OFTN SK2............................172 D4
WHIT OL12.............................19 H4
Ashcombe Dr *BOLE* BL2.............50 D5
RAD M26................................52 A1
Ashcott Av *WYTH/NTH* M22....168 C5
Ashcott Cl *HOR/BR* BL6.............47 E4
Ashcroft *WILM/AE* SK9............198 C5
Ashcroft Av *SLFD* M6..............113 H2
Ashcroft St *CHAD* OL9..............90 B2
Ashdale Av *BOLS/LL* BL3...........47 F4
Ashdale Cl *RDSH* SK5.............160 A1
Ashdale Crs *DROY* M43...........117 C4
Ashdale Dr *CHD/CHDH* SK8....183 E3
DID/WITH M20....................158 A1
Ashdene *AUL* OL6....................119 H3
OLDE OL4..............................74 D3
Ashdene Crs *BOLE* BL2.............27 F5
Ashdene Ri *OLD* OL1..................60 C2
Ashdene Rd *BNG/LEV* M19.....158 A4
DID/WITH M20....................143 F5
WILM/AE SK9.......................198 C5
Ashdown Cl *CHAD* OL9..............73 D3

WALK M28.............................97 F1
Ashgrove *MILN* OL16................43 G5
Ash Hill Dr *MOSL* OL5.............109 F2
Ashia Cl *MILN* OL16...................30 B5
Ashill Wk *CSLFD* M5 *...............5 G2
Ash Leigh Dr *BOL* BL1...............33 E5
Ashington Dr *TOT/BURYW* BL8...36 D5
Ashkirk St *GTN* M18.................130 C3
Ashlands *SALE* M33.................154 B1
Ashlands Av *NEWH/MOS* M40...96 B3
WALK M28.............................96 B3
Ashlands Dr *DTN/ASHW* M34...132 B2
Ashlands Rd
HALE/TIMP WA15................154 A5
Ash La *HALE/TIMP* WA15........178 D3
Ashlar Dr *WGTN/LGST* M12....115 C5
Ash Lawns *BOL* BL1...................48 A2
Ashlea Gv *OLDE* OL4.................93 C1
Ashleigh Cl *ROY/SHW* OL2........75 F2
Ash Leigh Dr *BOL* BL1................33 E5
Ashleigh Rd *HALE/TIMP* WA15...166 C1
Ashley Av *BOLE* BL2...................50 A1
OLDTF/WHR M16.................127 G4
SWIN M27..............................98 C4
URM M41.............................137 G1
Ashley Cl *ROCH* OL11................42 B2
Ashley Court Dr
NEWH/MOS M40................105 E1
Ashley Crs *SWIN* M27................98 C5
Ashley Dr *BRAM/HZG* SK7......183 H4
SALE M33............................153 H4
SWIN M27..............................98 C4
Ashley Gdns *HYDE* SK14.........146 B4
MPL/ROM SK6....................186 C4
Ashley La *BKLY* M9..................103 C2
Ashley Ms *HYDE* SK14 *..........146 B4
WHTF M45.............................70 A5
Ashleymill La *ALT* WA14 *.......177 G4
Ashley Rd *ALT* WA14...............177 C1
DROY M43...........................117 F3
OFTN SK2............................199 E1
WILM/AE SK9.......................199 E1
Ashley St *ANC* M4.......................7 H1
CHAD OL9..............................8 C3
HYDE SK14..........................133 H4
SLFD M6..............................112 D3
Ashlor St *BURY* BL9 *.................4 C7
Ashlyn Gv *RUSH/FAL* M14.......143 F3
Ashlynne *AUL* OL6...................119 H2
Ashmeade *HALE/TIMP* WA15...178 C3
Ashmond Rd *OLDE* OL4............93 E1
Ashmoor Rd
WYTH/NTH M22...................180 C3
Ashmore Av *EDGY/DAV* SK3...170 C2
Ashmount Dr *WHIT* OL12.........10 C1
Ashness Dr *BOLE* BL2................35 H4
BRAM/HZG SK7...................183 H4
MDTN M24.............................71 G5
Ashover Av
WGTN/LGST M12 *..............129 C2
Ashover St *ECC* M30................126 B5
Ashover Wy *STRET* M32..........126 E5
Ashridge Cl *HOR/BR* BL6...........46 D3
Ashridge Dr *DUK* SK16............133 E1
ECC M30..............................110 C5
Ash Rd *DROY* M43...................117 G3
DTN/ASHW M34...................131 H4
FWTH BL4..............................65 H1
PART M31............................150 C3
POY/DIS SK12......................195 G4
SWIN M27..............................99 G3
Ashstead Rd *SALE* M33...........154 D5
Ash St *BKLY* M9.........................3 G6
BOLE BL2................................3 G6
BURY BL9...............................5 H4
DTN/ASHW M34...................132 A1
EDGY/DAV SK3...................171 G1
FAIL M35..............................104 D2
HEY OL10..............................40 C3
MDTN M24.............................92 A1
OLD OL1................................76 C4
ROCH OL11............................43 E3
SLFD M6..............................113 E3
Ashton Av *ALT* WA14..............165 H3
Ashton Crs *CHAD* OL9...............90 B4
Ashton Field Dr *WALK* M28........81 H3
Ashton Hill La *DROY* M43........117 H5
Ashton La *MDTN* M24...............71 H5
SALE M33............................138 D1
Ashton New Rd *OP/CLY* M11...116 A1
Ashton Old Rd *OP/CLY* M11....115 H5
Ashton Pl *BRAM/HZG* SK7......185 F3
Ashton Rd *BKLY* M9...................88 A2
DROY M43...........................105 H4
DTN/ASHW M34...................133 E4
FAIL M35..............................105 H4
HYDE SK14..........................133 C3
MPL/ROM SK6....................146 C5
OLDS OL8..............................9 F6
PART M31............................151 F2
Ashton Rd East *FAIL* M35.........105 F3
Ashton Rd West *FAIL* M35.......105 E3
Ashton St *BOLS/LL* BL3..............67 E1
CHAD OL9..............................90 A4
DUK SK16............................120 D2
HEY OL10..............................40 D2
MPL/ROM SK6....................175 G5
ROCH OL11............................42 D1
Ash Tree Av *DROY* M43............117 G3
Ash Tree Dr *DUK* SK16............120 C4
Ash Tree Gv *CHM* M8...............102 B1
HYDE SK14..........................134 A1
Ashurst Av *OP/CLY* M11..........116 C3
Ashurst Cl *BOLE* BL2..................35 H5
HYDE SK14..........................148 C2
Ashurst Dr *EDGY/DAV* SK3......171 E4
Ashurst Gv *BOL* BL1...................48 A2
Ashurst Rd *WYTH/NTH* M22....181 G1
Ashville Ter *NEWH/MOS* M40....74 C4
Ash Wk *CHAD* OL9 *................74 A1
MDTN M24.............................88 C1
Ashwater Gv *BOLE* BL2 *...........4 C7
Ashway Cl *OLD* OL1.................119 F2
Ashway Clough North
OFTN SK2 *.........................173 G4

Ashway Clough South
OFTN SK2 * **173** E6
Ashwell Rd *NTHM/RTH M23*...**168** A2
Ashwell St *BOLE BL2 ** **35** G5
Ashwood *ALT WA14*..................**177** E4
CHAD OL9....................................**73** H5
RAD M26.....................................**67** E5
Ashwood Av *DID/WITH M20* ...**156** D2
DTN/ASHW M34........................**131** F5
RAMS BL0....................................**17** E1
SALE M33..................................**153** H3
WALK M28...................................**81** H2
Ashwood Crs *MPL/ROM SK6*...**175** E2
Ashwood Dr *OL OL15*..................**20** C5
ROY/SHW OL2............................**58** D4
TOT/BURYW BL8.........................**26** C5
Ashworth Av *BOLS/LL BL3*.........**67** F1
DTN/ASHW M34........................**132** B1
URM M41...................................**137** O1
Ashworth Cl *ALT WA14*.............**177** E3
CHAD OL9....................................**90** C3
LIT OL15......................................**20** D1
Ashworth Gdns *UPML OL3*........**95** E2
Ashworth La *BOL BL1*.................**34** A1
HYDE SK14................................**135** G5
Ashworth Ms *HEY OL10*.............**40** B4
Ashworth St *CHH M8*.................**101** H5
DTN/ASHW M34........................**132** B4
FAIL M35...................................**104** C4
FWTH BL4.....................................**66** A4
HEY OL10....................................**40** B4
RAD M26.....................................**52** D5
TOT/BURYW BL8.........................**37** H3
Asia St *BOLS/LL BL3*....................**35** F1
Askern Av *WYTH/NTH M22*........**180** C1
Askett Cl *NEWH/MOS M40*........**104** A4
Aspell Cl *MDTN M24*...................**72** C4
Aspen Cl *HALE/TIMP SK9*...........**167** F4
WHTN BL5.....................................**62** A2
Aspen Gdns *WHIT OL12 ** **28** D2
Aspen Gn *DTN/ASHW M34*.......**147** F1
The Aspens *CHD/CHDH SK8 ** ...**169** F3
Aspen Wy *MPL/ROM SK6*..........**187** F5
Aspen Wd *HYDE SK14*...............**134** A5
Aspenwood Cl *MPL/ROM SK6*...**174** D2
Aspenwood Dr *BKLY M9*............**102** D2
Aspenwood Dr *OLD OL9*.............**73** H5
Aspenwood Dr *SALE M33*..........**153** F2
Aspinall Cl *WALK M28*.................**81** E4
Aspinall Crs *WALK M28*...............**81** E5
Aspinall St *HEY OL10*..................**41** F4
MDTN M24...................................**71** H4
RUSH/FAL M14..........................**128** D5
Aspin La *ANC M4*...........................**7** G1
Aspland Rd *HYDE SK14*.............**148** B4
Aspull St *OLD OL4*.......................**92** B2
Asquith Av *DUK SK16*.................**133** G2
Asquith St *ROY/SHW OL2*..........**59** F1
WHIT OL12 * **11** H5
Assheton Av *DTN/ASHW M34* ...**118** C5
Assheton Cl *AUL OL6*.................**119** G2
Assheton Crs
NEWH/MOS M40.......................**117** E1
Assheton Rd *NEWH/MOS M40*...**117** E1
ROY/SHW OL2............................**59** G2
Assheton St *MDTN M24*...............**72** D2
Assheton Wy *MDTN M24*............**72** D4
Assisi Gdns *WGTN/LGST M12*...**129** F2
Assumption Rd *MDTN M24*.........**72** A1
Astan Av *DROY M43*...................**117** E2
Astbury Av *DTN/ASHW M34*.....**118** C4
Astbury Cl *BURY BL9*...................**53** H1
HALE/TIMP WA15 * **178** C5
OLDE OL4......................................**93** E1
Astbury Crs *EDGY/DAV SK3*.....**171** G3
Astbury St *RAD M26*.....................**68** C3
Aster Av *FWTH BL4*......................**65** F3
Aster St *OLD OL1*.........................**75** F3
Astley Cl *ROY/SHW OL2*..............**59** G2
Astley Gdns *DUK SK16*...............**119** G5
Astley Gv *STLY SK15*...................**120** C2
Astley Hall Dr *RAMS BL0*.............**16** D4
Astley La *BOL BL1*.........................**33** H1
Astley Rd *BOLE BL2*......................**35** F1
STLY SK15..................................**120** C3
Astley St *BOL BL1*.........................**33** H4
DUK SK16..................................**119** G5
HTNM SK4..................................**159** G2
OP/CLY M11...............................**116** D4
STLY SK15..................................**120** D5
Aston Av *RUSH/FAL M14*...........**142** C2
Aston Cl *EDGY/DAV SK3*............**171** F3
Astor Rd *BNG/LEV M19*..............**143** G4
SALE M50..................................**112** B4
Atcham Gv *BKLY M9*.....................**87** G1
Athenian Gdns *BRO M7*.............**101** F5
Athens St *STKP SK1*......................**13** K4
Atherfield *BOLE BL2*.....................**35** F2
Atherleigh Gv *NEWH/MOS M40*...**90** A5
Atherstone *WHIT OL12*.................**10** B4
Atherstone Av *CHH M8*................**87** F5
Atherstone Cl
TOT/BURYW BL8.........................**37** H2
Atherton Av *HYDE SK14*............**135** H5
Atherton Cl *FAIL M35*..................**105** G5
Atherton Gv *HYDE SK14*............**135** H4
Atherton La *IRL M44*...................**150** D1
Atherton St *CSLFD M3*...................**6** B6
ECC M30....................................**110** D4
EDGY/DAV SK3...........................**12** C6
OLDE OL4.....................................**92** D2
Athole St *ORD M5*.......................**113** E4
Atholl Av *STRET M32*..................**125** E4
Atholl Cl *BOLS/LL BL3*...................**47** G3
Atholl Dr *HEY OL10*.......................**55** F1
Athol Rd *BRAM/HZG SK7*...........**193** G2
OLDTF/WHR M16.......................**142** A2
Athol St *AUL OL6*.........................**106** A4
ECC M30....................................**110** D4
GTN M18....................................**130** D5
HTNM SK4..................................**159** G3
RAMS BL0....................................**16** D1
WHIT OL12...................................**11** G2

Atkinson Av *BOLS/LL BL3*............**65** G1
Atkinson St *SALE M33*................**139** G5
URM M41...................................**138** D1
Atkinson St *CHAD OL9*..................**8** C1
CSLFD M5......................................**6** C5
ROCH OL11..................................**42** B4
STKP SK1......................................**13** K7
Atkin St *WALK M28*......................**82** A5
Atlanta Av *MANAIR M90*............**179** H4
Atlantic St *ALT WA14*................**164** D3
Atlas Pk *WYTH/NTH M22 ** **181** E5
Atlas St *AUL OL7*..........................**119** F1
DUK SK16 * **120** A5
OLDE OL8......................................**9** F5
Atlow Dr *NTHM/RTH M23*...........**168** A4
Attenburys La *ALT WA14*..........**165** H1
Attenburys Park Est
ALT WA14 * **165** H1
Attercliffe Rd *CCHDY M21*.........**141** E4
Attewell St *OP/CLY M11 ** **116** B5
Attleboro Rd
NEWH/MOS M40.........................**103** G5
Attlee Wy *WGTN/LGST M12*.....**115** H4
Attock Cl *CHAD OL9*......................**8** D4
Attwood Rd *HALE/TIMP WA15*...**166** C4
Attwood St *WGTN/LGST M12*...**129** H5
Atwood Rd *DID/WITH M20*.........**157** F1
Atwood St *CMANE M1*...................**7** F7
Auberson Rd *BOLS/LL BL3*..........**64** C1
Aubrey Rd *RUSH/FAL M14*.........**142** D2
Aubrey St *ROCH OL11*...................**43** E1
SALO M50...................................**126** D1
Auburn Av *HYDE SK14*...............**148** A3
MPL/ROM SK6.............................**161** G2
Auburn Dr *URM M41*...................**139** E2
Auburn Rd *DTN/ASHW M34*.......**131** H2
OLDTF/WHR M16.......................**127** H4
Auburn St *BOLS/LL BL3*................**48** C5
CMANE M1....................................**7** H6
Auckland Dr *SLFD M6*.................**100** D5
Auckland Rd *BNG/LEV M19*.......**143** H5
Audax Wk *NEWH/MOS M40*......**116** C1
Auden Cl *OP/CLY M11*................**117** E4
Audenshaw Hall Gv
DTN/ASHW M34.........................**131** G1
Audenshaw Rd
DTN/ASHW M34.........................**131** H1
Audlem Cl *NEWH/MOS M40*......**115** G3
Audley Av *STRET M32*................**125** E4
Audley Rd *BNG/LEV M19*...........**144** B1
Audley St *AUL OL6*.......................**120** D5
MOSL OL5...................................**109** E2
Audlum Ct *BURY BL9*......................**5** H3
Audrey Av *GTN M18*...................**130** D3
Audrey St *BKLY M9*.....................**103** G3
Augusta Cl *WHIT OL12*.................**10** E2
Augusta St *WHIT OL12*................**10** D1
Augustine Webster Cl
BKLY M9....................................**103** F2
Augustus St *ANC M4*..................**114** D1
BOLS/LL BL3.................................**49** F5
Augustus Wy *HULME M15*...........**8** A7
Auriga Wk *BRO M7*......................**113** H2
Austell Rd *WYTH/NTH M22*........**180** C3
Austen Av *BURY BL9*....................**53** G3
Austen Rd *ECC M30*....................**111** E4
Austen Dr *DID/WITH M20*..........**157** H2
Austin Gv *BNG/LEV M19*............**143** H3
Autumn St *BRUN/LGST M13*......**128** D4
Avallon Cl *TOT/BURYW BL8*........**26** B4
Avalon Dr *DID/WITH M20*...........**169** H1
Avebury Cl *BRO M7*......................**102** A3
Avebury Rd *NTHM/RTH M23*......**167** H4
Avens Rd *PART M31*....................**151** E3
Avenue St *BOL BL1*.......................**34** A1
STKP SK1.....................................**13** H1
The Avenue *BOLE BL2*...................**3** J5
BRO M7......................................**101** F5
BURY BL9......................................**38** C1
CHD/CHDH SK8..........................**181** F3
ECC M30....................................**111** E4
HALE/TIMP WA15......................**178** A4
MPL/ROM SK6.............................**161** G5
ROY/SHW OL2............................**59** F1
SALE M33..................................**153** G3
URM M41...................................**137** G1
WALK M28...................................**97** F3
WHTN BL5.....................................**62** A3
WILM/AE SK9.............................**200** D4
Averhill Walk *BRO M7*.................**96** C2
Averill St *NEWH/MOS M40*.......**104** C5
Averon Rd *OLD OL1*.......................**60** C5
Aveson Av *CCHDY M21*.............**141** E4
Avian Dr *RUSH/FAL M14*............**142** D5
Aviary Rd *WALK M28*....................**97** F4
Aviator St *WYTH/NTH M22*........**180** C1
Aviemore Cl *RAMS BL0*................**26** B4
Avis St *ROY/SHW OL2*..................**59** H2
Avocet Dr *ALT WA14*..................**165** E1
IRL M44.......................................**122** B1
Avonbrook Dr
NEWH/MOS M40.........................**90** A5
Avoncliff Cl *BOL BL1*.....................**33** G3
Avon Ct *MILN OL16*.......................**31** H5
MPL/ROM SK6.............................**174** D4
WALK M28...................................**81** H1
Avondale *SWIN M27*......................**84** B5
Avondale Av *BRAM/HZG SK7*....**185** G2
BURY BL9......................................**5** J3
Avondale Crs *URM M41*..............**124** B5
Avondale Dr *RAMS BL0*................**26** A1
SLFD M6......................................**99** G5
Avondale Rd *WILM/AE SK9*.......**199** G4
BOL BL1.......................................**33** H4
BRAM/HZG SK7..........................**185** G2
EDGY/DAV SK3...........................**12** A6
FWTH BL4.....................................**65** F3
STRET M32.................................**126** B4
WHTF M45....................................**69** F3
Avondale St *BOL BL1*...................**33** H4
CHH M8......................................**102** B3
OLDS OL8......................................**91** F3
Avon Dr *BURY BL9*........................**53** F5
Avon Gdns *BNG/LEV M19*..........**144** A5
Avonhead Cl *BOL BL1*.................**23** F4
Avonlea Dr *BNG/LEV M19*..........**143** G5
Avonlea Rd *DROY M43*...............**117** G4
SALE M33..................................**153** G3
Avonleigh Gdns *OLD OL1 ** **76** B3
Avon Rd *BNG/LEV M19*..............**143** H5
CHAD OL9....................................**74** A4

CHD/CHDH SK8..........................**181** G5
FWTH BL4.....................................**83** E2
HALE/TIMP WA15......................**177** H4
HEY OL10....................................**40** B4
ROY/SHW OL2............................**59** F5
OLDS OL8......................................**91** G3
Avon St *BOL BL1*...........................**33** E5
EDGY/DAV SK3...........................**171** H2
OLDS OL8......................................**91** G3
Avril Cl *RDSH SK5*.......................**145** F3
Avro Cl *RUSH/FAL M14*..............**142** D2
Avroe Rd *ECC M30*......................**123** G1
Avro Wy *MANAIR M90*...............**179** G5
Awburn Rd *HYDE SK14*..............**149** G2
Axbridge Wk
NEWH/MOS M40.........................**115** G3
Axford Cl *BRO M7*.......................**102** A4
Axon Sq *OLDTF/WHR M16*.........**128** A4
Aycliffe Av *CCHDY M21*.............**156** C1
Aycliffe Gv *BRUN/LGST M13*.....**129** F5
Aylesbury Av *DTN/ASHW M34*...**146** D2
URM M41...................................**124** D4
Aylesbury Cl *ORD M5*.................**113** F4
Aylesbury Crs *MDTN M24*..........**73** F2
Aylesby Av *GTN M18*.................**130** A4
Aylesford Rd *RUSH/FAL M14*.......**2** D1
Aylesford Wk *BOL BL1 ** **2** D1
Aylsham Cl *MPL/ROM SK6*.........**161** G1
Aylsham Ms *SWIN M27*................**98** C5
Aylwin Dr *SALE M33*..................**154** C3
Ayr Av *OLDS OL8*.........................**91** G4
Ayr Cl *BRAM/HZG SK7*...............**185** H2
Ayres Rd *OLDTF/WHR M16*........**127** F4
Ayr Gv *HEY OL10*...........................**55** F1
Ayrshire Rd *BRO M7*...................**100** D4
Ayr St *BOLE BL2*............................**34** C2
Aysgarth Av *CHD/CHDH SK8*....**169** H3
GTN M18....................................**130** D2
MPL/ROM SK6.............................**162** C2
Aysgarth Cl *SALE M33*...............**153** H3
Ashford Cl *ALT WA14*................**165** E3
Ayton Gv *RUSH/FAL M14*...........**129** F4
Aytoun St *CMANE M1*....................**7** H5
Azalea Av *GTN M18*....................**130** C2

B

Babbacombe Gv *BKLY M9*..........**87** G2
Babbacombe Rd *OFTN SK2*......**172** D5
Back Abingdon Rd *BOLE BL2*....**34** D5
Back Acton St *CMANE M1 ** **7** H6
Back Adcroft St *STKP SK1*...........**13** H7
Back Adrian Rd *BOL BL1*.............**33** F4
Back Adrian Rd East *BOL BL1 ** **33** F4
Back Ainscow St *BOL BL1*..............**33** F4
Back Ainsworth La *BOLE BL2 ** **3** K1
Back Ainsworth La East
BOL BL1 * **49** H1
Back Ainsworth Rd North
TOT/BURYW BL8.........................**37** H4
Back Ainsworth Rd South
TOT/BURYW BL8.........................**37** H4
Back Ainsworth St *BOL BL1*.........**33** F4
Back Albert St *BURY BL9*................**5** H4
Back Albion Pl *BURY BL9*..............**38** C2
Back Alder St *BOLS/LL BL3*...........**65** E1
Back Alexander Rd *BOLE BL2*....**34** D5
Back Alexandra St
BOLS/LL BL3.................................**48** B5
Back Alfred St *BOLS/LL BL3*.........**49** G5
Back Alice St *BOLS/LL BL3 ** **48** B4
BOLS/LL BL3.................................**67** E1
Back Alicia St *BOLS/LL BL3*..........**50** A5
Back All Saints' St *BOL BL1 ** **3** F3
Back Alston St *BOLS/LL BL3*.........**64** D1
Back Andrew St *BURY BL9*............**5** H4
Back Andrew St North
BURY BL9......................................**5** H5
Back Anglia Gv *BOLS/LL BL3*........**48** B5
Back Annis Rd *BOLS/LL BL3 ** **64** C1
Back Anson St *BOL BL1 ** **34** A3
Back Apple Ter *BOL BL1 ** **33** G4
Back Argo St *BOLS/LL BL3*...........**48** C5
Back Argyle St *BURY BL9*..............**38** C1
Back Arlington st *BOLS/LL BL3 ** **65** F4
Back Arnold St *BOL BL1*...............**33** H3
Back Arnold Ter *BOL BL1 ** **32** C5
Back Ashbee st *BOL BL1*.............**33** H3
Back Ashford Wk *BOL BL1 ** **2** C1
Back Ashley St *ANC M4*..................**7** F3
Back Ash St *BOLE BL2*...................**3** G6
BURY BL9......................................**5** H4
Back Ashton St *BOLS/LL BL3 ** **48** A5
Back Ashworth La *BOL BL1 ** **34** A1
Back Ashworth St
TOT/BURYW BL8.........................**37** H3
Back Astley St *BOL BL1 ** **34** A4
Back Augustus St
BOLS/LL BL3 * **49** F5
Back Augustus St West
BOLS/LL BL3 * **49** E5
Back Avenue St *BOL BL1 ** **2** A2
Back Avondale St *BOL BL1*..........**33** F5
Back Baldwin St *BOLS/LL BL3 ** **48** D4
Back Baldwin St North
BOLS/LL BL3 * **48** D4
Back Balloon St *ANC M4 ** **7** F2
Back Banbury Rd *BOLE BL2*........**34** D5
Back Bank St *CHH M8*.................**114** D1
Back Bantry St *BOLS/LL BL3 ** **48** D5
Back Barbara St *BOLS/LL BL3*.......**48** C5
Back Bark St *BOL BL1 ** **2** D4
Back Bashall st *BOL BL1 ** **34** A1
Back Baxendale St *BOL BL1 ** **33** H2
Back Bayley St *BOL BL1*...............**34** A4
Back Baythorpe St *BOL BL1 ** **34** A4
Back Baytorpe St North
BOL BL1 * **34** A3
Back Beaconsfield St
BOLS/LL BL3 * **2** A7
Back Bedford St *BOLE BL2 ** **3** J1
Back Beech St *BOL BL1*.................**34** A4

Back Beechwood St
BOLS/LL BL3 * **65** E1
Back Belbeck St
TOT/BURYW BL8.........................**37** H4
Back Bell La *BURY BL9*.....................**5** G3
Back Belmont Rd *BOL BL1 ** **5** G3
Back Belmont Rd East
BOL BL1.......................................**33** H1
Back Bennett's La East
BOL BL1.......................................**33** F4
Back Bennett's La East
BOL BL1 * **33** F4
Back Benson St *BURY BL9*..............**5** G6
Back Bentinck St *BOL BL1*..........**33** E5
Back Bentley St *BOLE BL2*...........**49** H4
Back Bertrand Rd *BOL BL1*.........**48** B1
Back Beverley Rd *BOL BL1*..........**48** B1
Back Birch St *BURY BL9*................**5** F2
Back Blackbank St *BOL BL1 ** **34** A4
Back Blackburn Rd *BOL BL1 ** **34** A4
Back Blackburn Rd West
BOL BL1 * **33** H3
EDGW/EG BL7 * **22** D3
Back Blackburn St *BOL BL1*..........**34** A3
Back Blackwood St
BOLS/LL BL3.................................**49** F5
Back Bolton Rd North
TOT/BURYW BL8.........................**37** H5
Back Bolton Rd South
TOT/BURYW BL8.........................**37** H5
Back Bolton St *BURY BL9*..............**34** A4
Back Bolton St South *BURY BL9 ** ...**4** C4
Back Bolton St West *BURY BL9*....**5** H4
Back Boundary St *BOL BL1 ** **33** G4
Back Bowen St *BOL BL1 ** **34** A4
Backbower La *HYDE SK14*.........**148** B3
Back Bowness Rd
BOLS/LL BL3 * **48** C5
Back Bradford Rd
BOLS/LL BL3 * **65** F1
Back Bradford Rd West
BOLS/LL BL3 * **65** F1
Back Bradford St East
BOLE BL2 * **3** K5
Back Bradford St South
BOLE BL2 * **3** J5
Back Bradford St West
BOLE BL2 * **3** H6
Back Bradshaw Rd East
BOLE BL2 * **34** D2
Back Bradshaw Brow West
BOLE BL2 * **34** D2
Back Bradshawgate *BOL BL1 ** **3** F5
Back Bradshaw Rd East
BOLE BL2 * **35** E1
Back Brandon St *BOLS/LL BL3*.....**48** C5
Back Brandon St North
BOLS/LL BL3 * **48** C5
Back Brandwood St
BOLS/LL BL3 * **48** B5
Back Bridgeman St
BOLS/LL BL3 * **48** D5
Back Bridge St *BOLE BL2 ** **2** E5
CSLFD M3.......................................**6** D4
RAMS BL0....................................**16** D2
Back Brierley St *BURY BL9*............**5** F1
Back Brierley St South
BURY BL9 * **53** F1
Back Brigade St *BOL BL1 ** **48** B2
Back Brindley St *BOL BL1 ** **34** A2
Back Brink's Pl *BOL BL1 ** **2** C4
Back Bristol Av *BOLE BL2 ** **34** D5
Back Bristol St *BOLS/LL BL3*..........**48** B4
Back Broach St *BOLS/LL BL3 ** **48** C5
Back Broad o' th' La *BOL BL1 ** **33** H2
Back Broad St *BURY BL9*.................**4** D5
Back Bromwich St *BOLE BL2 ** **3** J6
Back Brookfield St *BOLE BL2 ** **3** J4
Back Brook St North *BURY BL9 ** **5** G1
Back Broom St *BOLE BL2 ** **3** H4
MILN OL16..................................**45** E2
Back Burnaby St *BOLS/LL BL3 ** **48** C5
Back Burnham Av *BOL BL1 ** **32** D5
Back Bury New Rd *BOLE BL2*......**35** E1
Back Bury New Rd East
BOLE BL2 * **3** J5
Back Bury Old Rd *BOLE BL2 ** **35** H4
Back Bury Rd *BOLE BL2*..............**50** A2
Back Bury Rd East *BOLE BL2 ** **50** A2
Back Bury Rd South *BOLE BL2 ** **50** A2
Back Bushell St *BOLS/LL BL3 ** **48** A5
Back Byrom St
TOT/BURYW BL8.........................**37** G2
Back Byrom St South
TOT/BURYW BL8 * **37** G2
Back Calder Rd *BOLS/LL BL3 ** **64** D1
Back Caledonia St *BOLS/LL BL3 ** ..**48** B5
Back Calvert Rd *BOLS/LL BL3 ** **64** C1
Back Cambridge St *AULW OL7 ** **119** E4
Back Camp St *BRO M7 ** **101** G5
Back Canada St *BOL BL1 ** **33** G4
Back Canning St *BURY BL9*............**4** E1
Back Carl St *BOL BL1*...................**33** G4
Back Carter St *BOLS/LL BL3 ** **49** F5
Back Castle St *BOLE BL2 ** **3** J5
Back Cateaton St *BURY BL9 ** **5** H4
Back Cecilia St *BOLS/LL BL3 ** **49** F5
Back Cecil St *BOLE BL2 ** **108** D2
MOSL OL5 * **108** D2
Back Cedar St *BURY BL9*..............**5** J3
Back Cedar St North *BURY BL9 ** **5** J3
Back Cemetery Rd East
BOLE BL2 * **3** K4
Back Cestrian St *BOLS/LL BL3 ** **65** E1
Back Chalfont St *BOL BL1 ** **33** H2
Back Chapel St *BNG/LEV M19 ** **144** B1
BRAM/HZG SK7 * **185** F1
TOT/BURYW BL8 * **19** H1
WHIT OL12 * **19** H1
Back Charles Holden St
BOL BL1 * **2** A6
Back Chaucer St *BOL BL1 ** **33** G5
Back Cheapside *BOL BL1 ** **2** D5
Back Chesham Rd North
BURY BL9......................................**38** D2
Back Chesham Rd South
BURY BL9......................................**38** D2
Back Chester St *BURY BL9 ** **38** D2
Back China La *CMANE M1 ** **7** H5

Back Chorley New Rd *BOL BL1*.....**2** A3
Back Chorley New Rd North
BOL BL1 * **48** A2
Back Chorley Old Rd *BOL BL1 ** **32** D5
Back Chorley Old Rd North
BOL BL1 * **33** G5
Back Chorley Old Rd South
BOL BL1 * **32** D5
Back Chorley St *BOL BL1 ** **2** C3
Back Chorley St East *BOL BL1 ** **2** C3
Back Chorley St East *BOL BL1 ** **48** B5
Back Church Av *BOLS/LL BL3 ** **32** D4
Back Church Rd *BOL BL1 ** **33** F4
Back Church Rd North *BOL BL1 ** ...**33** F4
Back Church St *BOL BL1 ** **2** D3
BOLS/LL BL3.................................**66** D1
Back Clarendon Rd *BOLE BL2 ** **48** B1
Back Clarke St *BOL BL1 ** **48** B1
Back Clay St East
EDGW/EG BL7 * **23** F4
Back Clay St West
EDGW/EG BL7 * **23** F4
Back Clegg's Buildings
BOL BL1 * **33** G5
Back Clegg St *BOLE BL2 ** **49** H2
Back Clifton St *BURY BL9 ** **53** E5
Back Cloister St *BOL BL1 ** **33** F4
Back Clyde St *BOL BL1 ** **33** H4
Back Cobden St *BOL BL1 ** **33** G4
Back Colenso Rd *BOLE BL2 ** **50** A2
Back College Land *CSLFD M3 ** **6** D4
Back College Wy *BOLS/LL BL3 ** **2** B6
Back Columbia Rd *BOL BL1 ** **48** B1
Back Coniston St *BOL BL1 ** **34** A4
Back Coop St *BOL BL1 ** **33** H2
Back Cornall St
TOT/BURYW BL8.........................**37** H3
Back Corson St *BOLS/LL BL3 ** **66** A2
Back Cottam St
TOT/BURYW BL8.........................**37** H3
Back Cotton St *BOL BL1 ** **33** G4
Back Cottonfield *WHIT OL12*......**14** B2
Back Cox Green Rd North
EDGW/EG BL7 * **23** E3
Back Crawford Av *BOLE BL2 ** **35** E1
Back Crawford St *BOLE BL2 ** **3** J6
Back Crescent Av *BOL BL1 ** **2** B3
Back Crescent Rd *BOLS/LL BL3 ** ...**49** E5
Back Crescent Rd West
BOLS/LL BL3 * **65** E1
Back Croft La *BOLS/LL BL3 ** **49** G5
Back Cromer Av *BOLE BL2 ** **34** D5
Back Crostons Rd
TOT/BURYW BL8.........................**4** A3
Back Croston St *BOLS/LL BL3 ** **48** C5
Back Crumpsall St
TOT/BURYW BL8.........................**37** H3
Back Cundey St *BOL BL1 ** **33** H3
Back Curzon Rd *BOL BL1 ** **32** D5
Back Cyril St *BOLS/LL BL3 ** **49** F4
Back Daisy St *BOLS/LL BL3 ** **48** C5
Back Darley St *FWTH BL4 ** **66** B4
Back Darwen Rd North
EDGW/EG BL7 * **23** E3
Back Darwen Rd South
EDGW/EG BL7 * **23** G4
Back Darwin St *BOL BL1 ** **33** G4
Back Deal St *BOLS/LL BL3 ** **65** E1
Back Deane Church La
BOLS/LL BL3 * **48** A5
Back Deane Church La West
BOLS/LL BL3 * **48** A5
Back Deane Rd North
BOLS/LL BL3 * **2** B7
Back Delamere St South
BURY BL9 * **38** D1
Back Denton St *BURY BL9 ** **38** C1
Back Derby St *BOLS/LL BL3 ** **48** D4
BURY BL9......................................**5** F4
Back Design St *BOLS/LL BL3 ** **48** C5
Back Devonshire Rd *BOL BL1 ** **32** D5
Back Devon St North
BURY BL9 * **53** F1
Back Devon St South
BURY BL9 * **53** G1
Back Dijon St *BOLS/LL BL3 ** **48** B5
Back Dijon St North
BOLS/LL BL3 * **48** B5
Back Doffcocker Brow
BOL BL1 * **32** C5
Back Dorset St *BOL BL1 ** **3** H5
Back Dougill St *BOL BL1 ** **33** E5
Back Dougill St South *BOL BL1 ** **33** E5
Back Drake St *MILN OL16*...........**10** D7
Back Drummond St *BOL BL1 ** **33** H2
Back Ducie Av *BOL BL1 ** **48** B2
Back Duckworth St *BURY BL9 ** **38** D2
Back Duncan St *BRO M7 ** **101** F3
Back Dunstan St *BOLE BL2 ** **49** H2
Back Duxbury St *BOL BL1 ** **33** G4
Back Earnshaw St
BOLS/LL BL3 * **64** B1
Back Eastbank St *BOL BL1 ** **34** A3
Back East St *BURY BL9*...................**5** F6
Back Eckersley St *BOL BL1 ** **33** H3
Back Edditch Gv *BOLE BL2 ** **34** D5
Back Eden St *BOL BL1 ** **33** H5
Back Edgmont Av
BOLS/LL BL3 * **48** C5
Back Eldon St *BURY BL9*...............**4** E1
Back Ellesmere St *BOLS/LL BL3 ** **2** A7
Back Elm St *BURY BL9 ** **5** J5
Back Elmwood Gv *BOL BL1 ** **48** B1
Back Elmwood Gv West
BOL BL1 * **48** B1
Back Elsworth St *CSLFD M3*.......**114** D2
Back Empire Rd *BOLE BL2 ** **35** E5
Back Empress St *BOL BL1 ** **33** E5
Back Ena St *BOLS/LL BL3 ** **65** F1
Back Eskrick St *BOL BL1 ** **33** G4
Back Eskrick St East *BOL BL1 ** **33** G4
Back Eskrick St South *BOL BL1 ** ...**33** G4
Back Eskrick St West *BOL BL1 ** **33** G4
Back Essingdon St *BOLS/LL BL3 ** ..**48** D5

Back Essingdon St South
  BOLS/LL BL3 .... 48 C5
Back Eustace St BOLS/LL BL3 ... 65 F1
Back Euxton St BOLS/LL BL3 .... 48 C5
Back Everton St North
  BOL1 * 34 A4
Back Ewart St BOL1 * 34 A4
Back Fairhaven Rd BOL BL1 ..... 34 A3
Back Fair St BOLS/LL BL3 .... 64 B2
Back Fenton St
  TOT/BURYW BL8 .... 37 H3
Back Fern St East BOLS/LL BL3 .. 48 B3
Back Fir St BURY BL9 .... 5 J4
Back Fletcher St BURY BL9 ...... 5 C4
  RAD M26 * 67 E5
Back Flora St BOLS/LL BL3 ...... 48 D5
Back Florence Av BOL BL1 ...... 34 A2
Back Fortune St BOLS/LL BL3 ... 49 C4
Back Foundry St BURY BL9 ...... 5 F5
Back Frances St BOL BL1 .... 33 G4
Back Frank St BOL BL1 .... 33 G5
  BURY BL9 .... 5 F6
Back Fylde St BOLS/LL BL3 ...... 66 A2
Back Gainsborough Av
  BOLS/LL BL3 .... 64 B1
Back Garside Gv BOL BL1 .... 33 F4
Back Garston St BURY BL9 ...... 38 D2
Back Gaskell St BOL BL1 .... 2 B3
Back Gaskell St East BOL BL1 * .. 2 B3
Back Gaythorne St BOL BL1 ..... 34 A3
Back George Barton St
  BOLE BL2 * 3 K1
Back George St BOLS/LL BL3 .... 49 F5
  CMANE M1 .... 7 F5
Back Gibraltar St BOLS/LL BL3 .. 2 B7
Back Gibraltar St South
  BOLS/LL BL3 .... 2 A7
Back Gigg La BURY BL9 .... 5 G6
Back Gilmour St MDTN M24 .... 72 D4
Back Gilnow Gv BOL BL1 .... 2 A6
Back Gilnow La West
  BOLS/LL BL3 .... 48 B3
Back Gilnow Rd BOL BL1 .... 48 B3
Back Glen Av BOLS/LL BL3 ...... 48 A4
Back Glenboro Av
  TOT/BURYW BL8 .... 37 G4
Back Glen Bott St BOL BL1 * 33 G4
Back Gloster St BOLE BL2 .... 3 H5
Back Goldsmith St
  BOLS/LL BL3 .... 48 C5
Back Goodlad St
  TOT/BURYW BL8 .... 37 G2
Back Gordon Av BOLS/LL BL3 ... 48 B4
Back Gorses St BOLE BL2 .... 49 H4
Back Grafton St ALT WA14 ...... 165 G5
  BOL BL1 .... 2 A4
Back Grantham Cl BOL BL1 ..... 33 H5
Back Grasmere St BOL BL1 ...... 34 A4
Back Greaves St OLD OL1 * 9 H4
Back Greenhalgh St
  BOLS/LL BL3 * 66 D1
Back Greenland Rd
  BOLS/LL BL3 .... 65 G2
Back Green La BOLS/LL BL3 ..... 65 G2
Back Green La South
  BOLS/LL BL3 .... 65 G2
Back Green St MDTN M24 ...... 73 E3
Back Gregory Av BOLE BL2 ...... 50 B1
Back Grendon St BOLS/LL BL3 .. 64 B1
Back Gresham St BOL BL1 .... 34 A3
Back Grosvenor St STLY SK15 ... 120 D4
Back Grove St BOL BL1 .... 2 E1
Back Hadwin St BOL BL1 .... 2 E1
Back Halliwell La CHH M8 * 102 A3
Back Halliwell Rd BOL BL1 ...... 33 H1
Back Halliwell Rd South
  BOL BL1 .... 33 G4
Back Halstead St BRO M7 .... 38 D2
  BURY BL9 .... 38 D2
Back Hampson St
  NEWH/MOS M40 .... 115 C1
Back Hanson St BOL BL1 .... 38 C2
Back Hargreaves St BOL BL1 .... 33 H4
Back Harper's La South
  BOL BL1 .... 33 E4
Back Hartington Rd BOL BL1 * .. 48 B1
Back Harvey St
  TOT/BURYW BL8 .... 37 H3
Back Haslam St BURY BL9 * 5 H3
Back Hatfield Rd BOL BL1 .... 33 F5
Back Hawthorne Rd
  BOLS/LL BL3 * 48 C5
Back Hawthorne Rd East
  BOLS/LL BL3 .... 48 A4
Back Hawthorn Rd West
  BOLS/LL BL3 .... 48 A4
Back Haydn St BOL BL1 .... 33 G4
Back Haydock St BOL BL1 .... 2 E2
Back Hayward St
  TOT/BURYW BL8 .... 37 H3
Back Hengist St BOLE BL2 ...... 49 H2
Back Hennon St BOL BL1 .... 33 G5
Back Henrietta St
  BOLS/LL BL3 .... 48 A5
Back Henry Lee St
  BOLS/LL BL3 .... 64 B1
Back Heywood St East
  BURY BL9 .... 5 G5
Back Heywood St West
  BURY BL9 .... 5 G6
Back High Bank St BOLE BL2 .... 49 H2
Back Higher Darcy St
  BOLE BL2 .... 3 J5
Back Higher Shady La West
  EDCW/EG BL7 .... 23 G4
Back Higher Swan La
  BOLS/LL BL3 .... 64 C1
Back Higher Swan La West
  BOLS/LL BL3 .... 64 C1
Back High St South
  BOLS/LL BL3 .... 48 D5
Back High St West
  BOLS/LL BL3 .... 48 D5
Back Hilden St BOLE BL2 .... 3 H5
Back Hilkirk St BOL BL1 .... 33 G4
Back Hilton St BRO M7 .... 101 G3
  BURY BL9 .... 5 F1

Back Hind St BOLE BL2 .... 49 H2
Back Holland St BOL BL1 .... 34 A2
Back Holland St East
  BOL BL1 .... 34 A2
Back Holly Pl BOL BL1 .... 33 H2
Back Holly St BOL BL1 .... 34 A2
  BURY BL9 .... 5 H4
Back Holly St South BURY BL9 .. 5 H4
Back Hopefield St BOLS/LL BL3 .. 63 H2
Back Hope St BRO M7 .... 101 G5
  OLD OL1 * 76 A5
Back Horbury St
  TOT/BURYW BL8 .... 37 H4
Back Horeb St East
  BOLS/LL BL3 .... 48 C4
Back Hornby St BURY BL9 ...... 38 C1
Back Hornby St East BURY BL9 .. 4 E2
Back Hornby St West
  BURY BL9 .... 4 E2
Back Horne St North
  BURY BL9 .... 53 F1
Back Horne St South
  BURY BL9 .... 53 F1
Back Horsa St BOLE BL2 .... 3 J1
Back Horsa St North BOLE BL2 .. 3 J1
Back Hotel St BOL BL1 * 2 E4
Back Hough La East
  EDGW/EG BL7 .... 23 F4
Back Howarden St BOL BL1 ..... 33 H1
Back Howcroft St
  BOLS/LL BL3 .... 48 C5
Back Howe St BRO M7 .... 101 F3
Back Hughes St BOL BL1 .... 33 G4
Back Hulbert St
  TOT/BURYW BL8 .... 37 H5
Back Hulme St ORD M5 .... 113 H4
  TOT/BURYW BL8 .... 4 A2
Back Hulton La BOLS/LL BL3 .... 63 H2
Back Hulton La South
  BOLS/LL BL3 .... 63 H2
Back Hulton La West
  BOLS/LL BL3 .... 47 H5
Back Huntley Mount Rd
  BURY BL9 .... 5 J2
Back Hurst St BOLS/LL BL3 ..... 64 B1
  BURY BL9 .... 5 G6
Back Huxley St BOL BL1 .... 33 F4
Back Ingham St BURY BL9 ...... 5 G6
Back Ingham St East BURY BL9 .. 5 G6
Back Irlam St BOL BL1 .... 33 H1
Back Irlam St North BOL BL1 * .. 33 H1
Back Ivy Bank Rd BOL BL1 ...... 33 H1
Back Ivy St BOL BL1 .... 33 F5
Back Ivy Rd West BOL BL1 * 33 F4
Back James St BOLS/LL BL3 .... 67 E1
Back Jauncey St BOL BL1 .... 48 B4
Back John Brown St BOL BL1 * .. 2 B3
Back John Cross St
  BOLS/LL BL3 .... 48 D5
Back Johnston St BOL BL1 ...... 3 F6
Back Junction St CMANE M1 .... 7 J4
Back Keighley St BOL BL1 .... 33 F4
Back Kendal Rd BOL BL1 .... 48 B1
Back Kershaw St BOL BL1 .... 5 H5
Back Kingholm Gdns BOL BL1 * . 33 G5
Back Kingsley St BOL BL1 .... 33 G4
Back King St BOL BL1 .... 2 D4
  OLDS OL8 .... 9 F4
Back King St North
  EDGW/EG BL7 .... 23 E3
Back King St South BOLE BL2 ... 35 E1
Back Knight St
  TOT/BURYW BL8 .... 37 H4
Back Knowl St STLY SK15 .... 121 E5
Back Knowsley Rd BOL BL1 * ... 33 E4
Back Knowsley St BOL BL1 ..... 2 E4
  BURY BL9 .... 4 D5
Back Kylemore Av
  BOLS/LL BL3 .... 48 A4
Back La AULW OL7 .... 118 D1
  BOL BL1 .... 2 C3
  DROY M43 .... 106 A5
  HALE/TIMP WA15 .... 188 A2
  HYDE SK14 .... 135 H5
  MOSL OL5 .... 108 C2
  OLDE OL4 .... 77 H5
  WHIT OL12 .... 14 B3
  WHTN BL5 .... 80 A1
Back Lark St BOL BL1 .... 3 F3
Back Latham St BOL BL1 .... 34 A4
Back Lathom St BURY BL9 ...... 38 D2
Back Laurel St BURY BL9 .... 5 J4
Back Lawn St BOL BL1 .... 33 F5
Back Leachfield St BOL BL1 ..... 33 G5
Back Leach St BOLS/LL BL3 ..... 48 D5
Back Lee Av BOLS/LL BL3 ...... 64 D1
Back Lee St UPML OL3 .... 79 E4
Back Lena St BOL BL1 .... 34 A4
Back Lenora St BOLS/LL BL3 * .. 48 A4
Back Lever Edge La
  BOLS/LL BL3 .... 64 B2
  BOLS/LL BL3 .... 65 E1
Back Lever Edge La South
  BOLS/LL BL3 .... 64 D1
Back Lever St BOLS/LL BL3 ..... 49 E5
Back Lever St North
  BOLS/LL BL3 .... 50 D5
Back Lever St South
  BOLS/LL BL3 * 48 D5
Back Lightburne Av BOL BL1 ... 48 A2
Back Lilly St BOL BL1 .... 2 C1
Back Lincoln Rd BOL BL1 * 48 B1
Back Lindley St BOLS/LL BL3 * .. 67 E1
Back Linton Av BURY BL9 ...... 38 C1
Back Longden St BOL BL1 ...... 48 B1
Back Longfield Rd
  BOLS/LL BL3 .... 64 A1
Back Long La BOLE BL2 .... 50 B2
Back Longsight North
  BOLE BL2 .... 35 F1
Back Longsight South
  BOLE BL2 .... 35 E1
Back Lonsdale St
  TOT/BURYW BL8 .... 37 H4
Back Lord St BOLS/LL BL3 ...... 67 E1
  BURY BL9 .... 5 F6
Back Loxham St BOLS/LL BL3 ... 66 A2
Back Lumsden St BOLS/LL BL3 .. 48 D4
Back Luton St BURY BL9 .... 49 F5
Back Lytton St BOL BL1 .... 33 G5

Back Mackenzie St BOL BL1 .... 33 G2
Back Malvern Av BOL BL1 ...... 32 D5
  BURY BL9 .... 38 C1
Back Manchester Old Rd
  BURY BL9 .... 4 C7
Back Manchester Rd
  BOLE BL2 .... 3 J5
  BOLS/LL BL3 .... 65 H2
  BURY BL9 .... 4 C5
Back Manchester Rd South
  BOLS/LL BL3 .... 49 F5
Back Manchester Rd West
  BOLS/LL BL3 .... 49 G5
Back Manchester St
  HEY OL10 * 41 F5
Back Manor St BURY BL9 ...... 5 G4
Back Maple St BOLS/LL BL3 * .. 48 C4
Back Marion St South
  BOLS/LL BL3 .... 65 E1
Back Market St BOLS/LL BL3 ... 67 E1
  RAD M26 .... 67 E5
Back Market St West BURY BL9 . 4 D4
Back Markland Hill BOL BL1 .... 32 C5
Back Markland Hill La East
  BOL BL1 * 32 C5
Back Markland Hill La West
  BOL BL1 .... 32 C5
Back Marlborough St BOL BL1 .. 2 A3
Back Marsh Fold La BOL BL1 * .. 48 B1
Back Mary St BOLS/LL BL3 ..... 48 C4
Back Mason St BURY BL9 ...... 2 E6
  TOT/BURYW BL8 .... 37 H3
Back Massie St
  CHD/CHDH SK8 * 170 A3
Back Mawdsley St BOL BL1 ..... 2 E5
Back Maxwell St BOL BL1 .... 33 H2
Back Maybank St BOLS/LL BL3 .. 48 C5
Back Mayfield Av BOLS/LL BL3 .. 65 C1
Back Mayor St BOL BL1 .... 2 A6
  TOT/BURYW BL8 .... 37 H3
Back Maze St BOLS/LL BL3 ..... 49 H4
Back McDonna St BOL BL1 ..... 33 F3
Back McKean St BOLS/LL BL3 ... 48 D5
Back McKean St North
  BOLS/LL BL3 .... 49 F5
Back Melbourne St
  BOLS/LL BL3 .... 48 B4
Back Melbourne St STLY SK15 .. 120 D3
Back Mellor Gv BOL BL1 * 33 E5
Back Mellor Gv West BOL BL1 * . 33 E5
Back Melrose Av BOL BL1 ...... 32 D5
Back Melville St BOLS/LL BL3 ... 65 F1
Back Mercia St BOLS/LL BL3 ... 48 B4
Back Meredith St BOLS/LL BL3 .. 65 E1
Back Mere Gdns BOL BL1 ...... 2 C2
Back Merlin Gv BOL BL1 * 33 E5
Back Merton St
  TOT/BURYW BL8 .... 4 A2
Back Methwold St
  BOLS/LL BL3 .... 48 B4
Back Milford Rd BOLS/LL BL3 .. 64 D1
Back Miller St BOL BL1 .... 33 H2
Back Millet St BURY BL9 .... 4 C5
Back Mill St North
  EDGW/EG BL7 * 23 E3
Back Mill St South
  EDGW/EG BL7 .... 23 E3
Back Milner Av BURY BL9 ...... 38 C1
Back Minorca St BOLS/LL BL3 * . 48 D5
Back Monmouth Av BURY BL9 . 38 C1
Back Moor HYDE SK14 .... 135 H4
Back Moorfield Gv BOLE BL2 ... 34 C5
Back Moorgate West BURY BL9 . 5 G3
Back Mornington Rd East
  BOLS/LL BL3 .... 48 B1
Back Morris Green La
  BOLS/LL BL3 .... 64 B2
Back Morris Green La East
  BOLS/LL BL3 .... 64 B2
Back Moss Ter BOL BL1 .... 2 E3
Back Mostyn Av BURY BL9 ..... 38 C1
Back Mowbray St BOL BL1 ..... 33 E5
Back Murton Ter BOL BL1 ...... 34 A2
Back Musgrave Rd BOL BL1 .... 33 E5
Back Musgrave Rd North
  BOL BL1 .... 48 B1
Back Myrtle St BOL BL1 .... 5 J4
Back Myrtle St South BURY BL9 . 5 J5
Back Nebo St BOLS/LL BL3 ..... 48 C5
Back Nelson St South
  BURY BL9 * 53 G1
Back Nevada St BOL BL1 .... 33 H5
Back New George St
  TOT/BURYW BL8 .... 37 H4
Back Newhall La BOL BL1 ...... 32 D5
Back Newport Rd
  BOLS/LL BL3 .... 49 F5
Back Newport St BOL BL1 ..... 2 E6
Back Newton St BOL BL1 .... 2 E6
Back Nixon Rd BOLS/LL BL3 ... 64 B1
Back Normanby St
  BOLS/LL BL3 .... 64 B2
Back Norris St BOLS/LL BL3 .... 66 D1
Back Northern Gv BOL BL1 ..... 33 F5
Back Nunnery Rd
  BOLS/LL BL3 .... 48 B5
Back Nut St BOL BL1 .... 33 G4
Back Oak St RAD M26 .... 68 B5
Back Olga St BOL BL1 .... 3 J1
Back Olga St North BOL BL1 * .. 33 G4
Back Olive Bank
  TOT/BURYW BL8 .... 37 G2
Back Oram St BURY BL9 .... 38 D2
Back Oriel St BOLS/LL BL3 ..... 48 B4
Back Ormrod St BURY BL9 ..... 5 H5
Back Osborne Gv BOL BL1 ..... 33 F5
Back o' th' Low Rd OLDE OL4 .. 77 E4
Back Oxford Gv North
  BOL BL1 .... 33 F5
Back Oxford St BURY BL9 ...... 5 G6
Back Packer St BOL BL1 .... 33 F4
Back Palace St BOL BL1 .... 33 G4
Back Parade BURY BL9 * 5 G6
Back Parkdale Rd BOLE BL2 .... 34 D5
Back Parkfield St
  BOLS/LL BL3 .... 65 F1

Back Parkhills Rd North
  BURY BL9 .... 53 F1
Back Parkinson St
  BOLS/LL BL3 * 48 B4
Back Park Rd BOL BL1 .... 2 A5
Back Park St BURY BL9 .... 2 A3
Back Park Vw BOL BL1 .... 23 E5
Back Park View Rd
  BOLS/LL BL3 * 48 B4
Back Parsonage St BURY BL9 .. 5 H3
Back Partington St
  BOLS/LL BL3 .... 64 B2
Back Patience St WHIT OL12 * .. 29 F2
Back Patterson St
  BOLS/LL BL3 .... 47 H5
Back Peabody St
  BOLS/LL BL3 * 48 D5
Back Peace St BOLS/LL BL3 .... 48 C4
Back Pedder St BOL BL1 .... 33 F5
Back Peel St TOT/BURYW BL8 .. 37 H4
Back Peers St BURY BL9 .... 4 C5
Back Penarth Rd
  BOLS/LL BL3 .... 48 A5
Back Pennington Rd
  BOLS/LL BL3 .... 65 E1
Back Percy St BURY BL9 .... 32 D5
Back Peter St BURY BL9 .... 5 G3
Back Peveril St BOLS/LL BL3 ... 64 A1
Back Phoenix St BOL BL1 ...... 4 C5
Back Piccadilly CMANE M1 ..... 7 H5
Back Pikes La West
  BOLS/LL BL3 .... 48 B4
Back Pine St BOL BL1 .... 34 J4
  BURY BL9 .... 34 J4
Back Pleasant St BOL BL1 ..... 2 D2
Back Pool Fold CMANW M2 * .. 6 E4
Back Poplar Av BOL BL1 .... 34 A2
Back Porter St BURY BL9 ...... 38 C2
Back Portland St AUL OL6 ..... 119 F3
Back Portugal St BOLE BL2 .... 3 J5
Back Primrose St BOL BL1 ..... 34 A2
Back Primula St BOL BL1 ...... 34 A2
Back Proctor St
  TOT/BURYW BL8 .... 37 H5
Back Progress St BOL BL1 ..... 34 A5
Back Quebec St BOLS/LL BL3 .. 48 B4
Back Queensgate BOL BL1 ..... 48 B1
Back Queen St BOL BL1 * 2 D5
Back Radcliffe Rd East
  BOLE BL2 .... 3 J4
Back Raimond St BOL BL1 ..... 33 F5
Back Rainshaw St BOL BL1 .... 33 H1
Back Rake St BURY BL9 .... 38 D2
Back Randal St BOLS/LL BL3 * . 48 B5
Back Range St BOLS/LL BL3 ... 48 D5
Back Raphael St BOL BL1 ...... 33 G5
Back Raven St BURY BL9 ...... 5 H5
Back Rawson Rd BOL BL1 ..... 33 F5
Back Rawson Rd North
  BOL BL1 .... 33 F5
Back Raymond Av BURY BL9 .. 38 C1
Back Red Bank ANC M4 .... 114 D2
Back Redhill Gv BOL BL1 ...... 2 C2
Back Regent St BURY BL9 ..... 4 C5
Back Ribblesdale Rd
  BOLS/LL BL3 .... 48 C5
Back Richard Burch St
  BURY BL9 .... 5 F2
Back Richelieu St BOLS/LL BL3 . 49 F5
Back Rigby La North
  BOLE BL2 .... 23 H5
Back Rigby La South BOLE BL2 . 23 H5
Back Rishton La BOLS/LL BL3 .. 65 E1
Back Rishton La East
  BOLS/LL BL3 .... 65 E1
Back Rochdale Old Rd North
  BURY BL9 .... 5 K2
Back Rochdale Old Rd South
  BURY BL9 .... 5 K2
Back Rochdale Rd South
  BURY BL9 .... 5 G4
Back Rock Av BOL BL1 .... 33 F5
Back Roscow Av BOLE BL2 .... 50 B1
Back Rose Bank BURY BL9 .... 38 C2
Back Romer St BOLE BL2 ...... 49 H2
Back Rosamond St
  BOLS/LL BL3 .... 48 B5
Back Roseberry St
  BOLS/LL BL3 .... 48 B5
Back Rossini St BOL BL1 .... 33 G3
Back Rowena St BOLS/LL BL3 .. 65 F1
Back Rowland St
  BOLS/LL BL3 .... 64 A1
Back Royal Av BURY BL9 ...... 38 C1
Back Royds St MILN OL16 ..... 43 F1
Back Rudolph St BOLS/LL BL3 . 65 E1
Back Rumworth St
  BOLS/LL BL3 .... 48 C5
Back Rushton Rd BOL BL1 ..... 33 E5
Back Russell St BOLS/LL BL3 ... 66 D1
Back Russell St BOL BL1 .... 48 B4
Back Rutland Gv BOL BL1 ..... 33 F5
Back Ryefield St BOL BL1 ..... 3 G1
Back St Anne's St BURY BL9 ... 38 C2
Back St Ann St BOL BL1 .... 33 H5
Back St Augustine St
  BOL BL1 .... 33 G4
Back St George's Rd ANC M4 * . 7 H1
Back St George's Rd North
  BOL BL1 .... 2 B3
Back St Helens Rd
  BOLS/LL BL3 .... 48 A5
Back St Helens Rd South
  BOLS/LL BL3 .... 64 A2
Back St James's St OLD OL1 * .. 76 A5
Back St Mark's La CHH M8 * ... 102 A2
Back St Mary's Pl BURY BL9 ... 4 D4
Back St Philip's Av
  BOL BL1 .... 33 G4
Back St Thomas St East
  BOL BL1 * 33 G4
Back Salford St BURY BL9 ..... 38 D2
Back Salisbury St BOLS/LL BL3 . 2 B6
Back Salisbury Ter BOLE BL2 .. 50 A2

Back Sandon St West
  BOLS/LL BL3 .... 48 C5
Back Sankey St BURY BL9 ..... 4 B4
Back Sapling Rd BOLS/LL BL3 . 64 A2
Back Sapling Rd South
  BOLS/LL BL3 .... 64 A2
Back Scholes St
  TOT/BURYW BL8 .... 37 H3
Back Scott St OLDS OL8 * 9 F7
Back Scowcroft St BOLE BL2 .. 3 J1
Back Settle St BOLS/LL BL3 ... 64 C1
Back Settle St North
  BOLS/LL BL3 .... 64 D1
Back Seymour Rd BOL BL1 ... 34 A3
Back Sharman St BOLS/LL BL3 . 49 G4
Back Shaw-Street BURY BL9 .. 5 J5
Back Shepherd St BURY BL9 .. 5 F5
Back Sherwood St BOL BL1 ... 34 A3
Back Shipton St BOL BL1 ..... 33 E5
Back Silverdale Rd BOL BL1 .. 48 B2
Back Silver St BURY BL9 ...... 4 D5
Back Skipton St BOLE BL2 .... 49 H1
Back Smethurst La
  BOLS/LL BL3 .... 64 A2
Back Smethurst La West
  BOLS/LL BL3 .... 64 A2
Back Sofa St BOL BL1 .... 33 E5
Back Soho St BOL BL1 .... 2 E6
Back Somerset Rd BOL BL1 ... 48 A2
Back Somerville St BOL BL1 * . 33 F5
Back South Cross St East
  BURY BL9 .... 5 F5
Back South Pde CSLFD M3 ... 6 D4
Back South St BOLS/LL BL3 ... 66 D1
Back South Vw BOLE BL2 .... 49 H2
Back Spa Rd BOL BL1 .... 2 A6
Back Spa Rd North BOL BL1 .. 2 A6
Back Spa Rd West BOL BL1 * . 2 A6
Back Spear St ANC M4 * 7 H3
Back Springfield St
  BOLS/LL BL3 .... 49 G5
Back Spring Gdns BOL BL1 ... 2 E6
  MDTN M24 .... 72 D2
Back Spring St East BURY BL9 . 5 F6
Back Spring St West BURY BL9 . 5 F6
Back Square St RAMS BL0 .... 16 D2
Back Stainsbury St
  BOLS/LL BL3 .... 48 B5
Back Stanley St RAMS BL0 ... 16 C3
Back Stephen St
  TOT/BURYW BL8 .... 37 H4
Back Stewart St BOL BL1 ..... 33 H5
Back Backstone St BOLE BL2 . 3 J1
Back Sunlight Rd BOL BL1 .... 48 B2
Back Sunning Hill St
  BOLS/LL BL3 .... 48 C5
Back Sunnyside Rd BOLS/LL BL3 33 F4
Back Swan La BOLS/LL BL3 ... 48 C5
Back Tavistock Rd BOL BL1 ... 33 F5
Back Teak St BURY BL9 ...... 5 J4
Back Tenterden St BURY BL9 . 4 C5
Back Thicketford Rd
  BOLE BL2 .... 34 C5
Back Thicketford Rd West
  BOLE BL2 .... 34 C5
Back Thomasson Cl BOL BL1 . 33 H5
Back Thomas St ANC M4 * ... 7 G3
Back Thorns Rd BOL BL1 ..... 33 H5
Back Thorn St BOL BL1 ...... 34 A4
Back Thorpe St BOL BL1 ..... 33 H1
Back Thurnham St
  BOLS/LL BL3 .... 64 B1
Back Tinline St BURY BL9 .... 4 C5
Back Tonge Moor Rd
  BOLE BL2 .... 34 C4
Back Tonge Moor Rd East
  BOLE BL2 .... 3 J1
Back Tonge Old Rd BOLE BL2 . 49 H2
Back Tong Rd BOLS/LL BL3 ... 48 C5
Back Tottington Rd
  TOT/BURYW BL8 .... 37 G2
Back Tottington Rd East
  .... 35 F1
Back Tottington Rd North
  .... 37 H3
Back Tottington Rd South
  .... 37 H3
Back Tudor St BOLS/LL BL3 .. 48 B5
Back Turner St ANC M4 ...... 7 H3
Back Turton Rd East BOLE BL2 34 D1
Back Turton Rd West
  BOLE BL2 .... 34 D2
Back Uganda St BOLS/LL BL3 . 64 B1
Back Ullswater St BOLS/LL BL3 34 A4
Back Union Rd BOLE BL2 ..... 3 H1
Back Unsworth St South
  BOLS/LL BL3 .... 48 C4
Back Uttley St BOL BL1 ...... 33 G4
Back Venice St BOLS/LL BL3 .. 48 B5
Back Vernon St BOL BL1 ..... 2 C3
  BURY BL9 .... 2 C3
Back Vernon St South
  BOL BL1 * 2 C3
Back Vickerman St BOL BL1 .. 33 G4
Back Victoria Gv BOL BL1 .... 33 F5
Back Victoria Gv North
  BOL BL1 .... 33 F5
Back Victory St East BOL BL1 . 48 B1
Back View St BOLS/LL BL3 ... 48 C4
Back Vincent St BOL BL1 ..... 48 B3
Back Viola St BOLS/LL BL3 ... 48 B3
Back Waldeck St BOL BL1 .... 48 B1
Back Walmersley Rd East
  BURY BL9 .... 5 F2
Back Walnut St BOL BL1 ..... 34 A3
Back Walshaw Rd North
  TOT/BURYW BL8 .... 37 H3
Back Walshaw Rd South
  TOT/BURYW BL8 .... 37 H3
Back Wapping St BOL BL1 ... 33 G3
Back Wardle St BOLE BL2 .... 49 G4
Back Wash La BURY BL9 ..... 5 H4
Back Water St EDGW/EG BL7 . 22 C1
  STKP SK1 * 13 H1
Back Waverley Rd BOL BL1 ... 33 H4

Back Webster St
*BOLS/LL BL3 ** 49 C5
Back Wellington Rd South
BURY BL9........53 F1
Back Westbank St *BOL BL1*....2 B3
Back Westbourne Av
BOLS/LL BL5........65 F1
Back Weston St North
Back Weston St South
BOLS/LL BL3........49 E5
Back Westwood Rd *BOL BL1 **..48 B1
Back Whittle Gv *BOL BL1 **....33 E5
Back Whittle St
*TOT/BURYW BL8 **........37 H3
Back Wigan Rd North
BOLS/LL BL3........47 H5
Back Wigan Rd South
BOLS/LL BL3........47 H5
Back Willows *BOLS/LL BL3*....48 A4
Back Willows La *BOLS/LL BL3*..48 A5
Back Willows La North
Back Willows La South
BOLS/LL BL3........48 B5
Back Wilmot St *BOL BL1*....33 F4
Back Wilton St *BOL BL1*....34 A3
Back Windermere St *BOL BL1*..34 A3
Back Windsor Gv *BOL BL1*....33 F5
Back Wolfenden St *BOL BL1 **..33 H4
Back Woodbine Rd
BOLS/LL BL3........64 B1
Back Woodfield St
*BOLS/LL BL3 **........65 F1
Back Woodgate St
*BOLS/LL BL3 **........65 F1
Back Wood St *TOT/BURYW BL8*..37 H3
Back Worcester St *BOL BL1*....33 H5
Back Wordsworth St *BOL BL1*..33 G4
Back Worsel St *BOLS/LL BL3*..48 B5
Back Worsel St North
*BOLS/LL BL3 **........48 B5
Back Wynne St *BOL BL1*....33 H4
Back Yates St *BOLE BL2*....4 E3
Bacon Av *DTN/ASHW M34*....147 E4
Bacup St *NEWH/MOS M40*....103 H2
Badby Cl *ANC M4*........115 G4
Baddeley Cl *EDGY/DAV SK3*..171 G4
Badder St *BOL BL1*........2 E3
Bader Dr *HEY OL10*........56 A2
Badger Cl *HYDE SK14*........133 H4
MILN OL16........43 H3
MPL/ROM SK6........187 E1
Badger Edge La *OLDE OL4*....77 H1
UPML OL3........61 H5
Badger Rd *ALT WA14*........165 F1
Badger St *BURY BL9*........69 H2
Badgers Wk *WYTH/NTH M22*..180 D3
Bagnall Cl *UPML OL3*........79 F3
WHIT OL12........28 C1
Bagot St *OP/CLY M11*........116 C4
SWIN M27........98 B1
Bagshaw St *HYDE SK14*....133 G3
Bagslate Moor La *ROCH OL11*..28 C3
Bagslate Moor Rd *ROCH OL11*..28 C4
Bagstock Av *POY/DIS SK12*..195 F5
Baguley Crs *EDGY/DAV SK3*..171 G5
MDTN M24........87 F1
Baguley Dr *BURY BL9*........69 H2
Baguley La *SALE M33*........155 F4
Baguley St *DROY M43*........118 A4
Baildon Rd *ROCH OL11*........29 E2
Baildon St
NEWH/MOS M40........103 H1
Bailey Fold *WHTN BL5*........62 C4
Bailey La *BOLE BL2*........3 F5
MANAIR M90........180 A3
PART M31........151 E2
Bailey St *OLD OL1 **........9 J3
OP/CLY M11........116 C4
PWCH M25........86 B2
Bailey Wk *ALT WA14*........177 F4
Baillie St *MILN OL16*........10 D5
RAD M26........53 F4
Baillie St East *MILN OL16*....101 F4
The Bails *BRO M7*........101 F4
Bainbridge Cl
*WGTN/LGST M12 **........129 E2
Bainbridge Rd *OLDE OL4*....76 C3
Bainburgh Clough *OLDS OL8*..92 D2
Baines Av *IRL M44*........136 B2
Baines St *BOL BL1*........48 A1
Bain St *SWIN M27*........99 E3
Baird St *CMANE M1*........7 J6
Baker St *FWTH BL4*........83 E1
HEY OL10........56 A1
HTNM SK4........159 H3
MDTN M24........73 E4
RAMS BL0........16 C3
STLY SK15........121 F4
Bakewell Av *AUL OL6*........108 A4
DTN/ASHW M34........147 E3
Bakewell Rd
BRAM/HZG SK7........185 F4
DROY M43........117 F3
ECC M30........103 H2
STRET M32........125 F5
Bakewell St *EDGY/DAV SK3*..12 C6
GTN M18........130 B4
Bala Cl *ORD M5*........113 F3
Balcary Gv *BOL BL1*........48 A1
Balcombe Cl
TOT/BURYW BL8........26 C4
Balderstone Rd *ROCH OL11*..43 F4
Baldock Rd *DID/WITH M20*..158 A3
Baldwin Rd *BNG/LEV M19*..143 H5
Baldwin St *ANC M4*........7 K7
BOLS/LL BL3........2 A7
OLDE OL4........76 B5
ROY/SHW OL2........60 A1

SLFD M6........100 C4
Balham Wk
*WGTN/LGST M12 **........129 G2
Balinge Wk *OL12*........10 B4
Ballantine St
NEWH/MOS M40........116 D1
Ballard Cl *LIT OL15*........21 E1
Ballard Wy *ROY/SHW OL2*....60 B2
Ballater Av *URM M41*........138 A2
Ballbrook Av *DID/WITH M20*..157 F1
Balleratt St *BNG/LEV M19*..131 E4
Ball Gn *STRET M32*........125 C3
Balliol Cl *MPL/ROM SK6*....162 B2
Balliol St *CHH M8*........102 B2
SWIN M27........98 D2
Balloon St *ANC M4*........7 F2
Balm St *MILN OL16*........10 E5
Ball Wk *HYDE SK14*........149 H2
Balmain Av *GTN M18*........130 B5
Balmain Rd *URM M41*........124 A5
Balmer Rd *NTHM/RTH M23*..167 H4
Balmfield St *CHH M8*........102 B5
Balmforth St *HULME M15*....127 G1
Balmoral Av *BOLS/LL BL3*....66 D1
CHD/CHDH SK8........182 D2
DTN/ASHW M34........132 A1
HYDE SK14........148 A3
ROCH OL11........29 E5
ROY/SHW OL2........59 C5
STRET M32........126 A5
URM M41........138 B2
WHTF M45........69 H5
Balmoral Cl *BURY BL9*........53 H4
MILN OL16........31 H5
TOT/BURYW BL8........26 B2
Balmoral Dr *ALT WA14*........166 A1
HEY OL10........40 A4
MPL/ROM SK6........186 D5
POY/DIS SK12........195 E4
STLY SK15........120 D2
Balmoral Gra *PWCH M25*....86 D4
Balmoral Gv *BRAM/HZG SK7*..185 G1
Balmoral Rd *FWTH BL4*....81 G1
HALE/TIMP WA15........165 H5
HTNM SK4........158 D3
RUSH/FAL M14........143 F5
SWIN M27........84 B5
URM M41........138 A2
Balmoral St *GTN M18*........130 B4
Balmoral Wy *WILM/AE SK9*..198 D4
Balmore Cl *BOLS/LL BL3*....63 H1
HEY OL10........40 A4
MPL/ROM SK6........186 D5
POY/DIS SK12........195 E4
Balsam Cl *BRUN/LGST M13*..128 F1
Balshaw Av *IRL M44*........136 B1
Balshaw Cl *BOLS/LL BL3*....2 A6
Balshaw St *IRL M44*........136 C1
Baltic Rd *ALT WA14*........164 D3
Baltic St *ORD M5*........112 D3
Baltimore St *NEWH/MOS M40*..103 C5
Bamber Av *SALE M33*........155 F3
Bamber Wk *BOLS/LL BL3 **..48 C4
Bamburgh Cl *RAD M26*........51 F4
Bamburgh Dr *AULW OL7*....106 B5
Bambury St *BURY BL9*........5 H4
Bamford Av *DTN/ASHW M34*..146 D3
HEY OL10........72 D2
Bamford Ct *BURY BL9*........39 H2
CHD/CHDH SK8........182 A4
Bamford Gdns
HALE/TIMP WA15........167 E4
Bamford Gv *AUL OL6*........108 A4
DID/WITH M20........157 F3
Bamford Ms *ROCH OL11*....28 B4
Bamford Prec *ROCH OL11 **..28 B4
Bamford Rd *DID/WITH M20*..157 F3
HEY OL10........40 D2
Bamford St *CHAD OL9*........74 D4
LIT OL15........20 C3
OP/CLY M11........116 C3
ROY/SHW OL2........59 F5
STKP SK1........13 G5
Bamford Wy *ROCH OL11*....28 C5
Bampton Cl *OFTN SK2*........172 C2
Bampton Rd *WYTH/NTH M22*..180 B3
Banbury Dr *ALT WA14*........165 H1
Banbury Ms *SWIN M27*........98 C1
Banbury Rd *FAIL M35*........117 F1
MDTN M24........88 C2
NTHM/RTH M23........167 G4
Banbury St *BOLE BL2*........34 D5
STKP SK1........13 G4
Bancroft Av *CHD/CHDH SK8*..169 H5
Bancroft Cl *MPL/ROM SK6*..162 C2
Bancroft Fold *HYDE SK14*..134 C3
Bancroft Rd
HALE/TIMP WA15........178 B1
SWIN M27........98 D1
Banff Gv *HEY OL10*........40 B5
Banff Rd *RUSH/FAL M14*....128 D4
Bangor Rd *CHD/CHDH SK8*..170 D8
Bangor St *AUL OL6*........120 B3
BOL BL1........2 D2
HULME M15........127 G3
*MILN OL16 **........11 G2
RDSH SK5........160 A2
Bank Barn La *WHIT OL12*....20 A2
Bank Bridge Rd *OP/CLY M11*..116 B2
Bank Cl *LIT OL15*........20 D5
Banker St *BOLS/LL BL3*........49 H4
Bankfield *HYDE SK14*........133 G3
Bank Fld *WHTN BL5*........62 B5
Bankfield Av *BRUN/LGST M13*..129 H3
DROY M43........117 H3
HTNM SK4........159 E4
IRL M44........150 C1
Bankfield Cl *BOLE BL2*........36 B5
Bankfield Dr *OLDS OL8*........92 A5
WALK M28........81 G3
Bankfield La *ROCH OL11*....28 B3
Bankfield Rd *CHD/CHDH SK8*..182 C3
FWTH BL4........82 A1
MPL/ROM SK6........162 A1
SALE M33........139 E5
Bankfield St *BKLY M9*........103 E1
BOLS/LL BL3........64 A1
HTNM SK4........159 H3
Bank Field St *RAD M26*....67 G5

Bank Hall *TOT/BURYW BL8*....37 H4
Bankhall La *HALE/TIMP WA15*..177 H4
Bankhall Rd *HTNM SK4*........158 D4
Bank Hey *WHTN BL5 **........62 A4
Bank Hill St *OLDE OL4*........76 A5
Bankhirst Cl *CHH M8*........102 B1
Bank House Rd *BKLY M9*....87 H4
Bankhouse Rd
TOT/BURYW BL8........37 H2
Banklands Cl *IRL M44*........150 C1
Bank La *LHULT M38*........81 E1
SLFD M6........100 A4
UPML OL3........95 C3
WHIT OL12........19 H1
Bankley St *BNG/LEV M19*..144 A2
Bankmill Cl *BRUN/LGST M13*..128 C1
Bank Pl *CSLFD M3*........114 A3
Bank Rd *CHH M8*........87 F5
MPL/ROM SK6........161 H3
STLY SK15........109 F5
Banks Cft *HEY OL10*........56 A2
Bankside *HALE/TIMP WA15*..149 F2
HYDE SK14........149 F2
Bank Side *WHTN BL5*........62 A4
Bankside Av *RAD M26*........53 E5
UPML OL3........79 F5
Bankside Cl *CHAD OL9*........8 C4
MPL/ROM SK6........165 G5
OLDS OL8........79 F4
WILM/AE SK9........199 G1
Bankside Ct *HTNM SK4 **....158 D4
Bankside Rd *DID/WITH M20*..158 D2
Banks La *STKP SK1*........172 C1
Bank Stanway Av *BOLS/LL BL3*..2 B7
Bank St *AUL OL6*........119 G3
BOL BL1
BRO M7........102 A2
CHD/CHDH SK8........170 B3
CSLFD M3........114 A3
DROY M43........117 G5
DTN/ASHW M34........132 C2
DTN/ASHW M34........147 F3
FWTH BL4........66 A4
HEY OL10........40 C4
HYDE SK14........133 G5
MPL/ROM SK6........162 A1
OP/CLY M11........116 B3
RAD M26........68 C2
RAMS BL0........17 F1
ROCH OL11........43 F2
ROY/SHW OL2........59 H2
SALE M33........154 D1
TOT/BURYW BL8........37 E2
WHTF M45........69 F3
Bank Top *AUL OL6*........119 H3
OLDE OL4........40 C3
Bank Top Gv *BOL BL1*........34 B1
Bank Top Pk *OLDE OL4*........92 C1
Bank Top St *HEY OL10*........40 C3
Bankwell St *HULME M15*....127 H3
Bank Wd *BOL BL1*........47 G2
Banky La *SALE M33*........138 C5
Bannach Dr *CHAD OL9*........74 B4
Bannatyne Cl
NEWH/MOS M40........104 D1
Banner Dale Cl
BRUN/LGST M13........129 G4
Bannerman Av *PWCH M25*..86 A4
Bannerman Rd *DROY M43*..118 A4
Banner Wk *OP/CLY M11*....116 A4
Bannister Dr *CHD/CHDH SK8*..182 C2
Bannister St *BOLE BL2*........50 B1
OFTN SK2........172 D3
Bann St *EDGY/DAV SK3*........13 E5
Banstead Av *RUSH/FAL M14*..142 D2
Bantry Av *BKLY M9*........87 G4
Bantry St *BOLS/LL BL3*........48 D4
Baptist St *ANC M4*........10 E1
Barathea Cl *ROCH OL11*....41 H3
Barbara Rd *BOLS/LL BL3*....63 H2
Barbara St *BOLS/LL BL3*....48 C5
Barberry Bank *EDGW/EG BL7*..22 C1
Barberry Cl *ALT WA14*........165 E2
Barber St *OP/CLY M11*....130 D1
Barbican St *DID/WITH M20*..142 D4
Barbon Wk *ANC M4*........7 K3
Barchester Av *BOLE BL2*....35 F5
Barcicroft Rd *BNG/LEV M19*....158 B2
Barclay Rd *POY/DIS SK12*....195 F5
Barclays Av *SLFD M6*........100 A4
Barcliffe Av *NEWH/MOS M40*..89 G5
Barclyde St *ROCH OL11*........42 D1
Barcombe Cl *OLDE OL4*........76 C2
STRET M32........125 F5
Bardell Cl *POY/DIS SK12*....195 E4
Bardon Cl *BOL BL1*........33 G5
Bardon Rd *NTHM/RTH M23*..167 G3
Bardsea Av *WYTH/NTH M22*..180 C3
Bardsley Av *FAIL M35*........105 E3
Bardsley Cl *BOLE BL2*........35 E1
HYDE SK14........149 G1
Bardsley Gate Av *STLY SK15*..135 H4
Bardsley St *CHAD OL9*........8 D4
HTNM SK4........159 G3
*MDTN M24 **........72 D3
NEWH/MOS M40........104 C5
*OLDE OL4 **........92 D2
Bardsley Vale Av *OLDS OL8*..106 C2
Bare St *BOL BL1*........3 H3
Barff Rd *ORD M5*........112 B3
Barfold Cl *OFTN SK2*........173 H4
Barfoot Aqueduct
STRET M32........140 A4
Bar Gap Rd *OLD OL1*........9 H1
Baring St *CMANE M1*........7 J7
Barker St *BURY BL9*........4 C7

CSLFD M3........114 C1
HEY OL10........40 C5
Barke St *LIT OL15*........20 C5
Bark St *BOL BL1*........2 D4
FWTH BL4........88 E2
Bark St East *BOL BL1*........2 E3
Bark Wk *HULME M15*........128 A2
Barkway Rd *STRET M32*....139 G2
Barkwell La *MOSL OL5*........108 C1
Barlea Av *NEWH/MOS M40*..104 C1
Barley Brook Meadow
BOL BL1........23 E5
Barleycorn Cl *SALE M33*....155 H3
Barley Cft *CHD/CHDH SK8*..182 C4
Barley Croft Rd *HYDE SK14*..133 H3
Barleycroft St
OLDTF/WHR M16........128 A4
Barley Dr *BRAM/HZG SK7*..183 H5
Barley Hall St *HEY OL10*....56 A2
Barlow Cl *BURY BL9*........38 C1
Barlow Ct *WALK M28*........82 B4
Barlow Crs *MPL/ROM SK6*..175 E5
Barlow Fold *BURY BL9*........53 G4
Barlow Fold Cl *BURY BL9*....53 G4
Barlow Fold Rd
MPL/ROM SK6........145 F3
RDSH SK5........145 F3
Barlow Hall Rd *CCHDY M21*..156 B1
Barlow La *ECC M30*........110 D3
Barlow La North *RDSH SK5*..145 F3
Barlow Moor Cl *WHIT OL12*..28 B1
Barlow Moor Ct
DID/WITH M20........157 E2
Barlow Moor Rd *CCHDY M21*..141 F4
Barlow Park Av *BOL BL1*....33 G1
Barlow Pl *BRUN/LGST M13*..128 D1
Barlow Rd *ALT WA14*........165 E1
BNG/LEV M19........144 C2
DUK SK16........120 A5
ORD M5........113 H4
STRET M32........125 E5
WILM/AE SK9........199 E1
Barlow's Cft *CSLFD M3*........6 C3
Barlow St *BURY BL9*........5 F3
ECC M30........111 E5
HEY OL10........56 B1
OLDE OL4........9 K5
RAD M26........68 C1
WALK M28........82 A3
Barlow Wood Dr
PL/ROM SK6........187 G1
Barmeadow *UPML OL3*........78 C2
Barmhouse Cl *HYDE SK14*..134 B5
Barmhouse La *HYDE SK14*..134 B5
Barmhouse Ms *HYDE SK14*..134 B5
Barmouth St *OP/CLY M11*..116 A5
Barmouth Wk *OLDS OL8*....90 D5
Barnaby Rd *POY/DIS SK12*..195 E5
Barnacre Av *BOLE BL2*........50 C2
NTHM/RTH M23........179 G1
Barnard Av *HTNM SK4*........159 E3
WHTF M45........70 A4
Barnard Cl *AULW OL7*........106 C5
Barnard Rd *GTN M18*........130 A5
Barnbrook St *BURY BL9*....5 G3
Barnby St *WGTN/LGST M12*..129 H5
Barn Cl *URM M41*........137 E1
Barnclose Rd *WYTH/NTH M22*..180 B4
Barn Ct *BOLE BL2 **........34 C4
Barncroft Gdns
*WYTH/NTH M22 **........180 B4
Barncroft Rd *FWTH BL4*....66 A4
Barnes Av *HTNM SK4*........158 D3
Barnes Cl *FWTH BL4*........65 E3
RAMS BL0........16 B5
Barnes St *FWTH BL4*........65 E3
Barnes Ter *FWTH BL4*........65 E3
Barneswell St
NEWH/MOS M40........104 B5
Barnet Rd *BOL BL1*........33 E4
Barnett Av *DID/WITH M20*..142 D5
Barnett Dr *CSLFD M3*........6 A2
Barnfield *URM M41*........138 B3
Barnfield Av *MPL/ROM SK6*..162 C3
Barnfield Cl *EDGW/EG BL7*..22 D1
ORD M5........113 G4
RAD M26........67 H1
Barnfield Crs *SALE M33*....154 A1
Barnfield Dr *WALK M28*....96 C4
WHTN BL5........79 H3
Barnfield Rd *BNG/LEV M19*..158 B2
HYDE SK14........134 C3
SWIN M27........83 E5
Barnfield Rd East
EDGY/DAV SK3........171 G5
Barnfield Rd West
EDGY/DAV SK3........171 G5
Barnfield St *DTN/ASHW M34*..132 A4
HEY OL10........30 A1
WHIT OL12........29 H1
Barnham Cl *TOT/BURYW BL8*..72 A1
Barnhill Av *PWCH M25*........86 A5
Barnhill Dr *PWCH M25*........86 A5
Barnhill Rd *PWCH M25*........86 A4
Barnhill St *RUSH/FAL M14*..128 B4
Barnley Cl *IRL M44*........122 C5
Barnsdale Cl *BOLE BL2*........36 B5
Barnsdale Dr *CHH M8*........102 B3
Barnsfold Av *RUSH/FAL M14*..143 E4
Barnsfold Rd *HALE/TIMP WA15*..187 E1
Barnside Av *WALK M28*....82 B5
Barnside Wy *FAIL M35*........105 H3
Barnsley St *STKP SK1*........13 K3
Barns Pl *HALE/TIMP WA15*..178 D4
Barnstable Dr
NEWH/MOS M40........102 D4

Barnstead Av *DID/WITH M20*........158 A1
Barnston Av *RUSH/FAL M14*..142 D1
Barnston Cl *BOL BL1*........34 A2
Barn St *BOL BL1*........2 E4
OLDS OL8........9 F4
Barnview Dr *IRL M44*........150 B1
Barnwell Cl *DTN/ASHW M34*..132 B3
Barnwell Cl *BOL BL1*........33 H5
Barnwood Rd
NTHM/RTH M23........179 H1
Barnwood Ter *BOL BL1*........33 H5
Baroness Gv *BRO M7*........113 H1
Baron Fold Crs *LHULT M38*....81 E2
Baron Fold Gv *LHULT M38*....81 E2
Baron Fold Rd *LHULT M38*....81 E2
Baron Gn *CHD/CHDH SK8*..182 A5
Baron Rd *HYDE SK14*........148 B4
Barons Ct *FAIL M35*........104 C4
Baron St *BURY BL9*........4 B6
ROCH OL11........
Baron Wk *BOLS/LL BL3*........67 F1
Barrack Hi *MPL/ROM SK6*..161 H4
Barrack Hill Cl *MPL/ROM SK6*..161 H3
Barrackhill Cl *MPL/ROM SK6*..161 H3
Barra Dr *URM M41*........124 A5
Barrack St *HULME M15*....127 G1
Barrass St *OP/CLY M11*....130 C1
Barratt Gdns *MDTN M24*....72 A1
Barrett Av *FWTH BL4*........66 C5
Barrett Ct *BURY BL9*........
Barr Hill Av *SLFD M6*........100 B5
Barrfield Rd *SLFD M6*........112 D1
Barrhill Cl *HULME M15*....127 G2
Barrie Wy *BOL BL1*........34 C2
Barrington Av *CHD/CHDH SK8*..182 D3
DROY M43........117 G4
Barrington Cl *ALT WA14*....165 G3
Barrington Rd *ALT WA14*....165 G3
Barrington St *OP/CLY M11*..116 D3
Barrisdale Cl *BOLS/LL BL3*..47 G4
Barrow Bridge Rd *BOL BL1*..32 D3
Barrowfield Rd
WYTH/NTH M22........179 H2
Barrowfields *MDTN M24*....72 D2
Barrow Hill Rd *CHH M8*....102 A3
Barrow La *HALE/TIMP WA15*..178 C5
Barrow Meadow
CHD/CHDH SK8........182 C4
Barrows Ct *BOL BL1*........2 E6
Barrowshaw Cl *WALK M28*....81 H5
Barrow St *CSLFD M3*........114 A4
Barrule Av *BRAM/HZG SK7*..185 F3
Barry Crs *WALK M28*........81 F5
Barry Lawson Cl *CHH M8 **..102 A3
Barry Ri *ALT WA14*........176 D2
Barry Rd *NTHM/RTH M23*..156 A4
RDSH SK5........160 A1
Barry St *OLD OL1*........9 G1
Barsham Dr *BOLS/LL BL3*..48 C4
Bar Ter *WHIT OL12*........18 B1
Bartlam Pl *OL1*........9 H3
Bartlemore St *OLD OL1*....75 H3
Bartlett Rd *ROY/SHW OL2*..59 H3
Bartlett St *OP/CLY M11*....130 A1
Bartley Rd *WYTH/NTH M22*..168 B1
Barton Av *URM M41*........138 B1
Barton Cl *WILM/AE SK9*....192 A5
Barton Dock Rd *STRET M32*..124 D1
Barton Fold *HYDE SK14*....147 H2
Barton Hall Av *ECC M30*..110 D4
Barton Highlevel Br
TRPK M17........124 A1
Barton La *ECC M30*........111 E5
Barton Moss Rd *ECC M30*..122 D1
Barton Rd *ECC M30*........110 D5
FWTH BL4........65 G5
HTNM SK4........158 B5
MDTN M24........72 C4
STRET M32........125 F5
SWIN M27........99 F3
URM M41........124 B4
Barton St *CHAD OL9*........
CSLFD M3........6 C7
Barway Rd *CCHDY M21*....140 D2
Barwell Rd *SALE M33*........153 H1
Barwell Sq *FWTH BL4*........65 G5
Barwick Pl *SALE M33*........154 B2
Basechurch Wk
*WGTN/LGST M12 **........129 G2
Bashall St *BOL BL1*........33 F4
Basil Ct *MILN OL16*........30 C5
Basildon Cl *BRUN/LGST M13*..128 E3
Basil St *BOLS/LL BL3*........48 D4
HTNM SK4........159 G3
RUSH/FAL M14........128 D5
Baslow Av *BNG/LEV M19*..144 B1
Baslow Dr *BRAM/HZG SK7*..185 G4
CHD/CHDH SK8........181 H4
Baslow Gv *RDSH SK5*........160 B3
Baslow Rd *DROY M43*........117 F2
DTN/ASHW M34........146 D3
Baslow St *OP/CLY M11*....115 H4
Bassenthwaite Cl
*WGTN/LGST M12 **........129 G2
Basset Av *SLFD M6*........100 A4
Bassett Wy *WHIT OL12*....29 H1
Bass La *BURY BL9*........16 C5
Bass St *BOL BL1*........34 C2
DUK SK16........119 G5
Basten Dr *BRO M7*........101 H4
Batchelor Cl *CCHDY M21*....142 A4
Bates Cl *ROCH OL11*........42 C5
Bateson Dr *OLDE OL4*........93 E1
Bateson St *STKP SK1*........13 J2
Bateson Wy *OLDS OL8 **....9 K5
Bates St *BRUN/LGST M13*..129 G4
DUK SK16........119 H5
Bath Cl *BRAM/HZG SK7*....185 H2
Bath Crs *CHD/CHDH SK8*..181 H4
OLDTF/WHR M16........127 F3
Bath St *ALT WA14*........177 G2
BOL BL1........2 E4

CHAD OL9 .... 8 B6
WHIT OL12 .... 11 F3
Batley St BKLY M9 .... 102 A3
MOSL OL5 .... 108 C1
Batsmans Dr SWIN M27 .... 83 H3
Battenberg Rd BOL BL1 .... 48 B1
Battersby Gv
    BRAM/HZG SK7 .... 185 F2
Battersby Ct OFTN SK2 * 173 E3
Battersby St BURY BL9 .... 39 G3
    OP/CLY M11 .... 130 D1
    ROCH OL11 .... 29 E5
Battersea Rd HTNM SK4 *
Battery La WILM/AE SK9 .... 198 A4
Batty St CHH M8 .... 102 D5
The Baum MILN OL16 .... 10 C5
Baxendale St BOL BL1 .... 33 H2
Baxter Gdns NTHM/RTH M23 ... 167 H2
Baxter Rd SALE M33 .... 154 C2
Baxter St OLDS OL8 .... 90 C5
Baybutt St RAD M26 * 68 D1
Baycroft Gv NTHM/RTH M23 ... 155 H5
Baydon Av BRO M7 .... 102 A4
Bayfield Gv
    NEWH/MOS M40 .... 103 H1
Bayle Cl HYDE SK14 .... 133 H3
Bayley Ct BOL BL1 .... 2 A2
Bayley St STLY SK15 .... 120 B3
Baysdale Av BOLS/LL BL3 * 4 A1
Bayston Wk WGTN/LGST M12 ... 129 G3
Bay St CHAD OL9 .... 3 D4
    HEY OL10 .... 40 C3
    WHIT OL12 .... 10 E2
Bayswater Av
    NEWH/MOS M40 .... 116 D1
Baythorpe St BOL BL1 .... 34 A5
Baytree Av CHAD OL9 .... 73 H4
    DTN/ASHW M34 .... 132 D4
Bay Tree Av WALK M28 .... 97 H5
Baytree Av MPL/ROM SK6 ..... 161 G2
Baytree Gv RAMS BL0 .... 26 C1
Baytree La MDTN M24 .... 73 G4
Baytree Wk WHIT OL12 .... 14 B4
Baywood St BKLY M9 .... 103 E2
Bazaar St SLFD M6 .... 115 F1
Bazley Rd WYTH/NTH M22 ..... 156 C5
Bazley St BOL BL1 .... 32 C3
Beacomfold MPL/ROM SK6 .... 163 G3
Beacon Av NTHM/RTH M23 .... 179 H2
Beacon Gv OLDS OL8 .... 92 B3
Beacon Rd MPL/ROM SK6 ..... 161 H5
    TRPK M17 .... 124 D1
Beaconsfield
    RUSH/FAL M14 * 143 E4
Beaconsfield Rd ALT WA14 ... 165 G2
Beaconsfield St BOLS/LL BL3 .... 2 A7
Beaconsfield Ter STLY SK15 ... 109 G3
Beacon Vw MPL/ROM SK6 ..... 175 E1
Beadham Dr BKLY M9 .... 87 F2
Beadle Av WHIT OL12 .... 20 A3
Bealbank Cl MILN OL16 .... 44 D3
Beal Cl HTNM SK4 .... 158 A3
Beal Crs MILN OL16 .... 11 K3
Bealcroft Cl MILN OL16 .... 31 F4
Beale Gv CCHDY M21 .... 141 F3
Bealey Av RAD M26 .... 53 H4
Bealey Cl GTN M18 .... 130 A2
    RAD M26 .... 53 E5
Bealey Dr BURY BL9 .... 53 E2
Beal La ROY/SHW OL2 .... 60 B3
Beaminster Rd HTNM SK4 .... 158 C3
Beaminster Wk
    BRUN/LGST M13 * 128 D2
Beamish Cl BRUN/LGST M13 ... 128 D2
Beamsley Rd WYTH/NTH M22 ... 180 A2
Beanfields WALK M28 .... 97 G5
Bean Leach Av OFTN SK2 ..... 173 G3
Bean Leach Dr OFTN SK2 ..... 173 G3
Bean Leach Rd
    OFTN SK2 .... 173 F5
Beard Rd GTN M18 * 130 B4
Beard St DROY M43 .... 117 G4
    ROY/SHW OL2 .... 75 F1
Beardwood Rd BKLY M9 .... 88 A3
Bearswood Cl HYDE SK14 .... 148 B2
Beathwaite Dr
    BRAM/HZG SK7 .... 183 F3
Beatrice Av CHD/CHDH SK8 ... 182 C2
    GTN M18 .... 131 E4
Beatrice Rd BOL BL1 .... 48 A3
    WALK M28 .... 98 A3
Beatrice St DTN/ASHW M34 ... 132 D5
    FWTH BL4 .... 65 H4
    ROCH OL11 .... 29 G4
    SWIN M27 .... 98 D1
Beatrice Wignall St
    DROY M43 * 117 H5
Beatson Wk ANC M4 .... 7 K4
Beattock Cl HULME M15 .... 127 C1
Beattock St HULME M15 .... 127 C1
Beauchamp St AUL OL6 .... 119 H2
Beaufont Dr OLDE OL4 .... 92 B2
Beaufort Av DID/WITH M20 ... 157 F1
    SALE M33 .... 154 D4
    SWIN M27 .... 98 C3
Beaufort Cl HYDE SK14 .... 149 G2
    WILM/AE SK9 .... 201 E3
Beaufort Rd AUL OL6 .... 120 A2
    HYDE SK14 .... 149 G1
    OFTN SK2 .... 173 E5
    SALE M33 .... 154 D3
Beaufort St CSLFD M5 .... 6 B7
    OLDM OL1 .... 110 C2
    PWCH M25 .... 86 B3
    WHIT OL12 .... 10 D4
Beauly Cl RAMS BL0 .... 26 B1
Beaumaris Crs
    BRAM/HZG SK7 .... 184 D4
Beaumonds Wy ROCH OL11 ... 28 C5
Beaumont Cha BOLS/LL BL3 ... 63 G5
Beaumont Cl LIT OL15 .... 20 C3
Beaumont Dr BOLS/LL BL3 .... 47 F4
Beaumont Rd CCHDY M21 ..... 141 F4
    HOR/BR BL6 .... 44 H5
Beaumont St AUL OL6 .... 119 H2
Beauvale Av OFTN SK2 .... 172 D2
Beaver Dr BURY BL9 .... 54 A5
Beaver Rd DID/WITH M20 ..... 157 G3
Beaver St CMANE M1 .... 7 F7

Bebbington Cl SALE M33 ...... 155 G4
Bebbington St OP/CLY M11 * ... 116 D4
Beccles Rd SALE M33 .... 154 C5
Beckenham Cl
    TOT/BURYW BL8 .... 37 G5
Beckenham Rd CHH M8 .... 102 B5
Becket Av BRO M7 .... 101 H4
Becket Mdw OLDE OL4 .... 92 A1
Beckett St BOL BL1 .... 18 D4
    OLDE OL4 .... 76 D5
Beckfield Rd NTHM/RTH M23 ... 167 H4
Beckfoot Dr BRUN/LGST M13 ... 129 F5
Beckford St NEWH/MOS M40 ... 103 F5
Beck Gv ROY/SHW OL2 .... 60 C4
    WALK M28 .... 97 G1
Beckhampton Cl
    BRUN/LGST M13 .... 128 D3
Beckley Av PWCH M25 .... 85 H5
Beckley Cl ROY/SHW OL2 ...... 59 H5
Beckside RDSH SK5 .... 145 G2
Beck St CSLFD M5 .... 6 B3
    OP/CLY M11 * 130 D1
Beckton Gdns
    WYTH/NTH M22 .... 180 B1
Becontree Av
    DTN/ASHW M34 .... 132 D4
Becontree Dr
    NTHM/RTH M23 .... 167 E3
Bedells La WILM/AE SK9 ...... 198 D4
Bede St BOL BL1 .... 33 F4
Bedford Av HYDE SK14 .... 133 H5
    OLDTF/WHR M16 .... 141 H1
    ROY/SHW OL2 .... 59 C2
    SALE M33 .... 155 E4
    SWIN M27 * 98 D3
    WALK M28 .... 96 D1
Bedford Dr HALE/TIMP WA15 ... 166 D3
Bedford St ECC M30 .... 111 F2
    OLDTF/WHR M16 .... 141 E1
    URM M41 .... 124 B4
Bedfordshire Cl CHAD OL9 .... 90 C2
Bedford St BOL BL1 .... 2 A3
    BURY BL9 .... 38 D2
    EDGW/EG BL7 .... 22 C1
    HEY OL10 .... 41 F4
    PWCH M25 .... 86 B2
    RDSH SK5 .... 145 E4
Bedlam Gn BURY BL9 .... 4 E4
Bedwell St OLDTF/WHR M16 ... 128 A5
Bedworth Cl BOLE BL2 .... 49 G4
Beechacre RAMS BL0 .... 17 E3
Beech Av BOLS/LL BL3 .... 67 E2
    BRAM/HZG SK7 .... 185 F2
    CHD/CHDH SK8 .... 169 C4
    DROY M43 .... 117 G4
    DTN/ASHW M34 .... 132 A4
    EDGY/DAV SK3 .... 172 A3
    FWTH BL4 .... 65 F4
    IRL M44 .... 122 D5
    MPL/ROM SK6 .... 174 C3
    OLD OL1 .... 74 B2
    OLDE OL4 .... 76 C4
    RAD M26 .... 68 A4
    SLFD M6 .... 113 G1
    UPML OL3 .... 95 E1
    URM M41 .... 138 C2
    WALK M28 .... 96 B4
    WHTF M45 .... 69 G5
    WHIT OL12 .... 14 B4
Beech Cl BOLE BL2 .... 23 H5
    PWCH M25 .... 86 B4
    WHIT OL12 .... 14 B4
    WILM/AE SK9 .... 201 E2
Beech Cottages WILM/AE SK9 ... 200 D5
Beech Ct WILM/AE SK9 .... 199 G4
Beech Crs POY/DIS SK12 ..... 195 F5
Beechcroft PWCH M25 .... 86 B5
Beechcroft Av BOLE BL2 .... 50 A3
Beechcroft Cl
    NEWH/MOS M40 .... 115 F2
Beechcroft Gv BOLE BL2 ...... 50 B3
Beechdale Cl
    NEWH/MOS M40 .... 104 B2
Beeches Ms DID/WITH M20 ... 156 D2
The Beeches BOL BL1 .... 29 G2
    DID/WITH M20 .... 157 E2
    MOSL OL5 .... 94 B5
Beechey Sq OLD OL1 .... 9 J2
Beechfield ALT WA14 .... 177 F1
    OLDE OL4 .... 76 D4
    SALE M33 .... 154 A4
Beechfield Av LHULT M38 ...... 81 F2
    RAD M26 .... 68 D3
    URM M41 .... 123 H5
    WILM/AE SK9 .... 198 B5
Beechfield Cl OLDE OL4 .... 93 E1
    ROCH OL11 .... 28 B5
Beechfield Dr BURY BL9 .... 53 G2
Beechfield Ms HYDE SK14 * ... 134 B5
Beechfield Rd BOL BL1 .... 47 G2
    CHD/CHDH SK8 .... 183 E4
    EDGY/DAV SK3 .... 172 A5
    MILN OL16 .... 44 B1
    SWIN M27 .... 98 D5
    WILM/AE SK9 .... 200 D5
Beech Gv AULW OL7 .... 119 E4
    LHULT M38 .... 80 D2
    RUSH/FAL M14 .... 143 F5
    SALE M33 .... 112 D1
    STLY SK15 .... 120 C5
    TOT/BURYW BL8 .... 26 B2
    WILM/AE SK9 .... 198 D4
Beech Grove Cl BURY BL9 .... 39 E2
Beech Hill Rd OLDE OL4 .... 93 H1
Beech Holme Gv STKP SK1 ... 172 D1
Beech Hurst Cl
    OLDTF/WHR M16 .... 141 H1
Beech La MPL/ROM SK6 .... 162 B4
    OLDE OL4 .... 76 C4
    WILM/AE SK9 .... 198 D4
Beech Ms CCHDY M21 .... 141 E3
    OFTN SK2 .... 172 B4
Beech Mt AULW OL7 .... 106 D4
Beechpark Av
    WYTH/NTH M22 .... 168 B2

Beech Rd CCHDY M21 .... 141 F3
    CHD/CHDH SK8 .... 183 E3
    EDGY/DAV SK3 .... 171 H3
    HALE/TIMP WA15 .... 177 H1
    MPL/ROM SK6 .... 187 E5
    SALE M33 .... 155 E2
    WILM/AE SK9 .... 201 E2
Beech St BOL BL1 .... 34 A4
    BURY BL9 .... 5 J4
    ECC M30 .... 110 C4
    FAIL M35 .... 100 D2
    MDTN M24 .... 72 C4
    MILN OL16 .... 44 D2
    OLD OL1 .... 9 L3
    RAD M26 .... 68 D3
    ROCH OL11 .... 29 C5
    SWIN M27 .... 99 E3
Beechcrest Rd CHD/CHDH SK8 ... 171 E4
Beech Vw HYDE SK14 .... 148 C1
Beech Wk MDTN M24 .... 88 C1
    STRET M32 .... 140 A3
Beechway MPL/ROM SK6 ...... 187 E5
    WILM/AE SK9 .... 198 C5
Beechwood ALT WA14 .... 177 E3
    ROY/SHW OL2 .... 60 C1
Beechwood Av CCHDY M21 ... 141 G4
    LIT OL15 .... 20 D5
    MPL/ROM SK6 .... 162 B4
    RAMS BL0 .... 17 E2
    STLY SK15 .... 121 F1
    URM M41 .... 123 F5
Beechwood Ct
    TOT/BURYW BL8 .... 37 G1
Beechwood Dr HYDE SK14 .... 148 B2
    MOSL OL5 .... 94 B5
    MPL/ROM SK6 .... 175 F5
    ROY/SHW OL2 .... 58 D3
    SALE M33 .... 153 F2
    WALK M28 .... 96 B5
    WILM/AE SK9 .... 199 H2
Beechwood Gv
    CHD/CHDH SK8 .... 182 D4
Beechwood La STLY SK15 .... 121 F1
Beechwood Rd OLDS OL8 ...... 91 G5
    PWCH M25 .... 86 C4
Beechwood St BOLS/LL BL3 ... 116 C5
Beede St OP/CLY M11 .... 116 C5
Beehive Av BOLS/LL BL3 .... 50 D5
Beehive Gn WHTN BL5 .... 62 C3
Beehive St OLDS OL8 .... 91 G4
Beeley St HYDE SK14 .... 148 A1
    SLFD M6 .... 101 F5
Beenham Cl SALE M33 .... 153 F3
Beeston Av BRO M7 .... 101 E4
    HALE/TIMP WA15 .... 166 A3
Beeston Gv EDGY/DAV SK3 ... 171 H4
    WHTF M45 .... 70 A5
Beeston Rd SALE M33 .... 153 H2
    WILM/AE SK9 .... 192 A2
Beeston St BKLY M9 .... 103 F3
Beeth St OP/CLY M11 .... 130 D2
Beeton Gv BRUN/LGST M13 ... 129 F4
Beever St OLD OL1 .... 9 G2
    OLDTF/WHR M16 .... 127 F3
Begley Cl MPL/ROM SK6 ...... 161 G5
Begonia Av FWTH BL4 .... 65 E3
Belayse Cl BOL BL1 .... 33 E4
Belbeck St TOT/BURYW BL8 ... 37 H4
Belbeck St South
    TOT/BURYW BL8 * 37 G4
Belcroft Cl WYTH/NTH M22 ... 168 D1
Belcroft Dr LHULT M38 .... 80 D1
Belcroft Gv LHULT M38 .... 80 D1
Belding Av NEWH/MOS M40 ... 105 E1
Beldon Rd BKLY M9 .... 87 E1
Belfairs Cl AULW OL7 .... 107 E4
Belfield Cl MILN OL16 .... 11 K4
Belfield La MILN OL16 .... 11 J6
Belfield La MILN OL16 .... 11 H4
Belfield Old Rd MILN OL16 .... 11 H4
Belfield Rd DID/WITH M20 .... 157 G3
    MILN OL16 .... 11 H4
    PWCH M25 .... 86 D4
Belford Av DTN/ASHW M34 ... 131 F5
Belford Dr BOLS/LL BL3 .... 64 A1
Belford Rd STRET M32 .... 126 A5
Belfort Dr ORD M5 .... 113 G5
Belfry Cl WILM/AE SK9 .... 199 G2
Belgate Cl WGTN/LGST M12 ... 129 H4
Belgium St ROCH OL11 .... 28 B4
Belgrave Av MILN OL16 .... 105 G2
    MPL/ROM SK6 .... 175 E3
    OLDS OL8 .... 91 G3
    URM M41 .... 138 C1
Belgrave Crs ECC M30 .... 111 G2
    OFTN SK2 .... 172 C5
Belgrave Dr RAD M26 .... 52 B5
Belgrave Gdns BOL BL1 .... 33 H4
Belgrave Rd ALT WA14 .... 177 F1
    IRL M44 .... 150 C1
    NEWH/MOS M40 .... 104 D1
    OLDS OL8 .... 91 G3
    SALE M33 .... 154 B2
Belgrave St South BOL BL1 ... 33 H4
Belgravia Gdns CCHDY M21 ... 141 E3
    HALE/TIMP WA15 .... 177 H4
Belgravia Ms ROY/SHW OL2 ... 60 B2
Belhaven Rd CHH M8 .... 87 E5
Bellairs St BOLS/LL BL3 .... 64 B1
Bella St BOLS/LL BL3 .... 48 B5
Bell Clough Rd DROY M43 .... 118 A2
Bell Crs OP/CLY M11 .... 116 A5
Belldale Cl HTNM SK4 .... 158 D4
Belle Isle Av WHIT OL12 .... 18 C2
Bellerby Cl WHTF M45 .... 69 F4
Belle Vue Av WYTH/NTH M22 ... 180 D4
Belle Vue Av WGTN/LGST M12 ... 129 G3
Belle Vue Ter BURY BL9 .... 4 C6
Bellfield Av CHD/CHDH SK8 ... 185 E5
    OLDS OL8 .... 91 G5
Bellfield Cl BKLY M9 .... 87 H5
Bellfield Vw BOL BL1 .... 34 B3

Bellhill Gdns SLFD M6 .... 113 E2
Bellingham Cl ROY/SHW OL2 ... 60 A1
Bellis Cl WGTN/LGST M12 ..... 115 H4
Bell La BURY BL9 .... 5 F5
Bellott St CHH M8 .... 102 B4
Bellott Wk OLD OL1 * 75 F4
Bellpit Cl WALK M28 .... 96 D5
Bells Croft Av
    NEWH/MOS M40 .... 104 A3
Bellshill Crs MILN OL16 .... 11 K3
Bell St DROY M43 .... 118 A3
    MILN OL16 .... 9 K2
    OLD OL1 .... 9 K2
Bell Ter ECC M30 .... 110 D5
Belmont Av DTN/ASHW M34 ... 132 A4
    OLDE OL4 .... 77 H2
    SLFD M6 .... 111 H1
    SWIN M27 .... 83 G2
Belmont Cl HTNM SK4 .... 159 H3
Belmont Dr MPL/ROM SK6 .... 163 G5
Belmont Rd BOL BL1 .... 22 C5
    CHD/CHDH SK8 .... 169 G3
    HALE/TIMP WA15 .... 177 H2
    SALE M33 .... 153 G5
    HTNM SK4 .... 159 H3
    OLDE OL4 .... 8 E1
    OLDE OL4 .... 92 D2
    SALO M50 .... 112 D1
Belmont Ter PART M31 * 137 F5
Belmont Vw BOLE BL2 .... 35 G2
Belmont Wk
    BRUN/LGST M13 .... 128 D2
Belmont Wy CHAD OL9 .... 74 D4
    HTNM SK4 .... 159 H3
    WHIT OL12 .... 10 E1
Belmore Rd SALE M33 .... 154 C5
Belper Rd ECC M30 .... 110 C5
    HTNM SK4 .... 154 A3
Belroy Ct PWCH M25 * 86 A4
Belsay Cl AULW OL7 .... 106 E5
Belsay Dr NTHM/RTH M23 .... 167 H5
Belsfield Ter AUL OL6 * 107 F2
Belstone Av
    NTHM/RTH M23 .... 179 H1
Belstone Cl BRAM/HZG SK7 ... 184 A2
Belthorne Av BKLY M9 .... 88 D5
Belton Av MILN OL16 .... 11 H4
Belton Cl STRET M32 .... 139 H2
Belton Wk NEWH/MOS M40 ... 104 A1
Belvedere Av RDSH SK5 .... 145 F1
    TOT/BURYW BL8 .... 26 B2
Belvedere Ct DUK SK16 .... 120 B5
Belvedere Ri OLD OL1 .... 75 F3
Belvedere Rd RUSH/FAL M14 ... 143 E3
    SLFD M6 .... 113 F2
Belvedere St SLFD M6 .... 113 G2
Belvoir Av BNG/LEV M19 ...... 144 A1
    BRAM/HZG SK7 .... 185 F4
Belvoir St BOLE BL2 .... 49 H2
    WHIT OL12 .... 29 G2
Belvor Av DTN/ASHW M34 .... 132 D1
Belwood Rd CCHDY M21 ...... 141 F4
Bembridge Cl BOLS/LL BL3 ... 128 D5
Bembridge Rd
    DTN/ASHW M34 .... 147 F3
Bempton Cl OFTN SK2 .... 173 H4
Bemrose Av ALT WA14 .... 165 F3
Bemsley Pl ORD M5 .... 113 G2
Benbecula Wy URM M41 ...... 124 C3
Benbow Av WGTN/LGST M12 ... 129 G3
Benbow St SALE M33 .... 154 C1
Ben Brierley Wy OLD OL1 * 9 H2
Bench Carr WHIT OL12 .... 10 A2
Benchill Court Rd
    WYTH/NTH M22 .... 168 D5
Benchill Dr WYTH/NTH M22 ... 168 D5
Benchill Rd WYTH/NTH M22 ... 168 B5
Bendall St OP/CLY M11 .... 117 F5
Ben Davies Ct
    MPL/ROM SK6 .... 162 B4
Bendemeer URM M41 .... 124 B4
Bendix St ANC M4 .... 7 H4
Benedict Cl BRO M7 .... 101 F5
Benedict Dr DUK SK16 .... 133 F2
Benfield Av NEWH/MOS M40 ... 89 H5
Benfield St HEY OL10 .... 41 F3
Benfleet Cl WGTN/LGST M12 ... 129 H2
Bengal La ANC M4 .... 7 J2
Bengal St ANC M4 .... 7 J2
    EDGY/DAV SK3 .... 172 C5
Benin Wk NEWH/MOS M40 .... 104 A1
Benjamin St AULW OL7 .... 119 F4
Benmore Cl HEY OL10 .... 40 B4
Benmore Rd BKLY M9 .... 88 C4
Bennet St RAD M26 .... 51 C5
Bennett Cl EDGY/DAV SK3 ... 172 A5
Bennett Dr BRO M7 .... 101 H4
Bennett St HYDE SK14 .... 133 H5
    STLY SK15 .... 121 F1
    STRET M32 .... 140 A2
    WGTN/LGST M12 .... 129 F2
Benny La DROY M43 .... 105 F4
Benson Cl BRO M7 .... 101 H5
Benson St BURY BL9 .... 5 K4
Bent St OP/CLY M11 .... 111 H4
Bentcliffe Wy ECC M30 .... 111 H4
Bentfield Crs MILN OL16 .... 31 K4
Bent Fold Dr BURY BL9 .... 69 H3
Bentgate Cl MILN OL16 .... 44 D3
Bentgate St MILN OL16 .... 44 D3
Bentham Cl TOT/BURYW BL8 ... 36 D5
Bent Hill St BOLS/LL BL3 * 48 A5
Bentinck Cl AULW OL7 .... 165 F5
Bentinck Rd ALT WA14 .... 165 F5
Bentinck St AUL OL6 .... 119 F5
    BOL BL1 .... 33 F4
    FWTH BL4 .... 66 A3
    HULME M15 .... 127 G1

WHIT OL12 .... 29 F2
Bent La CHH M8 .... 102 A3
    PWCH M25 .... 85 E5
Bent Lanes URM M41 .... 123 H3
Bentley Av MDTN M24 .... 57 G4
Bentley Cl RAD M26 .... 53 E5
Bentley Ct FWTH BL4 .... 66 A3
Bentley Fold TOT/BURYW BL8 ... 37 E2
Bentley Hall Rd
    TOT/BURYW BL8 .... 36 B2
Bentley La BURY BL9 .... 27 H2
Bentley Ms WHIT OL12 * 29 H1
Bentley Rd BRO M7 .... 101 H2
    CCHDY M21 .... 141 E2
    DTN/ASHW M34 .... 132 C5
Bentmeadows WHIT OL12 ..... 10 A2
Benton Dr MPL/ROM SK6 ..... 175 H1
Benton St BKLY M9 .... 103 G3
Bents Av MPL/ROM SK6 ...... 161 H3
    URM M41 .... 137 G2
Bents Farm Cl LIT OL15 * 20 D5
Bent Spur Rd FWTH BL4 ...... 82 D2
Bent St CHH M8 .... 102 B5
    RAD M26 .... 66 A1
Bentworth Wk BKLY M9 .... 103 F3
Beresford Av BOLS/LL BL3 .... 48 B4
Beresford Crs OLDE OL4 ...... 76 C4
    RDSH SK5 .... 145 E5
Beresford Rd
    BRUN/LGST M13 .... 129 G5
    STRET M32 .... 126 B4
Beresford St FAIL M35 .... 100 D3
    MILN OL16 .... 45 E2
    OLDE OL4 .... 76 C4
    RUSH/FAL M14 .... 128 B5
Berigan Cl WGTN/LGST M12 ... 129 F3
Berisford Cl HALE/TIMP WA15 ... 165 H2
Berkeley Av CHAD OL9 .... 90 A4
    RUSH/FAL M14 .... 129 F4
    STRET M32 .... 125 F3
Berkeley Cl HYDE SK14 .... 147 H2
    RAD M26 .... 51 F4
Berkeley Ct MILN OL16 .... 43 G2
    DTN/ASHW M34 .... 132 C5
Berkeley Crs HYDE SK14 ...... 119 F2
    BRAM/HZG SK7 .... 144 A1
Berkeley Dr MILN OL16 .... 44 C3
Berkeley Av ROY/SHW OL2 ... 59 E4
Berkeley Wk LIT OL15 .... 75 E2
Berkley Av BNG/LEV M19 ..... 144 A1
Berkshire Cl CHAD OL9 .... 90 C2
Berkshire Pl CHAD OL9 .... 53 G2
Berkshire Rd
    NEWH/MOS M40 .... 115 G2
    ROY/SHW OL2 .... 171 G3
Berlin St BOLS/LL BL3 .... 48 B3
Bermondsay St ORD M5 ...... 113 C5
Bernard Gv BOL BL1 .... 33 F4
Bernard St BKLY M9 .... 103 E2
    WHIT OL12 .... 29 G5
Berne Cl BRAM/HZG SK7 ...... 171 H5
    CHAD OL9 .... 8 A5
Bernice Av CHAD OL9 .... 90 C1
Bernice St BOL BL1 .... 33 F4
Berridale Cl
    OLDTF/WHR M16 * 141 H1
Berrie Gv BNG/LEV M19 ...... 144 A3
Berry Brow NEWH/MOS M40 ... 117 F1
    UPML OL3 .... 95 E2
Berry Cl WILM/AE SK9 .... 198 D5
Berrycroft La MPL/ROM SK6 ... 161 H5
Berry St CMANE M1 .... 7 J7
    ECC M30 .... 110 C5
    STLY SK15 .... 121 F5
    SWIN M27 .... 84 A5
Bertha Rd MILN OL16 .... 11 J7
Bertha St BOL BL1 .... 33 G4
    OP/CLY M11 .... 130 A1
    ROY/SHW OL2 .... 60 A4
Berte St ROCH OL11 .... 10 C5
Bertram St SALE M33 .... 155 F2
    WGTN/LGST M12 .... 129 H2
Bertrand Rd BOL BL1 .... 48 B2
Bert St BOLS/LL BL3 .... 64 A1
Berwick Av HTNM SK4 .... 139 G1
    URM M41 .... 139 G1
    WHTF M45 .... 69 H5
Berwick Cl HEY OL10 .... 40 B5
Berwick St MILN OL16 .... 11 J3
Berwyn Av BKLY M9 .... 87 H2
    CHD/CHDH SK8 .... 171 E4
    MDTN M24 .... 73 F4
Berwyn Cl OLDS OL8 .... 91 F4
Beryl Av TOT/BURYW BL8 ..... 34 A3
Beryl St BOL BL1 .... 34 A5
Besom La STLY SK15 .... 121 H2
Bessemer Rd IRL M44 .... 136 B5
Bessemer St OP/CLY M11 .... 130 B1
Bessemer Wy OLD OL1 .... 9 F2
Bessybrook Cl HOR/BR BL6 ... 45 F5
Beswicke Rd LIT OL15 .... 21 F5
Beswick St ANC M4 .... 4 D5
Beswick St LIT OL15 .... 21 F5
Beta Av STRET M32 .... 140 A2
Beta St BOL BL1 .... 2 D2
Bethany La MILN OL16 .... 104 D3
Bethel Av FAIL M35 .... 100 D4
Bethel St HEY OL10 .... 40 D4
Bethesda St OLDS OL8 .... 91 G3
Bethnal Dr RUSH/FAL M14 ... 142 C3
Betjeman Pl ROY/SHW OL2 ... 60 C2
Betleymere Rd
    CHD/CHDH SK8 .... 170 C5
Betley Rd RDSH SK5 .... 145 F2
Betley St CMANE M1 .... 7 K6

HEY OL10 * 40 D5
RAD M26.............................52 D5
Betnor Av STKP SK1.........160 C5
Betony CI WHIT OL12..........18 C5
Betsham St HULME M15.....128 A3
Bettwood Dr CHH M8............87 E5
Betula Gv BRO M7.............101 G3
Betula Ms ROCH OL11........28 A2
Bevan CI WGTN/LGST M12...115 H4
Bevendon Sq BRO M7.........101 H4
Beveridge St RUSH/FAL M14...128 D3
Beverley Av DTN/ASHW M34...147 E1
URM M41.........................124 D4
Beverley CI WHTF M45.........70 A3
Beverley PI MILN OL16 * 10 C5
Beverley Rd BOL BL3............48 B1
BOLS/LL BL3......................66 C1
OFTN SK2.........................172 D1
SWIN M27...........................99 H3
Beverley St BKLY M9.........103 F1
Beverly CI OLDE OL6.........107 E4
Beverly Rd RUSH/FAL M14...143 F4
Beverston Dr BRO M7.........101 H4
Bevill Sq CSLFD M3..............6 B2
Bevis Gn BURY BL9.............27 G3
Bewick St BOLE BL2.............34 B3
Bewley St OLDS OL8............91 E5
Bexhill Av HALE/TIMP WA15...166 A3
Bexhill Dr BRUN/LGST M13...129 E5
Bexhill Rd EDGY/DAV SK3...171 H5
Bexhill Wk CHAD OL9..........90 C1
Bexington Rd
   OLDTF/WHR M16.............127 G5
Bexley CI URM M41............124 A4
Bexley Dr LHULT M38...........81 H4
   TOT/BURYW BL8..............37 C5
Bexley Sq CSLFD M3.............6 A3
Bexley St CHAD OL9..............8 B6
Beyer CI GTN M18................130 B3
Bibby La BNG/LEV M19........143 H5
Bibby St BURY BL9................5 G4
HYDE SK14 *....................133 G3
Bibury Av WYTH/NTH M22...180 A1
Bickerdike Av
   WGTN/LGST M12.............130 A5
Bickershaw Dr WALK M28.....81 H5
Bickerstaffe CI ROY/SHW OL2...59 H4
Bickerton Rd BRAM/HZG SK7...184 C3
Bickerton Rd ALT WA14.......165 E4
Biddall Dr NTHM/RTH M23...168 A3
Biddisham Wk
   NEWH/MOS M40 *...........115 G3
Biddulph Av OFTN SK2........172 D4
Bideford Dr BOLE BL2..........50 D3
   NTHM/RTH M25...............167 G3
Bideford Rd OFTN SK2........160 D5
   ROCH OL11.......................42 A3
Bidston Av RUSH/FAL M14...128 C3
Bidston CI ROY/SHW OL2 *...37 E4
   TOT/BURYW BL8..............37 E4
Bidston Dr WILM/AE SK9.....192 B5
Biggin Gdns HEY OL10..........56 B2
Bignor St CHH M8...............102 B4
Bilbao St BOL BL1................48 B1
Bilberry St MILN OL16...........11 H3
Bilbrook St ANC M4.............115 E2
Bilberry CI WHTF M45..........70 A4
Billing Av WGTN/LGST M12...128 D1
Billinge CI BOL BL1................2 E2
Billington Rd SWIN M27.......100 B2
Bill Williams CI OP/CLY M11...116 D5
Billy La SWIN M27................38 A5
Billy's La CHD/CHDH SK8....182 D5
Bilson Dr EDGY/DAV SK3....171 E2
Binbrook Wk BOLS/LL BL3....48 D5
Bindloss Av ECC M30.........111 H2
Bingham Dr NTHM/RTH M23...167 G3
Bingham St SWIN M27..........99 F1
Bingley CI OP/CLY M11.......116 A5
Bingley Dr URM M41...........123 C4
Bingley Rd MILN OL16..........11 K7
Bingley Sq MILN OL16..........11 K7
Bingley Wk BRO M7............100 C2
   FWTH BL4..........................66 A5
Binns Nook Rd WHIT OL12....10 E1
Binns PI ANC M4....................7 J4
Binsley CI STLY SK15.........120 B4
Binsley CI IRL M44..............136 C2
Binstead CI RUSH/FAL M14...129 F5
Birbeck St MOSL OL5 *........94 B3
Birchacre Gv RUSH/FAL M14...143 F4
Birchall CI DUK SK16..........133 G2
Birchall Gn MPL/ROM SK6....161 H1
Birchall Wy HULME M15......128 A3
Birch Av FAIL M35..............105 E5
   HTNM SK4........................159 E2
   IRL M44...........................150 C4
   MDTN M24.........................72 D5
   MPL/ROM SK6..................162 C4
   OLD OL1............................74 B2
   OLDS OL8..........................91 E5
   SALE M33.........................156 C4
   SLFD M6..........................112 D1
   TOT/BURYW BL8................37 H1
   WHIT OL12.........................20 A4
   WHTF M45..........................85 C1
   WHTN BL5..........................62 A5
   WILM/AE SK9....................198 C4
Birch CI WHIT OL12..............18 B3
Birch Crs MILN OL16............44 D3
Birchdale ALT WA14...........177 E2
Birchdale Av CHD/CHDH SK8...182 C1
Birch Dr BRAM/HZG SK7.....184 D2
   OLDE OL4..........................92 D2
   SWIN M27..........................99 G2
Birchenall St NEWH/MOS M40...103 G2
Birchenlea St CHAD OL9.......90 B4
The Birches MOSL OL5.......108 C1
   SALE M33........................153 H5
Birchfield BOLE BL2..............24 B5
Birchfield Av ROY/SHW OL2...42 B1
Birchfield Dr ROCH OL11......43 H1
   WALK M28..........................96 B3
Birchfield Gv BOLS/LL BL3....47 F5
Birchfield Ms HYDE SK14 *...147 H1

Birchfield Rd EDGY/DAV SK3...170 D2
Birchfields HALE/TIMP WA15...178 A3
   OLDE OL4............................93 E3
Birchfields Av
   BRUN/LGST M13..............143 G1
Birchfields Rd
   BRUN/LGST M13..............129 F5
Birchfold CI LHULT M58.........81 G3
Birchgate Wk BOLS/LL BL3....48 D4
Birch Gv DTN/ASHW M34.....132 B5
   DTN/ASHW M34................132 C2
   HALE/TIMP WA15.............167 H4
   PWCH M25..........................85 H1
   RAMS BL0...........................16 B5
Birch Hall CI OLDE OL4.........92 D3
Birch Hall La BRUN/LGST M13...143 G1
Birch Hey CI WHIT OL12.......19 H4
Birch Hill Crs WHIT OL12.......20 B4
Birch Hill Wy WHIT OL12......20 A2
Birchington Rd
   OLDTF/WHR M20..............142 C3
Birchinlee Av ROY/SHW OL2...74 C1
Birchin PI ANC M4 *................7 G3
Birch La BRUN/LGST M13.....129 F4
   DUK SK16........................120 A5
Birchlea HALE/TIMP WA15....166 A5
Birch-lea CI BURY BL9..........53 C2
Birchleaf Gv ORD M5..........112 B3
Birch Mt WHIT OL12...............2 B4
Birch Polygon RUSH/FAL M14...129 E5
Birch Rd CHD/CHDH SK8.....169 F4
   CHH M8.............................102 C1
   FWTH BL4...........................82 C3
   GOL/RIS/CUL WA3............150 A4
   MDTN M24...........................73 F2
   PART M31........................152 C3
   POY/DIS SK12..................195 G5
   SWIN M27............................98 C5
   UPML OL3...........................79 F5
   WALK M28...........................97 F1
   WHIT OL12..........................19 H2
Birch St AULW OL7.............118 D4
   BOLE BL2.............................5 J7
   BURY BL9..............................5 F2
   DROY M43 *.....................118 A5
   HEY OL10...........................41 E5
   RAD M26.............................54 F4
   STLY SK15........................108 D5
   WGTN/LGST M12..............129 F2
   WHIT OL12..........................19 H2
Birch Tree Av HYDE SK14 *...147 G1
Birch Tree Av BRAM/HZG SK7...185 H5
Birch Tree CI ALT WA14.......165 E2
Birch Tree Dr WYTH/NTH M22...180 C1
Birchvale Av MPL/ROM SK6...162 C5
Birchway BRAM/HZG SK7.....185 G5
   MPL/ROM SK6..................187 E5
Birchwood CHAD OL9............73 H5
   DROY M43 *.....................118 A2
Birchwood Crs HYDE SK14...134 B2
Birchwood Dr
   NEWH/MOS M40...............103 E4
   WILM/AE SK9...................199 G5
Birchwood Rd MDTN M24......73 H4
Birchwood Wy DUK SK16 *...133 G2
Bird Hall Av CHD/CHDH SK8...171 F5
Birdhall Gv BNG/LEV M19....144 A3
Bird Hall La EDGY/DAV SK3...171 E2
Bird Hall Rd CHD/CHDH SK8...171 H4
Bird Hall Dr NTHM/RTH M23...179 H1
Birdlip Dr MDTN M24............72 B2
Birkby Dr MDTN M24............72 B2
Birkdale CI BRAM/HZG SK7...184 D2
   HEY OL10............................56 A1
   HYDE SK14........................133 H5
Birkdale Dr SALE M33.........153 H4
   TOT/BURYW BL8................37 G4
Birkdale Gdns BOLS/LL BL3...48 C4
Birkdale Gv ECC M30.........111 G5
   RDSH SK5..........................160 A1
Birkdale PI SALE M33..........139 F5
Birkdale Rd MILN OL16.........43 H2
   RDSH SK5..........................160 A1
Birkdale St CHH M8............102 B3
Birkenhills Dr BOLS/LL BL3....47 F4
Birkett CI BOL BL1.................22 C5
Birkett Dr BOL BL1................22 C5
Birkinbrook CI WHTF M45......69 H3
Birks Av OLDE OL4................77 E4
Birks Dr TOT/BURYW BL8......51 G5
Birkworth Ct OFTN SK2.......173 E5
Birley CI HALE/TIMP WA15...166 A2
Birley Pk DID/WITH M20......157 E3
Birley St BOL BL1..................33 H2
   BURY BL9.............................38 B1
   WHIT OL12..........................10 E2
Birling Dr NTHM/RTH M23...168 A5
Birnham Gv HEY OL10...........40 B5
Birshaw Ct ROY/SHW OL2.....60 A4
Birtenshaw Crs EDGW/EG BL7...23 F3
Birties Av RDSH SK5...........131 E5
Birties CI CHD/CHDH SK8.....170 D5
   DUK SK16........................133 G2
Birtlespool Rd
   CHD/CHDH SK8................170 C5
Birtley Wk NEWH/MOS M40 *...115 F2
Birt St NEWH/MOS M40.......115 G1
Birwood Rd CHH M8..............87 G5
Biscay CI OP/CLY M11........116 A4
Bishopbridge CI BOLS/LL BL3...47 F5
Bishopdale CI OLDTF/WHR M16...127 H4
Bishopgate CI ROY/SHW OL2...59 E4
Bishopgate St CHAD OL9......90 B2
Bishop Marshall CI
   NEWH/MOS M40 *...........103 E5
Bishop Marshall Wy
   NEWH/MOS M40................56 A5
Bishops CI ALT WA14..........177 E3
   AULW OL7 *......................107 F6
   BOLS/LL BL3.......................65 F2
   CHD/CHDH SK8................170 D4
Bishopsgate CMANW M2........6 E6
Bishopsgate Wk MILN OL16...43 H2
Bishops Meadow MDTN M24...72 A1
Bishops Ms SALE M33.........139 E5
Bishop's Rd BOLS/LL BL3......65 F2

PWCH M25.............................86 B4
Bishop St MDTN M24..............73 G5
HULME M16...........................11 G2
STKP SK1................................13 J3
Bishopton CI BNG/LEV M19...144 C2
Bisley Av NTHM/RTH M23....167 G3
Bisley St OLDS OL8.................8 D5
Bismarck St OLDE OL4..........94 B2
Bispham Av BOLE BL2...........50 C2
Bispham CI TOT/BURYW BL8...37 G5
Bispham Gv BRO M7.............101 H3
Bispham St BOLE BL2............49 H1
Bittern CI POY/DIS SK12......194 B4
   ROCH OL11..........................28 C4
Bittern Dr DROY M43............118 B2
Blackbank St BOL BL1............34 A4
Blackberry CI ALT WA14.......165 E1
Blackberry La RDSH SK5......145 H4
Black Brook Rd HTNM SK4...144 C4
Blackburn Gdns
   DID/WITH M20...................157 F2
Blackburn PI ORD M5..........113 H4
Blackburn St CSLFD M3........114 B2
   OLDTF/WHR M16..............127 F3
   RAD M26..............................68 C2
Blackcap CI WALK M28..........96 C3
Blackcarr Rd NTHM/RTH M23...168 A4
Blackchapel Dr MILN OL16.....43 G3
Blackcroft CI SWIN M27..........98 D2
Blackdown Gv OLDS OL8.......91 F4
Blackett St WGTN/LGST M12 *...115 F5
Blackfield La BRO M7............101 F2
Blackford Av BURY BL9..........53 G5
Blackford Rd BNG/LEV M19...144 B4
Blackford Wk
   NEWH/MOS M40 *............115 G2
Blackfriars Rd CSLFD M3.........6 B2
Blackfriars St CSLFD M3..........6 D3
Blackhill CI BRUN/LGST M13...128 C1
Black Horse St BOL BL1...........2 E6
   FWTH BL4...........................66 B5
Blackleach Dr WALK M28.......82 A5
Blackledge St BOLS/LL BL3....48 B5
Blackley CI BURY BL9.............69 H2
Blackley New Rd BKLY M9.....87 E3
Blackley Park Rd BKLY M9....103 E1
Blackley St MDTN M24............71 G5
   OLDTF/WHR M16..............127 F3
Blacklock St CSLFD M3.........114 C1
Blackmore Rd STRET M32....125 G3
Black Moss Rd ALT WA14....164 B2
Blackpits Rd ROCH OL11........28 A2
Blackpool St OP/CLY M11....116 C3
Blackrod Dr TOT/BURYW BL8...37 F5
Black Sail Wk OLD OL1 *........75 F3
Blackshaw La BOLS/LL BL3....48 B3
   ROY/SHW OL2.....................60 C5
   WILM/AE SK9...................200 C4
Blackshaw St EDGY/DAV SK3...15 F5
Blacksmith La ROCH OL11.....42 A2
Blackstock St
   BRUN/LGST M13..............128 D4
Blackstone Av MILN OL16......11 K4
Blackstone Edge Old Rd
   LIT OL15..............................21 H2
Blackstone Rd OFTN SK2....173 E4
Blackthorn Av BNG/LEV M19...144 A4
Blackthorne CI WHIT OL12.....29 H1
Blackthorne Dr SALE M33....155 G4
Blackthorne Rd HYDE SK14...148 A5
Blackthorn Ms WHIT OL12.....29 H1
Blackthorn Rd OLDS OL8.....105 H2
Blackwin St WGTN/LGST M12...116 A4
Blackwood Dr
   NTHM/RTH M23.................167 E1
Blackwood St BOLS/LL BL3....49 F5
Bladen CI CHD/CHDH SK8.....170 D5
Bladon CI CMANE M1 *............7 H6
Blair Av LHULT M38................81 G3
Blair CI BRAM/HZG SK7.......184 D4
   ROY/SHW OL2.....................60 A2
   SALE M33..........................153 F5
Blairhall Av NEWH/MOS M40...103 H3
Blair La BOLE BL2...................35 E5
Blairmore Dr BOLS/LL BL3....63 C5
Blair Rd OLDTF/WHR M16....142 A2
Blair St EDGW/EG BL7...........23 E3
   FWTH BL4.............................82 D1
   OLDTF/WHR M16..............127 G3
   WGTN/LGST M12 *.............29 G2
Blakedown Wk
   WGTN/LGST M12..............129 F3
Blake Dr OFTN SK2..............173 F3
Blakefield Dr WALK M28.........97 F1
Blake Gdns BOL BL1..............33 G4
Blakelock St ROY/SHW OL2...59 F4
Blakemere Av SALE M33......155 F3
Blakemore Wk
   WGTN/LGST M12 *............115 H4
Blake St EDGW/EG BL7..........23 F3
   EDGW/EG BL7.....................22 E2
   MILN OL16............................11 H3
Blakeswell CI URM M41........123 E5
Blakey CI BOLS/LL BL3..........47 F4
Blakey St WGTN/LGST M12...129 H4
Blanchard St HULME M15.....127 H4
Blanche St WHIT OL12............10 E1
Blanche Wk OLD OL1 *............9 J1
Bland CI FAIL M35................104 D3
Blandford Av WALK M28.........82 A5
Blandford CI TOT/BURYW BL8...38 A1
Blandford Ct STLY SK15.......120 D3
Blandford Dr NEWH/MOS M40...89 F5
Blandford Rd ECC M30...........12 A1
   HTNM SK4............................12 A1
   SLFD M6............................100 C4
Blandford St AUL OL6...........119 F2
   STLY SK15.........................120 D3
Bland St PWCH M25................86 A5
Bland Wk HULME M15 *.........78 A6
Blanefield CI CCHDY M21......142 A4
Blantyre Av WALK M28...........82 B5
Blantyre Rd SWIN M27............99 G4

Blantyre St ECC M30............110 B2
HULME M15..........................127 G1
SWIN M27..............................98 C2
Blanwood Dr CHH M8...........102 C3
Blaven CI EDGY/DAV SK3....173 E4
Blazemoss Bank OFTN SK2...173 A4
Bleackley St TOT/BURYW BL8...37 G5
Bleadale CI WILM/AE SK9.....199 G1
Blue Hey Rd WYTH/NTH M22...181 E2
Bleakley St WHTF M45............69 G2
Bleak St BOLE BL2..................34 C4
Bleasby St OLDE OL4..............76 B5
Bleasdale CI HOR/BR BL6.......46 A1
Bleasdale Rd BOL BL1............32 C4
   WYTH/NTH M22.................180 A1
Bleasdale St ROY/SHW OL2...59 E4
Bledlow CI ECC M30.............111 F2
Blenheim Av
   OLDTF/WHR M16..............141 H1
Blenheim CI ALT WA14.........177 G3
   HEY OL10.............................53 C4
   HEY OL10.............................41 F4
   POY/DIS SK12...................195 C5
   WILM/AE SK9...................199 G3
Blenheim Rd BOLE BL2..........50 B2
   CHD/CHDH SK8................183 C2
   OLDTF/WHR M16..............126 C5
Blenheim St ROCH OL11........42 A3
   WHIT OL12 *........................29 F2
Blenheim Wy AUL OL1............76 C1
Blenmar CI RAD M26..............68 C1
Blériot St BOLS/LL BL3...........64 C1
Bletchley CI BRUN/LGST M13...129 E3
Bletchley Rd HTNM SK4.......158 B5
Blethyn St BOLS/LL BL3.........64 A2
Blinco Rd URM M41...............124 C5
Blind La WGTN/LGST M12......129 E1
Blindsill Rd FWTH BL4............65 E5
Blisworth Av ECC M30..........111 F5
Blisworth CI ANC M4............115 G4
Block La CHAD OL9................90 C2
Blodwell St SLFD M6.............113 E3
Blomley St BOLE BL2..............42 B4
Bloomfield Dr BURY BL9.........70 A1
   WALK M28............................96 B3
Bloomfield Rd FWTH BL4.......82 A1
Bloomfield St BOL BL1............33 H5
Bloomsbury Gv
   HALE/TIMP WA15.............166 B3
Bloomsbury La
   HALE/TIMP WA15.............166 B3
Bloom St CMANE M1................7 G6
   CSLFD M3............................12 B6
   EDGY/DAV SK3...................12 B6
   RAMS BL0............................16 B4
Blossom PI MILN OL16............10 C5
Blossom St ANC M4 *...............7 J3
   ORD M5..............................113 H4
   WGTN/LGST M12..............129 F2
Blucher St AULW OL7...........106 D4
   ORD M5..............................113 H4
   WGTN/LGST M12..............129 F2
Blueball La PWCH M25...........71 E3
Blue Bell Av NEWH/MOS M40...103 H1
Bluebell CI HYDE SK14.........135 E2
Bluebell Dr ROCH OL11..........42 A3
Bluebell Gv CHD/CHDH SK8...170 D5
Blueberry Dr ALT WA14.........176 D2
Bluefields ROY/SHW OL2.......60 C1
Blue Ribbon Wk SWIN M27.....99 F1
Bluestone Dr HTNM SK4......158 B3
Bluestone Rd
   NEWH/MOS M40...............104 B4
   RDSH SK5..........................145 G1
Blundell La STLY SK15.........135 C2
Blundell St BOL BL1................2 D4
Blundering La STLY SK15.....135 E2
Blunn St OLDS OL8................91 E5
Blyborough CI SLFD M6........112 D1
Blyth Av LIT OL15 *.................20 D1
Blythe Av HALE/TIMP WA15...167 G3
Blythe Av BRAM/HZG SK7....193 F1
Blyton St HULME M15...........128 C3
Boad St CMANE M1...................7 H5
Boardale Dr MDTN M24.........72 B3
Boardman CI BOL BL1............33 H4
   RDSH SK5..........................146 B1
Boardman Fold CI MDTN M24...88 D2
Boardman Fold Rd MDTN M24...88 D2
Boardman La MDTN M24.........71 C4
Boardman Rd CHH M8............87 E5
Boardman St ECC M30..........110 C3
   HYDE SK14........................147 H1
Boardale St AUL OL6.............120 A1
   BOL BL1................................2 A6
Boar Green CI
   NEWH/MOS M40...............104 B3
Boarshaw Clough MDTN M24...73 E2
Boarshaw Clough Wy
   MDTN M24............................73 E2
Boarshaw Crs MDTN M24.......73 C1
Boarshaw La MDTN M24.........73 D3
Boarshurst La UPML OL3.......79 C2
Boat La IRL M44...................136 D1
Bobbin Wk ANC M4 *................7 K4
Bob Brook CI
   NEWH/MOS M40...............104 B4
Bob Massey CI OP/CLY M11...116 C2
Bob's La IRL M44..................150 C2
Boddens Hill Rd HTNM SK4...158 B1
Boddington Rd ECC M30......110 A4
Bodiam Rd TOT/BURYW BL8...26 C4
Bodley St OP/CLY M11.........116 C2
Bodmin Crs RDSH SK5.........160 D2
Bodmin Dr BRAM/HZG SK7...184 A5
Bodmin Rd SALE M33..........155 C1

Bolam CI NTHM/RTH M23.....155 G5
Boland Dr RUSH/FAL M14.....143 F3
Bolbury Crs SWIN M27.........100 A2
Bolderod Pl OLD OL1 *............9 J1
Bolderstone Pl OFTN SK2....173 F5
Bold St ALT WA14................177 G1
   BOL BL1.................................2 E6
   BURY BL9..............................5 H4
   HULME M15........................127 H3
   SWIN M27............................84 B5
Bolesworth CI CCHDY M21...140 D3
Boleyn Ct HEY OL10...............40 D5
Bolholt Ter TOT/BURYW BL8...37 G2
Bolivia St ORD M5.................112 A5
Bollin Av ALT WA14..............177 E4
Bollin CI FWTH BL4................82 D1
Bollin Ct HULME M15............127 G2
Bollin Dr ALT WA14..............165 H1
   SALE M33..........................154 B2
Bollings Yd BOL BL1 *..............3 F6
Bollington Rd HTNM SK4......159 G1
   NEWH/MOS M40...............115 G3
Bollington St AULW OL7.......119 F4
Bollin Hi WILM/AE SK9.........198 B7
Bollin Sq ALT WA14 *............177 E3
Bollin Wk WHTF M45..............70 B2
   WILM/AE SK9....................199 G3
Bollinway HALE/TIMP WA15...178 B4
Bolshaw Rd CHD/CHDH SK8...191 G1
Bolshaw Farm La
   CHD/CHDH SK8................191 H1
Bolshaw Rd CHD/CHDH SK8...191 G1
Bolton Av BNG/LEV M19......158 A4
Bolton CI POY/DIS SK12......195 E3
   PWCH M25............................85 G5
Bolton Rd BOLE BL2...............34 D1
   FWTH BL4.............................66 A2
   FWTH BL4.............................66 B5
   ROCH OL11...........................41 H2
   SLFD M6...............................99 H4
   SWIN M27.............................99 H2
   TOT/BURYW BL8..................25 F1
   TOT/BURYW BL8..................52 B1
   WALK M28.............................82 A3
   WHTN BL5.............................62 A4
Bolton Rd West RAMS BL0.....16 C4
Bolton St CSLFD M3.................6 C2
   OLDE OL4..............................9 K4
   RAD M26..............................15 C5
   RAMS BL0............................16 C5
   RDSH SK5..........................145 E4
   TOT/BURYW BL8...................4 A4
Bombay Rd EDGY/DAV SK3...171 F2
Bombay St ALT WA14...........120 A1
   CMANE M1.............................7 J6
Bonar CI EDGY/DAV SK3 *.....12 A5
Bonar Rd EDGY/DAV SK3......12 A6
Boncarn Dr NTHM/RTH M23...167 H5
Bonchurch Wk
   WGTN/LGST M12..............130 A2
Bondmark Rd GTN M18........130 B2
Bond Sq BRO M7..................101 H4
Bond St BURY BL9...................5 H4
   WGTN/LGST M12...............7 K7
   WHIT OL12............................11 F1
Bongs Rd OFTN SK2............173 G3
Bonhill Wk OP/CLY M11......116 C3
Bonington Ri MPL/ROM SK6...175 C1
Bonis Crs OFTN SK2............172 D5
Bonny Brow St MDTN M24.....71 G5
Bonsall St HULME M15........128 B2
Bonscale Crs MDTN M24.......72 B1
Bonville Cha ALT WA14.........164 D4
Bonville Rd ALT WA14..........164 D4
Boodle St AUL OL6...............119 G2
Boond St ANC M4.................115 G4
Boonfields EDGW/EG BL7 *.....6 C2
Booth Av RUSH/FAL M14.....143 F4
Booth Bridge CI MDTN M24...71 H5
Boothby Rd SWIN M27..........98 D1
Boothby St OFTN SK2.........172 D5
Booth CI STLY SK15.............120 C4
   TOT/BURYW BL8..................4 D4
Boothcote DTN/ASHW M34...132 A2
Booth Dr URM M41..............123 C3
Boothfield ECC M30............110 B2
Boothfield Rd
   WYTH/NTH M22.................168 C3
Booth Hall Dr TOT/BURYW BL8...37 H5
Booth Hall Rd BKLY M9..........88 D4
Booth Hill La OLD OL1............74 F5
Booth Rd ALT WA14.............165 F5
   BOLS/LL BL3.........................67 E2
   DTN/ASHW M34.................131 H1
   OLDTF/WHR M16..............127 F5
   SALE M33..........................139 H5
Boothroyden Rd BKLY M9......87 H1
Boothroyden Ter BKLY M9.....87 H1
Boothshall Wy WALK M28.......96 C4
Booth's Hall Gv WALK M28.....96 C4
Booth's Hall Rd WALK M28.....96 C4
Booth's Hall Wy WALK M28.....96 C4
Boothstown Dr WALK M28.......96 C4
Booth St AUL OL6 *..............119 G3
   BOL BL1...............................33 F3
   CHAD OL9..............................6 E5
   CMANW M2............................6 E5
   DTN/ASHW M34.................132 C3
   HYDE SK14........................147 H1
   MDTN M24............................89 C1
   OLDE OL4..............................92 D1
   STLY SK15.........................120 C5
   TOT/BURYW BL8..................37 F1
Booth St East
   BRUN/LGST M13..............128 C2
Booth St West HULME M15...128 B2
Booth Wy TOT/BURYW BL8...37 F1
Boot La BOL BL1....................32 A5
Bootle St CMANW M2..............6 D5
Bordale Av BKLY M9............103 G3

Bordan St OP/CLY M11 116 A5
Border Brook La WALK M28 96 B3
Border Wy BURY BL9 53 H3
Bordley Wk NTHM/RTH M23 155 F5
Bordon Rd EDGY/DAV SK3 171 E2
Boringdon Cl
NEWH/MOS M40 * 104 A4
Borland Av NEWH/MOS M40 104 C1
Borough Av RAD M26 53 E4
SWIN M27 99 F1
Borough Rd HALE/TIMP WA15 165 H5
SALQ M50 112 C4
Borough St STLY SK15 120 D4
The Borrans WALK M28 * 96 A5
Borron St STKP SK1 13 K1
Borrowdale Av BOL BL1 47 H1
CHD/CHDH SK8 169 G5
Borrowdale Cl ROY/SHW OL2 59 E3
Borrowdale Crs AULW OL7 119 E1
DID/WITH M20 156 D2
Borrowdale Dr BURY BL9 69 H1
ROCH OL11 42 A2
Borrowdale Rd MDTN M24 72 B2
OFTN SK2 172 C3
Borsden St SWIN M27 98 C1
Borth Av OFTN SK2 172 D2
Borwell St GTN M18 130 C3
Boscobel Rd BOLS/LL BL3 65 G2
Boscombe Av ECC M30 110 D5
Boscombe Dr BRAM/HZG SK7 184 D2
Boscombe St RDSH SK5 145 F1
RUSH/FAL M14 142 D1
Boscow Rd BOLS/LL BL3 66 D2
Bosden Av BRAM/HZG SK7 185 F1
Bosden Cl WILM/AE SK9 192 A2
Bosden Fold STKP SK1 13 H5
Bosdenfold Rd
BRAM/HZG SK7 185 F1
Bosden Hall Rd
BRAM/HZG SK7 185 F1
Bosdin Rd East URM M41 * 137 G2
Bosdin Rd West URM M41 137 G2
Bosley Av DID/WITH M20 142 C3
Bosley Cl WILM/AE SK9 192 A5
Bosley Dr POY/DIS SK12 195 H4
Bosley Rd EDGY/DAV SK3 170 D1
Bossall Av BKLY M9 88 B3
Bossington Cl OFTN SK2 172 D1
Bostock Wk
BRUN/LGST M13 * 128 C1
Boston Cl BRAM/HZG SK7 183 G5
FAIL M35 105 E2
Boston Ct SALQ M50 112 D5
Boston St BOL BL1 * 33 H4
HULME M15 128 A3
HYDE SK14 133 H5
OLDS OL8 91 G3
Boswell Av DTN/ASHW M34 118 C4
Boswell Wy MDTN M24 57 G5
Bosworth Cl WHTF M45 70 B4
Bosworth Sq ROCH OL11 * 42 C2
Bosworth St OP/CLY M11 116 B5
ROCH OL11 42 C1
Botanical Av
OLDTF/WHR M16 126 D3
Botany Cl HEY OL10 40 C3
Botany La AUL OL6 119 H1
Botany Rd ECC M30 110 B1
MPL/ROM SK6 147 E5
Botesworth Gn MILN OL16 44 D1
Botham Cl HULME M15 128 B3
Bothwell Rd
NEWH/MOS M40 * 115 F2
Bottesford Av DID/WITH M20 157 E1
Bottomfield Cl OLD OL1 75 H3
Bottomley Side BKLY M9 87 H5
Bottom o' th' Moor BOLE BL2 35 E4
OLD OL1 9 K3
Bottom St HYDE SK14 134 A5
Boulden Dr TOT/BURYW BL8 37 H1
Boulder Dr NTHM/RTH M23 179 H2
Boulderstone Rd STLY SK15 120 D1
The Boulevard
BRAM/HZG SK7 185 F2
DID/WITH M20 142 A5
Boundary Cl MOSL OL5 108 D4
MPL/ROM SK6 162 B1
Boundary Dr BOLE BL2 50 D4
Boundary Gdns BOL BL1 * 33 G4
OLD OL1 75 F4
Boundary Gv NTHM/RTH M23 155 G4
Boundary La HULME M15 128 B2
Boundary Park Rd OLD OL1 74 D3
Boundary Rd CHD/CHDH SK8 170 C3
IRL M44 122 D5
SWIN M27 99 E2
Boundary St BOL BL1 33 G4
BOLE BL2 51 E4
LIT OL15 20 D2
ROCH OL11 42 D1
WGTN/LGST M12 129 H3
Boundary St West
HULME M15 128 B2
Boundary Ter
WYTH/NTH M22 * 191 E1
The Boundary SWIN M27 83 G3
Boundary Wk ROCH OL11 43 E1
Boundry Gn DTN/ASHW M34 132 B3
Bourdon St NEWH/MOS M40 115 G2
Bourget St BRO M7 102 A2
Bournbrook Av LHULT M38 81 F1
Bourne Av SWIN M27 99 E3
Bourne Dr NEWH/MOS M40 104 A1
Bournelea Av BNG/LEV M19 143 G5
Bourne Rd ROY/SHW OL2 59 H1
Bourne St CHAD OL9 90 C5
HTNM SK4 159 H2
WILM/AE SK9 198 C4
Bourneville Dr
TOT/BURYW BL8 37 F4
Bournville Av HTNM SK4 159 H2
Bournville Gv BNG/LEV M19 144 B2
Bourton Cl TOT/BURYW BL8 37 G3
Bourton Dr GTN M18 130 A4
Bowden Cl HYDE SK14 149 G2
ROCH OL11 57 G1
Bowden La MPL/ROM SK6 174 D2
Bowden Rd SWIN M27 99 F3
Bowden St BRAM/HZG SK7 185 F1
DTN/ASHW M34 132 B5
Bowdon Av RUSH/FAL M14 142 B2
Bowdon Ri ALT WA14 177 G2
Bowdon Rd ALT WA14 177 F1
Bowdon St EDGY/DAV SK3 12 E6
Bowen Cl BRAM/HZG SK7 194 A2
Bowen St BOL BL1 33 E5
Bower Av BRAM/HZG SK7 185 E3
HTNM SK4 159 F3
WHIT OL12 20 A4
Bower Ct HYDE SK14 134 B3
Bower Cup Fold STLY SK15 121 H1
Bowerfield Av BRAM/HZG SK7 185 E4
Bowerfield Crs
BRAM/HZG SK7 185 F4
Bowerfold La HTNM SK4 12 C1
Bower Gdns STLY SK15 121 G5
Bower Gv STLY SK15 121 F3
Bower Rd HALE/TIMP WA15 177 H3
Bowers Av URM M41 124 A4
Bowers St RUSH/FAL M14 143 F4
Bower St BRO M7 * 101 H3
NEWH/MOS M40 103 G5
OLD OL1 9 K2
RDSH SK5 145 F1
Bower Ter DROY M43 118 B2
Bowery Av CHD/CHDH SK8 192 C1
Bowes Cl TOT/BURYW BL8 37 G1
Bowes St RUSH/FAL M14 128 A5
Bowfell Dr MPL/ROM SK6 186 D4
Bowfell Gv BKLY M9 87 G4
Bowfell Rd URM M41 138 B1
Bowgreave Av BOLE BL2 50 C2
Bow Green Rd ALT WA14 176 D3
Bowgreen Wk HULME M15 127 G2
Bowker Av DTN/ASHW M34 147 F3
Bowker Bank Av CHH M8 87 E5
Bowker Cl ROCH OL11 28 B2
Bowkers Rw BOL BL1 3 F5
Bowker St BRO M7 101 G4
HYDE SK14 133 H5
RAD M26 68 B1
WALK M28 81 G4
Bowlacre Rd HYDE SK14 147 H5
Bowland Av GTN M18 131 F4
Bowland Cl AUL OL6 107 F3
OFTN SK2 173 F4
ROY/SHW OL2 59 F2
TOT/BURYW BL8 36 D3
Bowland Dr BOL BL1 32 B4
Bowland Gv MILN OL16 44 C2
Bowland Rd DTN/ASHW M34 131 G5
MPL/ROM SK6 162 A1
NTHM/RTH M23 167 G3
Bow La ALT WA14 176 D4
CMANW M2 6 E5
HEY OL10 40 D4
Bowlee Cl WHTF M45 69 H3
Bowler St BNG/LEV M19 144 B3
ROY/SHW OL2 60 A2
Bowlers Wk WHIT OL12 30 A1
Bowley Av WYTH/NTH M22 179 H2
Bowling Green Cl CHAD OL9 90 B3
Bowling Green St HEY OL10 41 E4
HYDE SK14 147 G1
Bowling Green Wy ROCH OL11 28 C5
Bowling Rd GTN M18 130 D5
Bowling St CHAD OL9 90 C5
Bowman Crs AUL OL6 120 A2
Bow Meadow Gra
WGTN/LGST M12 129 G4
Bowmont Cl CHD/CHDH SK8 170 D5
Bowness Av CHD/CHDH SK8 183 E3
HTNM SK4 145 E5
IRL M44 150 C2
WHIT OL12 29 F2
Bowness Dr SALE M33 154 A1
Bowness Rd AULW OL7 119 E1
BOLS/LL BL3 48 C5
BOLS/LL BL3 50 C5
MDTN M24 72 A3
Bowness St OP/CLY M11 131 E1
STRET M32 126 A5
Bowring St BRO M7 * 101 F5
Bowscale Cl BRUN/LGST M13 129 G4
Bowstone Hill Rd BOLE BL2 36 A1
Bow St BOL BL1 2 E4
CMANW M2 6 D5
DUK SK16 119 H3
EDGY/DAV SK3 12 A5
OLD OL1 9 H3
ROCH OL11 42 C3
Bowyer Gdns BOLS/LL BL3 63 G1
Boxgrove Rd SALE M33 153 H1
Boxhill Dr NTHM/RTH M23 * 155 H5
Box St LIT OL15 20 D3
RAMS BL0 * 17 E2
Boxtree Av GTN M18 130 C5
Boyd St WGTN/LGST M12 129 H1
Boyd's Wk DUK SK16 133 F1
Boyer St OLDTF/WHR M16 127 E3
Boyle St BOL BL1 32 D5
CHH M8 102 C4
Boysnope Whf ECC M30 123 E4
Brabant Rd CHD/CHDH SK8 183 E2
Brabham Cl CCHDY M21 141 F3
Brabham Ms SWIN M27 98 B3
Brabyns Av MPL/ROM SK6 162 C3
Brabyns Brow MPL/ROM SK6 175 F2
Brabyns Rd HYDE SK14 148 A4
Bracadale Dr EDGY/DAV SK3 171 H5
Bracewell Cl WGTN/LGST M12 129 H3
Bracken Av WALK M28 82 B4
Bracken Cl BOL BL1 22 C5
DROY M43 118 B3
HEY OL10 56 A1
MPL/ROM SK6 175 H2
OLDE OL4 93 E1
SALE M33 153 F1
Bracken Dr NTHM/RTH M23 168 A4
Brackenhurst Av MOSL OL5 109 F1
Brackenlea Dr BKLY M9 87 H5
Bracken Lea Fold WHIT OL12 29 E1
Brackenlea Pl EDGY/DAV SK3 171 G4
Brackenside RDSH SK5 145 G3
Brackenwood Cl
ROY/SHW OL2 74 D2
Brackenwood Dr
CHD/CHDH SK8 170 A5
Brackenwood Ms
WILM/AE SK9 199 H1
Brackley Av HULME M15 127 G1
Brackley Dr MDTN M24 88 D2
Brackley Ldg ECC M30 * 111 G2
Brackley Rd ECC M30 111 E1
HTNM SK4 159 G1
WHTN BL5 63 H4
Brackley Sq OLD OL1 * 9 K1
Brackleys St FWTH BL4 66 A4
Brackley St FWTH BL4 66 A4
OLD OL1 * 9 J1
WALK M28 81 H3
Bracondale Av BOL BL1 33 E4
Bradbourne Cl BOLS/LL BL3 48 D4
Bradburn Cl ECC M30 111 E4
Bradburn Rd IRL M44 136 A4
Bradburn St ECC M30 111 E4
Bradburn Wk CHH M8 102 C4
Bradbury Av ALT WA14 164 D4
Bradbury's La UPML OL3 95 G4
Bradbury St AULW OL7 * 119 F1
HYDE SK14 148 A2
RAD M26 68 B2
Bradda Mt BRAM/HZG SK7 184 A2
Braddan Av SALE M33 154 D3
Bradden Cl ORD M5 113 F4
Braddocks Cl WHIT OL12 20 A4
Braddon Av URM M41 124 C5
Braddon Rd MPL/ROM SK6 161 H1
Braddon St OP/CLY M11 116 D4
Braddyll Rd WHTN BL5 63 G4
Brade Cl OP/CLY M11 116 D5
Bradfield Av SLFD M6 112 B3
Bradfield Cl RDSH SK5 145 E1
Bradfield Rd URM M41 139 F1
Bradford Av BOLS/LL BL3 65 G1
Bradford Crs BOLS/LL BL3 * 49 F5
Bradford Park Dr BOLE BL2 3 K6
Bradford Rd BOLS/LL BL3 65 F2
ECC M30 111 F1
NEWH/MOS M40 115 H2
Bradford St BOLE BL2 3 H5
FWTH BL4 66 A5
OLD OL1 75 F4
Bradford Ter BURY BL9 4 B7
Bradgate Av CHD/CHDH SK8 182 A3
Bradgate Cl WYTH/NTH M22 168 D1
Bradgate Rd ALT WA14 164 D4
SALE M33 154 C4
Bradgate St AULW OL7 119 F4
Bradgreen Rd ECC M30 110 D2
Bradley Av BRO M7 101 E3
Bradley Cl HALE/TIMP WA15 165 H2
Bradley Dr BURY BL9 70 A2
Bradley Fold Rd BOLE BL2 51 E3
Bradley Green Rd HYDE SK14 134 A2
Bradley La MILN OL16 45 E2
RAD M26 51 E4
STRET M32 139 G4
Bradleys Count CMANE M1 * 7 H4
Bradley Smithy Cl WHIT OL12 29 H1
Bradley St CMANE M1 7 H3
MILN OL16 45 E2
Bradney Cl BKLY M9 87 G3
Bradnor Rd WYTH/NTH M22 168 C2
Bradshaw Av DID/WITH M20 142 D4
FAIL M35 104 D5
WHTF M45 69 F2
Bradshaw Brow BOLE BL2 34 D2
Bradshaw Crs MPL/ROM SK6 175 F2
Bradshaw Fold Av NEWH/MOS M40 89 G4
Bradshawgate BOL BL1 3 F5
Bradshaw Hall Dr BOLE BL2 23 H5
Bradshaw Hall Fold BOLE BL2 * 24 A5
Bradshaw Hall La CHD/CHDH SK8 182 A4
Bradshaw La STRET M32 140 B3
Bradshaw Mdw BOLE BL2 24 A5
Bradshaw Rd BOLE BL2 24 A4
MPL/ROM SK6 175 E2
TOT/BURYW BL8 25 F5
Bradshaw St ANC M4 * 7 F2
BRO M7 101 H4
FWTH BL4 66 A5
HEY OL10 41 F4
OLD OL1 9 H3
RAD M26 68 A1
Bradshaw St North BRO M7 101 G3
Bradstock Rd OLDTF/WHR M16 127 H5
Bradstone Rd CHH M8 102 A5
Bradwell Av DID/WITH M20 142 B5
STRET M32 125 F5
Bradwell Dr CHD/CHDH SK8 181 H5
Bradwell Pl BOLE BL2 34 C5
Bradwell Rd BRAM/HZG SK7 185 F4
Bradwen Av CHH M8 102 B1
Bradwen Cl DTN/ASHW M34 147 E2
Brady St STKP SK1 13 J1
Braemar Av STRET M32 139 G1
URM M41 138 A2
Braemar Dr BURY BL9 39 G4
Braemar Gv HEY OL10 40 B5
Braemar La WALK M28 96 C4
Braemar Rd BRAM/HZG SK7 185 G1
RUSH/FAL M14 143 G3
SALE M33 153 F4
Braemore Cl ROY/SHW OL2 59 F1
Braemore Dr HYDE SK14 149 H2
Brae Side OLDS OL8 91 F5
Braeside STRET M32 * 139 G2
Braeside Cl OFTN SK2 173 G4
Braeside Gv BOLS/LL BL3 47 F4
Braewood Cl BURY BL9 39 F3
Bragenham St GTN M18 130 B3
Brailsford Rd BOLE BL2 34 D3
RUSH/FAL M14 143 G3
Braintree Rd WYTH/NTH M22 180 D4
Braithwaite Rd MDTN M24 56 A5
Brakehouse Cl MILN OL16 31 F5
Brakenhurst Dr BRO M7 * 102 A4
Brakesmere Gv WALK M28 81 E3
Braley St CMANE M1 * 128 C1
Bramall Cl BURY BL9 70 A2
Bramall St HYDE SK14 133 G4
Bramble Av OLDE OL4 76 C3
ORD M5 127 F1
Bramble Cl LIT OL15 20 C3
Bramble Cft HOR/BR BL6 62 B1
Brambling Cl DTN/ASHW M34 118 B3
OFTN SK2 173 H5
Bramcote Av BOLE BL2 49 G4
NTHM/RTH M23 168 A3
Bramdean Av BOLE BL2 35 F1
Bramfield Wk HULME M15 * 127 G1
Bramhall Av BOLE BL2 35 H2
Bramhall Cl DUK SK16 133 G2
HALE/TIMP WA15 167 E3
MILN OL16 31 F5
SALE M33 155 F3
Bramhall La EDGY/DAV SK3 172 A5
Bramhall La South
BRAM/HZG SK7 193 H1
Bramhall Moor La
BRAM/HZG SK7 184 D2
Bramhall Park Rd
BRAM/HZG SK7 183 F3
Bramhall St BOLS/LL BL3 65 G1
GTN M18 * 130 D3
Bramham Rd MPL/ROM SK6 175 F5
Bramley Av BNG/LEV M19 144 A3
STRET M32 139 H1
Bramley Cl BRAM/HZG SK7 193 H1
SWIN M27 98 B4
WILM/AE SK9 200 A1
Bramley Crs HTNM SK4 159 E5
Bramley Dr BRAM/HZG SK7 193 H1
TOT/BURYW BL8 26 D4
Bramley Meade BRO M7 101 H3
Bramley Rd BOL BL1 23 E5
BRAM/HZG SK7 193 H1
ROCH OL11 28 B3
Bramley St BRO M7 101 H5
Brammay Dr TOT/BURYW BL8 36 D1
Brampton Rd BOLS/LL BL3 63 H1
BRAM/HZG SK7 184 A2
Bramway BRAM/HZG SK7 183 F5
MPL/ROM SK6 187 E5
Bramwell Dr BRUN/LGST M13 128 D2
Bramwell St STKP SK1 172 C1
Bramworth Av RAMS BL0 16 C2
Brancaster Rd CMANE M1 128 B1
Branch Cl TOT/BURYW BL8 4 B2
Branch Rd LIT OL15 31 F2
Brancker St WHTN BL5 62 D4
Brandish Cl BRUN/LGST M13 129 E4
Brandle Av TOT/BURYW BL8 37 H2
Brandlehow Dr MDTN M24 71 H2
Brandlesholme Rd
TOT/BURYW BL8 26 D5
Brandon Av CHD/CHDH SK8 181 G3
DTN/ASHW M34 131 E5
ECC M30 111 H1
WYTH/NTH M22 168 B1
Brandon Brow OLD OL1 * 75 F4
Brandon Cl TOT/BURYW BL8 38 A1
WILM/AE SK9 192 A5
Brandon Crs ROY/SHW OL2 59 H1
Brandon Rd SLFD M6 99 G5
Brandon St BOLS/LL BL3 48 C5
MILN OL16 31 F5
Brandram Rd PWCH M25 * 86 A3
Brandsby Gdns ORD M5 * 113 F5
Brandwood OLD OL1 73 H3
Brandwood Av CCHDY M21 156 C2
Brandwood Cl WALK M28 96 B2
Brandwood St BOLS/LL BL3 48 B5
Branfield Av CHD/CHDH SK8 182 A3
Branksome Av PWCH M25 85 H3
Branksome Dr BKLY M9 87 G1
CHD/CHDH SK8 182 A3
SLFD M6 99 F5
Branksome Rd HTNM SK4 159 E5
Brannach Dr CHAD OL9 74 B4
Bransby Av BKLY M9 88 B3
Branscombe Dr SALE M33 153 F1
Branscombe Gdns
BOLS/LL BL3 * 50 A4
Bransdale Av ROY/SHW OL2 58 D5
Bransdale Cl BOLS/LL BL3 47 G5
Bransford Rd OP/CLY M11 117 E5
URM M41 124 B5
Branson St ANC M4 115 G3
Branson Wk
HALE/TIMP WA15 166 D3
Branston Rd NEWH/MOS M40 89 G5
Brantfell Gv BOLE BL2 50 C1
Brantingham Rd CCHDY M21 141 F2
Brantwood Cl ROY/SHW OL2 58 D5
Brantwood Dr BOLE BL2 50 C1
Brantwood Rd BRO M7 101 G2
CHD/CHDH SK8 182 C3
HTNM SK4 159 F2
Brantwood Ter BKLY M9 * 103 G3
Brassey St AUL OL6 119 G1
MDTN M24 72 D3
Brassica Cl ECC M30 110 B1
Brassington Av CCHDY M21 141 F4
ORD M5 113 G5
Brassington Rd HTNM SK4 158 B2
Brathay Cl BOLE BL2 35 G5
WHTF M45 70 B4
Brattice Dr SWIN M27 99 H2
Bratton Wk
BRUN/LGST M13 * 129 E2
Brattray Dr MDTN M24 72 B1
Braunston Cl ECC M30 111 F5
Bray Av ECC M30 110 C2
Braybrook Dr BOL BL1 47 E2
Bray Cl CHD/CHDH SK8 182 B2
Brayford Rd WYTH/NTH M22 180 C3
Brayshaw Cl HEY OL10 40 C5
Brayside Rd DID/WITH M20 158 A2
Braystan Gdns
CHD/CHDH SK8 169 G3
Braystones Cl
HALE/TIMP WA15 167 E3
Brayston Fold MDTN M24 71 H4
Brayton Av DID/WITH M20 157 H4
SALE M33 153 G1
Brazennose St CMANW M2 6 D5
Brazil Pl CMANE M1 7 G7
Brazil St CMANE M1 7 G7
Brazley Av BOLS/LL BL3 65 F1
Breach House La KNUT WA16 188 B5
Bread St GTN M18 130 D2
Brechvale Cl POY/DIS SK12 195 F4
Breckland Cl STLY SK15 121 G3
Breckland Dr BOL BL1 47 E2
Breckles Pl BOLS/LL BL3 * 48 C4
Breck Rd ECC M30 110 C3
Brecon Av BNG/LEV M19 143 H4
CHD/CHDH SK8 182 B3
DTN/ASHW M34 146 D2
URM M41 123 E5
Brecon Cl POY/DIS SK12 195 G3
ROY/SHW OL2 58 D3
Brecon Crs AUL OL6 107 E4
Brecon Dr BURY BL9 53 F2
Brecon Wk OLDS OL8 * 90 C5
Bredbury Dr FWTH BL4 66 B4
Bredbury Gn MPL/ROM SK6 161 H5
Bredbury Park Wy
MPL/ROM SK6 146 C5
Bredbury Rd RUSH/FAL M14 142 D1
Bredbury St CHAD OL9 90 C1
HYDE SK14 * 133 G3
Bredon Wy OLDS OL8 91 F4
Breeze Hill Rd OLDE OL4 92 C2
Breeze Mt PWCH M25 86 A5
Breightmet Dr BOLE BL2 50 B2
Breightmet Fold La BOLE BL2 50 C2
Breightmet St BOLE BL2 3 F6
Brellafield Dr ROY/SHW OL2 44 C5
Brenbar Crs WHIT OL12 14 C4
Brenchley Dr NTHM/RTH M23 155 H4
Brencon Av NTHM/RTH M23 154 D5
Brendall Cl OFTN SK2 173 H4
Brendon Av NEWH/MOS M40 103 H3
RDSH SK5 145 F5
Brendon Dr DTN/ASHW M34 118 C4
Brendon Hills ROY/SHW OL2 74 D1
Brennan Cl HULME M15 128 B3
Brennan Ct OLDS OL8 90 D5
Brennock Cl OP/CLY M11 116 A5
Brentbridge Rd
DID/WITH M20 142 D4
Brent Cl BOLE BL2 51 E4
POY/DIS SK12 194 C3
Brentfield Av CHH M8 102 A4
Brentford Av BOL BL1 33 E4
Brentford Rd RDSH SK5 145 F5
Brentford St BKLY M9 103 F3
Brent Moor Rd
BRAM/HZG SK7 184 B2
Brentnall St STKP SK1 13 G7
Brentnor Rd NEWH/MOS M40 89 F5
Brenton Av SALE M33 154 B2
Brent Rd HTNM SK4 12 B3
NTHM/RTH M23 155 H4
Brentwood SALE M33 154 B2
SLFD M6 112 D2
Brentwood Av ALT WA14 165 H2
URM M41 138 D1
WALK M28 98 A4
Brentwood Cl LIT OL15 20 C5
OLDTF/WHR M16 128 A5
RDSH SK5 161 E1
STLY SK15 121 F3
Brentwood Ct PWCH M25 85 G4
Brentwood Crs ALT WA14 165 H3
Brentwood Dr
CHD/CHDH SK8 169 G4
ECC M30 111 E1
FWTH BL4 65 G2
Brentwood Rd SWIN M27 98 C4
Brereton Cl ALT WA14 177 F3
Brereton Dr WALK M28 97 G3
Brereton Gv IRL M44 136 A5
Brereton Rd ECC M30 110 A4
WILM/AE SK9 192 B4
Breslyn St CSLFD M3 6 E1
Brethren's Ct DROY M43 117 H5
Bretland Gdns HYDE SK14 149 G2
Brettargh St SLFD M6 113 F1
Brett Rd WALK M28 96 A4
Brett St WYTH/NTH M22 156 D5
Brewer's Gn BRAM/HZG SK7 185 E1
Brewer St CMANE M1 7 H4
Brewerton Rd OLDE OL4 92 B2
Brewery St ALT WA14 165 G5
STKP SK1 13 H1
Brewster St BKLY M9 * 103 E2
MDTN M24 72 D2
Brian Av DROY M43 * 118 B2
Brian Redhead Ct
HULME M15 127 H1
Brian Rd FWTH BL4 65 F2
Brian St ROCH OL11 42 A4
Briaracre Ter AUL OL6 * 107 F2
Briar Av BRAM/HZG SK7 185 G2
GOL/RIS/CUL WA3 150 A4
OLDE OL4 76 C3
Briar Cl SALE M33 153 F2
URM M41 123 H5
WHIT OL12 28 D2
Briar Crs WYTH/NTH M22 168 D4
Briardene DTN/ASHW M34 * 132 D4
Briardene Gdns
WYTH/NTH M22 168 D5
Briarfield EDGW/EG BL7 22 C1
Briarfield Rd CHD/CHDH SK8 183 E1
DID/WITH M20 143 F5
FWTH BL4 65 F3
HALE/TIMP WA15 166 D3
HTNM SK4 145 E5
UPML OL3 78 D2
WALK M28 97 G3
Briar Gv CHAD OL9 74 C3
MPL/ROM SK6 161 H1
Briar Hill Av LHULT M38 80 D3
Briar Hill Cl LHULT M38 80 D3
Briar Hill Gv LHULT M38 80 D3
Briar Hill Wy SLFD M6 * 113 F2
Briar Hollow HTNM SK4 159 E5
Briarlands Av SALE M33 154 A4
Briarlands Cl BRAM/HZG SK7 193 G1
Briarlea Gdns BNG/LEV M19 158 B1
Briarley Gdns MPL/ROM SK6 147 G5
Briarmere Wk CHAD OL9 8 A2
Briars Mt HTNM SK4 158 D4
Briars Pk BRAM/HZG SK7 183 F3
Briarstead Cl
BRAM/HZG SK7 183 G5
Briar St BOLE BL2 * 50 A2
ROCH OL11 29 G5
Briarwood WILM/AE SK9 199 F3
Briarwood Av DROY M43 117 F2
NTHM/RTH M23 167 E1
Briarwood Cha
CHD/CHDH SK8 183 E3

Briarwood Crs *MPL/ROM* SK6 ...175 E5
Brice St *DUK* SK16 ....119 G5
Brickbridge Rd
  MPL/ROM 175 F4
Brickfield St *MILN* OL16 ....30 C1
Brickhill La *HALE/TIMP* WA15 ...188 C5
Brickkiln Rw *ALT* WA14 ....177 F3
Brickley St *CSLFD* M3 ....114 D2
Brick St *ANC* M4 * 7 G3
  BURY BL9 ....8 E3
Bridcam St *CHH* M8 ....102 B5
Briddon St *CSLFD* M3 ....114 C2
Brideoak St *CHH* M8 ....102 B4
  OLDE OL4 ....76 D4
Bridestowe Av *HYDE* SK14 ......134 D5
Bride St *BOL* BL1 ....33 H4
Bridge Av *MPL/ROM* SK6 ....161 H1
Bridge Bank Rd *LIT* OL15 ....20 C5
Bridge Cl *PART* M31 ....151 E3
  RAD M26 ....68 C2
Bridgecrest Ct
  CHD/CHDH SK8 * 182 D2
Bridge Dr *CHD/CHDH* SK8 ......170 A5
  WILM/AE SK9 ....192 A4
Bridgefield Av *WILM/AE* SK9 ...199 F1
Bridgefield Crs *OLDE* OL4 ....93 E1
Bridgefield Dr *BURY* BL9 ....39 G4
Bridgefield St *RAD* M26 ....68 C1
  ROCH OL11 ....29 G4
  STKP SK1 ....13 F3
Bridgefold Rd *ROCH* OL11 ....29 F4
Bridgefoot Cl *WALK* M28 ....95 G2
Bridge Gv *HALE/TIMP* WA15 ....166 A2
Bridge Hall Dr *BURY* BL9 ....39 F4
Bridge Hall Fold *BURY* BL9 ....39 G4
Bridge Hall La *BRAM/HZG* SK7 ..184 B3
Bridgelea Ms *DID/WITH* M20 ...142 D5
Bridgelea Rd *DID/WITH* M20 ....142 D5
Bridgeman Pl *BOLE* BL2 ....3 K5
Bridgeman St *BOLS/LL* BL3 ....48 D5
Brindale Rd *RDSH* SK5 ....160 D2
Brindle Cl *SLFD* M6 ....113 E1
Brindle Heath Rd *SLFD* M6 ......113 E1
Brindley Av *BKLY* M9 ....87 G2
  MPL/ROM SK6 ....174 D4
  SALE M33 ....140 A5
  WALK M28 ....96 B4
Brinell Dr *IRL* M44 ....151 E1
Brinkburn Rd *BRAM/HZG* SK7 ..185 H1
Brinklow Cl *OP/CLY* M11 ....130 D1
Brinkshaw Av
  WYTH/NTH M22 ....180 D2
Brinks La *BOLE* BL2 ....50 D2
Brinksway *BOL* BL1 ....46 D2
  EDGY/DAV SK3 ....11 E5
Brinksworth Cl *BOLE* BL2 ....50 D1
Brinnington Crs *RDSH* SK5 ......160 C2
Brinnington Rd *RDSH* SK5 ....160 D2
  STKP SK1 ....160 B3
Brinsop Sq *WGTN/LGST* M12 ..130 A2
Brinsworth Dr *CHH* M8 ....102 B4
Briony Av *HALE/TIMP* WA15 ....178 D2
Briony Cl *ROY/SHW* OL2 ....75 F2
Brisbane Cl *BRAM/HZG* SK7 ....194 A2
Brisbane St *BRUN/LGST* M13 ...128 C2
Briscoe La *NEWH/MOS* M40 .....116 B1
Briscoe Ms *BOLS/LL* BL3 ....49 F5
Briscoe St *OLD* OL1 ....76 C1
Bristle Hall Wy *WHTN* BL5 ....62 A2
Bristle St *HULME* M15 ....128 B2
Bristol Av *AUL* OL6 ....107 E3
  BNG/LEV M19 ....144 B3
  BOLE BL2 ....34 D5
Bristol St *BRO* M7 ....101 H3
Bristowe St *OP/CLY* M11 ....117 E2
Britain St *BURY* BL9 ....53 F3
Britannia Av *ROY/SHW* OL2 ....60 B1
Britannia Cl *RAD* M26 ....68 D1
Britannia Sa *AULW* OL7 ....119 E5
Britannia Wy *BOLE* BL2 ....34 B4
Britnall Av *WGTN/LGST* M12 ...129 F5
Britton St *MILN* OL16 ....11 G4
Brixham Av *CHD/CHDH* SK8 ....182 C5
Brixham Dr *SALE* M33 ....138 D5
Brixham Wk *BRAM/HZG* SK7 ...184 B5
  BRUN/LGST M13 ....128 D3
Brixton Av *DID/WITH* M20 ......142 C5
Broach St *BOLS/LL* BL3 ....48 D5
Broadacre *STLY* SK15 ....135 F2
Broad Acre *WHIT* OL12 ....28 B1
Broadacre Pl *WILM/AE* SK9 .....200 A2
Broadbent Av *AUL* OL6 ....120 A5
  DUK SK16 ....120 A5
Broadbent Cl *ROY/SHW* OL2 .....59 G4
  STLY SK15 ....109 F4
Broadbent Dr *BURY* BL9 ....27 G3
Broadbent Gv *HYDE* SK14 ......149 G2
Broadbent Rd *OLD* OL1 ....76 B2
Broadbent St *HYDE* SK14 ....133 G4
  SWIN M27 ....98 C3
Broadbottom Rd *HYDE* SK14 ...149 H1
Broadcarr La *MOSL* OL5 ....108 B3
Broadfield Cl
  DTN/ASHW M34 ....147 E1
Broadfield Dr *LIT* OL15 ....20 C5
Broadfield Gv *RDSH* SK5 ....130 D5
Broadfield Rd *RDSH* SK5 ....130 D5
  RUSH/FAL M14 ....128 D5
Broadfield Stile *MILN* OL16 ....29 H5
Broadfield St *HEY* OL10 ....40 C5
  MILN OL16 ....29 H5
Broadford Rd *BOLS/LL* BL3 ....47 G4
Broadgate *CHAD* OL9 ....89 H5
  MDTN M24 ....89 G1
  UPML OL3 ....78 B3

Broadgate Meadow
  SWIN M27 * 99 E3
Broadgreen Gdns *FWTH* BL4 ....66 A2
Broadhalgh Av *ROCH* OL11 ......28 D4
Broadhalgh Rd *ROCH* OL11 .....28 D5
Broadheath Cl *WHTN* BL5 ....62 B3
Broadhey Vw *ROY/SHW* OL2 ....74 D4
Broad Hill Cl *BRAM/HZG* SK7 ..184 B3
Broadhill Rd *BNG/LEV* M19 ......143 G5
  STLY SK15 ....120 D1
Broadhurst *DTN/ASHW* M34 ...132 D5
Broadhurst Av *OLD* OL1 ....74 D5
Broadhurst Ct *BOLS/LL* BL3 ......48 C5
Broadhurst Gv *AUL* OL6 ....107 F4
Broadhurst St *BOLS/LL* BL3 ......48 C5
  EDGY/DAV SK3 ....171 H2
Broad Ing *ROCH* OL11 * 29 E2
Broadlands Rd *WALK* M28 ....98 A4
Broad La *HALE/TIMP* WA15 .....178 C4
Broadlea Gv *WHIT* OL12 ....14 D5
Broad Lea *URM* M41 ....124 D5
Broadlea Gv *WHIT* OL12 ....29 F1
Broadley Av *WYTH/NTH* M22 ..168 C5
Broadmeadow *EDGW/EG* BL7 ...23 G5
Broadmeadow Av
  OLDTF/WHR M16 ....142 B2
Broadmoss Dr *BKLY* M9 ....88 D4
Broadmoss Rd *BKLY* M9 ....88 D4
Broadmount Ter *CHAD* OL9 * 90 C3
Broadoak Av *WALK* M28 ....96 A3
  WYTH/NTH M22 ....168 B4
Broadoak Crs *AUL* OL6 ....119 H5
Broad Oak Crs *OLDS* OL8 ....91 H5
Broadoak Dr *WYTH/NTH* M22 ...168 C4
Broad Oak La *BURY* BL9 ....39 G5
  DID/WITH M20 ....169 H1
Broad Oak Pk *ECC* M30 ....111 E1
  WALK M28 ....98 A4
Broadoak Rd *AUL* OL6 ....107 F4
  BOLS/LL BL3 ....65 F2
  ROCH OL11 ....42 A3
  WYTH/NTH M22 ....168 B5
Broadoaks *BURY* BL9 ....39 G3
Broadoaks Rd *SALE* M33 ....154 B2
  URM M41 ....138 D2
Broad Oak Ter *BURY* BL9 ....39 H5
Broad o' th' La *BOL* BL1 ....33 H2
Broadstone Av *OLDE* OL4 ....61 E5
Broadstone Cl *PWCH* M25 ....85 H5
  WHIT OL12 ....28 D2
Broadstone Hall Rd North
  RDSH SK5 ....144 D5
Broadstone Hall Rd South
  HTNM SK4 ....145 E5
Broadstone Rd *BOLE* BL2 ....35 E1
  HTNM SK4 ....144 D5
Broad St *BURY* BL9 ....4 D5
  MDTN M24 ....71 H5
  SLFD M6 ....112 B2
  STRET M32 ....13 K7
Broad Wk *MILN* OL16 ....44 A4
Broadway *BRAM/HZG* SK7 ......184 A2
  CHAD OL9 ....74 C3
  CHAD OL9 ....90 A4
  CHD/CHDH SK8 ....183 F5
  DROY M43 ....117 H5
  FAIL M35 ....104 C2
  FWTH BL4 ....65 F2
  HALE/TIMP WA15 ....178 B3
  HYDE SK14 ....133 E3
  IRL M44 ....136 A3
  OFTN SK2 ....172 D2
  PART M31 ....151 F2
  ROY/SHW OL2 ....75 F1
  SALE M33 ....153 G5
  SALQ M50 ....112 D5
  URM M41 ....123 H4
  WALK M28 ....97 E1
  WILM/AE SK9 ....199 G4
Broadway North *DROY* M43 ....117 H5
Broadway St *OLDS* OL8 ....91 G3
The Broadway *MPL/ROM* SK6 ...161 G2
Broadwell Dr *BKLY* M9 ....103 F3
Broadwood *HOR/BR* BL6 ....46 D2
Broadwood Cl *ROY/SHW* OL2 ...58 D5
Brocade Cl *CSLFD* M3 ....114 A2
Broche Cl *ROCH* OL11 ....42 A3
Brock Av *BOLE* BL2 ....50 C2
Brock Dr *CHD/CHDH* SK8 ....182 D4
Brockenhurst Dr *BOLE* BL2 ......35 G5
Brockford Dr *BKLY* M9 ....88 B2
Brocklebank Rd *RUSH/FAL* M14 ...143 E4
  RUSH/FAL M14 ....142 D1
Brocklehurst Av *BURY* BL9 ....27 F3
Brocklehurst St *BKLY* M9 ....103 H2
Brockley Av *RUSH/FAL* M14 ....142 D1
Brock St *CMANE* M1 * 7 J4
The Brock *ROY/SHW* OL2 ....59 G1
Brockway *MILN* OL16 ....43 H5
Brockdr Dr *BOLE* BL2 ....50 C3
Brock St *NEWH/MOS* M40 ......105 G2
Brodie Cl *ECC* M30 ....110 C3
Brogan St *GTN* M18 ....130 C4
Brogden Dr *CHD/CHDH* SK8 ...169 G4
Brogden Gv *SALE* M33 ....154 B3
Brogden Ter *SALE* M33 ....154 B3
Bromborough Av
  DID/WITH M20 ....142 C5
Bromfield *WHIT* OL12 ....10 C4
Bromfield Av *BKLY* M9 ....103 E1
Bromleigh Av *CHD/CHDH* SK8 ..169 G3
Bromley Av *ROY/SHW* OL2 ......58 D3
  URM M41 ....137 G2
Bromley Crs *AUL* OL6 ....107 E4
Bromley Cross Rd
  EDGW/EG BL7 ....23 G4
Bromley Rd *SALE* M33 ....154 A1
Bromley St *ANC* M4 * 115 E2
  CHAD OL9 ....90 B5
  DTN/ASHW M34 * 132 C5
Bromlow St *OP/CLY* M11 ....116 D4
Brompton Av *FAIL* M35 ....105 G2
Brompton Rd *HTNM* SK4 ....158 D4

Brompton St *OLDE* OL4 ....92 C1
Brompton Wy *WILM/AE* SK9 ...191 H2
Bromsgrove Av *ECC* M30 ....110 C3
Bromshill Dr *BRO* M7 ....101 H4
Bromwich St *BOLE* BL2 ....3 J7
Bronington Cl
  WYTH/NTH M22 ....168 D2
Bronte Av *BURY* BL9 ....37 G5
Bronte Cl *BOL* BL1 ....33 G5
  OLD OL1 ....60 C5
  WHIT OL12 ....28 D2
Bronte St *HULME* M15 ....128 B3
Bronville Cl *OLD* OL1 ....74 C5
Brookash Rd *WYTH/NTH* M22 ..181 F4
Brook Av *BNG/LEV* M19 ....144 B1
  DROY M43 ....117 F4
  HALE/TIMP WA15 ....165 H5
  HTNM SK4 ....159 E2
  ROY/SHW OL2 ....60 A1
  SWIN M27 ....99 E3
  UPML OL3 ....79 E4
  WILM/AE SK9 ....192 A4
Brook Bank *BOLE* BL2 * 36 B5
Brookbank Cl *MDTN* M24 ....73 E5
Brookbottom Rd *RAD* M26 ....53 A3
Brook Ct *HALE/TIMP* WA15 .....165 H5
  WHTF M45 ....70 A4
Brookcot Rd *NTHM/RTH* M23 ..167 G2
Brookcroft Av
  WYTH/NTH M22 ....168 C4
Brookcroft Rd
  WYTH/NTH M22 ....168 C4
Brookdale *WHIT* OL12 ....18 D5
Brookdale Av *DTN/ASHW* M34 ..132 B1
  NEWH/MOS M40 ....117 E1
Brookdale Cl *BOL* BL1 ....34 A4
  MPL/ROM SK6 ....161 G3
Brookdale Pk *LHULT* M38 * 81 G1
Brookdale Ri *BRAM/HZG* SK7 ..184 A2
Brookdale Rd *BRAM/HZG* SK7 ..184 A2
  CHD/CHDH SK8 ....169 G4
Brookdale St *FAIL* M35 ....104 D3
Brookdean Cl *BOL* BL1 ....34 A4
Brookdene Rd *BNG/LEV* M19 ...143 G5
  BURY BL9 ....69 H5
Brook Dr *MPL/ROM* SK6 ....175 E5
  WHTF M45 ....70 A4
Brooke Av *WILM/AE* SK9 ....192 A3
  WYTH/NTH M22 ....168 D2
Brooke Wy *WILM/AE* SK9 ....192 A3
Brook Farm Cl *PART* M31 ....150 D5
Brookfield *PWCH* M25 ....86 A3
  ROY/SHW OL2 ....59 G1
Brookfield Av *BOLE* BL2 ....36 B5
  CCHDY M21 ....141 G4
  HALE/TIMP WA15 ....166 A1
  MPL/ROM SK6 ....161 G2
  POY/DIS SK12 ....194 D3
  ROY/SHW OL2 ....75 F1
  SLFD M6 ....112 B2
  STRET M32 ....13 K7
Brookfield Cl *STKP* SK1 ....13 K7
Brookfield Crs
  CHD/CHDH SK8 ....170 A5
Brookfield Dr
  HALE/TIMP WA15 ....166 B2
  LIT OL15 ....20 C2
  SWIN M27 ....98 D1
  WALK M28 ....96 A4
Brookfield Gdns
  WYTH/NTH M22 ....168 C3
Brookfield Gv *AUL* OL6 ....120 A3
  CHD/CHDH SK8 ....183 F4
  CHH M8 ....102 B1
  ECC M30 ....110 C1
Brookfield St *BOLE* BL2 ....3 J4
  OLDS OL8 ....9 G6
Brookfold *FAIL* M35 ....104 D2
Brookfold La *BOLE* BL2 ....35 G2
  SALE M33 ....148 C1
Brook Fold La *HYDE* SK14 ....149 H1
Brookfold Rd *HTNM* SK4 ....159 G1
Brook Gdns *BOLE* BL2 ....35 F2
  HEY OL10 ....40 D4
Brook Green La *GTN* M18 ....131 E5
Brook Gv *IRL* M44 ....136 C1
Brookhead Av
  DID/WITH M20 * 142 C5
Brookhead Dr
  CHD/CHDH SK8 ....170 D4
Brookhey Av *BOLS/LL* BL3 ....65 E1
Brook Hey *WHIT* OL12 ....14 D5
Brookhey Dr *PART* M31 ....152 B2
Brookhill St
  NEWH/MOS M40 ....115 H2
Brookhouse Av *ECC* M30 ....110 B4
  FWTH BL4 ....65 E2
Brook House La *BOLE* BL2 ....35 F3
  TOT/BURYW BL8 ....26 A3
Brookhouse Mill La
  TOT/BURYW BL8 ....26 A3
Brookhurst La *LHULT* M38 ....80 D1
Brookhurst Rd *GTN* M18 ....130 C4
Brookland Av
  DTN/ASHW M34 ....146 C1
  FWTH BL4 ....65 H5
Brookland Gv *BOL* BL1 ....32 D4
  DID/WITH M20 ....142 C5
Brooklands Cl
  DTN/ASHW M34 ....132 A4
  HTNM SK4 ....159 G1
  IRL M44 ....136 B1
  MOSL OL5 ....94 B2
Brooklands Ct *ROCH* OL11 ....29 F5
Brooklands Dr *DROY* M43 ....118 B2
  OLDE OL4 ....61 H5
Brooklands Pde
  OLDE OL4 * 93 G1
Brooklands Rd
  BRAM/HZG SK7 ....185 G3
  NTHM/RTH M23 ....166 D1

  PWCH M25 ....86 D5
  RAMS BL0 ....26 A1
  RDSH SK5 ....145 E1
  SALE M33 ....153 H3
  SWIN M27 ....98 C4
Brooklands Station Ap
  SALE M33 ....154 B3
Brooklands St *ROY/SHW* OL2 ...59 E4
The Brooklands *HEY* OL10 ....40 A2
Brookland St *MILN* OL16 * 43 G3
Brook La *BURY* BL9 ....53 H4
  HALE/TIMP WA15 ....165 H5
  MILN OL16 ....43 G3
  OLDE OL4 ....91 H5
  OLDS OL8 ....78 C3
  UPML OL3 ....78 C3
  WILM/AE SK9 ....200 C2
Brooklawn Dr *DID/WITH* M20 ..157 G2
  PWCH M25 ....86 C5
Brookleigh Rd *DID/WITH* M20 ..143 F5
Brooklet Cl *OLDE* OL4 ....93 F2
Brooklyn Av *LIT* OL15 ....20 D1
  OLDTF/WHR M16 ....140 B4
  URM M41 ....137 G1
Brooklyn Crs *CHD/CHDH* SK8 ..170 A4
Brooklyn Rd *CHD/CHDH* SK8 ..170 A4
  OFTN SK2 ....172 D3
Brooklyn St *BOL* BL1 ....2 B1
  OLD OL1 ....76 B3
Brook Meadow *WHTN* BL5 * 62 B4
Brook Rd *CHD/CHDH* SK8 ....170 A3
  HTNM SK4 ....159 F1
  RUSH/FAL M14 ....142 C3
  URM M41 ....123 H5
Brooks Av *BRAM/HZG* SK7 ......185 E1
  HYDE SK14 ....148 A2
  RAD M26 ....52 A3
Brooksbottom Cl *RAMS* BL0 ......16 D4
Brooks Dr *CHD/CHDH* SK8 ......181 H2
  FAIL M35 ....104 D4
  HALE/TIMP WA15 ....167 E3
  HALE/TIMP WA15 ....179 F4
Brooks End *ROCH* OL11 ....28 B2
Brookshaw St *BURY* BL9 ....5 G4
  OP/CLY M11 ....116 B4
Brookside *BOLE* BL2 ....35 E1
  CHD/CHDH SK8 ....170 A5
  HYDE SK14 ....134 D5
  RAMS BL0 ....16 D3
Brookside Crs *MDTN* M24 ....89 F1
  TOT/BURYW BL8 ....26 A3
  WALK M28 ....82 B4
Brookside Dr *HYDE* SK14 ....134 B5
  PWCH M25 ....101 G2
Brookside La *MPL/ROM* SK6 ...186 D5
Brookside Rd *BOLE* BL2 ....50 A1
  CHD/CHDH SK8 ....169 F3
  NEWH/MOS M40 ....103 H1
  SALE M33 ....155 H3
Brooksmouth *TOT/BURYW* BL8 ...4 A5
Brook's Pl *WHIT* OL12 ....10 A4
Brook's Rd *OLDTF/WHR* M16 ...127 F5
Brooks St *STKP* SK1 ....13 H7
Brookstone Cl *CCHDY* M21 ......141 H5
Brook St *BOL* BL1 ....2 E6
  BRAM/HZG SK7 ....185 F2
  BURY BL9 ....5 G1
  CHAD OL9 ....74 C4
  CHD/CHDH SK8 ....170 C3
  FAIL M35 ....105 E3
  FWTH BL4 ....66 B3
  HYDE SK14 ....133 H5
  LIT OL15 ....21 F3
  OLD OL1 ....66 D5
  RAD M26 ....68 D1
  ROY/SHW OL2 ....75 E1
  SALE M33 ....154 D1
  SLFD M6 ....113 G1
  WHIT OL12 ....19 H2
  WHTN BL5 ....62 A3
Brook St East *AUL* OL6 ....119 F3
Brook St West *AUL* OL6 ....119 F3
Brookthorn Cl *OFTN* SK2 ....173 G4
Brookthorpe Av
  BNG/LEV M19 ....143 G5
Brookthorpe Rd
  TOT/BURYW BL8 ....37 F3
Brookwater Cl
  TOT/BURYW BL8 ....26 A5
Brookway
  HALE/TIMP WA15 ....166 A3
  LIT OL15 ....20 D4
  OLDE OL4 ....92 D2
  WHIT OL12 ....34 B1
Brookway Av *BNG/LEV* M19 ....158 B2
Brookway Cl *CHH* M8 ....102 D2
  SALE M33 ....153 H3
Brookwood Cl
  DTN/ASHW M34 ....147 E4
Broom Av *BNG/LEV* M19 ....144 B3
  BRO M7 ....101 H2
  RDSH SK5 ....145 F5
Broome Gv *FAIL* M35 ....105 E4
Broomehouse Av *IRL* M44 ......136 A5
Broome St *CHAD* OL9 ....90 C4
Broomfield *SWIN* M27 ....100 A4
  RDSH SK5 ....145 F5
Broomfield Cl *BOLE* BL2 ....51 F1
  RDSH SK5 ....145 F5
Broomfield Crs *MDTN* M24 ....72 A3
  OFTN SK2 ....172 B5
Broomfield Dr *CHH* M8 ....102 A3
  RDSH SK5 ....145 F5
Broomfield La
  HALE/TIMP WA15 ....177 H2
Broomfield Rd *BOLS/LL* BL3 .....48 B4
  HTNM SK4 ....159 F2
Broomfields
  DTN/ASHW M34 ....132 D3
Broomfield Sq *ROCH* OL11 * 43 E1
Broomfield Ter *MILN* OL16 ....45 E2

Broomgrove La DTN/ASHW M34 ...132 D4
Broomhall Rd BKLY M9 ...87 F2
SWIN M27 ...100 A4
Broomhill Dr BRAM/HZG SK7 ...185 C5
Broomhurst Av OLDS OL8 ...91 E5
Broom La BNG/LEV M19 ...144 B3
BRO M7 ...101 G2
Broom Rd HALE/TIMP WA15 ...177 F1
PART M31 ...151 E4
Broomstair Rd
DTN/ASHW M34 ...132 C2
Broom St MILN OL16 ...45 E2
SWIN M27 ...99 E5
TOT/BURYW BL8 ...4 A4
Broomville Av SALE M33 ...154 C2
Broom Wy WHTN BL5 ...62 B2
Broomwood Rd
HALE/TIMP WA15 ...166 D4
Broomwood Wk
HULME M15 * ...128 A2
Broseley Av DID/WITH M20 ...158 A3
Broseley Rd OLDTF/WHR M16 ...141 E1
Brotherdale Cl ROY/SHW OL2 ...59 E4
Brotherod Hall Rd WHIT OL12 ...29 F1
Brotherton Cl HULME M15 ...127 C1
Brotherton Dr CSLFD M3 ...6 A2
Brougham St WALK M28 ...81 H5
Broughton Av LHULT M38 ...81 F3
Broughton Cl MDTN M24 ...72 A2
Broughton La BRO M7 ...101 G5
Broughton Rd RDSH SK5 ...160 A2
SLFD M6 ...113 F2
Broughton Rd East SLFD M6 ...113 G1
Broughton St BOL BL1 ...33 C4
CHH M8 ...102 A5
Broughville Dr DID/WITH M20 ...169 H1
Brow Av MDTN M24 ...89 E1
Brow East BOLE BL2 ...34 D2
Browfield Av ORD M5 ...127 E1
Browfield Wy OLD OL1 ...75 E3
Browmere Dr DID/WITH M20 ...157 E4
Brownacre St DID/WITH M20 ...142 D5
Brown Bank Rd LIT OL15 ...20 B5
Browncross St CSLFD M3 ...6 B4
Brown Edge Rd OLDE OL4 ...92 D5
Brownhill Dr OLDE OL4 ...92 D5
Brownhill La UPML OL3 ...79 E5
Brownhills Ct CCHDY M21 * ...141 F5
Brownhill St TOT/BURYW BL8 ...37 F1
Brownhill Vw WHIT OL12 ...10 D2
Browning Av DROY M43 ...117 H4
Browning Cl BOL BL1 ...33 C5
Browning Rd MDTN M24 ...73 E2
OLD OL1 ...76 A3
RDSH SK5 ...144 D2
SWIN M27 ...98 D2
Browning St CSLFD M3 ...6 A3
HULME M15 ...127 G2
Brownlea Av CHD/CHDH SK8 ...181 F5
Brownlea Av DUK SK16 ...133 F1
Brownley Court Rd
WYTH/NTH M22 ...168 D4
Brown Lodge St LIT OL15 ...20 C5
Brownlow Av ROY/SHW OL2 ...75 H1
Brownlow Cl POY/DIS SK12 ...195 F5
Brownlow Wy BOL BL1 * ...2 C1
Brownrigg Cl MDTN M24 ...71 H3
Brownside Cl MILN OL16 ...19 H5
Browns La WILM/AE SK9 ...199 H2
Brownslow Wk
BRUN/LGST M13 * ...128 C1
Browns Rd BOLE BL2 ...51 E3
Brown St ALT WA14 ...177 C1
BOL BL1 ...3 F4
CHAD OL9 ...74 B5
CSLFD M3 ...6 C4
FAIL M35 ...104 D3
HEY OL10 ...40 D5
LIT OL15 ...20 D5
MDTN M24 ...72 D2
OLD OL1 ...9 K2
RAD M26 ...52 A3
RAMS BL0 ...16 C3
SLFD M6 ...113 F2
STKP SK1 ...13 F2
WILM/AE SK9 ...200 D4
Brownsville Rd HTNM SK4 ...159 E1
Brownville Gv DUK SK16 ...133 H1
Brownwood Av STKP SK1 ...160 C5
Brownwood Cl SALE M33 ...154 C5
Brows Av NTHM/RTH M23 ...155 H4
Brow St ROCH OL11 ...43 F2
Broxton Av BOLS/LL BL3 ...66 A1
Broxton St NEWH/MOS M40 ...116 A2
Bruce Dr ROCH OL11 ...130 C3
Brundage Rd WYTH/NTH M22 ...180 C2
Brundretts Rd CCHDY M21 ...141 F5
Brundrett St STKP SK1 ...13 K6
Brunel Av ORD M5 ...113 G4
Brunel Cl STRET M32 ...140 C1
Brunel St BOL BL1 ...33 C3
Brunet Wk WGTN/LGST M12 * ...129 G2
Brunstead Cl NTHM/RTH M23 ...167 E3
Brunswick Ct BOL BL1 ...3 J6
Brunswick Rd ALT WA14 ...165 G2
DID/WITH M20 ...145 E5
Brunswick Sq OLD OL1 * ...9 G4
Brunswick St
BRUN/LGST M13 ...128 D2
BURY BL9 ...4 E5
DUK SK16 ...119 H5
HEY OL10 ...40 D4
MILN OL16 ...11 F4
MOSL OL5 ...109 E2
OLD OL1 ...9 H4
ROY/SHW OL2 ...60 A1
STRET M32 ...140 A3
Brunton Rd RDSH SK5 ...145 F5
Brunt St RUSH/FAL M14 ...128 C5
Bruntwood Av
CHD/CHDH SK8 ...181 F3
Bruntwood La
CHD/CHDH SK8 ...170 B5
Brushes Av STLY SK15 ...121 G2
Brushes Rd STLY SK15 ...121 G1
Brussels Rd EDGY/DAV SK3 ...171 G3

Bruton Av STRET M32 ...139 H2
Bryan Rd OLDE OL4 * ...141 F1
Bryan St OLDE OL4 ...76 B3
Bryant Cl BRUN/LGST M13 ...128 C5
Bryantsfield BOL BL1 ...47 E3
Bryce St HYDE SK14 ...133 C4
Brydges Rd MPL/ROM SK6 ...174 D4
Brydon Av WGTN/LGST M12 ...128 D1
Brydon Cl SLFD M6 ...113 F3
Brynbridge Gv SALE M33 ...154 A5
Brynden Av DID/WITH M20 ...157 H1
Bryn Dr RDSH SK5 ...160 A1
Brynford Av BKLY M9 ...87 F2
Bryngs Dr BOLE BL2 ...35 G2
Brynhall Cl RAD M26 ...51 H4
Brynheys Cl LHULT M38 ...81 F2
Bryn Lea Ter BOL BL1 ...32 C2
Brynorme Vw CHH M8 ...87 F5
Brynton Rd BRUN/LGST M13 ...143 G1
Bryn Wk BOL BL1 ...2 E2
Bryone Dr OFTN SK2 ...172 C4
Bryony Cl WYTH/NTH M22 ...180 B3
Buchanan St RAMS BL0 ...16 C2
SWIN M27 ...99 E1
Buchan St OP/CLY M11 ...115 H5
Buckden Rd HTNM SK4 ...144 D4
Buckfast Av OLDS OL8 ...92 B4
Buckfast Cl CCHDY M21 ...141 F2
CHD/CHDH SK8 ...183 E5
HALE/TIMP WA15 ...178 C1
POY/DIS SK12 ...195 E2
Buckfast Rd MDTN M24 ...56 C5
SALE M33 ...138 D5
Buckfield Av ORD M5 ...127 E1
Buckhurst Rd BNG/LEV M19 ...162 A5
Buckingham Av SLFD M6 ...112 C3
WHTF M45 ...69 H5
Buckingham Dr DUK SK16 ...134 A2
TOT/BURYW BL8 ...52 C1
Buckingham Park Cl
ROY/SHW OL2 ...60 A1
Buckingham Rd ALT WA14 ...154 A5
CCHDY M21 ...141 F2
CHD/CHDH SK8 ...182 C2
DROY M43 ...118 A3
HTNM SK4 ...159 F1
IRL M44 ...150 B1
POY/DIS SK12 ...195 E4
PWCH M25 ...86 A5
STLY SK15 ...120 D2
STRET M32 ...126 C3
SWIN M27 ...84 B5
WILM/AE SK9 ...198 C4
Buckingham Rd West
HTNM SK4 ...158 D2
OFTN SK2 * ...172 B5
ORD M5 ...113 E4
Buckingham Wy
HALE/TIMP WA15 ...166 B3
WHTN BL5 ...62 A2
Buckland Av BKLY M9 ...87 E2
Buckland Gv HYDE SK14 ...148 C5
Buckland Rd SLFD M6 ...112 C1
Buck La SALE M33 ...139 E5
Buckley Av GTN M18 ...130 B4
Buckley Brook St WHIT OL12 ...30 C1
Buckley Cha MILN OL16 ...44 S4
Buckley Cl HYDE SK14 ...148 A4
Buckley Dr MPL/ROM SK6 ...161 H5
Buckley Farm La WHIT OL12 ...19 G5
Buckley Flds WHIT OL12 ...30 B1
Buckley Hill La MILN OL16 ...44 B5
Buckley La FWTH BL4 ...65 H5
WHIT OL12 ...19 G5
WHTF M45 ...85 F4
Buckley Rd GTN M18 ...130 A4
Buckley Sq FWTH BL4 ...81 H1
Buckley St BURY BL9 ...5 F2
CHAD OL9 ...74 B5
DROY M43 ...117 H5
DTN/ASHW M34 ...132 A1
HEY OL10 ...41 E5
MILN OL16 ...10 E4
OLDE OL4 ...92 D2
OP/CLY M11 ...130 D1
RDSH SK5 ...145 G2
STLY SK15 ...120 C5
UPML OL3 ...79 E4
Buckley Vw WHIT OL12 ...19 G5
Bucklow Cl PART M31 ...151 F2
Bucklow Dr
WYTH/NTH M22 ...168 D1
Buckstones Rd OLD OL1 ...45 G5
ROY/SHW OL2 ...45 F5
Buckthorn Cl CCHDY M21 ...141 H5
HALE/TIMP WA15 ...167 F4
Buckton Dr STLY SK15 ...109 F5
Buckton Vale Ms STLY SK15 ...109 F5
Buckton Vale Rd STLY SK15 ...109 F4
Buckwood Cl BRAM/HZG SK7 ...185 H1
Buddleia Gv BRO M7 * ...101 G4
Bude Av RDSH SK5 ...160 C1
URM M41 ...138 B3
Bude Cl BRAM/HZG SK7 ...184 A5
Budsworth Av DID/WITH M20 ...142 D4
Budworth Rd SALE M33 ...155 F5
Buersil Av MILN OL16 ...43 G3
Buersil St MILN OL16 ...43 G4
Buerton Av BKLY M9 ...87 F2
Bugle St CMANE M1 * ...6 C7
Buile Dr BKLY M9 ...88 C3
Buile Hill Av LHULT M38 ...81 H3
Buile Hill Dr ORD M5 ...112 C2
Buile Hill Gv LHULT M38 ...81 G2
Buile St BRO M7 ...101 H3
Bulford Av WYTH/NTH M22 ...180 A2
Bulkeley Rd CHD/CHDH SK8 ...170 D5
POY/DIS SK12 ...195 F4
WILM/AE SK9 ...191 H4
Bulkeley St EDGY/DAV SK3 ...12 C5
Bullcote Gn ROY/SHW OL2 ...59 H5
Bullcote La ROY/SHW OL2 ...60 A5
Buller Ms TOT/BURYW BL8 ...37 G5

Buller Rd BRUN/LGST M13 ...143 H1
Buller St BOLS/LL BL3 ...65 H2
DROY M43 ...118 A5
TOT/BURYW BL8 ...37 H5
Bullfinch Dr BURY BL9 ...39 E1
Bull Hill Crs RAD M26 ...68 C4
Bullock St STKP SK1 ...172 A2
Bullows Rd LHULT M38 ...81 E1
Bulteel St BOLS/LL BL3 ...64 B2
ECC M30 ...110 C2
Bulwer St MILN OL16 ...11 F4
The Bungalows
BRAM/HZG SK7 * ...173 G5
Bunkers Hill MPL/ROM SK6 ...162 A5
WHTF M45 ...85 F4
Bunkers Hill La HYDE SK14 ...149 C2
Bunkershill Rd MPL/ROM SK6 ...174 A1
Bunsen St CMANE M1 * ...7 H4
Bunting Ms WALK M28 ...96 C5
Bunyan Cl OLD OL1 ...60 C5
Bunyan St WHIT OL12 ...10 E4
Bunyard St CHH M8 ...102 A5
Burbage Rd NTHM/RTH M23 ...179 H2
Burbridge Cl OP/CLY M11 ...115 H5
Burchall Fld MILN OL16 ...11 H6
Burdale Dr SLFD M6 ...112 A1
Burdett Wy WGTN/LGST M12 ...129 F5
Burdith Av RUSH/FAL M14 ...142 C1
Burdon Av WYTH/NTH M22 ...168 D5
Burford Av BRAM/HZG SK7 ...193 F2
OLDTF/WHR M16 ...141 H1
URM M41 ...124 D5
Burford Crs WILM/AE SK9 ...198 B5
Burford Dr BOLS/LL BL3 ...48 D4
OLDTF/WHR M16 ...141 H1
SWIN M27 ...84 B5
Burford Gv SALE M33 ...153 H5
Burford Rd OLDTF/WHR M16 ...141 H1
Burgess Av AUL OL6 ...107 F5
Burgess Dr FAIL M35 ...105 E3
Burghley Av OLDE OL4 ...92 C1
Burghley Cl RAD M26 ...51 E4
STLY SK15 ...120 D3
Burghley Dr RAD M26 ...51 E4
Burgin Wk NEWH/MOS M40 ...115 F1
Burgundy Dr TOT/BURYW BL8 ...26 A4
Burke St BOL BL1 ...33 G4
Burkitt St HYDE SK14 ...148 A1
Burland Cl BRO M7 ...101 G5
Burleigh Cl BRAM/HZG SK7 ...184 B3
Burleigh Ms CCHDY M21 ...155 H1
Burleigh Rd STRET M32 ...126 B4
Burleigh St HULME M15 ...128 C3
Burlescombe Cl ALT WA14 ...165 E3
Burley Crs OLD OL1 ...59 H5
Burlington Av OLDS OL8 ...91 F3
Burlington Cl HTNM SK4 ...159 E3
Burlington Dr EDGY/DAV SK3 ...172 A5
Burlington Gdns
EDGY/DAV SK3 ...172 A5
Burlington Ms EDGY/DAV SK3 ...172 A5
Burlington Rd ALT WA14 ...165 C5
DID/WITH M20 ...143 E4
ECC M30 ...111 C1
Burlington St AULW OL7 ...119 E3
BRUN/LGST M13 ...128 C3
ROCH OL11 ...43 C4
Burman St OP/CLY M11 ...131 E1
Burnaby St BOLS/LL BL3 ...48 C4
OLDS OL8 ...8 B7
Burnage Av BNG/LEV M19 ...143 H3
Burnage Hall Rd
BNG/LEV M19 ...143 G4
Burnage La BNG/LEV M19 ...158 A4
Burnage Range
BNG/LEV M19 ...144 A2
Burn Bank UPML OL3 ...94 B2
Burnbray Av BNG/LEV M19 ...69 H1
Burnden Rd BOLS/LL BL3 ...49 C4
Burnedge Cl WHIT OL12 ...14 C3
Burnedge Fold Rd OLDE OL4 ...94 A1
Burnedge La OLDE OL4 ...93 H1
Burnell Cl NEWH/MOS M40 ...115 F2
Burnet Cl MILN OL16 ...44 B5
Burnett Av ORD M5 ...113 G5
Burnett Cl NEWH/MOS M40 ...115 E2
Burnfield Rd GTN M18 ...130 C5
Burnham Av BOL BL1 ...49 E3
RDSH SK5 ...145 F2
Burnham Cl CHD/CHDH SK8 ...182 C2
Burnham Dr BNG/LEV M19 ...144 B3
URM M41 ...124 B5
Burnham Rd
DTN/ASHW M34 ...131 F5
Burnley La CHAD OL9 ...74 B2
Burnley Rd BURY BL9 ...27 F3
Burnley St CHAD OL9 ...74 C5
FAIL M35 ...105 F3
Burnmoor Rd BOLE BL2 ...50 C1
Burnsall Av WHTF M45 ...69 E4
Burnsall Gv ROY/SHW OL2 ...59 E5
Burns Av BURY BL9 ...53 C3
CHD/CHDH SK8 ...182 D4
SWIN M27 ...98 C1
Burns Cl OLDS OL8 ...60 D4
OP/CLY M11 ...116 A4
Burns Crs OFTN SK2 ...173 F2
Burns Fold DUK SK16 ...134 B1
Burns Gdns PWCH M25 ...85 G4
Burns Gv DROY M43 ...117 H3
Burnside HALE/TIMP WA15 ...179 F5
ROY/SHW OL2 ...60 C1
STLY SK15 ...135 E1
Burnside Av HTNM SK4 ...145 E5
SLFD M6 ...99 G5
Burnside Cl HEY OL10 ...40 A5
MPL/ROM SK6 ...161 G3
RAD M26 ...67 G1
STLY SK15 ...135 E1
WILM/AE SK9 ...199 E3
Burnside Crs MDTN M24 ...72 B1
Burnside Dr BNG/LEV M19 ...143 G4
Burnside Rd BKLY M9 ...88 B1
CHD/CHDH SK8 ...169 F4
MILN OL16 ...44 B5
Burns Rd DTN/ASHW M34 ...147 G4
LHULT M38 ...81 G1

Burns St BOLS/LL BL3 ...2 E7
HEY OL10 ...41 E5
Burnthorp Av BKLY M9 ...87 C4
Burnthorpe Cl ROCH OL11 ...28 B5
Burran Rd WYTH/NTH M22 ...180 C4
Burrows Av CCHDY M21 ...141 F5
Burrs Cl TOT/BURYW BL8 ...26 D5
Burrs Lea Cl BURY BL9 ...27 F5
Burrswood Av BURY BL9 ...27 F5
Burrswood Dr BURY BL9 ...27 F5
Burslem Av DID/WITH M20 ...142 C3
Burstead St GTN M18 ...130 D2
Burstock St ANC M4 ...115 E2
Burston St GTN M18 ...130 C2
Burton Av DID/WITH M20 ...142 D5
HALE/TIMP WA15 ...154 B5
TOT/BURYW BL8 ...37 F2
Burton Dr POY/DIS SK12 ...195 E3
Burton Gv WALK M28 ...96 A2
Burton Rd DID/WITH M20 ...157 F2
Burton St HTNM SK4 ...159 H3
MDTN M24 ...72 C4
OLDE OL4 ...92 D1
WHTF M45 ...85 C5
Burtonwood Cl MDTN M24 ...72 C3
Burtree St WGTN/LGST M12 * ...129 H2
Burwell Cl BOLS/LL BL3 ...48 C5
WHIT OL12 ...18 C5
Burwell Gv NTHM/RTH M23 ...167 G2
Bury & Bolton Rd RAD M26 ...51 G1
Bury & Rochdale Old Rd
HEY OL10 ...40 D1
Bury Av OLDTF/WHR M16 ...141 G1
Bury New Rd BOL BL1 ...51 F2
BOLE BL2 ...51 E2
BRO M7 ...101 G1
BURY BL9 ...17 G4
BURY BL9 ...39 C4
PWCH M25 ...85 C4
RAD M26 ...51 C5
SWIN M27 ...98 D2
Bury Old Rd BOLE BL2 ...3 J4
BOLE BL2 ...36 A5
BRO M7 ...101 H1
BURY BL9 ...17 C4
BURY BL9 ...39 C1
HEY OL10 ...40 D1
NEWH/MOS M40 ...103 C1
SALQ M50 ...112 C4
Bury Pl OP/CLY M11 ...116 C3
Bury Rd BOLE BL2 ...50 A2
RAD M26 ...52 C5
ROCH OL11 ...42 C3
TOT/BURYW BL8 ...26 B5
Bury St CSLFD M3 ...6 C2
HEY OL10 ...40 C4
MOSL OL5 ...108 D2
RAD M26 ...52 C5
RDSH SK5 ...160 A5
Bushell St BOLS/LL BL3 ...48 A5
Bushey Dr NTHM/RTH M23 ...167 H4
Busheyfield Cl HYDE SK14 ...133 C3
Bush St NEWH/MOS M40 ...103 F5
Busk Rd CHAD OL9 ...74 D4
Busk Wk CHAD OL9 ...74 D4
Butcher La BURY BL9 ...4 E4
NTHM/RTH M23 ...167 E2
ROY/SHW OL2 ...58 D4
Bute Av OLDS OL8 ...91 G4
Bute St BOL BL1 ...33 C5
NEWH/MOS M40 ...103 C1
SALQ M50 ...112 C4
Butler La NEWH/MOS M40 ...115 C2
Butler St ANC M4 ...115 C3
BURY BL9 ...16 B4
Butley St BRAM/HZG SK7 ...173 F5
Butman St GTN M18 ...131 E2
Buttercup Av WALK M28 * ...95 G4
Buttercup Dr EDGY/DAV SK3 ...171 G5
OLDE OL4 ...76 C4
ROCH OL11 ...42 A3
Butterfield Cl CHD/CHDH SK8 ...183 E5
Butterfield Rd WHTN BL5 ...63 E3
Butterhouse La UPML OL3 ...79 E2
Butter La CSLFD M3 ...6 D4
Butterley Cl DUK SK16 ...134 A1
Buttermere Av HEY OL10 ...56 A1
SWIN M27 ...99 E4
Buttermere Cl BOLS/LL BL3 ...50 C5
STRET M32 ...125 H5
Buttermere Dr
HALE/TIMP WA15 ...188 D1
BURY BL9 ...38 D2
RAMS BL0 ...16 C1
Buttermere Gv
ROY/SHW OL2 ...59 E2
Buttermere Rd AULW OL7 ...119 E1
CHD/CHDH SK8 ...181 H5
FWTH BL4 ...64 D4
OLDE OL4 ...76 C4
PART M31 ...150 D3
Buttermill Cl IRL M44 ...122 C5
Butterstile Av PWCH M25 ...100 C1
Butterstile Cl PWCH M25 ...100 C1
Butterstile La PWCH M25 ...85 H4
Butterwick Cl
WGTN/LGST M12 ...130 A5
Butterworth Hall MILN OL16 ...44 B5
Butterworth La CHAD OL9 ...74 C5
Butterworth St CHAD OL9 ...74 C5
LIT OL15 ...20 D5
MDTN M24 ...73 F5
OLDE OL4 ...76 B5
Butterworth Wy UPML OL3 ...79 E2
Butteryhouse La
HALE/TIMP WA15 ...179 F2
Butt Hill Av PWCH M25 ...86 A4
Butt Hill Ct PWCH M25 ...86 A4
Butt Hill Dr PWCH M25 ...86 A4
Butt Hill Rd PWCH M25 ...86 A4
Butt La OLDE OL4 ...95 F3
Button Hole ROY/SHW OL2 ...60 C2
Button La NTHM/RTH M23 ...155 G4
Buttress St GTN M18 ...130 D2
The Butts Av MILN OL16 ...11 H5
Buxted Rd OLD OL1 ...60 A5
Buxton Av AUL OL6 ...108 A4
DID/WITH M20 ...142 B5
Buxton Crs MILN OL16 ...43 G2
SALE M33 ...155 E5

Buxton La DROY M43 ...117 F5
MPL/ROM SK6 ...174 D4
Buxton Pl OLDS OL8 * ...9 F7
Buxton Rd BRAM/HZG SK7 ...185 E5
OFTN SK2 ...172 D5
STRET M32 ...125 F5
Buxton St BRAM/HZG SK7 ...185 E1
CHD/CHDH SK8 ...169 F4
HEY OL10 ...7 J7
HEY OL10 ...41 E5
TOT/BURYW BL8 ...37 H4
WHIT OL12 ...14 C2
Bye Rd RAMS BL0 ...17 F1
Byfield Rd WYTH/NTH M22 ...168 B5
Byland Av CHD/CHDH SK8 ...193 E1
OLDE OL4 ...92 C3
Byland Cl BOL BL1 ...33 H4
Bylands Cl POY/DIS SK12 ...195 E3
Bylands Fold DUK SK16 ...133 G2
Byng Av IRL M44 ...150 B2
Byng St FWTH BL4 ...66 A4
Byng St East BOL BL1 ...56 B1
Byrcland Cl WGTN/LGST M12 ...115 H5
Byre Cl SALE M33 ...155 H3
Byrom Av BNG/LEV M19 ...144 B3
Byrom St ALT WA14 ...177 C1
CSLFD M3 ...6 C6
OLDTF/WHR M16 ...127 G4
ORD M5 ...113 F5
Byron Av DROY M43 ...117 H5
PWCH M25 ...85 G4
RAD M26 ...51 C5
SWIN M27 ...98 D2
Byron Dr CHD/CHDH SK8 ...170 C3
Byron Gv RDSH SK5 ...145 E4
Byron Rd DTN/ASHW M34 ...146 D3
MDTN M24 ...73 E2
STRET M32 ...126 B5
TOT/BURYW BL8 ...26 A1
Byron St ECC M30 ...111 E5
OLDS OL8 ...90 C5
ROY/SHW OL2 ...59 F5
Byron Wk FWTH BL4 ...81 G1
Byrth Rd OLDS OL8 ...106 C2

C

Cabin La OLDE OL4 ...77 F1
Cablestead Wk OP/CLY M11 ...116 A5
Cable St ANC M4 ...7 G2
BOL BL1 ...3 F2
Cabot Pl RDSH SK5 ...160 A2
Cabot St BRUN/LGST M13 * ...128 C2
Caddington Rd CCHDY M21 ...141 G3
Cadishead Wy IRL M44 ...136 C4
Cadman Cl WYTH/NTH M22 ...181 E1
Cadogan Pl BRO M7 * ...101 H1
Cadogan St RUSH/FAL M14 ...128 B4
Cadum Wk BRUN/LGST M13 ...128 D2
Caen Av NEWH/MOS M40 ...89 F4
Caernarvon Cl
TOT/BURYW BL8 ...26 A2
Caernavon Dr
BRAM/HZG SK7 ...184 D3
Caesar St ROCH OL11 ...43 F4
Cairn Dr ROCH OL11 ...43 F4
SLFD M6 ...113 H1
Cairngorm Dr BOLS/LL BL3 ...47 F4
Cairns Pl AUL OL6 ...107 C5
Cairn Wk OP/CLY M11 * ...116 A4
Cairnwell Rd CHAD OL9 ...74 B4
Caister Av WHTF M45 ...69 H5
Caister Cl URM M41 ...137 E2
Caistor Cl OLDTF/WHR M16 ...142 A3
Caistor St STKP SK1 ...160 C3
Caistor Wk OLD OL1 ...9 G1
Caithness Cl NTHM/RTH M23 ...167 H5
Caithness Dr BOLS/LL BL3 ...47 G4
Caithness Rd HEY OL10 ...41 F1
Cakebread St
WGTN/LGST M12 ...128 D1
Calbourne Crs
WGTN/LGST M12 ...130 A3
Calcutta Rd EDGY/DAV SK3 ...171 F2
Caldbeck Av BOL BL1 ...32 C5
SALE M33 ...155 F1
Caldbeck Dr FWTH BL4 ...64 D5
Caldecott Rd BKLY M9 ...87 H1
Calder Av IRL M44 ...136 B2
LIT OL15 ...20 D1
WYTH/NTH M22 ...168 C1
Calderbank Av URM M41 ...123 A5
Calderbank St
WYTH/NTH M22 ...168 D3
Calderbrook Dr
CHD/CHDH SK8 ...170 D5
Calderbrook Wy OLDE OL4 ...62 B2
Calder Cl BURY BL9 ...27 H3
POY/DIS SK12 ...195 E5
RDSH SK5 ...160 B1
Calder Ct URM M41 ...123 E4
Calder Crs WHTF M45 ...70 A2
Calder Dr FWTH BL4 ...82 B4
SWIN M27 ...98 D1
WALK M28 ...81 H5
Calder Gv ROY/SHW OL2 ...59 H1
Calder Rd BOLS/LL BL3 ...64 D1
Caldershaw La WHIT OL12 ...28 B2
Caldershaw Rd WHIT OL12 ...28 C2
St MILN OL16 ...11 H5
ORD M5 ...113 H5
Caldervale Av CCHDY M21 ...156 B2
Caldewood Cl
TOT/BURYW BL8 ...26 A5
Caldey Rd NTHM/RTH M23 ...167 F1
Caldon Cl ECC M30 ...111 E5
Caldwell St RDSH SK5 ...145 E2
Caldy Dr RAMS BL0 ...16 C1
WILM/AE SK9 ...192 A4
Caledon Av NEWH/MOS M40 ...103 H2
Caledonian Dr ECC M30 ...111 H5
Caledonia St BOLS/LL BL3 ...48 B4
RAD M26 ...52 C5

Caledonia Wy STRET M32 ...125 F3
Cale Gn OFTN SK2 ...172 A3
Cale St OFTN SK2 ...172 A2
Caley St BOL BL1 ...32 C4
  CMANE M1 * ...128 B1
Calf Hey LIT OL15 ...20 C2
Calf Hey Cl RAD M26 ...67 H1
Calf Hey North ROCH OL11 ...48 F1
Calf Hey Rd ROY/SHW OL2 ...60 C1
Calf Hey South ROCH OL11 ...43 F2
Calf La MOSL OL5 ...94 B3
Calgarth Dr BRAM/HZG SK7 ...72 A1
Calgary St GTN M18 ...130 B3
Calico Cl CSLFD M3 ...6 B3
Calico Crs STLY SK15 ...109 H4
Callaghan Wk HEY OL10 ...40 D5
Calland Av HYDE SK14 ...134 A5
Callender St RAMS BL0 ...16 C2
Calliards Rd MILN OL16 ...20 B4
Callingdon Rd CCHDY M21 ...156 C1
Callington Cl HYDE SK14 ...149 G1
Callington Dr HYDE SK14 ...149 G1
Callis Rd BOLS/LL BL3 ...48 B3
Callum Wk BRUN/LGST M13 * ...128 D2
Calluna Ms DID/WITH M20 ...157 F2
Caltha St RAMS BL0 ...16 C2
Calthorpe Av BKLY M9 ...102 D3
Calton Av DID/WITH M20 ...100 D3
Calve Croft Rd
  WYTH/NTH M22 ...180 D3
Calver Av ROC OL11 ...110 D5
Calver Cl URM M41 ...123 E5
Calver Hey Cl WHTN BL5 ...62 D2
Calverleigh Cl BOLS/LL BL3 ...63 H2
Calverley Av BNG/LEV M19 ...143 H4
Calverley Cl WILM/AE SK9 ...199 F1
Calverley Wy WHIT OL12 ...18 D4
Calverly Rd CHD/CHDH SK8 ...170 D4
Calverton Dr
  NEWH/MOS M40 ...104 B3
Calvert Rd BOLS/LL BL3 ...65 E1
Calvert St ORD M5 ...112 C3
Calver Wk NEWH/MOS M40 * ...115 F2
Calvine Wk NEWH/MOS M40 * ...115 F2
Cambeck Cl WHTF M45 ...70 A3
Cambell Rd ECC M30 ...110 C3
Camberley Cl BRAM/HZG SK7 ...184 B5
  TOT/BURYW BL8 ...37 E5
Camberley Dr ROCH OL11 ...28 C5
Camber La GTN M18 ...130 B3
Camberwell Dr AULW OL7 ...106 D5
Camberwell St CHH M8 ...114 D1
  OLDS OL8 * ...91 F3
Camberwell Wy ROY/SHW OL2 ...58 D5
Camborne Rd HYDE SK14 ...135 F5
Camborne St RUSH/FAL M14 ...142 D1
Cambourne Wk HTNM SK4 ...158 C3
Cambo Wk HTNM SK4 ...158 C3
Cambrai Crs ECC M30 ...110 B3
Cambrian Cl CSLFD M3 ...6 D2
  ROY/SHW OL2 ...74 D2
Cambrian Rd EDGY/DAV SK3 ...12 B6
Cambrian St NEWH/MOS M40 ...115 H3
Cambria Sq BOLS/LL BL3 ...48 B4
Cambria St BOLS/LL BL3 ...48 B4
  OLDE OL4 ...76 B5
Cambridge Av
  OLDTF/WHR M16 ...141 G1
  ROCH OL11 ...28 D5
  WILM/AE SK9 ...198 C3
Cambridge Cl FWTH BL4 ...65 E3
  SALE M33 ...153 G3
Cambridge Dr BOLS/LL BL3 ...131 F5
  DTN/ASHW M34 ...131 F5
  MPL/ROM SK6 ...162 B3
Cambridge Gv ECC M30 ...111 G3
  WHTF M45 ...69 H4
Cambridge Rd BKLY M9 ...103 G1
  CHD/CHDH SK8 ...169 G3
  DROY M43 ...117 G2
  FAIL M35 ...105 E5
  HALE/TIMP WA15 ...177 H2
  HOR/BR BL6 ...46 C3
  HTNM SK4 ...159 F1
  URM M41 ...138 D2
Cambridge St AULW OL7 ...119 E4
  BRO M7 ...114 B1
  CHAD OL9 ...8 A6
  CMANE M1 * ...128 A1
  DUK SK16 ...119 H4
  OFTN SK2 ...172 B5
  STLY SK15 ...110 D3
Camden Av NEWH/MOS M40 ...116 D1
Camden Cl NEWH/MOS M40 ...116 D1
Camden St MOSL OL5 ...108 D1
Camelford Cl HULME M15 * ...128 B2
Cameron Ct ROY/SHW OL2 ...59 E3
Cameron St BOL BL1 ...33 G1
  CMANE M1 * ...6 D7
  TOT/BURYW BL8 ...37 H5
Camrose Gdns BOL BL1 ...33 H5
Camrose Wk
  BRUN/LGST M13 * ...129 E3
Cams Acre Cl RAD M26 ...67 H1
Cams La RAD M26 ...67 H2
Canada St BOL BL1 ...33 H1
  NEWH/MOS M40 ...115 H1
  OFTN SK2 ...172 B3
Canal Bank ECC M30 ...110 D2
Canal Bridge La DROY M43 ...117 E4

Canal Cottages Yd ANC M4 * ...115 F4
Canal Rd ALT WA14 ...165 H2
Canal Side ECC M30 ...110 D2
Canal St CHAD OL9 ...90 C4
  CMANE M1 ...7 G6
  DROY M43 ...117 H5
  HEY OL10 ...56 B1
  HYDE SK14 ...133 G5
  LIT OL15 ...21 E3
  MPL/ROM SK6 ...175 F3
  ORD M5 * ...113 H4
  ROCH OL11 ...43 F1
  STKP SK1 ...13 H5
  STLY SK15 * ...120 D4
Canberra Rd BRAM/HZG SK7 ...194 A2
Canberra St OP/CLY M11 ...116 D3
Canberra Wy ROCH OL11 ...43 F3
Candahar St BOLS/LL BL3 ...65 F1
Candleford Pl OFTN SK2 ...173 F5
Candleford Rd
  DID/WITH M20 * ...142 D5
Candlestick Ct BURY BL9 ...39 G2
Canley Cl CHAD OL9 ...74 B4
Canley Cl STKP SK1 ...13 H6
Canmore Cl BOLS/LL BL3 ...63 H1
Cannel Fold WALK M28 ...96 C3
Canning Dr BURY BL9 ...33 H4
Canning St BOL BL1 * ...33 H4
  BURY BL9 ...4 B3
  HTNM SK4 ...13 F1
Cannock Dr HTNM SK4 ...158 D4
Cannon Ct CSLFD M3 ...6 E3
Cannon St BOLS/LL BL3 ...48 C4
  CHAD OL9 ...8 E4
  CSLFD M3 ...114 A5
  ECC M30 ...111 F4
  RAD M26 ...52 A4
  RAMS BL0 ...16 B4
Cannon St North BOLS/LL BL3 * ...2 E7
Cann St TOT/BURYW BL8 ...26 D1
Canon Av ALT WA14 ...177 E3
Canon Flynn Ct MILN OL16 ...11 K6
Canon Green Dr CSLFD M3 ...6 B2
Canon's Cl BOL BL1 ...33 E4
Canons Gv NEWH/MOS M40 ...103 F5
Canonsleigh Cl CHH M8 ...101 H5
Canon St BURY BL9 ...5 G1
  MILN OL16 ...11 G1
Canonsway SWIN M27 ...98 D3
Canon Tighe Ct CHAD OL9 * ...74 B5
Cansfield Ct FWTH BL4 ...82 D1
Canterbury Cl DUK SK16 ...133 G2
  ROCH OL11 ...28 D4
Canterbury Crs MDTN M24 ...73 G2
Canterbury Dr NEWH/MOS M40 ...86 B5
  TOT/BURYW BL8 ...38 A2
Canterbury Gdns ORD M5 ...111 H3
Canterbury Gv BOLS/LL BL3 ...64 C1
Canterbury Pk DID/WITH M20 ...157 E3
Canterbury Rd
  HALE/TIMP WA15 ...178 D1
  STKP SK1 ...160 C5
  URM M41 ...124 A5
Canterbury St AUL OL6 ...119 H1
Cantrell St OP/CLY M11 ...116 C4
Canute Rd STRET M32 ...126 B5
Canute St BOLE BL2 ...34 D5
  ORD M5 * ...113 G3
  RAD M26 ...67 H1
Cape Gdns ROY/SHW OL2 ...60 A3
Capella Wk BRO M7 ...113 H1
Capenhurst Ct
  NTHM/RTH M23 ...167 G5
  POY/DIS SK12 ...195 G3
Capesthorne Cl
  BRAM/HZG SK7 ...185 G4
Capesthorne Dr
  ROY/SHW OL2 ...59 G2
Capesthorne Rd
  BRAM/HZG SK7 ...185 G4
  DUK SK16 ...133 G2
  HALE/TIMP WA15 ...167 E3
  MPL/ROM SK6 ...186 D5
  WILM/AE SK9 ...198 B5
Cape St DID/WITH M20 ...143 E4
Capital Rd OP/CLY M11 ...130 C1
Capitol Cl BOL BL1 ...32 D3
Capricorn Wy SLFD M6 ...89 E4
Capstan St BKLY M9 ...103 F2
Captain Clarke Rd HYDE SK14 ...133 E4
Captain Fold HEY OL10 * ...41 F4
Captain Fold Rd LHULT M38 ...81 E2
Captain Lees Gdns WHTN BL5 ...62 B4
Captain Lees Rd WHTN BL5 ...62 B4
Captain's Clough Rd BOL BL1 ...33 E4
Capton Cl BRAM/HZG SK7 ...184 B2
Carberry Rd GTN M18 ...130 D3
Carden Av SWIN M27 ...98 C3
  URM M41 ...137 G1
Cardenbrook Gv
  WILM/AE SK9 ...198 B5
Cardew Av WYTH/NTH M22 ...168 D5
Cardiff Cl OLDS OL8 ...105 G1
Cardiff St BRO M7 ...101 H3
Cardigan Dr BURY BL9 ...53 F2
Cardigan Rd OLDS OL8 ...90 D5
Cardigan St ROY/SHW OL2 ...59 F5
  SLFD M6 * ...112 D4
  WHIT OL12 ...18 D5
Cardinal Ms MDTN M24 ...72 A2
Cardinal St CHH M8 ...102 C4
  OLDE OL4 ...9 J3
Carding Gv CSLFD M3 ...6 C2
Cardroom Rd ANC M4 ...7 K4
Cardus St BNG/LEV M19 ...144 A2
Cardwell Gdns BOL BL1 * ...33 H4
Cardwell Rd ECC M30 ...109 G4
Cardwell St OLDS OL8 ...91 G4
Carey Cl BRO M7 ...114 A1
Carey Wk HULME M15 * ...128 A3
Carfax Fold WHIT OL12 * ...19 E4
Carfax St GTN M18 ...130 C3
Carill Av NEWH/MOS M40 ...103 H1
Carill Dr RUSH/FAL M14 ...143 F3
Carina Pl BRO M7 ...113 H1
Carisbrook Av URM M41 ...138 C2
  WHTF M45 ...85 H1

Carisbrook Dr SWIN M27 ...99 F4
Carisbrooke Av
  BRAM/HZG SK7 ...185 E3
Carisbrooke Dr BOL BL1 ...34 A3
Carisbrook St BKLY M9 ...117 E3
Carleton Rd POY/DIS SK12 ...196 B5
Carley Gv BKLY M9 ...87 H3
Carlford Gv PWCH M25 ...85 G3
Carlile St EDGY/DAV SK3 ...12 C6
Carlin Ga HALE/TIMP WA15 ...166 B3
Carling Dr WYTH/NTH M22 ...180 D2
Carlingford Cl
  EDGY/DAV SK3 ...171 H4
Carlisle Cl BOLS/LL BL3 ...66 C5
  MPL/ROM SK6 ...161 H5
  WHTF M45 ...69 H4
Carlisle Crs AUL OL6 ...107 F3
Carlisle Dr ALT WA14 ...165 H1
  IRL M44 ...136 C1
Carlisle St CHAD OL9 ...90 D3
  EDGW/EG BL7 ...23 E1
  SWIN M27 ...84 A5
  WILM/AE SK9 ...200 D5
Carloon Rd NTHM/RTH M23 ...156 A5
Carlow Dr WYTH/NTH M22 ...180 D2
Carl St BOL BL1 ...33 G4
Carlton Av BOLS/LL BL3 ...47 H5
  BRAM/HZG SK7 ...193 G2
  CHD/CHDH SK8 ...182 C1
  MPL/ROM SK6 ...162 C3
  OLDE OL4 ...77 E3
  PWCH M25 ...86 D3
  WHTF M45 ...69 E3
  WILM/AE SK9 ...191 H5
Carlton Cl BOLE BL2 ...35 F3
  WALK M28 ...81 G4
Carlton Crs HALE/TIMP WA15 ...178 C3
  STKP SK1 ...13 K2
  URM M41 ...138 D2
Carlton Dr CHD/CHDH SK8 ...169 F3
  PWCH M25 ...86 D5
Carlton Pl BRAM/HZG SK7 ...185 H3
  PWCH M25 ...85 H5
Carlton Range GTN M18 * ...131 E4
Carlton Rd AUL OL6 ...107 F5
  BOL BL1 ...33 G4
  HALE/TIMP WA15 ...178 C4
  HTNM SK4 ...158 D4
  HYDE SK14 ...148 B4
  OLDTF/WHR M16 ...127 G5
  SALE M33 ...139 G5
  SLFD M6 ...112 D1
  URM M41 ...138 D2
  WALK M28 ...81 H4
Carlton St BOLE BL2 ...3 G6
  BURY BL9 ...53 G1
  ECC M30 ...111 E2
  FWTH BL4 ...66 A3
  OLDTF/WHR M16 ...127 G4
Carlton Wy
  GOL/RIS/CUL WA3 ...150 B1
  ROY/SHW OL2 ...59 G2
Carlyle Cl CHH M8 ...102 B4
Carlyle St BURY BL9 ...4 E4
Carlyn Av SALE M33 ...155 E2
Carmel Av ORD M5 ...127 F1
Carmel Ct ORD M5 ...113 H5
Carmel Dr BRAM/HZG SK7 ...184 A5
Carmichael Cl PART M31 ...150 D3
Carmichael St EDGY/DAV SK3 ...12 C7
Car Mill Ms WILM/AE SK9 ...191 G5
Carmine Fold MDTN M24 ...72 C2
Carmona Dr PWCH M25 ...85 H5
Carmona Gdns BRO M7 * ...101 H1
Carmoor Rd BRUN/LGST M13 ...128 C3
Carnaby St BKLY M9 ...103 G1
Carna Rd RDSH SK5 ...145 E1
Carnarvon St BRO M7 * ...101 H5
  CSLFD M3 ...90 C5
  STKP SK1 ...13 K5
Carnation Rd FWTH BL4 ...65 F3
  OLDE OL4 ...92 D3
Carnegie Av BNG/LEV M19 ...144 B1
Carnegie Cl SALE M33 ...153 G5
Carnforth Av CHAD OL9 ...90 B1
Carnforth Dr SALE M33 ...154 B3
  TOT/BURYW BL8 ...26 B1
Carnforth Rd CHD/CHDH SK8 ...183 F1
  HTNM SK4 ...144 C5
Carnforth Sq MDTN M24 ...57 G2
Carnforth St RUSH/FAL M14 ...128 C5
Carnoustie BOLS/LL BL3 ...63 H1
Carnoustie Cl
  NEWH/MOS M40 ...104 B3
  WILM/AE SK9 ...199 G2
Carnoustie Dr CHD/CHDH SK8 ...181 H5
  RAMS BL0 ...16 C2
Carnwood Cl
  NEWH/MOS M40 ...117 E1
Carolina Wy SALO M50 ...112 D4
Caroline St AUL OL6 ...119 H2
  BOLS/LL BL3 ...48 C5
  BRO M7 ...114 B1
  EDGY/DAV SK3 ...12 D7
  IRL M44 ...136 A3
  STLY SK15 ...120 D4
Carpenters La ANC M4 ...7 G3
Carpenters Wk DROY M43 ...117 H4
Carpenters Wy MILN OL16 ...43 G2
Carradale Dr SALE M33 ...153 F1
Carr Av PWCH M25 ...85 G5
Carr Bank Av BKLY M9 ...87 E4
Carr Bank Rd RAMS BL0 ...16 C1
Carrbrook Cl STLY SK15 ...109 G4
Carrbrook Dr ROY/SHW OL2 ...75 E3
Carrbrook Rd STLY SK15 ...109 H4
Carrbrook Ter RAD M26 ...52 D5
Carr Brow MPL/ROM SK6 ...187 F5
Carr Cl STKP SK1 ...172 C1
Carr Dr FWTH BL4 ...65 E3
Carrfield Av EDGY/DAV SK3 ...172 B5
  HALE/TIMP WA15 ...167 E4

  LHULT M38 ...80 D3
Carrfield Gv LHULT M38 ...80 D3
Carr Fold RAMS BL0 ...16 C1
Carrgate Rd DTN/ASHW M34 ...147 F2
Carrgreen Cl BNG/LEV M19 ...146 D5
Carrhill Quarry Cl MOSL OL5 ...93 H5
Carrhill Rd MOSL OL5 ...93 H5
Carrhouse La MOSL OL5 * ...93 H5
Carr House Rd OLDE OL4 ...77 E5
Carriage Dr LIT OL15 ...21 E1
  NEWH/MOS M40 ...103 E5
The Carriages ALT WA14 ...177 E3
Carrick Gdns MDTN M24 ...56 C5
Carrie St BOL BL1 ...33 F4
Carrigart PWCH M25 ...85 H4
Carrill Gv East BNG/LEV M19 ...144 C1
Carrington Dr MILN OL16 ...20 A5
Carrington Dr BOLS/LL BL3 ...49 E5
Carrington Field St OFTN SK2 ...13 K6
Carrington La SALE M33 ...138 D5
  STKP SK1 ...160 C4
Carrington Rd RUSH/FAL M14 ...143 E3
  STKP SK1 ...160 C4
Carrington St CHAD OL9 ...90 C4
  SWIN M27 ...99 G1
Carrington Ter SWIN M27 * ...99 G1
Carr La HALE/TIMP WA15 ...178 C2
  OLDE OL4 ...93 H1
Carr Lea OLDE OL4 ...93 H1
Carr Mill Ms WILM/AE SK9 ...199 E1
Carr Rd HALE/TIMP WA15 ...178 C2
  IRL M44 ...136 D1
Carrs Av CHD/CHDH SK8 ...170 D3
Carrsdale Dr BKLY M9 ...87 H5
Carrsfield Rd WYTH/NTH M22 ...180 C2
Carrslea Cl RAD M26 ...56 C5
Carr St AUL OL6 ...107 H5
  RAMS BL0 ...16 C1
  SWIN M27 ...98 C3
  WILM/AE SK9 ...200 A5
Carrsvale Av URM M41 ...124 A5
Carrswood Rd
  NTHM/RTH M23 ...166 D1
Carruthers Cl HEY OL10 ...41 G5
Carruthers St ANC M4 ...115 G4
Carrwood HALE/TIMP WA15 ...178 C5
Carrwood Av BRAM/HZG SK7 ...193 H1
Carrwood Hey RAMS BL0 ...16 B4
Carrwood Rd BRAM/HZG SK7 ...183 G2
  WILM/AE SK9 ...198 C2
Carsdale Rd WYTH/NTH M22 ...180 D1
Carslake Av BOL BL1 ...47 H1
Carslake Rd NEWH/MOS M40 ...103 E5
Carson Rd BNG/LEV M19 ...144 A3
Carstairs Av OFTN SK2 ...172 B5
Carstairs Cl CHH M8 ...102 A3
Carter Cl DTN/ASHW M34 * ...146 D1
Carter Pl HYDE SK14 ...133 G3
Carter St BOLS/LL BL3 ...49 F5
  BRO M7 * ...101 G5
  FWTH BL4 ...66 B5
  HYDE SK14 ...133 G3
  MOSL OL5 ...108 D2
  SALQ M50 ...112 B4
  STLY SK15 ...121 E5
Cartford Cl OLDS OL8 ...91 G3
Cartleach Gv WALK M28 ...81 E5
Cartleach La WALK M28 ...80 D5
Cartmel Av MILN OL16 ...44 C2
  RDSH SK5 ...144 D1
Cartmel Cl BOLS/LL BL3 ...63 E2
  BRAM/HZG SK7 ...184 D1
  BURY BL9 ...69 H1
  CHD/CHDH SK8 ...181 H1
  OLDS OL8 ...91 E4
Cartmel Crs BOLE BL2 ...34 D4
  CHAD OL9 ...90 C5
Cartmel Dr HALE/TIMP WA15 ...167 E3
Cartridge Cl WYTH/NTH M22 ...168 D4
Cartridge St HEY OL10 ...40 D4
Cartwright Rd CCHDY M21 ...141 E3
Cartwright St
  DTN/ASHW M34 ...132 C2
  HYDE SK14 ...132 D2
Carver Av PWCH M25 ...86 B3
Carver Cl OLDTF/WHR M16 ...127 E3
Carver Dr MPL/ROM SK6 ...161 G5
Carver Rd HALE/TIMP WA15 ...177 H2
  MPL/ROM SK6 ...161 G5
Carver St OLDTF/WHR M16 ...128 A3
Carville Rd BKLY M9 ...88 A4
Cascade Dr BRO M7 ...101 H5
Cashgate Ct OLDS OL8 ...90 D5
Cashmere Rd EDGY/DAV SK3 ...171 F2
Cashmoor Wk
  WGTN/LGST M12 ...129 G2
Caspian Rd ALT WA14 ...164 D3
Cass Av ORD M5 ...113 F5
Cassandra Ct
  BRUN/LGST M13 ...128 C3
Cassidy Gdns MDTN M24 ...56 A5
Casson Ga WHIT OL12 ...10 B2
Casson St FAIL M35 ...105 E2
Casterton Wy WALK M28 ...96 B5
Castle Av DTN/ASHW M34 ...146 C1
  ROCH OL11 ...29 H5
Castlebrook Cl BURY BL9 ...54 B5
Castle Cl AUL OL6 ...118 A3
Castle Ct BOLE BL2 ...34 C3
Castle Croft BOLE BL2 ...3 J5
Castlecroft Rd BURY BL9 ...53 G1
Castledene Av SLFD M6 ...112 D2
Castleford Cl BOLE BL2 ...2 B2
Castleford St OLD OL1 ...114 A5
Castle Gv RAMS BL0 ...16 A4
Castle Hall Cl STLY SK15 ...120 D4
Castle Hall Ct STLY SK15 ...120 D4
Castle Hall Vw STLY SK15 ...120 D4

Castle Hey Cl BURY BL9 ...70 B1
Castle Hill Crs ROCH OL11 ...29 H5
Castle Hill Rd BKLY M9 ...102 D1
Castle Hill Rd MPL/ROM SK6 * ...146 D5
Castle Hill Rd BURY BL9 ...39 G2
  PWCH M25 ...86 C5
Castle Hill St BOLE BL2 ...34 C4
Castle La STLY SK15 ...109 G2
Castlemere Dr ROY/SHW OL2 ...60 C1
Castlemere Rd BKLY M9 ...87 H4
Castlemere St ROCH OL11 ...29 H5
Castlemere Ter ROCH OL11 ...29 H5
Castle Mill La
  HALE/TIMP WA15 ...188 B2
Castlemoor Av BRO M7 ...101 E2
Castle Quay HULME M15 ...127 H1
Castlerea Cl ECC M30 ...111 E5
Castlerigg Cl HTNM SK4 ...144 D4
Castlerigg Dr MDTN M24 ...71 G2
Castle Rd BURY BL9 ...54 B5
Castle Shaw Rd OFTN SK2 ...173 F4
Castle St BOLE BL2 ...3 J6
  BURY BL9 ...26 D1
  CSLFD M3 ...6 B7
  ECC M30 ...111 G3
  EDGY/DAV SK3 ...12 C7
  HYDE SK14 ...133 G5
  MDTN M24 ...73 G5
  STLY SK15 ...120 D4
Castleton Av STRET M32 ...125 G5
Castleton Dr MPL/ROM SK6 ...197 E1
Castleton Gv AUL OL6 ...108 A4
Castleton Rd BRAM/HZG SK7 ...185 F3
  BRO M7 ...101 H2
  ROY/SHW OL2 ...58 C1
  STRET M32 ...125 F4
Castleton Rd South
  ROCH OL11 ...42 C4
Castleton St ALT WA14 ...165 F2
  BOLE BL2 ...34 C4
  CHAD OL9 ...8 A5
Castleton Wk OP/CLY M11 * ...116 D5
Castleway HALE/TIMP WA15 ...178 D5
  ROCH OL11 ...42 A4
  SLFD M6 ...112 D1
Castle Wy WHIT M27 ...84 B5
Castlewood Gdns OFTN SK2 ...172 D4
Castlewood Rd BRO M7 ...100 D2
Castlewood Sq BOLE BL2 ...34 D5
Catchdale Cl BKLY M9 ...87 H2
Catches Cl ROCH OL11 ...29 E3
Catches La ROCH OL11 ...29 E3
Caterham Av BOLS/LL BL3 ...63 G2
Caterham St ANC M4 ...115 G4
Catfield Wk HULME M15 * ...127 G1
Catford Rd NTHM/RTH M23 ...155 H5
Cathedral Ap CSLFD M3 ...6 E2
Cathedral Cl DUK SK16 ...133 G2
Cathedral Gdns ANC M4 ...6 E2
Cathedral Rd CHAD OL9 ...74 B3
Cathedral St CSLFD M3 ...6 E3
Catherine Houses
  HTNM SK4 ...158 C4
Catherine Rd ALT WA14 ...177 F1
  CHH M8 ...101 H4
  MPL/ROM SK6 ...161 G5
  SWIN M27 ...98 B3
Catherine St BRAM/HZG SK7 ...64 A2
  BRAM/HZG SK7 ...173 F5
  BURY BL9 ...53 F3
  ECC M30 ...110 D2
  HYDE SK14 ...133 G5
  OLDS OL8 ...92 D1
  OP/CLY M11 ...130 D1
Catherston Cl
  OLDTF/WHR M16 ...127 H5
Cathrine St East
  DTN/ASHW M34 ...132 A5
Cathrine St West
  DTN/ASHW M34 ...132 A5
Catlow La ANC M4 * ...7 G3
Catlow St BRO M7 ...114 B1
Caton Cl BURY BL9 ...53 F1
Caton St MILN OL16 ...30 A5
Cato St RAMS BL0 ...16 B4
Catterall Crs BOLE BL2 ...24 A5
Catterick Av DID/WITH M20 ...142 B5
  SALE M33 ...153 F4
Catterick Rd BOLS/LL BL3 ...66 C3
  DID/WITH M20 ...157 H3
Catterwood Dr
  MPL/ROM SK6 ...163 G4
Cattlin Wy OLDS OL8 ...90 D5
The Causeway ALT WA14 ...165 G5
  CHAD OL9 ...89 G2
Causewood Cl OLDE OL4 ...60 D5
Causey Dr MDTN M24 ...71 G2
Cavanagh Dr BRUN/LGST M13 ...129 E2
Cavan Cl EDGY/DAV SK3 ...170 C2
Cavell St CMANE M1 * ...7 H4
Cavell Wy ORD M5 ...113 H4
Cavendish Gdns BOLS/LL BL3 ...64 B1
Cavendish Gv ECC M30 ...111 F2
Cavendish Ms WILM/AE SK9 ...198 D5
Cavendish Pl AUL OL6 ...119 F2
Cavendish Rd ALT WA14 ...177 E3
  BRAM/HZG SK7 ...185 E3
  BRO M7 ...101 G1
  DID/WITH M20 ...142 B5
  ECC M30 ...111 F2
  HTNM SK4 ...159 H4
  OLDS OL8 ...42 D5
  STRET M32 ...126 B4
  URM M41 ...139 E1
  WALK M28 ...98 A4
Cavendish St AUL OL6 ...119 F2
  HULME M15 ...128 B2
Cavendish Wy ROY/SHW OL2 ...74 D2
Cavenham Gv ROCH OL11 ...48 B1
Caversham Dr BKLY M9 ...103 F2
Cawdor Ct FWTH BL4 ...65 H2

Cawdor Pl *HALE/TIMP* WA15......166 D3
Cawdor Rd *RUSH/FAL* M14.....143 E2
Cawdor St *ECC* M30........110 D4
FWTH BL4.............65 C2
HULME M15..............127 C1
SWIN M27.............98 C2
WALK M28.............82 B5
Cawley Av *PWCH* M25..........85 C5
Cawley Ter *BKLY* M9 *.......87 F2
Cawood Sq *RDSH* SK5..........146 A5
Cawston Wk *CHH* M8.........102 B4
Caxton Rd *RUSH/FAL* M14...142 D2
Caxton St *CSLFD* M3 *..........6 C3
HEY OL10...............41 E4
ROCH OL11..............42 B4
Caxton Wy *ORD* M5..........113 G4
Caygill St *CSLFD* M3............6 C2
Cayley St *MILN* OL16.........11 C7
Caythorpe St *RUSH/FAL* M14..128 B5
Cayton St *WGTN/LGST* M12..129 H5
The Ceal *MPL/ROM* SK6.....165 G4
Cecil Av *SALE* M33..........153 H5
Cecil Dr *URM* M41..........137 C1
Cecil Gv *OLD* H.............130 C4
Cecilia St *BOLS/LL* BL3.........89 F1
Cecil Rd *BKLY* M9...........88 A5
ECC M30.............111 F4
HALE/TIMP WA15.......177 H2
STRET M32...............140 A2
Cecil St *BOLE* BL2............5 J5
BURY BL9..............8 A6
DUK SK16.............119 G5
EDGY/DAV SK3 *.........12 E7
HULME M15..............128 C3
LIT OL15................20 D3
MOSL OL5.............108 D2
OLDS OL8................8 E7
ROCH OL11..............43 E1
ROY/SHW OL2............58 D5
STLY SK15.............121 E4
Cedar Av *ALT* WA14.........165 F5
AUL OL6.............107 G5
BOLS/LL BL3.............67 E2
BRAM/HZG SK7........185 F2
HEY OL10.................40 D5
STLY SK15.............121 F2
WHTF M45..............85 C1
Cedar Bank Cl *MILN* OL16.....31 E4
Cedar Cl *POY/DIS* SK12.....195 F4
Cedar Ct *HALE/TIMP* WA15 *..166 C4
Cedar Crs *CHAD* OL9.........74 C4
RAMS BL0..............16 D1
Cedar Dr *DROY* M43.........118 A3
SWIN M27.............83 C3
URM M41.............138 C2
Cedar La *DTN/ASHW* M34....132 B2
DUK SK16.............120 C5
FWTH BL4..............65 C4
HTNM SK4.............159 F1
PWCH M25.............85 H1
ROY/SHW OL2............60 A5
RUSH/FAL M14.........143 F3
Cedar La *MILN* OL16..........44 D3
OLDE OL4..............94 A1
Cedar Lawn
CHD/CHDH SK8 *..........182 D2
Cedar Ms *AULW* OL7.........106 D5
Cedar Pl *BRO* M7.............113 H1
Cedar Rd *CHD/CHDH* SK8......169 F4
FAIL M35.............105 E4
HALE/TIMP WA15.......177 H1
MDTN M24..............73 F4
MPL/ROM SK6.........174 D5
OFTN SK2.............172 C5
PART M31.............150 D3
SALE M33.............154 B2
Cedars Rd *WYTH/NTH* M22....180 C1
Cedar St *AUL* OL6...........120 A1
BURY BL9................5 H5
HYDE SK14.............133 G3
OLDE OL4................79 F4
WHIT OL12..............10 D2
Cedar Vw *AUL* OL6..........107 H5
Cedarwood Av *HTNM* SK4......158 D5
Cedarwood Cl
WYTH/NTH M22..........168 D1
Cedar Wood Ct *BOL* BL1 *......47 C1
OLDE OL4.................76 B5
Cedric Rd *CHH* M8...........86 D5
Cedric St *ORD* M5...........112 C3
Celandine Cl *LIT* OL15........20 D3
Celia St *CHH* M8...........102 D2
Cellini Sq *BOL* BL1............33 C5
Celtic St *STKP* SK1...........13 K5
Cemetery La *BURY* BL9........55 C1
Cemetery Rd *BOLE* BL2.........3 K4
DROY M43.............117 G4
DTN/ASHW M34.........132 C2
DTN/ASHW M34.........146 D2
FAIL M35.............105 E4
FWTH BL4..............66 C3
MOSL OL5.............109 G3
ORD M5.............112 D4
RAD M26..............52 B4
RAMS BL0..............16 B4
ROY/SHW OL2............58 D4
SWIN M27..............98 D1
Cemetery Rd North
SWIN M27..............83 H5
Cemetery St *MDTN* M24........72 D3
Cennick Cl *OLDE* OL4..........92 C1
Ceno St *OLD* OL1.............9 H3
Centaur Cl *SWIN* M27.........84 A5
Centenary Ct *BOLS/LL* BL3.....49 E5
Centenary Wy *SALQ* M50.....111 H4
TRPK M17.............112 A5
Central Av *BNG/LEV* M19....144 A1
BURY BL9................8 B2
FWTH BL4..............65 F4
LIT OL15................21 E2
SALE M33.............155 C5
SLFD M6.............100 B5
SWIN M27..............85 F2
UPML OL3..............78 E2
URM M41.............124 D2
WALK M28.............81 H2
Central Dr *BRAM/HZG* SK7....185 G2
BURY BL9..............27 G3

CHD/CHDH SK8..........182 A4
CHH M8.............102 C1
MPL/ROM SK6.........162 B5
RDSH SK5.............146 B4
SWIN M27..............99 G5
URM M41.............138 D1
Central Park Est *TRPK* M17 *..125 H2
Central Rd *DID/WITH* M20....157 F1
MANX M90.............190 B4
PART M31.............151 E3
Central St *BOL* BL1............2 F4
CMANW M2................6 E6
RAMS BL0..............16 C2
Central Wy *ALT* WA14.......165 C5
Centre Gdns *BOL* BL1.........33 C5
Centre Park Rd *BOL* BL1........2 D1
Centre Vale Cl *LIT* OL15.......21 F1
Centurion Gv *BRO* M7.......101 H5
Century Gdns *WHIT* OL12......10 C4
Century Ldg *FWTH* BL4........65 H4
Cestrian St *BOLS/LL* BL3........65 E1
Ceylon St *NEWH/MOS* M40...103 H4
OLDE OL4..............92 C2
Chadbury Cl *HOR/BR* BL6......62 D1
Chadderton Dr *BURY* BL9......69 H2
Chadderton Fold *OLD* OL1.....74 A2
Chadderton Hall Rd *CHAD* OL9..74 A3
Chadderton Park Rd *CHAD* OL9..74 A3
Chadderton Prec *CHAD* OL9 *..74 C5
Chadderton St *ANC* M4..........7 H2
Chadderton Wy *CHAD* OL9......74 A5
OLD OL1................74 D3
Chaddesley Wk *OP/CLY* M11 *..116 B5
The Chaddock Level *WALK* M28..96 B5
Chadkirk Rd *MPL/ROM* SK6...162 B5
Chadvil Rd *CHD/CHDH* SK8....169 H4
Chadwell Rd *OFTN* SK2......173 F2
Chadwick Cl *MILN* OL16.........44 D1
RUSH/FAL M14 *........128 C5
WILM/AE SK9...........199 F2
Chadwick Fold *BURY* BL9......27 G4
Chadwick Hall Rd *ROCH* OL11..29 E5
Chadwick La *MILN* OL16........43 H4
ROCH OL11.............41 H4
Chadwick Rd *ECC* M30.......111 F3
URM M41.............138 D3
Chadwick St *AUL* OL6........120 B5
BOLE BL2................3 H6
BOLS/LL BL3.............67 E1
BURY BL9..............39 H2
MILN OL16..............11 E4
MPL/ROM SK6.........175 E4
ROCH OL11..............29 C4
STKP SK1..............13 G6
SWIN M27..............99 E2
Chaffinch Cl *DROY* M43......118 D2
OLDE OL4..............92 D3
WYTH/NTH M22........169 E4
Chaffinch Dr *BURY* BL9........39 F2
Chaffinch Gv *STLY* SK15.....109 F3
Chain Bar La *HYDE* SK14.....149 H1
Chain Rd *BKLY* M9.............88 A2
Chain St *CMANE* M1............7 F5
Chalcombe Gra
WGTN/LGST M12 *......129 C5
Chale Cl *NEWH/MOS* M40....115 C2
Chale Dr *MDTN* M24...........89 F1
Chale Gn *BOLE* BL2............35 F3
Chalfont Av *URM* M41 *......139 E1
Chalfont Cl *OLDS* OL8.........92 A3
Chalfont Dr *CHH* M8.........102 B3
WALK M28.............81 F3
Chalfont St *BOL* BL1............54 A4
Chalford Rd *NTHM/RTH* M23...179 H1
Challenor Sq
WGTN/LGST M12 *......129 H2
Challum Dr *CHAD* OL9..........74 B4
Chamber Hall Cl *OLDS* OL8.....91 E3
Chamberhall St *BURY* BL9.......5 H2
Chamber House Dr *ROCH* OL11..42 A3
Chamberlain Dr *WILM/AE* SK9..199 C1
Chamberlain St *BOLS/LL* BL3.....2 B7
Chamber Rd *OLDS* OL8.........90 D4
ROY/SHW OL2............59 H2
Chambers Ct *HYDE* SK14......135 H5
Chambers Field Ct *ORD* M5....113 F4
Champness Hall *MILN* OL16 *..107 D7
Chancel Av *ORD* M5.........113 H5
Chancel Cl *DUK* SK16..........133 F2
Chancel La *WILM/AE* SK9......199 E2
Chancellor La
WGTN/LGST M12 *......115 C5
Chancel Ms *STKP* SK1.........13 J3
Chancel Pl *CMANE* M1 *........7 K5
MILN OL16..............10 C7
Chancery La *BOL* BL1............3 F5
CMANW M2................6 E5
ROY/SHW OL2 *.........60 B2
UPML OL3..............78 D2
Chancery St *OLDE* OL4.........92 B1
Chancery Wk *CHAD* OL9.......74 D4
Chandley St *CHD/CHDH* SK8 *..170 A3
Chandos Gv *ORD* M5.........112 C3
Chandos Rd *CCHDY* M21......141 C2
HTNM SK4.............144 B5
PWCH M25.............86 A5
Chandos Rd South
CCHDY M21.............141 C2
Chandos St *ROY/SHW* OL2.....60 B2
Change Wy *CSLFD* M3............6 B1
Channing Ct *MILN* OL16 *.......30 C5
Channing Sq *MILN* OL16........30 C5
Channing St *MILN* OL16........30 C5
The Chanters *WALK* M28........96 D3
Chantlers Av
TOT/BURYW BL8..........37 F5
Chantry Cl *RDSH* SK5.........145 E4
Chapel Aly *BOL* BL1 *...........2 E4
Chapel Ct *BURY* BL9...........54 A5
DUK SK16.............119 H5
Chapel Cft *ROY/SHW* OL2......59 E5
Chapel Dr *AUL* OL6..........107 H5
Chapelfield *DROY* M43........118 D5
Chapelfield Cl *STLY* SK15.....121 C1
Chapelfield Dr *WALK* M28......81 G4
Chapel Field Rd
DTN/ASHW M34.........132 C5

Chapelfield Rd
WGTN/LGST M12.......115 F3
Chapelfield St *BOL* BL1.........33 H3
Chapel Gdns *TOT/BURYW* BL8..25 H2
Chapel Ga *MILN* OL16.........31 C5
Chapel Gn *DTN/ASHW* M54....132 C5
Chapel Gv *URM* M41.........139 E1
Chapel HI *LIT* OL15...........21 E2
Chapelhill Dr *BKLY* M9.........87 H4
Chapel La *BKLY* M9...........87 G4
HALE/TIMP WA15.......178 D5
PART M31.............151 E3
ROY/SHW OL2............59 E5
SALE M33.............139 E5
TOT/BURYW BL8..........16 A4
WILM/AE SK9...........198 C4
Chapel Meadow *WALK* M28......96 C3
Chapel Pl *BOLS/LL* BL3.........64 A4
URM M41.............111 E5
Chapel Rd *IRL* M44..........136 C1
OLDS OL8..............90 D4
PWCH M25.............100 C1
SALE M33.............154 C1
SWIN M27..............98 B3
UPML OL3..............94 D1
WILM/AE SK9...........200 D4
WYTH/NTH M22........168 C1
Chapel St *AUL* OL6..........119 H2
BNG/LEV M19...........144 A2
BOL BL1.................3 G3
BOLS/LL BL3.............66 D1
BRAM/HZG SK7........185 F1
BURY BL9................4 E4
CHD/CHDH SK8..........68 A5
DROY M43.............118 A4
DTN/ASHW M34.........132 C2
DUK SK16.............119 H5
ECC M30.............110 D4
FWTH BL4..............66 B4
HEY OL10 *..............41 E4
HTNM SK4.............158 A5
HYDE SK14.............147 H2
MDTN M24..............72 C4
MOSL OL5.............108 C4
MPL/ROM SK6.........162 A1
OLDE OL4..............92 D1
PWCH M25.............85 C5
ROCH OL11..............43 F2
ROY/SHW OL2............59 E5
ROY/SHW OL2 *.........60 A2
STLY SK15.............120 C5
SWIN M27..............99 F1
TOT/BURYW BL8..........26 A4
UPML OL3..............79 E4
WALK M28.............96 A4
WHIT OL12..............14 B5
WHIT OL12..............19 H1
WILM/AE SK9...........200 D3
Chapeltown Rd *EDGW/EG* BL7...23 G3
RAD M26..............68 D2
Chapeltown St *CMANE* M1.......7 K6
Chapel Vw *DUK* SK16.........119 H5
Chapel View *HYDE* SK14......148 A4
Chapel Wk *OLD* OL1...........75 E5
Chapel Wks *CHD/CHDH* SK8....193 E1
URM M41.............138 C1
Chapelway Gdns
ROY/SHW OL2............59 E3
Chaplin Cl *SLFD* M6.........112 D1
Chapman Ms *GTN* M18 *......130 C3
Chapman Rd *HYDE* SK14......149 C2
Chapman St *BOL* BL1..........33 E5
GTN M18.............130 C2
Chappell Rd *DROY* M43.......118 A1
Chappeltown Rd *RAD* M26......68 A3
Chapter St *NEWH/MOS* M40...116 A1
Charcoal Rd *ALT* WA14......176 C1
Charcoal Woods *ALT* WA14....176 D1
Chard Dr *WYTH/NTH* M22....180 C3
Chardin Av *MPL/ROM* SK6....175 H1
Chard St *RAD* M26............68 B1
Charges St *AULW* OL7........119 F4
Chariot St *OP/CLY* M11......117 E5
Charlbury Av *PWCH* M25.......86 C4
RDSH SK5.............145 F5
Charlbury Wy *ROY/SHW* OL2...59 H4
Charlecote Rd *POY/DIS* SK12..195 E3
Charles Av *DTN/ASHW* M34...131 F1
MPL/ROM SK6.........162 A1
Charles Ct *BOL* BL1 *..........3 F3
Charles Halle Rd
RUSH/FAL M14.........128 B3
Charles Holden St *BOL* BL1.....2 A6
Charles La *MILN* OL16..........44 D1
Charles Ms *MILN* OL16.........44 D1
Charles Morris Cl *FAIL* M35...105 G2
Charles Shaw Cl *OLDE* OL4....76 D3
Charles St *AULW* OL7.........119 C5
BOL BL1.................3 F4
BRAM/HZG SK7........185 E1
BURY BL9................5 F2
CHAD OL9................8 B5
CMANE M1................7 F4
DROY M43.............117 F4
DTN/ASHW M34.........132 C3
EDGW/EG BL7...........22 C1
FWTH BL4..............66 B3
HEY OL10................41 E4
IRL M44.............136 B1
LIT OL15................20 D3
ROY/SHW OL2............59 E5
SLFD M6................13 H1
STKP SK1..............13 J7
SWIN M27..............99 F2
WHTF M45..............69 G5
Charleston Cl *SALE* M33......153 C4
Charleston St *OLDS* OL8......124 A5
Charleston St *OLDS* OL8........9 F1
Charlestown Rd *BKLY* M9......88 A5
Charlestown Rd East
OFTN SK2.............184 D1
Charlestown Rd West
EDGY/DAV SK3 *.......184 A1
Charlestown Wy *CHD/CHDH* SK8..119 F2
Charles Whittaker St
WHIT OL12..............18 D1
Charlesworth Av *BOLS/LL* BL3..65 C2
DTN/ASHW M34.........146 D3

Charlesworth St *OP/CLY* M11...116 A5
STKP SK1...............13 G7
Charlock Sq *ALT* WA14.......165 E1
Charlotte La *OLDE* OL4.........94 B2
Charlotte Pl *HALE/TIMP* WA15..178 A1
Charlotte St *BOL* BL1............3 H5
CHD/CHDH SK8..........170 A4
CMANW M2................7 F5
MILN OL16..............43 G3
RAMS BL0..............16 C3
STKP SK1..............160 C5
Charlton Av *ECC* M30........111 E4
HYDE SK14.............134 B4
PWCH M25.............86 A4
Charlton Dr *SALE* M33.......154 D2
SWIN M27..............99 C5
Charlton Fold *WALK* M28.......81 H2
Charlton Pl *CMANE* M1.......128 C1
Charlton Rd *BNG/LEV* M19....144 B1
Charminster Dr *CHH* M8......102 C2
Charmouth Wk
WYTH/NTH M22........181 E1
Charnley Cl *NEWH/MOS* M40..115 H2
Charnley St *WHTF* M45........69 G4
Charnock Dr *BOL* BL1...........2 D1
Charnville Rd *CHD/CHDH* SK8..169 E5
Charnwood *MPL/ROM* SK6....187 E5
Charnwood Av
DTN/ASHW M34.........131 C5
Charnwood Cl *AUL* OL6.......107 F3
ROY/SHW OL2............59 C1
WALK M28.............81 H5
Charnwood Crs
BRAM/HZG SK7........185 E4
MPL/ROM SK6.........162 D1
Charter Av *RAD* M26..........68 C5
Charter Rd *BNG/LEV* M19 *....144 B2
Charter St *CSLFD* M3.........114 C2
RAMS BL0..............16 A4
Chartist Wk *OP/CLY* M11 *....116 B4
Chartwell Cl *SLFD* M6.......113 E3
Chartwell Dr *NTHM/RTH* M23..167 E2
Chase Briar Wd
CHD/CHDH SK8 *........183 E3
Chasefield *ALT* WA14.........176 D2
Chaseley Rd *SLFD* M6.......112 D1
WHIT OL12..............10 A4
The Chase *WALK* M28..........97 H5
Chasewood *BNG/LEV* M19 *....144 A2
Chassen Av *URM* M41 *......138 A1
Chassen Ct *URM* M41.........138 B2
Chassen Rd *BOL* BL1............48 A2
URM M41.............138 B2
Chataway Rd *CHH* M8.........102 C2
Chatburn Av *ROCH* OL11.......57 C2
Chatburn Gdns *HEY* OL10......40 B5
Chatburn Rd *BOL* BL1...........32 C3
CCHDY M21.............141 C3
Chatburn Sq *ROCH* OL11.......57 C1
Chatcombe Rd
WYTH/NTH M22........179 H2
Chatfield Rd *CCHDY* M21....141 F3
Chatford Cl *BRO* M7.........114 B1
Chatham Ct *DID/WITH* M20...142 C5
Chatham Gdns *BOLS/LL* BL3....48 D4
Chatham Gv *DID/WITH* M20...142 C5
Chatham Pl *BOLS/LL* BL3 *.....48 C4
Chatham Rd *GTN* M18.........130 D5
OLDTF/WHR M16.........127 F5
Chatham St *CMANE* M1..........7 G6
EDGY/DAV SK3 *.......12 C5
HYDE SK14.............147 H4
STKP SK1..............160 D5
Chatley Rd *ECC* M30.........110 A4
Chatley St *CSLFD* M3........114 C1
Chatsworth Av *PWCH* M25......86 A5
Chatsworth Cl *BURY* BL9.......53 H4
DROY M43.............117 E2
HALE/TIMP WA15.......166 D4
ROY/SHW OL2............60 C1
URM M41.............139 E1
Chatsworth Gv
OLDTF/WHR M16........141 H1
Chatsworth Ms
BRAM/HZG SK7........183 G2
Chatsworth Rd
BRAM/HZG SK7........185 G3
DROY M43.............117 F3
ECC M30.............111 C1
GTN M18.............130 B3
MPL/ROM SK6.........197 E1
RAD M26..............51 H4
STRET M32.............125 E5
WALK M28.............80 A5
WILM/AE SK9...........200 B1
Chatsworth St *OLDE* OL4.......92 B2
WHIT OL12..............10 B5
Chattenden St
NEWH/MOS M40.........89 C5
Chatterton Cl *DID/WITH* M20..143 E5
Chattock St *OLDTF/WHR* M16..127 H1
Chatton Cl *TOT/BURYW* BL8....37 E5
Chatwood Rd
NEWH/MOS M40.........89 C5
Chaucer Av *DROY* M43.......117 H4
DTN/ASHW M34.........147 E4
RDSH SK5.............144 D3
Chaucer Ms *STKP* SK1.......160 C5
Chaucer Pl *DUK* SK16.........118 D4
WGTN/LGST M12........129 F4
Chaucer Rd *MDTN* M24........73 E2
Chaucer St *BOL* BL1............33 C5
OLDS OL8................9 F4
ROCH OL11..............43 E2
Chaucer Wk *BRUN/LGST* M13..128 D2
Chauncy Rd *NEWH/MOS* M40..104 D2
Chaytor Av *NEWH/MOS* M40..104 A3
Cheadle Av *BRO* M7..........100 D3
Cheadle Old Rd
EDGY/DAV SK3 *.......171 C2
Cheadle Pl *CHD/CHDH* SK8 *..171 E4
Cheadle Point *CHD/CHDH* SK8..170 C3
Cheadle Rd *CHD/CHDH* SK8...170 B5
Cheadle Sq *BOL* BL1............2 D5
Cheadle St *OP/CLY* M11......116 D5
Cheam Wd *CHD/CHDH* SK8...182 B4
Cheap Side *MDTN* M24.........72 D2
Cheapside *CMANW* M2...........6 E4

OLD OL1..................9 F3
Cheapside Sq *BOL* BL1 *........2 E5
Cheddar St *GTN* M18.........130 C5
Cheddington Cl
CHD/CHDH SK8..........182 D5
Chedlee Dr *CHD/CHDH* SK8....182 B3
Chedlin Dr *NTHM/RTH* M23...167 H5
Chedworth Crs *LHULT* M38.....81 F1
Chedworth Dr
NTHM/RTH M23.........168 A3
Chedworth Gv *BOLS/LL* BL3 *..48 D4
Cheeryble St *DROY* M43......117 C5
Cheetham Fold Rd
HYDE SK14.............147 H5
Cheetham Hill Rd *ANC* M4......7 F1
DUK SK16.............133 G2
Cheetham Pl *MPL/ROM* SK6...161 C2
Cheetham St *FAIL* M35.......105 F2
MILN OL16..............10 C5
NEWH/MOS M40 *.......103 F5
OLD OL1 *...............9 G4
RAD M26..............52 D5
ROY/SHW OL2............59 E5
Cheetwood Rd *CHH* M8......102 A5
Cheetwood St *BRO* M7........114 B1
Chelbourne Dr *OLDS* OL8......90 C5
Chelburn St *STLY* SK15.......121 G3
Chelford Av *BOL* BL1...........33 H1
Chelford Cl *HALE/TIMP* WA15..165 H3
MDTN M24..............73 F2
Chelford Dr *SWIN* M27........83 H5
Chelford Gv *EDGY/DAV* SK3...171 F4
Chelford Rd *OLDTF/WHR* M16..127 F5
SALE M33.............155 F4
WILM/AE SK9...........192 A2
Chellow Dene *MOSL* OL5.....108 C1
Chells St *BRUN/LGST* M13....129 G4
Chelmer Cl *WHTF* M45.........62 A3
Chelmer Gv *HEY* OL10..........40 B5
Chelmsford Av
NEWH/MOS M40.........116 C1
Chelmsford Rd *EDGY/DAV* SK3..8 E6
Chelmsford St *OLD* OL1........8 E6
Chelsea Av *RAD* M26..........51 C5
Chelsea Cl *ROY/SHW* OL2......60 A2
Chelsea Rd *BOLS/LL* BL3.......64 B1
NEWH/MOS M40.........104 B5
URM M41.............137 E2
Chelsea St *BURY* BL9..........53 C4
ROCH OL11..............57 E1
Chelsfield Gv *CCHDY* M21....141 H3
Chelston Av *NEWH/MOS* M40..89 C5
Chelston Dr *CHD/CHDH* SK8...182 B3
Cheltenham Crs *BRO* M7......101 H5
Cheltenham Dr *SALE* M33....154 D2
Cheltenham Gn *MDTN* M24....71 H1
Cheltenham Rd *CCHDY* M21...141 F1
EDGY/DAV SK3 *.......12 A4
MDTN M24..............88 D1
Cheltenham St *OLD* OL1........76 A3
ROCH OL11..............42 C2
SLFD M6.............113 F1
Chelwood Cl *BOL* BL1...........34 A1
Chelwood Dr *DROY* M43......117 C3
Chelwood Ms *HOR/BR* BL6 *....46 C2
Chendre Rd *BKLY* M9..........89 E4
Cheney Cl *OP/CLY* M11 *......130 C1
Chepstow Av *SALE* M33......153 F3
Chepstow Cl *ROCH* OL11.......28 C5
Chepstow Dr *BRAM/HZG* SK7..185 H2
OLD OL1................76 A3
Chepstow Rd *CCHDY* M21....141 H1
SWIN M27..............84 B5
Chepstow St South
CMANE M1 *.............6 E7
Chequers Rd *CCHDY* M21....141 H4
Cherington Cl
NTHM/RTH M23.........156 A4
WILM/AE SK9...........192 C4
Cherington Rd
CHD/CHDH SK8..........169 H5
Cheriton Av *SALE* M33......154 D1
Cheriton Cl *HYDE* SK14.......149 F1
Cheriton Dr *BOLE* BL2..........50 D3
Cheriton Ri *OFTN* SK2........173 H5
Cheriton Rd *URM* M41........137 F1
Cherrington Dr *ROCH* OL11....57 C1
Cherry Av *AUL* OL6..........106 D5
BURY BL9................8 B3
OLDS OL8................92 B4
Cherry Cl *BURY* BL9.........173 F2
OFTN SK2.............173 F2
Cherrycroft *MPL/ROM* SK6...162 D5
Cherry Dr *SWIN* M27..........99 H1
Cherry Gv *ROCH* OL11.........28 C3
ROY/SHW OL2............59 E5
STLY SK15.............120 D5
Cherry Hall Dr *ROY/SHW* OL2..59 F2
Cherry Hinton *OLD* OL1 *......75 H4
Cherry Holt Av *HTNM* SK4....158 C2
Cherry La *SALE* M33.........153 F4
Cherry Orchard Cl
BRAM/HZG SK7........183 G3
Cherry St *PWCH* M25..........86 B2
Cherry Tree Av *FWTH* BL4......66 A5
POY/DIS SK12.........195 G4
Cherry Tree Cl
HALE/TIMP WA15.......166 C4
MPL/ROM SK6.........174 D4
WILM/AE SK9...........199 H2
Cherry Tree Dr
BRAM/HZG SK7........185 H4
Cherry Tree La *MPL/ROM* SK6..162 D4
OFTN SK2.............172 D4
TOT/BURYW BL8..........37 H5
Cherry Tree Rd
CHD/CHDH SK8..........182 C5
NTHM/RTH M23.........167 G3
Cherry Tree Wk *STRET* M32...139 H2
Cherry Tree Wd *BOL* BL1.......34 D1
Cherry Wk *CHD/CHDH* SK8...183 F4
Cherrywood *CHAD* OL9.........73 D5

Cherrywood Av WHTN BL5 ....63 H5
Cherrywood Cl WALK M28........96 C2
Chertsey Cl GTN M18............130 D3
ROY/SHW OL2 ....60 A1
Chervil Cl RUSH/FAL M14....142 D2
Chervil Cl RUSH/FAL M14....143 E3
Cherwell Av HEY OL10.............40 B3
Cherwell Cl CHD/CHDH SK8....182 D5
OLDS OL8............................105 H1
WHTF M45............................69 H4
Cherwell Rd WHTN BL5............62 A2
Chesham Av BOL BL1................33 H4
ROCH OL11............................57 G2
URM M41.............................128 B2
WYTH/NTH M22....................168 B5
Chesham Cl WILM/AE SK9.......200 C1
Chesham Crs BURY BL9...............5 H2
Chesham Fold Rd BURY BL9.......5 K2
Chesham Pl ALT WA14............177 F2
Chesham Rd BURY BL9..............39 E1
ECC M30 *............................110 D5
OLDE OL4..............................92 B1
WILM/AE SK9.......................200 C1
Cheshire Cl STRET M32..........119 F2
Cheshire Ct RAMS BL0..............17 E2
Cheshire Ring Canal Wk
ALT WA14............................177 H5
MPL/ROM SK6.....................147 F5
MPL/ROM SK6.....................162 D5
POY/DIS SK12......................196 C3
Cheshire Rd PART M31...........150 C4
Cheshire Sq STLY SK15...........109 F5
The Cheshires MOSL OL5..........15 F4
Cheshire St MOSL OL5............109 E2
Chesney Av CHAD OL9..............89 H5
Chesshyre Av ANC M4.............115 G4
Chessington Ri SWIN M27.........84 B4
Chester Av BOLS/LL BL3...........51 E5
DUK SK16............................133 H1
HALE/TIMP WA15................178 A2
ROCH OL11............................28 D3
SALE M33............................155 E5
STLY SK15............................121 G2
URM M41.............................124 D5
WHTF M45............................69 H5
Chester Cl BOLS/LL BL3...........51 E5
IRL M44..............................150 C1
WILM/AE SK9.......................199 H1
Chester Dr RAMS BL0...............16 B4
Chesterfield Gv AUL OL6..........120 A2
Chesterfield St OLDE OL4.........92 A1
Chestergate EDGY/DAV SK3......12 E4
Chester Hill Rd BURY BL9.........13 F3
STKP SK1.............................13 F3
Chester Rd BRAM/HZG SK7....195 G5
HULME M15.........................127 H1
OLDTF/WHR M16..................127 F3
POY/DIS SK12......................185 E5
POY/DIS SK12......................194 C3
STRET M32............................140 A3
Chester St BURY BL9................38 D2
CHAD OL9...............................8 A2
DTN/ASHW M34...................146 D1
EDGY/DAV SK3......................12 C4
HULME M15.........................128 A1
PWCH M25.............................85 H2
SWIN M27.............................86 D5
Chesterton Dr BOLS/LL BL3......47 F4
Chesterton Gv DROY M43.........117 H3
Chesterton Rd
NTHM/RTH M23...................167 E1
Chester Wk BOL BL1.................33 H4
Chester Wks MPL/ROM SK6....161 H5
Chestnut Av BURY BL9...............5 J4
CCHDY M21.........................141 F3
CHD/CHDH SK8...................170 B4
DROY M43...........................117 F2
IRL M44..............................150 C1
TOT/BURYW BL8....................37 F1
WALK M28.............................82 A5
WHTF M45............................69 G5
Chestnut Cl BOLS/LL BL3..........48 A5
OLDE OL4..............................76 C4
STLY SK15............................120 D5
WILM/AE SK9.......................199 H2
Chestnut Crs OLDS OL8............91 H5
Chestnut Dr BURY BL9..............27 G4
POY/DIS SK12......................195 G3
SALE M33............................153 G5
WHTN BL5.............................62 A5
Chestnut Fold RAD M26............52 B5
Chestnut Gdns
DTN/ASHW M34...................146 C1
HEY OL10..............................40 D5
Chestnut Gv FAIL M35............105 E4
RAD M26..............................51 H5
Chestnut Rd ECC M30............110 B1
Chestnut St CHAD OL9..............90 B4
Chesworth Av LIT OL15.............13 C5
Chesworth Cl STKP SK1............13 G5
Chesworth Fold STKP SK1.........13 G6
Chetham Cl ORD M5 *..............127 E1
Chetwyn Av EDGW/EG BL7........23 F4
Chetwynd Av URM M41............138 C2
Chetwynd Cl SALE M33...........139 E5
Chevassut St HULME M15........127 H2
Chevington Dr HEY OL10.........103 E4
HTNM SK4............................158 A5
Cheviot Av CHD/CHDH SK8....182 C2
OLDS OL8..............................91 F4
ROY/SHW OL2........................74 D1
Cheviot Cl BOL BL1...................33 G3
CHAD OL9..............................90 A4
HTNM SK4............................159 G3
MDTN M24............................73 G4
MILN OL16............................31 H5
RAMS BL0..............................112 D2
SLFD M6...............................112 B4
TOT/BURYW BL8.....................37 F3
Cheviot Rd BRAM/HZG SK7....184 C3
Cheviots Rd ROY/SHW OL2........59 H1
Cheviot St CSLFD M3...............114 C2
Chevithorne Cl ALT WA14.......165 G4
Chevril Cl HULME M15............128 B2
Chevron Cl ROCH OL11............42 A3
SLFD M6...............................113 G3
Chevron Pl ALT WA14.............165 G2
Chew Brook Dr UPML OL3.........95 E2
Chew Moor La WHTN BL5.........62 B2

Chew V DUK SK16...................134 A1
UPML OL3...............................95 E2
Chew Valley Rd UPML OL3........95 G3
Chicago Av MANAIR M90........180 A5
Chichester Cl LIT OL15.............20 C5
Chichester Ct LIT OL15 *..........20 C5
SALE M33............................155 C3
Chichester Crs CHAD OL9..........74 B3
Chichester Rd South
HULME M15 *......................127 H3
Chichester St MILN OL16..........11 G7
Chidlow Av DID/WITH M20.....142 C4
Chidwall Rd WYTH/NTH M22...180 A2
Chief St OLDE OL4......................9 K5
Chiffon Wy CSLFD M3.............114 A2
Chigwell Cl WYTH/NTH M22...168 D4
Chilcote Av SALE M33.............153 H2
Childwall Cl BOLS/LL BL3..........64 D2
Chilham Rd ECC M30..............111 G1
WALK M28.............................82 B5
Chilham St BOLS/LL BL3...........64 A2
SWIN M27.............................98 D4
Chilmark Dr NTHM/RTH M23...167 H3
Chiltern Av URM M41.............123 E5
Chiltern Cl BRAM/HZG SK7....184 C5
RAMS BL0..............................16 D4
ROY/SHW OL2........................59 G1
WALK M28.............................97 F2
Chiltern Dr BOLE BL2...............34 C5
HALE/TIMP WA15................178 A2
OFTN SK2.............................172 B5
ROY/SHW OL2........................58 D5
SWIN M27.............................99 E4
TOT/BURYW BL8.....................37 G2
Chiltern Gdns SALE M33.........166 D1
Chiltern Rd RAMS BL0..............16 D4
Chilton Av CHAD OL9...............90 B1
Chilton Dr MDTN M24..............73 F5
Chilworth St RUSH/FAL M14...142 D1
Chime Bank CHH M8...............102 D5
Chimes Ct OLDE OL4.................93 G2
China La BOL BL1......................2 E1
CMANE M1..............................7 H5
Chingford Wk
BRUN/LGST M13 *...............129 G4
Chinley Av NEWH/MOS M40...103 H2
STRET M32...........................125 F4
Chinley Cl BRAM/HZG SK7......183 H1
HTNM SK4............................159 E3
SALE M33............................155 E3
Chinley St SLFD M6...................99 F5
Chinwell Vw BNG/LEV M19 *...144 A2
Chip Hill Rd BOLS/LL BL3..........47 H5
Chippendale Pl AUL OL6..........107 H5
Chippenham Av OFTN SK2.......172 D2
Chippenham Ct ANC M4...........115 F3
Chippenham Rd ANC M4..........115 F3
Chipping Fold MILN OL16..........44 C1
Chipping Rd BOL BL1................32 C4
Chipstead Av
WGTN/LGST M12..................129 F3
Chirmside St TOT/BURYW BL8...37 G5
Chiselden Av WYTH/NTH M22..180 D2
Chiselhurst St CHH M8............102 B3
Chisholme Cl TOT/BURYW BL8...26 A1
Chisholm St OP/CLY M11.........130 C1
Chisledon Av BRO M7 *...........102 A4
Chislehurst Av URM M41.........124 C5
Chislehurst Cl TOT/BURYW BL8...37 G5
Chiswick Dr RAD M26...............51 E4
Chiswick Rd DID/WITH M20.....157 H5
Chisworth Cl BRAM/HZG SK7....34 C3
Chisworth St BOLE BL2.............34 A5
Choir St BRO M7.....................114 B1
Chokeberry Cl ALT WA14 *.......165 G1
Cholmondeley Av ALT WA14 *...165 H1
Cholmondeley Rd SALE M33....112 A1
Chomlea Mnr SLFD M6 *...........112 B1
Choral Gv BRO M7..................101 G5
Chorley Cl TOT/BURYW BL8.......37 E5
Chorley Hall Cl WILM/AE SK9...200 C4
Chorley Hall La
WILM/AE SK9.......................200 D4
HOR/BR BL6...........................46 B1
Chorley New Rd BOL BL1..........47 F2
Chorley Old Rd BOL BL1..............2 A2
Chorley Rd SALE M33..............155 F4
SWIN M27...............................98 C1
Chorley St BOL BL1.....................2 C3
STRET M32...........................126 C3
Chorley Wood Av
BNG/LEV M19 *....................143 H5
Chorlton Dr CHD/CHDH SK8...170 B3
Chorlton Fold ECC M30..............98 C5
Chorlton Gn STKP SK1............172 C2
Chorlton Pl CHORLTON *..........141 F2
Chorlton Rd HULME M15.........127 H2
Chorlton St CMANE M1...............7 G5
OLDTF/WHR M16..................127 F3
Chorlton Ter
BRUN/LGST M13 *...............128 C2
Chretien Rd WYTH/NTH M22...156 D4
Christchurch Av ORD M5.........113 G3
Christ Church Cl BOLE BL2 *......35 G3
Christ Church La BOLE BL2 *.....35 G4
Christchurch Rd SALE M33......153 F1
Christie Rd STRET M32............140 C1
Christie St STKP SK1.................13 K7
Christine St ROY/SHW OL2........60 A2
Christleton Av HTNM SK4........159 G3
Christopher Acre ROCH OL11....28 B2
Christopher St
NEWH/MOS M40..................117 E1
ORD M5...............................113 H4
Chronnell Dr BOLE BL2.............50 B1
Chudleigh Cl ALT WA14..........165 E5
BRAM/HZG SK7....................184 B1
Chudleigh Rd CHH M8...............87 F5
Chulsey Gate La HOR/BR BL6....46 A3
Chulsey St BOLS/LL BL3............64 A1
Church Av BOLS/LL BL3.............48 B5
DTN/ASHW M34...................131 H5
HYDE SK14............................148 B3
MDTN M24..............................72 C4
NEWH/MOS M40..................104 B3
SLFD M6...............................112 A1
Church St East OLDE OL4..........76 D4
RAD M26..............................52 D5
Church Ter MILN OL16..............44 D1
OLD OL1..................................9 G3

Church Brow ALT WA14...........177 E2
HYDE SK14............................147 H2
HYDE SK14............................147 H2
Church Ct RAD M26...................61 G5
RAMS BL0..............................16 C3
WILM/AE SK9.......................192 A4
Church Ct BURY BL9 *.............119 G4
DUK SK16............................119 G4
Church Cft BURY BL9................46 A4
Churchdale Rd BKLY M9............87 G3
Church Dr PWCH M25...............85 G3
Churchfield Rd SLFD M6..........100 A5
Churchfields ALT WA14............177 E3
DTN/ASHW M34...................132 B1
SALE M33............................153 H3
Churchfield Wk
OP/CLY M11 *......................116 B5
Churchgate BOL BL1....................3 F4
STKP SK1.............................13 G3
URM M41.............................139 E2
Churchgate Buildings
CMANE M1..............................7 K6
Church Gn RAD M26..................53 E5
SLFD M6...............................113 G2
Church Gv BRAM/HZG SK7......185 F2
Churchill Av BOLE BL2...............36 C5
Churchill Cl HEY OL10..............56 B1
Churchill Crs MPL/ROM SK6...174 C2
RDSH SK5.............................145 G3
Churchill Dr BOLS/LL BL3.........67 F1
Churchill Rd ALT WA14............165 G2
Churchill St BOLE BL2................49 H2
HTNM SK4..............................9 J5
OLDE OL4................................9 J5
WHIT OL12.............................29 F2
Churchill St East OLDE OL4........9 K5
Churchill Wy SLFD M6.............113 F3
TRPK M17............................125 E1
Church La BKLY M9..................103 F3
BNG/LEV M19.......................143 H5
BRAM/HZG SK7....................193 F5
BRO M7..................................101 F4
MILN OL16..............................10 C7
MOSL OL5..............................94 A2
MPL/ROM SK6.....................162 B4
MPL/ROM SK6.....................174 D3
NEWH/MOS M40....................89 E5
OLD OL1..................................9 G3
PWCH M25.............................85 H4
SALE M33............................139 E5
UPML OL3..............................79 G3
WHTF M45............................69 H4
WILM/AE SK9.......................200 D5
Churchley Cl EDGY/DAV SK3...170 D3
Churchley Rd EDGY/DAV SK3...170 D2
Church Meadow BURY BL9.........54 B5
HYDE SK14............................133 H5
MILN OL16..............................9 K6
Church Mdw BOLE BL2..............35 G3
Church Ms
DTN/ASHW M34...................132 B5
Church Rd BKLY M9...................33 E4
CHD/CHDH SK8...................169 F4
CHD/CHDH SK8...................170 D3
FWTH BL4...............................66 B4
HALE SK14..............................12 D1
MDTN M24..............................73 G5
MILN OL16..............................30 C5
NEWH/MOS M40....................90 C3
ROY/SHW OL2........................60 A3
SALE M33............................155 E2
UPML OL3..............................79 F4
UPML OL3..............................95 E4
URM M41.............................138 A3
URM M41.............................138 D2
WALK M28.............................82 A4
WILM/AE SK9.......................192 A4
WYTH/NTH M22...................156 D5
Church Rd East SALE M33.......154 D2
Church Rd West
SALE M33............................154 D2
Churchside FWTH BL4...............65 G5
Church Side BKLY M9................88 A5
Church Stile MILN OL16............10 C7
Churchston Av
BRAM/HZG SK7....................184 B2
Church St ALT WA14...............165 G4
ANC M4....................................7 G3
AUL OL6................................120 B1
BOLE BL2................................35 E1
BOLE BL2................................36 C5
BOLS/LL BL3...........................66 C1
BURY BL9.................................5 G5
DTN/ASHW M54 *.................132 C1
DUK SK16............................119 G5
ECC M30...............................111 F3
FAIL M35..............................105 F2
HEY OL10..............................41 E4
HTNM SK4............................159 H3
HYDE SK14............................147 H2
LIT OL15.................................21 E3
MDTN M24 *...........................72 C4
MILN OL16..............................20 A5
MILN OL16..............................45 E2
MPL/ROM SK6.....................161 H1
MPL/ROM SK6.....................175 E4
OLDE OL4................................92 D2
RAD M26................................68 C2
RAMS BL0..............................16 D2
ROY/SHW OL2........................59 E5
STLY SK15............................120 D3
STRET M32...........................140 A1
SWIN M27...............................98 D2
SWIN M27...............................99 G2
TOT/BURYW BL8.....................37 E1
WHIT OL12............................10 A7
WILM/AE SK9.......................198 E3
WILM/AE SK9.......................199 E3

SALE M33 *...........................139 G5
WILM/AE SK9.......................192 A3
Churchtown Av BOLE BL2.........50 C2
Church Vw HYDE SK14............133 H5
IRL M44..................................28 B1
WHIT OL12.............................28 B1
Church Wk ALT WA14.............165 G4
FWTH BL4...............................65 H4
STLY SK15............................120 D2
SWIN M27...............................84 A3
TOT/BURYW BL8 *...................25 G2
Churchwood Rd
DID/WITH M20....................157 G3
Churnet St NEWH/MOS M40...103 E5
Churnett Cl WHTN BL5..............62 A2
Churning Ter IRL M44..............122 C5
Churston Av BKLY M9................88 B3
Churton Av SALE M33.............153 H5
Churton Rd GTN M18..............130 B3
Churwell Av HTNM SK4...........158 C2
Cicero St BKLY M9 *..................103 F2
OLD OL1..................................9 H1
Cinamon St WHIT OL12.............29 G3
Cinder Hill La OLD OL1..............74 B1
Cinder St ANC M4.......................7 K2
Cinnabar Dr MDTN M24.............72 C2
Cinnamon Cl WYTH/NTH M22..168 D1
Cipher St ANC M4........................7 K1
Circle South TRPK M17............126 B2
The Circuit CHD/CHDH SK8....182 D1
DID/WITH M20....................157 G5
EDGY/DAV SK3....................171 F3
WILM/AE SK9.......................198 A5
Circular Rd DID/WITH M20......157 G1
DTN/ASHW M34...................146 C2
PWCH M25.............................101 E1
Circus St CMANE M1 *................7 H5
Cirencester Cl LHULT M38.........81 F1
Ciss La URM M41....................139 E1
Citrus Wy SLFD M6.................113 F5
City Av DTN/ASHW M34 *.......146 C1
City Gdns DTN/ASHW M34 *...146 C1
City Rd HULME M15.................127 G2
WALK M28.............................80 D5
City Rd East HULME M15.........128 A1
City Wk SWIN M27....................99 G1
Clacton Wk BRUN/LGST M13 *..128 D2
Clague St OP/CLY M11............116 A4
Claife Av NEWH/MOS M40........89 E5
Clammerclough Rd FWTH BL4...66 A2
Clandon Av ECC M30...............110 C3
Clapgate MPL/ROM SK6..........161 H5
Clapgate Rd ROCH OL11...........28 B2
Clapham St NEWH/MOS M40...104 B2
Clara Gorton Ct MILN OL16 *.....90 C5
Clara St CHAD OL9...................90 C5
ROCH OL11............................43 E1
WHIT OL12.............................10 A5
Clare Av WILM/AE SK9............191 H4
Clarebank BOL BL1....................47 G2
Clare Cl TOT/BURYW BL8..........38 A1
Claremont Av ALT WA14.........165 G1
HTNM SK4............................159 F1
MPL/ROM SK6.....................174 B3
Claremont Ct BOL BL1 *............35 H5
Claremont Dr ALT WA14 *.......165 H1
LHULT M38.............................81 E2
Claremont Gdns AUL OL6........120 B1
Claremont Gv
HALE/TIMP WA15................177 H1
Claremont Range GTN M18 *...131 E4
Claremont Rd
CHD/CHDH SK8...................182 D4
MILN OL16..............................44 C1
OFTN SK2.............................172 C5
OLDTF/WHR M16..................127 F3
ROCH OL11............................29 F4
SALE M33............................154 C1
SLFD M6...............................112 B1
Claremont St AUL OL6.............120 A1
CHAD OL9...............................74 D3
FAIL M35..............................105 E2
OLDS OL8..............................99 H4
SLFD M6.................................99 H4
Clarence Av AUL OL6..............119 G3
OLDS OL8.............................143 E3
TRPK M17............................125 E2
WHTF M45............................69 H5
OLDE OL4..............................92 B1
Clarence Ct BOL BL1 *................2 C3
Clarence Rd AUL OL6...............119 G3
BRUN/LGST M13...................129 F5
HALE/TIMP WA15................177 H1
HTNM SK4............................159 E1
SWIN M27...............................98 B3
Clarence St BOL BL1...................2 C3
BRO M7................................114 A1
FWTH BL4...............................66 B3
HYDE SK14............................133 H4
ROY/SHW OL2........................75 H1
STLY SK15............................120 D4
WHIT OL12.............................29 G1
Clarendon Av
HALE/TIMP WA15................165 H4
HTNM SK4............................159 E3
Clarendon Cottages
WILM/AE SK9 *....................191 F4
Clarendon Crs ECC M30...........111 G2
SALE M33............................155 E1
Clarendon Pl HYDE SK14.........148 A1
Clarendon Rd BOLE BL2............49 H2
BRAM/HZG SK7....................185 G5
DTN/ASHW M34...................131 H3
ECC M30...............................111 G2
HYDE SK14............................148 A1
IRL M44..............................136 A4
OLDTF/WHR M16..................141 G1
SALE M33............................155 E2
SWIN M27...............................98 B3
URM M41.............................123 H5
Clarendon Rd West
CCHDY M21.........................141 F4
Clarendon St BOLS/LL BL3........48 D5
BURY BL9.................................5 G1

DUK SK16............................119 G5
HULME M15.........................128 A2
HYDE SK14............................43 C2
MOSL OL5...........................109 E2
RDSH SK5.............................160 A3
WHTF M45............................69 G4
Clare Rd BNG/LEV M19...........144 A3
RDSH SK5 *.........................160 A2
Clare St CMANE M1.................128 C1
DTN/ASHW M34...................132 B4
ORD M5................................113 H4
Claribel St OP/CLY M11...........115 H5
Claridge Rd CCHDY M21..........141 E2
Clarion St ANC M4.......................7 J3
Clark Av GTN M18...................130 D3
Clarke Av ORD M5...................127 E1
Clarke Brow MDTN M24............72 D3
Clarke Crs HALE/TIMP WA15...178 C1
LHULT M38.............................81 E2
Clarkes Cft BURY BL9................39 F3
Clarke's La LHULT M38..............29 C3
Clarke St AULW OL7 *.............119 E5
BOL BL1.................................48 B1
HEY OL10..............................11 G1
Clarksfield Rd OLDE OL4...........92 B1
Clarksfield St OLDE OL4............92 C1
Clark's Hi PWCH M25................85 H3
Clarkson Cl DTN/ASHW M34....146 C1
Clark Wy HYDE SK14...............133 C5
Clarkwell Cl OLD OL1..................8 E1
Claude Av SWIN M27.................98 C2
Claude Rd CCHDY M21............141 E4
Claude St CHH M8...................102 B1
ECC M30...............................110 C1
SWIN M27...............................98 C2
Claudia Sq STLY SK15.............109 F5
Claughton Av BOLE BL2............50 C2
WALK M28.............................96 D2
Claughton Rd TOT/BURYW BL8...37 E1
Claverton Rd NTHM/RTH M23..167 E4
Claxton Av BKLY M9...................88 A4
Clay Bank DROY M43..............117 F4
Claybank Dr TOT/BURYW BL8...25 H4
Clay Bank St HEY OL10..............40 D3
Claybar Dr ECC M30...............111 F2
Claybrook Wy OP/CLY M11 *...116 B4
Claycourt Rd HULME M15........127 H2
Claycroft Av ECC M30..............110 C1
Claydon Dr RAD M26.................51 E4
Clayfield Dr ROCH OL11............28 C5
Claygate Dr BKLY M9.................88 A2
Clay La HALE/TIMP WA15........166 D5
NTHM/RTH M23...................167 G5
OLD OL1................................76 A3
WILM/AE SK9.......................191 H2
Claymere Av ROCH OL11...........28 B3
Claymore St BOLS/LL BL3.........65 E1
GTN M18.............................130 D2
Clay St EDGW/EG BL7...............23 F1
LIT OL15.................................20 C3
OLDS OL8..............................91 F3
Claythorpe Wk PWCH M25........86 D5
Clayton Av BOLE BL2.................49 G4
DID/WITH M20....................157 G3
Claytonbrook Rd
OP/CLY M11.........................116 D4
Clayton Cl HULME M15...........127 H3
TOT/BURYW BL8....................37 E5
Clayton Hall Rd OP/CLY M11...116 D3
Clayton La OP/CLY M11...........116 C5
Clayton La South
WGTN/LGST M12..................129 H1
Clayton St BOLE BL2.................49 H4
CHAD OL9...............................90 B4
DTN/ASHW M34...................146 D1
DUK SK16............................120 A5
FAIL M35..............................104 D3
OP/CLY M11.........................116 C2
WHIT OL12.............................11 G1
Cleabarrow Dr WALK M28........96 B3
Cleadon Av GTN M18...............130 B4
Cleadon Dr South
TOT/BURYW BL8.....................25 H4
Clearwater Dr DID/WITH M20..157 E1
Cleavley St ECC M30...............110 C1
Clee Av BRUN/LGST M13........143 H1
Cleethorpes Av BKLY M9...........87 G4
Cleeve Rd NTHM/RTH M23......155 H4
OLDE OL4..............................92 B1
Clegg Hall Rd MILN OL16..........31 E1
Clegg Pl AUL OL6...................120 A1
Clegg's Buildings BOL BL1 *.......81 F2
Clegg's La LHULT M38...............81 F2
Clegg St BOLE BL2.....................6 D3
DROY M43...........................117 G4
LIT OL15.................................20 C1
MILN OL16..............................44 D1
MPL/ROM SK6.....................161 G3
OLD OL1..................................9 H4
WHIT OL12.............................93 E3
WHTF M45............................69 G5
Cleggswood Av LIT OL15...........20 D5
Clelland St FWTH BL4................66 B5
Clement Ct MILN OL16 *............30 C5
Clementina St WHIT OL12.........10 C7
Clementine Cl SLFD M6...........113 C3
Clement Rd MPL/ROM SK6.....175 G2
Clement Royds St CSLFD M3 *....7 J1
Clement Stott Cl BKLY M9..........88 D5
Clement St HTNM SK4.............159 H3
Cleminson St CSLFD M3.............6 A3
Clemshaw Cl HEY OL10.............40 D5
Clerewood Av CHD/CHDH SK8..181 G5
Cleveley Br BURY BL9.................4 E4
Cleveland Av BNG/LEV M19.....144 B1
HYDE SK14............................147 G1
SLFD M6...............................112 A1
Cleveland Cl RAMS BL0...............16 C3
Cleveland Dr MILN OL16............31 H5
Cleveland Gdns BOLS/LL BL3....48 A5
Cleveland Gv ROY/SHW OL2.....74 D2
Cleveland Rd CHH M8................87 G5

HALE/TIMP WA15............178 A1
HTNM SK4........................158 D2
Cleveland St BOLS/LL BL3 *....48 A5
Cleveleys Av BOLE BL2..........49 H1
BURY BL9.........................53 F2
CCHDY M21.......................101 G4
CHD/CHDH SK8.................181 G5
MILN OL16........................43 G3
Cleveleys Gv DROY M43..........101 H3
Clevis Ct HEY OL10...............40 C5
Clevlands CI ROY/SHW OL2.......59 H1
Cleworth Rd MDTN M24...........72 C2
Cleworth St HULME M15..........127 C4
Cleworth Wk HULME M15 *.......127 C1
Clibran St CHH M8.................102 C4
Clifden Dr WYTH/NTH M22.......180 D2
Cliff Av BRO M7....................101 F4
BURY BL9.........................27 E1
TOT/BURYW BL8.................25 H4
Cliff Crs BRO M7...................101 F4
Cliff Dl STLY SK15................120 C5
Cliffdale Dr CHH M8...............102 B1
Cliff Hill Rd ROY/SHW OL2.......159 E2
Cliffmere CI CHD/CHDH SK8.....182 C1
Clifford Av DTN/ASHW M34.....158 E3
HALE/TIMP WA15................166 B3
Clifford Rd BOLS/LL BL3 *.......194 D3
POY/DIS SK12....................194 D3
WILM/AE SK9.....................198 C4
Clifford St ECC M30...............110 C5
ROCH OL11........................43 E4
SWIN M27..........................99 G2
Cliff Rd WILM/AE SK9.............199 E2
Cliff Side WILM/AE SK9...........199 E2
Cliff St MILN OL16................11 G2
Clifton Av CHD/CHDH SK8........181 F2
ECC M30...........................111 F2
HALE/TIMP WA15................165 H4
OLDE OL4 *........................92 A2
RUSH/FAL M14...................143 F3
Clifton CI HEY OL10...............40 D5
OLDE OL4 *........................92 A2
OLDTF/WHR M16.................127 G3
Clifton Ct FWTH BL4..............65 G2
Clifton Crs ROY/SHW OL2........75 H1
Clifton Dr CHD/CHDH SK8........166 E4
CHD/CHDH SK6...................181 E2
MPL/ROM SK6....................175 E2
SWIN M27..........................83 G5
WILM/AE SK9.....................200 D4
Clifton Gv OLDTF/WHR M16......127 G3
SWIN M27..........................83 G5
Clifton House Rd SWIN M27......83 H4
Clifton Park Rd OFTN SK2........172 B4
Clifton Pl PWCH M25..............85 H2
Clifton Rd CCHDY M21............141 G3
ECC M30............................111 F2
HTNM SK4.........................158 D2
MDTN M24.........................57 G3
PWCH M25.........................85 F3
SALE M33..........................154 C3
URM M41...........................138 A1
Clifton St AUL OL6................119 F2
BOL BL1............................2 C5
BURY BL9.........................38 C2
FAIL M35...........................105 F1
FWTH BL4..........................65 G2
FWTH BL4..........................66 C5
MILN OL16.........................31 C5
NEWH/MOS M40...............116 A1
OLDTF/WHR M16.................127 G3
ROCH OL11 *.....................43 F1
UPML OL3 *.......................79 E4
WILM/AE SK9....................200 D4
Clifton Vw SWIN M27..............83 H5
Cliftonville Dr SWIN M27.........99 G4
Cliftonville Rd MILN OL16........58 D1
Clinton Av RUSH/FAL M14.......142 C1
Clinton Gdns RUSH/FAL M14...142 C1
Clinton St AUL OL6 *.............121 G2
Clinton Wk OLDE OL4 *...........9 J5
Clippers Quay SALQ M50........126 D2
Clipsley Crs OLDE OL4............61 E5
Cliston Wk BRAM/HZG SK7.....184 D2
Clitheroe Cl HEY OL10............41 E3
Clitheroe Dr TOT/BURYW BL8....37 E4
Clitheroe Rd BRUN/LGST M13...129 G5
Clito St HEY OL10..................40 C5
Clive Av WHTF M45................69 E3
Clivedale Pl BOL BL1..............3 F5
Clively Av SWIN M27..............99 G1
Clive Rd FAIL M35.................104 D3
Clive St ANC M4...................7 H1
AULW OL7.........................106 D5
BOL BL1............................3 J4
OLDS OL8..........................91 E5
Clivia Gv BRO M7 *................101 G4
Clock House Av DROY M43......117 F2
Clockhouse Ms DROY M43 *.....117 F2
Clock St CHAD OL9................90 C5
Clock Tower CI SALE M33........148 A2
WALK M28..........................81 E4
Cloister CI DUK SK16.............133 F2
Cloister Rd HTNM SK4............158 D2
The Cloisters CHD/CHDH SK8....170 D4
MILN OL16.........................11 H2
SALE M33..........................155 E2
Cloister St BKLY M9..............103 G2
BOL BL1............................33 F4
Clopton Wk HULME M15..........127 H2
Closes Farm BOLS/LL BL3........64 A2
The Close ALT WA14...............165 H4
BOLE BL2............................34 C3
DTN/ASHW M34..................132 A4
MDTN M24.........................73 E1
MPL/ROM SK6....................163 G5
STLY SK15.........................121 E3
TOT/BURYW BL8.................26 D5
Clothorn Rd DID/WITH M20.....157 E3
Cloudstock Gv LHULT M38.......80 D2
Clough Av MPL/ROM SK6........175 H3
SALE M33..........................153 H3
WHTN BL5.........................62 A4
WILM/AE SK9....................191 G5
Clough Bank BKLY M9 *..........88 A5
Cloughbank RAD M26.............67 F5
Clough Dr PWCH M25.............85 E4
Clough End Rd HYDE SK14......149 H2
Cloughfield Av ORD M5...........113 G5

Cloughfold RAD M26..............67 E5
Clough Fold Rd HYDE SK14.....147 H2
Clough Ga HYDE SK14 *..........148 B3
OLDS OL8...........................91 E5
Clough Gv WHTF M45.............69 E2
Clough House La WHIT OL12......19 G2
Clough La HEY OL10...............40 D2
OLDE OL4 *........................94 B1
PWCH M25.........................85 G3
Clough Meadow BOL BL1.........47 E3
Clough Meadow Rd RAD M26....67 H1
Clough Park Av OLDE OL4.......94 B1
Clough Rd BKLY M9...............103 G2
DROY M43.........................118 A3
FAIL M35............................105 F3
MDTN M24.........................72 D2
ROY/SHW OL2....................60 C3
Cloughs Av CHAD OL9............73 G4
Clough Side MPL/ROM SK6.....175 H2
Clough St FWTH BL4..............66 C5
MDTN M24.........................73 E2
NEWH/MOS M40................116 D1
RAD M26............................68 D3
WHIT OL12.........................19 H2
Clough Ter LIT OL15 *............20 D1
The Clough AULW OL7............106 D4
BOL BL1 *...........................47 F1
RDSH SK5.........................145 H5
Clough Top Rd BKLY M9.........88 D5
Clovelly Av OLDS OL8.............90 D5
Clovelly Rd CCHDY M21..........141 H4
OFTN SK2..........................172 D1
SWIN M27..........................98 B3
Clovelly St NEWH/MOS M40 *...104 C5
OLDS OL8..........................42 A3
Clover Av EDGY/DAV SK3........171 G5
Cloverbank Av BNG/LEV M19....158 A2
Clover Crs OLDE OL8.............92 B4
Clover Cft SALE M33..............155 E5
Cloverdale Sq BOL BL1..........32 D5
Clover Hall Crs MILN OL16......11 K3
Cloverley Dr
     HALE/TIMP WA15............166 B5
Clover Rd HALE/TIMP WA15....166 B4
     MPL/ROM SK6.................162 D3
Clover St NEWH/MOS M40 *....104 C5
Clover Vw MILN OL16.............11 H5
Clowes St CHAD OL9.............90 B5
     CSLFD M3........................6 C3
     WGTN/LGST M12............129 H2
Club St OP/CLY M11...............131 E1
Clumber Rd POY/DIS SK12......195 H4
Clumber Rd GTN M18.............131 E4
     POY/DIS SK12..................195 F4
Clunton Av BOLS/LL BL3.........48 A5
Clutha Rd EDGY/DAV SK3.......172 A5
Clwyd Av EDGY/DAV SK3........171 G2
Clyde Av WHTF M45...............85 C1
Clyde Ct MILN OL16...............30 C5
Clyde Rd DID/WITH M20.........157 E2
     EDGY/DAV SK3................12 B7
     RAD M26.........................52 A4
Clydesdale St OLDS OL8.........91 F5
Clyde St AULW OL7...............119 E4
     BOL BL1..........................33 H4
     OLD OL1...........................76 B3
Clyne Ter RAD M26 *..............52 A4
Clyne St STRET M32...............126 C3
Coach La ROCH OL11.............41 F1
Coalbrook Wk
     WGTN/LGST M12............115 G5
Coalburn St WGTN/LGST M12....129 H3
Coal Pit La OLDS OL8.............90 D5
Coalshaw Green Rd CHAD OL9....90 B4
Coatbridge St OP/CLY M11.......116 D4
Cobalt Av URM M41...............125 E2
Cobb Ci CHH M8...................86 D4
Cobbett's Wy WILM/AE SK9.....200 C1
Cobbie Bank BKLY M9............87 H4
Cobden St AUL OL6 *.............120 A3
     BKLY M9..........................103 F1
     BOL BL1............................33 C3
     BURY BL9.........................5 G4
     CHAD OL9........................74 C5
     EDGW/EG BL7 *...............22 C1
     HEY OL10..........................41 E5
     OLDE OL4.........................76 C3
     RAD M26..........................52 A5
     SLFD M6...........................113 G1
Coberley Av URM M41............123 G4
Cob Hall Rd STRET M32..........140 A2
Cobham Av BOLS/LL BL3.........64 C1
     NEWH/MOS M40...............89 F5
Cobourg St CMANE M1...........7 H4
Coburg Av BRO M7................85 C4
Cochrane Av WGTN/LGST M12....129 F3
Cochrane St BOLS/LL BL3........49 E4
Cock Brow HYDE SK14............149 E4
Cock Clod St RAD M26............68 D1
Cockcroft Rd ORD M5.............113 H5
Cockcroft St BKLY M9.............103 E1
Cockerell Springs BOLE BL2 *....3 L6
Cocker HI STLY SK15..............121 E3
Cocker La OLDE OL4..............94 C1
Cockers La STLY SK15............121 H5
Cocker St LHULT M38.............81 F1
Cockey Moor Rd BOLE BL2......36 C5
Cock Hall La WHIT OL12.........14 A1
Cockhall La WHIT OL12..........14 A4
Coconut Gv SLFD M6.............113 F5
Codale Dr BOLE BL2...............50 C1
Coddington Av OP/CLY M11......117 F5
Coe St BOLS/LL BL3...............49 E4
Coghlan CI OP/CLY M11..........116 C3
Cohen St ROY/SHW OL2.........59 H2
Colborne Av ECC M30.............110 C5
     MPL/ROM SK6..................162 A4
     RDSH SK5........................131 G5
Colbourne Av CHH M8............102 A1
Colbourne Gv HYDE SK14.......135 F5
Colbourne Wy BOLE BL2.........50 C1
Colchester Av NTHM/RTH M23...155 F1
Colchester Dr FWTH BL4.........65 E3
Colchester PI HTNM SK4.........159 F3
Colchester Wk OLD OL1..........9 C3
Colclough CI NEWH/MOS M40...104 A4
Coldfield Dr NTHM/RTH M23....167 G3
Cold Greave CI MILN OL16......45 F2
Coldhurst Dr OLD OL1...........75 F4

Coldstream Av BKLY M9..........88 A3
Colebrook Dr
     NEWH/MOS M40...............103 H4
Colebrook Rd
     HALE/TIMP WA15............166 B3
Coleby Av OLDTF/WHR M16.....127 F4
     WYTH/NTH M22...............181 E3
Coledale Dr MDTN M24...........71 H2
Coleford Gv BOL BL1..............2 C6
Colemore Av DID/WITH M20.....158 A3
Colenso Ct BOLE BL2 *...........49 H2
Colenso Gv HTNM SK4............159 E3
Colenso St OLDS OL8.............91 E4
Coleport CI CHD/CHDH SK8.....182 D1
Coleridge Av MDTN M24.........73 F1
     RAD M26.........................67 H1
Coleridge CI RDSH SK5..........145 C2
Coleridge Rd LIT OL15............31 G1
     OLD OL1..........................60 D5
     OLDTF/WHR M16.............127 F5
     RDSH SK5.......................145 E2
     TOT/BURYW BL8.............26 A1
Colesbourne CI LHULT M38.....81 F1
Coleshill St NEWH/MOS M40....115 H2
Cole St NEWH/MOS M40.........102 D5
Colgate Crs RUSH/FAL M14.....142 D2
Colgate La ORD M5...............126 D2
Colgrove Av NEWH/MOS M40....89 F5
Colina Dr BRO M7.................101 H5
Colindale Av BKLY M9............88 B3
Colindale CI BOLS/LL BL3 *......48 B4
Colin Murphy Rd HULME M15...127 H1
Colin Rd HTNM SK4................159 H2
Colinton CI BOL BL1...............33 C5
Colinwood CI BURY BL9..........69 G1
Coll Dr URM M41...................124 C3
Collard St OLDS OL8..............91 E4
College Av OLDS OL8..............91 H4
College CI BOLS/LL BL3...........2 D7
     OFTN SK2.........................172 C3
     WILM/AE SK9...................198 B2
College Dr OLDTF/WHR M16....141 G1
College Rd ECC M30...............91 E3
     OLDS OL8........................91 E3
     OLDTF/WHR M16..............141 H1
     WHIT OL12.......................29 G4
College Wy BOLS/LL BL3..........2 C7
Collegiate Wy SWIN M27.........84 D5
Collen Crs TOT/BURYW BL8....26 C5
Collett St OLD OL1.................76 B4
Colley St MILN OL16...............11 F3
     STRET M32.......................126 C3
Collier Av MILN OL16..............31 G4
Collier CI HYDE SK14.............149 C2
Collier HI OLDS OL8...............91 E4
Collier Hill Av OLDS OL8.........90 D4
Collier's Ct ROCH OL11...........43 G5
Colliers Row Rd BOL BL1.........32 A1
Collier St CSLFD M5...............6 C2
     CSLFD M3.........................6 A7
     SWIN M27.........................98 D3
Colliery St OP/CLY M11...........116 B4
Collin Av GTN M18.................130 D4
Collingburn Av ORD M5..........127 E1
Colling CI IRL M44.................136 C2
Collinge Av MDTN M24...........71 H2
Collinge St HEY OL10.............40 D4
     MDTN M24.......................73 G5
     ROY/SHW OL2 *...............60 A2
     TOT/BURYW BL8..............37 G2
Collingham St CHH M8...........114 D1
Colling St RAMS BL0 *............16 D1
Collington CI WGTN/LGST M12...129 H3
Collingwood Av DROY M43......117 F2
Collingwood CI POY/DIS SK12...195 H4
Collingwood Dr SWIN M27.......99 C4
Collingwood Rd
     BNG/LEV M19...................143 H2
     BNG/LEV M19 St ROCH OL11..57 F1
Collingwood Wy OLD OL1 *......75 G4
Collins St TOT/BURYW BL8......37 G2
Collins Wy CHAD OL9.............90 D4
Collop Dr HEY OL10...............56 B2
Collyhurst Av WALK M28.........82 B5
Collyhurst Rd
     NEWH/MOS M40...............115 E1
Collyhurst St
     NEWH/MOS M40...............127 E1
Colman Gdns ORD M5............127 E1
Colmore Dr BKLY M9..............88 D3
Colmore Gv BOLE BL2............34 C2
Colne Rd OLDS OL8...............34 C3
Colne St ROCH OL11..............43 C6
Colonial Rd OFTN SK2............172 B3
Colshaw Dr WILM/AE SK9.......199 C1
Colshaw Rd NTHM/RTH M23....167 H4
Colson Dr MDTN M24.............72 C5
Colt Hill La UPML OL3............78 D5
Coltsfoot Dr ALT WA14...........165 E1
Columbia Av OPCL M11..........117 G4
Columbia Rd BOL BL1.............48 B1
Columbia St OLDS OL8..........91 C3
Columbine CI WHIT OL12.........18 B5
Columbine St OP/CLY M11.......130 C1
Colville Gv HALE/TIMP WA15....166 D5
Colville Gv HALE/TIMP WA15....166 D5
     SALE M33........................153 H5
Colville Rd OLD OL1...............75 F3
Colwell Av STRET M32............139 H2
Colwick Av ALT WA14.............165 H3
Colwith Av BOLE BL2.............35 F5
Colwyn Av MDTN M24............88 D1
     RUSH/FAL M14.................158 A1
Colwyn Crs RDSH SK5............160 A1
Colwyn Rd BRAM/HZG SK7....182 B3
     CHD/CHDH SK8................182 B3
     SWIN M27.........................98 B4
Colwyn St CHAD OL9.............74 A4
     ROCH OL11......................42 A4
     SLFD M6...........................113 G2
Combe CI OP/CLY M11............116 C2
Combermere Av
     DID/WITH M20..................142 A4
Combermere CI
     CHD/CHDH SK8................170 C5
Combermere St DUK SK16......119 H4
Comer Ter SALE M33..............154 D2
Comet St CMANE M1...............7 J5
Commercial Av
     CHD/CHDH SK8................192 B2

Commercial Brow HYDE SK14...133 H4
Commercial Rd
     BRAM/HZG SK7................185 E1
Commercial St CHAD OL9.......8 B5
     HULME M15......................127 H1
     HYDE SK14.......................133 H3
Common La PART M31............151 H2
Common Side Rd WALK M28.....96 A3
Community St AULW OL7........119 E4
Como St BOLS/LL BL3 *..........48 E5
Compass Av CLSP M13...........130 A2
Compass St OP/CLY M11.........130 C1
Compstall Av RUSH/FAL M14...142 D2
Compstall Gv GTN M18............130 D2
Compstall Mills Est
     MPL/ROM SK6..................163 G4
Compstall Rd MPL/ROM SK6....162 C4
Compton CI URM M41.............137 E2
Compton Dr
     NTHM/RTH M23 *.............179 H2
Compton Fold ROY/SHW OL2....45 E5
Compton Wy MDTN M24.........73 F1
Comus St ORD M5.................113 H5
Concert La CMANW M2 *.........7 K6
Concord PI SLFD M6 *............100 D5
Concord Rd DTN/ASHW M34....118 B2
Condor PI SLFD M6................100 D5
Conduit St AUL OL6................119 H3
     OLD OL1...........................76 C1
Conewood Wk
     BRUN/LGST M13...............128 D2
Coney Gv NTHM/RTH M23.......167 H2
Coneymead STLY SK15...........120 D1
Congham Rd EDGY/DAV SK3....172 B1
Congleton Av RUSH/FAL M14...142 C1
Congleton CI RUSH/FAL M14....142 C1
Congleton St BRAM/HZG SK7....200 D5
Congou St CMANE M1.............7 K6
Congreave St OLD OL1............8 E1
Coningsby Dr BKLY M9............103 E2
Conisber CI EDGW/EG BL7......23 E2
Conisborough ROCH OL11 *.....29 H5
Conisborough PI WHTF M45....70 A5
Coniston BOL BL1 *...............34 A3
Coniston Av BKLY M9.............103 E2
     FWTH BL4..........................64 D5
     HALE/TIMP WA15.............133 F4
     LHULT M38.......................81 E3
     OLDS OL8..........................91 E4
     SALE M33..........................154 D4
     WHTF M45..........................69 G4
Coniston CI BOLS/LL BL3........74 E5
     CHAD OL9.........................90 B5
     DTN/ASHW M34................145 H1
     RAMS BL0 *......................16 D1
Coniston Dr BURY BL9...........53 F2
     CHD/CHDH SK8................169 C3
     MPL/ROM SK6.................186 D4
     PART M31........................150 D2
     RDSH SK5........................145 F5
     STRET M32.......................125 H5
     SWIN M27.........................99 E4
     URM M41.........................137 G3
Coniston Gv AULW OL7..........119 F1
     HEY OL10.........................56 A1
     LHULT M38.......................81 E3
     ROY/SHW OL2..................59 H2
Coniston Rd NEWH/MOS M40....88 D5
     SLFD M6...........................113 C1
Coniston Wk
     HALE/TIMP WA15.............167 E4
Conmere Sq HULME M15.........128 A1
Connaught Av BNG/LEV M19....143 H4
     MILN OL16........................43 G3
     WHTF M45.........................69 H5
Connaught CI WILM/AE SK9....199 F1
Connaught Sq BOLE BL2........34 C5
Connaught St BOLS/LL BL3......48 A4
     TOT/BURYW BL8...............37 G5
Connel CI BOLE BL2...............35 F5
Connell Rd NTHM/RTH M23.....167 H3
Connell Wy HEY OL10 *..........41 E4
Connery Crs AUL OL6.............107 G4
Connie St OP/CLY M11............116 D5
Connington Av EDGW/EG BL7....23 E3
Connington Av BKLY M9..........103 E1
Connington CI ROY/SHW OL2....58 C4
Connor Wy CHD/CHDH SK8....169 E5
Conrad CI OLD OL1................75 H4
Conran St BKLY M9................103 E3
Consett Av NTHM/RTH M23.....155 F2
Consort Av ROY/SHW OL2.......58 D3
Consort CI DUK SK16.............133 F2
Consort PI ALT WA14.............177 E1
Constable CI BOL BL1............175 G1
Constable Dr WILM/AE SK9.....199 H2
     WILM/AE SK9....................199 H2
Constable St GTN M18...........130 D2
Constance Gdns ORD M5 *.....113 H4
Constance Rd BOLS/LL BL3.....48 B4
     PART M31.........................151 E3
Constance St
     HULME M15......................127 H1
Constantine Rd MILN OL16.....10 D6
Constantine St OLDE OL4.......92 A2
Constantine St WYTH/NTH M22..156 D5
Convamore Rd
     BRAM/HZG SK7................195 G1
Convent Gv ROCH OL11.........42 C4
Convent St OLDE OL4.............92 B5
Conway Av BOL BL1...............34 B2
     IRL M44............................136 B3
     SWIN M27.........................84 C5
     WHTF M45.........................69 G5
Conway CI HEY OL10..............40 D3
     MDTN M24........................72 D5
     OLDTF/WHR M16 *............126 D5
     RAMS BL0..........................26 D1
Conway Crs TOT/BURYW BL8....37 E1
Conway Dr BRAM/HZG SK7.....184 D3
     BURY BL9...........................39 G4
     HALE/TIMP WA15..............166 D3
     STLY SK15.........................120 D3
Conway Gv CHAD OL9............74 A4
Conway Rd CHD/CHDH SK8....182 B2
     SALE M33..........................155 G3

URM M41............................124 C4
     RAD M26...........................66 A5
Conway St FWTH BL4.............66 B5
     RDSH SK5.........................159 H2
Conyngham Rd
     RUSH/FAL M14................129 C4
Cooke St BRAM/HZG SK7........185 E1
     DTN/ASHW M34................132 C5
     FAIL M35..........................105 E2
     FWTH BL4..........................66 B5
     HYDE SK14 *....................133 H3
Cook St BURY BL9.................5 F5
     CSLFD M3.........................6 B3
     DTN/ASHW M34................132 C2
     ECC M30...........................110 D3
     EDGY/DAV SK3.................12 C2
     MILN OL16.........................11 G2
     OLDE OL4..........................76 D5
Cook Ter MILN OL16...............11 C2
Coomassie St HEY OL10.........40 B8
     RAD M26............................68 B1
Coombes Av HYDE SK14.........148 D2
     MPL/ROM SK6...................175 E4
Coombes St OFTN SK2............172 C4
Coombes Vw HYDE SK14........149 H3
Co-operation St FAIL M35.......105 E3
Co-operative St
     BRAM/HZG SK7................185 F1
     LHULT M38........................80 D2
     OLDE OL4..........................93 E1
     RAD M26............................52 A5
     SLFD M6...........................113 E3
     UPML OL3 *.......................79 E4
Cooper Fold MDTN M24.........56 D5
Cooper La BKLY M9...............88 A2
     MDTN M24........................56 D5
Cooper St BRAM/HZG SK7.....185 G1
     BURY BL9...........................4 D4
     CMANW M2........................6 E5
     DROY M43.........................117 F4
     DUK SK16..........................119 G3
     STRET M32.........................13 H7
     OLDE OL4..........................77 F5
     STRET M32........................140 B2
     WHIT OL12.........................20 A4
Coopers Wk MILN OL16...........30 D1
Cooper Ter MILN OL16............11 G4
Coop St ANC M4....................7 H2
     BOL BL1............................33 H2
Copage Dr MPL/ROM SK6.......161 G2
Cope Bank BOL BL1...............33 F5
Cope Bank West BOL BL1 *.....3 F4
Cope CI OP/CLY M11..............130 D1
Copeland Av SWIN M27..........99 H1
Copeland CI MDTN M24..........71 H3
Copeland Ms BOL BL1............47 H2
Copeland St HYDE SK14..........133 H5
Copeman CI BRUN/LGST M13...128 D2
Copenhagen Sq MILN OL16 *....11 F5
     NEWH/MOS M40................103 H4
Cope St BOL BL1...................33 F5
Copgrove Rd CCHDY M21.......141 G4
Copley Av STLY SK15..............121 F3
Copley Park Ms STLY SK15......121 F3
Copley Rd CCHDY M21............141 E1
Copley St ROY/SHW OL2.........60 A1
Copperas La DROY M43..........117 F5
Copperas St ANC M4..............7 G3
Copperbeech CI
     WYTH/NTH M22................156 D5
Copper Beech Dr STLY SK15....121 G2
Copperfield Cl ALT WA14 *......177 F1
Copperfield Rd
     CHD/CHDH SK8................193 G2
     POY/DIS SK12...................195 E5
Copperfields HOR/BR BL6.......62 C1
Copper La WHTF M45.............68 C5
Coppice Av POY/DIS SK12......197 F1
     SALE M33..........................153 G4
Coppice CI HOR/BR BL6..........62 C1
     MPL/ROM SK6...................162 A2
Coppice Ct CHD/CHDH SK8.....181 G4
Coppice Dr WHIT OL12............18 E1
     WYTH/NTH M22................156 C5
Coppice La POY/DIS SK12.......197 F1
Coppice Rd POY/DIS SK12......196 A4
Coppice St OLDS OL8.............8 C6
The Coppice BKLY M9.............88 D5
     BOLE BL2..........................35 E1
     HALE/TIMP WA15..............178 C4
     PWCH M25.........................85 H3
     ROCH OL11........................42 D4
     WALK M28.........................97 G2
     WHTF M45..........................98 B5
Coppice Wk DTN/ASHW M34....146 B1
Coppice Wy WILM/AE SK9.......192 B4
Coppingford Cl WHIT OL12......129 G2
Copping St WGTN/LGST M12...129 G2
The Coppins WILM/AE SK9......200 B1
Coppleridge Dr CHH M8..........87 F5
Copplestone Dr SALE M33......153 F1
Copp St ROY/SHW OL2...........60 C3
Copse Av WYTH/NTH M22......180 D1
The Copse EDGW/EG BL7.......23 H1
     HALE/TIMP WA15..............175 H1
     MPL/ROM SK6...................142 D4
Copse Dr BURY BL9...............27 C5
Copson St DID/WITH M20.......142 D4
Copster Av OLDS OL8.............91 A4
Copster Hill Rd OLDS OL8.......91 F4
Copster PI OLDS OL8..............91 F4
Copthall La CHH M8................102 A2
Copthorne CI HEY OL10..........56 A1
Copthorne Crs
     BRUN/LGST M13...............143 C1
Copthorne Dr BOLE BL2..........50 B3
Coptrook
     TOT/BURYW BL8...............37 E1
Coptrod Head CI WHIT OL12....18 D4
Coral Av CHD/CHDH SK8........182 D3
Coral Rd CHD/CHDH SK8.........182 D3
Coral St BRUN/LGST M13........128 D2
Coram St GTN M18.................131 E2
Corbar Rd OFTN SK2..............172 C4
Corbel Wy ECC M30................111 E2
Corbett St MILN OL16.............11 F4
     OP/CLY M11......................116 B4

Corbrook Rd CHAD OL9 73 H3
Corby St WGTN/LGST M12 129 H2
Corcoran Dr MPL/ROM SK6 163 E4
Corda Av WYTH/NTH M22 168 C1
Cordingley Av DROY M43 117 G5
Cordova Av DTN/ASHW M34 131 E5
Corelli St NEWH/MOS M40 116 A1
Corfe Cl URM M41 137 E2
Corfe Crs BRAM/HZG SK7 185 E3
Corinthian Av BRO M7 101 F5
Corkland Cl AUL OL6 120 A3
Corkland Rd CCHDY M21 141 F3
Corkland St AUL OL6 120 B3
Cork St BURY BL9 5 H4
WGTN/LGST M12 115 G5
Corley Av EDGY/DAV SK3 170 C2
Corley Wk OP/CLY M11 * 116 A4
Cormallen Gv FAIL M35 105 F3
Cormorant Cl LHULT M38 81 H4
Cornall St TOT/BURYW BL8 37 H3
Cornbrook Arches
HULME M15 127 F1
Cornbrook Cl WHIT OL12 19 H2
Cornbrook Gv
OLDTF/WHR M16 127 G3
Cornbrook Park Rd
HULME M15 127 F2
Cornbrook St
OLDTF/WHR M16 127 G3
Cornbrook Wy
OLDTF/WHR M16 127 G3
Corn Cl BRUN/LGST M13 128 D3
Cornell St ANC M4 7 J2
Corner Brook HOR/BR BL6 62 B1
Corner Cft WILM/AE SK9 200 D1
Corner St AUL OL6 119 H3
Cornet St BRO M7 101 G5
Cornfield STLY SK15 135 F1
Cornfield Cl BURY BL9 27 G4
SALE M33 * 155 G3
Cornfield Dr
WYTH/NTH M22 180 B1
Cornfield Rd MPL/ROM SK6 162 D3
Cornfield St MILN OL16 44 D1
Cornford Av GTN M18 130 A5
Corn Hey Rd SALE M33 153 F4
Cornhill Av URM M41 124 A5
Corn Hill La DTN/ASHW M34 131 F3
Cornhill Rd URM M41 124 A5
Cornhill St OLD OL1 76 B2
Cornish Wy ROY/SHW OL2 75 G1
Cornishway WYTH/NTH M22 180 C4
Cornlea Dr WALK M28 96 D3
Corn Mill Cl WHIT OL12 19 H4
Corn Mill La STLY SK15 121 E4
Corn St FAIL M35 104 B4
OLDE OL4 9 K3
Cornwall Av BNG/LEV M19 144 B3
WHTN BL5 63 G4
Cornwall Cl MPL/ROM SK6 186 D5
Cornwall Crs RDSH SK5 146 A5
Cornwall Dr BURY BL9 53 H1
Cornwall Rd CHD/CHDH SK8 181 G4
DROY M43 117 H2
IRL M44 150 C1
Cornwall St CHAD OL9 90 C2
ECC M30 110 D4
OP/CLY M11 130 C1
Cornwell Cl WILM/AE SK9 199 G2
Corona Av HYDE SK14 133 H5
OLDS OL8 91 E4
Coronation Av DUK SK16 133 H1
HEY OL10 56 B1
HYDE SK14 148 A2
Coronation Gdns RAD M26 51 H5
Coronation Rd AUL OL6 107 F4
DROY M43 117 G2
FAIL M35 104 D4
RAD M26 51 H5
Coronation Sq
WGTN/LGST M12 115 F5
Coronation St BOL BL1 2 E5
DTN/ASHW M34 131 H5
OP/CLY M11 * 116 D5
ORD M5 113 G5
RDSH SK5 159 H2
SWIN M27 99 F1
Corporation Rd
DTN/ASHW M34 132 A3
ROCH OL11 29 G5
Corporation St BOL BL1 2 E4
CMANW M2 6 E4
HYDE SK14 * 147 H1
MDTN M24 72 D4
STKP SK1 13 H2
STLY SK15 120 D4
Corran Cl ECC M30 110 C3
Correction Brow
POY/DIS SK12 196 B1
Corrie Cl DTN/ASHW M34 146 D2
Corrie Crs FWTH BL4 83 G3
Corrie Dr FWTH BL4 83 G3
Corrie Rd SWIN M27 84 B4
Corrie St LHULT M38 81 F3
Corrie Wy MPL/ROM SK6 161 F1
Corrigan St GTN M18 130 D2
Corringham Rd BNG/LEV M19 144 C4
Corring Wy BOL BL1 34 C2
Corriss Av BKLY M9 87 F2
Corry St HEY OL10 41 F4
Corson St BOLS/LL BL3 66 A2
Corwen Av BKLY M9 103 F2
Corwen Cl OLDS OL8 90 C5
Cosgrove Crs FAIL M35 104 D5
Cosgrove Rd FAIL M35 104 D5
Cosham Rd WYTH/NTH M22 181 E1
Costobadie Cl HYDE SK14 135 G5
Cotaline Cl ROCH OL11 42 A3
Cotefield Av BOLS/LL BL3 65 E1
Cotefield Cl MPL/ROM SK6 * 175 E4
Cotefield Rd WYTH/NTH M22 180 A2
Cote Green La MPL/ROM SK6 163 G5
Cote Green Rd MPL/ROM SK6 163 H5
Cote La LIT OL15 20 C2
MOSL OL5 94 B4
Cotford Rd BOL BL1 34 A1
Cotham St CSLFD M3 114 C2
Cotman Dr MPL/ROM SK6 175 H1
Cotswold Av BRAM/HZG SK7 184 C3
CHAD OL9 90 B2
ROY/SHW OL2 59 G1
URM M41 123 G5
Cotswold Cl PWCH M25 86 B2
RAMS BL0 16 D4
Cotswold Crs MILN OL16 31 H4
TOT/BURYW BL8 37 G3
Cotswold Dr ROY/SHW OL2 74 C1
SLFD M6 113 E2
Cotswold Rd HTNM SK4 159 G3
Cottage Cft BOLE BL2 35 E1
Cottage Gdns MPL/ROM SK6 161 E3
Cottage Gv WILM/AE SK9 198 B5
The Cottages OLDE OL4 * 77 E5
Cottam Crs MPL/ROM SK6 175 G2
Cottam Gv SWIN M27 99 F3
Cottam St OLD OL1 75 E4
TOT/BURYW BL8 37 H3
Cottenham La BRO M7 114 B1
Cottenham St
BRUN/LGST M13 128 C2
Cotterdale Cl
OLDTF/WHR M16 141 H1
Cotteril Cl SALE M33 154 D5
Cotterill St SLFD M6 113 F3
Cotter St WGTN/LGST M12 128 D1
Cottesmore Cl WHIT OL12 18 B2
Cottesmore Dr CHH M8 102 D2
Cottesmore Gdns
HALE/TIMP WA15 178 D4
Cottingham Dr AUL OL6 119 H1
Cottingham Rd
WGTN/LGST M12 129 F2
Cottingley Cl BOL BL1 33 G1
Cotton Cl HYDE SK14 148 A2
Cottonfield Rd DID/WITH M20 143 E5
Cottonfields EDGW/EG BL7 23 E4
Cotton Fold MILN OL16 30 D5
Cotton Hl DID/WITH M20 157 H1
Cotton La DID/WITH M20 143 E5
Cotton Mill Crs CHAD OL9 90 C3
Cotton St ANC M4 7 J3
BOL BL1 33 G4
Cotton St East AUL OL6 119 G2
Cotton St West AUL OL6 119 F3
Cotton Tree Cl OLDE OL4 76 C4
Cotton Tree St HTNM SK4 12 E3
Cottonwood Dr SALE M33 153 F1
Cottrell Rd HALE/TIMP WA15 179 E5
Coucill Sq FWTH BL4 66 B4
Coulsden Dr BKLY M9 88 A4
Coulthart St AUL OL6 119 G2
Coulthurst St RAMS BL0 16 C2
Coulton Cl OLD OL1 9 K1
OLD OL1 75 H4
Councillor La CHD/CHDH SK8 170 C4
Councillor St
WGTN/LGST M12 115 H4
Countess Av CHD/CHDH SK8 192 B2
Countess Gv BRO M7 101 G5
Countess La RAD M26 51 G4
Countess Pl PWCH M25 86 B3
Countess Rd DID/WITH M20 157 G3
Countess St AUL OL6 120 A3
OFTN SK2 172 B4
Counthill Dr CHH M8 86 D5
Counthill Rd OLDE OL4 76 C3
Count St MILN OL16 43 F2
County Av AUL OL6 120 B1
County Rd LHULT M38 81 F3
County St CMANW M2 6 E5
OLDS OL8 90 D5
Coupland Cl OLDE OL4 61 E5
WHIT OL12 14 B5
Coupland St HULME M15 128 B3
WHIT OL12 14 C5
Courier St GTN M18 130 D2
Course Vw OLDE OL4 92 D4
Court Dr NEWH/MOS M40 117 F1
Courtfield Av BKLY M9 * 88 A3
Courthill St STKP SK1 13 K5
Courtney Gn WILM/AE SK9 192 A5
Courtney Pl ALT WA14 176 D3
Court St BOLE BL2 3 H5
UPML OL3 79 E4
Courts Vw SALE M33 154 D1
Courtyard Dr WALK M28 81 E4
The Courtyard BOL BL1 * 34 A5
HEY OL10 * 41 G5
Cousin Flds EDGW/EG BL7 23 H4
Covell Rd POY/DIS SK12 195 E2
Covent Gdn STKP SK1 13 G4
Coventry Av EDGY/DAV SK3 170 C2
Coventry Gv CHAD OL9 74 B3
Coventry Rd RAD M26 52 A4
Coventry St ROCH OL11 30 A5
Coverdale Av BOL BL1 47 H1
ROY/SHW OL2 58 D4
Coverdale Cl HEY OL10 40 D5
Coverdale Crs
WGTN/LGST M12 129 E2
Coverham Av OLDE OL4 92 C3
Coverhill Rd OLDE OL4 93 G2
Covert Rd OLDE OL4 92 D4
WYTH/NTH M22 168 D4
The Cove HALE/TIMP WA15 178 A1
Covington Pl WILM/AE SK9 199 E4
Cowan St NEWH/MOS M40 115 G3
Cowburn St CSLFD M3 114 D2
HEY OL10 41 F5
Cowdals Rd HOR/BR BL6 46 C5
Cowesby St RUSH/FAL M14 128 B5
Cowhill La AUL OL6 119 H2
Cowie St ROY/SHW OL2 60 A1
Cow La BOLS/LL BL3 64 A2
BRAM/HZG SK7 173 E5
FAIL M35 104 D3
HALE/TIMP WA15 188 A2
OLDE OL4 76 B5
ORD M5 113 H4
SALE M33 140 C5
WILM/AE SK9 199 F3
Cow Lees WHTN BL5 62 B3
Cowley Rd BOL BL1 34 A1
Cowley St NEWH/MOS M40 104 B4
Cowling St BRO M7 100 C2
Cowlishaw ROY/SHW OL2 59 H4
Cowlishaw La ROY/SHW OL2 59 H4
Cowlishaw Rd HYDE SK14 163 E1
Cowm Park Wy North
WHIT OL12 14 B3
Cowm Park Wy South
WHIT OL12 14 B5
Cowm Top La ROCH OL11 42 D4
Cown Edge Wy GLSP SK13 149 H5
HYDE SK14 147 H5
MPL/ROM SK6 175 H5
MPL/ROM SK6 187 F3
OFTN SK2 173 H5
Cowper St AUL OL6 119 H2
MDTN M24 73 G5
Coxton Rd WYTH/NTH M22 180 D3
Crabbe St ANC M4 114 D2
Crab La BKLY M9 87 G3
Crabtree Av
HALE/TIMP WA15 179 E5
Crabtree La OP/CLY M11 117 E5
Crabtree Rd OLD OL1 76 A4
Craddock Rd SALE M33 154 D4
Craddock St MOSL OL5 108 D1
Cradley Av OP/CLY M11 117 E5
Crag Av BURY BL9 27 E1
Cragg Fold BURY BL9 * 27 E1
Cragg Rd OLD OL1 74 B2
Cragie St CHH M8 102 A5
Crag La BURY BL9 27 E1
Cragside Wy WILM/AE SK9 199 F4
Craig Av TOT/BURYW BL8 37 G5
URM M41 123 H5
Craig Cl HTNM SK4 159 E5
Craighall Av BNG/LEV M19 143 H3
Craighall Rd BOL BL1 22 D5
Craiglands MILN OL16 43 G4
Craigmore Av DID/WITH M20 156 C2
Craignair Ct SWIN M27 * 99 H2
Craig Rd GTN M18 130 B4
HTNM SK4 158 D5
Craigslands Av
NEWH/MOS M40 103 H4
Craig Wk OLDS OL8 9 F7
Craigweil Av DID/WITH M20 157 H3
Craigwell Rd PWCH M25 86 C5
Cramer St NEWH/MOS M40 * 103 G5
Crammond Cl
NEWH/MOS M40 104 C4
Cramond Cl BOL BL1 33 G5
Cramond Wk BOL BL1 33 G5
Crampton Dr
HALE/TIMP WA15 178 D4
Crampton La PART M31 137 F5
Cranage Rd BNG/LEV M19 144 B3
Cranark Cl BOL BL1 47 H2
Cranberry Cl ALT WA14 165 E1
Cranberry Dr BOLS/LL BL3 47 G5
DTN/ASHW M34 131 H5
Cranberry Rd PART M31 151 E3
Cranberry St OLDE OL4 92 A2
Cranbourne Av
CHD/CHDH SK8 183 E2
Cranbourne Cl
HALE/TIMP WA15 166 B3
Cranbourne Rd AULW OL7 107 E5
CCHDY M21 141 F3
HTNM SK4 159 E2
OLDTF/WHR M16 127 F4
ROCH OL11 28 B5
Cranbourne St ORD M5 113 H4
Cranbourne Ter AUL OL6 107 E5
Cranbrook Dr PWCH M25 86 B5
Cranbrook Gdns AULW OL7 * 119 G1
Cranbrook Rd ECC M30 110 B1
GTN M18 130 D5
Cranbrook St AULW OL7 119 G1
OLDE OL4 92 B1
RAD M26 52 D4
Cranbrook Wk CHAD OL9 * 90 B1
Crandon Dr DID/WITH M20 169 H1
Cranesbill Cl WYTH/NTH M22 180 B3
Crane St BOLS/LL BL3 * 64 A1
WGTN/LGST M12 115 F5
Cranfield Cl NEWH/MOS M40 115 G3
Cranford Av DID/WITH M20 158 A2
SALE M33 140 A5
STRET M32 126 C5
WHTF M45 69 F2
Cranford Cl SWIN M27 99 G4
WHTF M45 69 F2
Cranford Dr IRL M44 122 A5
Cranford Gdns MPL/ROM SK6 175 E2
URM M41 * 123 F5
Cranford Rd URM M41 123 F5
WILM/AE SK9 198 D1
Cranford St BOLS/LL BL3 64 B2
Cranham Cl TOT/BURYW BL8 37 G3
Cranham Close Crs
LHULT M38 * 81 F1
Cranham Rd WYTH/NTH M22 179 H2
Cranleigh Av HTNM SK4 158 C2
Cranleigh Cl OLDE OL4 76 D3
Cranleigh Dr BRAM/HZG SK7 185 H4
CHD/CHDH SK8 170 C3
SALE M33 154 B1
SALE M33 154 D5
WALK M28 97 F2
Cranlington Dr CHH M8 102 A4
Cranmer Ct HEY OL10 40 D5
Cranmere Av BNG/LEV M19 144 C1
Cranmere Dr SALE M33 153 G4
Cranmer Rd DID/WITH M20 157 G2
Cranston Dr DID/WITH M20 169 G1
SALE M33 155 F3
Cranston Gv CHD/CHDH SK8 169 E4
Cranswick St RUSH/FAL M14 128 B5
Crantock Dr CHD/CHDH SK8 181 H4
STLY SK15 121 G2
Crantock St WGTN/LGST M12 130 A5
Cranwell Dr BNG/LEV M19 158 B2
Cranworth St STLY SK15 121 E4
Craston Rd BRUN/LGST M13 143 G1
Crathie Ct BOL BL1 33 E5
Craven Av ORD M5 113 G5
Craven Ct ALT WA14 * 165 F2
Craven Dr ALT WA14 165 F1
ORD M5 126 D2
Craven Gdns ROCH OL11 * 42 D1
Cravenhurst Av
NEWH/MOS M40 116 C1
Craven Pl BOL BL1 32 B4
OP/CLY M11 116 D3
Craven Rd ALT WA14 165 F2
RDSH SK5 * 145 F5
Craven St AUL OL6 * 107 G5
BURY BL9 5 K2
OLD OL1 75 F3
ORD M5 113 H4
Craven Ter SALE M33 154 D2
Cravenwood AUL OL6 108 A4
Cravenwood Rd CHH M8 102 B2
Crawford Av BOLE BL2 3 J6
WALK M28 97 G2
Crawford St AUL OL6 120 A3
BOLE BL2 3 H5
ECC M30 111 E2
MILN OL16 43 F1
NEWH/MOS M40 * 104 B5
Crawley Av ECC M30 111 H2
WYTH/NTH M22 180 C1
Crawley Gv OFTN SK2 172 C3
Craydon St OP/CLY M11 116 D5
Crayfield Rd BNG/LEV M19 144 B3
Crayford Rd NEWH/MOS M40 116 C1
The Cray MILN OL16 31 F5
Cray Wk BRUN/LGST M13 * 128 C1
Creaton Wy MDTN M24 56 A5
Creden Av WYTH/NTH M22 180 D1
Crediton Cl ALT WA14 165 E3
HULME M15 128 A3
Crediton Dr BOLE BL2 50 D2
Cresbury St
WGTN/LGST M12 * 129 E1
Crescent ORD M5 113 H3
Crescent Av BOL BL1 2 B3
CHH M8 * 102 B2
FWTH BL4 81 H1
PWCH M25 86 A5
SWIN M27 99 G2
WHTN BL5 63 H4
Crescent Cl DUK SK16 119 H4
EDGY/DAV SK3 172 B4
Crescent Dr CHH M8 102 C1
LHULT M38 81 G2
Crescent Fold HYDE SK14 * 149 H3
Crescent Gv BNG/LEV M19 * 144 A2
PWCH M25 86 A5
Crescent Pk HTNM SK4 12 A3
Crescent Range
RUSH/FAL M14 128 D5
Crescent Rd ALT WA14 164 D3
BOLS/LL BL3 65 G1
CHAD OL9 89 H5
CHD/CHDH SK8 169 H3
CHH M8 102 B2
DUK SK16 119 H4
FWTH BL4 82 C1
HALE/TIMP WA15 177 H2
ROCH OL11 42 A2
STKP SK1 160 C3
WILM/AE SK9 201 E3
Crescent St CHH M8 102 D2
The Crescent ALT WA14 164 D4
BNG/LEV M19 144 A2
BOLE BL2 35 G2
BOLS/LL BL3 67 E2
BURY BL9 5 G3
CHD/CHDH SK8 169 H3
DROY M43 117 G4
EDGW/EG BL7 23 F3
EDGY/DAV SK3 172 B5
HALE/TIMP WA15 166 A2
IRL M44 122 C5
MDTN M24 72 B4
MOSL OL5 108 C1
MPL/ROM SK6 161 E2
PWCH M25 86 A3
RAD M26 51 G4
ROY/SHW OL2 59 H3
STLY SK15 135 E2
URM M41 123 G5
WHIT OL12 * 14 B5
Crescent Wy EDGY/DAV SK3 172 B4
Cressfield Wy CCHDY M21 141 H4
Cressingham Rd BOLS/LL BL3 63 H1
STRET M32 139 H2
Cressington Cl ORD M5 * 112 D3
Cresswell Gv DID/WITH M20 157 F1
Crestfold LHULT M38 81 F3
Crest St CSLFD M3 6 E1
The Crest DROY M43 131 F1
Crete St OLDS OL8 91 G3
Crewe Rd NTHM/RTH M23 167 F1
Crib Fold UPML OL3 78 D2
Crib La UPML OL3 78 D2
Criccieth Rd EDGY/DAV SK3 170 D2
Criccieth St OLDTF/WHR M16 128 A4
Cricketfield La WALK M28 81 H4
Cricket's La AUL OL6 119 H2
Cricket's La North AUL OL6 119 H2
Cricket St BOLS/LL BL3 48 D4
DTN/ASHW M34 * 132 D4
Cricket Vw MILN OL16 44 C1
Cricklewood Rd
WYTH/NTH M22 180 B2
Crimble La ROCH OL11 41 F1
Crimble St WHIT OL12 29 G3
Crime La OLDS OL8 106 A3
Crimsworth Av
OLDTF/WHR M16 141 F1
Crinan Wk NEWH/MOS M40 115 G2
Cringlebarrow Cl WALK M28 96 A5
Cringle Cl BOLS/LL BL3 47 F5
Cringle Dr CHD/CHDH SK8 169 H5
Cringleford Wk
WGTN/LGST M12 129 G3
Cringle Hall Rd BNG/LEV M19 143 H3
Cringle Rd BNG/LEV M19 144 B4
Cripple Gate La ROCH OL11 42 D5
Crispin Rd WYTH/NTH M22 180 D4
Critchley Cl HYDE SK14 148 B2
Criterion St RDSH SK5 145 F1
Croal St BOL BL1 2 A6
Croasdale Av RUSH/FAL M14 142 D2
Croasdale Cl ROY/SHW OL2 59 F4
Croasdale St BOL BL1 2 E1
Crocus Dr ROY/SHW OL2 59 H4
Crocus St BOL BL1 34 A2
Croft Av PWCH M25 71 E4
Croft Bank BRO M7 * 101 F5
GTN M18 130 D3
Croft Brow OLDS OL8 91 F5
Croft Cl HALE/TIMP WA15 188 D1
Croft Dr TOT/BURYW BL8 25 H5
Croft Edge UPML OL3 94 D2
Crofters Brook RAD M26 52 D5
Crofters Gn WILM/AE SK9 198 C4
The Crofters SALE M33 155 G3
Crofters Wk BOLE BL2 23 H5
Croft Ga BOLE BL2 35 F2
Croft Gates Rd MDTN M24 72 A5
Croft Gv LHULT M38 81 E2
Croft Head ROY/SHW OL2 59 E5
Croft Head Dr MILN OL16 31 G4
Croft Hill Rd NEWH/MOS M40 103 H1
Croftlands RAMS BL0 16 B5
Croftlands Rd WYTH/NTH M22 168 D5
Croft La BOLS/LL BL3 49 G4
BURY BL9 53 H4
RAD M26 52 D5
Croftleigh Cl WHTF M45 69 F2
Crofton Av HALE/TIMP WA15 166 B1
Crofton St OLDS OL8 91 F4
OLDTF/WHR M16 127 G4
RUSH/FAL M14 128 C5
Croft Rd CHD/CHDH SK8 183 E1
SALE M33 155 F4
WILM/AE SK9 200 B1
Crofts Bank Rd URM M41 124 B4
Croftside Av WALK M28 82 B4
Croftside Cl WALK M28 82 B4
Croftside Gv WALK M28 82 B4
Croftside Wy WILM/AE SK9 199 F4
Croft St BOLS/LL BL3 49 G5
BRO M7 101 F5
BURY BL9 5 G4
FAIL M35 105 F1
HYDE SK14 147 H1
LHULT M38 81 E2
OP/CLY M11 116 C4
STLY SK15 121 E3
WHIT OL12 19 H5
The Croft BURY BL9 53 H3
HYDE SK14 135 H4
OLDS OL8 91 F5
PART M31 137 F5
Croichbank TOT/BURYW BL8 25 E1
Cromar Rd BRAM/HZG SK7 185 G1
Cromarty Av CHAD OL9 90 A4
Cromarty Wk OP/CLY M11 116 A4
Crombie Av WYTH/NTH M22 168 C1
Crombouke Fold WALK M28 96 C3
Cromdale Av BOL BL1 48 A1
BRAM/HZG SK7 185 G1
Cromer Av BOLE BL2 34 D5
DID/WITH M20 142 D5
DTN/ASHW M34 131 F5
Cromer Rd CHD/CHDH SK8 170 B3
SALE M33 154 D3
TOT/BURYW BL8 38 A1
Cromer St MDTN M24 72 D3
OP/CLY M11 * 117 E4
ROY/SHW OL2 * 60 A2
STKP SK1 13 K2
WHIT OL12 10 B3
Cromford Av STRET M32 125 G5
Cromford Cl BOL BL1 2 C1
Cromford Gdns BOL BL1 34 A4
Cromford St OLD OL1 75 H4
Cromhurst St CHH M8 102 B2
Cromley Rd MPL/ROM SK6 186 D5
OFTN SK2 184 B1
Crompton Av BOLE BL2 50 B1
MILN OL16 43 G3
Crompton Circuit
ROY/SHW OL2 45 H5
Crompton Cl BOL BL1 34 B2
MPL/ROM SK6 175 E2
RAD M26 68 C4
Crompton Pl BOL BL1 * 3 F5
RAD M26 68 C1
Crompton Rd BNG/LEV M19 144 A4
HOR/BR BL6 46 A1
RAD M26 66 D4
Crompton St AUL OL6 120 B1
BOL BL1 3 G3
BURY BL9 4 D4
CHAD OL9 8 A3
FWTH BL4 66 B5
OLD OL1 75 F4
ROY/SHW OL2 60 A2
ROY/SHW OL2 * 75 F1
SWIN M27 98 D2
WALK M28 82 C5
Crompton V BOLE BL2 50 A1
Crompton Wy BOLE BL2 34 D3
ROY/SHW OL2 60 A3
Cromwell Av CHD/CHDH SK8 169 F3
MPL/ROM SK6 174 C3
OLDTF/WHR M16 141 G1
RDSH SK5 145 G1
Cromwell Gv BNG/LEV M19 144 A2
BRO M7 101 F5
Cromwell Range
RUSH/FAL M14 143 F1
Cromwell Rd
BRAM/HZG SK7 193 G1
ECC M30 110 D3
IRL M44 136 A4
MPL/ROM SK6 146 B5
PWCH M25 86 B3
ROY/SHW OL2 58 D3
SLFD M6 113 F1
STRET M32 140 C2
SWIN M27 98 D1
WHTF M45 69 E2
Cromwell St BOL BL1 2 C6
HEY OL10 41 E5
HTNM SK4 159 G3
OLD OL1 9 G5
Crondall St RUSH/FAL M14 128 B5
Cronkeyshaw Av WHIT OL12 10 B1
Cronkeyshaw Rd WHIT OL12 10 B2
Cronshaw St BNG/LEV M19 144 B3
Crookhill Dr CHH M8 102 A3
Crookilley Wy
MPL/ROM SK6 161 E1
STKP SK1 160 C3
Crook St BOLS/LL BL3 2 E7
HYDE SK14 147 H1
MILN OL16 10 E5
Crosby Av WALK M28 82 C5
Crosby Rd BOL BL1 48 A1
NEWH/MOS M40 104 C5

RAD M26 .....51 H2
SLFD M6 * 100 A5
Crosby St OFTN SK2 .....172 A2
WHIT OL12 .....30 A1
Crosfield Av BURY BL9 .....26 D1
Crosfield Gv GTN M18 .....130 C4
Crossacres Rd WYTH/NTH M22 .....169 E5
Cross Acres Rd WYTH/NTH M22 .....180 D1
Crossav PWCH M25 .....85 H1
Crossbank Av OLDE OL4 .....75 H5
Crossbank Cl BRUN/LGST M13 .....129 E3
Crossbank St OLDS OL8 .....8 E5
Crossbridge Rd HYDE SK14 .....148 C1
Crossbrook Wy MILN OL16 .....44 D1
Crosby Cl MDTN M24 .....88 C2
Crosscliffe St OLDTF/WHR M16 .....128 A4
Crossdale Rd BKLY M9 .....88 B3
BOLE BL2 .....50 C1
Crossefield Rd CHD/CHDH SK8 .....182 D1
Crossen St BOLS/LL BL3 .....49 H4
Crossfell Av BKLY M9 .....87 G2
Cross Field St ROY/SHW OL2 .....45 F5
Crossfield Cl DTN/ASHW M34 .....147 E1
STLY SK15 .....120 D4
WHIT OL12 .....19 H1
Crossfield Dr RAD M26 .....67 H1
SWIN M27 .....98 D1
Crossfield Gv MPL/ROM SK6 .....163 G5
OFTN SK2 .....172 C5
Crossfield Pl ROCH OL11 .....43 F5
Crossfield Rd ECC M30 .....122 D4
HALE/TIMP WA15 .....178 C2
WHIT OL12 .....19 H2
WILM/AE SK9 .....192 A3
Crossfields EDGW/EG BL7 .....23 G5
Crossford Dr BURY BL9 .....53 G5
Crossford Br SALE M33 .....140 A4
Crossford Ct SALE M33 * 139 H5
Crossford Dr BOLS/LL BL3 .....47 F4
Crossford St STRET M32 .....140 B2
Crossgate Av WYTH/NTH M22 .....168 C3
Crossgates Ms HTNM SK4 .....158 B4
Crossgates Rd MILN OL16 .....31 G4
Cross Glebe St AUL OL6 * 119 H2
Cross Gv HALE/TIMP WA15 .....166 C1
Crosshill St OLDTF/WHR M16 .....128 A4
Cross Keys St ANC M4 .....7 H2
Cross Knowle Vw URM M41 .....123 H4
Crossland Rd CCHDY M21 .....141 E3
DROY M43 .....117 H3
Crosslands PWCH M25 .....85 H4
Crosslands Rd WALK M28 .....96 A4
Cross La DROY M43 .....118 C1
GTN M18 .....130 C3
MPL/ROM SK6 .....174 D4
ORD M5 .....113 F4
RAD M26 .....52 D5
TOT/BURYW BL8 .....16 B3
Cross La East PART M31 .....151 F3
Cross La West PART M31 .....150 D4
Crosslee Rd BKLY M9 .....88 C3
Cross Lees WHIT OL12 .....19 F5
Crossley Ct ANC M4 .....115 G4
Crossley Crs AUL OL6 .....107 H4
Crossley Rd BNG/LEV M19 .....144 A4
SALE M33 .....139 G5
Crossley St BOLS/LL BL3 .....50 D5
GTN M18 .....130 A2
MILN OL16 .....11 K5
ROY/SHW OL2 .....60 D2
ROY/SHW OL2 .....75 F2
STLY SK15 .....120 C3
Crossmead Dr BKLY M9 .....88 B2
Crossmeadow Cl ROCH OL11 .....28 D5
Crossmoor Crs MPL/ROM SK6 .....162 D4
Crossmoor Dr BOLE BL2 .....3 K2
Crossmoor Gv MPL/ROM SK6 .....162 B4
Cross Ormrod St BOLS/LL BL3 .....2 B7
Cross Rd CCHDY M21 .....141 F4
CHD/CHDH SK8 .....181 G5
Cross St ALT WA14 .....165 G5
AUL OL6 .....107 G5
AUL OL6 .....119 F3
BOL BL1 .....3 F2
BOLS/LL BL3 .....67 E1
BURY BL9 .....4 E4
CMANW M2 .....6 E4
CSLFD M3 .....6 C3
DTN/ASHW M34 .....132 B5
EDGW/EG BL7 .....23 G5
FWTH BL4 .....66 A3
FWTH BL4 .....41 F5
HEY OL10 .....41 F5
HYDE SK14 .....147 H1
MDTN M24 .....72 C4
MILN OL16 .....31 G4
MOSL OL5 .....93 H5
OLDE OL4 .....76 A5
OLDE OL4 .....93 F1
OLDTF/WHR M16 .....127 G3
RAMS BL0 .....16 D2
ROCH OL11 .....42 B4
SALE M33 .....154 C1
STLY SK15 .....121 G1
STRET M32 .....140 B1
SWIN M27 .....85 E5
URM M41 .....138 C2
WALK M28 .....98 B3
WHIT M45 .....69 F5
The Cross TOT/BURYW BL8 * 26 A5
Crosswaite Rd OFTN SK2 .....173 E3
Crossway BRAM/HZG SK7 .....193 H2
DID/WITH M20 .....157 G3
DROY M43 .....131 F1
OFTN SK2 .....172 B5
Crossways OLDS OL8 .....106 A1
Croston Cl WILM/AE SK9 .....201 F4
Crostons Rd TOT/BURYW BL8 .....4 A3
Croston St BOLS/LL BL3 .....48 B5
Croston Wk OP/CLY M11 .....115 H4
Croton St HTNM SK4 .....158 D3
Croughton Cl OP/CLY M11 * 130 C1
Crowborough Wk HULME M15 .....128 A3
Crowcroft Rd BRUN/LGST M13 .....144 A1

Crowden Rd NEWH/MOS M40 .....89 E5
Crow HI STLY SK15 .....109 F5
Crow HI North MDTN M24 .....88 C1
Crowhill Rd AULW OL7 .....119 E1
Crow HI South MDTN M24 .....88 C1
Crow Hill Vw OLDE OL4 .....93 E3
Crowland Gdns CHD/CHDH SK8 .....193 G1
Crowland Rd BOLE BL2 .....34 D4
NTHM/RTH M23 .....179 G1
Crow La RAMS BL0 .....16 D2
Crowley La OLDE OL4 .....76 C3
Crowley Rd BKLY M9 .....103 G2
HALE/TIMP WA15 .....166 C5
Crown Ct BRAM/HZG SK7 .....184 D1
Crowneast St ROCH OL11 .....29 F4
Crown Gdns MILN OL16 .....43 F1
Crowngreen Rd ECC M30 .....111 F4
Crown HI MOSL OL5 .....109 E2
Crownhill Dr DROY M43 .....117 H5
Crown La ANC M4 .....7 G1
Crown Passages HALE/TIMP WA15 .....177 H2
Crown Point Av NEWH/MOS M40 * 104 B5
Crown Rd HEY OL10 .....40 C4
Crown Sq CSLFD M3 .....6 C5
Crown St AUL OL6 .....119 G3
BOL BL1 .....3 F4
CSLFD M5 .....6 C2
DTN/ASHW M34 .....132 B5
FAIL M35 .....105 E2
HULME M15 .....127 H1
MILN OL16 .....43 G1
MPL/ROM SK6 * 161 G2
NEWH/MOS M40 .....104 B5
ROY/SHW OL2 * 60 A2
Crowsdale Pl OFTN SK2 .....173 F5
Crowshaw Dr WHIT OL12 .....18 D5
Crowswood Dr STLY SK15 .....109 E5
Crowther Av ORD M5 .....113 F5
Crowther St GTN M18 .....130 C3
LIT OL15 .....20 B4
MILN OL16 .....43 G2
Crowthorn Dr NTHM/RTH M23 .....179 H2
Crowthorn Rd AULW OL7 .....119 E4
HTNM SK4 .....144 D4
Crowton Av SALE M33 .....153 G4
Croxdale Cl AULW OL7 .....106 C5
Croxton Av MILN OL16 .....11 J5
Croxton Cl MPL/ROM SK6 .....174 D4
SALE M33 .....153 G4
Croyde Cl BOLE BL2 .....35 G4
NTHM/RTH M22 .....180 C5
Croydon Av ROCH OL11 .....57 G2
ROY/SHW OL2 .....60 B4
Croydon Dr NEWH/MOS M40 .....116 D1
Croydon Sq ROCH OL11 .....57 G1
Crummock Cl BOLS/LL BL3 .....66 C1
Crummock Dr BRAM/HZG SK7 .....72 B1
Crummock Rd CHD/CHDH SK8 .....181 G1
FWTH BL4 .....64 D5
Crumpsall La CHH M8 .....102 A1
Crumpsall St BOL BL1 .....34 B2
Crumpsall V CHH M8 .....87 H5
Crumpsall Wy CHH M8 .....102 C1
Crundale Rd BOL BL1 .....23 E5
Cruttenden Rd OFTN SK2 .....172 D5
Cryer St DROY M43 .....118 C3
Cubley Rd BRO M7 .....101 H2
Cuckoo Gv PWCH M25 .....86 A1
Cuckoo La BURY BL9 .....39 F4
PWCH M25 .....86 A1
Cuddington Av DID/WITH M20 .....142 C3
Cuddington Crs EDGY/DAV SK3 .....171 G3
Cudworth Rd BKLY M9 .....87 F2
Culand St WGTN/LGST M12 .....129 F2
Culbert Av DID/WITH M20 .....157 H5
Culcheth Av MPL/ROM SK6 .....175 E3
Culcheth La NEWH/MOS M40 .....116 D1
Culcheth Rd ALT WA14 .....177 C1
Culford Cl WGTN/LGST M12 .....129 F3
Culham Cl BOL BL1 * 33 G4
Cullen Gv BKLY M9 .....88 B4
Cullercoats Wk WGTN/LGST M12 * 130 A5
Culmere Rd WYTH/NTH M22 .....180 C3
Culmos Av BOLS/LL BL3 .....47 H3
NEWH/MOS M40 .....104 D1
Culvercliff Wk CSLFD M3 * 6 C6
Culver Rd EDGY/DAV SK3 .....171 G4
Culvert St MILN OL16 .....43 G4
Culverwell Dr ORD M5 .....113 G5
Cumber Cl WILM/AE SK9 .....200 A1
Cumber Dr WILM/AE SK9 .....200 A1
Cumberland Av DUK SK16 .....120 B5
HEY OL10 .....40 A1
IRL M44 .....150 B1
RDSH SK5 .....160 D2
SWIN M27 .....84 A5
Cumberland Cl BURY BL9 .....53 F3
Cumberland Dr ALT WA14 .....176 C4
OLD OL1 .....75 E3
Cumberland Gv AULW OL7 .....119 G1
Cumberland Rd BKLY M9 .....103 E1
PART M31 .....150 C4
ROCH OL11 .....43 E4
SALE M33 .....154 C1
URM M41 .....138 C2
Cumberland St BRO M7 .....114 A1
STLY SK15 .....120 C3
Cumber La WILM/AE SK9 .....200 A1
Cumbrae Gdns ORD M5 .....112 D4
Cumbrae Rd BNG/LEV M19 .....144 C2
Cumbrian Cl BRUN/LGST M13 * 128 D2
ROY/SHW OL2 .....59 G1
Cumbria Wk SLFD M6 .....113 H1
Cummings St OLDS OL8 .....90 D5
Cunard Cl BRUN/LGST M13 .....128 D2
Cunliffe Dr ROY/SHW OL2 .....60 C2
Cundey St BOL BL1 * 33 F5
Cundiff Rd CCHDY M21 .....141 F5

Cundy St HYDE SK14 .....133 H4
Cunliffe Av RAMS BL0 .....16 C1
Cunliffe Brow BOL BL1 .....33 E5
Cunliffe Dr SALE M33 .....154 C5
Cunliffe St EDGY/DAV SK3 .....12 B5
HYDE SK14 .....133 H4
RAMS BL0 .....16 D1
Cunningham Dr BURY BL9 .....70 A3
WYTH/NTH M22 .....181 F4
Cunningham Wy OLD OL1 * 75 F4
Curate St STKP SK1 .....13 K4
Curlew Cl ROCH OL11 .....28 C4
Curlew Dr IRL M44 .....122 B4
Curlew Rd OLDE OL4 .....92 D3
Currier La AUL OL6 .....119 H5
Curteis Cl WALK M28 .....98 B3
Curtis Rd BNG/LEV M19 .....144 A2
HTNM SK4 .....158 D4
Curtis St BOLS/LL BL3 .....64 B2
Curzon Av RUSH/FAL M14 .....129 F4
Curzon Cl ROCH OL11 .....43 E4
Curzon Dr HALE/TIMP WA15 .....166 D3
Curzon Gn OFTN SK2 .....175 E1
Curzon Ms WILM/AE SK9 .....198 D4
Curzon Rd AUL OL6 .....119 H1
BOL BL1 .....48 B2
BRO M7 .....101 G3
CHD/CHDH SK8 .....181 G5
OFTN SK2 .....175 E1
POY/DIS SK12 .....195 F5
ROCH OL11 .....43 E4
SALE M33 .....154 C1
STRET M32 .....125 F5
Curzon St MOSL OL5 .....108 D1
OLD OL1 .....9 G3
Cutacre La WHTN BL5 .....80 C1
Cutgate Cl NTHM/RTH M23 .....155 F5
Cutgate Rd WHIT OL12 .....29 E2
Cuthbert Av BNG/LEV M19 .....144 B1
Cuthbert Mayne Ct MILN OL16 .....29 H5
Cuthbert Rd CHD/CHDH SK8 .....170 B5
Cuthbert St BOLS/LL BL3 .....63 H2
Cutland St NEWH/MOS M40 .....103 H4
Cutland Wy LIT OL15 .....20 D4
Cut La WHIT OL12 .....28 C2
Cutler Hill Rd FAIL M35 .....105 H5
Cutnook La IRL M44 .....122 A3
Cutter Cl ORD M5 .....113 F5
Cycle St OP/CLY M11 .....116 A5
Cyclone St OP/CLY M11 .....116 A5
Cygnus Av BRO M7 .....113 H2
Cymbal Ct RDSH SK5 .....159 H1
Cynthia Dr MPL/ROM SK6 .....175 E4
Cypress Av DROY M43 .....117 H2
OLDE OL4 .....74 C4
Cypress Cl EDGY/DAV SK3 .....12 A5
Cypress Gdns MILN OL16 .....31 E4
Cypress Gv DTN/ASHW M34 .....132 D5
FWTH BL4 * 66 C5
Cypress Oaks STLY SK15 .....121 G2
Cypress Rd DROY M43 .....117 H2
ECC M30 .....110 B1
OLDE OL4 .....76 C4
Cypress St MDTN M24 .....73 F4
Cypress Wy MPL/ROM SK6 .....187 F5
Cyprus Cl OLDE OL4 .....92 C2
Cyprus St ORD M5 .....113 G4
STRET M32 .....140 B1
Cyril St BOLS/LL BL3 .....49 G4
ROY/SHW OL2 .....60 C4
RUSH/FAL M14 .....128 C5
Cyrus St NEWH/MOS M40 .....115 H3

D

Daccamill Dr SWIN M27 .....99 E4
Dacre Av OLDTF/WHR M16 .....141 F1
Dacre Cl MDTN M24 .....71 G3
Dacre Rd ROCH OL11 .....43 E3
Dacres Av UPML OL3 .....94 C3
Dacres Dr UPML OL3 .....94 C3
Dacres Rd UPML OL3 .....94 C3
Daffodil Cl WHIT OL12 .....18 D5
Daffodil Rd FWTH BL4 .....65 G3
Daffodil St BOL BL1 .....34 A1
Dagenham Rd RUSH/FAL M14 * 128 D5
Dagmar St WALK M28 .....81 H3
Dagnall Av CCHDY M21 .....141 F5
Dahlia Cl BNG/LEV M19 .....143 H5
WHIT OL12 .....18 C5
Daimler St CHH M8 .....102 B4
Dain Cl DUK SK16 .....120 D5
Daine Av NTHM/RTH M23 .....156 A5
Dainton St WGTN/LGST M12 .....129 E1
Daintry Cl HULME M15 .....128 A2
Daintry Rd CHAD OL9 .....8 B2
Dairydale Cl IRL M44 .....123 F5
Dairyground Rd BRAM/HZG SK7 .....183 H5
Dairyhouse La ALT WA14 .....165 G2
Dairy House La BRAM/HZG SK7 .....193 E4
Dairy House Rd BRAM/HZG SK7 .....193 E2
Dairy St CHAD OL9 .....74 C5
Daisy Av BRUN/LGST M13 .....129 F1
FWTH BL4 .....65 F3
Daisy Bank NEWH/MOS M40 .....104 B5
Daisy Bank La CHD/CHDH SK8 .....181 F4
Daisy Bank Rd RUSH/FAL M14 .....129 F4
WHTN BL5 .....80 B3
Daisyfield Ct TOT/BURYW BL8 .....38 B3
Daisyhill Cl SALE M33 .....155 F2
Daisy Hill Rd MOSL OL5 .....109 H3
Daisy Ms EDGY/DAV SK3 .....171 G5
Daisy St BOLS/LL BL3 .....48 C4
CHAD OL9 .....8 C2
CHAD OL9 .....74 B4
OFTN SK2 .....172 D2
TOT/BURYW BL8 .....37 H4
Daisy Wy MPL/ROM SK6 .....187 G5
Dakerwood Cl NEWH/MOS M40 .....104 B5
Dakley St OP/CLY M11 .....130 B1
Dakota Av SALQ M50 .....112 D5

Dakota South SALQ M50 .....113 E5
Dalbeattie St BKLY M9 .....103 H1
Dalberg St WGTN/LGST M12 .....129 E1
Dalbury Dr NEWH/MOS M40 .....102 D5
Dalby Av SWIN M27 .....98 D3
Dalby Gv STKP SK1 .....13 K3
Dale Av BRAM/HZG SK7 .....184 A4
ECC M30 .....110 D2
MOSL OL5 .....94 B4
Daleacre Ms SWIN M27 * 83 E1
Dalebeck Cl WHTF M45 .....70 A4
Dale Brook Av DUK SK16 .....133 G2
Dalebrook Ct HTNM SK4 .....12 B1
Dalebrook Rd SALE M33 .....154 D5
Daleford Sq BRUN/LGST M13 * 128 C1
Dalegarth Av BOL BL1 .....46 D2
Dale Gv AULW OL7 .....106 D5
HALE/TIMP WA15 .....166 B2
IRL M44 .....136 D3
Dalehead Dr ROY/SHW OL2 .....60 C2
Dale Lee WHTN BL5 .....62 B4
Dale Rd MDTN M24 .....73 E2
MPL/ROM SK6 .....186 B5
Dale Av CHH M8 .....87 E5
WHTF M45 .....69 H2
Dalesbrook Cl BOLS/LL BL3 .....50 D5
Dales Brow BOL BL1 .....23 E5
SWIN M27 * 98 C4
Dales Brow Av AULW OL7 .....106 D5
Dales Gv WALK M28 .....97 G1
Dales La WHTF M45 .....70 B2
Dalesman Cl BKLY M9 .....103 H1
Dalesman Dr OLD OL1 .....76 C1
Dalesman Wk HULME M15 * 128 A2
Dales Park Dr SWIN M27 * 98 C4
Dale St AUL OL6 .....108 B4
CMANE M1 .....7 H4
EDGY/DAV SK3 .....171 G2
FWTH BL4 .....66 B3
MDTN M24 .....73 F1
MILN OL16 .....11 J6
MILN OL16 .....31 G5
RAD M26 .....68 B2
ROY/SHW OL2 .....60 C4
STLY SK15 .....120 D3
SWIN M27 .....98 C4
TOT/BURYW BL8 .....37 H2
WHTF M45 .....69 F5
Dale St East AUL OL6 .....119 F3
Dale St West AUL OL6 .....119 F3
Daleswood Av WHTF M45 .....69 G3
Dale Vw DTN/ASHW M34 .....147 E4
HYDE SK14 .....147 H3
LIT OL15 .....31 G1
Dalham Av BKLY M9 .....88 D5
Dalkeith Gv BOLS/LL BL3 .....47 G4
Dalkeith Rd RDSH SK5 .....145 F4
Dalkeith St GTN M18 .....130 A2
Dallas Ct SALQ M50 .....112 D5
Dalley Av BRO M7 .....114 A1
Dallimore Rd NTHM/RTH M23 .....167 F5
Dalmahoy Cl NEWH/MOS M40 .....104 B2
Dalmain Cl CHH M8 .....102 A4
Dalmeny Ter ROCH OL11 .....43 E2
Dalmorton Rd CCHDY M21 .....141 H5
Dalny St BRUN/LGST M13 .....144 B2
Dalston Av FAIL M35 .....105 G2
Dalston Dr BRAM/HZG SK7 .....193 F2
DID/WITH M20 .....157 H4
Dalton Av MILN OL16 .....31 E4
RUSH/FAL M14 .....142 C1
STRET M32 .....125 E4
WHTF M45 .....69 H5
Dalton Cl MILN OL16 .....31 E4
RAMS BL0 .....16 B4
Dalton Dr SWIN M27 .....100 A3
Dalton Fold WHTN BL5 .....62 A3
Dalton Gdns URM M41 .....124 A5
Dalton Gv HTNM SK4 .....159 F2
Dalton Rd BKLY M9 .....88 A2
MDTN M24 .....71 G5
Dalton St ANC M4 .....7 K1
CHAD OL9 .....74 C5
ECC M30 .....111 E2
FAIL M35 .....104 D2
OLD OL1 .....76 A5
SALE M33 .....140 A5
TOT/BURYW BL8 .....37 H2
Daltry Cl OLD OL1 .....75 H4
Dalveen Av URM M41 .....124 B4
Dalveen Dr HALE/TIMP WA15 .....166 A2
Damask Av CSLFD M3 .....114 A3
Dame Hollow CHD/CHDH SK8 .....182 A4
Dameral Cl CHH M8 .....102 B4
Damery Ct BRAM/HZG SK7 .....183 H4
Damery Rd BRAM/HZG SK7 .....183 H4
Dam Head Dr BKLY M9 .....88 C2
Dam Head Fold WHTN BL5 .....62 A3
Damien St BNG/LEV M19 .....144 B1
Damson Gn MDTN M24 .....71 G4
Dan Bank MPL/ROM SK6 .....174 B5
Danby Cl HYDE SK14 .....134 A4
Danby Pl HYDE SK14 .....134 A4
Danby Rd BOLS/LL BL3 .....64 D1
HYDE SK14 .....134 A4
Dane Av EDGY/DAV SK3 .....170 D1
PART M31 .....151 E2
Dane Bank MDTN M24 .....73 E5
Danebank Ms DTN/ASHW M34 .....145 H1
Danebank Wk BRUN/LGST M13 * 128 C1
Danebridge Cl FWTH BL4 .....66 B4
Dane Cl BRAM/HZG SK7 .....185 G2
Dane Dr WILM/AE SK9 .....199 E4
Danefield Ct CHD/CHDH SK8 .....182 A4
Danefield Rd SALE M33 .....140 A5
Daneholme Rd BNG/LEV M19 .....158 B1
Dane Ms SALE M33 .....140 A5
Dane Rd DTN/ASHW M34 .....140 A5
SALE M33 .....140 A5
Danesbury Ri CHD/CHDH SK8 .....170 A4
Danesbury Rd BOLE BL2 .....34 C2

Danesmoor Dr BURY BL9 .....38 D2
Danesmoor Rd DID/WITH M20 .....157 F1
Danes Rd RUSH/FAL M14 .....143 F1
Daneswood Av BKLY M9 * 88 C3
Daneswood Cl WHIT OL12 .....14 A5
Daneswood Meadow WHIT OL12 .....14 A5
Danett Cl WGTN/LGST M12 .....129 H2
Danforth Gv BNG/LEV M19 .....144 B3
Daniel Adamson Av PART M31 .....150 C3
Daniel Adamson Rd SALQ M50 .....112 C5
Daniel Fold WHIT OL12 .....29 E1
Daniel's La STKP SK1 * 13 G2
Daniel St BRAM/HZG SK7 .....185 F2
HEY OL10 * 40 C4
OLD OL1 .....76 B4
ROY/SHW OL2 .....75 H1
WHIT OL12 .....14 C4
Danisher La OLDS OL8 .....106 C2
Dannywood Cl HYDE SK14 .....147 F2
Danson St NEWH/MOS M40 .....115 H2
Dantall Av BKLY M9 .....88 D5
Dante Cl ECC M30 .....111 H1
Danty St DUK SK16 * 119 G4
Danwood Cl DTN/ASHW M34 .....147 F2
Darbishire St BOL BL1 .....3 G1
Darby Rd IRL M44 .....136 C5
Darbyshire Cl BOL BL1 .....48 B1
Darbyshire St RAD M26 .....68 B2
Darcy St BOLE BL2 .....49 H4
Darden Cl HTNM SK4 .....158 B3
Darell Wk CHH M8 .....102 C4
Daresbury Av URM M41 .....123 E4
Daresbury Cl EDGY/DAV SK3 .....171 G4
SALE M33 .....155 G3
Daresbury Rd CCHDY M21 .....140 D2
Daresbury St CHH M8 .....102 B3
Dargai St OP/CLY M11 .....117 E4
Dargle Rd SALE M33 .....139 H5
Darian Av WYTH/NTH M22 .....180 C4
Dark La MOSL OL5 .....94 A5
UPML OL3 .....78 D4
Darley Av BOL BL1 .....32 A4
CCHDY M21 .....156 B3
FWTH BL4 .....64 D5
GTN M18 .....130 D5
Darley Gv BRAM/HZG SK7 .....185 G5
OLDTF/WHR M16 .....127 F5
ROCH OL11 .....43 E2
Darley Rd BRAM/HZG SK7 .....185 G5
Darley St BOL BL1 .....33 G5
OP/CLY M11 .....115 H4
SALE M33 .....154 C2
STRET M32 .....126 B4
Darley Ter BOL BL1 .....33 G5
Darlington Cl TOT/BURYW BL8 .....37 G2
Darlington Rd DID/WITH M20 .....157 E1
ROCH OL11 .....43 E5
Darliston Av BKLY M9 .....87 F2
Darnall Av DID/WITH M20 .....142 C3
Darnbrook Dr WYTH/NTH M22 .....180 A3
Darncombe Cl OLDTF/WHR M16 .....128 A4
Darnley Av WALK M28 .....96 D1
Darnley St OLDTF/WHR M16 .....127 G4
Darnton Gdns AUL OL6 .....120 B2
Darnton Rd AUL OL6 .....120 B2
Darras Rd GTN M18 .....130 D5
Dart Cl CHAD OL9 .....74 A4
Dartford Av ECC M30 .....110 C3
RDSH SK5 .....145 H5
Dartford Cl WGTN/LGST M12 .....128 C2
Dartford Rd URM M41 .....138 C2
Dartington Cl BRAM/HZG SK7 .....184 A1
NTHM/RTH M23 .....167 E3
Dartmouth Cl OLDS OL8 .....91 G3
Dartmouth Crs RDSH SK5 .....160 D1
Dartmouth Rd CCHDY M21 .....141 G3
WHTF M45 .....69 H5
Dartnall Cl POY/DIS SK12 .....197 F1
Darton Av NEWH/MOS M40 .....115 H2
Darvel Cl BOLE BL2 .....50 C3
Darwell Av ECC M30 .....110 C5
Darwen Rd EDGW/EG BL7 .....23 E5
Darwen St OLDTF/WHR M16 .....127 F3
Darwin Gv BRAM/HZG SK7 .....193 H1
Darwin St AULW OL7 .....119 F3
BOL BL1 .....34 B2
HYDE SK14 .....134 B2
OLDE OL4 .....92 B2
Dashwood Rd PWCH M25 .....85 G2
Datchett Ter ROCH OL11 .....43 E2
Dauntesy Av SWIN M27 * 100 A3
Davehall Av WILM/AE SK9 .....198 D3
Davenfield Ct DID/WITH M20 .....157 G3
Davenfield Rd DID/WITH M20 .....157 G3
Davenham Rd RDSH SK5 .....145 F1
SALE M33 .....139 E5
WILM/AE SK9 .....200 B1
Davenhill Rd BNG/LEV M19 .....144 A3
Davenport Av DID/WITH M20 .....142 D4
WILM/AE SK9 .....201 F2
Davenport Dr MPL/ROM SK6 .....147 F5
Davenport Fold BOLE BL2 .....35 H2
Davenport Fold Rd BOLE BL2 .....35 H1
Davenport Gdns BOLE BL2 .....3 H1
Davenport Park Rd OFTN SK2 .....172 B4
Davenport Rd BRAM/HZG SK7 .....185 E1
Davenport St BOL BL1 .....2 C3
DROY M43 .....117 H3
DTN/ASHW M34 .....118 D5
Daventry Rd CCHDY M21 .....141 H3
ROCH OL11 .....43 E2
Daveyhulme St WHIT OL12 .....11 G2
Daveylands URM M41 .....123 G3

WILM/AE SK9 .... 199 G4
Davey La *WILM/AE* SK9 .... 200 D5
David Brow *BOLS/LL* BL3 .... 63 H2
David Cl *DTN/ASHW* M34 * 147 E2
David Lewis Cl *MILN* OL16 .... 30 D5
David's Farm Cl *MDTN* M24 .... 73 F5
Davids La *OLDE* OL4 .... 77 E5
David's Rd *DROY* M43 .... 117 F3
David St *DTN/ASHW* M34 .... 147 E2
RDSH SK5 .... 145 E3
TOT/BURYW BL8 .... 37 H5
WHIT OL12 .... 10 D2
David St North *WHIT* OL12 .... 10 D2
Davies Av *CHD/CHDH* SK8 .... 191 C1
Davies Rd *MPL/ROM* SK6 .... 161 E3
PART M31 .... 151 F3
Davies Sq *RUSH/FAL* M14 .... 128 B4
Davies St *AULW* OL7 .... 119 E4
FWTH BL4 .... 66 D5
OLD OL1 .... 8 D1
Davis St *ECC* M30 .... 111 H4
Davy Av *SWIN* M27 .... 85 E5
Davyhulme Rd *MILN* M32 .... 125 H5
URM M41 .... 123 F4
Davyhulme Rd East
STRET M32 .... 126 A5
Davy St *NEWH/MOS* M40 * 115 F1
Dawlish Av *CHAD* OL9 .... 74 A3
CHD/CHDH SK8 .... 182 C4
DROY M43 .... 117 F3
RDSH SK5 .... 160 D1
Dawlish Cl *BRAM/HZG* SK7 .... 183 H5
GOL/RIS/CUL WA3 .... 150 A3
HYDE SK14 .... 135 F5
Dawlish Rd *CCHDY* M21 .... 141 G3
SALE M33 .... 153 H2
Dawnay St *OP/CLY* M11 * 130 A1
Dawn St *ROY/SHW* OL2 * 60 A3
Dawson La *BOL* BL1 .... 2 A5
Dawson Rd *AUL* WA14 .... 165 G2
CHD/CHDH SK8 .... 182 A4
Dawson St *BURY* BL9 .... 38 D2
CSLFD M3 .... 6 A7
CSLFD M3 * 6 D2
HEY OL10 .... 40 D4
HYDE SK14 .... 148 A2
OLDE OL4 .... 92 D2
STKP SK1 .... 160 C3
SWIN M27 .... 99 F2
Day Dr *FAIL* M35 .... 105 E4
Day Gv *HYDE* SK14 .... 135 H5
Daylesford Cl *CHD/CHDH* SK8 .... 169 H5
Daylesford Crs
CHD/CHDH SK8 .... 170 A5
Daylesford Rd
CHD/CHDH SK8 .... 170 A5
Deacon Cl *ALT* WA14 .... 177 E3
Deacons Cl *STKP* SK1 .... 13 J3
Deacons Crs *TOT/BURYW* BL8 .... 37 F1
Deacons Dr *SLFD* M6 .... 100 A4
Deacon St *MILN* OL16 .... 11 G2
Deal Av *RDSH* SK5 .... 145 H5
Deal Cl *NEWH/MOS* M40 .... 104 C5
Dealey Rd *BOLS/LL* BL3 .... 47 H5
Deal St *BOLS/LL* BL3 .... 65 E1
BUR BL9 .... 5 J3
CSLFD M3 * 6 C2
HYDE SK14 .... 148 A1
Deal Wk *CHAD* OL9 .... 90 B1
Dean Av *NEWH/MOS* M40 .... 104 A4
OLDTF/WHR M16 .... 127 E5
Deanbank Av *BNG/LEV* M19 .... 143 H5
Dean Bank Dr *MILN* OL16 .... 43 G5
Dean Cl *FWTH* BL4 .... 65 E4
PART M31 .... 151 E2
WHTF M45 .... 69 E5
WILM/AE SK9 .... 199 F1
Dean Ct *BOL* BL1 .... 3 F2
HULME M15 .... 127 G2
Deancourt *ROCH* OL11 .... 42 D2
Deane Av *ALT* WA14 .... 177 E3
WILM/AE SK9 .... 199 F1
Deane Av *BOLS/LL* BL3 .... 48 A4
CHD/CHDH SK8 .... 170 C4
Deane Church La *BOLS/LL* BL3 .... 48 A5
Deane Rd *BOLS/LL* BL3 .... 48 A4
Deanery Wy *STKP* SK1 .... 13 G2
Deane Wk *BOLS/LL* BL3 .... 2 C7
Dean La *BRAM/HZG* SK7 .... 184 A5
Dean Moor Rd *BRAM/HZG* SK7 .... 184 D2
Dean Rd *CSLFD* M3 .... 6 C1
GTN M18 .... 130 D4
IRL M44 .... 136 A5
Dean Row Rd *WILM/AE* SK9 .... 199 F1
Deanscourt Av *SWIN* M27 .... 98 D3
Deansgate *BOL* BL1 .... 2 E4
HULME M15 .... 127 H1
Deansgate La
HALE/TIMP WA15 .... 165 H2
Deanshut Rd *OLDS* OL8 .... 90 D5
Deans Rd *SWIN* M27 .... 98 D3
Dean St *AUL* OL6 .... 119 F2
CMANE M1 .... 7 J4
FAIL M35 .... 104 D3
MILN OL16 .... 11 G3
MOSL OL5 .... 108 C1
RAD M26 .... 68 A1
STLY SK15 .... 120 D4
Deansway *SWIN* M27 .... 98 D3
Deanswood Dr *BKLY* M9 .... 87 E1
Dean Ter *AUL* OL6 .... 107 E1
Deanwater Ct
BRUN/LGST M13 .... 128 C3
Deanwater Ct
CHD/CHDH SK8 * 182 A5
STRET M32 * 140 A3
Deanway *NEWH/MOS* M40 .... 103 H2
URM M41 .... 137 F1
WILM/AE SK9 .... 199 F2
Dearden Av *LHULT* M38 .... 81 F2
Dearden Fold
TOT/BURYW BL8 * 37 H5
Deardens St *TOT/BURYW* BL8 .... 37 H5
Dearden St *BOLS/LL* BL3 .... 50 D5

Hulme M15 .... 127 H2
LIT OL15 .... 21 E2
STLY SK15 * 120 D3
Dearmans Pl *CSLFD* M3 .... 6 C5
Dearnaley Cl *LIT* OL15 .... 20 C4
Dearnalay Wy *CHAD* OL9 .... 90 C1
Dearne Dr *STRET* M32 .... 140 C1
Dearnley Cl *LIT* OL15 .... 20 C4
Debdale Av *GTN* M18 .... 131 E4
Debdale La *GTN* M18 .... 131 E4
Debenham Av
NEWH/MOS M40 .... 116 D1
Debenham Ct *HALE/TIMP* WA15 * 66 A5
De Brook Cl *URM* M41 .... 137 G2
Dee Av *HALE/TIMP* WA15 .... 167 E4
Dee Dr *FWTH* BL4 .... 82 A2
Deepcar St *BNG/LEV* M19 .... 144 A1
Deepdale *OLDE* OL4 .... 92 C1
Deepdale Av *DID/WITH* M20 .... 142 C3
MILN OL16 .... 30 D5
ROY/SHW OL2 .... 58 D5
Deepdale Cl *RDSH* SK5 .... 145 F2
Deepdale Dr *SWIN* M27 .... 100 A3
Deepdale Rd *BOLE* BL2 .... 35 G5
Deeping Av *OLDTF/WHR* M16 .... 141 H1
Deeplish Rd *ROCH* OL11 .... 43 E1
Deeplish St *ROCH* OL11 .... 43 E1
Deeracre Av *OFTN* SK2 .... 172 D3
Deerfold Cl *GTN* M18 * 130 C3
Deerhurst Dr *CHH* M8 .... 102 A4
Deeroak Cl *GTN* M18 * 130 A2
Deerpark Rd
OLDTF/WHR M16 .... 127 H5
Deerwood V *HYDE* SK14 .... 149 G2
Defence St *BOLS/LL* BL3 * 2 B7
Deganwy Gv *RDSH* SK5 .... 160 A1
Degas Cl *BRO* M7 .... 101 E2
Delacourt Rd *RUSH/FAL* M14 .... 142 C3
Delafield Av *WGTN/LGST* M12 .... 144 A1
Delaford Av *SALE* M33 .... 97 F3
Delaford Cl *EDGY/DAV* SK3 .... 171 H5
Delahays Dr *HALE/TIMP* WA15 .... 178 D2
Delahays Range *GTN* M18 .... 131 E2
Delahays Rd *HALE/TIMP* WA15 .... 178 D2
Delaine Rd *DID/WITH* M20 .... 143 E5
Delamere Av *ROY/SHW* OL2 .... 60 C1
SALE M33 .... 155 F3
SLFD M6 .... 99 H5
STRET M32 .... 140 B1
SWIN M27 .... 84 C5
WHTF M45 .... 69 F4
Delamere Cl *BRAM/HZG* SK7 * 185 H1
MPL/ROM SK6 .... 162 B1
STLY SK15 .... 109 F4
Delamere Rd *BNG/LEV* M19 .... 144 A3
BRAM/HZG SK7 .... 185 H1
CHD/CHDH SK8 .... 169 G4
DTN/ASHW M34 .... 145 H1
MILN OL16 .... 43 H2
OFTN SK2 .... 172 C5
URM M41 .... 137 H1
Delamere St *AUL* OL6 .... 119 G4
BURY BL9 .... 5 H5
OLDS OL8 .... 92 A3
OP/CLY M11 .... 131 E1
Delamer Rd *ALT* WA14 .... 177 E1
Delaunays Rd *CHH* M8 .... 87 C5
SALE M33 .... 154 A2
Delbooth Av *URM* M41 .... 123 F4
Delfur Rd *BRAM/HZG* SK7 .... 184 A5
Delhi Rd *IRL* M44 .... 136 B5
Delius Cl *ARD* M3 * 101 G2
Dell Av *WHIT* OL12 .... 29 F2
Dell Av *WALK* M28 .... 100 A3
Dellcot Cl *PWCH* M25 .... 86 C5
SLFD M6 .... 99 G5
Dellcot La *WALK* M28 .... 97 G6
Dell Gdns *WHIT* OL12 .... 29 E1
Dellhide Cl *OLDE* OL4 .... 93 F1
Dell Meadow *WHIT* OL12 .... 18 B3
Dell Av *WHIT* OL12 .... 18 A4
Dell Side *MPL/ROM* SK6 .... 161 F3
Dellside Gv *WALK* M28 .... 82 B4
Dell Side Wy *WHIT* OL12 .... 29 F1
The Dell *BOLE* BL2 .... 34 D1
Delph Brook Wy *EDGW/EG* BL7 .... 22 C1
Delph Hl *BOL* BL1 .... 32 B4
Delph Hill Cl *BOL* BL1 .... 32 B4
Delph Av *WALK* M28 .... 82 A5
Delph La *BOLE* BL2 .... 36 B5
Delph New Rd *UPML* OL3 .... 78 C2
Delph Rd *UPML* OL3 .... 61 H2
Delph St *BOLS/LL* BL3 .... 48 C4
MILN OL16 .... 31 G5
The Delph *WALK* M28 * 97 C4
Delside Av *NEWH/MOS* M40 .... 103 H2
Delta Cl *ROY/SHW* OL2 .... 75 E2
Delta Rd *DTN/ASHW* M34 .... 132 D2
Delvers Rd *ALT* WA14 .... 165 G1
Delvino Wk *RUSH/FAL* M14 .... 128 B4
Delwood Gdns
WYTH/NTH M22 .... 168 C5
De-massey Cl
MPL/ROM SK6 .... 147 F5
Demesne Cl *STLY* SK15 .... 121 F4
Demesne Crs *STLY* SK15 .... 121 F4
Demesne Dr *STLY* SK15 .... 121 F4
Demesne Rd *OLDTF/WHR* M16 .... 142 C1
Demmings Rd *CHD/CHDH* SK8 .... 170 C4
Dempsey Dr *BURY* BL9 .... 70 A2
Denbigh Cl *BRAM/HZG* SK7 .... 184 D4
Denbigh Dr *ROY/SHW* OL2 .... 59 C3
Denbigh Pl *ORD* M5 .... 113 F4
Denbigh Rd *BOLS/LL* BL3 .... 49 H4
DTN/ASHW M34 .... 146 D2
SWIN M27 .... 84 B5
Denbigh St *HTNM* SK4 .... 159 G3
OLDS OL8 .... 91 G4
Denbigh Wk *HULME* M15 * 127 H3
Denbury Dr *ALT* WA14 .... 165 E4
Denbury Gn *BRAM/HZG* SK7 .... 184 D3
Denbydale Wy *ROY/SHW* OL2 .... 58 C5
Denby La *HTNM* SK4 .... 159 G2
Denby Rd *DUK* SK16 .... 133 F1
Dencombe St
BRUN/LGST M13 .... 129 G4
Dene Bank *BOLE* BL2 .... 34 D1
Dene Brow *DTN/ASHW* M34 .... 147 F3
Dene Ct *HTNM* SK4 .... 12 A1

Dene Dr *MDTN* M24 .... 72 C5
Denefield Cl *MPL/ROM* SK6 .... 163 G5
Deneford Rd *DID/WITH* M20 .... 157 F4
Dene Hollow *RDSH* SK5 .... 145 G3
Denehurst St
WGTN/LGST M12 * 129 G2
Dene Pk *DID/WITH* M20 .... 157 F3
Dene Rd *DID/WITH* M20 .... 157 F3
Dene Rd West *DID/WITH* M20 .... 157 E3
Deneside Crs *BRAM/HZG* SK7 .... 185 G1
Dene St *BOLE* BL2 .... 34 D1
Deneway *BRAM/HZG* SK7 .... 185 F5
HTNM SK4 .... 158 B1
MPL/ROM SK6 .... 187 E5
Deneway Cl *HTNM* SK4 .... 12 A2
Deneway Ms *HTNM* SK4 .... 12 A1
Denewell Cl *BRUN/LGST* M13 .... 129 E3
Denham Cl *BOL* BL1 .... 34 B1
Denham Dr *BRAM/HZG* SK7 .... 183 G5
IRL M44 .... 136 A4
Denham St *ALT* WA14 .... 165 G5
CHAD OL9 .... 74 D4
MILN OL16 .... 44 C1
Denmark Wy *CHAD* OL9 .... 74 A5
Denmore Rd
NEWH/MOS M40 .... 89 F5
Dennington Dr *URM* M41 .... 124 B4
Dennison Av *DID/WITH* M20 .... 142 D4
Dennison Rd *CHD/CHDH* SK8 .... 182 D4
Denshaw Av *DTN/ASHW* M34 .... 132 A3
Denshaw Cl *BNG/LEV* M19 .... 158 B3
Denshaw Rd *UPML* OL3 .... 61 H4
Densmead Wk
NEWH/MOS M40 * 115 F2
Densmore St *FAIL* M35 * 104 D3
Denson Rd *HALE/TIMP* WA15 .... 166 C1
Denstone Av *ECC* M30 .... 111 F2
SALE M33 .... 153 H5
URM M41 .... 124 B5
Denstone Crs *BOLE* BL2 .... 35 E4
Denstone Rd *RDSH* SK5 .... 160 B1
SLFD M6 .... 100 A5
URM M41 .... 137 G2
Dentdale Cl *BOL* BL1 .... 47 E3
Denton Hall Farm Rd
DTN/ASHW M34 .... 146 A1
Denton La *CHAD* OL9 .... 90 B2
Denton Rd *BOLE* BL2 .... 51 E3
DTN/ASHW M34 .... 132 B5
Denton St *BURY* BL9 .... 4 B5
HEY OL10 .... 40 D5
WHIT OL12 .... 10 C3
Denver Av *NEWH/MOS* M40 .... 115 G2
Denver Dr *HALE/TIMP* WA15 .... 166 B3
Denville Crs *WYTH/NTH* M22 .... 180 D1
Denzell Gdns *ALT* WA14 .... 176 D1
Depleach Rd *CHD/CHDH* SK8 .... 170 A4
Deptford Av *NTHM/RTH* M23 .... 179 H1
De Quincey Rd *ALT* WA14 .... 165 G2
Deramore St *AUL* OL6 .... 120 B2
Deramore St *RUSH/FAL* M14 .... 128 C5
Derby Av *SLFD* M6 .... 112 D3
Derby Cl *IRL* M44 .... 150 B1
SALE M33 .... 154 D3
Derby Gv *BNG/LEV* M19 .... 144 B2
Derby Range *BRAM/HZG* SK7 .... 185 G4
Derby Rd *AUL* OL6 .... 120 A2
HTNM SK4 .... 145 E5
RAD M26 .... 66 D4
RUSH/FAL M14 .... 143 E4
SALE M33 .... 139 E5
URM M41 .... 124 C5
WHTF M45 .... 69 E3
Derbyshire Av *STRET* M32 .... 125 G5
Derbyshire Gv *STRET* M32 .... 125 G5
Derbyshire La *STRET* M32 .... 125 F5
Derbyshire La West
STRET M32 .... 125 F5
Derbyshire Rd
NEWH/MOS M40 .... 117 E1
PART M31 .... 151 G3
POY/DIS SK12 .... 196 C2
Derbyshire Rd South
SALE M33 .... 155 E4
Derbyshire Rw *BOL* BL1 * 33 H3
Derbyshire St *OP/CLY* M11 .... 130 B2
Derby St *ALT* WA14 .... 165 G1
AULW OL7 .... 106 C5
BOLS/LL BL3 .... 48 C4
BURY BL9 .... 5 F4
CHAD OL9 .... 8 A7
CHH M8 .... 101 H5
DTN/ASHW M34 .... 132 A4
EDGY/DAV SK3 .... 12 D6
FAIL M35 .... 105 G3
HEY OL10 .... 40 C4
MOSL OL5 .... 109 E2
MPL/ROM SK6 .... 175 G4
PWCH M25 .... 85 H5
RAMS BL0 .... 17 E2
ROCH OL11 .... 30 C5
Dereham Cl *TOT/BURYW* BL8 .... 38 A1
Derg St *SLFD* M6 .... 113 E3
Derker St *OLD* OL1 .... 9 K1
Dermot Murphy Cl
DID/WITH M20 .... 142 B5

Dernford Av *BNG/LEV* M19 .... 158 C1
Derry Av *WYTH/NTH* M22 .... 168 D5
Derwen Rd *EDGY/DAV* SK3 .... 171 H5
Derwent Av *AULW* OL7 .... 119 F1
CCHDY M21 .... 156 C1
DROY M43 .... 117 H4
HALE/TIMP WA15 * 166 A1
HEY OL10 .... 56 A1
WHTF M45 .... 69 E4
Derwent Cl *BOLS/LL* BL3 .... 51 E5
DTN/ASHW M34 .... 145 H1
PART M31 .... 151 E2
WALK M28 .... 81 G5
WHTF M45 .... 69 E4
Derwent Dr *BRAM/HZG* SK7 .... 185 H1
BURY BL9 .... 53 G2
CHAD OL9 .... 89 H1
FWTH BL4 .... 83 E2
LIT OL15 .... 31 G1
ROY/SHW OL2 .... 58 D5
SALE M33 .... 154 D4
WILM/AE SK9 .... 199 H2
Derwent Rd *FWTH* BL4 .... 65 F5
MDTN M24 .... 72 B1
MPL/ROM SK6 .... 186 D4
URM M41 .... 126 A5
Derwent St *CHH* M8 .... 102 D4
DROY M43 .... 117 E4
ORD M5 .... 113 H5
Derwent Ter *STLY* SK15 .... 120 C1
Design St *BOLS/LL* BL3 .... 64 A1
Desmond Rd *WYTH/NTH* M22 .... 168 D5
Dettinger St *SLFD* M6 .... 100 B5
Deva Cl *BRAM/HZG* SK7 .... 184 A5
POY/DIS SK12 .... 194 C3
Deva Sq *CHAD* OL9 .... 89 H1
Deva St *HULME* M15 .... 128 C3
Devine Cl *CSLFD* M3 .... 131 E4
ROY/SHW OL2 .... 59 E3
Devisdale Gra *ALT* WA14 * 177 E1
Devisdale Rd *ALT* WA14 .... 165 E5
Devoke Av *WALK* M28 .... 82 B5
Devoke Gv *FWTH* BL4 .... 65 F5
Devoke Rd *WYTH/NTH* M22 .... 180 A2
Devon Av *BNG/LEV* M19 .... 143 H3
WHTF M45 .... 69 F3
Devon Cl *BOLS/LL* BL3 .... 51 E5
RDSH SK5 .... 160 D2
SLFD M6 .... 100 C5
Devon Dr *BOLE* BL2 .... 36 B5
Devonport Crs *ROY/SHW* OL2 .... 59 F2
Devon Rd *DROY* M43 .... 117 H2
FAIL M35 .... 104 D4
IRL M44 .... 150 C1
PART M31 .... 150 D4
Devon St *HEY* OL10 .... 40 D5
URM M41 .... 137 G2
Devonshire Cl *HEY* OL10 .... 40 D5
URM M41 .... 137 G2
Devonshire Dr *WILM/AE* SK9 .... 201 F3
Devonshire Park Rd
OFTN SK2 .... 172 B4
Devonshire Pl *PWCH* M25 .... 85 H2
Devonshire Rd *ALT* WA14 .... 165 E2
BOL BL1 .... 33 F5
BRAM/HZG SK7 .... 185 G4
CCHDY M21 .... 141 G3
ECC M30 .... 111 F3
HTNM SK4 .... 158 C3
ROCH OL11 .... 55 H4
SLFD M6 .... 99 H1
WALK M28 .... 81 G5
Devonshire St *BRO* M7 .... 101 H4
WGTN/LGST M12 .... 129 E2
Devonshire St East
FAIL M35 * 104 C3
Devonshire St North
WGTN/LGST M12 .... 129 E1
Devonshire St South
BRUN/LGST M13 .... 129 E3
Devon St *BOLE* BL2 .... 3 J1
BURY BL9 .... 5 G3
CHAD OL9 .... 90 C3
FWTH BL4 .... 66 A4
ROCH OL11 .... 42 C5
SWIN M27 .... 84 A5
Devon Wy *OLDS* OL8 .... 90 D4
Dewar Cl *OP/CLY* M11 .... 116 B4
Dewes Av *SWIN* M27 .... 84 C5
Dewey St *OP/CLY* M11 .... 130 C2
Dewhirst Rd *WHIT* OL12 .... 14 C4
Dewhirst Wy *WHIT* OL12 .... 19 E4
Dewhurst Clough Rd
EDGW/EG BL7 .... 22 B2
Dewhurst Rd *BOLE* BL2 .... 35 F3
Dewhurst St *CHH* M8 .... 102 B2
HEY OL10 * 41 F4
Dewint Av *MPL/ROM* SK6 .... 163 F5
Dew Meadow Cl *WHIT* OL16 .... 29 F5
Dewsnap Cl *DUK* SK16 .... 133 F2
Dewsnap La *DUK* SK16 .... 133 H2
HYDE SK14 .... 133 H2
Dexter Rd *BKLY* M9 .... 87 F2
Deyne Av *PWCH* M25 .... 86 A4
RUSH/FAL M14 .... 128 D4
Deyne St *ORD* M5 .... 112 D3
Dial Ct *FWTH* BL4 .... 66 B3
Dial Park Rd *OFTN* SK2 .... 173 E5
Dialstone La *OFTN* SK2 .... 172 D2
Diamond St *OFTN* SK2 .... 172 D2
Diamond Ter *MPL/ROM* SK6 .... 187 E5
Dicken Gn *ROCH* OL11 .... 43 E3
Dicken Green La *ROCH* OL11 .... 43 E3
Dickens Cl *CHD/CHDH* SK8 .... 193 E2
Dickens La *POY/DIS* SK12 .... 195 F4
Dickenson Rd *RUSH/FAL* M14 .... 128 C5
Dickens Rd *ECC* M30 .... 110 C1
Dickens St *HEY* OL10 * 41 E5
OLD OL1 .... 60 D5
Dickinson Cl *BOL* BL1 * 33 H5
Dickinson St *BOL* BL1 .... 33 H5
CMANE M1 .... 7 F6

Didcot Av *DTN/ASHW* M34 .... 146 D2
Didley Sq *WGTN/LGST* M12 * 129 F2
Didsbury Pk *DID/WITH* M20 .... 157 H5
Didsbury Rd *HTNM* SK4 .... 158 A4
Digby Rd *ROCH* OL11 .... 43 E2
Dig Gate La *MILN* OL16 .... 44 B3
Diggles La *ROCH* OL11 .... 28 B5
Diggle St *ROY/SHW* OL2 .... 60 A3
Dijon St *BOLS/LL* BL3 .... 2 A7
Dilham Ct *BOL* BL1 .... 48 B1
Dillmoss Wk *HULME* M15 * 127 G2
Dillon Dr *WGTN/LGST* M12 .... 129 F3
Dilston Cl *HEY* OL10 .... 40 A4
Dilworth Cl *HEY* OL10 * 40 A4
Dilworth Ct *OFTN* SK2 .... 173 F4
Dilworth St *HULME* M15 .... 128 A3
Dingle Av *ROY/SHW* OL2 .... 45 F5
WILM/AE SK9 .... 200 A2
Dingle Bank Rd
BRAM/HZG SK7 .... 183 G5
Dingle Cl *MPL/ROM* SK6 .... 162 C4
Dingle Dr *DROY* M43 .... 118 A2
Dingle Rd *MDTN* M24 .... 88 B1
Dingle Ter *AUL* OL6 .... 92 A5
The Dingle *BRAM/HZG* SK7 .... 184 B5
HYDE SK14 .... 148 A5
Dingle Wk *BOL* BL1 .... 2 E2
Dinmor Rd *WYTH/NTH* M22 .... 180 C4
Dinnington Dr *CHH* M8 .... 102 A4
Dinorwic Cl *NEWH/MOS* M40 .... 104 A4
Dinsdale Dr *BOLS/LL* BL3 .... 48 C4
Dinting Av *DID/WITH* M20 .... 142 C4
Dinton St *HULME* M15 .... 127 F1
Dirty La *OLDE* OL4 .... 77 G3
Dirty Leech *WHIT* OL12 .... 19 E2
Discovery Pk *HTNM* SK4 * 159 F1
Disley Av *DID/WITH* M20 .... 142 B5
Disley St *ROCH* OL11 .... 42 C2
Distaff Rd *POY/DIS* SK12 .... 194 C3
Ditton Brook *WHTN* BL5 .... 62 A3
Ditton Mead Cl *WHIT* OL12 .... 30 C1
Division St *BOLS/LL* BL3 .... 65 E1
WHIT OL12 .... 11 C1
Dixon Av *BRO* M7 .... 101 G4
Dixon Cl *SALE* M33 .... 155 E4
Dixon Closes *ROCH* OL11 .... 28 B4
Dixon Dr *WGTN/LGST* M12 .... 83 H5
Dixon Green Dr *FWTH* BL4 .... 65 H4
Dixon Rd *DTN/ASHW* M34 .... 147 F2
Dixon St *AUL* OL6 .... 120 A1
IRL M44 .... 136 B1
MDTN M24 .... 72 D2
NEWH/MOS M40 .... 104 A4
OLD OL1 .... 9 F1
OLDE OL4 .... 76 D4
SLFD M6 .... 100 C4
Dobb Hedge Cl
HALE/TIMP WA15 .... 188 D1
Dobbin Dr *ROCH* OL11 .... 43 E5
Dobbinetts La
HALE/TIMP WA15 .... 179 E1
Dobcross Cl *BRUN/LGST* M13 .... 144 A1
Dobcross New Rd *UPML* OL3 .... 78 D3
Dobhill St *FWTH* BL4 .... 66 A4
Dobroyd St *CHH* M8 .... 102 B2
Dobson Cl *BRUN/LGST* M13 .... 129 E2
Dobson Rd *BOL* BL1 .... 48 B2
Dobson St *BOL* BL1 .... 33 C4
Doctor Fold La *HEY* OL10 .... 55 H4
Doctor La *OLDE* OL4 .... 77 E5
Doctors La *BURY* BL9 .... 4 B5
Dodd Cft *MILN* OL16 .... 43 G4
Doddington La *ORD* M5 .... 113 F5
Doddington Wk
DTN/ASHW M34 * 146 C2
Dodge Fold *OFTN* SK2 .... 173 F3
Dodge Hill *HTNM* SK4 .... 13 F1
Dodgson St *MILN* OL16 .... 30 B5
Dodworth Cl *HULME* M15 .... 128 A3
Doe Brow *SWIN* M27 .... 83 H3
Doe Hey Gv *FWTH* BL4 .... 65 G2
Doe Hey Rd *BOLS/LL* BL3 .... 65 G2
Doffcocker Brow *BOL* BL1 .... 32 C5
Doffocker La *BOL* BL1 .... 32 C5
Dogford Rd *ROY/SHW* OL2 .... 59 E4
Dog Hill Lne *ROY/SHW* OL2 .... 60 D2
Dolbey St *ORD* M5 .... 112 D4
Dolefield *CSLFD* M3 .... 6 D4
D Olivera Ct *MDTN* M24 .... 72 B2
Dollond St *BKLY* M9 .... 103 F1
Dolphin Pl *WGTN/LGST* M12 .... 128 C1
Dolphin St *WGTN/LGST* M12 .... 128 D1
Doman St *BOLS/LL* BL3 .... 49 E4
Dombey Rd *POY/DIS* SK12 .... 195 E5
Domestic Ap *MANM* M90 .... 180 B5
The Dome *ALT* WA14 * 165 C5
Domett St *BKLY* M9 .... 87 H5
Dominic Cl *NTHM/RTH* M23 .... 155 F5
Donald Av *HYDE* SK14 .... 148 A2
Donald St *CMANE* M1 * 7 G7
Dona St *STKP* SK1 .... 13 K5
Don Av *SLFD* M6 .... 112 B3
Doncaster Av *DID/WITH* M20 .... 142 C4
Doncaster Cl *BOLS/LL* BL3 .... 66 C1
OLD OL1 .... 60 C5
Doncaster Wk *OLD* OL1 * 9 G2
Donhead Wk
BRUN/LGST M13 * 128 C3
Donleigh St *NEWH/MOS* M40 .... 104 C5
Donnington Rd *GTN* M18 .... 29 H5
Donnington Av
CHD/CHDH SK8 .... 170 C4
Donnington Gdns *WALK* M28 * 82 A4
Donnington Rd *GTN* M18 .... 130 D3
RAD M26 .... 51 H5
Donnison St *WGTN/LGST* M12 .... 129 G2
Donovan Av *NEWH/MOS* M40 .... 115 F1
Don St *BOLS/LL* BL3 .... 64 C1
MDTN M24 .... 72 C5
Doodson Av IRL M44 .... 136 B1
Doodson Sq *FWTH* BL4 .... 66 A4
Dooley La *MPL/ROM* SK6 .... 174 A2
Dooley's La *WILM/AE* SK9 .... 190 A5

Dorac Av CHD/CHDH SK8........191 H1
Dora St RAMS BL0.....................16 B4
Dorchester Av BOLE BL2.........35 F5
  DTN/ASHW M34.....................146 D2
  PWCH M25...............................86 B5
  URM M41................................125 E5
Dorchester CI
  HALE/TIMP WA15..................178 D1
  WILM/AE SK9.........................199 C2
Dorchester Ct
  CHD/CHDH SK8......................183 E3
  SALE M33...............................154 C4
Dorchester Dr
  NTHM/RTH M23....................155 F5
  ROY/SHW OL2...........................75 E2
Dorchester Gv HEY OL10.........55 H1
Dorchester Rd
  BRAM/HZG SK7.......................184 C3
  SWIN M27.................................99 F4
Dorclyn Av URM M41..............138 D1
Dorfield CI MPL/ROM SK6.......161 F5
Doric Av WYTH/NTH M22.........161 E4
Doric CI OP/CLY M11..............116 A4
Doris Av BOLE BL2.....................50 A2
Doris Rd EDGY/DAV SK3.............12 A6
Dorket St MDTN M24.................72 D2
Dorking Av NEWH/MOS M40...116 B1
Dorking CI BOL BL1...................34 A4
  STKP SK1...............................172 C2
Dorlan Av GTN M18.................131 E4
Dorland Gv GTN M18...............172 C2
Dorman St OP/CLY M11...........130 C1
Dormer St BOL BL1...................34 A3
Dorney St GTN M18..................130 C3
Dorning Rd ECC M30...............111 E4
Dorning St ECC M30................111 F4
  FWTH BL4.................................65 H2
  TOT/BURYW BL8.......................37 G2
Dorothy Av BRAM/HZG SK7.....185 E1
Dorothy St BRO M7..................102 A3
Dorres St BOL BL1.....................16 C3
Dorrington Rd EDGY/DAV SK3..170 C2
  SALE M33...............................153 G2
Dorris St BNG/LEV M19.............144 B3
  BOLS/LL BL3.............................64 B1
Dorrit CI POY/DIS SK12...........195 F5
Dorset Av BRAM/HZG SK7........183 G3
  CHD/CHDH SK8......................171 F5
  DTN/ASHW M54.......................118 B5
  FWTH BL4................................65 H4
  RDSH SK5...............................160 D1
  ROY/SHW OL2...........................59 G2
  RUSH/FAL M14.......................142 C1
Dorset CI FWTH BL4...................65 H4
  HEY OL10................................40 B5
Dorset Dr BURY BL9..................53 H1
Dorset Rd ALT WA14................165 E5
  BNG/LEV M19........................144 C2
  DROY M43..............................117 G2
  FAIL M35................................105 E5
  IRL M44..................................150 C1
Dorset St AUL OL6...................120 A3
  BOL BL1.....................................3 G5
  CHAD OL9..................................8 A7
  ROCH OL11................................30 A5
  STRET M32.............................140 B2
  SWIN M27................................84 A5
Dorsey St ANC M4 *....................7 H3
Dorstone CI NEWH/MOS M40..116 C1
Dorwood Av BKLY M9.................87 H2
Dougall Wk WGTN/LGST M12..129 F2
Doughty Av ECC M30...............111 G2
Douglas Av STRET M32.............126 A5
  TOT/BURYW BL8.......................37 G4
Douglas Gn SLFD M6..................70 B3
Douglas Gn SLFD M6..............100 D5
Douglas Rd BRAM/HZG SK7.....185 F1
  EDGY/DAV SK3.......................171 H5
  WALK M28...............................98 B3
Douglas St AUL OL6.................120 A2
  BOL BL1...................................33 H1
  BRO M7..................................101 C4
  FAIL M35................................105 H1
  HYDE SK14............................148 A1
  NEWH/MOS M40.....................103 H3
  OLD OL1.....................................9 J1
  RAMS BL0...............................16 C2
  SWIN M27................................99 F2
Doulton St NEWH/MOS M40....104 B2
Dounby Av ECC M30................110 C3
Douro St NEWH/MOS M40.......103 C5
Douthwaite Dr MPL/ROM SK6.162 D5
Dove Bank Rd BOLS/LL BL3.......50 C5
Dovebrook CI STLY SK15............85 H3
Dovecote CI EDG/EG BL7...........23 E3
Dovecote La LHULT M38.............80 D4
Dovecote OLDE OL4...................77 E5
Dovecote Ms CCHDY M21........141 E4
Dovedale Av DID/WITH M20.....142 C4
  DROY M43..............................117 F3
  ECC M30................................111 F2
  PWCH M25................................86 C4
  URM M41................................137 F1
Dovedale CI MPL/ROM SK6.....186 D5
Dovedale Dr WHIT OL12............20 A2
Dovedale Rd BOL BL1.................33 G5
  OFTN SK2...............................173 E2
Dovedale St FAIL M35..............104 D3
Dove Dr BURY BL9.......................5 K1
Dovehouse CI WHTF M45...........69 E4
Doveleys Rd SLFD M6...............112 C1
Dover CI TOT/BURYW BL8..........26 B2
Dovercort Av HTNM SK4............158 C5
Dovercourt Av HTNM SK4 *......158 C3
Dover Gv BOLS/LL BL3................48 C4
Doveridge Gdns SLFD M6.........113 E2
Dove Rd BOLS/LL BL3.................48 A5
Dover Pk URM M41.....................124 B4
Dover Rd SWIN M27...................84 B5
Dover St BRUN/LGST M13.......128 C2
  CHAD OL9.................................8 B6
  ECC M30................................110 C3
  FWTH BL4...............................65 H2
  MILN OL16.............................11 H1
  RDSH SK5..............................145 E4
Dovestone Crs DUK SK16.........134 A1
Dovestone Wk
  NEWH/MOS M40 *.................104 D1

Doveston Rd SALE M33............139 H5
Dove St BOL BL1........................33 H2
  OLDE OL4.................................92 C2
  ROCH OL11..............................43 E3
Dow Fold TOT/BURYW BL8........37 E5
Dowland CI NTHM/RTH M23 *..155 C4
Dow La TOT/BURYW BL8............37 E5
Dowling St ROCH OL11..............30 A5
Downesway WILM/AE SK9.......200 C4
Downes Wy WYTH/NTH M22....168 D5
Downfield CI RAMS BL0.............16 B2
Downfields RDSH SK5...............145 G2
Downgreen Rd BOLE BL2............35 F5
Downhall Gn BOL BL1..................2 E2
Downham Av BOLE BL2...............49 H1
Downham Cha
  HALE/TIMP WA15....................166 C3
Downham CI ROY/SHW OL2........74 D2
Downham Crs PWCH M25............86 D4
Downham Gdns PWCH M25.........86 C4
Downham Rd HEY OL10..............40 B4
Downham Rd N HEY OL10..........159 G1
Downham Wk
  NTHM/RTH M23......................167 E1
Downhill CI OLD OL1....................28 D1
Downing CI AULW OL7...............106 C4
Downing St AULW OL7..............106 C4
  CMANE M1.............................128 C1
Downley CI WHIT OL12................28 D1
Downley Dr ANC M4..................115 F3
Downs Dr ALT WA14.................165 H1
Downshaw Rd AULW OL7..........106 D4
The Downs ALT WA14...............177 C1
  CHD/CHDH SK8......................182 A1
  MDTN M24..............................89 E1
  PWCH M25................................85 H4
Dowry CI OLDE OL4....................76 D5
Dowry Rd OLDE OL4....................91 G4
Dowson Rd HYDE SK14............148 A3
Dowson St BOLE BL2...................3 H5
Dow St HYDE SK14....................133 C3
Doyle Av OLD OL1.......................60 D5
Doyle Av MPL/ROM SK6...........161 E3
Doyle CI OLD OL1........................60 D5
Doyle Rd BOLS/LL BL3................63 F1
Drake Av FWTH BL4....................82 A1
  IRL M44..................................136 A5
  WYTH/NTH M22.....................180 A2
Drake CI OLD OL1.......................75 G4
Drake Ct RDSH SK5...................159 H2
Drake Hall ALT WA14...............165 E1
Drake St MILN OL16...................10 C6
  OLD OL1...................................30 A5
Draycott St BOL BL1...................34 A4
Draycott St East BOL BL1............34 A4
Drayfields DROY M43................118 C3
Drayford CI NTHM/RTH M23.....155 C4
Drayton CI BOL BL1....................33 C4
  SALE M33...............................153 C4
  WILM/AE SK9.........................199 C1
Drayton Dr CHD/CHDH SK8......181 C5
Drayton Gv HALE/TIMP WA15..166 B5
Drayton St HULME M15............127 H3
Drayton Wk OLDTF/WHR M16...127 C2
Dresden St NEWH/MOS M40....104 B2
Drewett St NEWH/MOS M40.....115 H1
Dreyfus Av OP/CLY M11...........116 D3
Driffield St ECC M30..................110 D5
  RUSH/FAL M14.......................128 B5
Drinkwater Rd PWCH M25.......100 C1
Driscoll St BRUN/LGST M13.....129 G5
The Drive BRO M7 *.....................88 C2
  BURY BL9.................................38 C1
  CHD/CHDH SK8......................171 F5
  DID/WITH M20.......................157 H3
  HALE/TIMP WA15...................179 E4
  MPL/ROM SK6.........................60 A4
  PWCH M25................................86 A3
  RDSH SK5...............................160 D2
  SALE M33...............................153 H5
Droitwich Rd NEWH/MOS M40.115 C1
Dronfield Rd SLFD M6..............112 C1
  WYTH/NTH M22.....................168 C1
Droughts La PWCH M25.............70 C4
Droylsden Rd DTN/ASHW M34..118 A4
  NEWH/MOS M40.....................104 C5
Drummond St BOL BL1 *.............2 D4
Drury La CHAD OL9....................90 B4
Drury St BNG/LEV M19.............144 A2
Dryad CI OLDTF/WHR M16.........33 G5
Drybrook CI BRUN/LGST M13...129 F3
Dryburgh Av BOL BL1..................33 G3
Dryden Av CHD/CHDH SK8.......170 B3
  SWIN M27................................98 C3
Dryden CI DUK SK16.................134 C1
  MPL/ROM SK6........................175 E5
Dryden Rd OLDTF/WHR M16....127 F5
Dryden St BRUN/LGST M13......128 B2
Dryhurst Wk HULME M15.........128 B2
Drymoss OLDS OL8...................106 C1
Drysdale Vw BOL BL1.................33 H2
Drywood Av WALK M28...............97 H5
Ducal St ANC M4.......................115 E1
Duchess Park CI ROY/SHW OL2..60 A4
Duchess st LHH M8.....................102 C2
Duchess Av ROY/SHW OL2........59 H1
Duchess St BOLS/LL BL3.............48 A5
Duchy Av WALK M28...................95 F5
  WHTN BL5.................................63 H4
Duchy Bank SLFD M6...............100 A4
Duchy Rd SLFD M6...................100 B5
Duchy St EDGY/DAV SK3...........12 D7
  SLFD M6...................................113 E3
Ducie Av BOL BL1........................33 H1
Ducie St CMANE M1.....................7 H5
  OLDS OL8.................................91 C5
  RAD M26.................................52 A4
  WHTF M45...............................69 C4
Duckshaw La FWTH BL4............65 E4
Duckworth Rd PWCH M25..........85 C4
Duckworth St BURY BL9.............38 D2
  ROY/SHW OL2...........................60 B2
Duddon Av BOLE BL2.................35 C5
Duddon CI WHTF M45.................69 F4
Dudley Av BOLE BL2...................34 C5
  WHTF M45...............................69 C4
Dudley CI HULME M15..............127 H3
Dudley Rd HALE/TIMP WA15....166 C2
  IRL M44..................................150 C2

OLDTF/WHR M16.....................127 G5
  SALE M33...............................140 A5
  SWIN M27..................................99 E1
Dudley St BRO M7.......................102 A4
  ECC M30................................110 D4
  OLDE OL4.................................92 C1
Dudlow Wk HULME M15 *.........127 G2
Dudwell CI BOL BL1....................33 F5
Duerden St BOLS/LL BL3 *..........63 H2
Duffield Ct MDTN M24 *...............88 C2
Duffield Gdns MDTN M24.............88 C2
Duffield Rd MDTN M24................88 C2
  SLFD M6................................100 A5
Duffins CI WHIT OL12.................18 C5
Dugdale Av BKLY M9..................88 B3
Dugie St RAMS BL0......................16 C1
Duke Av CHD/CHDH SK8..........192 C1
Duke CI OLDTF/WHR M16.........127 G3
Dukefield St WYTH/NTH M22...168 D1
Duke PI CSLFD M3........................6 B7
Duke Rd BOLE BL2.....................36 B5
  HYDE SK14............................134 A3
Dukes Platting AUL OL6............108 A3
Duke St AUL OL6 *....................119 G3
  BOL BL1......................................2 D3
  BRO M7..................................101 C5
  CSLFD M3...................................6 B7
  CSLFD M3...................................6 B7
  DTN/ASHW M54.....................132 B5
  ECC M30................................110 D1
  FAIL M35................................105 F2
  HEY OL10.................................40 C4
  LHULT M38..............................81 F2
  LIT OL15.................................20 D5
  MOSL OL5...............................109 F1
  RAD M26...................................68 C2
  RAMS BL0.................................16 B4
  ROY/SHW OL2.........................60 B3
  STKP SK1.................................13 G4
  STLY SK15..............................120 C4
  WALK M28...............................83 E5
  WHIT OL12...............................10 C2
  WILM/AE SK9.........................201 E3
Duke St North BOL BL1................2 D2
Dukes Wk HALE/TIMP WA15.....166 C4
Dukinfield Rd HYDE SK14.........133 F3
Dulford Wk BRUN/LGST M13 *..128 D3
Dulgar St OP/CLY M11...............116 C5
Dulverton Gdns BOLS/LL BL3 *..67 E2
Dulverton St NEWH/MOS M40..104 A4
Dulwich CI SALE M33................153 G3
Dulwich St ANC M4...................115 E2
Dumbarton CI RDSH SK5..........145 E5
Dumbarton Dr HEY OL10............40 B5
Dumbarton Rd RDSH SK5.........145 F5
Dumbell St SWIN M27.................84 A5
Dumber La SALE M33................139 F5
Dumers CI RAD M26...................53 E5
Dumers La RAD M26....................53 E5
Dumfries Hollow HEY OL10........41 G3
Dunbar Av NTHM/RTH M23.......179 H1
Dunbar Dr BOLS/LL BL3..............64 D1
Dunbar Gv HEY OL10..................55 E1
Dunbar St OLD OL1.......................8 E1
Dunblane Av BOLS/LL BL3...........64 D1
  HTNM SK4..............................159 F2
Dunbane Gv HEY OL10................55 F1
Duncan Rd BRUN/LGST M13....129 C5
Duncan St BRO M7....................101 H4
  DUK SK16...............................133 E2
  ORD M5......................................7 G7
  RAD M26...................................67 H1
Dunchurch CI HOR/BR BL6.........47 E3
Dunchurch Rd SALE M33..........153 H2
Dun CI CSLFD M3...........................6 A4
Duncombe CI BRAM/HZG SK7..184 B1
Duncombe Dr
  NEWH/MOS M40.....................116 A1
Duncombe Rd BOLS/LL BL3........64 D2
Duncombe St BRO M7...............101 H4
Duncote Gv ROY/SHW OL2.........59 G4
Dundee CI HEY OL10...................40 A5
Dundee La RAMS BL0..................16 C2
Dundonald Rd
  CHD/CHDH SK8......................182 C5
  DID/WITH M20.......................157 H3
Dundonald St OFTN SK2...........172 A3
Dundraw CI MDTN M24...............70 C1
Dundrennan CI POY/DIS SK12..195 E2
Dunecroft DTN/ASHW M54 *.....132 D4
Dunedin Dr SLFD M6..................100 C5
Dunedin Rd TOT/BURYW BL8.....26 A1
Dunelm Dr SALE M33................155 E5
Dunham Lawn ALT WA14..........165 E5
Dunham Ms ALT WA14 *............176 C3
Dunham Rd ALT WA14..............176 C2
  DUK SK16...............................133 C2
  PART M31...............................152 A5
  WILM/AE SK9.........................192 A2
Dunham St HULME M15............127 H2
  OLDE OL4.................................76 D4
Dunkeld Rd NTHM/RTH M23....167 G3
Dunkerley Av FAIL M35.............105 F3
Dunkerley St AULW OL7...........106 C5
  OLDE OL4.................................76 B5
  ROY/SHW OL2 *.......................59 F5
Dunkery Rd WYTH/NTH M22....180 C3
Dunkirk La HYDE SK14..............133 F2
Dunkirk Ri WHIT OL12................10 A6
Dunkirk Rd WHTF M45................69 C3
Dunkirk St DROY M43...............118 A4
Dunley CI WGTN/LGST M12.....129 H3
Dunlin CI BOLE BL2......................49 E1
  OFTN SK2...............................173 H4
  POY/DIS SK12.........................194 B4
  ROCH OL11..............................28 C4
Dunlin Dr IRL M44.....................122 B5
Dunlop Av ROCH OL11................42 D5
Dunlop St CSLFD M3.....................6 D4
Dunmail Dr MDTN M24................72 B1
Dunmaston Av
  HALE/TIMP WA15...................167 G3
Dunmore Rd CHD/CHDH SK8...169 G3
Dunmow Ct OFTN SK2..............173 H4
Dunnisher Rd
  NTHM/RTH M23......................168 A5
Dunnock CI OFTN SK2..............173 C4
Dunollie Rd SALE M33..............155 F3
Dunoon CI HEY OL10...................40 B5
Dunoon Dr BOL BL1....................33 C1

Dunoon Rd RDSH SK5...............145 F4
Dunrobin CI HEY OL10.................40 B5
Dunscar CI WHTF M45...............69 E4
Dunsdale Dr BKLY M9................88 A5
Dunsfold Dr NTHM/RTH M23....167 E1
Dunsley Av NEWH/MOS M40.....89 C5
Dunsmore CI
  OLDTF/WHR M16....................127 C4
Dunsop Dr BOL BL1.....................32 D4
Dunstable WHIT OL12.................10 B4
Dunstable St BNG/LEV M19.....144 B2
Dunstall Rd WYTH/NTH M22....168 D4
Dunstan St BOLE BL2..................49 H2
Dunster Av DTN/ASHW M54.....132 D1
Dunster Av BKLY M9...................88 B5
  RDSH SK5...............................160 D1
  SWIN M27..................................84 C5
Dunster CI BRAM/HZG SK7......184 D3
Dunster Dr URM M41................137 E2
Dunster PI WALK M28..................96 A3
Dunster Rd WALK M28................96 A3
Dunsters Av TOT/BURYW BL8....37 H4
Dunston St OP/CLY M11...........116 D5
Dunton Gn RDSH SK5...............145 E4
Dunvegan Rd BRAM/HZG SK7..185 C5
Dunwood Av ROY/SHW OL2.......60 B1
Dunwoods Parte Cts
  ROY/SHW OL2...........................45 F5
Durant St ANC M4........................7 H1
Durban CI ROY/SHW OL2...........59 H3
Durban Rd AULW OL7...............118 D4
  OLDS OL8.................................90 D4
  ROCH OL11..............................42 B4
Durden Ms ROY/SHW OL2..........60 A3
Durham Av URM M41................124 D5
Durham CI BOLS/LL BL3.............51 E5
  DUK SK16...............................133 G2
  MPL/ROM SK6.......................161 H5
Durham Crs FAIL M35...............105 F4
Durham Dr AUL OL6..................107 G2
  BURY BL9.................................53 H1
  RAMS BL0.................................16 B5
Durham Rd SLFD M6...................96 C1
Durham St BKLY M9 *.................105 F3
  BOL BL1...................................34 A4
  CHAD OL9................................90 D3
  DROY M43..............................117 H5
  RDSH SK5..............................145 E1
  ROCH OL11.............................43 F1
Durley Av CHH M8.....................102 C3
  HALE/TIMP WA15...................166 C2
Durling St WGTN/LGST M12.....128 D1
Durn St LIT OL15.......................21 F3
Durnford Av URM M41.............139 G1
Durnford CI WHIT OL12..............28 A1
Durnford St MDTN M24...............72 C3
Durnlaw CI LIT OL15....................21 F3
Durn St LIT OL15........................21 F3
Duty St BOL BL1..........................33 H1
Duxbury Av BOLE BL2..................35 F1
  BOLS/LL BL3............................50 D4
Duxbury Dr BURY BL9.................39 F4
Duxbury St BOL BL1....................33 C2
Dyche St ANC M4..........................7 H2
Dye House La MILN OL16............19 H5
Dye La ROY/SHW OL2.................59 G3
Dyers Ct LIT OL15.......................20 D2
Dyers St OP/CLY M11................116 D5
  ORD M5......................................7 F7
Dymchurch Av RAD M26..............67 F5
Dymchurch St
  NEWH/MOS M40.....................116 D1
Dysarts CI MOSL OL5..................94 B4
Dysart St AUL OL6.....................120 A5
  OFTN SK2...............................172 C4
Dyserth Gv RDSH SK5...............160 A1
Dyson CI FWTH BL4....................66 A4
Dyson Gv OLDE OL4....................77 E4
Dyson St FWTH BL4....................66 A5
  MOSL OL5.................................93 C3

E

Eades St SLFD M6......................113 F2
Eadington St CHH M8................102 B1
Eafield Av MILN OL16.................31 G4
Eafield CI MILN OL16...................31 G4
Eafield Rd LIT OL15.....................20 D5
  MILN OL16...............................11 K2
Eagar St NEWH/MOS M40.......104 B4
Eagle Dr SLFD M6......................100 D5
Eagle St ANC M4..........................7 G2
  BOLE BL2....................................3 H4
  CHAD OL9..................................8 E3
  ROCH OL11..............................21 F3
Eagles Brook Wy BOL BL1..........34 A3
Eagley Av RAD M26.....................53 E3
Eagley Dr TOT/BURYW BL8........37 F5
Eagley Vw TOT/BURYW BL8.......37 F5
Eagley Wy BOL BL1......................18 D5
Eaiees Rd LIT OL15....................21 E1
Ealing Av RUSH/FAL M14.........142 D1
Ealinger Wy SWIN M27...............98 C4
Ealing PI BNG/LEV M19............144 A3
Ealing Rd EDGY/DAV SK3...........12 B2
Eames Av RAD M26.....................66 D4
Earby Gv BKLY M9........................87 H1
Earle Rd BRAM/HZG SK7.........183 H2
Earlesdon Crs LHULT M38...........81 F2
Earlesfield CI SALE M33............153 C4
Earle St AULW OL7....................119 F4
Earl Rd CHD/CHDH SK8............159 F2
  HTNM SK4..............................159 F2
  RAMS BL0.................................16 C2
Earlston Av DTN/ASHW M54.....131 H4
Earl St BRO M7..........................114 A1
  BURY BL9.................................38 C4
  DTN/ASHW M54.......................12 C6
  EDGY/DAV SK3.........................12 C6
  HEY OL10.................................40 D5
  MOSL OL5...............................108 C1
  PWCH M25................................85 E4
  RAMS BL0.................................17 E2
  ROCH OL11..............................57 F1
Earl Ter CHD/CHDH SK8 *.........159 F2

SALE M33 *..............................154 D1
Earls Wy FAIL M35.....................106 C1
Earlswood Wk BOLS/LL BL3 *......64 E5
Earl Wk WGTN/LGST M12 *......129 C4
Early Bank STLY SK15...............121 F5
Early Bank Rd HYDE SK14........134 C2
Earnshaw Av HTNM SK4...........160 C5
  WHIT OL12................................21 F2
Earnshaw CI AULW OL7 *.........106 C5
Earnshaw St BOLS/LL BL3 *........64 B3
Easby CI CHD/CHDH SK8.........193 E1
  POY/DIS SK12.........................195 E2
Easby Rd MDTN M24...................71 H4
Easedale CI URM M41...............123 C5
Easedale Rd BOL BL1..................47 H1
  NEWH/MOS M40.....................104 B3
East Aisle Rd TRPK M17............125 H4
East Av BNG/LEV M19.................144 A5
  CHD/CHDH SK8......................182 A4
  STLY SK15..............................120 D2
  WHTF M45...............................69 F2
Eastbank St BOL BL1...................47 H1
Eastbourne Gv BOL BL1.............33 G3
East Central Dr SWIN M27...........99 C3
Eastchurch CI FWTH BL4.............66 A5
Eastcombe Av BRO M7...............101 E3
Eastcote Rd RDSH SK5.............160 A1
East Crs MDTN M24.....................72 C5
Eastdale PI ALT WA14 *.............165 C2
East Downs Rd ALT WA14..........182 C2
  CHD/CHDH SK8......................182 C2
East Dr BURY BL9........................54 A5
  MPL/ROM SK6........................187 E1
  SLFD M6..................................100 B5
  SWIN M27..................................99 F3
Easterdale OLDE OL4.................92 E1
Eastern Av SWIN M27..................85 E5
Eastern By-Pass OP/CLY M11...116 D3
  OP/CLY M11............................117 E5
Eastern Cir BNG/LEV M19.........144 A5
Eastfield SLFD M6......................112 D1
Eastfield Av MDTN M24................72 D5
  NEWH/MOS M40.....................115 H2
Eastfields RAD M26...................51 H4
Eastford Sq NEWH/MOS M40...115 E1
Eastgate WHIT OL12...................18 D1
Eastgate St AULW OL7..............119 F4
East Gate St MILN OL16.............10 D5
East Gra OP/CLY M11...............116 D2
East Gv BRUN/LGST M13.........128 D3
Eastgrove Av BOL BL1.................22 D5
Eastham Av BURY BL9.................27 F5
East Hill St OLDE OL4..................9 K5
Eastholme Dr BNG/LEV M19....144 B4
Easthope CI DID/WITH M20......142 D4
East Lancashire Rd SWIN M27....99 C4
  WALK M28...............................96 A3
Eastlands BKLY M9 *..................88 A2
East Lea DTN/ASHW M54..........132 D5
Eastleigh Av BRO M7.................101 H2
Eastleigh Dr NEWH/MOS M40..115 C2
Eastleigh Rd CHD/CHDH SK8...181 C3
  PWCH M25................................86 D4
East Lynn Dr WALK M28..............82 C2
East Meade BOLS/LL BL3............64 D2
  CCHDY M21............................141 F4
  PWCH M25................................86 C5
  SWIN M27..................................98 D4
East Moor WALK M28....................94 B4
Eastmoor Dr NEWH/MOS M40..117 E1
Eastmoor Gv BOLS/LL BL3..........64 A2
East Newton St ANC M4............115 F2
Easton CI MDTN M24....................73 F5
Easton Dr CHD/CHDH SK8........170 D4
Easton Rd DROY M43................117 F3
East Ordsall La CSLFD M3...........6 A4
Eastover Av MPL/ROM SK6.......173 H1
East Park CI BRUN/LGST M13...128 D2
Eastpark CI BRUN/LGST M13....128 D2
East Philip St CSLFD M3............114 B2
East Rd BOL BL1.........................33 H2
  GTN M18.................................130 A5
  MANAIR M90..........................180 A5
  STLY SK15..............................121 G4
  STRET M32.............................125 C4
  URM M41................................125 E5
  WGTN/LGST M12...................129 H5
East Row BKLY M9.....................160 C1
East St AUL OL6.........................120 A1
  BURY BL9.................................38 C4
  DTN/ASHW M34.....................132 C2
  LIT OL15.................................21 F3
  MILN OL16...............................10 E6
  MDTN M24................................68 C1
  RAD M26...................................19 H2
East Union St
  OLDTF/WHR M16....................127 F2
East V MPL/ROM SK6...............175 F4
East Vw BURY BL9.....................16 D5
  MDTN M24................................72 A5
Eastville Gdns BNG/LEV M19...158 B1
East Wk EDGW/EG BL7..............22 C1
Eastward Av WILM/AE SK9.......198 C4
East Wy BOL BL1.........................34 C3
  OLD OL1...................................75 F3
Eastway MDTN M24.....................60 A3
  ROY/SHW OL2...........................60 A3
  SALE M33...............................154 A5
  URM M41................................123 F5
Eastwood Av DROY M43.............117 F4
  NEWH/MOS M40.....................104 A4
  URM M41................................138 D1
  WALK M28.................................81 F4
Eastwood CI BOLS/LL BL3...........63 H1
  BURY BL9....................................5 J4
Eastwood Gv
  NEWH/MOS M40.....................105 E1
Eastwood St
  DTN/ASHW M54.....................132 A1
  LIT OL15.................................21 E5
Eastwood Ter BKLY M9 *............87 H1
Eaton CI CHD/CHDH SK8.........182 C1
  DUK SK16...............................133 C2

POY/DIS SK12............195 H4
Eaton Dr AULW OL7 ....119 E1
  HALE/TIMP WA15......166 B1
  WILM/AE SK9.............200 C3
Eaton Rd ALT WA14 ....177 F5
  CHH M8.......................102 A1
Eaves La CHAD OL9 ....154 B2
Ebbage CI STKP SK1............13 J6
Ebberstone Rd RUSH/FAL M14...142 C1
Ebden St CMANE M1 *............7 H7
Ebor CI ROY/SHW OL2............59 H1
Ebor Rd WYTH/NTH M22 *......168 D5
Ebor St LIT OL15 ....21 E3
Ebsworth St NEWH/MOS M40....103 G2
Ebury St RAD M26..................68 A1
Ecclesbridge Rd
  MPL/ROM SK6..................175 E4
Eccles CI OP/CLY M11............116 D5
Eccleshall St OP/CLY M11......116 D4
Eccles New Rd SALQ M50......112 A3
Eccles Old Rd SLFD M6............112 B2
Eccles Rd SWIN M27................99 E4
Eccleston Av BOLE BL2............34 C5
  RUSH/FAL M14................142 C2
  SWIN M27.....................98 C3
Eccleston CI TOT/BURYW BL8...37 H1
Eccleston PI BRO M7............101 G2
Eccleston Rd EDGY/DAV SK3....171 H5
Eccleston St FAIL M35 *......105 F2
Eccto St CMANE M1 *...............1
Eckersley CI NTHM/RTH M23...167 G3
Eckersley Rd BOL BL1............33 H3
Eckersley St BOLS/LL BL3........48 B5
Eckford St CHH M8................102 C4
Eclipse CI MILN OL16............11 J6
Edale Av DTN/ASHW M34......132 A1
  DTN/ASHW M34..............146 D3
  NEWH/MOS M40..............103 H2
  RDSH SK5......................145 G2
  URM M41......................138 B2
Edale CI ALT WA14 ....177 F3
  BRAM/HZG SK7................185 E3
  CHD/CHDH SK8................182 A5
  IRL M44........................136 C2
Edale Gv AUL OL6................108 B4
  SALE M33......................153 H4
Edale Rd BOLS/LL BL3 *......47 H5
  FWTH BL4......................64 D5
  STRET M32....................125 G5
Edale St SLFD M6................101 E5
Edbrook Wk
  BRUN/LGST M13 *............129 E3
Eddie Colman CI
  NEWH/MOS M40 *............104 A5
Eddisbury Av DID/WITH M20...142 B3
  URM M41......................123 E4
Edditch Gv BOLE BL2............49 H2
Edystone CI ORD M5............113 F4
Eden Av BOL BL1.................33 H3
  MPL/ROM SK6..................186 D5
Edenbridge Dr RAD M26..........67 E5
Edenbridge Rd
  CHD/CHDH SK8................171 E5
  NEWH/MOS M40..............116 C1
Eden CI HEY OL10................40 B3
  HULME M15....................128 B3
  STKP SK1.......................13 J5
  WILM/AE SK9..................198 B5
Edendale Dr WYTH/NTH M22...180 C3
Edenfield La WALK M28..........110 A1
Edenfield Rd PWCH M25..........86 D4
  ROCH OL11....................28 A1
  ROCH OL11....................28 D2
Edenfield St ROCH OL11........29 F2
Eden Gv BOL BL1.................33 H3
Edenhall Av BNG/LEV M19....143 H3
Edenhurst Dr
  HALE/TIMP WA15............166 C4
Edenhurst Rd OFTN SK2..........172 C3
Eden Park Rd CHD/CHDH SK8...182 B4
Eden PI CHD/CHDH SK8............170 A3
Edensor Dr HALE/TIMP WA15...178 D1
Eden St BOL BL1.................33 H3
  WHIT OL12.....................9 F2
Edenvale WALK M28..............96 B3
Eden Wy ROY/SHW OL2..........59 H1
Edgar St BOLS/LL BL3............48 D4
  MILN OL16.....................30 D1
  RAMS BL0......................16 C3
Edgar St West RAMS BL0.........16 C3
Edgbaston Dr
  OLDTF/WHR M16................126 D5
Edge Ct WYTH/NTH M22..........169 G3
Edgedale Av EDGY/DAV SK3....158 H1
Edgefield Av BKLY M9.............87 H4
Edge Fold FWTH BL4...............64 B3
Edge Fold Crs WALK M28 *......97 E2
Edge Fold Rd WALK M28 *......96 C2
Edge Gn WALK M28 *............96 C2
Edge Hill Av ROY/SHW OL2......75 F2
Edgehill Cha WILM/AE SK9......199 H3
Edge Hill Rd BOLS/LL BL3.......64 A1
  ROY/SHW OL2.................75 F1
Edgehill Rd SLFD M6...............112 B2
Edgehill St ANC M4 *...............7 G3
Edge La DROY M43...............117 F4
  STRET M32....................135 F5
Edge La EDGY/DAV SK3...........171 F2
Edge Lane Rd OLD OL1............75 H4
Edge Lane St ROY/SHW OL2....59 F5
Edgeley Fold EDGY/DAV SK3...171 F2
Edgeley Rd EDGY/DAV SK3.....171 F3
  URM M41.......................138 A3
Edgemoor ALT WA14..............176 D2
Edgemoor Dr ROCH OL11 *......41 C1
  RAD M26.......................51 H4
Edgemoor Rd ROCH OL11........41 C1
Eg ANC M4 *....................7 J2
Edge Vw OLD OL1.................73 H5
Edgeware Av RUSH/FAL M14...143 E4
Edgeware Rd CHAD OL9..........89 H4
  ECC M30........................110 B1
Edgewater ORD M5................112 C3
Edgeway WILM/AE SK9............199 E5
Edgeworth Av BOLE BL2..........36 C5
Edgeworth Dr RUSH/FAL M14...143 C4

Edgware Av BOLS/LL BL3.......48 C5
Edgware Rd NEWH/MOS M40..116 C1
Edgworth CI HEY OL10............40 B4
Ediliom Rd CHH M8................86 D5
Edinburgh CI CHD/CHDH SK8...170 C3
Edinburgh Dr MPL/ROM SK6...162 B2
Edinburgh Rd BOLS/LL BL3.....66 D2
Edinburgh Sq
  NEWH/MOS M40...............115 G1
Edinburgh Wy ROCH OL11......42 C2
Edington WHIT OL12 *............10 B4
Edison Rd ECC M30................110 D5
Edison St OP/CLY M11............130 D1
Edith Av RUSH/FAL M14..........142 C1
Edith Cavell CI OP/CLY M11....116 D4
Edith St BOL BL1..................48 B3
  FWTH BL4......................66 A5
  OLDS OL8......................91 G4
Edlin CI WGTN/LGST M12 *......129 F3
Edlingham ROCH OL11 *.........29 H5
Edlington CI SALE M33............153 G3
Edmonds St MDTN M24............71 H3
Edmonton Rd EDGY/DAV SK3...172 B5
  NEWH/MOS M40...............116 B1
Edmund CI BOLS/LL BL3 *......3 H4
Edmunds Ct BOLS/LL BL3 *......2 B2
Edmunds Fold LIT OL15............20 C2
Edmund St CSLFD M5 *............7 H3
  DROY M43......................117 H5
  FAIL M35.......................105 E2
  RAD M26.......................52 D5
  ROY/SHW OL2..................60 B2
  SLFD M6........................112 D2
  WHIT OL12.....................10 A4
Edna St HYDE SK14...............147 H1
Edson Rd CHH M8..................87 E4
Edstone CI BOLS/LL BL3...........47 G5
Edward Av CCHDY M21............140 D4
  ROY/SHW OL2.................75 F2
Edward St BOL BL1................34 B1
Edwards CI MPL/ROM SK6.......174 D4
Edwards Dr WHTF M45.............70 A4
Edward St AUL OL6................120 B3
  BKLY M9........................103 F2
  BOLS/LL BL3...................48 C4
  BRO M7.........................114 B1
  BURY BL9.......................4 E6
  CHAD OL9......................8 A5
  DROY M43......................117 H5
  DTN/ASHW M34...............132 A1
  DUK SK16.......................133 F2
  FWTH BL4......................65 H5
  HYDE SK14....................133 F5
  MDTN M24......................72 D3
  MILN OL16......................11 F4
  MPL/ROM SK6.................163 F5
  PART M31......................150 B2
  RAD M26.......................85 H2
  RAD M26.......................68 C2
  SALE M33......................155 F2
  STKP SK1.......................13 G3
  STLY SK15.....................121 E4
  WHIT OL12.....................14 C3
  WHIT OL12.....................20 A4

Eileen Gv RUSH/FAL M14.......143 E1
Eileen Gv West
  RUSH/FAL M14................142 D1
Elaine Av BKLY M9................89 E5
Elbe St WGTN/LGST M12.........115 F5
Elbow St BNG/LEV M19..........130 B5
Elbut La BURY BL9................40 A1
Elcho Ct ALT WA14................177 E2
Elcho Rd ALT WA14................177 E1
Elcot CI NEWH/MOS M40.........102 D5
Elderberry Wy WILM/AE SK9...199 H2
Elder CI OFTN SK2................173 E1
  NEWH/MOS M40...............107 G3
Eldercot Gv BOLS/LL BL3 *.....47 H5
Eldercot Rd BOLS/LL BL3.......47 H5
Eldercroft Rd
  HALE/TIMP WA15............166 D4
Elder Dr BOLS/LL BL3.............50 B4
Elderfield Dr MPL/ROM SK6...161 G2
Eldermount Rd BKLY M9..........88 A5
Elder Rd OLDE OL4................92 D1
Elder St MILN OL16...............11 H4
Elderwood CHAD OL9.............73 H5
Eldon CI DTN/ASHW M34........132 B1
Eldon PI ECC M30................110 D4
Eldon Prec OLDS OL8...............9 F6
Eldon Rd BOLE BL2................34 C5
  BURY BL9.......................4 E1
  OLDS OL8......................9 G6
Eldon Street East OLDS OL8.....9 G6
Eldridge Dr NEWH/MOS M40...105 H5
Eleanor Rd CCHDY M21..........140 D3
  ROY/SHW OL2..................75 F2
Eleanor St BOL BL1.................34 B1
  OLD OL1.........................75 E4
Electo St OP/CLY M11............130 D1
Elevator Rd TRPK M17............126 B2
Eleventh St TRPK M17............126 A2
Elf Mill CI EDGY/DAV SK3.......171 H3
Elford Gv GTN M18.................131 E3
Elgar St WGTN/LGST M12........129 H5
Elgin Av DID/WITH M20...........158 A3
Elgin Rd DUK SK16................133 F2
  OLDE OL4......................92 A1
Elgin St AULW OL7................119 F1
  BOL BL1.........................33 H4
  STLY SK15.....................121 E4
Elgol CI EDGY/DAV SK3..........172 A4
Elgol Dr BOLS/LL BL3..............57 F4
Elham CI RAD M26.................67 F5
Elim St LIT OL15...................20 C2
Eliot Rd ECC M30..................111 E4
Eli St CHAD OL9....................90 B4
Eliza Ann St ECC M30............110 D4
  NEWH/MOS M40...............115 F1
Elizabethan Wy MILN OL16......31 F5
  DTN/ASHW M34...............132 B3
  ROY/SHW OL2..................74 D1
Elizabeth Av CHAD OL9..........90 B4
Elizabeth CI STRET M32..........140 B1
Elizabeth Ct HTNM SK4...........12 A1
Elizabeth Gv ROY/SHW OL2....60 A3
Elizabeth Rd PART M31...........150 D2
Elizabeth Slinger Rd
  DID/WITH M20.................158 D2
Elizabeth St AUL OL6 ....119 G1
  CHH M8.........................102 B5
  DTN/ASHW M34...............132 A5
  HEY OL10......................40 D4
  HYDE SK14....................133 G5
  RAD M26.......................68 B1
  ROCH OL11....................43 E1
  SWIN M27......................99 F1
  WHTF M45.....................85 H2
  RAMS BL0......................17 E2
Elkanagh Gdns SLFD M6.........113 E2
Elkstone Av LHULT M38...........81 F1
Elladene Pk CCHDY M21.........141 G3
Ellanby CI NEWH/MOS M40....128 C5
Elland CI BURY BL9................5 J3
Ellaston Dr URM M41..............138 D1
Ellastone Rd SLFD M6.............112 B1
Ellbourne Rd BKLY M9............87 F4
Ellenbrook CI
  WGTN/LGST M12..............130 A2
Ellenbrook Rd WALK M28........96 C2
Ellendale Gra WALK M28.........96 C2
Ellen Gv FWTH BL4................83 G2
Ellenhall CI BKLY M9..............103 G2
Ellenroad Ap MILN OL16.........28 D1
Ellenrod Dr WHIT OL12...........28 B1
Ellenrod La WHIT OL12...........28 C1
Ellen St BOL BL1...................33 E5
  CHAD OL9......................8 C1
  DROY M43......................118 A5
  HTNM SK4.....................159 G3
Ellen Wilkinson Crs
  WGTN/LGST M12..............129 H3
Elleray CI BOLS/LL BL3............67 F1
Elleray Rd MDTN M24.............85 H4
  SLFD M6........................100 A5
Ellerbeck CI BOLE BL2.............35 E1
Ellerbeck Crs WALK M28.........96 C5
Ellerby Av SWIN M27..............84 D4
Ellesmere Av AUL OL6............107 F5
  ECC M30........................111 F3
  WALK M28.....................81 H4
Ellesmere Cir URM M41..........124 C1
Ellesmere CI DUK SK16...........131 H4
Ellesmere Dr CHD/CHDH SK8...170 D4
Ellesmere Gdns BOLS/LL BL3...64 B4
Ellesmere Rd ALT WA14.........165 G3
  BOLS/LL BL3...................64 B4
  CCHDY M21....................141 F1
  ECC M30........................111 F1
  EDGY/DAV SK3................170 D2
Ellesmere Rd North
  HTNM SK4.....................159 F1

Ellesmere Rd South
  CCHDY M21....................141 G3
Ellesmere St BOLS/LL BL3 *......2 A7
  ECC M30........................111 E4
  FAIL M35.......................105 E2
  FWTH BL4......................66 A4
  HULME M15....................8 A7
  LHULT M38....................81 H4
  ROCH OL11....................43 E1
  SWIN M27......................99 F1
Ellesmere Ter RUSH/FAL M14...143 E1
Ellingham CI OP/CLY M11........116 A4
Elliot Dr SALE M33................153 H2
Elliot CI OLD OL1.................9 K1
Elliot St BOL BL1..................33 F3
  OLDE OL4......................92 D1
Elliott Av HYDE SK14.............133 G3
Elliott Dr SALE M33................153 H2
Elliott St FWTH BL4...............65 H5
  LIT OL15.......................10 E4
Ellis Crs WALK M28................81 G4
Ellis Dr CHH M8...................102 B1
Ellis Fold WHIT OL12...............28 C1
Ellis La MDTN M24.................71 G4
Ellis St BOLS/LL BL3..............47 H4
  CHH M8........................114 D1
  HULME M15...................127 H2
  HYDE SK14....................148 B1
  TOT/BURYW BL8................37 G4
Elliston Sq WGTN/LGST M12...129 F1
Ellonby Ri HOR/BR BL6...........46 D4
Ellor St SLFD M6...................113 E2
Ellwood Dr STKP SK1..............160 C5
Elly Clough ROY/SHW OL2......74 D1
Elm Av BNG/LEV M19.............143 H2
Elmbank Av DID/WITH M20....156 D2
Elmbank Rd MDTN M24...........71 H4
Elm Beds Rd POY/DIS SK12....196 B5
Elmbridge Wk BOLS/LL BL3 *...3 H4
  NEWH/MOS M40...............116 B1
Elm CI HYDE SK14.................155 H4
  POY/DIS SK12.................195 G4
Elm Crs WALK M28.................97 G1
Elmdale Av CHD/CHDH SK8...181 G2
Elmdale Wk HULME M15 *......128 B2
Elm Dr STRET M32................140 A3
  STRET M32....................125 G5
Elmfield Av WYTH/NTH M22...168 D1
  DTN/ASHW M34...............118 B5
  EDGY/DAV SK3................172 A4
  WILM/AE SK9..................201 E3
Elmfield St BOL BL1................34 A4
  CHH M8........................102 B5
Elmgate Gv BNG/LEV M19.....144 A2
Elm Gv AUL OL6....................107 F5
  DID/WITH M20.................157 F2
  DROY M43......................117 F5
  DTN/ASHW M34...............132 B4
  EDGW/EG BL7..................23 G5
  FWTH BL4......................65 G4
  HYDE SK14....................148 A1
  MILN OL16.....................44 D3
  OLDE OL4......................77 H3
  PWCH M25.....................85 H1
  ROCH OL11....................29 E5
  SALE M33......................139 G5
  SWIN M27......................98 A1
  URM M41.......................139 E1
  WHIT OL12.....................19 H3
  WILM/AE SK9..................200 D3
Elmham Wk NEWH/MOS M40...103 F5
Elmhurst Dr BNG/LEV M19......158 C1
Elmira Wy ORD M5.................126 D2
Elmley CI OFTN SK2..............173 H4
Elmore Wd LIT OL15...............20 C2
Elmpark Ga WHIT OL12............18 A5
Elmpark Gv WHIT OL12............18 A5
Elmpark V WHIT OL12.............18 A5
Elmpark Vw WHIT OL12...........18 A5
Elmridge Dr HALE/TIMP WA15...178 D4
Elm Rd BOLS/LL BL3................64 D3
  CHD/CHDH SK8................169 F4
  DID/WITH M20.................157 F2
  FWTH BL4......................82 C2
  HALE/TIMP WA15............177 H1
  MPL/ROM SK6.................161 G2
  WHIT OL12.....................18 B5
Elm Rd South EDGY/DAV SK3...170 D2
Elmscott Wk BRUN/LGST M13...129 E3
Elmsdale Av BKLY M9.............87 H2
Elmsfield Av ROCH OL11..........42 B1
Elmsleigh Rd CHD/CHDH SK8...181 F3
Elms Rd HTNM SK4................159 H1
  STLY SK15.....................121 G2
  WHTF M45.....................69 G5
Elms St WHTF M45..................69 G5
The Elms LIT OL15.................20 B4
  MOSL OL5......................108 C1
Elmstone CI BKLY M9.............87 H2
Elmstone Gv BOL BL1..............2 E1
Elm St BURY BL9....................5 J5
  ECC M30........................111 E4
  FAIL M35.......................111 H1
  FWTH BL4......................66 A3
  HEY OL10......................41 E4
  MDTN M24......................74 F4
  RAMS BL0......................17 E1
  SWIN M27......................99 F1
  WHIT OL12.....................10 D2
  WHTF M45.....................69 G5
Elm Tree CI DUK SK16.............134 A1
  FAIL M35.......................105 G5
Elm Tree Dr DUK SK16............134 A1
  WYTH/NTH M22................180 C1
Elmtree Dr HTNM SK4.............159 E4
Elm Tree Rd MPL/ROM SK6....160 D3

Ellesmere Rd North
  HTNM SK4.....................159 F1

Elmwood SALE M33................153 F2
Elmwood Dr ROY/SHW OL2.....58 D4
Elmwood Gv BKLY M9.............103 G3
  BOL BL1........................48 B1
  FWTH BL4......................81 H1
Elsa Rd BNG/LEV M19.............144 C2
Elsdon Dr GTN M18................130 C2
Elsdon Gdns BOLE BL2............34 C5
Elsdon Rd BRUN/LGST M13....143 H1
Elsfield CI BOL BL1 *..............33 H1
Elsham CI BOL BL1.................33 H1
Elsham Dr WALK M28..............81 G4
Elsinore Av IRL M44................136 C2
Elsinore CI FAIL M35..............105 G3
Elsinore Rd OLDTF/WHR M16...126 D4
Elsinore St BOLE BL2..............49 H2
Elsma Rd NEWH/MOS M40......117 F1
Elsmore Rd RUSH/FAL M14....142 C2
Elson St TOT/BURYW BL8........37 G2
Elsted Rd UPML OL3................94 B2
Elstree Av NEWH/MOS M40....104 D2
Elswick Av BOLS/LL BL3..........48 A4
  BRAM/HZG SK7................183 H5
  CCHDY M21....................156 C2
Elsworth CI RAD M26..............68 C3
Elsworth Dr
  NEWH/MOS M40...............115 H2
Elterwater CI TOT/BURYW BL8...37 G2
Elterwater Rd FWTH BL4.........64 C5
Eltham Av OFTN SK2..............172 D4
Eltham Dr URM M41................124 B4
Eltham St BNG/LEV M19.........144 A1
  FWTH BL4......................65 E4
Elton Av BNG/LEV M19...........143 A3
  FWTH BL4......................65 E4
Elton Brook CI
  TOT/BURYW BL8...............37 G3
Elton CI WHTF M45.................69 H4
  WILM/AE SK9..................199 H1
Elton Dr BRAM/HZG SK7.........185 E4
Elton Rd SALE M33.................153 G4
Elton's Yd BRO M7.................114 A2
Elton St BRO M7...................114 A2
  ROCH OL11....................126 C3
Elton Vale Rd TOT/BURYW BL8...37 G4
Elvate Crs CHH M8.................114 A1
Elverdon CI HULME M15..........127 H3
Elverston St WYTH/NTH M22...156 D5
Elverston Wy AUL OL6............8 A1
Elvey St NEWH/MOS M40.......103 G5
Elvington Crs WALK M28.........96 D2
Elwick CI OLDTF/WHR M16.....128 A1
Elwyn Av WYTH/NTH M22.......168 C2
Ely Av STRET M32.................125 E5
Ely CI WALK M28.....................96 C2
Ely Crs FAIL M35...................105 E5
Ely Dr TOT/BURYW BL8 *.......48 A1
Ely Gv BOL BL1 *...................2 D1
Elysian St OP/CLY M11...........116 D5
Ely St CHAD OL9...................8 A4
Emaline Gra SLFD M6.............112 D3
Ember St OP/CLY M11 *..........117 E3
Embla Wk BOLS/LL BL3............49 F5
Emblem St BOLS/LL BL3.........48 C4
Embleton CI BOLE BL2.............35 F2
  BOLE BL2......................35 F5
Embsay CI BOL BL1.................33 E5
Emerald Dr OLD OL1................76 D1
Emerald Rd WYTH/NTH M22...181 E5
Emerald St BOL BL1................34 A3
  DTN/ASHW M34...............132 B5
Emerson Av ECC M30..............111 H2
Emerson Dr MDTN M24............72 A3
Emerson St ORD M5................112 C3
Emery Av CCHDY M21............141 G5
Emery CI ALT WA14................165 G2
  HTNM SK4.....................158 D2
Emily Beavan CI OP/CLY M11...48 C4
Emily CI FAIL M35..................105 F1
Emily PI DROY M43................117 G4
Emley St BNG/LEV M19..........144 B2
Emlyn Gv CHD/CHDH SK8.......170 D3
Emlyn St FWTH BL4................65 H4
  SWIN M27......................98 C2
  WALK M28.....................82 A4
Emmanuel CI BOLS/LL BL3 *....48 C4
Emmanuel PI BOLS/LL BL3 *....48 C4
  WHIT OL12.....................91 G4
Emmerson St SWIN M27...........99 E1
Emmett St East
  NEWH/MOS M40...............103 F5
Emmott Wy OLD OL1 *............76 D4
Empire Rd BOLE BL2................50 A1
  DUK SK16.....................133 F2
Empire St CHH M8..................114 C1
Empress Av MPL/ROM SK6.....175 E4
Empress Dr HTNM SK4...........159 G4
Empress St BOL BL1................33 H4
  CHH M8........................102 A2
  OLDTF/WHR M16..............127 F2
Emsworth CI BOLE BL2...........35 E3
Ena Crs SLFD M6..................99 E4
Ena St BOLS/LL BL3................64 B1
  OLD OL1.......................76 D3
Enbridge St ORD M5...............113 F5
Encombe PI CSLFD M3 *.........114 A3
Endcott CI GTN M18................130 A2
Enderley Rd NEWH/MOS M40...104 B4
Endsleigh Rd DID/WITH M20...143 E5
Endsley Av WALK M28.............96 D1
Energy St NEWH/MOS M40 *...115 H2
Enfield Av BNG/LEV M19.........144 A5
  OLDS OL8......................91 F4
Enfield CI BOL BL1.................33 H5
  BURY BL9......................4 E1
  ECC M30........................111 E5
Enfield Dr OP/CLY M11...........117 E3
Enfield Rd ECC M30...............111 E1
  SWIN M27......................98 D4

Enfield St HYDE SK14 * ...148 A4
  WALK M28 ...82 A2
Enford Av WYTH/NTH M22 ...179 H2
Engell Cl GTN M18 ...130 B3
Engine Fold Rd WALK M28 ...81 F4
Engine St CHAD OL9 ...90 C3
Enginedene BOL BL1 ...22 C5
Enid Cl BRO M7 ...101 H5
Ennerdale Av BOLE BL2 ...35 G5
  CCHDY M21 ...156 C2
  ROY/SHW OL2 ...58 D2
  SWIN M27 ...99 E4
Ennerdale Cl BOLS/LL BL3 ...66 C1
Ennerdale Dr BURY BL9 ...69 H2
  CHD/CHDH SK8 ...181 G1
  HALE/TIMP WA15 ...166 B2
  SALE M33 ...153 H1
Ennerdale Gv AULW OL7 ...106 C5
  FWTH BL4 ...64 D4
Ennerdale Rd MDTN M24 ...162 A2
  MPL/ROM SK6 ...162 A2
  PART M31 ...150 D3
  ROCH OL11 ...42 A2
  STKP SK1 ...172 C2
  STRET M32 * ...125 H5
Ennerdale Ter STLY SK15 ...120 D2
Ennis Cl NTHM/RTH M23 ...167 F4
Ennismore Av ECC M30 ...111 H5
Enstone Dr
  NEWH/MOS M40 ...104 C1
Enticott Rd IRL M44 ...150 B1
Entwisle Av URM M41 ...124 A5
Entwisle Rd MILN OL16 ...10 E5
Entwisle Rw FWTH BL4 * ...66 A3
  MILN OL16 ...31 F5
  SWIN M27 ...98 C1
Entwistle St BOLE BL2 ...3 K2
Enver Rd CHH M8 ...102 C2
Enville Rd ALT WA14 ...177 F1
  NEWH/MOS M40 ...104 A1
  SLFD M6 ...100 B4
Enville St AUL OL6 ...119 H2
  BKLY M9 ...88 A4
  DTN/ASHW M34 ...132 B1
Enys Cl AUL OL6 ...107 F5
  CHAD OL9 * ...73 H4
Epping Cl SALE M33 ...153 F1
Epping Rd
  DTN/ASHW M34 ...145 H1
Epping St HULME M15 ...128 A2
Eppleworth Ri SWIN M27 ...84 B4
Epsom Av BNG/LEV M19 ...143 H5
  SALE M33 ...153 F4
  WILM/AE SK9 ...192 B3
Epsom Cl
  BRAM/HZG SK7 ...185 G2
  ROCH OL11 ...28 B3
Epworth St ANC M4 ...115 F4
Equitable St MILN OL16 ...44 C1
  OLDE OL4 ...76 C4
Era St BOLE BL2 ...50 A2
  SALE M33 ...154 C2
Ercall Av WGTN/LGST M12 ...129 F2
Erica Av OLDE OL4 ...61 E5
Erica Cl RDSH SK5 ...145 F3
Erica Dr BNG/LEV M19 ...158 B2
Eric Brook Cl RUSH/FAL M14 ...128 B5
Eric Bullows Cl
  WYTH/NTH M22 ...180 B3
Eric St LIT OL15 ...20 D2
  OLDE OL4 ...92 D2
Erin Cl CHAD OL9 ...90 C2
Erin St OP/CLY M11 ...130 D1
Erith Cl RDSH SK5 ...145 H5
Erith Rd OLDE OL4 ...92 A1
Erlesmere Av DTN/ASHW M34 ...132 D4
Erlesmere Cl OLDE OL4 ...61 F5
Erlington Av
  OLDTF/WHR M16 ...127 E5
Ermen Rd ECC M30 ...110 D5
Ermington Dr CHH M8 ...102 A4
Erneley Cl WGTN/LGST M12 ...130 A5
Ernest St BOL BL1 ...2 A5
  CHD/CHDH SK8 ...169 H3
  OFTN SK2 ...172 B3
  PWCH M25 ...85 G3
Ernest Ter WHIT OL12 ...11 G2
Ernlouen Av BOL BL1 ...47 H1
Ernocroft Gv GTN M18 ...130 C2
Ernocroft Rd MPL/ROM SK6 ...163 G5
Errington Cl BOLS/LL BL3 ...47 G4
Errington Dr BRO M7 ...114 A1
Errol Av BKLY M9 ...87 F2
  WYTH/NTH M16 ...180 B4
Errwood Crs BNG/LEV M19 ...144 A3
Errwood Rd BNG/LEV M19 ...144 A5
Erskine Cl BOLS/LL BL3 ...47 F4
Erskine Rd BKLY M9 ...88 B2
  PART M31 ...151 E3
Erskine St HULME M15 ...127 G2
  MPL/ROM SK6 ...163 G4
Erwin St NEWH/MOS M40 ...104 A4
Erwood Rd BNG/LEV M19 ...144 A5
Eryngo St STKP SK1 ...13 K4
Escott St OLDTF/WHR M16 ...127 H5
Esher Dr SALE M33 ...166 C1
Esk Cl URM M41 ...123 H4
Eskdale CHD/CHDH SK8 ...169 H5
Eskdale Av BOLE BL2 ...35 G4
  BRAM/HZG SK7 ...195 F2
  DID/WITH M20 ...142 C4
  MPL/ROM SK6 ...162 A1
  OLDS OL8 ...91 E3
  ROCH OL11 ...42 A2
  ROY/SHW OL2 ...59 E2
  UPML OL3 ...95 G2
Eskdale Cl BURY BL9 ...69 H1
Eskdale Dr HALE/TIMP WA15 ...166 D2
  MDTN M24 ...72 C1
Eskdale Gv FWTH BL4 ...65 F4
Eskdale Ms UPML OL3 * ...95 F1
Eskrick St BOL BL1 ...33 G4
Eskrigge Cl BRO M7 ...102 A2
Esmond Rd CHH M8 ...102 B3
Esmont Dr MDTN M24 ...72 B1
The Esplanade MILN OL16 ...10 E5
Essex Av BURY BL9 ...39 H5
  DID/WITH M20 ...157 G2

DROY M43 ...117 H2
  EDGY/DAV SK3 ...171 E1
Essex Cl FAIL M35 ...105 E5
  ROY/SHW OL2 ...59 G2
Essex Gdns IRL M44 ...150 B2
Essex Rd GTN M18 ...131 E5
  RDSH SK5 ...160 D1
Essex St CMANW M2 ...6 E5
  OLDS OL8 ...30 A5
Essex Wy OLDTF/WHR M16 ...127 E5
Essingdon St BOLS/LL BL3 ...48 C5
Essington Dr
  NEWH/MOS M40 * ...103 E4
Estate St OLDS OL8 ...91 G3
Estate St South OLDS OL8 ...91 G3
Est Bank Rd RAMS BL0 ...16 B5
Esther St OLDE OL4 ...76 B5
Estonfield Dr URM M41 ...139 F1
Eston St BRUN/LGST M13 ...129 G4
Eswick St OP/CLY M11 ...116 D4
Etchells Rd CHD/CHDH SK8 ...182 A3
Etchells St STKP SK1 ...13 G3
Etchell St
  NEWH/MOS M40 * ...102 D5
Ethel Av BKLY M9 ...88 A3
  SWIN M27 ...99 G2
Ethel St MILN OL16 * ...30 C5
  BOLS/LL BL3 ...2 A7
  OLDS OL8 ...91 G4
  OLDS OL8 ...14 C3
Ethel Ter BNG/LEV M19 ...144 A2
Etherley Cl IRL M44 ...136 C1
Etherow Av
  MPL/ROM SK6 ...162 D4
  NEWH/MOS M40 * ...90 A5
Etherstone St CHH M8 ...102 D2
Eton Av OLDS OL8 ...91 F4
  ROCH OL11 ...29 E5
Eton Ct OLDTF/WHR M16 ...127 G3
Eton Dr CHD/CHDH SK8 ...181 H2
Eton Hill Rd RAD M26 ...52 D4
Eton Wy North RAD M26 ...52 D4
Eton Wy South RAD M26 ...52 D4
Etruria Cl BRUN/LGST M13 ...129 F3
Ettington Cl
  TOT/BURYW BL8 ...37 F3
Ettrick Cl OP/CLY M11 ...130 C1
Euclid Cl OP/CLY M11 ...115 H4
Europa Ga TRPK M17 ...126 A3
Europa Wy EDGY/DAV SK3 ...171 F5
  RAD M26 ...66 D5
  TRPK M17 ...126 A3
Eustace St BOLS/LL BL3 ...65 F1
  OLDS OL8 ...74 C3
Euston Av BKLY M9 ...88 D4
Euxton Cl TOT/BURYW BL8 ...37 F5
Evan Cl DID/WITH M20 ...157 F3
Evans Cl DID/WITH M20 ...157 F3
Evans Rd ECC M30 ...110 B4
Evanton Cl OP/CLY M11 ...120 A1
  CSLFD M3 ...73 E4
  MDTN M24 ...73 E4
  OLD OL1 ...9 G1
Evan St NEWH/MOS M40 ...103 F5
Eva Rd EDGY/DAV SK3 ...170 D2
Eva St RUSH/FAL M14 ...128 D5
  WHIT OL12 ...10 C1
Evelyn St OLD OL1 ...76 A3
  RUSH/FAL M14 ...143 F5
Evening St FAIL M35 ...105 E2
Evenley Cl OP/CLY M11 * ...130 C2
Everard Cl WALK M28 ...96 C2
Everard St ORD M5 ...127 F1
Everbrom Rd BOLS/LL BL3 ...63 H2
Everest Av AULW OL7 ...107 E5
Everest Cl HYDE SK14 ...134 B4
Everest Rd HYDE SK14 ...134 B4
Everest St ROCH OL11 ...43 H4
Everett St HYDE SK14 * ...142 D5
Everglade OLDS OL8 ...106 D1
Evergreen Cl BOLE BL2 * ...35 E3
Eveleigh Dr BRO M7 ...102 A4
Eversden Cl BRO M7 ...114 B1
Everside Dr CHH M8 ...101 H4
Eversley Rd DID/WITH M20 ...157 F3
Everton Rd OLDS OL8 ...91 E4
  RDSH SK5 ...145 F1
Everton St SWIN M27 ...98 D2
Every St ANC M4 ...115 G4
  BURY BL9 ...4 E1
  RAMS BL0 ...17 G2
Evesham Av HTNM SK4 ...159 E3
  NTHM/RTH M23 ...167 E2
Evesham Cl BOLS/LL BL3 ...2 B7
  MDTN M24 ...89 E2
Evesham Dr FWTH BL4 ...65 G2
Evesham Drive WILM/AE SK9 ...191 H5
Evesham Gdns MDTN M24 * ...88 D2
Evesham Gv AUL OL6 ...107 F3
  SALE M33 ...155 F2
Evesham Rd BKLY M9 ...88 D5
  CHD/CHDH SK8 ...170 D5
Evesham Wk BOLS/LL BL3 * ...48 C4
  MDTN M24 ...89 E2
  OLDS OL8 ...91 F4
Eveside Cl CHD/CHDH SK8 * ...171 E5
Evie St OLDS OL8 ...91 G5
Ewan St GTN M18 ...130 C2
Ewart Av ORD M5 ...113 F4
Ewart St BOL BL1 ...33 H4
Ewhurst Av SWIN M27 ...98 A4
Ewing Cl CHH M8 ...102 B1
Ewood OLDS OL8 ...106 D2
Ewood Dr TOT/BURYW BL8 ...52 B1
Exbourne Rd WYTH/NTH M22 ...180 B3
Exbury WHIT OL12 ...10 B4
Exbury St RUSH/FAL M14 ...143 F4
Excalibur Wy IRL M44 ...136 B4
Excelsior Gdns HEY OL10 ...56 C1
Excelsior Ter LIT OL15 ...20 C5
Exchange Quay ORD M5 ...126 D2
Exchange St BOL BL1 * ...2 D4
  CSLFD M3 ...6 C3
Exchange St OLDE OL4 ...12 E4
Exeter Av BOLE BL2 ...34 C4
  DTN/ASHW M34 ...146 D2

ECC M30 ...111 H1
  FWTH BL4 ...65 E3
  RAD M26 ...51 G4
Exeter Cl CHD/CHDH SK8 ...182 C4
  DUK SK16 ...133 F1
Exeter Dr AUL OL6 ...107 G3
  IRL M44 ...136 D1
Exeter Gv ROCH OL11 ...43 E1
Exeter Rd BOLE BL2 ...35 F3
  HALE/TIMP WA15 ...166 B3
  RDSH SK5 ...160 D1
Exeter St ROCH OL11 ...43 E1
  SLFD M6 ...112 C3
Exford Dr BOLE BL2 ...50 D3
Exit Rd West MANAIR M90 ...180 A5
Exmoor Cl ALT WA14 ...207 F3
Exmouth Av RDSH SK5 ...160 D1
Exmouth Pl MILN OL16 ...43 F3
Exmouth Rd SALE M33 ...153 G1
Exmouth Sq MILN OL16 * ...43 F2
Exmouth St MILN OL16 ...43 F3
Exmouth Wk
  OLDTF/WHR M16 ...127 H5
Eyam Gv OFTN SK2 ...173 E5
Eyam Rd BRAM/HZG SK7 ...185 F4
Eycott Dr MDTN M24 ...72 A3
Eyebrook Rd ALT WA14 ...176 D3
Eynford Av RDSH SK5 ...160 D1
Eyre St HULME M15 ...128 B3

F

Faber St ANC M4 ...114 D2
Factory Brow MDTN M24 ...71 H5
Factory La BKLY M9 ...103 E3
  CSLFD M3 ...114 A4
Factory St MDTN M24 ...72 C4
  RAD M26 ...68 C1
  RAMS BL0 ...16 D1
Failsworth Rd FAIL M35 ...105 G3
Fair Acres BOLE BL2 ...35 F3
Fairacres Rd MPL/ROM SK6 ...186 D4
Fairbairn Dr MDTN M24 ...73 F4
Fairbottom St OLD OL1 ...9 H3
Fairbourne Av WILM/AE SK9 ...200 C5
  WILM/AE SK9 ...201 E2
Fairbourne Cl WILM/AE SK9 ...200 C1
Fairbourne Dr
  HALE/TIMP WA15 ...154 C5
  WILM/AE SK9 ...200 C1
Fairbourne Rd BNG/LEV M19 ...144 C2
  DTN/ASHW M34 ...146 C1
Fairbrook Dr SLFD M6 ...112 D5
Fairbrother St ORD M5 ...127 F1
Fairburn Cl URM M41 ...123 H4
Fairclough St BOLS/LL BL3 ...49 H5
  OP/CLY M11 ...116 B3
Fairfax Av DID/WITH M20 ...142 B5
  HALE/TIMP WA15 ...166 B3
Fairfax Cl MPL/ROM SK6 ...174 C2
  WILM/AE SK9 ...200 C5
Fairfax Rd PWCH M25 ...85 G5
Fairfield Av CHD/CHDH SK8 ...182 C2
  DROY M43 ...131 F1
  MPL/ROM SK6 ...161 H2
Fairfield Dr BURY BL9 ...39 G3
Fairfield Rd DROY M43 ...117 H5
  FWTH BL4 ...65 E4
  HALE/TIMP WA15 ...166 D4
  IRL M44 ...150 B1
  MDTN M24 ...72 B3
  OP/CLY M11 ...130 D1
Fairfields EDGW/EG BL7 ...23 G5
  OLDS OL8 ...91 F5
Fairfield Sq DROY M43 ...117 H5
Fairfield St CMANE M1 ...7 J7
  SLFD M6 ...100 A5
Fairford Cl RDSH SK5 ...145 G4
Fairford Dr BOLS/LL BL3 ...48 D4
Fairford Wy RDSH SK5 ...160 A1
  WILM/AE SK9 ...199 G3
Fairhaven CCHDY M21 ...141 F4
  WHTF M45 ...69 E4
  WHTN BL5 ...62 C4
Fairhaven Cl BRAM/HZG SK7 ...184 A5
Fairhaven St WGTN/LGST M12 ...129 G2
Fairhills IRL M44 ...136 C3
Fairholme Av URM M41 ...138 C1
Fairholme Rd DID/WITH M20 ...158 A1
  HTNM SK4 ...159 F5
Fairhope Av SLFD M6 ...112 A1
Fairhurst Dr WALK M28 ...81 H5
Fairisle Cl OP/CLY M11 ...116 A4
Fairlands Rd BURY BL9 ...27 G4
Fairlands St ROCH OL11 ...43 G4
Fairlawn HTNM SK4 ...159 E3
Fairlawn Cl RUSH/FAL M14 ...128 B4
Fairlea DTN/ASHW M34 ...157 H4
Fairlee Av DID/WITH M20 ...118 B4
Fairleigh Av SLFD M6 ...112 B2
Fairless Rd ECC M30 ...111 E4
Fairlie Av BOLS/LL BL3 ...47 G4
Fairlie Dr HALE/TIMP WA15 ...166 C1
Fairlyn Cl WHTN BL5 ...63 H5
Fairlyn Dr WHTN BL5 ...63 H5
Fairman St OLDTF/WHR M16 ...128 A5
Fairmead Rd
  NTHM/RTH M23 ...156 B5
Fairmile Dr DID/WITH M20 ...169 H1
Fairmount Av BOLE BL2 ...50 B1
Fairmount Rd SWIN M27 ...98 A4
Fairoak Ct BOLS/LL BL3 ...48 C4
Fair Oak Rd BNG/LEV M19 ...158 C1
Fairstead Wk OP/CLY M11 ...131 E1
Fair St BOLS/LL BL3 * ...64 B2
  CMANE M1 ...7 K5
  SWIN M27 ...99 F1
Fairview Av BNG/LEV M19 ...144 B1
  DTN/ASHW M34 ...145 G2
Fairview Cl CHAD OL9 ...73 H4
  MPL/ROM SK6 ...175 E2
Fairview Rd DTN/ASHW M34 ...145 G2
  HALE/TIMP WA15 ...166 D4

Fairway BRAM/HZG SK7 ...193 G1
  CHD/CHDH SK8 ...169 G5
  MPL/ROM SK6 ...117 H5
  PWCH M25 ...84 C1
  ROCH OL11 ...42 A5
  SWIN M27 ...99 H3
  WHIT OL12 ...18 B1
Fairway Av BOLE BL2 ...35 F3
  NTHM/RTH M23 ...167 E2
Fairway Crs ROY/SHW OL2 ...59 E3
Fairway Dr SALE M33 ...153 H4
Fairway Rd BURY BL9 ...69 H1
  OLDE OL4 ...92 D3
The Fairways WHTF M45 ...68 C3
The Fairways NEWH/MOS M40 ...104 C2
  OFTN SK2 ...173 E2
Fairwood Rd NTHM/RTH M23 ...167 E2
Fairy La CHH M8 ...101 H5
  SALE M33 ...153 H5
  SALE M33 ...156 A3
Fairy St TOT/BURYW BL8 ...37 H4
Fairywell Cl WILM/AE SK9 ...199 G1
Fairywell Dr SALE M33 ...154 B5
Fairywell Rd
  HALE/TIMP WA15 ...166 C2
Faith St BOL BL1 ...32 D5
Falcon Av URM M41 ...139 E1
Falcon Cl BURY BL9 ...5 H1
  WHIT OL12 ...28 A1
Falcon Crs SWIN M27 ...84 C5
Falcon Dr CHAD OL9 ...8 A1
  IRL M44 ...122 C5
  LHULT M38 ...81 F2
Falcon St OLDS OL8 ...9 F6
Falconwood Cha WALK M28 ...96 C4
Falfield Dr CHH M8 ...102 C5
Falinge Fold WHIT OL12 ...29 G2
Falinge Ms WHIT OL12 ...10 A5
Falinge Rd WHIT OL12 ...10 A5
Falkirk Dr BOLE BL2 ...50 C3
Falkirk St OLDE OL4 ...76 B5
Falkland Av NEWH/MOS M40 ...115 G1
  ROCH OL11 ...29 F3
Falkland Cl OLDE OL4 ...60 D5
Falkland Rd BOLE BL2 ...50 D2
Fall Birch Rd HOR/BR BL6 ...46 A1
Fallons Rd WALK M28 ...98 B1
Fallow Av GTN M18 ...144 D1
Fallowfield Av ORD M5 ...113 G5
Fallowfield Dr WHIT OL12 ...29 E1
Fallow Fields Dr RDSH SK5 ...145 G2
The Fallows CHAD OL9 ...90 B2
Falls Gv CHD/CHDH SK8 ...181 F1
Falmer Cl GTN M18 ...131 E2
  TOT/BURYW BL8 ...26 C5
Falmer Dr WYTH/NTH M22 ...180 C3
Falmouth Av SALE M33 ...153 C1
  URM M41 ...123 F5
Falmouth Crs RDSH SK5 ...136 D1
Falmouth Rd IRL M44 ...136 D1
Falmouth St NEWH/MOS M40 ...116 A1
  OLDS OL8 ...91 G3
Falsgrave Cl NEWH/MOS M40 ...103 H5
Falshaw Dr BURY BL9 ...5 J1
Falstaff Ms MPL/ROM SK6 ...161 H4
Falston Av NEWH/MOS M40 ...89 G5
Falstone Av RAMS BL0 ...16 D4
Falterley Rd NTHM/RTH M23 ...167 F1
Fancroft Rd WYTH/NTH M22 ...168 B4
Faraday Av CHH M8 ...102 B1
  SWIN M27 ...85 E5
Faraday Dr BOL BL1 ...33 G1
Faraday Ri WHIT OL12 ...29 E2
Faraday St CMANE M1 ...7 H4
Farcroft Av RAD M26 ...52 D4
Farcroft St WYTH/NTH M22 ...167 G1
Far Cromwell Rd
  MPL/ROM SK6 ...146 B5
Fardale ROY/SHW OL2 ...59 G3
Farden Dr NTHM/RTH M23 ...167 E1
Farewell Cl ROCH OL11 ...42 B4
Far Hey Cl RAD M26 ...67 H1
Farholme ROY/SHW OL2 ...59 E3
Faringdon ROCH OL11 ...29 F5
Faringdon Wk BOLS/LL BL3 ...48 C4
Farland Pl BOLS/LL BL3 ...64 A1
Farlands Dr DID/WITH M20 ...169 G2
Farlands Ri MILN OL16 ...31 G5
Far La GTN M18 ...131 F4
Farley Av GTN M18 ...131 F4
Farley Ct CHD/CHDH SK8 ...170 C5
Farley Rd SALE M33 ...154 D4
Farley Wy RDSH SK5 ...145 E2
Farleigh Cl WHTN BL5 ...62 B2
Farm Av STRET M32 ...125 H3
Farm Cl WHTN BL5 ...44 C5
  TOT/BURYW BL8 ...26 A5
Farmers Cl SALE M33 ...154 C5
Farmer St HTNM SK4 ...159 G3
Farmfield SALE M33 ...139 F5
Farm Hl PWCH M25 * ...85 H2
Farmlands Wk OLD OL1 * ...60 A2
Farm La HYDE SK14 ...133 G5
  POY/DIS SK12 ...197 F1
  PWCH M25 ...85 G2
  WALK M28 ...97 G5
Farm Rd OLDS OL8 ...91 G5
Farmside Av IRL M44 ...122 B5
Farmstead Cl FAIL M35 ...105 H4
Farm St FAIL M35 ...105 H1
  HEY OL10 ...56 B1
  CHAD OL9 ...8 B1
  MILN OL16 ...11 J2
Farmway MDTN M24 ...72 C5
Farm Yd BNG/LEV M19 ...145 E1
Farnborough Av OLDS OL8 ...91 F5
Farnborough Rd BOL BL1 ...22 D5
  NEWH/MOS M40 ...115 G2
Farndale Sq LHULT M38 ...81 E4
Farndon Av BRAM/HZG SK7 ...173 G5
Farndon Cl SALE M33 ...153 H3
Farndon Dr HALE/TIMP WA15 ...166 B3
Farndon Rd RDSH SK5 ...145 E1

Farnham Av BKLY M9 ...88 A2
Farnham Cl BOL BL1 * ...23 H4
  CHD/CHDH SK8 ...182 C5
Farnham Dr IRL M44 ...136 C2
Farnley Cl WHIT OL12 ...28 C1
Farnley St WGTN/LGST M12 * ...129 F2
Farnsworth Cl AULW OL7 ...107 E5
Farnworth Dr RUSH/FAL M14 ...143 E1
Farnworth St BOLS/LL BL3 * ...48 D5
  HEY OL10 ...40 D4
Farrand Rd OLDS OL8 ...90 C5
Farrant Rd WGTN/LGST M12 ...129 H5
Farrant St DROY M43 ...117 G5
Farrell St BRO M7 ...114 B2
Farrer Rd BRUN/LGST M13 ...143 H1
Far Ridings MPL/ROM SK6 ...162 C3
Farrier Cl SALE M33 ...155 C3
Farriers La ROCH OL11 ...42 C3
Farrier St SLFD M6 * ...112 C2
Farrowdale Av ROY/SHW OL2 ...60 A3
Farrow St ROY/SHW OL2 ...60 A3
Farrow St East ROY/SHW OL2 ...60 A3
Far St EDGY/DAV SK3 ...60 A3
Far Woodseats La GLSP SK13 ...149 H5
Fastnet St OP/CLY M11 ...116 B5
Faulkenhurst Ms OLD OL1 ...74 D3
Faulkenhurst St OLD OL1 ...74 D3
Faulkner Dr HALE/TIMP WA15 ...166 C3
Faulkner Rd STRET M32 ...140 C2
Faulkner St BOLS/LL BL3 ...48 D4
  CMANE M1 ...7 F6
  MILN OL16 ...10 D6
Faversham Brow OLD OL1 * ...75 F4
Faversham St
  NEWH/MOS M40 ...104 A1
Fawborough Rd
  NTHM/RTH M23 ...155 G5
Fawcett St BOLE BL2 ...3 K4
Fawley Av HYDE SK14 ...147 H2
Fawley Gv WYTH/NTH M22 ...168 C5
Fawns Keep STLY SK15 ...135 F2
  WILM/AE SK9 ...199 G3
Fay Av BKLY M9 ...88 D3
Faywood Dr MPL/ROM SK6 ...175 F5
Fearney Side BOLS/LL BL3 ...66 C1
Fearnhead Cl FWTH BL4 ...66 B4
Fearnhead St BOLS/LL BL3 ...48 B5
Fearn St HEY OL10 ...40 D4
Featherstall Brook Vie
  LIT OL15 ...20 D3
Featherstall Rd LIT OL15 ...20 D3
Featherstall Rd North
  CHAD OL9 ...8 C5
Featherstall Rd South
  CHAD OL9 ...8 C5
Federation St ANC M4 ...7 F2
  PWCH M25 ...85 G2
Feldom Rd NTHM/RTH M23 ...155 G4
Fellbridge Cl WHTN BL5 ...63 E5
Fellbrigg Cl GTN M18 ...130 D3
Fellfoot Cl WALK M28 ...96 A5
Fellpark Rd NTHM/RTH M23 ...155 H4
Fells Gv WALK M28 ...97 G1
Fellside BOLE BL2 ...35 H2
Fellside Cl TOT/BURYW BL8 * ...26 C2
Fellside Gdns LIT OL15 ...20 C1
Fellside Gn STLY SK15 ...120 D2
Fell St TOT/BURYW BL8 ...37 H4
Felltop Dr RDSH SK5 ...145 G5
Felskirk Rd WYTH/NTH M22 ...180 B1
Felsted BOL BL1 ...47 F1
Felt Ct DTN/ASHW M34 ...146 A1
Felthorpe Dr CHH M8 ...102 A4
Felton Av WYTH/NTH M22 ...180 B1
Felton Cl BURY BL9 ...5 H5
Felton Wk BOL BL1 ...33 H4
Fencegate Av HTNM SK4 ...159 C1
Fence St OFTN SK2 ...173 E5
Fenchurch Av
  NEWH/MOS M40 ...116 D1
Fencot Dr WGTN/LGST M12 ...129 H4
Fenella St BRUN/LGST M13 ...129 F4
Fenham Cl NEWH/MOS M40 * ...130 A5
Fenmore Av WYTH/NTH M22 ...180 A1
Fennel St ANC M4 ...3 G3
Fenners Cl BOLS/LL BL3 ...64 C1
Fenney St BRO M7 ...101 G5
Fenney St East BRO M7 ...101 H4
Fenn St HULME M15 ...127 H2
Fenside Rd WYTH/NTH M22 ...168 D4
Fenton Av BRAM/HZG SK7 ...172 D5
Fenton Ms ROCH OL11 * ...42 D1
Fenton St OLDE OL4 ...92 A1
  ROCH OL11 ...42 D1
  ROY/SHW OL2 ...60 A4
  TOT/BURYW BL8 ...37 G1
  WGTN/LGST M12 ...129 H3
  MDTN M24 ...72 A3
Fenwick Cl WHTN BL5 ...62 B2
Fenwick St HULME M15 ...128 B2
  ROCH OL11 ...10 A7
Ferdinand St
  NEWH/MOS M40 * ...115 G1
Fereday St WALK M28 ...81 H3
Ferguson Gdns WHIT OL12 ...19 E5
Ferguson Wy OLDE OL4 ...76 C3
Fermacre SALE M33 ...154 D1
Fernally St HYDE SK14 ...133 H5
Fern Av URM M41 ...138 A1
Fern Bank
  NEWH/MOS M40 * ...104 B3
Fernbank RAD M26 * ...68 A4
Fern Bank STLY SK15 ...121 F5
Fern Bank STLY SK15 ...121 F5
Fern Bank Dr
  NTHM/RTH M23 ...167 F1
Fern Bank St DTN/ASHW M34 ...148 A3
Fernbrae Av BNG/LEV M19 ...158 A2
Fernbrook Cl
  BRUN/LGST M13 ...129 E3
Fern Cl MDTN M24 ...73 G4
Ferncliffe Dr WHIT OL12 ...18 C1
  OLDE OL4 ...93 E1
Fern Clough BOL BL1 ...47 G2
Fernclough Rd BKLY M9 ...103 G4
Fern Crs STLY SK15 ...121 F5
Ferndale Av HTNM SK4 ...158 C3
Ferndale Av MILN OL16 ...43 H5
  OFTN SK2 ...172 C5

WHTF M45 68 D5
Ferndale Cl OLDE OL4 92 C3
Ferndale Gdns BNG/LEV M19 143 G5
Ferndale Rd SALE M33 154 C4
Fern Dene WHIT OL12 29 E1
Ferndene Rd DID/WITH M20 157 G1
WHTF M45 70 B5
Ferndown Av BRAM/HZG SK7 184 D3
CHAD OL9 73 G5
Ferndown Dr IRL M44 122 B5
Ferndown Rd BOLE BL2 35 F3
NTHM/RTH M23 167 E1
Ferney Field Rd MDTN M24 89 H1
Ferngate Dr DID/WITH M20 142 D5
Ferngrove BURY BL9 39 E2
Fernhill MPL/ROM SK6 175 G3
Fernhill Av BOLS/LL BL3 47 H5
Fernhill Dr GTN M18 130 A4
Fernhills EDGW/EG BL7 22 D1
Fernhill St BURY BL9 4 E2
Fernholme Ct OLDS OL8 90 D3
Fernhurst Rd DID/WITH M20 157 H1
Fernhurst St OLD OL1 74 D3
Fernie St ANC M4 * 114 D2
Fern Isle Cl WHIT OL12 18 A2
Fern Lea CHD/CHDH SK8 181 G3
Fernlea HALE/TIMP WA15 178 A3
Fernlea Av OLD OL1 74 D3
Fernlea Cl WHIT OL12 29 E1
Fernlea Crs SWIN M27 98 D3
Fern Lea Gv LHULT M38 81 E3
Fernleigh Av BNG/LEV M19 144 C2
Fernleigh Dr
OLDTF/WHR M16 * 127 F3
Fernley Av DTN/ASHW M34 147 E1
Fernley Rd OFTN SK2 172 C3
Fern Lodge Dr AUL OL6 107 G5
Fernone WILM/AE SK9 192 A4
Ferns Gv BOL BL1 48 A2
Fernside RAD M26 83 E1
Fernside Av DID/WITH M20 158 A1
Fernside Gv WALK M28 * 82 B3
Fernside Wy WHIT OL12 28 D2
Fernstead BOLS/LL BL3 48 B3
Fern St BOLS/LL BL3 48 B3
BURY BL9 4 E2
CHAD OL9 74 B4
CHH M8 114 D1
FWTH BL4 66 B3
OLDS OL8 8 D6
RAMS BL0 17 E2
ROCH OL11 29 G5
WHIT OL12 19 H2
Fernthorpe Av UPML OL3 79 F3
Fern Vw HALE/TIMP WA15 167 F4
Fernview Dr RAMS BL0 26 C2
Fernwood MPL/ROM SK6 175 H2
Fernwood Av GTN M18 130 C5
Fernwood Gv WILM/AE SK9 199 F2
Ferrand Ldg LIT OL15 21 F1
Ferrand Rd LIT OL15 21 E2
Ferring Wk CHAD OL9 * 90 C1
Ferris St OP/CLY M11 117 E5
Ferrous Wy IRL M44 136 B5
Ferryhill Rd IRL M44 136 C1
Ferrymasters Wy IRL M44 136 C2
Ferry Rd IRL M44 136 D1
Ferry St OP/CLY M11 115 H5
Fettler Cl SWIN M27 98 D4
Feversham Cl ECC M30 111 G1
Fewston Cl BOL BL1 33 H1
Fiddlers La IRL M44 122 C5
Field Bank Gv BNG/LEV M19 144 B2
Field Cl BRAM/HZG SK7 193 G3
MPL/ROM SK6 174 C4
Fieldcroft ROCH OL11 29 E4
Fielden Av CCHDY M21 141 F2
Fielden Ct CCHDY M21 156 C1
Fielden Rd DID/WITH M20 157 E1
Fielders Wy SWIN M27 83 H3
Fieldfare Av NEWH/MOS M40 116 C1
Fieldfare Wy AULW OL7 106 D3
Fieldhead Av ROCH OL11 28 D4
TOT/BURYW BL8 37 F5
Fieldhead Ms WILM/AE SK9 199 H2
Fieldhead Rd WILM/AE SK9 199 E2
Field House La MPL/ROM SK6 175 F4
Fieldhouse Rd WHIT OL12 10 D1
Fielding Av POY/DIS SK12 195 F5
Fielding St ECC M30 110 D4
MDTN M24 72 D2
Field La AUL OL6 107 G5
Field Pl DID/WITH M20 157 G3
Field Rd MILN OL16 31 E4
SALE M33 139 E5
Fieldsend Cl STLY SK15 121 G5
Fields End Fold ECC M30 122 D4
Fields Farm Cl HYDE SK14 149 F2
Fields Farm Rd HYDE SK14 149 G1
Fieldside Cl BRAM/HZG SK7 193 G3
Fields New Rd CHAD OL9 90 B2
Field St DROY M43 117 G5
FAIL M35 104 D3
GTN M18 130 D2
HYDE SK14 133 G3
MPL/ROM SK6 161 G3
ROCH OL11 43 F2
SLFD M6 113 E3
Fieldsway OLDS OL8 91 F5
Field Vale Dr RDSH SK5 145 G2
Fieldvale Rd SALE M33 153 H5
Field View Wk
OLDTF/WHR M16 142 B1
Field Wk HALE/TIMP WA15 * 178 C1
Fieldway MILN OL16 43 G3
Fife Av CHAD OL9 90 A3
Fifield Cl OLDS OL8 91 H4
Fifth Av BOL BL1 48 A2
BOLS/LL BL3 50 C5
BURY BL9 39 G2
DUK SK16 133 E1
OLDS OL8 90 D5
OP/CLY M11 116 D3
TRPK M17 125 H3
Fifth St BOL BL1 32 C2
TRPK M17 125 H3
Filbert St OLD OL1 76 B3
Filby Wk NEWH/MOS M40 115 H1
Fildes St MDTN M24 73 G5
Filey Av OLDTF/WHR M16 141 H1
URM M41 123 H4
Filey Dr SLFD M6 100 A4
Filey Rd OFTN SK2 172 D2
RUSH/FAL M14 143 F3
Filey St MILN OL16 30 D1
Filton Av BOLS/LL BL3 48 C4
Finance St LIT OL15 20 B3
Finborough Cl
OLDTF/WHR M16 127 H4
Finchale Dr HALE/TIMP WA15 178 C3
Finchley Av NEWH/MOS M40 116 D1
Finchley Cl TOT/BURYW BL8 37 G5
Finchley Gv NEWH/MOS M40 103 H1
Finchley Rd HALE/TIMP WA15 177 H1
RUSH/FAL M14 142 D3
Finchwood Rd
WYTH/NTH M22 168 D4
Findon Rd NTHM/RTH M23 167 H3
Finger Post BOLS/LL BL3 50 D5
Finghall Rd URM M41 138 B1
Finishing Wk ANC M4 * 115 F4
Finland Rd EDGY/DAV SK3 171 G2
Finlan Rd MDTN M24 57 H4
Finlay St FWTH BL4 * 66 A4
Finney Cl WILM/AE SK9 191 H5
Finney Dr CCHDY M21 141 E4
WILM/AE SK9 191 H5
Finney La CHD/CHDH SK8 181 F4
Finney St BOLS/LL BL3 * 49 E5
Finningley Rd BKLY M9 87 G1
Finny Bank Rd SALE M33 139 G5
Finsbury Av NEWH/MOS M40 116 D1
Finsbury Cl OLDS OL8 92 A3
Finsbury Rd RDSH SK5 145 E3
Finsbury St ROCH OL11 42 C1
Finsbury Wy WILM/AE SK9 192 B5
Finstock Cl ECC M30 110 C4
Fintry Gv ECC M30 111 E4
Fir Av BRAM/HZG SK7 183 H4
Firbank Cl AULW OL7 119 E3
Firbank Rd NTHM/RTH M23 179 H1
Fir Bank Rd ROY/SHW OL2 59 E3
Firbarn Cl MILN OL16 31 E4
Firbeck Dr ANC M4 115 G3
Fir Cl POY/DIS SK12 195 F4
Fircroft Rd OLDS OL8 91 H5
Firdale Av NEWH/MOS M40 104 D1
Firdale Wk CHAD OL9 8 A2
Firecrest Cl WALK M28 96 C2
Firefly Cl CSLFD M3 114 A4
Fire Station Sq ORD M5 * 113 H3
Fire Station Yd ROCH OL11 30 A5
Firethorn Av BNG/LEV M19 143 H5
Firethorn Cl WHTN BL5 62 A2
Firethorn Dr HYDE SK14 148 C1
Firfield Gv WALK M28 82 C4
Fir Gv BNG/LEV M19 144 A2
CHAD OL9 74 C4
Firgrove Av MILN OL16 31 E3
Firgrove Gdns MILN OL16 31 E3
Fir La ROY/SHW OL2 59 E3
Fir Rd BRAM/HZG SK7 183 H4
DTN/ASHW M34 132 D5
FWTH BL4 65 G4
MPL/ROM SK6 174 D5
SWIN M27 98 D4
Firs Av AUL OL6 119 G1
FAIL M35 104 D3
OLDTF/WHR M16 141 F1
Firsby Av MPL/ROM SK6 161 G2
Firsby St BNG/LEV M19 144 A2
Firs Gv CHD/CHDH SK8 169 F5
Firs Rd CHD/CHDH SK8 181 F1
SALE M33 153 H1
First Av BOLS/LL BL3 50 C5
OLDS OL8 91 E5
OP/CLY M11 117 E3
STLY SK15 109 F5
SWIN M27 98 C5
TOT/BURYW BL8 26 A5
TRPK M17 126 A3
The Firs ALT WA14 177 E2
Fir St BOL BL1 34 A4
BURY BL9 5 H4
ECC M30 111 E4
FAIL M35 104 D3
HEY OL10 41 F5
HTNM SK4 12 E2
NEWH/MOS M40 115 G1
OLDTF/WHR M16 * 127 F4
RAD M26 67 E1
RAMS BL0 17 E1
ROY/SHW OL2 59 E4
SLFD M6 113 E3
First St BOL BL1 32 C2
Firs Wy SALE M33 153 F3
Firswood Dr HYDE SK14 134 B5
ROY/SHW OL2 58 D4
SWIN M27 98 D4
Firswood Mt CHD/CHDH SK8 169 F5
Firth St OLD OL1 9 H4
Fir Tree Av OLDS OL8 91 H5
SALE M33 153 F2
WALK M28 96 C4
Fir Tree Cl DUK SK16 120 C5
Fir Tree Crs DUK SK16 120 C5
Fir Tree Dr HYDE SK14 133 H3
Fir Tree La DUK SK16 134 A1
Firvale Av CHD/CHDH SK8 181 G3
Firwood Av FWTH BL4 81 H1
URM M41 139 G2
Firwood Cl OFTN SK2 172 D1
Firwood Crs RAD M26 68 C3
Firwood Gv BOLE BL2 34 C4
Firwood La BOLE BL2 34 D3
Firwood Pk CHAD OL9 73 H5
Fishbourne Sq
RUSH/FAL M14 * 128 D5
Fisherfield WHIT OL12 28 C2
Fishermore Rd
URM M41 137 G1
Fisher St OLD OL1 9 H1
Fishwick St MILN OL16 30 B5
Fistral Av CHD/CHDH SK8 181 H4
Fistral Crs STLY SK15 121 G2
Fitton Av CCHDY M21 141 F5
Fitton Crs SWIN M27 84 A4
Fitton Hill Rd OLDS OL8 91 H4
Fitton St MILN OL16 11 F4
ROY/SHW OL2 59 G2
Fitzgeorge St
NEWH/MOS M40 102 D5
Fitzgerald Cl PWCH M25 85 G5
Fitzgerald Wy SLFD M6 * 113 E2
Fitzhugh St BOL BL1 * 34 B1
Fitzroy St AULW OL7 119 E4
DROY M43 118 A5
STLY SK15 121 G2
Fitzwarren St SLFD M6 113 E3
Fitzwilliam St BRO M7 114 A1
Five Quarters RAD M26 51 H4
Flagcroft Dr NTHM/RTH M23 168 A4
Flagg Wood Av
MPL/ROM SK6 174 C2
Flag Rw ANC M4 * 115 E2
Flagship Av ORD M5 * 113 G5
Flake La ROY/SHW OL2 59 E5
Flamborough Wk
RUSH/FAL M14 * 128 C5
Flamingo Cl WGTN/LGST M12 129 H2
Flamstead Av
NTHM/RTH M23 167 F3
Flannel St WHIT OL12 10 E4
Flashfields PWCH M25 100 C1
Flash St NEWH/MOS M40 104 B4
Flatley Cl HULME M15 128 B2
Flavian Wk OP/CLY M11 * 116 C5
Flaxcroft Rd WYTH/NTH M22 180 A2
Flaxfield Av STLY SK15 121 G3
Flaxman Ri OLD OL1 60 B5
Flaxpool Cl OLDTF/WHR M16 127 H4
Flax St CSLFD M3 6 A1
RAMS BL0 16 B4
Fleece St MILN OL16 10 C6
OLDE OL4 * 76 A5
Fleeson St RUSH/FAL M14 128 D5
Fleet St AUL OL6 119 G3
GTN M18 131 E2
HYDE SK14 133 H4
OLDE OL4 76 B5
Fleetwood Rd WALK M28 81 F4
Fleming Cl WHIT OL12 20 A3
Fleming Pl CHAD OL9 8 D4
Fleming Rd WYTH/NTH M22 180 C2
Flemish Rd DTN/ASHW M34 147 F1
Fletcher Av SWIN M27 84 B4
Fletcher Cl CHAD OL9 8 C4
HEY OL10 41 E4
Fletcher Dr ALT WA14 177 F3
POY/DIS SK12 197 E1
Fletcher Fold Rd BURY BL9 53 G3
Fletcher Sq CMANE M1 * 7 K5
Fletcher's Rd LIT OL15 20 B5
Fletcher St AUL OL6 119 H2
BOLS/LL BL3 48 D4
BOLS/LL BL3 67 E1
BURY BL9 5 G4
FWTH BL4 66 A4
NEWH/MOS M40 103 G5
RAD M26 52 D5
ROCH OL11 43 F1
STKP SK1 13 G3
Fletsand Rd WILM/AE SK9 199 F4
Fletton Cl WHIT OL12 29 H1
Fletton Ms WHIT OL12 29 F1
Flint Cl BRAM/HZG SK7 184 D3
OP/CLY M11 * 116 C3
Flint St DROY M43 118 A3
EDGY/DAV SK3 13 F7
OLD OL1 76 B4
Flitcroft Ct BOLS/LL BL3 * 49 E5
Flitcroft St OLDE OL4 92 B3
Flixton Rd URM M41 137 H2
Floatshall Rd NTHM/RTH M23 167 G3
Floats Rd NTHM/RTH M23 167 F4
Flora St BKLY M9 87 H4
OLD OL1 9 F2
Florence Av BOL BL1 34 A2
Florence Ct EDGY/DAV SK3 * 171 E2
Florence Park Ct
DID/WITH M20 157 H2
Florence St BOLS/LL BL3 * 48 C5
DROY M43 118 A5
ECC M30 110 C4
FAIL M35 105 E2
HTNM SK4 13 F1
MILN OL16 30 C5
SALE M33 139 H5
Florida St OLDS OL8 8 E6
Florin Gdns SLFD M6 113 E2
Florist St EDGY/DAV SK3 171 H2
Flowery Bank OLDS OL8 92 A3
Flowery Fld OFTN SK2 184 B1
Flowery Field Gn HYDE SK14 133 F4
Floyd Av CCHDY M21 141 G5
Floyer Rd BKLY M9 88 B3
Foden La BRAM/HZG SK7 193 G4
Foggbrook Cl OFTN SK2 173 G3
Fogg La BOLS/LL BL3 66 B1
Fog La BNG/LEV M19 158 A2
DID/WITH M20 157 G2
Fold Av DROY M43 118 A3
Fold Crs STLY SK15 109 G4
Fold Gdns WHIT OL12 18 A5
Fold Gn CHAD OL9 90 B1
Fold Ms BRAM/HZG SK7 185 F1
Fold Rd RAD M26 67 F5
Folds Rd BOL BL1 3 G3
Fold St BOL BL1 * 3 F5
BURY BL9 4 B4
HEY OL10 41 F4
NEWH/MOS M40 103 H2
The Fold BKLY M9 88 A4
ROY/SHW OL2 59 H5
URM M41 123 H5
Fold Vw EDGW/EG BL7 22 D2
OLDS OL8 91 H5
Foleshill Av BKLY M9 103 E3
Foley Gdns HEY OL10 56 B2
Foliage Crs RDSH SK5 160 C1
Foliage Gdns RDSH SK5 160 D1
Foliage Rd RDSH SK5 160 C2
Folkestone Rd OP/CLY M11 117 E3
Folkestone Rd East
OP/CLY M11 117 E3
Folkestone Rd West
OP/CLY M11 116 D3
Follows St GTN M18 130 C2
Folly La SWIN M27 98 C5
Folly Wk WHIT OL12 10 D3
Fonthill Gv SALE M33 154 A5
Fontwell Cl OLDTF/WHR M16 127 F5
Fontwell La OLD OL1 75 H3
Fontwell Rd BOLS/LL BL3 66 D2
Fooley Cl DROY M43 117 F5
Foot Mill Crs WHIT OL12 29 G1
Foot Wood Crs WHIT OL12 29 G1
Forber Crs GTN M18 130 B5
Forbes Cl SALE M33 155 E4
STKP SK1 172 C1
Forbes Pk BRAM/HZG SK7 183 G5
Forbes Rd STKP SK1 160 C5
Forbes St MPL/ROM SK6 161 G2
Fordbank Rd DID/WITH M20 157 F4
Ford Gdns ROCH OL11 29 E5
Ford Gv HYDE SK14 135 H4
Fordham Gv BOL BL1 48 B1
Ford La DID/WITH M20 157 F4
SLFD M6 113 F1
WYTH/NTH M22 156 D5
Ford Ldg DID/WITH M20 157 G4
Ford's La BRAM/HZG SK7 193 G1
Ford St CSLFD M3 6 A3
DUK SK16 133 F2
EDGY/DAV SK3 12 C4
RAD M26 66 D4
WGTN/LGST M12 129 E2
Foreland Cl NEWH/MOS M40 103 E5
Forest Cl DUK SK16 133 F2
Forest Ct URM M41 123 E5
Forest Dr HALE/TIMP WA15 166 A3
SALE M33 153 H4
WHTN BL5 62 B4
Forester Hill Av BOLS/LL BL3 65 E1
Forester Hill Cl BOLS/LL BL3 65 E1
Forest Gdns PART M31 150 C3
Forest Range BNG/LEV M19 144 A2
Forest Rd BOL BL1 33 E3
Forest St AUL OL6 119 H1
ECC M30 110 B1
OLDS OL8 91 G5
Forest Vw WHIT OL12 29 G1
Forest Wy EDGW/EG BL7 23 H5
Forfar St BOL BL1 33 H1
Forge St OLDE OL4 76 A5
Formby Av CCHDY M21 141 H4
Formby Dr CHD/CHDH SK8 181 G4
Formby Rd SLFD M6 100 B5
Forrester Dr ROY/SHW OL2 60 C1
STLY SK15 120 D4
Forresters Gn TRPK M17 126 B2
Forrester St WALK M28 97 H2
Forrest Rd DTN/ASHW M34 147 F2
Forshaw Av GTN M18 131 E3
Forsyth St WHIT OL12 28 B1
Fortescue Rd OFTN SK2 173 E2
Forth Pl RAD M26 52 A4
Forth Rd RAD M26 52 A4
Forton Av BOLE BL2 50 B2
Fortran Cl ORD M5 113 F4
Fort Rd PWCH M25 86 C5
Fortrose Av BKLY M9 87 G4
Fortuna Gv BNG/LEV M19 143 H3
Fortune St BOLS/LL BL3 49 G4
Fortyacre Dr MPL/ROM SK6 161 F3
Forum Gv BRO M7 101 H5
Fosbrook Av DID/WITH M20 157 H2
Foscarn Dr NTHM/RTH M23 168 A4
Fossgill Av BOLE BL2 34 D1
Foster Ct BURY BL9 39 G2
Foster La BOLE BL2 35 G5
Foster St DTN/ASHW M34 132 C5
OLDE OL4 92 B1
RAD M26 68 A1
Fotherby Dr BKLY M9 88 A4
Foulds Av TOT/BURYW BL8 37 F4
Foundry La ANC M4 7 H3
Foundry St BOLS/LL BL3 49 E4
BOLS/LL BL3 66 D1
BURY BL9 5 F5
DUK SK16 119 H5
HEY OL10 40 D4
OLDS OL8 8 E5
RAD M26 68 B1
Fountain Av
HALE/TIMP WA15 178 C2
Fountain Gdns OLD OL1 * 75 E3
Fountain Pl WHTF M45 69 G5
Fountains Av BOLE BL2 34 D5
Fountains Rd CHD/CHDH SK8 193 F1
STRET M32 125 E5
Fountain St AUL OL6 120 B2
BURY BL9 5 H5
CMANW M2 7 F5
ECC M30 111 E5
HYDE SK14 134 A5
MDTN M24 72 C4
OLD OL1 9 F3
TOT/BURYW BL8 37 H4
Fountain St North BURY BL9 5 G4
Fountains Wk CHAD OL9 * 90 B2
DUK SK16 133 F2
Fouracres Rd
NTHM/RTH M23 167 G4
Four Lane Ends URM M41 137 G3
Four Lanes HYDE SK14 135 H4
Four Stalls End LIT OL15 20 D4
Fourth Av BOL BL1 48 A2
BOLS/LL BL3 50 C5
BURY BL9 39 F2
CHAD OL9 90 B2
OLDS OL8 90 D5
OP/CLY M11 116 D2
STLY SK15 109 F4
SWIN M27 98 C5
Fourth St BOL BL1 32 C2
TRPK M17 125 H3
Fourways TRPK M17 125 F2
Four Yards CMANW M2 6 E5
Fovant Crs RDSH SK5 145 E2
Fowler Av GTN M18 131 E1
Fowler St OLDS OL8 90 D4
Fownhope Av SALE M33 154 A3
Fownhope Rd SALE M33 154 A3
Foxall Cl MDTN M24 71 H5
Foxall St MDTN M24 71 H5
Foxbank St BRUN/LGST M13 129 F4
Fox Bench Cl BRAM/HZG SK7 193 F1
Foxbench Wk CCHDY M21 141 H5
Fox Cl HALE/TIMP WA15 166 A3
Foxcroft St LIT OL15 20 C3
Foxdale St OP/CLY M11 116 D4
Foxdenton Dr STRET M32 125 E5
Foxdenton La MDTN M24 89 H1
Foxendale Wk BOLS/LL BL3 * 48 D4
Foxfield Cl TOT/BURYW BL8 37 G1
Foxfield Dr OLDS OL8 105 H1
Foxfield Rd NTHM/RTH M23 179 H1
Foxfold Cl WALK M28 96 A3
Foxglove Ct WHIT OL12 18 C5
Foxglove Dr ALT WA14 165 F1
BURY BL9 39 G3
Foxglove La STLY SK15 120 C2
Foxhall Rd DTN/ASHW M34 132 A4
HALE/TIMP WA15 165 H3
Foxham Dr BRO M7 101 H4
Foxhill ALT WA14 164 D4
Fox Hl ROY/SHW OL2 59 F1
Foxhill Cha OFTN SK2 173 H4
Foxhill Dr STLY SK15 121 F5
Foxhill Rd ECC M30 110 A4
Fox Hill Rd ROCH OL11 57 G1
Foxholes Cl WHIT OL12 10 E2
Foxholes La WHIT OL12 11 G1
Foxholes Rd HYDE SK14 147 H3
WHIT OL12 10 E2
Foxlair Rd WYTH/NTH M22 180 A1
Foxland Rd CHD/CHDH SK8 169 G5
Foxley Gv BOLS/LL BL3 2 B6
Fox Park Rd OLDS OL8 105 H1
Fox Platt Rd MOSL OL5 * 108 C1
Fox Platt Ter MOSL OL5 108 D2
Fox St BURY BL9 5 F2
ECC M30 111 G3
EDGY/DAV SK3 12 C6
HEY OL10 40 D4
MILN OL16 11 G4
MILN OL16 31 F5
OLDS OL8 90 D5
Foxton St MDTN M24 71 H5
Foxwood Dr HYDE SK14 133 H4
MOSL OL5 94 A5
Foxwood Gdns BNG/LEV M19 158 B1
Foynes Cl NEWH/MOS M40 * 103 E5
Framingham Rd SALE M33 154 C4
Frampton Cl MDTN M24 73 E5
Fram St BKLY M9 103 G2
SLFD M6 * 112 D3
Frances Av CHD/CHDH SK8 169 F3
Frances St BOL BL1 33 G4
BRUN/LGST M13 128 C2
CHD/CHDH SK8 170 B3
EDGY/DAV SK3 13 F5
HYDE SK14 133 F5
IRL M44 150 D1
MILN OL16 20 A5
OLD OL1 75 H3
Frances St West HYDE SK14 133 F5
Francis Av ECC M30 111 F3
WALK M28 82 C5
Francis Rd DID/WITH M20 157 H1
IRL M44 136 B3
Francis St CSLFD M3 114 C2
DTN/ASHW M34 147 F3
ECC M30 111 E2
FAIL M35 105 E3
FWTH BL4 65 H3
Frankby Cl SWIN M27 * 99 H3
Frank Fold HEY OL10 40 B4
Frankford Av BOL BL1 33 F4
Frankford Sq BOL BL1 * 33 F4
Frankland Cl OP/CLY M11 116 C3
Franklin Cl OLD OL1 9 F1
Franklin Rd DROY M43 117 H4
Franklin St ECC M30 111 E3
MILN OL16 43 G1
OLD OL1 9 F1
Franklyn Av URM M41 137 G1
Franklyn Rd GTN M18 130 D2
Frank Perkins Wy IRL M44 136 B4
Frank St BOL BL1 33 G5
BURY BL9 5 F6
FAIL M35 104 D3
HYDE SK14 148 A1
SLFD M6 113 F1
Frankton Rd WHTF M45 69 G5
Franton Rd OP/CLY M11 116 C3
Fraser Av SALE M33 155 F3
Fraser Pl TRPK M17 126 A3
Fraser Rd CHH M8 102 A1
Fraser St AUL OL6 119 H2
MILN OL16 43 G2
ROY/SHW OL2 59 H1
SWIN M27 99 F1
Frecheville Ct BURY BL9 4 C7
Freckleton Av CCHDY M21 156 B2
Freckleton Dr TOT/BURYW BL8 52 A1
Frederick Av ROY/SHW OL2 * 59 H4
Frederick Rd SLFD M6 113 G2
Frederick St AUL OL6 120 B3
CHAD OL9 74 C4
CSLFD M3 6 B3
DTN/ASHW M34 132 C3
FWTH BL4 66 A4
LIT OL15 20 D2
OLDS OL8 8 C7
RAMS BL0 16 C3
Frederick Ter BKLY M9 * 103 E1
Fred Tilson Cl RUSH/FAL M14 128 B5
Freehold St ROCH OL11 42 D1
Freeman Av AUL OL6 120 A2
Freeman Rd DUK SK16 133 F2
Freeman Sq HULME M15 * 128 B2
Freemantle St EDGY/DAV SK3 12 B5
Freesia Av WALK M28 81 E4
Freestone Cl
TOT/BURYW BL8 4 B2
Freetown Cl RUSH/FAL M14 128 B4
Freetrade St ROCH OL11 42 D1
Fremantle Av GTN M18 130 C5
French Av OLD OL1 76 B3
STLY SK15 121 F4
French Barn La BKLY M9 87 H4
French Gv BOLS/LL BL3 50 A4
French St AUL OL6 120 A1
STLY SK15 121 F4
Fresca Rd OLD OL1 60 C5
Freshfield CHD/CHDH SK8 181 C3
Freshfield Av BOLS/LL BL3 64 C2
HYDE SK14 147 H2

PWCH M25 86 B1
Freshfield Cl FAIL M35 105 F4
MPL/ROM SK6 163 G5
Freshfield Gv BOLS/LL BL3 65 E2
Freshfield Rd HTNM SK4 158 C4
Freshfields RAD M26 51 G4
Freshpool Wy
WYTH/NTH M22 168 D3
Freshville St CMANE M1 * 7 J6
Freshwater Dr AUL OL6 107 H5
DTN/ASHW M34 147 F3
Freshwater St GTN M18 130 D2
Freshwinds Ct OLDE OL4 92 C3
Fresnel Cl HYDE SK14 134 C2
Frewland Av EDGY/DAV SK3 172 A5
Freya Gv ORD M5 113 H5
Friars Cl ALT WA14 177 E3
WILM/AE SK9 198 B2
Friars Crs ROCH OL11 43 E4
Friar's Rd SALE M33 154 C2
Friendship Av GTN M18 * 130 D4
Frieston WHIT OL12 10 B4
Frieston Rd ALT WA14 153 H5
Friezland Cl STLY SK15 109 F5
Friezland La UPML OL3 94 D3
Frimley Gdns WYTH/NTH M22 180 C1
Frinton Av NEWH/MOS M40 * 89 G4
Frinton Cl SALE M33 154 A5
Frinton Rd BOLS/LL BL3 64 A1
Frith Rd DID/WITH M20 157 H1
Frobisher Cl BRUN/LGST M13 129 E3
Frobisher Pl RDSH SK5 159 H2
Frodesley Wk
WGTN/LGST M12 * 129 G2
Frodsham Av HTNM SK4 159 F3
Frodsham Rd SALE M33 155 F4
Frodsham St RUSH/FAL M14 * 128 C5
Frogley St BOLE BL2 * 34 C3
Frogmore Av HYDE SK14 148 A4
Frome Av OFTN SK2 172 D4
URM M41 138 B3
Frome Dr CHH M8 102 C3
Frome St OLDE OL4 92 B1
Frostlands St
OLDTF/WHR M16 127 H5
Frost St ANC M4 * 115 G4
OLDS OL8 91 F3
Froxmer St GTN M18 130 B2
Fulbrook Dr CHD/CHDH SK8 192 D1
Fulford St OLDTF/WHR M16 127 F4
Fulham Av NEWH/MOS M40 104 A5
Fulham St OLDE OL4 92 B1
Fullerton Rd HTNM SK4 159 E4
Full Pot La ROCH OL11 28 B3
Fulmar Cl POY/DIS SK12 194 B3
Fulmar Dr OFTN SK2 173 G4
SALE M33 153 F4
Fulmards Cl WILM/AE SK9 199 F3
Fulmar Gdns ROCH OL11 28 C4
Fulmer Dr ANC M4 115 F3
Fulmere Ct SWIN M27 98 C4
Fulneck Sq DROY M43 117 H5
Fulshaw Av WILM/AE SK9 198 D4
Fulshaw Ct WILM/AE SK9 198 D5
Fulshaw Pk WILM/AE SK9 198 D5
Fulshaw Pk South
WILM/AE SK9 200 C1
Fulstone Ms OFTN SK2 172 C3
Fulwood Av BKLY M9 88 C3
Fulwood Cl TOT/BURYW BL8 37 E5
Furbarn La ROCH OL11 28 A3
Furbarn Rd ROCH OL11 28 A3
Furlong Rd WYTH/NTH M22 180 A2
Furnace St DUK SK16 119 G4
HYDE SK14 133 F4
Furness Av AULW OL7 106 C5
BOLE BL2 34 C4
HEY OL10 40 D3
LIT OL15 20 D2
OLDS OL8 92 B3
WHTF M45 69 H4
Furness Cl MILN OL16 31 F5
POY/DIS SK12 194 D3
Furness Gv HTNM SK4 158 D5
Furness Quay SALQ M50 126 D1
Furness Rd BOL BL1 48 A2
CHD/CHDH SK8 193 F1
MDTN M24 72 C1
RUSH/FAL M14 143 E2
URM M41 124 C5
Furness Sq BOLE BL2 34 C4
Furnival Rd GTN M18 130 B2
Furnival St RDSH SK5 145 E1
Furrow Dr ECC M30 110 C1
Further Fld ROCH OL11 28 A2
Further Heights Rd WHIT OL12 10 B1
Further Hey Cl OLDE OL4 76 D5
Further La HYDE SK14 135 F5
Further Pits ROCH OL11 29 F4
Furze Av WHTN BL5 62 A5
Furzegate MILN OL16 43 H3
Furze La OLDE OL4 76 C3
Fushia Gv BRO M7 * 101 G4
Fylde Av BOLE BL2 50 B2
CHD/CHDH SK8 181 H4
Fylde Rd HTNM SK4 158 D4
Fylde St BOLS/LL BL3 66 A2
Fylde St East BOLS/LL BL3 66 A2

G

Gable Av WILM/AE SK9 198 D3
Gable Dr MDTN M24 72 B3
The Gables SALE M33 * 154 C3
Gable St BOLE BL2 * 35 E1
OP/CLY M11 116 A5
Gabriel's Ter MDTN M24 73 F5
The Gabriels ROY/SHW OL2 59 G2
Gaddum Rd ALT WA14 176 D3
DID/WITH M20 157 H3
Gadwall Cl WALK M28 97 E2
Gail Av HTNM SK4 12 C1
Gail Cl FAIL M35 104 D5
WILM/AE SK9 201 E3
Gainford Av CHD/CHDH SK8 169 G5
Gainford Gdns
NEWH/MOS M40 104 A1
Gainford Rd RDSH SK5 145 F2
Gainford Wk BOLS/LL BL3 * 48 D5
Gainsborough Av BOLS/LL BL3 64 B1
DID/WITH M20 * 157 H1
MPL/ROM SK6 175 G1
OLDS OL8 91 F3
STRET M32 * 126 C5
Gainsborough Cl
WILM/AE SK9 199 G2
Gainsborough Dr
CHD/CHDH SK8 170 C3
ROCH OL11 42 D3
Gainsborough Rd CHAD OL9 73 H4
DTN/ASHW M34 118 C4
RAMS BL0 26 B2
Gainsborough St BRO M7 101 H3
Gairloch Av STRET M32 139 H1
Gair Rd RDSH SK5 160 A2
Gair St HYDE SK14 133 G4
Gaitskell Cl WGTN/LGST M12 115 H4
Galbraith Rd DID/WITH M20 157 H3
Galbraith St CMANE M1 * 7 G7
Galbraith Wy ROCH OL11 28 B3
Gale Cl LIT OL15 21 F1
Gale Dr MDTN M24 72 A2
Gale Rd PWCH M25 85 G4
Gales Ter ROCH OL11 42 D1
Gale St HEY OL10 40 C4
WHIT OL12 19 E5
Galgate Cl HULME M15 127 H1
TOT/BURYW BL8 37 E5
Galindo St BOLE BL2 34 D2
Galland St OLDE OL4 76 C5
Galloway Cl BOLS/LL BL3 47 F4
HEY OL10 40 A5
Galloway Dr SWIN M27 84 A3
Galloway Rd SWIN M27 * 98 C4
Gallowsclough Rd STLY SK15 135 F2
Galston St OP/CLY M11 116 B5
Galsworthy Av CHH M8 102 B5
Galvin Rd BKLY M9 87 G4
Galway St OLD OL1 9 G4
Gambleside Cl WALK M28 96 C2
Gambrel Bank Rd AUL OL6 107 E4
Gambrel Gv AUL OL6 107 E4
Game St OLDE OL4 92 B2
Gamma Wk OP/CLY M11 116 C3
Gandy La WHIT OL12 18 B4
Gantock Wk RUSH/FAL M14 128 D5
Ganton Av WHTF M45 69 E5
Garbrook Av BKLY M9 87 H2
Garden Av DROY M43 118 A3
STRET M32 140 B1
SWIN M27 98 C3
Garden City RAMS BL0 26 B1
Garden Cl LIT OL15 31 G1
Gardenfold Wy DROY M43 118 A3
Garden La ALT WA14 165 G4
CSLFD M3 6 C2
CSLFD M3 6 D4
MILN OL16 10 E5
WALK M28 96 B4
Garden Ms AUL OL6 * 120 A3
Garden Rw HEY OL10 40 C2
The Gardens BOL BL1 23 E5
Garden St DTN/ASHW M34 132 C2
ECC M30 111 F4
FWTH BL4 66 B4
HEY OL10 40 D3
HYDE SK14 133 H4
MILN OL16 45 E2
OFTN SK2 * 172 D4
OLD OL1 9 K2
RAMS BL0 16 D2
TOT/BURYW BL8 26 A4
Garden Ter ROY/SHW OL2 58 D2
Garden Wk AUL OL6 119 H1
Garden Wall Cl ORD M5 113 H5
Garden Wy LIT OL15 31 G1
Gardner Rd PWCH M25 85 G3
Gardner St SLFD M6 113 F2
WGTN/LGST M12 130 A2
Garfield Av BNG/LEV M19 144 B2
Garfield Cl ROCH OL11 28 B3
Garfield Gv BOLS/LL BL3 2 B7
Garfield St BOLS/LL BL3 64 B1
STKP SK1 * 13 J1
Garforth Av ANC M4 115 F3
Garforth Crs DROY M43 118 B2
Garforth Ri BOL BL1 47 H2
Garforth St CHAD OL9 8 A2
Gargrave Av BOL BL1 32 C4
Gargrave St BRO M7 100 C2
OLDE OL4 92 A1
Garland Rd WYTH/NTH M22 180 D1
Garlick St CHAD OL9 8 E4
GTN M18 130 C3
HYDE SK14 * 134 A5
Garnant Cl BKLY M9 103 G2
Garner Av HALE/TIMP WA15 154 B5
Garner Cl ALT WA14 177 G2
Garner Dr ECC M30 * 110 D2
ORD M5 112 C2
Garner's La EDGY/DAV SK3 171 G5
EDGY/DAV SK3 172 A4
Garnet St OLD OL1 9 F5
Garnett Cl HYDE SK14 135 G5
Garnett Rd HYDE SK14 135 G5
Garnett St BOL BL1 33 H3
RAMS BL0 16 C3
STKP SK1 13 G4
Garratt Wy GTN M18 130 B3
Garret Gv ROY/SHW OL2 60 B2
Garrett Wk EDGY/DAV SK3 12 A5
Garrick Gdns WYTH/NTH M22 168 C5
Garsdale Cl BURY BL9 53 H2
Garsdale La BOL BL1 47 E2
Garside Gv BOL BL1 33 F4
Garside Hey Rd
TOT/BURYW BL8 26 D5
Garside St BOL BL1 2 C5
DTN/ASHW M34 * 146 D1
HYDE SK14 148 A2
Garstang Av BOLE BL2 50 B3
Garstang Dr TOT/BURYW BL8 37 E5
Garston Cl HTNM SK4 159 F3
Garston St BURY BL9 38 D2
Garswood Dr TOT/BURYW BL8 26 C5
Garswood Rd BOLS/LL BL3 64 D2
RUSH/FAL M14 142 C1
Garth Av HALE/TIMP WA15 165 H3
Garthland Rd BRAM/HZG SK7 185 G1
Garthorne Cl
OLDTF/WHR M16 127 H4
Garthorp Rd NTHM/RTH M23 155 F5
Garth Rd MPL/ROM SK6 175 F3
OFTN SK2 172 D2
WYTH/NTH M22 168 C5
The Garth ORD M5 112 C3
Garthwaite Av OLDS OL8 91 F4
Gartside St AULW OL7 * 118 D4
CSLFD M3 6 C5
OLDE OL4 92 A2
Garwick Rd BOL BL1 33 E3
Gascoyne St RUSH/FAL M14 128 C5
Gaskell Cl LIT OL15 * 20 D2
Gaskell Ri OLD OL1 60 D4
Gaskell Rd ALT WA14 165 G3
ECC M30 111 F4
Gaskell St BOL BL1 2 C2
DUK SK16 * 119 G4
NEWH/MOS M40 104 B5
SWIN M27 84 A5
Gaskill St HEY OL10 40 B4
Gas St AUL OL6 119 G2
BOL BL1 2 C5
FWTH BL4 66 A3
HEY OL10 41 E4
HTNM SK4 12 E3
ROCH OL11 10 A7
Gatcombe Sq RUSH/FAL M14 128 D5
Gateacre Wk NTHM/RTH M23 167 F2
Gate Field Cl RAD M26 67 H1
Gatehead Cft UPML OL3 78 C1
Gatehead Ms UPML OL3 78 C1
Gatehead Rd UPML OL3 78 C1
Gatehouse LIT OL15 * 21 G2
Gatehouse Rd WALK M28 81 F3
Gate Keeper Fold AULW OL7 106 D3
Gatemere Cl WALK M28 96 C2
Gatesgarth Rd MDTN M24 71 H2
Gateshead Cl RUSH/FAL M14 128 C4
Gate St DUK SK16 132 D2
OP/CLY M11 116 D5
ROCH OL11 43 E1
Gateway Crs CHAD OL9 89 H3
Gateway Rd GTN M18 * 130 B2
The Gateways SWIN M27 99 E1
The Gateway
NEWH/MOS M40 103 G4
Gathill Cl CHD/CHDH SK8 182 C3
Gathurst St GTN M18 130 D2
Gatley Av RUSH/FAL M14 142 C2
Gatley Brow OLD OL1 * 75 F4
Gatley Gn CHD/CHDH SK8 169 F4
Gatley Rd CHD/CHDH SK8 169 H4
SALE M33 155 F3
Gatling Av WGTN/LGST M12 144 A1
Gatwick Av NTHM/RTH M23 168 A3
Gavin Av ORD M5 113 F4
Gawsworth Av
DID/WITH M20 157 H5
Gawsworth Cl BRAM/HZG SK7 193 H2
EDGY/DAV SK3 171 G4
HALE/TIMP WA15 167 E3
POY/DIS SK12 195 G5
ROY/SHW OL2 59 G2
Gawsworth Ms
CHD/CHDH SK8 169 G4
Gawsworth Rd SALE M33 155 F4
Gawthorne Cl BRAM/HZG SK7 184 D2
Gawthorpe Cl BURY BL9 53 H4
Gaydon Rd SALE M33 153 G2
Gaythorne St BOL BL1 34 A3
Gaythorn St ORD M5 113 H4
Geddington Rd ALT WA14 165 F1
Gee Cross Fold HYDE SK14 148 A4
Gee La ECC M30 110 C2
Gee St EDGY/DAV SK3 12 D7
Gellfield La UPML OL3 79 G3
Gemini Rd SLFD M6 113 H1
Gencoyne Dr BOL BL1 22 C5
Gendre Rd EDGW/EG BL7 22 D3
Geneva Rd BRAM/HZG SK7 183 G1
Geneva Ter ROCH OL11 29 F3
Geneva Wk CHAD OL9 8 A4
Genista Gv BRO M7 * 101 G4
Geoffrey St BURY BL9 5 G1
RAMS BL0 16 B4
WHTN BL5 63 G4
George Barton St BOLE BL2 3 J1
George La MPL/ROM SK6 161 H2
George Leigh St ANC M4 7 H3
George Mann Cl
WYTH/NTH M22 180 B3
George Richards Wy
ALT WA14 165 E2
George Rd RAMS BL0 16 C3
George's Cl POY/DIS SK12 195 F4
George Sq OLD OL1 9 F4
George's Rd HTNM SK4 12 D2
SALE M33 154 C3
George's Rd West
POY/DIS SK12 195 F4
George St AUL OL6 119 H2
BURY BL9 5 F5
CHAD OL9 74 B5
CMANE M1 7 F6
DTN/ASHW M34 132 D5
ECC M30 110 D4
FAIL M35 105 E2
FWTH BL4 65 G5
HEY OL10 40 C3
IRL M44 122 C5
LIT OL15 * 21 E3
MILN OL16 10 E4
MILN OL16 20 A5
MILN OL16 31 E4
MOSL OL5 108 D1
MPL/ROM SK6 163 G4
OLD OL1 9 F4
PWCH M25 101 E1
RAD M26 68 A1
ROY/SHW OL2 45 F5
STKP SK1 13 J3
STLY SK15 120 D3
URM M41 139 E1
WHIT OL12 14 B5
WHTF M45 69 F3
WHTN BL5 62 A4
WILM/AE SK9 200 D4
George St East STKP SK1 172 C1
George St North BRO M7 102 A2
George St South BRO M7 101 H2
George St West STKP SK1 172 C1
Georgette Dr CSLFD M3 6 C1
Georgia Av DID/WITH M20 142 B5
Georgiana St FWTH BL4 65 G3
Georgina Ct BOLS/LL BL3 64 A2
Georgina St BOLS/LL BL3 64 A2
Gerald Av CHH M8 102 B2
Gerald Rd SLFD M6 100 D5
Germain Cl BKLY M9 87 H2
Gerrard Av HALE/TIMP WA15 166 B1
Gerrards Cl IRL M44 136 C1
Gerrards Gdns HYDE SK14 148 A4
Gerrards Hollow HYDE SK14 147 H4
The Gerrards HYDE SK14 147 H4
Gerrard St FWTH BL4 66 B4
ROCH OL11 43 F5
SLFD M6 113 F2
STLY SK15 121 E4
Gerrards Wd HYDE SK14 147 H4
Gertrude Cl ORD M5 113 F5
Gervis Cl NEWH/MOS M40 * 103 E5
Ghyll Gv WALK M28 82 B5
Giants Seat Gv SWIN M27 100 A2
Gibbon Av WYTH/NTH M22 180 C2
Gibbon St BOLS/LL BL3 48 C4
OP/CLY M11 116 B3
Gibb Rd WALK M28 98 A3
Gibbs St ORD M5 114 A4
Gib La NTHM/RTH M23 168 B1
Gibraltar La DTN/ASHW M34 147 F3
Gibraltar St BOLS/LL BL3 2 A7
OLDE OL4 92 C2
Gibsmere Cl
HALE/TIMP WA15 167 E3
Gibson Av GTN M18 131 E1
Gibson Gv WALK M28 81 F4
Gibson La WALK M28 81 F4
Gibson Pl ANC M4 114 D2
Gibsons Rd HTNM SK4 159 E2
Gibson St BOLE BL2 34 D5
MILN OL16 11 K4
OLDE OL4 * 92 B1
Gibson Wy ALT WA14 165 F1
Gibwood Rd WYTH/NTH M22 168 B1
Gidlow St GTN M18 130 D2
Gifford Av BKLY M9 88 C3
Gigg La BURY BL9 53 H1
Gilbertbank MPL/ROM SK6 161 H2
Gilbert Rd HALE/TIMP WA15 177 H3
Gilbert St ECC M30 110 C5
HULME M15 127 H1
SLFD M6 * 113 E4
WALK M28 96 D1
Gilbrook Wy MILN OL16 43 G4
Gilchrist Rd IRL M44 136 A5
Gilda Brook Rd ECC M30 111 H4
Gilda Crs ECC M30 111 H2
Gildenhall FAIL M35 105 F3
Gilderdale Cl ROY/SHW OL2 60 A1
Gilderdale St BOLS/LL BL3 49 F4
Gildersdale Dr BKLY M9 87 G1
Gildridge Rd
OLDTF/WHR M16 142 A2
Gilesgate RUSH/FAL M14 128 C5
Giles St WGTN/LGST M12 129 H4
Gillbent Rd CHD/CHDH SK8 192 D1
Gillbrook Rd DID/WITH M20 157 G4
Gillemere Gv
ROY/SHW OL2 60 B2
Gillers Gn WALK M28 81 H5
Gillford Av BKLY M9 103 G2
Gillingham Rd ECC M30 110 C3
Gillingham Sq OP/CLY M11 116 A5
Gill St BKLY M9 103 G1
STKP SK1 160 C3
Gillwood Dr MPL/ROM SK6 161 G5
Gilman Cl BKLY M9 * 87 H5
Gilman St BKLY M9 87 H5
Gilmerton Dr
NEWH/MOS M40 * 104 B5
Gilmore Dr PWCH M25 86 A2
Gilmore St EDGY/DAV SK3 13 F7
Gilmour St MDTN M24 72 D4
Gilmour Ter BKLY M9 103 G1
Gilnow Gdns BOL BL1 48 B3
Gilnow Gv BOL BL1 2 A6
Gilnow La BOLS/LL BL3 48 B3
Gilnow Rd BOL BL1 48 B3
Gilpin Rd URM M41 139 F2
Giltbrook Av
NEWH/MOS M40 115 H1
Gilwell Dr NTHM/RTH M23 167 G5
Gilwood Gv MDTN M24 56 C5
Gingham Pk RAD M26 51 H4
Gipsy La OFTN SK2 172 D3
ROCH OL11 42 B3
Girton St BRO M7 114 B1
Girvan Av NEWH/MOS M40 89 G5
Girvan Cl BOLS/LL BL3 64 B1
Gisborn Dr SLFD M6 100 C5
Gisburn Av BOL BL1 32 B4
Gisburn Dr TOT/BURYW BL8 36 D3
Gisburne Av NEWH/MOS M40 89 G5
Gisburn Rd ROCH OL11 43 F3
Givendale Dr CHH M8 87 F5
Givvons Fold OLDE OL4 76 C3
Glabyn Av HOR/BR BL6 46 A1
Glade Brow OLDE OL4 * 93 F1
Gladeside Rd WYTH/NTH M22 168 B5
Glade St BOL BL1 48 B2
The Glade BOL BL1 2 A1
HTNM SK4 158 D5
Gladewood Cl
WILM/AE SK9 199 F2
Gladstone Cl BOL BL1 * 33 H4
Gladstone Ct HULME M15 127 H4
Gladstone Crs ROCH OL11 43 F3
Gladstone Gv HTNM SK4 158 D3
Gladstone Ms HTNM SK4 * 159 H3
Gladstone Pl FWTH BL4 65 H3
Gladstone Rd ALT WA14 165 G3
ECC M30 111 F3
FWTH BL4 65 H3
URM M41 139 E1
Gladstone St BOL BL1 33 H4
BURY BL9 5 J3
OFTN SK2 172 D5
OLDE OL4 92 A1
SWIN M27 99 F2
Gladstone Terrace Rd
UPML OL3 94 D3
Gladwyn Av DID/WITH M20 156 D2
Gladys St BOLS/LL BL3 66 A2
Glaisdale OLDE OL4 92 C1
Glaisdale Cl BOLE BL2 34 D4
Glaisdale St BOLE BL2 34 C4
Glaister La BOLE BL2 35 E5
Glamis Av HEY OL10 56 B2
OP/CLY M11 116 D2
STRET M32 139 G1
Glamorgan Pl CHAD OL9 8 A6
Glandon Dr CHD/CHDH SK8 183 F5
Glanford Av BKLY M9 87 F4
Glanvor Rd EDGY/DAV SK3 12 A6
Glasshouse St ANC M4 7 K1
Glasson Wk CHAD OL9 90 B1
Glass St FWTH BL4 * 66 B5
Glastonbury WHIT OL12 10 B4
Glastonbury Av
CHD/CHDH SK8 193 F1
HALE/TIMP WA15 178 C2
Glastonbury Dr POY/DIS SK12 195 E2
Glastonbury Rd STRET M32 125 E5
Glaswen Gv RDSH SK5 160 A2
Glazebrook Cl HEY OL10 40 D5
Glazebury Dr NTHM/RTH M23 168 A4
WHTN BL5 62 A2
Glazedale Av ROY/SHW OL2 58 D5
Glaze Wk WHTF M45 70 B2
Gleaves Av BOLE BL2 35 H2
Gleaves Rd ECC M30 111 F4
Gleave St BOL BL1 * 3 F3
SALE M33 139 H5
Glebeland Rd BOLS/LL BL3 47 H4
Glebelands Rd
NTHM/RTH M23 167 G3
PWCH M25 85 H2
SALE M33 139 G5
Glebe La OLD OL1 76 D1
Glebe Rd URM M41 138 D1
Glebe St BOLE BL2 3 G6
CHAD OL9 90 B4
RAD M26 68 C1
ROY/SHW OL2 60 A2
STKP SK1 13 K4
Gleden St NEWH/MOS M40 115 H3
Gledhall St STLY SK15 120 D3
Gledhill Av ORD M5 126 D1
Gledhill Cl ROY/SHW OL2 44 D5
Gledhill St DID/WITH M20 142 D4
Gledhill Wy EDGW/EG BL7 23 F3
Glemsford Cl
NEWH/MOS M40 * 104 A4
Glenacre Gdns GTN M18 130 D5
Glenart ECC M30 111 F2
Glen Av BKLY M9 103 F1
BOLS/LL BL3 48 A4
FWTH BL4 83 E1
SALE M33 139 G5
SWIN M27 98 C2
WALK M28 97 H2
Glenavon Dr ROY/SHW OL2 59 G1
WHIT OL12 18 C5
Glenbarry Cl BRUN/LGST M13 128 C2
Glenbarry St WGTN/LGST M12 115 G5
Glenbeck Rd WHTF M45 69 F3
Glenboro Av TOT/BURYW BL8 37 G4
Glen Bott St BOL BL1 33 G4
Glenbourne Pk
BRAM/HZG SK7 193 G2
Glenbrook Gdns FWTH BL4 66 A2
Glenbrook Rd BKLY M9 87 F2
Glenburn St BOLS/LL BL3 64 C1
Glenby Av WYTH/NTH M22 181 E1
Glencastle Rd GTN M18 130 B3
Glen Cl GOL/RIS/CUL WA3 150 A4
Glencoe Cl HEY OL10 39 H5
Glencoe Dr BOLE BL2 50 C3
SALE M33 153 F4
Glencoe Pl ROCH OL11 29 G4
Glencoe St OLDS OL8 * 90 D5
Glen Cottages BOL BL1 * 32 B4
Glencross Av
OLDTF/WHR M16 141 E1
Glendale SWIN M27 99 G1
Glendale Av BNG/LEV M19 143 H5
BURY BL9 69 G1
Glendale Ct OLDS OL8 91 G3
Glendale Dr BOLS/LL BL3 47 G3
Glendale Rd ECC M30 111 H2
GTN M18 130 B4
WALK M28 96 A3
Glendene Av BRAM/HZG SK7 193 G2
DROY M43 118 B2
Glenden Foot WHIT OL12 29 G1
Glendevon Cl BOLS/LL BL3 47 G5
Glendevon Pl WHTF M45 70 A5
Glendinning St SLFD M6 112 D3
Glendon Ct OLD OL1 60 D5
Glendon Crs AUL OL6 107 E3
Glendore ORD M5 112 B3
Glendower Dr
NEWH/MOS M40 102 D5
Gleneagles BOLS/LL BL3 63 G1
Gleneagles Av HEY OL10 56 A1
Gleneagles Cl BRAM/HZG SK7 184 B5
WILM/AE SK9 199 G2
Gleneagles Rd
CHD/CHDH SK8 181 H3
URM M41 123 F4
Gleneagles Wy RAMS BL0 16 C3
Glenfield ALT WA14 165 E5
Glenfield Cl OLDE OL4 92 C1
Glenfield Dr POY/DIS SK12 195 E4
Glenfield Rd HTNM SK4 159 G2
Glenfield Sq FWTH BL4 65 G2
Glenfyne Rd SLFD M6 100 A5
Glen Gdns WHIT OL12 19 E5
Glengarth UPML OL3 79 E5
Glengarth Dr HOR/BR BL6 46 D3
Glen Gv MDTN M24 89 F1
ROY/SHW OL2 59 E4
Glenhaven Av URM M41 138 C1
Glenholme Rd BRAM/HZG SK7 183 C5
Glenhurst Rd BNG/LEV M19 * 158 B1
Glenilla Av WALK M28 97 F3

Glenlea Dr DID/WITH M20 169 G1
Glenmere Cl PWCH M25 85 G1
Glenmere Rd DID/WITH M20 169 H1
Glenmoor Rd STKP SK1 13 J4
Glenmore Av DID/WITH M20 156 D2
FWTH BL4 65 F2
Glenmore Cl BOLS/LL BL3 47 F4
ROCH OL11 41 F1
Glenmore Dr CHH M8 102 C3
FAIL M35 105 G2
Glenmore Gv DUK SK16 119 H5
Glenmore Rd TOT/BURYW BL8 26 A1
Glenmore St BURY BL9 4 C6
Glenmuir Cl IRL M44 136 C1
Glenolden St OP/CLY M11 117 E3
Glenridding Cl OLD OL1 75 H3
Glenridge Cl BOL BL1 34 A4
Glen Ri HALE/TIMP WA15 166 B4
Glen Rd OLDE OL4 92 B1
Glen Royd WHIT OL12 29 F2
Glensdale Dr NEWH/MOS M40 104 D1
Glenshee Dr BOLS/LL BL3 47 G4
Glenside Av GTN M18 130 C5
Glenside Dr BOLS/LL BL3 65 E2
MPL/ROM SK6 162 A1
WILM/AE SK9 199 F4
Glenside Gdns FAIL M35 105 F3
Glenside Gv WALK M28 82 B4
Glen St RAMS BL0 16 C1
SALQ M50 126 D1
The Glen BOL BL1 47 F2
MDTN M24 89 E1
Glenthorn Av BKLY M9 88 A1
Glenthorne St BOL BL1 33 H5
Glenthorn Gv SALE M33 154 C3
Glentrool Ms BOL BL1 47 H2
Glent Vw STLY SK15 120 D1
Glentwood ALT WA14 177 G3
Glenvale Cl RAD M26 68 C1
Glen Vw ROY/SHW OL2 59 E4
Glenville Rd CHH M8 102 A5
Glenville Wy DTN/ASHW M34 147 E1
Glenwood Av HYDE SK14 133 G3
Glenwood Cl RAD M26 68 C2
Glenwood Dr BKLY M9 103 F3
MDTN M24 73 G2
Glenwood Gv OFTN SK2 184 C1
Glenwyn Av BKLY M9 88 B3
Globe Cl OLDTF/WHR M16 127 G3
Globe La DUK SK16 133 E1
Globe Sq DUK SK16 132 D1
Globe St OLDE OL4 76 A5
Glodwick Rd OLDE OL4 92 A2
Gloster St BOLE BL2 3 H5
Gloucester Av BNG/LEV M19 144 B3
HEY OL10 55 H2
MPL/ROM SK6 175 E3
WHIT OL12 20 A4
WHTF M45 69 G4
Gloucester Cl AUL OL6 107 G2
Gloucester Dr SALE M33 153 G2
Gloucester Pl SLFD M6 113 F2
Gloucester Ri DUK SK16 134 B1
Gloucester Rd CHD/CHDH SK8 181 H5
DROY M43 117 H2
DTN/ASHW M34 145 G1
HYDE SK14 148 A3
MDTN M24 88 D1
POY/DIS SK12 195 E4
SLFD M6 112 B1
URM M41 138 D2
Gloucester St CMANE M1 * 128 A1
ORD M5 113 H5
SLFD M6 113 F1
Gloucester St North CHAD OL9 8 A7
Glover Dr HYDE SK14 148 A1
Glyn Av HALE/TIMP WA15 178 B2
Glynne St FWTH BL4 65 H4
Glynrene Dr SWIN M27 83 F5
Glynwood Pk FWTH BL4 65 H3
Goadsby St ANC M4 7 G2
Goats Gate Ter WHTF M45 * 69 E2
Godbert Av CCHDY M21 156 B1
Goddard St OLDS OL8 91 G3
Godfrey Av DROY M43 117 E2
Godfrey Range GTN M18 131 E4
Godfrey Rd SLFD M6 99 H5
Godlee Dr SWIN M27 98 D3
Godley Cl OP/CLY M11 130 B1
Godley Hill Rd HYDE SK14 134 C5
Godley St HYDE SK14 133 H4
Godmond Hall Dr WALK M28 96 A5
Godolphin Cl ECC M30 111 F1
Godson St OLD OL1 75 F3
Godwin St GTN M18 130 D2
Golborne Av DID/WITH M20 142 B4
Goldbourne Dr ROY/SHW OL2 60 A1
Goldbrook Cl HEY OL10 41 F5
Goldcrest Cl WALK M28 96 C3
WYTH/NTH M22 169 E4
Goldenhill Av OP/CLY M11 116 D2
Golden St ECC M30 111 E4
ROY/SHW OL2 60 D1
Goldfinch Dr BURY BL9 39 F1
Goldfinch Wy DROY M43 118 B2
Goldie Av WYTH/NTH M22 181 E3
Goldrill Av BOLE BL2 50 C1
Goldrill Gdns BOLE BL2 50 C1
Goldsmith Av OLD OL1 60 D5
ORD M5 112 C3
Goldsmith Rd RDSH SK5 144 D2
Goldsmith St BOLS/LL BL3 48 C5
Gold St CMANE M1 * 7 G5
Goldsworthy Rd URM M41 137 G1
Goldsworth Rd OLD OL1 76 C1
Goldsworthy Rd URM M41 123 F5
Golf Rd HALE/TIMP WA15 178 A1
SALE M33 155 G2
Golfview Dr ECC M30 111 E1
Goodacre HYDE SK14 134 C2
Gooden St HEY OL10 41 F5
Goodiers Dr ORD M5 113 F5
Goodier St
NEWH/MOS M40 103 F5
SALE M33 154 B2
Goodier Vw HYDE SK14 134 A3
Goodison Cl BURY BL9 70 A1
Goodlad St TOT/BURYW BL8 37 G2
Goodman St BKLY M9 103 F1
Goodrich ROCH OL11 * 29 H5
Goodridge Av
WYTH/NTH M22 180 B2
Goodrington Rd
WILM/AE SK9 192 B5
Goodshaw Rd WALK M28 96 D2
Good Shepherd Cl MILN OL16 11 F5
Goodwill Cl SWIN M27 99 E3
Goodwin Sq BKLY M9 * 103 E3
Goodwin St BOL BL1 3 G3
Goodwood Av
NTHM/RTH M23 167 E1
SALE M33 153 F2
Goodwood Cl BOLS/LL BL3 66 C1
Goodwood Crs
HALE/TIMP WA15 166 D3
Goodwood Dr EDGY/DAV SK3 171 H5
OLD OL1 75 H3
SWIN M27 99 G3
Goodwood Rd MPL/ROM SK6 174 D4
Goole St OP/CLY M11 116 B5
Goose Cote Hl EDGW/EG BL7 22 D2
Goose Gn ALT WA14 165 G5
Goose La WHIT OL12 10 C4
Goosetrey Cl WILM/AE SK9 199 H1
Goostrey Av DID/WITH M20 142 B3
Gordon Av BNG/LEV M19 144 B2
BOLS/LL BL3 48 B4
BRAM/HZG SK7 185 E1
CHAD OL9 90 B4
OLDE OL4 92 B1
Gordon Ct LIT OL15 21 E2
Gordon Pl DID/WITH M20 157 G1
Gordon Rd ECC M30 111 E2
SALE M33 139 H5
SWIN M27 98 B4
Gordon St AUL OL6 * 120 A1
BRO M7 114 A1
BURY BL9 4 C1
CHAD OL9 90 A3
GTN M18 130 D2
HTNM SK4 13 F1
HYDE SK14 148 A1
MILN OL16 45 E3
OLDE OL4 93 E1
OLDTF/WHR M16 127 G4
ROCH OL11 43 F1
ROY/SHW OL2 60 B2
STLY SK15 121 E4
Gordon Ter BKLY M9 * 103 F2
Gordon Wy HEY OL10 40 A5
Gore Av FAIL M35 105 G3
ORD M5 112 C3
Gorebrook Ct
WGTN/LGST M12 129 H4
Gore Cl BURY BL9 39 F5
Gore Crs ORD M5 112 C2
Goredale Av GTN M18 130 D5
Gore Dr ORD M5 112 C2
Gorelan Rd GTN M18 * 130 C3
Gore St CMANE M1 7 H5
CSLFD M3 6 B4
SLFD M6 113 F2
Goring Av GTN M18 130 C2
Gorrells Wy ROCH OL11 42 C3
Gorrels Cl ROCH OL11 42 C3
Gorrel St ROCH OL11 43 F1
Gorse Av DROY M43 118 B3
MOSL OL5 109 F1
MPL/ROM SK6 174 D3
OLDS OL8 92 B4
STRET M32 126 C5
Gorse Bank BURY BL9 39 F3
Gorse Bank Rd
HALE/TIMP WA15 178 D5
Gorse Crs STRET M32 126 C5
Gorse Dr LHULT M38 81 E1
STRET M32 126 C5
Gorsefield Cl RAD M26 52 B5
Gorsefield Dr SWIN M27 99 E3
Gorsefield Hey WILM/AE SK9 199 H2
Gorse Hall Cl DUK SK16 * 134 A1
Gorse Hall Dr STLY SK15 120 D5
Gorse Hall Rd DUK SK16 133 H1
Gorselands CHD/CHDH SK8 193 E2
Gorse La STRET M32 126 C5
Gorse Rd MILN OL16 31 G5
SWIN M27 98 D4
WALK M28 82 B5
Gorses Mt BOLE BL2 49 H4
Gorse Sq PART M31 150 C3
Gorses Rd BOLS/LL BL3 50 A4
Gorse St CHAD OL9 90 A3
STRET M32 126 B5
The Gorse ALT WA14 177 E4
Gorseway RDSH SK5 160 C2
Gorsey Av WYTH/NTH M22 168 B5
Gorsey Bank Rd
EDGY/DAV SK3 171 E1
Gorsey Brow MPL/ROM SK6 161 H4
Gorsey Clough Wk
TOT/BURYW BL8 37 E1
Gorsey Dr WYTH/NTH M22 168 B5
Gorseyfields DROY M43 117 H5
Gorsey Hill St HEY OL10 41 E5
Gorsey La ALT WA14 165 E4
AUL OL6 108 A4
Gorsey Mount St STKP SK1 13 H4
Gorsey Rd WILM/AE SK9 198 C3
WYTH/NTH M22 168 B5
Gorsey Wy AUL OL6 107 H4
Gorsley Bank LIT OL15 21 F1
Gorston Wk WYTH/NTH M22 180 B4
Gort Cl BURY BL9 69 H3
Gorton Crs DTN/ASHW M34 131 H5
Gorton Gv WALK M28 81 H2
Gorton La WGTN/LGST M12 129 H2
Gorton Rd OP/CLY M11 129 G1
RDSH SK5 145 F3
Gorton St AULW OL7 119 E4
BOLE BL2 3 G6
CHAD OL9 90 C1
CSLFD M3 * 6 D2
ECC M30 110 B4
FWTH BL4 65 G5
HEY OL10 41 E5
Gortonvilla Wk
WGTN/LGST M12 129 G2
Gosforth Cl OLD OL1 75 H3
TOT/BURYW BL8 37 H1
Goshen La BURY BL9 53 G3
Gosport Sq BRO M7 101 G5
Goss Hall St OLDE OL4 * 92 B1
Gotha Wk BRUN/LGST M13 * 128 D2
Gotherage Cl MPL/ROM SK6 162 D4
Gotherage La MPL/ROM SK6 162 D4
Gothic Cl MPL/ROM SK6 163 E4
Gough St EDGY/DAV SK3 12 D4
HEY OL10 * 41 F4
Goulden Rd DID/WITH M20 157 F1
Goulden St ANC M4 7 H2
SLFD M6 112 D3
Goulder Rd GTN M18 130 D5
Gould St DTN/ASHW M34 132 B5
OLD OL1 76 A4
Gourham Dr CHD/CHDH SK8 182 C2
Govan St WYTH/NTH M22 156 D5
Gowan Dr MDTN M24 72 A3
Gowanlock's St BOL BL1 33 H4
Gowan Rd OLDTF/WHR M16 142 A2
Gower Av BRAM/HZG SK7 184 D1
Gowerdale Rd RDSH SK5 160 D1
Gower Hey Gdns HYDE SK14 148 A2
Gower Rd HTNM SK4 159 G2
HYDE SK14 147 H2
Gowers St MILN OL16 11 G4
Gower St AUL OL6 * 119 H2
BOL BL1 2 A3
FWTH BL4 65 H3
OLD OL1 9 J2
SWIN M27 99 F1
Gowran Pk OLDE OL4 92 C1
Gowy Cl WILM/AE SK9 199 H1
Goyt Av MPL/ROM SK6 175 E5
Goyt Crs MPL/ROM SK6 161 G3
STKP SK1 160 C3
Goyt Rd MPL/ROM SK6 175 E5
STKP SK1 160 C3
Goyt Valley Rd MPL/ROM SK6 161 G4
Goyt Wy MPL/ROM SK6 163 E5
Grace St WHIT OL12 11 F1
Grace Wk ANC M4 115 G4
Gracie Av OLD OL1 76 A3
Gradwell St EDGY/DAV SK3 12 D5
Grafton Av ECC M30 111 H1
Grafton Ct MILN OL16 * 30 C5
The Graftons ALT WA14 * 165 G5
Grafton St ALT WA14 165 G5
AUL OL6 120 A3
BOL BL1 47 H1
BRUN/LGST M13 128 C3
BURY BL9 53 G1
FAIL M35 105 E2
HTNM SK4 159 H3
MILN OL16 30 C5
OLD OL1 60 D5
STLY SK15 121 G2
Graham Crs IRL M44 150 B2
Graham Dr POY/DIS SK12 187 H5
Graham Rd SLFD M6 112 B1
STKP SK1 172 C1
Graham St AULW OL7 119 E4
BOL BL1 * 2 E2
OP/CLY M11 116 B5
Grainger Av WGTN/LGST M12 129 H5
Grains Rd ROY/SHW OL2 60 B2
UPML OL3 61 G4
Grain Vw ORD M5 * 113 F5
Gralam Cl SALE M33 155 F5
Grammar School Rd OLDS OL8 90 C5
Grampian Cl CHAD OL9 90 B2
Grampian Wy ROY/SHW OL2 59 H1
Granada Ms
OLDTF/WHR M16 * 142 A2
Granada Rd DTN/ASHW M34 131 F5
Granary La WALK M28 110 A1
Granary Wy SALE M33 154 A4
Granby Rd CHD/CHDH SK8 183 E4
HALE/TIMP WA15 154 B5
OFTN SK2 172 C4
STRET M32 140 C2
SWIN M27 98 B3
Granby Rw CMANE M1 7 H7
Granby St CHAD OL9 90 B5
TOT/BURYW BL8 37 E2
Grandale St RUSH/FAL M14 * 128 D5
Grand Central Sq STKP SK1 * 13 F5
Grandidge St ROCH OL11 42 D1
Grand Union Wy ECC M30 111 E5
Granford Cl ALT WA14 * 165 G2
Grange Av BNG/LEV M19 143 H3
BOLS/LL BL3 67 F1
CHD/CHDH SK8 182 C1
ECC M30 111 E1
HALE/TIMP WA15 166 C2
HALE/TIMP WA15 178 B2
HTNM SK4 159 F1
MILN OL16 44 C2
OLDS OL8 90 D3
STRET M32 140 B1
SWIN M27 83 G5
URM M41 137 G1
Grange Cl HYDE SK14 148 B2
Grange Ct OLDS OL8 * 90 D3
Grange Crs URM M41 138 C2
Grange Dr BKLY M9 88 C4
ECC M30 111 E1
Grangeforth Rd CHH M8 102 A2
Grange Gv WHTF M45 69 G4
Grange La DID/WITH M20 157 G4
Grange Park Av AUL OL6 108 A4
CHD/CHDH SK8 170 A4
WILM/AE SK9 198 D2
Grangepark Rd BKLY M9 88 C4
Grange Park Rd
CHD/CHDH SK8 170 A4
EDGW/EG BL7 23 H5
Grange Pl IRL M44 150 C1
Grange Rd ALT WA14 177 F3
BOLS/LL BL3 48 A4
BRAM/HZG SK7 184 B2
CCHDY M21 141 E1
ECC M30 110 A1
EDGW/EG BL7 23 H4
FWTH BL4 65 F3
HALE/TIMP WA15 166 C2
MDTN M24 57 G3
SALE M33 154 A2
TOT/BURYW BL8 37 G4
URM M41 138 C2
WHIT OL12 14 C3
Grange Rd North HYDE SK14 148 B1
Grange Rd South HYDE SK14 148 B2
Grange St CHAD OL9 8 E2
FAIL M35 104 C4
SLFD M6 112 D3
The Grange HYDE SK14 148 B2
OLD OL1 * 76 A4
RUSH/FAL M14 128 D5
Grangethorpe Dr
BNG/LEV M19 143 G4
Grangethorpe Rd
RUSH/FAL M14 143 E1
URM M41 138 C2
Grangeway WILM/AE SK9 192 A3
Grangewood EDGW/EG BL7 23 H4
Grangewood Dr BKLY M9 103 E3
Granite St OLD OL1 76 A4
Gransden Dr CHH M8 102 D4
Granshaw St
NEWH/MOS M40 115 H2
Gransmoor Av OP/CLY M11 131 E1
Gransmoor Rd OP/CLY M11 131 E1
Grantchester Pl FWTH BL4 65 E3
Grantchester Wy BOLE BL2 35 F5
Grant Cl BKLY M9 88 A5
Grantham Cl BOL BL1 * 33 H5
Grantham Dr TOT/BURYW BL8 38 A1
Grantham Rd HTNM SK4 12 B2
Grantham St OLDE OL4 9 K6
Grants La RAMS BL0 16 D2
Grant St FWTH BL4 65 G2
ROCH OL11 42 C4
Granville Av BRO M7 101 H2
Granville Cl CHAD OL9 8 A2
Granville Ct MILN OL16 45 E3
Granville Gdns DID/WITH M20 157 F4
Granville Rd BOLS/LL BL3 64 B1
CHD/CHDH SK8 171 F4
DTN/ASHW M34 118 A4
HALE/TIMP WA15 166 D3
RUSH/FAL M14 143 E3
URM M41 124 D5
WILM/AE SK9 198 C5
Granville St AUL OL6 120 A3
CHAD OL9 8 A1
ECC M30 111 E2
FWTH BL4 66 A3
OLD OL1 75 F3
WALK M28 81 H4
Granville Wk CHAD OL9 8 A1
Grasmere Av BOLS/LL BL3 50 D5
FWTH BL4 65 E5
HEY OL10 56 A1
HTNM SK4 145 E5
SWIN M27 83 F5
URM M41 137 G2
WHTF M45 68 D5
Grasmere Cl STLY SK15 120 D1
Grasmere Crs BRAM/HZG SK7 183 H4
ECC M30 110 C1
MPL/ROM SK6 186 D3
Grasmere Dr BURY BL9 53 H2
Grasmere Gv AULW OL7 119 E1
Grasmere Rd CHD/CHDH SK8 181 G1
HALE/TIMP WA15 166 D3
OLDE OL4 92 B1
PART M31 150 D3
ROY/SHW OL2 59 E3
SALE M33 154 D4
STRET M32 126 A5
SWIN M27 99 E4
WILM/AE SK9 200 D4
Grasmere St BOL BL1 34 A4
WGTN/LGST M12 130 A5
WHIT OL12 10 C2
Grasmere Wk MDTN M24 72 C2
Grason Av WILM/AE SK9 199 F1
Grasscroft RDSH SK5 146 A5
Grasscroft Cl RUSH/FAL M14 142 B1
Grasscroft Rd STLY SK15 120 D4
Grassfield Av BRO M7 101 F4
Grassholme Dr OFTN SK2 173 H4
Grassingham Gdns SLFD M6 113 E2
Grassington Av
NEWH/MOS M40 103 H1
Grassington Ct
TOT/BURYW BL8 36 D2
Grassington Dr BURY BL9 39 H5
Grassington Pl BOLE BL2 34 B5
Grass Md DTN/ASHW M34 147 E3
Gratrix Av ORD M5 127 E1
Gratrix La SALE M33 155 G3
Gratrix St GTN M18 130 D4
Gratten Ct WALK M28 81 H3
Gravel Bank Rd
MPL/ROM SK6 147 F5
Gravel La CSLFD M3 6 D2
WILM/AE SK9 198 C5
Gravel Wks OLDE OL4 76 A5
Gravenmoor Dr BRO M7 101 H4
Graver La NEWH/MOS M40 104 C5
Gray Cl HYDE SK14 135 G5
Graymar Rd LHULT M38 81 F3
Graymarsh Dr POY/DIS SK12 195 F5
Graysands Rd
HALE/TIMP WA15 178 A1
Grayson Av WHTF M45 69 H5
Grayson Rd LHULT M38 81 G3
Grayson Wy UPML OL3 95 E1
Gray St BOL BL1 2 D2
Gray St North BOL BL1 2 E2
Graythorpe Wk ORD M5 * 113 F4
Graythorp Wk RUSH/FAL M14 128 C5
Graythwaite Rd BOL BL1 32 C4
Grazing Dr IRL M44 122 D5
Greame St OLDTF/WHR M16 128 A5
Great Ancoats St ANC M4 7 H3
CMANE M1 115 G5
Great Bent Cl WHIT OL12 20 A4
Great Bridgewater St
CMANE M1 6 D7
Great Cheetham St East
BRO M7 101 H4
Great Cheetham St West
BRO M7 101 F5
Great Clowes St BRO M7 101 G3
Great Ducie St CHH M8 114 C1
CSLFD M3 6 E1
Great Eaves Rd RAMS BL0 16 D1
Great Egerton St STKP SK1 13 F2
Greatfield Rd WYTH/NTH M22 168 A5
Great Flatt WHIT OL12 29 E2
Great Gable Cl OLD OL1 75 H4
Great Gates Cl ROCH OL11 43 F2
Great Gates Rd ROCH OL11 43 F4
Great George St CSLFD M3 114 A3
MILN OL16 10 D7
Great Hall Cl RAD M26 52 B5
Great Heaton Cl MDTN M24 * 71 H5
Great Holme BOLS/LL BL3 65 E1
Great Howarth WHIT OL12 19 G4
Great Jackson St HULME M15 127 H1
Great John St CSLFD M3 6 B6
Great Jones St
WGTN/LGST M12 129 H2
Great Lee WHIT OL12 18 C5
Great Lee Wk WHIT OL12 29 G1
Great Marlborough St
CMANE M1 6 E7
Great Marld Cl BOL BL1 32 C4
Great Meadow ROY/SHW OL2 44 C5
Great Moor St BOL BL1 2 E6
OFTN SK2 172 C4
Great Newton St
NEWH/MOS M40 104 B5
Great Norbury St HYDE SK14 147 H1
Great Portwood St STKP SK1 13 H1
Great Southern St
RUSH/FAL M14 128 C5
Great Stone Cl RAD M26 * 67 G1
Great Stone Rd STRET M32 126 C4
Great Stones Cl EDGW/EG BL7 22 D1
Great St CMANE M1 115 F5
Great Underbank STKP SK1 13 G3
Great Western St
OLDTF/WHR M16 127 H4
Greave MPL/ROM SK6 162 C2
Greave Av ROCH OL11 29 E3
Greave Fold MPL/ROM SK6 162 C2
Greave Rd STKP SK1 172 D1
Greaves Av FAIL M35 104 D4
Greaves Rd WILM/AE SK9 198 B2
Greaves St MOSL OL5 93 H5
OLD OL1 9 H4
OLDE OL4 93 E1
ROY/SHW OL2 * 60 B2
Greave St ROY/SHW OL2 60 B2
Grebe Cl POY/DIS SK12 194 C3
Grecian Crs BOLS/LL BL3 49 E5
Grecian St BRO M7 101 F5
Grecian St North BRO M7 101 F5
Grecian Ter BRO M7 * 101 F5
Gredle Cl URM M41 139 F1
Greeba Rd NTHM/RTH M23 167 F3
Greek St CMANE M1 * 128 C1
EDGY/DAV SK3 13 F6
Green Acre WHTN BL5 62 A5
Greenacre Cl RAMS BL0 17 F1
Greenacre La WALK M28 110 A1
Green Acre Pk BOL BL1 * 34 A5
Greenacres Dr BNG/LEV M19 158 B2
Greenacres Rd OLDE OL4 76 B5
Green Av BOLS/LL BL3 65 G1
LHULT M38 80 D2
SWIN M27 99 E3
Green Bank BOLE BL2 35 F3
Greenbank FWTH BL4 65 H3
Greenbank Av CHD/CHDH SK8 169 F4
HTNM SK4 158 B4
SWIN M27 * 98 C4
UPML OL3 79 F3
Greenbank Crs MPL/ROM SK6 175 E5
Greenbank Dr LIT OL15 20 C5
Greenbank Rd BOLS/LL BL3 * 48 A5
CHD/CHDH SK8 169 F3
MPL/ROM SK6 163 G5
RAD M26 52 A4
SALE M33 153 H1
SLFD M6 112 D2
WHIT OL12 10 E1
Green Bank Ter HTNM SK4 13 F1
Greenbank Ter MDTN M24 73 F3
Greenbeech Cl MPL/ROM SK6 174 D2
Green Booth Cl DUK SK16 134 A1
Green Bridge Cl ROCH OL11 * 43 E2
Greenbridge La UPML OL3 94 D2
Green Brook Cl BURY BL9 38 D2
Greenbrook St BURY BL9 38 D2
Greenbrow Rd
NTHM/RTH M23 179 G1
Greenburn Dr BOLE BL2 35 F4
Green Cl CHD/CHDH SK8 169 F3
Greencourt Dr LHULT M38 81 E3
Green Cts ALT WA14 177 E1
Green Cft MPL/ROM SK6 162 C3
Greencroft Meadow
ROY/SHW OL2 59 G4
Greencroft Rd ECC M30 110 C1
Greencroft Wy MILN OL16 20 A5
Greendale Dr BKLY M9 88 B4
RAD M26 68 C3
Greendale Gv DTN/ASHW M34 147 F3
Green Dr BNG/LEV M19 143 H2
HALE/TIMP WA15 166 B2
HOR/BR BL6 46 D2
WILM/AE SK9 192 A5
Green End BNG/LEV M19 158 B1
DTN/ASHW M34 147 F3
Green End Rd BNG/LEV M19 158 B1
Greenfield Av ECC M30 123 H1
URM M41 138 D1
Greenfield Cl EDGY/DAV SK3 171 H3
HALE/TIMP WA15 166 D3
TOT/BURYW BL8 37 F5
WHTN BL5 62 B3
Greenfield Ct HEY OL10 41 E5
Greenfield La MILN OL16 20 A5
ROCH OL11 43 F2
ROY/SHW OL2 60 A3
Greenfield St DTN/ASHW M34 132 A1
HYDE SK14 147 H1
ROCH OL11 43 F2
Green Fold GTN M18 131 E2
Greenfold Av FWTH BL4 65 G5
Greenford Cl
CHD/CHDH SK8 171 E5
Greenford Rd CHH M8 102 B3
Green Gables Cl
CHD/CHDH SK8 181 G3
Greengate CSLFD M3 6 D2

HALE/TIMP WA15 179 E5
HYDE SK14 147 H3
MDTN M24 89 F2
NEWH/MOS M40 89 F4
Greengate Cl WHIT OL12 20 A4
Greengate East
NEWH/MOS M40 89 F4
Greengate La BOLE BL2 50 C1
PWCH M25 85 H3
Greengate Rd
DTN/ASHW M34 132 D4
Greengate St OLDE OL4 9 J6
Greengate West CSLFD M3 6 B1
Greengrove Bank MILN OL16 19 H5
Greenhalgh Moss La
TOT/BURYW BL8 37 G1
Greenhalgh St FAIL M35 104 B4
HTNM SK4 13 F1
Greenhalgh Wk ANC M4 7 K3
Green Hall Ms WILM/AE SK9 199 E4
Greenham Rd
NTHM/RTH M23 155 G5
Greenhaven Cl WALK M28 82 C4
Greenheys BOLE BL2 35 F3
DROY M43 117 H3
Greenheys Crs
TOT/BURYW BL8 25 H2
Greenheys La HULME M15 128 A3
Greenheys La West
HULME M15 128 A3
Greenheys Rd LHULT M38 80 D1
Greenhill OLD OL1 9 J4
PWCH M25 85 H3
Greenhill Av BOLS/LL BL3 48 A4
FWTH BL4 81 H1
ROY/SHW OL2 44 B5
SALE M33 139 G5
WHIT OL12 10 A4
Greenhill La BOLS/LL BL3 47 G5
Greenhill Pas OLD OL1 9 J4
Green Hill Rd HYDE SK14 134 B5
Greenhill Rd CHH M8 102 B3
HALE/TIMP WA15 166 D3
MDTN M24 73 F5
TOT/BURYW BL8 37 F5
Green Hill St EDGY/DAV SK3 12 C7
Green Hill Ter EDGY/DAV SK3 12 C7
Greenhill Ter OLDE OL4 9 J5
Green Hollow Fold STLY SK15 121 G1
Greenholm Cl
NEWH/MOS M40 104 C1
Greenhow St DROY M43 117 G5
Greenhurst Crs OLDS OL8 91 H5
Greenhurst La AUL OL6 107 H4
Greenhurst Rd AUL OL6 107 G3
Greenhythe Rd
CHD/CHDH SK8 191 H1
Greening Rd BNG/LEV M19 144 B1
Greenland Rd BOLS/LL BL3 65 E2
Greenlands Cl CHD/CHDH SK8 182 B4
Greenland St CHH M8 102 A3
SLFD M6 * 112 D3
Green La AUL OL6 107 E5
BOLS/LL BL3 65 E1
BRAM/HZG SK7 185 E1
ECC M30 110 D3
FAIL M35 117 F1
FWTH BL4 66 D5
GTN M18 130 C2
HALE/TIMP WA15 166 C5
HEY OL10 41 F4
HEY OL10 * 56 B1
HTNM SK4 12 C2
HYDE SK14 148 C2
IRL M44 150 C1
MDTN M24 73 E3
MDTN M24 73 G5
MPL/ROM SK6 162 A5
OLDE OL4 77 F2
OLDS OL8 91 F5
POY/DIS SK12 196 B3
SALE M33 139 E5
WHIT OL12 * 10 B4
WHTF M45 69 G3
WILM/AE SK9 199 E3
WILM/AE SK9 200 C5
Green La North
HALE/TIMP WA15 166 C5
Greenlea Av GTN M18 130 C5
Greenleach La WALK M28 97 G2
Greenleaf Cl WALK M28 96 A4
Greenleas HOR/BR BL6 46 D3
Greenlees St WHIT OL12 10 C4
Greenleigh Cl BOL BL1 33 G1
Greenmans La UPML OL3 94 D4
Green Meadow WHIT OL12 20 A4
Green Mdw MPL/ROM SK6 175 E2
Green Meadows Dr
MPL/ROM SK6 175 E2
Green Meadows Wk
WYTH/NTH M22 180 D3
Greenmount Cl
TOT/BURYW BL8 26 A1
Greenmount Ct BOL BL1 47 H1
Greenmount Dr HEY OL10 56 C2
TOT/BURYW BL8 16 A5
Greenmount La BOL BL1 47 G1
Greenmount Pk FWTH BL4 82 D1
Greenoak RAD M26 67 F5
Greenoak Dr SALE M33 154 D5
WALK M28 81 H2
Greenock Cl BOLS/LL BL3 47 F4
Greenpark Cl TOT/BURYW BL8 25 H2
Greenpark Rd
WYTH/NTH M22 156 C5
Green Park Vw OLD OL1 76 C2
Green Pastures HTNM SK4 158 B5
Green Rd PART M31 150 D3
Greenroyd Av BOLE BL2 35 F4
Greenroyde ROCH OL11 * 42 D1
Greensbridge Gdns WHTN BL5 62 A3
Greenshank Cl ROCH OL11 * 28 C4
Greenside BOLE BL2 36 B5
HTNM SK4 158 D5
WALK M28 97 H5
Greenside Av FWTH BL4 82 C1
OLDE OL4 76 C2
Greenside Cl DUK SK16 120 D5
Greenside Crs DROY M43 117 G2
Greenside Dr ALT WA14 177 H3
IRL M44 136 B2
TOT/BURYW BL8 26 A3
Greenside La DROY M43 117 F2
Greenside Pl DTN/ASHW M34 147 E3
Greenside St OP/CLY M11 116 C4
Greenside Vw HYDE SK14 134 A3
Greenside Wy MDTN M24 89 F2
Greenson Dr MDTN M24 72 B5
Greenstead Av CHH M8 102 B2
The Greens WHIT OL12 14 B4
Greenstone Dr SLFD M6 100 C5
Green St BOL BL1 3 F4
ECC M30 110 C5
EDGY/DAV SK3 172 A3
FWTH BL4 65 H3
HYDE SK14 148 A2
MDTN M24 73 F3
OLDS OL8 8 D5
RAD M26 68 B1
RUSH/FAL M14 143 G4
STRET M32 140 A3
TOT/BURYW BL8 37 E2
WILM/AE SK9 200 D4
The Green CHD/CHDH SK8 182 C4
HTNM SK4 12 A1
MPL/ROM SK6 187 F1
OLDS OL8 91 H4
ROCH OL11 42 B3
SWIN M27 84 C5
TOT/BURYW BL8 26 A2
WALK M28 97 G5
WILM/AE SK9 192 B4
Greenthorne Av HTNM SK4 144 D4
Green Tree Gdns
MPL/ROM SK6 162 A4
Greenvale ROCH OL11 28 A3
Greenvale Dr CHD/CHDH SK8 169 H3
Greenview Cha OLDE OL4 93 G2
Greenview Dr DID/WITH M20 169 H1
ROCH OL11 28 C3
Green Villa Pk WILM/AE SK9 200 B1
Green Wk ALT WA14 176 D1
CHD/CHDH SK8 169 F3
HALE/TIMP WA15 166 A2
OLDTF/WHR M16 141 G1
STRET M32 139 H1
Green Wks PWCH M25 86 B4
Greenwatch Cl ECC M30 110 D4
Green Wy BOL BL1 34 C3
ROCH OL11 42 A5
Greenway ALT WA14 164 D4
BRAM/HZG SK7 193 G1
HYDE SK14 147 H2
MDTN M24 88 B2
MPL/ROM SK6 162 D5
ROY/SHW OL2 44 C5
WILM/AE SK9 198 D4
WYTH/NTH M22 168 D1
Greenway Av BNG/LEV M19 144 B3
Green Way Cl BOL BL1 34 C2
Greenway Cl SALE M33 153 G3
TOT/BURYW BL8 37 G3
Greenway Dr MOSL OL5 93 H5
Greenway Rd CHD/CHDH SK8 191 H1
HALE/TIMP WA15 154 B5
Greenways AULW OL7 106 C4
NEWH/MOS M40 104 C1
Greenwich Cl
NEWH/MOS M40 117 E1
ROCH OL11 28 C5
Greenwood Av AUL OL6 107 F5
OFTN SK2 172 D3
SWIN M27 99 G1
WALK M28 81 H4
Greenwood Cl
HALE/TIMP WA15 167 E4
Greenwood Dr WILM/AE SK9 199 G2
Greenwood Rd
WYTH/NTH M22 168 B4
Greenwoods La BOLE BL2 35 G2
Greenwood St ALT WA14 165 G5
FWTH BL4 66 A4
LIT OL15 21 E3
MILN OL16 10 D7
OLDE OL4 76 B4
OLDS OL8 * 106 C1
SLFD M6 113 E1
Greenwood V BOL BL1 33 H3
Greenwood V South BOL BL1 * 34 A3
Greer St OP/CLY M11 116 D5
Greetland Dr BKLY M9 88 C3
Gregge St HEY OL10 41 F5
Greg Ms WILM/AE SK9 191 G5
Gregory Av BOLE BL2 50 B1
MPL/ROM SK6 162 A5
Gregory St HYDE SK14 133 H3
OLDS OL8 90 D4
WGTN/LGST M12 129 G2
Gregory Wy RDSH SK5 145 F5
Gregson Fld BOLS/LL BL3 48 D5
Gregson Rd RDSH SK5 145 E5
Gregson St OLD OL1 9 H4
Greg St RDSH SK5 145 E5
Greiley Wk RUSH/FAL M14 128 C5
Grendale Av BRAM/HZG SK7 185 F3
STKP SK1 160 C5
Grendon Av OLDS OL8 91 F4
Grendon St BOLS/LL BL3 64 B1
Grendon Wk WGTN/LGST M12 129 H2
Grenfell Rd DID/WITH M20 157 F3
Grenham Av HULME M15 127 G2
Grenville Rd BRAM/HZG SK7 184 D1
Grenville St DUK SK16 119 H5
EDGY/DAV SK3 12 C5
STLY SK15 121 G1
Gresford Cl CCHDY M21 141 E3
Gresham Cl WHTF M45 69 E5
Gresham Dr CHAD OL9 8 B3
Gresham St BOL BL1 34 A3
DTN/ASHW M34 132 C4
Gresham Wk HTNM SK4 159 H3
Gresham Wy SALE M33 154 B5
Gresty Av WYTH/NTH M22 181 E3
Greswell St DTN/ASHW M34 132 B4
Greta Av CHD/CHDH SK8 191 H1
Greton Cl BRUN/LGST M13 129 F4
Gretton Cl ROY/SHW OL2 59 G5
Greville St BRUN/LGST M13 129 F5
Grey Cl MPL/ROM SK6 161 H2
Greyfriars Rd WYTH/NTH M22 180 A2
Greyhound Dr SLFD M6 101 E5
Grey Knotts WALK M28 96 B5
Greylag Crs WALK M28 97 E2
Greylands Cl SALE M33 153 H2
Greylands Rd DID/WITH M20 169 H1
Grey Mare La OP/CLY M11 116 B5
Greymont Rd BURY BL9 27 G5
Grey Rd ALT WA14 165 F4
Greystoke Av BNG/LEV M19 144 C2
HALE/TIMP WA15 167 E3
SALE M33 154 C3
Greystoke Crs WHTF M45 69 F2
Greystoke Dr BOL BL1 22 C5
MDTN M24 72 A2
WILM/AE SK9 200 D3
Greystoke La FAIL M35 104 C4
Greystoke St STKP SK1 13 K4
Greystone Av CCHDY M21 142 B3
Grey St AUL OL6 119 H2
DTN/ASHW M34 132 A5
MDTN M24 72 C3
PWCH M25 86 B3
STLY SK15 121 F4
WGTN/LGST M12 129 F2
Greyswood Av CHH M8 102 A4
Greytown Cl SLFD M6 100 C5
Greywood Av BURY BL9 5 K4
Grierson St BOL BL1 33 H3
OLDTF/WHR M16 127 H4
Griffe La BURY BL9 70 B1
Griffin Cl BURY BL9 5 J1
Griffin Ct CSLFD M3 * 6 B3
Griffin Gv BNG/LEV M19 144 A3
Griffin La CHD/CHDH SK8 182 A5
Griffin Rd FAIL M35 104 C3
Griffin St BRO M7 101 F4
Griffiths Cl BRO M7 * 114 A1
Griffiths St NEWH/MOS M40 104 B5
Grimes St WHIT OL12 28 C2
Grime St RAMS BL0 16 B4
Grimscott Cl BKLY M9 * 103 G1
Grimshaw Av FAIL M35 105 F2
Grimshaw Cl MPL/ROM SK6 161 H2
Grimshaw La MDTN M24 73 E5
NEWH/MOS M40 103 G5
Grimshaw St FAIL M35 * 104 D2
STKP SK1 13 K3
Grimstead Cl NTHM/RTH M23 167 F3
Grindall Av NEWH/MOS M40 89 E5
Grindley Av CCHDY M21 156 C1
Grindlow St BRUN/LGST M13 129 F3
Grindon Av BRO M7 100 D3
Grindrod St RAD M26 52 B5
Grindsbrook Rd RAD M26 52 A2
Grinton Av BRUN/LGST M13 143 G1
Grisdale Dr MDTN M24 72 B2
Grisdale Rd BOLS/LL BL3 48 B4
Grisebeck Wy OLD OL1 9 F2
Grisedale Av ROY/SHW OL2 58 D1
Grisedale Cl GTN M18 130 B4
MDTN M24 72 A1
Grisedale Rd ROCH OL11 42 A2
Gristlehurst La BURY BL9 40 A1
Grizebeck Cl GTN M18 130 B2
Grizedale Cl BOL BL1 32 C4
STLY SK15 109 F3
Grizedale Rd MPL/ROM SK6 162 A2
Groby Pl ALT WA14 165 F4
Groby Rd ALT WA14 165 F5
CCHDY M21 141 F3
DTN/ASHW M34 132 B1
Groby Rd North
DTN/ASHW M34 118 C5
Groby St OLDS OL8 91 H4
STLY SK15 121 F4
Groom St CMANE M1 128 C1
Grosvenor Av WHTF M45 69 F4
Grosvenor Cl WALK M28 81 H2
WILM/AE SK9 200 D1
Grosvenor Ct AULW OL7 119 F4
CHD/CHDH SK8 170 A3
Grosvenor Crs HYDE SK14 147 G2
Grosvenor Dr POY/DIS SK12 194 D4
WALK M28 81 H2
Grosvenor Gdns BRO M7 114 A1
STLY SK15 * 120 D4
WYTH/NTH M22 168 D3
Grosvenor House Sq
STLY SK15 120 D4
Grosvenor Pl AULW OL7 * 119 F4
Grosvenor Rd ALT WA14 165 H3
CHD/CHDH SK8 171 F5
ECC M30 110 B2
HTNM SK4 158 D3
HYDE SK14 147 H2
MPL/ROM SK6 175 E2
OLDTF/WHR M16 141 H1
SALE M33 154 A1
SWIN M27 99 G3
URM M41 138 C1
WALK M28 81 H2
WHTF M45 69 F3
Grosvenor Sq SALE M33 154 B2
Grosvenor St AULW OL7 119 F4
BOLE BL2 3 G7
BOLS/LL BL3 50 D5
BRAM/HZG SK7 185 E1
BRUN/LGST M13 128 C1
BURY BL9 53 G1
DTN/ASHW M34 132 A4
EDGY/DAV SK3 13 G6
FWTH BL4 66 C4
HEY OL10 40 D5
PWCH M25 86 B3
RAD M26 68 A1
ROCH OL11 42 B5
STLY SK15 120 D4
STRET M32 140 B1
SWIN M27 84 A5
Grosvenor Wy ROY/SHW OL2 75 E2
Grotton Hollow OLDE OL4 93 G1
Grotton Mdw OLDE OL4 93 G2
Grouse St WHIT OL12 10 C2
Grove Av FAIL M35 104 D5
WILM/AE SK9 198 D3
Grove Bank OLDE OL4 94 B2
Grove Cl RUSH/FAL M14 128 D5
Grove Ct BRAM/HZG SK7 * 185 F1
SALE M33 155 E2
Grove Hl WALK M28 96 A4
Grovehurst SWIN M27 98 A4
Grove La CHD/CHDH SK8 193 E2
DID/WITH M20 157 G4
HALE/TIMP WA15 166 B3
HALE/TIMP WA15 178 B1
Grove Ms WALK M28 * 82 A4
Grove Rd HALE/TIMP WA15 177 H1
MDTN M24 73 E2
STLY SK15 121 G1
UPML OL3 79 E5
Grove St AULW OL7 106 B5
BOL BL1 33 G4
BRAM/HZG SK7 * 185 F1
BRO M7 101 H5
DROY M43 117 G5
DUK SK16 120 A4
FWTH BL4 66 B4
HEY OL10 41 F4
OLD OL1 9 K2
ROCH OL11 42 D1
UPML OL3 95 E2
WILM/AE SK9 * 199 E3
The Grove ALT WA14 * 165 G4
BOLE BL2 49 G4
BOLS/LL BL3 67 E1
CHD/CHDH SK8 192 D1
DID/WITH M20 157 G5
ECC M30 111 G4
OFTN SK2 171 H2
ROY/SHW OL2 59 H3
SALE M33 154 C3
UPML OL3 78 C3
URM M41 137 H2
Grove Wy WILM/AE SK9 199 E3
Grovewood Cl AULW OL7 106 B5
Grundey St BRAM/HZG SK7 185 F2
Grundy Av PWCH M25 85 F5
Grundy Cl BURY BL9 5 G7
Grundy La BURY BL9 * 53 F1
Grundy Rd FWTH BL4 66 B5
Grundy St BOLS/LL BL3 48 C5
HEY OL10 56 B1
HTNM SK4 158 B4
WALK M28 82 C4
Guardian Cl WHIT OL12 20 A3
Guardian Ms
NTHM/RTH M23 * 154 D5
Guernsey Cl BNG/LEV M19 * 144 A5
Guest Rd PWCH M25 85 H1
Guide La AULW OL7 118 D5
Guide Post Sq
BRUN/LGST M13 * 129 E2
Guide Post St BRUN/LGST M13 129 E2
Guide St SALQ M50 112 B4
Guido St BOL BL1 33 G4
FAIL M35 104 D3
Guild Av WALK M28 82 A5
Guildford Av CHD/CHDH SK8 192 D1
Guildford Cl STKP SK1 172 C2
Guildford Dr AUL OL6 107 F3
Guildford Gv MDTN M24 73 F1
Guildford Rd BNG/LEV M19 144 B1
BOL BL1 33 E4
DUK SK16 134 B1
SLFD M6 112 A1
URM M41 124 D4
Guildford St MILN OL16 * 10 E7
Guildhall Cl HULME M15 128 B3
Guild St EDGW/EG BL7 23 G5
Guilford Rd ECC M30 110 C4
Guinness Rd TRPK M17 111 H5
Guiseley Cl BURY BL9 27 F3
Gullane Cl NEWH/MOS M40 104 B3
Gull Cl POY/DIS SK12 194 C4
Gulvain Pl CHAD OL9 74 A4
Gunson St NEWH/MOS M40 115 F2
Gun St ANC M4 7 J3
Gurner Av ORD M5 127 E1
Gurney St ANC M4 115 G4
Gutter La RAMS BL0 16 C1
Guy Fawkes St ORD M5 127 E1
Guywood La MPL/ROM SK6 162 B3
Gwelo St OP/CLY M11 116 B3
Gwenbury Av STKP SK1 160 C5
Gwendor Av CHH M8 87 E4
Gwladys St STLY SK15 109 F4
Gylden Cl HYDE SK14 134 C3
Gypsy La ROCH OL11 42 B3

H

Habergham Cl WALK M28 96 D3
Hackberry Cl ALT WA14 165 E1
Hacken Bridge Rd BOLS/LL BL3 50 A5
Hacken La BOLS/LL BL3 49 H5
Hackford Cl BOL BL1 48 B1
TOT/BURYW BL8 38 A1
Hacking St BRO M7 101 H4
BURY BL9 5 G5
PWCH M25 85 H3
Hackle St OP/CLY M11 116 D3
Hackleton Cl ANC M4 115 G4
Hackness Rd CCHDY M21 141 E3
Hackney Av NEWH/MOS M40 116 D1
Hackney Cl RAD M26 52 B4
Haddington Dr BKLY M9 88 B4
Haddon Av NEWH/MOS M40 104 D1
Haddon Cl BURY BL9 53 H4
MPL/ROM SK6 196 D1
WILM/AE SK9 200 C3
Haddon Gv HALE/TIMP WA15 166 A2
RDSH SK5 145 E4
SALE M33 154 B3
Haddon Hall Rd DROY M43 117 F3
Haddon Rd BRAM/HZG SK7 185 F3
CCHDY M21 156 C1
CHD/CHDH SK8 181 H5
ECC M30 110 D5
WALK M28 98 B5
Haddon St ROCH OL11 42 D1
SLFD M6 101 E5
STRET M32 126 A4
Haddon Wy ROY/SHW OL2 60 B1
Hadfield Av CHAD OL9 90 C2
Hadfield Cl RUSH/FAL M14 129 E5
Hadfield Crs AUL OL6 107 H5
Hadfield St BRO M7 101 H4
DUK SK16 132 D1
OLDS OL8 91 F4
OLDTF/WHR M16 127 F2
Hadleigh Cl BOL BL1 23 F5
Hadley Av BRUN/LGST M13 143 G1
Hadley Cl CHD/CHDH SK8 182 C3
Hadley St SLFD M6 101 E5
Hadlow Gn RDSH SK5 145 H5
Hadlow Wk
NEWH/MOS M40 * 115 H2
Hadwin St BOL BL1 2 E1
Hafton Rd BRO M7 101 E4
Haggate ROY/SHW OL2 74 D1
Haggate Crs ROY/SHW OL2 74 D1
Hagley Rd ORD M5 126 D2
The Hags BURY BL9 53 H4
Hague Rd DID/WITH M20 157 F1
Hague St AUL OL6 119 H1
NEWH/MOS M40 103 G5
OLDE OL4 76 D4
Haig Av IRL M44 150 B2
Haig Ct TOT/BURYW BL8 37 G5
Haigh Av HTNM SK4 159 H1
Haigh Hall Cl RAMS BL0 16 C4
Haigh La CHAD OL9 73 H3
Haigh Pk HTNM SK4 159 H1
Haigh St BOL BL1 2 E2
ROCH OL11 30 B5
Haig Rd STRET M32 126 A5
TOT/BURYW BL8 37 G4
Haile Dr WALK M28 96 A4
Hailsham Cl TOT/BURYW BL8 26 D4
Hail St RAMS BL0 * 16 B4
Halbury Wk BOL BL1 * 34 A4
Halcyon Cl WHIT OL12 29 E1
Haldon Rd DID/WITH M20 158 A1
Hale Av POY/DIS SK12 195 E5
Hale Bank WHTN BL5 62 A2
Hale La FAIL M35 104 D2
Hale Low Rd
HALE/TIMP WA15 178 A1
Hale Rd HALE/TIMP WA15 177 H1
HALE/TIMP WA15 178 D4
HTNM SK4 159 F3
Hales Cl DROY M43 117 G2
Halesden Rd HTNM SK4 159 G1
Halesworth Wk
NEWH/MOS M40 * 115 F1
Hale Vw ALT WA14 * 177 G2
Haley Cl RDSH SK5 145 F3
Haley St CHH M8 102 B3
Half Acre RAD M26 52 A3
Half Acre Dr ROCH OL11 29 F5
Half Acre La ROCH OL11 29 E5
Half Acre Ms ROCH OL11 29 E5
Half Acre Rd ROCH OL11 29 E5
Halfacre Rd WYTH/NTH M22 168 C5
Half Edge La ECC M30 111 G2
Half Moon La OFTN SK2 173 F3
Halford Dr NEWH/MOS M40 104 A2
Half St CSLFD M3 * 6 C1
Halifax Rd MILN OL16 11 G2
Halifax St AUL OL6 119 G1
Haliwell St LIT OL15 21 F3
Hallacres La CHD/CHDH SK8 182 B4
Hallam Rd NEWH/MOS M40 104 A5
Hallam St OFTN SK2 172 B3
RAD M26 53 E5
Hallas Gv NTHM/RTH M23 156 A5
Hall Av HALE/TIMP WA15 166 A2
RUSH/FAL M14 129 E5
SALE M33 139 E5
STLY SK15 108 D5
Hall Bank ECC M30 110 D3
Hallbottom St HYDE SK14 134 A3
Hallbridge Gdns BOL BL1 34 B3
Hall Cl HYDE SK14 135 H3
The Hall Coppice
EDGW/EG BL7 22 C2
Hallcroft PART M31 151 E2
Hallcroft Gdns MILN OL16 31 F5
Hall Dr HYDE SK14 135 H3
MDTN M24 88 C1
Hall Farm Av URM M41 124 A5
Hall Farm Cl BRAM/HZG SK7 185 H1
Hall Fold WHIT OL12 14 B5
Hall Gdns WHIT OL12 29 F1
Hallgate Dr CHD/CHDH SK8 181 F2
Hallgate Rd STKP SK1 172 C1
Hall Green Cl DUK SK16 * 119 H4
Hall Green Rd DUK SK16 119 H4
Hall Gv RUSH/FAL M14 129 E5
Halliday Rd NEWH/MOS M40 116 C1
Halliford Rd NEWH/MOS M40 103 H4
Hallington Cl BOLS/LL BL3 49 E5
Hall i' th' Wood La BOL BL1 34 B2
Halliwell Av OLDS OL8 91 F4
Halliwell La CHH M8 102 A3
Halliwell Rd BOL BL1 33 G4
PWCH M25 100 C1
Halliwell St BOL BL1 * 33 G4
CHAD OL9 * 105 F1
MILN OL16 31 F4
WHIT OL12 10 A5
Halliwell St West CHH M8 * 102 A3
Hall La FWTH BL4 66 B1
MPL/ROM SK6 147 F5
NTHM/RTH M23 168 A3
PART M31 151 E2
Hall Lee Dr WHTN BL5 62 B3
Hall Meadow CHD/CHDH SK8 182 B3
Hall Moss La BRAM/HZG SK7 193 F3
Hall Moss Rd BKLY M9 88 D4
Hallows Av CCHDY M21 156 B1
Hallows Farm Av WHIT OL12 29 G1
Hall Pool Dr OFTN SK2 173 F2
Hall Rd ALT WA14 177 F3
AUL OL6 107 F5
BRAM/HZG SK7 183 G3
RUSH/FAL M14 129 E5
WILM/AE SK9 192 B4
WILM/AE SK9 198 D3
Hallroyd Brow OLD OL1 * 75 F4
Hallstead Av LHULT M38 80 D3
Hallstead Gv LHULT M38 80 D3
Hall St AUL OL6 120 B3
BOLS/LL BL3 66 A2
BURY BL9 26 D2
CHD/CHDH SK8 170 A3
CMANW M2 6 E6

FAIL M35 ....104 C4
HYDE OL10 ....41 E5
MDTN M24 * 72 D4
OLDE OL4 ....76 A5
RAD M26 ....52 A3
ROY/SHW OL2 ....59 E5
STKP SK1 ....172 C1
SWIN M27 ....84 A5
TOT/BURYW BL8 ....36 D1
TOT/BURYW BL8 ....37 H2
WHIT OL12 ....11 G1
Hallsville Rd BNG/LEV M19 ....144 C2
Halls Wy URML OL5 ....94 D1
Hallsworth Rd ECC M30 ....110 B4
Hallview Wy WALK M28 ....81 E4
Hallwood Av SLFD M6 ....112 B1
Hallwood Rd NTHM/RTH M23 ...167 H5
WILM/AE SK9 ....192 B4
Hall Wood Rd WILM/AE SK9 ....192 B5
Hallworth Av DTN/ASHW M34 ..118 A4
Hallworth Rd CHH M8 ....102 C2
Halmore Rd NEWH/MOS M40 ...115 F1
Halsall Cl BURY BL9 ....25 G3
Halsall Dr BOLS/LL BL3 ....64 D2
Halsbury Cl WGTN/LGST M12 ..129 F2
Halsey Cl CHAD OL9 ....89 H4
Halshaw La FWTH BL4 ....66 C5
Halsted Dr BKLY M9 ....88 B4
Halstead Av CCHDY M21 ....141 E4
SLFD M6 ....100 B5
Halstead Dr IRL M44 ....150 D5
Halstead Gv BURY BL9 ....38 D1
BURY BL9 ....38 D1
Halstead Wk BURY BL9 * 38 D1
Halstock Rd NEWH/MOS M40 ..105 E5
Halstone Av WILM/AE SK9 ....200 B1
Halston St HULME M15 ....127 H2
Halter Cl RAD M26 ....58 D5
Halter St BOLE BL2 ....34 C5
HEY OL10 ....40 C4
RAD M26 ....52 D5
RAMS BL0 ....26 C1
Hamerton Rd
NEWH/MOS M40 ....115 F1
Hamilcar Av ECC M30 ....111 F3
Hamilton Av ECC M30 ....111 F4
IRL M44 ....150 C2
ROY/SHW OL2 ....74 C1
Hamilton Cl PWCH M25 ....85 H4
TOT/BURYW BL8 ....37 G3
Hamilton Crs HTNM SK4 ....159 E5
Hamilton Gv
OLDTF/WHR M16 ....127 G3
Hamilton Ms ECC M30 * 110 C2
PWCH M25 * 85 H4
Hamilton Rd BRUN/LGST M13 ..129 G5
PWCH M25 ....85 H4
WHTF M45 ....69 F4
Hamilton Sq HTNM SK4 ....159 H5
Hamilton St AULW OL7 ....117 H5
BOL BL1 ....33 H2
BRO M7 * 38 C2
BURY BL9 ....38 D1
CHAD OL9 ....74 B5
ECC M30 ....110 C2
OLDE OL4 ....9 K4
OLDTF/WHR M16 ....127 G3
STLY SK15 ....120 C3
SWIN M27 ....98 C1
Hamilton Wy HEY OL10 ....39 H5
Hamlet Dr SALE M33 ....139 E5
The Hamlet HOR/BR BL6 ....46 C1
Hammerstone Rd GTN M18 .....130 B2
Hammett Rd CCHDY M21 ....141 E5
Hammond Av HTNM SK4 ....159 H1
Hamnet Cl BOL BL1 ....2 C4
Hamnett St HYDE SK14 * 147 H1
OP/CLY M11 ....117 E4
Hamon Rd HALE/TIMP WA15 ...165 H5
Hampden Crs GTN M18 ....130 B3
Hampden Gv ECC M30 ....111 E3
Hampden Rd PWCH M25 ....86 A3
ROY/SHW OL2 ....60 C3
SALE M33 ....155 E3
Hampden St HEY OL10 ....41 E5
ROCH OL11 ....30 A5
Hampshire Cl BURY BL9 ....53 H1
Hampshire Rd CHAD OL9 ....90 C2
DROY M43 ....117 H3
PART M31 ....150 C4
RDSH SK5 ....160 D1
Hampshire St ECC M30 ....110 C4
Hampson Crs WILM/AE SK9 .....191 H5
Hampson Fold RAD M26 ....52 A5
Hampson Mill La BURY BL9 ......53 G4
Hampson Rd BOL BL1 ....107 H4
STRET M32 ....140 A1
Hampson St CSLFD M3 ....6 A6
DROY M43 ....117 H3
ECC M30 ....110 C4
NEWH/MOS M40 ....115 G1
ORD M5 ....114 A4
RAD M26 ....68 D1
SALE M33 ....155 E2
STKP SK1 * 172 C1
SWIN M27 ....99 F5
Hampstead Av URM M41 ....137 G2
Hampstead Dr OFTN SK2 ....172 D4
Hampstead La OFTN SK2 ....172 D4
Hampton Gv ALT WA14 ....165 H3
BURY BL9 ....27 G5
CHD/CHDH SK8 ....182 B2
Hampton Rd BOLS/LL BL3 ....65 F1
CCHDY M21 ....140 D2
FAIL M35 ....105 F2
IRL M44 ....150 C2
URM M41 ....138 D2
Hampton St OLDS OL8 ....91 E3
Hamsell Rd BRUN/LGST M13 ..128 C5
Hancock La RUSH/FAL M14 .....128 C5
Hancock St STRET M32 ....140 D3
Handel Av URM M41 ....138 A1
Handel Ms SALE M33 ....154 D2
Handel St BOL BL1 ....33 G3
Handforth Gv
BRUN/LGST M13 ....143 G1
Handforth Rd RDSH SK5 ....160 A1
WILM/AE SK9 ....199 H1
Handley Av RUSH/FAL M14 .....142 D2
Handley Cl EDGY/DAV SK3 ....171 F4
Handley Gdns BOL BL1 ....48 A1
Handley Rd BRAM/HZG SK7 ....183 H1
Handley St BURY BL9 ....53 G1
WHIT OL12 ....29 G3
Hands La ROCH OL11 ....28 D4
Handsworth St
WGTN/LGST M12 ....129 E1
Hanging Chadder La
ROY/SHW OL2 ....58 D2
Hankinson Cl PART M31 ....151 E4
Hankinson Wy SLFD M6 ....113 F2
Hanley Cl MDTN M24 ....88 D2
Hanlith Ms BNG/LEV M19 ....143 H5
Hanlon St CHH M8 ....102 A1
Hannah Baldwin Cl
OP/CLY M11 ....116 A5
Hannah St WGTN/LGST M12 ...144 A1
Hannerton Rd ROY/SHW OL2 ....60 C2
Hannesburg Gdns
NTHM/RTH M23 ....167 G5
Hannet Rd WYTH/NTH M22 .....180 C3
Hanover Ct BRO M7 ....101 G3
WALK M28 * 98 A4
Hanover Crs RUSH/FAL M14 ....129 E4
Hanover Gdns BRO M7 ....101 H2
Hanover Rd ALT WA14 ....165 E2
Hanover St ANC M4 ....7 F2
BOL BL1 ....36 C5
LIT OL15 ....20 C5
MOSL OL5 ....93 H5
ROCH OL11 ....42 B4
STLY SK15 ....120 C3
Hanover St North
DTN/ASHW M34 ....118 D5
Hanover St South
DTN/ASHW M34 * 118 D5
Hansby Cl OLD OL1 ....75 F3
Hansdon Cl CHH M8 ....102 B4
Hanson Cl MDTN M24 ....72 D5
Hanson Ms STKP SK1 ....160 C4
Hanson Pk MDTN M24 * 103 H5
Hanson St BURY BL9 ....38 C2
MDTN M24 ....72 D4
OLDE OL4 ....76 B5
Hanworth Cl BRUN/LGST M13 ..128 C2
Hapton Av STRET M32 ....140 B2
Hapton Pl HTNM SK4 * 159 H5
Hapton St BNG/LEV M19 ....144 A2
Harbern Cl ECC M30 ....111 E1
Harbord St MDTN M24 ....72 D4
Harboro Gv SALE M33 ....154 A2
Harboro Rd SALE M33 ....155 H2
Harboro Wy SALE M33 ....154 A2
Harbour Farm Rd HYDE SK14 ..133 H5
Harbour La MILN OL16 ....44 C5
Harbour La North MILN OL16 ....31 C5
Harbourne Av WALK M28 ....96 D2
Harbourne Cl WALK M28 ....96 D2
Harbury Cl BOLS/LL BL3 ....63 H3
Harbury Crs WYTH/NTH M22 ...168 A4
Harcles Dr RAMS BL0 ....26 C1
Harcombe Rd DID/WITH M20 ...143 E4
Harcourt Av URM M41 ....139 F2
Harcourt Cl URM M41 ....165 G3
Harcourt Rd SALE M33 ....139 G5
Harcourt St OLD OL1 ....76 A4
RDSH SK5 ....145 F3
STRET M32 ....126 B5
WALK M28 ....82 A2
Hardberry Pl OFTN SK2 ....173 E5
Hardcastle Av CCHDY M21 ......141 G5
Hardcastle Cl BOLE BL2 ....23 H5
Hardcastle Gdns BOLE BL2 ....23 H5
Hardcastle Rd EDGY/DAV SK3 ..171 G2
Hardcastle St BOL BL1 ....34 A4
Harden Dr BOLE BL2 ....35 E4
Harden Hills ROY/SHW OL2 ....60 C1
Harden Pk WILM/AE SK9 ....200 D2
Hardfield Rd MDTN M24 ....89 H1
Hardfield St HEY OL10 ....41 E4
Hardicker St HTNM SK4 ....144 B4
Hardie Av FWTH BL4 ....65 G5
Harding St ANC M4 ....115 G4
CSLFD M3 ....6 A5
HYDE SK14 ....133 G3
SLFD M6 ....113 F1
STKP SK1 ....160 C5
Hard La WHIT OL12 ....15 F5
Hardman Av MPL/ROM SK6 ......86 C5
PWCH M25 ....86 C5
Hardman Cl RAD M26 ....52 A3
Hardman La FAIL M35 ....104 D2
Hardman Rd RDSH SK5 ....145 E1
Hardman's EDGW/EG BL7 ....23 E4
Hardman's Ms EDGW/EG BL7 ...23 E4
Hardman St ANC M4 ....85 G1
CHAD OL9 ....90 C4
CSLFD M3 ....6 A4
EDGY/DAV SK3 ....12 D5
FAIL M35 ....104 C3
FWTH BL4 ....66 B5
HEY OL10 ....41 E4
RAD M26 ....52 A3
Hardon Gv BRUN/LGST M13 ....143 H1
Hardrush Fold FAIL M35 ....105 F4
Hardshaw Cl
BRUN/LGST M13 * 128 C2
Hardwick Cl MPL/ROM SK6 .....197 E1
RAD M26 ....51 E4
Hardwick Rd ROCH OL11 ....42 D2
Hardwick Rd PART M31 ....151 F3
Hardwick St AULW OL7 ....119 E5
Hardwood Cl CHH M8 ....102 B3
Hardy Av CCHDY M21 ....141 E5
Hardy Dr BRAM/HZG SK7 ....183 G5
HALE/TIMP WA15 ....166 A2
Hardy Gv SWIN M27 ....98 C5
WALK M28 ....97 G2
Hardy La CCHDY M21 ....141 G5
Hardy Mill Rd BOLE BL2 ....35 G3
Hardy St AUL OL6 ....107 H4
ECC M30 ....110 C4
OLDE OL4 ....9 K6
Hardywood Rd
DTN/ASHW M34 ....147 F4
Harebell Av WALK M28 * 81 E4
Harebell Cl WHIT OL12 ....18 C5
Harecastle Av ECC M30 ....111 F5
Haredale Dr CHH M8 ....102 C4
Hare Dr BURY BL9 ....54 A5
Harefield Av ROCH OL11 ....42 D1
Harefield Dr DID/WITH M20 .....157 F4
HEY OL10 ....41 G4
WILM/AE SK9 ....198 D5
Harefield Rd WILM/AE SK9 ......192 B3
Harehill Cl BRUN/LGST M13 ....128 C1
Hare Hill Rd HYDE SK14 ....134 D5
LIT OL15 ....20 D2
Hareshill Rd HEY OL10 ....55 H2
Hare St ANC M4 * 7 G3
ROCH OL11 ....28 B5
Harewood Av ROCH OL11 ....28 A2
SALE M33 ....153 G2
Harewood Cl ROCH OL11 ....28 A2
Harewood Dr ROY/SHW OL2 .....58 D4
Harewood Gv RDSH SK5 ....145 E3
Harewood Rd IRL M44 ....136 D1
ROY/SHW OL2 ....60 B1
RUSH/FAL M14 ....142 C1
Harewood Wy SWIN M27 ....84 A5
Harford Cl BRAM/HZG SK7 ......184 B3
Hargate Av WHIT OL12 ....28 D1
Hargate Cl BURY BL9 ....26 D1
Hargate Dr HALE/TIMP WA15 ..178 B3
IRL M44 ....122 B5
Hargrave Cl BKLY M9 ....87 H1
Hargreaves St
HALE/TIMP WA15 ....166 D3
Hargreaves's St ANC M4 ....114 D2
BOL BL1 * 33 H4
CHAD OL9 ....8 B4
OLD OL1 ....9 F2
ROY/SHW OL2 ....75 F2
Harkerside Cl CCHDY M21 ....115 H5
Harkness St WGTN/LGST M12 ..128 D1
Harland Dr CHH M8 ....102 C3
Harland Wy WHIT OL12 ....28 D1
Harlech Av WHTF M45 ....86 A1
Harlech Dr BRAM/HZG SK7 .....184 D2
Harleen Gv OFTN SK2 ....173 E2
Harlesden Crs BOLS/LL BL3 * 48 A4
Harley Av BOLE BL2 ....35 E3
BOLE BL2 ....36 C5
RUSH/FAL M14 ....142 C1
Harley Ct MDTN M24 ....72 C3
SALE M33 ....154 D1
Harley St AUL OL6 ....119 G2
OP/CLY M11 ....116 A5
Harling Rd WYTH/NTH M22 .....168 C2
Harlow Dr GTN M18 ....130 C5
Harlyn Av BRAM/HZG SK7 ......184 A5
Harmer Cl NEWH/MOS M40 ....103 H5
Harmol Gv AULW OL7 ....106 C4
Harmony St OLDE OL4 ....9 J6
Harmsworth Dr HTNM SK4 .....159 E1
Harmsworth St SLFD M6 ....112 D1
Harold Av DUK SK16 ....120 A4
GTN M18 ....131 E4
Haroldene St BOLE BL2 ....34 C4
Harold Lees Rd HEY OL10 ....41 G3
Harold Priestnall Cl
NEWH/MOS M40 ....104 A5
Harold St BOL BL1 ....33 G4
BOLE BL2 ....35 E3
FAIL M35 * 104 D3
MDTN M24 ....72 B4
MILN OL16 ....30 D1
OLDTF/WHR M16 ....127 F2
PWCH M25 ....85 G3
STKP SK1 ....160 A3
Harper Cl EDGY/DAV SK3 ....13 F7
Harper Fold Rd RAD M26 ....67 H1
Harper Green Rd FWTH BL4 ....65 G3
Harper Pl AUL OL6 ....119 H2
Harper Rd WYTH/NTH M22 .....168 D2
Harpers La BOL BL1 ....33 E4
Harper Sq ROY/SHW OL2 ....60 B2
Harper St EDGY/DAV SK3 ....12 E7
FWTH BL4 ....65 E4
OLDS OL8 ....91 F5
ROCH OL11 ....42 D1
Harpford Cl BOLE BL2 ....50 D4
Harpford Dr BOLE BL2 ....50 D4
Harp Rd TRPK M17 ....111 H5
Harp St OP/CLY M11 ....130 B1
Harpurhey Rd CHH M8 ....102 D2
Harridge Av STLY SK15 ....121 G3
WHIT OL12 ....18 B5
Harridge St WHIT OL12 ....18 B5
The Harridge WHIT OL12 ....18 B5
Harrier Cl WALK M28 ....97 E2
WYTH/NTH M22 ....180 B3
Harriet St IRL M44 ....150 D1
WALK M28 ....82 A4
Harriett St ANC M4 ....115 F3
MILN OL16 ....10 E7
Harringay Rd
NEWH/MOS M40 ....104 A5
Harrington Cl BURY BL9 ....53 H3
Harrington Rd ALT WA14 ....165 E2
Harrington St GTN M18 ....130 D3
Hart St ALT WA14 ....165 H2
Harris Av DTN/ASHW M34 ....131 G5
URM M41 ....124 C3
Harris Cl DTN/ASHW M34 ....131 G5
Harris Dr BURY BL9 ....39 H5
HYDE SK14 ....134 D4
Harrison Av BNG/LEV M19 ......144 B1
Harrison Cl WHIT OL12 ....28 C2
Harrison Dr MPL/ROM SK6 ....162 B1
Harrison St ANC M4 ....115 G4
BRO M7 ....114 A1
ECC M30 ....110 B5
HYDE SK14 ....148 B3
LHULT M38 ....81 F3
OFTN SK2 ....172 A2
OLD OL1 ....9 G4
RAMS BL0 ....16 D2
STLY SK15 ....120 C3
Harris St BOLS/LL BL3 ....2 C7
BRO M7 ....114 B1
Harrogate Av PWCH M25 ....86 C5
Harrogate Cl OP/CLY M11 ....130 C1
Harrogate Dr RDSH SK5 ....145 E3
Harrogate Rd RDSH SK5 ....145 E2
Harrop Edge Rd HYDE SK14 ....135 F5
Harrop Rd OLDS OL8 ....106 D1
Harrop Rd HALE/TIMP WA15 ...178 A2
Harrop St BOLS/LL BL3 ....47 H5
GTN M18 ....131 E2
STLY SK15 ....120 C3
WALK M28 ....81 G4
Harrow Av BNG/LEV M19 ....144 A5
OLDS OL8 ....91 E4
ROCH OL11 ....28 D5
Harrowby Dr
NEWH/MOS M40 ....103 E5
Harrowby Fold FWTH BL4 ....65 H3
Harrowby La FWTH BL4 ....65 H3
Harrowby Rd BOL BL1 ....32 C4
BOLS/LL BL3 ....63 H1
SWIN M27 ....98 D4
Harrowby St FWTH BL4 ....65 G4
Harrow Cl BURY BL9 ....53 G4
WILM/AE SK9 ....199 G2
Harrow Dr SALE M33 ....154 D3
Harrow Ms ROY/SHW OL2 ....60 A2
Harrow Rd BOL BL1 ....48 A2
SALE M33 ....154 B4
Harrow St CHH M8 ....102 C1
ROCH OL11 * 43 F1
Harrycroft Rd MPL/ROM SK6 ...162 A1
Harry Hall Gdns BRO M7 * 113 H1
Harry Rd BOLE BL2 ....35 F4
Harry Rowley Cl
WYTH/NTH M22 * 180 B2
Harry St OLD OL9 * 8 B5
ROCH OL11 ....42 B4
ROY/SHW OL2 ....75 F2
Harry Thorneycroft Wk
OP/CLY M11 ....115 H5
Harrytown MPL/ROM SK6 ....161 H4
Hart Av DROY M43 ....115 G5
Hart Ct MOSL OL5 ....93 G5
Hart Dr BURY BL9 ....54 A5
Harter St CMANE M1 ....7 F6
Hartfield Cl BRUN/LGST M13 ..128 C2
Hartford Av HEY OL10 ....40 A4
HTNM SK4 ....144 D5
WILM/AE SK9 ....198 C5
Hartford Cl HEY OL10 ....40 A4
Hartford Gdns
HALE/TIMP WA15 ....167 E4
Hartford Rd SALE M33 ....153 G5
URM M41 ....124 D4
Hartford Sq CHAD OL9 * 8 B5
Hartford St DTN/ASHW M34 * ..132 C3
Hart Hill Dr ORD M5 ....112 D2
Harthill St CHH M8 ....102 A5
Hartington Cl URM M41 ....139 E1
Hartington Dr BRAM/HZG SK7 ..185 F4
OP/CLY M11 ....116 B4
Hartington Rd ALT WA14 ....165 G2
BOL BL1 ....48 A1
BRAM/HZG SK7 ....193 H1
CCHDY M21 ....141 F5
CHD/CHDH SK8 ....182 B4
ECC M30 ....110 B2
MPL/ROM SK6 ....196 D1
OFTN SK2 ....173 E5
Hartington St
RUSH/FAL M14 ....128 A3
Hartis Av BRO M7 ....101 H4
Hartland Cl OFTN SK2 ....172 D1
POY/DIS SK12 ....195 E4
Hartland St HEY OL10 ....41 E4
Hartlebury ROCH OL11 * 42 A4
Hartlepool Cl RUSH/FAL M14 ..128 C5
Hartley Av PWCH M25 ....86 B4
Hartley Gv IRL M44 ....122 C4
Hartley Hall Gdns
OLDTF/WHR M16 ....127 E3
Hartley La ROCH OL11 ....42 C5
Hartley Rd ALT WA14 ....165 H2
CCHDY M21 ....141 E2
Hartley St EDGY/DAV SK3 * 171 H2
HEY OL10 ....41 E4
MILN OL16 ....11 G6
NEWH/MOS M40 ....103 G1
STLY SK15 ....121 F1
WHIT OL12 ....19 H2
Hart Mill Cl MOSL OL5 ....93 H4
Harton Av GTN M18 ....130 D5
Harton Cl ROY/SHW OL2 ....59 H5
Hart Rd RUSH/FAL M14 ....142 D2
Hartshead Av AUL OL6 ....120 B1
OP/CLY M11 ....131 F1
Hartshead Crs FAIL M35 ....105 H4
Hartshead Rd AUL OL6 ....107 H4
Hartshead St OLDE OL4 ....93 H3
Hartshead Vw HYDE SK14 ......148 B2
Hartspring Av SWIN M27 ....99 F3
Hart St ALT WA14 ....165 H2
CMANE M1 ....7 G6
DROY M43 ....117 H3
Hartswood Cl
DID/WITH M20 ....143 F5
Hartswood Rd DID/WITH M20 ..143 F5
Hartwell Cl BOLE BL2 ....34 C4
OP/CLY M11 ....116 A5
Harvard Cl MPL/ROM SK6 ....162 B1
Harvard Gv SLFD M6 ....112 B2
Harvard St ALT WA14 ....113 A3
ROCH OL11 ....43 F2
Harvest Cl SALE M33 ....155 H3
SLFD M6 ....100 B5
Harvest Pk BOL BL1 ....33 G3
Harvey St BOL BL1 ....33 G3
TOT/BURYW BL8 ....37 H3
WHIT OL12 ....11 C1
Harwin Cl DTN/ASHW M34 ......147 E1
Harwich Cl BNG/LEV M19 * 144 A5
RDSH SK5 ....146 A5
Harwin Cl WHIT OL12 ....18 C5
Harwood Cl SLFD M6 ....96 B3
Harwood Crs TOT/BURYW BL8 ...25 H4
Harwood Dr TOT/BURYW BL8 ...25 H4
Harwood Gv BOL BL2 * 3 F2
Harwood Meadow BOLE BL2 .....35 G3
Harwood Rd BNG/LEV M19 .....143 G5
BOLE BL2 ....36 A2
HTNM SK4 ....159 H3
LIT OL15 ....20 C3
Harwood St BOLE BL2 ....35 F3
WHIT OL12 ....11 C1
Haselhurst Wk
NTHM/RTH M23 ....155 H4
Hasguard Cl BOL BL1 ....47 G2
Haslam Brow BURY BL9 ....53 F1
Haslam Rd BOL BL1 ....47 F2
Haslam Hey Cl BOLE BL2 * 36 B5
TOT/BURYW BL8 ....37 E4
Haslam St BOLS/LL BL3 ....48 C4
BURY BL9 ....38 D2
MDTN M24 * 73 F5
WHIT OL12 ....29 G3
Haslemere Av
HALE/TIMP WA15 ....188 D3
Haslemere Dr CHD/CHDH SK8 ...182 D3
Haslemere Rd DID/WITH M20 ..143 F5
URM M41 ....138 B2
Haslington Rd
WYTH/NTH M22 ....180 D2
Hasper Av DID/WITH M20 ....142 C4
Hassall Av DID/WITH M20 ....142 B5
Hassall St STLY SK15 ....121 E4
Hassop Av BRO M7 ....100 D3
Hassop Cl OP/CLY M11 ....115 H4
Hassop Rd RDSH SK5 ....145 G2
Hastings Av CCHDY M21 ....141 E3
WHTF M45 ....70 A5
Hastings Cl CHD/CHDH SK8 ....183 F2
STKP SK1 ....172 C2
WHTF M45 ....70 A5
Hastings Dr URM M41 ....123 E4
Hastings Rd BOL BL1 ....48 A1
ECC M30 ....110 B1
PWCH M25 ....86 B2
Hastings St ROCH OL11 ....43 E1
Haston Cl RDSH SK5 ....160 A2
Hasty La HALE/TIMP WA15 .....179 G5
Hatchett Rd WYTH/NTH M22 ...180 D3
Hatchmere Cl CHD/CHDH SK8 ..170 C5
HALE/TIMP WA15 ....167 E3
Hatfield Rd BOL BL1 ....33 F5
Hathaway Dr BOL BL1 ....34 B1
Hathaway Gdns
MPL/ROM SK6 ....161 G3
Hatherley Rd BURY BL9 ....69 H1
DID/WITH M20 ....157 H1
Hatherlow MPL/ROM SK6 ....161 H4
Hatherlow La BRAM/HZG SK7 ..185 E2
Hatherop Cl ECC M30 ....110 C4
Hathersage Rd
BRUN/LGST M13 ....128 D2
Hathershaw La OLDS OL8 ....91 G4
Hatro Ct URM M41 ....139 G2
Hatters Ct STKP SK1 ....13 H6
Hattersley Rd East
HYDE SK14 ....149 G1
Hattersley Rd West
HYDE SK14 ....149 F2
Hatter St ANC M4 ....7 H2
Hatton Gv BOL BL1 ....34 B1
Hattons Ct STRET M32 ....140 A1
Hattons Rd TRPK M17 ....125 G2
Hatton St STKP SK1 ....13 F2
WGTN/LGST M12 ....129 H5
Haugh Hill Rd OLDE OL4 ....76 D1
Haugh La MILN OL16 ....45 E2
Haughton Cl MPL/ROM SK6 ....147 E5
Haughton Dr WYTH/NTH M22 ..156 C5
Haughton Green Rd
DTN/ASHW M34 ....147 F3
Haughton Hall Rd
DTN/ASHW M34 ....132 D5
Haughton St
DTN/ASHW M34 ....132 C3
HYDE SK14 ....148 A2
Havana Cl OP/CLY M11 ....116 A4
Haveley Rd WYTH/NTH M22 ...156 B4
Havelock Dr BOL BL1 ....114 A1
Havelock St OLDS OL8 ....9 G7
Havenbrook Gv RAMS BL0 * 16 B5
Haven Cl BRAM/HZG SK7 ....184 D5
OLDE OL4 ....62 A5
RAD M26 ....51 G4
Haven Dr DROY M43 ....117 F3
Haven La OLDE OL4 ....76 D1
Havencroft Av ECC M30 ....111 G5
Havenside Cl OLDE OL4 ....76 D1
Haven St SLFD M6 ....112 D4
The Haven
HALE/TIMP WA15 ....178 A1
Haverfield Rd BKLY M9 ....88 B4

Haverford St WCTN/LGST M12.....129 G2
Haverhill Gv BOLE BL2.....34 C4
Haversham Av CHH M8.....86 D5
Havers Rd GTN M18.....130 D3
Havisham Cl HOR/BR BL6.....46 C5
Hawarden Av OLDTF/WHR M16.....141 G1
Hawarden Rd ALT WA14.....165 G3
Haw Clough La UPML OL3.....95 C1
Hawarden Gn OFTN SK2.....175 F5
Hawes Av FWTH BL4.....64 D5
  RUSH/FAL M14.....143 G4
  SWIN M27 *.....99 E4
Hawes Cl OFTN SK2.....172 B5
  TOT/BURYW BL8.....37 G1
Haweswater Cl DTN/ASHW M34.....145 G1
Haweswater Crs BURY BL9.....54 A4
Haweswater Dr MDTN M24.....72 B2
Hawfinch Gv WALK M28.....97 E2
Hawk Cl BURY BL9.....5 J1
Hawker Av BOLS/LL BL3.....46 C5
Hawkeshead Rd CHH M8.....102 C4
Hawke St STLY SK15.....121 F4
Hawk Green Rd MPL/ROM SK6.....187 E1
Hawkhurst Rd BRUN/LGST M13.....129 G5
Hawkins St RDSH SK5.....159 H2
Hawkridge Dr NTHM/RTH M23.....155 H4
Hawk Rd IRL M44.....122 B5
Hawkshaw Ct ORD M5.....113 F4
Hawkshead Dr BOLS/LL BL3.....63 H1
  MDTN M24.....72 B3
  ROY/SHW OL2.....59 E3
Hawkshead Rd ROY/SHW OL2.....59 H1
Hawksley St OLDS OL8.....90 D4
Hawksmoor Dr ROY/SHW OL2.....60 A1
Hawkstone Av DROY M43.....117 F2
  WHTF M45.....69 F1
Hawkstone Cl BOLE BL2.....35 F3
Hawkswick Dr NTHM/RTH M23.....155 H4
Hawkswick Dr
Hawk Yard La UPML OL3.....95 G2
Hawley Dr HALE/TIMP WA15.....178 C4
Hawley Gn WHIT OL12.....29 C1
Hawley La HALE/TIMP WA15.....178 C4
Hawley St BNG/LEV M19.....144 B2
Haworth Av RAMS BL0.....26 C1
Haworth Cl BURY BL9.....53 G5
Haworth Dr STRET M32.....125 F5
Haworth Rd GTN M18.....130 B4
Haworth St OLD OL1.....75 G3
  RAD M26.....68 C1
  TOT/BURYW BL8.....37 E2
Hawthorn Cl HALE/TIMP WA15.....166 A2
Hawthorn Crs OLDS OL8.....91 G5
  ROY/SHW OL2.....60 A3
Hawthorn Dr BNG/LEV M19.....143 H4
  IRL M44.....150 D1
  SLFD M6.....111 H1
  STLY SK15.....120 C5
  SWIN M27.....99 H5
Hawthorne Av FWTH BL4.....65 C4
Hawthorne Dr AULW OL7.....119 E4
  CHAD OL9.....74 C4
  MPL/ROM SK6.....161 F2
  POY/DIS SK12.....196 B3
Hawthorne Rd BOLS/LL BL3.....48 A5
Hawthorne St BOLS/LL BL3.....48 A4
Hawthorn Gv BRAM/HZG SK7.....193 F1
  HTNM SK4.....159 E3
  HYDE SK14.....147 H2
  WILM/AE SK9.....199 E3
Hawthorn La CCHDY M21 *.....141 G3
  SALE M33.....138 D5
  WILM/AE SK9.....198 D5
Hawthorn Pk WILM/AE SK9.....198 D5
Hawthorn Rd CHD/CHDH SK8.....169 F4
  DROY M43.....118 B3
  DTN/ASHW M34.....131 G4
  FWTH BL4.....83 E2
  HALE/TIMP WA15.....177 H1
  HTNM SK4.....104 D1
  NEWH/MOS M40.....105 C1
  OLDS OL8.....28 B5
  ROCH OL11.....140 C3
  STRET M32.....62 A5
Hawthorn Rd South DROY M43.....118 B3
The Hawthorns DTN/ASHW M34.....132 A2
Hawthorn St DTN/ASHW M34.....132 B2
  GTN M18.....130 C2
  WILM/AE SK9.....198 D4
Hawthorn Ter HTNM SK4.....159 E3
Hawthorn Vw WILM/AE SK9 *.....198 D3
Hawthorn Wk LIT OL15.....20 C5
  SWIN M27 *.....198 D3
Hawthorpe Gv UPML OL3.....79 E4
Haxby Rd GTN M18.....130 C5
Haybarn Rd NTHM/RTH M23.....168 A2
Hayburn Rd GTN M18.....172 D1
Hay Cft CHD/CHDH SK8.....135 F1
Haycock Cl STLY SK15.....182 B4
Haydn Av RUSH/FAL M14.....128 C2
Haydock Av SALE M33.....153 F4
Haydock Cl STRET M32.....126 C4
Haydock Dr BRAM/HZG SK7.....184 A2
  HALE/TIMP WA15.....166 C4
  WALK M28.....96 B4
Haydock La EDGW/EG BL7.....23 G3
Haydock St BOL BL1.....2 E2

Haye's Rd IRL M44.....150 D1
Hayeswater Rd URM M41.....124 B5
Hayfield Av MPL/ROM SK6.....161 H2
Hayfield Cl MDTN M24.....73 F1
  OLDE OL4.....61 G3
  TOT/BURYW BL8.....4 E4
  WGTN/LGST M12.....129 F2
Hayfield Rd MPL/ROM SK6.....161 H2
  SLFD M6.....112 A1
Hayfield St SALE M33.....154 B2
Hayfield Wk HALE/TIMP WA15.....166 D3
Hayle Cl OLD OL1.....60 C5
Hayley St WGTN/LGST M12 *.....129 F4
Hayling Cl TOT/BURYW BL8.....26 D5
Hayling Rd SALE M33.....153 H1
Haymaker Ri WHIT OL12.....19 H2
Haymans Wk BRUN/LGST M13.....128 C1
Haymarket St BURY BL9.....4 D5
The Haymarket BURY BL9.....4 E4
Haymill Av LHULT M38.....81 F1
Haymond Cl SLFD M6.....100 D4
Haynes St BOLS/LL BL3.....64 A1
  WHIT OL12.....10 D4
Haysbrook Av LHULT M38.....80 C2
Haysbrook Cl AUL M34.....106 D5
Haythorp Av WYTH/NTH M22.....180 D1
Hayward Av BOLS/LL BL3.....67 F1
Hayward St TOT/BURYW BL8.....37 H5
Hazel Av AUL OL6.....107 H4
  BURY BL9.....5 K4
  CHD/CHDH SK8.....170 B4
  LHULT M38.....80 D2
  MILN OL16.....44 D5
  MPL/ROM SK6.....162 C4
  OLDTF/WHR M16.....141 H1
  RAD M26.....66 D4
  RAMS BL0.....26 C2
  SALE M33.....154 C3
  SWIN M27.....99 F5
  TOT/BURYW BL8.....37 E1
  WHTN BL5.....62 A5
Hazelbadge Cl POY/DIS SK12.....194 D3
Hazelbadge Rd POY/DIS SK12.....194 D3
Hazelbank Av DID/WITH M20.....142 D4
Hazelbottom Rd CHH M8.....102 C3
Hazel Cl DROY M43.....118 B3
  MPL/ROM SK6.....174 D5
Hazelcroft WILM/AE SK9.....200 D5
Hazel-dene Cl BURY BL9.....53 G2
Hazeldene Rd NEWH/MOS M40.....104 D1
Hazel Dr POY/DIS SK12.....173 E5
  POY/DIS SK12.....195 G4
  WYTH/NTH M22.....181 F4
Hazelfields WALK M28.....98 A3
Hazel Gv CHAD OL9.....74 C4
  FWTH BL4.....65 C4
  ORD M5.....112 B3
  RAD M26.....68 A4
  URM M41.....139 E1
Hazel Hall La TOT/BURYW BL8.....36 C5
Hazelhurst Ct BOL BL1 *.....33 H4
  RAMS BL0.....16 C4
Hazelhurst Dr MDTN M24.....56 C5
Hazelhurst Fold WALK M28.....98 B3
Hazelhurst Rd AUL OL6.....105 H5
  STLY SK15.....120 D1
  WALK M28.....98 A3
Hazel La OLDS OL8.....91 E5
Hazelmere Av ECC M30.....110 C1
Hazel Mt EDGW/EG BL7.....22 D2
Hazel Rd ALT WA14.....165 G4
  CHD/CHDH SK8.....183 E5
  MDTN M24.....73 E2
  STLY SK15.....121 F2
  WHTF M45.....70 A4
Hazel St BRAM/HZG SK7.....185 H4
  DTN/ASHW M34.....132 B2
  RAMS BL0.....16 B4
Hazel Ter BKLY M9 *.....88 A3
Hazelwell SALE M33.....154 C3
Hazelwood Av BOLE BL2.....35 F3
Hazelwood Cl HYDE SK14.....148 C1
Hazelwood Ct URM M41.....27 G4
  DTN/ASHW M34.....132 B2
Hazelwood Rd BOL BL1.....54 B5
  BRAM/HZG SK7.....185 F2
  HALE/TIMP WA15.....177 H2
  OFTN SK2.....172 B5
  WILM/AE SK9.....199 G2
  WYTH/NTH M22.....180 C4
Hazlemere FWTH BL4.....66 D5
Headingley Dr OLDTF/WHR M16.....126 D5
Headingley Rd RUSH/FAL M14.....142 B3
Headingley Wy BOLS/LL BL3.....64 C1
Headlands Dr PWCH M25.....85 H5
Headlands Rd BRAM/HZG SK7.....184 A5
Headlands St WHIT OL12.....10 A2
Heady Hill Cl HEY OL10.....40 B5
Heady Hill Rd HEY OL10.....40 B5
Heald Av RUSH/FAL M14.....128 C5
Heald Cl ALT WA14.....177 F2
  LIT OL15.....20 C5
  WHIT OL12.....18 B5
Heald Dr ALT WA14.....177 F2
  WHIT OL12.....18 B5
Heald Gn CHD/CHDH SK8.....181 F1
  RUSH/FAL M14.....128 C5
Heald La LIT OL15.....20 D5
Heald Pl RUSH/FAL M14.....128 C5
Heald Rd ALT WA14.....177 F2
Healds Gn CHAD OL9.....74 A1
Heald St STKP SK1.....13 J1
Healdwood Rd MPL/ROM SK6.....162 B2
Healey Av HEY OL10.....41 F3
Healey Cl BRO M7.....101 F2
  NTHM/RTH M23.....155 G4
Healey Gv WHIT OL12.....18 B3
Healey La WHIT OL12.....18 B3
Healey St MILN OL16.....29 H5
Healing St ROCH OL11.....43 F1
Heanor Av DTN/ASHW M34.....147 E3
Heap Br BURY BL9.....39 G4
Heap Brow BURY BL9.....39 G5

Heape St ROCH OL11.....42 B5
Heaplands TOT/BURYW BL8.....26 A2
Heap Rd WHIT OL12.....28 A1
Heaps Farm Ct STLY SK15.....121 G5
Heap St BOLS/LL BL3.....48 D5
  BURY BL9.....39 C5
  OLDE OL4.....76 B4
  RAD M26.....68 C1
  WHTF M45 *.....69 G5
Heapworth Av RAMS BL0.....16 B5
Heapy Ct TOT/BURYW BL8.....37 E4
Heath Av BRO M7.....113 H1
  RAMS BL0.....26 C2
Heathbank Rd BKLY M9.....87 H2
  CHD/CHDH SK8.....182 C4
  EDGY/DAV SK3.....171 E2
Heathcliffe Wk BRUN/LGST M13.....128 D3
Heath Cl BOLS/LL BL3.....64 A2
Heathcote Av HTNM SK4.....159 F5
Heathcote Rd GTN M18.....130 B4
Heath Crs OFTN SK2.....172 A4
Heather Av DROY M43.....118 B3
  ROY/SHW OL2.....59 G1
Heather Bank LIT OL15 *.....21 G2
  TOT/BURYW BL8 *.....25 H4
Heather Brow STLY SK15.....135 F1
Heather Cl OLDE OL4.....76 D3
Heatherdale Dr CHH M8.....102 B4
Heatherfield BOL BL1.....33 G1
Heatherfield Ct WILM/AE SK9.....199 H2
Heather Gv DROY M43.....118 A5
Heatherlands WHIT OL12.....14 C1
Heather Lea DTN/ASHW M34.....147 E1
Heather Rd ALT WA14.....177 H1
Heatherside RDSH SK5.....160 B4
  STLY SK15.....121 G3
Heatherside Av MOSL OL5.....109 F1
Heatherside Rd RAMS BL0.....16 A5
The Heathers OFTN SK2.....172 C5
Heather St OP/CLY M11.....116 C3
Heather Wy MPL/ROM SK6.....174 D4
  SALE M33.....153 C1
Heath Farm La PART M31.....151 F4
Heathfield BOLE BL2.....35 G2
  FWTH BL4.....66 B3
  WALK M28.....97 G5
  WILM/AE SK9.....198 D5
Heathfield Av CHD/CHDH SK8.....169 G4
  DTN/ASHW M34.....146 B1
  SWIN M27.....99 F4
Heathfield Cl SALE M33.....155 G3
Heathfield Dr BOLS/LL BL3.....64 A2
  SWIN M27.....99 F4
Heathfield Rd BURY BL9.....69 C1
  OFTN SK2.....172 A3
Heathfield St NEWH/MOS M40.....104 B5
Heathland Rd BRO M7.....101 E1
Heathlands Dr PWCH M25.....100 D1
Heathland Ter EDGY/DAV SK3.....171 H7
Heathea Cl BOL BL1.....2 C5
Heath Pl BRO M7 *.....113 H1
Heath Rd ALT WA14.....177 C2
  HALE/TIMP WA15.....166 A3
  OFTN SK2.....172 A3
Heathside Gv WALK M28.....82 A4
Heathside Park Rd EDGY/DAV SK3.....171 H7
Heathside Rd DID/WITH M20.....157 H1
  EDGY/DAV SK3.....170 D2
Heath St CHH M8.....102 A3
  ROCH OL11.....29 C5
The Heath AULW OL7.....106 D3
  MDTN M24.....89 E1
Heathwood UPML OL3.....79 F4
Heathwood Rd BNG/LEV M19.....158 B2
Heatley Rd MILN OL16.....31 E5
Heaton Av BOL BL1.....32 C5
  BOLE BL2.....35 F1
  BRAM/HZG SK7.....185 G1
  FWTH BL4.....65 H4
Heaton Ct BURY BL9.....53 H4
Heaton Dr BURY BL9.....53 H4
Heaton Fold BURY BL9.....53 F1
Heaton Grange Dr BOL BL1.....47 H2
Heaton Gv BURY BL9.....53 F2
Heaton La HTNM SK4.....12 E5
Heaton Moor Rd HTNM SK4.....158 C5
Heaton Mt BOL BL1.....32 C5
Heaton Park Rd BKLY M9.....87 F2
Heaton Park Rd West BKLY M9.....87 F2
Heaton Rd BOLE BL2.....51 E4
  DID/WITH M20.....143 E4
  HDR/BR BL6.....47 E5
  HTNM SK4.....159 C3
Heatons Gv WHTN BL5.....62 B2
Heaton St BRO M7.....100 B5
  DTN/ASHW M34.....132 A5
  MDTN M24.....44 D1
  MILN OL16.....44 D1
  PWCH M25.....86 B3
Heaviley Gv HULME M15 *.....172 B3
Hebble Butt Cl MILN OL16 *.....11 G5
Hebburn Dr TOT/BURYW BL8.....37 H1
Hebburn Wk RUSH/FAL M14.....128 C4
Hebden Av MPL/ROM SK6.....161 H2
  SLFD M6.....112 B2
Heber Pl LIT OL15 *.....21 E3
Heber St RAD M26.....68 B1
Hebron St ROY/SHW OL2.....75 H1
Hector Av MILN OL16.....11 G4
Hector Rd BRUN/LGST M13.....129 G5
Hedera Cl HTNM SK4.....158 B5
Hedge Rows WHIT OL12.....14 B3
The Hedgerows HYDE SK14.....134 B5
Hedges St FAIL M35.....105 F2
Hedley St BOL BL1.....33 H4
Heginbottom Crs AUL OL6.....107 F5
Heights Av WHIT OL12.....10 A1
Heights Cl WHIT OL12.....10 A1
Heights La OLD OL1.....74 A2
  WHIT OL12.....10 A1

Helena St SLFD M6.....99 H5
Helen St BRO M7.....101 F5
  ECC M30.....110 C5
  FAIL M35.....66 A4
Heensville Av SLFD M6.....100 C5
Helga St NEWH/MOS M40.....104 A1
Helias Cl WALK M28.....81 E4
Hellidon Cl WGTN/LGST M12.....129 F2
Helmclough Wy WALK M28.....96 D2
Helmet St CMANE M1.....115 F5
Helmsdale WALK M28.....81 H5
Helmsdale Av BOLS/LL BL3.....47 G3
Helmsdale Cl RAMS BL0.....16 B5
Helmshore Av OLDE OL4.....76 C1
Helmshore Wk BRUN/LGST M13.....128 C1
Helmshore Wy ROY/SHW OL2.....60 A1
Helsby Cl OLDE OL4.....93 F1
Helsby Gdns BOL BL1.....34 A2
Helsby Rd SALE M33.....155 F4
Helsby Wk WGTN/LGST M12.....115 H5
Helston Cl BRAM/HZG SK7.....184 A1
  IRL M44.....136 D1
Helston Dr ROY/SHW OL2.....59 C5
Helston Gv CHD/CHDH SK8.....181 H4
Helvellyn Dr MDTN M24.....72 A2
Helvellyn Wk OLD OL1 *.....9 G5
Hembury Av BNG/LEV M19.....143 H5
Hembury Cl MDTN M24.....73 E2
Hemley St OFTN SK2.....172 D5
  RUSH/FAL M14.....128 B5
Hemming Dr ECC M30.....111 F4
Hemmington Dr BKLY M9.....103 E3
Hemmons Rd WGTN/LGST M12.....144 B3
Hempcroft Rd HALE/TIMP WA15.....166 D4
Hemphaw La STKP SK1.....13 J7
Hempshaw St BKLY M9.....103 C3
Hemsley St South BKLY M9.....103 F2
Hemswell Cl SLFD M6.....112 D1
Hemsworth Rd BOL BL1.....2 B2
  GTN M18.....130 C5
Henbury Dr MPL/ROM SK6.....147 F5
Henbury La CHD/CHDH SK8.....192 A3
Henbury Rd WILM/AE SK9.....192 A3
Henbury St OFTN SK2.....172 D5
  RUSH/FAL M14.....128 B5
Henderson Av SWIN M27.....99 F1
Henderson St BNG/LEV M19.....144 B3
  LIT OL15.....11 C1
  WHIT OL12.....11 C1
Hendham Cl BRAM/HZG SK7.....184 A2
Hendham Dr ALT WA14.....165 E4
Hendham V BKLY M9.....102 D3
Hendon Dr BURY BL9.....53 G4
  EDGY/DAV SK3.....170 D2
Hendon Rd BKLY M9.....87 H3
Hendriff Pl WHIT OL12 *.....10 C2
Hengist St BOLE BL2.....49 H7
  GTN M18.....130 C4
Henley Av CHD/CHDH SK8.....182 C2
  IRL M44.....136 A5
  OLDTF/WHR M16.....127 E5
Henley Cl TOT/BURYW BL8.....26 D1
  HALE/TIMP WA15.....166 A2
Henley Gv BOLS/LL BL3.....64 B1
Henley Pl BNG/LEV M19.....158 B1
Henley St CHAD OL9.....90 B4
  OLD OL1.....75 E4
  WHIT OL12.....11 F1
Henley Ter ROCH OL11.....42 D1
Henniker Rd BOLS/LL BL3.....63 H2
Henniker St SWIN M27.....98 D5
  WALK M28.....97 E1
Hennon St BOL BL1.....33 G5
Henrietta St AUL OL6.....119 C1
  BOLS/LL BL3.....48 A5
  OLDTF/WHR M16.....127 F3
Henry Herman St BOLS/LL BL3.....63 H1
Henry Lee St BOLS/LL BL3 *.....64 B1
Henry St ANC M4.....7 H5
  BOLE BL2.....3 G4
  DROY M43.....117 H4
  DTN/ASHW M34.....147 F3
  ECC M30.....110 D4
  FAIL M35.....105 E3
  HALE/TIMP WA15.....166 A1
  LIT OL15.....20 C5
  MDTN M24.....72 C4
  MILN OL16.....30 A5
  OLDTF/WHR M16.....127 F3
  PWCH M25.....86 B3
  RAMS BL0.....17 E1
  STKP SK1.....172 C1
  WHIT OL12.....19 H1
Henshaw Ct OLDTF/WHR M16.....127 E4
Henshaw La CHAD OL9.....90 A5
Henshaw St OLD OL1.....9 F3
  STRET M32.....140 B1
Henshaw Wk BOL BL1.....33 H4
Henson Gv HALE/TIMP WA15.....166 B5
Henthorn St ROY/SHW OL2.....59 C5
Henton Wk NEWH/MOS M40.....115 F1
Henty Cl ECC M30.....110 C4
Henwick Hall Av RAMS BL0.....16 A5
Henwood Rd DID/WITH M20.....157 H1
Hepley Rd POY/DIS SK12.....195 H4
Hepple Cl HTNM SK4.....158 C3
Heppleton Rd NEWH/MOS M40.....89 G5
Hepton St OLD OL1.....8 E2
Hepworth St HYDE SK14.....148 A1
Herbert St BOLS/LL BL3.....67 F1
  CHAD OL9 *.....74 C5
  DROY M43.....102 A5
  DROY M43.....117 G4
  DTN/ASHW M34.....146 C4
  EDGY/DAV SK3.....12 A6
  OLDE OL4.....76 C3
  PWCH M25.....85 C3
  RAD M26.....52 A4
  STRET M32.....140 B1

Hereford Dr BURY BL9.....53 C1
  PWCH M25.....86 B5
  SWIN M27.....99 E4
  WILM/AE SK9.....192 B4
Hereford Gv URM M41.....48 A1
Hereford Rd BOL BL1.....170 D5
  CHD/CHDH SK8.....99 F5
  ECC M30.....160 D1
  RDSH SK5.....34 A4
Hereford St BOL BL1.....8 A6
  CHAD OL9.....43 F1
  ROCH OL11.....154 C2
  SALE M33.....73 F3
Hereford Wy MDTN M24.....73 F3
  STLY SK15.....135 E1
Herevale Gra WALK M28.....96 C3
Herevale Hall Dr RAMS BL0.....16 C4
Heristone Av DTN/ASHW M34.....132 B5
Heritage Gdns DID/WITH M20.....157 G4
Herle Dr WYTH/NTH M22.....180 B3
Hermitage Av MPL/ROM SK6.....163 E4
Hermitage Gdns MPL/ROM SK6.....163 E4
Hermitage Rd CHH M8.....102 B1
  HALE/TIMP WA15.....178 B1
Hermon Av OLDS OL8.....91 F5
Herne St OP/CLY M11.....116 B5
Heron Av DUK SK16.....133 H1
Heron Ct SLFD M6.....112 C3
Herondale Cl NEWH/MOS M40.....104 A5
Heron Dr DTN/ASHW M34.....118 B4
  IRL M44.....122 B5
  POY/DIS SK12.....194 B4
Heron Ml OLDS OL8 *.....91 E4
Heron St EDGY/DAV SK3.....12 D6
  HULME M15.....127 H5
  OLDS OL8.....90 D4
  SWIN M27.....99 F1
Herries St AUL OL6.....120 A1
Herristone Rd CHH M8.....87 F5
Herrod Av HTNM SK4.....159 H2
Herschel St NEWH/MOS M40.....103 H2
Hersey St SLFD M6 *.....112 D3
Hertford Rd BKLY M9.....103 E1
Hertfordshire Park Cl ROY/SHW OL2.....60 A1
Hertford St AULW OL7.....119 F4
Hesford Av BKLY M9.....103 C3
Hesketh Av BOL BL1.....34 A1
  DID/WITH M20.....157 F5
  ROY/SHW OL2.....59 H1
Hesketh Rd MILN OL16.....11 J6
  SALE M33.....154 A3
Hesketh St HTNM SK4.....159 H3
Hessel St SALO M50.....112 C4
Hester Wk HULME M15 *.....128 A2
Heston Av BRUN/LGST M13.....143 G1
Heston Dr URM M41.....124 D5
Heswall Av DID/WITH M20.....142 D4
Heswall Dr TOT/BURYW BL8.....36 D1
Heswall Rd RDSH SK5.....145 F2
Hetherington Wk WGTN/LGST M12.....129 G4
Hethorn St NEWH/MOS M40.....104 B5
Hetton Av BRUN/LGST M13.....143 G1
Heversham Av ROY/SHW OL2.....60 C2
Hewart Dr BURY BL9.....39 F4
Hewitt Av DTN/ASHW M34.....131 E5
Hewitt St HULME M15.....128 A1
Hewlett Rd CCHDY M21.....141 E2
Hewlett St BOLE BL2.....3 C5
  TOT/BURYW BL8.....32 C5
Hexham Av BOL BL1.....8 A2
  OFTN SK2.....172 D4
Hexham Rd GTN M18.....130 A4
Hexon Cl SLFD M6.....111 G3
Hey Bottom La WHIT OL12.....19 F2
Heybrook Cl WHIT M45.....70 B4
Heybrook Rd MILN OL16 *.....11 G3
Heybury Cl OP/CLY M11.....116 A5
Hey Crs OLDE OL4.....77 E5
Hey Cft WHTF M45.....68 D5
Heyes Av HALE/TIMP WA15.....166 C2
Heyes Gv RAD M26.....52 B5
Heyes La ALT WA14.....201 E3
Heyes Leigh HALE/TIMP WA15 *.....166 C2
Heyes Ter HALE/TIMP WA15 *.....166 C1
Heyford Av NEWH/MOS M40.....89 C5
Heyheads New Rd STLY SK15.....109 F5
Hey Hill Cl ROY/SHW OL2.....59 H4
Heyland Rd NTHM/RTH M23.....167 H3
Heyridge Dr WYTH/NTH M22.....156 C5
Heyrod St CMANE M1.....7 K6
  STLY SK15.....121 G2
Heyrose Wk HULME M15 *.....127 G2
Heys Av MPL/ROM SK6.....162 D3
  NTHM/RTH M23.....155 H5
  SWIN M27.....83 C5
Heys Cl North SWIN M27.....83 F5
Heyscroft Rd DID/WITH M20.....158 D4
  HTNM SK4.....158 D4
Heysham Av DID/WITH M20.....142 B4
Heyside ROY/SHW OL2.....59 H5
Heyside Av ROY/SHW OL2.....59 H5
Heyside Cl STLY SK15.....9 5 F6
Heys La HEY OL10.....40 B4
  MPL/ROM SK6.....162 D3
Heys Rd AUL OL6.....120 A2
  PWCH M25.....86 A2
Heys St MILN OL16.....11 J5
Heys Vw PWCH M25.....86 A3
The Heys AUL OL6.....120 A2
  PWCH M25.....86 A3
  RDSH SK5.....145 G2
Heythrop Cl WHTF M45.....69 F3
Heywood Av OLDE OL4.....77 F4
  SWIN M27.....99 H3
Heywood Cl WILM/AE SK9.....201 E3
Heywood Fold Rd OLDE OL4.....77 E5
Heywood Gdns BOLS/LL BL3.....48 D5
  PWCH M25.....86 A3
Heywood Gv SALE M33.....139 G5

Heywood Hall Rd HEY OL10.....41 E3
Heywood La OLDE OL4.....77 F5
Heywood Old Rd HEY OL10.....55 H5
 MDTN M24.....71 H4
Heywood Park Vw
 BOLS/LL BL3.....48 D4
Heywood Rd PWCH M25.....86 A4
 ROCH OL11.....42 A4
 SALE M33.....154 C5
 WILM/AE SK9.....201 E3
Heywoods Hollow BOL BL1.....34 A3
Heywood St BOL BL1.....2 E2
 BOLS/LL BL3.....67 E1
 BURY BL9.....5 G6
 CHH M8.....102 B4
 FAIL M35.....104 C3
 OLDE OL4.....76 D4
 SWIN M27.....98 D2
Heywood Wy SLFD M6.....113 E2
Heyworth Av MPL/ROM SK6.....162 C3
Hexworth St ORD M5 *.....112 D4
Hibbert Av DTN/ASHW M34.....132 C3
 HYDE SK14.....148 A2
Hibbert Crs FAIL M35.....105 F3
Hibbert La MPL/ROM SK6.....175 E4
Hibbert St BOL BL1.....33 A4
 HTNM SK4.....159 H1
 OLDE OL4.....77 E5
 RUSH/FAL M14.....128 D5
Hibernia St BOLS/LL BL3.....88 B4
Hibernia Wy STRET M32.....125 F3
Hibson Av WHIT OL12.....28 E1
Hibson Cl WHIT OL12.....19 H2
Hickenfield Rd HYDE SK14.....134 A3
Hicken Pl HYDE SK14.....134 A3
Hickton Dr ALT WA14.....165 E4
Higginshaw La OLD OL1 *.....75 H2
Higginshaw Rd OLD OL1.....75 C3
Higginson Rd RDSH SK5.....145 E4
Higgs Cl OLDE OL4.....77 C5
Higham Cl ROY/SHW OL2.....59 H4
Higham La HYDE SK14.....148 B3
Higham St CHD/CHDH SK8.....182 D4
Higham Vw OLDE OL4.....113 F2
High Ash Gv DTN/ASHW M34.....132 A1
High Av BOLE BL2 *.....50 B2
High Bank ALT WA14.....165 C4
 EDGW/EG BL7.....23 E4
 GTN M18.....130 D3
High Bank Av STLY SK15.....135 E1
Highbank Crs OLDE OL4.....94 B2
High Bank Cl BOLE BL2.....33 E4
Highbank Dr DID/WITH M20.....169 G1
High Bank Gra HOR/BR BL6.....46 C1
High Bank Gv PWCH M25.....86 B4
High Bank La HOR/BR BL6.....46 C1
High Bank Rd DROY M43.....117 G5
 HYDE SK14.....134 A5
 SWIN M27.....99 G2
Highbank Rd BURY BL9.....69 C1
 MILN OL16.....45 F3
High Bank St BOLE BL2.....49 H2
High Barn Cl ROCH OL11.....42 C1
High Barn La WHIT OL12.....14 B2
High Barn Rd MDTN M24.....72 C2
 ROY/SHW OL2.....59 C5
High Barn St ROY/SHW OL2.....59 F5
The Beeches BOL BL2.....51 F4
High Bent Av CHD/CHDH SK8.....192 D1
Highbridge Cl BOLE BL2.....50 D3
Highbury IRL M44.....136 C2
 URM M41.....137 C1
Highbury Rd HTNM SK4.....144 C5
 OLDTF/WHR M16.....142 A2
Highbury Wy ROY/SHW OL2.....59 E3
Highclere Av CHH M8.....102 A4
Highcliffe Rd CHH M8.....87 E5
Highcliffe Rd BKLY M9.....87 F3
Highclove La WALK M28.....96 A5
High Crest Av CHD/CHDH SK8.....169 E4
Highcroft BOL BL1.....34 B5
Highcroft Av DID/WITH M20.....156 D2
High Croft Cl DUK SK16.....120 C5
Highcroft Rd MPL/ROM SK6.....162 C5
Highdales Rd NTHM/RTH M23.....168 A4
High Elm Dr HALE/TIMP WA15.....178 D4
High Elm Rd
 HALE/TIMP WA15.....178 D5
High Elms CHD/CHDH SK8.....193 E2
Higher Ainsworth Rd RAD M26.....51 H2
Higher Ardwick
 WGTN/LGST M12.....128 C1
Higher Arthurs UPML OL3.....95 E1
Higher Bank Rd LIT OL15.....20 D5
Higher Barlow Rw STKP SK1.....13 H5
Higher Bents La
 MPL/ROM SK6.....161 G3
Higher Bridge St BOL BL1.....2 C2
Higher Cambridge St
 HULME M15.....128 B3
Higher Carr La UPML OL3.....79 C5
Higher Chatham St
 HULME M15 *.....128 B2
Higher Cleggswood Av
 LIT OL15.....20 D5
Higher Cft ECC M30.....110 D5
 WHTF M45.....84 D1
Higher Crossbank OLDE OL4.....77 H5
Higher Cross La WHIT OL12.....79 F5
Higher Damshead WHTN BL5.....62 A4
Higher Darcy St BOLE BL2.....49 H1
Higher Dean St RAD M26.....67 H1
Higher Downs ALT WA14.....177 F1
Higher Fold La RAMS BL0.....16 D3
Higher Fold Farm
 MPL/ROM SK6.....186 D3
Higher Fold La RAMS BL0.....17 F1
Higher Fullwood OLDE OL4.....60 C5
Higher Gn AUL OL6.....119 H1
Higher Henry St HYDE SK14.....147 H2
Higher Hillgate STKP SK1.....13 H5
Higher House Cl CHAD OL9.....90 B3
Higher La WHTF M45.....69 F4
Higher Lime Rd OLDS OL8.....105 H2
Higher Lomax La HEY OL10.....40 C3
Higher Lydgate Pk OLDE OL4.....93 H1

Higher Market St FWTH BL4.....66 B4
Higher Mdw BNG/LEV M19.....144 C2
Higher Ormond St
 HULME M15 *.....128 B2
Higher Oswald St ANC M4.....7 G2
Higher Pk ROY/SHW OL2.....45 F5
Higher Pit La BOLE BL2.....51 H1
Higher Ridings EDGW/EG BL7.....23 E4
Higher Ri ROY/SHW OL2.....44 D5
Higher Rd URM M41.....139 E1
Higher Rw BURY BL9.....5 J2
Higher Shady La EDGW/EG BL7.....23 H4
Higher Shore Rd LIT OL15.....20 B1
Higher Summerseat RAMS BL0.....26 C2
Higher Swan La BOLS/LL BL3.....48 C5
Higher Tame St STLY SK15.....121 E5
Higher Turf La OLDE OL4.....77 G4
Higher Turf Pk ROY/SHW OL2.....75 F1
Higher Wharf St BOLE BL2.....119 G3
Higher Wheat La MILN OL16.....11 E5
Higher Wood St MDTN M24.....72 C2
Highfield CHD/CHDH SK8.....181 H1
 SALE M33.....154 D3
Highfield Av BOLE BL2.....35 H3
 HEY OL10.....40 B4
 RAD M26.....66 C4
Highfield Cl EDGY/DAV SK3.....172 A5
 HYDE SK14.....134 A2
 STRET M32.....140 A3
Highfield Dr ECC M30.....111 E2
 FWTH BL4.....65 F5
 MDTN M24.....72 C5
 MOSL OL5.....108 D2
 ROY/SHW OL2.....59 H5
 SWIN M27.....99 H5
 URM M41.....124 B5
Highfield Est WILM/AE SK9.....199 F1
Highfield Gdns HYDE SK14.....134 A5
Highfield Gln AUL OL6.....108 A5
Highfield La BURY BL9.....69 G1
Highfield Pk HTNM SK4.....158 C4
Highfield Park Rd
 MPL/ROM SK6.....161 F2
Highfield Pkwy
 BRAM/HZG SK7.....193 G3
Highfield Pl GTN M18 *.....131 E4
 PWCH M25.....85 H2
Highfield Range BNG/LEV M19.....144 C2
 BOL BL1.....33 E4
 BRAM/HZG SK7.....184 A1
 BRAM/HZG SK7.....185 H2
 CHD/CHDH SK8.....182 C3
 ECC M30.....111 E1
 FWTH BL4.....65 F5
 HALE/TIMP WA15.....166 C4
 HALE/TIMP WA15.....178 B2
 LHULT M38.....81 E2
 MILN OL16.....31 H5
 MPL/ROM SK6.....175 F5
 POY/DIS SK12.....194 B5
 PWCH M25.....85 H1
 ROCH OL11.....28 B2
 SLFD M6.....113 E2
 STRET M32.....140 A3
Highfield St BRO M7.....102 A3
 CHAD OL9.....8 D5
 DTN/ASHW M34.....132 C2
 DUK SK16.....119 G4
 EDGY/DAV SK3.....12 A5
 FAIL M35.....82 D1
 MDTN M24.....73 E4
Highfield Ter BKLY M9.....103 E2
 OLDE OL4.....76 C2
Highgate BOLS/LL BL3.....62 D2
Highgate Av URM M41.....123 H4
Highgate Crs GTN M18.....130 C4
Highgate Dr LHULT M38.....80 D2
 ROY/SHW OL2.....58 D2
Highgate La LHULT M38.....80 D2
 WHIT OL12.....18 B2
Highgate Rd ALT WA14.....165 E5
High Gates SALE M33.....155 F1
Highgrove HALE/TIMP WA15.....154 B5
Highgrove Cl BOL BL1.....34 A3
High Grove Rd
 CHD/CHDH SK8.....169 H4
 OLDE OL4.....94 B2
The Highgrove BOL BL1 *.....32 A5
High Houses BOL BL1 *.....22 C5
High Hurst Cl MDTN M24 *.....71 H5
Highland Rd EDGW/EG BL7.....23 H5
Highlands OL.....74 D1
 ROY/SHW OL2.....74 D1
Highlands Dr OFTN SK2.....173 G3
Highlands Rd OFTN SK2.....173 G3
 ROCH OL11.....41 E1
 ROY/SHW OL2.....59 E3
The Highlands MOSL OL5 *.....108 C1
High La CCHDY M21.....141 F3
 MPL/ROM SK6.....162 A2
High Lea CHD/CHDH SK8.....169 H4
High Lee La OLDE OL4.....61 G5
High Legh Rd OP/CLY M11.....117 E5
High Level Rd ROCH OL11.....30 B5
High Meadow
 CHD/CHDH SK8 *.....182 B4
Highmeadow RAD M26.....68 A3
High Mdw EDGW/EG BL7.....23 G3
Highmead St GTN M18.....130 C3
Highmere Dr CHH M8 *.....102 B4
High Moor Crs OLDE OL4.....76 D3
Highmore Dr BKLY M9.....88 B4
High Mt BOLE BL2.....35 F3
High Peak Rd AUL OL6.....108 B4
 OLDE OL4.....18 B2
High Peak St
 NEWH/MOS M40.....104 A4
Highshore Dr CHH M8.....102 A3
High Stile La OLDE OL4.....79 G2
High Stile St FWTH BL4.....66 B5
Highstone Dr CHH M8.....102 D4
High St ALT WA14.....165 G5
 ANC M4.....7 G3
 BOLS/LL BL3.....48 D5

BOLS/LL BL3.....67 E1
BRAM/HZG SK7.....185 G2
CHD/CHDH SK8.....170 A3
DROY M43.....117 H4
HEY OL10.....40 B3
HYDE SK14.....134 A5
LIT OL15.....20 C5
MDTN M24.....72 D5
MOSL OL5.....94 A5
OLD OL1.....9 G5
OLDE OL4.....92 D1
ROY/SHW OL2.....59 F5
ROY/SHW OL2.....60 A3
STKP SK1.....13 J3
STLY SK15.....120 D4
TOT/BURYW BL8.....37 E3
UPML OL3.....79 F4
WALK M28.....81 H4
WHIT OL12.....10 C5
Highthorne Gn ROY/SHW OL2.....58 D1
High View St BOL BL1.....34 A1
 BOLS/LL BL3 *.....48 B5
Highwood ROCH OL11.....28 B2
Highwood Cl BOLE BL2 *.....35 G5
High Wood Fold
 MPL/ROM SK6.....175 H1
Highworth Dr BOLS/LL BL3 *.....48 D4
Highworth Dr
 NEWH/MOS M40.....89 G5
Higifield Av SALE M33.....154 D3
Higson Av CCHDY M21.....141 F4
 ECC M30.....110 D5
 MPL/ROM SK6.....161 G4
Hilary Av CHD/CHDH SK8.....182 A4
 OLDS OL8.....106 C1
Hilary Cl HTNM SK4.....12 C3
Hilary Gv FWTH BL4.....65 H5
Hilary Rd WYTH/NTH M22.....180 A3
Hilary St ROCH OL11 *.....42 C5
Hilbre Av ROY/SHW OL2.....75 F2
Hilbury Av BKLY M9.....103 E1
Hilda Av CHD/CHDH SK8.....170 B4
 TOT/BURYW BL8.....26 A5
Hilda Gv RDSH SK5.....160 A2
Hilda St BOLS/LL BL3.....49 F5
 CHAD OL9 *.....8 A2
 HEY OL10.....41 E4
Hilden St OLDTF/WHR M16.....127 C4
Hildenborough Dr BURY BL9.....70 A2
Hilditch Cl NTHM/RTH M23.....168 A3
Hilary Av OLDE OL4.....93 H1
Hilliam Cl URM M41.....139 F2
Hilliard St CHH M8 *.....102 A5
Hillary Av AULW OL7.....107 E5
Hillary Rd HYDE SK14.....134 B3
Hillbank Cl BOL BL1.....33 F3
Hill Bank Cl STLY SK15.....109 C5
Hillbank St MDTN M24.....57 C3
Hillbre Wy WILM/AE SK9.....192 A3
Hillbrook Av NEWH/MOS M40 *.....89 E5
Hillbrook Rd BRAM/HZG SK7.....193 G1
 STKP SK1.....172 D1
Hill Brow BRAM/HZG SK7.....184 A1
Hill Cl OLDE OL4.....92 B2
Hillcote Wk GTN M18 *.....130 A2
Hill Cot Rd BOL BL1.....34 A1
Hill Court Ms MPL/ROM SK6.....162 A4
Hillcourt Rd MPL/ROM SK6.....162 A4
 MPL/ROM SK6.....186 D5
Hillcourt St CMANE M1.....128 B1
Hill Crs BKLY M9 *.....87 G5
Hillcrest HYDE SK14.....148 B4
Hill Crest Av HTNM SK4.....158 D4
Hillcrest Av HEY OL10.....40 B3
Hillcrest Crs HEY OL10.....40 B3
Hillcrest Dr BNG/LEV M19.....144 C4
 DTN/ASHW M34.....147 E4
Hillcrest Rd BRAM/HZG SK7.....184 A3
 OFTN SK2.....172 D3
 PWCH M25.....85 G3
 ROCH OL11.....42 C4
 OLDS OL8.....106 D2
Hillcroft Cl CHH M8.....102 B2
Hillcroft Rd ALT WA14.....164 D4
Hilldale Av BKLY M9.....88 A3
Hill Dr WILM/AE SK9.....192 B4
Hill End MPL/ROM SK6.....162 C2
Hillend La HYDE SK14.....149 H2
Hillend Pl NTHM/RTH M23.....155 H4
Hillend Rd NTHM/RTH M23.....155 H4
Hill Farm Cl OLDS OL8.....90 B3
Hillfield ORD M5.....112 C3
Hillfield Cl BRUN/LGST M13.....129 E3
Hillfield Dr BOLE BL2.....34 C5
 WALK M28.....96 B3
Hillfield Wk BOLE BL2.....34 C5
Hillgate Av ORD M5.....127 E1
Hillgate St AUL OL6.....119 H1
Hillier St BKLY M9.....103 F2
Hillier St North BKLY M9.....103 F2
Hillingdon Cl OLDS OL8.....106 C2
Hillingdon Dr NEWH/MOS M40.....89 E5
Hillingdon Rd STRET M32.....140 C2
 WHTF M45.....68 D5
Hillington Rd EDGY/DAV SK3.....12 A6
 SALE M33.....153 H2
Hillkirk Dr WHIT OL12.....18 E5
Hillkirk St OP/CLY M11.....115 H4
Hill La BKLY M9.....88 A4
 BOLE BL2.....3 H2
Hillman Cl NEWH/MOS M40.....115 F2
Hill Mt DUK SK16.....120 D5
Hill Ri ALT WA14.....164 D4
 MPL/ROM SK6.....162 A4
 RAMS BL0.....16 B4
Hillsborough Dr BURY BL9.....70 A2
Hill's Ct TOT/BURYW BL8.....27 E3
Hillsdale Gv BOLE BL2.....35 F3
Hill Side BOL BL1.....33 H1
Hillside Av BRO M7.....100 D2
 EDGW/EG BL7.....23 G4
 FWTH BL4.....65 H5
 HYDE SK14.....148 B5
 OLDE OL4.....78 B5
 OLDE OL4.....93 G2
 ROY/SHW OL2.....59 F4

ROY/SHW OL2.....60 C2
STLY SK15.....109 G4
UPML OL3.....79 F1
WALK M28.....81 H3
WHIT OL12.....69 F2
Hillside Cl BOLE BL2.....35 G5
 BOLS/LL BL3.....63 E2
 BRAM/HZG SK7.....184 B5
 NEWH/MOS M40.....103 H1
Hillside Crs AUL OL6.....108 A5
 BURY BL9.....69 E1
Hillside Dr MDTN M24.....72 C5
 SWIN M27.....100 A4
Hillside Gv MPL/ROM SK6.....163 G5
Hillside Rd HALE/TIMP WA15.....178 B1
 MPL/ROM SK6.....162 B1
 OFTN SK2.....173 F2
 RAMS BL0.....16 B3
Hillside Vw DTN/ASHW M34.....147 E4
 HALE/TIMP WA15.....18 C4
Hillside Wk WHIT OL12.....14 D1
Hills La BURY BL9.....70 B2
Hillspring Rd OLDE OL4.....93 F1
Hillstone Av WHIT OL12.....18 B4
Hillstone Cl TOT/BURYW BL8.....26 A1
Hill St ALT WA14.....165 G5
 BRO M7.....101 G4
 BURY BL9.....70 B2
 DID/WITH M20.....142 D4
 HALE/TIMP WA15.....178 B1
 MDTN M24.....72 D1
 MILN OL16.....10 E7
 OLDE OL4.....76 A5
 ROY/SHW OL2.....60 B3
 TOT/BURYW BL8.....37 E2
 WILM/AE SK9.....199 E2
Hill Top BOLS/LL BL3.....48 C4
 HALE/TIMP WA15.....178 B1
 MPL/ROM SK6.....162 A3
Hill Top Av CHD/CHDH SK8.....183 E4
 PWCH M25.....86 A3
 WILM/AE SK9.....199 E2
Hilltop Av BKLY M9.....88 A4
 WHTF M45.....70 A4
Hill Top Ct CHD/CHDH SK8.....183 E4
Hill Top Dr HALE/TIMP WA15.....178 B2
 ROCH OL11.....41 H3
Hilltop Dr MPL/ROM SK6.....174 B2
 ROY/SHW OL2.....75 F2
 TOT/BURYW BL8.....25 H5
Hilltop Gv WHTF M45.....70 A4
Hill Top Rd WALK M28.....80 B5
Hill Vw STLY SK15.....135 E2
Hill View Cl OLD OL1.....1 H1
Hillview Rd BOL BL1 *.....33 H2
 DTN/ASHW M34.....146 C1
Hillwood Av CHH M8.....87 G3
Hillyard St TOT/BURYW BL8.....37 H3
Hilly Cft EDGW/EG BL7.....23 E3
Hilmarton Cl BOLE BL2.....35 F1
Hilrose Av URM M41.....139 F1
Hilson Av URM M41.....138 D1
Hilton Av URM M41.....138 D1
Hilton Ct EDGY/DAV SK3 *.....12 C5
Hilton Crs AUL OL6.....107 F5
 PWCH M25.....86 A5
Hilton Dr AUL OL6.....107 F5
 IRL M44.....150 B1
 PWCH M25.....85 H4
Hilton Fold La MDTN M24.....73 E3
Hilton Gv POY/DIS SK12.....195 G4
Hilton La PWCH M25.....81 G4
 WALK M28.....81 H4
Hilton Rd BRAM/HZG SK7.....184 B1
 BURY BL9.....53 G1
 POY/DIS SK12.....195 G2
 WYTH/NTH M22.....181 E1
Hiltons Cl OLDS OL8.....8 E7
Hiltons Farm Cl
 DTN/ASHW M34.....132 B3
Hilton Sq SWIN M27.....99 E4
Hilton St ANC M4.....7 G3
 BOLE BL2.....49 H2
 BRO M7.....101 H5
 BOLE BL2.....5 F1
 EDGY/DAV SK3.....12 D5
 HYDE SK14 *.....134 A3
 LHULT M38.....81 E3
Hilton St North BRO M7.....101 G4
Hilton Wk MDTN M24.....116 D2
Himley Rd OP/CLY M11.....116 D2
Hinchcombe Cl CHAD OL9.....6 B4
Hinchley Rd BRAM/HZG SK7.....184 A1
Hinchley Wy SWIN M27.....84 A5
Hindburn Cl WHTF M45.....69 F2
Hindburn Dr WALK M28.....96 B2
Hinde St NEWH/MOS M40.....103 H2
Hind Hill St HEY OL10.....40 C4
Hinde Dr ROY/SHW OL2.....74 D1
Hindle St RAD M26.....67 G1
Hindley Av WYTH/NTH M22.....180 A2
Hindley St AULW OL7.....119 E4
 STKP SK1.....13 K7
Hindsford Cl NTHM/RTH M23.....155 E5
Hind St BOLE BL2.....50 A1
 TOT/BURYW BL8.....37 H5
Hind St BOLE BL2.....50 A1
Hinkler Av BOLS/LL BL3.....62 D2
Hinton WHIT OL12.....10 B4
Hinton Cl ROCH OL11.....28 B3
Hinton St HYDE SK14.....148 C3
Hinton St ANC M4 *.....7 H1
 OLDS OL8.....9 H5

Hobson Ct DTN/ASHW M34.....132 B2
Hobson Crs DTN/ASHW M34.....132 B2
Hobson Moor Rd HYDE SK14.....135 H2
Hobson St FAIL M35.....104 C4
 OLD OL1.....9 G5
 OP/CLY M11.....131 F1
 STKP SK1.....145 E1
Hockenhull Cl
 WYTH/NTH M22.....180 D2
Hockerley Cl SALE M33.....153 E1
Hockley Cl POY/DIS SK12.....195 C4
Hockley Paddock
 POY/DIS SK12.....195 G4
Hockley Rd NTHM/RTH M23.....167 G4
 POY/DIS SK12.....195 C4
Hodder Av LIT OL15.....20 C2
Hodder Bank OFTN SK2.....173 F4
Hodder Wy WHTF M45.....70 B4
Hoddesdon St CHH M8.....102 C3
Hodge Clough Rd OLDE OL4.....60 C5
Hodge La WHIT OL12.....149 H5
 SLFD M6.....113 E4
Hodge Rd OLD OL1.....76 C1
 WALK M28.....82 A5
Hodge St BKLY M9.....103 G1
Hodgson Dr HALE/TIMP WA15.....168 B1
Hodgson St AUL OL6.....119 F3
 CHH M8.....102 A5
Hodnett Av URM M41.....137 G2
Hodson Fold OLDS OL8.....106 D1
Hodson Rd SWIN M27.....83 H5
Hogarth Rd MPL/ROM SK6.....175 C1
Hogarth Rd MPL/ROM SK6.....175 C1
Holbeach Cl TOT/BURYW BL8.....38 A1
Holbeck Av WHIT OL12.....18 C4
Holbeck Gv RUSH/FAL M14.....129 H5
Holbeton Cl CHH M8.....101 H5
Holborn Av FAIL M35.....105 C3
Holborn Dr CHH M8.....102 C5
Holborn Gdns ROCH OL11.....42 C1
Holborn Sq ROCH OL11.....42 C1
Holborn St ROCH OL11.....42 C1
 STKP SK1.....13 C4
Holbrook Av LHULT M38.....81 F1
Holcombe Cl ALT WA14.....165 E5
 FWTH BL4.....82 D2
 OLDE OL4.....77 F5
 SLFD M6.....113 F5
Holcombe Ct RAMS BL0.....16 B5
Holcombe Crs FWTH BL4.....82 D1
Holcombe Lee RAMS BL0.....16 B5
Holcombe Old Rd
 TOT/BURYW BL8.....16 A5
Holcombe Rd BOLS/LL BL3.....48 C4
 RUSH/FAL M14.....143 C4
 TOT/BURYW BL8.....26 A1
Holcombe View Cl OLDE OL4.....76 C2
Holden Av BOL BL1.....22 D5
 BURY BL9.....26 D1
 OLDTF/WHR M16.....142 A2
 RAMS BL0.....16 B5
Holden Clough Dr AULW OL7.....106 D3
Holden Fold La ROY/SHW OL2.....74 D2
Holden Rd BRO M7.....101 C1
Holden St AUL OL6.....107 F5
 OLDS OL8.....91 C4
 OLD OL1.....11 F1
Holder Av BOLS/LL BL3.....51 E4
Holderness Dr ROY/SHW OL2.....74 D2
Holdgate Cl HULME M15.....127 H5
Holdsworth St SWIN M27.....99 C3
Holebottom AUL OL6.....107 F4
Hole House Fold
 MPL/ROM SK6.....162 A4
Holford Av RUSH/FAL M14.....142 D1
Holford St WH MILN OL16.....11 K3
Holiday La OFTN SK2.....173 C3
Holkar Mdw EDGW/EG BL7.....23 C5
Holker Cl BRUN/LGST M13.....129 F4
 POY/DIS SK12.....195 C3
Holkham Cl ANC M4 *.....115 F3
Holland Cl POY/DIS SK12.....195 F4
Holland Gv AUL OL6.....107 E4
Holland Rd WHIT OL12.....10 B5
Holland Rd BRAM/HZG SK7.....183 H5
 CHH M8.....87 E5
Holland St BOL BL1.....34 A2
 DTN/ASHW M34.....132 A4
 HEY OL10.....41 E4
 MILN OL16.....20 A4
 MOS M40.....52 D5
 SLFD M6.....100 C5
 WHIT OL12.....10 A6
Holland St East
 DTN/ASHW M34.....132 A4
Holland St West
 DTN/ASHW M34.....131 H4
Hollies La WILM/AE SK9.....175 F4
The Hollies CHD/CHDH SK8 *.....169 G4
 DID/WITH M20.....157 C3
Hollin Acre WHTN BL5.....62 A2
Hollin Bank HTNM SK4.....144 D4
Hollin Crs UPML OL3.....94 B3
Hollin Dr MDTN M24.....56 B5
Hollinhey Av WYTH/NTH M22.....181 E3
Hollinhey Rd
 WYTH/NTH M22.....181 D3
Hollin Gn MDTN M24.....72 D1
Hollinghurst Av
 NEWH/MOS M40.....90 A3
Hollingworth Cl STKP SK1.....13 C5
Hollingworth Dr
 MPL/ROM SK6.....187 E1
Hollingworth Rd LIT OL15.....21 E4
 MPL/ROM SK6.....161 F2
Hollingworth St CHAD OL9.....90 C4
Hollinhall St OLDE OL4.....76 D5
Hollin La MDTN M24.....56 B5
 RAD M26.....52 D5
 SLFD M6.....100 C5
 WHIT OL12.....10 A4
Hollinhurst Dr HOR/BR BL6.....46 D2
Hollinhurst Rd RAD M26.....68 C3

Hollin La MDTN M24 .... 56 C5
  ROCH OL11 .... 28 B5
  WILM/AE SK9 .... 191 E2
Hollins FWTH BL4 * 64 C4
Hollins Av HYDE SK14 .... 148 A4
Hollin St OLDE OL4 .... 77 E4
Hollins Brook Cl BURY BL9 * 54 A3
Hollins Brook Wy BURY BL9 .... 54 A3
Hollins Brow BURY BL9 .... 53 C5
Hollins Cl BURY BL9 .... 54 A5
Hollinscough Cl
  WYTH/NTH M22 .... 168 D4
Hollinscroft Av
  HALE/TIMP WA15 .... 167 E4
Hollins Green Rd
  MPL/ROM SK6 .... 175 E3
Hollins Gv SALE M33 .... 154 B2
  WGTN/LGST M12 .... 129 H5
Hollins La BURY BL9 .... 53 H4
  MOSL OL5 .... 109 E1
  MPL/ROM SK6 .... 175 E3
  MPL/ROM SK6 .... 175 H1
  UPML OL3 .... 95 G2
Hollins Ms BURY BL9 .... 54 B5
Hollins Mt MPL/ROM SK6 .... 175 G1
Hollins Rd OLDE OL4 .... 77 E4
  OLDS OL8 .... 90 D5
  OLDS OL8 .... 91 G4
Hollins St BOLE BL2 .... 3 J7
  OLDE OL4 .... 93 E1
  STLY SK15 .... 120 C5
Hollinswood Rd BOLE BL2 .... 50 B4
  WALK M28 .... 96 C4
Hollinwell Cl MDTN M24 .... 56 C5
Hollinwood Av CHAD OL9 .... 90 B5
  NEWH/MOS M40 .... 89 G5
Hollinwood La MPL/ROM SK6 .... 187 G2
Holloway Dr WALK M28 .... 98 B1
Hollowbrook Wy WHIT OL12 .... 29 G1
Hollow End RDSH SK5 .... 145 H4
Hollowfield ROCH OL11 .... 28 A2
Hollow Mdw RAD M26 .... 83 F1
Hollowspell WHIT OL12 .... 19 H5
The Hollows
  CHD/CHDH SK8 * 181 H3
Hollow Vale Dr RDSH SK5 .... 145 G3
Holly Av CHD/CHDH SK8 .... 170 A4
  URM M41 .... 138 B1
  WALK M28 .... 82 B5
Holly Bank DROY M43 .... 118 B2
  NEWH/MOS M40 .... 104 B5
  ROY/SHW OL2 .... 59 E4
Hollybank Rd DUK SK16 .... 120 C5
Holly Bank Rd WILM/AE SK9 .... 199 E1
Hollybank St RAD M26 .... 68 A1
Hollybrook Dene
  MPL/ROM SK6 .... 162 D4
Hollybush St GTN M18 .... 130 D2
Holly Cl HALE/TIMP WA15 .... 166 B3
Holly Ct HYDE SK14 .... 148 C1
Hollycroft Av BOLE BL2 .... 50 B4
Holly Dene Dr HOR/BR BL6 .... 46 C2
Holly Dr SALE M33 .... 154 B2
Hollyedge Dr PWCH M25 .... 85 H5
Holly Gra ALT WA14 .... 177 G2
  BRAM/HZG SK7 .... 184 A1
Holly Gv BOL BL1 .... 33 F5
  CHAD OL9 .... 74 C4
  DTN/ASHW M34 .... 132 D5
  FWTH BL4 .... 65 F4
  HOR/BR BL6 .... 46 C4
  OLDE OL4 .... 76 D4
  SALE M33 .... 155 E2
  STLY SK15 .... 120 B5
Hollyhedge Av
  WYTH/NTH M22 .... 168 C4
Hollyhedge Court Rd
  WYTH/NTH M22 .... 168 D4
Hollyhedge Rd
  NTHM/RTH M23 .... 168 A4
Hollyhey Dr NTHM/RTH M23 .... 156 A5
Hollyhouse Dr MPL/ROM SK6 .... 161 H1
Holly House Dr URM M41 .... 137 F1
Hollyhurst WALK M28 .... 98 A4
Holly La OLDS OL8 .... 90 D5
  WILM/AE SK9 .... 199 E5
Holly Mill Crs BOL BL1 .... 34 A2
Hollymount Av OFTN SK2 .... 172 D4
Hollymount Dr OFTN SK2 .... 172 D4
  OLDE OL4 .... 76 D4
Hollymount Gdns OFTN SK2 .... 173 E4
Hollymount Rd OFTN SK2 .... 172 D4
Holly Oak Gdns HEY OL10 .... 40 C5
Holly Rd BRAM/HZG SK7 .... 193 H2
  HTNM SK4 .... 159 F1
  MPL/ROM SK6 .... 186 D5
  POY/DIS SK12 .... 195 F4
  SWIN M27 .... 98 A5
Holly Rd North WILM/AE SK9 .... 198 D4
Holly Rd South WILM/AE SK9 .... 198 C4
Holly Royde Cl DID/WITH M20 .... 142 C5
Holly St BOL BL1 .... 34 A2
  BURY BL9 .... 5 H3
  BURY BL9 .... 16 D5
  DROY M43 .... 117 E3
  MILN OL16 .... 43 G4
  STKP SK1 .... 13 K4
  TOT/BURYW BL8 .... 26 D2
  WGTN/LGST M12 .... 115 H5
Hollythorn Av CHD/CHDH SK8 .... 183 F5
Hollyway WYTH/NTH M22 .... 168 D1
Hollywood Rd BOL BL1 .... 33 E4
Hollywood Wy HTNM SK4 .... 158 A1
Holmbrook Wk HTNM SK4 .... 102 B4
Holm Ct SLFD M6 .... 113 F2
Holmcroft Rd GTN M18 .... 144 D1
Holmdale Av BNG/LEV M19 .... 158 B1
Holme Av TOT/BURYW BL8 .... 37 H1
Holme Beech Gv OFTN SK2 * 172 D2
Holme Crs ROY/SHW OL2 .... 74 D2
Holme Park Gdns WALK M28 .... 154 C2
Holme Park Wy FAIL M35 .... 105 G3
Holme Rd DID/WITH M20 .... 157 E3
Holmes Cottages BOL BL1 * 33 F3
Holmes Rd WHIT OL12 .... 29 G4

Holmes St BOLS/LL BL3 .... 49 E5
  CHD/CHDH SK8 .... 170 B3
  OFTN SK2 .... 13 F7
  WHIT OL12 .... 19 H5
  WHIT OL12 .... 19 H5
Holme St HYDE SK14 .... 147 H1
Holmeswood Cl WILM/AE SK9 .... 199 F2
Holmeswood Rd BOLS/LL BL3 .... 64 C2
Holmfield Av BKLY M9 .... 103 G3
  PWCH M25 .... 86 B4
Holmfield Av West BKLY M9 .... 103 G4
Holmfield Cl HTNM SK4 .... 159 G3
Holmfield Dr CHD/CHDH SK8 .... 183 E4
Holmfield Gn BOLS/LL BL3 .... 63 G3
Holmfirth Rd UPML OL3 .... 95 G3
Holmfirth St BRUN/LGST M13 .... 129 G4
Holmlea Rd DROY M43 .... 117 F3
Holmleigh Av BKLY M9 .... 103 F1
Holmpark Rd OP/CLY M11 .... 131 E1
Holmside Gdns BNG/LEV M19 .... 158 A2
Holmwood ALT WA14 .... 176 D1
Holmwood Rd DID/WITH M20 .... 157 G1
Holroyd St MILN OL16 .... 10 E7
  OP/CLY M11 * 116 B5
Holset Dr ALT WA14 .... 165 E4
Holst Av CHH M8 .... 102 B4
Holstein Av WHIT OL12 .... 18 B4
Holtby St BKLY M9 .... 103 F1
Holthouse Rd TOT/BURYW BL8 .... 36 D1
Holt La FAIL M35 .... 105 F3
Holt Lane Ms FAIL M35 .... 105 F3
Holts La OLDE OL4 .... 92 C3
  WILM/AE SK9 .... 191 E4
Holts Ter WHIT OL12 .... 10 B1
Holt St ALT WA14 .... 165 F2
  BOLS/LL BL3 .... 48 C4
  DTN/ASHW M34 .... 118 D5
  ECC M30 .... 110 D5
  MILN OL16 .... 44 D1
  NEWH/MOS M40 .... 103 G5
  OLDE OL4 .... 76 B4
  RAMS BL0 .... 16 C5
  STKP SK1 .... 13 G6
  SWIN M27 .... 84 A5
  WHIT OL12 .... 14 B4
Holt West RAMS BL0 .... 16 C5
Holt Town NEWH/MOS M40 .... 116 A2
Holwick Rd NTHM/RTH M23 .... 155 G5
Holwood Dr OLDTF/WHR M16 .... 142 A3
Holy Harbour St BOL BL1 * 33 F4
Holyhurst Wk BOL BL1 * 33 H4
Holyoake Rd WALK M28 .... 82 A5
Holyoake St DROY M43 .... 118 B3
Holyoak St NEWH/MOS M40 .... 104 B4
Holyrood Cl PWCH M25 .... 86 B1
Holyrood Dr PWCH M25 .... 86 B1
  SWIN M27 .... 98 B3
Holyrood Gv PWCH M25 .... 86 B1
Holyrood Rd PWCH M25 .... 86 B2
Holyrood St
  NEWH/MOS M40 .... 117 E1
  OLD OL1 .... 75 H3
Holywell St RUSH/FAL M14 .... 128 D3
Homebury Dr OP/CLY M11 * 116 C3
Home Dr MDTN M24 .... 88 C1
Home Farm Av HEY OL10 .... 149 H2
Homelands Cl SALE M33 .... 154 A4
Homelands Rd SALE M33 .... 154 A4
Homer Dr MPL/ROM SK6 .... 175 C1
Homerton Rd
  NEWH/MOS M40 .... 116 C1
Homestead Cl PART M31 .... 151 F2
Homestead Crs BNG/LEV M19 .... 158 A3
Homestead Gdns WHIT OL12 .... 20 A3
Homestead Rd POY/DIS SK12 .... 197 H1
Hometel RUSH/FAL M14 .... 143 E2
Homewood Av
  WYTH/NTH M22 .... 156 C5
Homewood Rd
  WYTH/NTH M22 .... 156 B5
Honduras St OLDE OL4 .... 9 K3
Hondwith Cl BOLE BL2 .... 34 C1
Honeycombe Cottages
  CHD/CHDH SK8 * 170 B4
Honey St CHH M8 .... 114 D1
Honeysuckle Cl
  MPL/ROM SK6 .... 161 H1
  NTHM/RTH M23 .... 155 E5
Honeysuckle Dr STLY SK15 .... 121 E5
Honeysuckle Wv WHIT OL12 .... 18 C5
Honeywell La OLDS OL8 .... 91 G4
Honeywood Cl RAMS BL0 .... 16 B5
Honford Rd WYTH/NTH M22 .... 168 A5
Hong Kong Av
  HALE/TIMP WA15 .... 179 H4
Honister Dr MDTN M24 .... 72 C2
Honister Rd BKLY M9 .... 103 G3
Honister Wv ROCH OL11 .... 42 A2
Honiton Av HYDE SK14 .... 149 E1
Honiton Cl CHAD OL9 .... 74 A1
Honiton Dr BOLE BL2 .... 50 D3
Honiton Gv RAD M26 .... 51 G4
Honiton Wy ALT WA14 .... 164 D5
Honor St BRUN/LGST M13 .... 129 F1
Hood Sq OLDE OL4 .... 93 F2
Hood St ANC M4 .... 7 J3
Hoole Cl CHD/CHDH SK8 .... 170 D4
Hooley Range HTNM SK4 .... 159 E3
Hooper St EDGY/DAV SK3 .... 13 F4
  OLDE OL4 .... 93 E2
  WGTN/LGST M12 .... 115 G5
Hooton St BOLS/LL BL3 .... 64 B1
  NEWH/MOS M40 .... 115 H2
Hopcroft Cl BKLY M9 .... 87 C1
Hope Av BOLE BL2 .... 35 F1
  BOLE BL2 .... 81 G3
  LHULT M38 .... 81 C4
  STRET M32 .... 125 C5
Hope Carr Rd SALE M33 .... 154 C3

Hope Rd PWCH M25 .... 85 H5
  RUSH/FAL M14 .... 129 E4
  SALE M33 .... 154 C3
Hopes Carr STKP SK1 .... 13 H4
Hope St AUL OL6 .... 107 G5
  BRAM/HZG SK7 .... 184 D1
  BRO M7 .... 101 G3
  CMANE M1 .... 7 H5
  DTN/ASHW M34 .... 132 B3
  DUK SK16 .... 119 H5
  HEY OL10 .... 56 C1
  HTNM SK4 .... 12 D3
  LHULT M38 .... 81 F3
  OLD OL1 .... 76 A5
  ORD M5 .... 113 H4
  RAMS BL0 .... 16 C3
  ROY/SHW OL2 .... 60 A2
  SWIN M27 .... 99 F2
  WHIT OL12 .... 10 C4
Hope Ter DUK SK16 .... 119 G5
Hopkin Av OLD OL1 .... 76 A4
Hopkins Fld ALT WA14 .... 177 E3
Hopkinson Av
  DTN/ASHW M34 .... 132 B3
Hopkinson Cl UPML OL3 .... 79 H4
Hopkinson Rd BKLY M9 .... 88 A2
Hopkins St HYDE SK14 .... 133 H4
Hopkin St OLD OL1 .... 9 H3
  WGTN/LGST M12 .... 129 H5
Hoppet La DROY M43 .... 118 B3
Hopton Av WYTH/NTH M22 .... 180 D1
Hopwood Av ECC M30 .... 111 E2
  HEY OL10 .... 40 A5
Hopwood Cl BURY BL9 .... 69 G1
Hopwood Rd MDTN M24 .... 56 D5
Hopwood St CSLFD M3 * 6 C2
  NEWH/MOS M40 .... 104 A4
  SWIN M27 .... 99 F2
Horace Barnes Cl
  RUSH/FAL M14 .... 128 B5
Horace Gv HTNM SK4 .... 159 H2
Horace St BOL BL1 .... 33 C4
Horatio St GTN M18 .... 131 E2
Horbury Av GTN M18 .... 130 C5
Horbury Dr TOT/BURYW BL8 .... 37 H4
Horeb St BOLS/LL BL3 .... 48 C4
Horest La UPML OL3 .... 61 G1
Horley Cl TOT/BURYW BL8 .... 26 C1
Hornbeam Cl
  HALE/TIMP WA15 .... 167 F4
  SALE M33 .... 153 F1
Hornbeam Ct SLFD M6 .... 113 F2
Hornbeam Rd BNG/LEV M19 .... 144 B1
Hornby Av BKLY M9 .... 88 B2
Hornby Dr BOLS/LL BL3 .... 63 F2
Hornby Rd STRET M32 .... 126 C4
Hornby St BURY BL9 .... 4 E4
  CHH M8 .... 114 C1
  HEY OL10 .... 41 E5
  MDTN M24 .... 72 D4
  OLDS OL8 .... 8 D6
Horncastle Cl TOT/BURYW BL8 .... 38 A1
Horncastle Rd
  NEWH/MOS M40 .... 104 A4
Hornchurch Ct HEY OL10 .... 56 B2
Hornchurch St HULME M15 .... 127 H2
Horne Dr ANC M4 .... 115 H3
Horne St BURY BL9 .... 53 G1
Hornsea Cl CHAD OL9 .... 74 A3
  TOT/BURYW BL8 .... 37 E4
Hornsea Rd OFTN SK2 .... 173 H4
Hornsea Wk OP/CLY M11 * 116 B4
Horridge Fold Av WHTN BL5 .... 63 G2
Horridge Fold EDGW/EG BL7 * 23 H1
Horrobin Fold EDGW/EG BL7 * 23 H1
Horrobin La EDGW/EG BL7 .... 23 H1
Horrocks Fold Av BOL BL1 .... 22 C5
Horrocks St BOLS/LL BL3 .... 47 H4
  RAD M26 * 52 C5
Horsa St BOLE BL2 .... 3 J1
Horsedge St OLD OL1 .... 9 H1
Horsefield Av WHIT OL12 .... 18 B2
Horsefield Cl CCHDY M21 .... 142 A4
Horseforth La UPML OL3 .... 94 D5
Horseshoe La EDGW/EG BL7 .... 23 F3
  MDTN M24 .... 90 A1
Hotel Rd MANAIR M90 .... 180 B5
Hotel St BOL BL1 .... 2 E5
Hothersall Rd RDSH SK5 .... 145 F4
Hotspur Ct RUSH/FAL M14 .... 128 D3
Hough Cl OLDS OL8 .... 91 E5
Hough End Av CCHDY M21 .... 141 G5
Houghton Av OLDS OL8 .... 91 E5
Houghton La SWIN M27 .... 98 C5
Houghton Rd CHH M8 .... 102 B1
Houghton St BOLS/LL BL3 .... 64 A2
  BURY BL9 .... 4 D2
  SWIN M27 .... 99 E3
  SWIN M27 .... 100 A4
Hough Wk BRO M7 .... 114 A2
Houldsworth Av ALT WA14 .... 165 H2
Houldsworth Ml RDSH SK5 .... 145 E4

Houldsworth St CMANE M1 .... 7 H3
  RAD M26 .... 52 A4
  RDSH SK5 .... 145 E4
Houseley Av CHAD OL9 .... 90 B4
Houson St OLDS OL8 .... 9 G6
Houston Pk SALQ M50 .... 113 E4
Hove Cl TOT/BURYW BL8 .... 26 A2
Hoveden Rd CHH M8 .... 114 C1
Hove Dr RUSH/FAL M14 .... 143 E3
Hove St BOLS/LL BL3 .... 48 B4
Hove St North BOLS/LL BL3 * 48 B4
Hovey Cl CHH M8 .... 102 A3
Hovingham St MILN OL16 .... 11 C5
Hovis St OP/CLY M11 .... 116 D5
Howard Av BOLS/LL BL3 .... 47 H5
  CHD/CHDH SK8 .... 182 D5
  ECC M30 .... 111 E2
  FWTH BL4 .... 66 C5
Howard Cl MPL/ROM SK6 .... 161 E4
Howard Ct AUL OL6 .... 119 G2
  HALE/TIMP WA15 * 166 C3
Howard Dr HALE/TIMP WA15 .... 178 B3
Howard Hl BURY BL9 .... 53 H5
Howardian Cl OLDS OL8 .... 91 F5
Howard La DTN/ASHW M34 .... 132 C4
Howard Pl MILN OL16 .... 10 E4
Howard Rd WYTH/NTH M22 .... 156 C5
Howards La MOSL OL5 .... 109 F1
Howard St AULW OL7 .... 119 F2
  BOL BL1 .... 34 A5
  CHH M8 .... 102 C2
  OLDE OL4 .... 76 D4
  ORD M5 .... 113 F5
  RAD M26 .... 68 C1
  ROY/SHW OL2 .... 59 H2
  STKP SK1 .... 13 G1
  STLY SK15 .... 121 G1
  STRET M32 .... 140 B1
  WHIT OL12 .... 10 B4
Howarth Av WALK M28 .... 96 D2
Howarth Cross St MILN OL16 .... 30 C1
Howarth Dr IRL M44 .... 136 B2
Howarth Farm Wy
  WHIT OL12 .... 19 H5
Howarth Sq MILN OL16 .... 11 F5
Howarth St FWTH BL4 .... 66 C4
  LIT OL15 .... 21 E5
  OLDTF/WHR M16 .... 127 F4
  WHTN BL5 .... 62 A4
Howbridge Cl WALK M28 .... 96 D2
Howbro Dr AULW OL7 .... 105 H4
Howclough Cl WALK M28 .... 82 C5
How Clough Dr WALK M28 .... 82 C5
Howcroft Cl BOL BL1 .... 2 C3
Howcroft St BOLS/LL BL3 .... 48 C4
Howden Cl RDSH SK5 .... 145 E1
Howden Rd BKLY M9 .... 87 H2
How Dr RAMS BL0 .... 26 C1
Howell Cft North BOL BL1 * 2 E5
Howell Cft South BOL BL1 * 2 E5
Howells Av SALE M33 .... 154 D4
Howe St AULW OL7 .... 118 D5
  BRO M7 .... 101 F3
Howgill Crs OLDS OL8 .... 91 F4
Howgill St OP/CLY M11 .... 117 E4
How Lea Dr BURY BL9 .... 27 G5
Howsin Av BOLE BL2 .... 34 C2
Howton Cl WGTN/LGST M12 .... 129 H4
Howty Cl WILM/AE SK9 .... 199 G1
Hoxton Cl MPL/ROM SK6 .... 161 H2
Hoy Dr URM M41 .... 124 C3
Hoylake Cl NEWH/MOS M40 .... 104 C2
Hoylake Rd EDGY/DAV SK3 .... 170 D1
  SALE M33 .... 155 G4
Hoyland Cl WGTN/LGST M12 .... 129 G2
Hoyle Av OLDS OL8 .... 8 E6
Hoyles Ct RAD M26 .... 51 F5
Hoyle's Ter MILN OL16 .... 31 F5
Hoyle St RAD M26 .... 68 C3
  WHIT OL12 .... 14 C2
Hoyle Wk BRUN/LGST M13 * 128 C2
Hucclecote Av
  WYTH/NTH M22 .... 180 B2
Hucklow Av NTHM/RTH M23 .... 179 F3
Hudcar La BURY BL9 .... 5 G1
Huddart Cl ORD M5 .... 113 G5
Hudderfield Rd OLDE OL4 .... 76 B4
  OLDE OL4 .... 77 F4
  STLY SK15 .... 121 F3
  UPML OL3 .... 79 F1
Hudson Rd BOLS/LL BL3 .... 64 A1
  HYDE SK14 .... 148 A4
Hudson St CHAD OL9 .... 90 B5
Hudsons Wk ROCH OL11 .... 29 E4
Hudswell Cl WHTF M45 .... 69 F4
Hughenden Ct
  TOT/BURYW BL8 .... 26 A4
Hughes Cl BURY BL9 .... 4 C4
  FAIL M35 .... 104 D2
Hughes St BOL BL1 .... 33 G4
  OP/CLY M11 .... 115 H5
Hughley Cl ROY/SHW OL2 .... 59 G5
Hugh Lupus St BOL BL1 .... 34 E1
Hugh Oldham Dr BRO M7 .... 101 F4
Hugh St MILN OL16 .... 10 E5
Hughtrede St MILN OL16 .... 43 G3
Hugo St FWTH BL4 .... 65 G2
  NEWH/MOS M40 .... 103 H4
  ROCH OL11 .... 42 A5
Hulbert St MDTN M24 .... 73 E3
Hull Sq CSLFD M3 .... 114 A3
Hully St STLY SK15 .... 120 D5
Hulme Hall Av CHD/CHDH SK8 .... 166 D2
Hulme Hall Cl CHD/CHDH SK8 .... 182 D3
Hulme Hall Crs CHD/CHDH SK8 .... 182 D4
Hulme Hall La
  NEWH/MOS M40 .... 115 H1
  HULME M15 .... 127 G1
Hulme Pl ORD M5 * 113 H4
Hulme Rd BOLS/LL BL3 .... 64 B5
  DTN/ASHW M34 .... 133 E3
  HTNM SK4 .... 159 G1
  RAD M26 .... 66 D1
  SALE M33 .... 155 E2

Hulme St AUL OL6 .... 120 A1
  BOL BL1 .... 3 F3
  HULME M15 .... 127 H1
  OLDS OL8 .... 91 F3
  ORD M5 .... 113 H4
  STKP SK1 .... 172 C2
  TOT/BURYW BL8 .... 4 A2
Hulton Av WALK M28 .... 81 G4
Hulton Cl BOLS/LL BL3 .... 63 H1
Hulton Dr BOLS/LL BL3 .... 63 H1
  OLDTF/WHR M16 .... 127 H4
Hulton La BOLS/LL BL3 .... 63 H1
Hulton St DTN/ASHW M34 .... 132 B4
  FAIL M35 .... 104 C3
  ORD M5 .... 126 D1
Humber Dr BURY BL9 .... 27 H5
Humber Rd MILN OL16 .... 31 H5
Humberstone Av HULME M15 .... 127 H1
Humber St CHH M8 .... 102 B3
  SALQ M50 .... 112 C4
Humber St BNG/LEV M19 .... 144 B5
  MILN OL16 .... 43 F1
Humphrey Crs URM M41 .... 139 G1
Humphrey La URM M41 .... 139 G1
Humphrey Pk URM M41 .... 139 G2
Humphrey Rd
  OLDTF/WHR M16 .... 127 E3
Humphrey St CHH M8 .... 102 A2
Huncoat Av HTNM SK4 .... 159 G1
Huncote Dr BKLY M9 .... 103 F1
Hunger Hill Av BOLS/LL BL3 .... 63 F1
Hunstanton Dr
  TOT/BURYW BL8 .... 38 A1
Hunston Rd SALE M33 .... 154 A3
Hunt Av ALT WA14 .... 107 E5
Hunter Dr RAD M26 .... 52 B4
Hunters Cl MPL/ROM SK6 .... 175 C1
Hunters Ct STLY SK15 .... 121 C5
Hunters HI BURY BL9 .... 16 A5
Hunters La MILN OL16 .... 10 C5
Hunters Ms SALE M33 .... 154 B2
  WILM/AE SK9 .... 199 F3
Hunterston Av ECC M30 .... 111 H3
Hunt Fold Dr TOT/BURYW BL8 .... 26 A2
Huntingdon Crs RDSH SK5 * 160 D1
Huntingdon Wy
  DTN/ASHW M34 .... 133 H4
Huntington Av
  DID/WITH M20 .... 142 C4
Huntley Av HTNM SK4 .... 159 H1
Huntley Mount Rd BURY BL9 .... 5 J1
Huntley Rd CHH M8 .... 86 C5
  EDGY/DAV SK3 .... 171 E2
Huntley St BKLY M9 .... 5 K2
Huntly Cha WILM/AE SK9 .... 199 G4
Huntly Rd BURY BL9 .... 54 A2
Huntly Wy HYDE SK14 .... 146 C5
Huntroyde Av BOLE BL2 .... 3 K1
Hunts Bank CSLFD M3 .... 6 E2
Huntsham Cl ALT WA14 .... 165 E3
Hunt Sq BKLY M9 .... 100 A5
Huntsman Dr IRL M44 .... 136 B4
Huntspill Rd ALT WA14 .... 165 C2
Hunts Rd SLFD M6 .... 100 A5
Hunt St BKLY M9 .... 103 E1
Hurdlow Av BRO M7 .... 100 D5
Hurdsfield Rd OFTN SK2 .... 172 D5
Hurford Av GTN M18 .... 130 C1
Hurlbote Cl WILM/AE SK9 .... 192 A2
Hurley Dr CHD/CHDH SK8 .... 182 B2
Hurlston Rd BOLS/LL BL3 .... 64 C2
Hurst Av CHD/CHDH SK8 .... 193 F1
  SALE M33 .... 153 F3
Hurstbank Av BNG/LEV M19 * 158 A2
Hurst Bank Rd AUL OL6 .... 120 B1
Hurstbourne Av OP/CLY M11 .... 116 C2
Hurst Brook Cl AUL OL6 .... 119 H1
Hurstbrook Dr STRET M32 .... 139 F1
Hurst Cl WHTN BL5 .... 62 B5
Hurstead Gn WHIT OL12 .... 20 A4
Hurstead Rd MILN OL16 .... 31 G5
Hurstfield Rd WALK M28 .... 96 C2
Hurstfold Av BNG/LEV M19 .... 158 A3
Hurst Green Cl RAD M26 .... 52 A4
Hurst Gv AUL OL6 .... 107 H5
Hurst Hall Dr AUL OL6 .... 107 H5
Hursthead Rd CHD/CHDH SK8 .... 183 E5
Hursthead Wk
  BRUN/LGST M13 .... 128 C1
Hurst Lea Ct WILM/AE SK9 .... 200 D2
Hurst Meadow MILN OL16 .... 43 G4
Hurst St BOLS/LL BL3 .... 64 B1
  BURY BL9 .... 5 H6
  CHAD OL9 .... 132 D2
  DUK SK16 .... 132 D2
  RDSH SK5 .... 145 E4
  ROCH OL11 .... 41 H1
  WALK M28 .... 81 H1
Hurstvale Av CHD/CHDH SK8 .... 181 G3
Hurstville Rd CCHDY M21 .... 141 F5
Hurstway Dr BKLY M9 .... 88 B4
Hurstwood AUL OL6 .... 108 A4
  BOL BL1 .... 23 E5
Hurstwood Cl OLDS OL8 .... 92 B3
Hurstwood Gv OFTN SK2 .... 173 G3
Hus St DROY M43 .... 117 G5
Husteads La UPML OL3 .... 78 B3
Hutchins La OLDE OL4 .... 76 D5
Hutchinson Rd ROCH OL11 .... 28 A2
Hutchinson St ROCH OL11 .... 29 E5
Hutchinson Wy RAD M26 .... 68 B2
Hutton Av AUL OL6 .... 120 B3
  WALK M28 .... 96 A4
Huxley Av CHH M8 .... 102 B4
Huxley Cl BRAM/HZG SK7 .... 183 H5
Huxley Dr BRAM/HZG SK7 .... 183 H5
Huxley St ALT WA14 .... 165 G2
  BOL BL1 .... 33 E2
  OLDE OL4 .... 92 B2
Huxton Gn BRAM/HZG SK7 .... 184 B2
Hyacinth Cl EDGY/DAV SK3 .... 171 G4
Hyacinth Wk PART M31 .... 150 D4
Hyde Dr WALK M28 .... 81 H5
Hyde Fold Cl BNG/LEV M19 .... 143 H5
Hyde Gv BRUN/LGST M13 .... 128 C3
  SALE M33 .... 154 C2
  WALK M28 .... 81 H5

Hyde Pl *BRUN/LGST* M13 ....128 D3
Hyde Rd *DTN/ASHW* M34 ....132 C5
GTN M18 ....131 E4
HYDE SK14 ....135 G5
MDTN M24 ....89 H1
MPL/ROM SK6 ....162 A1
WALK M28 ....81 F3
WGTN/LGST M12 ....129 E2
Hyde Sq *MDTN* M24 ....72 B4
Hyde St *BOLS/LL* BL3 * 64 B1
DROY M43 ....118 B1
DUK SK16 ....120 A5
Hydon Brook Wk *ROCH* OL11 ....42 B2
Hydra Cl *BRO* M7 ....113 H2
Hydrangea Cl *SALE* M33 ....155 F5
Hyldavale Av *CHD/CHDH* SK8 ....169 G3
Hylton Dr *CHD/CHDH* SK8 ....185 H4
Hypatia St *BOLE* BL2 ....3 K4
Hythe Cl *RUSH/FAL* M14 ....128 D5
Hythe Rd *EDGY/DAV* SK3 ....171 E1
Hythe St *BOLS/LL* BL3 * 47 H5
Hythe Wk *CHAD* OL9 * 90 C1

Ibsley *WHIT* OL12 ....10 B4
Ice House Cl *WALK* M28 ....81 E4
Iceland St *SLFD* M6 ....112 D5
Idonia St *BRO* M7 ....33 G3
Ilex Gv *BRO* M7 ....101 G4
Ilford St *OP/CLY* M11 ....116 C3
Ilfracombe St
    NEWH/MOS M40 ....104 C4
Ilkley Cl *CHAD* OL9 ....90 C1
Ilkley Crs *RDSH* SK5 ....145 E3
Ilkley Dr *URM* M41 ....123 H4
Ilkley St *NEWH/MOS* M40 ....103 H1
Ilk St *OP/CLY* M11 ....116 C3
Illingworth Av *STLY* SK15 ....121 F4
Illona Dr *BRO* M7 ....100 D2
Ilminster *ROCH* OL11 * 29 H5
Imperial Ter *SALE* M33 * 139 C5
Ina Av *BOL* BL1 ....32 C5
Ince Cl *DID/WITH* M20 ....142 D4
    HTNM SK4 ....159 H3
Ince St *HTNM* SK4 ....159 H3
Inchcape Dr *BKLY* M9 ....87 C3
Inchfield Cl *ROCH* OL11 ....28 B3
Inchfield Rd *NEWH/MOS* M40 ....105 H3
Inchley Rd *BRUN/LGST* M13 ......128 C2
Inchwood Ms *OLDE* OL4 ....60 D5
Incline Rd *OLDS* OL8 ....90 C5
Independent St *BOLS/LL* BL3 .....66 D1
Indigo St *SLFD* M6 ....66 A5
Indus Rd *BRO* M7 ....113 H1
Industrial St *WHTN* BL5 ....62 A5
Industry Rd *WHIT* OL12 ....10 C3
Industry St *CHAD* OL9 ....90 B3
    LIT OL15 ....21 E5
    ROCH OL11 ....28 B2
    WHIT OL12 ....14 C3
Infant St *PWCH* M25 * 86 B3
Infirmary St *BOL* BL1 ....3 F5
Ingham Rd *ALT* WA14 ....155 C5
Inghams La *LIT* OL15 ....21 E3
Ingham St *BURY* BL9 ....5 G6
    NEWH/MOS M40 ....117 F1
    OLD OL1 ....9 J3
Inghamwood Cl *BRO* M7 ....102 A5
Ingleby Av *BKLY* M9 ....80 B2
Ingleby Cl *ROY/SHW* OL2 ....59 H1
Ingleby St *BRO* M7 ....62 A2
Ingleby Wy *ROY/SHW* OL2 ....59 H1
Ingledene Av *BRO* M7 ....101 F5
Ingledene Gv *BOL* BL1 * 32 D4
Ingle Dr *OFTN* SK2 ....172 D2
Inglefield *ROCH* OL11 ....28 B2
Inglehead Cl *DTN/ASHW* M34 ....147 E1
Inglenook Cl *PART* M31 ....151 F4
Ingle Rd *CHD/CHDH* SK8 ....170 D3
Ingles Fold *WALK* M28 ....96 C2
Inglesham Cl *NTHM/RTH* M23 ....168 A3
Ingleton Av *CHH* M8 ....102 C1
Ingleton Cl *CHD/CHDH* SK8 ......169 H3
    ROY/SHW OL2 ....59 E4
Ingleton Ms *TOT/BURYW* BL8 ....37 C2
Ingleton Rd *EDGY/DAV* SK3 ......12 A6
Inglewhite Cl *BURY* BL9 ....53 C2
Inglewood Cl *AULW* OL7 * 119 H3
    BURY BL9 ....39 F2
    PART M31 ....150 D2
Inglewood Hollow *STLY* SK15 ...121 F5
Inglewood Rd *CHAD* OL9 ....73 H3
Inglewood Wk
    BRUN/LGST M13 * 128 D3
Inglis St *LIT* OL15 ....21 E2
Ingoe Cl *HEY* OL10 ....41 G3
Ingoldsby Av *BRUN/LGST* M13 ...129 E4
Ingram Dr *HTNM* SK4 ....158 B4
Ings Av *WHIT* OL12 ....29 E1
Ings La *WHIT* OL12 ....29 F2
Inkerman St *NEWH/MOS* M40 ....105 E5
    NEWH/MOS M40 ....10 C5
Ink St *MILN* OL16 ....10 D6
Inman St *BURY* BL9 ....53 F1
    DTN/ASHW M34 ....132 C5
Innes St *WGTN/LGST* M12 ....130 A5
Innis Av *NEWH/MOS* M40 ....104 B5
Institute St *BOL* BL1 ....3 H4
Instow Cl *BRUN/LGST* M13 ....129 E3
    CHAD OL9 ....74 A3
Intake La *UPML* OL3 ....94 D4
International Ap
    MANAIR M90 ....180 A5
Interlink Wk *WALK* M28 ....98 C1
Inverbeg Dr *BOLE* BL2 ....50 D2
Inverlael Av *BOL* BL1 ....48 A1
Inverness Av *BKLY* M9 ....88 D3
Inverness Rd *DUK* SK16 ....133 H1
Inwood Wk *CHH* M8 * 102 B4
Iona Pl *BOLE* BL2 ....34 D4
Iona Wy *URM* M41 ....124 C3
Ionian Gdns *BRO* M7 ....101 F5

Ipswich St *ROCH* OL11 ....43 E1
Iqbal Cl *WGTN/LGST* M12 ....129 H3
Ireby Cl *MDTN* M24 ....71 H2
Iredine St *OP/CLY* M11 ....116 D4
Irene Av *HYDE* SK14 ....133 H4
Iris Av *FWTH* BL4 ....65 F3
    FWTH BL4 ....82 C2
Iris St *OLDS* OL8 ....91 G5
    RAMS BL0 ....16 C2
Irkdale St *CHH* M8 ....102 D4
Irk Vale Dr *OLD* OL1 ....73 H5
Irlam Av *ECC* M30 ....111 E4
Irlam Rd *IRL* M44 ....136 D2
    SALE M33 ....154 D1
    URM M41 ....137 E2
Irlam Sq *SLFD* M6 ....100 A5
Irlam St *BOL* BL1 ....33 H5
    NEWH/MOS M40 ....103 F5
Irlam Wharf Rd *IRL* M44 ....136 C5
Irma St *BOL* BL1 ....34 A5
Iron St *DTN/ASHW* M34 * 132 C5
    NEWH/MOS M40 ....115 H2
Irvin Dr *WYTH/NTH* M22 ....181 F4
Irvine Av *WALK* M28 ....96 B4
Irving Cl *OFTN* SK2 ....184 B1
Irving St *BOL* BL1 ....33 H4
    OLDS OL8 ....90 C5
Irvin St *NEWH/MOS* M40 ....104 B4
Irwell *ECC* M30 ....111 C4
    LHULT M38 ....81 G3
Irwell Gv *ECC* M30 ....111 C4
Irwell Pl *ECC* M30 ....111 C4
    ORD M5 ....113 H4
Irwell Sculpture Trail *BRO* M7 ...101 F4
Irwell St *BURY* BL9 ....4 C5
    CSLFD M5 ....6 B4
    SLFD M6 ....114 B1
    RAD M26 ....66 D5
    RAD M26 ....68 C2
    RAMS BL0 ....16 D2
Irwell Valley Wy *BURY* BL9 ....16 D4
Irwin Dr *WILM/AE* SK9 ....191 H2
Irwin Rd *ALT* WA14 ....165 F1
Irwin St *DTN/ASHW* M34 ....132 B5
Isaac Cl *ORD* M5 ....113 H4
Isabel Wk *BOLS/LL* BL3 ....48 B1
Isabella Cl *OLDTF/WHR* M16 .....127 F4
Isabella St *WHIT* OL12 ....10 D1
Isabel Wk *BOLS/LL* BL3 ....48 C4
Isaiah St *OLDS* OL8 ....91 G3
Isca St *OP/CLY* M11 ....116 B4
Isherwood Dr *MPL/ROM* SK6 ....174 C3
Isherwood Rd *PART* M31 ....137 H5
Isherwood St *HEY* OL10 ....41 F5
    RAD M26 ....43 F1
Isis Cl *BRO* M7 ....100 D2
Islington Rd *OFTN* SK2 ....172 D5
Islington St *CSLFD* M3 ....6 A3
Islington Wy *CSLFD* M3 ....114 A4
Isobel Cl *ECC* M30 ....110 C4
    OLDTF/WHR M16 ....128 A4
Ivanhoe Ct *BOLS/LL* BL3 ....65 H2
Ivanhoe St *BOLS/LL* BL3 ....65 H2
    OLD OL1 ....76 B3
Iveagh Ct *MILN* OL16 ....30 C5
Ivor St *ROCH* OL11 ....42 A3
Ivy Bank Cl *BOL* BL1 ....33 H1
Ivy Bank Rd *BOL* BL1 ....33 H1
Ivy Cl *DROY* M43 ....117 G2
Ivy Cottages *WHIT* OL12 * 29 F2
Ivy Dr *MDTN* M24 ....88 C1
Ivygreen Dr *OLDE* OL4 ....93 E1
Ivygreen Rd *CCHDY* M21 ....140 D5
Ivy Gv *FWTH* BL4 ....65 E5
    FWTH BL4 ....66 C5
    LHULT M38 ....81 E5
Ivyleaf Sq *BRO* M7 ....101 H4
Ivylea Rd *BNG/LEV* M19 ....158 B2
Ivy Rd *BOL* BL1 ....33 H1
    ROY/SHW OL2 ....59 H2
    TOT/BURYW BL8 ....37 C4
    WHTN BL5 ....62 A5
Ivy St *BOLS/LL* BL3 ....48 B5
    ECC M30 ....111 E4
    NEWH/MOS M40 ....103 H2

Jack Brady Cl *NTHM/RTH* M23 ...167 F5
Jackdaw Rd *TOT/BURYW* BL8 ....26 A1
Jack La *DROY* M43 ....118 B3
    URM M41 ....123 G5
Jackman Av *HEY* OL10 ....56 A2
Jackroom Dr *ANC* M4 * 7 K4
Jackson Av *DUK* SK16 ....120 A5
Jackson La *HALE/TIMP* WA15 ...166 D2
    OLDS OL8 ....8 D5
Jackson Ct *URM* M41 ....123 H5
Jackson Crs *HULME* M15 ....127 H3
Jackson Gdns *DTN/ASHW* M34 ..146 B1
Jackson Ms *OLDE* OL4 ....76 C3
Jacksons Edge Rd
    POY/DIS SK12 ....195 E5
Jacksons La *BRAM/HZG* SK7 ....184 C4
Jacksons Rw *CMANW* M2 ....6 D5
Jackson St *AUL* OL6 ....119 G1
    CHD/CHDH SK8 ....170 B5
    FAIL M35 ....104 D2
    FWTH BL4 ....64 A4
    FWTH BL4 ....66 C5
    HYDE SK14 ....147 H1
    MDTN M24 ....73 E3
    MILN OL16 ....30 C5
    OLDE OL4 ....76 A5
    RAD M26 ....66 D5
    SALE M33 ....155 E1
    STRET M32 ....139 G5
    WALK M28 ....81 H3
    WHIT OL12 ....19 H2
Jack St *BOLE* BL2 ....34 C5
Jack Taylor Ct *WHIT* OL12 * 11 G3

Jacob Bright Ms *WHIT* OL12 ......10 C1
Jacobite Cl *BRO* M7 ....101 F1
Jacobsen Av *HYDE* SK14 ....134 A4
James Andrew St *MDTN* M24 * ..73 E3
James Brindley Basin
    ....7 K5
James Butterworth Ct
    MILN OL16 ....30 C5
James Butterworth St
    MILN OL16 ....30 C5
James Cl *DUK* SK16 ....120 B5
James Corbett Rd *SALO* M50 ....112 B4
James Dr *HYDE* SK14 ....148 A1
James Henry Av *ORD* M5 ....113 G5
James Hill St *LIT* OL15 ....21 E3
James Leech St *STKP* SK1 ....13 F5
James Leigh St *CMANE* M1 ....7 F7
Jameson St *ROCH* OL11 ....42 A4
James Pl *ROY/SHW* OL2 ....60 A1
James's Ct *SALE* M33 ....76 C3
James St *BOLS/LL* BL3 ....67 E1
    BURY BL9 ....4 E6
    DROY M43 ....118 A3
    DTN/ASHW M34 * 118 D5
    DTN/ASHW M34 * 132 D5
    EDGY/DAV SK3 * 120 B5
    FAIL M35 ....105 F2
    FWTH BL4 ....66 C4
    HEY OL10 ....41 E4
    LIT OL15 ....20 C3
    MPL/ROM SK6 ....115 G2
    NEWH/MOS M40 ....105 E1
    OLD OL1 ....114 A4
    PWCH M25 ....85 H2
    RAD M26 ....68 C2
    ROY/SHW OL2 ....59 H4
    SALE M33 ....155 E2
    WHIT OL12 ....10 E3
    WHIT OL12 ....14 C3
James St North *RAD* M26 ....68 C2
James St South *CHAD* OL9 * 74 B5
Jamieson Cl *CHH* M8 ....101 H5
Jammy St *CHAD* OL9 ....8 A5
Jane St *CHAD* OL9 ....90 C1
    OLD OL1 ....10 A4
Janus Dr *OLD* OL1 ....75 E3
Japan St *BRO* M7 ....102 A3
Jardine Wy *CHAD* OL9 ....90 A3
Jarvis Cl *OLDE* OL4 ....9 K5
Jasmine Av *DROY* M43 ....118 B3
Jasmine Cl *NTHM/RTH* M23 ......155 F5
Jasmine Ct *BOLS/LL* BL3 ....64 D1
Jason St *ANC* M4 ....115 E2
Jauncey St *BOLS/LL* BL3 ....48 B4
Jayton Av *DID/WITH* M20 ....169 G2
Jean Cl *BNG/LEV* M19 ....143 F5
Jedburgh Av *BOL* BL1 ....48 A1
Jefferson Wy *WHIT* OL12 ....19 E5
Jeffreys Dr *DUK* SK16 ....120 A5
Jehlum Cl *CHH* M8 ....102 C3
Jellicoe Av *IRL* M44 ....136 A5
Jenkinson St *HULME* M15 ....128 B2
Jennaby Wk *BOL* BL1 * 33 H4
Jennings Av *ORD* M5 ....113 F5
Jennings Cl *HYDE* SK14 ....134 C3
    ORD M5 ....113 F5
Jennison Cl *GTN* M18 * 130 C1
Jenny La *BRAM/HZG* SK7 ....193 H4
Jenny Lind Cl *BOLS/LL* BL3 ......65 H2
Jenny St *OLDS* OL8 ....90 D5
Jepheys Pl *WHIT* OL12 * 10 D2
Jepheys St *WHIT* OL12 ....10 D2
Jepson St *OFTN* SK2 ....172 B3
Jericho Rd *BURY* BL9 ....39 H3
Jermyn St *WHIT* OL12 ....10 E4
Jerrold St *LIT* OL15 ....21 E3
Jersey Rd *RDSH* SK5 ....144 D1
Jersey St *ANC* M4 ....7 J3
Jerusalem Pl *CMANW* M2 * 6 D6
Jesmond Av *PWCH* M25 ....86 A5
Jesmond Dr *TOT/BURYW* BL8 ...25 H4
Jesmond Gv *CHD/CHDH* SK8 ....183 E4
Jesmond Rd *BOL* BL1 ....33 E2
Jespersen St *OLD* OL1 ....9 G2
Jessamine Av *BRO* M7 ....114 A1
Jessel Cl *BRUN/LGST* M13 ....128 C3
Jessie St *BOLS/LL* BL3 ....48 B4
    NEWH/MOS M40 ....103 H4
Jessop Dr *MPL/ROM* SK6 ....175 E5
Jessop Forge *BOLS/LL* BL3 ......66 D1
Jethro St *BOLE* BL2 ....34 D2
    BOLE BL2 ....49 H1
Jimmy McMullen Wk
    RUSH/FAL M14 * 128 B5
Jinnah Cl *OLDE* OL4 ....92 B2
    OP/CLY M11 ....116 D5
J J Thomson Ms
    RUSH/FAL M14 ....130 A1
Joan St *NEWH/MOS* M40 ....103 H5
Jobling St *OP/CLY* M11 ....115 H4
Jocelyn St *NEWH/MOS* M40 .....103 F4
Joddrell St *CSLFD* M3 ....6 C5
Joel La *HYDE* SK14 ....148 B4
Johannesburg Gdns
    OLDS OL8 ....167 C5
John Ashworth St *WHIT* OL12 ...11 G2
John Atkinson Ct *ORD* M5 * 112 C3
John Av *CHD/CHDH* SK8 ....170 B4
John Beeley Av *OP/CLY* M11 ....117 E5
John Booth St *OLDE* OL4 ....93 E2
John Brown St *BOL* BL1 * 2 D3
John Clynes Av
    NEWH/MOS M40 * 115 F2
John Cross St *BOLS/LL* BL3 ......48 D5
John Dalton St *CMANW* M2 ......6 D5
John Foran Cl
    NEWH/MOS M40 * 104 A4
John Gilbert Wy *TRPK* M17 ......126 B3
John Heywood St
    OP/CLY M11 ....116 C3
John Kennedy Gdn
    HYDE SK14 ....135 H1
John Kennedy Rd *HYDE* SK14 ...135 C5
John Knott St *OLDE* OL4 ....93 E1

Jura Gv *HEY* OL10 ....40 C5
Jurby Av *BKLY* M9 ....87 H3
Jury St *CHH* M8 ....114 C1
Justin Cl *BRUN/LGST* M13 ....128 C1
Jutland Av *ROCH* OL11 ....29 F5
Jutland St *CMANE* M1 ....7 J5

K

Kale St *BRUN/LGST* M13 ....128 C1
Kalima Gv *BRO* M7 ....101 G4
Kansas Av *SALO* M50 ....112 D5
Kara St *SLFD* M6 ....112 D5
Kate St *RAMS* BL0 ....16 C1
Kathan Cl *MILN* OL16 ....11 H7
Katherine Rd *OFTN* SK2 ....172 D4
Katherine St *AULW* OL7 ....119 E3
Kathleen Gv *RUSH/FAL* M14 .....143 E1
Kathleen St *WHIT* OL12 ....29 E1
Kay Av *MPL/ROM* SK6 ....161 E3
Kay Brow *HEY* OL10 ....40 D4
    RAMS BL0 ....16 D2
Kayfields *BOLE* BL2 ....35 F2
Kays Gdns *CSLFD* M3 * 6 A2
Kay St *BOL* BL1 ....3 F3
    BOLS/LL BL3 ....66 D1
    BURY BL9 ....5 H2
    HEY OL10 ....40 C5
    OP/CLY M11 ....129 G1
    ROCH OL11 ....42 D1
    SLFD M6 ....100 C4
    STLY SK15 ....120 D4
Kays Wood Rd *MPL/ROM* SK6 ...174 C3
Keadby Cl *ECC* M30 ....111 E5
Keal Dr *IRL* M44 ....122 C4
Kearsley Dr *BOLS/LL* BL3 ....65 C1
Kearsley Hall Rd *RAD* M26 ....67 F5
Kearsley Rd *CHH* M8 ....87 E4
    RAD M26 ....67 F4
Kearsley V *ECC* M30 ....110 C3
Kearsley V *RAD* M26 ....67 G4
Kearton Dr *ECC* M30 ....111 H4
Keary Cl *GTN* M18 ....130 C2
Keaton Cl *SLFD* M6 ....112 C1
Keats Av *DROY* M43 ....117 H3
    DTN/ASHW M34 ....147 E3
    OLD OL1 ....28 D2
Keats Crs *RAD* M26 ....51 H5
Keats Fold *DUK* SK16 ....134 C1
Keats Ms *NTHM/RTH* M23 ....166 D1
Keats Rd *ECC* M30 ....111 E4
    OP/CLY M11 * 116 D4
    TOT/BURYW BL8 ....76 A3
Keb La *OLDS* OL8 ....106 D2
Keble Av *OLDS* OL8 ....91 H5
Kedleston Av *RUSH/FAL* M14 ....129 F4
Kedleston Gn *OFTN* SK2 ....173 E2
Keele Cl *NEWH/MOS* M40 ....115 F2
Keele Wk *NEWH/MOS* M40 * 115 F1
Keepers Dr *WHIT* OL12 ....18 B2
The Keep *BOL* BL1 ....47 F2
Keighley Av *DROY* M43 ....117 H2
Keighley Cl *TOT/BURYW* BL8 ....37 E4
Keighley St *BOL* BL1 ....33 H4
Keilder Ms *BOL* BL1 ....47 F2
Keith Dr *EDGY/DAV* SK3 ....171 E2
Keith Wk *NEWH/MOS* M40 ....115 G2
Kekoro Av *DTN/ASHW* M34 ......132 A1
Kelbrook Ct *OFTN* SK2 * 172 D3
Kelbrook Rd *OP/CLY* M11 ....116 C5
Kelby Av *NTHM/RTH* M23 ....168 A2
Keld Cl *TOT/BURYW* BL8 ....37 G1
Kelfield Av *SALE* M33 ....155 H4
Kelbrook Crs *BRO* M7 * 100 D2
Kellers Rw *WALK* M28 * 23 E5
Kellett St *BOL* BL1 ....11 C5
    MILN OL16 ....31 G5
Kelling Wk *HULME* M15 * 127 C1
Kelmarsh Cl *OP/CLY* M11 * 53 C5
Kelsall Dr *DROY* M43 ....117 C2
    HALE/TIMP WA15 ....166 D3
Kelsall Rd *CHD/CHDH* SK8 ....170 D4
Kelsall St *SALE* M33 ....154 B2
    WGTN/LGST M12 ....129 G2
Kelso Cl *OLDS* OL8 ....106 C1
Kelstern Av *BRUN/LGST* M13 ....129 F5
Kelstern Sq *BRUN/LGST* M13 ....129 F5
Kelton Cl *RDSH* SK5 ....160 A1
Kelverlow St *OLDE* OL4 ....92 B1
Kelvin Av *MDTN* M24 ....71 C5
    SALE M33 ....154 C2
Kelvindale Dr
    HALE/TIMP WA15 ....166 D2
Kelvin Gv *CHH* M8 ....102 B4
Kelvington Dr *BKLY* M9 ....103 E4
Kelvin St *ANC* M4 ....7 G3
    AULW OL7 ....119 E5
Kembe Av *NTHM/RTH* M23 ....156 B5
Kemmel Av *WYTH/NTH* M22 .....168 D4
Kemp Av *ROCH* OL11 ....42 C1
Kempnough Hall Rd
    WALK M28 ....97 G3
Kemp Rd *MPL/ROM* SK6 ....175 H1
Kempsey Ct *CHAD* OL9 ....74 D3
Kempsford Cl
    NTHM/RTH M23 ....168 A3
Kempster Gdns *BRO* M7 ....114 A1
Kempston Gdns *BOL* BL1 * 33 H4
Kempt St *NEWH/MOS* M40 ....133 H4
Kempton Av *BOLS/LL* BL3 ....66 D2
    SALE M33 ....153 H2
Kempton Cl *BRAM/HZG* SK7 ....185 H2
    DROY M43 ....118 B3
Kempton Wy *CHAD* OL9 ....8 A3
Kemsing Wk *ORD* M5 * 113 F3
Kenchester Av *OP/CLY* M11 .....117 F4
Kendal Av *AUL* OL6 ....119 E1
    DTN/ASHW M34 ....147 E2
    HYDE SK14 ....133 F3

SALE M33 ....154 D3
URM M41 ....125 F4
WHIT OL12 ....28 B1
Kendal Cl HALE/TIMP WA15...167 E4
HEY OL10 ....56 B1
Kendal Dr BRAM/HZG SK7 ...193 F2
BURY BL9 ....53 E2
CHD/CHDH SK8 ....169 H5
ROY/SHW OL2 ....60 C2
Kendal Gdns MPL/ROM SK6 ...162 A2
Kendal Gv WALK M28 ....82 C5
WHTF M45 ....69 G4
Kendal Rd CHH M8 ....87 E4
Kendal Rd BOL BL1 ....48 B1
RAMS BL0 ....26 A1
SLFD M6 ....99 H5
STRET M32 ....126 A5
Kendal Rd West RAMS BL0...26 A1
Kendon Gv DTN/ASHW M34 ...132 B5
Kendrew Rd BOLS/LL BL3 ....47 H5
Kenilworth ROCH OL11 * 29 H5
Kenilworth Av CHAD OL9 ....73 H3
CHD/CHDH SK8 ....182 D1
DID/WITH M20 ....157 E1
SWIN M27 ....84 C4
WHTF M45 ....85 H1
WILM/AE SK9 ....192 A5
Kenilworth Cl MPL/ROM SK6..175 E1
OLDE OL4 ....93 E3
RAD M26 ....52 A3
Kenilworth Dr
BRAM/HZG SK7 ....185 E4
Kenilworth Gv
DTN/ASHW M34 ....118 D5
MILN OL16 ....58 D1
SALE M33 ....153 H5
URM M41 ....137 F2
Kenilworth Sq BOL BL1 ....33 E5
Kenion Rd ROCH OL11 ....28 D5
Kenion St MILN OL16 ....10 D7
Kenley Dr HEY OL10 ....56 C2
Kenley Ldg BRAM/HZG SK7 *..185 G5
Kenley Wk CHH M8 * 102 D4
Kenmay Av BOLS/LL BL3 ....47 G3
Kenmere Gv NEWH/MOS M40 ..104 A1
Kenmor Av TOT/BURYW BL8...52 B1
Kenmore Cl WHTF M45 ....70 A4
Kenmore Dr
HALE/TIMP WA15 ....178 B1
Kenmore Rd SALE M33 ....153 F5
WHTF M45 ....70 A4
WYTH/NTH M22 ....168 C2
Kenmore Wy WHTF M45 ....70 A4
Kennard Cl BKLY M9 ....105 G1
Kennedy Dr BOLS/LL BL3 ....67 F1
BURY BL9 ....70 A2
Kennedy Rd ORD M5 ....112 B3
Kennedy St HYDE SK14 ....149 H1
Kennedy St CMANW M2 * 6 E5
OLDS OL8 ....8 B7
Kennedy Wy DTN/ASHW M34..146 B1
Kennerley Rd OTH SK1 ....12 B2
Kennerley's La WILM/AE SK9..198 D5
Kennet Cl WHTN BL5 ....62 A3
WILM/AE SK9 ....192 A5
Kenneth Sq BRO M7 ....101 H4
Kennett Dr MPL/ROM SK6 ....161 G2
Kennett Rd NTHM/RTH M23...179 H1
Kenninghall Rd
WYTH/NTH M22 ....180 C1
Kennington Av
NEWH/MOS M40 ....116 C1
Kennington Fold
BOLS/LL BL3 ....64 C1
Kenny Cl OLDE OL4 ....92 D2
Kensington Av AUL OL6 ....120 B1
CHAD OL9 ....73 H3
HYDE SK14 * 148 A2
RAD M26 ....51 G5
ROY/SHW OL2 ....58 D3
RUSH/FAL M14 ....129 E4
Kensington Ct MILN OL16 ....31 H5
TOT/BURYW BL8 ....26 D2
Kensington Ct BOL BL1 * 2 B3
HYDE SK14 ....148 A2
WILM/AE SK9 ....198 D4
Kensington Dr ORD M5 ....112 C2
TOT/BURYW BL8 ....52 B1
Kensington Gdns
HALE/TIMP WA14 ....165 H1
DTN/ASHW M34 ....131 G4
STLY SK15 ....120 D4
Kensington Rd
CCHDY M21 ....141 E1
EDGY/DAV SK3 ....171 E2
FAIL M35 ....105 G2
OLDS OL8 ....91 E3
Kensington St BOL BL1 ....2 C4
HYDE SK14 ....148 A2
ROCH OL11 ....42 D2
RUSH/FAL M14 ....128 B5
Kenslow Av CHH M8 ....87 E5
Kensworth Cl BOL BL1 * 33 G5
Kensworth Dr BOL BL1 ....90 B1
Kent Av CHAD OL9 ....90 B1
CHD/CHDH SK8 ....171 F5
DROY M43 ....117 F4
Kent Cl WALK M28 ....81 F3
Kent Ct BOL BL1 ....2 D3
Kent Dr BURY BL9 ....53 C1
FWTH BL4 ....83 E1
Kentford Dr
NEWH/MOS M40 ....115 F1
Kentford Rd BOL BL1 ....2 D1
Kentmere Av WHIT OL12 ....19 C5
Kentmere Cl CHD/CHDH SK8..181 C1
Kentmere Dr NTHM M24 ....72 B1
Kentmere Gv FWTH BL4 ....65 G5
Kentmere Rd BOLE BL2 ....35 G5
HALE/TIMP WA15 ....167 E3
Kentmore Cl HTNM SK4 ....158 B4
WGTN/LGST M12 ....129 H1
Kenton Av GTN M18 ....130 D5
Kenton Cl BOL BL1 ....33 G5
DTN/ASHW M34 ....132 A1
Kenton Rd ROY/SHW OL2 ....59 H2
Kenton St OLDS OL8 ....92 A2

Kent Rd DTN/ASHW M34 ....145 G1
EDGY/DAV SK3 ....171 E1
FAIL M55 ....104 D4
IRL M44 ....150 B1
PART M31 ....150 D4
Kent Rd East RUSH/FAL M14 ..129 E5
Kent Rd West RUSH/FAL M14 ..128 D5
Kentsford Dr RAD M26 ....51 F4
Kentstone Av BNG/LEV M19 ..158 A3
Kent St BOL BL1 ....2 D2
BRO M7 ....114 A1
CMANW M2 * 6 E4
OLDS OL8 ....91 C3
ROCH OL11 ....30 A5
SWIN M27 ....84 A5
Kentucky St OLDE OL4 ....92 B1
Kentwell Cl DUK SK16 ....133 F1
Kenwick Dr NEWH/MOS M40 ..89 H5
Kenwood Av BNG/LEV M19 ...143 H5
BRAM/HZG SK7 ....193 G2
CHD/CHDH SK8 ....169 F3
HALE/TIMP WA15 ....178 B2
Kenwood Cl STRET M32 ....140 C1
Kenwood La WALK M28 ....97 C5
Kenwood Rd BOL BL1 ....33 E3
OLD OL1 * 9 H1
RDSH SK5 ....145 E1
STRET M32 ....140 C2
Kenworthy Av AUL OL6 ....107 C5
Kenworthy Cl HYDE SK14 ....149 G1
Kenworthy Gdns UPML OL3....79 E4
Kenworthy La
WYTH/NTH M22 ....156 C4
Kenworthy St MILN OL16 ....11 J6
STLY SK15 ....120 D4
Kenwright St ANC M4 ....7 G2
Kenwyn St NEWH/MOS M40...115 H2
Kenyon Av DUK SK16 ....133 H1
OLDS OL8 ....91 G4
SALE M33 ....155 F4
Kenyon Cl HYDE SK14 ....134 A3
Kenyon Crs BURY BL9 ....27 G5
Kenyon Fold ROCH OL11 ....41 F3
Kenyon Gv LHULT M38 ....80 D5
Kenyon La MDTN M24 ....73 H4
NEWH/MOS M40 ....103 H2
PWCH M25 ....86 B3
Kenyon Rd BOLE BL2 ....36 C4
Kenyon St AUL OL6 ....119 E2
BURY BL9 ....5 C2
DUK SK16 ....133 H1
GTN M18 ....130 D2
HEY OL10 ....40 D3
RAMS BL0 ....16 D1
Kenyon Ter LHULT M38 ....80 D4
Kenyon Wy LHULT M38 ....81 E4
TOT/BURYW BL8 ....37 E1
Keppel Rd CCHDY M21 ....141 F2
Keppel St AUL OL6 ....119 H2
Kepplecove Meadow
WALK M28 ....96 A5
Kepwick Dr WYTH/NTH M22 ..180 D3
Kerenhappuch St RAMS BL0....16 C5
Kerfoot Cl WYTH/NTH M22 ...168 D1
Kermoor Av BOL BL1 ....22 D5
Kerne Gv WYTH/NTH M23 ....155 H5
Kerrera Dr ORD M5 * 112 C4
Kerridge Dr MPL/ROM SK6 ...161 G2
Kerris Cl WYTH/NTH M22 ....168 C5
Kerr St BKLY M9 * 88 A4
Kerry Gv BOLE BL2 ....3 K2
Kersal Av LHULT M38 ....81 G3
SWIN M27 ....99 H2
Kersal Bank BRO M7 ....101 F2
Kersal Cl PWCH M25 ....100 D1
Kersal Crag BRO M7 ....101 F1
Kersal Dr HALE/TIMP WA15 ..166 D2
Kersal Hall Av BRO M7 ....100 D2
Kersal Rd PWCH M25 ....100 C1
Kersal Vale Rd PWCH M25 ....100 C1
Kersal Wy BRO M7 ....101 E3
Kerscott Rd NTHM/RTH M23..155 C4
Kersh Av BNG/LEV M19 ....144 B3
Kershaw Av BOLS/LL BL3 ....50 D5
PWCH M25 ....85 G2
SALE M33 ....155 E4
Kershaw Dr CHAD OL9 ....89 G3
Kershaw Gv DTN/ASHW M34 ..118 A5
Kershaw La DTN/ASHW M34 ..118 B5
Kershaw Rd FAIL M35 ....104 C4
Kershaw St AULW OL7 ....119 E5
BOLE BL2 ....34 D1
BOLS/LL BL3 ....48 C4
BURY BL9 ....5 G5
HEY OL10 ....40 C4
ROY/SHW OL2 ....59 E4
ROY/SHW OL2 ....60 C2
WHIT OL12 ....10 C4
Kershaw St East ROY/SHW OL2..60 A2
Kershaw Wk WGTN/LGST M12..129 E2
Kershope Gv ORD M5 ....113 F5
Kersley St OLDE OL4 ....92 A1
Kerwin Wk OP/CLY M11 * 116 B5
Kerwood Dr ROY/SHW OL2 ....75 F1
Kesteven Rd BKLY M9 ....103 E3
Keston Av BKLY M9 ....88 D4
DROY M43 ....117 H4
Keston Crs RDSH SK5 ....145 H5
Keston Rd OLD OL1 ....76 B3
Kestor St BOLE BL2 ....3 J4
Kestrel Av DTN/ASHW M34....118 B4
FWTH BL4 ....65 E5
LHULT M38 ....81 F2
OLDE OL4 ....92 B2
SWIN M27 ....84 C5
Kestrel Cl HYDE SK14 ....133 H4
MPL/ROM SK6 ....187 F1
PWCH M25 ....85 H1
Kestrel Dr BURY BL9 ....5 L1
IRL M44 ....122 B5
Kestrel Rd TRPK M17 ....111 G5
Kestrel St BOL BL1 * 3 G3
Kestrel Wk WGTN/LGST M12..129 H2
Keswick Av AULW OL7 ....106 C5
CHAD OL9 ....74 B5
DTN/ASHW M34 ....133 G4
HYDE SK14 ....133 F4
OLDS OL8 ....91 H3

URM M41 ....137 G2
Keswick Cl BRUN/LGST M13...129 E4
MDTN M24 ....72 A2
STLY SK15 ....120 D1
Keswick Dr BRAM/HZG SK7...193 F2
BURY BL9 ....53 E2
Keswick Gv SLFD M6 ....113 E2
Keswick Rd HALE/TIMP WA15...167 E3
HTNM SK4 ....144 D4
MPL/ROM SK6 ....186 D4
STRET M32 ....125 H5
WALK M28 ....82 C5
Keswick St BOL BL1 ....34 A4
ROCH OL11 ....42 A4
Kettering Rd BNG/LEV M19 ...144 B1
Kettleshulme Wy
POY/DIS SK12 ....195 H5
Ketton Cl OP/CLY M11 ....130 D1
Kevin Av ROY/SHW OL2 ....75 F2
Kevin St BNG/LEV M19 ....144 B3
Kew Av HYDE SK14 ....148 A2
Kew Dr CHD/CHDH SK8 ....182 D2
URM M41 ....124 C5
Kew Gdns NEWH/MOS M40....103 H1
Kew Rd FAIL M35 ....105 F2
OLDE OL4 ....92 A1
ROCH OL11 ....43 E5
Key Cl DTN/ASHW M34 ....147 E3
Keymer St OP/CLY M11 ....115 H5
Keynsham Rd OP/CLY M11 ....116 C2
Keystone Cl SLFD M6 ....112 D1
Key West Cl OP/CLY M11 ....116 C2
Keyworth Wk
NEWH/MOS M40 ....115 H1
Khartoum St
OLDTF/WHR M16 ....127 C4
OP/CLY M11 ....117 E3
Kibbles Brow EDGW/EG BL7....23 C3
Kibboth Crew RAMS BL0 ....16 C1
Kibworth Cl WHTF M45 ....69 E4
Kidderminster Wy CHAD OL9...74 A3
Kidd Rd MPL/ROM SK6 ....147 H5
Kiel Cl ECC M30 ....111 F3
Kielder Hl MDTN M24 ....56 C5
Kilbride Av BOLE BL2 ....50 A5
Kilburn Av BKLY M9 ....88 A2
Kilburn Cl CHD/CHDH SK8....181 H5
Kilburn Rd EDGY/DAV SK3.....12 E7
RAD M26 ....51 G5
Kilburn St OLD OL1 ....76 B3
Kilcoby Av SWIN M27 ....100 B2
Kildale Cl BOLS/LL BL3 ....47 F5
Kildare Crs ROCH OL11 ....43 F4
Kildare Rd CCHDY M21 ....141 H3
SWIN M27 ....98 D3
Kildare St FWTH BL4 ....65 H5
Kildonan Dr BOLS/LL BL3 ....47 G3
Killer St RAMS BL0 * 16 D2
Killon St BURY BL9 ....5 L7
Kilmaine Av BKLY M9 ....89 E4
Kilmaine Dr BOLS/LL BL3 ....47 F4
Kilmington Dr CHH M8 ....102 A4
Kilmory Dr BOLE BL2 ....50 C3
Kiln Bank La WHIT OL12 ....14 D5
Kilnbrook Cl OLDE OL4 ....93 C3
Kiln Brow EDGW/EG BL7 ....23 H3
Kiln Cft MPL/ROM SK6 ....162 A4
Kiln Croft La WILM/AE SK9 ...192 B3
Kilner Cl BURY BL9 ....53 G1
Kilnerdeyne Ter MILN OL16 *...29 H3
Kilner Wk NEWH/MOS M40 ...115 F1
Kiln Fld EDGW/EG BL7 ....23 E3
Kiln Hill Cl MDTN M24 ....72 A1
Kiln Hill La OLD OL1 ....74 A2
Kilnhurst Wk BOL BL1 * 2 B3
Kiln La MILN OL16 ....31 H4
Kilnside Dr BKLY M9 ....103 E3
Kiln St RAMS BL0 ....16 C3
Kiln Wk WHIT OL12 ....29 H1
Kilnwick Cl GTN M18 ....130 A5
The Kilphin HOR/BR BL6 ....46 C1
Kilrush Av ECC M30 ....111 E5
Kilsby Cl FWTH BL4 ....65 G2
Kilsby Wk NEWH/MOS M40...115 F1
Kilton Wk NEWH/MOS M40 ...115 F1
Kilvert Dr SALE M33 ....154 A1
Kilvert St TRPK M17 ....126 D3
Kilworth Av SALE M33 ....154 A3
Kilworth Dr HOR/BR BL6 ....47 E3
Kilworth St ROCH OL11 ....42 C1
Kimberley Av MPL/ROM SK6 ...85 H1
Kimberley St BRO M7 * 101 H5
EDGY/DAV SK3 ....171 H2
OLDS OL8 ....90 D4
Kimberley Wk HULME M15 * ..127 G1
Kimble Cl TOT/BURYW BL8 ....26 A1
Kimbolton Cl
WGTN/LGST M12 ....129 H1
Kinburn Rd BNG/LEV M19 ....158 A4
Kincardine Rd
BRUN/LGST M13 ....128 D2
Kincraig Cl BOLS/LL BL3 ....47 F5
Kinder Av AUL OL6 ....108 B4
OLDE OL4 ....92 C2
Kinder Dr MPL/ROM SK6 ....175 F3
Kinder Fold STLY SK15 ....135 G2
Kinders Crs UPML OL3 ....95 G2
Kinders Fold LIT OL15 ....21 F3
Kinders La UPML OL3 ....95 F1
Kinders Ms UPML OL3 * 95 E2
Kinder St EDGY/DAV SK3 ....12 C5
STLY SK15 ....120 D3
Kinderton Av DID/WITH M20..143 E1
Kinder Wy MDTN M24 ....72 C2
Kineton Wk BRUN/LGST M13..129 G2
King Albert St ROY/SHW OL2...60 A2
King Edward Rd HYDE SK14...148 A4
King Edward St BNG/LEV M19..144 B2
ECC M30 ....110 D3
ORD M5 ....113 H1

King George Rd HYDE SK14 ...148 A2
Kingham Dr ANC M4 ....115 F3
Kingholm Gdns BOL BL1 * 33 G5
King La OLD OL1 ....60 D5
Kingmoor Av RAD M26 ....52 C5
King's Acre ALT WA14 ....176 D3
Kings Av CHD/CHDH SK8 ....169 F5
CHH M8 ....102 B2
WHTF M45 ....69 F2
Kingsbridge Av BOLE BL2 ....36 C5
Kingsbridge Cl
MPL/ROM SK6 ....174 D2
Kingsbridge Dr DUK SK16 ....133 E1
Kingsbridge Rd BKLY M9 ....102 D3
OLDS OL8 * 92 A2
Kingsbrook Rd
OLDTF/WHR M16 ....142 A3
Kingsbury Av BOL BL1 ....22 D4
Kingsbury Cl
TOT/BURYW BL8 ....26 B5
Kingsbury Dr WILM/AE SK9....199 G2
Kingsbury Rd OP/CLY M11 ....116 D3
Kingscliffe St BKLY M9 ....103 F3
King's Cl BRAM/HZG SK7 ....184 A2
GTN M18 ....131 E2
ROY/SHW OL2 ....59 G5
WILM/AE SK9 ....198 D4
Kings Ct RDSH SK5 ....160 A5
Kingscourt Av BOL BL1 ....33 F4
Kings Crs OLDTF/WHR M16 ...127 E5
Kingsdale Cl BURY BL9 ....53 H2
Kingsdale Rd GTN M18 ....131 F4
BNG/LEV M19 ....157 G1
Kingsdown Dr BOL BL1 ....2 E1
Kingsdown Gdns
BOL BL1 * 2 E1
Kingsdown Rd
WYTH/NTH M22 ....180 B3
Kings Dr CHD/CHDH SK8 ....182 D1
HTNM SK4 ....158 D3
MDTN M24 ....72 A4
MPL/ROM SK6 ....174 D2
Kingsfield Dr
DID/WITH M20 ....157 H4
Kingsfold Av
NEWH/MOS M40 ....115 F1
Kingsford St ORD M5 ....112 C3
Kingsgate BOL WYTH/NTH M22..180 B3
Kings Gv STRET M32 ....126 C5
WHIT OL12 ....19 H4
Kingsheath Av OP/CLY M11 ...116 C2
Kingshill Rd CCHDY M21 ....141 E3
Kingsholme Rd
WYTH/NTH M22 ....180 B2
Kingsland Cl NEWH/MOS M40..115 F2
Kingsland Rd EDGY/DAV SK3 ...170 D2
FWTH BL4 ....65 E3
Kingsleigh Rd HTNM SK4 ....158 C2
Kingsley Av BKLY M9 ....103 G3
BRO M7 ....101 G5
HTNM SK4 ....159 H2
STRET M32 ....126 C5
URM M41 ....138 B1
WHTF M45 ....69 H5
Kingsley Cl AUL OL6 ....108 B5
DTN/ASHW M34 ....146 B2
Kingsley Dr CHD/CHDH SK8 ...182 D1
OLDE OL4 ....76 D5
Kingsley Gv DTN/ASHW M34..118 B5
Kingsley Rd
HALE/TIMP WA15 ....166 C2
MDTN M24 ....73 E2
OLDE OL4 ....92 B1
SWIN M27 ....98 C1
WALK M28 ....82 C4
WYTH/NTH M22 ....168 C1
Kingsley St BOL BL1 ....33 G4
TOT/BURYW BL8 ....37 G4
King's Lynn Cl
DID/WITH M20 ....157 G3
Kingsmead Ms BKLY M9 ....87 H2
Kingsmere Av BNG/LEV M19 ..143 H2
Kingsmill Av BNG/LEV M19 ...144 B3
Kingsnorth Rd URM M41 ....123 E5
King's Rd AUL OL6 ....107 G3
BRAM/HZG SK7 ....185 F1
CCHDY M21 ....141 H3
CHD/CHDH SK8 ....182 D1
CHH M8 ....89 H4
IRL M44 ....136 A5
MILN OL16 ....43 G1
MPL/ROM SK6 ....161 H5
OLDS OL8 ....9 H7
OLDTF/WHR M16 ....126 D5
PWCH M25 ....85 H3
ROY/SHW OL2 ....59 H3
SALE M33 ....154 A2
STRET M32 ....140 C1
Kings St WHTN BL5 ....62 A4
Kings Ter STRET M32 ....126 C5
Kingston Av BOLE BL2 ....34 D5
CHAD OL9 ....90 B3
DID/WITH M20 ....157 G5
OLDE OL4 ....92 C2
Kingston Cl BRO M7 ....101 G2
HYDE SK14 ....149 G1
ROY/SHW OL2 ....60 A2
SALE M33 ....153 G4
TOT/BURYW BL8 ....52 C1
Kingston Dr ROY/SHW OL2 ....60 A2
SALE M33 ....155 E1
URM M41 ....138 B3
Kingston Gdns HYDE SK14 ....133 E5
Kingston Gv BKLY M9 ....88 C3
Kingston Hill CHD/CHDH SK8..182 D5
Kingston Mi EDGY/DAV SK3 *..12 D7
Kingston Pl CHD/CHDH SK8 ...182 D2
Kingston Rd
DID/WITH M20 ....157 G5
DTN/ASHW M34 ....132 A1
FAIL M35 ....105 E3
RAD M26 ....52 D3
WILM/AE SK9 ....191 H3

King St BOL BL1 ....2 D4
BOLE BL2 ....35 E1
BRO M7 ....101 H3
CMANW M2 ....6 E4
CSLFD M3 ....6 C2
DROY M43 ....117 H5
DTN/ASHW M34 ....132 C2
DUK SK16 ....119 C5
ECC M30 ....111 E5
EDGW/EG BL7 ....23 E3
FAIL M35 ....104 C4
FWTH BL4 ....66 A4
HEY OL10 ....41 E5
HYDE SK14 ....133 C5
MDTN M24 ....72 D3
MILN OL16 ....10 E1
MOSL OL5 ....109 E1
OLDS OL8 ....9 F4
RAD M26 ....68 C2
RAMS BL0 ....16 D2
SLFD M6 ....100 A5
STLY SK15 ....120 D3
WHIT OL12 ....10 C4
King St East ROCH OL11 ....42 D1
STKP SK1 ....13 G1
King Street Rbt OLDS OL8 ....9 F6
King St South ROCH OL11 ....42 D1
King St West CSLFD M3 ....6 D4
HTNM SK4 ....12 D3
Kings Vw HTNM SK4 * 12 B3
Kingsway ALT WA14 ....165 G4
BNG/LEV M19 ....143 G4
BRAM/HZG SK7 ....184 A2
CHD/CHDH SK8 ....169 H5
DID/WITH M20 ....158 A4
DUK SK16 ....133 H1
FWTH BL4 ....82 C1
MDTN M24 ....56 B5
MILN OL16 ....30 D5
MPL/ROM SK6 ....161 F3
STRET M32 ....99 H4
SWIN M27 ....99 G2
Kingsway Av BNG/LEV M19 ...143 H2
Kingsway Cl OLDS OL8 ....8 F7
Kingsway Crs BNG/LEV M19 ..158 B1
Kingsway Pk URM M41 ....124 C4
Kingswear Dr BOL BL1 ....33 F5
Kingsway Rd RDSH SK5 ....145 F2
Kingswood Rd ECC M30 ....110 C1
MDTN M24 ....72 C1
PWCH M25 ....85 G2
Kingthorpe Gdns
BOLS/LL BL3 * 48 D5
King William St ECC M30 ....110 B2
SALQ M50 ....113 F5
Kingwood Av BOL BL1 ....47 G4
Kinlay Rd FWTH BL4 ....65 E3
Kinley Cl WGTN/LGST M12 ...129 G2
Kinloch Dr BOL BL1 ....48 A2
Kinloch Gdns OLDS OL8 ....91 G3
Kinloch St OLDS OL8 ....91 H1
OP/CLY M11 ....116 B3
Kinmel Av RDSH SK5 ....160 D2
Kinnaird Crs STKP SK1 ....13 J3
Kinnaird Rd DID/WITH M20....157 H1
Kinnerly Gv WALK M28 ....96 B1
Kinross Av OFTN SK2 ....172 B4
Kinross Cl RAMS BL0 ....26 B1
Kinross Dr BOLS/LL BL3 ....47 G4
Kinross Rd RUSH/FAL M14 ....129 F5
Kinsey Av NTHM/RTH M23 ....167 G2
Kinsley Dr WALK M28 ....81 H5
Kintore Av BRAM/HZG SK7....185 G5
Kintyre Av ORD M5 ....112 D4
Kintyre Cl OP/CLY M11 * 116 D4
Kintyre Dr BOLS/LL BL3 ....47 F4
Kinver Rd NEWH/MOS M40 ....89 F5
Kipling Av DROY M43 ....117 H2
DTN/ASHW M34 ....147 E4
Kipling Cl OFTN SK2 ....173 F2
Kipling Rd OLD OL1 ....59 H5
Kipling St BRO M7 ....101 G4
Kippax St RUSH/FAL M14 ....128 C5
Kirby Av CHAD OL9 ....89 C4
SALE M33 ....154 D4
SWIN M27 ....98 C5
Kirkbank St CHAD OL9 ....8 D1
Kirkburn Vw TOT/BURYW BL8...26 A1
Kirkby Av NEWH/MOS M40 ...104 A3
Kirkby Cl BURY BL9 ....53 F2
Kirkby Dr SALE M33 ....155 E3
Kirkby Rd BOL BL1 ....48 A1
Kirkdale Av NEWH/MOS M40...89 G5
Kirkdale Dr ROY/SHW OL2 ....59 H4
Kirkebrok Rd BOLS/LL BL3 ....47 H5
Kirkfell Dr MPL/ROM SK6 ....175 G3
Kirkgate Cl NEWH/MOS M40 *...115 F1
Kirkhall La BOL BL1 ....48 B1
Kirkham Av GTN M18 ....130 C2
Kirkham Cl DTN/ASHW M34 ..132 C5
Kirkham Rd CHD/CHDH SK8...181 H4
Kirkham St BOLE BL2 ....34 D5
CHAD OL9 ....8 D2
LHULT M38 ....80 D2
SALQ M50 ....112 D4
Kirkhaven Sq
NEWH/MOS M40 ....115 H1
Kirkhill Gra WHTN BL5 ....62 B2
Kirkhope Dr BOL BL1 ....33 C5
Kirkhope Wk BOL BL1 ....33 C5
Kirklands BOLE BL2 ....35 E4
SALE M33 ....154 B4
Kirklee Av CHAD OL9 ....74 B3
Kirklee Rd ROCH OL11 ....43 E4
Kirklees St TOT/BURYW BL8....26 D4
Kirkley St HYDE SK14 ....147 H2
Kirklinton Dr BKLY M9 ....88 A1
Kirkman Av ECC M30 ....110 D5
Kirkman Cl GTN M18 ....130 A3
Kirkmanshulme La
GTN M18 ....130 A3
WGTN/LGST M12 ....129 H4
Kirkman St BURY BL9 ....69 G1
Kirkstall WHIT OL12 * 10 C6
Kirkstall Av HEY OL10 ....40 D3
LIT OL15 ....20 D1

Kirkstall Cl POY/DIS SK12 ....195 E3
Kirkstall Rd MDTN M24 ....72 C1
URM M41 ....124 D5
Kirkstall Sq BRUN/LGST M13 ....128 E3
Kirkstead Rd CHD/CHDH SK8 ....183 F5
Kirkstile Pl SWIN M27 ....83 H5
Kirkstone Av WALK M28 ....97 G1
Kirkstone Cl OLD OL1 ....75 C3
Kirkstone Dr MDTN M24 ....72 B2
ROY/SHW OL2 ....58 D5
Kirkstone Rd HYDE SK14 ....133 F3
NEWH/MOS M40 ....116 A1
Kirk St GTN M18 ....130 C3
Kirkwall Dr BOLE BL2 ....49 G4
Kirkway BKLY M9 ....88 D1
MDTN M24 ....88 D1
URM M41 ....43 E4
Kirkwood Dr
NEWH/MOS M40 ....115 F1
Kirtley Av ECC M30 ....111 E2
Kirtlington Cl ROY/SHW OL2 .....59 H4
Kitchener Av IRL M44 ....150 B2
Kitchener St BOLS/LL BL3 ....65 C1
TOT/BURYW BL8 ....37 H5
Kitchen Wy FWTH BL4 ....65 E3
Kitchen St MILN OL16 ....10 E5
Kitepool St ECC M30 * 110 B2
Kitter St WHIT OL12 ....19 H5
Kitt's Moss La BRAM/HZG SK7 ..193 G1
Kitty Wheeldon Gdns
SALE M33 * 154 B1
Kiverton Cl WALK M28 ....81 G5
Kiwi St SLFD M6 ....113 G5
Knaresborough Cl RDSH SK5 ....145 E2
Knarr Barn La UPML OL3 ....78 A1
Knarr La UPML OL3 ....78 B2
Knight Crs MDTN M24 ....72 A1
Knightley Wk
NEWH/MOS M40 ....103 E5
Knightsbridge STKP SK1 ....13 H5
WILM/AE SK9 ....199 G1
Knight's Cl PWCH M25 ....86 A2
Knight St AULW OL7 ....119 E3
BOL BL1 ....2 A4
DID/WITH M20 ....157 G4
HYDE SK14 ....148 B2
TOT/BURYW BL8 * 37 H4
Knightswood BOLS/LL BL3 ....63 G1
Knightswood Rd CHH M8 ....102 B3
Kniveton Cl WGTN/LGST M12 ...129 G2
Kniveton St HYDE SK14 * 195 C5
Knole Av POY/DIS SK12 ....195 C5
Knoll St BRO M7 ....101 G3
ROCH OL11 ....42 A3
The Knoll MOSL OL5 ....108 C4
ROY/SHW OL2 ....60 B3
Knott Fold HYDE SK14 ....147 H3
Knott Hill La UPML OL3 ....78 B1
Knott La BOL BL1 ....32 C4
HYDE SK14 ....147 H3
Knott Lanes OLDS OL8 ....106 B2
Knott St ORD M5 ....112 C4
Knowe Av WYTH/NTH M22 ......180 C3
Knowl Cl
DTN/ASHW M34 ....145 C1
RAMS BL0 ....16 D4
Knowldale Wy
WGTN/LGST M12 ....129 F3
Knowle Av AULW OL7 ....119 F1
Knowle Dr PWCH M25 ....85 H5
Knowle Pk WILM/AE SK9 ....199 H4
Knowle Rd
MPL/ROM SK6 ....175 H3
Knowles Edge St BOL BL1 * 33 F4
Knowles St
RAD M26 ....52 B5
The Knowles OLDS OL8 ....105 H5
Knowl Hill Dr WHIT OL12 ....28 B1
Knowl Rd MILN OL16 ....31 E5
ROY/SHW OL2 ....60 B3
Knowls La OLDE OL4 ....93 E2
Knowl St OLDS OL8 ....90 D5
STLY SK15 ....121 G5
Knowl Syke St WHIT OL12 ....19 H1
Knowl Top La UPML OL3 ....79 G5
Knowl Vw LIT OL15 ....31 C1
TOT/BURYW BL8 ....26 B5
Knowsley Av OFTN SK2 ....172 D2
ORD M5 * 113 G5
URM M41 ....124 B4
Knowsley Crs STKP SK1 ....172 C1
Knowsley Dr OLDE OL4 ....77 F5
SWIN M27 ....77 E5
Knowsley Gra BOL BL1 ....47 E2
ORD M5 * 113 G5
Knowsley Rd BOL BL1 ....33 E4
BOLE BL2 ....36 B5
BRAM/HZG SK7 ....183 G5
STKP SK1 ....172 C1
WHTF M45 ....69 G4
Knowsley St BOL BL1 * 4 C7
BURY BL9 ....7 H2
CHH M8 ....114 D1
WHIT OL12 ....10 B4
Knowsley Ter OLDE OL4 * 77 F5
STKP SK1 * 172 C1
Knutsford Av HTNM SK4 ....144 D4
SALE M33 ....155 F2
Knutsford Rd GTN M18 ....130 B4
WILM/AE SK9 ....198 C5
Knutsford St SLFD M6 ....112 D3
Knutshaw Crs BOLS/LL BL3 ....63 E2
Krokus Sq CHAD OL9 * 74 B5
Kylemore Av BOLS/LL BL3 ....48 A4
Kyle Rd BRAM/HZG SK7 * 185 G3
Kynder St
DTN/ASHW M34 ....132 C5

L

Labrador Quay SALQ M50 ....126 C1
Labtec St SWIN M27 ....99 G1

Laburnum Av AUL OL6 ....107 F4
CHAD OL9 ....74 C3
DTN/ASHW M34 ....118 B4
ECC M30 ....110 B5
FAIL M35 ....105 E4
HYDE SK14 ....147 H3
SWIN M27 ....60 A3
STLY SK15 ....120 C5
SWIN M27 ....98 D4
TOT/BURYW BL8 ....26 A4
WHTF M45 ....85 C1
Laburnum Cl
HALE/TIMP WA15 ....166 C4
Laburnum Gv PWCH M25 ....85 H2
Laburnum La
HALE/TIMP WA15 ....177 H4
MILN OL16 ....44 D3
Laburnum Pk BOLE BL2 ....34 D1
Laburnum Rd
DTN/ASHW M34 ....131 E5
FWTH BL4 ....65 H4
GTN M18 ....130 C4
IRL M44 ....150 C1
MDTN M24 ....73 F4
OLDS OL8 ....105 H2
URM M41 ....124 A4
Laburnum St BOL BL1 * 2 A3
SLFD M6 ....113 C3
Laburnum Wy EDGY/DAV SK3 ..171 E1
LIT OL15 ....20 C5
Lacerta Ms BRO M7 ....113 H2
Lacey Av WILM/AE SK9 ....199 E3
Lacey Gn WILM/AE SK9 ....199 F1
Lacey Gv WILM/AE SK9 ....199 F1
Lackford Dr NEWH/MOS M40 ...115 F1
Lacrosse Av OLDS OL8 ....90 D5
Lacy Gv STRET M32 ....140 B2
Lacy St STKP SK1 ....13 G5
STRET M32 ....140 B2
Lacy Wk WGTN/LGST M12 ....115 G3
Ladbrooke Cl AUL OL6 ....119 H1
Ladbrooke Rd AUL OL6 ....107 F5
Lady Bridge La BOL BL1 ....47 C2
Ladybridge Rd CHD/CHDH SK8 ..183 F1
Ladybridge Rd
CHD/CHDH SK8 ....183 F1
Ladybrook Av
HALE/TIMP WA15 ....166 C2
Ladybrook Rd BRAM/HZG SK7 ..183 F5
Ladyfield St WILM/AE SK9 ....199 E3
Ladyhill Vw WALK M28 ....96 D2
Ladyhouse Cl MILN OL16 ....44 D2
Ladyhouse La MILN OL16 ....30 D5
Lady Kelvin Rd ALT WA14 ....165 F3
Ladymere Dr WALK M28 ....96 C2
Lady Rd OLDE OL4 ....93 E2
Ladyshore Cl ORD M5 ....113 C4
Ladyshore Rd BOLS/LL BL3 ....67 E3
Ladysmith Av BURY BL9 ....38 D1
Ladysmith Rd AUL OL6 ....108 A5
DID/WITH M20 ....157 H4
STLY SK15 ....120 C1
Ladysmith St EDGY/DAV SK3 ...171 H2
OLDS OL8 ....90 D4
The Ladysmith AUL OL6 ....108 A5
Ladythorn Av MPL/ROM SK6 .....175 H1
Ladythorn Crt PWCH M25 ....85 H5
Ladythorn Crs
BRAM/HZG SK7 ....194 A1
Ladythorne Av PWCH M25 ....85 H5
Ladythorne Dr PWCH M25 ....85 H5
Ladythorn Gv BRAM/HZG SK7 ..194 A1
Ladythorn Rd BRAM/HZG SK7 ..193 H1
Ladywell Av LHULT M38 ....81 F3
Ladywell Cl BRAM/HZG SK7 .....184 B2
Lagos Cl RUSH/FAL M14 ....128 D4
Laindon Rd RUSH/FAL M14 ......129 F5
Lake Bank LIT OL15 ....20 D5
Lake Dr MDTN M24 ....71 F1
Lakelands Crs BURY BL9 ....53 C5
Lakeland Dr ROY/SHW OL2 * 58 D1
Lakelands Dr BOLS/LL BL3 ....47 C4
Lakenheath Dr BOL BL1 ....23 E5
Lake Rd DTN/ASHW M34 ....132 C4
STLY SK15 ....120 C1
TRPK M17 ....125 F3
Lake Side BURY BL9 ....53 C3
LIT OL15 ....31 H1
Lakeside CHD/CHDH SK8 ....119 E1
Lakeside Av AULW OL7 ....118 C1
BOLS/LL BL3 ....82 A2
WALK M28 ....82 A2
Lakeside Cl GTN M18 ....131 E2
Lakeside Dr POY/DIS SK12 ....195 F2
Lakeside Gn OFTN SK2 ....172 D3
Lakeside Ri BKLY M9 ....87 F4
Lakeside Wy BURY BL9 ....4 E6
Lakes Rd DUK SK16 ....119 H5
MPL/ROM SK6 ....175 C4
Lake St BOLS/LL BL3 * 64 D1
OFTN SK2 ....172 C4
Lakeswood DUK SK16 ....119 G5
Lake Vw BKLY M9 ....88 D5
Lakin St NEWH/MOS M40 ....103 H3
Laleham Gn BRAM/HZG SK7 ....183 G1
Lamb Cl WGTN/LGST M12 ....129 C3
Lamb Ct CSLFD M3 * 6 B3
Lambert Dr SALE M33 ....138 D5
Lamberton Dr
NTHM/RTH M23 ....167 F3
Lambert St AULW OL7 ....119 E4
Lambeth Av FAIL M35 ....105 F2
Lambeth Gv MPL/ROM SK6 ......161 H1

Lambeth Rd NEWH/MOS M40 ...116 D1
RDSH SK5 ....145 F4
Lambeth Ter ROCH OL11 ....42 C1
Lamb La CSLFD M3 ....6 B3
Lambourn Cl BOLS/LL BL3 ....48 D4
SWIN M27 ....195 E3
Lambourne Cl
WYTH/NTH M22 ....180 C4
Lambourne Gv MILN OL16 ....44 C1
Lambourn Rd URM M41 ....123 E4
Lambton Rd CCHDY M21 ....141 H5
WALK M28 ....98 B4
Lambton St BOLS/LL BL3 ....64 B2
OLDE OL4 ....110 C1
Lamerton Wy WILM/AE SK9 .....192 B5
Lamorna Cl BRO M7 ....101 E2
Lamphey Cl BOL BL1 ....47 E1
Lamplight Wy SWIN M27 ....100 B3
Lamport Cl CMANE M1 ....128 C1
Lamport Ct CMANE M1 ....128 C1
Lampson St CHH M8 ....114 B1
Lampton Cl ALT WA14 ....165 G2
Lamshomle Cl BNG/LEV M19 ...144 A1
Lanark Av WYTH/NTH M22 ....168 C1
Lanark Cl BRAM/HZG SK7 ....185 H2
HEY OL10 ....40 D5
Lanbury Dr CHH M8 ....102 A5
Lancashire Cl CHAD OL9 ....8 A6
Lancashire Hl HTNM SK4 ....159 H3
Lancashire Rd PART M31 ....150 D4
Lancashire St
NEWH/MOS M40 ....103 G5
Lancaster Av FAIL M35 ....104 D3
FWTH BL4 ....65 E4
RAMS BL0 ....16 B4
SALE M33 ....120 C2
URM M41 ....124 D5
WHTF M45 ....69 H5
Lancaster Cl BOL BL1 ....3 C5
BRAM/HZG SK7 ....185 E4
RAMS BL0 ....16 B4
Lancaster Dr BOLS/LL BL3 ....51 E5
BURY BL9 ....27 C3
PWCH M25 ....86 B5
Lancaster Rd DID/WITH M20 .....157 F3
DROY M43 ....118 B2
DTN/ASHW M34 ....146 D2
IRL M44 ....150 B1
SLFD M6 ....112 A1
WILM/AE SK9 ....199 H1
Lancaster St CHAD OL9 ....90 B4
MOSL OL5 ....108 C4
RAD M26 ....67 H1
STKP SK1 ....13 J1
Lancaster Wk BOL BL1 * 33 H4
Lancelot Rd WYTH/NTH M22 ....181 E2
Lancelyn Dr WILM/AE SK9 ....199 G2
Lanchester Dr BOLS/LL BL3 ....48 C4
Lanchester St
NEWH/MOS M40 ....115 H2
Lancing Av DID/WITH M20 ....158 A3
Lancing Wk CHAD OL9 ....90 B1
Landau Dr WALK M28 ....81 E4
Landcross Rd RUSH/FAL M14 ...143 E2
Landeans Rd ROY/SHW OL2 ....59 H3
Lander Gv BKLY M9 ....88 C4
Landkey Cl NTHM/RTH M23 ......155 G4
Landmark Ct BOL BL1 ....32 C5
Landos Rd NEWH/MOS M40 ......115 F2
Landrace Dr WALK M28 ....96 C4
Landsberg Rd FAIL M35 ....105 G2
Landseer Dr MPL/ROM SK6 ......161 H2
Landseer St OLDE OL4 ....9 J6
Lands End Rd MDTN M24 ....71 G5
Lane Brow OLDE OL4 ....93 G2
Lane Dr OLDE OL4 ....93 G2
Lane End CHH M8 ....86 C1
HEY OL10 ....56 C1
Lane End Cl FAIL M35 ....105 F4
Lane End Rd BNG/LEV M19 ......158 A2
Lane Ends MPL/ROM SK6 ....162 C5
Lanegate HYDE SK14 ....147 G1
Lane Head Rd OLDE OL4 ....93 F4
Lane Meadow ROY/SHW OL2 .....59 H3
Lane North BOLS/LL BL3 * 48 A5
Laneside Av ROY/SHW OL2 ....60 C2
Laneside Cl LIT OL15 ....20 D5
Laneside Dr BRAM/HZG SK7 ....184 B3
Laneside Rd DID/WITH M20 ......169 H1
The Lane BOL BL1 ....47 E2
Lanfield Dr CHH M8 ....102 A3
Langcroft Dr
NEWH/MOS M40 ....104 B5
Langdale Av BNG/LEV M19 ....144 B3
MILN OL16 ....58 D1
OLDS OL8 ....91 E3
Langdale Cl CHD/CHDH SK8 .....181 H1
DTN/ASHW M34 ....145 H4
HALE/TIMP WA15 ....165 H4
MPL/ROM SK6 ....186 D4
Langdale Dr BURY BL9 ....69 H1
MDTN M24 ....72 C1
WALK M28 ....81 F5
Langdale Rd BRAM/HZG SK7 ....193 F2
HTNM SK4 ....144 C5
MPL/ROM SK6 ....162 A1
PART M31 ....150 D3
RUSH/FAL M14 ....128 D5
SALE M33 ....155 H5
STRET M32 ....125 H5
Langden Cl ROY/SHW OL2 ....59 H1
Langdon Cl BOL BL1 ....33 H4
Langdon St BKLY M9 ....87 H3
Langford Dr IRL M44 ....136 C2
Langford Gdns BOLS/LL BL3 .....48 A5
Langford Rd DID/WITH M20 .....142 C5
HTNM SK4 ....159 F2
Langford St
DTN/ASHW M34 * 132 C5
Langham Cl BOL BL1 ....23 F1
Langham Ct STRET M32 ....125 F4
Langham Gv
HALE/TIMP WA15 ....166 C1

Langham Rd ALT WA14 ....177 F2
HTNM SK4 ....159 E5
OLDS OL8 ....91 F3
SLFD M6 ....113 G3
Langham St AULW OL7 ....106 D5
Langholm Dr BOLE BL2 ....50 C3
Langholme Cl HULME M15 * 127 G1
Langholme Pl ECC M30 ....110 C3
Langholme Wy HEY OL10 ....40 A5
Langland Cl BNG/LEV M19 ....144 D1
Langland Dr ECC M30 ....124 D1
Langsett Av SLFD M6 ....112 B2
Langshaw Rd BOLS/LL BL3 ....48 B4
Langshaw St
NEWH/MOS M40 ....103 H4
SLFD M6 ....113 E4
Langshaw Wk BOLS/LL BL3 * 48 B4
Langside Av BKLY M9 ....88 B3
Langside Dr BOLS/LL BL3 ....47 F5
Langston Gn BRAM/HZG SK7 ...184 B5
Langston St CSLFD M3 * 7 C1
Langthorne St BNG/LEV M19 ....144 D3
Langthorne Wk BOLS/LL BL3 ......2 A7
Langton Cl FAIL M35 ....105 G2
Langton St HEY OL10 ....40 D3
SLFD M6 ....112 D3
Langton Ter ROCH OL11 ....42 D2
Langtree Cl WALK M28 ....96 C2
Langworthy Av LHULT M38 ....81 C3
Langworthy Rd
NEWH/MOS M40 ....103 H5
SLFD M6 ....113 E2
Lanhill Dr CHH M8 ....102 D4
Lankro Wy TRPK M17 ....111 G4
Lansdale Gdns BNG/LEV M19 ...158 B1
Lansdale St ECC M30 ....110 B5
Lansdown Cl CHD/CHDH SK8 ...183 G4
Lansdowne Cl BOLE BL2 * 34 C5
RAMS BL0 ....16 C3
Lansdowne Ct CHAD OL9 ....90 C1
Lansdowne Dr WALK M28 ....96 D2
Lansdowne Rd ALT WA14 ....165 G3
BOLE BL2 ....34 A4
CHAD OL9 ....8 A4
CHH M8 ....111 E2
ECC M30 ....110 D2
SALE M33 ....137 G3
URM M41 ....137 G3
Lansdowne Rd North
URM M41 ....123 F5
Lansdowne St ROCH OL11 ....29 F4
Lanstead Dr NEWH/MOS M40 ..115 H3
Lapwing Cl ROCH OL11 ....28 B4
Lapwing La DID/WITH M20 ......157 G1
RDSH SK5 ....146 A5
Larch Av CHD/CHDH SK8 ....182 D3
RAD M26 ....68 C3
STRET M32 ....125 G5
SWIN M27 ....98 D4
Larch Cl FAIL M35 ....105 E4
MPL/ROM SK6 ....166 D1
NTHM/RTH M23 ....166 C4
POY/DIS SK12 ....195 F4
The Larches MOSL OL5 ....109 E1
Larch Gv CHAD OL9 ....74 C4
SWIN M27 ....83 E5
Larch Rd DTN/ASHW M34 ....132 D5
ECC M30 ....124 D1
PART M31 ....150 D3
Larch St BURY BL9 ....5 K4
OLDS OL8 ....91 E3
Larchview Rd MDTN M24 ....73 F4
Larchway BRAM/HZG SK7 ....193 H2
MILN OL16 ....31 F4
MPL/ROM SK6 ....187 E5
Larchwood CHAD OL9 ....73 G5
Larchwood Cl SALE M33 ....153 H3
Larchwood Dr WILM/AE SK9 ....199 H2
Larchwood St BOL BL1 ....34 A4
Larke Ri DID/WITH M20 ....157 E3
Larkfield Av LHULT M38 ....81 F3
Larkfield Cl AULW OL7 ....107 E3
TOT/BURYW BL8 ....37 E2
Larkfield Gv BOLE BL2 ....3 H7
Larkfield Ms LHULT M38 ....81 F3
Larkhall Ri WYTH/NTH M22 ......168 D4
Lark Hl FWTH BL4 ....66 A5
Larkhill Cl HALE/TIMP WA15 ....166 C3
Lark Hill La OLDE OL4 ....78 D1
Larkhill Pl WHIT OL12 ....10 B2
Lark Hill Rd EDGY/DAV SK3 ......171 F4
UPML OL3 ....78 C2
Larkhill Vw CHD/CHDH SK8 .....102 C4
Larkhill Wk CHH M8 ....102 C4
Larkside Av WALK M28 ....79 G4
Larkspur Cl BOL BL1 ....34 B5
Langford Gdns BOLS/LL BL3 .....183 C1
Lark St BOL BL1 ....2 F4
FWTH BL4 ....66 A5
OLD OL1 * 76 C1
Larkswood Dr OFTN SK2 ....175 G4
STLY SK15 ....121 H1
Larmuth Av CCHDY M21 ....156 D2
Larne Av EDGY/DAV SK3 ....171 E2
STRET M32 ....140 A1

Larne St OP/CLY M11 ....116 B5
Larwood Av HTNM SK4 ....158 D5
Lascar Av ORD M5 ....113 F5
Lashbrook Cl
NEWH/MOS M40 ....115 C1
Lassell Fold HYDE SK14 ....134 C2
Lassell St OP/CLY M11 * 131 E1
Lastingham St
NEWH/MOS M40 ....104 B4
Latchford St AULW OL7 ....119 F1
Latchmere Rd RUSH/FAL M14 ..143 E3
Latham Ct MPL/ROM SK6 ....161 G1
Latham St BOL BL1 ....34 A4
OP/CLY M11 ....131 E1
Lathbury Rd BKLY M9 ....103 E4
Lathom Gv SALE M33 ....155 F3
Lathom Hall Av OLDE OL4 * 77 F3
Lathom Rd DID/WITH M20 ....143 F4
IRL M44 ....136 B3
Latimer St OLDE OL4 ....9 K5
Latin St MILN OL16 * 29 F4
Latrigg Crs MDTN M24 ....71 H2
Latrobe St DROY M43 ....117 H5
Lauderdale Crs
BRUN/LGST M13 ....128 D2
Launceston Cl BRAM/HZG SK7 ..184 A5
OLDS OL8 ....92 B5
Launceston Rd RAD M26 ....51 G4
Laundry St SLFD M6 ....113 C1
Laura St BURY BL9 ....26 D1
Laureate Wy DTN/ASHW M34 ..147 E4
Laurel Av BOLS/LL BL3 ....50 B5
CHAD OL9 ....73 G4
CHD/CHDH SK8 ....170 A4
RUSH/FAL M14 ....142 C1
Laurel Bank HYDE SK14 ....147 G3
STLY SK15 ....121 E5
Laurel Bank Gdns BKLY M9 * 88 A3
Laurel Ct BOL BL1 ....48 B2
MILN OL16 ....30 C5
Laurel Dr HALE/TIMP WA15 .....166 C5
LHULT M38 ....81 E3
Laurel Gn DTN/ASHW M34 ....147 E1
Laurel Gv BNG/LEV M19 ....158 D3
DTN/ASHW M34 ....112 B3
Laurel Gv SLFD M6 ....112 B3
Laurel Rd HTNM SK4 ....159 E2
Laurels Dr LIT OL15 ....31 C1
The Laurels MOSL OL5 ....109 E1
Laurel St BOL BL1 ....5 J4
BURY BL9 ....12 E2
HTNM SK4 ....73 G4
OLDE OL4 ....4 D4
TOT/BURYW BL8 ....26 A5
Laurel Wy BRAM/HZG SK7 ....183 H4
DID/WITH M20 ....142 D4
Lavender Cl NTHM/RTH M23 ....166 C5
SALE M33 ....153 F1
Lavender Rd FWTH BL4 ....65 F3
OLDE OL4 ....92 D3
Lavenders Brow STKP SK1 * 13 G5
Lavender Wk HYDE SK14 * 148 C6
Lavenham Av OP/CLY M11 ....117 E4
Lavenham Cl BRAM/HZG SK7 ...185 E4
BURY BL9 ....69 G1
Laverton Cl BURY BL9 ....39 H5
Lavington Av CHD/CHDH SK8 ...170 D4
Lavington Gv CTN M18 ....130 A4
Lavinia St ECC M30 ....110 C3
Lavister Av BNG/LEV M19 ....158 A3
Lawefield Crs SWIN M27 ....83 G2
Lawers Av CHAD OL9 ....74 B4
Lawflat WHIT OL12 ....19 H1
Lawler Av ORD M5 ....127 E2
Lawnbank Cl MDTN M24 ....72 B3
Lawndale Cl RAD M26 ....68 C4
Lawngreen Av CCHDY M21 ....141 E4
Lawnside Ms DID/WITH M20 .....157 F1
The Lawns ALT WA14 ....177 F3
Lawn St BOL BL1 ....2 F4
Lawnswood ROCH OL11 ....42 B2
Lawnswood Dr SWIN M27 ....99 F4
Lawnswood Park Rd
SWIN M27 ....99 F3
Lawrence Cl WHIT OL12 ....28 D2
Lawrence Pl POY/DIS SK12 ....195 E5
Lawrence Rd ALT WA14 ....165 F3
BRAM/HZG SK7 ....185 F1
URM M41 ....123 F5
Lawrence St BURY BL9 ....53 G5
EDGY/DAV SK3 * 16 C3
Lawson Av CHD/CHDH SK8 ......169 G4
Lawson Cl MDTN M24 ....56 D5
WALK M28 ....98 B3
Lawson Gv SALE M33 ....139 G5
Lawson Rd BOL BL1 ....33 F3
BKLY M9 ....87 H5
BOL BL1 ....33 H2
Law St ROCH OL11 ....41 B1
Lawton Av BRAM/HZG SK7 ....183 H4
Lawton Cl MPL/ROM SK6 ....161 G5
Lawton Moor Rd
NTHM/RTH M23 ....155 H5
Lawton Rd HTNM SK4 ....159 F2
Lawton St DROY M43 ....118 C5
OP/CLY M11 ....130 C1
STLY SK15 ....121 E4
WHIT OL12 ....10 E1
Laxey Rd NEWH/MOS M40 * 104 A3
Laxfield Dr URM M41 ....123 E5
Laxford Gv BOLS/LL BL3 * 47 F3
Laxley Cl CHAD OL9 ....90 C2
Layard St AUL OL6 ....119 F2
Laycock Av BOLE BL2 ....34 A3
STLY SK15 ....121 H1
Laycock Crs FAIL M35 ....105 F3
Laycock Dr DUK SK16 ....134 B1
Laycock Gv FAIL M35 ....105 F3
Laycock St MILN OL16 ....20 A5

Layfield Cl TOT/BURYW BL8 .....25 G3
Laystall St CMANE M1 ....7 J4
Laythe Barn Cl MILN OL16 ....31 F5
Layton Av HYDE SK14 ....133 E5
Layton Cl STKP SK1 ....13 J5
Layton Dr FWTH BL4 ....82 C1
    MPL/ROM SK6 ....162 B3
Layton St NEWH/MOS M40 ....115 G3
Leabank St BNG/LEV M19 ....144 A2
Leabrook Dr NEWH/MOS M40 ....104 D2
Leaburn Dr AULW OL7 ....30 D1
Leach Cl MILN OL16 ....30 D1
Leach St BOLS/LL BL3 ....48 D4
    FWTH BL4 ....66 B3
    GTN M18 ....130 A3
    MILN OL16 ....30 C5
    PWCH M25 ....85 G3
    ROY/SHW OL2 ....60 B5
Leach Wk OLDE OL4 ....76 D4
Leaconfield Dr WALK M28 ....97 G3
Lea Ct FAIL M35 ....104 D5
Leacroft Av BOLE BL2 ....50 A4
Leacroft Rd CCHDY M21 ....156 C1
Leadale Ri OLDE OL4 * 93 F1
Leader Williams Rd IRL M44 ....136 B2
Lea Dr BKLY M9 ....88 C4
Leafield Av DID/WITH M20 ......158 B2
Leafield Cl RAD M26 ....67 H1
Leafield Dr CHD/CHDH SK8 .....192 C1
    WALK M28 ....96 B4
Leafield Rd POY/DIS SK12 .....197 H1
Leaford Av DTN/ASHW M34 ......132 A4
Leaford Cl DTN/ASHW M34 ......132 A4
Leaf St BOLE BL2 ....49 G4
    HULME M15 ....128 A2
    RDSH SK5 ....145 G4
Leagate OLDHM M41 ....133 G2
Lea Gate Cl BOLE BL2 ....35 E1
League St MILN OL16 ....31 G1
Leaholme Cl NEWH/MOS M40 ...104 C5
Leah St LIT OL15 ....21 E3
Leak St OLDTF/WHR M16 ....127 F2
Leamington Av RAD M26 ....67 F1
    DID/WITH M20 ....157 E2
Leamington Rd ECC M30 ....110 C2
    RDSH SK5 ....145 E4
    URM M41 ....124 A5
Leamington St OLDE OL4 ....76 B4
    OP/CLY M11 ....130 C1
    WHIT OL12 ....10 B4
Lea Mount Dr BURY BL9 ....39 G2
Leam St AUL OL6 ....120 A1
Leamore Cl BKLY M9 ....88 D5
Leander Dr ROCH OL11 ....42 C5
Lea Rd CHD/CHDH SK8 ....181 G3
    HTNM SK4 ....159 E2
Leaside Av OLD OL1 ....74 B2
Leaside Cl WHIT OL12 ....29 G1
Leaside Dr DID/WITH M20 ....158 A1
Leaside Gv WALK M28 ....82 B4
Leaside Wy WILM/AE SK9 ....199 F4
The Leas HALE/TIMP WA15 ......178 C1
Leaton Av NTHM/RTH M23 ......167 H3
Leavale Cl LHULT M38 ....65 E2
Lea Ww ROY/SHW OL2 ....74 D1
Leaway OL12 * 19 H2
Lecester Rd CHH M8 ....102 C4
Leckenby Cl WALK M28 ....96 B4
Leconfield Dr BKLY M9 ....88 B4
Leconfield Rd ECC M30 ....110 A1
Lecturers Cl BOLS/LL BL3 ....49 E4
Ledbrooke Cl ORD M5 ....127 E1
Ledburn Cl HULME M15 ....127 G2
Ledbury Av URM M41 ....124 A5
Ledbury Cl MDTN M24 ....88 D1
Ledbury Rd FAIL M35 *.........117 F1
Ledge Ley CHD/CHDH SK8 .....182 C4
Ledsham Av BKLY M9 ....87 F2
Ledson Rd NTHM/RTH M23 .....167 H4
Ledward La ALT WA14 ....177 E2
Lee Av ALT WA14 ....165 F2
    BOLS/LL BL3 ....64 C1
Lee Bank WHTN BL5 ....62 B4
Leech Av AUL OL6 ....107 H5
Leech Brook Av
    DTN/ASHW M34 ....132 B3
Leech Brook Cl
    DTN/ASHW M34 ....132 B2
Leech St HYDE SK14 ....148 B1
    STLY SK15 ....120 D4
Lee Cl IRL M44 ....136 B2
Lee Ct WYTH/NTH M22 * 168 D1
Lee Crs STRET M32 ....140 C1
Lee Dale Cl
    DTN/ASHW M34 ....147 E1
Leeds Cl BURY BL9 ....70 A2
Leefields Cl UPML OL3 ....79 E4
Lee Ga BOLE BL2 ....35 E1
Leegate Cl HTNM SK4 ....158 C2
Leegate Dr BKLY M9 ....88 B2
Leegate Gdns HTNM SK4 ....158 C2
Leegate Rd HTNM SK4 ....158 D2
Leegrange Rd BKLY M9 ....103 F1
Lee Gv FWTH BL4 ....65 E4
Leek St RAD M26 ....67 H1
Leemans Hill St
    TOT/BURYW BL8 ....37 F1
Lees Av DTN/ASHW M34 ....146 C1
Lees Brook Pk OLDE OL4 ....92 C1
Lees Gv OLDE OL4 ....92 C2
Lees Hall Crs RUSH/FAL M14 ...158 D5
Leeside HTNM SK4 ....158 D5
Lees Park Av DROY M43 ....118 B3
Lees Rd AUL OL6 ....107 G1
    OLDE OL4 ....93 E3
Lees St AUL OL6 ....119 G1
    DROY M43 ....118 B3
    GTN M18 ....130 D2
    MDTN M24 ....73 G5
    MOSL OL5 * 93 H5
    OLDS OL8 ....106 C2
    OLDS OL8 ....120 D3
    SWIN M27 ....99 E1
Lees St East ROY/SHW OL2 .....60 A2
Leestone Rd WYTH/NTH M22 ...168 D3

Lee St BURY BL9 ....27 G3
    LIT OL15 ....21 E2
    MDTN M24 ....72 C1
    OLDS OL8 ....8 E6
    STKP SK1 ....13 G4
    UPML OL3 ....79 E4
Leesway OLDE OL4 ....92 D2
Leesway Dr DTN/ASHW M34 ....147 E1
Leeswood Av CCHDY M21 ......141 G5
Leewood SWIN M27 ....83 G3
Left Bank CSLFD M3 ....6 C4
Le Gendre St BOLE BL2 ....34 D5
Legh Cl POY/DIS SK12 ....195 F4
Legh Dr DTN/ASHW M34 ....118 A4
    MPL/ROM SK6 ....147 F5
Legh Rd BRO M7 ....101 G2
    POY/DIS SK12 ....197 F1
    SALE M33 ....155 F3
Legh St BRO M7 ....101 G2
    ECC M30 ....110 D4
Legion Gv BRO M7 ....101 H4
Legwood Ct URM M41 ....138 C1
Leicester Av BRO M7 * 102 A2
    DROY M43 ....117 G2
    DTN/ASHW M34 ....146 D2
    HALE/TIMP WA15 ....166 B1
Leicester Rd BRO M7 ....101 H5
    FAIL M35 ....105 E5
    HALE/TIMP WA15 ....177 H2
    SALE M33 ....154 C1
    WHTF M45 ....69 F3
Leicester St AULW OL7 ....119 G1
    OLDE OL4 ....92 A1
    RDSH SK5 ....145 E1
    ROCH OL11 ....43 F1
Leigh Av MPL/ROM SK6 ....174 D3
    SWIN M27 ....98 C5
Leighbrook Rd
    RUSH/FAL M14 ....142 D3
Leigh Cl TOT/BURYW BL8 ....25 H4
Leigh Fold HYDE SK14 ....133 H5
Leigh La TOT/BURYW BL8 ....37 F5
Leigh Rd HALE/TIMP WA15 .....179 F4
    WALK M28 ....96 B4
    WHTN BL5 ....62 A5
    WILM/AE SK9 ....198 A5
Leigh St FWTH BL4 ....66 A4
    HEY OL10 ....40 C4
    HYDE SK14 ....148 A1
    MILN OL16 ....31 E4
    TOT/BURYW BL8 ....37 E2
Leighton Av BOL BL1 ....48 A1
    LIT OL15 ....31 G1
Leighton Dr MPL/ROM SK6 ....175 H1
Leighton Rd OLDTF/WHR M16 ...127 F4
Leighton St NEWH/MOS M40 ...103 H2
Leinster Rd SWIN M27 ....98 D3
Leinster St FWTH BL4 ....65 H4
Leith Av SALE M33 ....155 H3
Leith Pl OLDS OL8 ....91 F5
Leith Rd SALE M33 ....155 F2
Le Mans Crs BOL BL1 ....2 E5
Lemnos St OLD OL1 ....9 J2
Lena St BOL BL1 ....14 A4
    CMANE M1 ....7 H5
Len Cox Wk ANC M4 * 7 H3
Lenfield La LIT OL15 ....75 F3
Leng Rd NEWH/MOS M40 ......104 C5
Lenham Ct RDSH SK5 ....145 H5
Lenham Gdns BOLE BL2 ....50 B5
Lennox Gdns BOLS/LL BL3 ......47 G4
Lennox St AUL OL6 ....119 H2
Lenora St BOLS/LL BL3 ....48 A5
Lenten Gv HEY OL10 ....56 B2
Lentmead Dr NEWH/MOS M40 ..103 H1
Lenton Gdns WYTH/NTH M22 ..168 D4
Lentworth Dr WALK M28 ....81 H2
Leominster Dr
    WYTH/NTH M22 ....180 D1
Leominster Rd MDTN M24 * 89 E1
Leonardin Cl ROY/SHW OL2 .....59 G1
Leonard St BOLS/LL BL3 ....64 D1
    ROCH OL11 ....42 B5
Leopold Av DID/WITH M20 .....157 F1
Leopold St ROCH OL11 ....43 G2
Lepp Crs TOT/BURYW BL8 ....26 D5
Leroy Dr BKLY M9 ....88 A5
Lerryn Dr BRAM/HZG SK7 ......193 G2
Lesley Rd URM M41 ....139 G2
Leslie Av BURY BL9 ....69 G2
    CHAD OL9 ....90 C4
Leslie Gv HALE/TIMP WA15 ....166 B3
Leslie Hough Wy SLFD M6 .....113 G2
Leslie St BOLE BL2 ....3 J1
    RUSH/FAL M14 ....128 C5
Lester Rd LHULT M38 ....80 D2
Lester St STRET M32 ....140 B1
Letchworth Av ROCH OL11 .....43 F1
Letchworth St RUSH/FAL M14 ..128 C5
Letham St OLDS OL8 ....91 G5
Levedale Rd BKLY M9 ....88 E3
Leven Cl FWTH BL4 ....83 E2
Levenhurst Rd CHH M8 ....102 A3
Levens Cl CHD/CHDH SK8 .....169 G5
Levens Dr BOLE BL2 ....35 F5
Levenshulme Rd GTN M18 .....130 C4
Levenshulme Ter
    BNG/LEV M19 * 144 A2
Levens Rd BRAM/HZG SK7 .....184 D2
Levens St NEWH/MOS M40 ....103 H3
    SLFD M6 ....101 G5
Levens Wk CHAD OL9 ....90 B2
Lever Av SWIN M27 ....84 C5
Lever Bridge Pl BOLS/LL BL3 ...49 H4
Lever Dr BOLS/LL BL3 ....48 D4
Lever Edge La BOLS/LL BL3 .....64 D3
Leverett Cl ALT WA14 ....164 D4
Lever Gv BOLE BL2 ....49 F4
Lever Hall Rd BOLE BL2 ....50 A2
Leverhulme Av BOLS/LL BL3 ....65 F5
Lever St BOLS/LL BL3 ....49 E5
    BOLS/LL BL3 ....50 D5
    BRAM/HZG SK7 ....185 E2
    CMANE M1 ....7 H4
    HEY OL10 ....41 E3
    MDTN M24 ....72 D3
    RAMS BL0 ....16 D2
Lever Wk MDTN M24 ....72 C5
Levington Dr OLDS OL8 ....106 D2

Levi St BOL BL1 ....32 C5
Lewes Av DTN/ASHW M34 .....146 D1
Lewis Av BKLY M9 ....103 F1
    URM M41 ....124 C3
Lewis Dr HEY OL10 ....40 A5
Lewisham Av
    NEWH/MOS M40 ....116 C1
Lewisham Cl ROY/SHW OL2 * ...58 D3
Lewis Rd DROY M43 ....117 F3
    RDSH SK5 ....145 F2
Lewis St ECC M30 ....111 E4
    HEY OL10 * 41 F5
    NEWH/MOS M40 ....115 G2
    ROY/SHW OL2 ....60 A4
Lewtas St ECC M30 ....111 F4
Lexton Av CHH M8 ....87 G5
Leybourne Av BNG/LEV M19 ...144 B1
Leybourne St BOL BL1 ....33 H4
Leybrook Rd WYTH/NTH M22 ..180 B1
Leyburn Av OLDTF/WHR M16 ...127 F4
    STRET M32 ....140 A1
    URM M41 ....138 A2
Leyburn Cl WHTF M45 ....69 F4
Leyburn Gv MPL/ROM SK6 ....162 B4
Leyburn Rd NEWH/MOS M40 ...89 F5
Leycett Dr NTHM/RTH M23 ....155 H5
Leycroft St CMANE M1 ....7 J6
Ley Dr HEY OL10 ....56 B2
Leyfield Av MPL/ROM SK6 .....162 B4
Leyfield Rd MILN OL16 ....31 E5
Ley Hey Av MPL/ROM SK6 .....162 B4
Ley Hey Rd MPL/ROM SK6 .....162 B4
Leyland Av CHD/CHDH SK8 ....169 G3
    DID/WITH M20 ....158 A3
    IRL M44 ....122 C4
Leylands La HYDE SK14 ....149 G5
Leyland St BURY BL9 ....53 G5
    HYDE SK14 ....12 E3
Ley La MPL/ROM SK6 ....175 H1
Leys Rd ALT WA14 ....146 D5
Leyton Av NEWH/MOS M40 ....104 A3
Leyton Cl FWTH BL4 ....65 E3
Leyton Dr BURY BL9 ....53 G4
Leyton St WHIT OL12 ....30 A1
Leywell Dr OLD OL1 ....76 C1
Leywell Rd BKLY M9 ....103 G2
Library La CHAD OL9 ....8 D1
Library St WHTN BL5 ....62 A4
Libra St BOL BL1 ....33 G4
Lichens Crs OLDS OL8 ....91 H4
Lichfield Av AUL OL6 ....107 G3
    BOLE BL2 ....34 C4
    HALE/TIMP WA15 ....178 D2
    RDSH SK5 ....145 E4
Lichfield Cl FWTH BL4 ....74 B3
    CHH M8 ....102 C3
    PWCH M25 ....86 B5
    SWIN M27 ....99 E4
    TOT/BURYW BL8 ....4 B1
Lichfield Rd ECC M30 ....111 G1
    RAD M26 ....51 G4
    URM M41 ....124 C4
Lichfield St SLFD M6 ....100 C5
Lichfield Ter MILN OL16 ....43 H1
Lichfield Wk MPL/ROM SK6 ....161 H5
Lidbrook Wk WGTN/LGST M12 ..129 F2
Liddington Hall Dr RAMS BL0 ...18 B1
Lidgate Cl LHULT M38 ....81 H2
Lidgard St CHH M8 ....102 B1
Liffey Av WYTH/NTH M22 ......180 D1
Lifton Av NEWH/MOS M40 .....115 H1
Light Alders La POY/DIS SK12 ..187 F5
Lightborne Rd SALE M33 ......155 E2
Lightbounds Rd BOL BL1 ....32 C5
Lightbourne Av SWIN M27 ......99 E5
Lightbowne Rd
    NEWH/MOS M40 ....103 H4
Lightburn Av LIT OL15 ....20 D1
Lightburne Av BOL BL1 ....48 A2
Lightfoot Wk OP/CLY M11 * 115 H5
Lighthorne Av EDGY/DAV SK3 ..170 C2
Lighthorne Gv EDGY/DAV SK3 ..170 C2
Lighthorne Rd EDGY/DAV SK3 ..170 C2
Light Oaks Rd SLFD M6 ....112 A1
Lightowlers La LIT OL15 ....21 G1
Lightwood WALK M28 ....96 C2
Lightwood Cl FWTH BL4 ....66 B3
Lignum Av CHAD OL9 ....74 C4
Lilac Av BURY BL9 ....53 E2
    HYDE SK14 ....147 H5
    MILN OL16 ....44 D3
    SWIN M27 ....99 F2
Lilac Ct SLFD M6 ....113 F5
Lilac Gv CHAD OL9 ....74 C4
    NEWH/MOS M40 ....103 H1
    PWCH M25 ....85 H1
Lilac La OLDS OL8 ....91 E5
Lilac Rd HALE/TIMP WA15 .....178 B1
    ROCH OL11 ....43 E4
Lilac St OFTN SK2 ....172 A3
Lilac View Cl ROY/SHW OL2 ....60 C3
Lilac View Rd ROY/SHW OL2 ...60 B3
Lila St BKLY M9 ....103 G3
Lilburn Ct RAMS BL0 ....16 C4
Lilford St LEIGH M16 ....11 F7
Lilford Cl WGTN/LGST M12 ....129 H2
Lillian Gv RDSH SK5 ....145 F3
Lillian St OLDTF/WHR M16 ....127 F4
Lilly St BOL BL1 ....2 A2
    HYDE SK14 ....148 B3
Lilmore Av CHH M8 ....102 D4
    NEWH/MOS M40 ....104 B4
Lily Av FWTH BL4 ....65 E3
Lily Cl EDGY/DAV SK3 ....171 G4
Lily Hill St WHTF M45 ....69 F2
Lily La BKLY M9 ....103 G3
Lily Lanes AUL OL6 ....107 H2
Lily St ECC M30 ....110 C4
    MDTN M24 ....73 G4
    MILN OL16 ....11 J5
    OLD OL1 ....75 F3
    ROY/SHW OL2 ....60 A1
Lima St BURY BL9 ....5 K2
Limber Cir CHH M8 ....102 D4
Lime Av SWIN M27 ....98 B4
    WHTF M45 ....69 E4
    WHTF M45 ....69 F3
Lime Bank St WGTN/LGST M12 .115 G5
Limebrook Cl OP/CLY M11 .....130 D1

Lime Cl DUK SK16 ....133 G2
    MILN OL16 ....111 F2
Lime Ct SLFD M6 * 115 F2
Lime Crs OLDTF/WHR M16 ....127 E4
Limeditch Rd FAIL M35 ....105 G2
Lime Fld MILN OL16 ....31 F4
Limefield MDTN M24 ....72 B5
    MOSL OL5 ....93 G5
Limefield Av FWTH BL4 ....66 A3
Limefield Brow BURY BL9 ....27 G4
Limefield Cl BOL BL1 ....32 D2
Limefield Rd BOL BL1 ....33 H1
    BRO M7 ....101 G1
    BURY BL9 ....27 G4
    RAD M26 ....67 G1
Limefield Ter BNG/LEV M19 ....144 A2
Lime Gdns DUK SK16 ....119 G5
    MDTN M24 ....72 B5
Lime Ga OLDS OL8 ....90 D5
Lime Gn OLDS OL8 ....106 A1
Lime Green Rd OLDS OL8 .....105 H3
Lime Gv AUL OL6 ....107 F5
    BURY BL9 ....5 G3
    CHD/CHDH SK8 ....170 A3
    DTN/ASHW M34 ....132 C4
    HALE/TIMP WA15 ....166 C3
    MILN OL16 ....40 D3
    LIT OL15 ....20 D5
    OLDTF/WHR M16 ....127 E4
    PWCH M25 ....85 H1
    RAMS BL0 ....17 E1
    ROY/SHW OL2 ....59 E3
    STLY SK15 ....120 D2
    WALK M28 ....68 A4
    WHTF M45 ....97 E1
Limehurst Av AULW OL7 ......106 C4
Limehurst Ct OLDS OL8 ....106 A1
Limehurst Rd AULW OL7 ......106 C4
Lime Kiln La MPL/ROM SK6 ...175 H4
Limekiln La WGTN/LGST M12 ..115 C5
Lime La OLDS OL8 ....105 H1
Lime Rd STRET M32 ....140 B2
Limers Ga WHIT OL12 ....9 J1
Limerston Dr NEWH/MOS M40 .105 G5
Limesdale Cl BOLE BL2 ....50 C5
Limeside Rd OLDS OL8 ....90 D5
Limestead Av CHH M8 ....102 B2
The Limes MOSL OL5 ....108 C1
Lime St BURY BL9 ....5 H5
    DUK SK16 ....119 G5
    ECC M30 ....111 E4
    FWTH BL4 ....66 B4
    MPL/ROM SK6 ....161 F2
    NEWH/MOS M40 ....115 G2
    OLD OL1 ....74 D3
    ROCH OL11 ....42 B7
Lime Tree Cl URM M41 ....139 E2
Lime Tree Gv FAIL M35 ....105 G3
Limetrees Rd MDTN M24 ....72 A2
Limley Gv CCHDY M21 ....141 G4
Linacre Av BOLS/LL BL3 ....64 D2
Linby St HULME M15 ....127 H1
Lincoln Av BNG/LEV M19 ......144 B2
    BOLS/LL BL3 ....64 D3
    CHD/CHDH SK8 ....181 G5
    DROY M43 ....117 H2
    DTN/ASHW M34 ....146 D2
    STRET M32 ....150 B2
Lincoln Cl AUL OL6 ....107 G2
    ROCH OL11 ....30 B5
Lincoln Dr BURY BL9 * 53 G1
    HALE/TIMP WA15 ....166 C4
    LIT OL15 ....21 E5
Lincoln Gv BOLE BL2 ....35 G2
    BRUN/LGST M13 ....128 D3
    SALE M33 ....155 F2
Lincoln Leach Ct ROCH OL11 *..43 E1
Lincoln Mnr BRO M7 * 101 H5
Lincoln Rd BOL BL1 ....48 A1
    FAIL M35 ....105 F4
    MDTN M24 ....89 F2
    WILM/AE SK9 ....199 H1
Lincoln St BRUN/LGST M13 ....128 C2
    CHAD OL9 ....90 C2
    ECC M30 ....110 D4
    NEWH/MOS M40 ....104 B2
    ROCH OL11 ....29 G5
Lincoln Towers
    WGTN/LGST M12 * 129 G4
Lincombe Rd WYTH/NTH M22 .180 B4
Lincroft Rd SALE M33 * 185 E3
Lindale Av BOL BL1 ....47 G1
    DTN/ASHW M34 ....132 A1
    HALE/TIMP WA15 ....165 H4
    OLDE OL4 ....76 C4
    RAMS BL0 ....17 E2
    URM M41 ....124 A4
Lindale Cl WALK M28 ....80 B3
Lindale Dr MDTN M24 ....72 B1
Lindale Ri OLDE OL4 * 60 C2
Lindbury Av OFTN SK2 ....172 D2
Linden Av BOLS/LL BL3 ....50 D2
    DTN/ASHW M34 ....132 A1
    HALE/TIMP WA15 ....165 H4
    OLDE OL4 ....76 C4
    RAMS BL0 ....17 E2
    SLFD M6 ....100 B4
    SWIN M27 ....98 D3
Linden Cl DTN/ASHW M34 .....132 D5
Linden Crs DTN/ASHW M34 ....37 E1
Linden Dr ORD M5 ....113 E5
Linden Gv BRAM/HZG SK7 ....193 G5
    OFTN SK2 ....172 C5
    RUSH/FAL M14 ....143 F3
Linden Ms WALK M28 ....96 A4
Linden Pk BNG/LEV M19 ......144 A5
Linden Rd CHD/CHDH SK8 ....169 H4
    DID/WITH M20 ....157 F2
    DTN/ASHW M34 ....132 D5
    STLY SK15 ....135 E1
    WALK M28 ....96 A4
Linden Wk BOLE BL2 * 35 E1
Linden Wy MPL/ROM SK6 .....187 F5
Lindenwood CHAD OL9 ....73 H4
Lindeth Av GTN M18 ....130 C4
Lindfield Dr BOL BL1 ....33 H5
Lindfield Est North
    WILM/AE SK9 ....198 D4
Lindfield Est South
    WILM/AE SK9 ....198 D4

Lindfield Rd RDSH SK5 ....145 F2
Lindinis Av ORD M5 ....113 F3
Lindisfarne WHIT OL12 ....10 B5
Lindisfarne Cl SALE M33 ......154 C5
Lindisfarne Dr POY/DIS SK12 ..195 E3
Lindisfarne Pl BOLE BL2 ....34 D4
Lindisfarne Rd AULW OL7 .....106 B5
Lindley Gv EDGY/DAV SK3 ....171 G4
Lindley St BOLS/LL BL3 * 67 E1
    FWTH BL4 ....83 E1
Lindleywood Rd
    RUSH/FAL M14 ....143 G3
Lindon Wv DROY M43 ....117 F5
Lindop Rd HALE/TIMP WA15 ..178 A3
Lindow Cl TOT/BURYW BL8 .....26 D5
Lindow Ct MPL/ROM SK6 * 161 E3
Lindow Fold Dr WILM/AE SK9 .198 B4
Lindow La WILM/AE SK9 ....198 B4
Lindow Rd OLDTF/WHR M16 ..141 F1
Lindow St SALE M33 ....155 G3
Lindrick Av WHTF M45 ....85 E1
Lindrick Cl NEWH/MOS M40 ..104 B3
Lindrick Ter BOLS/LL BL3 * 48 C4
Lindsay Av BNG/LEV M19 .....143 H2
    CHD/CHDH SK8 ....183 E3
    SWIN M27 ....98 D3
Lindsay Cl OLDE OL4 * 76 C2
Lindsay Rd BNG/LEV M19 .....143 H3
Lindsay St STLY SK15 ....121 E5
Lindsell Rd ALT WA14 ....165 F1
Lindsgate Dr
    HALE/TIMP WA15 ....166 C2
Lindum Av OLDTF/WHR M16 ..127 F4
Lindum St RUSH/FAL M14 .....128 C5
Lindwall Cl NTHM/RTH M23 ...158 A4
Linehan Cl HTNM SK4 ....158 A4
Linenholme ROY/SHW OL2 * 74 D2
Linen Ct CSLFD M3 ....114 A2
Lines Rd DROY M43 ....118 A4
    IRL M44 ....136 D2
Linfield Cl BOLE BL2 ....35 E2
Linfield St OP/CLY M11 ....116 C4
Linford Av NEWH/MOS M40 ....89 F5
Lingard La BRAM/HZG SK7 .....161 E1
Lingard Rd WYTH/NTH M22 ...156 D5
Lingard St RDSH SK5 ....145 F3
Lingcrest Rd NEWH/MOS M40 .144 C4
Lingdale Rd CHD/CHDH SK8 ...182 C2
Lingfield Av BRAM/HZG SK7 ...185 G2
    SALE M33 ....153 E4
Lingfield Cl FWTH BL4 ....65 H5
    TOT/BURYW BL8 ....26 D4
Lingfield Rd OP/CLY M11 ......116 B2
Lingholme Dr MDTN M24 ....71 H2
Lingmell Cl BOL BL1 ....47 C1
    MDTN M24 ....72 A2
    URM M41 ....123 G4
Lingmoor Cl MDTN M24 ....71 H2
Lingmoor Rd BOL BL1 ....32 C5
Lingmoor Wk HULME M15 * ...128 A3
Lings Wk WYTH/NTH M22 .....180 D3
Linhope Cl HTNM SK4 ....158 B3
Link Av URM M41 ....139 G2
Linkfield Dr WALK M28 ....96 A4
Link La OLDS OL8 ....91 F5
Link Rd OLDE OL4 ....153 G4
    SALE M33 ....153 G4
Links Av FAIL M35 ....105 G5
Links Crs PWCH M25 ....86 D5
Links Dr HOR/BR BL6 ....46 A5
Linksfield DTN/ASHW M34 ....132 C3
Linkside Av ROY/SHW OL2 .....59 E4
Links Pl AUL OL6 ....107 H4
Links Rd AUL OL6 ....107 H4
    HEY OL10 ....56 A1
    HOR/BR BL6 ....44 C2
    MPL/ROM SK6 ....162 C3
    MPL/ROM SK6 ....175 E2
    WILM/AE SK9 ....200 B2
The Links NEWH/MOS M40 ....104 B3
Links Vw PWCH M25 ....100 D1
    ROCH OL11 ....29 E5
Links Wy CHAD OL9 ....86 C5
Linksway CHD/CHDH SK8 .....169 F5
    PWCH M25 ....86 C5
    SWIN M27 ....99 F3
Linksway Cl HTNM SK4 ....158 D1
Linksway Dr BURY BL9 ....69 H1
The Link RDSH SK5 ....145 G5
    ROY/SHW OL2 ....44 C5
    WILM/AE SK9 ....192 A4
Linley Av BURY BL9 ....53 F4
Linley Dr OLDE OL4 ....92 C3
Linley Gv RAMS BL0 ....16 C4
Linley Rd CHD/CHDH SK8 .....183 E4
    SALE M33 ....155 E4
Linnell Dr ROCH OL11 ....28 B3
Linnet Cl DTN/ASHW M34 .....132 D3
    OFTN SK2 ....173 G4
    WGTN/LGST M12 ....129 G4
Linnet Dr BURY BL9 ....5 K1
    IRL M44 ....122 B3
Linnet Hl ROCH OL11 ....29 F5
Linnet's Wood Ms WALK M28 ..82 B4
Linney La ROY/SHW OL2 ....60 B2
Linney Rd BRAM/HZG SK7 ....183 G2
Linn St CHH M8 ....102 B1
Linslade Gdns BOLS/LL BL3 ....48 D4
Linsley St CSLFD M3 ....6 C2
Linstead Dr CHH M8 ....102 C4
Linthorpe Wk BOLS/LL BL3 ....48 D4
Linton Av BURY BL9 ....38 C1
    DTN/ASHW M34 ....115 C3
Linton Cl ANC M4 ....115 G5
Linton Rd SALE M33 ....140 A5
Linton Wk BRO M7 ....101 H5
Linwood Gv WGTN/LGST M12 .144 A1
Linwood St NEWH/MOS M40 ..104 B4
Lion Brow BKLY M9 ....88 A5
Lion Fold La BKLY M9 ....88 A5
Lions Dr SWIN M27 ....99 F3
Lion St BKLY M9 ....88 A5
Lisbon St WHIT OL12 ....29 E3
Lisburn Av CCHDY M21 ....141 G5
    SALE M33 ....154 B5
Lisburne Av OFTN SK2 ....173 E5
Lisburne Cl OFTN SK2 ....173 E5
Lisburne La OFTN SK2 ....172 D5

Lisburn Rd NEWH/MOS M40 .... 103 H2
Liscard Av RUSH/FAL M14 .... 142 D2
Lisetta Av OLDE OL4 * 92 A2
Liskeard Av RUSH/FAL OL2 .... 59 H5
Liskeard Cl MILN OL16 .... 11 J3
Liskeard Cl BRAM/HZG SK7 .... 184 A5
Lisle St WHIT OL12 .... 10 E4
Lismore Av BOLS/LL BL3 .... 47 G4
EDGY/DAV SK3 .... 171 E2
Lismore Rd DUK SK16 .... 133 G1
Lismore Wy URM M41 .... 124 C3
Lissadel St SLFD M6 .... 113 F1
Lisson Gv HALE/TIMP WA15 .... 177 H2
Lister Rd MDTN M24 .... 87 G1
Lister St BOLS/LL BL3 .... 64 A1
Liston St DUK SK16 .... 120 C5
Litcham Cl CMANE M1 .... 128 E1
Litchfield Gv WALK M28 .... 98 A3
Litherland Av WYTH/NTH M22 .... 180 D2
Litherland Rd BOLS/LL BL3 .... 64 D2
SALE M33 .... 155 F3
Little 66 BURY BL9 .... 54 A3
Little Ancoats St CMANE M1 .... 7 H5
Little Bank St OLDE OL4 .... 92 A1
Littlebourne Wk BOL BL1 .... 23 F5
Littlebrook Cl CHD/CHDH SK8 .... 171 F5
Little Brow RAD SALE M33 .... 158 S5
Little Brow EDGY/EC BL7 .... 23 F4
Little Clegg Rd LIT OL15 .... 20 C5
Littledale Wk WHIT OL12 .... 10 A5
Little David St CMANE M1 .... 7 H6
Little Ees La SALE M33 .... 139 F4
Little Egerton St STKP SK1 .... 13 F2
Littlefields HYDE SK14 .... 135 H4
Little Flatt WHIT OL12 .... 29 E2
Little Gn MDTN M24 .... 73 E3
Littlegreen Gdns SLFD M6 .... 113 G2
Little Harwood Lee BOLE BL2 .... 35 E3
Littlehaven Cl WGTN/LGST M12 .... 129 F3
Little Heath La ALT WA14 .... 164 A4
Little Hey St ROY/SHW OL2 .... 60 A5
Littlehills Cl MDTN M24 .... 72 B3
Little Holme St ANC M4 .... 115 G4
Little Holme Wk BOLS/LL BL3 * 49 E5
Little Howarth Wy
WHIT OL12 .... 19 H4
Little John St CSLFD M3 .... 6 B6
Little Lever St CMANE M1 .... 7 H4
Little Meadow Rd EDGW/EG BL7 * 23 E4
Little Moor Clough
EDGW/EG BL7 .... 22 D1
Little Moor Cottages
WHIT OL12 .... 172 C1
Little Moor La OLDE OL4 .... 76 B4
Little Moss La SWIN M27 .... 84 A5
Littlemoss Rd DROY M43 .... 118 B2
Little Nelson St ANC M4 * 7 G1
Little Oak Cl OLDE OL4 .... 75 G2
Little Peter St HULME M15 .... 128 A1
Little Pitt St CMANE M1 * 7 J4
Little Quay St CSLFD M3 .... 6 D5
Little Stones Rd EDGW/EG BL7 .... 22 D1
Littleton Rd BRO M7 .... 100 D2
Little Underbank STKP SK1 .... 13 G3
Littlewood Av BURY BL9 .... 38 C1
Littlewood Rd
WYTH/NTH M22 .... 168 C5
Littlewood St SLFD M6 .... 112 D5
Littondale Cl ROY/SHW OL2 .... 59 H5
Liverpool Cl RDSH SK5 .... 145 E4
Liverpool Rd CSLFD M3 .... 6 A6
ECC M30 .... 110 C4
ECC M30 .... 123 E2
IRL M44 .... 150 D3
Liverpool St RDSH SK5 .... 145 E4
SLFD M6 .... 112 D5
Liverstudd Av RDSH SK5 .... 145 E4
Livesey St ANC M4 .... 115 F3
BNG/LEV M19 .... 144 A5
OLD OL1 .... 76 B4
Livingston Av
WYTH/NTH M22 .... 180 A2
Livingstone Av MOSL OL5 .... 108 C1
Livingstone St OLDE OL4 .... 92 D2
Livsey St BOL BL1 .... 33 H3
Livsey La HEY OL10 .... 40 B4
Livsey St MILN OL16 .... 10 E7
WHTF M45 .... 69 G4
Lizmar Ter BKLY M9 .... 103 E1
Llanberis Rd CHD/CHDH SK8 .... 182 B3
Lloyd Av CHD/CHDH SK8 .... 169 F3
Lloyd Gdns ALT WA14 .... 177 G1
Lloyd Rd BNG/LEV M19 .... 144 A5
Lloyd Sq ALT WA14 .... 165 G5
Lloyd St ALT WA14 .... 165 G5
CMANW M2 .... 6 E5
HEY OL10 .... 41 E5
HTNM SK4 .... 12 D1
ROCH OL11 .... 42 C2
WHIT OL12 .... 14 B4
Lloyd St South
RUSH/FAL M14 .... 142 C2
Lobden Crs WHIT OL12 .... 14 B1
Lobelia Av FWTH BL4 .... 65 F3
Lobley Cl WHIT OL12 .... 30 C1
Lochawe Cl HEY OL10 .... 40 B5
Lochinver Gv HEY OL10 .... 40 B5
Lochmaddy Cl
BRAM/HZG SK7 .... 185 G3
Lock Cl HEY OL10 .... 56 B1
Lockett Gdns CSLFD M3 .... 6 A2
Lockett St SLFD M6 .... 114 B1
SLFD M6 .... 100 D5
Lockhart Cl WGTN/LGST M12 .... 129 F2
Lockhart St ROCH OL11 .... 43 G1
Lockingate St AUL OL6 .... 107 F4
Locking Gate Ri OLDE OL4 .... 76 D3
Lock Keepers Ms SWIN M27 .... 100 A2
Locklands La IRL M44 .... 136 A1
Lock La HOR/BR BL6 .... 46 D5
PART M31 .... 150 B3
Lock Rd ALT WA14 .... 165 F3
Lockside MPL/ROM SK6 .... 175 F3
Lockside Vw MOSL OL5 .... 94 B4
Locksley Cl HTNM SK4 .... 12 C1
Lockton Cl RDSH SK5 .... 145 E5
Lockton Ct CMANE M1 * 128 C1

Lockwood St
WGTN/LGST M12 .... 130 A3
Lodge Av URM M41 .... 139 E1
Lodge Bank Rd LIT OL15 .... 20 C5
Lodge Brow RAD M26 .... 68 C2
Lodge Cl DUK SK16 .... 133 H1
Lodge Ct HTNM SK4 .... 158 C4
HYDE SK14 .... 135 H4
Lodge Farm Cl
BRAM/HZG SK7 .... 183 H2
Lodge Fold DROY M43 .... 118 A3
Lodge Gn DUK SK16 .... 133 H1
Lodge La DUK SK16 .... 120 A5
DUK SK16 .... 133 G4
Lodgepole Cl ECC M30 .... 110 A5
Lodge Rd RAD M26 .... 68 C2
Lodgeside Cl DROY M43 .... 118 A3
Lodge St AULW OL7 .... 119 E4
HYDE SK14 .... 133 H3
LIT OL15 .... 21 E3
MDTN M24 .... 72 D3
NEWH/MOS M40 .... 103 F5
RAMS BL0 .... 16 D2
WHIT OL12 .... 19 H2
Lodge Vw DROY M43 .... 118 A3
Loen Crs BOL BL1 .... 33 F3
Loganberry Av SLFD M6 .... 113 E2
Logan St BOL BL1 .... 33 H1
Logwood Av TOT/BURYW BL8 .... 4 A2
Loisine Cl ROCH OL11 .... 41 H3
Lokfu Gdns CHH M8 .... 101 H5
Lomas Cl BNG/LEV M19 .... 144 A3
Lomas St EDGY/DAV SK3 .... 12 D7
FAIL M35 .... 105 F1
MDTN M24 .... 73 E3
Lomax's Buildings BOLE BL2 .... 3 F6
Lomax St BOL BL1 .... 33 H4
BURY BL9 .... 5 G3
CMANE M1 .... 7 K4
RAD M26 .... 67 G1
WHIT OL12 .... 10 D4
WHTF M45 .... 69 F2
Lombard Cl MPL/ROM SK6 .... 161 G2
Lombard Gv RUSH/FAL M14 .... 143 E3
Lombard St OLD OL1 .... 9 G3
RAD M26 .... 67 G1
Lombardy Ct SLFD M6 * 113 F2
Lomond Av HALE/TIMP WA15 .... 178 B1
STRET M32 .... 126 A5
Lomond Cl OFTN SK2 .... 184 B1
Lomond Dr TOT/BURYW BL8 .... 37 E3
Lomond Pl BOLS/LL BL3 .... 47 F3
Lomond Rd WYTH/NTH M22 .... 181 E2
Lomond Ter MILN OL16 * 13 G4
London Pl STKP SK1 .... 13 G4
London Rd BRAM/HZG SK7 .... 173 E5
CMANE M1 .... 7 J7
OLD OL1 .... 76 A3
SWIN M27 .... 200 D4
London Rd North
POY/DIS SK12 .... 195 G5
London Rd South
POY/DIS SK12 .... 195 G5
London Sq STKP SK1 .... 13 G4
London St BOLS/LL BL3 .... 48 D5
SLFD M6 .... 113 G1
WHTF M45 .... 69 G5
Long Acres Dr WHIT OL12 .... 14 C4
Longacres La WHIT OL12 .... 14 C3
Longacres Rd
HALE/TIMP WA15 .... 178 D5
Longbow Ct BRO M7 * 7 K6
Longbridge Rd TRPK M17 .... 125 F2
Long Clawy FWTH BL4 .... 65 G4
Longcliffe Wk BOL BL1 * 34 A4
Long Clough ROY/SHW OL2 .... 74 D2
Longcrag Wk HULME M15 * 128 A3
Longcroft Dr ALT WA14 .... 165 E5
Longcroft Gv DTN/ASHW M34 .... 118 A5
NTHM/RTH M23 .... 167 H2
Long Croft La CHD/CHDH SK8 .... 182 C4
Longdale Cl ROY/SHW OL2 .... 58 D5
Longdale Dr HYDE SK14 .... 135 H5
Longden Av OLDE OL4 .... 76 D1
Longden Rd WGTN/LGST M12 .... 144 A4
Longden St BOL BL1 .... 48 B1
Longfellow Av BOLS/LL BL3 .... 64 A4
Longfellow Crs OLDE OL1 .... 60 C5
Longfield BURY BL9 .... 38 D2
Longfield Av CHD/CHDH SK8 .... 181 H5
HALE/TIMP WA15 .... 166 D3
URM M41 .... 138 B1
Longfield Cl HYDE SK14 .... 133 H2
Longfield Crs OLDE OL4 .... 76 B3
Longfield Dr URM M41 .... 138 B1
Longfield La OLDE OL4 .... 76 C3
Longfield Pk ROY/SHW OL2 .... 59 H4
Longfield Rd BOLS/LL BL3 .... 64 A2
NTHM/RTH M23 .... 167 G1
ROY/SHW OL2 .... 59 H4
Longford Av BOL BL1 .... 33 F4
STRET M32 .... 140 C1
Longford Cl STRET M32 .... 126 B5
Longford Gdns STRET M32 .... 140 C1
Longford Pl RUSH/FAL M14 .... 129 G4
Longford Rd CCHDY M21 .... 141 E2
RDSH SK5 .... 145 F2
STRET M32 .... 126 B5
Longford Rd West
BNG/LEV M19 .... 144 D2
Longford St GTN M18 .... 130 C2
HEY OL10 .... 40 D4
Long Grain Pl OFTN SK2 .... 173 E4
Longham Cl BRAM/HZG SK7 .... 172 C1
Long Hey HALE/TIMP WA15 .... 178 B1
Longhey Rd WYTH/NTH M22 .... 168 C4
Long Hl ROCH OL11 .... 42 C2
Longhirst Cl BOL BL1 .... 33 E3
Longhurst La MPL/ROM SK6 .... 188 C1
Longhurst Rd BKLY M9 .... 87 G3
Longlands Av WHIT OL12 .... 30 A2
Longlands Dr HYDE SK14 .... 134 C5
Long La BOLE BL2 .... 52 A5
BURY BL9 .... 5 K2
CHAD OL9 .... 90 A4
OFTN SK2 .... 184 D2
UPML OL3 .... 78 D2

Longlevens Rd
WYTH/NTH M22 .... 180 B2
Longley Dr WALK M28 .... 98 A4
Longley La WYTH/NTH M22 .... 168 D2
Longley St OLDE OL1 .... 9 G5
ROY/SHW OL2 .... 60 A4
RAD M26 .... 82 A5
Long Marl Dr WILM/AE SK9 .... 192 C5
Longmead Av BRAM/HZG SK7 .... 183 H4
Long Meadow EDGW/EG BL7 .... 23 H4
HYDE SK14 .... 134 A2
Longmeadow Gv
DTN/ASHW M34 .... 146 C1
Longmead Pas HYDE SK14 .... 133 C5
Longmead Rd SLFD M6 .... 100 A5
Longmere Av WYTH/NTH M22 .... 180 C1
Long Millgate CSLFD M3 .... 6 E2
Longnor Rd BRAM/HZG SK7 .... 185 F5
CHD/CHDH SK8 .... 182 A5
Longport Av DID/WITH M20 .... 142 C4
Longridge EDGW/EG BL7 .... 23 H5
Longridge Av STLY SK15 .... 120 D1
Longridge Crs BOL BL1 .... 32 C4
Longridge Dr HEY OL10 .... 40 A4
TOT/BURYW BL8 .... 52 B1
Long Rw STLY SK15 .... 109 G3
Long Rushes ROY/SHW OL2 .... 59 G1
Longshaw Av SWIN M27 .... 98 B1
Longshaw Dr LHULT M38 .... 81 F5
Longshaw Ford Rd BOL BL1 .... 32 C1
Longshut La OFTN SK2 .... 13 G7
Longshut La West OFTN SK2 .... 13 G7
Longsides
HALE/TIMP WA15 .... 178 D5
Longsight BOLE BL2 .... 35 E1
Longsight La BOLE BL2 .... 35 E2
CHD/CHDH SK8 .... 192 C2
Longsight Rd BOLE BL2 .... 35 E3
Longsight St HTNM SK4 .... 12 C2
Longson St BOL BL1 .... 3 H3
Long St GTN M18 .... 130 D2
MDTN M24 .... 72 D3
SWIN M27 .... 99 E3
Longton Av DID/WITH M20 .... 157 F1
Longton Rd BKLY M9 .... 87 H3
SLFD M6 .... 99 H5
Longton St BURY BL9 .... 53 C5
Longtown Gdns BOL BL1 * 33 H4
Longview Dr SWIN M27 .... 98 B1
Longwall Av WALK M28 .... 96 D2
Longwood Cl MPL/ROM SK6 .... 162 D5
Longwood Rd TRPK M17 .... 125 E2
WYTH/NTH M22 .... 180 D1
Longworth Cl URM M41 .... 137 F2
Longworth Clough
EDGW/EG BL7 .... 22 C1
Longworth La EDGW/EG BL7 .... 22 C3
Longworth St BOLE BL2 .... 6 C6
CMANW M2 .... 6 C6
Lonsdale Av MILN OL16 .... 43 G1
RDSH SK5 .... 131 E5
SWIN M27 .... 99 F3
URM M41 .... 124 A4
Lonsdale Gv BNG/LEV M19 .... 144 B1
BOL BL1 .... 48 A1
OLDS OL8 .... 90 C5
Lonsdale Rd
NEWH/MOS M40 .... 104 B4
TOT/BURYW BL8 .... 37 H4
Loom St ANC M4 .... 7 J3
Loonies Ct STKP SK1 * 13 G5
Lord Byron Sq SALQ M50 * 113 E5
Lord Kitchener Ct
EDGY/DAV SK3 * 171 H3
Lord La FAIL M35 .... 117 F1
Lord Napier Dr ORD M5 .... 126 D1
Lord North St
NEWH/MOS M40 .... 115 H1
Lords Av BOLS/LL BL3 .... 48 B4
Lordsfields Av AULW OL7 .... 119 G1
Lords Fold BOL BL1 * 32 C4
Lord Sheldon Wy AULW OL7 .... 118 D3
Lordship Cl BKLY M9 .... 103 G1
Lordsmead St HULME M15 .... 127 H1
Lord's Stile La EDGW/EG BL7 .... 23 G4
Lord's St IRL M44 .... 150 B1
Lord St ANC M4 .... 114 D2
AUL OL6 .... 119 G1
BURY BL9 .... 5 F5
DTN/ASHW M34 .... 131 F4
FWTH BL4 .... 66 B4
MDTN M24 .... 73 E4
OLD OL1 .... 9 G2
RAD M26 .... 68 B1
STKP SK1 .... 13 G4
Loretto Rd URM M41 .... 139 F2
Lorgill Cl EDGY/DAV SK3 .... 171 H4
Loring St NEWH/MOS M40 .... 104 B5
Lorland Rd EDGY/DAV SK3 .... 171 E2
Lorna Gv CHD/CHDH SK8 .... 169 E3
Lorna Rd CHD/CHDH SK8 .... 183 E2
Lorna Wy IRL M44 .... 136 C5
Lorne Av ROY/SHW OL2 .... 74 C1
Lorne Gv EDGY/DAV SK3 .... 171 H3
URM M41 .... 139 E1
Lorne Rd RUSH/FAL M14 .... 143 E3
Lorne St BOL BL1 .... 33 F4
BRUN/LGST M13 .... 128 D3
ECC M30 .... 110 C5
FWTH BL4 .... 65 H2
HEY OL10 .... 40 D5
MOSL OL5 .... 108 D1
OLDE OL4 .... 91 F5
WHIT OL12 .... 19 G5
Lorne Wy HEY OL10 .... 40 A5
Lorraine Cl HEY OL10 .... 56 B1
Lorraine Rd
HALE/TIMP WA15 .... 166 B4
Lorton Cl MDTN M24 .... 71 H2
WALK M28 .... 96 A4
Lorton Gv BOLE BL2 .... 50 C1

Lostock Av BNG/LEV M19 .... 144 B2
BRAM/HZG SK7 .... 183 G3
POY/DIS SK12 .... 194 C3
SALE M33 .... 155 F2
URM M41 .... 124 A5
Lostock Cl HEY OL10 .... 40 C3
Lostock Dr BURY BL9 .... 27 G5
Lostock Gv STRET M32 .... 125 G5
Lostock Hall Rd POY/DIS SK12 .... 194 C4
Lostock Junction La
HOR/BR BL6 .... 46 D3
Lostock Park Dr HOR/BR BL6 .... 46 D3
Lostock Rd ORD M5 .... 112 D3
POY/DIS SK12 .... 194 D5
URM M41 .... 124 C4
Lostock St NEWH/MOS M40 .... 115 G2
Lostock Wy WILM/AE SK9 .... 192 A3
Lothian Av ECC M30 .... 110 C2
Lottery Rw BOL BL1 .... 3 F5
Lottery St EDGY/DAV SK3 .... 12 D4
Lottie St SWIN M27 .... 99 F2
Loughborough Cl SALE M33 .... 153 G3
Loughfield URM M41 .... 138 A1
Loughrigg Av ROY/SHW OL2 .... 58 D1
Louisa St BOL BL1 .... 33 G4
OP/CLY M11 .... 117 E5
WALK M28 .... 82 A3
Louise Av BURY BL9 .... 38 C2
Louise Cl WHIT OL12 .... 19 G5
Louise Gdns WHIT OL12 .... 19 G5
Louise St WHIT OL12 .... 19 G5
Louvaine Av BOL BL1 .... 32 C2
Louvain St FAIL M35 .... 104 D3
Lovalle St BOL BL1 .... 48 A1
Lovat Rd BOLE BL2 .... 50 C2
Love La HTNM SK4 .... 12 D4
Lovell Ct CHH M8 .... 86 C5
Lovell Dr HYDE SK14 .... 134 A4
Lovers La OLDE OL4 .... 93 H1
Lowbrook Av BKLY M9 .... 89 E4
Lowcroft Crs CHAD OL9 .... 89 E4
Low Crompton Rd
ROY/SHW OL2 .... 59 F3
Lowcross Rd
NEWH/MOS M40 .... 115 G1
Low Gn ROY/SHW OL2 .... 59 H4
Lower Albion St CMANE M1 .... 7 H7
Lower Alma St DUK SK16 .... 119 G4
Lowerbank DTN/ASHW M34 .... 146 B5
Lower Bank St BURY BL9 .... 4 C5
Lower Beechwood ROCH OL11 .... 42 C1
Lower Bennett St HYDE SK14 .... 133 H3
Lower Bents La
MPL/ROM SK6 .... 161 G2
Lower Birches OLDE OL4 .... 93 E3
Lower Bridgeman St BOLE BL2 .... 3 G7
Lower Broadacre STLY SK15 .... 135 F2
Lower Brook La WALK M28 * 97 H5
Lower Brook St CMANE M1 .... 7 H6
Lower Broughton Rd
BRO M7 .... 101 F5
Lower Bury St HTNM SK4 .... 12 C3
Lower Byrom St CSLFD M3 .... 6 B6
Lower Carr La UPML OL3 .... 78 C1
Lower Carrs AUL OL6 .... 107 G5
STKP SK1 .... 13 G4
Lower Chatham St
CMANE M1 .... 128 A1
Lower Cft WHTF M45 .... 84 D1
Lowercroft Rd
TOT/BURYW BL8 .... 37 E4
Lower Crossbank OLDE OL4 .... 93 H4
Lower Darcy St BOLE BL2 .... 49 H4
Lower Dingle OLDE OL4 .... 60 B5
Lower Falinge WHIT OL12 .... 10 C4
Lowerfield Dr OFTN SK2 .... 173 G4
Lowerfields OLDS OL8 .... 92 A3
Lower Flds UPML OL3 .... 78 D5
Lowerfields Rd ROY/SHW OL2 .... 60 A1
Lower Fold DTN/ASHW M34 .... 147 E1
MPL/ROM SK6 .... 175 E5
Lowerfold Av ROY/SHW OL2 .... 59 H5
Lowerfold Cl WHIT OL12 .... 18 B4
Lowerfold Crs WHIT OL12 .... 18 B4
Lowerfold Dr WHIT OL12 .... 18 B4
Lowerfold Wy WHIT OL12 .... 18 B4
Lower Frenches Dr UPML OL3 .... 94 D1
Lower Goodwin Cl BOLE BL2 .... 35 F3
Lower Gn AUL OL6 .... 119 H1
MDTN M24 .... 88 C2
WHIT OL12 .... 30 C1
Lower Hardman St CSLFD M3 .... 6 E5
Lower Hey La MOSL OL5 .... 94 B4
Lower Hillgate STKP SK1 .... 13 H4
Lower House Dr HOR/BR BL6 .... 46 D2
Lower House La WHIT OL12 .... 19 G1
Lower House St OLD OL1 .... 76 A4
Lower House Wk
EDGW/EG BL7 .... 23 F3
Lower Jowkin La ROCH OL11 .... 28 A4
Lower Landedmans WHTN BL5 .... 62 A3
Lower La MILN OL16 .... 43 H5
Lowerlea POY/DIS SK12 .... 197 H1
Lower Lime Rd OLDS OL8 .... 105 H3
Lower Marlands
EDGW/EG BL7 .... 22 D3
Lower Md EDGW/EG BL7 .... 23 E3
Lower Meadow Rd
WILM/AE SK9 .... 192 B3
Lower Moat Cl HTNM SK4 .... 159 H3
Lower Monton Rd ECC M30 .... 111 F3
Lower Mosley St CMANE M1 .... 6 D7
Lower Moss La HULME M15 .... 127 H1
WHTF M45 .... 69 G4
Lower New Rw WALK M28 .... 96 B1
Lower Ormond St CMANE M1 .... 128 B1
Lower Park Crs POY/DIS SK12 .... 194 C1
Lower Park Rd POY/DIS SK12 .... 194 C1
RUSH/FAL M14 .... 128 D5
Lower Rawson St FWTH BL4 .... 66 B3
Lower Seedley Rd SLFD M6 .... 112 D2
Lower Sheriff St WHIT OL12 .... 10 A5
Lower St FWTH BL4 .... 65 H5
MILN OL16 .... 43 H3
Lower Strines Rd
MPL/ROM SK6 .... 175 F4
Lower Sutherland St
SWIN M27 .... 98 D2
Lower Tenterfield ROCH OL11 .... 28 D1
Lower Tong EDGW/EG BL7 .... 23 E4
Lower Turf La OLDE OL4 .... 77 G4
Lower Tweedale St ROCH OL11 .... 30 A5

Lower Victoria St CHAD OL9 .... 74 C5
Lower Wharf St AUL OL6 .... 119 E3
Lower Wheat End MILN OL16 .... 11 H5
Lower Woodhill Rd
TOT/BURYW BL8 .... 4 B3
Lowerwood La BOLE BL2 .... 34 C5
Lowes Rd BURY BL9 .... 27 G5
Lowestead Rd OP/CLY M11 .... 116 D3
The Lowes ALT WA14 .... 177 E3
Lowestoft St RUSH/FAL M14 .... 142 D1
Loweswater Av
CHD/CHDH SK8 .... 181 G1
FWTH BL4 .... 65 E5
Lowfield Av AUL OL6 .... 108 A5
DROY M43 .... 117 G2
Lowfield Gv OFTN SK2 .... 172 A2
Lowfield Rd EDGY/DAV SK3 .... 171 H5
Low Grove La UPML OL3 .... 94 B2
Low Hl WHIT OL12 .... 10 C1
Lowhouse Cl MILN OL16 .... 31 H4
Lowick Av BOLS/LL BL3 .... 65 F1
Lowick Cl BRAM/HZG SK7 .... 185 G2
Lowland Gv AULW OL7 .... 100 D4
Lowland Rd OFTN SK2 .... 172 C5
Lowlands Cl MDTN M24 .... 89 F3
Lowndes Cl OFTN SK2 .... 172 C2
Lowndes La OFTN SK2 .... 172 C2
Lowndes St BOL BL1 .... 48 A1
Lowndes Wk
BRUN/LGST M13 * 128 C2
Lownorth Rd WYTH/NTH M22 .... 180 D4
Lowood Av URM M41 .... 123 G4
Lowry Cl WHTF M45 .... 69 E2
Lowry Dr MPL/ROM SK6 .... 175 G1
SWIN M27 .... 99 E1
Lowry Gv HYDE SK14 .... 135 G5
Lowry Houses ECC M30 * 111 F3
Lowry Wk BOL BL1 .... 33 G5
Lowside Av BOL BL1 .... 46 D3
MPL/ROM SK6 .... 147 G5
Lowside Dr OLDE OL4 .... 92 A2
Lowry's PI WHIT OL12 .... 10 B1
Lowstern Cl EDGW/EG BL7 .... 23 E2
The Lows OLDE OL4 .... 92 A2
Lowther Av OFTN SK2 .... 130 A5
HALE/TIMP WA15 .... 166 B3
Lowther Cl MPL/ROM SK6 .... 85 H4
Lowther Crs MDTN M24 .... 72 B3
Lowther Gdns URM M41 .... 123 E5
Lowther Rd CHH M8 .... 102 B1
PWCH M25 .... 85 G1
ROCH OL11 .... 42 D2
Lowther St BOLS/LL BL3 .... 65 F2
Lowton Av RUSH/FAL M14 .... 142 C1
Lowton Av BKLY M9 .... 103 G3
Lowton Rd SALE M33 .... 153 G4
Lowton St RAD M26 .... 52 B5
Low Wood Cl BRAM/HZG SK7 .... 183 F3
Low Wood Rd
DTN/ASHW M34 .... 131 H4
Loxford Cl HULME M15 .... 128 A1
Loxford St HULME M15 .... 128 B1
Loxham St BOLS/LL BL3 .... 66 A2
Lttn Cl CMANE M1 * 128 C1
Lubeck St BKLY M9 .... 103 F2
Lucas Rd FWTH BL4 .... 65 F4
Lucas St BURY BL9 .... 5 H2
OLDE OL4 .... 76 A5
Lucas Wk OP/CLY M11 .... 116 A5
Lucerne Cl CHAD OL9 .... 8 A5
Lucerne Rd BRAM/HZG SK7 .... 183 H1
Lucien Cl WGTN/LGST M12 .... 129 F3
Lucknow St ROCH OL11 .... 43 H2
Lucy St BOL BL1 .... 32 D5
BRO M7 .... 101 G5
EDGY/DAV SK3 .... 12 E6
HULME M15 .... 127 G2
Ludford Gv SALE M33 .... 154 B4
Ludgate Hl ANC M4 .... 7 H1
Ludgate Rd NEWH/MOS M40 .... 116 D1
ROCH OL11 .... 43 F4
Ludgate St ANC M4 .... 7 G1
WHTF M45 .... 86 A1
Ludlow Pk OLDE OL4 .... 92 C1
Ludlow Rd OFTN SK2 .... 172 D1
Lugano Rd BRAM/HZG SK7 .... 183 H1
Luke Rd DROY M43 .... 117 H3
Lullington Cl WYTH/NTH M22 .... 180 B3
Lullington Rd SLFD M6 .... 112 C1
Lulworth Cl TOT/BURYW BL8 .... 26 D5
Lulworth Crs FAIL M35 .... 105 G2
Lulworth Gdns
NTHM/RTH M23 .... 167 G3
Lulworth Rd BOLS/LL BL3 .... 110 D3
ECC M30 .... 110 D3
MDTN M24 .... 73 E2
Lumb Carr Av RAMS BL0 .... 16 A4
Lumb Carr Rd RAMS BL0 .... 16 A5
Lumb Cl BRAM/HZG SK7 .... 193 H1
Lumber La WALK M28 .... 97 F2
Lumb La BRAM/HZG SK7 .... 193 H1
DROY M43 .... 103 H4
DTN/ASHW M34 .... 118 B4
Lumley Cl RUSH/FAL M14 .... 128 D4
Lumn Hollow HYDE SK14 .... 148 A1
Lumn Rd HYDE SK14 .... 148 A1
Lumn's La SWIN M27 .... 84 C5
Lumn St BURY BL9 .... 27 G5
Lumsdale Rd STRET M32 .... 125 F4
Lumsden St BOLS/LL BL3 * 48 C4
Lum St BOL BL1 .... 3 G3
Lunwood BOL BL1 .... 48 A1
Lund Av RAD M26 .... 68 C4
Lund St TRPK M17 .... 127 F2
Lundy Av CCHDY M21 .... 156 B1
Lune Cl WHTF M45 .... 69 H1
Lune Dr WHTF M45 .... 69 H1
Lune Gv HEY OL10 .... 40 B3
Lune St OLDS OL8 .... 91 G3

Lune Wy RDSH SK5 ....160 A1
Lunn Av GTN M18................131 E2
Lupin Av FWTH BL4..............65 F3
Lupin Cl OLD OL1...............76 D1
Lupton St CSLFD M3 * 6 A5
 DTN/ASHW M34.................132 C4
Lurden Wk CHAD OL9 * 90 B3
Lurgan Av SALE M33.............154 D3
Lutener Av ALT WA14............165 F1
Luton Dr NTHM/RTH M23.........167 H5
Luton Rd RDSH SK5.............145 F3
Luton St BOLS/LL BL3..........37 G5
 TOT/BURYW BL8...............37 G5
Luxhall Wk NEWH/MOS M40......104 A5
Luxor Gv DTN/ASHW M34........131 E5
Luzley Brook Rd ROY/SHW OL2..59 H4
Luzley Rd OL..................108 C5
Lyceum Pas MILN OL16.........10 C6
Lyceum Pl HULME M15..........128 B1
Lychgate Ct OLDE OL4.........92 D4
Lychgate Ms HTNM SK4 * 158 B4
Lydbrook Cl BOL BL1..........2 C6
Lydden Av OP/CLY M11.........117 E2
Lydford ROCH OL11 * 29 H5
Lydford Gdns BOLE BL2........50 C4
Lydford St SLFD M6...........113 G1
Lydford Wk
 BRUN/LGST M13 * 128 D2
Lydgate Av BOLE BL2..........50 B1
Lydgate Cl DTN/ASHW M34......147 F2
 STLY SK15...................109 F4
 WHTF M45....................69 H4
Lydgate Dr OLDE OL4..........92 B2
Lydgate Rd DROY M43..........117 F2
 SALE M33....................154 D4
Lydiate Cl BOLS/LL BL3.......65 G2
Lydiat La WILM/AE SK9........200 D5
Lydney Av CHD/CHDH SK8.......181 H5
Lydney Rd URM M41............123 E5
Lyefield Wk MILN OL16........30 C5
Lyme Av WILM/AE SK9..........199 E1
Lyme Clough Wy MDTN M24......56 C5
Lymefield Dr WALK M28........96 B3
Lymefield Gv OFTN SK2........172 C3
Lyme Gv ALT WA14.............165 F5
 DROY M43....................117 G5
 MPL/ROM SK6.................162 A4
 OFTN SK2....................13 C7
Lyme Rd BRAM/HZG SK7.........185 F3
 POY/DIS SK12................187 F5
 POY/DIS SK12................196 D4
Lymes Alt WA14...............177 F3
Lyme St BRAM/HZG SK7 * 185 E1
 HTNM SK4....................158 B4
Lymewood Dr POY/DIS SK12....197 G1
 WILM/AE SK9.................199 H2
Lymington Ct MDTN M24........89 C2
Lymington Dr
 NTHM/RTH M23................167 E1
Lymm Cl EDGY/DAV SK3.........171 C3
 WALK M28....................81 H6
Lyncombe Cl CHD/CHDH SK8.....193 E1
Lyndale Av RDSH SK5..........131 E5
 SWIN M27....................98 C4
Lyndale Dr LIT OL15..........20 D2
Lyndene Av WALK M28..........97 H2
Lyndene Gdns CHD/CHDH SK8....169 G3
Lyndene Rd WYTH/NTH M22......168 C4
Lyndhurst Av AUL OL6.........107 E5
 BRAM/HZG SK7................184 D3
 CHAD OL9....................90 A2
 DTN/ASHW M34 * 132 B5
 IRL M44.....................122 C5
 MPL/ROM SK6.................161 G2
 PWCH M25....................86 D4
 ROCH OL11...................57 C1
 SALE M33....................154 A5
 URM M41.....................124 B4
Lyndhurst Cl WILM/AE SK9.....198 A5
Lyndhurst Dr
 HALE/TIMP WA15..............178 B2
Lyndhurst Rd DID/WITH M20....157 F2
 OLDS OL8....................91 E4
 RDSH SK5....................145 E1
 STRET M32...................139 H1
Lyndhurst St SLFD M6.........112 D3
Lyndhurst Vw DUK SK16 *......119 H4
Lyndon Cl OLDE OL4...........77 C4
 TOT/BURYW BL8...............26 A5
Lyndon Rd IRL M44............136 B2
Lyne Edge Crs DUK SK16.......134 A1
Lyne Edge Rd DUK SK16........134 B2
Lyne Vw HYDE SK14............134 B2
Lyngard Cl WILM/AE SK9.......199 C1
Lyngate Cl STKP SK1..........13 G5
Lyn Gv HEY OL10..............40 B3
Lynham Dr HEY OL10...........56 A1
Lynmouth Av DID/WITH M20.....157 E2
 OLDS OL8....................91 G4
 RDSH SK5....................145 E4
 ROY/SHW OL2.................74 D1
 URM M41.....................138 B5
Lynmouth Cl CHAD OL9.........73 H3
 RAD M26.....................52 D5
Lynmouth Gv PWCH M25.........85 G4
Lynn Av SALE M33.............140 A5
Lynndene Ct HEY OL10 * 40 D3
Lynn Dr DROY M43.............117 F3
Lynn St CHAD OL9.............90 B1
Lynnwood Dr ROCH OL11........73 H3
Lynnwood Rd BNG/LEV M19......158 A4
Lynroyle Wy ROCH OL11........42 C3
Lynsted Av BOLS/LL BL3.......65 F1
Lynthorpe Rd NEWH/MOS M40....89 E1
Lynton Av HYDE SK14..........136 A5
 IRL M44.....................136 A5
 OLDS OL8....................90 D5
 ROCH OL11...................42 A3
 SWIN M27....................98 C4
 URM M41.....................137 E1
Lynton Cl CHAD OL9...........74 A3
Lynton Crs WALK M28..........97 E2
Lynton Dr BNG/LEV M19........143 H4
 MPL/ROM SK6.................161 G2
 PWCH M25....................86 D6
Lynton Gv HALE/TIMP WA15.....166 B4
Lynton La WILM/AE SK9........200 D3
Lynton Lea RAD M26...........52 D5
Lynton Ms WILM/AE SK9........200 D3

Lynton Park Rd
 CHD/CHDH SK8................182 C4
Lynton Rd BOLS/LL BL3........64 B2
 CCDHY M21...................141 F3
 CHD/CHDH SK8................169 H4
 HTNM SK4....................159 E1
 SWIN M27....................99 E1
Lynton St RUSH/FAL M14 *.....142 D1
Lyntonvale Av
 CHD/CHDH SK8................169 F3
Lynway Dr DID/WITH M20.......157 C1
Lynway Gv MDTN M24...........73 E2
Lynwell Rd ECC M30...........111 E3
Lynwood HALE/TIMP WA15.......178 B4
Lynwood Av BOLS/LL BL3.......65 G2
 ECC M30.....................111 E3
 OLDTF/WHR M16...............141 G1
Lynwood Cl AULW OL7..........106 D3
Lynwood Dr OLDE OL4..........76 D5
Lynwood Gv BOLE BL2..........35 E2
 DTN/ASHW M34................118 B4
 HTNM SK4....................144 C5
 SALE M33....................154 D1
Lyon Gv WALK M28.............97 H2
Lyon Rd ALT WA14.............165 F2
 FWTH BL4....................82 B2
Lyons Dr TOT/BURYW BL8.......37 F5
Lyons Fold SALE M33..........139 H5
Lyons Rd TRPK M17............125 E1
Lyon St ROY/SHW OL2..........60 A2
Lyra Pl BRO M7...............113 H2
Lysander Cl RUSH/FAL M14.....142 C3
Lytham Av CCHDY M21..........141 G4
Lytham Cl AUL OL6............106 A3
Lytham Dr BRAM/HZG SK7.......184 B5
 HEY OL10....................40 C5
Lytham Rd CHD/CHDH SK8.......181 G3
 RUSH/FAL M14................142 A1
 URM M41.....................137 F1
Lytham St EDGY/DAV SK3.......172 A3
 WHIT OL12...................18 D5
Lytherton Av IRL M44.........150 C2
Lyth St RUSH/FAL M14.........142 B1
Lytton Av CHH M8.............102 B4
Lytton Rd DROY M43...........117 H3
Lytton St BOL BL1............33 G4

M

Mabel Av BOLS/LL BL3.........65 F1
 WALK M28....................97 H3
Mabel Rd FAIL M35............105 F1
Mabel's Brow FWTH BL4........66 B5
Mabel St BOL BL1.............48 B1
 NEWH/MOS M40................104 C5
 WHIT OL12...................29 C1
Mabfield Rd RUSH/FAL M14.....143 E2
Mableden Cl CHD/CHDH SK8.....182 A4
Mabs Ct AUL OL6..............120 A3
Macaulay St ROCH OL11........42 B5
 ROY/SHW OL2.................59 F5
Macauley Rd
 OLDTF/WHR M16...............141 F1
 RDSH SK5....................144 D2
Macclesfield Rd
 BRAM/HZG SK7................185 C4
 WILM/AE SK9.................199 F4
Macdonald Av FWTH BL4........65 F5
Macdonald Rd IRL M44.........136 A4
Macdonald St OLDS OL8........91 C3
Macefin Av CCHDY M21.........155 C2
Macfarren St
 WGTN/LGST M12...............129 H5
Mackenzie Gv BOL BL1.........33 G2
Mackenzie Rd BRO M7..........101 E4
Mackenzie St BOL BL1.........33 G2
 WGTN/LGST M12...............129 H5
Mackenzie Wk OLD OL1 * 60 D4
Mackeson Dr AUL OL6..........120 B1
Mackeson Rd AUL OL6..........120 B1
Mackintosh Wy OLD OL1 *......9 G2
Mackworth St HULME M15.......127 G3
Maclaren Dr CHH M8...........101 H1
Maclure Rd ROCH OL11.........30 A5
Macnair Cl MPL/ROM SK6 *.....175 F4
Macnair Ms MPL/ROM SK6 *.....175 E3
 MPL/ROM SK6.................175 E3
Madams Wood Rd WALK M28.....81 E4
Maddison Rd DROY M43.........117 C5
Madeley Cl ALT WA14..........177 H4
Madeley Dr CHAD OL9..........90 C1
Madeley Gdns BOL BL1.........33 H4
Maden Sq LIT OL15............21 E3
Maden Wk OLD OL9 *...........74 C4
Madison Av CHD/CHDH SK8......182 D2
Madison Gdns WHTN BL5.......62 A2
Madison Pk WHTN BL5..........62 A2
Madison St GTN M18...........130 D2
Madras Rd EDGY/DAV SK3 *.....171 F2
Mafeking Av BURY BL9.........38 D1
Mafeking Rd BOLE BL2 *.......50 B2
Mafeking St OLDS OL8.........90 D4
Magdala St HEY OL10 *........56 B1
 OLD OL1.....................75 H4
Magda Rd OFTN SK2............172 D4
Magenta Av IRL M44...........136 A5
Magnolia Cl SALE M33.........138 C5
Magnolia Dr CHH M8...........102 B4
Magpie Cl DROY M43...........118 B2
Magpie La OLDE OL4...........92 D3
Magpie Wk OP/CLY M11 *.......116 A4
Maher Gdns HULME M15.........127 H4
Mahood St STKP SK1...........12 D7
Maida St BNG/LEV M19.........144 B1
Maiden Cl AULW OL7...........106 C4
Maidford Cl ANC M4 *.........7 H3
 STRET M32...................138 C5
Maidstone Av CCHDY M21.......141 G2
Maidstone Ms CCHDY M21.......141 E2
Maidstone Rd BNG/LEV M19....158 A4
Main Av BNG/LEV M19..........143 H4
 TRPK M17....................125 H4

Main Dr ALT WA14.............176 B1
 OLD OL1.....................75 E3
Maine Rd RUSH/FAL M14........142 C1
Mainprice Cl SLFD M6.........113 E1
Main Rd CHAD OL9.............8 B2
 SWIN M27....................85 E4
Main St FAIL M35.............105 E2
 HYDE SK14...................133 G4
Mainwaring Dr WILM/AE SK9....199 G2
Mainwaring Ter
 NTHM/RTH M23................155 H4
Mainway MDTN M24.............89 F1
Mainway East MDTN M24........89 F1
Mainwood Rd
 HALE/TIMP WA15..............166 D4
Maismore Rd WYTH/NTH M22.....179 H3
Maitland Av CCHDY M21........156 B2
Maitland Cl WHIT OL12........19 H5
Maitland St STKP SK1.........172 C2
Maizefield Cl CHAD OL9 *.....74 C4
Major St CMANE M1............7 G6
 MILN OL16...................31 G5
 RAMS BL0....................16 C2
Makin St CMANE M1 *..........7 G7
Makkah Cl NEWH/MOS M40.......103 H5
Malaga Av MANAIR WN5.........180 A5
Malakoff St STLY SK15........120 B5
Malbrook Wk
 BRUN/LGST M13 * 128 D2
Malby St OLD OL1.............9 G1
Malcolm Av SWIN M27..........84 B5
Malcolm Dr SWIN M27..........84 B5
Malcolm St ROCH OL11.........42 C3
Malden Gv NTHM/RTH M23.......166 D1
Maldon Cl BOLS/LL BL3........66 D1
 OFTN SK2....................173 H4
Maldon Crs SWIN M27..........99 E4
Maldon Dr ECC M30............111 F1
Maldon St ROCH OL11..........43 E1
Maldwyn Av BOLS/LL BL3.......64 A2
 CHH M8......................87 F5
Maleham St BRO M7 *..........101 H4
Malgam Dr DID/WITH M20.......169 C1
Malham Cl ROY/SHW OL2........59 E3
Malham Ct OFTN SK2...........173 E3
Malham Dr WHTF M45...........69 H4
Mallard Cl DUK SK16..........133 H1
 OFTN SK2....................173 H4
 OLDS OL8....................91 E3
Mallard Crs POY/DIS SK12.....194 B3
Mallard Gn ALT WA14..........165 E1
Mallards Reach
 MPL/ROM SK6.................162 A4
Mallard St CMANE M1..........128 B1
Mallet Crs BOL BL1...........32 C4
Malling Rd NTHM/RTH M23......167 H5
Mallison St BOL BL1..........34 A3
Mallory Av AULW OL7..........107 E5
Mallory Rd HYDE SK14.........134 B4
Mallow Cft MILN OL16.........43 H2
Mallowdale Wk WALK M28.......96 C2
Mallowdale Av
 RUSH/FAL M14................142 D3
Mallowdale Cl BOL BL1........47 E3
Mallowdale Rd OFTN SK2.......173 F4
Mallow St HULME M15..........127 H2
The Mall BURY BL9............4 E5
 STLY SK15...................135 F2
Mally Gdns MOSL OL5..........108 D1
Malmesbury Rd POY/DIS SK12...195 E3
Malmesbury Rd
 CHD/CHDH SK8................193 E1
Malpas Cl CHD/CHDH SK8.......170 D4
 WILM/AE SK9.................199 H1
Malpas Dr ALT WA14...........153 H5
Malpas St OLD OL1............9 H2
 WGTN/LGST M12...............129 H2
Malpas Wk
 OLDTF/WHR M16 * 127 G3
Malrae HALE/TIMP WA15 *......177 H3
Malsham Rd NTHM/RTH M23......155 H4
Malta St MDTN M24............73 G5
Malta St AUL OL6.............92 C1
 OLDE OL4....................92 C1
Maltby Ct OLDE OL4...........93 E2
Maltby Dr BOLS/LL BL3........64 B2
Maltby Rd NTHM/RTH M23.......167 G3
Maltings La ROCH OL11........42 B5
Malton Av BOLS/LL BL3........64 B2
 CCHDY M21...................141 H1
 WHTF M45....................69 F3
Malton Dr ALT WA14...........164 D3
 BRAM/HZG SK7................185 E1
Malton Rd HTNM SK4...........158 D2
Malton St OLDS OL8...........91 E4
Malt St HULME M15............127 G2
Malus Ct SLFD M6 *...........113 F2
Malvern Av AUL OL6...........107 F3
 BOL BL1.....................32 C5
 BURY BL9....................5 C5
 CHD/CHDH SK8................169 E4
 DROY M43....................118 B3
 URM M41.....................138 B1
Malvern Cl FWTH BL4..........65 E3
 HTNM SK4....................158 C4
 MILN OL16...................31 H4
 PWCH M25....................86 B2
 ROY/SHW OL2.................59 G1
 ROY/SHW OL2.................74 D1
 SWIN M27....................100 A4
Malvern Dr ALT WA14..........165 E4
 SWIN M27....................100 A4
Malvern Gv DID/WITH M20......142 C5
 SLFD M6.....................112 D2
 WALK M28....................81 H6
Malvern Rd MDTN M24..........88 D2
Malvern Rw HULME M15 *.......127 F2
Malvern St OLDS OL8..........8 D6
Malvern St East ROCH OL11....29 F4
Malvern St West ROCH OL11....29 F4
Manby Rd GTN M18.............130 A4
Manby Sq GTN M18.............130 A4
Manchester Chambers
 OLD OL1.....................9 F3
Manchester New Rd
 MDTN M24....................88 C1
 PART M31....................151 E3
Manchester Old Rd BURY BL9...4 C7
 MDTN M24....................71 H5

Manchester Rd ALT WA14.......165 G3
 BOLE BL2....................49 F4
 BOLS/LL BL3.................65 H1
 BURY BL9....................17 F5
 BURY BL9....................53 F5
 CCHDY M21...................141 F2
 DID/WITH M20................170 A1
 DROY M43....................118 B3
 DTN/ASHW M34................131 F4
 DTN/ASHW M34................131 C1
 DTN/ASHW M34................132 B5
 GOL/RIS/CUL WA3.............150 A4
 HEY OL10....................56 A5
 HTNM SK4....................159 C1
 HYDE SK14...................133 E5
 MDTN M24....................57 C2
 MOSL OL5....................108 D3
 OLDS OL8....................90 D3
 PART M31....................151 F2
 RAMS BL0....................16 C1
 ROCH OL11...................29 H5
 ROY/SHW OL2.................59 H4
 SWIN M27....................84 A4
 SWIN M27....................98 C1
 WHTN BL5....................62 A2
 WILM/AE SK9.................199 F2
Manchester Rd East
 LHULT M38...................81 F3
Manchester Rd North
 DTN/ASHW M34................131 H4
Manchester Rd South
 DTN/ASHW M34................131 H5
Manchester Rd West
 LHULT M38...................80 D2
Manchester St CHAD OL9.......8 C6
 HEY OL10....................41 E4
 OLDTF/WHR M16...............127 F3
 ROCH OL11...................42 A5
Mancunian Rd
 DTN/ASHW M34................147 E3
Mancunian Wy
 WGTN/LGST M12...............128 D1
Mandalay Gdns
 MPL/ROM SK6.................174 C2
Mandarin Gn ALT WA14.........165 E1
Mandarin Wk SLFD M6 *........113 F2
Mandeville St BNG/LEV M19....144 B3
Mandley Av NEWH/MOS M40 *....89 C5
Mandley Cl BOLS/LL BL3.......51 E4
Mandley Park Av BRO M7.......101 H4
Mandon Cl RAD M26............51 H4
Manesty Cl MDTN M24..........56 B5
Manet Cl BRO M7..............101 E2
Mangle St CMANE M1...........7 H4
Mango Pl SLFD M6.............113 F2
Manifold Dr MPL/ROM SK6......197 E1
Manifold St SLFD M6..........101 E5
Manilla Wk OP/CLY M11........116 A4
Manipur St OP/CLY M11........115 H5
Manley Av SWIN M27...........84 A3
Manley Cl BURY BL9...........26 D1
Manley Crs WHTN BL5.........62 D3
Manley Gv BRAM/HZG SK7......193 H1
Manley Rd CCHDY M21.........141 G2
 OLDS OL8....................91 F3
 ROCH OL11...................42 B3
 SALE M33....................153 H5
Manley St BRO M7.............101 C4
Manley Ter BOL BL1 *.........33 H2
Manningham Rd BOLS/LL BL3....48 A4
Mannington Dr BKLY M9.......102 D4
Mannock St OLDS OL8..........90 B6
The Manns UPML OL3...........94 C2
Manor Av BOLS/LL BL3.........67 F1
 OLDTF/WHR M16...............141 H1
 SALE M33....................138 D2
Manor Cl CHAD OL9............8 A1
 CHD/CHDH SK8................183 F4
 DTN/ASHW M34................147 F1
 OLDE OL4....................76 D5
 WILM/AE SK9.................198 B5
Manor Ct STRET M32...........139 H2
Manor Dr CCHDY M21..........156 C2
 ROY/SHW OL2.................75 F1
Manor Farm Cl AULW OL7......106 C5
Manor Farm Ri OLDE OL4.......77 F4
Manorfield Cl BOL BL1.......32 D5
Manor Gate Rd BOLE BL2......50 D1
Manor Hill Rd MPL/ROM SK6....175 E3
Manor Rd BNG/LEV M19........144 B1
 CHD/CHDH SK8................182 B5
 DROY M43....................117 F4
 DTN/ASHW M34................131 C1
 HALE/TIMP WA15..............165 H5
 HYDE SK14...................134 C1
 MDTN M24....................88 C1
 MPL/ROM SK6.................162 A1
 OLDE OL4....................92 B3
 RDSH SK5....................160 C1
 ROY/SHW OL2.................59 H2
 SALE M33....................154 C1
 SLFD M6.....................112 C1
 STRET M32...................139 H2
 SWIN M27....................99 E4
Manor St BOL BL1.............3 G4
 BURY BL9....................5 G4
 DTN/ASHW M34................132 C1
 FWTH BL4....................66 B4
 HYDE SK14...................133 F5
 MDTN M24....................72 D1
 MOSL OL5....................93 H5
 RAMS BL0....................16 C1
 ROY/SHW OL2.................75 H2
 WGTN/LGST M12...............128 D1
Manor Vw MPL/ROM SK6.........147 F5
The Manse MOSL OL5...........108 D2
Mansell Av BKLY M9...........88 A3
Mansfield Av DTN/ASHW M34....132 A3
 RAMS BL0....................26 C2
Mansfield Cl AULW OL7........119 E4
 DTN/ASHW M34................132 A3
Mansfield Crs
 DTN/ASHW M34................132 A4
Mansfield Dr BKLY M9.........88 B3
Mansfield Gra ROCH OL11.....29 F5
Mansfield Rd BOL BL1........33 E5
 BKLY M9.....................88 B3
 HYDE SK14...................148 A2
 MOSL OL5....................109 F1
 OLDS OL8....................92 A2
 ROCH OL11...................28 B4
 URM M41.....................138 A2
Mansfield St AULW OL7........118 D5
Mansford Dr NEWH/MOS M40.....103 G5
Manshaw Crs DTN/ASHW M34....131 F1
Manshaw Rd OP/CLY M11........131 F1
Mansion Av WHTF M45..........69 F1
Manson Av HULME M15..........127 G2
Manstead Wk
 NEWH/MOS M40 * 115 H3
Manston Dr CHD/CHDH SK8......182 D2
Manswood Dr CHH M8...........102 B3
Manthorpe Av WALK M28.......97 H3
Mantley La UPML OL3..........89 E4
 DTN/ASHW M34................131 F1
Manton Cl BRO M7.............102 A4
Manvers St RDSH SK5..........159 H3
Manwaring St FAIL M35........104 D5
Maple Av BOL BL1.............33 E5
 BURY BL9....................5 K4
 CCHDY M21...................141 E3
 CHD/CHDH SK8................182 C2
 DTN/ASHW M34................118 A4
 DTN/ASHW M34................132 B5
 ECC M30.....................110 D1
 HALE/TIMP WA15..............166 A5
 MPL/ROM SK6.................195 C4
 POY/DIS SK12................195 C4
 STLY SK15...................120 B6
 STRET M32...................140 D2
 WHTF M45....................69 C5
Maple Cl FWTH BL4............82 C4
 MDTN M24....................73 C4
 OFTN SK2....................172 C3
 ROY/SHW OL2.................59 C1
 SLFD M6.....................113 E2
Maplecroft STKP SK1..........13 C7
Mapledon Rd BKLY M9..........103 G2
Maplefield Dr WALK M28......96 C5
Maple Gv FAIL M35............104 D5
 NEWH/MOS M40................89 H5
 PWCH M25....................85 H3
 RAMS BL0....................17 E3
 TOT/BURYW BL8...............37 F1
 WALK M28....................96 D3
Maple Rd BRAM/HZG SK7.......193 H2
 CHAD OL9....................74 C3
 FWTH BL4....................65 F4
 NTHM/RTH M23................166 D1
 PART M31....................166 D1
 SWIN M27....................98 D4
 WILM/AE SK9.................201 E3
Maple Rd West
 NTHM/RTH M23................166 D1
Maple St BOLE BL2............34 D4
 BOLS/LL BL3.................48 C4
 OLDS OL8....................90 D4
 ROCH OL11...................30 D5
Maple Wk NTHM/RTH M23........166 D1
 ROY/SHW OL2.................74 D1
Maplewood Cl BKLY M9.........87 H5
Maplewood Ct SLFD M6 *.......113 F2
Maplewood Gdns BOL BL1 *.....33 H4
Maplewood Gv STLY SK15......121 G2
Maplewood House BOL BL1.....33 H5
Maplewood Rd WILM/AE SK9....199 H2
Mapley Av WYTH/NTH M22......168 C1
Maplin Cl BRUN/LGST M13......128 C2
Maplin Dr OFTN SK2..........173 H4
Marble St CMANW M2...........7 F4
 OLD OL1.....................9 H1
Marbury Av RUSH/FAL M14.....142 D2
Marbury Cl EDGY/DAV SK3.....170 D2
 URM M41.....................123 E5
Marbury Rd HTNM SK4.........144 D4
 WILM/AE SK9.................199 E1
Marcer Rd NEWH/MOS M40......115 G3
March Av HTNM SK4............158 D2
Marchbank
 CHD/CHDH SK8................169 H3
March Dr TOT/BURYW BL8......38 A1
Marchers Ms ECC M30.........110 C4
Marchioness St GTN M18 *....112 C1
Marchmont Cl
 BRUN/LGST M13...............129 E2
March St MILN OL16...........11 F6
Marcliffe Av CCHDY M21......141 H2
Marcliffe Dr BNG/LEV M19....144 C2
 ROCH OL11...................29 E5
Marcliff Gv HTNM SK4........159 E4
Marcroft Pl ROCH OL11.......43 F2
Marcus Gv RUSH/FAL M14......143 E1
Marcus St BOL BL1............33 E5
Mardale Av DID/WITH M20.....157 H1
 ROY/SHW OL2.................60 A2
 SWIN M27....................98 B4
 URM M41.....................123 G5
Mardale Cl BOLE BL2..........35 E1
 OLDE OL4....................76 C5
 PWCH M25....................86 D5
 STLY SK15...................120 D2
Mardale Dr BOLE BL2..........35 C5
 CHD/CHDH SK8................169 C3
 MDTN M24....................72 B5
Mardale Rd SWIN M27..........98 C4
Marden Rd NTHM/RTH M23......167 H4
Mardyke WHIT OL12...........10 B5
Marfield Av CHAD OL9........90 B2
Marford Cl WYTH/NTH M22.....168 C3
Marford Crs SALE M33........153 H4
Margaret Ashton Cl BKLY M9...103 G3
Margaret Av MILN OL16.......11 J7

Margaret Rd *DROY* M43 * 117 F3
DTN/ASHW M34 ....132 D4
Margaret Sands St
HULME M15 ....127 G2
Margaret St *AUL* OL6 ....119 F3
BURY BL9 ....5 F6
HEY OL10 ....40 C4
OLDS OL8 ....90 C5
RDSH SK5 ....145 E4
ROY/SHW OL2 ....60 A3
Margate Av *NEWH/MOS* M40 ...104 A5
Margate Rd *RDSH* SK5 ....145 E4
Margrove Av *HOR/BR* BL6 ....46 D4
Margrove Cl *FAIL* M35 ....105 H5
Margrove Rd *SLFD* M6 ....112 B1
Margroy Cl *WHIT* OL12 ....11 F1
Marguerita Rd
NEWH/MOS M40 ....117 E1
Marham Cl *CCHDY* M21 * 142 A5
Margham St *SALE* M33 ....133 G2
Maria St *BOL* BL1 ....33 H4
Marie Cl *DTN/ASHW* M34 ......146 D1
Marie St *BRO* M7 ....101 H5
Marigold St *ROCH* OL11 ....43 E2
Mariman Dr *CHH* M8 ....87 F5
Marina Av *DTN/ASHW* M34 .....147 E2
Marina Cl *WILM/AE* SK9 ....192 A2
Marina Crs *OP/CLY* M11 ....116 C2
Marina Dr *MPL/ROM* SK6 ......178 F2
Marina Rd *DROY* M43 ....118 A3
MPL/ROM SK6 ....161 F2
Marine Av *PART* SK1 ....150 C3
Marion St *BOLS/LL* BL3 ....65 H2
OLDS OL8 ....91 G4
Marjorie Cl *GTN* M18 ....130 A2
Mark Av *SLFD* M6 ....115 C1
Markenfield Dr *ROY/SHW* OL2 ..59 G2
Market Pde *BURY* BL9 ....4 E5
Market Pl *AUL* OL6 ....119 G2
BURY BL9 ....4 D4
HYDE SK14 ....135 H5
MDTN M24 ....72 D3
OLD OL1 ....9 F3
RAMS BL0 ....16 D1
STKP SK1 ....13 G2
Market St *ALT* WA14 ....165 C5
BOL BL1 ....2 D4
BOLS/LL BL3 ....66 D1
BURY BL9 ....4 D5
CMANE M1 ....7 E4
DROY M43 ....118 A3
DTN/ASHW M34 ....132 C5
FWTH BL4 ....66 A3
HEY OL10 ....40 D4
HYDE SK14 ....135 H4
HYDE SK14 ....148 A2
MDTN M24 ....72 C3
MOSL OL5 ....67 F4
RAD M26 ....67 G4
ROY/SHW OL2 ....60 A3
STLY SK15 ....120 C5
SWIN M27 ....99 F1
TOT/BURYW BL8 ....26 A5
WHIT OL12 ....18 B2
Market Wk *SALE* M33 * 54 C2
Market Wy *SLFD* M6 ....113 E2
Markham Cl *BRUN/LGST* M13 ..129 E3
Markham St *HYDE* SK14 ....135 G2
Markington St *RUSH/FAL* M14 .128 B3
Markland Hill *BOL* BL1 ....47 E1
Markland Hill La *BOL* BL1 ....32 C5
Markland St *BOL* BL1 ....2 E6
HYDE SK14 ....148 A1
RAMS BL0 * 16 D2
Mark La *ROY/SHW* OL2 ....60 C3
Marks St *RAD* M26 ....68 B1
Mark St *CHAD* OL9 ....8 D2
WHIT OL12 ....96 A5
Marland Av *CHD/CHDH* SK8 ...182 C2
OLDS OL8 ....90 D3
ROCH OL11 ....42 A2
Marland Cl *ROCH* OL11 ....42 A1
Marland Crs *RDSH* SK5 ....145 F3
Marland Fold *ROCH* OL11 ......42 A2
Marland Fold La *OLDS* OL8 ....106 C1
Marland Gn *ROCH* OL11 ....42 A2
Marland Hill Rd *ROCH* OL11 ...42 B1
Marland St *CHAD* OL9 ....90 B4
Marland Wy *STRET* M32 ....126 A3
Marlborough Av
CHD/CHDH SK8 ....183 E3
OLDTF/WHR M16 ....141 G2
WILM/AE SK9 ....201 E3
Marlborough Cl *AULW* OL7 ....118 D5
DTN/ASHW M34 ....146 C2
MPL/ROM SK6 ....174 C2
RAMS BL0 ....17 H1
Marlborough Dr *FAIL* M35 .....104 D4
HTNM SK4 ....159 G2
Marlborough Gdns *FWTH* BL4 ..65 E4
Marlborough Rd *ALT* WA14 ....177 C2
BRO M7 ....102 A4
ECC M30 ....111 H1
HYDE SK14 ....148 A3
IRL M44 ....122 C5
ROY/SHW OL2 ....75 F2
SALE M33 ....154 C2
STRET M32 ....125 G3
URM M41 ....125 C5
Marlborough St *AULW* OL7 ....119 E4
BOL BL1 ....33 F3
HEY OL10 ....56 B1
OLDS OL8 ....90 C5
WHIT OL12 ....29 F2
Marlbrook Wk *BOLS/LL* BL3 ....49 E5
Marlcroft Av *HTNM* SK4 ....159 E4
Maricroft La *NTHM/RTH* M23 ..167 H2
Marld Crs *BOL* BL1 ....33 F3
Marle Av *MOSL* OL5 ....109 F1
Marle Cft *WHTF* M45 ....84 D1
Marle Ri *MOSL* OL5 ....109 F1
Marler Rd *HYDE* SK14 ....133 H4
Marley Cl *HALE/TIMP* WA15 ...166 A2
Marley Dr *SALE* M33 ....139 G5
Marleyer Cl *NEWH/MOS* M40 ..104 B3

Marleyer Ri *MPL/ROM* SK6 ....173 H1
Marley Rd *BNG/LEV* M19 ......144 B3
Marley St *STKP* SK1 ....195 F5
Marlfield Rd
HALE/TIMP WA15 ....179 E5
ROY/SHW OL2 ....59 F1
Marlfield St *BKLY* M9 ....103 F1
Marfield Cl *OFTN* SK2 ....173 H4
Marlinford Dr
NEWH/MOS M40 ....104 B5
Marlor St *DTN/ASHW* M34 .....132 B4
Marlow Cl *BOLE* BL2 ....35 C5
CHD/CHDH SK8 ....182 C2
URM M41 ....124 A4
Marlow Dr *ALT* WA14 ....176 C2
IRL M44 ....122 B5
SWIN M27 ....98 D4
WILM/AE SK9 ....191 H1
Marlowe Dr *DID/WITH* M20 ....157 G2
Marlowe Wks *MPL/ROM* SK6 ..161 F4
Marlow Rd *BKLY* M9 ....103 G1
Marlwood Rd *BOL* BL1 ....32 C4
Marmion Dr *CCHDY* M21 ......141 E3
Marne Av *AUL* OL6 ....108 A5
WYTH/NTH M22 ....168 D4
Marne Crs *ROCH* OL11 ....29 F4
Marnland Gv *BOLS/LL* BL3 * ...47 E5
Maroon Rd *WYTH/NTH* M22 ...181 E5
Marple Av *BOL* BL1 ....34 B2
Marple Cl *OLDS* OL8 ....91 E5
Marple Gv *STRET* M32 ....125 H5
Marple Hall Dr *MPL/ROM* SK6 .174 C3
Marple Old Rd *OFTN* SK2 .....173 F4
Marple Rd *OFTN* SK2 ....173 E2
OFTN SK2 ....173 H5
Marple St *HULME* M15 ....127 G3
Marquis Av *BURY* BL9 ....38 B2
Marquis Dr *CHD/CHDH* SK8 ...182 A5
Marquis St *BNG/LEV* M19 ....144 D2
Marrick Av *CHD/CHDH* SK8 ...169 H4
Marriotts Ct *CMANW* M2 ....7 F4
Marriott St *DID/WITH* M20 ....142 D5
STKP SK1 ....13 H6
Marron Pl *CMANW* M2 * 6 C6
Mars Av *BOLS/LL* BL3 ....64 B1
Marsden Cl *AULW* OL7 ....106 B5
Marsden Dr *HALE/TIMP* WA15 .166 D3
Marsden Rd *BOL* BL1 ....2 D4
MPL/ROM SK6 ....162 B3
Marsden St *BURY* BL9 ....6 E4
CMANW M2 ....6 C4
ECC M30 ....110 D2
MDTN M24 ....73 F5
WALK M28 ....96 A4
Marsett Cl *WHIT* OL12 ....28 A2
Marshall Ct *AUL* OL6 ....120 A3
OLD OL1 * 75 F4
Marshall Stevens Wy
TRPK M17 ....125 C3
Marshall St *ANC* M4 ....7 H2
MILN OL16 ....11 H7
WGTN/LGST M12 ....129 F4
Marsham Cl *BRUN/LGST* M13 .129 F4
Marsham Dr *MPL/ROM* SK6 ...174 C5
Marsham Rd *BRAM/HZG* SK7 .184 C3
Marshbrook Dr *BKLY* M9 .....102 D1
Marshbrook Rd *URM* M41 .....124 B5
Marshdale Rd *BOL* BL1 ....47 G1
Marshfield Rd
BRUN/LGST M13 * 128 D2
Marshfield Wk
BRUN/LGST M13 * 128 D2
Marsh Fold La *BOL* BL1 ....48 B1
Marsh Hey Cl *LHULT* M38 ....81 E1
Marsh La *FWTH* BL4 ....65 F4
Marsh Rd *BOLS/LL* BL3 ....50 D5
LHULT M38 ....81 G3
Marsh St *WALK* M28 ....82 C4
Marsland Av
HALE/TIMP WA15 ....166 C1
Marsland Cl
DTN/ASHW M34 ....131 C5
Marsland Rd
HALE/TIMP WA15 ....166 C3
MPL/ROM SK6 ....174 D2
SALE M33 ....154 B3
Marslands *UPML* OL3 ....79 E1
Marsland St
BRAM/HZG SK7 * 185 G2
Marsland St North *BRO* M7 ...101 H3
Marsland St South *BRO* M7 ...102 A3
Marsland Ter *STKP* SK1 ....172 C1
Mars St *CHAD* OL9 ....8 B2
Marston Cl *FAIL* M35 ....105 G4
HOR/BR BL6 ....46 A1
WHTF M45 ....70 B4
Marston Dr *IRL* M44 ....136 D1
Marston Rd *BRO* M7 ....101 H2
STRET M32 ....140 C1
Marston St North
CMANE M1 ....6 E4
Marsworth Dr *ANC* M4 ....115 F3
Martens Rd *IRL* M44 ....150 D1
Martha St *SALE* M33 ....159 E4
Martham Dr *OFTN* SK2 ....173 H4
Martha's Ter *MILN* OL16 ....19 H5
Martha St *BOLS/LL* BL3 * 48 C5
OLD OL1 ....8 D1
Martin Av *BOLS/LL* BL3 ....64 A2
OLDE OL4 ....92 B2
Martin Cl *DTN/ASHW* M34 ....132 C3
OFTN SK2 ....173 G4
Martindale Cl *ROY/SHW* OL2 ...59 F4
Martindale Crs *MDTN* M24 ....72 A1
WGTN/LGST M12 ....129 F2
Martindale Gdns *BOL* BL1 ....33 H4
Martin Dr *IRL* M44 ....122 B4
Martingale Cl *RAD* M26 ....52 B4
Martingale Wy *DROY* M43 ....118 C2
Martin Gv *FWTH* BL4 ....66 B5
Martin La *WHIT* OL12 ....29 G5
Martin Rd *SWIN* M27 ....98 D3
Martinscroft Rd
NTHM/RTH M23 ....167 H4
Martins Fld *WHIT* OL12 ....28 C2

Martin St *BURY* BL9 ....39 G3
DTN/ASHW M34 ....132 C1
HYDE SK14 ....185 H3
ORD M5 ....112 C3
Martlesham Wk *ANC* M4 * 7 G3
Martlet Av *POY/DIS* SK12 .....197 H1
Martlet Cl *RUSH/FAL* M14 ....142 C2
Martock Av *WYTH/NTH* M22 ..180 D1
Marton Av *BOLE* BL2 ....49 H1
DID/WITH M20 ....157 H4
Marton Gra *PWCH* M25 ....86 D5
Marton Dr *EDGY/DAV* SK3 ...171 C3
Marton Gv *HTNM* SK4 ....145 E5
Marton Pl *SALE* M33 ....154 B2
Marwood Cl *ALT* WA14 ....165 E3
RAD M26 ....66 D4
Marwood Dr *NTHM/RTH* M23 .179 G1
Maryfield Ct
OLDTF/WHR M16 ....142 A3
Mary France St *HULME* M15 ..127 H2
Mary Hulton Ct *WHTN* BL5 .....62 B4
Maryland Av *BOLE* BL2 ....50 A2
Marylon Dr *WYTH/NTH* M22 ..168 D1
Maryport Dr
HALE/TIMP WA15 ....167 E2
Mary St *CHD/CHDH* SK8 ....170 A3
CSLFD M3 ....114 C2
DROY M43 ....118 A4
DTN/ASHW M34 ....132 C4
DUK SK16 ....119 C5
FWTH BL4 ....66 A5
HEY OL10 ....40 D4
HYDE SK14 ....133 F5
MILN OL16 ....11 H3
RAMS BL0 ....16 C3
STKP SK1 ....13 J2
Masboro St *CHH* M8 ....102 A3
Masbury Cl *BOL* BL1 ....22 D4
Masefield Av *PWCH* M25 ......85 H5
RAD M26 ....51 H5
Masefield Cl *DUK* SK16 ....134 C1
Masefield Crs *DROY* M43 .....117 H4
Masefield Dr *FWTH* BL4 ....65 E2
HTNM SK4 ....158 D4
Masefield Gv *RDSH* SK5 ....145 G2
Masefield Rd *BOLS/LL* BL3 .....51 E5
DROY M43 ....117 H4
OLD OL1 ....76 A2
Mason Gdns *BOLS/LL* BL3 ....2 C7
Mason St *ANC* M4 ....7 H2
AULW OL7 ....119 E4
BURY BL9 ....5 G5
EDCW/EG BL7 * 22 D2
HEY OL10 ....40 C4
MILN OL16 ....11 H3
Massey Av *AUL* OL6 ....107 F4
FAIL M35 ....105 G2
Massey Cft *WHIT* OL12 ....18 B1
Massey Rd *HALE/TIMP* WA15 .165 H5
SALE M33 ....155 F2
Massey St *BURY* BL9 ....5 H2
STKP SK1 ....13 G4
WILM/AE SK9 ....200 D4
Massey Wk *WYTH/NTH* M22 ..181 E3
Massie St *CHD/CHDH* SK8 ....170 A3
Matham Wk *HULME* M15 * ...128 A1
Mather Av *ECC* M30 ....111 F3
PWCH M25 ....101 F1
WHTF M45 ....69 G2
Mather Cl *WHTF* M45 ....69 C3
Mather Fold Rd *WALK* M28 ....96 B1
Mather Rd *BURY* BL9 ....27 C4
ECC M30 ....111 F3
Mather St *BOLS/LL* BL3 * 2 D7
FAIL M35 ....104 C3
FWTH BL4 ....66 B1
RAD M26 ....68 B1
Mather Wy *SLFD* M6 ....113 F2
Matisse Wy *BRO* M7 ....101 E2
Matley Cl *GTN* M18 ....134 C3
Matley Gv *STLY* SK15 ....146 A5
Matley La *STLY* SK15 ....134 D2
Matlock Av *AUL* OL6 ....108 A4
BRO M7 ....100 D3
DID/WITH M20 ....142 D5
DTN/ASHW M34 ....147 E5
URM M41 ....138 B3
Matlock Cl *FWTH* BL4 ....66 B3
SALE M33 ....154 D2
Matlock Rd *CHD/CHDH* SK8 ..181 H5
RDSH SK5 ....145 F5
STRET M32 ....125 F5
Matlock St *ECC* M30 ....110 D5
Matt Busby Cl *SWIN* M27 .....99 G3
Matthew Cl *OLDS* OL8 ....92 B3
Matthew Moss La *ROCH* OL11 .42 A3
Matthews Av *FWTH* BL4 ....66 C5
Matthews La *BNG/LEV* M19 ..144 B1
Matthew's St
WGTN/LGST M12 ....129 C5
Mattison St *MPL/ROM* SK6 ...175 F3
Mattison St *OP/CLY* M11 .....130 D1
Maudsley St *BURY* BL9 ....4 C6
Maud St *BOLE* BL2 ....34 D1
WHIT OL12 ....10 E1
Mauldeth Rd *BKLY* M9 ....87 H5
Mauldeth Cl *HTNM* SK4 ....143 G5
BNG/LEV M19 ....158 C2
Mauldeth Rd *DID/WITH* M20 ..143 A2
Mauldeth Rd West
DID/WITH M20 ....142 A3
Maunby Gdns *LHULT* M38 ......81 H4
Maureen Av *CHH* M8 ....86 A2
Maureen St *WHIT* OL12 ....11 F1
Maurice Cl *DUK* SK16 ....120 B5
Maurice Dr *SLFD* M6 ....113 E1
Maurice St *SLFD* M6 ....113 E1
Mavis Gv *MILN* OL16 ....31 H5
Mavis St *ROCH* OL11 ....42 B5
Mawdsley Dr *CHH* M8 ....102 D2
Mawdsley St *BOL* BL1 ....3 G3
Maxwell Av *OFTN* SK2 ....172 D4
Maxwell St *BOL* BL1 ....33 H2
BURY BL9 ....5 J3
Max Woosnam Wk
RUSH/FAL M14 ....128 B5
Mayall St *MOSL* OL5 ....108 D1

Mayall St East *OLDE* OL4 * 76 B5
May Av *CHD/CHDH* SK8 ......193 G1
HTNM SK4 ....12 A2
Maybank St *BOLS/LL* BL3 .....48 A5
Maybreck Cl *BOLS/LL* BL3 .....84 B4
Mayberth Av *CHH* M8 ....87 F5
Maybreck Cl *BOLS/LL* BL3 .....88 B4
Mayburn Cl *MDTN* M24 ....89 F2
Maybury Cl *RAMS* BL0 ....16 C3
Maybury St *GTN* M18 ....130 D2
Maycroft Av *DID/WITH* M20 ..157 H1
May Dr *BNG/LEV* M19 ....143 H5
Mayer St *OFTN* SK2 * 172 D2
Mayes Gdns *ANC* M4 ....115 G4
Mayes St *ANC* M4 ....7 G2
Mayfair Av *RAD* M26 ....51 G5
SLFD M6 ....112 A2
URM M41 ....138 B1
WHTF M45 * 69 G5
Mayfair Cl *DUK* SK16 ....120 C5
POY/DIS SK12 ....195 F2
Mayfair Ct *HALE/TIMP* WA15 .166 C2
Mayfair Crs *FAIL* M35 ....105 G2
Mayfair Dr *IRL* M44 ....136 C1
ROY/SHW OL2 ....75 E2
SALE M33 ....153 H4
Mayfair Gdns *ROCH* OL11 .....42 C1
Mayfair Ms *DID/WITH* M20 ....157 H1
Mayfair Pk *DID/WITH* M20 * ..157 H2
Mayfair Rd *WYTH/NTH* M22 ..168 D5
Mayfield *BOLE* BL2 ....35 G1
Mayfield Av *BOLS/LL* BL3 ......65 C1
DTN/ASHW M34 ....147 E4
FWTH BL4 ....65 H5
OLDTF/WHR M16 ....141 G4
RDSH SK5 ....160 A1
SALE M33 ....155 F2
SWIN M27 ....99 B5
Mayfield Cl *HALE/TIMP* WA15 .166 C2
RAMS BL0 ....26 B1
Mayfield Gv *GTN* M18 ....130 A1
WALK M28 ....82 A4
Mayfield Houses *RAD* M26 ....67 F2
Mayfield Rd *BRAM/HZG* SK7 ..193 H5
BRO M7 ....101 C1
HALE/TIMP WA15 ....166 C3
MPL/ROM SK6 ....161 C5
OLD OL1 ....76 A3
OLDTF/WHR M16 ....127 H5
RAMS BL0 ....26 B1
Mayfield St *DTN/ASHW* M34 ..132 B3
MILN OL16 ....11 H3
Mayfield Ter *MILN* OL16 ....11 H3
Mayflower Av *ORD* M5 ....113 F5
Mayford Rd *BNG/LEV* M19 ...144 A1
Maygate *CHAD* OL9 ....75 E4
May Gv *BNG/LEV* M19 ....144 B1
Mayhill Dr *SLFD* M6 ....111 H1
WALK M28 ....82 A4
Mayhurst Av *CCHDY* M21 ....156 C3
Maylorlowe Av *RDSH* SK5 ....160 D2
Mayor's Rd *HALE/TIMP* WA15 .165 H5
Mayor St *BOL* BL1 ....2 B6
TOT/BURYW BL8 ....37 F3
Mayo St *WGTN/LGST* M12 ....115 G5
Maypool Dr *RDSH* SK5 ....145 F5
May Rd *CHD/CHDH* SK8 ......182 C5
OLDTF/WHR M16 ....127 C5
SWIN M27 ....99 G4
May St *BOLE* BL2 ....3 H5
ECC M30 ....110 D1
HEY OL10 * 56 B1
NEWH/MOS M40 ....104 B5
OLDS OL8 ....90 D3
RAD M26 ....68 B1
Mayton St *OP/CLY* M11 ....116 B5
Mayville Dr *DID/WITH* M20 ...157 G3
Maywood Av *DID/WITH* M20 ..169 G1
Maze St *BOLS/LL* BL3 ....50 A6
McConnell Rd
NEWH/MOS M40 ....103 H3
McCready Dr *ORD* M5 * 113 C5
McDonna St *BOL* BL1 ....33 F3
McEvoy St *BOL* BL1 ....34 A4
McKean St *BOLS/LL* BL3 ....49 F5
McKie Cl *OLDS* OL8 ....91 H4
McLaren Ct *CCHDY* M21 ......141 E2
McLean Dr *IRL* M44 ....122 B4
McNaught St *MILN* OL16 ......30 C5
Meachin Av *CCHDY* M21 ......156 B1
Meade Cl *URM* M41 ....124 A5
Meade Gv *BRUN/LGST* M13 ..129 G5
Meade Hill Rd *CHH* M8 ....86 D4
PWCH M25 ....86 D4
The Meade *BOLS/LL* BL3 ....64 D2
WILM/AE SK9 ....199 E2
Meadfoot Av *PWCH* M25 ......85 H3
Meadfoot Rd *GTN* M18 ....130 C3
Meadland Gv *BOL* BL1 ....34 A2
Meadow Av *HALE/TIMP* WA15 .179 E1
SWIN M27 ....99 G1
Meadowbank *AULW* OL7 ......106 D4
Meadow Bank *CCHDY* M21 ...166 D2
HALE/TIMP WA15 ....166 B2
HTNM SK4 ....158 D2
MPL/ROM SK6 ....161 C3
Meadowbank Cl *FAIL* M35 ....105 F4
Meadow Bank Cl *OLDE* OL4 ..92 D3
Meadowbank Rd *BOLS/LL* BL3 ..64 A2
Meadowbrook Cl *BURY* BL9 ...39 F2
HOR/BR BL6 ....45 F4
Meadow Brook Wy
CHD/CHDH SK8 ....171 E5
Meadow Brow *WILM/AE* SK9 ..200 C4
Meadow Cl *BOLS/LL* BL3 ....67 E2
DTN/ASHW M34 ....147 E4
HALE/TIMP WA15 ....179 E1
HEY OL10 ....40 D4
MOSL OL5 ....94 B4
MPL/ROM SK6 ....161 H1
MPL/ROM SK6 ....187 G4
STRET M32 ....126 B1
WILM/AE SK9 ....200 B3
Meadow Crs *CCHDY* M21 .....141 H3
Meadow Cft *BRAM/HZG* SK7 .185 F1
WHTF M45 ....84 D1

Meadowcroft *HYDE* SK14 .....135 G4
RAD M26 ....52 A4
WHTN BL5 ....62 A5
Meadowcroft La *OLD* OL1 .....75 H5
ROCH OL11 ....25 H5
Meadowfield *HOR/BR* BL6 .....46 C2
MILN OL16 ....43 G5
Meadowfield Ct *HYDE* SK14 ..133 G4
Meadowfield Dr *WALK* M28 ...96 C4
Meadow Fold *UPML* OL3 ....78 B3
Meadowgate *URM* M41 ....138 D2
WALK M28 ....97 G2
Meadowgate Rd *SLFD* M6 ....112 B3
Meadow Head Av *WHIT* OL12 ..18 C2
Meadow La BOLE* BL2 ....50 A1
DTN/ASHW M34 ....147 E4
DUK SK16 ....120 A5
OLDS OL8 ....91 F5
WALK M28 ....97 G5
Meadow Ri *ROY/SHW* OL2 .....60 A5
Meadow Rd *BRO* M7 ....113 H5
MDTN M24 ....88 B1
URM M41 ....138 D2
Meadows *BRAM/HZG* SK7 ....193 D2
Meadowside *BRAM/HZG* SK7 ..165 F2
MILN OL16 ....43 G5
Meadowside Av *BOLE* BL2 .....49 H1
IRL M44 ....136 C1
WALK M28 ....82 B3
WYTH/NTH M22 ....168 C5
Meadowside Cl *RAD* M26 .....168 C5
Meadows La *BOLE* BL2 ....35 G3
Meadows Rd *CHD/CHDH* SK8 .181 G3
CHD/CHDH SK8 ....182 C4
HTNM SK4 ....143 A5
SALE M33 ....140 A5
The Meadows *MDTN* M24 ......89 D3
MPL/ROM SK6 ....162 A2
OLDE OL4 ....93 F1
PWCH M25 ....86 B4
RAD M26 ....51 H4
UPML OL3 ....79 E5
WHIT OL12 ....14 B4
Meadow St *HYDE* SK14 ....148 A2
OFTN SK2 ....172 D4
The Meadow *BOL* BL1 ....28 E2
Meadow Vw *WHIT* OL12 ....18 B2
Meadow Wk *FWTH* BL4 ....65 H5
LIT OL15 * 20 C3
Meadow Wy
HALE/TIMP WA15 ....178 C1
NEWH/MOS M40 ....103 H1
TOT/BURYW BL8 ....25 H5
WILM/AE SK9 ....200 B3
Meadscroft Dr *WILM/AE* SK9 .200 C4
Meads Gv *FWTH* BL4 ....64 B1
The Meads *CCHDY* M21 * 141 F4
ORD M5 * 112 D3
Meadway *BRAM/HZG* SK7 ....193 H2
BURY BL9 ....53 C5
CHAD OL9 ....89 H5
DUK SK16 ....133 H1
MPL/ROM SK6 ....187 E4
POY/DIS SK12 ....194 C2
ROCH OL11 ....42 A3
SALE M33 ....153 H4
STLY SK15 ....135 F2
The Meadway *HEY* OL10 ....40 C3
NEWH/MOS M40 ....115 G2
Meech St *OP/CLY* M11 ....116 D5
Meek St *ROY/SHW* OL2 ....75 H2
Meerbrook Rd *EDGY/DAV* SK3 .170 D1
Mee's Sq *ECC* M30 ....111 E5
Megna Cl *CHAD* OL9 ....8 B2
Melandra St *HYDE* SK14 .....149 C1
Melandra Cr *RDSH* SK5 ....145 F5
Melanie Dr *RDSH* SK5 ....145 F5
Melba St *OP/CLY* M11 ....117 F5
Melbecks Wk *NTHM/RTH* M23 .155 G4
Melbourne Av *CHAD* OL9 ......74 B5
MANAIR M90 ....180 D1
STRET M32 ....140 B1
Melbourne Cl *ROCH* OL11 .....43 F4
Melbourne Rd *BOLS/LL* BL3 ...48 A4
BRAM/HZG SK7 ....193 H1
RAD M26 ....43 G4
Melbourne St *BOLS/LL* BL3 ....3 G5
BRO M7 ....101 G5
CHAD OL9 ....74 C5
DTN/ASHW M34 ....146 C1
RDSH SK5 ....145 F3
STLY SK15 ....120 C4
SWIN M27 ....99 G2
Melbourne St North *AUL* OL6 .119 H4
Melbourne St South *AUL* OL6 .119 H4
Melbury Av *DID/WITH* M20 ...158 A2
Melbury Dr *HOR/BR* BL6 ......45 E4
Melbury Rd *CHD/CHDH* SK8 ..193 E1
Meldon Rd *BRUN/LGST* M13 ..143 G1
Meldrum St *OLDS* OL8 ....91 G3
Melford Av *NEWH/MOS* M40 ..104 D1
Melford Gv *OLDE* OL4 ....92 D4

Melford Rd BRAM/HZG SK7 185 G3
Melfort Av STRET M32 140 C2
Meliden Crs BOL BL1 * 33 E5
  WYTH/NTH M22 180 D2
Melksham Cl ORD M5 113 C3
Mellalieu St MDTN M24 72 B3
  ROY/SHW OL2 75 F2
Melland Av CCHDY M21 156 B1
Melland Rd GTN M18 130 B5
Meller Rd BRUN/LGST M13 143 H1
Melling Av CHAD OL9 73 H3
  HTNM SK4 145 E5
Mellor Av CHAD OL9 92 B1
Melling St WGTN/LGST M12 129 H4
Mellington Av DID/WITH M20 169 H1
Mellodew Dr OLD OL1 76 C1
Mellor Brow HEY OL10 40 C4
Mellor Cl AUL OL6 120 B3
Mellor Ct OFTN SK2 173 F2
Mellor Dr BURY BL9 53 E2
  WALK M28 96 C1
Mellor Gv BOL BL1 33 E5
Mellor Rd AUL OL6 120 C1
  CHD/CHDH SK8 183 E5
Mellors Rd TRPK M17 125 C1
Mellor St DROY M43 117 G4
  ECC M30 111 E4
  FAIL M35 104 C3
  NEWH/MOS M40 115 G2
  OLDE OL4 92 D1
  OLDS OL8 90 D5
  PWCH M25 85 G5
  RAD M26 68 C2
  ROCH OL11 29 G4
  ROY/SHW OL2 59 E4
  STRET M32 125 G2
Mellor Wy CHAD OL9 90 A1
Mellowstone Dr CCHDY M21 142 B5
Melloy Pl CHH M8 114 D1
Melon Pl SLFD M6 113 G3
Melrose WHIT OL12 10 B5
Melrose Av BOL BL1 32 C5
  DID/WITH M20 157 H3
  ECC M30 110 B1
  EDGY/DAV SK3 * 170 C2
  HEY OL10 40 C3
  LIT OL15 20 D1
  SALE M33 154 C3
  TOT/BURYW BL8 37 H3
Melrose Cl WHTF M45 69 G2
Melrose Ct CHAD OL9 89 E1
Melrose Crs EDGY/DAV SK3 171 F1
  HALE/TIMP WA15 178 C5
  POY/DIS SK12 196 C2
Melrose Gdns RAD M26 51 H4
Melrose Rd BOLS/LL BL3 66 C1
  RAD M26 51 H4
Melrose St NEWH/MOS M40 104 B5
  OLD OL1 76 A3
  RAMS BL0 26 C1
  ROCH OL11 29 G4
Melsomby Rd
  NTHM/RTH M23 155 H4
Meltham Av DID/WITH M20 142 C1
Meltham Cl HTNM SK4 158 B5
Meltham Pl BOLS/LL BL3 * 48 B5
Melton Av DTN/ASHW M34 131 F1
  URM M41 122 D5
Melton Cl HEY OL10 40 C5
  WALK M28 81 H5
Melton Dr BURY BL9 53 H4
Melton Rd CHH M8 101 H1
Melton St BKLY M9 103 C1
  HEY OL10 40 C5
  RAD M26 52 A5
  RDSH SK5 160 A2
Melverley Rd BKLY M9 87 F2
Melville Cl OP/CLY M11 130 D1
Melville Rd FWTH BL4 82 C1
  IRL M44 150 B1
  STRET M32 125 C5
Melville St AUL OL6 119 C1
  BOLS/LL BL3 49 F5
  CSLFD M3 6 A3
  OLDE OL4 92 D2
  ROCH OL11 42 C5
Melvin Av WYTH/NTH M22 168 D5
Melyncourt Rd HYDE SK14 * 135 F5
Memorial Cottages
  SWIN M27 * 84 A4
Memorial Rd WALK M28 82 A4
Menai Gv CHD/CHDH SK8 170 D5
Menai Rd EDGY/DAV SK3 171 H3
Menai St BOLS/LL BL3 * 48 A5
Mendip Av WYTH/NTH M22 169 E1
Mendip Cl BOLE BL2 50 D2
  CHAD OL9 90 B2
  CHD/CHDH SK8 182 A5
  HTNM SK4 159 H3
  ROY/SHW OL2 74 D1
Mendip Crs TOT/BURYW BL8 37 F3
Mendip Dr BOLE BL2 50 D2
  MILN OL16 31 H5
Mendip Rd OLDS OL8 91 E4
Mendips Cl ROY/SHW OL2 59 H3
Menston Av NEWH/MOS M40 104 D1
Mentmore Rd MILN OL16 31 E5
Mentone Crs WYTH/NTH M22 168 D5
Mentone Rd HTNM SK4 159 E3
Mentor St BRUN/LGST M13 143 H1
Mercer La ROCH OL11 28 B3
Mercer Rd GTN M18 130 C3
  HEY OL10 56 A2
Mercer St BNG/LEV M19 126 D2
  DROY M43 118 A3
Merchants Quay SALQ M50 126 D1
Mercian Ml AUL OL6 * 119 G2
Mercian Wy EDGY/DAV SK3 171 E2
Mercia St BOLS/LL BL3 48 B4
Mercury Pk URM M41 * 125 E2
Mercury Wy URM M41 125 E3
Mere Av DROY M43 117 F5
  MDTN M24 88 D1
  SLFD M6 112 D3
Merebank Cl ROCH OL11 28 B3
Mere Bank Cl WALK M28 81 H4
Mere Cl BURY BL9 53 H4
  DTN/ASHW M34 145 H1
  SALE M33 155 G3

Mereclough Av WALK M28 97 G1
Meredew Av WALK M28 98 D4
Meredith St BOLS/LL BL3 65 E1
Mere Dr DID/WITH M20 157 G2
  SWIN M27 83 H5
Merefield Av ROCH OL11 42 D1
Merefield Rd
  HALE/TIMP WA15 166 D4
Merefield St ROCH OL11 42 D1
Merefield Ter ROCH OL11 * 42 D1
Mere Fold WALK M28 81 C4
Mere Gdns BOL BL1 2 C2
Merehall Cl BOL BL1 2 C2
Merehall Dr BOL BL1 2 C2
Merehall St BOL BL1 2 B1
Mereland Av DID/WITH M20 157 H2
Mere La ROCH OL11 43 E1
Meremanor WALK M28 97 G1
Merepool Cl MPL/ROM SK6 174 B2
Mere Side STLY SK15 120 C1
Mereside Cl CHD/CHDH SK8 170 C5
Mereside Gv WALK M28 82 B4
Mere St ROCH OL11 30 A5
  WHIT OL12 10 C5
Mere Wk BOL BL1 2 C2
Merewood Av
  WYTH/NTH M22 168 C3
Meriden Cl RAD M26 52 A3
Meriden Gv HOR/BR BL6 47 E5
Meridiam Pl DID/WITH M20 157 F2
Meridian Cl MILN OL16 11 K7
Meriton Rd WILM/AE SK9 191 H3
Merlewood Av BNG/LEV M19 144 C4
  DTN/ASHW M34 118 A4
  UPML OL3 79 E4
Merlewood Dr SWIN M27 98 B4
Merlin Cl LIT OL15 31 H1
  OFTN SK2 173 H5
  OLDS OL8 106 D2
Merlin Dr SWIN M27 84 C5
Merlin Gv BOL BL1 33 E5
Merlin Rd IRL M44 122 B4
  MILN OL16 31 G5
Merlyn Av DID/WITH M20 157 H2
  DTN/ASHW M34 146 D1
  SALE M33 154 D1
Merrick Av WYTH/NTH M22 168 D5
Merrick St HEY OL10 41 F5
Merridale Rd
  NEWH/MOS M40 104 B1
The Merridale
  HALE/TIMP WA15 178 B4
Merrill St ANC M4 115 C4
Merriman St OLDTF/WHR M16 127 H4
Merrion St FWTH BL4 65 H2
Merrow Wk CMANE M1 * 128 C1
Merrybent Cl OFTN SK2 173 E5
Merrybower Rd BRO M7 101 H2
Merrydale Av ECC M30 111 F1
Merryman Hall WHIT OL12 * 30 C1
Merseybank Av CCHDY M21 156 C2
Mersey Cl WHTF M45 70 A3
Mersey Crs DID/WITH M20 156 C3
Mersey Dr PART M31 151 F2
  WHTF M45 70 A3
Mersey Mdw DID/WITH M20 157 E3
Mersey Rd DID/WITH M20 157 E5
  HTNM SK4 158 C4
  SALE M33 139 H5
Mersey Rd North FAIL M35 105 F1
Mersey Sq STKP SK1 3 J4
Mersey St DROY M43 117 F5
  STKP SK1 13 K1
Mersey Vw URM M41 * 137 G3
Merseyway STKP SK1 13 F2
Merston Dr DID/WITH M20 169 F1
Merton Av BRAM/HZG SK7 185 G4
  MPL/ROM SK6 161 H2
  OLDS OL8 91 E4
Merton Cl BOLS/LL BL3 * 48 B4
Merton Dr DROY M43 117 F4
Merton Gv CHAD OL9 89 G4
  HALE/TIMP WA15 166 C5
Merton Rd EDGY/DAV SK3 * 171 E2
  POY/DIS SK12 194 C3
  PWCH M25 86 B2
  SALE M33 154 D1
Merton St TOT/BURYW BL8 4 C2
Merville Av NEWH/MOS M40 103 C1
Mervyn Rd BRO M7 100 D4
Mervyn St URM M41 137 G2
Merwood Av CHD/CHDH SK8 182 A4
Merwood Gv RUSH/FAL M14 129 F4
Meshaw Cl NTHM/RTH M23 155 F5
Mesnefield Av BRO M7 100 D2
Mesne Lea Gv WALK M28 * 97 F2
Mesnefield Rd WALK M28 97 E2
Metcalfe Ct LHULT M38 * 81 E3
Metcalfe Dr MPL/ROM SK6 162 A4
Metcalf Gdns UPML OL3 79 E4
Metfield Pl BOL BL1 * 48 B1
Methuen St WGTN/LGST M12 130 A5
Methwold St BOLS/LL BL3 * 48 B5
The Mews BOL BL1 48 A1
  CHD/CHDH SK8 169 G4
  NEWH/MOS M40 115 H2
  PWCH M25 86 A4
  SALE M33 * 154 D3
  WHTF M45 69 F1
Mexborough St OLDE OL4 76 C4
Meyer St EDGY/DAV SK3 172 A3
Meyrick Rd SLFD M6 113 F2
Miall St ROCH OL11 30 D5
Micawber Rd POY/DIS SK12 195 F5
Michael St MDTN M24 72 C4
Michigan Av SALQ M50 115 H4
Mickleby Wk NEWH/MOS M40 115 F2
Micklehurst Av DID/WITH M20 156 D2
Micklehurst Gn OFTN SK2 173 F4
Micklehurst Rd MOSL OL5 109 F1
Middlebourne St SLFD M6 112 D3
Middlebrook Dr HOR/BR BL6 46 D5
Middle Fld ROCH OL11 14 C3
Middlefields CHD/CHDH SK8 171 E5
Middlegate NEWH/MOS M40 89 G4
Middle Ga OLDS OL8 91 F5
Middle Gn AUL OL6 119 H1

Middleham St RUSH/FAL M14 142 C1
Middle Hl WHIT OL12 19 E4
Middle Hillgate STKP SK1 13 H4
Middlesex Dr BURY BL9 55 E1
Middlesex Rd BKLY M9 88 A5
  RDSH SK5 146 A5
Middlesex Wk CHAD OL9 8 D4
Middlestone Dr BKLY M9 103 E3
Middle St WHIT OL12 14 B4
Middleton Av FAIL M35 105 E3
Middleton Dr BURY BL9 69 C1
Middleton Old Rd BKLY M9 88 A1
Middleton Rd BKLY M9 87 E2
  CHAD OL9 73 H5
  CHAD OL9 73 H5
  CHH M8 87 E5
  HEY OL10 56 B4
  RDSH SK5 145 F1
  ROY/SHW OL2 74 C1
Middleton Wy MDTN M24 72 C4
Middleway OLDE OL4 93 C2
Middlewood Dr HTNM SK4 158 D5
Middlewood Gn CHAD OL9 74 B5
Middle Wood La LIT OL15 20 B2
Middlewood Rd
  MPL/ROM SK6 186 C5
  POY/DIS SK12 195 E3
Middlewood St ORD M5 113 H4
Midford Av ECC M30 110 C3
Midford Dr BOL BL1 28 D5
Midge Hall Dr ROCH OL11 28 D5
Midge Hi MOSL OL5 94 A3
Midgley Av GTN M18 130 D2
Midgley Crs AUL OL6 120 D1
Midgley Dr MILN OL16 43 G4
Midgley St SWIN M27 98 C4
Midgrove La UPML OL3 78 C1
Midhurst Av
  NEWH/MOS M40 * 116 C1
Midhurst Cl CHD/CHDH SK8 182 C4
Midhurst St ROCH OL11 43 E1
Midland Rd BRAM/HZG SK7 183 H1
  RDSH SK5 145 F1
Midland St WGTN/LGST M12 129 E1
Midland Ter ALT WA14 * 177 G2
Midland Wk BRAM/HZG SK7 * 183 H1
Midlothian St OP/CLY M11 116 C3
Midville Rd OP/CLY M11 116 D2
Midway CHD/CHDH SK8 182 B3
Midway St WGTN/LGST M12 144 A1
Milan St BRO M7 101 H4
Milbourne Rd BURY BL9 27 G5
Milburn Av NTHM/RTH M23 156 A4
Milburn Dr BOLE BL2 50 C1
Milbury Dr LIT OL15 31 H1
Milden Cl DID/WITH M20 157 H2
Mildred Av OLDE OL4 93 C2
  PWCH M25 86 B5
  ROY/SHW OL2 75 F2
Mildred St BRO M7 101 F5
Mile End La OFTN SK2 172 D5
  TOT/BURYW BL8 37 E5
Miles St BOL BL1 33 G4
  HYDE SK14 148 B1
  OLD OL1 76 A4
  WGTN/LGST M12 129 H1
Milford Av OLDS OL8 90 D5
Milford Brow OLDE OL4 76 C5
Milford Crs LIT OL15 21 F2
Milford Dr BNG/LEV M19 144 C4
Milford Gv OFTN SK2 172 D2
Milford Rd BOLS/LL BL3 64 D1
  HEY OL10 40 C5
Milford St BKLY M9 * 87 G4
  SLFD M6 112 D4
  WHIT OL12 10 C2
Milkstone Pl ROCH OL11 * 30 A5
Milkstone Rd ROCH OL11 30 A5
Milk St CMANW M2 7 F4
  HYDE SK14 147 H1
  RAMS BL0 16 C3
  ROY/SHW OL2 60 A5
  TOT/BURYW BL8 4 D1
Milkwood Gv GTN M18 130 C4
Millais St NEWH/MOS M40 103 H2
Millard St CHAD OL9 74 B5
Millbank Gdns BOL BL1 * 3 H3
Millbank St CMANE M1 7 K5
  HEY OL10 40 C4
Millbeck Gv BOLS/LL BL3 * 48 D5
Millbeck Rd MDTN M24 72 A2
Millbeck St HULME M15 128 B2
Millbrae Gdns ROY/SHW OL2 59 G2
Millbrook Av DTN/ASHW M34 146 B2
Millbrook Bank ROCH OL11 * 28 A2
Millbrook Cl ROY/SHW OL2 60 C3
Millbrook Fold BRAM/HZG SK7 185 H5
Millbrook Rd NTHM/RTH M23 155 F5
Millbrook St STKP SK1 13 G5
Mill Brow AUL OL6 107 F1
  CHH M8 87 H5
  OLD OL1 76 A4
  RAD M26 68 A4
Mill Court Dr RAD M26 67 E4
Millcrest Cl WALK M28 96 A5
Mill Cft BOL BL1 2 B2
  ROY/SHW OL2 60 B3
Milldale Cl HOR/BR BL6 46 D2
Millers Brook Cl HEY OL10 * 41 E3
Millers Ct ORD M5 111 H3
Millers St ECC M30 110 D4
Millett St BURY BL9 17 E1
  RAMS BL0 26 D1

Mill Ga MILN OL16 30 C1
  OLDS OL8 91 E4
Millgate ANC M4 * 7 F5
  DUK SK16 * 51 G5
  STKP SK1 13 H2
Millgate La DID/WITH M20 157 G5
Mill Green St
  WGTN/LGST M12 * 115 G5
Millhall Cl HULME M15 128 A2
Millhead Av NEWH/MOS M40 115 H3
Mill Hl BOLE BL2 * 3 H3
  LHULT M38 80 D1
Mill Hill Caravan Pk BOLE BL2 3 H3
Mill Hill Gv HYDE SK14 149 H1
Mill Hill Hollow POY/DIS SK12 185 E5
Mill Hill St BOLE BL2 3 H3
Millhouse Av NTHM/RTH M23 167 H5
Mill House Cl WHIT OL12 20 A4
Milliner Ct OFTN SK2 * 173 E2
Millington Wk HULME M15 127 G2
Mill La AUL OL6 119 G3
  BRAM/HZG SK7 185 G4
  CHAD OL9 90 D3
  CHD/CHDH SK8 183 E1
  DTN/ASHW M34 147 F2
  FAIL M35 104 B3
  HALE/TIMP WA15 189 F3
  MOSL OL5 95 H1
  ROCH OL11 43 E1
  RDSH SK5 145 G4
  ROY/SHW OL2 58 D5
  TOT/BURYW BL8 37 G2
  UPML OL3 78 B1
  WYTH/NTH M22 156 D5
Millom Av NTHM/RTH M23 156 A5
Millom Cl MILN OL16 31 H5
Millom Ct HALE/TIMP WA15 * 167 E3
Millom Dr BURY BL9 69 G2
Millom Pl CHD/CHDH SK8 181 G1
Millow St ANC M4 7 F1
Millpond Av BOLS/LL BL3 65 F1
Mill Pond Cl ROY/SHW OL2 60 A3
Mills Farm Cl OLDS OL8 106 D1
Mills Hill Rd MDTN M24 73 G1
Mills St HEY OL10 40 C4
  WHIT OL12 14 C2
Millstone Cl MPL/ROM SK6 161 H5
Millstone Rd BOL BL1 23 F2
Millstream La
  NEWH/MOS M40 117 F2
Mill St ALT WA14 165 H4
  BOL BL1 33 G4
  BRAM/HZG SK7 185 E1
  EDGW/EG BL7 23 E3
  FAIL M35 104 B3
  FWTH BL4 65 E3
  HYDE SK14 133 H5
  MOSL OL5 94 D1
  OP/CLY M11 116 B5
  RAD M26 68 A4
  ROY/SHW OL2 59 G5
  SLFD M6 113 H1
  STLY SK15 121 F4
  TOT/BURYW BL8 26 A3
  UPML OL3 96 B5
  WHTN BL5 62 C4
  WILM/AE SK9 199 E3
Mills Way BRAM/HZG SK7 183 H5
Millwall Cl GTN M18 130 C3
Millway HALE/TIMP WA15 178 D5
Millwell La BOL BL1 2 E4
Millwood
  CHD/CHDH SK8 182 B4
Millwood Ct BURY BL9 53 G3
Millwood Ter HYDE SK14 * 147 G1
Millwright St
  NEWH/MOS M40 104 A5
Mill Yd BURY BL9 5 G3
Milne St CHAD OL9 8 B4
  CHAD OL9 74 C5
  OLD OL1 75 H4
  ROCH OL11 42 B4
  ROY/SHW OL2 60 C3
Milngate Cl MILN OL16 43 H3
Milnholme BOL BL1 33 E3
Milnrow Cl BRUN/LGST M13 128 C1
Milnrow Rd LIT OL15 31 C1
  MILN OL16 11 H6
  ROY/SHW OL2 45 F5
Milnthorpe Rd BOLE BL2 50 B3
Milnthorpe St SLFD M6 100 D5
Milnthorpe Wy
  WGTN/LGST M12 129 F2
Milo St BKLY M9 * 88 A4
Milsom Av BOLS/LL BL3 51 E5
Milstead Wk NEWH/MOS M40 116 A1
Milton Av BOLS/LL BL3 51 E5
  DROY M43 118 A3
  IRL M44 136 A5
  ORD M5 * 112 C3
  STLY SK15 121 H1
Milton Cl DUK SK16 134 C1
  MPL/ROM SK6 174 C5
  STRET M32 126 B5
Milton Ct BNG/LEV M19 158 B2
Milton Crs CHD/CHDH SK8 169 H4
  FWTH BL4 81 G1
Milton Dr CHAD OL9 90 B1
  HALE/TIMP WA15 178 C4
  POY/DIS SK12 195 G3
  SALE M33 139 G5
Milton Gv OLDTF/WHR M16 127 G4
  SALE M33 139 G5
Milton Pl SLFD M6 113 F2

Milton Rd BRAM/HZG SK7 183 H5
  DTN/ASHW M34 118 C4
  PWCH M25 86 B2
  RAD M26 51 G5
  STRET M32 126 B5
  SWIN M27 98 C1
Milton St BRO M7 101 E3
  ECC M30 111 E3
  HYDE SK14 133 G4
  MDTN M24 72 C5
  MILN OL16 10 D6
  MOSL OL5 94 D5
  RAMS BL0 16 C2
  ROY/SHW OL2 59 G5
Milverton Av HYDE SK14 149 E1
Milverton Cl HOR/BR BL6 47 E4
Milverton Dr BRAM/HZG SK7 193 E2
Milverton Rd RUSH/FAL M14 129 E5
Milverton Wk HYDE SK14 149 E1
Milwain Dr HTNM SK4 144 C5
Milwain Rd BNG/LEV M19 143 E3
  STRET M32 140 A2
Mimosa Dr SWIN M27 84 A5
Mincing St ANC M4 * 7 G1
Minden Cl DID/WITH M20 157 H2
  TOT/BURYW BL8 37 G4
Minden Pde BURY BL9 4 E5
Minden St SLFD M6 100 B4
Minehead Av DID/WITH M20 144 B4
  URM M41 138 B3
Minerva Rd DUK SK16 119 H3
  FWTH BL4 65 E3
Mine St HEY OL10 41 E2
Minnie St BOLS/LL BL3 * 48 A5
  WHIT OL12 * 14 C3
Minoan Gdns BRO M7 101 F5
Minorca Cl ROCH OL11 28 B3
Minorca St BOLS/LL BL3 48 D5
Minor St FAIL M35 105 G3
  OLDS OL8 8 F6
  ROCH OL11 42 B5
Minshull St CMANE M1 7 G5
Minshull St South CMANE M1 7 H6
Minstead Cl HYDE SK14 148 C2
Minster Cl BOLE BL2 34 C4
  DUK SK16 135 G2
Minster Dr ALT WA14 176 D3
  CHD/CHDH SK8 144 B4
  URM M41 123 H5
Minsterley Pde
  WYTH/NTH M22 * 180 B3
Minster Rd BKLY M9 103 G2
  BOLE BL2 34 D4
Minster Wy CHAD OL9 74 B3
Minstrel Cl SWIN M27 98 C5
Minton St NEWH/MOS M40 104 B2
  OLDE OL4 9 J6
Minto St AULW OL7 119 F1
Mirabel St CSLFD M3 6 D1
Mirfield Av BKLY M9 88 A5
  HTNM SK4 159 E4
  OLDS OL8 91 F3
Mirfield Dr ECC M30 111 E1
  MDTN M24 72 C3
  URM M41 124 B4
Mirfield Rd BKLY M9 88 A5
Miriam St BOLS/LL BL3 * 48 A5
  FAIL M35 104 D5
Mission St HEY OL10 40 D4
Missouri Av SALQ M50 112 D4
Mistletoe Gv CSLFD M3 * 6 A1
Mitcham Av BKLY M9 88 D4
Mitchell Cl CHD/CHDH SK8 * 169 E3
Mitchell Hey WHIT OL12 10 A6
Mitchells Quay FAIL M35 104 D3
Mitchell St ECC M30 110 D2
  MILN OL16 19 H5
  NEWH/MOS M40 104 A5
  OLD OL1 75 E4
  OP/CLY M11 129 C1
  TOT/BURYW BL8 37 G2
  WHIT OL12 29 G3
Mitchenson Gdns SLFD M6 113 C2
Mitford Rd RUSH/FAL M14 143 E4
Mitford St STRET M32 140 A2
Mitre Rd BRUN/LGST M13 129 C4
Mitre St BOL BL1 33 F3
  FAIL M35 105 E2
Mitton Cl HEY OL10 40 A4
  TOT/BURYW BL8 37 E4
Mizpah Gv TOT/BURYW BL8 37 G4
Mizzy Rd WHIT OL12 10 B2
Moadlock MPL/ROM SK6 162 B2
Moat Av WYTH/NTH M22 168 B5
Moatfield Gdns BOL BL1 2 A2
Moat Gdns WYTH/NTH M22 168 B5
Moat Hall Av ECC M30 110 A2
Moat Rd WYTH/NTH M22 168 B5
Mobberley Gv BNG/LEV M19 158 B2
Mobberley Rd BOLE BL2 50 A1
Mocha Pde BRO M7 114 A2
Modbury Cl BRAM/HZG SK7 184 B3
Model Cottages
  HALE/TIMP WA15 * 167 E5
Mode Wheel Rd South
  SALQ M50 112 C4
Modwen Rd ORD M5 * 127 E2
Moelfre Dr CHD/CHDH SK8 183 E5
Moffat Cl BOLE BL2 50 C3
Moisant St BOLS/LL BL3 64 C1
Mold St BOL BL1 33 H3
  OLD OL1 75 F4
Molesworth St MILN OL16 11 G7
Mollets Wd
  DTN/ASHW M34 132 D3
Mollington Rd
  WYTH/NTH M22 180 D4
Mollis Gv OLD OL1 76 D1
Molyneux Rd BNG/LEV M19 144 C2
  WHTN BL5 62 C3
Molyneux St WHIT OL12 29 G3
Mona Av CHD/CHDH SK8 182 C3
  STRET M32 125 H5
Monaco Dr WYTH/NTH M22 156 C4
Monarch Cl IRL M44 136 A5
  ROY/SHW OL2 75 F2
Mona Rd CHAD OL9 90 C2
Monart Rd BKLY M9 103 F1

Mona St HYDE SK14 148 A1
SLFD M6 113 F1
Mona Wy IRL M44 136 D3
Mond Rd IRL M44 122 C4
Money Ash Rd
HALE/TIMP WA15 177 G1
Monfa Av OFTN SK2 172 B5
Monica Av CHH M8 87 E5
Monica Gv BNG/LEV M19 143 H3
Monks Cl MILN OL16 31 F5
Monksdale Av URM M41 138 B1
Monks Hall Gv ECC M30 111 G3
Monks La BOLE BL2 35 E4
Monkton Av GTN M18 130 B5
Monkwood Dr BKLY M9 * 103 F2
Monmouth Av BURY BL9 38 C1
SALE M33 154 A1
Monmouth Rd
CHD/CHDH SK8 183 E3
Monmouth St CHAD OL9 8 A7
GTN M18 130 D2
MDTN M24 73 F4
ROCH OL11 30 A5
Monroe Cl SLFD M6 112 D1
Monsal Av BRO M7 100 D3
OFTN SK2 173 E2
Monsall Cl BURY BL9 69 H2
Monsall Rd NEWH/MOS M40 103 F4
Monsall St NEWH/MOS M40 103 E5
OLDS OL8 91 F4
Mons Av ROCH OL11 29 F3
Montague Rd AUL OL6 120 A2
OLDTF/WHR M16 126 D3
SALE M33 154 C2
Montague St BOLS/LL BL3 * 64 A1
Montague Wy STLY SK15 120 D3
Montagu Rd OFTN SK2 173 E2
Montagu St MPL/ROM SK6 163 G4
Montana Sq OP/CLY M11 130 D1
Montcliffe Crs
OLDTF/WHR M16 142 B2
Monteagle St BKLY M9 87 G3
Montford St SALQ M50 113 E5
Montgomery ROCH OL11 * 29 H5
Montgomery Dr BURY BL9 70 A2
Montgomery Rd
BRUN/LGST M13 143 H1
Montgomery St OLDS OL8 90 C5
ROCH OL11 42 C2
Montgomery Wy RAD M26 51 F4
Monton Av ECC M30 111 F2
Montondale ECC M30 110 D2
Montonfields Rd ECC M30 110 D2
Monton Gn ECC M30 111 E1
Monton La ECC M30 111 F3
Monton Mill Gdns ECC M30 110 D2
Monton Rd ECC M30 111 E2
RDSH SK5 160 D2
Monton St BOLS/LL BL3 64 D1
RAD M26 68 A1
RUSH/FAL M14 128 B4
Montpellier Rd
WYTH/NTH M22 180 C2
Montreal St BNG/LEV M19 144 B2
OLDS OL8 91 G3
Montrose Av BOLE BL2 34 D5
DID/WITH M20 157 E1
DUK SK16 133 F1
OFTN SK2 184 B1
RAMS BL0 26 B1
STRET M32 139 H1
Montrose Crs BNG/LEV M19 144 A2
Montrose Dr EDGW/EG BL7 23 H4
Montrose St ROCH OL11 57 F1
Montserrat Rd BOL BL1 32 B4
Moon Gv RUSH/FAL M14 143 F1
Moon St CHAD OL9 8 B2
Moor Bank La MILN OL16 44 A2
Moorbank La MILN OL16 44 B3
Moorby Av BNG/LEV M19 158 B2
Moorby St OLD OL1 9 J1
Moorby Wk BOLS/LL BL3 * 48 D4
Moor Cl RAD M26 51 H4
Moorclose St MDTN M24 73 F4
Moorcock Av SWIN M27 99 G2
Moor Crs UPML OL3 79 E1
Moorcroft ROCH OL11 43 E3
Moorcroft Dr BNG/LEV M19 158 C2
Moorcroft Rd
NTHM/RTH M23 155 G5
Moorcroft St DROY M43 * 117 H4
OLDS OL8 90 D5
Moordale Av OLDE OL4 76 D3
Moordale St DID/WITH M20 157 F1
Moordown Cl CHH M8 102 C4
Moor Edge Rd MOSL OL5 109 G1
Mooredge Ter ROY/SHW OL2 75 F2
Moor End WYTH/NTH M22 168 C1
Moor End Av BRO M7 101 F2
Moore's Ct BOL BL1 48 B1
Moore St MILN OL16 10 D7
Moorfield WALK M28 96 A3
WALK M28 97 G2
Moorfield Av DID/WITH M20 143 E4
DTN/ASHW M34 147 E2
LIT OL15 20 D1
STLY SK15 135 E1
Moorfield Cha FWTH BL4 66 A5
Moorfield Cl IRL M44 * 122 C5
SWIN M27 98 C4
Moorfield Dr HYDE SK14 * 133 H3
WILM/AE SK9 198 B5
Moorfield Gv BOLE BL2 34 C5
HTNM SK4 159 E2
SALE M33 155 E3
Moorfield Hts STLY SK15 109 F3
STLY SK15 109 H4
Moorfield Ms ROY/SHW OL2 * 60 A2
Moorfield Pl WHIT OL12 * 10 B2
Moorfield Rd DID/WITH M20 157 E2
IRL M44 122 C5
OLDS OL8 90 C5
SLFD M6 100 A5
SWIN M27 98 B4
Moorfield St DID/WITH M20 142 D4
Moor Ga BOLE BL2 35 E1
Moorgate BURY BL9 5 F3
Moorgate Av DID/WITH M20 142 B5
ROCH OL11 28 D4
Moorgate Ct BOLE BL2 3 K1
Moorgate Dr STLY SK15 109 F4
Moorgate La LIT OL15 20 B1
Moorgate Ms STLY SK15 * 109 F3
Moorgate Rd RAD M26 51 H1
STLY SK15 109 F3
Moorgate St UPML OL3 79 E4
Moorhead St ANC M4 7 J1
Moorhey Rd LHULT M38 81 E1
Moorhey St OLDE OL4 92 A1
Moor Hl ROCH OL11 28 C2
Moorhouse Farm MILN OL16 31 F5
Moor House Fold MILN OL16 31 F5
Moorings Rd TRPK M17 112 A5
The Moorings MOSL OL5 94 B4
WALK M28 97 H5
Moorland Av CHH M8 87 E5
DROY M43 117 F4
MILN OL16 31 H5
ROCH OL11 28 C2
SALE M33 154 D3
UPML OL3 78 C1
WHIT OL12 18 B2
Moorland Crs WHIT OL12 18 C1
Moorland Dr CHD/CHDH SK8 182 C4
LHULT M38 81 F1
Moorland Gv BOL BL1 32 D4
Moorland Rd DID/WITH M20 157 G3
OFTN SK2 172 B5
STLY SK15 109 F5
Moorlands Av URM M41 * 124 A5
Moorlands Crs MOSL OL5 109 E1
Moorlands Dr MOSL OL5 94 B4
Moorlands St ROY/SHW OL2 60 B2
Moorland St WHIT OL12 10 B2
Moorlands Vw BOLS/LL BL3 63 H2
Moorland Ter WHIT OL12 28 D2
Moor La BOL BL1 2 D5
BRAM/HZG SK7 193 G4
BRO M7 100 D2
NTHM/RTH M23 155 H4
UPML OL3 79 F2
URM M41 123 H5
WILM/AE SK9 198 B5
Moor Nook SALE M33 155 E3
Moor Park Av ROCH OL11 42 A4
Moor Park Rd
DID/WITH M20 * 157 H5
Moor Rd NTHM/RTH M23 167 F1
TOT/BURYW BL8 16 B2
Moorsholme Av
NEWH/MOS M40 103 H3
Moorside HALE/TIMP WA15 * 166 D2
ROCH OL11 43 E3
SWIN M27 98 C3
Moorside Av BOL BL1 32 D4
BOLE BL2 36 C5
DROY M43 118 B2
FWTH BL4 65 G5
OLDE OL4 61 E5
Moorside Ct DTN/ASHW M34 132 C4
Moorside Crs DROY M43 118 B3
Moorside La DTN/ASHW M34 132 D4
Moor Side La RAMS BL0 17 H1
Moorside Rd BRO M7 101 F1
CHH M8 * 102 B1
HTNM SK4 158 D4
MOSL OL5 109 F1
SWIN M27 98 C2
TOT/BURYW BL8 36 D1
URM M41 123 F5
Moorside St DROY M43 118 A3
Moorside Vw TOT/BURYW BL8 26 A5
Moorsley Dr BKLY M9 88 C3
Moor St BURY BL9 5 F3
ECC M30 110 C4
HEY OL10 40 C4
OLD OL1 * 76 A5
ROY/SHW OL2 59 H3
SWIN M27 99 E3
Moorsview RAMS BL0 16 C2
Moorton Av BNG/LEV M19 143 H4
Moorton Pk BNG/LEV M19 143 H4
Moortop Cl BKLY M9 87 H2
Moor Top Pl HTNM SK4 159 E3
Moor View Cl WHIT OL12 28 C2
Moorville Rd SLFD M6 99 H5
Moorway Dr BKLY M9 88 D3
Moorwood Dr OLDS OL8 92 B3
SALE M33 153 H3
Mora Av CHAD OL9 74 C3
Moran Cl WILM/AE SK9 192 A5
Moran Wk HULME M15 128 A2
Morar Dr BOLE BL2 50 D2
Morar Rd DUK SK16 133 G1
Mora St BKLY M9 103 G3
Moravian Cl DUK SK16 119 H4
Moravian Fld DROY M43 * 117 H5
Moray Cl RAMS BL0 16 B4
Moray Rd CHAD OL9 90 B3
Morbourne Cl
WGTN/LGST M12 129 F2
Morecambe Cl
NEWH/MOS M40 104 A4
Morely St OLDE OL4 76 D3
Moresby Dr DID/WITH M20 169 G1
Moreton Av BRAM/HZG SK7 193 H2
SALE M33 153 H3
STRET M32 140 B1
WHTF M45 69 G3
Moreton Cl DUK SK16 133 G2
Moreton Dr POY/DIS SK12 195 G3
TOT/BURYW BL8 37 G3
WILM/AE SK9 192 B4
Moreton La OFTN SK2 172 D2
Moreton St CHAD OL9 74 A4
Morgan Pl RDSH SK5 160 A2
Morgan St LIT OL15 21 E3
Morillon Rd IRL M44 122 B4
Morland Rd OLDTF/WHR M16 127 F4
Morley Av RUSH/FAL M14 142 C2
SWIN M27 98 D4
Morley Green Rd
WILM/AE SK9 190 B5
Morley Rd RAD M26 51 G5
Morley St BOLS/LL BL3 2 B6
BURY BL9 53 G1
MILN OL16 11 G3
WHTF M45 69 G4
Morley Wy UPML OL3 95 E2
Morna Wk WGTN/LGST M12 115 G5
Morningside Cl MILN OL16 * 30 C5
OP/CLY M11 131 E1
Morningside Dr
DID/WITH M20 169 H1
Mornington Av
CHD/CHDH SK8 170 A5
Mornington Crs
RUSH/FAL M14 142 C3
Mornington Rd BOL BL1 48 A1
CHD/CHDH SK8 170 A5
ROCH OL11 43 F3
SALE M33 155 E1
Morpeth Cl AULW OL7 118 D1
WGTN/LGST M12 129 F3
Morpeth St SWIN M27 98 D4
Morrell Rd WYTH/NTH M22 168 D1
Morris Fold Dr HOR/BR BL6 46 D3
Morris Gn BOLS/LL BL3 64 B2
Morris Green La BOLS/LL BL3 64 B1
Morris Green St BOLS/LL BL3 * 64 B2
Morris Gv URM M41 137 G3
Morrison St BOLS/LL BL3 64 D1
Morris St BOL BL1 3 G4
DID/WITH M20 142 D4
OLDE OL4 9 K6
RAD M26 53 F4
Morrowfield Av CHH M8 102 A3
Morse Rd NEWH/MOS M40 104 A5
Mortar St OLDE OL4 76 B5
Mortfield Gdns BOL BL1 2 A2
Mortfield La BOL BL1 2 A2
Mortimer Av BKLY M9 88 B3
Mortimer St OLD OL1 75 H3
Mortlake Cl WALK M28 81 E4
Mortlake Dr NEWH/MOS M40 104 A5
Mort La TYLD M29 80 D5
Morton St FAIL M35 104 B3
HTNM SK4 159 H2
MDTN M24 72 D3
RAD M26 68 C2
Mort St FWTH BL4 65 G4
Morven Av BRAM/HZG SK7 185 G1
Morven Dr NTHM/RTH M23 167 H4
Morven Gv BOLE BL2 50 C2
Morville Rd CCHDY M21 141 H2
Morville St CMANE M1 * 7 K6
Moscow Rd EDGY/DAV SK3 171 G2
Moscow Rd East
EDGY/DAV SK3 171 H2
Mosedale Cl NTHM/RTH M23 167 F3
Mosedale Rd MDTN M24 72 A2
Moseldene Rd OFTN SK2 173 E4
Moseley Rd BNG/LEV M19 143 H3
CHD/CHDH SK8 182 C1
RUSH/FAL M14 143 G3
Moseley St EDGY/DAV SK3 12 E6
Mosley Av BURY BL9 38 C1
RAMS BL0 26 C1
Mosley Cl HALE/TIMP WA15 166 A2
Mosley Rd HALE/TIMP WA15 166 C3
TRPK M17 125 H4
Mosley Rd North TRPK M17 112 B5
Mosley St CMANE M1 7 F5
CMANW M2 * 6 E5
RAD M26 52 A5
Mossack Av WYTH/NTH M22 180 C3
Moss Av MILN OL16 30 D5
Moss Bank BRAM/HZG SK7 193 F2
CHH M8 102 B2
Moss Bank Av DROY M43 118 B3
Moss Bank Cl BOL BL1 33 G2
Moss Bank Ct DROY M43 * 118 B3
Mossbank Gv HEY OL10 40 D3
Moss Bank Gv SWIN M27 83 F5
Moss Bank Pk BOL BL1 * 32 C3
Moss Bank Rd SWIN M27 83 G5
Moss Bank Wy BOL BL1 32 B5
Mossbray Av BNG/LEV M19 158 A2
Moss Bridge Rd MILN OL16 30 C5
Mossbrook Dr LHULT M38 80 D1
Moss Brook Rd BKLY M9 103 F3
Moss Cl RAD M26 51 G4
Mossclough Ct BKLY M9 103 F3
Moss Colliery Rd SWIN M27 83 H4
Mosscot Wk BRUN/LGST M13 128 D2
Moss Croft Cl URM M41 123 F5
Mossdale Av BOL BL1 47 E2
Mossdale Rd NTHM/RTH M23 155 G5
SALE M33 153 H5
Mossdown Rd ROY/SHW OL2 75 H1
Moss Farm Cl MDTN M24 89 E1
Mossfield Cl BURY BL9 5 K2
HTNM SK4 159 E4
Mossfield Ct BOL BL1 2 C2
Mossfield Dr BKLY M9 88 D3
Mossfield Rd FWTH BL4 65 G4
FWTH BL4 82 C2
HALE/TIMP WA15 167 E3
SWIN M27 83 H5
Mossgate Rd ROY/SHW OL2 44 C5
Moss Grange Av
OLDTF/WHR M16 * 127 G5
Moss Gn PART M31 137 H5
Moss Gv ROY/SHW OL2 44 B5
Mossgrove Rd
HALE/TIMP WA15 166 A3
Mosshall Cl HULME M15 127 G2
Moss Hall Rd BURY BL9 39 G5
Moss Hey Dr NTHM/RTH M23 156 B5
Moss Hey St ROY/SHW OL2 60 B3
Moss House La WALK M28 96 B5
Moss House Ter BKLY M9 * 102 D1
Mossland Cl HEY OL10 56 A1
Mossland Gv BOLS/LL BL3 63 E2
Moss La AULW OL7 118 D3
BOL BL1 32 D3
BRAM/HZG SK7 193 F2
FWTH BL4 83 E2
HALE/TIMP WA15 165 H5
HALE/TIMP WA15 166 A2
HYDE SK14 149 H3
IRL M44 150 C1
LYMM WA13 150 D5
MDTN M24 88 C2
MILN OL16 30 B5
PART M31 151 F3
ROY/SHW OL2 75 H1
SALE M33 153 E3
SALE M33 153 G3
SWIN M27 98 C1
URM M41 124 D3
WALK M28 82 C4
WHIT OL12 18 A1
WHTF M45 69 G4
WILM/AE SK9 190 D1
WILM/AE SK9 201 E4
Moss La East
OLDTF/WHR M16 127 H4
Moss La West HULME M15 127 H4
RUSH/FAL M14 128 B4
Moss Lea BOL BL1 33 G2
Mosslee Av CHH M8 87 E4
Mossley Rd AUL OL6 119 H2
MOSL OL5 94 A3
Moss Meadow Rd SLFD M6 * 112 B1
Mossmere Rd CHD/CHDH SK8 170 D5
Moss Mill St MILN OL16 43 G1
Moss Park Rd STRET M32 139 G1
Moss Pl BURY BL9 * 53 F1
Moss Rd SALE M33 153 E2
STRET M32 125 H5
WILM/AE SK9 201 F3
Moss Rose WILM/AE SK9 201 E3
Moss Rw BURY BL9 4 E6
Moss Shaw Wy RAD M26 51 H4
Moss Side La MILN OL16 43 H1
Moss St BRO M7 101 G5
BURY BL9 4 D5
BURY BL9 27 E1
DROY M43 118 A3
FWTH BL4 66 B3
HEY OL10 40 D4
MILN OL16 30 C5
OLDE OL4 76 D4
Moss St West AULW OL7 119 E3
Moss Ter MILN OL16 30 B5
The Moss MDTN M24 89 E1
Moss Vale Crs STRET M32 125 E4
Moss Vale Rd STRET M32 125 E5
URM M41 139 E1
Moss View Rd BOLE BL2 50 B1
PART M31 151 F3
Mossway MDTN M24 88 C2
Moss Wy SALE M33 153 H2
Mosswood Pk DID/WITH M20 169 G1
Mosswood Rd WILM/AE SK9 199 H1
Mossylea Cl MDTN M24 89 E2
Moston Bank Av BKLY M9 103 F3
Moston La BKLY M9 103 F2
NEWH/MOS M40 103 H2
Moston La East
NEWH/MOS M40 104 D1
Moston Rd MDTN M24 89 G1
RDSH SK5 145 F4
Moston St BRO M7 102 A3
Mostyn Av BURY BL9 38 C1
CHD/CHDH SK8 182 B3
RUSH/FAL M14 143 G3
Mostyn Rd BRAM/HZG SK7 184 D3
Mostyn St DUK SK16 120 C5
Motcombe Farm Rd
CHD/CHDH SK8 181 G3
Motcombe Gv CHD/CHDH SK8 181 F1
Motcombe Rd CHD/CHDH SK8 181 F2
Motherwell Av BNG/LEV M19 144 A2
Mottershead Av BOLS/LL BL3 50 D5
Mottershead Rd
WYTH/NTH M22 168 A5
Mottram Av CCHDY M21 156 B1
Mottram Cl CHD/CHDH SK8 170 D4
Mottram Dr HALE/TIMP WA15 166 B4
Mottram Fold STKP SK1 13 G5
Mottram Old Rd HYDE SK14 148 C3
STLY SK15 135 E1
Mottram Rd HYDE SK14 148 B1
SALE M33 155 F3
STLY SK15 121 F4
WILM/AE SK9 201 E4
Mottram St STKP SK1 13 G5
Mough La CHAD OL9 89 G4
Mouldsworth Av
DID/WITH M20 142 C4
HTNM SK4 144 D5
Moulton St CHH M8 114 B1
Mouncey St CMANE M1 * 128 B1
Mountain Ash WHIT OL12 18 A5
Mountain Ash Cl SALE M33 153 F1
WHIT OL12 18 A5
Mountain Gv WALK M28 81 H3
Mountain St MOSL OL5 108 D1
NEWH/MOS M40 117 E1
STKP SK1 13 K2
WALK M28 81 H3
Mount Av LIT OL15 20 D1
WHIT OL12 20 B4
Mountbatten Av DUK SK16 134 A2
Mountbatten Cl BURY BL9 70 A2
Mountbatten St GTN M18 130 B3
Mount Carmel Crs ORD M5 * 127 F1
Mount Dr MPL/ROM SK6 175 E4
URM M41 139 F1
Mountfield PWCH M25 86 A3
Mountfield Rd
BRAM/HZG SK7 193 H2
EDGY/DAV SK3 171 F2
Mountfield Wk OP/CLY M11 116 A4
Mount Fold MDTN M24 72 D5
Mountford Av CHH M8 * 87 E5
Mount Gv CHD/CHDH SK8 169 E4
Mount La UPML OL3 78 B3
Mountmorres Cl WHTN BL5 63 G5
Mount Pleasant BOLS/LL BL3 * 49 H4
BRAM/HZG SK7 185 E1
BURY BL9 17 G5
MDTN M24 71 H4
PWCH M25 70 D4
WILM/AE SK9 199 E1
Mount Pleasant Rd
DTN/ASHW M34 146 D1
FWTH BL4 65 E4
Mount Pleasant St AUL OL6 119 H2
DTN/ASHW M34 132 C2
OLDE OL4 * 76 A5
Mount Pleasant Wk RAD M26 52 B5
Mount Rd GTN M18 * 130 A3
HTNM SK4 12 B1
HYDE SK14 148 C5
MDTN M24 72 D5
PWCH M25 70 B5
Mountroyal Cl HYDE SK14 134 A3
Mount St Joseph's Rd
BOLS/LL BL3 48 A4
Mountside Cl WHIT OL12 10 C1
Mountside Crs PWCH M25 85 G3
Mount Sion Houses RAD M26 * 67 G2
Mount Sion Rd RAD M26 67 H2
Mount Skip La LHULT M38 81 F3
Mount St BOL BL1 33 H5
CMANW M2 6 E6
CSLFD M3 6 A2
ECC M30 110 D5
HEY OL10 41 E5
HYDE SK14 148 A1
RAMS BL0 16 C1
ROCH OL11 42 B5
ROY/SHW OL2 75 F1
SWIN M27 99 E3
WHIT OL12 10 A5
The Mount ALT WA14 165 G4
HALE/TIMP WA15 178 D4
Mount View Rd ROY/SHW OL2 60 C3
Mount Zion Rd BURY BL9 53 G4
Mousell St CHH M8 114 D1
Mowbray Av PWCH M25 86 B5
SALE M33 154 D3
Mowbray St AULW OL7 119 E3
BOL BL1 * 33 E5
OLD OL1 9 H4
ROCH OL11 42 A3
STKP SK1 13 H5
Mow Halls La UPML OL3 78 D3
Moxley Rd CHH M8 101 H1
Moyse Av TOT/BURYW BL8 37 E1
Mozart Cl ANC M4 115 F3
Muirfield Av MPL/ROM SK6 161 H2
Muirfield Cl BOLS/LL BL3 63 G1
HEY OL10 41 E5
NEWH/MOS M40 104 B3
WILM/AE SK9 199 G2
Mulberry Cl CHD/CHDH SK8 181 H5
RAD M26 68 B2
ROCH OL11 42 D1
Mulberry Ct SLFD M6 * 113 F2
Mulberry Ms HTNM SK4 12 E1
Mulberry Mount St
EDGY/DAV SK3 13 F6
Mulberry Rd SLFD M6 113 F3
Mulberry St AUL OL6 * 119 H2
CMANW M2 6 D5
Mulberry Wk DROY M43 117 F5
SALE M33 138 D5
Mule St BOLE BL2 3 H3
Mulgrave Rd WALK M28 97 H2
Mulgrave St BOLS/LL BL3 64 B2
SWIN M27 98 C1
Mullacre Rd WYTH/NTH M22 168 C3
Mull Av WGTN/LGST M12 129 F3
Mulliner St BOL BL1 * 34 A5
Mullion Cl BNG/LEV M19 144 D1
Mullion Dr HALE/TIMP WA15 165 H2
Mullion Wk CHH M8 102 C4
Mulmount Cl OLDS OL8 90 D4
Mumps Rbt OLD OL1 9 K3
Munday St ANC M4 115 G4
Municipal Cl HEY OL10 * 41 E4
Munn Rd BKLY M9 87 G2
Munro Av WYTH/NTH M22 181 E2
Munster St ANC M4 * 7 F1
Muriel St BRO M7 101 G5
HEY OL10 41 F4
MILN OL16 43 G1
Murieston Rd
HALE/TIMP WA15 177 H2
Murrayfield ROCH OL11 28 B5
Murray Rd BURY BL9 4 E5
Murray St ANC M4 7 K3
BRO M7 101 G4
Musabbir Sq MILN OL16 * 10 E4
Musbury Av CHD/CHDH SK8 183 E2
Museum St CMANW M2 6 E6
Musgrave Gdns BOL BL1 48 B1
Musgrave Rd BOL BL1 48 B1
WYTH/NTH M22 180 C1
Muslin St ORD M5 113 H4
Muter Av WYTH/NTH M22 181 E2
Mutual St HEY OL10 41 F3
Myerscroft Cl
NEWH/MOS M40 104 C2
Myrrh St BOL BL1 33 H3
Myrtle Bank PWCH M25 100 D1
Myrtle Cl OLDS OL8 9 F7
Myrtle Gdns BURY BL9 5 J4
Myrtle Gv DROY M43 118 B3
DTN/ASHW M34 131 E5
PWCH M25 86 A5
WHTF M45 69 E2
Myrtleleaf Gv ORD M5 * 112 C3
Myrtle Pl BRO M7 113 H1
Myrtle Rd MDTN M24 73 F3
PART M31 150 C4
Myrtle St BOL BL1 2 B3
EDGY/DAV SK3 171 E1
OLDTF/WHR M16 * 127 F4
OP/CLY M11 115 H5
Myrtle St North BURY BL9 5 J4
Myrtle St South BURY BL9 5 J5
My St ORD M5 112 D4
Mytham Rd BOLS/LL BL3 67 E1
Mythholme Av IRL M44 150 B3
Mytton Rd BOL BL1 33 E3
Mytton St HULME M15 127 H3

N

Nabbs Fold TOT/BURYW BL8 16 A5
Nabbs Wy TOT/BURYW BL8 26 B2
Naburn Cl RDSH SK5 146 A5
Naburn St BRUN/LGST M13 129 E4
Nada Rd CHH M8 102 A1
Nadine St SLFD M6 112 D2
Nadin St OLDS OL8 91 F4
Nairn Cl NEWH/MOS M40 * 115 H2
Nallgate MILN OL16 43 H4
Nall St BNG/LEV M19 144 B4
MILN OL16 31 F5
Nameplate Cl ECC M30 110 C3
Nancy St HULME M15 127 G2

Nandywell *BOLS/LL* BL3........67 E1
Nangreave Rd *OFTN* SK2.......172 C3
Nan Nook Rd *NTHM/RTH* M23...155 G5
Nansen Av *ECC* M50................132 C2
Nansen Cl *STRET* M32..............126 B4
Nansen Rd *CHD/CHDH* SK8.......169 F5
Nansen St *OP/CLY* M11...........115 H5
  SLFD M6.........................112 D5
  STRET M32......................126 B4
Nansmoss La *WILM/AE* SK9.......198 A1
Nantwich Av *WHIT* OL12............19 E5
Nantwich Rd *RUSH/FAL* M14.......142 C3
Nantwich Wk *BOLS/LL* BL3 *.......48 D5
Napier Cl *HULME* M15 *.............127 F2
Napier Gn *ORD* M5..................127 E1
Napier Rd *CCHDY* M21.............141 F3
  ECC M30.........................110 D2
  HTNM SK4........................159 E3
Napier St *BRAM/HZG* SK7.........185 E1
  HYDE SK14......................148 A2
  ROY/SHW OL2....................60 A1
  SWIN M27.........................98 C3
Napier St East *OLDS* OL8...........8 D6
Napier St West *OLDS* OL8...........8 D7
Naples Rd *EDGY/DAV* SK3.........171 E3
Naples St *ANC* M4.....................7 H1
Narbonne Av *ECC* M30.............111 H1
Narbuth Dr *CHH* M8................102 A3
Narrowgate Brow
  The Narrows ALT OL4.............59 E2
The Narrows ALT OL4................165 F5
Naseby Av *BKLY* M9..................88 C3
Naseby Pl *PWCH* M25...............86 B2
Naseby Rd *RDSH* SK5..............145 E3
Naseby Wk *WHTF* M45..............70 B4
Nash Rd *TRPK* M17..................111 F5
Nash St *HULME* M15...............127 H2
Nasmyth Av *DTN/ASHW* M34......132 D4
Nasmyth Rd *ECC* M30..............110 D5
Nasmyth St *CHH* M8................102 D5
Nately Rd *OLDTF/WHR* M16 *....141 E1
Nathan Dr *CSLFD* M3...................6 B2
Nathans Rd *WYTH/NTH* M22.....168 B5
National Dr *ORD* M5................113 F5
Naunton Rd *MDTN* M24..............75 E5
Naval St *ANC* M4.......................7 K3
Nave Ct *SLFD* M6....................113 C1
Navenby Av *OLDTF/WHR* M16....127 F4
Navigation Rd *ALT* WA14..........165 G2
Naylor St *NEWH/MOS* M40.......115 G2
  OLD OL1 *...........................9 F2
Nazeby Wk *CHAD* OL9.................8 B7
Naze Ct *OLD* OL1 *..................75 F4
Neal Av *ALT* OL6....................120 A2
  CHD/CHDH SK8....................181 F4
Neale Av *UPML* OL3..................95 F2
Neale Rd *CCHDY* M21..............141 E4
Near Birches Pde *OLDE* OL4......92 D5
Nearbrook Rd
  WYTH/NTH M22..................168 B5
Nearcroft Rd *NTHM/RTH* M23...167 H3
Near Hey Cl *RAD* M26...............67 H1
Nearmaker Av
  WYTH/NTH M22..................168 B5
Nearmaker Rd
  WYTH/NTH M22..................168 B5
Neary Wy *URM* M41.................124 B3
Neasden Gv *BOLS/LL* BL3 *........48 B4
Neath Av *NTHM/RTH* M23........168 C2
Neath Cl *POY/DIS* SK12.............195 E2
  WHTF M45.........................70 B5
Neath Fold *BOLS/LL* BL3.............64 C1
Neath St *CHAD* OL9....................8 D3
Nebo St *BOLS/LL* BL3.................48 C5
Nebraska St *BOL* BL1................33 H5
Needam Av *OP/CLY* M11..........116 C5
Needham Av *CCHDY* M21.........141 F3
Needwood Cl
  NEWH/MOS M40..................103 G5
Needwood Rd *MPL/ROM* SK6....162 B1
Neenton Sq *WGTN/LGST* M12...129 H1
Neild St *CMANE* M1......................7 J7
  OLDS OL8..........................91 F3
Neill St *BRO* M7......................114 B1
Neilson Cl *MDTN* M24................73 F5
Neil Carrs *RAMS* BL0................17 F1
Neile St *HEY* OL10....................40 C4
Neil La *CCHDY* M21.................142 A5
Neil St *BOL* BL1........................34 A2
Nelson Av *ECC* M30................111 E2
  POY/DIS SK12....................195 H4
Nelson Dr *DROY* M43..............117 E3
  IRL M44............................136 A5
Nelson Fold *SWIN* M27...............99 F1
Nelson Rd *BKLY* M9...................88 B5
Nelson Sq *BOL* BL1......................3 F5
Nelson St *BOLS/LL* BL3..............49 F4
  BOLS/LL BL3 *...................67 E1
  BRAM/HZG SK7.................173 G5
  BRO M7...........................101 G5
  BRUN/LGST M13.................53 C1
  BURY BL9.........................53 C1
  DTN/ASHW M34.................132 C2
  DTN/ASHW M34 *...............132 C4
  ECC M30..........................111 E3
  FWTH BL4...........................66 B4
  HEY OL10...........................41 E5
  HYDE SK14........................148 A1
  LIT OL15.............................20 D5
  MDTN M24..........................75 F5
  MILN OL16.........................10 D7
  NEWH/MOS M40.................115 G1
  OLDE OL4...........................92 D2
  ORD M5............................112 D4
  STRET M32.........................140 B2
Nelson Wy *CHAD* OL9................90 B3
Nelstrop Crs *HTNM* SK4...........144 C5
Nelstrop Rd *HTNM* SK4............144 C5
Nelstrop Rd North
  BNG/LEV M19....................144 D3
Nepaul Rd *BKLY* M9..................103 F1
Neptune Gdns *BRO* M7 *..........113 H1
Nesbit St *BOLE* BL2....................34 C3
Nesfield Rd *NTHM/RTH* M23....155 G4
Neston Av *BOL* BL1....................34 A1
  DID/WITH M20..................142 C5
  SALE M33........................155 F4
Neston Cl *ROY/SHW* OL2...........60 C4
Neston Gv *EDGY/DAV* SK3.......171 G4

Neston Rd *MILN* OL16...............43 H2
  TOT/BURYW BL8...................37 E2
Neston St *OP/CLY* M11...........131 E1
Neston Wy *WILM/AE* SK9.........192 A4
Netherbury Cl *GTN* M18............130 B5
Nethercote Av
  NTHM/RTH M23.................168 A3
Nethercroft *ROCH* OL11.............28 B3
Nethercroft Rd
  HALE/TIMP WA15................166 D4
Netherfield Cl *OLDS* OL8.............90 D3
Netherfield Rd *BOLS/LL* BL3.......64 D2
Netherfields *WILM/AE* SK9.......200 D5
Netherhey La *ROY/SHW* OL2.......74 D2
Nether Hey St *OLDS* OL8............92 A1
Netherhouse Rd
  ROY/SHW OL2......................59 H2
Netherland St *SALQ* M50.........113 E4
Netherlees *OLDE* OL4................92 C2
Nether St *HYDE* SK14..............148 B3
  WGTN/LGST M12 *................7 K7
Netherton Rd *RUSH/FAL* M14...142 C2
Netherwood Dr *BKLY* M9..........103 F3
Netherwood Fld *FAIL* M35.........105 G2
Netherwood Rd
  WYTH/NTH M22.................168 B2
Netherwood Wy *WHTN* BL5.......62 B2
Netley Av *WHIT* OL12.................19 E5
Netley Gv *OLDS* OL8...................92 B5
Netley Rd *NTHM/RTH* M23.......167 H5
Nettlebarn Rd
  WYTH/NTH M22.................168 B4
Nettleford Rd *CCHDY* M21........142 A3
Nettleton Gv *BKLY* M9.............103 G1
Nevada St *BOL* BL1 *.................33 H5
Nevendon Dr *NTHM/RTH* M23..167 G5
Nevile Rd *BRO* M7.....................101 E2
Neville Cardus Wk
  RUSH/FAL M14..................143 E1
Neville Cl *BOL* BL1 *....................2 D5
Neville Dr *IRL* M44...................122 B4
Neville Rd *BRAM/HZG* SK7.......185 E1
  CHAD OL9............................8 A5
Nevill Rd *BRAM/HZG* SK7.........183 H2
Nevin Av *CHD/CHDH* SK8.........182 B3
Nevin Cl *BRAM/HZG* SK7.........184 B5
Nevin Rd *NEWH/MOS* M40.......104 C1
Nevis Gv *BOL* BL1......................33 G1
Nevis St *ROCH* OL11..................43 F4
New Allen St *NEWH/MOS* M40...115 F2
Newall Rd *NTHM/RTH* M23.......179 G1
Newall St *CHAD* OL9..................90 C5
  LIT OL15............................21 E2
Newark Av *RAD* M26...................81 H1
  RUSH/FAL M14...................128 C5
Newark Park Wy
  ROY/SHW OL2......................58 D3
Newark Rd *RDSH* SK5..............160 C1
  SWIN M27............................99 E3
  WHIT OL13...........................19 E5
Newark Sq *WHIT* OL12...............19 E5
New Bailey St *CSLFD* M3...............6 B4
Newbank Cha *CHAD* OL9............74 B4
Newbank Cl *MDTN* M24..............73 E2
  UPML OL3...........................93 E6
New Bank St *WGTN/LGST* M12..129 F3
New Barn Cl *ROY/SHW* OL2.......59 H2
New Barn La *ROCH* OL11............42 D1
New Barns Av *CCHDY* M21.......141 G5
New Barn St *BOL* BL1................43 F1
  MILN OL16...........................43 F1
  ROY/SHW OL2......................59 H2
New Barton St *SLFD* M6.............99 H5
Newbeck St *ANC* M4....................7 G2
New Beech Rd *HTNM* SK4........158 B4
New Beech St *HTNM* SK4..........133 G5
Newberry Gv *EDGY/DAV* SK3...171 G4
Newbold Hall Dr *MILN* OL16........11 J6
Newbold Moss *MILN* OL16.........11 H6
Newbold St *MILN* OL16..............11 H6
  TOT/BURYW BL8...................37 H4
Newbourne Cl
  BRAM/HZG SK7..................185 E1
Newbreck Rd *OLDE* OL4.............76 B4
Newbridge Gdns *BOLE* BL2........35 F2
Newbridge Gdns *BURY* BL9.........53 F4
Newbridge La *STKP* SK1.............13 J5
New Bridge St *CSLFD* M5.............6 E1
Newburn Wk *MOSL* OL5 *.........109 E2
New Briggs Fold
  EDGW/EG BL7.......................22 D1
New Broad La *MILN* OL16...........43 H5
Newbrook Av *CCHDY* M21.........156 C5
New Buildings Pl *MILN* OL16.......10 C5
Newburn Av *BKLY* M9..................88 B5
Newbury Av *SALE* M33..............153 F2
Newbury Cl *CHD/CHDH* SK8.....192 D1
Newbury Dr
  HALE/TIMP WA15................166 A3
Newbury Dr *ECC* M30................110 C2
  URM M41...........................124 B3
Newbury Gv *HEY* OL10...............55 H1
Newbury Rd *BOLS/LL* BL3............66 C1
  CHD/CHDH SK8..................181 H5
Newbury Wk *BOL* BL1 *.................2 D3
Newby Cl *BURY* BL9....................53 H2
Newby Dr *ALT* WA14................165 G3
  CHD/CHDH SK8..................169 F4
  MDTN M24...........................73 F4
  SALE M33..........................155 E3
Newby Rd *BOLE* BL2...................35 F5
  BRAM/HZG SK7..................184 D2
  HTNM SK4............................12 A2
Newcastle St *HULME* M15.........128 A1
Newchurch *OLDS* OL8...............106 D2
New Church Ct *WHTF* M45..........69 G5
Newchurch Pl *ROCH* OL11...........42 B5
New Church Rd *BOL* BL1............32 C4
New Church St *RAD* M26............68 C1
Newchurch St *OP/CLY* M11.......116 A5
New Church Wk *CHD/CHDH* SK8..181 F1
New Cns Rd *WALK* M28...............96 B2
Newcliffe Rd *BKLY* M9................88 C3
New Coin St *ROY/SHW* OL2........75 E1
New Colliers Bw *BOL* BL1 *..........32 B1
Newcombe Cl *OP/CLY* M11.......116 A4
Newcombe Dr *LHULT* M38...........81 E1

Newcombe Rd *RAMS* BL0..........26 B2
Newcombe St *CSLFD* M5 *........114 C2
New Copper Moss
  HALE/TIMP WA15................166 A5
Newcroft *FAIL* M35..................105 G4
Newcroft Crs *URM* M41...........139 F2
Newcroft Dr *BKLY* M9..............102 D1
  EDGY/DAV SK3...................171 G3
  URM M41..........................139 F2
Newcroft Rd *URM* M41............139 F2
New Cross St *ORD* M5.............112 B5
Newdale Rd *WGTN/LGST* M12..144 B1
Newearth Rd *WALK* M28.............96 C2
New Earth St *MOSL* OL5.............94 A5
  OLDE OL4............................92 B2
New Ellesmere Ap *WALK* M28.....81 H5
New Elm Rd *CSLFD* M3..............6 A7
New Field Cl *MILN* OL16............11 J5
  RAD M26............................67 H1
Newfield Head La *MILN* OL16......45 E1
Newfield Vw *MILN* OL16.............31 H5
New Forest Rd
  NTHM/RTH M23.................166 D1
Newgate *MILN* OL16..................10 C6
Newgate Cottages
  WHTN BL5...........................63 H3
Newgate Dr *LHULT* M38.............81 E1
Newgate Rd *SALE* M33..............153 E2
  WILM/AE SK9....................198 A3
New George St
  TOT/BURYW BL8...................37 H3
  CHD/CHDH SK8..................181 G5
Newhall Av *BOLE* BL2.................51 E3
  ECC M30...........................111 E1
New Hall Cl *SALE* M33..............155 G2
New Hall Dr *NTHM/RTH* M23....155 H4
New Hall La *BOL* BL1..................47 H1
New Hall Ms *BOL* BL1.................32 A5
New Hall Pl *BOL* BL1...................47 H1
New Hall Rd *BRO* M7...............101 G3
  BURY BL9............................39 H2
  SALE M33 *.......................155 C3
Newhall Rd *RDSH* SK5..............145 G1
Newham Av *BOL* BL1.................33 H5
Newham Av *TOT/BURYW* BL8.....37 C5
Newhart Gv *WALK* M28...............81 E5
Newhaven Av *OP/CLY* M11.......131 E1
Newhaven Cl *CHD/CHDH* SK8...183 F2
  TOT/BURYW BL8...................37 H4
Newhey Av *WYTH/NTH* M22.....168 C4
New Hey Rd *CHD/CHDH* SK8....181 G5
Newhey Rd *MILN* OL16...............44 D2
  WYTH/NTH M22.................168 C5
New Heys Wy *BOLE* BL2.............24 A5
New Holder St *BOL* BL1................2 C5
Newholme Gdns *WALK* M28.......81 H4
Newholme Rd *DID/WITH* M20....156 D1
New Houghton Cl *LIT* OL15 *.......19 H2
Newhouse Crs *ROCH* OL11.........28 B3
Newhouse Rd *HEY* OL10.............56 A1
New Houses *OLDE* OL4...............77 H4
Newington Av *CHH* M8...............87 E4
Newington Dr *BOL* BL1 *..............2 E1
  TOT/BURYW BL8...................52 B1
Newington Wk *BOL* BL1 *............2 E1
New Islington *ANC* M4.................7 J3
New Kings Head Yd *CSLFD* M5 *...6 D2
Newland Dr *WHTN* BL5...............63 G5
Newlands *FAIL* M35.................117 F1
Newlands Av *BOLE* BL2..............35 G5
  BRAM/HZG SK7..................183 H3
  CHD/CHDH SK8..................182 D5
  ECC M30...........................110 A5
  IRL M44............................122 A5
  WHIT OL12.........................19 E5
Newlands Cl *CHD/CHDH* SK8....182 D5
  WHIT OL12.........................19 E5
Newlands Dr *DID/WITH* M20.....169 H1
  PWCH M25...........................85 H2
  SWIN M27............................99 E3
Newlands Rd *CHD/CHDH* SK8...170 B3
  NTHM/RTH M23.................167 G1
Newland St *CHH* M8.................102 C1
New La *BOLE* BL2.......................35 E5
  MDTN M24...........................72 D3
  ROY/SHW OL2......................59 E5
New Lane Ct *BOLE* BL2...............35 F4
New Lawns *RDSH* SK5..............145 G2
Newlea Cl *BOL* BL1......................53 F4
New Lees St *AUL* OL6...............107 C5
New Lester Wy *LHULT* M38.........80 D3
Newport Av *RDSH* SK5..............145 G4
Newport Rd *BOLS/LL* BL3..........145 E2
  CCHDY M21.......................141 H1
  DTN/ASHW M34.................147 F3
Newport St *BOL* BL1.....................2 E6
  BOLS/LL BL3..........................3 F6
  FWTH BL4............................66 A5
  MDTN M24...........................73 F3
  OLDS OL8............................91 F5
  RUSH/FAL M14...................128 C5
  SLFD M6...........................112 D3

TOT/BURYW* BL8.....................37 F1
Newquay Av *BOLE* BL2...............36 C5
  RDSH SK5.........................145 E4
Newquay Dr *BRAM/HZG* SK7...184 A5
New Quay St *CSLFD* M3...............6 A5
New Radcliffe St *OLD* OL1.............8 E3
New Raven Ct *BOLS/LL* BL3 *.......66 D1
New Ridd Ri *HYDE* SK14...........147 H3
New Riven Ct *BOLS/LL* BL3 *.......66 D1
New Rd *LIT* OL15........................20 B4
  OLDS OL8............................91 F3
  RAD M26..............................68 D2
  WHIT OL12...........................14 A5
New Royd Av *OLDE* OL4..............77 F3
Newry Rd *ECC* M30..................111 F5
Newry St *BOL* BL1......................33 G5
Newsam Ct *BOLS/LL* BL3 *............2 A7
Newsham Rd *EDGY/DAV* SK3...171 H5
Newsham Wk
  WGTN/LGST M12................130 A5
Newsholme St *CHH* M8.............102 A3
New Springs *BOL* BL1 *...............33 F1
Newstead *WHIT* OL12................10 E5
Newstead Av *AUL* OL6..............107 G2
  DID/WITH M20...................158 A1
Newstead Cl *POY/DIS* SK12......195 E2
Newstead Dr *BOLS/LL* BL3..........63 H2
Newstead Gv *MPL/ROM* SK6....161 G3
Newstead Rd *URM* M41............124 D5
Newstead Ter
  HALE/TIMP WA15................166 A2
New St *ALT* WA14.....................164 A2
  BOLS/LL BL3..........................2 D6
  DROY M43..........................118 A3
  ECC M30...........................110 D4
  LIT OL15............................20 C4
  MILN OL16...........................44 D1
  NEWH/MOS M40.................115 H1
  OLDE OL4............................68 C2
  RAD M26..............................68 C2
  STLY SK15.........................120 B2
  SWIN M27............................99 F1
  WHIT OL12...........................29 H1
New Tempest Rd *HOR/BR* BL6....46 D5
New Ter *HYDE* SK14 *..............148 A2
New Thomas St *SLFD* M6 *........113 F1
Newton Av *DID/WITH* M20........157 G2
  WGTN/LGST M12................129 C4
Newton Crs *MDTN* M24..............72 A1
Newton Dr *TOT/BURYW* BL8.......37 F5
New Tong Fld *EDGW/EG* BL7......23 E4
Newton Hall Rd *HYDE* SK14.......133 F2
Newton Rd *ALT* WA14...............165 H2
  FAIL M35...........................104 D5
  HYDE SK14........................133 G2
  MDTN M24...........................71 G5
  URM M41...........................138 C1
  WALK M28............................98 B1
Newton St *AUL* OL6..................119 H2
  BOL BL1...............................27 G5
  CMANE M1...........................7 H4
  DROY M43..........................118 B2
  EDGY/DAV SK3...................171 H4
  FAIL M35 *.........................105 F3
  HYDE SK14........................133 C4
  MILN OL16...........................43 G1
  STLY SK15.........................120 C3
  STRET M32........................140 B2
Newton Ter *BOL* BL1 *...............33 H4
Newton Wk *BOL* BL1 *...............33 H4
Newton Wood Rd *DUK* SK16......133 F2
Newtown Av *DTN/ASHW* M34...146 D1
  OP/CLY M11.......................116 C5
  SWIN M27............................82 A1
Newtown St *PWCH* M25..............86 B3
  ROY/SHW OL2......................60 A3
New Union St *ANC* M4..................7 J4
New Vernon St *BURY* BL9.............5 F1
New Viaduct St
  NEWH/MOS M40.................115 H3
Newville Dr *DID/WITH* M20........158 A1
New Vine St *HULME* M15 *.........128 A2
New Wakefield St *CMANE* M1.......6 E7
New Wy *WHIT* OL12....................14 A4
New York *BOLS/LL* BL3...............47 G5
New York St *HEY* OL10...............40 C4
New Zealand Rd *STKP* SK1...........13 K2
Ney St *AULW* OL7....................106 C4
Niagara St *OFTN* SK2...............172 B3
Nicholas Cft *ANC* M4....................7 F3
Nicholas Owen Cl
  OP/CLY M11.......................116 D5
Nicholas St *OLDS* OL8.................91 F3
Nicholas St *BOLE* BL2..................3 H3
  CMANW M2...........................6 F4
Nicholls St *SLFD* M6.................113 F2
Nicholson Rd *OLDE* OL4...............76 D3
Nicholson Sq *DUK* SK16 *..........119 G5
Nicholson St *HTNM* SK4.............13 E1
  OLDE OL4............................93 E4
  ROCH OL11...........................43 E1
Nichols St *SLFD* M6 *................113 G2
Nickleby Rd *POY/DIS* SK12.......195 F4
Nicolas Rd *CCHDY* M21............141 E2
Nield Rd *DTN/ASHW* M34.........146 B3
Nield's Brow *ALT* WA14...........177 F2
Nield St *MOSL* OL5....................93 G5
Nigel Rd *BKLY* M9.....................103 G3
Nigher Moss Av *MILN* OL16........10 K7
Nightingale Cl *WILM/AE* SK9....199 E1
Nightingale Dr
  DTN/ASHW M34.................118 B3
Nightingale Gdns
  NTHM/RTH M23.................155 H5
Nile St *AULW* OL7....................119 E5
  BOLS/LL BL3........................49 E4
  MILN OL16...........................10 E5
  OLD OL1..............................9 K4
Nile Ter *BRO* M7......................101 G5
Nimble Nook *CHAD* OL9.............90 A4
Nina Dr *NEWH/MOS* M40...........89 F4
Nine Acre Dr *ORD* M5................112 B5
Ninehouse La *BOLS/LL* BL3.........49 E5
Ninfield Rd *NTHM/RTH* M23......168 A5
Ninth Av *OLDS* OL8..................106 A1
Nipper La *WHTF* M45..................69 F3
Nisbet Av *WYTH/NTH* M22........180 D1

Niven St *WGTN/LGST* M12........128 D1
Nixon Rd *BOLS/LL* BL3...............64 B1
Nixon Rd South *BOLS/LL* BL3.....64 B1
Nixon St *EDGY/DAV* SK3............13 F6
  FAIL M35...........................104 D5
  OLDS OL8............................42 A3
No 11 Pas *CHD/WITH* M20 *......157 E1
Noble Meadow *WHIT* OL12..........20 A4
Noble St *BOLS/LL* BL3.................48 D4
  OLDS OL8............................91 G3
Noel Dr *SALE* M33....................155 E2
Noel St *BOL* BL1..........................2 D4
Nolan St *BKLY* M9....................103 F3
Nona St *SLFD* M6.....................112 D3
Nook Farm Av *WHIT* OL12..........19 E5
Nook Flds *BOLE* BL2...................35 F4
Nook La *AUL* OL6.....................107 H4
The Nook *ECC* M30...................110 D2
  URM M41...........................138 D2
  WALK M28............................97 G2
Noon Sun Cl *UPML* OL3..............94 D3
Noon Sun St *WHIT* OL12..............19 E5
Norbet Wk *BKLY* M9 *...............103 F3
Norbreck Av *CCHDY* M21..........141 F4
  CHD/CHDH SK8..................170 D3
Norbreck St *BOLE* BL2................49 H1
Norburn Rd *BRUN/LGST* M13....129 H4
  OLDE OL4............................93 H1
  SALE M33..........................154 A2
Norbury Av *SLFD* M6................100 A5
Norbury Ct *NEWH/MOS* M40 *...115 F1
Norbury Crs *BRAM/HZG* SK7....185 E2
Norbury Dr *BRAM/HZG* SK7......175 E3
Norbury Gv *BOL* BL1 *................34 A2
  BRAM/HZG SK7..................185 E2
  SWIN M27............................99 E1
Norbury Hollow Rd
  BRAM/HZG SK7..................186 A4
Norbury La *OLDS* OL8................92 C4
Norbury Ms *MPL/ROM* SK6 *....174 D3
Norbury St *BRO* M7..................101 H4
  BRAM/HZG SK7..................185 E2
  SWIN M27............................99 F1
Norcot Wk *HULME* M15 *...........127 G2
Norcross Cl *OFTN* SK2..............173 E4
Nordale Pk *WHIT* OL12...............28 A1
Nordek Dr *ROY/SHW* OL2...........59 H2
Nordek Rd *ROY/SHW* OL2...........58 D4
Norden Av *DID/WITH* M20.........142 C5
Norden Ct *BOLS/LL* BL3...............48 D5
Norden Rd *ROCH* OL11...............41 E1
Nordens Dr *CHAD* OL9...............74 A4
Nordens Rd *CHAD* OL9...............74 B4
Noreen Av *PWCH* M25................86 B2
Norfield Cl *DUK* SK16...............119 H5
Norfolk Av *DROY* M43..............131 F5
  DTN/ASHW M34.................130 D4
  HEY OL10............................40 A4
  HTNM SK4..........................144 C5
  WHTF M45............................69 H4
Norfolk Cl *BOLS/LL* BL3..............51 E5
  IRL M44............................150 D1
  ROY/SHW OL2......................59 G2
Norfolk Crs *FAIL* M35...............104 D4
Norfolk Dr *FWTH* BL4.................66 A3
Norfolk Gdns *URM* M41............123 E5
Norfolk Rd *GTN* M18................130 D4
Norfolk St *CHAD* OL9..................90 D3
  CMANW M2...........................6 E4
  HYDE SK14........................147 H1
  NEWH/MOS M40.................100 D5
  SALE M33..........................154 C3
  WALK M28............................82 A1
Norfolk Wy *ROY/SHW* OL2..........75 E2
Norford Wy *ROCH* OL11..............28 B4
Norgate St *DID/WITH* M20........157 C3
Norlan Av *DTN/ASHW* M34........132 B2
Norleigh Rd *WYTH/NTH* M22....168 C1
Norley Dr *STRET* M32...............126 C5
Norley Cl *OLD* OL1......................74 C2
Norley Dr *BNG/LEV* M19...........144 C1
Norman Av *BRAM/HZG* SK7......184 D1
Normanby Cha *ALT* WA14.........165 E3
Normanby Gv *SWIN* M27.............99 F1
Normanby Rd *WALK* M28.............96 D1
Normanby St *BOLS/LL* BL3.........49 E5
  RUSH/FAL M14...................128 D4
  SWIN M27............................98 D1
Norman Cl *MDTN* M24.................73 F3
Normandale Av *BOL* BL1.............32 D5
Normandy Crs *RAD* M26..............68 A4
Norman Gv *RDSH* SK5..............145 E4
  WGTN/LGST M12 *..............129 H4
Norman Rd *ALT* WA14...............165 F3
  AUL OL6............................107 F4
  BRO M7.............................101 G3
  HTNM SK4..........................159 E3
  RUSH/FAL M14...................143 F1
  SALE M33..........................155 C5
Norman Rd West *BKLY* M9 *......103 G3
Norman's Pl *ALT* WA14.............165 G5
Norman St *BURY* BL9....................5 J1
  FAIL M35...........................105 F1
  HYDE SK14........................148 A1
  MDTN M24 *.........................73 F3
  OLD OL1..............................9 K4
Normanton Av *SLFD* M6............112 B2
Normanton Dr *BKLY* M9..............88 B3
Normanton Rd
  EDGY/DAV SK3...................170 D2
Norman Weall Ct
  MDTN M24 *.........................72 D2
Norreys Av *URM* M41................123 F5
Norris Av *HTNM* SK4.................144 C2
Norris Bank Ter *HTNM* SK4.........12 A3
Norris Hill Dr *HTNM* SK4...........144 D1
Norris Rd *SALE* M33.................154 D4
Norris St *BOLS/LL* BL3................66 D1
  BOLS/LL BL3........................66 D1
  FWTH BL4............................65 H5
Northallerton Rd *BRO* M7..........101 E4

Northampton Rd
NEWH/MOS M40 103 F4
North Av BNG/LEV M19 143 H4
BURY BL9 54 A5
FWTH BL4 65 F4
STLY SK15 120 D2
TOT/BURYW BL8 26 A1
UPML OL3 95 F2
URM M41 124 D1
North Back Rock BURY BL9 4 E4
Northbank Gdns
BNG/LEV M19 143 G5
North Blackfield La BRO M7 101 F2
Northbourne St SLFD M6 112 D3
Northbrook Av CHH M8 87 E3
North Cir WHTF M45 85 H1
North Clifden La BRO M7 101 H4
Northcliffe Rd OFTN SK2 172 D1
Northcombe Rd
EDGY/DAV SK3 171 H4
Northcote Av WYTH/NTH M22 180 C1
Northcote Rd BRAM/HZG SK7 184 A5
North Crs NEWH/MOS M40 89 G4
OP/CLY M11 117 E2
North Cft OLDS OL8 91 H4
Northdale Rd BKLY M9 87 G2
North Dean St SWIN M27 99 F1
Northdene Dr ROCH OL11 28 C5
Northdown Av HULME M15 127 G2
MPL/ROM SK6 162 B1
North Downs Rd
CHD/CHDH SK8 182 C1
Northdowns Rd ROY/SHW OL2 59 G1
North Dr DTN/ASHW M34 118 B4
SWIN M27 99 G3
Northenden Rd
CHD/CHDH SK8 169 F4
SALE M33 154 D2
Northend Rd STLY SK15 121 F2
Northen Gv DID/WITH M20 157 E2
Northern Av SWIN M27 84 D4
Northern Gv BOL BL1 33 F5
Northern Service Rd
NTHM/RTH M23 * 167 G4
Northfield Av NEWH/MOS M40 90 A5
Northfield Dr WILM/AE SK9 199 G2
Northfield Rd BURY BL9 27 G5
NEWH/MOS M40 90 A5
Northfield St BOLS/LL BL3 48 B4
Northfleet Rd ECC M30 110 A5
North Ga OLDS OL8 91 F4
Northgate WHIT OL12 18 B1
Northgate La OLD OL1 60 D5
Northgate Rd EDGY/DAV SK3 12 A5
North George St CSLFD M3 114 A2
North Gv BRUN/LGST M13 129 E3
URM M41 138 C2
WALK M28 81 H4
North Hill St CSLFD M3 6 A1
Northland Rd BKLY M9 88 D4
BOL BL1 23 E5
Northlands RAD M26 51 H4
North La WHIT OL12 10 D4
Northleach Cl TOT/BURYW BL8 37 F3
Northleigh Dr PWCH M25 * 86 C4
Northleigh Rd
OLDTF/WHR M16 127 E5
North Lonsdale St STRET M32 * 126 B5
North Md CCHDY M21 141 F4
Northmoor Rd
WGTN/LGST M12 129 H4
North Nook OLDE OL4 77 E4
Northolme Gdns
BNG/LEV M19 158 B2
Northolt Ct OP/CLY M11 * 117 E3
Northolt Dr BOLS/LL BL3 49 E5
Northolt Fold HEY OL10 56 B2
Northolt Rd NTHM/RTH M23 155 H5
North Pde CSLFD M3 6 D4
MILN OL16 45 F2
SALE M33 155 E4
North Park Rd
BRAM/HZG SK7 183 H2
North Phoebe St ORD M5 113 G5
North Pl STKP SK1 13 G3
Northridge Rd BKLY M9 88 A1
North Ri UPML OL3 95 E2
North Rd DTN/ASHW M34 118 C4
HALE/TIMP WA15 178 B4
MANAIR M90 190 B1
OP/CLY M11 116 D3
PART M31 152 A2
PWCH M25 85 G2
STRET M32 125 G4
Northside Av URM M41 137 H2
North Star Dr CSLFD M3 6 A4
Northstead Av
DTN/ASHW M34 147 F1
North St AUL OL6 119 F3
CHH M8 114 D1
HEY OL10 40 C4
MDTN M24 72 D2
MILN OL16 10 E4
RAD M26 52 D5
ROY/SHW OL2 75 E1
WHIT OL12 14 B4
Northumberland Av
AULW OL7 119 G1
Northumberland Cl
OLDTF/WHR M16 127 F3
Northumberland Crs
OLDTF/WHR M16 * 127 F3
Northumberland Rd
OLDTF/WHR M16 127 F4
PART M31 150 D4
RDSH SK5 145 H5
Northumberland St BRO M7 101 G3
Northumberland Wy
WYTH/NTH M22 168 D3
Northumbria St BOLS/LL BL3 48 B4
Northurst Dr CHH M8 87 E4
North Vale Rd
HALE/TIMP WA15 166 A3
North Veiw WHTF M45 69 F2
North View Cl OLDE OL4 93 H2
Northward Rd WILM/AE SK9 198 C4
North Wy BOL BL1 34 C2
HYDE SK14 148 A1
RDSH SK5 146 A5
Northway DROY M43 117 H5
North Western St
BNG/LEV M19 144 A3
CMANE M1 7 K6
Northwold Dr BKLY M9 89 E4
BOL BL1 47 F1
Northwood BOLE BL2 35 E2
Northwood Crs BOLS/LL BL3 * 48 B4
Northwood Gv SALE M33 154 C2
Norton Av DTN/ASHW M34 131 F5
SALE M33 153 G1
URM M41 124 C4
WGTN/LGST M12 130 A5
Norton Gra PWCH M25 86 C4
Norton Gv HTNM SK4 159 E5
Norton Rd WHIT OL12 19 E5
Norton St BOL BL1 34 A3
BRO M7 101 H3
CMANE M1 115 F5
CSLFD M3 6 D2
NEWH/MOS M40 115 H1
Norview Dr DID/WITH M20 169 G2
Norville Av NEWH/MOS M40 89 G4
Norway Gv RDSH SK5 * 160 A2
Norway St BOL BL1 * 33 G4
SLFD M6 112 D3
STRET M32 126 B5
Norwell Rd WYTH/NTH M22 168 D4
Norwich Av CHAD OL9 74 B3
DTN/ASHW M34 146 D2
ROCH OL11 28 D4
Norwich Cl AUL OL6 107 G2
DUK SK16 134 B1
Norwich Dr TOT/BURYW BL8 4 A2
Norwich Rd STRET M32 125 E5
Norwich St ROCH OL11 43 F1
Norwick Cl BOLS/LL BL3 47 F5
Norwood PWCH M25 86 A5
Norwood Av BRAM/HZG SK7 193 F2
BRO M7 101 E2
CHD/CHDH SK8 182 D1
DID/WITH M20 158 A2
MPL/ROM SK6 186 C5
Norwood Cl ROY/SHW OL2 59 H1
WALK M28 97 F2
Norwood Crs ROY/SHW OL2 75 F2
Norwood Dr
HALE/TIMP WA15 167 E4
SWIN M27 98 C3
Norwood Gv BOL BL1 * 48 B1
Norwood Rd CHD/CHDH SK8 169 G3
OFTN SK2 172 C5
STRET M32 140 C2
Nottingham Av RDSH SK5 160 D1
Nottingham Cl RDSH SK5 146 A5
Nottingham Dr AUL OL6 107 E3
BOL BL1 2 C1
FAIL M35 105 F5
RDSH SK5 146 A5
Nowell Rd MDTN M24 72 D1
Nudger Cl UPML OL3 77 G2
Nudger Gn UPML OL3 78 D2
Nuffield Cl BOL BL1 33 E5
Nuffield Rd WYTH/NTH M22 168 D5
Nugent Rd BOLS/LL BL3 64 D1
Nugget St OLDE OL4 * 92 A1
Nuneaton Dr
NEWH/MOS M40 115 G2
Nuneham Av DID/WITH M20 143 E4
Nunfield Cl NEWH/MOS M40 89 E5
Nunnery Rd BOLS/LL BL3 48 A5
Nunthorpe Dr CHH M8 102 D2
Nursery Av HALE/TIMP WA15 177 H4
Nursery Cl OFTN SK2 173 E2
SALE M33 155 E2
Nursery Dr POY/DIS SK12 195 E3
Nursery Gdns MILN OL16 11 K5
Nursery Gv PART M31 151 E2
Nursery La EDGY/DAV SK3 170 D2
WILM/AE SK9 198 C4
Nursery Rd CHD/CHDH SK8 182 C3
FAIL M35 105 F4
HTNM SK4 12 A1
PWCH M25 85 H1
URM M41 124 A4
Nursery St OLDTF/WHR M16 128 A5
SLFD M6 113 E2
Nuthatch Av WALK M28 97 E2
Nuthurst Rd NEWH/MOS M40 104 B1
Nutsford V WGTN/LGST M12 129 H4
Nut St BOL BL1 * 33 G4
Nuttall Av BOLS/LL BL3 67 F1
WHTF M45 69 G4
Nuttall Cl RAMS BL0 16 D3
Nuttall Hall Rd RAMS BL0 17 E4
Nuttall La RAMS BL0 16 D4
Nuttall Ms WHTF M45 69 G4
Nuttall Rd RAMS BL0 17 E4
Nuttall Sq BURY BL9 53 G4
Nuttall St BURY BL9 5 G6
IRL M44 136 A5
MILN OL16 10 E7
OLDS OL8 * 92 A3
OLDTF/WHR M16 127 F3
OP/CLY M11 129 H1
Nutt La PWCH M25 70 D4

O

Oadby Cl WGTN/LGST M12 129 H4
Oadby Pl RDSH SK5 131 E5
Oak Av BOLS/LL BL3 67 E1
CCHDY M21 141 F3
CHD/CHDH SK8 182 C2
HTNM SK4 159 E4
IRL M44 150 C1
MDTN M24 72 D5
MPL/ROM SK6 162 B4
RAMS BL0 26 B1
ROY/SHW OL2 59 E3
WHTF M45 69 G5
WILM/AE SK9 198 C5
Oak Bank BKLY M9 103 E2
PWCH M25 100 C1
Oak Bank Av BKLY M9 103 G1
Oakbank Av CHAD OL9 73 H4
Oak Bank Cl WHTF M45 70 A4
Oakbank Dr BOL BL1 22 C5
Oakbarton HOR/BR BL6 46 D5
Oakcliffe Rd NTHM/RTH M23 167 H2
WHIT OL12 19 H4
Oak Cl HYDE SK14 135 H4
WHIT OL12 14 C1
WILM/AE SK9 198 C4
Oak Coppice BOL BL1 47 H2
Oakcroft STLY SK15 135 F1
Oakcroft Wy WYTH/NTH M22 168 D3
Oakdale BOLE BL2 35 E2
Oakdale Cl WHTF M45 69 E4
Oakdale Ct UPML OL3 78 B1
Oakdale Dr CHD/CHDH SK8 181 G2
DID/WITH M20 157 H5
Oak Dene UPML OL3 94 D3
Oakdene WALK M28 98 A4
Oakdene Av CHD/CHDH SK8 181 G5
HTNM SK4 159 G1
Oakdene Crs MPL/ROM SK6 175 E2
Oakdene Gdns MPL/ROM SK6 175 E2
Oakdene Rd HALE/TIMP WA15 166 C1
MDTN M24 73 F4
MPL/ROM SK6 175 E2
Oakdene St BKLY M9 103 G2
Oak Dr BRAM/HZG SK7 183 F5
DTN/ASHW M34 131 F4
MPL/ROM SK6 174 C3
RUSH/FAL M14 143 F2
Oaken Bank Rd HEY OL10 56 C3
Oakenbottom Rd BOLE BL2 50 A3
Oaken Clough AULW OL7 106 C4
Oakenclough Cl WILM/AE SK9 192 A5
Oaken Clough Dr AULW OL7 106 C4
Oakenclough Dr BOL BL1 32 C4
Oakenrod Hl ROCH OL11 29 F4
Oakenshaw Av WHIT OL12 18 B2
Oakenshaw Vw WHIT OL12 18 B2
Oaker Av DID/WITH M20 156 D2
Oakes St FWTH BL4 66 C5
Oakfield DUK SK16 133 H2
PWCH M25 86 C4
SALE M33 154 B1
Oakfield Av CHD/CHDH SK8 170 B3
DROY M43 117 G4
OLDTF/WHR M16 126 D5
OLDTF/WHR M16 127 G5
STLY SK15 109 F4
Oakfield Cl BRAM/HZG SK7 193 H3
WILM/AE SK9 201 E2
Oakfield Dr LHULT M38 80 D2
Oakfield Gv FWTH BL4 81 H1
GTN M18 130 C4
Oakfield Rd DID/WITH M20 157 F3
EDGY/DAV SK3 172 A4
HALE/TIMP WA15 165 H4
HYDE SK14 133 H3
POY/DIS SK12 195 G3
WILM/AE SK9 201 E3
Oakfield St CHH M8 102 B4
HALE/TIMP WA15 165 H4
Oakfield Ter ROCH OL11 29 F3
Oakfold Av AUL OL6 107 G4
Oakford Av NEWH/MOS M40 115 F2
Oakford Wk BOLS/LL BL3 48 B5
Oak Gates EDGW/EG BL7 22 D2
Oak Gv AUL OL6 107 G4
CHD/CHDH SK8 170 B4
ECC M30 110 C4
POY/DIS SK12 195 E3
URM M41 139 E1
Oakham Av DID/WITH M20 142 C3
Oakham Cl TOT/BURYW BL8 38 B1
Oakham Ms BRO M7 101 F1
Oakham Rd DTN/ASHW M34 * 147 E2
Oak Hl LIT OL15 20 C3
Oakhill Cl BOLE BL2 50 D2
Oakhill Wy CHH M8 102 A3
Oakhouse Dr CCHDY M21 141 F4
Oakhurst Cha WILM/AE SK9 200 D3
Oakhurst Dr EDGY/DAV SK3 171 E4
Oakhurst Gdns PWCH M25 85 H3
Oakington Av
RUSH/FAL M14 * 128 C5
Oakland Av BNG/LEV M19 158 B2
OFTN SK2 172 D3
SLFD M6 111 H1
Oakland Gv BOL BL1 * 32 D4
Oaklands BOL BL1 47 G2
Oaklands Av CHD/CHDH SK8 182 D2
MPL/ROM SK6 175 H1
Oaklands Cl WILM/AE SK9 199 H1
Oaklands Dene HYDE SK14 148 C1
Oaklands Dr BRAM/HZG SK7 185 F3
HYDE SK14 148 C1
PWCH M25 86 A2
SALE M33 154 B1
Oaklands Pk OLDE OL4 94 B2
Oaklands Rd BRO M7 100 D3
ROY/SHW OL2 75 F2
SWIN M27 98 C4
UPML OL3 94 C2
Oak La WHTF M45 70 A4
WILM/AE SK9 198 C4
Oak Lea Av WILM/AE SK9 198 D5
Oaklea Rd SALE M33 139 E5
Oakleigh Av BNG/LEV M19 143 H4
BOLS/LL BL3 65 F2
HALE/TIMP WA15 166 B2
Oakleigh Cl HEY OL10 56 B2
Oakleigh Rd CHD/CHDH SK8 182 B4
Oakley Cl NEWH/MOS M40 104 B5
RAD M26 68 B4
Oakley Dr OLD OL1 60 C5
Oakley Pk BOL BL1 47 G2
Oakley St ORD M5 112 C4
Oakley Vls HTNM SK4 159 E3
Oak Ldg BRAM/HZG SK7 * 184 A5
Oakmere Av ECC M30 110 D1
Oakmere Cl WYTH/NTH M22 168 C5
Oakmere Rd CHD/CHDH SK8 170 C5
WILM/AE SK9 192 A2
Oak Ms WILM/AE SK9 199 F1
Oakmoor Dr BRO M7 100 D2
Oakmoor Rd NTHM/RTH M23 167 H3
Oak Mt DID/WITH M20 * 157 G4
Oak Rd BRO M7 101 F4
CHD/CHDH SK8 170 B3
DID/WITH M20 157 G1
FAIL M35 105 E4
HALE/TIMP WA15 177 H1
OLDS OL8 90 D5
PART M31 150 C4
SALE M33 155 E2
Oaks Av BOLE BL2 34 D2
Oak Shaw Cl BKLY M9 88 A5
Oakshaw Dr WHIT OL12 28 D2
Oaks La BOLE BL2 34 C1
The Oaks CHD/CHDH SK8 181 F2
HYDE SK14 134 B5
Oak St ANC M4 7 H3
BRAM/HZG SK7 185 E1
DTN/ASHW M34 132 C2
ECC M30 111 E4
EDGY/DAV SK3 171 E1
HEY OL10 40 C3
HYDE SK14 133 H4
LIT OL15 21 F3
MDTN M24 * 73 G5
MILN OL16 10 C7
MILN OL16 44 D3
RAMS BL0 * 16 C3
ROY/SHW OL2 60 B2
SWIN M27 99 F1
WHIT OL12 14 C1
Oak Tree Cl OFTN SK2 173 E1
Oak Tree Ct CHD/CHDH SK8 170 B4
Oak Tree Crs STLY SK15 120 D5
Oak Tree Dr DUK SK16 134 A1
Oak Vw OLD OL1 75 E3
Oak View Rd UPML OL3 95 E2
Oakville Dr SLFD M6 111 H1
Oakville Ter NEWH/MOS M40 103 G1
Oakway DID/WITH M20 169 H1
MDTN M24 56 C5
Oakwell Dr BRO M7 101 H1
BURY BL9 70 A1
Oakwell Man BRO M7 101 H1
Oakwood CHAD OL9 73 H5
SALE M33 153 F2
Oakwood Av CHD/CHDH SK8 169 G4
DTN/ASHW M34 132 B1
NEWH/MOS M40 104 C1
SWIN M27 83 H3
WALK M28 82 C5
WILM/AE SK9 198 B4
Oakwood Cl TOT/BURYW BL8 37 G3
Oakwood Ct ALT WA14 177 E4
Oakwood Dr BOL BL1 47 G1
SLFD M6 99 G5
WALK M28 82 C5
Oakwood La ALT WA14 176 D3
Oakwood Rd MPL/ROM SK6 162 C5
Oakworth Cft OLDE OL4 61 E5
Oakworth Dr BOL BL1 33 G1
Oakworth St BKLY M9 87 H4
Oatlands WILM/AE SK9 201 E5
Oatlands Rd WYTH/NTH M22 180 B2
Oat St STKP SK1 13 J7
Oban Av NEWH/MOS M40 116 C1
OLD OL1 76 A3
Oban Crs EDGY/DAV SK3 171 G5
Oban Dr SALE M33 155 F3
Oban Gv BOL BL1 33 H1
Oban St BOL BL1 * 33 G3
Oberlin St OLDE OL4 76 C5
ROCH OL11 42 C1
Occlestone Cl SALE M33 155 F5
Occupiers La
BRAM/HZG SK7 * 186 A3
Ocean St ALT WA14 165 E3
Ockendon Dr BKLY M9 103 F3
Octagon Ct BOL BL1 * 2 E5
Octavia Dr NEWH/MOS M40 116 D1
Odell St OP/CLY M11 * 130 A1
Odessa Av SLFD M6 112 A1
Odette St GTN M18 130 B4
Offerton Dr OFTN SK2 173 E2
Offerton Fold OFTN SK2 172 D2
Offerton Gn OFTN SK2 173 H3
Offerton La OFTN SK2 172 D1
Offerton Rd BRAM/HZG SK7 185 H1
OFTN SK2 173 H5
Offerton St STKP SK1 160 C4
Off Grove Rd STLY SK15 121 G1
Off Ridge Hill La STLY SK15 * 120 C3
Off Stamford St STLY SK15 * 121 G1
Ogbourne Wk
BRUN/LGST M13 128 D2
Ogden Cl HEY OL10 40 B4
WHTF M45 69 H3
Ogden Gv CHD/CHDH SK8 * 169 E5
Ogden La MILN OL16 45 G1
OP/CLY M11 130 C1
Ogden Rd BRAM/HZG SK7 193 G2
FAIL M35 105 E4
Ogden Sq DUK SK16 119 G5
Ogden St CHAD OL9 74 C4
DID/WITH M20 157 G3
MDTN M24 72 D4
OLDE OL4 * 92 C1
PWCH M25 86 B3
ROCH OL11 42 B4
SWIN M27 99 E3
Ogwen Dr PWCH M25 86 A2
Ohio Av SALQ M50 113 E5
Okehampton Cl RAD M26 51 F4
Okehampton Crs SALE M33 153 G1
Okeover Rd BRO M7 101 G2
Olaf St BOLE BL2 3 J1
Olanyian Dr CHH M8 101 H5
Old Bank Cl MPL/ROM SK6 161 H3
Old Bank St CMANW M2 6 E4
Old Bank Vw OLD OL1 60 B5
Old Barn Pl EDGW/EG BL7 23 F3
Old Barton Rd ECC M30 124 B1
Old Bent La WHIT OL12 19 F1
Old Birley St HULME M15 128 A3
Old Broadway
DID/WITH M20 157 H1
Old Brook Cl ROY/SHW OL2 60 C1
Oldbrook Fold
HALE/TIMP WA15 166 C5
Old Brow MOSL OL5 108 D2
Old Brow La MILN OL16 19 H5
Old Brown St MOSL OL5 108 D2
Oldbury Cl HEY OL10 56 A2
NEWH/MOS M40 115 G2
Oldcastle Av DID/WITH M20 142 C4
Old Chapel St EDGY/DAV SK3 12 B7
Old Church Ms DUK SK16 120 B5
Old Church St
NEWH/MOS M40 104 A4
OLD OL1 9 H3
Old Clay Dr WHIT OL12 20 A4
Old Clough La WALK M28 97 G2
Old Colliers Rw BOL BL1 * 32 B1
Oldcott Cl WALK M28 96 A5
Old Court St HYDE SK14 147 H1
The Old Ctyd
WYTH/NTH M22 * 169 E4
Old Cft OLDE OL4 93 F1
Old Croft Ms STKP SK1 172 C2
Old Crofts Bank URM M41 124 B5
Old Cross St AUL OL6 * 119 H2
Old Dairy Ms HYDE SK14 133 F3
Old Delph Rd ROCH OL11 28 C2
Old Doctors St
TOT/BURYW BL8 26 A4
Old Eagley Ms BOL BL1 23 E5
Old Edge La ROY/SHW OL2 75 F2
Old Elm St BRUN/LGST M13 * 128 D2
Oldershaw Dr BKLY M9 103 E4
Old Farm Crs DROY M43 117 G5
Old Farm Dr OFTN SK2 173 G3
Oldfield Cl WHTN BL5 62 A4
Oldfield Dr HALE/TIMP WA15 166 A3
Oldfield Gv SALE M33 154 D1
Oldfield Ms ALT WA14 165 F4
Oldfield Rd ALT WA14 164 D4
ORD M5 127 F1
PWCH M25 70 B5
SALE M33 154 D1
Oldfield St OP/CLY M11 116 C4
Old Gardens St STKP SK1 13 H5
The Old Gdn
HALE/TIMP WA15 166 C2
Oldgate Wk HULME M15 * 127 G2
Old Gn BOLE BL2 24 B5
Old Ground St RAMS BL0 * 16 D2
Old Hall Cl TOT/BURYW BL8 26 C4
Old Hall Clough HOR/BR BL6 46 D2
Old Hall Crs WILM/AE SK9 192 B4
Old Hall Dr GTN M18 130 C4
OFTN SK2 173 F3
Old Hall La BRUN/LGST M13 143 G1
HYDE SK14 135 H3
MPL/ROM SK6 175 H4
PWCH M25 71 E5
WALK M28 97 F3
WHTF M45 84 D1
Old Hall Rd BRO M7 101 G2
CHD/CHDH SK8 169 F3
NEWH/MOS M40 104 A3
SALE M33 155 F2
STRET M32 125 F4
WHTF M45 68 D5
Old Hall St DUK SK16 132 D1
FWTH BL4 66 B5
MDTN M24 72 D4
OP/CLY M11 * 130 D1
Old Hall St North BOL BL1 2 E5
Oldham Av STKP SK1 160 C5
Oldham Dr MPL/ROM SK6 161 H2
Oldham Rd ANC M4 7 J2
AULW OL7 119 F1
FAIL M35 105 F1
MDTN M24 72 C4
MILN OL16 10 D7
NEWH/MOS M40 115 G2
OLDE OL4 93 F1
OLDS OL8 106 C3
ROCH OL11 58 C1
ROY/SHW OL2 60 A5
ROY/SHW OL2 75 F2
UPML OL3 61 F3
UPML OL3 78 A3
Oldhams La BOL BL1 33 G1
Oldham St CMANE M1 7 G4
DROY M43 118 A3
DTN/ASHW M34 146 A1
HYDE SK14 147 H1
ORD M5 114 A4
RDSH SK5 * 145 E4
Oldham Wy CHAD OL9 8 D2
MILN OL16 44 C5
OLD OL1 9 J4
OLDE OL4 94 A2
Old Kiln La BOL BL1 32 A4
OLDE OL4 93 G3
Oldknow Rd MPL/ROM SK6 175 F3
Old La BURY BL9 27 G3
CHAD OL9 90 C3
LHULT M38 81 E2
OLDE OL4 77 E4
OLDE OL4 94 B1
OP/CLY M11 130 C1
Old Lansdowne Rd
DID/WITH M20 157 E2
Old Lees St AUL OL6 107 G5
Old Malt La DID/WITH M20 142 C4
Old Market Pl ALT WA14 165 G4
Old Market St BKLY M9 87 H5
Old Meadow Dr
DTN/ASHW M34 132 C3
Old Meadow La
HALE/TIMP WA15 178 D1
Old Medlock St CSLFD M3 * 6 A6
Old Mill Cl SWIN M27 99 G2
Old Mill La BRAM/HZG SK7 185 H4
OLDE OL4 93 F2
Old Mills Hl MDTN M24 73 G3
Old Mill St ANC M4 115 F4
Oldmill St WHIT OL12 10 C4
Old Moat La DID/WITH M20 142 D5
Oldmoor Rd MPL/ROM SK6 161 F1
Old Mount St ANC M4 7 G1
Old Nans La BOLE BL2 35 G4
Old Nursery Fold BOLE BL2 35 F2
Old Oak Cl BOLE BL2 51 E4
Old Oak Dr DTN/ASHW M34 132 D5
Old Oake Cl WALK M28 * 82 B5
Old Oak St DID/WITH M20 157 G3
Old Orch WILM/AE SK9 198 D3
The Old Orch
HALE/TIMP WA15 166 C1
Old Park La TRPK M17 124 B2
Old Parrin La ECC M30 110 C2
Old Pasture Cl OFTN SK2 173 F2
Old Quarry La
EDGW/EG BL7 23 E2

Old Rectory Gdns
CHD/CHDH SK8 170 A4
Old River Cl IRL M44 136 C1
Old Rd AUL OL6 108 A5
BKLY M9 88 A5
BOL BL1 33 H3
CHD/CHDH SK8 170 C3
DUK SK16 119 H5
FAIL M35 104 D3
HTNM SK4 159 H3
HYDE SK14 133 G4
HYDE SK14 135 G3
MILN OL16 20 B4
STLY SK15 121 F5
WILM/AE SK9 192 A4
WILM/AE SK9 199 E2
Old School Dr BKLY M9 * 87 H5
Old School La CHD/CHDH SK8 182 D4
Old School Ms DUK SK16 * 120 B5
Old Shaw St ORD M5 * 113 F5
The Old Stables
DTN/ASHW M34 132 C2
Old Station St ECC M30 110 D4
Oldstead Gv BOLS/LL BL3 47 G5
Old St AUL OL6 119 G3
OLDE OL4 92 C2
STLY SK15 120 D4
Old Swan Cl EDGW/EG BL7 * 22 D1
Old Thorn La UPML OL3 95 G1
Old Towns Cl TOT/BURYW BL8 26 A4
Old Vicarage Gdns WALK M28 82 A4
Old Wellington Rd ECC M30 111 F3
Old Wells Cl LHULT M38 81 F1
Oldwood Rd NTHM/RTH M23 179 H1
Old Wool La CHD/CHDH SK8 170 C5
Old York St HULME M15 127 H2
Olebrook Cl WGTN/LGST M12 129 E2
Oleo Ter IRL M44 122 D5
Olga St BOL BL1 33 G4
Olga Ter BKLY M9 * 88 A5
Olivant St BURY BL9 53 F1
Olive Bank TOT/BURYW BL8 37 G2
Oliver Cl LIT OL15 20 C3
Olive Rd HALE/TIMP WA15 166 B1
Oliver St EDGY/DAV SK3 13 G6
OP/CLY M11 * 116 A5
Olive Shapley Av
DID/WITH M20 157 G3
Olive St BOLS/LL BL3 48 C5
FAIL M35 104 D2
HEY OL10 41 F4
RAD M26 68 D1
ROCH OL11 * 42 B5
TOT/BURYW BL8 4 A4
Olivia Gv RUSH/FAL M14 129 E5
Ollerbarrow Rd
HALE/TIMP WA15 177 H2
Ollerbrook Ct BOL BL1 34 A4
Ollerton WHIT OL12 10 B5
Ollerton Av SALE M33 153 G1
Ollerton Dr FAIL M35 105 E4
Ollerton Rd WILM/AE SK9 192 A2
Ollerton St BOL BL1 23 E5
Ollier Av WGTN/LGST M12 144 A1
Olney ROCH OL11 * 29 H5
Olney Av WYTH/NTH M22 168 C3
Olney St BRUN/LGST M13 129 E4
Olsberg Cl RAD M26 52 D5
Olwen Crs RDSH SK5 145 F3
Olympic Ct SALQ M50 113 E5
Omer Av BRUN/LGST M13 143 H1
Omer Dr BNG/LEV M19 143 G4
Onchan Av OLDE OL4 92 A1
One Ash Cl WHIT OL12 10 C1
Onslow Av NEWH/MOS M40 104 D1
Onslow Cl OLD OL1 8 E1
Onslow Rd EDGY/DAV SK3 12 A6
Onslow St ROCH OL11 42 B2
Onward St HYDE SK14 147 H1
Oozewood Rd MDTN M24 58 B4
Opal Ct RUSH/FAL M14 * 143 F3
Opal St BNG/LEV M19 144 B3
Openshaw Fold Rd BURY BL9 53 E2
Openshaw La IRL M44 136 A5
Openshaw Pl FWTH BL4 65 G4
Openshaw St BURY BL9 5 G6
Orama Av SLFD M6 111 H1
Orama Ml WHIT OL12 * 14 B5
Oram St BURY BL9 38 D2
Orange Hill Rd PWCH M25 86 B2
Orange St SLFD M6 113 F2
Orbital Wy DTN/ASHW M34 132 A5
Orchard Av BOL BL1 34 A3
GTN M18 130 D4
PART M31 151 E2
WALK M28 96 C3
Orchard Cl CHD/CHDH SK8 183 F5
POY/DIS SK12 195 F4
WILM/AE SK9 198 C5
Orchard Ct OFTN SK2 * 173 E3
Orchard Dr HALE/TIMP WA15 178 B1
WILM/AE SK9 192 B5
Orchard Gdns BOLE BL2 35 G3
Orchard Gn WILM/AE SK9 201 E4
Orchard Gv DID/WITH M20 157 E1
ROY/SHW OL2 59 H2
Orchard Pl HALE/TIMP WA15 166 C2
POY/DIS SK12 * 195 E3
SALE M33 154 C1
Orchard Ri HYDE SK14 148 B3
Orchard Rd FAIL M35 105 E3
HALE/TIMP WA15 165 H4
MPL/ROM SK6 163 G4
Orchard Rd East
WYTH/NTH M22 156 C4
Orchard Rd West
WYTH/NTH M22 156 C4
Orchard St DID/WITH M20 157 E1
HEY OL10 41 F3
HYDE SK14 148 A1
SLFD M6 113 F1
STKP SK1 13 H3
Orchard V EDGY/DAV SK3 171 F3
Orchid Av FWTH BL4 65 G3
Orchid Cl IRL M44 136 A3
OLD OL1 75 E3
Orchid Dr BURY BL9 53 H2
Orchid Gdns CHD/CHDH SK8 169 E3
Orchid St BKLY M9 103 E3
Ordsall Av LHULT M38 81 G3
Ordsall Dr ORD M5 127 E1
Ordsall La ORD M5 114 A5
ORD M5 126 D2
Oregon Av OLD OL1 75 F3
Oregon Cl BRUN/LGST M13 128 D2
Orford Cl MPL/ROM SK6 186 D5
Orford Rd NEWH/MOS M40 104 B5
PWCH M25 85 H2
Oriel Av OLDS OL8 91 F4
Oriel Cl CHAD OL9 90 B3
OFTN SK2 172 C3
Oriel Rd DID/WITH M20 157 F2
Oriel St BOLS/LL BL3 48 B4
ROCH OL11 43 E1
Orient Rd SLFD M6 111 H1
Orient St BRO M7 102 A3
Oriole Cl WALK M28 96 C3
Oriole Dr WALK M28 96 C2
Orion Pl BRO M7 * 113 H1
Orkney Cl NTHM/RTH M23 167 H5
RAD M26 52 C5
Orkney Dr URM M41 124 C3
Orlanda Av SLFD M6 111 H1
Orlanda Dr BRO M7 102 A4
Orlando St BOLE BL2 49 F4
Orleans Wy OLD OL1 9 F2
Orley Wk OLD OL1 60 C5
Orme Av MDTN M24 72 D5
SLFD M6 112 A1
Orme Cl OP/CLY M11 115 H4
URM M41 139 F1
Ormerod Av ROY/SHW OL2 75 F1
Ormerod Cl MPL/ROM SK6 161 G5
Ormerod St HEY OL10 41 F5
Orme St OLDE OL4 9 J6
STKP SK1 * 160 C4
WILM/AE SK9 200 D4
Ormonde Av SLFD M6 112 A1
Ormonde Ct AUL OL6 119 H1
Ormond St BOLS/LL BL3 50 A4
BURY BL9 5 G3
Ormrod St BOLE BL2 34 D1
BOLS/LL BL3 2 D6
BURY BL9 5 H5
FWTH BL4 65 H4
Ormsby Av GTN M18 130 A4
Ormsby Cl EDGY/DAV SK3 171 H5
Ormsgill Cl HULME M15 128 A2
Orms Gill Pl OFTN SK2 * 173 F3
Ormsgill St HULME M15 128 A2
Ormskirk Av DID/WITH M20 142 B5
Ormskirk Cl TOT/BURYW BL8 52 A1
Ormskirk Rd RDSH SK5 145 F5
Ornatus St BOL BL1 * 34 A1
Orphanage St HTNM SK4 159 H3
Orpington Dr TOT/BURYW BL8 37 G5
Orpington Rd BKLY M9 103 F3
Orrell St OP/CLY M11 * 117 E5
TOT/BURYW BL8 4 A3
Orrel St SLFD M6 112 D3
Orrishmere Rd CHD/CHDH SK8 182 C1
Orron St LIT OL15 20 D3
Orsett Cl NEWH/MOS M40 115 F2
Orthes Gv HTNM SK4 159 G1
Orton Av NTHM/RTH M23 155 H5
Orton Rd NTHM/RTH M23 155 H5
Orvietto Av SLFD M6 111 H1
Orville Dr BNG/LEV M19 143 H4
Orwell Av DTN/ASHW M34 131 F5
WYTH/NTH M22 168 C3
Orwell Cl TOT/BURYW BL8 4 B2
WILM/AE SK9 192 A5
Orwell Rd BOL BL1 33 E4
Osborne Cl TOT/BURYW BL8 52 C1
Osborne Dr SWIN M27 99 H3
Osborne Gv BOL BL1 33 F5
CHD/CHDH SK8 181 F1
Osborne Rd BKLY M9 * 103 F3
BNG/LEV M19 143 H2
DTN/ASHW M34 132 C4
HALE/TIMP WA15 165 H4
HYDE SK14 148 A2
OFTN SK2 172 A2
OLDS OL8 8 C7
SLFD M6 * 111 H2
Osborne St CHAD OL9 8 B1
HEY OL10 41 E5
MPL/ROM SK6 160 D3
NEWH/MOS M40 115 F1
ROCH OL11 42 D1
ROY/SHW OL2 60 A3
SLFD M6 113 E2
Osborne Ter SALE M33 154 C2
Osbourne Cl FWTH BL4 66 A3
WILM/AE SK9 199 G4
Osbourne Pl ALT WA14 165 G5
Osbourne St DID/WITH M20 157 F3
Oscar St BOL BL1 * 33 F4
NEWH/MOS M40 103 H3
Oscott Av LHULT M38 81 F2
Oscroft Cl CHH M8 102 A4
Osmond St OLDE OL4 76 B5
Osmund Av BOLE BL2 50 A2
Osprey Cl DUK SK16 133 H1
HULME M15 127 H3
Osprey Dr DROY M43 118 B2
IRL M44 122 B5
WILM/AE SK9 199 F2
Osprey Wk BRUN/LGST M13 * 128 D2
Ossory St RUSH/FAL M14 128 C5
Osterley Rd BKLY M9 88 D4
Ostlers Ga DROY M43 118 C3
Ostrich La PWCH M25 86 B4
Oswald Cl SLFD M6 100 D5
Oswald La CCHDY M21 141 F2
Oswald Rd CCHDY M21 141 F1
Oswald St ANC M4 7 F1
BOLS/LL BL3 48 B5
CHAD OL9 75 E4
MILN OL16 11 F4
RDSH SK5 131 E5
ROY/SHW OL2 60 B1
Oswestry Cl TOT/BURYW BL8 25 H3
Otago Rd OLDE OL4 76 B3
Otago St OLDE OL4 * 76 B3
Othello Dr ECC M30 111 E3
Otley Av SLFD M6 112 B2
Otley Cl CHAD OL9 90 C1
Otley Gv EDGY/DAV SK3 171 G5
Otmoor Wy ROY/SHW OL2 59 H5
Otranto Av SLFD M6 112 A1
Ottawa Cl NTHM/RTH M23 167 G5
Ott Cl HULME M15 128 A2
Otterburn Pl OFTN SK2 173 E3
Otterbury Cl TOT/BURYW BL8 37 E4
Otter Dr BURY BL9 54 A5
CHH M8 101 H5
Otterspool Rd MPL/ROM SK6 162 A5
Oulder Hl ROCH OL11 28 D4
Oulder Hill Dr ROCH OL11 29 E4
Oulder Mt ROCH OL11 * 29 E4
Ouldfield Cl MILN OL16 * 30 C5
Oulton Av SALE M33 155 F1
Oulton St BOL BL1 34 B1
Oulton Wk NEWH/MOS M40 115 G3
Oundle Cl RUSH/FAL M14 128 D5
Ouse St SALQ M50 112 B4
Outram Cl MPL/ROM SK6 * 175 E5
Outram Rd DUK SK16 133 E2
Outram Sq DROY M43 * 117 H5
Outrington Dr OP/CLY M11 116 B5
Outwood Av SWIN M27 83 G3
Outwood Dr CHD/CHDH SK8 181 F4
Outwood Gv BOL BL1 33 H1
Outwood La MANAIR M90 180 B4
Outwood La West
MANAIR M90 180 A4
Outwood Rd CHD/CHDH SK8 181 G4
RAD M26 68 B3
Oval Dr DUK SK16 133 E1
The Oval CHD/CHDH SK8 181 G4
Overbridge Rd BRO M7 114 B1
Overbrook Av
NEWH/MOS M40 103 E5
Overbrook Dr PWCH M25 86 A4
Overdale SWIN M27 99 F4
Overdale Cl OLD OL1 75 F3
Overdale Crs URM M41 137 H1
Overdale Dr BOL BL1 47 H2
Overdale Rd MPL/ROM SK6 161 H5
WYTH/NTH M22 168 C4
Overdell Dr WHIT OL12 18 B5
Overdene Cl HOR/BR BL6 46 C3
Overens St OLDE OL4 76 A5
Overfield Wy WHIT OL12 30 A1
Overgreen BOLE BL2 35 F3
Overhill Dr WILM/AE SK9 199 H3
Overhill La WILM/AE SK9 199 H3
Overhill Rd CHAD OL9 74 A4
WILM/AE SK9 199 G3
Overlea Dr BNG/LEV M19 158 B1
Overlinks Dr SLFD M6 99 G5
Overstone Dr CHH M8 102 A3
Overton Av WYTH/NTH M22 168 C4
Overton Cl RAD M26 68 C3
Overton Crs BRAM/HZG SK7 173 F5
SALE M33 153 G4
Overton Rd WYTH/NTH M22 168 C4
Overt St ROCH OL11 43 E1
Overwood Rd
WYTH/NTH M22 168 C1
Owenington Gv LHULT M38 81 F2
Owens Cl CHAD OL9 73 H4
Owens Farm Dr OFTN SK2 173 F2
Owens Pk RUSH/FAL M14 * 143 F2
Owen St ECC M30 110 C4
EDGY/DAV SK3 12 D4
OLD OL1 76 D1
SLFD M6 100 D5
Owlerbarrow Rd
TOT/BURYW BL8 37 F3
Owler La CHAD OL9 89 G4
Owlwood Cl LHULT M38 80 D4
Owlwood Dr LHULT M38 80 D4
Oxbridge Cl SALE M33 153 G3
Oxbrow Wy WHTF M45 69 H4
Oxendale Dr MDTN M24 71 H3
Oxenhurst Gn OFTN SK2 173 F4
Oxford Av DROY M43 117 G2
ROCH OL11 28 D5
SALE M33 153 G2
WHTF M45 69 H4
Oxford Cl FWTH BL4 65 E4
Oxford Ct CMANW M2 * 6 E7
OLDTF/WHR M16 * 127 G3
Oxford Dr MDTN M24 73 F2
MPL/ROM SK6 162 B2
Oxford Gv BOL BL1 2 A2
Oxford Ml AULW OL7 * 119 E5
Oxford Pl MILN OL16 43 F1
RUSH/FAL M14 128 D4
Oxford Rd ALT WA14 177 G1
BOLS/LL BL3 66 C1
BRUN/LGST M13 128 C3
DUK SK16 120 A5
HOR/BR BL6 46 A1
SLFD M6 111 H1
Oxford St BOL BL1 2 E5
BURY BL9 5 G6
CHAD OL9 8 A7
CMANE M1 6 E6
ECC M30 111 F4
ROY/SHW OL2 60 A2
STLY SK15 121 F4
STLY SK15 121 G1
Oxford St East AULW OL7 119 E5
Oxford St West AULW OL7 119 E5
Oxford Wy HTNM SK4 159 G3
WHIT OL12 29 H1
Ox Ga BOLE BL2 35 E1
Ox Hey Cl RAMS BL0 16 D1
Ox Hey La HOR/BR BL6 46 A2
Oxney Rd RUSH/FAL M14 128 D4
Ox St RAMS BL0 16 C3
Oxton Av WYTH/NTH M22 168 B5
Oxton St OP/CLY M11 131 E1

P

Pacific Rd ALT WA14 164 D3
Pacific Wy SALQ M50 112 B5
Packer St BOL BL1 33 F4
MILN OL16 10 C6
Packwood Cha CHAD OL9 74 A4
Padbury Cl URM M41 123 E5
Padbury Wy BOLE BL2 35 F4
Padden Brook MPL/ROM SK6 162 A4
Paddington Av
NEWH/MOS M40 * 104 A5
Paddington Cl SLFD M6 113 F3
Paddison St SWIN M27 98 D3
Paddock Cha POY/DIS SK12 195 G1
Paddock La FAIL M35 105 E5
Paddock Rd HYDE SK14 * 147 H3
The Paddocks EDGY/DAV SK3 172 B4
Paddock St WGTN/LGST M12 128 D1
The Paddock BRAM/HZG SK7 183 G3
CHD/CHDH SK8 170 B4
HALE/TIMP WA15 166 C5
RAMS BL0 16 C1
UPML OL3 94 C3
WALK M28 97 F3
Paderborn Ct BOL BL1 2 C6
Padiham Cl BURY BL9 53 E2
Padstow Cl HYDE SK14 135 E5
Padstow Dr BRAM/HZG SK7 184 A5
Padstow St
NEWH/MOS M40 * 115 H2
Padstow Wk HYDE SK14 135 E5
Pagan St MILN OL16 10 D5
Paget St NEWH/MOS M40 103 E5
Pagnall Ct CHAD OL9 * 90 C2
Paignton Av BNG/LEV M19 143 H3
HYDE SK14 149 E1
Paignton Dr SALE M33 153 G1
Paignton Gv RDSH SK5 145 E4
Pailin Dr DROY M43 118 B3
Pailton Cl HOR/BR BL6 47 E3
Painswick Rd WYTH/NTH M22 180 A3
Paisley Pk FWTH BL4 66 A3
Paiton St BOL BL1 48 B2
Palace Gdns ROY/SHW OL2 75 E2
Palace Rd AUL OL6 107 H5
SALE M33 154 B1
Palace St BOL BL1 2 E3
BURY BL9 5 H5
CHAD OL9 8 B3
Palatine Av DID/WITH M20 142 D5
Palatine Cl IRL M44 136 B2
Palatine Crs DID/WITH M20 157 G1
Palatine Dr BURY BL9 27 G3
Palatine Rd DID/WITH M20 157 E3
ROCH OL11 28 D3
WYTH/NTH M22 156 D4
Palatine St BOL BL1 2 E4
DTN/ASHW M34 132 B3
MILN OL16 11 J7
RAMS BL0 16 D2
Paley St BOL BL1 3 F4
Palfrey Pl WGTN/LGST M12 128 D1
Palgrave Av NEWH/MOS M40 103 E5
Pall Ml CMANW M2 6 E5
Palma Av HALE/TIMP WA15 179 H4
Palm Cl SALE M33 153 F1
Palmer Av CHD/CHDH SK8 170 C3
Palmer Cl OLDS OL8 91 G3
Palmerston Av
OLDTF/WHR M16 141 H1
Palmerston Cl
DTN/ASHW M34 131 G5
RAMS BL0 16 C5
Palmerston Rd
DTN/ASHW M34 131 G5
OFTN SK2 184 C1
Palmerston St
WGTN/LGST M12 115 G5
Palmer St BRO M7 101 F5
DUK SK16 119 G4
SALE M33 154 B2
Palm Gv CHAD OL9 74 C4
Palm St BOL BL1 34 A3
BRUN/LGST M13 129 G5
DROY M43 117 E3
OLDE OL4 76 B4
Pandora St DID/WITH M20 157 F1
Panfield Rd WYTH/NTH M22 168 B5
Pangbourne Av URM M41 124 D5
Pangbourne Cl
EDGY/DAV SK3 171 F3
Pankhurst Wk
RUSH/FAL M14 128 C5
Panmure St OLDS OL8 91 G3
Pansy Rd FWTH BL4 65 F4
Paper Mill Rd EDGW/EG BL7 23 E4
Paprika Cl OP/CLY M11 130 C1
Parade Rd MANAIR M90 180 B5
Paradise St DTN/ASHW M34 132 C1
RAMS BL0 16 D2
Paramel Av BOLS/LL BL3 51 E4
Parbold Av DID/WITH M20 142 C4
Pargate Cha ROCH OL11 28 D3
Paris Av ORD M5 127 E1
Parish Vw ORD M5 113 G5
Paris St BOLS/LL BL3 48 A5
Park 66 BURY BL9 * 54 A3
Park Av ALT WA14 165 H1
BNG/LEV M19 143 H2
BOL BL1 * 33 H2
BRAM/HZG SK7 193 F2
BRO M7 102 A2
CHAD OL9 74 C3
CHD/CHDH SK8 182 C3
EDGY/DAV SK3 170 C2
FAIL M35 104 C2
HALE/TIMP WA15 178 A3
HYDE SK14 133 G4
MPL/ROM SK6 162 B4
OLDTF/WHR M16 127 F3
POY/DIS SK12 195 F3
PWCH M25 86 A3
RAD M26 53 E5
RAMS BL0 17 E2
SALE M33 139 G5
URM M41 138 C1
WHTF M45 85 E1
WILM/AE SK9 199 F2
Park Bridge Rd AULW OL7 106 D3
Parkbrook Rd
NTHM/RTH M23 168 A2
Park Brow Cl CCHDY M21 141 G4
Park Cl ALT WA14 166 A1
STLY SK15 120 C2
WHTF M45 85 G1
Park Cottages BOL BL1 * 33 F3
ROY/SHW OL2 59 G1
Park Court Ms
CHD/CHDH SK8 * 170 B5
Park Crs AUL OL6 120 B3
CHAD OL9 74 A3
RUSH/FAL M14 128 D5
WILM/AE SK9 199 E1
Parkdale CHAD OL9 74 C3
Parkdale Av DTN/ASHW M34 132 A1
GTN M18 130 B3
Parkdale Rd BOLE BL2 34 D5
Parkdene Cl BOLE BL2 35 E2
Park Dr ECC M30 111 E1
HALE/TIMP WA15 166 B2
HALE/TIMP WA15 178 A3
HTNM SK4 159 E4
HYDE SK14 133 G4
OLDTF/WHR M16 141 G1
WILM/AE SK9 199 E1
Park Edge WHTN BL5 62 B5
Parkend Rd NTHM/RTH M23 167 H4
Parker St BURY BL9 5 G5
CMANE M1 7 G5
Parkfield CHAD OL9 74 B3
DROY M43 117 H3
ECC M30 * 122 D4
ORD M5 112 C3
Parkfield Av FWTH BL4 65 H5
MPL/ROM SK6 175 E3
OLDS OL8 90 C5
PWCH M25 86 C4
RUSH/FAL M14 128 C5
URM M41 138 B2
Parkfield Dr MDTN M24 72 B4
Parkfield Rd ALT WA14 165 F5
BOLS/LL BL3 65 E1
CHD/CHDH SK8 182 C3
OLDE OL4 94 B1
Parkfield Rd North
NEWH/MOS M40 89 H5
Parkfield Rd South
DID/WITH M20 157 F2
Parkfields STLY SK15 121 G2
Parkfield St MILN OL16 43 G4
RUSH/FAL M14 128 C5
Parkgate CHAD OL9 74 C3
TOT/BURYW BL8 36 D1
Park Gate Av DID/WITH M20 142 D5
Park Gate Cl MPL/ROM SK6 161 F1
Parkgate Dr BOL BL1 34 A1
OFTN SK2 172 C5
SWIN M27 99 G3
Parkgate Rd ALT WA14 165 F1
Park Gates Av CHD/CHDH SK8 183 F3
Park Gates Dr CHD/CHDH SK8 183 F3
Park Gv BNG/LEV M19 144 A1
HTNM SK4 159 E2
RAD M26 52 A5
WALK M28 97 E2
Park Hl PWCH M25 * 86 C5
Parkhill Av CHH M8 87 G5
Park Hill Dr WHTF M45 69 F4
Park Hill Rd HALE/TIMP WA15 178 B3
Parkhills Cl BURY BL9 53 G1
Parkhills Rd BURY BL9 5 F7
BURY BL9 53 F1
Park Hill St BOL BL1 2 A3
Park House Bridge Est
SLFD M6 * 100 C3
Park House Bridge Rd
SLFD M6 100 C4
Parkhouse St OP/CLY M11 116 D5
Parkhurst Av
NEWH/MOS M40 104 D1
Parkin Cl DUK SK16 119 H5
Parkinson St BOLS/LL BL3 48 B4
BURY BL9 38 C1
Parkin St WGTN/LGST M12 129 H5
Parklake Av BRO M7 101 H2
Parklands ROY/SHW OL2 58 D3
ROY/SHW OL2 60 C1
WHTF M45 69 F4
Parklands Dr SALE M33 153 G4
Parklands Rd NTHM/RTH M23 167 G2
The Parklands HTNM SK4 159 H2
RAD M26 67 E4
Parklands Wy POY/DIS SK12 195 F3
Park La BRO M7 101 G2
DUK SK16 119 H5
HALE/TIMP WA15 178 B3
OLDS OL8 91 G5
POY/DIS SK12 195 F3
ROY/SHW OL2 59 F4
SLFD M6 99 H5
STKP SK1 172 C1
UPML OL3 95 F2
WHIT OL12 10 C5
WHTF M45 69 F5
Park Lane Ct WHTF M45 * 69 E5
Park La West SWIN M27 100 A3
Parkleigh Dr NEWH/MOS M40 89 H5
Park Ldg BNG/LEV M19 144 A2
Park Lodge Cl CHD/CHDH SK8 170 B5
Park Meadow WHTN BL5 62 B4
Park Ms OLDTF/WHR M16 141 G1
Parkmount Rd BKLY M9 103 F1
Park Pde AUL OL6 119 F3
ROY/SHW OL2 45 F5
Park Pl ANC M4 114 D2
HTNM SK4 158 C4
PWCH M25 86 B2
SLFD M6 111 H2
Park Range RUSH/FAL M14 129 E5
Park Ri MPL/ROM SK6 162 B3
Park Rd ALT WA14 176 D2
BOL BL1 2 A5
BOLS/LL BL3 50 C5
BURY BL9 4 D1
CHD/CHDH SK8 169 E3
CHD/CHDH SK8 170 B3
CHD/CHDH SK8 183 F3
DTN/ASHW M34 118 C5
DTN/ASHW M34 132 B5
DUK SK16 120 A4
ECC M30 111 E1
HALE/TIMP WA15 166 A1
HALE/TIMP WA15 178 A3
HTNM SK4 159 E1
HYDE SK14 133 G4
MDTN M24 72 C4
MPL/ROM SK6 162 B3
OLDS OL8 9 G6
PART M31 151 F3

POY/DIS SK12 ....197 E1
PWCH M25 ....86 C4
RAMS BL0 ....16 A5
SALE M33 ....139 G5
SLFD M6 ....111 H1
STRET M32 ....140 A1
WALK M28 ....96 D1
WHIT OL12 ....11 F2
WHTN BL5 ....62 A4
WHTN BL5 ....62 C5
WILM/AE SK9 ....198 C3
Park Rd North URM M41 ..124 B5
Park Rd South URM M41 ...138 C1
Park Rw BOL BL1 ....23 E5
Park Seventeen WHTF M45 ...69 G4
Parkside MDTN M24 ....88 B1
Park Side La ROY/SHW OL2 ...60 B1
ECC M30 ....110 D4
FAIL M35 ....104 D5
WALK M28 ....97 E1
Parkside Cl MPL/ROM SK6 ...186 C4
RAD M26 ....53 F5
Parkside Ms WHTF M45 ......68 C1
Parkside Rd RUSH/FAL M14 ...142 B1
SALE M33 ....36 C5
Parkside Wk BOLE BL2 * 34 D5
Parkside Wk BRAM/HZG SK7 ...183 H1
BURY BL9 ....4 E7
Parks Nook FWTH BL4 ....65 H5
Parks Sq AUL OL6 ....120 B1
OLDTF/WHR M16 ....141 E1
Parkstone Av BRO M7 ....101 H2
Parkstone Av GTN M18 ......131 E2
WHTF M45 ....85 E1
Parkstone Cl FWTH BL4 .....65 H3
Parkstone Dr SWIN M27 .....77 G4
Parkstone La ALT WA14 .....110 A1
Parkstone Rd IRL M44 ......122 B5
Park St AUL OL6 ....119 G3
  BOL BL1 ....2 A3
  BRO M7 ....101 F2
  CSLFD M3 ....114 A4
  DROY M43 ....118 D3
  DTN/ASHW M34 ....132 A5
  FWTH BL4 ....66 A3
  HEY OL10 ....56 B1
  MOSL OL5 ....30 A5
  MOSL OL5 ....108 D2
  MPL/ROM SK6 ....161 G3
  OLDS OL8 ....8 E6
  PWCH M25 ....86 B5
  RAD M26 ....52 D5
  ROY/SHW OL2 ....59 F5
  ROY/SHW OL2 ....53 G2
  STKP SK15 ....13 G2
  STLY SK15 ....121 E4
  SWIN M27 ....99 F3
Parksway BKLY M9 ....87 G1
  PWCH M25 ....86 D5
  SWIN M27 ....99 H4
Parks Yd BURY BL9 ....4 D2
Park Ter HEY OL10 ....41 E3
  MOSL OL5 ....95 F2
The Park OLDE OL4 ....94 A2
  UPML OL3 ....13 H5
Park Vw BKLY M9 ....102 D4
  CHAD OL9 ....74 B3
  DTN/ASHW M34 * 118 C5
  EDGY/DAV SK3 ....170 C2
  FWTH BL4 ....66 A3
  FWTH BL4 ....66 C5
  LIT OL15 ....21 E2
  STKP SK1 ....172 C2
Park View Ct BRAM/HZG SK7 ...86 A4
Park View Rd BOLS/LL BL3 * ...48 B5
  PWCH M25 ....86 A5
Park Wy STRET M32 ....125 F4
Parkway BRAM/HZG SK7 .....183 H2
  CHAD OL9 ....74 B3
  DTN/ASHW M34 ....131 H5
  EDGY/DAV SK3 ....170 C2
  LHULT M38 ....80 D4
  ROCH OL11 ....43 G2
  WILM/AE SK9 ....199 E4
Parkway GV LHULT M38 ......80 D3
Parkwood Dr WHTN BL5 ......63 G5
Parkwood Rd
  NTHM/RTH M23 ....168 D2
Parliament Pl BURY BL9 ......4 C7
Parliament St BURY BL9 ......4 C7
Parndon Dr OFTN SK2 ....172 D2
Parnell Av WYTH/NTH M22 ...168 C1
Parnham Cl RAD M26 ....51 E4
Parrbrook Cl BURY BL9 ......35 H3
Parr Cl FWTH BL4 ....65 G4
Parrenthorn Rd PWCH M25 ...70 B5
Parrfield Rd WALK M28 .....97 F3
Parr Fold BURY BL9 ....70 A2
Parr Fold Av WALK M28 .....96 D1
Parrin La ECC M30 ....96 D3
Parr La BURY BL9 ....69 H3
Parrot St BOLS/LL BL3 * 48 D4
  OP/CLY M11 ....130 D1
Parrs Mount Ms HTNM SK4 ...158 C4
Parr St ECC M30 ....111 E4
  OP/CLY M11 ....130 D1
Parrs Wood Av
  DID/WITH M20 ....157 H5
Parrs Wood La
  DID/WITH M20 ....158 A5
Parrs Wood Rd
  DID/WITH M20 ....157 H5
Parry Md MPL/ROM SK6 ......161 H2
Parry Rd WGTN/LGST M12 ...129 H4
Parslow Av CHH M8 ....102 B2
Parsonage Dr WALK M28 .....81 H5
  ORD M5 ....113 H4
Parsonage Gdns CSLFD M3 * ...6 C4
  MPL/ROM SK6 ....175 F5
Parsonage La
  CSLFD M3 * 6 D3
Parsonage Rd DID/WITH M20 ...143 E4
  HTNM SK4 ....159 E2
  RAD M26 ....67 F5
  URM M41 ....137 G2
Parsonage St BURY BL9 ....5 H4
  CHH M8 ....102 A1
  HTNM SK4 ....12 E2
  HULME M15 ....127 H5
  HYDE SK14 ....147 H1
Parsonage Wk MILN OL16 * ...31 G4
Parsonage Wy
  CHD/CHDH SK8 ....170 D4
Parsons Dr MDTN M24 ....72 C2
Parsons Fld SLFD M6 ....100 D5
Parson's La BURY BL9 ....35 H4
Parsons Wy BKLY M9 ....103 F3
Parth St BURY BL9 ....39 G5
Partington Cl FWTH BL4 .....65 H3
Partington La SWIN M27 .....98 D3
Partington Pk ROCH OL11 ...57 F1
Partington Pl SALE M33 ....154 C1
Partington St BOLS/LL BL3 ...64 B2
  ECC M30 ....111 E2
  FAIL M35 ....105 E3
  HEY OL10 ....40 C5
  NEWH/MOS M40 ....105 G5
  OLD OL1 * 9 J3
  ROCH OL11 ....42 A4
  WALK M28 ....98 B2
Partridge Av NTHM/RTH M23 ...168 A3
Partridge Cl ROCH OL11 .....28 C4
Partridge Ct OFTN SK2 .....172 C5
Partridge Ri DROY M43 ....118 C2
Partridge Rd FAIL M35 ....105 H4
Partridge St STRET M32 ....126 C3
Partridge Wy CHAD OL9 .....73 G4
Parvet Av DROY M43 ....117 G2
Pascal St BNG/LEV M19 ....144 A3
Passmonds Crs ROCH OL11 ...29 E3
Passmonds Wy ROCH OL11 ...29 E3
Pass St CHAD OL9 ....8 A4
The Pass MILN OL16 ....11 F5
Paston Rd WYTH/NTH M22 ...168 C2
Pasture Cl HEY OL10 ....40 C5
Pasturefield Cl SALE M33 ...155 G3
Pasture Field Rd
  NTHM/RTH M23 ....181 E3
Pasturegreen Wy IRL M44 ...122 C5
Pastures La OLDE OL4 ....77 G4
Patch Croft Rd
  WYTH/NTH M22 ....181 E3
Patchett St WGTN/LGST M12 ...129 G2
Patch La BRAM/HZG SK7 .....193 H2
Patey St WGTN/LGST M12 ...129 H5
Patience St WHIT OL12 .....29 F2
Patmos St RAMS BL0 ....17 E2
Paton Av BOLS/LL BL3 ......65 F1
Paton Ct BRO M7 * 113 H1
  WHIT OL12 ....18 C5
Patricia Dr WALK M28 ......82 B5
Patten St DID/WITH M20 ....143 E3
Patterdale Av AULW OL7 ....106 C5
  URM M41 ....124 A4
Patterdale Cl OLD OL1 ......75 H3
  ROCH OL11 ....42 A3
Patterdale Dr BURY BL9 .....53 F2
  MDTN M24 ....72 B2
Patterdale Rd AULW OL7 ...106 C5
  BOLE BL2 ....35 F2
  MPL/ROM SK6 ....162 A2
  PART M31 ....150 D3
  STKP SK1 ....172 C5
  WYTH/NTH M22 ....168 D1
Patterson Av CCHDY M21 ...141 E2
Patterson St BOLS/LL BL3 ...47 H5
  DTN/ASHW M34 ....132 C4
Pattishall Cl ANC M4 ....115 G4
Pattison Cl WHIT OL12 ......18 B5
Patton Cl BURY BL9 ....70 A2
Paulden Av NTHM/RTH M23 ...168 A3
  OLDE OL4 ....76 D3
Paulden Dr FAIL M35 ......105 F3
Paulette St BOL BL1 ....33 H4
Paulhan Rd DID/WITH M20 ...158 A2
Paulhan St BOLS/LL BL3 ....64 D1
Pavilion Dr AUL OL6 ....107 G5
The Pavilions CHD/CHDH SK8 ...170 A5
Pavilion Wk RAD M26 ....52 A5
Paxford Pl WILM/AE SK9 ...198 D5
Paythorne Gn OFTN SK2 ....173 F4
Peabody St BOLS/LL BL3 ....48 B5
Peace Gv BOLS/LL BL3 ......48 C4
  FAIL M35 ....105 F1
Peaceville Rd BNG/LEV M19 ...143 H2
Peach Bank MDTN M24 ....72 C4
Peach Rd OLDE OL4 ....76 C4
Peach St PWCH M25 ....86 B2
Peach Tree Cl BRO M7 * ...102 A4
Peach Tree Ct SLFD M6 * ...115 F5
Peacock Av CU GTN M18 ....130 B4
Peacock Cl GTN M18 ....130 B2
Peacock Dr CHD/CHDH SK8 ...191 G1
Peacock Gv GTN M18 ....130 C4
Peak Cl OLDE OL4 ....75 H4
Peakdale Av CHD/CHDH SK8 ...181 F5
Peakdale Rd DROY M43 .....117 F2
  MPL/ROM SK6 ....175 F5
Peaknaze Cl SWIN M27 ....99 G2
Peak St BOL BL1 ....33 G4
  CHAD OL9 ....8 B5
  CMANE M1 ....7 H4
  STKP SK1 ....13 J3
Pear Av BURY BL9 ....39 F3
Pearl Av BURY BL9 ....89 E1
Peardale Ct ECC M30 ....95 F3
Peart Av BRO M7 * 101 H1
Pearl Mill Cl OLDS OL8 ....92 A3
Pearl St BRAM/HZG SK7 ....173 F5
  DTN/ASHW M34 ....132 B5
  ROCH OL11 ....29 F3
Pearly Bank OLD OL1 ....60 C5
Pearn Rd BNG/LEV M19 .....158 C1
Pearson Cl MILN OL16 ......31 G4
  PART M31 ....151 F3
Pearson Gv OLDE OL4 ....92 D1
Pearson St BURY BL9 ....5 J2
  DUK SK16 ....133 F2
  MILN OL16 ....11 K4
  RDSH SK5 ....160 A5
Peart Av WN MPL/ROM SK6 ...147 G5
Pear Tree Cl MPL/ROM SK6 ...175 G1
  SLFD M6 ....113 F5
Pear Tree Ct SLFD M6 .....113 F5
Pear Tree Dr FWTH BL4 .....63 H2
  STLY SK15 ....121 E3
Peart St DTN/ASHW M34 ...132 B5
Peary St ANC M4 ....115 E2
Peaslake Cl MPL/ROM SK6 ...162 C4
Peatfield Av SWIN M27 ......85 G5
Peatfield Wk HULME M15 * ...128 A3
Pebble Cl STLY SK15 ....120 D1
Pebworth Cl MDTN M24 ......88 C2
Peckford Dr NEWH/MOS M40 ...103 H5
Peckforton Cl CHD/CHDH SK8 ...169 F4
Peckmill Cl WILM/AE SK9 ...192 B5
Pedder St BOL BL1 ....33 F5
Pedler Brow La WHIT OL12 ...20 B2
Pedley Wk BRUN/LGST M13 * ...128 C1
Peebles Dr NEWH/MOS M40 ...117 E1
Peel Av ALT WA14 ....177 H1
Peel Brow RAMS BL0 ....17 E2
Peel Cir URM M41 ....124 D2
Peel Cross Rd ORD M5 .....113 H4
Peel Dr LHULT M38 ....81 E5
  SALE M33 ....155 F2
Peelgate Dr CHD/CHDH SK8 ...181 F2
Peel Green Rd ECC M30 .....110 D5
Peel Gv WALK M28 ....97 F2
  WGTN/LGST M12 ....129 H4
Peel Hall Rd RAMS BL0 ......26 C1
  WYTH/NTH M22 ....181 E3
Peel La CHH M8 ....114 D1
  HEY OL10 ....40 C3
  LHULT M38 ....81 G5
Peel Moat Rd HTNM SK4 ....159 E1
Peel Mt RAMS BL0 ....16 D3
  SLFD M6 ....113 G2
Peel Park Crs LHULT M38 ...81 E3
Peel Rd HALE/TIMP WA15 ...177 H1
Peels Av OLDE OL4 ....77 F5
Peel St AUL OL6 ....107 F5
  CHAD OL9 ....74 C5
  DROY M43 ....117 G5
  DTN/ASHW M34 ....132 B2
  DTN/ASHW M34 ....132 B4
  ECC M30 ....119 H4
  FAIL M35 ....104 C4
  FWTH BL4 ....66 B4
  HEY OL10 ....40 C4
  LIT OL15 ....21 E3
  OFTN SK2 ....172 A5
  RAD M26 ....68 C2
  STLY SK15 ....120 D4
  WHIT OL12 ....10 A4
Peers Cl URM M41 ....123 E4
Peers St TOT/BURYW BL8 ....37 H4
Pegamoid St BOLE BL2 ......34 C5
Pegasus Ct ROCH OL11 * 29 F5
Pegasus Sq BRO M7 ....113 H2
Pegwell Dr BRO M7 ....101 H4
Pekin St AUL OL6 ....119 H1
Pelham Pl CHH M8 ....87 G5
Pelham St AULW OL7 ....118 D5
  BOLS/LL BL3 ....64 B1
  OP/CLY M11 ....116 C5
Pelican Cl RAD M26 ....51 G5
Pelton Av SWIN M27 ....85 G5
Pemberton St BOL BL1 ....33 H2
  LHULT M38 ....81 G3
  ROCH OL11 ....42 B4
Pemberton Wy ROY/SHW OL2 ...60 A1
Pembridge Fold MPL/ROM SK6 ...74 F4
Pembroke Av ECC M30 ....110 C2
  SALE M33 ....154 A1
Pembroke Cl BRUN/LGST M13 ...129 E2
Pembroke Ct
  BRAM/HZG SK7 * 185 F2
  HYDE SK14 ....10 C3
Pembroke Dr BURY BL9 ......70 C3
  OLDE OL4 ....92 C1
Pembroke St BOL BL1 ....2 D5
  BRO M7 ....101 H4
  LIT OL15 ....21 E2
  OLDS OL8 ....8 D5
  SLFD M6 ....112 C4
Pembry Cl RDSH SK5 ....160 C1
Pembury Cl WYTH/NTH M22 ...180 D1
Penarth Rd BOLS/LL BL3 ....48 A5
  WYTH/NTH M22 ....168 C1
Pencarrow Cl DID/WITH M20 ...157 F3
Pencombe Cl
  WGTN/LGST M12 ....129 H3
Pencroft Wy HULME M15 ...128 B3
Pendale Av CHH M8 ....102 C2
Pendeen Cl WYTH/NTH M22 ...180 D3
Pendennis ROCH OL11 * 29 F4
Pendennis Av HOR/BR BL6 ...47 E4
Pendennis Cl RAD M26 ....51 F4
Pendennis Rd HTNM SK4 ....159 F3
Pendle Av BOL BL2 ....35 G1
Pendlebury Cl PWCH M25 ....85 G5
Pendlebury Fold BOLS/LL BL3 ...63 E2
Pendlebury Rd
  CHD/CHDH SK8 ....169 F3
  SWIN M27 ....84 C5
Pendlebury St BOL BL2 ......34 A3
  TOT/BURYW BL8 ....37 G3
Pendle Cl OLDE OL4 ....92 C2
  TOT/BURYW BL8 ....37 G3
Pendlecroft Av SWIN M27 ...99 H3
Pendlegreen Cl OP/CLY M11 ...116 A5
Pendle Gv ROY/SHW OL2 ....74 D1
Pendle Rd DTN/ASHW M34 ...146 D2
Pendleton Gn SLFD M6 * ...113 E2
Pendleton Wy SLFD M6 ....113 F2
Pendle Av OLDE OL4 ....76 D5
Pendleway SWIN M27 ....99 F1
Pendragon Pl FAIL M35 ....105 F3
Penelope Rd SLFD M6 ......100 A5
Penerly Dr BKLY M9 ....103 E4
Penfield Cl CMANE M1 .....128 C1
Penfold Wk
  WGTN/LGST M12 * 129 G2
Pengwern Av BOLS/LL BL3 ...48 A4
Penhale Ms BRAM/HZG SK7 ...184 C4
Penistone Av BKLY M9 ......88 D4
  MILN OL16 ....30 D5
  SLFD M6 ....112 B2
Penketh Av GTN M18 ......130 A4
Penmere Gv SALE M33 .....153 H5
Penmoor Cha BRAM/HZG SK7 ...184 C3
Penmore Cl ROY/SHW OL2 ...60 B2
Pennant Dr PWCH M25 ......85 H2
Pennant St OLD OL1 ....76 A4
Pennell St OP/CLY M11 ....117 E4
Penn Gn CHD/CHDH SK8 ....183 E3
Penn House Cl
  BRAM/HZG SK7 ....183 H5
Pennine Av CHAD OL9 ....90 B2
Pennine Bridleway WHIT OL12 ...18 C3
Pennine Cl BKLY M9 ....88 C3
  TOT/BURYW BL8 ....37 F3
Pennine Ct STLY SK15 .....121 G2
Pennine Dr ALT WA14 .....165 E4
  AUL OL6 ....108 A4
  MILN OL16 ....31 H5
  OLDE OL4 ....19 H2
Pennine Gv AUL OL6 ....107 H4
Pennine Rd BRAM/HZG SK7 ...184 C3
  MPL/ROM SK6 ....147 G5
Pennine V ROY/SHW OL2 .....60 B1
Pennine Vw DTN/ASHW M34 ...132 B3
  MOSL OL5 ....109 E1
  ROY/SHW OL2 ....59 F5
  STLY SK15 ....108 C5
Pennington Cl LHULT M38 ...80 D3
Pennington Rd BOLS/LL BL3 ...63 G4
Pennington St CHAD OL9 .....90 C4
  TOT/BURYW BL8 ....38 D2
  WALK M28 ....96 A3
  WGTN/LGST M12 ....144 A1
Pennon Cl BRO M7 ....101 H4
Penn St FWTH BL4 ....65 H4
  HEY OL10 ....40 C3
  MILN OL16 ....10 E5
  NEWH/MOS M40 ....103 G2
  OLDS OL8 ....8 E7
Penny Bridge La URM M41 ...138 A1
Penny Meadow AUL OL6 ....119 H2
Pennymoor Dr ALT WA14 ...165 H1
Penrhos Av CHD/CHDH SK8 ...169 E5
Penrhyn Av BRAM/HZG SK7 ...182 B3
  MDTN M24 ....72 D5
Penrhyn Crs BRAM/HZG SK7 ...184 C3
Penrhyn Dr BRAM/HZG SK7 ...184 C3
  PWCH M25 ....86 A3
Penrice Cl RAD M26 ....51 C4
Penrice Fold WALK M28 .....96 C3
Penrith Av AULW OL7 ....106 C5
  BOL BL1 ....32 C5
  OLDS OL8 ....90 C5
  RDSH SK5 ....145 F2
  SALE M33 ....154 D4
  WHTF M45 ....82 C5
Penrith Cl PART M31 ......150 D2
Penrith St ROCH OL11 ......43 E1
Penrod Pl SLFD M6 ....113 G1
Penrose Cl CHH M8 ....102 B4
Penrose Gdns MDTN M24 ....73 E3
Penrose Wk MDTN M24 ......73 E3
Penroy Av DID/WITH M20 ...156 C3
Penruddock Wk
  BRUN/LGST M13 * 129 G1
Penry Av IRL M44 ....136 A5
Penryn Av ROY/SHW OL2 .....75 G1
  SALE M33 ....154 D5
Pensarn Av RUSH/FAL M14 ...143 G3
Pensarn Gv RDSH SK5 ......160 A2
Pensby Cl SWIN M27 * 99 H5
Pensford Ct BOLE BL2 ....35 E1
Pensford Rd NTHM/RTH M23 ...179 G1
Penshurst Rd RDSH SK5 ....145 H4
Penthorpe Dr ROY/SHW OL2 ...75 G1
Pentland Av NEWH/MOS M40 ...88 D5
Pentland Cl BRAM/HZG SK7 ...184 C1
Pentlands Av BRO M7 .....101 G4
Pentland Ter BOL BL1 * 33 H5
The Pentlands ROY/SHW OL2 ...59 E1
Pentland Wy HYDE SK14 ...134 C2
Pentwyn Gv NTHM/RTH M23 ...168 A2
Penwell Fold OLD OL1 * 9 J3
Penwortham St
  NEWH/MOS M40 ....116 A1
Penydarren Vw BOLS/LL BL3 ...65 H1
Penzance Rd NEWH/MOS M40 ...115 H2
Penzance St
  NEWH/MOS M40 ....115 H2
Peover Av SALE M33 ....155 F2
Peover Rd WILM/AE SK9 ...192 B2
Pepler Av NTHM/RTH M23 ...156 A4
Pepperhill Rd
  OLDTF/WHR M16 ....128 A3
Peppermint Cl MILN OL16 ...45 F2
Pepper Rd BRAM/HZG SK7 ...184 C2
Percival Cl CHH M8 ....87 E3
Percival Rd DROY M43 .....118 A2
Percy Dr ORD M5 ....127 E1
Percy St BOL BL1 ....34 A4
  BURY BL9 ....5 G5
  FWTH BL4 ....66 B5
  HULME M15 ....127 G2
  MILN OL16 ....43 G1
  OLDE OL4 ....76 B4
  RAMS BL0 ....16 C3
  STLY SK15 ....121 G2
Peregrine Crs DROY M43 ...118 D2
Peregrine Dr IRL M44 ......136 B4
Peregrine Rd OFTN SK2 ....173 H5
Perendale Rd OP/CLY M11 ...116 B3
Perendale Ri BOL BL1 ....23 F1
Pernham St OLDE OL4 ....76 D5
Perrin St HYDE SK14 ......147 H1
Perryn Wk HALE/TIMP WA15 ...134 B4
Perry Cl ROCH OL11 ....42 C1
Perrygate Av DID/WITH M20 ...142 C5
Perrymead PWCH M25 ....86 A1
Perry Rd HALE/TIMP WA15 ...166 C3
Pershore WHIT OL12 ....10 B5
Pershore Rd MDTN M24 .....90 B3
Perth Av CHAD OL9 ....90 B3
Perth Cl BRAM/HZG SK7 ...193 H2
Perth Rd ROCH OL11 ....43 G4
Perth St BOLS/LL BL3 ....64 C1
  ROY/SHW OL2 ....59 H5
  SWIN M27 ....98 C3
Peru St CSLFD M3 ....114 A3
Peterborough Cl AUL OL6 ...107 E4
Peterborough Dr BOL BL1 ....2 D1
Peterborough St GTN M18 ...131 E2
Peterborough Wk BOL BL1 * ...2 B1
Peterhead Cl BOL BL1 ....2 B1
Peterhead Wk ORD M5 * ...113 H4
Peterhouse Gdns
  MPL/ROM SK6 ....162 B2
Peterloo Ct SLFD M6 * 112 B2
Petersburg Rd EDGY/DAV SK3 ...171 F3
Petersfield Dr
  NTHM/RTH M23 ....167 E2
Petersfield Wk BOL BL1 * 2 C1
Peter St ALT WA14 ....177 G1
  BRAM/HZG SK7 ....185 E1
  BURY BL9 ....5 F2
  CMANE M1 ....6 E6
  DTN/ASHW M34 ....132 D5
  ECC M30 ....111 E4
  OLD OL1 ....9 G4
  STKP SK1 ....13 J1
Peterswood Cl
  WYTH/NTH M22 ....180 A1
Peterwood Gdns STRET M32 ...139 G2
Petheridge Dr
  WYTH/NTH M22 ....180 A3
Petrel Av POY/DIS SK12 ...194 B3
Petrel Cl DROY M43 ....118 B2
  EDGY/DAV SK3 ....171 G3
  ROCH OL11 ....28 C4
Petrie St WHIT OL12 ....10 C3
Petts Crs LIT OL15 ....20 D2
Petworth Cl WYTH/NTH M22 ...180 C3
Petworth Rd CHAD OL9 ......90 C1
Pevensey Rd SLFD M6 .....100 B5
Pevensey Wk CHAD OL9 .....90 C1
Peveril Cl WHTF M45 ....70 B5
Peveril Crs CCHDY M21 ...141 E1
Peveril Dr BRAM/HZG SK7 ...185 C4
Peveril Rd ALT WA14 ......165 F2
  OLD OL1 ....76 B3
  ORD M5 ....112 C3
Peveril St BOL BL1 ....64 A1
Peveril Ter HYDE SK14 ...148 B1
Pewsey Rd WYTH/NTH M22 ...181 E1
Pexwood OLD OL1 ....73 H3
Pheasant Cl WALK M28 .....96 C4
Pheasant Dr CCHDY M21 ...141 H4
Pheasant Ri ALT WA14 ....177 G5
Phelan Cl NEWH/MOS M40 ...102 D5
Phethean St BOLE BL2 ....3 H4
  FWTH BL4 ....65 H3
Philip Av DTN/ASHW M34 ...132 A3
Philip Dr SALE M33 ....154 A5
Philips Av FWTH BL4 ....66 A5
Philips Park Rd OP/CLY M11 ...115 H3
  WHTF M45 ....84 D2
Philip St BOLS/LL BL3 ....48 C4
  ECC M30 ....111 E4
  OLDE OL4 ....76 B4
  ROCH OL11 ....43 E1
Phillimore St OLDE OL4 .....92 C2
Phillips Park Rd WHTF M45 ...85 C1
Phipps St WALK M28 ....81 E5
Phoebe St BOLS/LL BL3 * ...48 B5
  ORD M5 ....113 F5
Phoenix Cl HEY OL10 ....41 G5
Phoenix Pk BURY BL9 ....3 G2
  CMANE M2 ....7 F4
  FWTH BL4 ....66 A5
  LIT OL15 ....21 E2
  OLD OL1 ....9 G5
  STKP SK1 ....29 F2
Phoenix Wy HULME M15 ...128 A3
  RAD M26 ....68 B2
  URM M41 ....124 D2
Phyllis St MDTN M24 ....73 F5
  OLD OL1 ....29 E2
Piccadilly CMANE M1 ....7 G3
  STKP SK1 ....13 G4
Piccadilly Plaza CMANE M1 ...7 G3
Piccadilly South CMANE M1 ...7 H6
Piccard Cl ANC M4 ....7 J1
Pickering Cl HALE/TIMP WA15 ...166 B2
  RAD M26 * 67 F5
  TOT/BURYW BL8 ....37 G1
  URM M41 ....138 B1
Pickering St HULME M15 ...127 H5
Pickford Av BOLS/LL BL3 ....67 F1
Pickford Ct DUK SK16 * 119 H5
Pickford La DUK SK16 .....119 H5
Pickford's Brow STKP SK1 ...13 G3
Pickhill La UPML OL3 ....7 J3
Pickhill Ms UPML OL3 ....79 E4
Pickmere Av DID/WITH M20 ...142 D3
Pickmere Cl DROY M43 .....118 A4
  EDGY/DAV SK3 ....171 F3
  SALE M33 ....155 G4
Pickmere Ct
  CHD/CHDH SK8 ....170 C4
Pickmere Ms UPML OL3 .....79 E4
Pickmere Rd WILM/AE SK9 ...192 A2
Pickup St CMANE M1 * 7 K6
  MILN OL16 ....10 E7
Pickwick Rd POY/DIS SK12 ...194 B4
Picton Cl CSLFD M3 ....6 B2
Picton Dr WILM/AE SK9 ....199 H1
Picton Sq OLDE OL4 ....9 J5
Picton St BRO M7 ....114 A2
Picton Wk OLDTF/WHR M16 ...128 A5
Pierce St OLD OL1 ....76 B3

Piercy St ANC M4 115 G4
FAIL M35 * 104 D3
Piethorne Cl MILN OL16 45 F2
Pigeon St CMANE M1 7 J4
Pigginshaw WILM/AE SK9 198 B2
Piggott St FWTH BL4 65 H5
Pike Av FAIL M35 105 H4
Pike Fold La BKLY M9 87 H4
Pike Rd BOLS/LL BL3 48 C5
Pike St ROCH OL11 43 E1
Pike View Cl OLDE OL4 92 A2
Pilgrim Dr OP/CLY M11 116 A4
Pilgrim Wy OLD OL1 76 C1
Pilkington Dr WHTF M45 70 A2
Pilkington Rd BKLY M9 88 D5
FWTH BL4 82 C1
RAD M26 52 A4
Pilkington St BOLS/LL BL3 48 D4
MDTN M24 73 F3
RAMS BL0 16 C3
Pilkington Wy RAD M26 68 B2
Pilling Fld EDGW/EG BL7 22 D2
Pilling St DTN/ASHW M34 132 C5
NEWH/MOS M40 103 G5
TOT/BURYW BL8 37 H3
WHIT OL12 29 G3
Pilning St BOLS/LL BL3 49 F5
Pilot St BURY BL9 5 F7
Pilsworth Rd BURY BL9 53 H3
Pilsworth Wy BURY BL9 53 H3
Pimblett St CSLFD M3 114 C2
Pimhole Fold BURY BL9 5 H6
Pimhole Rd BURY BL9 5 H5
Pimlico Cl BRO M7 * 101 G4
Pimlott Gv HYDE SK14 133 G3
PWCH M25 85 F5
Pimlott Rd BOL BL1 34 C3
Pimmcroft Wy SALE M33 155 G3
Pine Av WHTF M45 69 G5
Pine Cl DTN/ASHW M34 132 B2
MPL/ROM SK6 174 D5
Pine Gv DTN/ASHW M34 132 D5
DUK SK16 120 C5
ECC M30 111 F1
FWTH BL4 65 G4
PWCH M25 85 H1
ROY/SHW OL2 59 E3
RUSH/FAL M14 129 F4
SALE M33 138 D5
SWIN M27 98 C3
WALK M28 97 F2
Pinehurst Rd
NEWH/MOS M40 103 F5
Pine Ldg BRAM/HZG SK7 * 184 A5
Pine Meadow RAD M26 83 F1
Pine Rd BRAM/HZG SK7 184 A4
DID/WITH M20 157 F2
DUK SK16 120 B5
POY/DIS SK12 195 G4
Pine St AUL OL6 119 G1
BOL BL1 34 A4
BURY BL9 5 J4
CHAD OL9 74 B4
CMANE M1 7 F5
HEY OL10 41 E4
HYDE SK14 133 G3
LIT OL15 21 E2
MDTN M24 73 F5
MILN OL16 * 11 G7
MILN OL16 45 E3
MPL/ROM SK6 162 A1
Pine St North BURY BL9 5 J3
Pine St South BURY BL9 5 J5
Pinetop Cl CCHDY M21 141 H4
Pine Tree Rd OLDS OL8 106 A1
Pinetree St GTN M18 130 B3
Pineway OLDE OL4 93 E1
Pinewood ALT WA14 176 D2
CHAD OL9 73 H5
SALE M33 153 G2
Pinewood Cl BOL BL1 33 H4
DUK SK16 119 H4
HTNM SK4 158 D3
Pinewood Ct ALT WA14 177 H5
SALE M33 155 E1
Pinewood Rd CCHDY M21 * 141 E4
WILM/AE SK9 199 H2
The Pinewoods
MPL/ROM SK6 162 A1
Pinfold Av BKLY M9 88 D5
Pinfold Cl HALE/TIMP WA15 179 E5
Pinfold Dr CHD/CHDH SK8 182 D3
Pinfold La HALE/TIMP WA15 189 G1
MPL/ROM SK6 162 D2
WHTF M45 69 F4
Pinfold Rd WALK M28 96 D1
Pingate Dr CHD/CHDH SK8 192 D1
Pingate La CHD/CHDH SK8 192 D1
Pingate La South
CHD/CHDH SK8 192 D1
Pingot Av NTHM/RTH M23 156 A5
The Pingot IRL M44 122 C5
Pink Bank La
WGTN/LGST M12 129 H4
Pinnacle Dr EDGW/EG BL7 22 C1
Pinner Pl BNG/LEV M19 158 D1
Pinners Cl RAMS BL0 16 D1
Pinnington La STRET M32 * 140 B2
Pinnington Rd GTN M18 130 C3
Pintail Av EDGY/DAV SK3 171 G3
Pintail Cl WHIT OL12 29 E1
Pioneer Rd SWIN M27 85 E5
Pioneer St LIT OL15 21 E3
OP/CLY M11 116 C2
ROCH OL11 30 B5
Pioneer Vls MILN OL16 * 45 H1
Piperhill Av WYTH/NTH M22 156 C5
Pipers Cl ROCH OL11 28 A3
Pipers Ct IRL M44 122 D5
Pipewell Av GTN M18 130 B3
Pipit Cl DTN/ASHW M34 118 B3
Pitchcombe Rd
WYTH/NTH M22 180 A2
Pitcombe Cl BOL BL1 22 C4
Pitfield Gdns NTHM/RTH M23 167 G2
Pitfield La BOLE BL2 35 G3
Pitfield St BOLE BL2 3 J5
Pit La ROY/SHW OL2 44 A5
Pitman Cl OP/CLY M11 116 B5
Pits Farm Av ROCH OL11 29 F4
Pitsford Rd NEWH/MOS M40 103 F5
Pitshouse La WHIT OL12 * 28 B1
Pit St CHAD OL9 90 C3
DTN/ASHW M34 132 C5
Pittbrook St WGTN/LGST M12 129 E1
Pitt St EDGY/DAV SK3 12 D6
HEY OL10 40 D4
HYDE SK14 133 G5
OLDE OL4 9 K5
RAD M26 67 H1
WHIT OL12 10 D4
Pitt St East OLDE OL4 92 A2
Pixmore Av BOL BL1 34 C2
Place Rd ALT WA14 165 F3
Plain Pit St HYDE SK14 133 F3
Plainsfield Cl
OLDTF/WHR M16 128 A4
Plainsfield St
OLDTF/WHR M16 127 H4
Plane Ct SLFD M6 * 113 F3
Plane Rd FAIL M35 105 E5
Plane St OLDE OL4 76 A5
Plane Tree Cl MPL/ROM SK6 174 C4
Planetree Rd
HALE/TIMP WA15 178 B2
Plane Tree Rd PART M31 150 C3
Planet Wy DTN/ASHW M34 132 B3
Plantation Av WALK M28 81 H3
Plantation St AUL OL6 120 A4
GTN M18 130 D3
Plant Cl SALE M33 154 B1
Plant Hill Rd BKLY M9 87 H2
Plant St CMANE M1 * 7 H5
Plant Ter BKLY M9 * 88 A2
Plate St OLD OL1 9 H3
Plato St CHAD OL9 8 C2
Platt Av AUL OL6 107 F4
Plattbrook Cl RUSH/FAL M14 142 D2
Platt Cl MILN OL16 44 D1
Platt Hill Av BOLS/LL BL3 47 H5
Platting Gv AULW OL7 106 C5
Platting La ROCH OL11 43 F2
Platting Rd OLDE OL4 77 H5
Platt La RUSH/FAL M14 142 B2
UPML OL3 78 C2
Platts Dr IRL M44 136 C1
Platt St CHD/CHDH SK8 170 B3
DUK SK16 132 D1
OLDE OL4 93 E1
Plattwood Wk HULME M15 * 127 G2
Playfair Cl HEY OL10 56 B2
Playfair St BOL BL1 23 E5
RUSH/FAL M14 128 C4
Pleachway HTNM SK4 158 C4
Pleasant Gdns BOL BL1 2 C2
Pleasant Rd ECC M30 111 F4
Pleasant St BKLY M9 103 E3
HEY OL10 40 D2
ROCH OL11 42 B4
TOT/BURYW BL8 37 E2
Pleasant Wy CHD/CHDH SK8 193 F1
Pleasington Dr
NEWH/MOS M40 89 F5
TOT/BURYW BL8 36 D4
Plevna St BOLE BL2 3 H4
Plodder La FWTH BL4 64 C4
WHTN BL5 63 H4
Ploughbank Dr CCHDY M21 142 A4
Plough Cl URM M41 137 E2
Plough Flds WALK M28 96 A5
Plough St DUK SK16 120 A5
Plover Cl ROCH OL11 28 B4
Plover Dr ALT WA14 165 E1
BURY BL9 39 E2
IRL M44 122 B4
Plowden Av BOLS/LL BL3 64 B1
Plowden Rd WYTH/NTH M22 180 A2
Plowley Cl DID/WITH M20 157 G4
Plucksbridge Rd
MPL/ROM SK6 187 F1
Plumbley Dr OLDTF/WHR M16 127 F5
Plumbley St OP/CLY M11 * 130 D1
Plumley Cl EDGY/DAV SK3 172 A4
Plumley Rd WILM/AE SK9 192 A2
Plummer Av CCHDY M21 141 F5
Plumpton Cl ROY/SHW OL2 75 F3
Plumpton Dr BURY BL9 27 F5
Plumpton Rd ROCH OL11 58 C1
Plumpton Wk
BRUN/LGST M13 * 129 G4
Plum St OLDS OL8 8 C6
Plum Tree Ct SLFD M6 113 F3
Pluto Cl SLFD M6 * 113 H1
Plymouth Av BRUN/LGST M13 129 F3
Plymouth Cl AUL OL6 107 F5
Plymouth Dr BRAM/HZG SK7 184 A5
FWTH BL4 65 E4
Plymouth Gv
BRUN/LGST M13 129 E3
EDGY/DAV SK3 171 E2
RAD M26 51 G4
Plymouth Gv West
BRUN/LGST M13 129 F3
Plymouth Rd SALE M33 153 G1
Plymouth St OLDS OL8 91 G3
Plymouth Vw
BRUN/LGST M13 128 D2
Plymtree Cl CHH M8 86 D5
Pobgreen La UPML OL3 79 G3
Pochard Dr ALT WA14 165 E2
POY/DIS SK12 194 B3
Pochin St NEWH/MOS M40 115 H2
Pocket Nook Rd HOR/BR BL6 62 C1
Pocklington Dr
NTHM/RTH M23 167 G2
Podsmead Rd
WYTH/NTH M22 180 A2
Poise Brook Dr OFTN SK2 173 G4
Poise Brook Rd OFTN SK2 173 G4
Poise Cl BRAM/HZG SK7 185 H1
Poland St ANC M4 7 K2
DTN/ASHW M34 118 D5
Polden Cl OLDS OL8 91 F4
Poleacre La MPL/ROM SK6 147 G5
Polebrook Cl
WGTN/LGST M12 129 E2
Pole Ct BURY BL9 * 70 B1
Polefield Ap PWCH M25 86 A1
Polefield Cir PWCH M25 86 A1
Polefield Gdns PWCH M25 86 A1
Polefield Gra PWCH M25 86 A1
Polefield Gv PWCH M25 86 A1
Polefield Hall Rd PWCH M25 86 A1
Polefield Rd BKLY M9 88 A5
PWCH M25 70 A5
Pole La BURY BL9 70 B2
FAIL M35 105 E2
Pole St BOLE BL2 3 J1
Polesworth Cl
WGTN/LGST M12 129 H2
Police St ALT WA14 165 G4
CMANW M2 6 D4
ECC M30 110 D3
Pollard Ct OLD OL1 * 75 F4
Pollards La BURY BL9 26 D1
Pollard Sq PART M31 151 F3
Pollard St ANC M4 115 G4
Pollard St East ANC M4 115 G3
Pollen Cl SALE M33 154 D4
Pollen Rd ALT WA14 165 F3
Polletts Av RDSH SK5 146 A5
Pollit Cft MPL/ROM SK6 161 G5
Pollitt Av AUL OL6 107 F5
Pollitt Cl WGTN/LGST M12 * 129 G2
Pollitts Cl ECC M30 110 C3
Polonia Ct OLDS OL8 90 D4
Polperro Cl ROY/SHW OL2 59 H5
Polruan Rd CCHDY M21 141 E1
Polworth Rd BKLY M9 103 F1
Polygon Av BRUN/LGST M13 128 D2
Polygon Rd CHH M8 102 A1
Polygon St BRUN/LGST M13 128 D1
The Polygon BRO M7 101 F4
ECC M30 111 H3
Pomfret St SLFD M6 * 99 H5
WGTN/LGST M12 129 H2
Pomona Crs ORD M5 127 E1
Pomona Strd HULME M15 127 F2
ORD M5 126 D3
Pomona St ROCH OL11 43 E1
Ponds Cl CCHDY M21 * 141 F2
Pondwater Cl WALK M28 81 E4
Ponsford Av BKLY M9 88 D4
Ponsonby Rd STRET M32 126 A5
Pontefract Cl SWIN M27 99 G3
Pool Bank St MDTN M24 71 H5
Poolcroft SALE M33 155 G3
Poole Cl BRAM/HZG SK7 183 G3
Pooley Cl MDTN M24 71 G3
Poolfield Cl RAD M26 67 H1
Pool Fold FAIL M35 105 F4
Pool House Rd POY/DIS SK12 196 B2
Pool Rd GOL/RIS/CUL WA3 150 A3
Pool St BOL BL1 2 D4
OLDS OL8 91 G3
Pool Ter BOL BL1 32 D4
Poolton Rd BKLY M9 87 G3
Poorfield St OLDS OL8 9 F6
Poplar Av ALT WA14 165 G3
BNG/LEV M19 144 B4
BOL BL1 34 A2
BOLE BL2 23 H5
BURY BL9 5 K3
OLDE OL4 93 H3
OLDS OL8 91 E5
WILM/AE SK9 198 B5
Poplar Cl CHD/CHDH SK8 169 G4
Poplar Ct DTN/ASHW M34 * 132 C2
EDGY/DAV SK3 * 172 A4
Poplar Dr PWCH M25 85 H5
Poplar Gv AUL OL6 107 F5
GTN M18 130 C4
OFTN SK2 172 D5
RAMS BL0 17 E1
SALE M33 154 C3
URM M41 139 E1
Poplar Rd BNG/LEV M19 158 A3
DUK SK16 134 A1
ECC M30 111 F1
STRET M32 140 A3
SWIN M27 98 C3
WALK M28 82 B5
Poplars Rd STLY SK15 121 G2
The Poplars MOSL OL5 109 F1
Poplar St DTN/ASHW M34 132 C2
FAIL M35 104 C4
HTNM SK4 158 B4
Poplar Wk CHAD OL9 * 74 C4
Poplar Wy MPL/ROM SK6 187 F5
Poplin Dr CSLFD M3 6 C1
Poppy Cl CHAD OL9 73 G5
NTHM/RTH M23 155 F5
Poppyfield Vw ROCH OL11 28 B3
Poppythorn La PWCH M25 85 H2
Porchester Dr RAD M26 51 F4
Porchfield Sq CSLFD M3 6 C6
Porlock Av DTN/ASHW M34 118 B5
HYDE SK14 149 E1
Porlock Cl STKP SK1 172 D1
Porlock Rd NTHM/RTH M23 168 A3
URM M41 138 B3
Porritt Cl ROCH OL11 28 B5
Porritt St BURY BL9 5 J1
Porritt Wy RAMS BL0 16 D1
Portal Gv DTN/ASHW M34 147 F2
Porter Dr NEWH/MOS M40 103 E4
Porter St BURY BL9 38 C2
Portfield Cl BOL BL1 47 G1
Porthleven Dr
NTHM/RTH M23 167 F3
Portinscale Cl
TOT/BURYW BL8 37 G3
Portland Cl BRAM/HZG SK7 184 C3
Portland Crs BRUN/LGST M13 129 E4
Portland Gv HTNM SK4 159 E2
Portland Houses
MPL/ROM SK6 * 174 D4
Portland Pl AULW OL7 119 F4
Portland Rd ALT WA14 177 G1
BRUN/LGST M13 129 G5
ECC M30 111 G2
STRET M32 126 B5
SWIN M27 99 F3
WALK M28 81 H2
Portland St BOL BL1 33 H4
BURY BL9 5 G1
CMANE M1 7 F6
MILN OL16 10 D5
Portland St North AUL OL6 119 F2
Portland St South AUL OL6 119 F3
Portloe Rd CHD/CHDH SK8 181 G5
Portman Rd
OLDTF/WHR M16 127 H5
Portrea Cl EDGY/DAV SK3 171 H4
Portree Cl ECC M30 110 C3
Portrush Rd WYTH/NTH M22 180 D2
Portside Cl WALK M28 96 C5
Portsmouth Cl BRO M7 101 G5
Portsmouth St
BRUN/LGST M13 128 C3
Port Soderick Av ORD M5 113 F4
Portstone Cl
OLDTF/WHR M16 127 H4
Portstone St
OLDTF/WHR M16 * 127 H4
Port St CMANE M1 7 H4
OLDS OL8 91 G3
STKP SK1 12 E2
Portugal Rd PWCH M25 86 A5
Portugal St ANC M4 115 F2
AULW OL7 119 E5
BOLE BL2 3 J5
Portugal St East CMANE M1 7 K6
Portville Rd BNG/LEV M19 144 A2
Portway WYTH/NTH M22 180 B3
Portwood Pl RDSH SK5 13 G1
Posnett St EDGY/DAV SK3 12 A5
Postal St CMANE M1 * 7 H4
Postbridge Cl
BRUN/LGST M13 128 D2
Post Office St ALT WA14 165 G5
Potato Whf CSLFD M3 6 A7
Pot Hl AUL OL6 119 H1
Pot Hill Sq AUL OL6 * 119 H1
Potters La BKLY M9 103 F3
Potter St BURY BL9 5 H2
RAD M26 53 E5
Pottery La OP/CLY M11 116 B5
Pottinger St AULW OL7 119 E5
Pott St SWIN M27 84 A5
Poulton Av BOLE BL2 50 B2
Poulton St OP/CLY M11 130 D1
Poundswick La
WYTH/NTH M22 180 C1
Powder Mill Cl IRL M44 136 C2
Powell Av HYDE SK14 133 H5
Powell St OLDTF/WHR M16 127 F4
OP/CLY M11 117 E3
TOT/BURYW BL8 37 G5
Powicke Dr MPL/ROM SK6 161 G5
Powicke Wk MPL/ROM SK6 161 H5
Powis Rd URM M41 137 E2
Pownall Av BRAM/HZG SK7 194 A1
DID/WITH M20 142 C3
Pownall Rd ALT WA14 177 G1
CHD/CHDH SK8 182 D3
WILM/AE SK9 198 C2
Pownall St BRAM/HZG SK7 185 E1
Poynings Dr WYTH/NTH M22 180 B3
Poynt Cha WALK M28 96 C5
Poynter St NEWH/MOS M40 104 B1
Poynton St BURY BL9 5 G7
HULME M15 128 A2
Praed Rd TRPK M17 125 H3
The Precinct EDGY/DAV SK3 * 12 E7
OFTN SK2 * 173 E3
Preece Cl HYDE SK14 134 B4
Preesall Av CHD/CHDH SK8 181 G4
Preesall Cl TOT/BURYW BL8 52 A1
Premier Rd CHH M8 114 C1
Premier St OLDTF/WHR M16 127 G4
Prenton St OP/CLY M11 117 F5
Prenton Wy TOT/BURYW BL8 37 E1
Presall St BOLE BL2 * 49 H1
Prescot Cl BURY BL9 5 G7
Prescot Rd BKLY M9 103 E3
HALE/TIMP WA15 178 A2
Prescott Rd WILM/AE SK9 199 E1
Prescott St BOLS/LL BL3 * 48 B5
MILN OL16 30 D1
WALK M28 81 G4
Press St OP/CLY M11 130 C1
Presswood Ct SLFD M6 * 99 H4
Prestage St OLDTF/WHR M16 127 G4
WGTN/LGST M12 144 B1
Prestbury Av
HALE/TIMP WA15 165 H3
RUSH/FAL M14 142 B2
Prestbury Cl BURY BL9 5 G7
OFTN SK2 173 E5
Prestbury Dr MPL/ROM SK6 161 F3
OLD OL1 75 E3
Prestbury Rd BOL BL1 34 B1
WILM/AE SK9 199 H5
Prestfield Rd WHTF M45 69 H5
Presto Gdns BOLS/LL BL3 * 48 A5
Prestolee Rd BOLS/LL BL3 66 D3
RAD M26 67 F3
Preston Av ECC M30 111 H2
IRL M44 136 B4
Preston Cl ECC M30 * 111 H2
Preston Rd BNG/LEV M19 144 A3
Preston St BOLS/LL BL3 * 49 G5
GTN M18 130 B2
MDTN M24 72 D4
OLDE OL4 9 J5
WHIT OL12 29 F3
Presto St BOLS/LL BL3 48 A5
FWTH BL4 66 B3
Prestwich Cl OFTN SK2 172 C2
Prestwich Hills PWCH M25 85 H5
Prestwich Park Rd South
PWCH M25 85 H4
Prestwood Cl BOL BL1 33 F5
Prestwood Dr BOL BL1 33 G5
Prestwood Rd FWTH BL4 65 F3
SLFD M6 112 B1
Pretoria Rd BOLE BL2 50 B2
OLDS OL8 90 D4
Pretoria St WHIT OL12 * 29 F2
Prettywood BURY BL9 39 G4
Price St ANC M4 * 115 G4
BURY BL9 5 G7
DUK SK16 * 119 H5
FWTH BL4 66 A3
Prichard St STRET M32 140 B1
Prickshaw La WHIT OL12 18 A2
Pridmouth Rd DID/WITH M20 143 E5
Priest Av CHD/CHDH SK8 169 F5
Priestley Rd WALK M28 98 B2
Priestley Wy ROY/SHW OL2 60 C2
Priestnall Rd HTNM SK4 158 C3
Priest St STKP SK1 13 H7
Priestwood Av OLDE OL4 61 E5
Primrose Av FWTH BL4 65 F3
HYDE SK14 147 H4
MPL/ROM SK6 174 D3
UPML OL3 79 F3
URM M41 * 138 D1
WALK M28 81 G5
Primrose Bank ALT WA14 177 F3
OLDS OL8 8 E7
TOT/BURYW BL8 25 H4
WALK M28 81 G5
Primrose Cl BOLE BL2 35 H2
ORD M5 113 E3
Primrose Cottages
ALT WA14 * 177 F3
Primrose Crs HYDE SK14 147 H3
Primrose Dr BURY BL9 39 G3
DROY M43 118 B2
Primrose St ANC M4 7 J2
BOL BL1 * 34 A2
FWTH BL4 66 B5
OLDS OL8 9 F6
WHIT OL12 29 G3
Primrose Wk OLDS OL8 9 F6
Primula St BOL BL1 34 A2
Prince Albert Av
BNG/LEV M19 * 144 A1
Prince Charlie St OLD OL1 76 A4
Princedom St BKLY M9 103 F2
Prince Edward Av
DTN/ASHW M34 146 D1
OLDE OL4 76 B5
Prince George St OLD OL1 76 B3
Prince Mead Pl TRPK M17 125 G3
Prince Rd POY/DIS SK12 196 B2
Prince's Av BOLS/LL BL3 51 E5
DID/WITH M20 157 H2
IRL M44 122 D5
MPL/ROM SK6 161 H3
Princes Ct ECC M30 * 111 E2
Prince's Dr MPL/ROM SK6 174 D2
SALE M33 155 E3
Princes Rd ALT WA14 165 G3
HTNM SK4 158 D2
MPL/ROM SK6 161 H3
SALE M33 154 D3
Princess Av CHD/CHDH SK8 182 D1
DTN/ASHW M34 132 B5
FWTH BL4 82 C2
PWCH M25 86 B5
WHIT OL12 19 H4
Princess Cl DUK SK16 120 A5
HEY OL10 41 E5
MOSL OL5 109 F2
Princess Dr MDTN M24 72 B4
Princess Gv FWTH BL4 66 A4
Princess Pde BURY BL9 4 E5
RUSH/FAL M14 142 B2
Princess Pkwy
WYTH/NTH M22 156 B5
Princess Rd CHAD OL9 89 H4
DID/WITH M20 156 C3
HOR/BR BL6 46 C2
HULME M15 128 A3
MILN OL16 31 E4
PWCH M25 * 86 B3
ROY/SHW OL2 59 H3
URM M41 138 B1
WILM/AE SK9 198 C5
Princess St ALT WA14 165 F1
AUL OL6 120 A1
BOL BL1 3 F5
CMANW M2 6 E5
ECC M30 110 D3
FAIL M35 104 D3
HYDE SK14 148 A1
OLDE OL4 92 D1
RAD M26 67 H1
SLFD M6 113 F1
SWIN M27 99 F3
WHIT OL12 10 D3
Prince's St STKP SK1 13 F3
Prince St BOL BL1 2 D2
HEY OL10 41 E4
MILN OL16 43 G1
OLD OL1 9 J3
RAMS BL0 16 D2
Princes Wk BRAM/HZG SK7 184 B5
Princethorpe Cl HOR/BR BL6 47 E3
Princeton Cl SLFD M6 112 B2
Prinknash Rd
WYTH/NTH M22 180 C3
Printers Cl BNG/LEV M19 158 A4
Printers Dr STLY SK15 109 H3
Printers La EDGW/EG BL7 23 H5
Printer St OLD OL1 9 G4
OP/CLY M11 * 117 E5
Printon Av BKLY M9 87 G4
Printworks La BNG/LEV M19 144 C2
Printworks Rd STLY SK15 121 E2
Prior St OLDS OL8 92 A3
Priory Av BRO M7 101 F4
CCHDY M21 141 F3
Priory Cl DUK SK16 133 G2
OLDS OL8 91 E4
SALE M33 140 B5
Priory Ct RDSH SK5 145 E3
Priory Gv BRO M7 101 F4
CHAD OL9 90 B3
Priory La RDSH SK5 145 E3
Priory Pl BOLE BL2 34 D4
Priory Rd ALT WA14 177 E4
CHD/CHDH SK8 170 D4
SALE M33 155 E1
SWIN M27 98 D2
WILM/AE SK9 198 B2
Priory St ALT WA14 177 F4
The Priory BRO M7 101 F4
Pritchard St CMANE M1 * 7 G7
Privet St OLDE OL4 76 C3
Proctor St TOT/BURYW BL8 37 H5
Progress Av DTN/ASHW M34 132 C3
Progress St AUL OL6 119 F2
BOL BL1 34 A5
ROCH OL11 42 B5
Promenade St HEY OL10 41 F4
Propps Hall Dr FAIL M35 104 D4

Prospect Av *FWTH* BL4 .... 66 A5
  IRL M44 .... 136 A5
Prospect Ct *TOT/BURYW* BL8...... 26 A4
Prospect Dr *FAIL* M35 .... 105 E5
  HALE/TIMP WA15 .... 179 E5
Prospect Hl *BOLE* BL2 .... 35 C2
Prospect Pl *AUL* OL6 .... 107 C5
  FWTH BL4 .... 65 H5
  HEY OL10 .... 41 E3
Prospect Rd *AUL* OL6 .... 107 H5
  CHAD OL9 .... 8 A2
  IRL M44 .... 136 A5
Prospect St *BOL* BL1 .... 34 A5
  HEY OL10 .... 56 B1
  LIT OL15 * 21 E2
  ROCH OL11 .... 42 B5
Prospect Ter *TOT/BURYW* BL8..... 4 A1
Prospect V *CHD/CHDH* SK8 ...... 181 G3
Prospect Vw *SWIN* M27 .... 99 F3
Prout St *WGTN/LGST* M12 .... 129 H1
Provender Cl *ALT* WA14 .... 165 C1
Providence Av *ANC* M4............. 115 G4
  AUL OL6 .... 119 E4
  BOLS/LL BL3 .... 49 E4
  DTN/ASHW M34 .... 132 B3
Providence St *BNG/LEV* M19 .... 144 C2
Provident St *ROY/SHW* OL2 * 60 A2
Provident Wy
  HALE/TIMP WA15 .... 166 B2
Provis Rd *CCHDY* M21 .... 141 F4
Prubella Av *DTN/ASHW* M34 ..... 132 B3
Pryce St *BOL* BL1 .... 33 H5
Pryme St *HULME* M15............... 127 H1
Pudding La *HYDE* SK14 .... 134 D5
Puffin Av *POY/DIS* SK12 .... 194 B4
Puffingate Cl *STLY* SK15........... 109 F3
Pulborough Cl
  TOT/BURYW BL8 .... 26 C4
Pulford Av *CCHDY* M21 .... 141 F4
Pulford Rd *SALE* M33 .... 154 D3
Pullman Cl *BNG/LEV* M19 .... 144 B3
Pullman Dr *STRET* M32 .... 139 F1
Pullman St *ROCH* OL11............. 43 E1
Punch La *BOLS/LL* BL3 .... 63 E2
Punch St *BOLS/LL* BL3 .... 2 B7
Purbeck Cl *WYTH/NTH* M22 ..... 180 B3
Purbeck Dr *HOR/BR* BL6 .... 46 A1
  TOT/BURYW BL8 .... 26 C5
Purcell Cl *BOL* BL1 .... 33 G5
Purcell St *WGTN/LGST* M12 ..... 129 H5
Purdon St *BURY* BL9 .... 27 G5
Purley Av *NTHM/RTH* M23 .... 156 A4
Purley Dr *IRL* M44 .... 150 B1
Purple St *BOL* BL1 .... 3 J4
Purslow Cl *WGTN/LGST* M12 .... 114 A4
Putney Cl *OLD* OL1 .... 75 F3
Pygmate Dr *CHD/CHDH* SK8 .... 181 F2
Pygmate La *CHD/CHDH* SK8 .... 181 F2
Pym St *ECC* M30 .... 111 C3
  HEY OL10 .... 40 D5
  NEWH/MOS M40 .... 103 G2
Pyramid Ct *BRO* M7 .... 101 C4
Pyrus St *ECC* M30 .... 110 A5
Pytha Fold Rd
  DID/WITH M20 .... 158 A1

Q
The Quadrant *BKLY* M9............. 88 D4
  DROY M43 .... 117 G4
  MPL/ROM SK6..................... 161 H4
  STKP SK1 .... 160 C5
Quail Dr *IRL* M44 .... 122 B5
Quail St *OLDE* OL4 .... 92 B2
Quakers Fld
  TOT/BURYW BL8 .... 26 A3
Quantock Cl *HTNM* SK4............ 12 E1
Quantock Dr *OLDS* OL9.............. 91 C4
Quantock St
  OLDTF/WHR M16 * 127 H4
Quarmby Rd *GTN* M18 .... 131 E4
Quarry Bank Rd
  WILM/AE SK9 .... 191 E4
Quarry Clough *STLY* SK15........ 121 G5
Quarry Hts *STLY* SK15............. 120 C5
Quarry La *UPML* OL3 .... 78 A3
Quarry Pond Rd *WALK* M28 ...... 81 E4
Quarry Ri *MPL/ROM* SK6 .... 162 A4
  STLY SK15........................... 120 C5
Quarry Rd *FWTH* BL4 .... 66 D5
  MPL/ROM SK6..................... 162 A4
Quarry St *MPL/ROM* SK6 .... 162 A1
  RAD M26 .... 68 C1
  RAMS BL0 .... 17 E2
  STLY SK15........................... 120 C4
  WHIT OL12 .... 10 B3
Quarry Wk *OP/CLY* M11 * 116 A4
Quayside Cl *WALK* M28............. 96 C3
The Quays *SALQ* M50............. 126 C1
Quay St *CSLFD* M3..................... 6 B5
  CSLFD M3.............................. 6 C3
  HEY OL10 .... 41 F5
Quay Vw *ORD* M5 .... 113 F5
Quebec Pl *BOLS/LL* BL3 .... 48 D4
Quebec St *BOLS/LL* BL3 .... 48 C4
  CHAD OL9............................. 8 A5
  DTN/ASHW M34 .... 132 B4
Queen Alexandra Cl
  ORD M5 *........................... 113 H5
Queen Ann Dr *WALK* M28 .... 96 C3
Queenhill Dr *HYDE* SK14 .... 148 A4
Queenhill Rd
  WYTH/NTH M22 * 156 D5
Queen's Av *EDGW/EG* BL7 ...... 23 E3
  MPL/ROM SK6..................... 161 H3
  WHIT OL12 .... 19 H4
Queensbrook *BOL* BL1............... 2 C4
Queensbury Cl *BOL* BL1........... 33 G1
  WILM/AE SK9 .... 199 G2
Queensbury Pde
  NEWH/MOS M40 * 115 H2
  HYDE SK14 .... 148 A4
  MPL/ROM SK6...................... 96 A3
Queens Ct
  NEWH/MOS M40 .... 103 E5

Queens Dr *CHD/CHDH* SK8 ...... 182 D1
  HTNM SK4............................ 158 D4
  HYDE SK14 .... 148 B4
  PWCH M25............................ 86 B5
  ROCH OL11 .... 42 D3
Queensferry St
  NEWH/MOS M40................... 104 B4
Queensgate *BOL* BL1 .... 48 A1
  BRAM/HZG SK7.................... 193 H2
Queensgate Dr *ROY/SHW* OL2.. 58 D3
Queen's Gv *WGTN/LGST* M12.... 129 H4
Queensland Rd *GTN* M18......... 130 A3
Queensmere Dr *SWIN* M27....... 99 F2
Queens Pk *BOL* BL1 * 2 A5
Queen's Park *HEY* OL10 .... 41 E3
Queen's Pl *BURY* BL9 .... 26 D1
Queen's Rd *AUL* OL6................ 107 H5
  BOLS/LL BL3 .... 48 A5
  BRAM/HZG SK7.................... 185 F1
  CHAD OL9............................ 74 B5
  CHD/CHDH SK8.................... 170 C5
  CHH M8.............................. 102 C5
  HALE/TIMP WA15................ 177 H1
  LIT OL15 * 21 E3
  MPL/ROM SK6..................... 161 H3
  NEWH/MOS M40.................. 103 E5
  OLDS OL8 .... 9 J6
  SALE M33 .... 154 A2
  URM M41............................ 138 D2
  WILM/AE SK9 .... 198 D4
Queenston Rd
  DID/WITH M20..................... 157 F2
Queen St *AUL* OL6 .... 120 A2
  BOL BL1 .... 2 D5
  BURY BL9 .... 5 G4
  CHD/CHDH SK8.................... 170 B3
  CSLFD M3.............................. 6 C2
  CSLFD M3.............................. 6 C3
  DTN/ASHW M34 .... 132 B4
  DTN/ASHW M34 .... 132 C2
  DUK SK16 .... 119 G4
  ECC M30 *........................... 111 C4
  FAIL M35............................. 104 D3
  FWTH BL4 .... 66 A4
  HEY OL10 .... 41 F4
  HYDE SK14 .... 148 A2
  LHULT M38............................ 81 C4
  LIT OL15 * 21 E3
  MDTN M24........................... 72 C5
  MOSL OL5 .... 108 D1
  MPL/ROM SK6..................... 175 E3
  OLD OL1 .... 9 H3
  RAD M26 .... 68 D2
  RAMS BL0 .... 16 D2
  ROY/SHW OL2 .... 59 E5
  ROY/SHW OL2 .... 60 A3
  SLFD M6............................. 100 A5
  STLY SK15........................... 120 D3
  TOT/BURYW BL8 .... 37 F1
  WHIT OL12 .... 10 D4
Queen St West
  DID/WITH M20..................... 142 D4
Queens Vw *LIT* OL15................. 20 D5
Queensway *BNG/LEV* M19 .... 144 A4
  CHD/CHDH SK8.................... 181 H4
  DUK SK16 .... 134 A1
  FWTH BL4 .... 82 C1
  IRL M44 .... 136 B1
  MOSL OL5 .... 109 E3
  PART M31............................ 151 E2
  POY/DIS SK12 .... 195 E4
  ROCH OL11 .... 42 C3
  SWIN M27 .... 84 B5
  UPML OL3 .... 95 E1
  URM M41............................ 124 D4
  WALK M28............................ 96 C2
Queen Victoria St *ECC* M30....... 110 D3
  ROCH OL11 .... 43 F1
Quenby St *HULME* M15........... 127 C2
Quendon Av *BRO* M7 .... 114 D1
Quickedge La *OLDE* OL4 .... 93 G3
Quickedge Rd *MOSL* OL5.......... 93 H5
Quick Rd *MOSL* OL5................. 93 H5
Quick Vw *MOSL* OL5 .... 94 B4
Quill Ct *IRL* M44 .... 136 A5
Quilter Gv *BKLY* M9.................. 87 H5
Quinney Crs
  OLDTF/WHR M16................. 128 A5
Quinn St *OP/CLY* M11............. 116 B4
Quinton *WHIT* OL12 .... 10 E5
Quinton Wk *BRUN/LGST* M13 .. 128 C2

R
Rabbit La *HYDE* SK14............... 135 H2
Raby St *OLDTF/WHR* M16 .... 127 H4
  RUSH/FAL M14 .... 128 A4
Racecourse Rd *WILM/AE* SK9.. 198 C4
Racecourse Rd *WILM/AE* SK9.. 198 C4
Racefield Rd *ALT* WA14........... 165 F5
The Race *WILM/AE* SK9 .... 192 A5
Rachel St *WGTN/LGST* M12..... 115 F5
Rackhouse Rd
  NTHM/RTH M23.................... 156 A5
Radbourne Cl
  WGTN/LGST M12 .... 129 H2
Radbourne Gv *BOLS/LL* BL3...... 47 G5
Radcliffe Moor Rd *BOLE* BL2..... 51 E4
Radcliffe New Rd *RAD* M26....... 50 C5
Radcliffe Park Crs *SLFD* M6....... 99 H5
Radcliffe Park Rd *SLFD* M6........ 99 H5
Radcliffe Rd *BOLE* BL2............... 3 J5
  BOLS/LL BL3 .... 50 D5
  BURY BL9 .... 5 J7
  OLDE OL4 .... 76 C2
Radcliffe St *OLD* OL1................. 9 G2
  OLDE OL4 .... 93 F1
  ROY/SHW OL2 .... 59 F5
Raddenbury St *CHAD* OL9........ 74 D2
Radlan Gv *RAD* M26 .... 51 C5
Radford Cl *OFTN* SK2.............. 173 E2
Radford Dr *BKLY* M9 .... 103 F2
  IRL M44.............................. 121 H5
Radford St *BRO* M7................ 101 H1
Radium St *ANC* M4 .... 7 J2
Radlet Dr *HALE/TIMP* WA15 ... 166 B1

Radlett Wk *BRUN/LGST* M13 *.. 128 D3
Radley Cl *BOL* BL1................... 33 G5
  SALE M33 .... 153 G3
Radley St *DROY* M43 .... 117 F5
  OLDTF/WHR M16 .... 128 A5
Radnor Av *DTN/ASHW* M34 .... 131 G5
Radnor Dr
  CHD/CHDH SK8.................... 170 C5
Radnor St *CHAD* OL9................ 8 A4
  GTN M18............................ 130 B4
  HULME M15......................... 127 H3
  STRET M32......................... 140 B2
Radstock Cl *BOL* BL1............... 22 D4
  RUSH/FAL M14 .... 142 D2
Radstock Rd *STRET* M32.......... 140 A1
Raeburn Dr *MPL/ROM* SK6..... 175 G1
Rae St *EDGY/DAV* SK3............. 12 B5
Raglan Av *SWIN* M27 .... 84 C5
Raglan Cl *OP/CLY* M11 .... 116 B3
Raglan Dr *ALT* WA14 .... 165 H1
Raglan Rd *SALE* M33 .... 154 A3
  STRET M32.......................... 125 G5
Raglan St *BOL* BL1.................. 34 A5
  HYDE SK14 .... 147 C1
  ROCH OL11 .... 42 B5
Raglan Wk *HULME* M15 * 128 A2
Ragley Cl *POY/DIS* SK12........... 195 G3
Raikes La *BOLS/LL* BL3............. 49 C5
Raikes Rd *BOLS/LL* BL3............ 50 A4
Raikes Wy *BOLS/LL* BL3........... 50 A4
Railton Av *OLDTF/WHR* M16.... 127 C5
Railton Ter *BKLY* M9................ 103 C3
Railway Ap *ROCH* OL11 .... 43 F4
Railway Rd *CHAD* OL9................ 8 C5
  CHAD OL9............................ 90 B5
  STKP SK1 .... 13 F5
  STRET M32......................... 126 C3
  URM M41............................ 138 D1
Railway St *ALT* WA14.............. 165 G5
  BURY BL9 .... 26 C1
  DUK SK16 .... 13 F6
  FWTH BL4 .... 66 B3
  GTN M18............................ 130 B2
  HEY OL10 .... 41 F5
  HTNM SK4............................ 12 E3
  LIT OL15 .... 21 E3
  MILN OL16........................... 10 B5
  MPL/ROM SK6..................... 175 G3
  RAD M26 .... 68 B2
  RAMS BL0 .... 16 D2
Railway Ter *TOT/BURYW* BL8... 37 H5
Railway Vw *OLDE* OL4.............. 93 E1
  ROY/SHW OL2 .... 60 B1
Raimond St *BOL* BL1 .... 33 F3
Rainbow Cl *CCHDY* M21.......... 141 F4
Raincliff Av *RUSH/FAL* M14 .... 143 H1
Rainford Av *DID/WITH* M20..... 142 C3
  HALE/TIMP WA15................ 166 B4
Rainford St *BOLE* BL2 .... 23 H5
Rainforth St *BRUN/LGST* M13 . 129 C5
Rainham Dr *CHH* M8............... 102 B3
Rainham Wy *CHAD* OL9............ 90 C1
  RDSH SK5........................... 145 H5
Rainow Av *DROY* M43.............. 117 H3
Rainow Dr *POY/DIS* SK12........ 195 H5
Rainow Rd *EDGY/DAV* SK3...... 171 F3
Rainshaw St *BOL* BL1................ 34 A2
  OLDE OL4 *............................. 76 C4
Rainsough Av *PWCH* M25......... 100 C1
Rainsough Brow *PWCH* M25..... 100 C1
Rainsough Cl *PWCH* M25......... 100 D1
Rainwood *CHAD* OL9................ 73 H4
Raja Cl *CHH* M8...................... 102 C3
Rake Cl *BOLE* BL2..................... 24 B4
Rake La *SWIN* M27 .... 84 A4
Rake St *BURY* BL9 .... 38 C2
Rakewood Dr *OLDE* OL4 .... 60 D5
Rakewood Rd *LIT* OL15 .... 21 E5
Raleigh Cl *DID/WITH* M20....... 157 F1
  OLD OL1 .... 75 G4
Raleigh St *RDSH* SK5.............. 159 H2
  STRET M32......................... 140 B1
Ralph Av *HYDE* SK14................ 148 A5
Ralph Green St *CHAD* OL9........ 90 C5
Ralphs La *DUK* SK16............... 133 F1
Ralph St *BOL* BL1 .... 33 G4
  OP/CLY M11........................ 117 E4
  WHIT OL12 .... 10 E3
Ralston Cl *BRO* M7.................. 102 A2
Ralstone Av *OLDS* OL8............. 91 G3
Ramage Wk *WGTN/LGST* M12.. 115 H4
Ramillies Av *CHD/CHDH* SK8.. 183 E5
Ramp Rd East *MANAIR* M90..... 180 B5
Ramp Rd South *MANAIR* M90.. 180 B5
Ramp Rd West *MANAIR* M90.... 180 A5
Ramsay Av *FWTH* BL4............... 65 G5
Ramsay Pl *MILN* OL16.............. 10 E5
Ramsay St *BOL* BL1 .... 33 H2
  MILN OL16........................... 10 E5
Ramsay Ter *MILN* OL16 * 10 E5
Ramsbottom Rd
  TOT/BURYW BL8 .... 24 D1
Ramsdale Rd *BRAM/HZG* SK7.. 183 H4
Ramsdale St *CHAD* OL9............ 74 B5
Ramsden Cl *OLD* OL1................. 8 E2
Ramsden Crs *OLD* OL1.............. 8 E2
Ramsden Fold *SWIN* M27......... 84 A4
Ramsden Rd *WHIT* OL12........... 15 H5
Ramsden St *AUL* OL6.............. 119 C1
  BOLS/LL BL3 .... 50 A4
  OLD OL1 .... 8 E2
Ramsey Av *BNG/LEV* M19....... 144 B3
Ramsey Gv *TOT/BURYW* BL8... 37 G4
Ramsey St *CHAD* OL9................ 90 C2
  NEWH/MOS M40.................. 104 A3
  OLD OL1 .... 76 A4
Ramsgate Rd
  NEWH/MOS M40.................. 104 A4
  RDSH SK5........................... 145 H4
Ramsgate St *BRO* M7............. 101 H5
Ramsgill Cl *NTHM/RTH* M23... 155 H5
Ramsgreave Cl *BURY* BL9......... 53 E2
Ram St *LHULT* M38.................. 81 E3
Ramwell Gdns *BOLS/LL* BL3 *.. 48 C4
Ramwells Brow *EDGW/EG* BL7. 23 E3

Ramwells Ct *EDGW/EG* BL7 *.... 23 G3
Ramwells Ms *EDGW/EG* BL7 *.. 23 G3
Ranby Av *BKLY* M9................... 103 G2
Randale Dr *BURY* BL9................ 69 H2
Randal St *BOLS/LL* BL3............. 48 B5
Randerson St
  WGTN/LGST M12 .... 129 G2
Randlesham St *PWCH* M25........ 86 B3
Randolph Pl *EDGY/DAV* SK3..... 13 F7
Randolph Rd *FWTH* BL4............ 66 C5
Randolph St *BNG/LEV* M19..... 144 A1
  OLDS OL8............................ 90 D5
  OLDS OL8.............................. 8 A6
Rands Clough Dr *WALK* M28..... 96 C4
Rand St *OLD* OL1 .... 76 C3
Ranelagh Rd *SWIN* M27 .... 99 H3
Ranelagh St *OP/CLY* M11........ 116 C3
Raneley Gv *ROCH* OL11............ 43 F4
Ranford Rd *BNG/LEV* M19...... 144 A5
Range Dr *MPL/ROM* SK6......... 147 D5
Rangemore Av
  WYTH/NTH M22 * 168 C1
Range Rd *DUK* SK16................ 134 C2
  EDGY/DAV SK3.................... 171 H3
  OLDTF/WHR M16................. 127 H5
  STLY SK15........................... 121 E5
Range St *BOLS/LL* BL3.............. 48 C5
  OP/CLY M11........................ 116 D5
Rankine Ter *BOLS/LL* BL3 * 48 C5
Rannoch Rd *BOLE* BL2............. 50 C2
Ransfield Rd *CCHDY* M21........ 141 E1
Ranulph Ct *SLFD* M6 * 100 A5
Ranworth Av *HTNM* SK4......... 158 C4
Ranworth Cl *BOL* BL1................ 23 G1
  OP/CLY M11........................ 116 C5
Raper St *OLDE* OL4................... 76 B4
Raphael St *BOL* BL1.................. 33 F3
Rappax Rd *HALE/TIMP* WA15.. 178 B4
Rassbottom Brow *STLY* SK15... 120 C3
Rassbottom St *STLY* SK15....... 120 C3
Ratcliffe Av *MPL/ROM* SK6..... 136 C1
Ratcliffe St *BNG/LEV* M19...... 144 B2
  SLFD M6.............................. 13 C6
Rathan Rd *URM* M41............... 124 D4
Rathbone St *MILN* OL16........... 11 J7
Rathbourne Av *BKLY* M9 .... 88 A4
Rathen Rd *DID/WITH* M20...... 157 G1
Rathen Rd *NTHM/RTH* M23.... 155 C4
Rathmore Av
  NEWH/MOS M40.................. 103 H5
Rathvale Dr *WYTH/NTH* M22.. 180 B4
Rathybank Cl *BOL* BL1............. 33 F5
Rattenbury Ct *SLFD* M6............ 99 H5
Raveden Cl *BOL* BL1 .... 33 F3
Raveley Av *RUSH/FAL* M14..... 143 E3
Ravelston Dr *BKLY* M9............. 103 E4
Raven Av *CHAD* OL9................. 90 B2
Raven Cl *DROY* M43................ 118 B2
  HALE/TIMP WA15................ 154 C5
Ravendale Cl *WHIT* OL12........... 29 E2
Raven Dr *IRL* M44................... 122 B5
Ravenfield Gv *BOL* BL1 *........... 33 F2
Ravenhead Cl *RUSH/FAL* M14.. 143 F3
Ravenhead Sq *STLY* SK15....... 109 H3
Ravenhurst Dr *BOL* BL1............ 33 E1
Ravenna Av *NTHM/RTH* M23... 167 E2
Ravenoak Av *BNG/LEV* M19.... 144 B3
Ravenoak Dr *FAIL* M35............ 105 C2
Ravenoak Park Rd
  CHD/CHDH SK8.................... 183 C4
  OFTN SK2............................ 172 B5
Raven Rd *BOLS/LL* BL3 * 47 H5
Ravensbury St *OP/CLY* M11.... 116 C2
Ravenscar Crs
  WYTH/NTH M22................... 180 C4
Ravens Cl *PART* M31................ 150 B2
Ravenscraig Rd *LHULT* M38....... 81 C1
Ravensdale Gdns *ECC* M30...... 111 F2
Ravensdale St *RUSH/FAL* M14.. 128 D5
Ravens Holme *BOL* BL1............. 47 F1
Ravenside Pk *CHAD* OL9........... 90 B2
Ravenstonedale Dr
  ROY/SHW OL2 .... 59 F1
Ravenstone Dr *SALE* M33....... 155 F1
  UPML OL3 .... 79 F1
Raven St *BURY* BL9 .... 26 C4
  ROCH OL11 .... 43 G3
Ravensway *PWCH* M25............. 86 C5
Ravens Wd *BOL* BL1.................. 47 F1
Ravenswood Av *HTNM* SK4..... 158 D5
Ravenswood Dr *BKLY* M9 .... 88 B4
  BOL BL1 .... 33 G1
  CHD/CHDH SK8.................... 183 G4
Ravenswood Rd *STRET* M32.... 126 C5
  WILM/AE SK9 .... 200 C3
Raven Wy *SLFD* M6................ 113 C2
Ravenwood *CHAD* OL9.............. 73 C5
Ravenwood Dr
  DTN/ASHW M34 .... 132 B2
  HALE/TIMP WA15................ 179 E5
Ravine Av *BKLY* M9................. 103 G2
Rawcliffe Av *BOLE* BL2............. 50 C2
Rawcliffe St *RUSH/FAL* M14.... 128 C5
Rawdon Cl *BNG/LEV* M19....... 144 A1
Rawkin Cl *HULME* M15........... 127 H3
Rawlyn Rd *BOL* BL1 .... 32 C5
Rawpool Gdns
  NTHM/RTH M23.................... 167 H2
Rawson Av *FWTH* BL4............... 66 A3
Rawson Rd *BOL* BL1.................. 33 F5
Rawsons Rake
  TOT/BURYW BL8 .... 16 B2
Rawson St *FWTH* BL4............... 66 A3
Rawsthorne Av *GTN* M18........ 144 D1
Rawsthorne St *AUL* OL6.......... 119 F2
Raycroft Av *BKLY* M9................ 88 D5
Raydon Av *NEWH/MOS* M40 *.. 103 E4
Rayleigh Av *OP/CLY* M11......... 131 E1
Raymond Av *BURY* BL9............ 53 G2
  CHAD OL9............................ 90 B3
Raymond Rd *NTHM/RTH* M23.. 156 A4
Raymond St *SWIN* M27 .... 99 E1
Rayner La *AULW* OL7.............. 118 C4
Rayners Cl *STLY* SK15.............. 120 C4
Rayner St *STKP* SK1................ 172 C1

Raynham Av *DID/WITH* M20.... 157 G3
Raynham St *AUL* OL6............... 119 H2
Rayson Hill Dr *BKLY* M9............. 87 H5
Reabrock Av
  WGTN/LGST M12 .... 129 G2
The Reach *WALK* M28............... 82 B5
Read Cl *BURY* BL9 .... 53 E2
  ROY/SHW OL2 .... 60 A2
Reade Av *URM* M41................ 137 G2
Reading Cl *OP/CLY* M11.......... 116 B5
Reading Dr *SALE* M33............. 153 G2
Reading St *SLFD* M6................ 101 E5
Readitt Wk *OP/CLY* M11.......... 116 C5
Read St *HYDE* SK14................. 133 F5
Read St West *HYDE* SK14........ 133 F5
Reaney Wk
  WGTN/LGST M12 .... 129 H2
Reather Wk *NEWH/MOS* M40 .. 115 G2
Rebecca St *CHH* M8................ 102 B2
Recreation Av *FAIL* M35........... 105 F1
Recreation St *BOLE* BL2............ 35 F1
  BOLS/LL BL3 .... 48 D5
  PWCH M25............................ 86 A3
Rectory Av *CHH* M8................ 102 B1
  PWCH M25............................ 86 A3
Rectory Cl *DTN/ASHW* M34..... 147 E1
  RAD M26............................. 53 E5
Rectory Flds *STKP* SK1............... 13 J3
Rectory Gdns *PWCH* M25......... 85 H5
Rectory Gn *PWCH* M25............. 85 H5
  STKP SK1 .... 13 J3
Rectory Gv *PWCH* M25............. 86 A4
Rectory La *BURY* BL9................ 39 C5
  PWCH M25............................ 85 H5
  RAD M26 .... 68 C1
Rectory Rd *CHH* M8................ 102 A1
  MPL/ROM SK6...................... 72 C3
  PART M31........................... 150 D4
Redacre *POY/DIS* SK12............ 195 C1
Redacre Rd *GTN* M18.............. 130 D3
Red Bank *ANC* M4................... 114 D2
Red Bank Rd *RAD* M26............. 52 A4
Redbarn Cl *MPL/ROM* SK6...... 147 D5
Redbourne Dr *URM* M41......... 123 G4
Redbrick Ct *AULW* OL7........... 119 F4
Redbrook Av
  NEWH/MOS M40.................. 103 F5
Redbrook Cl *FWTH* BL4 * 66 B3
Redbrook Rd
  HALE/TIMP WA15................ 167 G3
  PART M31........................... 150 D4
Red Brook St *ROCH* OL11......... 29 G4
Redbrow Hollow
  MPL/ROM SK6...................... 163 F4
Redburn Rd *NTHM/RTH* M23.. 168 A2
Redby St *OP/CLY* M11............. 130 A1
Redcar Av *DID/WITH* M20....... 142 D5
  URM M41............................ 123 H4
Redcar Cl *BRAM/HZG* SK7....... 185 E4
  OLD OL1 .... 76 A3
Redcar Rd *BOL* BL1.................. 33 E2
  BOLS/LL BL3 .... 66 D1
  SWIN M27 .... 99 H5
Redcote St *NEWH/MOS* M40 ... 103 H2
Redcourt Av *DID/WITH* M20.... 157 G2
Redcroft Gdns *BNG/LEV* M19.. 158 B2
Redcroft Rd *SALE* M33............ 139 E5
Redcross St *WHIT* OL12............ 10 C4
Redcross St North *WHIT* OL12.. 10 C3
Reddaway Cl *SLFD* M6............. 100 D5
Reddish Cl *BOLE* BL2 .... 35 F1
Reddish La *GTN* M18............... 130 D5
Reddish Rd *RDSH* SK5............. 145 F5
Reddish Vale Rd *RDSH* SK5..... 145 G4
Redesmere Cl *DROY* M43......... 118 A4
  HALE/TIMP WA15................ 167 E3
Redesmere Dr
  CHD/CHDH SK8.................... 170 C5
  WILM/AE SK9 .... 199 G1
Redesmere Pk *URM* M41......... 138 B3
Redfearn Wd *WHIT* OL12.......... 29 E1
Redfern Av *SALE* M33.............. 155 F3
Redfern St *ANC* M4 .... 7 G2
Redfern Wy *ROCH* OL11........... 28 A2
Redfield Cl *OP/CLY* M11........... 116 A4
Redford Dr *BRAM/HZG* SK7.... 184 B2
Redford Rd *CHH* M8................. 87 E3
Redford St *TOT/BURYW* BL8.... 37 H5
Redgate *HALE/TIMP* WA15...... 167 E4
Redgate La *WGTN/LGST* M12.. 129 H5
Redgate Wk *CCHDY* M21 *....... 141 F2
Redgate Wy *FWTH* BL4............. 65 C5
Redgrave Pas *OLDE* OL4........... 76 C4
Redgrave St *OLDE* OL4............. 76 C4
Red Hall St *OLDE* OL4............... 92 B1
Redhill Dr *MPL/ROM* SK6........ 161 E3
Redhill Gv *BOL* BL1 .... 2 C1
Redhill St *ANC* M4..................... 7 J4
Redhouse La *MPL/ROM* SK6.... 162 B1
Redington Cl *WALK* M28........... 96 B5
Redisher Cl *RAMS* BL0.............. 16 A5
Redisher Cft *RAMS* BL0............. 16 A5
Redland Av *RDSH* SK5............. 160 A1
Redland Cl *LIT* OL15................. 21 E2
Redland Crs *CCHDY* M21......... 141 E5
Red La *BOLE* BL2...................... 35 C5
  POY/DIS SK12 .... 197 G2
  WHIT OL12 .... 11 C1
Red Lion St *ANC* M4 * 7 C3
Redmans Cl *ECC* M30............. 110 C4
Redmere Dr *BURY* BL9.............. 53 H1
Redmere Gv *RUSH/FAL* M14... 143 E3
Redmire Ms *DUK* SK16............ 134 A1
Redmond Cl *DTN/ASHW* M34.. 132 B1
Redmoor Sq *BRUN/LGST* M13. 128 C1
Redmoss Rw *SWIN* M27........... 100 A2
Red Pike Wk *OLD* OL1............... 75 H4
Redpoll Cl *WALK* M28................ 96 C3
Red Rock La *RAD* M26............... 83 C1
Red Rose Crs *BNG/LEV* M19.... 144 C4
Red Rose Rtl Pk *RAD* M26.......... 68 C1
Redruth St *RUSH/FAL* M14...... 142 C5
Redscar Av *BOLE* BL2 .... 23 H5

Redshaw Cl RUSH/FAL M14....143 F2
Redstart Gv WALK M28.........97 E2
Redstock Cl WHTN BL5.........62 B5
Redstone Rd BNG/LEV M19.....158 A3
Redthorn Av BNG/LEV M19.....143 H4
Redthorpe Cl BOLE BL2........34 C5
Redvale Rd BRO M7...........101 H4
Redvales Rd BURY BL9........53 F2
Redvers St OLD OL1...........8 D1
Redwater Cl WALK M28.........96 B4
Redwing Rd TOT/BURYW BL8....26 A1
Redwood CHAD OL9............75 G5
  SALE M33..................153 F2
  WHIT OL12..................18 A5
Redwood Dr CHH M8..........102 C5
  DTN/ASHW M34..............132 B2
  MPL/ROM SK6...............161 G3
Redwood La OLDE OL4..........93 G2
Redwood Park Gv MILN OL16...31 F4
Redwood Rd UPML OL3.........79 F5
Redwood St SLFD M6..........113 F1
Reeceton Gdns BOL BL1.......47 H2
Reedbank Rd M26.............65 G4
Reed Ct OLD OL1..............75 F4
Reedham Cl BOL BL1...........48 B1
Reedham Wk CHAD OL9.........90 D3
  NEWH/MOS M40.............115 G1
Reedley Dr WALK M28..........96 D2
Reedmace Cl WALK M28.........97 F1
Reedshaw Bank OFTN SK2.....175 E4
Reedshaw Rd BKLY M9........102 D4
Reed St GTN M18.............130 C2
  OLD OL1 *...................9 J3
Reeman Cl MPL/ROM SK6......161 H2
Reeve Cl OFTN SK2...........175 G4
Reeves Rd CCHDY M21........141 F4
Reevey Av BRAM/HZG SK7.....184 D4
Reform St WHIT OL12..........10 C4
Reform Wk OP/CLY M11.......116 C5
Regal Cl WHTF M45...........70 A4
Regal Fold WHIT OL12.........19 G4
Regan Av CCHDY M21.........141 H3
Regan St BOL BL1............33 G3
  RAD M26...................68 C2
Regatta Cl CHAD OL9..........90 B4
Regatta St SLFD M6...........100 C4
Regency Cl NEWH/MOS M40....103 G5
  OLDS OL8...................91 E3
Regency Ct
  HALE/TIMP WA15 *.........178 C3
  ROCH OL11..................28 C4
Regency Gdns
  HYDE SK14 *...............134 A4
Regency Ldg PWCH M25 *......85 H4
Regency Pk WILM/AE SK9.....198 C5
Regent Av LHULT M38.........81 H5
Regent Cl BRAM/HZG SK7.....193 H3
  CHD/CHDH SK8.............171 F5
  HEY OL10...................40 C5
  WILM/AE SK9...............198 C5
Regent Ct HTNM SK4.........159 F1
Regent Crs FAIL M35.........104 D4
  ROY/SHW OL7...............75 E2
Regent Dr DTN/ASHW M34.....146 B2
  HOR/BR BL6.................46 C2
Regent Pl RUSH/FAL M14.....128 D4
Regent Rd ALT WA14.........145 E6
  HOR/BR BL6.................46 C3
  OFTN SK2.................172 B3
  ORD M5...................113 G5
Regents Dr MOSL OL5.........109 E3
Regents HI HOR/BR BL6........46 D3
Regents Pk ORD M5 *........113 H5
Regent Sq ORD M5...........113 G5
The Regents WILM/AE SK9.....199 F2
Regent St BURY BL9...........4 E1
  ECC M30...................111 G1
  HEY OL10...................40 C5
  LIT OL15...................21 E3
  MDTN M24...................72 C2
  NEWH/MOS M40.............104 C5
  OLD OL1 *...................9 J3
  RAMS BL0...................16 B4
  WHIT OL12..................10 D2
Regent Wk FWTH BL4 *........66 A4
Regina Av STLY SK15.........120 D3
Reginald St BOLS/LL BL3 *.....63 H2
  ECC M50...................110 B5
  OP/CLY M11................131 E1
  SWIN M27...................98 C1
Reid Cl DTN/ASHW M34.......147 E3
Reigate Cl TOT/BURYW BL8.....37 C5
Reigate Rd URM M41.........137 G3
Reilly St HULME M15.........127 H2
Reins Lee Av OLDS OL8........91 H5
Reins Lee Rd AULW OL7........90 C5
Reliance St NEWH/MOS M40...104 B4
Rembrandt Wk OLD OL1.......60 C4
Rena Cl HTNM SK4...........159 G3
Rendel Cl STRET M32........140 B1
Renfrew Dr BOLS/LL BL3......63 G1
Rennie Cl STRET M32........140 B1
Renshaw Av ECC M30.........111 E4
Renshaw Dr BURY BL9.........5 F4
Renshaw St ECC M30.........111 E4
Renton Rd BOLS/LL BL3........64 A1
  STRET M32.................140 C1
  WYTH/NTH M22.............180 B2
Renwick Gv BOL BL3..........48 A5
Repton Av DROY M43.........117 F2
  DTN/ASHW M34.............131 F5
  HYDE SK14................133 H5
  NEWH/MOS M40.............104 D1
  OLDS OL8...................91 E4
  URM M41..................137 F1
Repton Cl SALE M33..........155 E3
Reservoir Rd EDGY/DAV SK3...171 E2
Reservoir St CSLFD M3.........6 C1
  MILN OL16..................11 J4
  SLFD M6..................113 E3
The Residences PWCH M25......86 B4
Retford Av WHTN BL5.........43 G3
Retford Cl TOT/BURYW BL8.....38 B1
Retford St OLDE OL4 *.........92 A2
Retiro St OLD OL1.............9 H3
The Retreat MPL/ROM SK6....162 A5
Reuben St HTNM SK4.........159 H2

Revers St TOT/BURYW BL8......4 A3
Reverton Gn BRAM/HZG SK7...184 B2
Revcine Wy HYDE SK14.......134 B3
Reynard Rd CCHDY M21......141 F4
Reynard St HYDE SK14 *......133 C5
Reynell Rd BRUN/LGST M13...143 H1
Reyner St AUL OL6 *...........4 D5
  CMANE M1...................7 F6
Reynolds Dr GTN M18........130 C2
  MPL/ROM SK6...............175 G1
  WHTN BL5...................63 G5
Reynolds Rd
  OLDTF/WHR M16............127 F4
Reynold St HYDE SK14.......147 H1
Rhine Cl TOT/BURYW BL8......26 A4
Rhine Dr CHH M8.............101 H5
Rhiwlas Dr BURY BL9..........53 G1
Rhodes Av OLDE OL4..........93 G2
  UPML OL3...................79 F5
Rhodes Bank OLD OL1..........9 J4
Rhodes Crs ROCH OL11........43 E5
Rhodes Dr BURY BL9..........69 G2
Rhodes HI OLDE OL4...........93 G2
Rhodes St HYDE SK14........133 F5
  NEWH/MOS M40.............115 H1
  OLD OL1....................9 J3
  OLDE OL4...................19 G5
Rhodes St North HYDE SK14..133 F5
Rhode St TOT/BURYW BL8......26 A5
Rhos Av CHD/CHDH SK8......182 C3
  MDTN M24...................71 H1
  RUSH/FAL M14.............143 G3
Rhos Dr BRAM/HZG SK7.......185 E3
Rhosleigh Av BOL BL1.........33 F2
Rialto Gdns BRO M7 *........101 H4
Ribble Av BOLE BL2...........50 B2
  CHAD OL9...................74 A5
  LIT OL15...................20 C2
Ribble Dr BURY BL9...........27 G3
  FWTH BL4...................83 E2
  WALK M28...................96 A4
  WHTF M45...................69 H5
Ribble Rd OLDS OL8...........90 D4
Ribblesdale Cl HEY OL10 *.....56 B2
Ribblesdale Dr
  NEWH/MOS M40.............102 D5
Ribblesdale Rd BOLS/LL BL3....48 C5
Ribble St ROCH OL11..........42 D2
Ribbleton Cl TOT/BURYW BL8...37 E5
Ribchester Dr BURY BL9........53 E2
Ribchester Gv BOLE BL2........35 G4
Ribston St HULME M15.......127 H2
Rice St CSLFD M3..............6 B7
Richard Burch St BURY BL9......5 F2
Richards Cl DTN/ASHW M34...132 B1
Richardson Cl WHTF M45......69 G3
Richardson Rd ECC M30......111 F3
Richardson St OP/CLY M11...130 D1
  STKP SK1..................172 B2
Richard St FAIL M35.........105 E3
  RAD M26...................68 A1
  RAMS BL0...................17 F1
  STKP SK1...................13 H1
Richbell Cl IRL M44.........136 B4
Richborough Cl BRO M7......101 H5
Richelieu St BOLS/LL BL3......49 F5
Richmond Av CHAD OL9.......90 D5
  PWCH M25...................85 G5
  ROY/SHW OL2...............59 E5
  URM M41..................139 E1
  WILM/AE SK9...............192 A2
Richmond Cl DUK SK16.......133 G2
  MILN OL16..................29 H5
  MOSL OL5.................109 F2
  ROY/SHW OL2...............59 E5
  SALE M33..................155 G3
  STLY SK15.................120 D4
  TOT/BURYW BL8.............26 A5
  WHTF M45...................69 E5
Richmond Crs MOSL OL5.....109 F2
Richmond Dr WALK M28.......98 B2
Richmond Gdns BOLS/LL BL3...65 G1
Richmond Gn ALT WA14.......177 E2
  BRAM/HZG SK7..............194 A1
Richmond Gv
  BRUN/LGST M13............129 F4
  CHD/CHDH SK8.............182 C3
  FWTH BL4...................65 F3
Richmond Gv East
  WGTN/LGST M12............129 F5
Richmond Hill Rd
  CHD/CHDH SK8.............169 H4
Richmond Rd ALT WA14......165 G4
  ALT WA14..................177 E2
  DTN/ASHW M34 *...........131 F5
  DUK SK16..................133 G2
  FAIL M35...................158 C4
  HTNM SK4..................158 D2
  RUSH/FAL M14.............143 F3
  TRPK M17..................125 F1
Richmond St AULW OL7.......119 E1
  BURY BL9...................53 F1
  CMANE M1...................7 G5
  CSLFD M5....................6 B1
  DROY M43 *...............118 B3
  DTN/ASHW M34.............131 F5
  HYDE SK14................148 A1
  STLY SK15.................120 D4
Richmond Wk CHAD OL9........8 C4
Ricroft Rd MPL/ROM SK6.....163 G3
Ridding Av WYTH/NTH M22...180 D1
Ridding Cl OFTN SK2.........173 E3
Riddings Ct HALE/TIMP WA15..166 B1
Riddings Rd HALE/TIMP WA15..166 B1
  HALE/TIMP WA15...........178 A3
Ridge Av HALE/TIMP WA15....188 D1
  MPL/ROM SK6..............175 F5
Ridge Cl MPL/ROM SK6.......162 D4
Ridge Crs MPL/ROM SK6......162 D5
  WHTF M45...................70 A4
Ridgecroft AULW OL7........107 F4
The Ridgedales OLD OL1.......60 D5
Ridge End Fold
  MPL/ROM SK6..............187 F3
Ridgefield CMANW M2.........6 D5
Ridgefield St FAIL M35.......104 D4

Ridgegreen WALK M28 *......96 B5
Ridge Gv WHIT OL12.........70 A4
Ridge Hill La STLY SK15......120 D2
Ridgemont Av HTNM SK4.....159 E4
Ridge Pk BRAM/HZG SK7.....193 G1
Ridge Rd MPL/ROM SK6......175 F5
Ridgeway BOL BL1 *...........2 E4
  SWIN M27...................99 G1
Ridgeway Gates BOL BL1.......2 E4
Ridgeway Rd
  HALE/TIMP WA15...........166 D1
Ridgeway St NEWH/MOS M40..115 G3
Ridgeway St East
  POY/DIS SK12..............187 H5
Ridgewood Av CHAD OL9......73 H4
  NEWH/MOS M40............103 F5
Ridgmont Dr WALK M28........96 A4
Ridgmont Rd BRAM/HZG SK7..193 H5
The Ridgway MPL/ROM SK6...161 H5
Riding Cl SALE M33.........155 E3
Riding Fold DROY M43.......118 B2
Riding Fold La WALK M28......97 H5
Riding Ga BOLE BL2...........24 B5
Riding Gate Ms BOLE BL2......24 B5
Ridings Ct UPML OL3..........78 D2
Ridings St NEWH/MOS M40...103 G5
  OP/CLY M11................115 H5
Riding St CSLFD M3............6 B4
Ridley Av SALE M33..........155 H5
Ridley Gv SALE M33.........155 C3
Ridley St OLDE OL4...........9 K5
Ridley Wk HULME M15........128 A3
Ridling La HYDE SK14........148 A1
Ridsdale Av DID/WITH M20...142 C1
Ridyard St LHULT M38.........81 H3
Rifield BOL BL1...............33 E3
Rifle Rd SALE M33...........155 G1
Rifle St OLD OL1..............9 G1
Riga Rd RUSH/FAL M14......143 E2
Riga St ANC M4...............7 G2
Rigby Ct BOLS/LL BL3.........48 E5
Rigby Gv LHULT M38..........80 C3
Rigby La BOLE BL2............35 E1
Rigby St ALT WA14...........177 C1
  BOLS/LL BL3................49 E5
  BRO M7...................101 G3
Rigel St ANC M4.............115 F2
Rigton Cl WGTN/LGST M12...129 H1
Rildene Wk ROCH OL11.........28 A3
Riley Cl SALE M33...........155 C3
Riley Ct BOL BL1.............34 A5
Riley Wood Cl MPL/ROM SK6 *.161 G5
Rimington Fold MDTN M24....56 A5
Rimmer Cl OP/CLY M11.......115 H5
Rimmington Cl BKLY M9.......88 D5
Rimsdale Cl CHD/CHDH SK8..181 F1
Rimworth Dr
  NEWH/MOS M40.............115 F1
Ringcroft Gdns
  NEWH/MOS M40.............104 C3
Ringley Cha WHTF M45........69 E4
Ringley Dr WHTF M45.........69 E4
Ringley Gv BOL BL1...........33 H1
Ringley Hey WHTF M45........69 E4
Ringley Meadow RAD M26.....67 F5
Ringley Old Brow RAD M26....67 F4
Ringley Pk WHTF M45.........69 E4
Ringley Rd RAD M26..........68 C4
Ringley Rd West RAD M26....67 H4
Ringley St BKLY M9...........98 B3
Ringlow Av SWIN M27.........98 B5
Ringlow Park Rd SWIN M27....98 B5
Ring Lows La WHIT OL12......19 F4
Ringmer Dr WYTH/NTH M22..180 B3
Ringmere Ct OLD OL1 *........75 H3
Ringmore Rd BRAM/HZG SK7..184 B2
Rings Cl FAIL M35...........105 E4
Ringstead Cl WILM/AE SK9...199 G1
Ringstead Dr
  NEWH/MOS M40.............115 F2
  WILM/AE SK9...............199 G1
Ringstone PWCH M25..........85 H4
Ringway Av SALE M33........155 F4
Ringway Rd MANAIR M90.....193 G5
Ringway Rd West
  WYTH/NTH M22.............180 B4
Ringwood Av BRAM/HZG SK7..184 B2
  DTN/ASHW M34.............118 B4
  HYDE SK14.................148 C2
  RAD M26...................66 A4
  RAMS BL0...................16 B4
  WGTN/LGST M12............144 B1
Ringwood Wy CHAD OL9........8 A1
Ripley Av OFTN SK2..........172 D5
Ripley Cl ANC M4 *...........7 K3
  BRAM/HZG SK7..............185 F4
Ripley Crs URM M41.........123 G5
Ripley St BOLE BL2...........34 C2
Ripon Av BOL BL1............32 C5
  OLD OL1 *.................60 C1
  HALE/TIMP WA15...........178 D3
Ripon Cl CHAD OL9...........73 H4
  RAD M26...................53 E4
  STKP SK1...................13 J4
  WHTF M45...................69 G2
Ripon Crs STRET M32........125 E5
Ripon Dr BOL BL1............32 C5
Ripon Gv SALE M33.........139 F5
Ripon Hall Av RAMS BL0......16 C5
Ripon Rd STRET M32........125 F5
Ripon St AUL OL6 *..........119 F2
  OLD OL1...................75 E4
Rippenden Av CCHDY M21....141 E1
Rippingham Rd
  DID/WITH M20.............142 D4
Rippleton Rd WYTH/NTH M22..168 D5
Ripponden Rd OLDE OL4.......76 C3
Ripponden St OLD OL1..........9 K3
The Rise OLDE OL4............77 E5
Rishton Av BOLS/LL BL3........49 F5
Rishton La BOLS/LL BL3.......48 D5
Rishworth Cl OFTN SK2......173 E4
Rishworth Dr
  NEWH/MOS M40.............104 D2

Rishworth Ri ROY/SHW OL2....44 C5
Rising La OLDS OL8............91 F5
Risley Av BKLY M9............87 E3
Risley St OLD OL1.............75 G4
Rissington Av
  NTHM/RTH M23.............168 A3
Rita Av RUSH/FAL M14 *.....128 C5
Ritson Cl GTN M18...........130 A2
Riva Rd BNG/LEV M19........158 A4
Riverbank UPML OL3..........78 C3
Riverbank Dr TOT/BURYW BL8...8 A1
Riverbanks BOLS/LL BL3.......49 H4
The Riverbank RAD M26......66 C4
Riverbrook Rd ALT WA14.....155 F5
Riverdale Rd BKLY M9.........87 F4
River La PART M31...........151 E2
Rivermead MILN OL16..........45 E3
Rivermead Av
  HALE/TIMP WA15...........188 C1
Rivermead Cl DTN/ASHW M34.147 E4
Rivermead Rd
  DTN/ASHW M34.............147 F4
Riverpark Rd
  NEWH/MOS M40.............116 B2
River Pl HULME M15..........127 H1
  MILN OL16 *................31 G5
Riverside Av DID/WITH M20 *...136 C2
Riverside Ct MPL/ROM SK6 *..175 F1
Riverside Dr BURY BL9........16 C5
  MILN OL16..................11 J1
  RAD M26...................67 E2
  URM M41..................138 B3
Riverside Gdns SALE M33...139 G5
Riverside Rd RAD M26........53 E5
Rivers La URM M41..........124 B3
Riversmeade EDGW/EG BL7....23 E2
Riverstone Dr
  NTHM/RTH M23.............167 E2
River St BOLE BL2............35 E3
  HEY OL10...................41 E2
  HULME M15................128 A1
  MILN OL16..................10 D6
  RAD M26...................67 E3
  RAMS BL0...................17 F3
  STKP SK1 *.................13 G3
  WGTN/LGST M12 *.........115 F5
  WILM/AE SK9...............199 E2
Riverton Rd DID/WITH M20...169 G2
River Vw RDSH SK5...........145 G4
River View Cl PWCH M25.....100 C2
Riverview Wk BOL BL1 *.......2 A6
Rivington Cl ROY/SHW OL2....59 G3
  TOT/BURYW BL8.............37 F5
Rivington Crs SWIN M27......99 H3
Rivington Dr ROY/SHW OL2...60 C2
  TOT/BURYW BL8.............37 F5
Rivington Gv AULW OL7......106 D1
  CCHDY M21................141 G2
Rivington Rd
  HALE/TIMP WA15...........178 A2
  OLDE OL4...................77 F5
  SLFD M6...................112 B1
Rivington St OLDS OL8.........75 G4
Rixton St BOL BL1...........33 H4
Rixtonleys Dr IRL M44.......136 D5
Roach Bank Rd BURY BL9.....54 B2
Roaches Ms MOSL OL5.........94 A4
Roaches Wy MOSL OL5.........94 B4
Roachill Cl ALT WA14.........10 E5
Roach Pl MILN OL16...........10 E5
Roach St BURY BL9............5 F5
  BURY BL9...................53 G5
Roach V MILN OL16............30 D1
Roachwood Cl CHAD OL9......73 H5
Roading Brook Rd BOLE BL2...36 C2
Road La WHIT OL12............18 C4
Roads Ford Av MILN OL16.....31 G4
Roan Wy WILM/AE SK9.......201 E5
Roaring Gate La
  HALE/TIMP WA15...........179 F1
Robert Hall St ORD M5......127 E1
Robert Lawrence Cl
  URM M41 *................138 A2
Robert Malcolm Cl
  NEWH/MOS M40.............103 E5
Robert Owen Gdns
  WYTH/NTH M22.............168 C1
Robert Salt Cl ALT WA14.....165 H3
Robertscroft Cl
  WYTH/NTH M22.............168 C1
Robertshaw Av CCHDY M21...141 F5
Robertson St RAD M26........52 B5
Roberts St ECC M30.........111 E4
Robert St BOLE BL2...........35 F1
  CHAD OL9...................8 C5
  DUK SK16..................119 C5
  FAIL M35...................105 F1
  HEY OL10...................56 B1
  HYDE SK14................147 C1
  NEWH/MOS M40.............103 C5
  OLDS OL8...................90 C5
  PWCH M25...................86 B3
  SALE M33..................155 F2
  WHTF M45...................69 H3
Robeson Wy
  WYTH/NTH M22.............169 G3
Robin Cft MPL/ROM SK6......161 E3
Robin Dr IRL M44...........122 B5
Robin Hood St CHH M8......102 A2
Robinia Cl ECC M30.........110 A5
Robin Rd AUL OL6............107 H1
  BURY BL9...................53 F5

Robinsbay Rd
  WYTH/NTH M22.............180 D5
Robins Ct BRAM/HZG SK7....183 H5
  BRAM/HZG SK7.............118 B2
Robins La BRAM/HZG SK7....183 H5
Robinson La AUL OL7.........119 E2
Robinson Pk STLY SK15.......120 B4
Robinson St CHAD OL9.........90 C1
  EDGY/DAV SK3..............12 D7
  HYDE SK14................134 A3
  MILN OL16..................10 E6
  OLDS OL8...................91 G4
  STLY SK15.................120 C4
Robin St OLD OL1 *...........75 G4
Robinsway ALT WA14.........177 F3
Robinswood Rd
  WYTH/NTH M22.............180 C3
Robson Av URM M41.........124 D1
Robson St OLD OL1............9 H4
Roby Rd ECC M30............110 D5
Roby St CMANE M1............7 H5
Roch Av HEY OL10............40 B4
Roch Bank BKLY M9...........88 A2
Rochbury Cl ROCH OL11.......28 C5
Roch Cl WHTF M45............70 A3
Roch Crs WHTF M45..........70 A3
Rochdale La HEY OL10........41 E4
Rochdale Old Rd BURY BL9....39 F3
Rochdale Rd BKLY M9........103 E3
  BURY BL9...................4 E4
  HEY OL10...................41 E4
  MDTN M24...................73 E1
  MILN OL16..................31 E4
  NEWH/MOS M40.............115 F1
  OLD OL1....................9 G1
  ROY/SHW OL2...............58 D5
Rochdale Rd East HEY OL10...41 G3
Rochdale Wy MILN OL16......44 B4
Roche Gdns CHD/CHDH SK8..193 H1
Rochester Av BOLE BL2......141 H5
  CCHDY M21................86 B5
  PWCH M25..................96 D1
  WALK M28...................96 D1
Rochester Cl AUL OL6........107 F3
  DUK SK16..................134 B1
Rochester Dr ALT WA14......165 H3
Rochester Gv BRAM/HZG SK7.185 F1
Rochester Rd URM M41......124 C4
Rochester Wy CHAD OL9......90 C1
Rochford Av WHTF M45.......69 E5
Rochford Cl WHTF M45.......69 E5
Roch Mills Crs ROCH OL11....42 B1
Roch Mills Gdns ROCH OL11...42 B1
Roch St MILN OL16............11 H2
Roch Valley Wy ROCH OL11...70 A3
Roch Wy WHTF M45...........70 A3
Rockall Wk OP/CLY M11.....116 A4
Rock Av BOL BL1..............33 F4
Rock Bank BRO M7 *.........100 D1
  MOSL OL5.................108 D1
Rockdove Av HULME M15....128 A1
Rocket Wy CSLFD M3...........6 A4
Rockfield Dr BKLY M9 *......103 E2
Rock Fold EDGW/EG BL7.......23 E2
Rockhampton St GTN M18....130 D3
Rockhouse Cl ECC M30.......110 A5
Rockingham Cl ROY/SHW OL2..59 F1
  WGTN/LGST M12............129 E2
Rockley Gdns SLFD M6.......113 G1
Rocklyn Av NEWH/MOS M40...89 F5
Rocklynes MPL/ROM SK6.....162 A4
Rockmead Dr BKLY M9........88 B4
Rock Rd URM M41............139 F1
Rock St AULW OL7 *.........106 C3
  BRO M7...................101 G4
  HEY OL10...................41 F5
  HYDE SK14................148 A4
  OP/CLY M11 *.............130 D1
  RAD M26...................68 C2
  RAMS BL0...................17 F1
Rock Ter EDGW/EG BL7........23 E2
  MOSL OL5..................94 A4
The Rock BURY BL9............4 D4
Rocky La ECC M30...........111 E1
Roda St BKLY M9.............103 E1
Rodborough Rd
  NTHM/RTH M23.............179 H1
Rodeheath Cl WILM/AE SK9...199 G3
Rodenhurst Dr
  NEWH/MOS M40.............103 H4
Rodepool Cl WILM/AE SK9....199 G3
Rodmell Av NEWH/MOS M40 *.103 E5
Rodmell Cl EDGW/EG BL7......23 E4
Rodmill Ct RUSH/FAL M14....143 E2
Rodmill Dr CHD/CHDH SK8..169 F5
Rodney Ct ANC M4.............7 K1
Rodney Dr MPL/ROM SK6.....161 F4
Rodney St ANC M4...........115 F3
  AUL OL6...................120 A1
  CSLFD M3..................114 A4
  ROCH OL11..................42 A4
Roebuck Gdns SALE M33 *...154 B2
Roebuck La OLDE OL4.........77 F1
  SALE M33..................154 B2
Roe Cross Gn HYDE SK14....135 G3
Roe Cross Rd HYDE SK14....135 G3
Roedean Gdns URM M41......137 F1
Roefield Ter WHIT OL12.......29 F3
Roe Gn WALK M28............97 H2
Roe Green Av WALK M28......97 H2
Roe La OLDE OL4.............92 D5
Roe St ANC M4...............7 K1
  WHIT OL12..................29 F2
Rogate Dr NTHM/RTH M23...167 H2
Roger Cl MPL/ROM SK6......161 G5
Rogerson Cl
  NEWH/MOS M40.............166 D2
Rogerstead BOLS/LL BL3 *.....48 B3
Roger St ANC M4..............7 H1
Roger Wy CHD/CHDH SK8....182 D2
Rokeby Av STRET M32.......140 A4
Roker Av BRUN/LGST M13...143 H1
Roker Park Av
  DTN/ASHW M34.............132 D4

Roland Rd BOLS/LL BL3 .....48 B4
RDSH SK5 .....145 F4
Rolla St CSLFD M5 .....6 C2
Rollesby Cl TOT/BURYW BL8 ...38 A1
Rolleston Av ANC M4 .....115 G3
Rollins La MPL/ROM SK6 .....163 F5
Rolls Crs HULME M15 .....127 H2
Rollswood Dr
NEWH/MOS M40 .....103 H4
Romana Sq ALT WA14 .....165 H1
Roman Rd FAIL M35 .....105 F2
HTNM SK4 .....13 F2
PWCH M25 .....100 C1
ROY/SHW OL2 .....75 E1
Roman St RAD M26 .....67 H1
Romer Av NEWH/MOS M40 * ...104 D1
Romer Rd NEWH/MOS M40 .....7 K1
Romer St BOLE BL2 .....49 H2
Romford Av DTN/ASHW M34 ..132 D4
Romford Cl OLDS OL9 .....9 F7
Romiley Crs BOLE BL2 .....50 A1
Romiley Rd SALE M33 .....139 E5
Romiley St BOLE BL2 .....50 A1
Romiley St SLFD M6 .....160 C4
STKP SK1 .....160 C4
Romley Av URM M41 .....124 C4
Romney Av ROCH OL11 .....42 D4
Romney Cha BOL BL1 .....33 H2
Romney Rd BOL BL1 .....32 B4
Romney St AUL OL6 .....119 H2
NEWH/MOS M40 .....103 H4
SLFD M6 .....100 D5
Romney Wy CHAD OL9 .....90 C1
Romney Wy RDSH SK5 .....145 H5
Romsey WHIT OL12 .....10 B5
Romsey Dr MDTN M24 .....72 C1
Romsey Gv WGTN/LGST M12 ..129 E1
Romsley Dr BOLS/LL BL3 .....64 B1
Rona Cl WGTN/LGST M12 .....129 C3
Ronaldsay Gdns ORD M5 .....112 D4
Ronald St OLDE OL4 .....76 B5
OP/CLY M11 .....117 F4
ROCH OL11 .....42 B5
Rondin Cl WGTN/LGST M12 ...129 F1
Rondin Rd WGTN/LGST M12 ..129 F1
Roocroft Cl BOL BL1 .....2 B1
Rookery Av GTN M18 .....131 E2
Rookery Cl STLY SK15 .....135 E1
Rookerypool Cl WILM/AE SK9 ..192 A5
Rooke St ECC M30 .....110 B5
Rookfield Av SALE M33 .....154 D1
Rookley Wk RUSH/FAL M14 * ..128 D5
Rook St HULME M15 .....127 H2
OLDE OL4 .....92 B2
RAMS BL0 .....16 D2
Rookswood Dr ROCH OL11 .....42 A3
Rookway MDTN M24 .....72 C5
Rookwood OLD OL1 .....73 H3
Rookwood Av
NTHM/RTH M23 .....167 G3
Rooley Moor Rd WHIT OL12 ...29 E1
Rooley St WHIT OL12 .....10 A4
Roosevelt Rd FWTH BL4 .....66 C5
Rooth St HTNM SK4 .....12 C2
Ropefield Wy WHIT OL12 .....18 D5
Rope St WHIT OL12 .....10 C4
Rosamond Dr CSLFD M3 .....6 A5
Rosamond St BOLS/LL BL3 ...48 D5
HULME M15 .....127 H5
Rosamond St West
HULME M15 .....128 B2
Rosary Cl OLDS OL8 .....106 C1
Rosary Rd OLDS OL8 .....106 D1
Roscoe Ct WHTN BL5 .....62 A5
Roscoe St EDGY/DAV SK3 .....12 D5
OLD OL1 .....9 J4
Roscow Av BOLE BL2 .....50 B1
Roscow Rd FWTH BL4 .....82 D1
Roseacre Dr CHD/CHDH SK8 ..181 H5
Rose Av IRL M44 .....136 B4
LIT OL15 .....20 C5
ROCH OL11 .....28 A1
Rosebank HOR/BR BL6 .....46 D2
Rosebank Cl BOLE BL2 .....36 B5
Rosebank Rd IRL M44 .....150 D1
NEWH/MOS M40 .....116 C1
Rosebay Cl ROY/SHW OL2 * ...59 G5
Roseberry Cl BOLS/LL BL3 .....48 B5
OLDS OL8 * 9 G7
Roseberry St OFTN SK2 .....173 E5
RUSH/FAL M14 .....128 A5
WHTN BL5 .....62 A4
Rosebury Av OLD OL1 .....60 A1
Rose Cottage Rd
NTHM/RTH M23 * 142 D4
Rose Crs IRL M44 .....136 B2
Rosecroft Cl EDGY/DAV SK3 ..171 H5
Rosedale Av BOL BL1 .....33 H1
Rosedale Cl OLD OL1 * 76 A5
Rosedale Ct DTN/ASHW M34 *.132 D4
Rosedale Rd NTHM/RTH M23 .159 G1
RUSH/FAL M14 .....142 C1
Rosedale Wy DUK SK16 .....133 F2
Rosefield Cl EDGY/DAV SK3 ..171 H4
Rosefield Crs MILN OL16 .....11 F7
Rosegarth Av DID/WITH M20 ..156 C2
Rose Gv FWTH BL4 .....66 C5
TOT/BURYW BL8 .....37 F4
Rosehay Av DTN/ASHW M34 ..146 D1
Rose Hey La FAIL M35 .....117 F1
Rose Hill BOLE BL2 .....49 F4
DTN/ASHW M34 .....132 A5
STLY SK15 .....120 C5
UPML OL3 .....78 C1
Rose Hill Av
NEWH/MOS M40 .....116 C1
Rose Hill Cl EDGW/EG BL7 .....23 F4
Rosehill Cl SLFD M6 .....113 E3
Rose Hill Rd AUL OL6 .....108 A5
Rosehill Rd SWIN M27 .....84 A5
Rose Hill St HEY OL10 .....40 C4
Roseland Av DID/WITH M20 ..157 C2
Roseland Dr PWCH M25 .....86 B1

Roselands Av SALE M33 .....154 A4
Rose La MPL/ROM SK6 .....174 D4
Rose Lea BOLE BL2 .....35 F2
Rosemary Dr HYDE SK14 .....147 H4
LIT OL15 .....20 C2
Rosemary Gv BRO M7 .....101 F5
Rosemary La STKP SK1 .....13 J4
WHTN BL5 .....80 A1
Rosemary Rd CHAD OL9 .....73 H4
Rosemount HYDE SK14 .....133 C3
Rose Mt MDTN M24 .....72 C2
Rosemount Crs HYDE SK14 ..133 C3
Roseneath BRAM/HZG SK7 ...185 G3
Roseneath Av BOLS/LL BL3 ...64 C1
Roseneath Gv BOLS/LL BL3 ...64 C1
Roseneath Rd BOLS/LL BL3 ..64 C1
URM M41 .....124 B5
Rosen Sq CHAD OL9 * 74 C5
Rose St BOLE BL2 .....49 F4
CHAD OL9 .....90 B4
MDTN M24 .....73 F4
Rose Ter STLY SK15 .....120 D4
Rosethorns Cl MDTN M24 .....56 C5
Rose V CHD/CHDH SK8 .....181 C3
Rosevale Av BNG/LEV M19 ...158 A1
Roseway BRAM/HZG SK7 .....184 A2
Rosewell Cl NEWH/MOS M40 ..115 G1
Rose Wd DTN/ASHW M34 .....132 C3
Rosewood Av DROY M43 .....118 B2
HTNM SK4 .....158 D5
TOT/BURYW BL8 .....26 B5
Rosewood Cl DUK SK16 .....133 G2
Rosewood Crs CHAD OL9 * ...74 C3
Rosewood Gdns
CHD/CHDH SK8 .....169 E3
Rosford Av RUSH/FAL M14 ...142 D1
Rosgill Cl HTNM SK4 .....158 B4
Rosgill Dr MDTN M24 .....72 A3
Rosina St OP/CLY M11 .....131 E1
Roslin St OP/CLY M11 .....117 E3
Roslyn Av URM M41 .....137 G3
Roslyn Rd EDGY/DAV SK3 ....171 H4
Rossall Av RAD M26 .....68 D4
STRET M32 .....125 H5
Rossall Cl BOLE BL2 .....49 H1
Rossall Dr BRAM/HZG SK7 ....194 A1
Rossall Rd BOLE BL2 .....49 H1
WHIT OL12 .....10 E1
Rossall St BOLE BL2 .....49 H1
Rossall Wy SLFD M6 .....113 F2
Ross Av CHAD OL9 .....90 A4
EDGY/DAV SK3 .....171 H4
WHTF M45 .....69 F4
Ross Dr SWIN M27 .....83 H3
Rossenclough Rd
WILM/AE SK9 .....199 C1
Rossendale Av BKLY M9 .....103 C1
Rossendale Cl ROY/SHW OL2 ..60 C2
Rossendale Rd
CHD/CHDH SK8 .....181 H4
Rossendale Wy WHIT OL12 ...31 G1
Rossett Av HALE/TIMP WA15 ..166 B1
WYTH/NTH M22 .....168 C3
Rossett Dr URM M41 .....123 C4
Ross Gv URM M41 .....138 C1
Rosshill Wk HULME M15 * 127 C2
Rossington St
NEWH/MOS M40 .....104 C5
Rossini St BOL BL1 * 34 C3
Rosslare Rd WYTH/NTH M22 .180 D2
Ross Lave La DTN/ASHW M34 .146 B3
Rosslyn Gv HALE/TIMP WA15 .166 B3
Rosslyn Rd CHD/CHDH SK8 ..182 A3
NEWH/MOS M40 .....103 H1
OLDTF/WHR M16 .....141 E1
Rossmere Av BKLY M9 .....103 C1
Rossmill La HALE/TIMP WA15 .178 D5
Ross St OLDS OL8 .....8 D6
Rostherne Av MPL/ROM SK6 ..186 D4
RUSH/FAL M14 .....142 C2
Rostherne Gdns BOLS/LL BL3 ..48 A5
SALE M33 .....155 C3
WILM/AE SK9 .....198 B5
Rostherne St ALT WA14 .....177 C1
SLFD M6 * 112 D4
Rosthernmere Rd
CHD/CHDH SK8 .....170 C5
Rosthwaite Cl MDTN M24 .....71 H5
Roston Rd BRO M7 .....101 H2
Rostrevor Rd WGTN/LGST M12 .129 F2
Rostron Av WGTN/LGST M12 ..129 F2
Rostron Rd RAMS BL0 .....16 C2
Rostron St BNG/LEV M19 .....144 B1
Rothay Cl BOLE BL2 .....35 G5
WHTF M45 .....69 E4
Rothay Dr MDTN M24 .....72 B1
RDSH SK5 .....145 F4
Rothbury Av AULW OL7 .....106 B5
Rothbury Cl TOT/BURYW BL8 ..37 E4
Rothbury Ct BOLS/LL BL3 .....2 D7
Rotherby Rd WYTH/NTH M22 .168 D5
Rotherdale Av
HALE/TIMP WA15 .....
Rotherwood Av STRET M32 ...126 B5
Rotherwood Rd WILM/AE SK9 .198 A1
Rothesay Av DUK SK16 .....133 F1
Rothesay Crs SALE M33 .....153 F4
Rothesay Rd BOLS/LL BL3 * ...64 A1
CHH M8 .....86 D3
OLD OL1 .....76 B3
Rothesay Ter MILN OL16 .....43 H2
Rothiemay Rd URM M41 .....137 G2
Rothley Av WYTH/NTH M22 ...168 C4
Rothman Cl NEWH/MOS M40 ..104 D1
Rothwell Crs LHULT M38 .....80 D2
Rothwell La LHULT M38 .....80 D2
Rothwell St BOLS/LL BL3 * ...48 D5
FAIL M35 .....104 A4
NEWH/MOS M40 .....104 A4
RAMS BL0 .....16 C2
ROY/SHW OL2 .....59 G1
WALK M28 .....81 G5
WHIT OL12 .....11 G2
Rottingdene Dr
WYTH/NTH M22 .....180 B3
Roughey Gdns
WYTH/NTH M22 .....168 B5

Rough Hey Wk MILN OL16 .....30 C5
Rough Hill La BURY BL9 .....39 H2
Roughlee Av SWIN M27 .....98 C3
Roughtown Ct MOSL OL5 .....94 A5
Roughtown Rd MOSL OL5 .....94 A5
Roundcroft BRUN/LGST M13 ..162 C3
Roundhey CHD/CHDH SK8 ...181 G4
Round Hey MOSL OL5 .....108 D2
Round Hill Wy BOL BL1 * 3 F2
Roundhill Wy OLDE OL4 .....76 D3
Round Thorn Rd MDTN M24 ...73 E5
Roundthorn Rd
NTHM/RTH M23 .....167 G3
OLDE OL4 .....92 B2
Roundway BRAM/HZG SK7 ...193 G1
Roundwood Rd
WYTH/NTH M22 .....168 C2
Rousdon Cl NEWH/MOS M40 * .103 E5
Rouse St ROCH OL11 .....42 B2
Roving Bridge Ri SWIN M27 ..100 A2
Rowan Av OLDTF/WHR M16 ...127 F5
SALE M33 .....154 C3
URM M41 .....124 C5
Rowan Cl DUK SK16 .....134 A1
Rowan Crs DUK SK16 .....134 A1
Rowan Dr BURY BL9 .....5 K3
CHD/CHDH SK8 .....183 F4
Rowanlea Pwch M25 * 86 B3
Rowan Lodge NEWH/MOS M40 ..89 F2
Rowans St BURY BL9 .....86 A4
Rowans Cl STLY SK15 .....121 F2
Rowanside Dr WILM/AE SK9 ..199 H2
Rowans St TOT/BURYW BL8 ...37 H2
The Rowans BOL BL1 .....47 F2
MOSL OL5 .....109 E1
Rowan St HYDE SK14 .....148 B2
Rowanswood Dr HYDE SK14 ..134 B5
Rowan Tree Dr SALE M33 .....154 C5
Rowan Tree Rd OLDS OL8 .....106 A1
Rowanwood CHAD OL9 .....73 H5
Rowany Cl PWCH M25 .....85 H5
Rowarth Av DTN/ASHW M34 ..147 E3
Rowarth Rd NTHM/RTH M23 ..179 G2
Rowbottom Wk OLDS OL8 * ...9 F7
Rowcon Cl DTN/ASHW M34 ...132 B3
Rowden Rd OLDE OL4 .....92 D3
Rowe Gn DTN/ASHW M34 .....132 C5
Rowena St BOLS/LL BL3 .....65 H2
Rowendale St HULME M15 * ...6 D7
Rowfield Dr NTHM/RTH M23 ..179 H1
Rowland Av URM M41 .....124 D5
Rowland Ct MILN OL16 * 30 C5
Rowlands Rd BURY BL9 .....27 F2
Rowland St MILN OL16 .....30 C5
Rowlandsway
WYTH/NTH M22 .....180 C2
Rowland Wy OLDE OL4 .....76 D5
Rowley Rd BRAM/HZG SK7 ...185 F4
Rowley St AUL OL6 .....107 G4
Rowood Av CHH M8 .....102 C2
NEWH/MOS M40 .....104 A2
RDSH SK5 .....145 F1
Rowrah Crs MDTN M24 .....71 G3
Rowsley Av BOL BL1 .....32 D5
DID/WITH M20 .....156 D2
Rowsley Gv RDSH SK5 .....145 G4
Rowsley Rd ECC M30 .....110 D5
STRET M32 .....125 F5
Rowsley St OP/CLY M11 .....115 H3
SLFD M6 .....101 E5
Rowson Ct SALE M33 * 155 F2
Rowton St BOLE BL2 .....34 C4
Roxalina St BOLS/LL BL3 .....48 D5
Roxburgh St GTN M18 .....130 C3
Roxbury Av OLDE OL4 .....92 C2
Roxby Cl WALK M28 .....81 G4
Roxholme Wk
WYTH/NTH M22 .....180 B4
Roxton Rd HTNM SK4 .....144 C5
Royal Av BURY BL9 .....38 C1
CCHDY M21 .....141 F4
DROY M43 .....118 A2
HEY OL10 .....41 E5
URM M41 .....138 D1
Royal Court Dr BOL BL1 .....2 B3
Royal Crs CHD/CHDH SK8 * ..181 H2
Royal Ex CMANW M2 * 6 E4
Royal Exchange Ar
CMANW M2 * 6 E4
Royal Gdns ALT WA14 .....176 C2
Royal George St
EDGY/DAV SK3 * 13 F6
Royal Oak Rd NTHM/RTH M23 ..167 H2
Royal Pde OLD OL1 .....75 F3
Royal St MILN OL16 .....30 C1
Royalthorn Dr
WYTH/NTH M22 .....168 B3
Royalthorn Rd
WYTH/NTH M22 .....168 C3
Royce Av HALE/TIMP WA15 ...165 H4
Royce Rd HULME M15 .....127 H2
Roydale St NEWH/MOS M40 ..115 H2
Royden Av BKLY M9 .....88 B3
Royds Cl BRUN/LGST M13 * ..129 E3
Royds Pl MILN OL16 .....43 G3
Royds St BURY BL9 .....39 G2
LIT OL15 .....21 F3
MILN OL16 .....43 G1
MILN OL16 .....44 D1
TOT/BURYW BL8 .....26 B4
Royds St West MILN OL16 .....43 F1
Royd St OLDS OL8 .....90 D3
Royland Av BOLS/LL BL3 .....65 F1
Royle Barn Rd ROCH OL11 .....42 B4
Royle Cl OFTN SK2 .....172 B4
Royle Green Rd
WYTH/NTH M22 .....168 D1
Royle Rd ROCH OL11 .....42 C3
Royle St DTN/ASHW M34 .....132 C3
OFTN SK2 .....172 B4
RUSH/FAL M14 .....143 F4
SLFD M6 * 113 E4
WALK M28 .....82 A5
Royley ROY/SHW OL2 .....74 D1
Royley Crs ROY/SHW OL2 .....74 D1
Royley Rd OLDS OL8 .....91 F5
Royon Dr EDGY/DAV SK3 .....171 E3

Royston Av BOLE BL2 .....3 K2
DTN/ASHW M34 .....131 E5
OLDTF/WHR M16 .....127 G5
Royston Cl TOT/BURYW BL8 ..26 A2
Royston Rd OLDTF/WHR M16...127 G5
URM M41 .....138 A3
Roy St BOLS/LL BL3 .....48 A5
ROY/SHW OL2 .....59 E5
Royton Av SALE M33 .....155 F4
Rozel Sq CSLFD M3 .....6 C6
Ruabon Rd DID/WITH M20 ....157 E4
Rubens Cl MPL/ROM SK6 .....175 H1
Ruby St BOL BL1 .....34 A3
BURY BL9 .....16 D5
DTN/ASHW M34 .....132 B5
HULME M15 .....128 B2
Rudcroft Cl BRUN/LGST M13 ..128 C2
Rudding St ROY/SHW OL2 * 59 F5
Ruddpark Rd WYTH/NTH M22 .180 C3
Rudd St NEWH/MOS M40 .....103 H3
Rudheath Av DID/WITH M20 ..142 C4
Rudman Dr ORD M5 .....126 C1
Rudman St AULW OL7 .....119 F4
WHIT OL12 .....10 A1
Rudolph St BOLS/LL BL3 .....65 E1
Rudston Av NEWH/MOS M40 ..89 E5
Rudyard Av MDTN M24 .....72 C3
Rudyard Gv HTNM SK4 .....144 D5
ROCH OL11 .....43 E4
SALE M33 .....153 H4
Rudyard Rd SLFD M6 .....100 B5
Rudyard St BRO M7 .....101 G4
Rufford Av HYDE SK14 .....148 B1
ROCH OL11 .....28 A5
Rufford Cl AUL OL6 .....107 F3
ROY/SHW OL2 .....59 G2
WHTF M45 .....69 H2
Rufford Dr BOLS/LL BL3 .....64 C2
WHTF M45 .....69 H2
Rufford Gv BOLS/LL BL3 .....64 C2
Rufford Pl GTN M18 * 131 E4
Rufford Rd OLDTF/WHR M16 ..127 G5
Rufus St RUSH/FAL M14 .....143 C4
Rugby Dr SALE M33 .....154 B4
Rugby Rd SLFD M6 .....111 H2
WHIT OL12 .....10 E5
Rugby St CHH M8 .....114 B1
Rugeley St SLFD M6 .....101 E5
Ruins La BOLE BL2 .....35 F2
Ruislip Av NEWH/MOS M40 ....03 F5
Ruislip Cl OLDS OL8 .....92 A3
Rumworth Rd HOR/BR BL6 ...46 D5
Rumworth St BOLS/LL BL3 ...48 C5
Runcorn St HULME M15 .....127 F1
Runger La HALE/TIMP WA15 ..179 G4
Runhall Cl WGTN/LGST M12 ..129 F2
Running Hill Ga UPML OL3 .....79 H5
Runnymeade SWIN M27 .....99 F4
Runnymede Cl EDGY/DAV SK3 ..171 F3
Runnymede Ct BOLS/LL BL3 ..59 C4
ROY/SHW OL2 .....59 F5
Rupert St BOLS/LL BL3 .....51 E1
NEWH/MOS M40 .....117 F1
RAD M26 .....68 C3
RDSH SK5 .....145 F3
WHIT OL12 .....29 F2
Ruscombe Fold MDTN M24 ....72 A4
Rush Acre Cl RAD M26 .....67 H1
Rushbank WALK M28 * 95 H1
Rushbrooke Av OP/CLY M11 ..116 D2
Rushbury Dr ROY/SHW OL2 ...59 H5
Rushcroft Ct BKLY M9 * 103 F1
Rushcroft Rd BNG/LEV M19 ..144 B1
Rushden Rd BNG/LEV M19 ...144 B1
Rushen St OP/CLY M11 .....116 C4
Rushey Cl HALE/TIMP WA15 ..179 E5
Rushey Fld EDGW/EG BL7 .....23 E3
Rushey Fold La BOL BL1 .....33 G4
Rusheylea Cl BOL BL1 * 33 E4
Rushey Rd WYTH/NTH M22 ...168 B4
Rushfield Dr BRUN/LGST M13 .129 E3
Rushfield Rd CHD/CHDH SK8 .192 D1
Rushford Av BNG/LEV M19 ...144 A1
Rushford Gv BOL BL1 * 33 G3
Rushford St WGTN/LGST M12 .129 H4
Rush Gv UPML OL3 .....79 E5
Rush Hill Rd UPML OL3 .....79 E5
Rush Hill Ter UPML OL3 .....79 E5
Rushlake Gdns ROCH OL11 * ..28 B3
Rushley Av BROM7 .....101 G4
Rushmere AUL OL6 .....119 E3
Rushmere Av BNG/LEV M19 ..144 B2
Rushmere Dr TOT/BURYW BL8 ..37 H1
Rushmere Wk
OLDTF/WHR M16 .....127 G5
Rushmoor Cl IRL M44 .....136 C1
Rush Mt ROY/SHW OL2 .....44 C5
Rusholme Gv RUSH/FAL M14 .128 D5
Rusholme Pl RUSH/FAL M14 ..128 D5
Rush St DUK SK16 .....134 C3
Rushton Cl MPL/ROM SK6 ...175 G5
Rushton Dr BRAM/HZG SK7 ..185 G5
MPL/ROM SK6 .....162 B3
Rushton Gv OLDE OL4 .....75 G4
Rushton Rd CHD/CHDH SK8 ..182 C5
EDGY/DAV SK3 .....170 D2
Rushton St DID/WITH M20 ....157 G4
DTN/ASHW M34 .....146 A4
WALK M28 .....95 G1
Rushwick Av
NEWH/MOS M40 .....103 H5
Rushworth Ct HTNM SK4 * ...159 F5
Rushycroft HYDE SK14 .....135 H4
Rushyfield Crs MPL/ROM SK6 .162 C3
Rushy Hill Vw OLD OL12 * 29 E2
Ruskin Av CHAD OL9 .....90 A1
DTN/ASHW M34 .....146 D2
FWTH BL4 .....64 D4
RUSH/FAL M14 .....128 A5
Ruskin Crs PWCH M25 * 85 H4
Ruskin Gdns MPL/ROM SK6 ...175 H3
Ruskin Gv MPL/ROM SK6 .....161 H3

Ruskington Dr BKLY M9 .....103 E3
Ruskin Rd BOLS/LL BL3 .....51 E5
DROY M43 .....117 H5
OLDTF/WHR M16 .....127 F5
PWCH M25 .....85 F4
RDSH SK5 .....145 G2
Ruskin St RAD M26 .....42 D4
RAD M26 .....52 D5
Rusland Ct OFTN SK2 * 172 C2
Rusland Dr BOLE BL2 .....35 F4
Rusland Wk MPL/ROM SK6 ...161 H4
OLDTF/WHR M16 .....141 H1
Russell Av HALE/TIMP WA15 ..155 E1
Russell Cl BOL BL1 .....48 B1
Russell Ct FWTH BL4 * 66 B4
LHULT M58 .....81 H4
Russell Dr IRL M44 .....150 C1
Russell Gdns HTNM SK4 .....159 E5
Russell Rd OLDTF/WHR M16 ..127 G5
PART M31 .....151 F3
SLFD 99 G5
Russell St AUL OL6 .....120 A1
BURY BL9 .....5 K5
CHAD OL9 * 74 C5
CHH M8 .....114 C1
DUK SK16 .....119 H5
ECC M30 .....111 F3
FWTH BL4 .....66 A5
HEY OL10 .....41 F5
LHULT M58 .....81 H4
MOSL OL5 .....108 D1
PWCH M25 .....86 B5
Russet Rd BKLY M9 .....103 E1
Russet Wy WILM/AE SK9 .....200 B2
Ruth Av NEWH/MOS M40 .....104 C1
Ruthen La OLDTF/WHR M16 ..126 C5
Rutherford Av RUSH/FAL M14.128 C5
Rutherford Cl HYDE SK14 .....147 H1
Rutherford Dr WHTN BL5 .....63 G5
Rutherglade
NEWH/MOS M40 .....102 D4
Rutherglen Dr BOLS/LL BL3 ...64 C2
Rutherglen Wk
NEWH/MOS M40 .....105 F5
Ruthin Av BKLY M9 .....87 H2
CHD/CHDH SK8 .....182 B2
MDTN M24 .....88 D1
Ruthin Cl OLDS OL8 .....90 C5
Ruth St BOL BL1 .....2 C3
BURY BL9 .....5 F1
GTN M18 .....130 C5
OLDE OL4 .....77 E2
WHIT OL12 .....14 C4
Rutland ROCH OL11 * 29 H5
Rutland Av DID/WITH M20 ....157 F1
OLDTF/WHR M16 .....126 D5
SWIN M27 .....98 A4
URM M41 .....139 E1
Rutland Cl AUL OL6 .....120 A3
BOLS/LL BL3 .....51 E5
CHD/CHDH SK8 .....169 G3
Rutland Ct DID/WITH M20 ....157 E1
Rutland Dr BRO M7 .....99 G1
BURY BL9 .....53 H1
Rutland Gv BOL BL1 .....33 E5
FWTH BL4 * 65 H5
Rutland La SALE M33 .....155 C3
Rutland Rd ALT WA14 .....165 G3
BRAM/HZG SK7 .....185 F4
DROY M43 .....117 F3
ECC M30 .....111 G2
IRL M44 .....150 C1
PART M31 .....150 D4
WALK M28 .....81 E4
Rutland St AUL OL6 .....120 A3
BOLS/LL BL3 .....48 C5
CHAD OL9 .....8 A7
DROY M43 .....118 A4
FAIL M35 * 105 E2
GTN M18 .....130 D2
HEY OL10 .....41 E3
HYDE SK14 .....133 G3
SWIN M27 .....98 D1
Rutland Wy ROY/SHW OL2 ....60 B1
Rutter's La
BRAM/HZG SK7 * 184 D2
Ryall Av ORD M5 .....113 G5
Ryall Av South ORD M5 .....113 G5
Ryan St OP/CLY M11 .....130 D1
Rydal Av BRAM/HZG SK7 .....184 D1
CHAD OL9 .....73 F4
DROY M43 .....117 F4
ECC M30 .....110 C1
HYDE SK14 .....133 F3
MDTN M24 .....71 H3
MPL/ROM SK6 .....186 D4
ROY/SHW OL2 .....58 D1
SALE M33 .....154 A1
URM M41 .....138 A3
Rydal Cl BURY BL9 .....53 G5
CHD/CHDH SK8 .....181 G1
DTN/ASHW M34 .....145 H1
Rydal Crs SWIN M27 .....99 E4
WALK M28 .....95 F1
Rydal Dr HALE/TIMP WA15 ...179 E4
Rydal Gv AULW OL7 .....119 E1
FWTH BL4 .....65 E3
HEY OL10 .....56 A1
WHTF M45 .....69 G4
Rydal Rd BOL BL1 .....47 H1
BOLS/LL BL3 .....51 E5
STRET M32 .....126 A5
Ryde Av DTN/ASHW M34 .....147 E3
HTNM SK4 .....159 E4
Ryder Av ALT WA14 .....165 G4
Ryder Brow GTN M18 .....130 C4
Ryderbrow Rd GTN M18 .....130 C4
Ryder St BOL BL1 .....33 F4
HEY OL10 .....41 E4
NEWH/MOS M40 .....115 G1
Ryde St BOLS/LL BL3 .....64 B1
Rydings La WHIT OL12 .....19 F2
Rydings Rd WHIT OL12 .....19 G3
Rydley St BOLE BL2 .....3 J6
Ryebank Gv AUL OL6 .....107 G5
Ryebank Ms CCHDY M21 * ...140 D2
Ryebank Rd CCHDY M21 .....140 D2

Rye Bank Rd
OLDTF/WHR M16 141 E1
Ryeburn Av WYTH/NTH M22 180 C1
Ryeburn Dr BOLE BL2 34 C1
Ryeburne St OLDE OL4 76 B5
Ryeburn Wk URM M41 123 G4
Rye Cft WHTF M45 68 D5
Rye Croft Av SLFD M6 112 B2
Ryecroft Av HEY OL10 41 F4
TOT/BURYW BL8 26 A5
Ryecroft Cl CHAD OL9 90 A4
Ryecroft Gv NTHM/RTH M23 167 H2
Ryecroft La DTN/ASHW M34 132 B1
WALK M28 110 A1
Ryecroft Rd STRET M32 140 A2
Ryecroft St AULW OL7 119 E4
Ryecroft Vw DTN/ASHW M34 118 B5
Ryedale Av NEWH/MOS M40 103 E5
Ryedale Cl HTNM SK4 159 E3
Ryefield Cl HALE/TIMP WA15 166 D4
Ryefield Rd SALE M33 153 F4
Ryefields ROCH OL11 28 D5
Ryefields Dr UPML OL3 79 F3
Ryefield St BOL BL1 3 G1
Rye Hl WHTN BL5 * 62 A4
Ryeland Cl MILN OL16 43 G2
Ryelands WHTN BL5 62 A4
Ryelands Ct WHTN BL5 * 62 A4
Rye St HEY OL10 41 F3
Rylance St OP/CLY M11 115 H4
Rylands St GTN M18 * 130 D2
Rylane Wk NEWH/MOS M40 103 E5
Ryley Av BOLS/LL BL3 48 A4
Ryleys La WILM/AE SK9 200 C4
Ryley St BOLS/LL BL3 * 2 A7
Rylstone Av CCHDY M21 156 C3
Ryther Gv BKLY M9 87 G2
Ryton Av GTN M18 130 B5

S

Sabden Cl BURY BL9 27 G4
HEY OL10 40 B4
NEWH/MOS M40 115 H2
Sabden Rd BOL BL1 32 B4
Sabrina St CHH M8 101 H5
Sackville Cl ROY/SHW OL2 44 D5
Sackville St AUL OL6 119 G2
BOLE BL2 * 49 H2
CMANE M1 7 G7
CSLFD M3 6 B3
ROCH OL11 42 B5
Saddleback Cl WALK M28 96 C4
Saddlecote WALK M28 110 B1
Saddlecote Cl CHH M8 102 C2
Saddle Gv DROY M43 118 C2
Saddle St BOLE BL2 34 C4
Saddlewood Av
BNG/LEV M19 158 A4
Sadie Av STRET M32 125 F4
Sadler Ct HULME M15 127 H3
Sadler St BOLS/LL BL3 49 F5
MDTN M24 72 C3
Saffron Dr OLDE OL4 76 C2
Sagars Rd WILM/AE SK9 191 H3
Sagar St CHH M8 114 C1
St Agnes Rd BRUN/LGST M13 143 H1
St Agnes St RDSH SK5 131 E5
St Aidan's Cl ROCH OL11 42 C1
St Aidan's Gv BRO M7 101 E4
St Albans Av AUL OL6 107 E4
HTNM SK4 159 F1
NEWH/MOS M40 104 A5
St Albans Cl OLDS OL8 91 G3
St Albans Crs ALT WA14 165 F1
St Alban's St MILN OL16 29 H5
St Alban's Ter CHH M8 102 A5
ROCH OL11 * 29 H5
St Aldates MPL/ROM SK6 161 G4
St Aldwyn's Rd
DID/WITH M20 157 G1
St Ambrose Gdns SLFD M6 * 113 E3
St Ambrose Rd OLD OL1 76 B3
St Andrew's Av DROY M43 117 F4
ECC M30 111 F4
HALE/TIMP WA15 165 H2
St Andrews Cl HTNM SK4 159 E2
LIT OL15 20 B4
MPL/ROM SK6 162 A5
RAMS BL0 16 D3
SALE M33 153 F5
St Andrews Ct BOL BL1 * 2 E5
St Andrew's Dr HEY OL10 41 E5
St Andrews Rd
CHD/CHDH SK8 181 H3
HOR/BR BL6 46 B2
HTNM SK4 159 E2
RAD M26 52 A3
STRET M32 139 H1
St Andrew's Sq CMANE M1 115 F5
St Andrew's St CMANE M1 7 K6
St Andrew's Vw RAD M26 52 A3
St Anne's Av ROY/SHW OL2 75 F1
SLFD M6 112 D2
St Anne's Ct DTN/ASHW M34 * 132 C2
SALE M33 154 D2
SLFD M6 * 113 E1
St Anne's Crs OLDE OL4 93 H2
St Anne's Dr DTN/ASHW M34 132 D4
St Annes Gdns HEY OL10 41 G4
St Annes Meadow
TOT/BURYW BL8 26 A4
St Annes Rd CCHDY M21 141 F4
DTN/ASHW M34 132 C2
DTN/ASHW M34 132 D4
St Annes St BURY BL9 * 38 C2
St Anns Cl PWCH M25 85 H4
St Anns Pas CMANW M2 6 E4
St Ann's Rd BRAM/HZG SK7 184 D3
MILN OL16 11 K5
PWCH M25 85 G4
St Ann's Rd North
CHD/CHDH SK8 181 G3
St Ann's Rd South
CHD/CHDH SK8 181 H3
St Ann's Sq CHD/CHDH SK8 181 H4
CMANW M2 6 E4
St Ann's St CMANW M2 6 D4
SALE M33 155 G3
SWIN M27 98 D2
St Ann St BOL BL1 33 H5
St Anthonys Dr MOSL OL5 94 A5
St Asaphs Dr AUL OL6 107 E4
St Aubin's Rd BOLE BL2 3 J7
St Augustine's Rd
EDGY/DAV SK3 171 E1
St Augustine St BOL BL1 33 G4
NEWH/MOS M40 103 F5
St Austell Dr CHD/CHDH SK8 181 G4
TOT/BURYW BL8 26 A1
St Austell Rd
OLDTF/WHR M16 142 A3
St Austells Dr PWCH M25 86 A2
SWIN M27 99 H4
St Barnabas's Dr LIT OL15 20 D2
St Barnabas Sq OP/CLY M11 116 C5
St Bartholomew's Dr ORD M5 113 H5
St Bartholomew St
BOLS/LL BL3 49 F5
St Bede's Av BOLS/LL BL3 64 A2
St Bees Cl CHD/CHDH SK8 181 G1
RUSH/FAL M14 128 B4
St Bees Rd BOLE BL2 34 D4
St Benedicts Av
WGTN/LGST M12 * 129 G2
St Benedict's Sq
WGTN/LGST M12 129 G2
St Bernard's Av SLFD M6 101 F5
St Boniface Rd BRO M7 113 H1
St Brannocks Rd CCHDY M21 141 G2
CHD/CHDH SK8 183 E5
St Brelades Dr BRO M7 102 A2
St Brendans Rd
DID/WITH M20 142 D4
St Brendans Rd North
DID/WITH M20 142 D4
St Brides Wy
OLDTF/WHR M16 127 G3
St Catherines Dr FWTH BL4 65 E4
St Catherine's Rd
DID/WITH M20 142 D4
St Chads Av MPL/ROM SK6 162 B4
St Chads Ct MILN OL16 10 D7
St Chads Crs OLDS OL8 106 A1
UPML OL3 79 F4
St Chads Gv MPL/ROM SK6 162 B4
St Chad's Rd DID/WITH M20 143 F4
St Chad's St CHH M8 * 114 D1
St Christopher's Av AUL OL6 107 H4
St Christophers Cl
DID/WITH M20 142 B5
St Christophers Dr
MPL/ROM SK6 161 H4
St Christopher's Rd AUL OL6 107 G4
St Clair Rd TOT/BURYW BL8 * 16 A5
St Clare Ter HOR/BR BL6 * 46 A1
St Clements Ct OLDS OL8 9 G6
St Clement's Dr ORD M5 127 E1
St Clements Fold URM M41 * 139 E1
St Clements Rd CCHDY M21 141 E4
St Cuthberts Fold OLDS OL8 106 D1
St Davids Av MPL/ROM SK6 162 A4
St David's Cl AUL OL6 107 G3
St David's Rd BRAM/HZG SK7 184 D3
CHD/CHDH SK8 170 D4
St Domingo Pl OLD OL1 * 9 F3
St Dominics Ms BOLS/LL BL3 64 B1
St Dominics Wy MDTN M24 72 D5
St Edmund Hall Cl RAMS BL0 16 D4
St Edmund's Rd
NEWH/MOS M40 103 F4
St Edmund St BOL BL1 2 D4
St Elisabeth's Wy RDSH SK5 145 E4
St Elmo Av OFTN SK2 173 E2
St Elmo Pk POY/DIS SK12 196 B3
St Ethelbert's Av BOLS/LL BL3 48 A4
St Gabriel's Cl ROCH OL11 42 C5
St George's Av
HALE/TIMP WA15 166 B1
HULME M15 * 127 G1
St George's Ct ALT WA14 165 E2
BOL BL1 2 E3
HYDE SK14 * 147 H1
STRET M32 * 140 A2
St George's Crs
HALE/TIMP WA15 166 B1
SLFD M6 * 111 H2
WALK M28 82 A5
St Georges Dr HYDE SK14 147 H2
NEWH/MOS M40 104 A3
St Georges Gdns
DTN/ASHW M34 147 E2
St George's Rd BOL BL1 2 B3
BURY BL9 54 B5
DROY M43 117 G2
PART M31 137 F5
ROCH OL11 28 C3
RUSH/FAL M14 143 G4
STRET M32 139 H1
St Georges Sq BOL BL1 3 F3
CHAD OL9 89 H4
St George's St BOL BL1 2 E3
STLY SK15 120 D2
St George's Wy SLFD M6 113 F1
St Germain St FWTH BL4 65 H4
St Giles Dr HYDE SK14 148 B1
St Gregorys Cl FWTH BL4 65 H5
St Gregorys Rd
WGTN/LGST M12 128 D1
St Helena Rd BOL BL1 2 C4
St Helens Cl
GOL/RIS/CUL WA3 150 A3
St Helens Rd BOLS/LL BL3 48 B5
WHTN BL5 63 H3
St Helier's Dr BRO M7 102 A2
St Heliers St BOLS/LL BL3 48 C5
St Hilarys Pk WILM/AE SK9 200 D4
St Hilda's Dr OLD OL1 75 E4
St Hilda's Rd DTN/ASHW M34 132 B2
OLDTF/WHR M16 127 F3
WYTH/NTH M22 156 C5
St Hilda's Vw DTN/ASHW M34 132 B3
St Hugh's Cl ALT WA14 165 H1
St Ignatius Wk ORD M5 * 113 G5
St Ives Av CHD/CHDH SK8 170 D3
St Ives Crs SALE M33 154 B5
St Ives Rd RUSH/FAL M14 142 D1
St James Av BOLE BL2 50 B1
TOT/BURYW BL8 37 G3
St James Cl MILN OL16 58 D1
St James Ct HALE/TIMP WA15 165 H5
SLFD M6 * 112 A2
St James Dr SALE M33 154 B3
WILM/AE SK9 198 D4
St James Rd HTNM SK4 159 E1
St James's Gv ALT WA14 154 A5
St James's Rd BRO M7 101 H4
St James's Sq CMANW M2 6 E5
St James's St OLD OL1 76 A5
St James's Ter HEY OL10 40 D4
St James St AUL OL6 120 A3
CMANE M1 7 F6
ECC M30 * 111 F3
FWTH BL4 65 G5
HEY OL10 40 D4
MILN OL16 31 G5
ROY/SHW OL2 60 A2
St James' Wy CHD/CHDH SK8 192 C1
St John's Av DROY M43 118 A3
St John's Cl BRO M7 101 G4
DUK SK16 120 B5
MPL/ROM SK6 162 A4
St Johns Ct BRO M7 * 101 G4
HOR/BR BL6 46 C5
HYDE SK14 134 A5
MILN OL16 * 30 C5
OLDE OL4 77 E5
RAD M26 68 C2
St John's Dr HYDE SK14 134 A5
MILN OL16 30 C5
St John's Gdns MOSL OL5 93 H5
St John's Rd ALT WA14 177 F1
BRAM/HZG SK7 184 C3
BRUN/LGST M13 129 G4
DTN/ASHW M34 132 C3
HOR/BR BL6 62 C1
HTNM SK4 158 B4
OLDTF/WHR M16 127 F4
WALK M28 96 A3
WILM/AE SK9 200 B2
St John's St BRO M7 101 G4
CHAD OL9 8 B6
FWTH BL4 66 B4
RAD M26 68 C2
St John St CSLFD M3 6 C6
DUK SK16 * 120 B5
ECC M30 111 E4
IRL M44 136 C1
OLDE OL4 92 D1
SWIN M27 100 A4
WALK M28 81 H3
St John's Wk CHAD OL9 8 B5
EDGY/DAV SK3 * 171 E1
St Johns Wd HOR/BR BL6 46 C5
St Josephs Av WHTF M45 70 B5
St Josephs Cl ROY/SHW OL2 60 B1
St Joseph's Dr MILN OL16 43 G2
ORD M5 113 G5
St Joseph St BOL BL1 33 G4
St Kilda Av FWTH BL4 82 C1
St Kildas Av DROY M43 117 G2
St Kilda's Dr BRO M7 102 A2
St Lawrence Quay SALQ M50 126 C1
St Lawrence Rd
DTN/ASHW M34 132 C5
St Leonard's Ct SALE M33 154 A2
St Leonards Dr
HALE/TIMP WA15 166 A3
St Leonard's Rd HTNM SK4 159 G1
St Leonard's St MDTN M24 72 D3
St Lesmo Rd EDGY/DAV SK3 12 A7
St Lukes Ct CHAD OL9 74 B5
St Luke's Rd SLFD M6 112 C3
St Luke St ROCH OL11 * 43 E1
St Margaret's Av
BNG/LEV M19 143 H5
St Margaret's Cl ALT WA14 165 F5
BOL BL1 * 48 A1
PWCH M25 86 B1
St Margarets Gdns OLDS OL8 * 90 D4
St Margaret's Rd ALT WA14 165 F5
BOL BL1 48 A1
CHD/CHDH SK8 170 D3
NEWH/MOS M40 89 G4
PWCH M25 86 B2
St Mark's Av ALT WA14 164 D4
ROY/SHW OL2 59 H5
St Mark's Cl ROY/SHW OL2 59 H5
St Mark's Crs WALK M28 97 E1
St Mark's La BRO M7 102 A2
St Marks Sq BURY BL9 5 F1
St Mark's St BNG/LEV M19 144 C2
BOLS/LL BL3 49 E4
MPL/ROM SK6 161 H2
St Mark St DUK SK16 119 G4
St Mark's Vw BOLS/LL BL3 * 49 E4
St Marks Wk BOLS/LL BL3 48 D5
St Martin's Av HTNM SK4 12 A2
St Martins Cl DROY M43 117 G2
HYDE SK14 * 148 B1
St Martin's Dr BRO M7 102 A2
St Martin's Rd
MPL/ROM SK6 175 F3
OLDS OL8 91 H5
SALE M33 138 D5
St Martin's St ROCH OL11 42 B5
St Mary's Av BOLS/LL BL3 47 H4
DTN/ASHW M34 147 E3
St Mary's Cl MILN OL16 43 G2
PWCH M25 85 H3
STKP SK1 13 J3
St Marys Ct
NEWH/MOS M40 104 A2
OLD OL1 * 9 F2
St Mary's Crest UPML OL3 95 F2
St Mary's Dr CHD/CHDH SK8 * 170 C3
RDSH SK5 160 A1
UPML OL3 95 F2
St Marys Est OLD OL1 9 G2
St Mary's Ga CMANE M1 6 E3
MILN OL16 10 B5
ROY/SHW OL2 * 60 A2
UPML OL3 * 79 E4
St Mary's Hall Rd CHH M8 102 A1
St Mary's Parsonage
CSLFD M3 6 D4
St Mary's Pl BURY BL9 4 C5
St Mary's Rd ALT WA14 177 E2
ECC M30 111 G3
HYDE SK14 133 H3
NEWH/MOS M40 104 A3
PWCH M25 85 H3
SALE M33 154 A1
WALK M28 81 H3
St Mary's St CSLFD M3 6 D4
HULME M15 127 H3
OLD OL1 9 G1
OLDTF/WHR M16 128 A4
St Mary's Wy OLD OL1 9 F2
STKP SK1 13 J6
St Matthews Ct STRET M32 * 140 A2
St Matthew's Dr OLD OL1 74 B2
St Matthews Gra BOL BL1 * 33 H5
St Matthew's Rd
EDGY/DAV SK3 12 D6
St Matthews Ter
EDGY/DAV SK3 * 12 D6
St Matthews Wk BOL BL1 * 33 H5
St Mawes Ct RAD M26 * 51 F4
St Michael's Av BOLS/LL BL3 65 G2
BRAM/HZG SK7 183 H5
St Michaels Cl TOT/BURYW BL8 52 B1
St Michaels Ct SALE M33 139 E5
St Michaels Gdns WHTF M45 70 A3
St Michael's Rd HYDE SK14 148 B1
St Michael's Sq ANC M4 * 7 G1
St Modwen Rd STRET M32 125 E3
St Nicholas Rd HULME M15 127 H1
St Osmund's Dr BOLE BL2 50 B2
St Osmund's Gv BOLE BL2 50 B2
St Oswald's Rd BNG/LEV M19 144 B1
St Pauls Cl STLY SK15 121 F3
St Paul's Ct RAD M26 68 B3
WALK M28 82 A5
St Paul's Hill Rd HYDE SK14 148 B1
St Paul's Rd BRO M7 101 F1
DID/WITH M20 143 E5
HTNM SK4 159 E2
WALK M28 * 82 B5
St Paul's St BURY BL9 5 H3
HYDE SK14 133 H5
RAMS BL0 * 16 D2
STKP SK1 160 B3
STLY SK15 121 F3
St Pauls Vls BURY BL9 5 H3
St Peter's Av BOL BL1 32 D4
St Peters Cl AULW OL7 119 E3
St Peters Ct STRET M32 * 126 B5
St Peter's Dr HYDE SK14 * 148 B1
St Petersgate STKP SK1 13 G3
St Peter's Rd BURY BL9 53 G3
SWIN M27 98 D3
St Peter's Sq CMANW M2 6 E6
STKP SK1 13 F3
St Peter's St AUL OL6 119 F3
MILN OL16 30 C5
St Peter's Ter FWTH BL4 66 A5
St Peter's Wy BOL BL1 3 F3
BOLE BL2 3 H7
BOLS/LL BL3 65 H1
St Philip's Av BOLS/LL BL3 48 C5
St Philip's Pl CSLFD M3 * 114 A3
St Philip's Rd GTN M18 130 C4
St Phillip's Dr ROY/SHW OL2 75 F3
St Saviour's Rd OFTN SK2 172 D4
Saintsbridge Rd
WYTH/NTH M22 180 B2
St Simons Cl OFTN SK2 172 D1
St Simon St CSLFD M3 6 B1
St Stephen's Av
DTN/ASHW M34 118 D5
St Stephen's Cl BOLE BL2 49 H4
BRUN/LGST M13 129 E3
St Stephens Ct BKLY M9 * 103 E3
St Stephens St OLD OL1 9 J1
St Stephen St CSLFD M3 6 B3
OLD OL1 9 J1
St Stephens Vw DROY M43 117 H3
St Teresa's Rd
OLDTF/WHR M16 126 D5
St Thomas Ct BURY BL9 5 H4
St Thomas' Pl CHH M8 114 D1
St Thomas's Cir OLDS OL8 8 D7
St Thomas's Pl STKP SK1 13 G6
St Thomas St BOL BL1 * 33 G4
St Thomas St North OLDS OL8 8 D6
St Thomas St South OLDS OL8 8 D7
St Vincent St ANC M4 115 F3
St Werburghs Rd CCHDY M21 141 G3
St Wilfred's Dr WHIT OL12 * 18 C4
St Wilfrids St HULME M15 127 H2
St Williams Av BOLS/LL BL3 64 D1
Salcombe Av BOLE BL2 36 C5
Salcombe Cl SALE M33 153 H1
Salcombe Gv BOLE BL2 50 C3
Salcombe Rd OFTN SK2 172 D1
OP/CLY M11 117 E5
Salcot Wk NEWH/MOS M40 * 115 F2
Sale Heys Rd SALE M33 154 A3
Sale La WALK M28 96 A2
Salem Gv OLDE OL4 92 C1
Sale Rd NTHM/RTH M23 155 H4
Sale St LIT OL15 21 E2
Salford Rd WHTN BL5 63 H4
Salford St BURY BL9 38 D2
OLDE OL4 92 B2
Salik Gdns ROCH OL11 43 E1
Salisbury Av HEY OL10 55 H1
Salisbury Crs AUL OL6 107 G3
Salisbury Dr DUK SK16 134 B1
PWCH M25 86 B5
Salisbury Rd CCHDY M21 141 F2
ECC M30 111 G1
OLDE OL4 92 A1
RAD M26 51 H4
SWIN M27 98 D3
URM M41 124 C4
WHTF M45 69 G4
Salisbury St BOLS/LL BL3 2 B6
MDTN M24 73 E3
RDSH SK5 145 F3
ROY/SHW OL2 59 G1
RUSH/FAL M14 128 B4
Salisbury Ter BOLS/LL BL3 67 F1
Salkeld St ROCH OL11 43 E1
Salmon Flds ROY/SHW OL2 75 G1
Salmon St ANC M4 7 G3
Salmesbury Hall Cl RAMS BL0 16 C4
Salop St BOLE BL2 3 G6
SLFD M6 113 F1
Saltash Cl WYTH/NTH M22 180 C3
Saltdene Rd WYTH/NTH M22 180 B3
Saltergate BOLS/LL BL3 47 G5
Saltergate Ms ORD M5 * 113 F3
Salterton Dr BOLS/LL BL3 63 G2
Salteye Rd ECC M30 110 B4
Saltford Av ANC M4 115 F3
Saltford Ct ANC M4 115 F3
Salthill Av HEY OL10 56 B2
Salthill Dr WYTH/NTH M22 180 D2
Salthouse Cl TOT/BURYW BL8 26 D5
Saltire Gdns BRO M7 101 H2
Saltney Av DID/WITH M20 142 B4
Saltram Cl RAD M26 51 F4
Saltrush Rd WYTH/NTH M22 180 C2
Salts Dr LIT OL15 20 D2
Salts St ROY/SHW OL2 60 A2
Saltwood Gv BOL BL1 2 E1
Salutation St HULME M15 128 A2
Sam Cowan Cl RUSH/FAL M14 128 B5
Samian Gdns BRO M7 101 F5
Samlesbury Cl DID/WITH M20 157 E3
ROY/SHW OL2 59 G2
Samouth Cl NEWH/MOS M40 115 G2
Sampson Sq RUSH/FAL M14 128 B4
Samson St MILN OL16 11 K4
Sam Swire St HULME M15 127 H3
Samuel La ROY/SHW OL2 59 F1
Samuel Ogden St CMANE M1 7 G7
Samuel St BNG/LEV M19 144 B3
BURY BL9 5 G2
FAIL M35 105 E2
HTNM SK4 159 G3
ROCH OL11 42 B4
Sanby Av GTN M18 130 B4
Sanby Rd GTN M18 130 B4
Sanctuary Cl HULME M15 128 C3
The Sanctuary HULME M15 127 H2
Sandacre Rd NTHM/RTH M23 168 A2
Sandal St NEWH/MOS M40 115 H2
Sandbach Av RUSH/FAL M14 142 B3
Sandbach Rd RDSH SK5 * 145 E1
SALE M33 155 G3
Sandbank Gdns WHIT OL12 14 B3
Sand Banks BOL BL1 23 E5
Sandbed La MOSL OL5 93 H5
Sandbrook Pk ROCH OL11 * 42 D2
Sandbrook Wy
DTN/ASHW M34 132 C3
ROCH OL11 42 D2
Sandby Dr MPL/ROM SK6 175 G1
Sanderling Rd OFTN SK2 173 H4
Sanderson Cl WALK M28 98 A2
Sanderson St BURY BL9 5 H3
NEWH/MOS M40 103 F5
Sanderstead Dr BKLY M9 88 B4
Sandfield Dr HOR/BR BL6 46 D3
Sandfield Rd MILN OL16 43 G1
Sandfold La BNG/LEV M19 144 C1
Sandford Av GTN M18 * 130 C2
Sandford Cl BOLE BL2 35 F3
Sandford Rd SALE M33 155 G3
Sandford Station La
RDSH SK5 144 D1
Sandford St RAD M26 53 E5
Sandgate Av OP/CLY M11 117 E3
RAD M26 67 E5
Sandgate Dr URM M41 124 C4
Sandgate Rd CHAD OL9 90 C1
WHTF M45 70 A5
Sandham St BOLS/LL BL3 49 E5
Sandham Wk BOLS/LL BL3 * 49 E5
Sandheys DTN/ASHW M34 132 C3
Sandheys Gv GTN M18 130 D4
Sandhill Cl BOLS/LL BL3 49 E5
Sandhill St HYDE SK14 134 A5
Sandhill Wk WYTH/NTH M22 180 A2
Sandhole La ROCH OL11 41 F1
Sand Hole La ROCH OL11 43 E5
Sand Hole Rd FWTH BL4 83 E1
Sandhurst Av DID/WITH M20 142 C5
Sandhurst Cl TOT/BURYW BL8 37 G3
Sandhurst Ct BOLE BL2 50 B3
Sandhurst Dr BOLE BL2 50 B3
WILM/AE SK9 199 F2
Sandhurst Rd DID/WITH M20 157 G4
OFTN SK2 172 C4
Sandhurst St OLDE OL4 92 B3
Sandhutton Rd BKLY M9 103 E1
Sandilands Rd
NTHM/RTH M23 167 E1
Sandileigh Av CHD/CHDH SK8 170 D3
DID/WITH M20 157 G1
HALE/TIMP WA15 178 A1
RDSH SK5 160 C2
Sandileigh Dr BOL BL1 34 C3
HALE/TIMP WA15 178 A1
Sandiway BRAM/HZG SK7 183 H2
HEY OL10 41 F4
IRL M44 136 C1
MPL/ROM SK6 161 G3
Sandiway Cl MPL/ROM SK6 175 E1
Sandiway Dr DID/WITH M20 157 F3
Sandiway Pl ALT WA14 165 G4
Sandiway Rd ALT WA14 165 G3
SALE M33 154 A2
WILM/AE SK9 192 A2
Sandon St BOLS/LL BL3 48 C5
Sandown Av SLFD M6 112 D3
Sandown Cl OLD OL1 75 H3
WILM/AE SK9 199 G2
Sandown Crs BOLS/LL BL3 66 D2
GTN M18 130 C5
Sandown Dr DTN/ASHW M34 147 F3
HALE/TIMP WA15 188 D1
SALE M33 153 H3
Sandown Gdns URM M41 138 A1
Sandown Rd BOLE BL2 35 G3
BRAM/HZG SK7 185 H3
BURY BL9 69 H2
EDGY/DAV SK3 171 E1
Sandown St GTN M18 130 D2
Sandpiper Cl DUK SK16 133 H1
FWTH BL4 65 E5
ROCH OL11 28 C4
Sandpiper Dr EDGY/DAV SK3 171 G3
Sandray Cl BOLS/LL BL3 47 G4

Sandray Gv ORD M5 ....112 D4
Sandridge CI FWTH BL4 ....66 B4
Sandridge Wk
  WGTN/LGST M12 ....129 F2
Sandringham Av
  DTN/ASHW M34 ....131 F5
  DTN/ASHW M34 ....132 A2
  STLY SK15 ....128 D2
Sandringham CI ALT WA14 ......176 C5
Sandringham Dr DUK SK16 ......134 A2
  HTNM SK4 ....158 D5
  MILN OL16 ....31 H5
  POY/DIS SK12 ....195 E4
  TOT/BURYW BL8 ....26 B2
Sandringham Gra PWCH M25 ....86 D4
Sandringham Rd
  BRAM/HZG SK7 ....185 G2
  CHD/CHDH SK8 ....182 D1
  HYDE SK14 ....148 A4
  MPL/ROM SK6 ....160 D5
  WALK M28 ....96 B4
Sandringham Wy GTN M18 ......130 B4
Sandringham Wy
  ROY/SHW OL2 ....58 D3
  WILM/AE SK9 ....198 D4
Sands Av CHAD OL9 ....73 H4
Sands CI HYDE SK14 ....149 F2
Sandsend CI CHH M8 ....101 H5
Sandsend Rd URM M41 ....124 B5
Sandstone Rd MILN OL16 ....31 G4
Sandstone Wy ECC/LEV BL3 .....47 H5
Sand St NEWH/MOS M40 ....115 F1
  STLY SK15 ....120 C5
Sandwell Dr SALE M33 ....139 H5
Sandwich CI WALK M28 ....82 A5
Sandwich Rd ECC M30 ....122 A4
Sandwich St BOLS/LL BL3 ....48 C4
Sandwood Av BOLS/LL BL3 ....47 F4
Sandy Acre MOSL OL5 ....108 D2
Sandy Bank ROY/SHW OL2 ....59 C1
Sandy Bank Av HYDE SK14 ......99 H2
Sandy Bank Rd CHH M8 ....102 A2
Sandy Bank Wk HYDE SK14 * ...149 F2
Sandybrook CI
  TOT/BURYW BL8 ....26 A5
Sandybrook Dr BKLY M9 ....87 H5
Sandy Brow BKLY M9 ....88 A5
Sandy CI BURY BL9 ....53 C5
Sandycroft Av
  WYTH/NTH M22 ....180 C1
Sandygate CI WHTN M27 ....98 D3
Sandy Gv DUK SK16 ....112 D2
  SLFD M6 ....112 D2
  SWIN M27 ....99 E2
Sandy Haven CI HYDE SK14 ....149 F2
Sandyhill Rd BKLY M9 ....87 H4
Sandyhills BOLS/LL BL3 ....47 H4
Sandylands Dr PWCH M25 ......100 C1
Sandy La DROY M43 ....141 F3
  DROY M43 ....118 B2
  DUK SK16 ....120 A5
  IRL M44 ....122 B5
  MDTN M24 ....73 E5
  MPL/ROM SK6 ....162 B3
  NTHM/RTH M23 ....167 E2
  OLDS OL8 * 8 D5
  PWCH M25 ....85 H5
  RDSH SK5 ....159 H3
  ROCH OL11 ....29 F4
  ROY/SHW OL2 ....59 E5
  SLFD M6 ....112 D2
  STRET M32 ....139 F2
  UPML OL3 ....79 E2
  WILM/AE SK9 ....198 A2
Sandy Meade PWCH M25 ....85 H4
Sandywarps IRL M44 ....136 C3
Sandyway PWCH M25 * 85 H4
Sangwell CI OP/CLY M11 ....130 C1
Sandywell St OP/CLY M11 ....117 E5
Sandy Wd SLFD M6 ....112 D2
Sangster Ct ORD M5 ....113 F5
Sankey Gv BKLY M9 ....87 G4
Sankey St BURY BL9 ....4 B4
Santiago St RUSH/FAL M14 .....128 C5
Santley St WGTN/LGST M12 ....129 H5
Santon Av RUSH/FAL M14 ......143 G4
Sapling Rd BOLS/LL BL3 ....64 B2
  SWIN M27 ....98 C5
Sarah Butterworth Ct
  MILN OL16 ....11 H7
Sarah Butterworth St
  MILN OL16 ....30 C5
Sarah St ECC M30 ....110 C4
  MDTN M24 ....72 C4
  OP/CLY M11 ....116 A5
  ROCH OL11 ....30 A5
Sargent Dr OLDTF/WHR M16 ...127 H4
Sargent Rd MPL/ROM SK6 .....161 E4
Sark Rd CCHDY M21 ....141 E1
Sarn Av WYTH/NTH M22 ....168 C5
Saturn Gv SLFD M6 ....113 H1
Saunton Av BOLE BL2 ....35 G4
Saunton Rd OP/CLY M11 ....117 E5
Sautridge CI MDTN M24 ....57 C2
Savernake Rd MPL/ROM SK6 ...162 B1
Savick Av BOLE BL2 ....50 B2
Saville Rd CHD/CHDH SK8 ......169 E5
  RAD M26 ....52 A2
Saville St BOLE BL2 ....3 C5
  MDTN M24 ....73 E2
Saviours Ter BOLS/LL BL3 * 48 B4
Savio Wy MDTN M24 ....72 D5
Savoy Ct WHTF M45 * 72 D3
Savoy Dr ROY/SHW OL2 ....75 E2
Savoy St OLDE OL4 ....92 A2
  ROCH OL11 ....10 C3
Sawley Av LIT OL15 ....20 D1
  OLDE OL4 ....92 C3
  WHTF M45 ....69 G2
Sawley Dr CHD/CHDH SK8 .....193 E1
Sawley Rd NEWH/MOS M40 ....115 G1
Sawmill Wy LIT OL15 * 104 D4
Saw St BOL BL1 ....34 B3
Sawyer Brow HYDE SK14 ....134 A4
Sawyer St TOT/BURYW BL8 ......37 C2
  WHIT OL12 ....10 C3
Saxby Av EDGW/EG BL7 ....23 C5
Saxby St SLFD M6 ....99 H5

Saxelby Dr CHH M8 ....102 C4
Saxfield Dr NTHM/RTH M23 ....168 B3
Saxon Av CHH M8 ....87 F5
  DUK SK16 ....119 H5
Saxon CI TOT/BURYW BL8 ....37 C4
Saxon Dr CHAD OL9 ....73 H4
  DROY M43 ....117 H3
  DTN/ASHW M34 ....132 B1
Saxonholme Rd ROCH OL11 .....57 F2
Saxon St DROY M43 ....118 A3
  MDTN M24 ....73 E4
  NEWH/MOS M40 ....115 H2
  OLDE OL4 ....76 B5
  MDTN M24 ....68 A1
Saxthorpe CI SALE M33 ....153 C1
Saxthorpe Wk
  WGTN/LGST M12 ....129 F3
Saxwood Av BKLY M9 ....103 E1
Saxwood CI WHIT OL12 ....28 C2
Scafell Av AULW OL7 ....119 E1
Scafell CI MPL/ROM SK6 ....186 D4
  OLD OL1 ....75 G3
Scale St ORD M5 ....113 G4
Scarborough St
  NEWH/MOS M40 ....103 H2
Scarcroft Rd WGTN/LGST M12 ..129 H3
Scardale Av BOL BL1 ....32 D5
Scarfield Dr ROCH OL11 ....28 B2
Scargill CI RUSH/FAL M14 * 143 E3
Scargill Rd BOLS/LL BL3 ....47 F5
Scarisbrick Av DID/WITH M20 ..158 A3
Scarisbrick St BNG/LEV M19 ...143 H5
Scarr Av RAD M26 ....68 D3
Scarr Dr WHIT OL12 ....30 A1
Scarr La ROY/SHW OL2 ....60 B2
Scarsdale Rd RUSH/FAL M14 ...129 E4
Scarsdale St SLFD M6 ....113 G2
Scarthwood CI BOLE BL2 ....35 F1
Scawfell Av BOLE BL2 ....34 C4
Schofield Av DROY M43 ....118 A4
  ECC M30 ....110 B4
Schofield St FAIL M35 * 105 E2
  HEY OL10 ....41 E5
  LIT OL15 ....21 F2
  MILN OL16 ....44 D1
  OLDS OL8 ....91 F4
  OP/CLY M11 ....116 D3
  ROCH OL11 ....43 F2
  ROY/SHW OL2 ....59 E4
Scholar Green Rd STRET M32 ...125 E5
Scholars Dr DID/WITH M20 ....142 C4
Scholars Wy MDTN M24 ....72 C4
Scholes La NEWH/MOS M40 ....89 H5
Scholes St CHAD OL9 ....90 B3
  FAIL M35 ....105 F1
  OLD OL1 ....9 J3
  ROCH OL11 ....42 B5
  SWIN M27 ....99 F2
  TOT/BURYW BL8 ....37 H3
Scholes Wk PWCH M25 ....86 B4
Scholey St BOLE BL2 ....49 F4
Scholfield Av URM M41 ....139 F2
School Av AUL OL6 ....107 G4
  STRET M32 ....126 C5
School Brow BURY BL9 ....4 F1
  MPL/ROM SK6 ....161 H4
  WALK M28 ....97 G4
School CI POY/DIS SK12 ....195 G4
School Ct ANC M4 ....7 K3
  EDGY/DAV SK3 ....172 A3
School Crs STLY SK15 ....120 D2
School Gv DID/WITH M20 ......143 E5
  PWCH M25 ....85 H5
School Gv West
  DID/WITH M20 * 143 E5
School HI BOL BL1 ....45 E2
School House Flats OLDS OL8 * ..90 D5
School La ALT WA14 ....164 A5
  BKLY M9 ....87 H5
  BURY BL9 ....27 F3
  DID/WITH M20 ....157 H3
  HTNM SK4 ....159 F1
  HYDE SK14 ....148 A4
  IRL M44 ....136 B1
  IRL M44 ....150 C1
  MILN OL16 ....10 C7
  MPL/ROM SK6 ....163 G5
  MPL/ROM SK6 ....165 G3
  PART M31 ....137 C5
  POY/DIS SK12 ....195 C4
  STLY SK15 ....109 F3
School Ms MILN OL16 * 45 E2
School Rd ECC M30 ....110 D5
  FAIL M35 ....105 G3
  HALE/TIMP WA15 ....178 A1
  OLDS OL8 ....90 C5
  SALE M33 ....153 H3
  STRET M32 ....140 A1
  WILM/AE SK9 ....192 A3
Schools HI CHD/CHDH SK8 .....182 A1
Schoolside CI CHH M8 ....102 C4
Schoolside La MDTN M24 ....71 H5
Schools Rd GTN M18 ....130 D3
School St ANC M4 ....7 C1
  BOLS/LL BL3 ....67 E1
  BRAM/HZG SK7 ....185 F2
  BURY BL9 ....5 J6
  ECC M30 ....110 C2
  EDGW/EG BL7 ....23 C4
  HEY OL10 ....40 D4
  LIT OL15 ....20 B3
  OLD OL4 ....93 F1
  OLDE OL4 ....93 F1
  RAD M26 ....68 C5
  RAMS BL0 ....16 C3
  UPML OL3 ....79 G3
  WHIT OL12 ....14 C3
School Wk OLDTF/WHR M16 ...127 G3
Schuter Rd RUSH/FAL M14 .....143 F2
Schwabe St MDTN M24 ....71 H4
Scobell St TOT/BURYW BL8 ......37 H4
Scoitock Wy OLD OL1 ....9 G2
Scorton Av BOLE BL2 ....35 F1
Scorton St BOL BL1 * 48 B1
Scotforth CI HULME M15 ....127 H1
Scotland Hall Rd
  NEWH/MOS M40 ....116 C1

Scotland St AUL OL6 ....119 H3
  NEWH/MOS M40 ....104 B5
Scott Av CCHDY M21 ....141 F1
Scott CI RDSH SK5 ....110 D2
Scott Ct RDSH SK5 ....160 A2
Scott Dr HALE/TIMP WA15 .....166 A5
  MPL/ROM SK6 ....175 G1
Scottfield OLDS OL8 ....9 F7
Scottfield Rd OLDS OL8 ....9 G7
Scott Ga DTN/ASHW M34 ......132 B1
Scottia Rd ECC M30 ....110 C5
Scott Rd DROY M43 ....117 H4
  DTN/ASHW M34 ....146 C2
  PWCH M25 ....85 G4
Scott St OLDS OL8 ....9 G7
  RAD M26 ....67 G5
Scottwood Wk NTHM/RTH M23 .167 G5
Scout Dr WYTH/NTH M22 ....180 A1
Scout Gn MDTN M24 ....72 D1
Scout Vw TOT/BURYW BL8 ......26 B5
Scovell St BRO M7 ....101 G4
Scowcroft La ROY/SHW OL2 .....59 H3
Scowcroft St BOLE BL2 ....3 J1
Scroggins La PART M31 ....151 E2
Scropton St NEWH/MOS M40 ..103 E5
Seabright Wk OP/CLY M11 * ...116 A4
Seabrook Crs URM M41 ....124 C4
Seabrook Rd NEWH/MOS M40 .116 D1
Seacombe Av RUSH/FAL M14 ..142 C2
Seacombe Gv EDGY/DAV SK3 ..171 E1
Seaford Rd BOLE BL2 ....24 B5
  NEWH/MOS M40 ....103 C5
Seaforth Av RAD M26 ....68 D3
Seaforth Wk CHAD OL9 * 90 C1
Seaforth Rd BOL BL1 ....33 H1
Seaham Dr TOT/BURYW BL8 ....37 H1
Seaham Wk RUSH/FAL M14 ...128 C5
Sealand CI SALE M33 ....155 F4
Sealand Dr ECC M30 ....110 B5
Sealand Rd NTHM/RTH M23 ...155 C4
Seale Av DTN/ASHW M34 ....132 A1
Sealey Wk NEWH/MOS M40 * ..115 H1
Seal Rd BRAM/HZG SK7 ....184 B5
Seamon's Dr ALT WA14 ....164 D4
Seamon's Rd ALT WA14 ....164 D3
Searby Rd GTN M18 ....130 A4
Searness Rd MDTN M24 ....71 H2
Seascale Av OP/CLY M11 ....116 C2
Seathwaite CI MDTN M24 ....71 H4
Seathwaite Rd FWTH BL4 ....65 E5
Seatoller Dr BOLE BL2 ....21 H3
Seaton Rd BRAM/HZG SK7 ....185 E3
Seaton Ms AULW OL7 ....118 D1
Seaton Rd BOL BL1 ....33 H1
Sebastian CI MPL/ROM SK6 ...175 G2
Sebastopol Wk ANC M4 * 7 K3
Second Av BOL BL3 ....48 A2
  BOLS/LL BL3 ....50 C5
  BURY BL9 ....39 G3
  OLDS OL8 ....90 D5
  OP/CLY M11 ....117 E3
  STLY SK15 ....109 F5
  SWIN M27 ....98 C5
  TRPK M17 ....126 A3
Second St BOL BL1 ....32 C2
Section St BOL BL1 ....32 C2
Sedan CI ORD M5 ....113 F4
Sedburgh CI SALE M33 ....153 G3
Sedbury CI NTHM/RTH M23 ....155 C5
Seddon Av BURY BL9 ....39 E4
Seddon CI RAD M26 ....52 B5
Seddon Gdns RAD M26 ....66 D4
Seddon La RAD M26 ....66 D4
Seddon Rd ALT WA14 ....177 G5
Seddon St BNG/LEV M19 * 144 B1
  BOLS/LL BL3 * 67 E1
  LHULT M38 ....81 E2
  RAD M26 ....68 B1
Sedgeborough Rd
  OLDTF/WHR M16 ....127 H5
Sedge CI RDSH SK5 ....145 G3
Sedgefield CI ORD M5 ....113 F3
Sedgefield Dr BOL BL1 ....33 E5
Sedgefield Pk OLDE OL4 ....92 C4
Sedgeford Rd RAD M26 ....68 A4
Sedgeford CI WILM/AE SK9 ....199 F1
Sedgeford Rd
  NEWH/MOS M40 ....103 E5
Sedgemoor CI
  CHD/CHDH SK8 ....183 E2
Sedgemoor V BOLE BL2 ....35 G4
Sedgemoor Wy OLD OL1 ....9 F2
Sedgley Av MILN OL16 ....43 G2
  PWCH M25 ....86 B5
Sedgley CI MDTN M24 ....73 F5
Sedgley Park Rd PWCH M25 .....86 B5
Sedgley St MDTN M24 ....73 F5
Seedfield Rd BURY BL9 ....38 B1
Seedley Av LHULT M38 ....81 C3
Seedley Park Rd SLFD M6 ......112 D3
Seedley Rd SLFD M6 ....112 D3
Seedley St RUSH/FAL M14 .....128 C5
Seedley Vw RD ORD M5 ....112 D2
Seedley View Rd ORD M5 ......112 D2
Seel St MOSL OL5 ....108 C1
Sefton CI BRUN/LGST M13 ....128 C2
  MDTN M24 ....72 C4
  OLD OL1 ....60 C5
Sefton Crs SALE M33 ....139 H5
Sefton Dr BURY BL9 ....27 H5
  SWIN M27 ....98 C5
  WALK M28 ....97 H4
Sefton Rd BOL BL1 ....33 E4
  CCHDY M21 ....141 F5
  MDTN M24 ....72 B4
  SALE M33 ....154 C1
Sefton St BURY BL9 ....27 G5
  CHAD OL9 ....90 B5
  CHH M8 ....102 B2
  HEY OL10 ....41 F5
  RAD M26 ....68 D5
  ROCH OL11 ....43 F2
  WHTF M45 ....69 C5
Segal CI BRO M7 ....101 G3
Selborne Rd CCHDY M21 ....141 F2
Selbourne CI WHTN BL5 ....62 B3

Selby Av CHAD OL9 ....74 A3
  WHTF M45 ....69 G3
Selby CI MILN OL16 ....31 F5
  POY/DIS SK12 * 195 E2
  RAD M26 ....52 B5
  STRET M32 ....125 E5
Selby Dr SLFD M6 ....112 A2
  URM M41 ....123 G3
Selby Gdns CHD/CHDH SK8 ...193 F1
Selby Rd MDTN M24 ....72 C5
  STRET M32 ....125 F5
  OP/CLY M11 ....116 B5
Selham Wk BRUN/LGST M13 * .128 C1
Selhurst Av OP/CLY M11 ....116 D3
Selkirk Av OLDS OL8 ....91 E3
Selkirk Dr BKLY M9 ....88 C4
Selkirk Rd BOL BL1 ....33 G1
  CHAD OL9 ....90 A3
Sellars Sq DROY M43 ....117 H5
Sellers Wy CHAD OL9 ....90 B4
Selsby Av ECC M30 ....110 C3
Selsey Av EDGY/DAV SK3 ......170 C2
  SALE M33 ....154 A3
Selsey Dr DID/WITH M20 ....169 H1
Selside Wk RUSH/FAL M14 ....143 E3
Selstead Rd WYTH/NTH M22 ..180 B3
Selston Rd BKLY M9 ....87 G3
Selworth Av SALE M33 ....155 F2
Selworthy Rd
  OLDTF/WHR M16 ....127 H4
Selwyn Av BKLY M9 ....103 E2
  OLDS OL8 ....8 E6
Selwyn CI OLDS OL8 * 8 E6
Selwyn Dr CHD/CHDH SK8 ....183 F5
Selwyn St BOLE BL2 ....2 A5
  OLDS OL8 ....8 E6
Senior Av RUSH/FAL M14 ......143 G4
Senior Rd ECC M30 ....110 A5
Senior St CSLFD M3 ....6 C1
Senior Vw HYDE SK14 * 133 H5
Sepal CI RDSH SK5 ....145 G2
Sepia Gv MDTN M24 ....72 C3
Sequoia St BKLY M9 ....103 F2
Sergeants La WHTF M45 ....69 E3
Serin CI OFTN SK2 ....173 G5
Serpentine Wk SLFD M6 ....113 F2
Service St HTNM SK4 ....171 F1
Sesame Gdns IRL M44 ....122 D5
Set St STLY SK15 ....120 C4
Settle CI TOT/BURYW BL8 ....37 G5
Settle St BOLS/LL BL3 ....64 D1
  BOLS/LL BL3 ....67 E2
  NEWH/MOS M40 ....115 E5
Seven Acres La WHIT OL12 .....28 B1
Seven Acres Rd WHIT OL12 .....28 B1
Sevenoaks Av HTNM SK4 ......158 D1
  URM M41 ....124 C4
Sevenoaks Dr BOLS/LL BL3 .....64 D1
  SWIN M27 ....98 C5
Sevenoaks Rd CHD/CHDH SK8 .169 G3
Sevenoaks Wk
  BRUN/LGST M13 * 128 D3
Seven Stiles Dr MPL/ROM SK6 .174 D2
Seventh Av OLDS OL8 ....105 H1
Severn CI ALT WA14 ....165 F3
  BURY BL9 ....23 E4
Severn Dr BRAM/HZG SK7 ....193 F1
  MILN OL16 ....31 F5
Severn Rd CHAD OL9 ....74 A4
  HEY OL10 ....40 B3
  OLDS OL8 ....105 G1
Severn Wy FWTH BL4 ....83 G2
  RDSH SK5 ....160 A1
Seville St ROY/SHW OL2 ....59 H4
  ROY/SHW OL2 ....75 F2
Sewell Wy LHULT M38 ....81 E3
Sewerby CI OLDTF/WHR M16 ..128 A4
Sewerby St OLDTF/WHR M16 ..127 F4
Sexa St OP/CLY M11 ....117 E5
Sexton St HEY OL10 ....40 C4
Seymour Av OP/CLY M11 ......117 E3
Seymour CI OLDTF/WHR M16 ..127 F3
Seymour Dr BOLE BL2 ....35 E4
Seymour Gv FWTH BL4 * 65 F3
  HALE/TIMP WA15 ....166 B4
  MILN OL16 ....43 G3
  MPL/ROM SK6 ....174 D3
  OLDTF/WHR M16 ....127 E4
  SALE M33 ....154 C2
Seymour PI
  OLDTF/WHR M16 * 127 E3
Seymour Rd BOL BL1 ....34 A3
  CHD/CHDH SK8 ....182 D4
  MILN OL16 ....102 A1
  OFTN SK2 ....172 D2
Seymour Rd South
  OP/CLY M11 ....117 E3
Seymour St BOLE BL2 ....35 E4
  DTN/ASHW M34 ....132 A5
  GTN M18 ....130 C2
  HEY OL10 ....40 B5
  RAD M26 ....68 C1
Shackleton Gv BOL BL1 ....32 C4
Shackleton St ECC M30 ....110 D2
Shackliffe Rd NEWH/MOS M40 .89 F5
Shaddock Av WHIT OL12 ....28 C2
Shade Av OLDE OL4 ....93 E2
Shadowbrook Av
  NTHM/RTH M23 ....167 H5
Shadowbrook CI OLD OL1 ....75 F3
Shadowmoss Rd
  WYTH/NTH M22 ....180 D4
Shadows La WHIT OL12 ....94 B3
Shadwell St East HEY OL10 .....41 F3
Shadwell St West HEY OL10 ....41 E3
Shadworth CI MOSL OL5 ....94 B3
Shady La EDGW/EG BL7 ....23 G5
  NTHM/RTH M23 ....167 F5
Shady Oak Rd OFTN SK2 ......173 G3
Shaftesbury Av
  CHD/CHDH SK8 ....170 C3
  ECC M30 ....110 D5
  HALE/TIMP WA15 ....166 A4
  HOR/BR BL6 ....46 A1
Shaftesbury Dr WYTH/NTH M22 .20 A2
Shaftesbury Gdns URM M41 ...137 E1
Shaftesbury Rd CHH M8 ....102 B2
  EDGY/DAV SK3 ....170 D3
  SWIN M27 ....99 E3

Shaftesbury Dr HEY OL10 ....55 H1
Shakespeare Av BURY BL9 ......53 G3
  DTN/ASHW M34 ....146 D3
  RAD M26 ....51 H5
  STLY SK15 ....121 H2
Shakespeare Crs DROY M43 ...117 H5
  ECC M30 ....111 E3
Shakespeare Dr
  CHD/CHDH SK8 ....170 C3
Shakespeare Rd DROY M43 ...117 H3
  MPL/ROM SK6 ....161 F5
  OLD OL1 ....75 F2
  PWCH M25 ....85 G4
  SWIN M27 ....98 C2
Shakespeare Wk
  BRUN/LGST M13 ....128 D3
Shakleton Av BKLY M9 ....88 D4
Shalbourne Rd WALK M28 ....81 H4
Shaldon Dr NEWH/MOS M40 ..117 F1
Shafleet CI BOLE BL2 ....35 F1
Shambles Sq CMANE M1 ....6 E4
Shamdon Av WYTH/NTH M22 ..156 C5
Shanklin Av URM M41 ....138 C1
Shanklin CI CCHDY M21 ....141 E2
  DTN/ASHW M34 * 147 F3
Shanklin Wk BOLS/LL BL3 ....49 H4
Shanley Ct CHAD OL9 ....74 C4
Shannon CI HEY OL10 ....40 B3
Shannon Rd WYTH/NTH M22 ..168 D5
Shap Av HALE/TIMP WA15 .....167 E4
Shap Dr WALK M28 ....82 C5
Sharcott CI OLDTF/WHR M16 ..128 A4
Shardlow CI NEWH/MOS M40 ..115 H1
Shargate CI WILM/AE SK9 .....199 F1
Sharman St BOLS/LL BL3 ....49 G4
Sharnford CI BOLE BL2 ....3 J7
Sharnford Sq
  WGTN/LGST M12 ....129 G3
Sharon Av OLDE OL4 ....94 A1
Sharon CI AULW OL7 ....118 D4
Sharples Av BOL BL1 ....22 D5
Sharples Dr TOT/BURYW BL8 ...37 G2
Sharples Hall Dr BOL BL1 ....35 E5
Sharples Hall Fold BOL BL1 .....34 A1
Sharples Hall Ms BOL BL1 ....23 E5
Sharples Hall St OLDE OL4 ......76 C3
Sharples Pk BOL BL1 ....33 G2
Sharples St HTNM SK4 ....159 H5
Sharp St ANC M4 ....7 H1
  MDTN M24 ....73 D4
  PWCH M25 ....85 H3
  TOT/BURYW BL8 ....37 G2
  WALK M28 ....82 B4
Sharrington Dr
  NTHM/RTH M23 ....167 F3
Sharston Rd WYTH/NTH M22 ..168 D2
Shaving La WALK M28 ....97 E1
Shaw Av HYDE SK14 ....148 A4
Shawbrook Av WALK M28 ....96 C2
Shawbrook Rd BNG/LEV M19 ..158 D1
Shawbury Ct SALE M33 ....154 A4
Shawbury Rd
  NTHM/RTH M23 ....168 A5
Shawbury St MDTN M24 ....73 F5
Shawclough CI WHIT OL12 ....18 C5
Shawclough Dr WHIT OL12 .....18 C5
Shawclough Ri WHIT OL12 ....29 G1
Shawclough Rd WHIT OL12 .....18 C5
Shawclough Wy WHIT OL12 .....18 B5
Shawcroft CI ROY/SHW OL2 ....59 H4
Shawcross Fold STKP SK1 ....13 G2
Shawcross La
  WYTH/NTH M22 ....169 E1
Shawcross St HYDE SK14 ......148 B3
  SLFD M6 ....113 E4
  STKP SK1 ....13 H6
Shawdene Rd
  WYTH/NTH M22 ....168 B1
Shawe Hall Av URM M41 ....138 A3
Shawe Hall Crs URM M41 ......138 A3
Shawe Rd URM M41 ....138 A1
Shawe Vw URM M41 ....138 A3
Shawfield CI RUSH/FAL M14 ...142 C3
Shawfield La ROCH OL11 ....43 G1
Shawfields STLY SK15 ....121 G2
Shawford Rd NEWH/MOS M40 ..89 F5
Shawgreen CI HULME M15 .....127 G2
Shaw Hall Av HYDE SK14 ......134 C3
Shaw Hall Bank Rd UPML OL3 ..94 C2
Shaw Hall CI UPML OL3 ....94 C2
Shaw Head Dr FAIL M35 ....105 E4
Shaw Heath EDGY/DAV SK3 ....12 E6
  OFTN SK2 ....172 A2
Shawheath CI HULME M15 .....127 G2
Shawhill Wk NEWH/MOS M40 ..7 J2
Shaw La MILN OL16 ....31 G3
Shawlea Av BNG/LEV M19 .....143 G5
Shaw Moor Av STLY SK15 .....121 F4
Shaw Rd HTNM SK4 ....159 F1
  MILN OL16 ....31 G3
  MILN OL16 ....43 E3
  OLD OL1 ....75 H3
  ROY/SHW OL2 ....59 G5
Shaw Rd South
  EDGY/DAV SK3 ....171 H3
Shaws Fold OLDE OL4 * 77 F5
Shaw's La UPML OL3 ....79 F5
Shaw St AUL OL6 ....120 A2
  BOLS/LL BL3 ....50 B4
  BURY BL9 ....5 J5
  CSLFD M3 ....6 E1
  FWTH BL4 * 65 H2
  HYDE SK14 ....135 H4
  MILN OL16 ....31 G3
  OLD OL1 ....9 F1
  OLDE OL4 ....92 D2
  ROY/SHW OL2 ....59 F5
  WHIT OL12 ....11 G1
Shay Av HALE/TIMP WA15 ....179 F5
Shayfield Av CHAD OL9 ....73 G3
  WYTH/NTH M22 ....168 C4
Shayfield Dr WYTH/NTH M22 ..168 C4
Shayfield Rd WYTH/NTH M22 ..168 C4
  WYTH/NTH M22 ....179 F3
Sheader Dr ORD M5 ....112 B3
Sheaf Field Wk RAD M26 ....52 D5
Sheard Av AUL OL6 ....107 G4
Shearer Wy SWIN M27 ....100 A3
Shearing Av WHIT OL12 ....28 C3

Shearsby Cl HULME M15 ....127 H2
Shearwater Dr WALK M28 ....81 H4
Shearwater Gdns ECC M30 ....110 B5
The Sheddings BOLS/LL BL3 ....49 G5
Shed St WHIT OL12 ....14 C4
Sheepfoot La OLD OL1 ....75 E3
  PWCH M25 ....86 C4
Sheepfoot Wk OLD OL1 ....75 E3
Sheep Gap WHIT OL12 ....29 E2
Sheep Gate Dr
  TOT/BURYW BL8 ....36 D1
Sheerness St GTN M18 ....130 C3
Sheffield Rd HYDE SK14 ....134 A5
Sheffield St CMANE M1 ....7 J6
  HTNM SK4 ....159 H3
Shefford Cl OP/CLY M11 ....116 A5
Sheiling Ct ALT WA14 ....165 F5
Shelbourne Av BOL BL1 ....33 E4
Shelderton Cl
  NEWH/MOS M40 ....103 H3
Sheldon Cl PART M31 ....151 E3
Sheldon Rd AULW OL7 ....107 E5
  POY/DIS SK12 ....196 D5
Sheldon St OP/CLY M11 ....116 B5
Sheldrake Cl DUK SK16 ....133 H1
Sheldrake Rd ALT WA14 ....165 E1
Shelfield Cl ROCH OL11 ....28 C2
Shelford Av GTN M18 ....130 A4
Shelley Av MDTN M24 ....73 F2
Shelley Gv DROY M43 ....117 H4
  HYDE SK14 ....133 G4
  STLY SK15 ....121 H1
Shelley Ri DUK SK16 ....134 C1
Shelley Rd CHAD OL9 ....90 A4
  LHULT M38 ....81 F2
  OLD OL1 ....76 B3
  PWCH M25 ....85 C4
  RDSH SK5 ....144 D2
  SWIN M27 ....98 B4
Shelley St NEWH/MOS M40 ....104 B2
Shelley Wk BOL BL1 ....33 G5
Shelton Av SALE M33 ....153 G2
Shenfield Wk
  NEWH/MOS M40 ....115 G2
Shenhurst Cl WILM/AE SK9 ....200 B1
Shentonfield Rd
  WYTH/NTH M22 ....168 D3
Shenton Park Av SALE M33 ....153 F5
Shenton St HYDE SK14 ....133 H4
Shepherd Cross St BOL BL1 ....33 F5
Shepherds Cl DTN/ASHW BL8 ....26 A2
Shepherd St BKLY M9 ....103 E1
  BURY BL9 ....5 F6
  HEY OL10 ....40 C4
  ROCH OL11 ....28 A2
  ROY/SHW OL2 ....59 F5
  TOT/BURYW BL8 ....26 A3
  WHIT OL12 * 10 C4
Shepherds Wy MILN OL16 ....44 B1
Shepley Av BOLS/LL BL3 ....48 B4
Shepley Cl BRAM/HZG SK7 ....185 E4
  DUK SK16 ....120 A5
Shepley Dr BRAM/HZG SK7 ....185 F4
Shepley La MPL/ROM SK6 ....175 G5
Shepley Rd DTN/ASHW M34 ....132 C2
Shepley St DTN/ASHW M34 ....132 C1
  FAIL M35 ....105 F1
  HYDE SK14 ....148 A1
  OLD OL1 ....92 D1
Shepton Cl BOL BL1 ....22 C4
Shepton Dr NTHM/RTH M23 ....179 H2
Sheraton Rd OLDS OL8 ....91 F3
Sherborne Rd EDGY/DAV SK3 ....170 D2
  URM M41 ....124 D5
Sherborne St CHH M8 ....114 C1
Sherborne St West CSLFD M3 ....114 B2
Sherbourne Cl
  CHD/CHDH SK8 ....193 E1
  OLDS OL8 ....92 B3
Sherbourne Dr HEY OL10 ....40 B3
Sherbourne Rd BOL BL1 ....32 D5
  MDTN M24 ....72 C1
Sherbourne St PWCH M25 * 85 H3
Sherbrook Cl SALE M33 ....154 A3
Sherbrooke Av UPML OL3 ....79 F3
Sherbrook Ri WILM/AE SK9 ....199 F4
Sherdley Ct CHH M8 ....102 B1
Sherdley Rd CHH M8 ....102 B1
Sherford Cl BRAM/HZG SK7 ....184 B2
Sheridan Wy CHAD OL9 * 89 H1
Sheriff St BOL BL2 ....34 C5
  MILN OL16 ....44 D1
  WHIT OL12 ....10 A5
Sheringham Dr HYDE SK14 ....133 E5
  SWIN M27 ....99 E4
  TOT/BURYW BL8 ....37 H1
Sheringham Pl BOLS/LL BL3 ....48 C4
Sheringham Rd
  DID/WITH M20 ....143 F4
Sherlock St RUSH/FAL M14 ....143 F4
Sherratt St ANC M4 ....7 J6
Sherrington St
  WGTN/LGST M12 ....129 H5
Sherway Dr HALE/TIMP WA15 ....166 D3
Sherwell Rd BKLY M9 ....87 G4
Sherwin Wy ROCH OL11 ....42 C5
Sherwood Av BRO M7 ....101 E3
  DROY M43 ....118 B3
  HTNM SK4 ....158 D5
  RAD M26 ....52 A1
  RUSH/FAL M14 ....142 D3
  SALE M33 ....154 D1
Sherwood Cl AUL OL6 ....107 F3
  MPL/ROM SK6 ....175 E5
  ORD M5 ....112 C2
  TOT/BURYW BL8 ....26 A4
Sherwood Dr SWIN M27 ....99 G3
Sherwood Rd
  DTN/ASHW M34 ....131 G5
  MPL/ROM SK6 ....162 C5
Sherwood St BOL BL1 ....34 A3
  OLD OL1 ....75 E4
  ROCH OL11 ....42 C4
  RUSH/FAL M14 ....143 G2
Sherwood Wy ROY/SHW OL2 ....59 F1
Shetland Rd NEWH/MOS M40 ....115 G2

Shetland Wy RAD M26 ....52 B4
  URM M41 ....124 C3
Shevington Gdns
  NTHM/RTH M23 ....156 A5
Shieldborn Dr BKLY M9 ....103 E3
Shield Cl OLDS OL8 ....8 E5
Shield Dr WALK M28 ....98 B2
Shield St EDGY/DAV SK3 ....12 E5
Shiel St WALK M28 ....82 A4
Shiers Dr CHD/CHDH SK8 ....170 B5
Shiffnall St BOL BL2 ....3 G6
Shilford Dr ANC M4 ....7 J1
Shillingford Rd FWTH BL4 ....65 H4
Shillingford St BOLE BL2 ....35 H3
Shillingten Cl WALK M28 ....81 E4
Shiloh La OLDE OL4 ....77 G2
Shilton Gdns BOLS/LL BL3 * 48 D4
Shilton St RAMS BL0 ....16 C5
Shipgate BOL BL1 ....3 F4
Shipla Cl CHAD OL9 ....8 E2
Ship La OLDE OL4 ....61 G4
Shipley Av SLFD M6 ....112 B2
Shipley Vw URM M41 ....123 G3
Shipper Bottom La RAMS BL0 ....17 F2
Shippey St RUSH/FAL M14 ....163 F4
Shipston Cl TOT/BURYW BL8 ....37 G3
Shipton St BOL BL1 ....33 E5
Shirburn ROCH OL11 * 29 H5
Shirebrook Dr RAD M26 ....52 C5
Shireburn Av BOLE BL2 ....49 H1
Shiredale Cl CHD/CHDH SK8 ....171 E5
Shiredale Dr BKLY M9 ....103 E3
Shiregreen Av
  NEWH/MOS M40 ....102 D5
Shirehills PWCH M25 ....85 H4
Shireoak Rd DID/WITH M20 ....143 F4
The Shires DROY M43 ....118 C2
  RAD M26 ....52 B4
Shirley Av BRO M7 ....100 D3
  CHAD OL9 ....89 H5
  CHD/CHDH SK8 ....191 H1
  DTN/ASHW M34 ....118 B5
  DTN/ASHW M34 ....131 E5
  ECC M30 ....110 D5
  HYDE SK14 ....133 G3
  MOSL OL5 ....94 A3
  STRET M32 ....126 C5
  SWIN M27 ....99 H3
Shirley Cl BRAM/HZG SK7 ....184 D2
Shirley Gv EDGY/DAV SK3 ....171 H4
Shirley Rd CHH M8 ....102 B3
Shirley St ROCH OL11 ....42 B3
Shoecroft Av DTN/ASHW M34 ....146 C1
Sholver Hill Cl OLD OL1 ....60 D5
Sholver La OLD OL1 ....60 C5
Shone Av WYTH/NTH M22 ....181 E2
Shore Av ROY/SHW OL2 ....45 F5
Shoreditch Cl HTNM SK4 ....159 E1
Shorefield Cl MILN OL16 ....31 C4
Shorefield Mt EDGW/EG BL7 ....22 D3
Shore Fold LIT OL15 ....20 C2
Shoreham Wk CHAD OL9 * 90 B1
Shore Hill LIT OL15 ....21 F2
Shore Lea LIT OL15 ....20 C2
Shore Mt LIT OL15 ....20 C2
Shore St MILN OL16 ....31 G5
  OLD OL1 ....9 K2
Shorewood BOL BL1 ....33 G1
Shorland St SWIN M27 ....98 B3
Shorrocks St TOT/BURYW BL8 ....37 E3
Short Av DROY M43 ....117 C5
Shortcroft St HULME M15 * 128 A1
Shortland Crs BNG/LEV M19 ....158 A3
Shortlands Av BURY BL9 ....5 F7
Short St BRAM/HZG SK7 ....185 E1
  BRO M7 * 100 D4
  CMANE M1 ....7 G4
  HEY OL10 ....40 C5
  HTNM SK4 ....159 H3
Short St East HTNM SK4 ....159 H3
Shotton Wk RUSH/FAL M14 * 128 C5
Shrewsbury Ct
  OLDTF/WHR M16 * 127 G3
Shrewsbury Gdns
  CHD/CHDH SK8 ....193 F1
Shrewsbury Rd BOL BL1 ....48 A1
  DROY M43 ....105 G3
  PWCH M25 ....85 H4
  SALE M33 ....154 B4
Shrewsbury St OLDE OL4 ....76 B4
  OLDTF/WHR M16 ....127 G3
Shrigley Cl WILM/AE SK9 ....199 G1
Shrigley Rd POY/DIS SK12 ....196 B5
Shrigley Rd North
  POY/DIS SK12 ....196 B4
Shropshire Av RDSH SK5 ....146 A5
Shropshire Rd FAIL M35 ....105 F4
Shropshire Sq
  WGTN/LGST M12 * 129 F2
Shrowbridge Wk
  WGTN/LGST M12 ....129 H2
Shudehill ANC M4 ....7 G2
Shudehill Rd WALK M28 ....96 B1
Shurmer St BOLS/LL BL3 ....48 B5
Shutt La UPML OL3 ....78 C2
Shuttle St ECC M30 * 111 C3
  RAD M26 ....68 D3
Shuttleworth Cl
  OLDTF/WHR M16 ....142 A4
Shutts La STLY SK15 ....121 C5
Siam St OP/CLY M11 ....116 A5
Sibley Rd HTNM SK4 ....159 E3
Sibley St GTN M18 ....130 C3
Sibson Rd CCHDY M21 ....141 E2
  SALE M33 ....154 B2
Sickle St CMANW M2 ....7 F4
  OLD OL1 ....9 J6
Sidbury Rd CCHDY M21 ....141 G1
Sidcup Rd NTHM/RTH M23 ....167 G4
Siddal St HEY OL10 ....56 B1
  OLD OL1 ....9 G1
  RAD M26 ....52 B5
  ROY/SHW OL2 ....60 A2
  WGTN/LGST M12 ....129 F2
Siddington Av DID/WITH M20 ....142 C4
  EDGY/DAV SK3 ....171 F3
Siddington Rd POY/DIS SK12 ....195 G5
  WILM/AE SK9 ....192 A2
Side Av ALT WA14 ....177 F3

Sidebotham St MPL/ROM SK6 ....161 G2
Sidebottom St DROY M43 * 117 G2
  OLDE OL4 ....76 D4
  STLY SK15 ....120 D3
Side St OLDS OL8 ....90 D5
  OP/CLY M11 ....116 C4
Sidford Cl BOLS/LL BL3 ....50 A4
The Sidings WALK M28 ....97 H5
Sidlaw Cl OLDS OL8 ....91 G5
Sidley Av BKLY M9 ....88 C3
Sidley St HYDE SK14 ....134 A5
Sidmouth Av URM M41 ....123 F5
Sidmouth Dr BKLY M9 ....88 A5
Sidmouth Gv CHD/CHDH SK8 ....182 C5
Sidmouth Rd SALE M33 ....153 C1
Sidmouth St CHAD OL9 ....90 C2
  DTN/ASHW M34 ....132 A1
Sidney Rd BKLY M9 ....103 E1
Sidney St BOLS/LL BL3 ....49 E4
  CMANE M1 ....128 B1
  CSLFD M3 ....6 A3
  CSLFD M3 * 6 D1
  OLD OL1 ....75 H3
Sidwell Wk ANC M4 * 115 G4
Siebers Bank WHIT OL12 * 29 G1
Siemens Rd IRL M44 ....150 D1
Sienna Cl IRL M44 ....136 A5
Signal Cl ECC M30 ....110 C3
Signal Dr NEWH/MOS M40 ....103 E4
Signet Wk CHH M8 ....102 C5
Silas St AUL OL6 * 107 H4
Silburn Wy MDTN M24 ....71 H5
Silchester Dr
  NEWH/MOS M40 ....103 E4
Silchester Wy BOLE BL2 ....35 F5
Silfield Cl OP/CLY M11 ....115 H4
Silkhey Gv WALK M28 ....97 E1
Silkin Cl BRUN/LGST M13 * 128 C1
Silkstone St OP/CLY M11 ....130 B1
Silk St ANC M4 ....7 J2
  CSLFD M5 ....114 A2
  MDTN M24 ....72 C4
  NEWH/MOS M40 ....104 B4
  ROCH OL11 ....42 C2
Sillavan Wy CSLFD M3 ....6 B3
Silsden Av BKLY M9 ....87 G2
Silton St BKLY M9 ....103 C3
Silverbirch Cl SALE M33 ....155 C4
Silver Birches DTN/ASHW M34 ....147 F2
Silver Birch Gv SWIN M27 ....99 G4
Silver Birch Ms DUK SK16 ....133 H1
Silverbirch Wy FAIL M35 ....105 E3
Silver Cl DUK SK16 ....133 E1
Silvercroft St HULME M15 ....127 H1
Silverdale SALE M33 ....154 B5
Silverdale Av CHAD OL9 ....90 A4
  DTN/ASHW M34 ....147 E1
  IRL M44 ....122 C4
  PWCH M25 ....86 D5
Silverdale Cl BURY BL9 ....6 B6
  MPL/ROM SK6 ....186 D4
Silverdale Dr OLDE OL4 ....93 E1
  WILM/AE SK9 ....200 D1
Silverdale Rd BOL BL1 ....48 B2
  CCHDY M21 ....141 G2
  CHD/CHDH SK8 ....169 G5
  FWTH BL4 ....65 F3
  HTNM SK4 ....159 F2
Silverdale St OP/CLY M11 ....131 G1
Silver HI MILN OL16 ....30 C5
Silver Hill Rd HYDE SK14 ....148 A2
Silver Jubilee Wk ANC M4 ....7 H2
Silverlea Dr BKLY M9 ....87 H5
Silvermere AUL OL6 ....107 H4
Silver Spring HYDE SK14 ....148 B3
Silverstone Dr
  NEWH/MOS M40 ....117 E1
Silverton Cl HYDE SK14 ....149 F1
Silverton Gv BOL BL1 ....34 A2
Silverwell La BOL BL1 ....3 F5
Silverwell St BOL BL1 ....3 G5
  NEWH/MOS M40 ....104 C5
Silverwell Yd BOL BL1 * 3 G5
Silverwood CHAD OL9 ....73 H5
Silverwood Av CCHDY M21 ....141 F5
Simeon St ANC M4 * 7 H1
  MILN OL16 ....30 C5
Simister Dr BURY BL9 ....69 H2
Simister Gn PWCH M25 ....70 D4
Simister La MDTN M24 ....71 F3
  PWCH M25 ....70 C4
Simister Rd FAIL M35 ....105 E3
Simister St BKLY M9 ....103 E3
Simkin Wy OLDS OL8 ....106 D1
Simms Cl CSLFD M3 ....114 A3
Simonbury Ct TOT/BURYW BL8 ....37 E4
Simon Freeman Cl
  BNG/LEV M19 ....144 C5
Simon La MDTN M24 ....71 F2
Simons Cl SALE M33 ....154 C3
Simonsway NTHM/RTH M23 ....179 H1
  WYTH/NTH M22 ....180 B2
Simpson Av SWIN M27 ....98 C2
Simpson Gv WALK M28 ....96 B4
Simpson Hl Cl HEY OL10 ....41 G3
Simpson Rd WALK M28 ....96 C4
Simpson St ANC M4 ....7 G1
  CHAD OL9 ....90 C3
  EDGY/DAV SK3 * 13 H4
  HYDE SK14 ....133 F5
  OP/CLY M11 ....116 B4
  WILM/AE SK9 ....198 C4
Sinclair St ROCH OL11 ....42 C3
Sinderland La ALT WA14 ....151 H5
Sinderland Rd ALT WA14 ....151 H5
  ALT WA14 ....165 E1
Sindsley Gv BOLS/LL BL3 ....64 D1
Sindsley Rd SWIN M27 ....83 G5
Singapore Av MANAIR M90 ....179 H4
Singleton Av BOLE BL2 ....50 A2
Singleton Cl BRO M7 ....101 F1

Singleton Gv WHTN BL5 ....62 C4
Singleton Rd BRO M7 ....101 F1
  HTNM SK4 ....159 E2
Singleton St RAD M26 ....51 G5
Sion St RAD M26 ....68 A2
Sirdar St OP/CLY M11 * 117 C5
Sirius Pl BRO M7 ....114 A2
Sir Matt Busby Wy TRPK M17 ....126 C3
Sir Richard Fairey Rd
  HTNM SK4 ....144 A4
Sir Robert Thomas Ct
  BKLY M9 * 103 E2
Siskin Rd OFTN SK2 ....173 G4
Sisley St BRO M7 ....101 F2
Sisson St FAIL M35 ....104 D3
Sisters' St DROY M43 ....117 H5
Sixpools Gv WALK M28 ....96 D2
Sixth Av BOL BL1 ....48 A2
  BOLS/LL BL3 ....59 G2
  OLDS OL8 ....105 H1
Sixth St TRPK M17 ....126 A3
Size St WHIT OL12 ....14 C4
Skagen Ct BOL BL1 ....2 D1
Skaife Rd SALE M33 ....155 F2
Skarratt Cl WGTN/LGST M12 ....129 G2
Skegness Cl TOT/BURYW BL8 ....38 A1
Skelton Gv BOLE BL2 ....49 H2
  BRUN/LGST M13 ....143 H2
Skelwith Av BOLS/LL BL3 ....65 E2
Skelwith Cl URM M41 ....123 H4
Skerry Cl BRUN/LGST M13 ....128 C1
Skerton Rd OLDTF/WHR M16 ....127 E4
Skilgate Cl MDTN M24 ....72 A1
Skip Pl ANC M4 ....114 D2
Skipton Av NEWH/MOS M40 ....104 C1
Skipton Cl BRAM/HZG SK7 ....184 D5
  RDSH SK5 ....145 E3
  TOT/BURYW BL8 ....37 E4
Skipton Dr URM M41 ....123 G3
Skipton St BOLE BL2 ....49 H2
  NEWH/MOS M40 ....104 B1
Skye Cl HEY OL10 ....40 A5
Skye Cft MPL/ROM SK6 ....186 A4
Skye Rd URM M41 ....124 C3
Slackcote La UPML OL3 ....61 H2
Slackey Brow FWTH BL4 ....83 F2
Slack Fold La FWTH BL4 ....64 C3
Slack Ga WHIT OL12 ....14 D5
Slack Hall OLDE OL4 ....77 E4
Slack La BOLE BL2 ....24 B4
  SWIN M27 ....99 F1
  WHTN BL5 ....62 A2
Slack Rd BKLY M9 ....102 D1
Slack St HYDE SK14 ....134 A4
  MILN OL16 ....10 E5
Slade Gv BRUN/LGST M13 ....143 H3
Slade Hall Rd WGTN/LGST M12 ....144 A1
Slade La BNG/LEV M19 ....143 H5
Slade Mt BNG/LEV M19 ....143 H5
Sladen St LIT OL15 ....10 C5
Slade St BOLS/LL BL3 ....48 C5
Slaidburn Av BOLE BL2 ....49 H2
Slaidburn Cl MILN OL16 ....44 B1
Slaidburn Dr TOT/BURYW BL8 ....36 D3
Slaithwaite Dr OP/CLY M11 ....115 H3
Slateacre Rd HYDE SK14 ....148 B5
Slate La ANC M4 ....115 F4
  DTN/ASHW M34 ....118 B5
Slaterfield BOLS/LL BL3 ....48 D4
Slater La BOL BL1 ....3 G2
Slater St BOL BL1 ....3 G2
  CHAD OL9 ....8 C3
  ECC M30 ....110 C3
  FAIL M35 ....105 E1
  FWTH BL4 ....66 A4
Slate Whf HULME M15 * 6 A7
Slawson Wy HEY OL10 ....41 G3
Sleaford Cl NEWH/MOS M40 ....115 G2
  TOT/BURYW BL8 ....38 A1
Sleddale Cl OFTN SK2 ....173 E4
Sledmere Cl BOL BL1 * 2 C5
  OP/CLY M11 ....116 B4
Sledmoor Rd NTHM/RTH M23 ....155 C5
Slimbridge Cl BOLE BL2 ....35 H5
Sloane Av OLDE OL4 ....76 D4
Sloane St AUL OL6 ....120 A2
  BOLS/LL BL3 * 48 A5
  OP/CLY M11 ....116 B3
Smallbridge Cl WALK M28 ....96 D2
Smallbrook Rd ROY/SHW OL2 ....45 F4
Smalldale Av
  OLDTF/WHR M16 ....128 A5
Smalley St ROCH OL11 ....42 B4
Smallfield Dr BKLY M9 ....103 E2
Smallridge Cl NEWH/MOS M40 ....115 G2
Smallshaw La AUL OL6 ....107 F5
Smallwood St NEWH/MOS M40 ....104 B4
Smart St WGTN/LGST M12 ....129 H5
Smeaton Cl STRET M32 ....140 C1
Smeaton St CHH M8 ....102 D4
Smedley Av BOLS/LL BL3 ....48 A5
Smedley La CHH M8 ....102 C4
Smedley Rd CHH M8 ....102 C4
Smedley St CHH M8 ....102 C4
Smethurst La BOLS/LL BL3 ....64 A2
Smethurst St BKLY M9 ....103 E1
  HEY OL10 ....40 C4
  RAD M26 ....67 G1
Smithfield Market WALK M28 ....31 G5
Smith Hl MILN OL16 ....31 G5
Smithies Av MDTN M24 ....72 D2
Smithies St HEY OL10 ....41 E4
Smithills Croft Rd BOL BL1 ....33 E5
Smithills Dean Rd BOL BL1 ....32 D3
Smithills Dr BOL BL1 ....33 E4
Smithills Hall Cl RAMS BL0 ....16 C4
Smith La EDGW/EG BL7 ....22 D1
Smiths Lawn WILM/AE SK9 ....198 D5
Smith's Rd BOLS/LL BL3 ....66 A1

Smith St AULW OL7 ....119 E4
  BURY BL9 ....5 G3
  CHD/CHDH SK8 * 170 C3
  DTN/ASHW M34 ....146 B1
  HEY OL10 ....41 E4
  HYDE SK14 ....133 C3
  LIT OL15 ....21 E3
  MILN OL16 ....10 D6
  MOSL OL5 ....95 C5
  OLDE OL4 ....76 D4
  OLDTF/WHR M16 ....127 F2
  RAMS BL0 ....16 C3
  WALK M28 ....82 A4
Smithybridge Rd LIT OL15 ....20 C5
Smithy Bridge Rd LIT OL15 ....31 H1
Smithy Cft EDGW/EG BL7 ....23 E3
Smithy Dr ALT WA14 ....176 A1
Smithy Fold WHIT OL12 ....29 F2
Smithy Fold Rd HYDE SK14 ....148 A3
Smithy Grn CHD/CHDH SK8 * 182 A4
  MPL/ROM SK6 ....162 A1
Smithy Gv AUL OL6 ....119 H1
Smithy Hl BOLS/LL BL3 ....47 H5
Smithy La ALT WA14 ....176 B1
  CSLFD M3 * 6 E3
  HYDE SK14 ....148 A2
  PART M31 ....151 E3
  UPML OL3 ....79 E4
Smithy St BRAM/HZG SK7 ....185 E1
  RAMS BL0 * 16 C3
Smyrna St HEY OL10 ....40 D5
  ORD M5 ....112 D4
  RAD M26 ....52 A5
Snape St RAD M26 * 52 A5
Snell St ANC M4 ....115 G4
Snipe Av ROCH OL11 ....43 F4
Snipe Cl POY/DIS SK12 ....194 B4
Snipe Rd OLDS OL8 ....92 A5
Snipe St BOLS/LL BL3 ....49 E4
Snipe Wy AULW OL7 ....119 E4
Snowden Av URM M41 ....138 B5
Snowden St BOL BL1 ....2 C3
  HEY OL10 ....56 B1
  OLDS OL8 ....91 G3
Snowdon Rd ECC M30 ....111 H1
Snowdon St ROCH OL11 ....43 F4
Snow Hill Rd BOLS/LL BL3 ....50 A4
Snydale Cl WHTN BL5 ....62 B2
Snydale Wy BOLS/LL BL3 ....63 E2
Soapstone Wy IRL M44 ....136 A5
Soap St ANC M4 ....7 G3
Society St ROY/SHW OL2 ....60 A2
Sofa St BOL BL1 ....33 E5
Soho St BOL BL1 ....2 E6
  OLDE OL4 * 8 H5
Solent Av BKLY M9 ....87 H5
Solent Dr BOLS/LL BL3 ....49 H4
Solness St BURY BL9 ....5 H2
Soloman Rd ALT WA14 ....153 F5
Solway Cl BOLS/LL BL3 ....64 C1
  OLDS OL8 ....8 A5
  SWIN M27 ....83 H3
Solway Rd WYTH/NTH M22 ....168 D5
Somerby Dr WYTH/NTH M22 ....180 B3
Somerdale Av BOL BL1 ....47 H2
Somerfield Rd BKLY M9 ....103 E1
Somerford Av DID/WITH M20 ....142 C3
Somerford Rd RDSH SK5 ....145 G1
Somersby Dr EDGW/EG BL7 ....23 E3
Somersby Wk BOLS/LL BL3 * 48 D4
Somerset Cl RDSH SK5 ....160 C2
Somerset Dr BURY BL9 ....53 C1
Somerset Gv ROCH OL11 ....28 D3
Somerset Pl SALE M33 ....139 H5
Somerset Rd ALT WA14 ....165 F5
  BOL BL1 ....48 A1
  DROY M43 ....117 H2
  ECC M30 ....111 H1
  FAIL M35 ....104 D4
Somerset Sq OLDE OL4 ....92 B1
Somers Rd RDSH SK5 ....145 E3
Somerton Av SALE M33 ....154 D3
  WYTH/NTH M22 ....180 B1
Somerton Rd BOLE BL2 ....50 C4
Somerville Gdns
  HALE/TIMP WA15 ....166 A3
Somerville Sq BOL BL1 ....33 F3
Somerville St BOL BL1 ....33 F3
Somerwood Wk
  WGTN/LGST M12 * 129 G2
Sonning Dr BOLS/LL BL3 ....63 G1
Sopwith Dr RUSH/FAL M14 ....142 C2
Sorby Rd IRL M44 ....136 C4
Sorrel Bank SLFD M6 ....113 E1
Sorrel Cl LIT OL15 ....20 C2
Sorrel Bank RDSH SK5 ....145 G5
Sorrel St HULME M15 ....127 H2
Sorrel Wy OLDE OL4 ....76 D2
Soudan Rd OFTN SK2 ....172 B3
Soudan St MDTN M24 ....72 F3
Souracre Fold STLY SK15 ....121 G2
South Acre Dr WILM/AE SK9 ....192 A4
Southall St CHH M8 ....114 C2
Southampton Cl BRO M7 ....101 C5
Southam St BRO M7 ....101 H3
South Av BNG/LEV M19 ....143 H4
  FWTH BL4 ....64 D3
  HEY OL10 ....40 C4
  SWIN M27 ....98 C5
  UPML OL3 ....94 B2
  URM M41 ....124 D2
South Back Rock BURY BL9 ....4 E4
South Bank Cl WILM/AE SK9 ....201 E3
Southbank Rd BNG/LEV M19 ....158 A1
South Bank Rd BURY BL9 ....4 C7
Southbourne Av URM M41 ....139 F1
Southbourne St SLFD M6 ....112 D3
Southbrook Av CHH M8 ....87 E4
Southbrook Gv BOLS/LL BL3 ....65 E1
Southcliffe Rd RDSH SK5 ....145 F5
South Cliffe St OP/CLY M11 ....130 B1
South Cl BURY BL9 ....69 H1
  WILM/AE SK9 ....198 C4
South Crs NEWH/MOS M40 ....89 G4
  OP/CLY M11 ....117 E3
South Cft OLDS OL8 ....92 A4
Southcross Rd GTN M18 ....130 C5

South Cross St *BURY* BL9 ....5 F5
South Croston St
　OLDTF/WHR M16 ....127 G4
Southdene Av *DID/WITH* M20 ...156 D2
Southdown Cl *HTNM* SK4 ....12 D1
　ROCH OL11 ....42 B2
Southdown Crs *BKLY* M9 ....88 C5
　CHD/CHDH SK8 ....182 C4
Southdown Dr *WALK* M28 ....96 A4
South Downs Dr *ALT* WA14 ....177 E3
South Downs Rd *ALT* WA14 ....177 F3
South Dr *BOLE* BL2 ....35 F3
　CCHDY M21 ....141 F5
　CHD/CHDH SK8 ....169 F5
　HALE/TIMP WA15 ....166 B2
　WILM/AE SK9 ....84 D5
Southend Av *HULME* M15 ....127 G2
Southend St *BOLS/LL* BL3 ....64 F1
Southern Ap *SWIN* M27 ....84 D5
Southerny Cl
　BRUN/LGST M13 * 129 G4
Southern Cl *BRAM/HZG* SK7 ....184 A3
　DTN/ASHW M34 ....146 C3
Southern Crs *BRAM/HZG* SK7 ...184 A3
Southern Rd *SALE* M33 ....139 G5
Southern St *CSLFD* M3 ....112 D3
　SLFD M6 ....112 D3
　WALK M28 ....82 A2
Southey Cl *LIT* OL15 ....31 G1
Southfield Av *BURY* BL9 ....27 F3
Southfield Cl *DUK* SK16 ....133 G2
Southfield Dr *WHTN* BL5 ....62 A5
Southfield Rd *RAMS* BL0 ....26 B1
Southfields Av *OP/CLY* M11 ....110 D3
Southfields Dr
　HALE/TIMP WA15 ....166 C2
Southfield St *BOLS/LL* BL3 ....49 G5
Southgarth Rd *SLFD* M6 ....112 D2
Southgate *BOLE* BL2 ....35 F2
　CCHDY M21 ....141 F4
　HTNM SK4 ....159 F1
　URM M41 ....78 D2
　WHIT OL12 ....18 A1
Southgate Av
　NEWH/MOS M40 * 116 B1
Southgate College Land
　CSLFD M5 ....6 D4
Southgate Ct *BURY* BL9 ....69 C1
　CHAD OL9 ....89 H4
Southgate St *OLD* OL1 ....9 H4
South Gv *BRUN/LGST* M13.........129 E3
　SALE M33 ....154 C3
　WALK M28 ....81 H5
　WILM/AE SK9 ....200 D4
Southgrove Av *BOL* BL1 ....22 D5
South Hi *OLDE* OL4 ....93 E2
South Hill St *OLDE* OL4 ....9 K5
South King St *CSLFD* M3 ....6 D4
　ECC M30 ....110 A5
Southlands Av *ECC* M30 ....110 A5
South Langworthy Rd
　ORD M5 ....113 E4
Southlea Rd *DID/WITH* M20 ....158 A1
Southleigh Dr *BOLE* BL2 ....50 D3
Southlink *OLDE* OL4 ....9 K4
South Lonsdale St *STRET* M32 ....126 B5
South Meadway *POY/DIS* SK12 ....194 C2
South Meade *CCHDY* M21 ....141 F4
　HALE/TIMP WA15 ....166 B2
　PWCH M25 ....86 C5
South Meadway
　MPL/ROM SK6 ....187 E5
Southmere Cl *BKLY* M9 ....89 F5
South Mesnefield Rd *BRO* M7 ....100 D3
Southmill St *CMANW* M2 ....6 D6
Southmoor Rd
　NTHM/RTH M23 ....167 F4
Southmoor Wk
　BOLS/LL BL3 * 48 D4
South Oak La *WILM/AE* SK9 ......198 C4
South Pde *BRAM/HZG* SK7 ....184 A2
　MILN OL16 ....10 C6
South Park Dr *POY/DIS* SK12 ....195 F5
South Park Rd
　CHD/CHDH SK8 ....169 G3
Southpool Cl *BRAM/HZG* SK7 ...184 B2
South Pump St *CMANE* M1 * 7 H4
South Radford St *BRO* M7 ....100 D3
South Rdg *DTN/ASHW* M34 ......132 C3
South Rd *ALT* WA14 ....177 F2
　ALT WA14 ....177 G4
　DID/WITH M20 ....157 G4
　STRET M32 ....125 F4
　SWIN M27 ....85 E5
South Royd St
　TOT/BURYW BL8 ....26 A4
Southsea St *OP/CLY* M11 ....130 C1
South Side *NEWH/MOS* M40 * 99 G4
　WILM/AE SK9 * 190 A3
South St *AULW* OL7 ....118 D5
　BOLS/LL BL3 ....64 D1
　MILN OL16 ....10 E5
　OLDS OL8 ....90 D5
　OP/CLY M11 ....90 C5
　RAMS BL0 ....17 E2
　WCTN/LGST M12 ....129 H2
　WILM/AE SK9 ....200 D4
South Ter *BURY* BL9 ....53 E2
South Terrace Ct *MILN* OL16 ......43 F1
South Vale Crs
　HALE/TIMP WA15 ....166 A4
South Vw *MPL/ROM* SK6 ....161 H5
　RDSH SK5 ....131 E5
　ROCH OL11 ....28 B5
　STLY SK15 ....109 G4
South View Gdns
　CHD/CHDH SK8 ....181 H1
South View Rd *MILN* OL16 ....20 B5
South View St *BOLE* BL2 ....49 H2
South View Ter *MILN* OL16 ....20 B4
Southview Wk *OLDE* OL4 * 76 D3
Southwark Dr *DUK* SK16 ....133 G2
Southway *ALT* WA14 ....177 H5
　AULW OL7 ....106 D4
　DROY M43 ....117 H5
　NEWH/MOS M40 ....90 A5
South Wy *OLDS* OL8 ....91 F5

Southwell Cl *BOL* BL1 ....2 C2
　MPL/ROM SK6 ....161 H5
Southwell Ct *STRET* M32 * 140 A2
Southwell Gdns *AUL* OL6 ....107 E3
Southwell St *BKLY* M9 ....103 F3
Southwick Rd
　NTHM/RTH M23 ....155 H4
South William St *CSLFD* M5 * 114 A4
Southwood Cl *BOLS/LL* BL3 ....65 E1
Southwood Dr *BKLY* M9 ....87 F2
South Woodley Gdns *RAD* M26 ...68 D4
Southwood Rd *OFTN* SK2 ....172 C5
Southyard St *BNG/LEV* M19 * ...144 B3
Sovereign St *SLFD* M6 ....113 F1
Sowerby Cl *TOT/BURYW* BL8 ......37 E4
Spa Cl *RDSH* SK5 ....145 E3
Spa Crs *LHULT* M38 ....81 F1
Spa Gv *LHULT* M38 ....81 F1
Spa La *LHULT* M38 ....81 F1
　OLDE OL4 ....92 C2
Spalding Dr *NTHM/RTH* M23 ....179 H2
Sparkford Av *NTHM/RTH* M23 ...155 E5
Sparkle St *CMANE* M1 ....7 J5
Spa Rd *NTHM/RTH* M23 ....167 G2
　BOL BL1 ....2 B6
Sparrow Cl *RDSH* SK5 ....145 E1
Sparrowfield Cl *STLY* SK15 ....109 F5
Sparrow Hl *MILN* OL16 ....10 B7
Sparrow St *ROY/SHW* OL2 ....75 F2
Sparta Av *WALK* M28 ....81 H5
Sparta Wk *OP/CLY* M11 ....116 B5
Sparth Bottoms Rd
　ROCH OL11 ....29 G5
Sparthfield Av *ROCH* OL11 ....42 D1
Sparthfield Rd *HTNM* SK4 ....159 G3
Sparth La *HTNM* SK4 ....159 G3
Sparth Rd *NEWH/MOS* M40 ......104 C5
Spath St *HULME* M15 * 128 C3
Spath La *BRAM/HZG* SK7 ....192 A2
Spath La East *CHD/CHDH* SK8 ...193 E2
Spath Rd *DID/WITH* M20 ....157 F3
Spath Wk *CHD/CHDH* SK8 ....193 E2
Spaw St *CSLFD* M3 ....113 H3
Spear St *CMANE* M1 ....7 H4
Spectator St *ANC* M4 ....115 G3
Spencer Av *BOLS/LL* BL3 ....67 F1
　OLDTF/WHR M16 ....133 G3
　WHIT OL12 ....69 F2
Spencer La *ROCH* OL11 ....41 F1
Spencer St *CHAD* OL9 ....90 C3
　DUK SK16 ....119 H4
　ECC M30 ....110 A4
　MOSL OL5 ....108 C1
　OLD OL1 ....9 K1
　RAD M26 * 52 D5
　RAMS BL0 ....16 C3
　RDSH SK5 ....145 F3
　TOT/BURYW BL8 ....37 H5
Spender Av *CHH* M8 ....102 B4
Spen Fold *LIT* OL15 ....20 B8
　TOT/BURYW BL8 ....52 B1
Spennithorne Rd *URM* M41 ....138 D1
Spenser Av *DTN/ASHW* M34 .....147 E3
　RAD M26 ....51 H5
Spenwood Rd *LIT* OL15 ....20 C3
Spey Cl *ALT* WA14 ....165 F3
Speyside Cl *WHTF* M45 * 69 H4
Spindle Av *STLY* SK15 ....121 F2
Spindle Cft *FWTH* BL4 ....66 A5
Spindle Hill *WHTF* M45 * 65 G2
Spindlepoint Dr *WALK* M28 ....96 D2
The Spindles *MOSL* OL5 ....109 E2
Spindle Wk *WHTN* BL5 ....62 A2
Spindlewood Cl *STLY* SK15 ....121 G3
Spingfield St *BOLS/LL* BL3 ....49 F5
Spingdale *LHULT* M38 ....80 C1
Spinks St *OLDE* OL4 ....92 A2
Spinners Gdns *WHIT* OL12 ....19 H4
Spinners Gn *WHIT* OL12 ....69 F2
Spinners La *POY/DIS* SK12 ....194 D5
Spinners Ms *BOL* BL1 * 2 D2
Spinners Wy *OLDE* OL4 ....61 E5
Spinney Dr *BURY* BL9 ....27 G5
　SALE M33 ....153 G3
Spinney Gv *DTN/ASHW* M34 .....132 C5
Spinney Nook *BOLE* BL2 ....35 E4
Spinney Rd *NTHM/RTH* M23 .....168 A2
The Spinney *CHD/CHDH* SK8 ..182 B1
　EDGW/EG BL7 ....23 H1
　OLDE OL4 ....77 H4
　URM M41 ....138 A1
　WALK M28 * 98 B4
　WHIT OL12 ....18 C5
　WHTF M45 ....69 F4
Spinningfields *BOL* BL1 * 2 A2
Spinningfield Wy *HEY* OL10 ....56 A2
Spinning Jenny Wk *ANC* M4 * ...115 F3
Spinning Meadow *BOL* BL1 ....2 B2
Spinning Mdw *BOL* BL1 * 2 B2
The Spinnings *BURY* BL9 * 16 C3
Spirk Wk *WCTN/LGST* M12 * 115 G5
Spirewood Gdns
　MPL/ROM SK6 ....161 H4
Spodden Fold *WHIT* OL12 ....14 B5
Spodegreen La *LYMM* OL12 ....29 G3
Spod Rd *WHIT* OL12 ....29 G2
Spokeshave Wy *MILN* OL16 ....30 D1
Sportside Av *WALK* M28 ....82 A4
Sportside Cl *WALK* M28 ....82 A4
Sportsmans Dr *OLDS* OL8 ....91 H4
Spotland Rd *WHIT* OL12 ....29 G3
Spotland Tops *WHIT* OL12 ....28 D2
Spreadbury St
　NEWH/MOS M40 ....103 H5
Spring Av *HYDE* SK14 ....148 B3
　WHTF M45 ....69 F2
Springbank *CHAD* OL9 ....74 B5
Spring Bank Av *AUL* OL6 ....107 E5
　DTN/ASHW M34 ....132 D2
Springbank Cl *MPL/ROM* SK6 ...147 G5
Spring Bank La *ROCH* OL11 ....28 B3
　STLY SK15 ....108 C5
Spring Bank PI *RDSH* SK5 * 145 G5
Spring Bank Rd *MPL/ROM* SK6 ...147 G5
Spring Bridge Rd
　OLDTF/WHR M16 ....142 B1
Springburn Cl *WALK* M28 ....96 B4

Spring Cl *AULW* OL7 ....106 D4
　OLDE OL4 ....92 C2
　RAMS BL0 ....16 C2
Spring Clough *WALK* M28 ....98 A5
Spring Clough Av *WALK* M28 ....82 C5
Spring Clough Dr *OLDS* OL8 ....92 B3
　WALK M28 ....82 C5
Springdale Gdns
　DID/WITH M20 ....157 F3
Springfield *BOL* BL1 ....33 E1
Springfield Av *BRAM/HZG* SK7 ..185 E1
　CHH M8 ....102 A3
　HTNM SK4 ....145 E4
　LIT OL15 ....20 D1
　MPL/ROM SK6 ....175 E3
Springfield Cl *FAIL* M35 ....104 D2
Springfield Dr *WILM/AE* SK9 .....198 A5
Springfield Gdns *FWTH* BL4 ....66 C1
Springfield La *CSLFD* M3 ....6 C1
　MILN OL16 ....136 E1
　MILN OL16 ....20 A5
　ROY/SHW OL2 ....58 D2
Springfield Rd *ALT* WA14 ....165 G4
　BOL BL1 ....33 E1
　CHD/CHDH SK8 ....169 G4
　DROY M43 ....117 G2
　FAIL M35 ....65 F3
　FWTH BL4 ....82 C1
　MDTN M24 ....72 A1
　RAMS BL0 ....26 B1
　SALE M33 ....154 C2
Springfield St *AUL* OL6 ....107 H5
　DTN/ASHW M34 ....132 D2
　HEY OL10 ....40 B4
Spring Gdns *BOLE* BL2 ....35 G2
　BRAM/HZG SK7 ....185 E1
　CMANW M2 ....7 F4
　HALE/TIMP WA15 ....166 D4
　HYDE SK14 ....133 G4
　MDTN M24 ....72 C1
　SLFD M6 ....113 E2
　STKP SK1 ....13 K4
Spring Garden St
　ROY/SHW OL2 ....59 E5
Spring Gv *UPML* OL3 ....95 F2
　WHTF M45 ....69 E3
Spring Hall Ri *OLDE* OL4 ....61 E5
Springhead Av *DID/WITH* M20 ...142 C4
　OLDE OL4 ....93 E2
Springhill *ROY/SHW* OL2 ....59 E5
Spring La *OLDE* OL4 ....93 E2
　RAD M26 ....68 C1
Springlawn *BOL* BL1 * 47 G1
Springlawns *BOL* BL1 * 47 G1
Spring Meadow La *UPML* OL3 .....79 F4
Spring Mill Wk *MILN* OL16 * 30 D1
Spring PI *WHIT* OL12 ....14 C3
Spring Ri *ROY/SHW* OL2 ....44 D5
Spring Rd *ALT* WA14 ....177 G2
　POY/DIS SK12 ....195 G5
Springside Av *WALK* M28 ....82 A4
Springside Cl *WALK* M28 * 82 B4
Springside Gv *WALK* M28 ....82 B4
Springside Rd *BURY* BL9 ....27 F5
Springside Vw
　TOT/BURYW BL8 ....26 A4
Springs Wk *HULME* M15 * 127 G2
Springs La *STLY* SK15 ....120 C1
Springs Rd *MDTN* M24 ....72 C5
The Springs *ALT* WA14 ....177 E2
　ROCH OL11 ....28 B4
Spring St *BOLS/LL* BL3 ....49 E4
　BURY BL9 ....5 F6
　FWTH BL4 ....66 A3
　MOSL OL5 ....108 C1
　OLDE OL4 ....76 B4
　RAMS BL0 ....16 C2
　STLY SK15 ....120 D5
　TOT/BURYW BL8 ....37 F2
　TOT/BURYW BL8 ....37 E2
　UPML OL3 * 79 E4
　WCTN/LGST M12 ....144 A1
　WILM/AE SK9 ....198 D5
Spring Vw
　TOT/BURYW BL8 ....26 D4
Springvale Cl *AULW* OL7 ....106 C5
Spring Vale Dr *TOT/BURYW* BL8 ...26 B5
Spring Vale St *TOT/BURYW* BL8 ...26 A5
Spring Vale Ter *LIT* OL15 ....21 E3
Spring Vale Wy *ROY/SHW* OL2 ....59 H4
Springville Av *BKLY* M9 ....103 G3
Springwater Av *RAMS* BL0 ....16 B5
Springwater Cl *BOLE* BL2 ....35 F3
Springwell Gdns *HYDE* SK14 .....149 G2
Springwood Av *OLDS* OL8 ....73 H4
　SWIN M27 ....99 G4
Springwood Crs
　MPL/ROM SK6 ....162 D4
Springwood Hall Rd *OLDS* OL8 ...91 H5
Springwood La *MPL/ROM* SK6 ...163 E4
Spring Wood St *RAMS* BL0 ....16 C1
Spruce Av *BURY* BL9 ....5 K4
Spruce Cl *SLFD* M6 ....113 F1
Spruce Crs *BURY* BL9 ....27 G4
Spruce St *HULME* M15 ....127 H2
　MILN OL16 ....11 F7
　RAMS BL0 ....16 B4
Sprucewood *CHAD* OL9 ....73 G4
Spurn La *UPML* OL3 ....79 H1
The Spur *OLDS* OL8 ....91 H5
Square Rd *RAMS* BL0 ....16 D2
The Square *DUK* SK16 ....134 A1
　HALE/TIMP WA15 ....178 D4
　SWIN M27 ....98 D2
　UPML OL3 ....79 E2
　WHTF M45 ....69 F4
Squire Rd *CHH* M8 ....102 A3
Squirrel Dr *ALT* WA14 ....165 F1

Squirrel's Jump *WILM/AE* SK9 ...201 E4
Stablefold *MOSL* OL5 ....108 D2
Stable Fold *RAD* M26 ....52 B5
Stabi-fold *WALK* M28 ....97 H5
Stableford Av *ECC* M30 ....110 D1
The Stablings *WILM/AE* SK9 ....198 B5
Stafford Rd *ECC* M30 ....111 F2
　FAIL M35 ....105 F5
　SWIN M27 ....82 B3
　WALK M28 ....96 D1
Stafford St *CHAD* OL9 ....90 B5
　TOT/BURYW BL8 ....38 A2
Stag Pasture Rd *OLDS* OL8 ....106 A1
Stainburne Rd *OFTN* SK2 ....172 D3
Stainburn Rd *OP/CLY* M11 ....116 C5
Staindale *OLDE* OL4 ....92 D1
Stainer St *WCTN/LGST* M12 .....129 H5
Stainforth Cl *TOT/BURYW* BL8 ....37 E3
Stainforth St *OP/CLY* M11 ....129 G1
Stainmoor Ct *OFTN* SK2 ....173 E3
Stainmore Av *AUL* OL6 ....107 F3
Stainton Av *BNG/LEV* M19 ....52 A5
Stainton Dr *MDTN* M24 ....72 A1
Stainton Rd *RAD* M26 ....51 H4
Staithes Rd *WYTH/NTH* M22 .....180 C4
Stakeford Dr *CHH* M8 ....102 D2
Stakehill La *MDTN* M24 ....59 H4
Staley Cl *STLY* SK15 ....121 F3
Staley Hall Crs *STLY* SK15 ....121 F2
Staley Hall Rd *STLY* SK15 ....121 F3
　OLDE OL4 ....93 E1
Stalham Cl
　NEWH/MOS M40 ....115 G2
Stalmine Av *CHD/CHDH* SK8 .....181 G4
Stalybridge Rd *STLY* SK14 ....135 H4
Stalyhill Dr *STLY* SK15 ....135 F1
Stamford Av *ALT* WA14 ....164 D3
　STLY SK15 ....120 C3
Stamford Cl *STLY* SK15 ....120 C3
Stamford Dr *FAIL* M35 ....105 G5
Stamford New Rd *ALT* WA14 .....165 F5
Stamford Park Rd
　HALE/TIMP WA15 ....177 H1
Stamford PI *SALE* M33 ....154 D2
Stamford Rd *ALT* WA14 ....177 F2
　BRO M7 ....101 E4
　BRUN/LGST M13 ....132 A1
　DTN/ASHW M34 ....132 A1
　MOSL OL5 ....93 H5
　OLDE OL4 ....77 F4
　PART M31 ....150 A4
　URM M41 ....138 C5
　WALK M28 ....98 B3
　WILM/AE SK9 ....200 D4
Stamford Sq *AUL* OL6 ....120 A3
Stamford St *ALT* WA14 ....165 F5
　HEY OL10 ....41 F5
　MILN OL16 ....30 C5
　MOSL OL5 ....108 C5
　OLDE OL4 ....92 D1
　SALE M33 ....139 G5
　STLY SK15 ....120 C3
　STLY SK15 ....120 D3
　SWIN M27 ....99 F1
Stamford St Central *AUL* OL6 ...119 H2
Stamford St East *AUL* OL6 .....119 H3
Stamford St West *AUL* OL6 ....119 H3
Stamford Wy *ALT* WA14 ....165 F5
Stampstone St *OLD* OL1 ....76 A5
Stanage Av *BKLY* M9 ....88 C3
Stanbank St *HTNM* SK4 ....159 H2
Stanbourne Dr *BOL* BL1 ....34 A2
Stanbrook St *BNG/LEV* M19 ....144 A1
Stanbury Cl *BURY* BL9 ....39 G5
Stanbury Dr *DUK* SK16 ....134 A1
Stanbury Wk
　NEWH/MOS M40 * 115 G2
Stancliffe Rd *WYTH/NTH* M22 ...168 D4
Stancross Rd *NTHM/RTH* M23 ...155 E5
Stand Av *WHTF* M45 ....68 C4
Stand Cl *WHTF* M45 ....68 C4
Standedge Rd *UPML* OL3 ....79 E1
Standfield Dr *WALK* M28 ....96 B4
Standish Rd *RUSH/FAL* M14 ....143 F3
Stand La *RAD* M26 ....68 C3
Standmoor Ct *WHTF* M45 * 68 C4
Standmoor Rd *WHTF* M45 ....68 C4
Standrick Hill Ri *STLY* SK15 ....109 E5
Standring Av *TOT/BURYW* BL8 ....37 G5
Stand Ri *RAD* M26 ....68 C4
Stanedge Cl *RAMS* BL0 ....16 D4
Stanhope Av *DTN/ASHW* M34 ...132 B3
Stanier Av *ECC* M30 ....111 F2
Stanier St *BKLY* M9 ....103 H1
Stanion Gv *DUK* SK16 ....119 H5
Stan Jolly Wk *OP/CLY* M11 * 116 A5
Stanley Av *BRAM/HZG* SK7 ....185 E1
　HYDE SK14 ....133 H4
　MPL/ROM SK6 ....162 A5
　RUSH/FAL M14 ....128 C3
Stanley Av North *PWCH* M25 ....85 H1
Stanley Av South *PWCH* M25 ....85 H1
Stanley Cl *WHTF* M45 ....69 G3
　WHTN BL5 ....62 B5
Stanley Ct *BURY* BL9 ....5 F3

Stanley Dr *CHD/CHDH* SK8 ....192 A1
　HALE/TIMP WA15 ....166 B4
　WHTF M45 ....85 G1
Stanley Gv *GTN* M18 ....130 A4
　URM M41 ....138 D1
　WCTN/LGST M12 ....129 H3
Stanley Hall La *POY/DIS* SK12 ...187 H5
Stanley Ms *BOLE* BL2 ....50 A2
Stanley Mt *SALE* M33 ....154 B3
Stanley Park Wk *BOLE* BL2 * 10 B4
Stanley PI *WHIT* OL12 ....33 G4
Stanley Rd *BOL* BL1 ....33 E5
　BRO M7 ....101 H2
　CHAD OL9 ....90 D4
　CHD/CHDH SK8 ....193 G5
　DTN/ASHW M34 ....131 G5
　ECC M30 ....110 D4
　FWTH BL4 ....64 D4
　HTNM SK4 ....159 E2
　OLDE OL4 ....77 G3
　OLDTF/WHR M16 ....142 A1
　RAD M26 ....51 H3
　SWIN M27 ....99 F2
　WALK M28 ....82 A5
Stanley St *BKLY* M9 ....103 F2
　CHAD OL9 ....74 C5
　CHH M8 ....114 D1
　CSLFD M3 ....6 B4
　HEY OL10 ....41 E5
　NEWH/MOS M40 ....105 C5
　OLDE OL4 ....92 D1
　OLDE OL4 ....93 E1
　OP/CLY M11 ....130 D1
　PWCH M25 ....86 B5
　RAMS BL0 ....16 D4
　STKP SK1 ....13 J2
　STLY SK15 ....120 C4
　WHIT OL12 ....10 B3
　WHTF M45 ....69 F4
Stanley St South *BOLS/LL* BL3 ......2 C6
Stanmore Av *STRET* M32 ....139 H1
Stanmore Dr *BOLS/LL* BL3 ....48 B4
Stannard Rd *ECC* M30 ....110 A4
Stanneybrook Cl *MILN* OL16 ....11 H5
Stanneylands Cl
　WILM/AE SK9 ....191 H5
Stanneylands Dr
　WILM/AE SK9 ....191 G5
Stanneylands Rd
　WILM/AE SK9 ....191 G3
Stannybrook Rd *FAIL* M35 ....106 A4
Stanrose Cl *EDGW/EG* BL7 ....22 D2
Stansbury PI *OFTN* SK2 ....173 F3
Stansby Gdns
　WCTN/LGST M12 ....129 F2
Stansfield Dr *ROCH* OL11 ....28 B2
Stansfield Rd *BOLE* BL2 ....3 J3
　FAIL M35 ....105 F1
　HYDE SK14 ....133 H4
Stansfield St *CHAD* OL9 ....90 C2
　NEWH/MOS M40 ....117 E1
　OLD OL1 ....75 H4
　OP/CLY M11 ....117 G5
Stanstead Av *DID/WITH* M20 .....142 C4
Stanton Av *BRO* M7 ....101 E4
　DID/WITH M20 ....156 D2
Stanton Gdns *HTNM* SK4 ....159 E5
Stanton St *CHAD* OL9 ....90 C4
　OP/CLY M11 ....116 D5
　STRET M32 ....126 A4
Stanway Av *BOLS/LL* BL3 * 2 B7
Stanway Cl *BOLS/LL* BL3 * 2 B7
　MDTN M24 ....89 E1
Stanway Dr *HALE/TIMP* WA15 ..178 A1
Stanway Rd *WHTF* M45 ....70 A4
Stanway St *BKLY* M9 ....105 F2
　STRET M32 ....126 A4
Stanwell Rd *NEWH/MOS* M40 ...104 B3
　SWIN M27 ....98 D3
Stanwick Av *RUSH/FAL* M14 ....87 F3
Stanworth Av *BOLE* BL2 ....50 B2
Stanworth Cl
　OLDTF/WHR M16 ....127 H5
Stanyard Ct *ORD* M5 ....113 F5
Starcliffe La *MDTN* M24 ....67 G5
Starkey Ct *NTHM/RTH* M23 * 167 G5
　SALE M33 ....155 F1
　TOT/BURYW BL8 ....37 F4
Staplehurst Rd
　NEWH/MOS M40 ....116 B1
Stapleton Av *BOL* BL1 ....47 F1
Stapleton St *SLFD* M6 ....99 G2
Starbeck Cl *TOT/BURYW* BL8 .....37 E4
Starcliffe St *BOLS/LL* BL3 ....66 A2
Starfield Av *LIT* OL15 ....31 G1
Star Gv *BRO* M7 ....101 H5
Starkey St *HEY* OL10 ....41 E5
Starkie Av *WALK* M28 ....97 H2
Starkie St *DROY* M43 ....118 D3
　WYTH/NTH M22 ....168 D3
Starling Dr *FWTH* BL4 ....65 E5
Starling Rd *RAD* M26 ....51 H1
Starmoor Dr *CHH* M8 ....102 B4
Starmount Cl *BOLE* BL2 ....35 E2
Starring Gv *LIT* OL15 ....20 C5
Starring La *LIT* OL15 ....20 B3
Starring Rd *LIT* OL15 ....20 B3
Starring Wy *LIT* OL15 ....20 B3
Stash Gv *NTHM/RTH* M23 ....168 A2
Statham Cl *DTN/ASHW* M34 ....132 D5
Statham Fold *HYDE* SK14 ....134 B4
Statham St *SLFD* M6 ....113 G3
Station Ap *CMANE* M1 ....7 F7
　MILN OL16 ....11 H5
Station Cl *HYDE* SK14 ....147 G1
Stationers Entry *MILN* OL16 ....10 C6
Station La *OLDE* OL4 ....93 G2
Station Rd *CHD/CHDH* SK8 ....183 E3
　DUK SK16 ....120 A1
　ECC M30 ....110 D4
　EDGY/DAV SK3 ....13 F4
　FWTH BL4 ....66 C5
　HTNM SK4 ....158 B5

HYDE SK14 ....148 D1
IRL M44 ....136 A4
LIT OL15 ....21 E3
MILN OL16 ....44 C1
MOSL OL5 ....109 E1
MPL/ROM SK6 ....162 A1
MPL/ROM SK6 ....175 E3
OLDE OL4 ....93 F2
RDSH SK5 ....145 E1
ROCH OL11 ....30 A5
STRET M32 ....126 A5
SWIN M27 ....99 E1
TOT/BURYW BL8 ....26 A2
UPML OL3 ....79 E4
URM M41 ....138 D2
WHIT OL12 ....14 C2
WHIT OL12 ....18 A3
WILM/AE SK9 ....191 F4
WILM/AE SK9 ....199 E3
Station St AUL OL6 ....119 G4
BOLS/LL BL3 ....3 F7
BRAM/HZG SK7 ....185 E2
OLDE OL4 ....93 E1
Station to Station Wk LIT OL15 ....21 E5
Station Vw BNG/LEV M19 ....144 A2
Staton Av BOLE BL2 ....49 H1
Staton St OP/CLY M11 ....116 D5
Statter St BURY BL9 ....7 F3
Staveleigh MI AUL OL6 * 119 G2
Staveley Av BOL BL1 ....22 D5
Staveley CI MDTN M24 ....72 E3
ROY/SHW OL2 ....60 C3
Staverton CI BRUN/LGST M13 ....128 C3
Staveton CI BRAM/HZG SK7 ....184 A1
Stavordale WHIT OL12 ....10 F7
Staycott St OLDTF/WHR M16 ....128 A4
Stayley Dr STLY SK15 ....121 F3
Stayley Rd MOSL OL5 ....109 E2
Stead St RAMS BL0 ....16 D2
Steadway UPML OL3 ....79 G3
Stedman CI OP/CLY M11 ....115 H4
Steele Gdns BOLE BL2 ....50 A4
Steeles Av HYDE SK14 ....133 H5
Steeple CI CHH M8 ....102 A5
Steeple Dr ORD M5 ....113 F5
Steeple Vw ROY/SHW OL2 ....59 E5
Stelfox Av FAIL/TIMP WA15 ....166 D2
RUSH/FAL M14 ....142 C2
Stelfox Av DTN/ASHW M34 * 132 C1
Stelfox St ECC M30 ....110 C5
Stella St BKLY M9 ....87 G3
Stelling St GTN M18 ....130 C3
Stenbury Cl RUSH/FAL M14 ....128 D5
Stenner La DID/WITH M20 ....157 E4
Stephen CI TOT/BURYW BL8 * 37 H4
Stephenson Av DROY M43 ....117 H4
Stephenson Rd STRET M32 ....140 C1
Stephenson St FAIL M35 ....105 F1
OLDE OL4 ....93 E1
Stephens Rd DID/WITH M20 ....157 H1
STLY SK15 ....120 D1
Stephens St BOLE BL2 ....49 G1
Stephen St CSLFD M3 ....114 C1
STKP SK1 ....172 C1
TOT/BURYW BL8 ....37 H4
URM M41 ....139 E1
Stephen St South
TOT/BURYW BL8 ....37 H5
Steps Meadow WHIT OL12 ....19 H4
Steptoe Dr OLD OL1 ....75 E3
Stern Av ORD M5 * 113 F5
Sterndale Rd EDGY/DAV SK3 ....171 H4
MPL/ROM SK6 ....162 A5
WALK M28 ....96 A4
Sterratt St BOL BL1 ....2 A5
Stetchworth Dr WALK M28 ....96 C3
Steuber Dr IRL M44 ....151 E1
Stevenson Dr OLD OL1 ....60 C5
Stevenson PI CMANE M1 ....7 H4
Stevenson Rd SWIN M27 ....98 D2
Stevenson Sq CMANE M1 ....7 H4
WHIT OL12 ....19 C5
Stevenson St WILM/AE SK9 ....200 D4
WALK M28 ....81 G4
Stewart Av FWTH BL4 ....65 G5
Stewart St AULW OL7 ....33 H5
BOL BL1 ....45 E3
MILN OL16 ....45 E3
TOT/BURYW BL8 ....37 H2
Steynton CI BOL BL1 ....47 G1
Stile CI URM M41 ....137 E1
Stiles Av MPL/ROM SK6 ....174 D2
Stillwater Dr OP/CLY M11 ....116 B3
Stilton Dr OP/CLY M11 ....116 B5
Stockdale Av
EDGY/DAV SK3 ....172 A4
Stockdale Gv BOLE BL2 ....35 C5
Stockdale Rd BKLY M9 ....88 C3
Stockfield Mt CHAD OL9 ....90 C1
Stockfield Rd CHAD OL9 ....74 C5
Stock Gv MILN OL16 ....31 G4
Stockholm Rd
EDGY/DAV SK3 ....171 G3
Stockholm St OP/CLY M11 ....116 C3
Stock La CHAD OL9 ....74 C5
Stockley Av BOLE BL2 ....35 F4
Stockley Wk HULME M15 * 127 G2

Stockport Rd AULW OL7 ....119 G5
BNG/LEV M19 ....144 A3
BRUN/LGST M13 ....129 E2
DTN/ASHW M54 ....146 C2
EDGY/DAV SK3 ....170 D2
HALE/TIMP WA15 ....166 A4
HYDE SK14 ....148 A2
HYDE SK14 ....149 G2
MOSL OL5 ....93 H5
MPL/ROM SK6 ....162 A4
MPL/ROM SK6 ....174 C3
OLDE OL4 ....93 H2
WGTN/LGST M12 ....129 F4
Stockport Rd East
MPL/ROM SK6 ....161 G2
Stockport Rd West
MPL/ROM SK6 ....160 D3
Stockport Village STKP SK1 * 13 F5
Stocksfield Dr BKLY M9 ....88 B4
LHULT M38 ....81 E2
Stocks Gdns STLY SK15 ....121 F4
Stocksgate WHIT OL12 ....29 E1
Stocks La STLY SK15 ....121 E4
Stocks St CHH M8 ....114 D1
Stocks St East CHH M8 ....114 D1
Stock St BOL BL4 ....38 B1
Stockton Av EDGY/DAV SK3 ....171 E1
Stockton Dr TOT/BURYW BL8 ....26 A1
Stockton Pk OLDE OL4 ....92 C1
Stockton Rd CCHDY M21 ....141 E3
FWTH BL4 ....65 H2
WALK M28 ....200 C1
Stockton St LIT OL15 ....20 D3
OLDTF/WHR M16 ....127 H4
SWIN M27 ....98 D3
Stoke Abbott CI
BRAM/HZG SK7 ....183 H5
Stokesay CI BURY BL9 ....53 C4
ROY/SHW OL2 ....59 H5
Stokesay Dr BRAM/HZG SK7 ....184 D3
Stokesay Rd SALE M33 ....153 H1
Stokes St OP/CLY M11 ....117 E4
Stoke St ALT WA14 * 30 C5
MILN OL16 * 164 D5
Stonall Av HULME M15 ....127 C2
Stoneacre HOR/BR BL6 ....46 A1
Stoneacre CI SWIN M27 ....99 E3
Stoneacre Rd
WYTH/NTH M22 ....180 B2
Stonebeck Rd
NTHM/RTH M23 ....167 G4
Stone Breaks Rd OLDE OL4 ....77 G5
Stonebridge CI HOR/BR BL6 ....46 C5
Stonechat CI DROY M43 * 118 B2
WALK M28 ....96 C2
Stonecliffe Av STLY SK15 ....120 D3
Stone CI RAMS BL0 ....16 B4
Stoneclough Rd RAD M26 ....67 E4
Stoneclough Rd FWTH BL4 ....66 C5
Stonedelph CI BOLE BL2 ....36 C5
Stonefield Dr CHH M8 ....101 H5
Stonefield St MILN OL16 ....44 C1
Stonehaven BOLS/LL BL3 ....63 G1
Stonehead St BKLY M9 ....103 G3
Stonehewer St RAD M26 ....68 C2
Stone Hill La WHIT OL12 ....28 D1
Stone Hill Rd FWTH BL4 ....82 A1
Stonehouse EDGW/EG BL7 ....23 C4
Stonehurst CI
WGTN/LGST M12 ....129 H2
Stonelands Wy OLDE OL4 ....93 F3
Stoneleigh Dr RAD M26 ....67 E5
Stoneleigh Rd OLDE OL4 ....77 G5
Stoneleigh St OLD OL1 ....76 A3
Stonelow CI HULME M15 ....128 A2
Stonemead Av
HALE/TIMP WA15 ....178 D5
Stonemead CI BOLS/LL BL3 ....49 F5
Stonemead Dr BKLY M9 ....88 A3
Stonepail CI CHD/CHDH SK8 ....169 E4
Stonepail Cottages
CHD/CHDH SK8 * 169 F4
Stonepail Rd CHD/CHDH SK8 ....169 E4
Stone Pale WHTF M45 ....69 C5
Stone PI RUSH/FAL M14 ....128 D5
Stone Row MPL/ROM SK6 ....175 F3
Stonesby CI OLDTF/WHR M16 ....127 H4
Stonesdale CI ROY/SHW OL2 ....59 F4
Stonesteads Dr EDGW/EG BL7 ....23 F3
Stonesteads Wy
EDGW/EG BL7 ....23 F3
Stone St BOLE BL2 ....3 J1
BOLE BL2 ....6 C7
Stoneswood Dr MOSL OL5 ....94 A5
Stoneswood Rd UPML OL3 ....78 B1
Stoney Bank RAD M26 ....67 F5
Stoney Bridge La
HALE/TIMP WA15 ....166 B2
Stoneyfield STLY SK15 ....120 D1
Stoneyfield CI
OLDTF/WHR M16 ....142 B1
Stoneygate Wk OP/CLY M11 ....130 C1
Stoneyhurst CI HULME M15 ....128 A2
Stoney La WILM/AE SK9 ....198 C5
Stoneyroyd WHIT OL12 * 14 C3
Stoneyside Av WALK M28 ....82 B3
Stoneyside Gv WALK M28 ....82 B4
Stonie Heyes Av WHIT OL12 ....19 C5
Stonyford Rd SALE M33 ....155 C2
Stonyhurst Av BOL BL1 ....33 H1
Stopes Rd BOLS/LL BL3 ....67 E1
Stopford Av LIT OL15 ....20 B4
Stopford St EDGY/DAV SK3 ....13 D1
OP/CLY M11 ....130 A1
Stores Cottages OLDE OL4 * 94 A1
Stores St PWCH M25 ....86 B3
Store St AULW OL7 ....106 D4
CMANE M1 ....7 K5
OFTN SK2 ....172 D5
OP/CLY M11 * 130 A1
RAD M26 ....53 E5
ROCH OL11 ....28 B2
ROY/SHW OL2 ....58 D2
Storeton CI WYTH/NTH M22 ....180 D2
Stortford Dr NTHM/RTH M23 ....156 A4
Stothard Rd STRET M32 ....139 H2
Stott Dr URM M41 ....137 F2
Stottfield ROY/SHW OL2 ....74 C1

Stott La BOLE BL2 ....34 C5
MDTN M24 ....56 C4
SLFD M6 ....112 A2
Stott Milne St CHAD OL9 ....90 B2
Stott Rd CHAD OL9 ....89 H4
SWIN M27 ....98 C4
Stott's La NEWH/MOS M40 ....104 C4
Stott St FAIL M35 ....104 C4
MILN OL16 ....44 C1
MILN OL16 ....44 C2
WHIT OL12 ....10 D3
Stourbridge Av LHULT M38 ....81 F1
Stour CI ALT WA14 ....165 F3
Stourport CI MPL/ROM SK6 ....161 H5
Stourport St OLD OL1 ....75 H3
Stovell Av WGTN/LGST M12 ....144 A1
Stovell Rd NEWH/MOS M40 ....103 H2
Stow CI TOT/BURYW BL8 ....38 A1
Stowell St BOL BL1 ....2 C1
Stowell St BOL BL1 ....33 H5
ORD M5 ....112 D4
Stow Gdns DID/WITH M20 ....142 C5
Stow Gdns OLDTF/WHR M16 ....128 B4
Stracey St NEWH/MOS M40 * 115 C1
Stradbroke CI GTN M18 ....130 A3
Strain Av BKLY M9 ....88 A3
Strand CI STRET M32 ....140 A3
The Strand ROCH OL11 ....43 E4
Strand Wy ROY/SHW OL2 ....75 C2
Strangford St RAD M26 ....51 C5
Strang St RAMS BL0 ....16 D2
Stranton Dr WALK M28 ....98 B2
Stratfield Av NTHM/RTH M23 ....155 C5
Stratford Av BOL BL1 ....33 E5
BURY BL9 ....27 F3
DID/WITH M20 ....157 E1
OLDS OL8 ....91 F4
ROCH OL11 ....42 D5
Stratford CI FWTH BL4 ....65 E3
Stratford Gdns MPL/ROM SK6 ....161 C3
Stratford Rd MDTN M24 ....89 E2
Strathblane CI DID/WITH M20 ....142 D4
Strathfield Dr OP/CLY M11 ....116 C3
Strathmere Av STRET M32 ....126 A5
Strathmore Av CCHDY M21 ....141 F1
DTN/ASHW M34 ....147 F1
Strathmore Rd BOLE BL2 ....35 F5
Stratton Rd OFTN SK2 ....172 D1
OLDTF/WHR M16 ....141 F1
SWIN M27 ....99 E1
Strawberry Bank SLFD M6 * 113 G2
Strawberry CI ALT WA14 ....165 E2
Strawberry Hill SLFD M6 ....113 G2
Strawberry Hill Rd BOLE BL2 ....49 G4
Strawberry La MOSL OL5 ....94 A3
WILM/AE SK9 ....198 A4
Strawberry Rd SLFD M6 ....113 F2
Stray St OP/CLY M11 ....117 F5
The Stray BOL BL1 ....34 A5
Streamside CI
HALE/TIMP WA15 ....166 C5
Stream Ter STKP SK1 ....160 C5
Streetbridge OLD OL1 ....74 B2
Street Bridge Rd OLD OL1 ....74 B2
Street Elmfield BOL BL1 ....34 A4
Streetgate LHULT M38 ....81 F2
Streethouse La UPML OL3 ....79 E4
Street Kirklees
TOT/BURYW BL8 ....26 A4
Street La RAD M26 ....55 H1
Stretford Av HULME M15 ....128 A3
OLDTF/WHR M16 ....127 F3
URM M41 ....138 D2
Stretton Av DID/WITH M20 ....157 H3
SALE M33 ....153 H2
STRET M32 ....139 H2
Stretton CI NEWH/MOS M40 ....103 C3
Stretton Rd BOLS/LL BL3 ....48 A5
RAMS BL0 ....26 D4
Striding Edge Wk OLD OL1 * 75 H3
Strines Rd MPL/ROM SK6 ....175 F4
Stringer Av HYDE SK14 ....149 H1
Stringer CI HYDE SK14 ....149 H1
Stroma Gdns URM M41 ....124 B3
Strong St BRO M7 ....114 B1
Stroud Av ECC M30 ....110 C2
Stroud CI MDTN M24 ....88 D2
Stuart Av IRL M44 ....136 B1
MPL/ROM SK6 ....146 B5
STRET M32 ....126 A5
Stuart Rd ALT WA14 ....165 E2
MILN OL16 ....30 C5
OLDS OL8 ....8 E7
OP/CLY M11 ....116 B3
Stuart St East OP/CLY M11 ....116 B3
Stuart Wk MDTN M24 ....72 C5
Stubbins CI NTHM/RTH M23 ....155 F5
Stubbs CI BRO M7 ....101 E2
Stubley Gdns LIT OL15 ....20 D3
Stubley La LIT OL15 ....20 C4
Stubley Mill Rd LIT OL15 ....20 B4
Studforth Wk HULME M15 * 128 A3
Studland Rd WYTH/NTH M22 ....181 C1
Studley CI ROY/SHW OL2 ....60 A5
Styal Av RDSH SK5 ....160 A1
STRET M32 ....125 F5
Styal Gv CHD/CHDH SK8 ....181 F1
Styal Rd CHD/CHDH SK8 ....181 F1
Styal Vw WILM/AE SK9 ....191 C5
Styhead Dr MDTN M24 ....72 A1
Style St ANC M4 ....7 H2
Styperson Wy POY/DIS SK12 ....195 F4
Sudbury CI CHD/CHDH SK8 ....181 H5
HOR/BR BL6 ....46 D5
Sudbury Dr CHD/CHDH SK8 ....189 F1
Sudden CI ROCH OL11 ....42 B2
Sudell St ANC M4 ....7 J1
Sudley Rd ROCH OL11 ....42 B1
Sudlow St MILN OL16 ....11 H1
Sudren St TOT/BURYW BL8 ....37 E3
Suffield St MDTN M24 ....72 B4
Suffolk Av DROY M43 ....117 H2
Suffolk CI BOLS/LL BL3 ....51 E4
Suffolk Dr RDSH SK5 ....146 A5
WILM/AE SK9 ....199 F1
Suffolk Rd ALT WA14 ....165 E5

Suffolk St CHAD OL9 ....90 C3
ROCH OL11 ....30 A5
SLFD M6 ....100 D5
Sugar La BOLE BL2 ....78 D2
Sugar Mill Sq ORD M5 * 112 C3
Sugden St AUL OL6 ....120 A2
Sulby Av STRET M32 ....140 C1
Sulby St NEWH/MOS M40 ....103 H2
RAD M26 ....67 E4
Sulgrave Av POY/DIS SK12 ....195 C3
Sullivan St WGTN/LGST M12 ....129 H5
Sultan St BURY BL9 ....53 C1
Sulway CI SWIN M27 * 99 F3
Sumac St OP/CLY M11 ....117 E3
Summer Av URM M41 ....139 E1
Summer Castle MILN OL16 ....10 D7
Summercroft CHAD OL9 ....90 C4
Summerdale Dr RAMS BL0 ....26 C1
Summerfield Av DROY M43 ....117 F2
Summerfield Dr MDTN M24 ....73 F2
Summerfield PI WILM/AE SK9 ....198 C5
Summerfield Rd BOLS/LL BL3 ....49 C5
WALK M28 ....81 H3
WYTH/NTH M22 ....180 C4
Summerfields Vw OLDS OL8 ....92 B4
Summer HI MOSL OL5 * 94 A1
Summerlea CHD/CHDH SK8 ....183 E4
Summer PI RUSH/FAL M14 ....143 E1
Summers Av STLY SK15 ....121 E5
Summerseat CI OLDE OL4 ....77 F5
ORD M5 * 113 F5
Summerseat La RAMS BL0 ....26 B1
Summershades La OLDE OL4 ....94 A1
Summershades Ri OLDE OL4 ....94 A1
Summers St CHAD OL9 ....8 A3
Summer St MILN OL16 ....10 F7
Summerville Av BKLY M9 ....103 C3
Summerville Rd SLFD M6 ....100 B5
Summit CI BURY BL9 ....40 A2
Summit St HEY OL10 ....40 A4
Sumner Av BOLE BL2 ....36 C5
Sumner St ROY/SHW OL2 ....60 A4
Sumner Wy URM M41 ....138 D1
Sunadale CI BOLS/LL BL3 ....48 A4
Sunbank CI WHIT OL12 ....29 C1
Sunbank La
HALE/TIMP WA15 ....189 E1
Sunbury CI DUK SK16 ....120 C5
WILM/AE SK9 ....192 B5
Sunbury Dr NEWH/MOS M40 ....117 E1
Sunderland Av OLDE OL4 ....119 H1
Sundew PI MDTN M24 ....73 C5
Sundial CI HYDE SK14 ....135 E5
Sundial Rd OFTN SK2 ....173 E3
Sundridge CI BOLS/LL BL3 ....63 H1
Sunfield MPL/ROM SK6 ....162 A3
Sunfield Av OLDE OL4 ....60 D5
Sunfield Crs ROY/SHW OL2 ....75 F1
Sunfield Dr ROY/SHW OL2 ....75 C1
Sunfield Rd OLD OL1 ....75 C3
Sunfield Wy OLDE OL4 ....76 D5
Sunflower Meadow IRL M44 ....136 C1
Sunhill CI MILN OL16 ....43 G4
Sunk La MDTN M24 ....72 C5
Sunlight Rd BOL BL1 ....33 H4
Sunningdale Av OP/CLY M11 ....116 C3
RAD M26 ....51 G4
SALE M33 ....155 F3
WHTF M45 ....68 D5
Sunningdale CI HYDE SK14 ....133 H3
TOT/BURYW BL8 ....52 B1
Sunningdale Dr
BRAM/HZG SK7 ....184 B5
HEY OL10 ....56 A1
IRL M44 ....122 A5
PWCH M25 ....85 E3
SLFD M6 ....99 F5
Sunningdale Rd
CHD/CHDH SK8 ....187 D5
DTN/ASHW M34 ....147 F2
URM M41 ....138 D2
Sunningdale Wk BOLS/LL BL3 * 48 B4
Sunning Hill St BOLS/LL BL3 ....48 C5
Sunny Av BURY BL9 ....38 C1
Sunny Bank OLDE OL4 ....92 D2
RAD M26 ....66 D4
WILM/AE SK9 ....200 A1
Sunny Bank Av DROY M43 ....117 C4
Sunnybank Av ECC M30 ....111 C2
HTNM SK4 ....158 C2
Sunny Bank Rd ALT WA14 ....177 F4
BRUN/LGST M13 ....129 F5
BURY BL9 ....69 H1
Sunny Bank Rd BOL BL1 ....33 F4
DROY M43 ....117 C4
Sunny Bower St
TOT/BURYW BL8 ....25 H5
Sunny Brow Rd GTN M18 ....130 B3
MDTN M24 ....72 B4
Sunny Dr PWCH M25 ....85 C3
Sunnyfield Rd HTNM SK4 ....159 E5
PWCH M25 ....70 B5
Sunnylea Av BNG/LEV M19 ....158 B1
Sunnymead Av BOL BL1 ....34 A2
Sunnymede V RAMS BL0 ....16 B5
Sunnyside AUL OL6 ....106 D5
Sunnyside CI DROY M43 * 117 C2
Sunnyside Crs AUL OL6 ....120 A3
Sunnyside Gv AUL OL6 ....120 A3
Sunnyside La DROY M43 ....117 C1
Sunnyside Rd BOL BL1 ....33 F4
DROY M43 ....117 H2
Sunnywood Dr
TOT/BURYW BL8 ....26 B5
Sunnywood La
TOT/BURYW BL8 ....26 B5
Sunset Av WYTH/NTH M22 ....156 C5
Sun St MOSL OL5 ....108 D1
RAMS BL0 ....16 C1
Sunwell Ter MPL/ROM SK6 ....187 E1
Surbiton Rd NEWH/MOS M40 ....116 C2
Surma CI CHAD OL9 ....8 C2
MILN OL16 ....43 G1
Surrey Av DROY M43 ....117 G2
ROY/SHW OL2 ....59 G2
Surrey CI BOLS/LL BL3 ....51 E5
Surrey Dr BURY BL9 ....53 G1
Surrey Park CI ROY/SHW OL2 * 60 A1
Surrey Rd BKLY M9 ....88 A5

Surrey St AUL OL6 ....107 G5
BKLY M9 * 87 H5
CHAD OL9 ....8 A7
Surrey Wy RDSH SK5 ....160 D2
Surtees Rd NTHM/RTH M23 ....155 H4
Sussex Av BURY BL9 ....39 H5
DID/WITH M20 ....157 G2
Sussex CI CHAD OL9 ....90 C1
SWIN M27 ....99 E2
Sussex Dr BURY BL9 ....53 G1
DROY M43 ....117 H2
Sussex PI HYDE SK14 ....134 A3
Sussex Rd EDGY/DAV SK3 ....171 E1
PART M31 ....150 D4
Sussex St BRO M7 ....114 A2
CMANW M2 ....6 E4
ROCH OL11 * 30 A5
Sutcliffe Av WGTN/LGST M12 ....144 A1
Sutcliffe St AULW OL7 ....119 E4
BOL BL1 ....33 H4
LIT OL15 ....21 E2
MDTN M24 ....73 F4
OLDS OL8 ....8 E5
ROY/SHW OL2 ....75 H1
Sutherland CI OLDS OL8 ....106 C1
Sutherland Gv FWTH BL4 ....65 H4
Sutherland Rd BOL BL1 ....47 H1
HEY OL10 ....40 A5
OLDTF/WHR M16 ....126 D5
Sutherland St ECC M30 ....110 C2
FWTH BL4 ....65 H4
SWIN M27 ....98 D1
Suthers St OLDE OL4 ....68 D3
Sutton Dr DROY M43 ....117 F2
Sutton Dwellings SLFD M6 ....113 G2
Sutton Rd BOLS/LL BL3 ....67 G1
GTN M18 ....130 D5
HTNM SK4 ....159 F3
POY/DIS SK12 ....195 H5
Suttons La MPL/ROM SK6 ....174 C4
Swailes St OLDE OL4 ....92 A1
Swaindrod La LIT OL15 ....21 H1
Swaine St EDGY/DAV SK3 ....12 E4
Swainsthorpe Dr BKLY M9 ....103 F2
Swain St WHIT OL12 ....10 B2
Swalecliff Av NTHM/RTH M23 ....155 H5
Swale CI WILM/AE SK9 ....192 B5
Swaledale CI ROY/SHW OL2 ....59 F4
Swale Dr ALT WA14 ....165 F3
Swallow Bank Dr ROCH OL11 * 42 A3
Swallow CI STLY SK15 ....109 C3
Swallow Dr BURY BL9 ....39 E2
IRL M44 ....122 B5
ROCH OL11 ....28 C4
Swallow La STLY SK15 ....109 C3
Swallow St OLDS OL8 ....91 E5
OP/CLY M11 ....116 A4
STKP SK1 ....13 H7
WGTN/LGST M12 * 144 A1
Swanage Av NTHM/RTH M23 ....155 E5
OFTN SK2 ....173 E5
Swanage CI TOT/BURYW BL8 ....26 D5
Swanage Rd ECC M30 ....110 A1
Swanbourne Gdns
EDGY/DAV SK3 ....171 F3
Swan CI POY/DIS SK12 ....194 C3
Swan Ct ROY/SHW OL2 * 60 A3
Swanhill CI GTN M18 ....131 E2
Swanley Av NEWH/MOS M40 ....103 F5
Swann La CHD/CHDH SK8 ....183 E3
Swann St BRO M7 ....114 B1
Swan Rd HALE/TIMP WA15 ....154 B5
TOT/BURYW BL8 ....26 B2
Swansea St OLDS OL8 ....92 A3
Swan St ANC M4 ....7 G2
AUL OL6 ....119 H2
WILM/AE SK9 ....199 E3
Swarbrick Dr PWCH M25 ....85 C5
Swayfield Av BRUN/LGST M13 ....129 C5
Swaylands Dr SALE M33 ....154 C5
Sweetbriar CI ROY/SHW OL2 ....60 A2
Sweet Briar La WHIT OL12 ....29 H1
Sweetloves Gv BOL BL1 ....33 H1
Sweetlove's La BOL BL1 ....33 H1
Sweetnam Dr OP/CLY M11 ....115 H4
Swettenham Rd WILM/AE SK9 ....192 A2
Swift CI MPL/ROM SK6 ....162 B1
Swift Rd OLD OL1 ....60 C4
ROCH OL11 ....28 C4
Swift St AUL OL6 ....107 G5
Swinbourne Gv
DID/WITH M20 ....143 E4
Swinburne Av DROY M43 ....117 H2
Swinburne Gn RDSH SK5 ....144 D2
Swinburn St BKLY M9 ....103 G1
Windells St HYDE SK14 ....133 H3
OP/CLY M11 * 117 E4
Swindon CI GTN M18 ....130 C3
Swinfield Av CCHDY M21 ....140 D3
Swinford Gv ROY/SHW OL2 ....59 H4
Swinside CI MDTN M24 ....71 H2
Swinside Rd BOLE BL2 ....50 C1
Swinstead Av
NEWH/MOS M40 ....103 F5
Swinton Crs BURY BL9 ....53 G1
Swinton Gv BRUN/LGST M13 ....128 D3
Swinton Hall Rd SWIN M27 ....99 F2
Swinton Park Rd SLFD M6 ....99 F5
Swinton St BOLE BL2 ....50 D2
Swiss Hl WILM/AE SK9 ....201 G4
Swithin Rd WYTH/NTH M22 ....180 D4
Swithland Rd ALT WA14 ....153 F5
Swythamley CI
EDGY/DAV SK3 ....170 D1
Swythamley Rd
EDGY/DAV SK3 ....170 D1
Sybil St LIT OL15 ....21 E2
Sycamore Av ALT WA14 ....164 D4
CHAD OL9 ....90 A3
DTN/ASHW M34 ....146 D1
HEY OL10 ....56 B1
MILN OL16 ....44 D3
OLDE OL4 ....76 C4
RAD M26 ....68 A4

Sycamore Cl AUL OL6 ....120 B3
DID/WITH M20 * 143 E4
DUK SK16 ....120 C5
LIT OL15 ....20 C3
WILM/AE SK9 ....199 E1
Sycamore Cr SLFD M6 ....113 F2
Sycamore Crs AUL OL6 ....107 F5
Sycamore Dr BURY BL9 ....27 C5
RAD M26 ....52 B4
Sycamore Gv FAIL M35 ....105 G3
Sycamore Ldg
BRAM/HZG SK7 ....184 A5
Sycamore Pl WHTF M45 ....85 G1
Sycamore Rd ECC M50 ....110 B1
MPL/ROM SK6 ....161 H2
PART M31 ....150 C3
TOT/BURYW BL8 ....37 E1
The Sycamores MOSL OL5 ....109 F1
OLDE OL4 ....76 D4
RAD M26 ....83 E1
STLY SK15 ....101 F5
Sycamore St EDGY/DAV SK3 ....171 E1
SALE M33 ....155 F2
Sycamore Wk CHD/CHDH SK8 ....123 H3
Syddal St DTN/ASHW M34 ....132 C5
Syddal Crs BRAM/HZG SK7 ....193 G3
Syddal Gn BRAM/HZG SK7 ....193 G2
Syddal Rd CHD/CHDH SK8 ....182 A4
Syddal St HYDE SK14 ....147 H1
Syddall Rd BRAM/HZG SK7 ....193 G2
Sydenham St OLD OL1 ....76 A3
MANAIR M90 ....179 H4
Sydney Av ECC M30 ....111 E3
Sydney Barnes Ct ROCH OL11 ....42 A4
Sydney Jones Ct
NEWH/MOS M40 ....104 B1
Sydney Rd BRAM/HZG SK7 ....194 A2
Sydney St FAIL M35 ....104 D3
MOSL OL5 ....109 E2
OFTN SK2 ....172 D2
SLFD M6 ....112 D3
STRET M32 ....140 B1
SWIN M27 ....98 C2
Syke La WHIT OL12 ....19 E4
Syke Rd WHIT OL12 ....19 F5
Sykes Av BURY BL9 ....54 A5
Sykes Cl UPML OL3 ....95 E2
Sykes Ct MILN OL16 * 30 C5
Sykes Meadow
EDGY/DAV SK3 ....171 G3
Sykes St BURY BL9 ....5 G2
MILN OL16 ....31 G5
MILN OL16 ....44 D2
RDSH SK5 ....145 F3
Sykes Wk BOL BL1 * 104 D5
HALE/TIMP WA15 ....166 A1
SALE M33 ....154 D3
URM M41 ....124 C5
WILM/AE SK9 ....198 C5
Sylvan Av FAIL M35
HALE/TIMP WA15 ....166 A1
SALE M33 ....154 D3
URM M41 ....124 C5
WILM/AE SK9 ....198 C5
Sylvan Cl MDTN M24 ....72 A2
Sylvandale Av BNG/LEV M19 ....144 A2
Sylvan Gv ALT WA14 ....165 G4
Sylvan St CHAD OL9 ....8 B2
Sylvester Av OFTN SK2 ....172 C5
Sylvester Cl HYDE SK14 ....149 G1
Sylvia Gv RDSH SK5 ....145 E4
Symms St SALE M33 ....113 G1
Symond Rd BKLY M9 ....88 B2
Symons Rd SALE M33 ....154 D1
Symons St BRO M7 ....101 H3
Syndall Av WGTN/LGST M12 ....129 E2
Syndall St WGTN/LGST M12 ....129 E2

T

Tabley Av RUSH/FAL M14 ....142 D1
Tabley Gdns MPL/ROM SK6 ....175 F5
Tabley Gv BRUN/LGST M13 ....143 H1
HALE/TIMP WA15 ....166 B1
RDSH SK5 ....145 E4
Tabley Mere Gdns
CHD/CHDH SK8 ....182 C1
Tabley Ms ALT WA14 ....165 G4
Tabley Rd BOLS/LL BL3 ....48 A5
SALE M33 * 155 F4
WILM/AE SK9 ....192 A2
Tabley St DUK SK16 ....120 B5
MOSL OL5 ....109 E2
SLFD M6 ....101 E5
Tabor St MDTN M24 ....72 C2
Tackler Cl SWIN M27 ....99 E3
Tadcaster Dr NEWH/MOS M40 ....103 E4
Tadman Gv ALT WA14 ....165 G4
Tadmor Cl LHULT M38 ....81 E5
Tagore Cl BRUN/LGST M13 ....129 F4
Tag Wood Vw RAMS BL0 ....16 B4
Tahir Cl CHH M8 ....102 C3
Tait Ms HTNM SK4 ....159 E3
Talavera St BRO M7 ....101 G5
Talbenny Ct BOL BL1 ....47 C1
Talbot Av AULD OL1 ....50 D5
Talbot Cl OLDE OL4 ....76 B4
Talbot Cl BOL BL1 ....34 A2
Talbot Gv OLDTF/WHR M16 ....127 E5
Talbot Rd ALT WA14 ....177 E2
HYDE SK14 ....133 H5
RUSH/FAL M14 ....155 G4
STRET M32 ....126 C4
WILM/AE SK9 ....201 E4
Talbot St AUL OL6 ....119 F2
BRAM/HZG SK7 ....173 E5
ECC M30 ....111 F4
MDTN M24 ....72 D2
ROCH OL11 ....30 A5
Talford Gv DID/WITH M20 ....157 F1
Talgarth Rd NEWH/MOS M40 ....115 F1
Talkin Dr MDTN M24 ....72 B1
Talland Wk BRUN/LGST M13 ....129 E3
Tallarn Cl DID/WITH M20 ....143 E4
Tallis Cl WGTN/LGST M12 ....129 H5
Tallow Wy IRL M44 ....136 C3
Tall Trees Cl ROY/SHW OL2 ....58 D5
Tall Trees Pl OFTN SK2 ....172 D3
Tallyman Wy SWIN M27 ....100 B3

Tamar Cl FWTH BL4 ....83 E2
WHTF M45 ....69 H4
Tamar Ct HULME M15 ....127 G2
Tamar Dr RNFM/RTH M23 ....167 H5
Tamarin Cl SWIN M27 ....98 B1
Tamebank MOSL OL5 ....94 A4
Tame Barn Cl MILN OL16 ....31 H1
Tame Gr STLY SK15 ....121 F2
Tame La UPML OL3 ....61 H2
Tamerton Dr CHH M8 ....102 B4
Tameside Ct DUK SK16 * 133 E1
Tame St ANC M4 ....115 G4
DTN/ASHW M34 ....132 C1
DTN/ASHW M34 ....132 C4
MOSL OL5 ....94 B4
STLY SK15 ....120 B4
UPML OL3 ....79 E4
Tame Valley Cl MOSL OL5 ....109 F1
Tamworth Av ORD M5 ....113 G5
WHTF M45 ....70 A5
Tamworth Av West ORD M5 * 113 F5
Tamworth Cl BRAM/HZG SK7 ....184 D4
HULME M15 * 127 H5
Tamworth Dr TOT/BURYW BL8 ....37 H1
Tamworth Gn STKP SK1 ....160 C4
Tamworth St CHAD OL9 ....8 A6
STKP SK1 ....160 C4
Tamworth Wk WBOL BL1 * 128 A4
Tandis Ct SLFD M6 * 111 H2
Tandle Hill Rd ROY/SHW OL2 ....58 C3
Tandlewood Ms
NEWH/MOS M40 ....104 B5
Tandlewood Pk ROY/SHW OL2 ....58 C3
Tanfield Dr RAD M26 ....67 E5
Tanfield Rd DID/WITH M20 ....169 G2
Tangmere Av HTNM SK4 ....158 B3
Tangmere Cl NEWH/MOS M40 * 89 F4
Tanhill Cl OFTN SK2 ....173 F5
Tanhill La OLDS OL8 ....91 H5
Tanhouse Rd URM M41 ....123 E5
Tanners Cft RAMS BL0 ....16 C2
Tanners Fold OLDS OL8 ....91 H5
Tanners Gn SLFD M6 ....113 E2
Tanner St RAMS BL0 ....16 C2
Tannett St HYDE SK14 * 133 G5
Tannery Wy ALT WA14 ....165 H2
Tannock Rd BRAM/HZG SK7 ....185 G3
Tanpits Rd BURY BL9 ....4 C3
Tansey Gv BRO M7 ....102 A4
Tansley Rd CHH M8 ....87 F5
Tanworth Wk BOL BL1 ....33 H4
Tan Yard Brow GTN M18 ....130 D4
Tanyard Dr HALE/TIMP WA15 ....188 D1
Tanyard Gn RDSH SK5 ....160 A1
Tanyard La HALE/TIMP WA15 ....188 C1
Taper St RAMS BL0 ....16 C2
Tapley Av POY/DIS SK12 ....195 F5
Taplin Dr GTN M18 ....130 B3
Taplow Gv CHD/CHDH SK8 ....182 C2
Taplow Wk RUSH/FAL M14 ....129 F5
Tarbet Dr BOLE BL2 ....50 C5
Tarbet Rd DUK SK16 ....133 F1
Tarbolton Crs
HALE/TIMP WA15 ....178 D1
Tariff St CMANE M1 ....7 J4
Tarleton Cl TOT/BURYW BL8 ....37 E5
Tarleton Pl BOLS/LL BL3 ....63 H1
Tarleton Wk
BRUN/LGST M13 * 128 D2
Tarnbrook Cl WHTF M45 ....70 D4
Tarnbrook Wk HULME M15 * 128 A5
Tarn Gv WALK M28 ....53 F5
Tarn Gv WALK M28 ....97 G1
Tarnside Cl MILN OL16 ....19 H5
OFTN SK2 * 172 D4
The Tarns CHD/CHDH SK8 ....181 G1
Tarporley Av RUSH/FAL M14 ....142 C3
Tarporley Cl EDGY/DAV SK3 ....171 F4
Tarran Gv DTN/ASHW M34 ....147 F2
Tarran Pl ALT WA14 ....165 G4
Tarrington Cl WGTN/LGST M12 ....129 H3
Tarvin St OP/CLY M11 ....116 C3
Tarvin Av DID/WITH M20 ....142 C4
HTNM SK4 ....144 D4
Tarvin Dr MPL/ROM SK6 ....161 F2
Tarvington Ct
NEWH/MOS M40 * 102 D4
Tarvin Rd CHD/CHDH SK8 ....170 D5
Tarvin Wk BOL BL1 ....33 H4
Tasle Aly CMANW M2 ....6 E5
Tatchbury Rd FAIL M35 ....105 F3
Tate St OLDS OL8 ....92 A5
Tatham Cl BRUN/LGST M13 ....129 G5
Tatham St MILN OL16 ....10 E7
Tatland Dr WYTH/NTH M22 ....181 E1
Tattersall Av BOL BL1 ....32 B4
Tattersall St CHAD OL9 ....8 C5
Tatton Cl BRAM/HZG SK7 ....173 G5
CHD/CHDH SK8 ....170 D5
Tatton Gdns MPL/ROM SK6 ....162 C1
Tatton Gv DID/WITH M20 ....142 D5
Tatton Ms DROY M43 ....118 A4
Tattonmere Gdns
CHD/CHDH SK8 ....170 D5
Tatton Pl SALE M33 ....154 C1
Tatton Rd DTN/ASHW M34 ....147 E2
SALE M33 ....154 C1
WILM/AE SK9 ....192 B2
Tatton Rd North HTNM SK4 ....159 F1
Tatton Rd South HTNM SK4 ....159 F1
Tatton St HULME M15 ....127 G2
HYDE SK14 ....148 A4
ORD M5 ....113 G5
STKP SK1 ....13 G5
STLY SK15 ....121 E3
Taunton Av AULW OL7 ....119 F1
ECC M30 ....110 C2
RDSH SK5 ....160 A1
URM M41 ....138 D3
Taunton Brook La
AULW OL7 ....106 C5
Taunton Cl BOL BL1 * 33 F5
BRAM/HZG SK7 ....185 H2
Taunton Dr FWTH BL4 ....65 E3
Taunton Gn AULW OL7 ....106 C5
Taunton Gv WHTF M45 ....85 H1
Taunton Hall Cl AULW OL7 ....106 C5
Taunton Lawns AULW OL7 ....119 F1
Taunton Pl AULW OL7 * 106 C5
Taunton Platting AULW OL7 * 106 C4

Taunton Rd AULW OL7 ....106 D5
CHAD OL9 ....74 B3
SALE M33 ....153 G2
Taunton St ANC M4 ....115 G4
Taurus St OLDE OL4 ....76 B4
Tavern Court Av SALE M35 ....105 F3
Tavery Cl ANC M4 ....115 F3
Tavistock Cl HYDE SK14 ....149 G1
Tavistock Dr CHAD OL9 ....74 A3
Tavistock Rd BOL BL1 ....2 A6
ROCH OL11 ....43 E3
SALE M33 ....153 G1
Tawton Av HYDE SK14 ....135 F5
Tay Cl OLDS OL8 ....8 E7
Tayfield Rd WYTH/NTH M22 ....180 B2
Taylor Av ROCH OL11 ....28 C5
Taylor Green Wy OLDE OL4 ....77 E5
Taylor La DTN/ASHW M34 ....132 A4
Taylor Rd ALT WA14 ....164 D4
URM M41 ....124 D1
Taylor's La BOLE BL2 ....51 E1
Taylorson St ORD M5 ....127 E1
Taylorson St South ORD M5 ....126 D2
Taylors Pl WHIT OL12 * 10 C3
Taylor St BOLS/LL BL3 * 126 B4
BURY BL9 ....3 F6
DROY M43 ....74 B5
DROY M43 ....117 G5
DTN/ASHW M34 ....132 C4
GTN M18 ....130 B2
HEY OL10 ....40 D5
HYDE SK14 ....134 A5
MDTN M24 ....72 D4
OLD OL1 ....76 B4
OLDS OL8 ....92 D1
PWCH M25 ....86 B5
RAD M26 ....66 B1
ROY/SHW OL2 * 59 E4
RUSH/FAL M14 ....128 D5
STLY SK15 ....121 E4
WHIT OL12 ....10 D2
WHIT OL12 ....14 C5
Taywood Rd BOLS/LL BL3 ....63 E2
Teak St BURY BL9 ....5 J4
Teal Av POY/DIS SK12 ....194 B3
Tealby Av OLDTF/WHR M16 ....127 F4
Tealby Rd GTN M18 ....130 A4
Teal Cl ALT WA14 ....165 E1
RDSH SK5 ....160 A1
Teal St BOLS/LL BL3 ....49 E5
Teasdale Cl CHAD OL9 ....74 B5
Tebbutt St ANC M4 ....7 J1
Tedder Cl BURY BL9 ....70 A2
Tedder Dr WYTH/NTH M22 ....181 E5
Teddington Rd
NEWH/MOS M40 ....104 B1
Ted Jackson Wk
OP/CLY M11 * 116 A5
Teer St ANC M4 ....115 G3
Teesdale Av URM M41 ....123 H4
Teesdale Cl OFTN SK2 ....173 F3
Tees St ROCH OL11 ....30 C5
Teignmouth Av
NEWH/MOS M40 * 115 F1
Teignmouth St
NEWH/MOS M40 * 115 F1
Telfer Av BRUN/LGST M13 ....143 G1
Telfer Rd BRUN/LGST M13 ....143 G1
Telford Av DTN/ASHW M34 ....132 B1
Telford Ms UPML OL3 ....79 E3
Telford Rd MPL/ROM SK6 ....162 C4
Telford St CHH M8 ....102 A3
Telford Wk OLDTF/WHR M16 ....127 G4
Telford Wy ROCH OL11 ....43 F4
Tellson Cl SLFD M6 ....100 A4
Tellson Crs SLFD M6 ....100 A4
Tell St WHIT OL12 ....29 G2
Temperance St BOLS/LL BL3 ....48 C4
WGTN/LGST M12 ....128 D1
Tempest Cha HOR/BR BL6 ....46 C5
Tempest Rd HOR/BR BL6 ....46 D5
Tempest Rd HOR/BR BL6 ....62 D1
WILM/AE SK9 ....201 F4
Tempest St BOLS/LL BL3 ....48 A5
Temple Cl OLDE OL4 ....76 D4
Templecombe Dr BOL BL1 ....22 C5
Temple Dr BOL BL1 ....33 F3
SWIN M27 ....99 F5
Temple La MILN OL16 ....19 G3
Temple Rd BOL BL1 ....33 F3
SALE M33 ....155 E2
Temple Sq CHH M8 ....102 B5
Temple St HEY OL10 ....41 E4
MDTN M24 ....73 E3
OLD OL1 * 76 A5
Templeton Cl ALT WA14 ....165 E3
Ten Acre Dr WHTF M45 ....69 E5
Ten Acre Dr WHTF M45 ....69 E5
Ten Acres La NEWH/MOS M40 ....103 G4
Tenax Rd TRPK M17 ....125 G1
Tenbury Cl SLFD M6 ....113 E2
Tenbury Dr MDTN M24 ....88 D2
Tenby Av BOL BL1 ....32 D5
DID/WITH M20 ....142 D5
STRET M32 ....126 B4
Tenby Dr OLDTF/WHR M16 ....127 F2
Tenby Gv OLDE OL4 ....76 D3
OLDS OL8 ....100 B5
Tenby Rd OFTN SK2 ....29 F2
Tenby St RAD M26 ....67 H1
EDGY/DAV SK3 ....90 C5
Tenby Ry EDGY/DAV SK3 ....171 E2
Tenement La BRAM/HZG SK7 ....183 G2
Teneriffe St BRO M7 ....101 G5
Tennis St BOL BL1 ....33 H3
OLDTF/WHR M16 ....127 F4
Tennyson Av BURY BL9 ....53 G3
DTN/ASHW M34 * 147 E4
DUK SK16 ....134 B1
RAD M26 ....66 C1
Tennyson Cl HTNM SK4 ....158 D5
Tennyson Gdns PWCH M25 ....85 G4
Tennyson Rd CHD/CHDH SK8 ....170 C3
DROY M43 ....117 H3
FWTH BL4 ....81 G1
MDTN M24 ....56 A4
RDSH SK5 ....144 D2
SWIN M27 ....98 C2

Tennyson St BOL BL1 ....33 H5
BRUN/LGST M13 ....128 D3
OLD OL1 ....76 B3
ROCH OL11 ....43 F1
Tensing Av AULW OL7 ....107 F5
Tensing St OLDS OL8 ....106 D2
Tentercroft WHIT OL12 ....10 A6
Tenterden St BURY BL9 ....4 B5
Tenterhill La ROCH OL11 ....28 A1
Tenters St BURY BL9 ....4 B5
Tenth St TRPK M17 ....126 A2
Terence St NEWH/MOS M40 ....104 C5
Terminal Rd East
MANAIR M90 ....180 A5
Terminal Rd North
MANAIR M90 ....180 B5
Terminal Rd South
MANAIR M90 ....180 A5
Tern Cl ALT WA14 ....165 E1
DUK SK16 ....133 H1
ROCH OL11 ....28 C4
Tern Dr POY/DIS SK12 ....194 C3
Ternhill Cl FWTH BL4 ....65 H4
Terrace St OLDE OL4 ....76 D4
The Terrace PWCH M25 ....86 A4
Terrington Cl CCHDY M21 ....142 A4
Tetbury Dr BOLE BL2 ....50 C1
Tetbury Rd WYTH/NTH M22 ....180 A5
Tetlow Gv ECC M30 ....110 D4
Tetlow La BRO M7 ....101 H2
Tetlow St CHAD OL9 * 8 D5
HYDE SK14 ....133 H5
MDTN M24 ....72 D4
NEWH/MOS M40 ....115 H1
OLDS OL8 ....91 G3
Teviot St BRUN/LGST M13 ....129 F4
Tewkesbury Av AUL OL6 ....107 F3
DROY M43 ....117 H2
HALE/TIMP WA15 ....178 D1
MDTN M24 ....72 C1
URM M41 ....124 C4
Tewkesbury Cl
CHD/CHDH SK8 ....193 E1
POY/DIS SK12 ....195 E3
Tewkesbury Dr PWCH M25 ....86 B5
Tewkesbury Rd
EDGY/DAV SK3 ....171 E3
NEWH/MOS M40 ....115 G2
Texas St AUL OL6 ....119 H3
Textile St WGTN/LGST M12 ....117 H1
Textilose Rd TRPK M17 ....125 G3
Thackeray Cl CHH M8 ....102 B4
Thackeray Rd OLD OL1 ....76 B3
Thames Cl BURY BL9 ....27 G4
OP/CLY M11 ....116 C5
Thames Ct HULME M15 ....6 A7
Thames Rd MILN OL16 ....31 H5
Thames St SLFD M6 ....30 C5
OLD OL1 * 9 J1
Thanet Cl BRO M7 ....101 H5
Thankerton Av
DTN/ASHW M34 ....118 C4
Thatcher Cl ALT WA14 ....177 F4
Thatcher St OLDS OL8 ....91 H4
Thatch Leach CHAD OL9 ....90 A2
Thatch Leach La WHTF M45 ....69 H5
Thaxmead Dr
NEWH/MOS M40 ....117 E1
Thaxted Dr OFTN SK2 ....173 H4
Thaxted Pl BOL BL1 ....48 B1
Theatre St OLD OL1 ....9 H3
Thekla St CHAD OL9 ....8 D1
Thelma St RAMS BL0 ....16 C2
Thelwall Av BOLE BL2 ....50 A1
RUSH/FAL M14 ....142 B3
Thelwall Cl HALE/TIMP WA15 ....165 H4
Thelwall Rd SALE M33 ....155 F3
Theobald Rd ALT WA14 ....177 G3
Theta Cl OP/CLY M11 ....116 C3
Thetford Cl WALK M28 ....133 F1
Thetford Dr CHH M8 ....102 C3
Thetford Rd BOLE BL2 * 38 A1
Thicketford Brow BOLE BL2 ....34 D4
Thicketford Cl BOLE BL2 ....34 D5
Thicketford Rd BOLE BL2 ....34 C4
Thimble Cl WHIT OL12 ....20 A4
The Thimbles WHIT OL12 ....20 A4
Third Av BOL BL1 ....48 A2
BOLS/LL BL3 ....50 C5
BOL BL3 ....89 G3
OLDS OL8 ....106 B5
OP/CLY M11 ....116 D3
STLY SK15 ....109 F5
TRPK M17 ....125 F2
Third St BOL BL1 ....32 C2
Thirlby Dr WYTH/NTH M22 ....180 C3
Thirlemere Rd STKP SK1 ....172 C2
Thirlmere Av AULW OL7 ....119 E1
STRET M32 ....138 D3
SWIN M27 ....99 F3
Thirlmere Cl WILM/AE SK9 ....200 C4
Thirlmere Dr BURY BL9 ....53 F2
MDTN M24 ....81 F1
Thirlmere Gv FWTH BL4 ....64 D4
ROY/SHW OL2 ....59 E3
Thirlmere Rd PART M31 ....150 D2
ROCH OL11 ....42 A2
URM M41 ....138 A5
WYTH/NTH M22 ....180 A5
Thirlspot Cl BOL BL1 ....22 D5
Thirlstone Av OLDE OL4 ....61 E5
Thirsfield Dr OP/CLY M11 ....116 D3
Thirsk Av CHAD OL9 ....73 G5
SALE M33 ....153 F3
Thirsk St TOT/BURYW BL8 ....37 G1
Thirsk Rd BOLS/LL BL3 ....63 G5
Thirsk St WGTN/LGST M12 ....128 D1
Thistle Bank CL BKLY M9 ....102 D1
Thistle Cl STLY SK15 ....121 G1
Thistledown Cl ECC M50 ....110 D5
Thistle Gn MILN OL16 ....31 F4
Thistle Sq PART M31 ....150 D4
Thistleton Rd BOLS/LL BL3 ....63 E2
Thistlewood Dr WILM/AE SK9 ....199 G3
Thistleyfields MILN OL16 * 31 F4
Thomas Cl DTN/ASHW M34 ....132 D4

Thomas Dr BOLS/LL BL3 ....48 C4
Thomas Gibbon Cl
STRET M32 * 140 A2
Thomas Henshaw Ct
ROCH OL11 ....42 B2
Thomas Holden St BOL BL1 * 2 C3
Thomas Johnson Cl ECC M50 * 110 D4
Thomas More Cl FWTH BL4 ....82 C1
Thomasson Cl BOL BL1 ....33 H5
Thomas St ANC M4 ....7 H4
BOLS/LL BL3 ....48 C4
CHH M8 ....102 A2
FWTH BL4 ....66 B4
HALE/TIMP WA15 ....165 H5
MILN OL16 ....10 E4
NEWH/MOS M40 ....115 G4
OFTN SK2 ....13 G7
OLDE OL4 ....92 D2
RAD M26 ....68 C1
ROY/SHW OL2 ....60 B3
ROY/SHW OL2 ....75 G1
STRET M32 ....126 A5
Thomas St West OFTN SK2 ....13 G7
Thomas Telford Basin
CMANE M1 ....7 J5
Thompson Av BOLE BL2 ....36 C5
WHTF M45 ....69 H5
Thompson Cl DTN/ASHW M34 ....131 G5
Thompson Dr DTN/ASHW M34 ....131 G5
Thompson Dr BURY BL9 ....27 F4
Thompson Fold STLY SK15 ....120 C3
Thompson La CHAD OL9 ....90 B3
Thompson Rd BOL BL1 ....33 E5
DTN/ASHW M34 ....131 G5
TRPK M17 ....111 F5
Thompson St ANC M4 ....7 H2
BOLS/LL BL3 ....49 E4
CSLFD M3 * 114 B2
NEWH/MOS M40 ....103 G5
Thomson Rd GTN M18 ....130 B4
Thomson St BRUN/LGST M13 ....128 D2
EDGY/DAV SK3 ....13 F6
Thoralby Cl WGTN/LGST M12 ....129 H3
Thorburn Dr WHIT OL12 ....18 A1
Thoresby Cl RAD M26 ....51 F4
Thoresway Rd
BRUN/LGST M13 ....129 F5
NEWH/MOS M40 ....115 G2
Thor Gv ORD M5 ....113 H5
Thorley Cl CHAD OL9 ....89 H5
Thorley Dr HALE/TIMP WA15 ....166 C4
URM M41 ....138 D1
Thorley La HALE/TIMP WA15 ....166 C3
HALE/TIMP WA15 ....179 G3
Thorley Ms BRAM/HZG SK7 ....184 A5
Thorley St FAIL M35 ....105 E2
Thornage Dr NEWH/MOS M40 ....133 F1
Thorn Av FAIL M35 ....105 E4
Thornbank BOLS/LL BL3 ....48 B5
Thorn Bank DROY M43 * 117 G2
Thornbeck Dr BOL BL1 ....32 C5
Thornbeck Rd BOL BL1 ....32 C5
Thornbridge Av CCHDY M21 ....141 F3
Thornbury ROCH OL11 * 29 H5
Thornbury Av HYDE SK14 ....135 F5
Thornbury Cl CHD/CHDH SK8 ....183 F1
Thornbury Rd STRET M32 ....126 B4
Thornbury Wy GTN M18 ....130 B3
Thornbush Wy MILN OL16 ....11 J5
Thorncliff Av OLDS OL8 ....91 F4
Thorncliffe Av OLDS OL8 ....91 F4
ROY/SHW OL2 ....58 D5
Thorncliffe Gv BNG/LEV M19 ....144 C2
Thorncliffe Pk ROY/SHW OL2 ....58 D5
Thorncliffe Rd BOL BL1 ....34 A1
Thorn Cl HEY OL10 ....40 C3
Thorncombe Rd
OLDTF/WHR M16 ....127 H5
Thorn Ct SLFD M6 ....113 G3
Thorncross Cl HULME M15 ....127 F1
Thorndale Cl ROY/SHW OL2 ....59 F4
Thorndale Gv
HALE/TIMP WA15 ....166 B4
Thorn Dr WYTH/NTH M22 ....181 F4
Thorne Av URM M41 ....123 H5
Thorneside DTN/ASHW M34 ....132 C3
Thorne St FWTH BL4 ....65 H5
Thorneycroft Av CCHDY M21 ....156 B1
Thorneycroft Rd
HALE/TIMP WA15 ....166 C4
Thorney Dr CHD/CHDH SK8 ....193 F1
Thorney Hill Cl OLDE OL4 ....9 K5
Thorneyholme Cl HOR/BR BL6 ....46 D3
Thorneylea WHIT OL12 ....14 B5
Thornfield Av AUL OL6 ....120 B2
Thornfield Crs LHULT M38 ....81 E2
Thornfield Dr SWIN M27 ....98 D3
LHULT M38 ....81 E2
Thornfield Hey WILM/AE SK9 ....199 H2
Thornfield Houses
CHD/CHDH SK8 * 182 D2
Thornfield Rd BNG/LEV M19 ....158 B1
BOL BL1 ....33 H1
TOT/BURYW BL8 ....25 G4
Thornfield St ORD M5 ....112 C4
Thorngate Rd CHH M8 ....102 B5
Thorn Gv CHD/CHDH SK8 ....183 E5
HALE/TIMP WA15 ....177 H1
RUSH/FAL M14 ....143 G2
SALE M33 ....154 C2
Thorngrove Av
NTHM/RTH M23 ....167 E2
Thorngrove Dr WILM/AE SK9 ....199 F4
Thorngrove Hl WILM/AE SK9 ....199 F4
Thorngrove Rd WILM/AE SK9 ....199 F4
Thornham Cl
TOT/BURYW BL8 ....26 D5
Thornham Ct ROY/SHW OL2 ....58 D1
Thornham Dr BOL BL1 ....23 E5
Thornham La MDTN M24 ....57 H3
MDTN M24 ....58 B2
ROY/SHW OL2 ....58 B1
Thornham New Rd
ROCH OL11 ....57 H1
Thornham Rd ROY/SHW OL2 ....59 E2
SALE M33 ....153 H4
Thornhill Dr WALK M28 ....97 F2

Thornhill Rd *DROY* M43 ....118 A3
  HTNM SK4.........158 C4
  RAMS BL0 *.........26 B2
Thornholme Cl *GTN* M18 ....130 A5
Thornholme Rd
  MPL/ROM SK6.........175 F5
Thornley Brow *ANC* M4 ....7 F3
Thorn Lea *BOLE* BL2 ....35 E2
Thornlea *DROY* M43 ....117 F4
  HALE/TIMP WA15.........166 A5
Thornlea Av *OLDS* OL8 ....105 H1
  SWIN M27 ....98 C4
Thorn Lea Cl *BOL* BL1 ....47 C2
Thornlea Dr *WHIT* OL12 ....29 E1
Thornleigh Rd *RUSH/FAL* M14.........142 D2
Thornley Av *BOL* BL1 ....33 F4
Thornley Cl *OLDE* OL4 ....93 F2
Thornley Crs *MPL/ROM* SK6.........161 H2
  OLDE OL4.........93 F2
Thornley La North *RDSH* SK5.........131 E5
Thornley La South *RDSH* SK5.........145 G2
Thornley Ms *BOL* BL1 *.........33 F4
Thornley Park Rd *OLDE* OL4 ....93 F2
Thornley Rd *DTN/ASHW* M34.........132 D4
  PWCH M25.........70 B5
Thornley St *HYDE* SK14.........148 A2
  MDTN M24.........73 E3
  RAD M26.........68 C2
Thornmere Cl *SWIN* M27.........83 F5
Thorn Rd *BRAM/HZG* SK7.........193 H2
  OLDS OL8.........92 B4
  SWIN M27.........98 D4
Thorns Av *BOL* BL1.........33 C3
Thorns Cl *BOL* BL1.........33 C3
Thornsett Cl *BKLY* M9 *.........103 C2
Thornsgreen Rd
  WYTH/NTH M22.........180 C4
Thorns Rd *BOL* BL1.........33 C3
The Thorns *CCHDY* M21.........141 F4
Thorn St *BOL* BL1.........34 A4
  BURY BL9.........16 D5
Thornton Av *BOL* BL1 *.........32 C5
  DTN/ASHW M34.........132 D4
  URM M41.........138 A1
Thornton Cl *BOLS/LL* BL3.........67 F2
  FWTH BL4.........65 F3
Thornton Crs *PWCH* M25.........85 C2
Thornton Dr *WILM/AE* SK9.........192 A4
Thornton Ga *CHD/CHDH* SK8.........169 F3
Thornton Pl *HTNM* SK4.........159 E2
Thornton Rd *CHD/CHDH* SK8.........181 H5
  RUSH/FAL M14.........142 C1
Thornton St *BOLE* BL2.........3 H4
  NEWH/MOS M40.........115 F1
  OLDE OL4.........9 H6
  ROCH OL11 *.........43 E1
Thornton St North
  NEWH/MOS M40.........115 G1
Thorntree Cl *WHIT* OL12.........103 F3
Thorntree Pl *WHIT* OL12.........29 G3
Thorn Vw *BURY* BL9.........5 H3
Thornway *BRAM/HZG* SK7.........183 F4
  MPL/ROM SK6.........187 E5
  WALK M28.........96 B3
Thornway Dr *AULW* OL7.........119 E3
Thornwood Av *GTN* M18.........130 D2
Thornydyke Av *BOL* BL1.........34 A1
Thorold Gv *SALE* M33.........155 F2
Thorpe Av *RAD* M26.........53 E4
  SWIN M27.........98 D1
Thorpebrook Rd
  NEWH/MOS M40.........103 H4
Thorpe Cl *DTN/ASHW* M34.........132 C4
  OLDE OL4.........77 F4
Thorpe Gv *HTNM* SK4.........144 D5
Thorpe Hall Gv *HYDE* SK14.........134 A2
Thorpe La *OLDE* OL4.........77 F4
Thorpeness Sq *GTN* M18.........130 C2
Thorpe St *BOL* BL1.........33 C4
  MDTN M24.........71 H5
  OLDTF/WHR M16.........127 F4
  RAMS BL0 *.........16 C3
Thorp Rd *NEWH/MOS* M40.........103 H4
  ROY/SHW OL2.........59 E5
Thorp St *ECC* M30.........110 C5
  WHTF M45.........69 F2
Thorsby Av *HYDE* SK14.........148 B1
Thorsby Cl *EDGW/EG* BL7.........23 E5
Thorsby Rd *HALE/TIMP* WA15.........166 A5
Thrapston Av *DTN/ASHW* M34.........118 C4
Threadfold Wy *EDGW/EG* BL7.........23 E4
Threaphurst La
  BRAM/HZG SK7.........186 B3
Threapwood Rd
  WYTH/NTH M22.........180 D3
Three Acre Av *ROY/SHW* OL2.........59 H5
Three Acres La
  CHD/CHDH SK8.........182 B5
Threlkeld Cl *MDTN* M24.........71 H3
Threlkeld Rd *BOL* BL1.........22 C4
  MDTN M24.........71 H3
Thresher Cl *SALE* M33.........155 C3
Threshfield Cl *BURY* BL9.........27 G4
Threshfield Dr
  HALE/TIMP WA15.........166 D2
Throstle Bank St *HYDE* SK14.........133 F4
Throstle Gv *MPL/ROM* SK6.........174 D4
  TOT/BURYW BL8.........37 H1
Throstle Hall Ct *MDTN* M24 *.........72 C3
Throstles La *DROY* M43.........118 B2
Thrum Fold *WHIT* OL12.........18 C4
Thrum Hall La *WHIT* OL12.........18 D5
Thrush Dr *BURY* BL9.........5 J1
Thrush St *WHIT* OL12.........29 F2
Thruxton Cl *OLDTF/WHR* M16.........127 H5
Thurcaston Rd *ALT* WA14 *.........165 E3
Thurland Rd *OLDE* OL4.........92 B1
Thurland St *ROY/SHW* OL2.........73 H4
Thurlby Av *BKLY* M9.........88 D2
Thurlby St *BRUN/LGST* M13.........129 E4
Thurleigh Rd *DID/WITH* M20.........157 E2
Thurlestone Av *BOLE* BL2.........36 C5
Thurlestone Dr
  BRAM/HZG SK7.........184 C2
  URM M41.........124 B5
Thurlestone Rd *ALT* WA14.........165 E3

Thurloe St *RUSH/FAL* M14.........128 D5
Thurlow St *SALO* M50.........113 E5
Thurlston Crs *CHH* M8.........102 C3
Thurlwood Av *DID/WITH* M20.........142 C4
Thurnham St *BOLS/LL* BL3.........64 B1
Thursfield St *SLFD* M6.........101 E5
Thurstane St *BOL* BL1.........33 F4
Thurston Cl *BURY* BL9.........69 H2
Thurston Clough Rd *OLDE* OL4.........78 A5
Thurston Gn *WILM/AE* SK9.........200 D4
Thynne St *BOLS/LL* BL3.........49 E4
  FWTH BL4.........65 H3
Tiber Av *OLDS* OL8.........105 H1
Tib La *CMANW* M2.........7 G4
Tib St *CMANE* M1.........7 G4
  DTN/ASHW M34.........146 D1
  RAMS BL0 *.........16 C2
Tideswell Av *NEWH/MOS* M40.........115 G2
Tideswell Cl *CHD/CHDH* SK8.........182 A4
Tideswell Rd *BRAM/HZG* SK7.........185 F4
  DROY M43.........117 F2
Tideway Cl *BRO* M7.........100 C2
Tidworth Av *ANC* M4.........115 C3
Tiflis St *WHIT* OL12.........10 B4
Tig Fold Rd *FWTH* BL4.........64 D4
Tilbury St *OLD* OL1.........75 F4
Tilby Cl *URM* M41.........137 G1
Tildsley St *BOLS/LL* BL3.........48 D5
Tile St *BURY* BL9.........4 E2
Tillard Av *EDGY/DAV* SK3.........171 E1
Tillerman Cl *SWIN* M27.........100 A2
Tillhey Rd *WYTH/NTH* M22.........180 C2
Tilney Av *STRET* M32.........140 C2
Tilshead Wk
  BRUN/LGST M13 *.........128 D2
Tilside Gv *HOR/BR* BL6.........46 C3
Tilson Rd *NTHM/RTH* M23.........167 G4
Tilton St *OLD* OL1.........76 B2
Timberbottom *BOLE* BL2.........34 D2
Timberhurst *BURY* BL9.........39 G4
Times St *MDTN* M24.........73 E4
Timothy Cl *SLFD* M6.........112 A2
Timperley Cl *OLDS* OL8.........91 H5
Timperley Fold *AUL* OL6.........107 F4
Timperley La *AUL* OL6.........107 E4
Timperley St *OP/CLY* M11.........116 D5
Timpson Rd *NTHM/RTH* M23.........167 F2
Timsbury Cl *BOLE* BL2.........50 C4
Timson St *FAIL* M35.........105 C3
Tindall St *ECC* M30.........110 C5
  RDSH SK5.........131 E5
Tindle St *WALK* M28.........82 C4
Tinline St *BURY* BL9.........5 H5
Tinningham Ct *OP/CLY* M11.........130 D1
Tinshill Cl *WGTN/LGST* M12.........129 H5
Tinsley Cl *NEWH/MOS* M40.........115 H3
Tinsley Gv *BOLE* BL2.........3 K2
Tin St *BOLS/LL* BL3 *.........48 D4
Tintagel Ct *RAD* M26.........51 F5
  STLY SK15.........120 C3
Tintern Av *BOLE* BL2.........34 C4
  DID/WITH M20.........157 E1
  HEY OL10.........40 D2
  OLDS OL8.........91 H5
  URM M41.........138 A3
  WHIT OL12.........29 H1
  WHTF M45.........69 G3
Tintern Cl *NTHM/RTH* M23.........72 C1
Tintern Dr *HALE/TIMP* WA15.........178 D2
Tintern Gv *STKP* SK1.........160 C5
Tintern Pl *HEY* OL10.........40 D2
Tintern Rd *BRAM/HZG* SK7.........186 C1
  CHD/CHDH SK8.........169 G4
  WILM/AE SK9.........199 F5
Tintern St *RUSH/FAL* M14.........142 D1
Tipperary St *STLY* SK15.........109 F5
Tipping St *ALT* WA14.........177 C1
Tipton Cl *CHD/CHDH* SK8.........171 E5
  RAD M26.........51 C4
Tipton Dr *NTHM/RTH* M23.........155 H4
Tiree Cl *BRAM/HZG* SK7.........185 C3
Tirza Av *BNG/LEV* M19.........143 H4
Titanian Ri *OLD* OL1.........60 C4
Titchfield Rd *OLDS* OL8.........92 B3
The Barn Cl *WHIT* OL12 *.........20 A4
Tithe Barn Crs *BOL* BL1.........34 C2
Tithebarn Rd
  HALE/TIMP WA15.........178 D4
Tithe Barn Rd *HTNM* SK4.........158 C2
Tithebarn St *BURY* BL9.........4 E4
Titherington Cl
  BNG/LEV M19 *.........144 D2
Titterington Av *CCHDY* M21.........141 F1
Tiverton Av *SALE* M33.........154 A3
Tiverton Cl *RAD* M26.........51 C4
Tiverton Dr *SALE* M33.........154 A3
Tiverton Pl *AULW* OL7.........106 D5
Tiverton Rd *URM* M41.........124 D4
Tiverton Wk *BOL* BL1 *.........33 F5
Tiviot Dl *STKP* SK1.........13 C2
Tiviot Wy *RDSH* SK5.........160 A3
Tivoli St *CSLFD* M3.........6 D5
Toad La *WHIT* OL12.........10 B5
Tobermory Cl
  OP/CLY M11.........117 E4
Tobermory Rd
  CHD/CHDH SK8.........181 H2
Todd St *BRO* M7.........101 C4
  BURY BL9.........4 E1
  CSLFD M3.........7 F2
  HEY OL10.........40 B4
  MILN OL16.........11 C2
Todmorden Rd *LIT* OL15.........21 F2
Toft Rd *GTN* M18.........130 B4
Toledo St *OP/CLY* M11.........117 E4
Tolland La *HALE/TIMP* WA15.........178 A4
Tollard Av *NEWH/MOS* M40.........103 G5
Tollard Cl *CHD/CHDH* SK8.........183 E5
Toll Bar St *STKP* SK1.........13 H5
  WGTN/LGST M12.........129 F2
Tollemache Rd *HYDE* SK14.........135 H3
Tollemache Rd *HYDE* SK14.........135 H3
Tollesbury Ct
  NEWH/MOS M40.........115 G1
Toll Gate Cl *BRUN/LGST* M13.........129 F4
Tollgate Wy *MILN* OL16.........11 J5
Toll St *RAD* M26.........51 H4
Tolworth Dr *CHH* M8.........102 C3
Tomcroft La *DTN/ASHW* M34.........146 B1
Tomlinson St *HULME* M15 *.........127 H2

Tomlinson St *HULME* M15.........127 H2
  NEWH/MOS M40.........89 F4
  ROCH OL11.........42 B2
Tomlin Sq *BOLE* BL2.........49 H2
Tommy Browell Cl
  RUSH/FAL M14.........128 B5
Tommy Johnson Wk
  RUSH/FAL M14.........128 B5
Tommy La *BOLE* BL2.........36 B5
Tommy Taylor Cl
  NEWH/MOS M40.........104 B5
Tom Shepley St *HYDE* SK14.........148 A1
Tonacliffe Rd *WHIT* OL12.........18 B3
Tonacliffe Ter *WHIT* OL12.........18 B1
Tonacliffe Wy *WHIT* OL12.........18 B2
Tonbridge Cl *TOT/BURYW* BL8.........26 D4
Tonbridge Rd *BNG/LEV* M19.........144 B3
  RDSH SK5.........145 F3
Tonge Bridge Wy *BOLE* BL2.........3 J4
Tonge Fold Rd *BOLE* BL2.........49 H2
Tonge Gn *STLY* SK15 *.........135 F2
Tonge Hall Cl *MDTN* M24.........73 E4
Tonge Meadow *MDTN* M24.........73 E4
Tonge Moor Rd *BOLE* BL2.........3 K1
Tong End *WHIT* OL12.........14 B3
Tonge Old Rd *BOLE* BL2.........49 H2
Tonge Park Av *BOLE* BL2.........34 D5
Tonge Roughs *MDTN* M24.........73 G4
Tonge St *HEY* OL10.........41 E4
  MILN OL16.........30 B5
  WGTN/LGST M12 *.........129 E1
Tongfields *EDGW/EG* BL7.........23 E5
Tonge Head Av *BOL* BL1.........34 C3
Tong La *WHIT* OL12.........14 B4
Tong Rd *BOLS/LL* BL3.........50 D5
Tong St *FWTH* BL4.........83 E2
Tonman St *CSLFD* M3.........6 C6
Toon Crs *TOT/BURYW* BL8.........26 D5
Tootal Dr *SLFD* M6.........112 B2
Tootal Gv *SLFD* M6.........112 B3
Tootal Rd *ORD* M5.........112 B3
Topbridge Wy *WHIT* OL12.........168 D1
Topfield Rd *WYTH/NTH* M22.........168 D3
Topgate Brow *SWIN* M27.........100 A2
Topham St *BURY* BL9.........53 H1
Topley St *HEY* OL10.........41 E4
  NEWH/MOS M40.........102 D4
Top o th Brow *BOLE* BL2.........24 B5
Top o' th' Cnd *OLDE* OL9.........90 D3
Top o' th' La *BOLS/LL* BL3 *.........50 A4
Top o' th' Meadows La
  OLDE OL4.........77 F3
Topping Fold Rd *BURY* BL9.........39 F3
Toppings Gn *EDGW/EG* BL7.........23 F2
The Toppings *MPL/ROM* SK6.........161 H5
Topping St *BOL* BL1.........33 H5
  BURY BL9.........5 F2
Topp St *FWTH* BL4.........66 B5
Topp Wy *BOL* BL1.........33 H4
Top Schwabe St *MDTN* M24.........71 F4
Topside *OLD* OL1.........75 F3
Top St *MDTN* M24.........72 B3
  OLDE OL4.........77 H6
Torah St *CHH* M8.........114 D1
Tor Av *TOT/BURYW* BL8.........26 A2
Torbay Dr *OFTN* SK2.........172 C2
Torbay Rd *CCHDY* M21.........141 C3
  URM M41.........139 F2
Torcross Rd *BKLY* M9.........87 G2
Tor Meg Ms *TOT/BURYW* BL8.........26 A1
Torkington Av *SWIN* M27.........99 E1
Torkington La *BRAM/HZG* SK7.........186 C1
Torkington Rd *BRAM/HZG* SK7.........185 H2
  CHD/CHDH SK8.........169 G4
  WILM/AE SK9.........199 E4
Torness Wk *OP/CLY* M11.........116 C4
Toronto Av *MANAIR* M90.........180 A5
Toronto Rd *OFTN* SK2.........172 B3
Toronto St *BOLE* BL2.........3 K4
Torquay Cl *BRUN/LGST* M13.........129 E3
Torquay Gv *OFTN* SK2.........172 C5
Torra Barn Cl *EDGW/EG* BL7.........22 D1
Torrax Cl *SLFD* M6.........99 C4
Torre Cl *MDTN* M24.........72 D1
Torrens St *SLFD* M6.........100 B3
Torridon Rd *BOLE* BL2.........50 C2
Torrin Cl *EDGY/DAV* SK3.........172 A4
Torrington Av *BKLY* M9.........88 D5
Torrington Dr *HYDE* SK14.........148 B4
Torrington Rd *SWIN* M27.........99 C4
Torrington St *HEY* OL10.........56 B1
Torrisdale Cl *BOLS/LL* BL3.........48 A4
Torside Wy *SWIN* M27.........84 B5
Torver Dr *BOLE* BL2.........50 C1
  MDTN M24.........72 A2
Torwood Rd *CHAD* OL9.........73 H4
Totland Cl *WGTN/LGST* M12.........129 H5
Totnes Av *BRAM/HZG* SK7.........184 B2
  CHAD OL9.........74 A3
Totnes Rd *CCHDY* M21.........141 G5
  SALE M33.........153 G1
Totridge Cl *OFTN* SK2.........173 E4
Tottenham Dr
  NTHM/RTH M23.........167 E2
Tottington Av *OLDE* OL4.........77 E5
Tottington La *PWCH* M25.........85 F2
Tottington Rd *BOLE* BL2.........35 F1
  EDGW/EG BL7.........24 A1
  TOT/BURYW BL8.........37 G2
Tottington St *OP/CLY* M11.........116 D5
Totton Rd *FAIL* M35.........105 E3
Touchet Hall Rd *MDTN* M24.........73 C1
Tours Av *NTHM/RTH* M23.........155 H4
Towcester Cl *ANC* M4.........115 G4
Tower Av *NTHM/RTH* M23.........103 E5
Tower Ct *TOT/BURYW* BL8.........26 A3
Towers Av *BOLS/LL* BL3.........47 H5
Towers Cl *POY/DIS* SK12.........195 G2
Tower Sq *BRUN/LGST* M13 *.........129 E2
Towers Rd *POY/DIS* SK12.........195 G2
Towers St *OLDE* OL4.........76 D5
Tower St *DUK* SK16.........120 A4
  HEY OL10.........40 D3
  HYDE SK14.........147 H2
  RAD M26.........31 H5
Towey Cl *GTN* M18.........130 C2
Towncliffe Wk *HULME* M15 *.........127 G2
Towncroft *DTN/ASHW* M34.........132 C4

Towncroft Av *MDTN* M24.........72 C2
Towncroft La *BOL* BL1.........47 F1
Townend St *HYDE* SK14.........148 A1
Townfield *URM* M41.........123 H5
Townfield Gdns *ALT* WA14.........165 G4
Townfield Rd *ALT* WA14 *.........165 G4
Town Fields Cl *BURY* BL9.........4 E6
Townfield St *OLDE* OL4 *.........76 A5
Townfield Wk *HULME* M15 *.........127 G2
Town Fold *MPL/ROM* SK6.........175 G2
Town Gate Dr *URM* M41.........137 E1
Town Hall La *CMANW* M2 *.........6 E4
Town House Rd *LIT* OL15.........21 E2
Town La *DTN/ASHW* M34.........146 B2
  DUK SK16.........131 H5
Townley Fold *HYDE* SK14.........134 C2
Townley Rd *MILN* OL16.........31 H5
Townley St *CHH* M8.........102 A5
  MDTN M24.........72 D3
  OP/CLY M11 *.........116 C4
Townley Ter *MPL/ROM* SK6.........175 F3
Townrow St *HEY* OL10 *.........41 F4
Townscliffe La *MPL/ROM* SK6.........175 F5
Townsend Rd *SWIN* M27.........99 E1
Townside Rw *BURY* BL9.........4 E6
Townsley Gv *AUL* OL6.........107 H5
Town St *MPL/ROM* SK6.........175 G5
Towton St *BKLY* M9.........103 F3
Towyn Av *ORD* M5.........113 F3
Toxteth St *OP/CLY* M11.........130 D1
Tracey St *CHH* M8.........102 B1
Traders Av *URM* M41.........123 H5
Trafalgar Av *DTN/ASHW* M34.........131 H1
  POY/DIS SK12.........195 H4
Trafalgar Cl *POY/DIS* SK12.........195 H4
Trafalgar Gv *BRO* M7 *.........101 G5
Trafalgar Pl *DID/WITH* M20.........157 E2
Trafalgar Rd *SALE* M33.........140 A5
  SLFD M6.........111 H2
Trafalgar Sq *AULW* OL7.........119 E4
Trafalgar St *BRO* M7 *.........101 G5
  MILN OL16.........10 D6
Trafford Av *URM* M41.........124 D5
Trafford Bank Rd
  OLDTF/WHR M16 *.........127 F3
Trafford Bvd *URM* M41.........124 B2
Trafford Dr *HALE/TIMP* WA15.........166 C1
  LHULT M38.........81 G2
Trafford Gv *FWTH* BL4.........83 B2
  STRET M32.........140 B2
Trafford Park Rd *TRPK* M17.........125 H1
Trafford Pl *OLDTF/WHR* M16.........127 G3
  WILM/AE SK9 *.........199 G4
Trafford Rd *ECC* M30.........111 E5
  SALO M50.........126 D2
  WILM/AE SK9 *.........199 G4
  WILM/AE SK9.........200 D4
Trafford St *CSLFD* M3.........6 C7
  FWTH BL4.........65 G5
  OLDS OL8.........9 F6
  ROCH OL11.........42 D2
Trafford Wharf Rd *TRPK* M17.........125 H1
Tragan Cl *OFTN* SK2.........173 E3
Tragan Dr *OFTN* SK2.........173 E3
Trail St *SLFD* M6.........112 D3
Tram St *OP/CLY* M11.........130 B1
Tramway Rd *AUL* OL6.........119 H3
  IRL M44.........136 B4
Tranby Cl *WYTH/NTH* M22.........130 A3
Tranmere Cl *GTN* M18.........130 A3
Tranmere Dr *WILM/AE* SK9.........192 B5
Tranmere Rd *EDGY/DAV* SK3.........171 H2
Transvaal St *OP/CLY* M11.........117 E4
Travis Brow *HTNM* SK4.........12 C3
Travis St *CMANE* M1.........7 K6
  HYDE SK14.........148 A1
  MILN OL16.........45 E2
  ROY/SHW OL2.........59 F2
Trawden Av *BOL* BL1.........33 F4
Trawden Dr *BURY* BL9.........27 F3
Trawden Gn *OFTN* SK2.........173 G3
Trawden Rd *LIT* OL15.........21 E2
Traylen Wy *WHIT* OL12.........19 F5
Traynor Cl *MDTN* M24.........72 C3
Tree Av *DROY* M43.........117 H2
Tree House Av *AULW* OL7.........106 C4
Treelands Wk *ORD* M5.........127 E2
Tree Tops *EDGW/EG* BL7.........16 B5
Treetops Av *RAMS* BL0.........16 B5
Treetops Cl *UPML* OL3 *.........78 C5
Trefoil Wy *LIT* OL15.........20 C2
Tregaer Fold *MDTN* M24.........73 H4
Trenam Pl *ORD* M5.........113 C3
Trenant Rd *SLFD* M6.........112 C1
Trenchard Dr *WYTH/NTH* M22.........181 E5
Trenchard St *FWTH* BL4.........65 H5
Trengrove St *WHIT* OL12 *.........29 F2
Trent Av *CHAD* OL9.........73 H4
  MILN OL16.........40 D3
  MILN OL16.........31 H5
Trent Bridge Wk
  OLDTF/WHR M16.........126 D5
Trent Cl *BRAM/HZG* SK7.........193 F1
  RDSH SK5.........160 D3
Trent Ct *HULME* M15 *.........127 G2
Trent Dr *BURY* BL9.........27 G3
  WALK M28.........81 G5
Trentham Av *FWTH* BL4.........65 H5
  SALE M33.........158 C3
Trentham Cl *FWTH* BL4.........65 H5
Trentham Gv
  NEWH/MOS M40.........103 H1
Trentham Lawns *SLFD* M6.........113 F1
Trentham Rd
  OLDTF/WHR M16.........126 D5
Trentham St *FWTH* BL4.........65 H5
  HULME M15.........127 F1
  SWIN M27 *.........98 D1
Trent Rd *ROY/SHW* OL2.........59 H1
Trent St *MILN* OL16.........44 A4
Trent Wk *DROY* M43.........118 A5
Tresco Av *STRET* M32.........140 C2
Trevelyan St *ECC* M30.........111 H3
Trevor Av *SALE* M33.........154 A4
Trevor Dr *NEWH/MOS* M40.........89 H5
Trevor Gv *STKP* SK1.........13 K5

Trevor Rd *ECC* M30.........110 C2
  SWIN M27.........98 D4
Trevor St *OP/CLY* M11.........123 C5
Trevor St *OP/CLY* M11.........42 A3
  ROCH OL11.........42 A3
The Triangle
  HALE/TIMP WA15.........166 C3
  HALE/TIMP WA15.........165 G2
Trident Rd *ECC* M30.........123 C1
Trillo Av *BOLE* BL2.........3 K7
Trimdon Cl *OP/CLY* M11.........116 C3
Trimingham Dr
  TOT/BURYW BL8.........27 E5
Trinity Av *NEWH/MOS* M40.........103 E5
Trinity Av *SALE* M33.........155 E2
Trinity Buildings *MOSL* OL5 *.........94 A5
Trinity Crs *DUK* SK16.........120 B5
Trinity Crs *WALK* M28.........82 B5
Trinity Gdns *EDGY/DAV* SK3.........184 A1
Trinity Gn *RAMS* BL0.........26 C1
Trinity Rd *SALE* M33.........154 D2
Trinity St *BOLS/LL* BL3.........2 D7
  BURY BL9.........4 E6
  MDTN M24.........72 C4
  MPL/ROM SK6.........175 E3
  OLD OL1.........75 F4
  STLY SK15.........120 D4
Trinity Wy *CSLFD* M3.........6 A5
Trippier Rd *ECC* M30.........110 A5
Tripps Ms *DID/WITH* M20.........157 E2
Triscombe Wy
  OLDTF/WHR M16.........127 H5
Tristam Cl *BRUN/LGST* M13.........128 D2
Trojan Gdns *BRO* M7.........101 H5
Troon Cl *BOLS/LL* BL3.........63 G1
  BRAM/HZG SK7.........184 B5
Troon Dr *CHD/CHDH* SK8.........181 H3
Troon Rd *NTHM/RTH* M23.........167 G3
Trough Ga *OLDS* OL8.........91 E5
Troutbeck Av *ANC* M4.........115 G4
Troutbeck Cl *TOT/BURYW* BL8.........25 E1
Troutbeck Dr *RAMS* BL0.........16 B5
Troutbeck Rd *CHD/CHDH* SK8.........181 C1
  HALE/TIMP WA15.........167 E4
Troutbeck Wy *ROCH* OL11.........42 A2
Trowbridge Dr
  NEWH/MOS M40.........104 B1
Trowbridge Rd
  DTN/ASHW M34.........147 E2
Trows La *ROCH* OL11.........42 C5
Trowtree Av *WGTN/LGST* M12.........129 F2
Troydale Dr *NEWH/MOS* M40.........103 H4
Troy Wk *ORD* M5.........127 E1
Trumpet St *CMANE* M1.........6 D7
Truro Av *AUL* OL6.........107 C3
  RDSH SK5.........160 D1
  STRET M32.........140 C1
Truro Cl *BRAM/HZG* SK7.........184 A5
  TOT/BURYW BL8.........26 D4
Truro Dr *SALE* M33.........153 C2
Truro Rd *AUL* OL6.........74 B5
Trust Rd *GTN* M18.........130 B5
Tucana Av *BRO* M7.........113 H2
Tudbury Wy *CSLFD* M3.........6 A2
Tudor Av *BKLY* M9.........87 H5
  BOL BL1 *.........48 A2
  CHAD OL9.........89 G4
  FWTH BL4.........65 G5
  STLY SK15.........121 C2
Tudor Cl *MOSL* OL5.........109 F1
  RDSH SK5.........145 E5
Tudor Ct *PWCH* M25.........86 B4
  WHIT OL12.........11 G2
Tudor Gn *WILM/AE* SK9.........199 H1
Tudor Gv *MDTN* M24.........72 A1
Tudor Hall St *ROCH* OL11.........42 A4
Tudor Rd *ALT* WA14.........165 E2
  WILM/AE SK9.........199 H1
Tudor St *BOLS/LL* BL3 *.........48 B5
  OLDS OL8.........8 E7
  ROY/SHW OL2.........60 A2
Tuffley Rd *NTHM/RTH* M23.........167 H5
Tugford Cl *OLDTF/WHR* M16.........127 H5
Tuley St *OP/CLY* M11.........129 C1
Tulip Av *FWTH* BL4.........82 C2
  FWTH BL4.........
Tulip Cl *CHAD* OL9.........73 H5
  EDGY/DAV SK3.........171 G4
  SALE M33.........153 F2
Tulip Dr *HALE/TIMP* WA15.........166 C5
Tulip Gv *WHIT* OL12.........18 D5
Tulip Rd *PART* M31.........150 D4
Tully Pl *BRO* M7.........114 B1
Tully St *BRO* M7.........101 H5
Tully St South *BRO* M7.........101 H4
Tulpen Sq *CHAD* OL9.........74 C5
Tulworth Rd *POY/DIS* SK12.........195 F3
Tumblewood Dr
  CHD/CHDH SK8.........170 B5
Tunbridge Sq *ORD* M5.........113 F3
Tunshill Rd *NTHM/RTH* M23.........155 F5
Tuns Rd *OLDS* OL8.........92 A5
Tunstall Rd *OLDE* OL4.........92 B1
Tunstall St *HTNM* SK4.........12 E4
  OP/CLY M11 *.........130 D1
Tunstead Av *DID/WITH* M20.........142 D5
Tunstead La *UPML* OL3.........95 G2
Turbary Wk *MILN* OL16.........31 E5
Turf Cl *ROY/SHW* OL2.........75 F1
Turf Hill Rd *MILN* OL16.........20 C1
Turf House Cl *LIT* OL15.........20 C1
Turfland Av *ROY/SHW* OL2.........75 F1
Turf La *CHAD* OL9.........90 B4
  ROY/SHW OL2.........75 G1
Turf Lea Rd *MPL/ROM* SK6.........175 G5
Turf Park Rd *ROY/SHW* OL2.........75 G1
Turf Pit La *OLDE* OL4.........61 E5
Turf St *RAD* M26.........68 A1
Turf Ter *LIT* OL15.........20 C2
Turfton Rd *ROY/SHW* OL2.........75 G1
Turks Rd *RAD* M26.........52 A5
Turley St *CHH* M8.........102 C4
Turnberry *BOLS/LL* BL3.........63 G1
Turnberry Dr *WILM/AE* SK9.........199 G2
Turnberry Wk *NEWH/MOS* M40.........103 H1
Turnbull Av *PWCH* M25.........70 B5

Turnbull Rd ALT WA14 .... 165 E1
  BRUN/LGST M13 .... 143 H1
Turnbury Cl SALE M33 .... 139 H5
Turnbury Rd WYTH/NTH M22 .. 168 D4
Turncliff Crs WILM/AE SK6 .... 174 C2
Turncroft La STKP SK1 .... 13 K4
  STKP SK1 .... 172 C1
Turncroft Wy WALK M28 .... 96 A3
Turnell Wy WALK M28 .... 97 H5
Turner Av FAIL M35 .... 104 D4
  IRL M44 .... 122 B3
Turner Bridge Rd BOLE BL2 .... 49 H1
Turner Dr URM M41 .... 139 F1
Turnerford Cl EDGW/EG BL7 .... 22 D2
Turner Gdns HYDE SK14 .... 133 H4
Turner La AUL OL6 .... 119 G1
  HYDE SK14 .... 134 A4
  MPL/ROM SK6 .... 146 D5
Turner Rd MPL/ROM SK6 .... 175 E4
Turner's Pl WHIT OL12 .... 18 D5
Turner St ANC M4 .... 7 G3
  AUL OL6 .... 119 G1
  BOL BL1 .... 3 H2
  BRO M7 .... 101 H3
  DTN/ASHW M34 .... 132 C3
  GTN M18 .... 130 C3
  OLDE OL4 .... 76 D4
  OLDTF/WHR M16 .... 127 F2
  OP/CLY M11 .... 116 D4
  STKP SK1 .... 13 G2
  WHIT OL12 .... 10 B2
Turnfield Cl MILN OL16 .... 20 A5
Turnfield Rd CHD/CHDH SK8 .. 181 H1
Turnhill Rd MILN OL16 .... 43 G5
Turn Moss Rd STRET M32 .... 140 D3
Turnough Rd MILN OL16 .... 31 G4
Turnpike Gn SLFD M6 * 113 E2
The Turnpike MPL/ROM SK6 .. 174 C2
Turnpike Wk OP/CLY M11 .... 115 H4
Turnstone Rd BOLE BL2 .... 3 G7
  OFTN SK2 .... 173 H4
Turn St AUL OL6 .... 120 A1
Turton Cl HEY OL10 .... 40 B4
  TOT/BURYW BL8 .... 52 B1
Turton Ct BOL BL1 .... 3 G2
Turton Hts BOLE BL2 .... 23 G5
Turton La PWCH M25 .... 85 G2
Turton Rd BOLE BL2 .... 23 H5
  TOT/BURYW BL8 .... 25 H5
Turton St BOL BL1 .... 3 F2
  OP/CLY M11 * 130 C1
Turves Rd CHD/CHDH SK8 .... 182 C3
Tuscan Rd DID/WITH M20 .... 169 G1
Tuscany Vw BRO M7 .... 101 E2
Tutbury St ANC M4 .... 115 J4
Tuxford Wk NEWH/MOS M40 .. 103 E5
Tweedale Av BKLY M9 .... 87 H2
Tweedale St ROCH OL11 .... 42 D1
Tweed Cl ALT WA14 .... 165 F5
  OLDS OL8 .... 9 F6
Tweedle Hill Rd BKLY M9 .... 87 F1
Tweenbrook Av
  NTHM/RTH M23 .... 179 H1
Tweesdale Cl WHTF M45 .... 70 A3
Twelve Yards Rd ECC M30 .... 123 E1
Twigworth Rd
  WYTH/NTH M22 .... 180 B2
Twillbrook Dr CSLFD M3 * 6 C1
Twinegate WHIT OL12 .... 18 D5
Twingates Cl ROY/SHW OL2 .. 60 A4
Twining Brook Rd
  CHD/CHDH SK8 .... 183 E1
Twining Rd ECC M30 .... 111 E5
Twinnies Rd WILM/AE SK9 .. 199 E1
Twin St HEY OL10 .... 41 F5
Twirl Hill Rd AUL OL6 .... 107 H2
Twisse Rd BOLE BL2 .... 50 C2
Twoacre Av WYTH/NTH M22 .. 168 B4
Two Acre Dr ROY/SHW OL2 .. 59 G1
Two Acre La OLDE OL4 .... 77 G2
Two Bridges Rd MILN OL16 .. 45 E3
Two Brooks La
  TOT/BURYW BL8 .... 25 E1
Two Trees La DTN/ASHW M34.. 147 E2
Twyford Cl DID/WITH M20 .. 157 E3
Tydeman Wk NEWH/MOS M40.. 44 D1
Tyldesley St RUSH/FAL M14 .. 128 D5
Tyler St WILM/AE SK9 .... 200 D4
Tymm St WILM/AE SK9 .... 104 D1
Tyndall Av NEWH/MOS M40.. 103 H1
Tyndall St OLDE OL4 .... 92 B2
Tyne Ct WALK M28 .... 81 H4
Tynedale Cl RDSH SK5 .... 159 H1
Tynesbank WALK M28 .... 81 H5
Tynesbank Cottages
  WALK M28 * 81 H4
Tyne St OLDE OL4 .... 76 B5
Tynwald St OLDE OL4 .... 76 B5
Tyrol Wk OP/CLY M11 .... 116 A5
Tyrone Cl NTHM/RTH M23 .. 167 E1
Tyrone Dr ROCH OL11 .... 41 G1
Tyro St OLDS OL8 * 91 G4
Tyrrell Rd HYDE SK14 .... 148 C2
Tyrrel Rd RDSH SK5 .... 145 F2
Tysoe Gdns CSLFD M3 .... 6 A2
Tyson St CHH M8 .... 102 A2
Tytherington Dr BNG/LEV M19.. 144 D2

U

Uganda St BOLS/LL BL3 .... 64 B2
Ukraine Rd BRO M7 .... 100 D4
Uldale Dr MDTN M24 .... 72 B3
Ullesthorpe WHIT OL12 .... 10 B5
Ulleswater Cl BOLS/LL BL3 .. 66 C1
Ulleswater St BOL BL1 .... 34 A4
Ullswater Av AUL OL6 .... 119 F1
  ROY/SHW OL2 .... 59 E3
  WHIT OL12 .... 29 F2
Ullswater Dr BURY BL9 * 53 F3
  FWTH BL4 .... 64 D5
  MDTN M24 .... 72 C1
Ullswater Gv HEY OL10 .... 56 A1
Ullswater Rd STKP SK1 .... 172 C2
  URM M41 .... 138 A2
  WILM/AE SK9 .... 191 H3
  WYTH/NTH M22 .... 180 A2
Ullswater Ter STLY SK15 .... 120 D1
Ulster Av ROCH OL11 .... 42 D1
Ulster Rd WYTH/NTH M20.. 100 B1
Ulundi St RAD M26 .... 68 A1
Ulverston Av CHAD OL9 .... 90 B1
  MDTN M20 .... 142 B4
Umberton Rd WHTN BL5 .... 63 G5
Uncouth Rd MILN OL16 .... 31 F4
Underhill RAD M26 .... 68 B4
Underhill Rd OLD OL1 .... 75 F3
Underhill Wk
  NEWH/MOS M40 .... 116 C1
Under La CHAD OL9 .... 90 C4
  OLDE OL4 .... 93 G3
Underwood WHIT OL12 .... 10 B6
Underwood Cl GTN M18 .... 131 E2
Underwood Rd HYDE SK14 .. 135 E5
  WILM/AE SK9 .... 201 F4
Underwood St DUK SK16 .... 119 G5
Underwood Wy ROY/SHW OL2.. 60 C1
Undsworth Ct HEY OL10 * 41 E4
Unicorn St ECC M30 .... 110 C5
Union Av BURY BL9 .... 4 E4
  BURY BL9 .... 4 E4
Union Buildings BOLE BL2 .... 3 F6
Union Ct BOLE BL2 * 34 D4
Union Rd AUL OL6 .... 119 H1
  BOLE BL2 .... 3 H1
  MPL/ROM SK6 * 175 E5
  WHIT OL12 .... 20 B4
Union St ANC M4 .... 7 G3
  AUL OL6 .... 119 G1
  BURY BL9 .... 4 E4
  CHAD OL9 .... 90 C3
  EDGW/EG BL7 .... 22 C1
  GTN M18 .... 130 D2
  HYDE SK14 .... 148 A1
  MDTN M24 .... 72 D3
  OLD OL1 .... 9 G4
  OLDE OL4 .... 92 D1
  RAMS BL0 .... 16 D2
  ROY/SHW OL2 .... 59 H4
  RUSH/FAL M14 * 128 C5
  SLFD M6 .... 113 F1
  STKP SK1 .... 13 G6
  SWIN M27 .... 98 D2
  WGTN/LGST M12 .... 128 D1
  WHIT OL12 .... 10 C4
  WHIT OL12 .... 14 B5
Union St West OLDS OL8 .... 8 E6
Union Ter BRO M7 * 102 A1
United Rd OLDTF/WHR M16.. 126 B3
Unity Cl HEY OL10 .... 40 C5
Unity Crs HEY OL10 .... 40 C5
Unity Dr BRO M7 .... 101 H4
Unity St HEY OL10 .... 40 C5
  HYDE SK14 * 13 J6
University Rd ORD M5 .... 113 G3
University Rd West ORD M5 * .. 113 G3
Unsworth St RAD M26 .... 52 A5
Unsworth Wy OLD OL1 * 9 H1
Unwin Av GTN M18 .... 130 C4
Upavon Rd WYTH/NTH M22 .. 181 E1
Upcast La WILM/AE SK9 .... 200 A3
Upland Dr LHULT M38 .... 81 E1
Upland Rd OLDS OL8 .... 91 F3
Uplands MDTN M24 .... 72 D5
Uplands Av RAD M26 .... 68 D2
Uplands Rd HYDE SK14 .... 148 C5
  URM M41 .... 137 G3
The Uplands MOSL OL5 .... 109 E1
Upper Brook St
  BRUN/LGST M13 .... 128 D3
  STKP SK1 .... 13 H4
Upper Camp St BRO M7 .... 101 G5
Upper Chorlton Rd
  OLDTF/WHR M16 .... 127 F5
Upper Cleminson St
  CSLFD M3 .... 114 A3
Upper Cliff Hi ROY/SHW OL2.. 45 F5
Upper Conran St BKLY M9 .. 103 F2
Upper Downs ALT WA14 .... 177 F1
Upper George St WHIT OL12 .. 10 D3
Upper Gloucester St SLFD M6.. 113 F2
Upper Hayes Cl MILN OL16.. 11 J5
Upper Helena St
  NEWH/MOS M40 .... 115 H3
Upper Hibbert La
  MPL/ROM SK6 .... 175 E5
Upper Kent Rd
  RUSH/FAL M14 .... 129 E5
Upper Kirby St ANC M4 .... 115 F4
Upper Lees Dr WHTN BL5 .... 62 B3
Upper Lloyd St
  RUSH/FAL M14 .... 128 B5
Upper Medlock St
  HULME M15 .... 128 A2
Uppermill Dr BNG/LEV M19.. 158 A3
Upper Monsall St
  NEWH/MOS M40 .... 103 F4
Upper Moss La HULME M15.. 127 H2
Upper Park Rd BRO M7 .... 101 H1
  BKLY M9 .... 128 D4
Upper Passmonds Gv
  ROCH OL11 .... 29 E3
Upper Stone Dr MILN OL16.. 31 E5
Upper West Gv
  BRUN/LGST M13 .... 129 E3
Upper Wharf St ORD M5 .... 113 H4
Upper Wilton St PWCH M25.. 86 B3
Uppingham Dr RAMS BL0 .... 16 C1
Upton ROCH OL11 .... 29 H5
Upton Av CHD/CHDH SK8 .. 182 C4
  HTNM SK4 .... 158 B2
Upton Cl MDTN M24 .... 88 D2
Upton Dr ALT WA14 .... 165 H1
Upton La BOL BL1 .... 47 G2
Upton Wy TOT/BURYW BL8 .. 37 E1
  WILM/AE SK9 .... 165 H5
Urban Rd
  HALE/TIMP WA15 .... 165 H5
  SALE M33 .... 154 B2
Urmson St OLDS OL8 .... 91 G4
Urmston La STRET M32 .... 139 G2
Urmston Dr URM M41 .... 139 E4
Urwick Rd MPL/ROM SK6 .. 162 A5
Usk Cl WHTF M45 .... 70 B5

Uttley St BOL BL1 .... 33 G4
  ROCH OL11 .... 28 C4
Uxbridge Av OP/CLY M11 .. 116 D3
Uxbridge St AUL OL6 .... 119 F2

V

Vaal St OLDS OL8 .... 90 D4
Valance Cl WGTN/LGST M12 .. 129 H2
Valdene Cl FWTH BL4 .... 66 A5
Valdene Dr FWTH BL4 .... 66 A5
  WALK M28 .... 97 E2
Vale Av BURY BL9 .... 53 E2
  HYDE SK14 .... 134 B5
  RAD M26 .... 67 F5
  SALE M33 .... 155 F1
  SWIN M27 .... 99 F1
Vale Cl BRAM/HZG SK7 .... 175 F5
  HTNM SK4 .... 158 C4
  MPL/ROM SK6 .... 162 D4
Vale Coppice RAMS BL0 .... 16 C5
Vale Cottages LIT OL15 .... 20 D5
Vale Crs CHD/CHDH SK8 .. 182 C2
Vale Dr CHAD OL9 .... 8 C5
  PWCH M25 .... 85 H5
Vale Edge RAD M26 .... 52 B4
Vale Head WILM/AE SK9 .... 192 A5
Vale La FAIL M35 .... 117 H1
Valencia Rd BRO M7 .... 101 E4
Valentia Rd BKLY M9 .... 88 A3
Valentine St FAIL M35 .... 104 D3
  OLDE OL4 .... 92 B1
Vale Park Wy CHH M8 .... 102 D3
Vale Rd HALE/TIMP WA15 .. 128 A1
Vale Rd ALT WA14 .... 177 E3
  DROY M43 .... 118 A2
  HALE/TIMP WA15 .... 166 B4
  HTNM SK4 .... 158 C5
  MPL/ROM SK6 .... 174 A1
  ROY/SHW OL2 .... 59 E5
  STLY SK15 .... 109 F4
  WILM/AE SK9 .... 198 B2
Vale Side MOSL OL5 .... 108 D2
Vale St AULW OL7 .... 106 D4
  BOLE BL2 .... 50 D2
  HEY OL10 .... 41 F4
  MDTN M24 .... 73 E4
  OP/CLY M11 .... 116 D3
  STKP SK1 .... 108 C1
The Vale MOSL OL5 .... 108 C1
Vale Top Av BKLY M9 .... 103 F3
Valetta Cl RUSH/FAL M14 .. 142 D3
Vale Vw ALT WA14 * 177 F3
Valewood Av HTNM SK4 .... 158 D5
Valletts La BOL BL1 .... 33 F5
Valley Av TOT/BURYW BL8.. 26 D1
Valley Cl CHD/CHDH SK8 .. 182 B1
  MOSL OL5 .... 94 C3
Valley Dr WILM/AE SK9 .... 191 H4
Valley Gv DTN/ASHW M34 .. 147 F1
Valley Ms UPML OL3 .... 95 F2
Valley Ml EDGW/EG BL7 * .. 23 E3
Valley Mill La BURY BL9 .... 5 F1
Valley New Rd ROY/SHW OL2.. 75 F1
Valley Park Rd PWCH M25.. 85 G2
Valley Ri ROY/SHW OL2 .... 59 E1
Valley Rd BRAM/HZG SK7 .. 184 A5
  CHD/CHDH SK8 .... 182 B1
  HYDE SK14 .... 149 G3
  MDTN M24 .... 73 E2
  MPL/ROM SK6 .... 161 E2
  ROY/SHW OL2 .... 59 E1
  URM M41 .... 136 D5
Valley Rd South URM M41 .. 137 F1
Valley Vw HYDE SK14 .... 134 B4
  WHIT OL12 .... 14 C1
Valley Wk OP/CLY M11 .... 116 A4
Valley Wy STLY SK15 .... 121 H4
Valpy Av BOLE BL2 .... 34 C3
Vancouver Quay SALQ M50.. 126 C1
Vandyke Av SLFD M6 .... 112 A2
Vandyke St WHIT OL12 .... 28 D2
Vane St ECC M30 .... 110 D3
Vannes Gv HYDE SK14 .... 135 G5
Vantomme St BOL BL1 .... 33 H2
Vant St OLDE OL4 .... 92 B3
Varden Gv EDGY/DAV SK3 .. 171 G4
Varden Rd POY/DIS SK12 .. 195 H4
Vardon Dr WILM/AE SK9 .. 199 G4
Varey St GTN M18 .... 130 C3
Varley Rd BOLS/LL BL3 .... 47 H5
Varley St NEWH/MOS M40.. 115 G1
Varna St OP/CLY M11 * 130 C1
Vauban Dr SLFD M6 .... 112 A2
Vaudrey Dr BRAM/HZG SK7.. 185 E2
  CHD/CHDH SK8 .... 182 D2
  HALE/TIMP WA15 .... 166 B4
Vaudrey La DTN/ASHW M34.. 147 E1
Vaudrey Rd MPL/ROM SK6 .. 161 H1
Vaudrey St STLY SK15 .... 120 D4
Vaughan Av NEWH/MOS M40.. 103 H2
Vaughan Gv OLDE OL4 .... 93 E1
Vaughan Rd ALT WA14 .... 165 F3
  CCHDY M21 .... 141 H3
  HTNM SK4 .... 159 G3
Vaughan St ECC M30 .... 110 C2
  ROY/SHW OL2 .... 75 F1
  WGTN/LGST M12 .... 129 H1
Vauxhall St NEWH/MOS M40.. 115 E1
Vavasour Ct MILN OL16 * 30 C5
Vawdrey Dr NTHM/RTH M23.. 155 G4
Vaynor WHIT OL12 .... 10 B4
Vega St CHH M8 .... 113 H2
Vela Wk BRO M7 * 113 H2
Velmere Av BKLY M9 .... 87 F2
Velour Cl CSLFD M3 .... 114 A2
Vendale Av SWIN M27 .... 98 C4
Venetia St
  NEWH/MOS M40 * 104 B5
Venice St BOLS/LL BL3 .... 48 B5
  CMANE M1 * 7 G7
Venlow Gdns CHD/CHDH SK8.. 183 E3
Ventnor Av BNG/LEV M19 .. 144 C3
  BOL BL1 .... 33 J1
  BURY BL9 .... 69 G1
  SALE M33 .... 139 H5
Ventnor Cl DTN/ASHW M34.. 147 F5

Ventnor Rd DID/WITH M20 .. 157 H3
  SLFD M6 .... 100 A1
Ventnor St ROCH OL11 .... 43 E1
  SLFD M6 .... 101 G5
Ventor St BKLY M9 .... 103 E2
Venture Scout Wy CHH M8.. 102 A4
Venture Wy POY/DIS SK12.. 195 G4
Venwood Ct PWCH M25 * .. 85 G5
Verbena Av FWTH BL4 .... 65 E4
Verbena Ct PART M31 .... 151 E3
Verdant La ECC M30 .... 110 A5
Verdun Av SLFD M6 .... 100 A3
Verdun Rd ECC M30 .... 110 C1
Verdure Av BOL BL1 * 47 F1
  SALE M33 .... 154 D5
Verdure Cl FAIL M35 .... 105 G2
Vere St SALQ M50 .... 113 E4
Verity Cl DID/WITH M20 .. 142 D5
  ROY/SHW OL2 .... 59 E5
Vermont St BOL BL1 .... 2 A2
Verne Av SWIN M27 .... 98 D2
Verne Dr OLD OL1 .... 60 D4
Verney Rd ROY/SHW OL2 .. 75 F2
Vernham Wk BOLS/LL BL3 .. 48 D5
Vernon Av ECC M30 * 111 G3
  STKP SK1 .... 160 C4
  STRET M32 .... 140 B2
Vernon Cl CHD/CHDH SK8 .. 182 D3
  POY/DIS SK12 .... 195 F5
Vernon Dr MPL/ROM SK6 .. 174 B2
  PWCH M25 .... 85 H5
Vernon Gv SALE M33 .... 155 F3
Vernon Pk HALE/TIMP WA15.. 166 D2
Vernon Rd BRO M7 .... 101 E4
  DROY M43 .... 117 F3
  POY/DIS SK12 .... 195 F5
  TOT/BURYW BL8 .... 26 A2
Vernon St AUL OL6 .... 119 H1
  BKLY M9 .... 103 F3
  BOL BL1 .... 2 C3
  BRAM/HZG SK7 .... 185 E1
  BRO M7 .... 101 G5
  BURY BL9 .... 4 E1
  FWTH BL4 .... 66 B4
  HYDE SK14 .... 148 A1
  MOSL OL5 .... 93 H5
  OLDTF/WHR M16 .... 127 F3
  STKP SK1 .... 96 B4
Vernon Wk BOL BL1 * 2 C3
  WHIT OL12 * 10 C3
  WHIT OL12 * 14 B5
  WHTN BL5 .... 62 A4
Veronica Dr NEWH/MOS M40.. 116 D1
Veronica Rd DID/WITH M20.. 157 H3
Verrill Av NTHM/RTH M23 .. 156 B5
Vesper St FAIL M35 .... 105 F2
Vesta St ANC M4 .... 115 H4
  RAMS BL0 .... 16 C2
Vestris Dr SLFD M6 .... 112 A2
Vetch Cl GOL/RIS/CUL WA3.. 150 A1
Viaduct Rd ALT WA14 .... 165 G2
Viaduct St CSLFD M3 .... 6 C2
  EDGY/DAV SK3 * 12 E4
  WGTN/LGST M12 .... 128 C1
Vicarage Av CHD/CHDH SK8.. 183 E4
Vicarage Cl BURY BL9 .... 27 F3
  DUK SK16 .... 108 C6
  SLFD M6 .... 99 G5
Vicarage Crs AUL OL6 .... 107 G5
Vicarage Dr DUK SK16 .... 108 C6
  MILN OL16 .... 19 H5
Vicarage Gdns
  EDGY/DAV SK3 * 12 E6
  HYDE SK14 .... 148 A1
Vicarage Gv ECC M30 .... 111 G3
Vicarage La ALT WA14 * 177 H5
  MDTN M24 .... 73 C5
  POY/DIS SK12 .... 195 F5
Vicarage Rd AULW OL7 .... 107 F5
  EDGY/DAV SK3 * 171 H3
  IRL M44 .... 136 C1
  SWIN M27 .... 98 C3
  URM M41 .... 124 A5
  WALK M28 .... 81 H3
Vicarage Rd North
  ROCH OL11 .... 42 B5
Vicarage Rd South
  ROCH OL11 .... 42 B5
Vicarage St BOLS/LL BL3 .. 48 C4
  OLDS OL8 .... 90 D5
  RAD M26 .... 50 D4
  ROY/SHW OL2 .... 60 A2
Vicarage Vw ROCH OL11 .. 42 C5
Vicar's Dr MILN OL16 .... 10 C7
Vicar's Ga MILN OL16 .... 11 G7
Vicars Hall Gdns WALK M28.. 96 A5
Vicars Hall La WALK M28 .. 96 A5
Vicars Rd CCHDY M21 * 141 E3
Vickerman St BOL BL1 .... 111 G3
Vicker Cl SWIN M27 .... 84 A5
Vicker Gv DID/WITH M20 .. 157 E3
Vickermann St BOL BL1 .... 33 G4
Vickers Rw FWTH BL4 .... 65 G4
Vickers St BOLS/LL BL3 .. 48 C4
  NEWH/MOS M40 .... 115 H2
Victor Av BURY BL9 .... 68 B1
Victoria Av BKLY M9 .... 87 H2
  BNG/LEV M19 .... 144 A3
  BRAM/HZG SK7 * 185 F1
  CHD/CHDH SK8 .... 182 D3
  DID/WITH M20 .... 157 H2
  ECC M30 .... 111 G2
  HALE/TIMP WA15 .... 166 C3
  MPL/ROM SK6 .... 161 G3
  SWIN M27 .... 99 F2
  WHTF M45 .... 69 H2
Victoria Av East BKLY M9 .. 88 C3
Victoria Bridge St
  CSLFD M3 .... 6 D2
Victoria Cl BRAM/HZG SK7.. 195 G1
  EDGY/DAV SK3 .... 12 C7
  WALK M28 .... 96 B4
Victoria Ct AULW OL7 .... 119 F3
  FWTH BL4 .... 65 H2
  ECC M30 .... 111 G2
Victoria Dr SALE M33 .... 155 E3
Victoria Gdns HYDE SK14 .. 134 A4
  ROY/SHW OL2 * 60 A2

Victoria Gv BOL BL1 .... 33 F5
  HTNM SK4 .... 159 F1
  RUSH/FAL M14 .... 143 E4
Victoria La SWIN M27 .... 98 C2
  WHTF M45 .... 69 G5
Victoria Ldg BRO M7 * 101 F5
Victoria Ms BURY BL9 .... 70 A2
Victoria Pk STKP SK1 * 172 C1
Victoria Pl TRPK M17 .... 125 E3
Victoria Rd ALT WA14 .... 177 G2
  BOL BL1 .... 47 E2
  ECC M30 .... 111 F2
  FWTH BL4 .... 82 D1
  HALE/TIMP WA15 .... 166 B2
  IRL M44 .... 136 B2
  OLDTF/WHR M16 .... 141 H1
  RUSH/FAL M14 .... 142 D3
  SALE M33 .... 155 E3
  SLFD M6 .... 111 H1
  STKP SK1 .... 160 C5
  STRET M32 .... 140 B1
  URM M41 .... 138 B1
  WILM/AE SK9 .... 198 D4
  WYTH/NTH M22 .... 168 C1
Victoria Sq ANC M4 * 7 J2
  ROY/SHW OL2 .... 2 E5
Victoria Station Ap CSLFD M3.. 6 E2
Victoria St ALT WA14 .... 165 G4
  AULW OL7 .... 119 F4
  BOLE BL2 .... 36 B5
  CHAD OL9 .... 8 A1
  CSLFD M3 .... 6 E2
  DTN/ASHW M34 .... 132 B5
  DUK SK16 .... 120 A5
  FAIL M35 .... 104 C4
  FWTH BL4 .... 65 H1
  HEY OL10 .... 41 E4
  HYDE SK14 .... 134 C3
  LIT OL15 .... 21 E3
  MDTN M24 .... 72 D4
  OLDE OL4 .... 92 D1
  OLD OL1 .... 106 C2
  OP/CLY M11 .... 116 D5
  RAD M26 .... 68 B1
  RAMS BL0 .... 16 C2
  ROY/SHW OL2 .... 60 C3
  STLY SK15 .... 120 C3
  STLY SK15 .... 121 C1
  TOT/BURYW BL8 .... 4 A4
  UPML OL3 .... 25 H4
  WHIT OL12 .... 10 C3
  WHIT OL12 * 14 B5
  WHTN BL5 .... 62 A4
Victoria St East AULW OL7 .. 119 F4
  WGTN/LGST M12 .... 129 G4
Victoria Ter CHAD OL9 .... 74 D3
Victoria Wk BRAM/HZG SK7.. 193 G1
Victor Mann St OP/CLY M11.. 131 F1
Victor St CSLFD M3 .... 6 A5
  HEY OL10 .... 56 B1
  NEWH/MOS M40 .... 115 F1
  OLDS OL8 .... 105 G1
Victory Gv DTN/ASHW M34.. 131 H4
Victory Rd BOLS/LL BL3 .. 50 D5
  IRL M44 .... 136 B3
Victory St BOL BL1 * 48 B1
  RUSH/FAL M14 .... 128 D5
Vienna Rd EDGY/DAV SK3.. 171 G3
Vienna Rd East EDGY/DAV SK3.. 171 G3
Viewlands Dr WILM/AE SK9.. 192 A5
View St BOLS/LL BL3 .... 48 C5
Vigo Av BOLS/LL BL3 .... 64 A1
Vigo St HEY OL10 .... 41 F5
  OLDE OL4 .... 92 C2
Viking Cl OP/CLY M11 .... 116 A3
Viking St BOLS/LL BL3 .... 49 F5
  ROCH OL11 .... 29 F3
Village Brow TRPK M17 .... 125 H2
Village Mnr UPML OL3 .... 79 E4
Village St BRO M7 .... 101 F5
The Village URM M41 .... 137 H3
Village Wy WILM/AE SK9 .. 199 D1
Village Wy (Ashburton Rd East)
  TRPK M17 .... 125 H2
Villa Rd OLDS OL8 .... 91 G3
Villdale Av OFTN SK2 .... 173 G2
Villiers Ct WHTF M45 * 85 H1
Villiers Dr OLDS OL8 .... 120 A3
Villiers St AUL OL6 .... 120 A3
  BURY BL9 .... 5 H2
  HYDE SK14 .... 134 D5
Vinca Gv BRO M7 .... 101 G4
Vincent Av CCHDY M21 .. 141 E2
  ECC M30 .... 76 B4
Vincent St BOL BL1 .... 2 A6
  HYDE SK14 .... 148 B2
  LIT OL15 .... 20 D2
  MDTN M24 .... 72 D2
  MILN OL16 .... 43 F1
  OP/CLY M11 .... 116 C5
Vine Av SWIN M27 .... 99 F2
Vine Cl ROY/SHW OL2 .... 60 A2
  SALE M33 .... 153 F1
Vine Ct MILN OL16 .... 30 C5
  STRET M32 .... 140 B2
Vine Fold NEWH/MOS M40.. 104 C2
Vine Gv OFTN SK2 .... 172 D3
Vine Pl ROCH OL11 .... 43 E1
Vinery Gv DTN/ASHW M34.. 132 B5
Vine St BRAM/HZG SK7 .. 185 F1
  BRO M7 .... 101 G4
  ECC M30 .... 110 D4
  OP/CLY M11 .... 130 D1
  PWCH M25 .... 86 B2
  RAMS BL0 .... 16 D4
  ROY/SHW OL2 * 60 A2
Vineyard St OLDE OL4 .... 76 A5
Viola St OP/CLY M11 .... 117 E3
Violet Av FWTH BL4 .... 65 F3
Violet St GTN M18 .... 131 E2
  HYDE SK14 .... 148 A2
  MDTN M24 .... 73 G5
Virgil St OLDTF/WHR M16 .. 127 F2
Virginia Cha CHD/CHDH SK8.. 182 C4

Virginia Cl NTHM/RTH M23......167 E2
Virginia St BOLS/LL BL3......48 A5
  ROCH OL11 *......42 D2
Viscount Dr CHD/CHDH SK8......182 A5
  MANAIR M90 *......179 G5
The Vista IRL M44......150 D2
Vivian St ROCH OL11......42 D1
Vixen Cl CCHDY M21......142 A4
Voltaire Av SLFD M6......112 A2
Vorlich Dr CHAD OL9......74 A4
Vulcan St OLD OL1......76 B4
Vyner Gv SALE M33......139 F5

W

Waddicor Av AUL OL6......107 H4
Waddington Cl
  TOT/BURYW BL8......36 D4
Waddington Fold MILN OL16......43 H4
Waddington Rd BOL BL1......32 D5
Waddington St CHAD OL9......8 B1
Wade Bank WHTN BL5......62 A4
Wadebridge Av
  NTHM/RTH M23......167 E2
Wadebridge Dr
  TOT/BURYW BL8......37 E4
Wadeford Cl ANC M4 *......115 F3
Wade Hill La UPML OL3......78 B4
Wade Rw UPML OL3......79 E4
Wadesmill Wk
  BRUN/LGST M13 *......128 C1
Wadeson Rd BRUN/LGST M13...128 C1
Wade St BOLS/LL BL3......65 E1
  MDTN M24......89 C1
Wade Wk OP/CLY M11......116 B5
Wadham Gdns MPL/ROM SK6...162 B1
Wadham Wy
  HALE/TIMP WA15......178 A3
Wadhurst Wk
  BRUN/LGST M13 *......128 C3
Wadsley St BOL BL1......2 C2
Wadlow Cl CSLFD M3 *......6 B1
Wadsworth Cl WILM/AE SK9...192 B4
Wadsworth Ms DROY M43......117 C4
Waggoners Crs SWIN M27......99 E3
Waggon Rd AULW OL7......107 E2
  BOLE BL2......50 A1
  MOSL OL5......108 D2
Wagner St BOL BL1......33 C3
Wagstaffe Dr FAIL M35......105 E3
Wagstaffe St MDTN M24......72 D3
Wagtail Cl WALK M28......97 E2
Waincliffe Av CCHDY M21......156 C2
Waingap Crs WHIT OL12......14 C5
Waingap Ri WHIT OL12......19 E4
Waingap Vw WHIT OL12......18 C1
Wainman St SLFD M6......101 E5
Wainwright Av
  DTN/ASHW M34......131 E5
Wainwright Cl OFTN SK2......172 B2
  OLDE OL4......77 F5
Wainwright Rd ALT WA14......165 E4
Wainwright St DUK SK16......120 B4
  OLDS OL8......9 F6
Waithlands Rd MILN OL16......30 C5
Wakefield Crs MPL/ROM SK6...161 H5
Wakefield Dr OLD OL1......54 C2
  SWIN M27......83 G3
Wakefield Rd EDGW/EG BL7...23 E4
Wakefield Rd STLY SK15......121 E3
Wakeling Rd DTN/ASHW M34..146 C3
Walcott Cl BRUN/LGST M13...129 E3
Wald Av RUSH/FAL M14......143 G4
Waldeck St BOL BL1......48 B1
Walden Av OLDE OL4......76 C2
Walden Cl RUSH/FAL M14......142 C3
Walden Crs BRAM/HZG SK7...184 D1
Walderton Av
  NEWH/MOS M40......103 H4
Waldon Av CHD/CHDH SK8...170 A4
Waldon Cl BOLS/LL BL3......48 B5
Wales St OLD OL1......76 B3
Walkdene Dr WALK M28......81 G4
Walkden Market Pl
  WALK M28 *......82 A4
Walkden Rd WALK M28......97 E1
Walkden St WHIT OL12......10 C3
Walker Av BOLS/LL BL3......65 E1
  FAIL M35 *......105 G4
  STLY SK15......121 F3
  WHTF M45......85 H1
Walker Cl FWTH BL4......82 D1
  HYDE SK14......148 B1
Walker Fold Rd BOL BL1......32 A2
Walker La HYDE SK14......148 B1
Walker Rd BKLY M9......88 B3
  CHAD OL9......90 A5
  ECC M30......110 B1
  IRL M44 *......136 B2
Walkers Cl UPML OL3......79 E4
Walkers Ct FWTH BL4......66 A4
Walker's Ct CSLFD M3......6 C2
Walker's La OLDE OL4......93 F1
Walker's Rd OLDS OL8......90 D5
Walker St BOL BL1......2 B6
  BURY BL9......5 F3
  DTN/ASHW M34......132 D4
  HEY OL10......40 D5
  MDTN M24......71 H5
  MILN OL16......11 F7
  OLDE OL4......8 C5
  RAD M26......68 D3
  STKP SK1......13 F5
Walkerwood Dr STLY SK15....122 C3
Walkmill UPML OL3......78 C3
Walk Mill Cl WHIT OL12......20 A4
The Walk MILN OL16......10 C6
The Walkway BOLS/LL BL3....47 G4
Wallace Av RUSH/FAL M14...143 F1
Wallace St OLDS OL8......91 G3
Wallasey Av RUSH/FAL M14...142 C2
Wallbank Dr WHIT OL12......18 A1
Wallbank Rd BRAM/HZG SK7..184 B3
Wallbrook Crs LHULT M38......81 F1
Wallbrook Rd BKLY M9......87 H5
The Walled Gdn SWIN M27.....98 C4

Waller Av RUSH/FAL M14......143 E3
Walley St BOL BL1......33 H3
Wallhead Rd MILN OL16......31 E4
Wall Hill Rd UPML OL3......78 C3
Wallingford Rd URM M41......124 D5
  WILM/AE SK9......191 H2
Wallis St CHAD OL9......90 B5
  NEWH/MOS M40 *......104 D5
Wallness La SLFD M6......113 H2
Wallshaw St OLD OL1......9 K3
Wallshaw St OLD OL1 *......9 G6
  SLFD M6......113 E3
Wall Wy GTN M18......130 D4
Wallwork Av CTN M18......103 F4
Wallwork St OP/CLY M11......117 F5
  RAD M26......52 B5
  RDSH SK5 *......145 F1
Wallworth Av GTN M18......130 C3
Walmer St BRAM/HZG SK7...184 B3
Walmersley
  MPL/ROM SK6 *......175 G3
Walmersley Old Rd BURY BL9...27 G1
Walmersley Rd BURY BL9......7 F1
  BURY BL9......27 F2
  NEWH/MOS M40......104 D1
Walmer St GTN M18......130 D2
  RUSH/FAL M14......128 C5
Walmer St East
  RUSH/FAL M14......128 D5
Walmley Gv BOLS/LL BL3......64 B1
Walmsley Av LIT OL15......20 C5
Walmsley Gv URM M41......138 D1
Walmsley Rd RDSH SK5......159 H3
  STLY SK15......120 D5
  TOT/BURYW BL8......37 G2
Walney Rd WYTH/NTH M22...168 C5
Walnut Av BURY BL9......5 K7
  OLDE OL4......76 C4
Walnut Cl HYDE SK14......148 C1
  SWIN M27......83 G3
  WILM/AE SK9......199 H2
Walnut Rd ECC M30......110 B1
  PART M31......150 C3
Walnut St BOL BL1......34 A3
  GTN M18......130 C2
Walnut Tree Rd
  EDGY/DAV SK3......170 D2
Walnut Wk STRET M32......140 A3
Walpole St MILN OL16......11 F7
Walsall St SLFD M6......100 D5
Walsden St OP/CLY M11......116 D3
Walsh Av BKLY M9......87 H5
Walshaw Brook Cl
  TOT/BURYW BL8......37 E2
Walshaw Dr SWIN M27......99 E3
Walshaw La TOT/BURYW BL8...37 E2
Walshaw Rd TOT/BURYW BL8...37 E2
Walshe St BURY BL9......90 C1
Walsingham Av
  DID/WITH M20......157 E2
  MDTN M24......88 D2
Walter Scott St OLD OL1......76 A4
Walters Dr OLDS OL8......91 H4
Walter St BKLY M9......103 E2
  GTN M18......130 D2
  OLD OL1......9 H4
  OLDTF/WHR M16......127 F4
  PWCH M25......85 G3
  RAD M26......52 A3
  WALK M28......82 A5
Waltham Dr CHD/CHDH SK8...145 G1
Waltham Rd OLDTF/WHR M16...142 A2
Waltham St OLDE OL4......92 D5
Walton Cl MDTN M24......71 H3
Walton Ct BOLS/LL BL3......49 E5
Walton Dr BURY BL9......27 F3
  MPL/ROM SK6......174 C2
Walton Hall Dr BNG/LEV M19..144 D2
Walton Houses FAIL M35 *....105 E2
Walton Pl FWTH BL4......66 B5
Walton Rd ALT WA14......165 E1
  BKLY M9......88 A2
  SALE M33......154 A5
Walton St AULW OL7......106 C5
  HEY OL10......56 A1
  MDTN M24 *......72 D2
  STKP SK1 *......13 J4
Walwyn Cl STRET M32......140 A3
Wandsworth Av OP/CLY M11...117 E3
Wansbeck Cl STRET M32......140 C2
Wansfell Wk ANC M4......115 C3
Wansford St RUSH/FAL M14...128 B5
Wanstead Av BKLY M9......88 D4
Wapping St BOL BL1......33 C4
Warbeck Cl RDSH SK5......145 G1
Warbeck Rd NEWH/MOS M40...89 G5
Warbreck Cl BOLE BL2......50 C2
Warbreck Dr URM M41......138 C2
Warbreck Gv SALE M33......155 E3
Warburton Bridge Rd
  GOL/RIS/CUL WA3......150 A5
Warburton Cl
  HALE/TIMP WA15......189 E1
  MPL/ROM SK6......161 H5
Warburton Dr
  HALE/TIMP WA15......189 E1
Warburton La PART M31......151 E3
Warburton Rd WILM/AE SK9...192 C5
Warburton St BOL BL1......34 A4
  DID/WITH M20......157 G3
  ECC M30......111 F4
  ORD M5......127 E2
Warburton Wy
  HALE/TIMP WA15......166 D2
Warcock Rd OLDE OL4......76 B5
Wardend Cl LHULT M38......81 F1
Warde St HULME M15......127 H2
Wardle Brook Av
  HYDE SK14......135 E5
Wardle Cl RAD M26......51 H4
  STRET M32......140 C1
Wardle Edge WHIT OL12......19 G5
Wardle Fold WHIT OL12......19 H4
Wardle Gdns WHIT OL12......19 H5
Wardle Rd SALE M33......154 C3
  WHIT OL12......19 H5

Wardle St BOLE BL2......49 C4
  LIT OL15......20 D2
  NEWH/MOS M40......115 H2
  OLDE OL4......92 A1
Wardley Av CCHDY M21......142 A3
Wardley Hall La WALK M28......81 C5
Wardley Hall Rd WALK M28......98 A1
Wardley St SWIN M27......99 E2
Wardlow St BOLS/LL BL3......48 A5
Ward Rd DID/WITH M20......157 C3
  DROY M43......118 A4
Wardsend Wk HULME M15 *...127 G2
Ward St BKLY M9......87 H5
  CHAD OL9......8 A3
  FAIL M35......104 D2
  HYDE SK14......148 A1
  MPL/ROM SK6......161 G3
  NEWH/MOS M40......103 G2
  OLD OL1......75 E4
  STKP SK1......13 J7
Wareham Gv ECC M30......110 D2
Wareham St CHH M8 *......102 C1
Wareings Yd ROCH OL11......43 F2
Wareing Wy BOLS/LL BL3......2 C6
Warford Av POY/DIS SK12......195 H5
Warford St ANC M4......115 G3
Warham St WILM/AE SK9......199 E3
The Warke WALK M28......97 G4
Warley Cl CHD/CHDH SK8......170 B3
Warley Gv DUK SK16......119 H5
Warley Rd OLDTF/WHR M16...126 D5
Warley St LIT OL15......21 E2
Warlingham Cl
  TOT/BURYW BL8......37 G5
Warlow Crest UPML OL3......94 D3
Warlow Dr UPML OL3......94 D3
Warmington Dr
  WGTN/LGST M12......129 F2
Warmley Rd NTHM/RTH M23...167 E1
Warne Av DROY M43......118 B3
Warnford Cl NEWH/MOS M40...117 E1
War Office Rd ROCH OL11......28 B5
Warren Av CHD/CHDH SK8......170 A4
Warren Bank BKLY M9......87 H4
Warren Bruce Rd TRPK M17...126 A2
Warren Cl BRAM/HZG SK7......183 G2
  DTN/ASHW M34......146 B4
  POY/DIS SK12......194 C3
Warren Dr HALE/TIMP WA15...179 E5
  SWIN M27......98 C5
Warrener St SALE M33......155 E3
Warren Hey WILM/AE SK9......199 H1
Warren La OLDS OL8......92 A3
Warren Lea MPL/ROM SK6......163 G4
  POY/DIS SK12......195 F2
Warren Rd CHD/CHDH SK8......182 D2
  EDGY/DAV SK3......171 G4
  TRPK M17 *......125 G2
  WALK M28......82 B4
Warren St BKLY M9......103 E1
  BRO M7......102 A2
  SLFD M6 *......113 C2
  TOT/BURYW BL8......37 G4
Warre St AUL OL6......119 C2
Warrington Rd BKLY M9......87 H3
Warrington St AUL OL6......119 C3
  OLDE OL4......92 A1
  STLY SK15......121 E4
Warsall Rd WYTH/NTH M22...168 D2
Warslow Dr SALE M33......155 F5
Warsop Av WYTH/NTH M22...168 D4
Warstead Wk
  BRUN/LGST M13 *......128 D3
Warth Fold Rd RAD M26......52 D3
Warth Rd BURY BL9......51 C6
Warton Cl BRAM/HZG SK7......184 B5
  TOT/BURYW BL8......37 E5
Warton Dr NTHM/RTH M23...167 H4
Warwick Av DID/WITH M20...157 E2
  DTN/ASHW M34......146 C2
  SWIN M27......83 G5
  WHTF M45......70 A5
Warwick Cl CHD/CHDH SK8...170 D5
  DUK SK16......133 F2
  HTNM SK4......159 F2
  MDTN M24......88 D2
  ROY/SHW OL2......59 G2
  TOT/BURYW BL8......26 B2
  WHTF M45......69 H5
Warwick Ct MDTN M24 *......72 D4
  OLDTF/WHR M16......127 G5
Warwick Dr BRAM/HZG SK7...185 E4
  HALE/TIMP WA15......177 H5
  SALE M33......155 E2
  URM M41......124 A4
Warwick Gdns BOLS/LL BL3...64 D1
Warwick Gv DTN/ASHW M34...118 B5
Warwick Rd AUL OL6......107 F5
  CHAD OL9......74 A4
  FAIL M35......105 E5
  HALE/TIMP WA15......177 H5
  HTNM SK4......159 F3
  IRL M44......150 C1
  MPL/ROM SK6......161 H4
  OLDTF/WHR M16......126 D4
  RAD M26......52 A3
  STRET M32......138 B3
  WALK M28......96 D1
Warwick Rd South
  OLDTF/WHR M16......126 D5
Warwick St ANC M4......7 H3
  BOL BL1......33 H2
  CHAD OL9......8 A7
  HULME M15......127 H1
  PWCH M25......85 H1
  SWIN M27......99 E1
  LIT OL11......11 G1

Washbrook Av WALK M28......96 C1
Washbrook Dr STRET M32......139 F1
Wash Ford TOT/BURYW BL8...37 G2
Washford Dr NTHM/RTH M23..167 F1
Washington Cl
  CHD/CHDH SK8......182 C4
Washington Ct BURY BL9......5 F2
Washington St BOLS/LL BL3...48 E3
  CHAD OL9......8 B3
Wash La BURY BL9......5 H3
Wash Ter TOT/BURYW BL8......37 C1
Washway Rd SALE M33......153 H5
Washwood Cl LHULT M38......81 G1
Wasnidge Wk HULME M15 *...128 A3
Wasp Av ROCH OL11......43 F3
Wasp Mill Dr WHIT OL12......19 H2
Wastdale Av BURY BL9......69 H1
Wastdale Rd NTHM/RTH M23..167 G5
Waste St OLD OL1 *......9 K2
Wastwater St OLD OL1......75 H3
Watchgate BRAM/HZG SK7...184 D4
Watchgate Cl MDTN M24......72 A1
Waterbridge WALK M28......97 H5
Watercroft ROCH OL11......28 A2
Waterdale Cl WALK M28......96 C5
Waterdale Dr WHTF M45......69 H5
Waterfield Cl BURY BL9......27 G4
Waterfield Wy FAIL M35......105 F4
Waterfold La BURY BL9......5 K7
Waterfoot Cottages
  HYDE SK14......135 H4
Waterford Av DID/WITH M20...156 B4
  MPL/ROM SK6......162 D4
Waterfront Quay SALO M50...126 C1
Watergate DTN/ASHW M34...118 B5
Watergate Dr WHTN BL5......79 E4
Watergate La WHTN BL5......64 B5
Water Grove Rd DUK SK16...134 A1
Waterhead OLDE OL4......76 D4
Waterhouse Av WHIT OL12...10 D3
Waterhouse Rd GTN M18......130 D4
Waterhouse St WHIT OL12...10 C5
Waterhouse Wy RDSH SK5...145 H4
Water La DROY M43......117 H4
  FWTH BL4......66 B5
  MILN OL16......44 D1
  RAD M26......68 A1
  WILM/AE SK9......198 D3
Water Lane St RAD M26......68 A1
Waterloo Ct BURY BL9......53 F1
Waterloo Gdns AUL OL6......107 H5
Waterloo Pl STKP SK1 *......13 H4
Waterloo Rd AUL OL6......107 H5
  BKLY M9......103 E1
  BRAM/HZG SK7......184 A3
  CHH M8......101 H4
  MPL/ROM SK6......162 D4
  POY/DIS SK12......195 H5
  STKP SK1......13 H4
  STLY SK15......120 D3
Waterloo St AUL OL6......120 A1
  BOL BL1 *......3 F4
  CHH M8......102 D2
  CMANE M1......7 F6
  OLD OL1......9 H4
  TOT/BURYW BL8......4 A4
Watermans Cl BKLY M9......103 G2
Waterman Vw MILN OL16......11 J4
Watermead SALE M33......154 B5
Watermead Cl EDGY/DAV SK3...171 H5
Watermeetings La
  MPL/ROM SK6......162 D4
Watermill Cl MILN OL16......31 E5
Water Mill Clough
  ROY/SHW OL2......74 D2
Watermill Ct AULW OL7......106 D5
Watermillock Gdns BOL BL1...34 A3
Waterpark Rd BRO M7......101 H2
Waters Edge AUL OL6......107 H5
  FWTH BL4......65 F2
  MPL/ROM SK6......175 F1
  WALK M28......82 C5
Watersedge Cl
  CHD/CHDH SK8......183 E1
Waters Edge Fold OLD OL1...58 A3
Watersfield Cl CHD/CHDH SK8...182 C4
Watersheddings St OLDE OL4...76 C3
Waterside HYDE SK14......149 F1
  MPL/ROM SK6......175 F5
  SALE M33......154 D1
  TRPK M17......126 C2
Waterside Av WHTF M45......69 H5
Waterside Cl CCHDY M21......156 C2
  HYDE SK14......149 F1
  OLD OL1......60 B5
  RAD M26......53 E5
Waterside Ct URM M41 *......137 F1
Waterside La MILN OL16......30 B5
Waterside Rd BURY BL9......26 D1
Waterside Vw DROY M43......117 F5
Waterslea ECC M30......110 D3
Watersmead Cl BOL BL1......34 A4
Watersmead St BOL BL1......34 A4
Watersmeet STRET M32......125 H4
Waters Meeting Rd BOL BL1...34 A3
Waters Nook Rd WHTN BL5...62 D4
Waterson Av NEWH/MOS M40...103 H4
Waters Reach MOSL OL5......94 B3
  POY/DIS SK12......195 G3
  TRPK M17......126 C2
Water Street RAD M26......68 B1
Water St AUL OL6......120 A1
  BKLY M9......103 C2
  BOL BL1......3 F4
  CSLFD M3......6 D6
  DTN/ASHW M34......132 C1
  EDGY/DAV SK3......12 C6
  HYDE SK14......133 G5
  MDTN M24......72 C4
  MILN OL16......11 F5
  ROY/SHW OL2......59 H5
  STLY SK15......121 G2
  WHIT OL12......14 A5

Waterton La MOSL OL5......93 G5
Waterview Cl MILN OL16......45 E3
Waterworks Rd OLDE OL4......76 D5
Watford Av RUSH/FAL M14...142 D1
Watkin Cl BRUN/LGST M13...128 C3
Watkins Dr PWCH M25......86 D4
Watkin St CSLFD M3 *......114 A2
  HYDE SK14......134 B3
Watling St LIT OL15......20 C5
  TOT/BURYW BL8......24 C1
  TOT/BURYW BL8......52 A1
Watlington Cl OLD OL1......76 C1
Watson Gdns WHIT OL12......18 B1
Watson Rd FWTH BL4......65 E4
Watson Sq STKP SK1......13 H4
Watson St DTN/ASHW M34...6 D7
  ECC M30......110 C5
  OLDE OL4......76 B4
  RAD M26......52 B5
  STRET M32......99 E1
Watton Cl SWIN M27 *......84 A5
Watts St BNG/LEV M19......144 B3
  CHAD OL9......91 E5
  WHIT OL12......10 D4
Waugh Av FAIL M35......105 E4
Wavell Dr BURY BL9......26 B4
Wavell Rd WYTH/NTH M22...180 C2
Waveney Dr ALT WA14......165 F3
  WILM/AE SK9......192 A5
Waveney Rd ROY/SHW OL2...59 H1
  WYTH/NTH M22......168 D5
Waverley Av STRET M32......126 B5
Waverley Crs DROY M43......117 H2
Waverley Dr CHD/CHDH SK8...193 E1
Waverley Gv BKLY M9......103 G3
  BOL BL1 *......33 H5
  EDGY/DAV SK3......12 B7
  HYDE SK14......147 H5
  MDTN M24......72 D1
  SALE M33......154 A3
  SWIN M27 *......99 H5
  WALK M28......96 C1
Waverley Rd West BKLY M9...103 G3
Waverley St OLD OL1......76 A4
  ROCH OL11......42 B5
Waverton Av HTNM SK4......144 D4
Waverton Rd RUSH/FAL M14...142 C2
Wayfarers Wy SWIN M27......98 D5
Wayfaring WHTN BL5......62 A2
Wayland Rd GTN M18......130 C5
Wayland Rd South GTN M18...130 C5
Wayne Cl DROY M43......118 B1
Wayne St OP/CLY M11......117 F5
Wayside Dr POY/DIS SK12...194 D3
Wayside Gdns BRAM/HZG SK7...182 B5
Wayside Gv WALK M28......82 B5
Weald Cl BRUN/LGST M13...128 D2
Wealdstone Gv BOLE BL2......34 C4
Weardale Rd BKLY M9......87 G2
Weaste Av LHULT M38......81 G3
Weaste Dr SLFD M6......112 C2
Weaste La ORD M5......112 C2
Weaste Rd ORD M5......112 C4
Weatherall St North BRO M7...102 A3
Weatherley Cl OLDS OL8......91 G5
Weatherley Dr MPL/ROM SK6...174 C3
Weaver Av WALK M28......81 F5
Weaver Cl ALT WA14......177 F3
Weaver Ct HULME M15 *......127 G2
Weaver Dr BURY BL9......27 G3
Weaverham
  BRUN/LGST M13......129 G5
Weavers Ct BOLS/LL BL3......48 D4
  MDTN M24......72 C3
Weavers Gn FWTH BL4......66 A5
Weavers La BRAM/HZG SK7...185 C1
Weavers Rd MDTN M24......72 C3
Webb Gv HYDE SK14......149 G2
Webb La STKP SK1......13 K4
Webb St TOT/BURYW BL8......37 G4
Webdale Dr NEWH/MOS M40...103 H5
Weber Dr BOLS/LL BL3......48 C4
Webster Gv PWCH M25......85 C5
Webster St BOLS/LL BL3......49 G4
  MOSL OL5......93 H5
  ... OL6......9 G6
Wedgewood St
  NEWH/MOS M40......116 A1
Wedgwood Rd SWIN M27......84 D5
Wedhurst St OLDE OL4......76 B5
Weedall Av ORD M5......113 C5
Weedon St MILN OL16......11 G5
Weeton Av BOLE BL2......50 C2
Weighbridge Ct IRL M44......122 C5
Weir Rd MILN OL16......31 F4
Weir St FAIL M35......104 D3
Welbeck Av CHAD OL9......89 G4
  LIT OL15......20 C2
  URM M41......124 D5
Welbeck Cl MILN OL16......31 F5
  WHTF M45......69 G2
Welbeck Gv BRO M7......101 H2
Welbeck Rd BOL BL1......34 A1
  ECC M30......111 F1
  HYDE SK14......148 B1
  MILN OL16......43 G2
  RDSH SK5......145 F3
  WALK M28......98 A4
Welburn Av WYTH/NTH M22...180 D1
Welburn St ROCH OL11......43 E1
Welbury Rd NTHM/RTH M23...155 G5
Welby St BRUN/LGST M13...129 E4
Welch Rd HYDE SK14......134 A4
Welcomb Cl MPL/ROM SK6...161 G2
Welcomb St OP/CLY M11......116 D4
Welcombe Pde OLDS OL8......92 C4
Welcroft St STKP SK1......13 H5
Weldon Av BOLS/LL BL3......64 A2
Weldon Crs EDGY/DAV SK3...171 H5
Weldon Dr BKLY M9......88 A2
Weldon Rd ALT WA14......165 F3
Weld Rd DID/WITH M20......143 F4
Welford Cl WILM/AE SK9......199 H2

Welford Gn RDSH SK5 ....160 A1
Welford Rd CHH M8 ....87 E3
Welford St SLFD M6 ....113 G1
Welkin Rd MPL/ROM SK6 ....160 D3
Wellacre Av URM M41 ....137 F1
Welland Av HEY OL10 ....40 A3
Welland Cl HULME M15 * 127 C2
Welland Ct HULME M15 ....127 G2
Welland Rd ROY/SHW OL2 ....59 H1
   WILM/AE SK9 ....192 A5
Welland St OP/CLY M11 ....117 E5
   STLY SK15 ....121 F5
Wellbank PWCH M25 * 85 G4
Wellbank Av AUL OL6 ....107 H4
Wellbank Cl BOLS/LL BL3 ....67 E1
Wellbank Vw WHIT OL12 ....28 C2
Wellbrow Ter WHIT OL12 ....29 G2
Wellens Wy NEWH/MOS M40 ....71 H5
Weller Av CCHDY M21 ....141 H4
   POY/DIS SK12 ....195 E5
Weller Cl POY/DIS SK12 ....195 E5
Wellesbourne Dr
   NTHM/RTH M23 ....167 G2
Wellesley Av GTN M18 ....130 C2
Wellfield Cl BURY BL9 ....53 F3
Wellfield La HALE/TIMP WA15 ....166 D5
Wellfield Pl ROCH OL11 ....43 F1
Wellfield Rd BOLS/LL BL3 ....48 B4
   CHH M8 ....102 B2
   NTHM/RTH M23 ....167 H2
   OFTN SK2 ....172 D3
Wellfield St ROCH OL11 ....43 F1
Wellgate Rd BNG/LEV M19 ....144 B3
Wellgreen Cl
   HALE/TIMP WA15 ....178 D1
Well Green Ldg
   HALE/TIMP WA15 * 178 D1
Well Gv WHTF M45 ....69 F1
Wellhead Cl HULME M15 ....128 A3
Wellhouse Dr NEWH/MOS M40 ....88 A5
Well-i-hole Rd UPML OL3 ....94 C5
Welling St BOLE BL2 ....3 J1
Wellington Av
   OLDTF/WHR M16 ....141 H1
Wellington Cl IDSALE M33 ....154 A3
Wellington Clough AULW OL7 ....106 C4
Wellington Ct OLDS OL8 * 91 E3
Wellington Crs
   OLDTF/WHR M16 ....127 F5
Wellington Dr HULME M15 ....127 G2
   OFTN SK2 ....172 A2
   MILN OL16 ....11 F5
Wellington Rd ALT WA14 ....177 C1
   BRAM/HZG SK7 ....186 A4
   BURY BL9 ....4 E7
   BURY BL9 ....53 F1
   CHH M8 ....102 C2
   ECC M30 ....111 F3
   HALE/TIMP WA15 ....166 A3
   OLDS OL8 ....90 D3
   OLDTF/WHR M16 ....142 A1
   RUSH/FAL M14 ....143 E4
   SWIN M27 ....99 E2
   UPML OL3 ....94 D1
Wellington Rd North
   BNG/LEV M19 ....144 B4
Wellington Rd South
   OFTN SK2 ....13 G7
Wellington Sq TOT/BURYW BL8 ....37 G5
Wellington St AUL OL6 ....119 G3
   BOLS/LL BL3 ....2 B6
   BRAM/HZG SK7 ....185 G1
   CHAD OL9 ....74 C4
   CSLFD M3 ....6 A2
   DTN/ASHW M34 ....132 C2
   FAIL M35 * 66 A4
   GTN M18 ....130 C3
   HYDE SK14 ....133 F5
   LIT OL15 ....21 E3
   MILN OL16 ....31 H5
   OLD OL1 ....9 H4
   RAD M26 ....52 D5
   STKP SK1 ....13 G4
   STRET M32 ....140 A2
   TOT/BURYW BL8 ....4 A6
   WHIT OL12 ....10 C5
Wellington St East BRO M7 ....101 G4
Wellington St West BRO M7 ....101 G4
Wellington Ter ORD M5 * 112 C3
Wellington Vls
   TOT/BURYW BL8 ....37 H5
Wellington Wk BOLS/LL BL3 ....2 C6
Well I' Th' La ROCH OL11 ....43 F1
Well La WHTF M45 ....69 G2
Well Mdw MPL/ROM SK6 ....161 F3
Wellmead Cl CHH M8 ....102 A5
Well Meadow HYDE SK14 ....133 G4
Well Mdw Av UPML OL3 ....79 F4
Wells Av CHAD OL9 ....74 B3
   PWCH M25 ....86 B5
Wells Cl CHD/CHDH SK8 ....181 H5
   DROY M43 ....117 G5
   MDTN M24 ....71 H5
Wells Dr DUK SK16 ....133 F2
Wells Dr BURY BL9 * 133 F2
   HTNM SK4 ....158 B4
Wells Rd OLD OL1 ....60 D4
Wells St BURY BL9 ....4 C7
Wellstock La LHULT M38 ....81 E1
Well St BOL BL1 ....3 F4
   BOLE BL2 ....36 B5
   HEY OL10 ....41 F5
   ROCH OL11 ....43 F1
Well St West RAMS BL0 ....16 C1
Wellwood Dr NEWH/MOS M40 ....103 H3
Wellyhole St OLDE OL4 ....9 G7
Welman Wy HALE/TIMP WA15 ....166 A5
Welney Rd OLDTF/WHR M16 ....127 E5
Welshpool Cl NTHM/RTH M23 ....155 H5
Weltdown Gdns ROY/SHW OL2 ....59 G1
Welton Av DID/WITH M20 ....157 H4
Welton Cl WILM/AE SK9 ....200 C1
Welton Dr WILM/AE SK9 ....200 B1
Welton Gv WILM/AE SK9 ....200 B1

Welwyn Cl URM M41 ....124 B3
Welwyn Dr SLFD M6 ....99 F5
Welwyn Wk NEWH/MOS M40 ....115 C3
Wembley Cl EDGY/DAV SK3 ....171 G4
Wembley Gv RUSH/FAL M14 ....143 E3
Wembury Rd GTN M18 ....130 B5
Wembury St BKLY M9 * 103 F5
Wembury St North BKLY M9 ....103 F2
Wemsley Gv BOLE BL2 ....34 C5
Wem St CHAD OL9 ....90 B3
Wemyss Av RDSH SK5 ....145 F2
Wendlebury Gn ROY/SHW OL2 ....59 H4
Wendon Rd NTHM/RTH M23 ....168 A4
Wendover Dr BOLS/LL BL3 ....47 F4
Wendover Rd NTHM/RTH M23 ....166 D2
   URM M41 ....138 C2
Wenfield Dr BKLY M9 ....88 D4
Wenlock Av AUL OL6 ....107 E5
Wenlock Cl OFTN SK2 ....173 H5
Wenlock Rd SALE M33 ....154 B4
Wenlock St SWIN M27 ....98 C2
Wenlock Wy WGTN/LGST M12 ....129 H2
Wenning Cl WHTF M45 ....70 A3
Wensleydale Av
   CHD/CHDH SK8 ....169 H5
Wensleydale Cl BURY BL9 ....69 H1
   NTHM/RTH M23 ....179 C1
   ROY/SHW OL2 ....58 D4
Wensley Dr BRAM/HZG SK7 ....185 E5
   DID/WITH M20 ....157 C1
Wensley Rd BRO M7 ....100 D1
   RDSH SK5 ....169 H3
Wensley Wy MILN OL16 ....30 C5
Wentbridge Rd BOL BL1 ....2 B3
Wentworth Av FWTH BL4 ....65 H5
   GTN M18 ....130 D3
   HEY OL10 ....56 A1
   IRL M44 * 122 B5
   SLFD M6 ....112 B2
   TOT/BURYW BL8 ....69 C5
   WHTF M45 ....69 E5
Wentworth Cl MDTN M24 ....72 B4
   MPL/ROM SK6 ....175 E1
   RAD M26 ....51 G5
Wentworth Dr
   BRAM/HZG SK7 ....184 B5
   SALE M33 ....154 A1
Wentworth Rd ECC M30 ....111 C1
   RDSH SK5 ....145 F2
   SWIN M27 ....98 C4
Wenworth Av URM M41 ....138 B2
Werneth Av HYDE SK14 ....148 B3
   RUSH/FAL M14 ....142 D1
Werneth Cl DTN/ASHW M34 ....146 D1
Werneth Hall Rd OLDS OL8 ....8 C7
Werneth Hollow
   MPL/ROM SK6 ....147 F5
Werneth Low Rd HYDE SK14 ....148 D4
   MPL/ROM SK6 ....162 C2
Werneth Ri HYDE SK14 ....148 B4
Werneth Rd HYDE SK14 ....148 B1
   MPL/ROM SK6 ....162 B1
Werneth St DTN/ASHW M34 ....132 C3
   STKP SK1 ....160 C3
Wesley Cl WHIT OL12 ....30 C1
Wesley Ct WALK M28 * 82 A3
Wesley Gn ORD M5 ....112 D4
Wesley Gn SALE M33 * 154 C3
Wesley Sq URM M41 ....138 A1
Wesley St BOLE BL2 ....3 J5
   BRAM/HZG SK7 ....185 F1
   ECC M30 ....110 D3
   EDGW/EG BL7 ....23 H2
   FAIL M35 ....105 F1
   FWTH BL4 ....66 B5
   HEY OL10 ....40 D4
   MILN OL16 ....31 F5
   OP/CLY M11 ....116 D5
   ROY/SHW OL2 ....75 F1
   STKP SK1 ....13 H4
   STRET M32 ....126 B5
   SWIN M27 ....99 E2
   TOT/BURYW BL8 ....25 H4
   WHIT OL12 * 19 G5
Wessenden Bank East
   OFTN SK2 ....173 E4
Wessenden Bank West
   OFTN SK2 ....173 E4
Wessex Park Cl ROY/SHW OL2 ....60 A1
Westage Gdns
   NTHM/RTH M23 ....167 H2
West Ashton St SALQ M50 ....113 G5
West Av ALT WA14 ....164 D4
   BNC/LEV M19 ....143 H4
   CHD/CHDH SK8 ....181 H5
   FWTH BL4 ....65 G4
   GTN M18 * 130 D3
   NEWH/MOS M40 ....104 C1
   STLY SK15 ....120 D3
   WALK M28 ....81 H4
   WHTF M45 ....69 F2
West Bank BOL BL1 ....32 D5
West Bank Rd DID/WITH M20 ....158 B1
   HOR/BR BL6 * 46 A5
West Bank St ORD M5 ....113 H5
Westbourne Av BOLS/LL BL3 ....65 F1
   SWIN M27 ....83 G2
   WHTF M45 ....69 H4
Westbourne Dr WILM/AE SK9 ....199 G2
Westbourne Gv BKLY M9 ....103 E2
   DID/WITH M20 ....142 C5
   RDSH SK5 ....145 F3
   SALE M33 ....154 B2
Westbourne Pk URM M41 ....124 C5
Westbourne Range
   GTN M18 ....131 G5
Westbourne Rd
   DTN/ASHW M34 ....146 C1
   ECC M30 ....110 C1
   RUSH/FAL M14 ....143 F3
   URM M41 ....138 D1

Westbrook Cl BOLE BL2 ....3 G7
   ROCH OL11 ....57 C1
Westbrook Ct BOLE BL2 * 3 G7
Westbrook Rd SWIN M27 ....98 D5
   TRPK M17 ....125 H1
Westbrook Sq
   WGTN/LGST M12 ....129 H2
Westbrook St BOLE BL2 ....3 H7
Westbury Av SALE M33 ....153 F5
Westbury Cl TOT/BURYW BL8 ....37 F5
   WHTN BL5 ....62 B3
Westbury Dr MPL/ROM SK6 ....174 D4
Westbury Rd CHH M8 ....102 B1
   ROY/SHW OL2 ....58 A3
Westbury St AUL OL6 ....119 H2
   HYDE SK14 ....133 F3
   ROY/SHW OL2 ....75 E2
Westby Cl BRAM/HZG SK7 ....184 B5
Westby Gv BOLE BL2 ....3 K3
West Canteen Rd TRPK M17 ....125 H4
West Central Dr SWIN M27 ....99 G5
West Charles St ORD M5 ....113 G4
West Church St HEY OL10 ....40 D4
Westcliffe Rd BOL BL1 ....23 E5
Westcombe Dr
   TOT/BURYW BL8 ....37 H2
Westcott Av DID/WITH M20 ....142 C5
Westcott Cl BOLE BL2 ....35 F1
Westcott Gv ROY/SHW OL2 ....59 H4
Westcourt Rd BOLS/LL BL3 ....64 C1
   SALE M33 ....154 B1
Westcraig Av NEWH/MOS M40 ....89 F4
West Craven St ORD M5 ....127 E1
West Crs MDTN M24 ....72 C5
Westcroft Rd DID/WITH M20 ....158 A2
West Crown Av ORD M5 ....113 G5
Westdale Gdns BNG/LEV M19 ....158 C1
Westdean Crs BNG/LEV M19 ....158 C1
West Dean St CWE M5 ....113 H4
West Downs Rd
   CHD/CHDH SK8 ....182 C1
West Dr BURY BL9 ....38 B1
   CHD/CHDH SK8 ....168 B5
   DROY M43 ....117 G4
   SLFD M6 ....100 C4
   SWIN M27 ....99 G3
West Duke St ORD M5 ....114 A4
West Egerton St ORD M5 ....113 C4
West End Av CHD/CHDH SK8 ....169 F5
West End St CHAD OL9 ....8 A5
Westend St FWTH BL4 ....65 G4
Westerdale OLDE OL4 ....92 B1
Westerdale Dr BOLS/LL BL3 ....47 H4
   ROY/SHW OL2 ....59 H3
Westerham Av ORD M5 ....113 F4
Westerham Cl TOT/BURYW BL8 ....26 C4
Wester Hill Rd OLDS OL8 ....106 A1
Westerling Wy
   OLDTF/WHR M16 ....127 H5
Western Access TRPK M17 * 111 C5
Western Av SWIN M27 ....85 E5
Western Cir BNG/LEV M19 ....143 H5
Western Rd URM M41 ....137 G2
Western St GTN M18 ....131 D2
   SLFD M6 ....112 D2
Westerton Ct BOLS/LL BL3 ....48 C4
Westfield SLFD M6 ....112 D1
   CHAD OL9 ....74 D4
Westfield Av MDTN M24 ....158 D2
Westfield Cl ROCH OL11 ....57 H3
Westfield Dr MPL/ROM SK6 ....162 B1
Westfield Gv DTN/ASHW M34 ....132 D3
Westfield Rd BOLS/LL BL3 ....64 A2
   CCHDY M21 ....141 F2
   CHD/CHDH SK8 ....182 C4
   DROY M43 ....117 F3
Westfields HALE/TIMP WA15 ....178 A4
Westfield St BRO M7 ....101 G1
   CHAD OL9 ....74 D4
Westgate HALE/TIMP WA15 ....177 H2
   SALE M33 ....154 B2
   URM M41 ....138 B2
   WHIT OL12 ....18 A1
   WILM/AE SK9 ....198 D5
Westgate Av BKLY M9 * 87 H5
   BOL BL1 ....48 B2
   BURY BL9 * 26 A1
   RAMS BL0 ....26 A1
Westgate Cl WHIT OL12 ....18 A1
Westgate Dr SWIN M27 ....99 E4
Westgate Rd SLFD M6 ....112 A1
   WILM/AE SK9 ....198 D5
Westgate St AULW OL7 ....117 G2
West Gn BRUN/LGST M13 ....129 E3
   MOSL OL5 ....108 D2
   SALE M33 ....154 C3
Westgrove Av BOL BL1 ....23 H2
West High St ORD M5 ....113 H5
West HI ROCH OL11 * 29 H5
Westholm Av HTNM SK4 ....144 B4
Westholme Rd DID/WITH M20 ....157 F2
   PWCH M25 ....70 D5
West Hope St ORD M5 ....113 G4
Westhulme Av OLD OL1 ....75 E3
Westhulme St OLD OL1 ....75 E3
Westhulme Wy OLD OL1 ....75 E3
Westinghouse Rd TRPK M17 ....125 H5
West King St CSLFD M3 ....6 B2
Westland Av BOL BL1 ....32 D5
   FWTH BL4 ....81 H1
   STKP SK1 ....160 C5
Westland Dr BKLY M9 ....88 A3
Westlands WHTF M45 ....85 G1
The Westlands SWIN M27 ....99 G4
West Lea DTN/ASHW M34 ....132 D5
Westlea Dr GTN M18 ....130 C5
Westleigh Dr PWCH M25 ....86 D4
Westleigh St BKLY M9 ....103 F1
West Malling Cl HEY OL10 ....56 C2
Westmarsh Cl BOL BL1 ....2 D1
West Marwood St BRO M7 ....101 H4
Westmead Dr
   HALE/TIMP WA15 ....166 C2
West Meade BOLS/LL BL3 ....64 D2
   CCHDY M21 ....141 E4
   PWCH M25 ....86 C5
   SWIN M27 ....99 G5
Westmeade Rd WALK M28 ....81 H2
West Meadow RDSH SK5 ....145 G2
Westmere Dr BKLY M9 ....102 D4
Westminster Cl ROY/SHW OL2 ....60 A1

Westminster Av AUL OL6 ....107 G3
   FWTH BL4 ....65 H4
   OLDTF/WHR M16 ....141 G1
   RAD M26 ....51 G5
   RDSH SK5 ....145 G4
   WHTF M45 ....69 G4
Westminster Cl
   MPL/ROM SK6 ....174 C2
   SALE M33 ....153 G3
Westminster Dr
   CHD/CHDH SK8 ....193 E1
   WILM/AE SK9 ....200 C1
Westminster Rd BOL BL1 ....33 H1
   ECC M30 ....111 F2
   FAIL M35 ....105 G2
   HALE/TIMP WA15 ....178 B1
   URM M41 ....124 C4
   WALK M28 ....82 A5
Westminster St
   BNG/LEV M19 * 144 B2
   BURY BL9 ....4 E5
   FWTH BL4 ....65 H4
   OLD OL1 ....76 A4
   ROCH OL11 ....42 C1
Westminster Wy DUK SK16 ....133 G2
Westmoreland Cl ALT WA14 ....177 E4
   BURY BL9 ....53 F3
Westmorland Av AULW OL7 ....119 G1
   DUK SK16 ....133 G2
Westmorland Dr RDSH SK5 ....146 A5
Westmorland Rd
   DID/WITH M20 ....157 F4
   PART M31 ....150 D4
   SALE M33 ....154 D4
   URM M41 ....138 C2
West Mosley St CMANW M2 * 7 F5
Westmount Cl
   NEWH/MOS M40 ....102 D4
West Oak PI CHD/CHDH SK8 * 182 C3
Weston Av NEWH/MOS M40 ....104 D1
   SWIN M27 ....99 H4
   URM M41 ....138 B2
Weston Dr CHD/CHDH SK8 ....171 G5
   DTN/ASHW M34 ....132 D5
Weston Gv HTNM SK4 ....144 C5
   WYTH/NTH M22 ....168 D4
Weston Rd IRL M44 ....136 C1
   WILM/AE SK9 ....199 G4
Weston St BOLS/LL BL3 ....49 E5
   MILN OL16 ....11 G5
   NEWH/MOS M40 * 103 H1
   OLDE OL4 ....92 B3
   RDSH SK5 ....159 H2
Westover Rd URM M41 ....124 B5
Westover St SWIN M27 ....98 D1
Westover MPL/ROM SK6 ....173 H1
West Pk ALT WA14 ....148 A4
West Park Av
   DTN/ASHW M34 ....147 F1
   POY/DIS SK12 ....194 B3
West Park Rd BRAM/HZG SK7 ....185 G2
West Park St ORD M5 ....127 E1
West Pl BNC/LEV M19 ....143 H4
Westray Crs ORD M5 ....113 G4
Westray Rd BRUN/LGST M13 ....143 G1
Westridge Cha
   ROY/SHW OL2 ....59 E4
West Rd ALT WA14 ....177 F2
   PWCH M25 ....86 D4
   STRET M32 ....125 F4
West Rw PWCH M25 ....100 C1
West Starkey St HEY OL10 ....40 D3
West St AUL OL6 ....119 G2
   BOL BL1 ....48 B2
   CHAD OL9 ....119 G4
   EDGY/DAV SK3 ....12 C5
   FAIL M35 ....104 D5
   FWTH BL4 ....66 A6
   HEY OL10 ....41 E4
   HYDE SK14 * 133 G3
   LIT OL15 ....20 C4
   MILN OL16 ....31 E4
   OLD OL1 ....9 H3
   OLDE OL4 ....77 G5
   RAMS BL0 ....16 C1
West Towers Ms
   STLF M6 ....113 H1
West Towers St SLFD M6 ....175 F5
West V RAD M26 ....52 B4
West Vale Rd
   HALE/TIMP WA15 ....166 A4
   WILM/AE SK9 * 198 D5
West View Gv WHTF M45 ....69 F3
West View Rd
   WYTH/NTH M22 ....168 D1
Westville Gdns BNG/LEV M19 ....158 B1
West Wk EDGW/EG BL7 ....23 G4
Westward Ho MILN OL16 ....31 G5
Westward Rd WILM/AE SK9 ....199 G1
West Wy BOL BL1 ....34 C5
   LHULT M38 ....81 F2
Westway DROY M43 ....117 H1
   OLDE OL4 ....60 A3
   ROY/SHW OL2 ....60 A3
Westwell Gdns BOL BL1 ....33 H4
Westwick Ter BOL BL1 * 33 G4
Westwood Av ALT WA14 ....165 F2
   BRO M7 ....100 A5
   IRL M44 ....136 A2
   NEWH/MOS M40 * 89 F4
   URM M41 ....139 F2
   WALK M28 ....80 D5
Westwood Cr FWTH BL4 ....66 A4
Westwood Crs ECC M30 ....109 H2
Westwood Dr CHAD OL9 ....154 C4
   OFTN SK2 ....173 E4
   SALE M33 ....153 H3
   SWIN M27 ....99 H4

Westwood Rd BOL BL1 ....48 B1
   CHD/CHDH SK8 ....181 G4
   OFTN SK2 ....172 C5
   STRET M32 ....139 H1
Westwood St RUSH/FAL M14 ....128 A4
Westwood Wy OLD OL1 ....75 E3
West Works Rd TRPK M17 ....125 H4
Westworth Cl BOL BL1 ....2 B2
Wetheral Dr BOLS/LL BL3 ....64 D1
Wetherall St BNG/LEV M19 * 144 B2
   ROY/SHW OL2 ....58 D4
Wetherby St OP/CLY M11 ....130 D1
Weybourne Av BKLY M9 ....88 B5
Weybourne Dr MPL/ROM SK6 ....161 G2
Weybourne Gv BOLE BL2 ....34 C4
Weybridge Rd ANC M4 ....115 F3
Weybrook Rd BNG/LEV M19 ....144 C4
Weycroft Cl BOLE BL2 ....50 D3
Weygates Dr
   HALE/TIMP WA15 ....188 D1
Weyhill Rd NTHM/RTH M23 ....167 H5
Weylands Gv SLFD M6 ....99 C5
Weymouth Rd AUL OL6 ....107 H4
   ECC M30 ....110 C2
Weymouth St BOL BL1 ....33 H4
   AUL OL6 ....34 A2
   BURY BL9 ....40 A1
Whalley Av BNG/LEV M19 ....144 B1
   BOL BL1 ....32 C3
   CCHDY M21 ....141 H3
   LIT OL15 ....20 D2
   OLDTF/WHR M16 ....127 C5
   SALE M33 ....154 B3
   URM M41 ....124 D5
Whalley Cl HALE/TIMP WA15 ....178 B2
   MILN OL16 ....31 F5
   WHTF M45 ....69 C3
Whalley Dr TOT/BURYW BL8 ....37 E4
Whalley Gdns WHIT OL12 ....29 E2
Whalley Gv AUL OL6 ....107 F3
   OLDTF/WHR M16 ....127 C5
Whalley Rd CHD/CHDH SK8 ....169 H5
   HALE/TIMP WA15 ....178 B2
   MDTN M24 ....40 B4
   OFTN SK2 ....172 D2
   OLDTF/WHR M16 ....127 C5
   WHIT OL12 ....29 E2
   WHTF M45 ....69 G3
Whalley St NEWH/MOS M40 ....115 G3
Wham Bar Dr HEY OL10 ....40 B4
Wham La WHIT OL12 ....18 C4
Wham St HEY OL10 ....40 C4
Whardf Cl CMANE M1 ....7 J5
Wharfedale ALT WA14 ....165 G2
Wharfedale Av
   NEWH/MOS M40 ....103 H1
Wharfedale Rd RDSH SK5 ....145 E3
Wharf End TRPK M17 ....126 D2
Wharf Rd ALT WA14 ....165 G2
   SALE M33 ....154 D1
Wharfside Av ECC M30 ....111 E5
   DUK SK16 ....119 H4
   HTNM SK4 ....159 H5
Wharmton Ri MOSL OL5 ....94 A1
Wharmton Vw MOSL OL5 ....94 B4
Wharton Av CCHDY M21 ....141 H4
Wharton La LHULT M38 ....80 D2
Wharton Ldg ECC M30 ....111 F2
Wheat Cl BRUN/LGST M13 ....128 D3
Wheatcroft ROY/SHW OL2 ....60 A5
Wheaters St BRO M7 ....113 H1
Wheaters St BRO M7 ....114 A1
Wheatfield STLY SK15 ....135 F1
Wheatfield Cl BURY BL9 ....27 G4
   MPL/ROM SK6 ....161 H2
Wheatfield St BOLE BL2 ....49 G4
Wheathill St ROCH OL11 ....43 F2
Wheatley Rd SWIN M27 ....83 C5
Wheatley Wk
   WGTN/LGST M12 ....129 C2
Wheeldale OLDE OL4 ....92 C1
Wheeldale Cl BOL BL1 ....33 H4
Wheelock Cl WILM/AE SK9 ....199 G1
Wheelton Cl TOT/BURYW BL8 ....37 F5
Wheelwright Cl
   MPL/ROM SK6 ....175 E1
   ROCH OL11 * 42 A2
Wheelwright Dr MILN OL16 ....19 H5
Whelan Av BURY BL9 ....53 F2
Whelan Cl BURY BL9 ....53 F2
Wheler St OP/CLY M11 ....117 E5
Whernside Av ANC M4 ....107 F5
   NEWH/MOS M40 ....103 H1
Whernside Cl HTNM SK4 ....13 F1
Whetstone Hill Cl OLD OL1 ....76 B2
Whetstone Hill La OLD OL1 ....76 B3
Whetstone Hill Rd OLD OL1 ....76 A2
Whewell Av RAD M26 ....53 E4
Whickham St ROCH OL11 ....28 C5
Whiley St BRUN/LGST M13 ....129 C4
Whimberry Cl SLFD M6 ....127 F1
Whimberry Wy
   DID/WITH M20 ....143 F5
Whimbrel Rd OFTN SK2 ....173 H4
Whinberry Rd ALT WA14 ....165 E2
Whinberry Wy OLDE OL4 ....60 D5
Whinchat Cl OFTN SK2 ....173 H5
Whinfell Dr MDTN M24 ....71 G3
Whinfield Cl HOR/BR BL6 * 64 D4
Whins Crest HOR/BR BL6 ....46 D2
Whinslee Dr HOR/BR BL6 ....46 D2
Whinstone Wy OLD OL1 ....73 H3
Whipp St HEY OL10 ....40 C5
Whirley Cl HTNM SK4 ....159 C1
Whiston Dr BOLE BL2 ....49 H4
Whiston Rd CHH M8 ....102 C2
Whitaker St MDTN M24 ....72 C4
Whitbrook Wy MDTN M24 ....57 F4
Whitburn Av BRUN/LGST M13 ....143 G1
Whitburn Cl BOLS/LL BL3 ....47 F5
Whitburn Dr
   TOT/BURYW BL8 ....37 H1
Whitburn Rd
   NTHM/RTH M23 ....167 H5

Whitby Av HEY OL10 40 D3
OLDTF/WHR M16 141 H1
RUSH/FAL M14 143 G3
SLFD M6 112 B2
URM M41 139 E1
Whitby Cl CHD/CHDH SK8 169 H3
POY/DIS SK12 194 D3
TOT/BURYW BL8 37 E4
Whitby Rd OLDS OL8 92 B4
RUSH/FAL M14 143 F3
Whitby St MDTN M24 73 F3
ROCH OL11 43 F1
Whitchurch Dr
OLDTF/WHR M16 127 G3
Whitchurch Gdns BOL BL1 33 H4
Whitchurch Rd
DID/WITH M20 142 B4
Whitchurch St BRO M7 114 B2
Whiteacre Rd AUL OL6 120 A1
Whiteacres SWIN M27 98 B3
White Bank Av RDSH SK5 160 D2
White Bank Rd OLDS OL8 106 A2
Whitebarn Rd WILM/AE SK9 201 E5
Whitebeam Cl
HALE/TIMP WA15 167 F4
MILN OL16 44 D3
SLFD M6 113 F2
Whitebeam Ct SLFD M6 * 113 F2
Whitebeam Wk WHTN BL5 62 A2
White Birk Cl TOT/BURYW BL8 26 A1
White Brook La UPML OL3 79 F4
Whitebrook Rd
RUSH/FAL M14 142 D2
Whitecar Av NEWH/MOS M40 104 D1
White Carr La BURY BL9 27 H2
Whitecarr La
HALE/TIMP WA15 179 F1
Whitechapel Cl BOLE BL2 50 B2
Whitechapel St
DID/WITH M20 157 G3
White City Wy
OLDTF/WHR M16 126 D3
Whitecliff Cl RUSH/FAL M14 128 D5
Whitecroft Av ROY/SHW OL2 60 C2
Whitecroft Dr TOT/BURYW BL8 37 E4
Whitecroft Gdns
BNG/LEV M19 158 B2
Whitecroft Rd BOL BL1 32 D5
MPL/ROM SK6 187 H2
Whitecroft St OLD OL1 76 B3
Whitefield HTNM SK4 159 G3
Whitefield Av ROCH OL11 28 C3
Whitefield Rd BURY BL9 53 F3
MPL/ROM SK6 161 F2
SALE M33 154 A1
Whitegate BOLS/LL BL3 62 D2
LIT OL15 20 B4
Whitegate Av CHAD OL9 90 A3
Whitegate Cl
NEWH/MOS M40 104 D1
Whitegate Dr BOL BL1 34 A1
ORD M5 112 C2
SWIN M27 84 C5
Whitegate La CHAD OL9 90 B3
Whitegate Pk URM M41 137 G1
Whitegate Rd CHAD OL9 89 G4
Whitegates Cl
HALE/TIMP WA15 166 C4
Whitegates La OLDE OL4 77 G2
Whitegates Rd
CHD/CHDH SK8 170 A4
MDTN M24 57 F5
Whitehall Cl WILM/AE SK9 198 D5
Whitehall La BOL BL1 22 C5
OLDE OL4 61 E5
Whitehall Rd DID/WITH M20 157 H3
SALE M33 154 C4
Whitehall St OLD OL1 9 H1
WHIT OL12 10 C3
White Hart Meadow
MDTN M24 72 D2
White Hart St HYDE SK14 133 G4
Whitehaven Gdns
DID/WITH M20 157 F4
Whitehaven Rd
BRAM/HZG SK7 193 F2
Whitehead Crs RAD M26 67 E5
TOT/BURYW BL8 37 H1
Whitehead Rd CCHDY M21 140 D3
SWIN M27 84 C5
Whitehead St
DTN/ASHW M34 132 C1
MILN OL16 * 31 F5
MILN OL16 45 G2
ROY/SHW OL2 59 G1
WALK M28 82 A3
White Hill Cl WHIT OL12 18 C4
Whitehill Dr
NEWH/MOS M40 103 H3
Whitehill St HTNM SK4 159 H2
RDSH SK5 160 A1
Whitehill St West HTNM SK4 159 G2
Whiteholme Av CCHDY M21 156 C2
White Horse Gdns SWIN M27 * 98 B4
White Horse Gv WHTN BL5 62 B2
White Horse Mdw MILN OL16 * 43 H4
Whitehouse Av OLDE OL4 92 B2
White House Av PWCH M25 86 D4
White House Cl HEY OL10 56 A2
Whitehouse Dr
HALE/TIMP WA15 178 C4
NTHM/RTH M23 167 H4
Whitehouse La ALT WA14 164 A2
Whitehurst Rd HTNM SK4 158 C2
Whitekirk Cl BRUN/LGST M13 128 C2
White Lady Cl WALK M28 81 E4
Whitelake Av URM M41 123 G5
Whitelake Vw URM M41 123 F5
Whiteland Av BOLS/LL BL3 48 A4
Whitelands DUK SK16 119 H3
Whitelands Rd AUL OL6 119 H3
Whitelea Dr EDGY/DAV SK3 171 G4
Whitelees Rd LIT OL15 20 D3
Whitelegge St
TOT/BURYW BL8 37 G2
Whiteley Dr MDTN M24 73 F5
Whiteley Pl ALT WA14 165 G3
Whiteley St CHAD OL9 90 C3
OP/CLY M11 116 C3
White Lion Brow BOL BL1 2 C5
Whitelow Rd BURY BL9 17 F3
CCHDY M21 141 E3
HTNM SK4 158 D3
Whitemoss WHIT OL12 * 29 E1
White Moss Av CCHDY M21 141 G3
White Moss Rd BKLY M9 88 B4
Whitemoss Rd East BKLY M9 88 C3
Whiteoak Cl MPL/ROM SK6 174 D2
Whiteoak Rd RUSH/FAL M14 143 E3
Whiteoak Vw BOLS/LL BL3 50 A4
Whites Cft SWIN M27 99 E2
Whiteside Cl ORD M5 112 C3
Whiteside Fold WHIT OL12 28 D2
Whitestone Cl HOR/BR BL6 47 E3
Whitestone Wk
BRUN/LGST M13 * 129 E3
White St HULME M15 127 G2
SLFD M6 112 D4
TOT/BURYW BL8 37 H5
White Swallows Rd SWIN M27 99 F4
Whitethorn Av BNG/LEV M19 144 A4
OLDTF/WHR M16 127 G5
Whitethorn Cl MPL/ROM SK6 174 D2
Whitewater Dr BRO M7 100 C3
Whiteway St BKLY M9 103 F3
Whitewell Cl BURY BL9 53 E2
MILN OL16 11 J4
Whitewillow Cl FAIL M35 105 F4
Whitfield Crs MILN OL16 45 E3
Whitfield Dr MILN OL16 44 B1
Whitfield Ri ROY/SHW OL2 44 D5
Whitfield St CSLFD M3 114 D2
Whiting Gv BOLS/LL BL3 47 F3
Whitland Av BOL BL1 47 G1
Whitland Dr OLDS OL8 90 C5
Whit La SLFD M6 100 D5
Whitley Gdns
HALE/TIMP WA15 166 D2
Whitley Pl HALE/TIMP WA15 166 C2
Whitley Rd HTNM SK4 159 E3
NEWH/MOS M40 115 F1
Whitley St BOLS/LL BL3 66 A2
Whitlow Av ALT WA14 165 E1
Whitman St BKLY M9 103 G2
Whitmore Rd RUSH/FAL M14 142 D2
Whitnall Cl OLDTF/WHR M16 127 H5
Whitnall St HYDE SK14 * 133 G3
Whitsand Rd WYTH/NTH M22 168 D4
Whitsbury Av GTN M18 130 C5
Whitstable Cl CHAD OL9 90 C1
Whitstable Rd
NEWH/MOS M40 * 104 B1
Whitsters Hollow BOL BL1 33 E3
Whitsundale WHTN BL5 62 A2
Whittaker Dr LIT OL15 31 G1
Whittaker Fold LIT OL15 * 21 H3
Whittaker La LIT OL15 21 G4
PWCH M25 86 B3
ROCH OL11 28 A2
Whittaker St AUL OL6 107 G5
CHAD OL9 74 C5
NEWH/MOS M40 103 H2
RAD M26 52 C5
ROCH OL11 * 28 B2
WGTN/LGST M12 115 G5
Whittingham Dr RAMS BL0 16 D5
Whittingham Gv OLD OL1 75 E4
Whittington St AULW OL7 119 F4
Whittlebrook Gv HEY OL10 56 B2
Whittle Dr ROY/SHW OL2 60 C1
WALK M28 82 A2
Whittle Gv BOL BL1 33 E5
WALK M28 82 B4
Whittle La HEY OL10 55 F4
Whittles Av DTN/ASHW M34 132 D5
Whittle's Cft CMANE M1 * 7 J5
Whittles St WHIT OL12 14 C1
Whittle St ANC M4 * 7 H3
LIT OL15 20 C3
SWIN M27 98 D3
TOT/BURYW BL8 * 37 H3
WALK M28 82 B4
Whitwell Wy GTN M18 130 B3
Whitworth Cl AUL OL6 119 H1
Whitworth La RUSH/FAL M14 143 F2
Whitworth Rake WHIT OL12 14 C5
Whitworth Rd WHIT OL12 10 C1
Whitworth Sq WHIT OL12 14 C5
Whitworth St CMANE M1 7 H6
MILN OL16 * 30 D1
MILN OL16 31 G5
OP/CLY M11 130 A1
Whitworth St East
OP/CLY M11 130 B1
Whitworth St West CMANE M1 6 E7
Whixhall Av WGTN/LGST M12 129 F2
Whoolden St FWTH BL4 65 H3
Whowell Fold BOL BL1 33 F3
Whowell St BOLS/LL BL3 2 C7
Wibbersley Pk URM M41 * 137 H1
Wichbrook Rd WALK M28 81 E4
Wicheaves Crs WALK M28 81 E4
The Wicheries WALK M28 81 E4
Wicken Bank HEY OL10 56 B2
Wickenby Dr SALE M33 154 B2
Wicken St OFTN SK2 172 D2
Wickentree Holt WHIT OL12 28 D1
Wickentree La FAIL M35 105 F1
Wicker La HALE/TIMP WA15 178 C4
Wicket Gv SWIN M27 83 H3
Wickliffe Pl ROCH OL11 30 A5
Wickliffe St BOL BL1 2 D3
Wicklow Av EDGY/DAV SK3 171 E2
Wicklow Dr WYTH/NTH M22 180 D2
Wicklow Gv OLDS OL8 91 F4
Widcombe Dr BOLE BL2 50 C4
Widdop St CHAD OL9 8 C3
Widecombe Cl URM M41 * 124 A4
Widgeon Cl POY/DIS SK12 194 C3
RUSH/FAL M14 142 D3
Widgeon Rd ALT WA14 165 E2
Widnes St OP/CLY M11 * 130 B1
Wigan Rd BOLS/LL BL3 63 F1
Wiggins Wk RUSH/FAL M14 * 128 D5
Wigley St WGTN/LGST M12 129 F1
Wigmore Rd CHH M8 102 C3
Wigmore St AUL OL6 120 A1
Wigsby Av NEWH/MOS M40 104 B1
Wigwam Cl POY/DIS SK12 194 D3
Wike St TOT/BURYW BL8 4 A3
Wilbraham Rd CCHDY M21 141 F3
OLDTF/WHR M16 142 A2
RUSH/FAL M14 142 D2
WALK M28 82 A4
Wilburn St ORD M5 114 A5
Wilby Av BOLS/LL BL3 50 D4
Wilby Cl TOT/BURYW BL8 * 38 A1
Wilby St CHH M8 102 C4
Wilcock Cl OLDTF/WHR M16 127 H4
Wilcott Dr SALE M33 153 H1
WILM/AE SK9 200 C1
Wilcott Rd CHD/CHDH SK8 169 F4
Wildbank Cha STLY SK15 135 F1
Wildbrook Cl LHULT M38 80 D4
Wildbrook Crs OLDS OL8 91 H4
Wildbrook Gv LHULT M38 80 D4
Wildbrook Rd LHULT M38 80 D3
Wildbrook Ter OLDS OL8 * 91 H4
Wild Clough HYDE SK14 148 B2
Wildcroft Av NEWH/MOS M40 103 H1
Wilders Moor Cl WALK M28 96 D2
Wilderswood Cl
DID/WITH M20 157 H1
Wilde St DTN/ASHW M34 132 C5
Wildhouse La LIT OL15 31 G2
Wildman La FWTH BL4 65 E4
Wildmoor Av OLDE OL4 92 D4
Wild Moor Wood Cl STLY SK15 109 E5
Wilds Pl RAMS BL0 * 16 C3
Wild St BRAM/HZG SK7 * 185 E2
DUK SK16 120 A5
HEY OL10 41 F4
MPL/ROM SK6 161 G4
OLD OL1 9 K2
OLDE OL4 92 D1
RAD M26 53 E5
ROY/SHW OL2 60 B3
Wildwood Cl OFTN SK2 172 B4
RAMS BL0 16 B4
Wilford Av SALE M33 154 B4
Wilfred Dr BURY BL9 5 J1
Wilfred Rd ECC M30 110 B5
WALK M28 82 A5
Wilfred St BRO M7 114 B1
EDGW/EG BL7 * 23 F4
NEWH/MOS M40 103 H2
Wilfrid St SWIN M27 99 E2
Wilkes St OLD OL1 76 C1
Wilkin Cft CHD/CHDH SK8 182 B4
Wilkins La WILM/AE SK9 190 D2
Wilkinson Av BOLS/LL BL3 50 D5
Wilkinson Rd BOL BL1 33 G1
HTNM SK4 12 E1
Wilkinson St AUL OL6 119 F2
HTNM SK4 12 E1
MDTN M24 72 C4
SALE M33 155 E2
Wilks Av WYTH/NTH M22 181 E2
Willand Cl BOLE BL2 50 D3
Willand Dr BOLE BL2 50 D4
Willan Rd BKLY M9 87 H3
ECC M30 111 F3
Willard St BRAM/HZG SK7 * 185 E1
Willaston Cl CCHDY M21 141 E4
Willbutts La ROCH OL11 29 F3
Willdale Cl OP/CLY M11 116 B3
Willdor Gv EDGY/DAV SK3 171 E3
Willenhall Rd NTHM/RTH M23 156 B4
Willerby Rd BRO M7 101 H5
Willesden Av BRUN/LGST M13 129 F5
Will Griffith Wk OP/CLY M11 115 H5
William Chadwick Cl
NEWH/MOS M40 115 F2
William Cl URM M41 138 C2
William Greenwood Cl
HEY OL10 40 D4
William Henry St ROCH OL11 43 F2
William Jessop Ct CMANE M1 7 K5
William Kay Cl
OLDTF/WHR M16 127 H4
William Lister Cl
NEWH/MOS M40 * 117 E1
Williams Crs CHAD OL9 90 A4
Williamson Av MPL/ROM SK6 161 H2
RAD M26 52 A3
Williamson La DROY M43 118 A5
Williamson St ANC M4 115 E2
AUL OL6 119 G3
RDSH SK5 145 E4
Williams Rd GTN M18 130 B3
NEWH/MOS M40 104 A3
Williams St BOLS/LL BL3 67 E1
GTN M18 130 B4
William St AULW OL7 119 F4
CSLFD M3 6 B3
DID/WITH M20 157 G3
FAIL M35 105 F1
LIT OL15 20 D3
MDTN M24 73 E4
MILN OL16 20 A4
RAD M26 52 C5
ROCH OL11 30 A5
STKP SK1 172 C2
WGTN/LGST M12 115 G5
WHIT OL12 14 B4
Willingdon Cl TOT/BURYW BL8 26 D4
Willingdon Dr PWCH M25 86 A2
Willis Rd EDGY/DAV SK3 171 H3
Willis St BOLS/LL BL3 48 B5
Willock St BRO M7 101 H4
Willoughby Av DID/WITH M20 157 H2
Willoughby Cl SALE M33 154 B1
Willow Av CHD/CHDH SK8 182 C2
MDTN M24 73 F5
RDSH SK5 160 A2
URM M41 139 E1
Willow Bank CHD/CHDH SK8 192 D1
OLDE OL4 76 D4
RUSH/FAL M14 143 E3
Willowbank RAD M26 68 B4
Willowbank Av BOLE BL2 3 K7
Willow Bank Cl OFTN SK2 173 E2
Willowbrook Av
NEWH/MOS M40 103 H3
Willow Cl BOLS/LL BL3 48 A5
BURY BL9 70 A2
DUK SK16 134 A1
POY/DIS SK12 195 F4
Willow Ct MPL/ROM SK6 175 E4
SALE M33 155 F1
Willowdale Av
CHD/CHDH SK8 181 G2
Willowdene Cl EDGW/EG BL7 23 E3
NEWH/MOS M40 102 D5
Willow Dr BURY BL9 70 A2
SALE M33 153 H4
WILM/AE SK9 192 A4
Willowfield Rd OLDE OL4 76 C2
Willow Fold DROY M43 118 A5
Willow Gv CHAD OL9 * 74 C4
DTN/ASHW M34 132 B5
GTN M18 * 130 D4
MPL/ROM SK6 175 E4
Willow Hey EDGW/EG BL7 23 H5
Willow Hill Rd CHH M8 102 B1
Willow Lawn CHD/CHDH SK8 * 182 D2
Willowmead Wy WHIT OL12 28 D1
Willowmoss Cl WALK M28 97 F1
Willow Ri LIT OL15 20 C5
Willow Rd ECC M30 110 B1
MPL/ROM SK6 187 E5
PART M31 150 D4
PWCH M25 85 H1
UPML OL3 79 F5
Willows Dr FAIL M35 117 G1
Willows End STLY SK15 121 G2
Willows La BOLS/LL BL3 48 B5
MILN OL16 31 F4
Willows Rd ORD M5 * 112 C3
The Willows BOLS/LL BL3 50 D4
CCHDY M21 141 E4
MOSL OL5 109 F1
PART M31 151 E3
Willow St BURY BL9 5 K4
CHH M8 114 B1
HEY OL10 41 E4
OLD OL1 9 K2
OP/CLY M11 116 B4
SWIN M27 98 C5
WALK M28 98 B3
Willow Tree Ms
CHD/CHDH SK8 181 G3
Willow Tree Rd ALT WA14 177 G2
Willow Wy BRAM/HZG SK7 183 F5
DID/WITH M20 157 H3
Willow Wood Cl AUL OL6 120 B2
Wilma Av BKLY M9 87 H3
Wilmcote Cl HOR/BR BL6 47 E3
Wilmcote Rd
NEWH/MOS M40 115 F1
Wilmington Rd STRET M32 * 139 H1
Wilmot St BOL BL1 33 F3
Wilmott St HULME M15 128 B2
Wilmslow Av BOL BL1 33 H1
Wilmslow Old Rd
HALE/TIMP WA15 189 G1
Wilmslow Park Rd
WILM/AE SK9 199 G3
Wilmslow Rd CHD/CHDH SK8 170 A5
CHD/CHDH SK8 182 A1
CHD/CHDH SK8 182 A4
DID/WITH M20 157 H5
HALE/TIMP WA15 189 G2
RUSH/FAL M14 143 E1
WILM/AE SK9 192 A2
WILM/AE SK9 200 D3
Wilmur Av BRO M7 101 H4
WHTF M45 69 H5
Wilpshire Av WGTN/LGST M12 130 A5
Wilshaw Gv AULW OL7 107 E4
Wilshaw La AULW OL7 106 D5
Wilson Av HEY OL10 40 B4
SWIN M27 99 G1
Wilson Crs AUL OL6 120 B1
Wilson Rd BKLY M9 103 E1
HTNM SK4 159 E2
Wilsons Pk NEWH/MOS M40 * 103 F5
Wilson St BOLS/LL BL3 * 2 E6
BRUN/LGST M13 128 D2
BURY BL9 5 G6
FWTH BL4 66 B4
HYDE SK14 148 A1
OLDS OL8 91 F3
OP/CLY M11 116 B5
RAD M26 52 A5
STRET M32 126 B4
UPML OL3 94 D2
WHIT OL12 10 C4
Wilson Wy OLD OL1 9 G2
Wilsthorpe Cl BNG/LEV M19 144 C5
Wilton Av CHD/CHDH SK8 181 H5
OLDTF/WHR M16 126 D5
PWCH M25 86 C5
SWIN M27 99 H3
Wilton Ct GTN M18 131 F4
Wilton Crs WILM/AE SK9 200 C3
Wilton Dr BURY BL9 53 H4
HALE/TIMP WA15 178 D4
Wilton Gdns RAD M26 52 D4
Wilton Gv DTN/ASHW M34 131 F4
HEY OL10 41 E5
Wilton Paddock
DTN/ASHW M34 131 F4
Wilton Pl CSLFD M3 * 114 A3
Wilton Rd BOL BL1 33 H1
CCHDY M21 141 F3
CHH M8 87 F5
SLFD M6 112 A1
Wilton St BOL BL1 34 A3
CHAD OL9 90 C4
DTN/ASHW M34 132 B4
HEY OL10 40 D4
MDTN M24 71 G5
PWCH M25 86 B3
RDSH SK5 145 F1
WHTF M45 69 G5
Wilton Ter WHIT OL12 10 A4
Wiltshire Av RDSH SK5 160 D2
Wiltshire Cl BURY BL9 53 H1
Wiltshire Rd CHAD OL9 90 C2
FAIL M35 105 E4
PART M31 150 D4
Wiltshire St BRO M7 101 H4
Wimberry Cl UPML OL3 95 E2
Wimbledon Dr EDGY/DAV SK3 171 F3
ROCH OL11 42 C1
Wimbledon Rd FAIL M35 105 G2
Wimborne Av URM M41 124 C4
Wimborne Cl CHD/CHDH SK8 171 F5
Wimbourne Av CHAD OL9 74 B3
Wimpole St AUL OL6 119 H2
OLD OL1 75 H4
Wimpory St OP/CLY M11 130 C1
Winbolt St OFTN SK2 172 D5
Wincanton Av
NTHM/RTH M23 167 E1
Wincanton Dr BOL BL1 22 C4
Wincanton Pk OLDE OL4 92 C1
Wince Cl MDTN M24 89 F1
Wincham Cl HULME M15 127 G2
Wincham Rd SALE M33 153 H4
Winchester Av AUL OL6 107 G3
CHAD OL9 74 A3
DTN/ASHW M34 146 D2
HEY OL10 55 H1
PWCH M25 86 B5
Winchester Cl ROCH OL11 28 C4
TOT/BURYW BL8 26 D4
WILM/AE SK9 198 B5
Winchester Dr HTNM SK4 159 E4
SALE M33 153 G2
Winchester Pk DID/WITH M20 157 E3
Winchester Rd DUK SK16 134 B1
ECC M30 111 H1
HALE/TIMP WA15 178 D3
RAD M26 51 G4
SLFD M6 112 B1
URM M41 124 C5
Winchester Wy BOLE BL2 35 E5
Wincle Av POY/DIS SK12 195 G5
Wincombe St RUSH/FAL M14 142 D1
Windale WALK M28 81 G4
Windcroft Cl OP/CLY M11 116 A5
Winder Dr ANC M4 115 F4
Windermere Av BOLS/LL BL3 50 D5
DTN/ASHW M34 145 G1
SALE M33 155 E3
SWIN M27 99 F3
Windermere Cl OP/CLY M11 116 B5
PWCH M25 85 F2
STRET M32 125 H5
Windermere Crs AULW OL7 * 119 E1
Windermere Dr BURY BL9 53 F2
RAMS BL0 16 D1
WILM/AE SK9 200 C4
Windermere Rd DUK SK16 119 H5
FWTH BL4 64 D5
HYDE SK14 133 F3
MDTN M24 71 H2
MPL/ROM SK6 186 C3
ROY/SHW OL2 59 E3
STKP SK1 172 C2
STLY SK15 120 D2
URM M41 * 138 C2
WILM/AE SK9 191 H3
Windermere St BOL BL1 34 A3
Winder St BOL BL1 2 E2
Winders Wy SLFD M6 113 G1
Windfields Cl CHD/CHDH SK8 183 E1
Wind Gate Ri STLY SK15 109 E5
Windham St MILN OL16 19 H5
Windle Av CHH M8 87 E4
Windle Ct OFTN SK2 173 F4
Windlehurst Dr WALK M28 96 C3
Windlehurst Old Rd
MPL/ROM SK6 187 E2
Windlehurst Rd
MPL/ROM SK6 186 C4
Windley St BOLE BL2 3 H2
Windmill Av ORD M5 127 E1
Windmill Cl DTN/ASHW M34 145 H1
Windmill Ct MILN OL16 * 30 C5
Windmill La DTN/ASHW M34 145 G1
Windmill Rd SALE M33 155 G3
WALK M28 81 H2
Windmill St CMANW M2 6 D6
MILN OL16 30 C5
Windover Cl WHTN BL5 63 H5
Windover St BOLS/LL BL3 47 H5
Windrush Av RAMS BL0 26 B1
Windrush Dr BKLY M9 103 E3
WHTN BL5 62 A3
The Windrush WHIT OL12 18 B4
Windsor Av BOLS/LL BL3 66 D1
CHAD OL9 90 B3
CHD/CHDH SK8 169 E4
FAIL M35 105 G2
HEY OL10 40 C4
HTNM SK4 158 D3
IRL M44 122 C5
LHULT M38 81 G2
SALE M33 139 H5
SWIN M27 84 B5
URM M41 137 H1
WHTF M45 69 H5
WILM/AE SK9 198 C4
Windsor Cl POY/DIS SK12 195 E3
TOT/BURYW BL8 26 B2
Windsor Crs PWCH M25 86 D4
Windsor Dr ALT WA14 166 A1
ALT WA14 176 C3
AULW OL7 119 E1
DTN/ASHW M34 118 C4
DUK SK16 134 A1
MPL/ROM SK6 174 D4
STLY SK15 120 D2
TOT/BURYW BL8 52 C1
Windsor Gv AUL OL6 107 F3
BOL BL1 33 F5
CHD/CHDH SK8 182 C4
MPL/ROM SK6 162 D4
RAD M26 67 E5
Windsor Rd BKLY M9 103 F3
BNG/LEV M19 143 H2
BRAM/HZG SK7 185 G2
DROY M43 117 E3
DTN/ASHW M34 131 F5
EDGW/EG BL7 23 F4
HYDE SK14 147 H4
MPL/ROM SK6 160 D3
NEWH/MOS M40 117 F1
OLDS OL8 8 C6
PWCH M25 86 D4
Windsor St FAIL M35 105 F3
GTN M18 130 B4
NEWH/MOS M40 117 F1
OFTN SK2 172 B3
OLD OL1 75 H3
ORD M5 113 G4
ROCH OL11 43 F1

Windsor Ter MILN OL16......11 K6
 MILN OL16......31 F5
Windybank BKLY M9......87 H2
Windy Harbour La
 EDGY/EG BL7......23 C3
Windyhill Dr BOLS/LL BL3......63 H1
Winfell Dr NEWH/MOS M40......115 C2
Winfield Av DID/WITH M20......158 A1
Winfield Dr GTN M18......130 C2
Winfield St MPL/ROM SK6......165 G5
Winfield St HYDE SK14......148 B1
Winford St BKLY M9......37 G2
Wingate Av TOT/BURYW BL8......37 C4
Wingate Dr DID/WITH M20......157 H4
 HALE/TIMP WA15......166 C4
 WHTF M45......69 F5
Wingate Rd HTNM SK4......159 F2
 LHULT M38......81 G3
Wingate St ROCH OL11......28 A2
Wingfield Av WILM/AE SK9......198 B4
Wingfield Dr SWIN M27......99 F4
 WILM/AE SK9......198 B4
Wingfield St STRET M32......126 A4
Wings Gv HEY OL10......56 A2
Winifred Av BURY BL9......40 A2
Winifred Rd DID/WITH M20......157 G3
 FWTH BL4......65 F5
 NEWH/MOS M40......104 A3
 OFTN SK2......172 B4
 URM M41......124 B5
Winifred St ECC M30......110 C4
 HYDE SK14......148 B3
 RAMS BL0......16 C3
 WHIT OL12......29 E2
Winmarith Dr
 HALE/TIMP WA15......179 E5
Winmarleigh Cl
 TOT/BURYW BL8......37 E5
Winnie St OP/CLY M11......103 H2
Winning Hill Cl GTN M18......130 C4
Winnington Gn OFTN SK2......173 E3
Winnington Rd
 MPL/ROM SK6......175 E1
Winnipeg Quay SALQ M50......126 C1
The Winnows
 DTN/ASHW M34......132 A5
Winscombe Dr
 NEWH/MOS M40......115 F1
Winser St CMANE M1......7 F7
Winsfield Rd BRAM/HZG SK7......185 E4
Winsford Dr ROCH OL11......41 G1
Winsford Gv BOLS/LL BL3......47 H4
Winsford Rd RUSH/FAL M14......142 D2
Winskill Rd IRL M44......136 C1
Winslade Cl BRAM/HZG SK7......184 B2
 OLDE OL4......76 C3
Winslade Ms FWTH BL4......66 A3
Winslow Rd NTHM/RTH M23......155 G4
Winslow Av HYDE SK14......149 H1
Winslow Pl BNG/LEV M19......143 H5
Winslow Rd BOLS/LL BL3......62 D2
Winslow St OP/CLY M11......116 D5
Winstanley Rd
 NEWH/MOS M40......115 G2
 SALE M33......154 D1
Winster Av BRO M7......101 E4
 DID/WITH M20......156 D2
 STRET M32......125 F5
Winster Cl BOLE BL2......35 C5
 WHTF M45......70 A4
Winster Dr BOLE BL2......35 F5
 MDTN M24......72 B2
Winster Gv OFTN SK2......172 D5
Winster Rd ECC M30......110 C5
Winston Av BOLS/LL BL3......67 F1
 ROCH OL11......28 B5
Winston Cl MPL/ROM SK6......174 C2
 RAD M26......51 H4
Winston Rd BKLY M9......103 C1
 SALE M33......154 A1
Winswell Cl OP/CLY M11......115 H4
Winterbottom Gv HYDE SK14......149 H1
Winterbottom St CHAD OL9......8 D5
Winterburn Av BOLE BL2......35 G3
 CHDY M21......156 B2
Winterdyne OFTN SK2......173 F4
Winterdyne St BKLY M9......103 F3
Winterfield Dr BOLS/LL BL3......63 H1
Winterford Av
 BRUN/LGST M13......129 G3
Winterford Rd BRO M7......101 H1
 MOSL OL5......109 F1
Wintermans Rd CCHDY M21......141 H5
Winterslow Av
 NTHM/RTH M23......155 E5
Winter St BOL BL1......33 F5
Winterton Cl WHTN BL5......62 B3
Winterton Rd RDSH SK5......145 G2
Winthrop Av NEWH/MOS M40......115 F3
Winton Av DTN/ASHW M34......132 A1
 NEWH/MOS M40......104 C1
Winton Cl BRAM/HZG SK7......183 G3
Winton Gn HOR/BR BL6......46 A1
Winton Gv BOLS/LL BL3......47 F5
Winton Rd AUL WA14......177 F2
 SLFD M6......100 D5
Winton St AUL OL6......119 G2
 LIT OL15......21 E4
 STLY SK15......121 E4
Winward St BOLS/LL BL3......47 H5
Winwood Dr MDTN M24......73 E2
Winwood Rd DID/WITH M20......169 H1
Wirral Cl SWIN M27......84 B5
Wisbech Dr NTHM/RTH M23......155 F5
Wisbeck Rd BOLE BL2......49 H1
Wiseley St OP/CLY M11......115 H5
Wiseman Ter PWCH M25......86 B3
Wishaw Sq CCHDY M21......142 A5
Wisley Cl RDSH SK5......145 F3
Wistaria Rd GTN M18......130 C3
Witham Av WYTH/NTH M22......168 D4
Witham Cl HEY OL10......55 G2
Witham St AUL OL6......120 B1
Withenfield Rd
 NTHM/RTH M23......167 G1
Withens Gn OFTN SK2......173 F3
Withington Gn MDTN M24......56 D5
Withington Rd CCHDY M21......141 H3
 OLDTF/WHR M16......127 G5

Withington St HEY OL10 *......56 B1
Withinlea Cl WHTN BL5......62 B2
Withins Av RAD M26......52 D4
Withins Cl BOLE BL2......50 B1
Withins Dr BOLE BL2......50 B1
Withins Gv BOLE BL2......50 B1
Withins Hall Rd FAIL M35......105 G4
Withins La BOLE BL2......50 B1
 RAD M26......52 D4
Withins Rd OLDS OL8......90 C5
Withins St RAD M26......52 D5
Withnell Br DTN/ASHW BL8......37 F5
Withnell Rd BNG/LEV M19......158 A3
Withycombe Pl SLFD M6......100 D5
Withy Gv ANC M4......7 F3
Withypool Dr OFTN SK2......172 D4
Withy Tree Gv
 DTN/ASHW M34 *......147 E1
Witley Dr SALE M33......138 D5
Witley Rd MILN OL16......11 H7
Wittenbury Rd NTHM SK4......159 E4
Witterage Cl
 WGTN/LGST M12 *......129 G2
Woburn Abbey UPML OL3 *......78 D3
Woburn Av BOLE BL2......34 D3
 NEWH/MOS M40......115 H5
Woburn Dr BURY BL9......53 G4
 HALE/TIMP WA15......178 C2
Woburn St OLDTF/WHR M16......141 E1
Wodens Av ORD M5......127 F1
Woden St ORD M5......127 F1
Woking Back Gdns BOL BL1......33 H5
Woking St BOL BL1......33 H5
Woking Ter BOL BL1 *......33 H5
Wolfenden St BOL BL1......33 H4
Wolfenden St BOL BL1......33 H4
Wolfreton Crs SWIN M27......84 B4
Wolseley Pl DID/WITH M20......157 G1
Wolseley Rd SALE M33......139 H5
Wolseley St MILN OL16......45 G2
 TOT/BURYW BL8......37 G5
Wolsey Dr ALT WA14......176 D3
Wolsey St HEY OL10......40 D5
 RAD M26......68 B1
Wolstenholme Av BURY BL9......27 G5
Wolstenvale Cl MDTN M24......73 E3
Wolver Cl LHULT M38 *......81 C1
Wolverton Av OLDS OL8......91 E4
Wolverton St OP/CLY M11......129 C1
Woodacre OLDTF/WHR M16......142 A2
Woodacres St WILM/AE SK9......198 C4
Woodall Cl SALE M33......155 E2
Woodark Cl OLDE OL4......93 E2
Woodbank BOLE BL2......35 C5
Woodbank Av MPL/ROM SK6......161 F3
 STKP SK1......172 C1
Woodbank Ct URM M41......124 A5
Woodbank Dr TOT/BURYW BL8......37 H2
Woodbank La OLDE OL4......93 E2
Woodbine Av IRL M44......150 C2
Woodbine Crs OFTN SK2......172 A2
Woodbine Rd BOLS/LL BL3......64 B1
Woodbine St MILN OL16......43 G1
Woodbine St East MILN OL16......43 G1
Woodbourne Rd HTNM SK4......144 C4
 SALE M33......154 B4
Woodbray Av BNG/LEV M19......158 B1
Woodbridge Av
 DTN/ASHW M34......132 A1
Woodbridge Gdns WHIT OL12......29 F1
Woodbridge Gv
 NTHM/RTH M23......155 H5
Woodbridge Rd URM M41......123 E5
Woodbrook Av OLDE OL4......77 G5
Wood Brook La OLDE OL4......77 G5
Woodbrook Rd WILM/AE SK9......201 E4
Woodburn Dr BOL BL1......33 E3
Woodburn Rd
 WYTH/NTH M22......168 C1
Woodbury Crs DUK SK16......133 E1
Woodbury Rd EDGY/DAV SK3......171 E2
Woodchurch WHIT OL12......29 H1
Woodcock Cl DROY M43......118 B2
 ROCH OL11......28 C4
Woodcote Av BRAM/HZG SK7......183 F3
Woodcote Rd ALT WA14......155 G5
 PART M31......152 D2
Wood Cottage Cl WALK M28......81 E4
Woodcott Bank BOL BL1......33 G2
Woodcott Gv SALE M33......92 D4
Woodcroft OFTN SK2......173 E5
Woodcroft Av BNG/LEV M19......158 B2
Wooded Cl BURY BL9......53 F1
Wood Edge Cl BOLS/LL BL3 *......65 H1
Wood End BRAM/HZG SK7......183 G2
Woodend ROY/SHW OL2......45 F5
Woodend Dr STLY SK15......135 E2
Woodend La HYDE SK14......147 G2
 STLY SK15......135 E1
 WHIT OL12......29 G3
Woodend Rd EDGY/DAV SK3......172 A5
 WYTH/NTH M22......168 C5
Woodend St OLD OL1......75 F3
 OLDE OL4......93 E2
Woodfield WHTN/NTH M22......147 H2
Woodfield Av HYDE SK14......147 H5
 MPL/ROM SK6......161 H2
 WHIT OL12......10 A1
Woodfield Cl OLDS OL8......90 D5
Woodfield Ct OFTN SK2......173 E5
Woodfield Crs MPL/ROM SK6......161 G4
Woodfield Dr WALK M28......96 C4
Woodfield Gv ECC M30......110 D4
 FWTH BL4......81 H1
 SALE M33......139 E5
Woodfield Ms HYDE SK14 *......147 H5
Woodfield Rd ALT WA14......165 H3
 CHD/CHDH SK8......183 E5
 CHH M8......102 B1
 MDTN M24......88 B1
 SLFD M6......99 H1
Woodfield St BOLS/LL BL3......65 H1
Wood Fold EDGW/EG BL7......23 H5
Woodfold Av BNG/LEV M19......144 A1
Woodfold Rd FAIL M35......105 F2

Woodford Av DTN/ASHW M34......132 D4
 ECC M30......110 C3
 ROY/SHW OL2......60 C2
Woodford Dr SWIN M27......83 H5
Woodford Gdns
 DID/WITH M20......157 F4
Woodford Gv BOLS/LL BL3......48 B5
Woodford Rd BRAM/HZG SK7......193 H2
 POY/DIS SK12......194 C2
Woodgarth Av
 NEWH/MOS M40......104 C5
Woodgarth Dr SWIN M27......98 D4
Woodgarth La WALK M28......97 G5
Woodgate Av BURY BL9......39 G2
Woodgate Cl MPL/ROM SK6......161 C3
Woodgate Dr PWCH M25......86 B1
Woodgate Hill Rd BURY BL9......39 G2
Woodgate Rd
 OLDTF/WHR M16......142 A2
Woodgate St BOLS/LL BL3......65 F1
Woodgrange Cl SLFD M6......112 D3
Woodgreen Dr RAD M26......68 B4
Wood Gv DTN/ASHW M34......132 C4
 MPL/ROM SK6......161 H1
 WHTF M45......69 F1
Woodhall Av DID/WITH M20......142 C4
 WHTF M45......85 E1
Woodhall Cl BOLE BL2......34 D3
 BRAM/HZG SK7......193 G2
Woodhall Crs RDSH SK5......160 B2
Woodhall Rd RDSH SK5......160 B2
Woodhall St FAIL M35......105 E2
Woodhalt Rd CHH M8......102 B2
Woodham Rd
 NTHM/RTH M23......155 G5
Woodham Wk BOLS/LL BL3......48 C4
Woodhead Cl OLDE OL4......76 D5
 RAMS BL0......16 D4
Woodhead Dr
 HALE/TIMP WA15......178 A3
Woodhead Rd
 HALE/TIMP WA15......178 A3
Woodhead St
 OLDTF/WHR M16......127 H4
Wood Hey Cl RAD M26......67 G1
Wood Hey Gv
 DTN/ASHW M34 *......147 E1
Woodhey Rd RAMS BL0......16 B5
Woodheys HTNM SK4......158 C2
Woodheys Dr SALE M33......155 C5
Woodheys Rd LIT OL15......31 H1
Woodhill Cl MDTN M24......72 C2
 WGTN/LGST M12......130 A4
Woodhill Dr PWCH M25......86 A5
Woodhill Fold TOT/BURYW BL8......4 B2
Woodhill Gv PWCH M25......86 A4
Woodhill Rd TOT/BURYW BL8......4 B1
 TOT/BURYW BL8......38 B2
Woodhill St TOT/BURYW BL8......4 A1
Woodhill V TOT/BURYW BL8......4 A2
Woodhouse La SALE M33......153 E5
 WYTH/NTH M22......180 C5
Woodhouse La East
 HALE/TIMP WA15......154 C5
Woodhouse Rd ROY/SHW OL2......45 F5
 URM M41......123 C4
Woodhouse St GTN M18......130 D3
Wooding Cl PART M31......151 F2
Woodlake Av CCHDY M21......156 B2
Woodland Av BOLS/LL BL3......65 C2
 BRAM/HZG SK7......185 F3
 GTN M18......130 D4
 HEY OL10......41 E2
 WHIT OL12......30 B1
Woodland Cl HEY OL10......41 E4
 WGTN/LGST M12......130 A3
 WHIT OL12......30 B1

Woodlands Vw MILN OL16......11 J5
Woodland Vw EDGW/EG BL7......23 G3
 HYDE SK14......134 A5
Wood La AULW OL7......107 E5
 HALE/TIMP WA15......166 B4
 MDTN M24......73 E5
 MPL/ROM SK6......174 C4
 PART M31......150 D3
Woodlark Cl CSLFD M3 *......6 A4
Woodlawn Ct
 OLDTF/WHR M16......127 F5
Woodlea CHAD OL9......73 C5
 WALK M28......97 F2
Woodlea Av BNG/LEV M19......158 B1
Woodlea Cha SWIN M27......83 G2
Woodleigh Ct TOT/BURYW BL8......37 G1
Woodleigh Dr DROY M43......118 B1
Woodleigh Rd OLDE OL4......77 F5
Woodley Av RAD M26......68 C5
Woodley Cl OFTN SK2......173 E2
Woodley St BURY BL9......53 C1
Woodman Dr BURY BL9......53 C1
Woodman St STKP SK1......13 F2
Woodmeadow Ct MOSL OL5......93 H5
Woodmere Dr BKLY M9......88 B4
Wood Mt HALE/TIMP WA15......166 C4
Woodmount Cl MPL/ROM SK6......162 D4
Woodnewton Cl GTN M18......130 D4
Woodpecker Pl WALK M28 *......97 E2
Woodridge Dr BOLE BL2......34 C5
Wood Rd HALE/TIMP WA15......166 C4
 OLDTF/WHR M16......127 F5
Wood Rd North
 OLDTF/WHR M16......127 F5
Woodrow Wk
 WGTN/LGST M12......129 G2
Woodrow Wy IRL M44......136 B3
Woodroyd Cl BRAM/HZG SK7......183 G1
Woodroyd Dr BURY BL9......39 F3
Woodruffe Gdns
 MPL/ROM SK6......173 H1
Woods Ct BOL BL1......3 F4
Woodseaves Cl IRL M44......136 D2
Woodsend Cir URM M41......123 E5
 URM M41......123 E5
Woodsend Rd URM M41......123 E5
Woodsend Rd South
 URM M41......137 G2
Woods Gv CHD/CHDH SK8......183 E5
Woodshaw Gv WALK M28......96 D2
Woodside HTNM SK4......158 C5
 MILN OL16......43 F4
 ROY/SHW OL2......60 C1
Woodside Av BNG/LEV M19......158 B2
 WALK M28......82 C5
Woodside Cl OLDE OL4......92 D1
Woodside Dr HYDE SK14......148 A2
 MPL/ROM SK6......186 D5
 RAMS BL0......16 D4
 SLFD M6......112 B2
Woodside La POY/DIS SK12......195 F3
Woodside Rd
 OLDTF/WHR M16......141 F1
Woodside St STLY SK15......109 F4
Woods La CHD/CHDH SK8......183 E5
 UPML OL3......78 D3
Woodsley Rd BOL BL1......32 C4
Woodsmoor Rd SWIN M27......98 B1
Wood Sq DROY M43......117 H5
 OLDE OL4......93 C4
 OLDE OL4......77 F1
 WHIT OL12......29 F1
Woodstock Av
 CHD/CHDH SK8......182 D5
 RDSH SK5......160 A1
 WALK M28......81 F5
Woodstock Crs
 MPL/ROM SK6......161 H1
Woodstock Dr BOL BL1......32 D5
 SWIN M27......99 E4
 TOT/BURYW BL8......37 H2
 WALK M28......97 H4
Woodstock Gn RDSH SK5......160 B1
Woodstock Rd ALT WA14......165 F1
 OLDTF/WHR M16......141 H1
 NEWH/MOS M40......104 B1
 OLDTF/WHR M16......127 E5
Woodstock St OLDE OL4......9 H6
Wood St ALT WA14......165 G5
 AUL OL6......119 G3
 BOL BL1......3 F5
 CHD/CHDH SK8......170 A3
 CSLFD M3......6 C5
 DTN/ASHW M34......133 F2
 DUK SK16......133 E1
 HYDE SK14......148 A1
 LIT OL15......21 E5
 MDTN M24......72 A2
 MILN OL16......45 F2
 OLD OL1......75 G4
 OP/CLY M11......130 A1
 RAD M26......68 B1
 RAMS BL0......17 E4
 ROY/SHW OL2......59 F2
 STLY SK15......121 E4
 TOT/BURYW BL8......37 H5
 WHTF M45......69 F3

Woodvale BOLS/LL BL3......64 C2
Woodvale Dr BOLS/LL BL3......64 C2
Woodvale Gdns BOLS/LL BL3......64 C2
Woodvale Gv BOLS/LL BL3......64 C2
Woodvale Rd HAD K6......68 C3
Woodvale Wk OP/CLY M11 *......116 A4
Wood Vw HEY OL10......40 D2
Woodville Dr MPL/ROM SK6......174 D5
 SALE M33......154 B1
 STLY SK15......121 G2
Woodville Gv RDSH SK5......145 F5
Woodville Rd ALT WA14......165 F5
 SALE M33......154 B1
Woodville Ter
 NEWH/MOS M40......103 G1
Woodward Cl BURY BL9......38 C1
Woodward Ct ANC M4 *......115 F3
Woodward Pl ANC M4......115 F3
Woodward Rd PWCH M25......85 G5
Woodward St ANC M4......115 F3
Woodwise La
 NTHM/RTH M23......155 F5
Wooden St ECC M30......101 H4
Woolcoat Cl OLD OL1 *......9 H4
Woollam Pl CSLFD M3......6 A6
Woolley Av POY/DIS SK12......195 F5
Woolley St CHH M8......114 C1
Woolmore Av OLD OL1......75 F3
Woolpack Gn SLFD M6 *......112 C3
Woolston Av WALK M28......79 E2
Wootton St HYDE SK14......133 G4
Worcester Cl AUL OL6......107 G2
 BURY BL9......53 H1
 MPL/ROM SK6......161 H5
Worcester Rd BOLS/LL BL3......66 C1
 CHD/CHDH SK8......170 D5
 MDTN M24......88 D2
 SALE M33......153 G3
 SLFD M6......112 B1
 SWIN M27......83 G5
Worcester St BOL BL1......33 H5
 BOL BL1......101 H4
 CHAD OL9......90 C2
 ROCH OL11......42 D2
 TOT/BURYW BL8......38 A2
Wordsworth Av BURY BL9......53 C3
 CHH M8......102 B4
 DROY M43......117 G3
 FWTH BL4......65 C5
 RAD M26......67 H1
Wordsworth Cl DUK SK16......134 B1
Wordsworth Crs AULW OL7......106 B5
 LIT OL15......31 G1
Wordsworth Gdns PWCH M25......85 G4
Wordsworth Rd
 DTN/ASHW M34......147 E4
 LHULT M38......81 F2
 OLD OL1......76 A3
 OLDTF/WHR M16......127 E5
 RDSH SK5......144 D2
 SWIN M27......98 C1
Wordsworth Wy ROCH OL11......28 B5
Workesleigh St
 NEWH/MOS M40......104 B4
World Wy MANAIR M90......180 A4
Worrall St EDGY/DAV SK3......12 E7
 NEWH/MOS M40......103 H4
 ORD M5......127 F1
 WHIT OL12......29 G1
Worsbrough Av WALK M28......81 H5
Worsefold St
 NEWH/MOS M40 *......103 G1
Worsel St BOLS/LL BL3......48 B5
Worsley Av NEWH/MOS M40......103 G1
Worsel St BOLS/LL BL3......81 F5
Worsley Brow WALK M28......97 F4
Worsley Ct RUSH/FAL M14......142 A4
Worsley Gv BNG/LEV M19......172 C2
 WALK M28......81 F5
Worsley Pl ROY/SHW OL2......59 H3
Worsley Rd BOLS/LL BL3......47 H5
 ECC M30......82 A1
 FWTH BL4......82 A1
Worsley Rd North WALK M28......82 A2
Worsley St BOLS/LL BL3 *......48 C4
 CSLFD M3......6 C7
 CSLFD M5 *......127 G1
 HULME M15......127 G1
 MILN OL16......11 G7
 OLDS OL8......92 A2
 SWIN M27......99 F5
 TOT/BURYW BL8......25 H4
Worston Av BOL BL1......32 C4
Worth Ct POY/DIS SK12......195 E5
Worthenbury Wk
 BRUN/LGST M13......129 F5
Worthing Gv OFTN SK2......173 E3
Worthing St RUSH/FAL M14......142 D1
Worthington Av HEY OL10......56 B2
 PART M31......151 E3
Worthington Cl HYDE SK14 *......149 G1
Worthington Dr BRO M7......101 G1
Worthington Rd
 DTN/ASHW M34......147 F2
 SALE M33......155 F2
Worthington St AULW OL7......106 C5
 BOLS/LL BL3......64 B1
 NEWH/MOS M40......104 B2
 STLY SK15......120 C4
Worthington Wy
 DTN/ASHW M34......132 B4
Wortley Av ORD M5......113 F5
Wortley Gv NEWH/MOS M40......89 E5
Wragby Cl TOT/BURYW BL8......38 A1
Wragby St BOL BL1......33 G3
Wrath Cl BOLE BL2......35 E3
Wray Cl WYTH/NTH M22......180 C1
Wray Gdns BNG/LEV M19......144 C3
Wray Pl MILN OL16......30 D5
Wrekin Av NTHM/RTH M23......179 H1
Wren Av SWIN M27......84 C4

Wrenbury Av DID/WITH M20 ....142 B4
Wrenbury Crs EDGY/DAV SK3 ...171 F4
Wrenbury Dr BOL BL1..............23 E5
  CHD/CHDH SK8 ....170 D3
  MILN OL16 ....43 H2
Wren CI DTN/ASHW M34 ....118 D3
  FWTH BL4 ....65 E4
  OFTN SK2 ....173 G4
Wren Dr BURY BL9.................39 E2
  IRL M44.................122 B4
Wren Gdns MDTN M24...........72 C3
Wren Gn MILN OL16............30 C5
Wren's Nest Av ROY/SHW OL2...60 B1
Wren St OLDE OL4...............92 B1
Wrenswood Dr WALK M28 ......96 D2
Wren Wy OP/CLY M11..........115 H5
Wrexham CI OLDS OLDS 90 C5
Wrigglesworth CI
  TOT/BURYW BL8..................37 E3
Wright Robinson CI
  OP/CLY M11...............115 H5
Wrights Bank North
  OFTN SK2................173 F4
Wrights Bank South
  OFTN SK2................173 E4
Wright St AUL OL6..............120 A1
  CHAD OL9..................90 B2
  DTN/ASHW M34............118 D5
  FAIL M35..................105 E2
  OLD OL1...................9 J3
  OLDTF/WHR M16............127 F5
  RAD M26...................68 A1
Wrigley Crs FAIL M35..........105 E3
Wrigley Fold MDTN M24........55 H5
Wrigley Head FAIL M35.........105 H4
Wrigley Head Crs FAIL M35 *...105 E2
Wrigley PI LIT OL15 *..........20 C5
Wrigley St AUL OL6............119 C1
  OLDE OL4..................76 A5
  OLDE OL4..................77 C4
  OLDE OL4..................93 E1
Wroe St CSLFD M3.............114 A4
  OLDE OL4..................93 E1
  SWIN M27..................84 A4
Wroe Ter SWIN M27 *...........84 A4
Wroxham CI ORD M5...........113 F4
Wroxham Av DTN/ASHW M34 ..131 F5
  URM M41..................124 A5
Wroxham Rd BKLY M9..........87 H4
Wuerdle CI MILN OL16..........20 B5
Wuerdle Farm Wy MILN OL16 ..20 B4
Wuerdle PI MILN OL16..........20 B4
Wuerdle St MILN OL16..........20 B4
Wyatt Av ORD M5..............127 F1
Wyatt St DUK SK16............119 H4
  HTNM SK4.................5 K6
Wybersley Rd MPL/ROM SK6...187 F3
Wychbury St ORD M5...........112 D3
Wychelm Rd PART M31..........151 E3

Wycherley Rd WHIT OL12........29 E1
Wych Fold HYDE SK14..........148 A4
Wych St AUL OL6 *............119 C3
Wychwood ALT WA14...........177 E5
Wychwood CI MDTN M24........73 E5
Wycliffe Av WILM/AE SK9......198 D4
Wycliffe Ct URM M41..........138 C1
Wycliffe St ECC M30..........110 D3
  HTNM SK4.................5 H3
Wycombe Av DTN/ASHW M18 ...130 D2
Wycombe CI URM M41..........124 B3
Wye Av FAIL M35..............105 E3
Wyecroft CI MPL/ROM SK6 .....162 A1
Wye St OLDS OL8...............8 D2
Wykeham Gv WHIT OL12.........29 E2
Wykeham Ms BOL BL1...........47 H2
Wykeham St RUSH/FAL M14 ....128 B5
Wyke Pk OLDE OL4..............92 C1
Wylam Wk WGTN/LGST M12 ....130 A5
The Wylde BURY BL9............4 D4
Wynchgate Rd
  BRAM/HZG SK7..............185 H1
Wyndale Dr FAIL M35..........105 E5
Wyndale Rd OLDS OL8...........91 G4
Wyndcliff Dr URM M41.........137 G2
Wyndham Av BOLS/LL BL3.......63 H2
  SWIN M27..................84 A5
Wyndham CI BRAM/HZG SK7....185 H5
Wyne CI BRAM/HZG SK7........185 H1
Wynfield Av WYTH/NTH M22 ...185 E5
Wynford Sq SALQ M50.........113 E4
Wyngate Rd CHD/CHDH SK8...182 C3
  HALE/TIMP WA15............178 A4
Wynne Av SWIN M27............84 A4
Wynne CI DTN/ASHW M34......146 D2
  OP/CLY M11...............116 A5
Wynne Gv DTN/ASHW M34......146 D2
Wynne St BOL BL1..............33 H4
  LHULT M38.................81 E1
  SLFD M6...................113 G1
Wynnstay Gv RUSH/FAL M14...148 B3
Wynnstay Rd SALE M33........154 C1
Wynyard Cl SALE M33.........155 E4
Wynyard Rd WYTH/NTH M22...180 B1
Wyre Dr WALK M28.............96 C5
Wyresdale Rd BOL BL1.........48 B1
Wyre St CMANE M1..............7 J7
  MOSL OL5.................108 C1
Wythall Av LHULT M38.........81 G1
Wythburn Av BOL BL1..........32 D5
  CHH M8..................102 D4
  URM M41.................124 A5
Wythburn Rd MDTN M24.........72 B1
  STKP SK1.................172 C2
Wythburn St ORD M5..........112 D3
Wythenshawe Pk
  NTHM/RTH M23 *............167 H1
Wythenshawe Rd
  NTHM/RTH M23.............167 F1
  SALE M33.................155 F2

Wythens Rd CHD/CHDH SK8......181 G4
Wythop Gdns ORD M5..........113 F4
Wyverne Rd NTHM/RTH M14 ....159 H1
Wyverne Av CCHDY M21.........141 H3
Wyville CI BRAM/HZG SK7......185 H2
Wyville Dr BKLY M9............87 G1
  SLFD M6....................6 B1
  SWIN M27...................98 D4

Y

Yale Rd GTN M18..............130 A3
Yarburgh St OLDTF/WHR M16...127 H5
Yardley Av STRET M32.........139 G2
Yardley CI STRET M32.........139 G2
Yarmouth Dr NTHM/RTH M23....156 A5
Yarnton CI ROY/SHW OL2.......59 H4
Yarn Wk ANC M4 *.............115 F4
Yarrow CI ROCH OL11...........43 E1
Yarrow PI BOL BL2.............10 B4
Yarwood Av NTHM/RTH M23....167 G2
Yarwood CI HEY OL10...........41 F3
Yarwoodheath La ALT WA14....176 B4
Yarwood St ALT WA14.........177 G1
  BURY BL9...................5 G4
Yasmin Gdns OLD OL1...........75 E4
Yates Dr WALK M28............81 F4
Yates St BOLE BL2..............3 H1
  MDTN M24.................71 H5
  OLD OL1...................75 E4
  STKP SK1.................160 C3
Yattendon Av
  NTHM/RTH M23.............167 E1
Yeadon Rd GTN M18...........130 C5
Yea Fold LIT OL15.............20 D5
Yealand Av HTNM SK4.........159 G3
Yealand CI ROCH OL11..........29 E5
Yeardsley CI BRAM/HZG SK7...183 H1
Yeb Fold NEWH/MOS M40 *.....104 A1
Yellow Lodge Dr WHTN BL5.....62 C3
Yeoford Dr ALT WA14.........165 E3
Yeoman CI
  BRAM/HZG SK7 *...........185 E1
Yeoman's CI MILN OL16.........31 G4
Yeoman Wk OP/CLY M11.......115 H4
Yeovil St OLDTF/WHR M16......128 A5
Yewbarrow Rd OLD OL1.........75 H4
Yew CI BOLS/LL BL3............48 A5
Yew Crs OLDE OL4..............76 C4
Yewdale SWIN M27.............84 B5
Yewdale Av BOLE BL2...........35 G4
Yewdale Dr FAIL M35.........105 G2
  MDTN M24.................72 B3
Yewdale Gdns BOLE BL2.........35 G4
Yew Dale Gdns ROCH OL11......42 A2

Yewdale Rd STKP SK1..........172 C3
Yewlands Av BKLY M9...........88 A2
Yew St BRO M7...............101 F4
  DTN/ASHW M34.............132 C3
  HEY OL10..................40 D5
  HULME M15.................127 H1
Yew Tree Av BNG/LEV M19 ....144 A3
  BRAM/HZG SK7.............185 H5
  RUSH/FAL M14.............128 B5
  WYTH/NTH M22.............156 C5
Yew Tree CI AULW OL7........106 D4
  MPL/ROM SK6..............174 D4
  WHIT OL12.................29 G5
Yew Tree Crs RUSH/FAL M14 ..142 D2
Yew Tree Dr HOR/BR BL6.......46 D3
  MDTN M24.................73 C5
  MPL/ROM SK6.............161 E3
  PWCH M25.................86 A3
  SALE M33.................155 F2
  URM M41.................123 G4
  WYTH/NTH M22.............156 C5
Yew Tree Gv BNG/LEV M19 ....144 A3
Yew Tree La BOL BL1...........33 H2
  DUK SK16................134 B1
Yewtree La NTHM/RTH M23 ....156 A4
  POY/DIS SK12.............195 G4
  WYTH/NTH M22.............156 C5
Yew Tree Park Rd
  CHD/CHDH SK8.............193 E1
Yew Tree Rd
  DTN/ASHW M34.............146 C2
  EDGY/DAV SK3.............184 A1
  RUSH/FAL M14.............142 D2
  SALE M33...................66 D1
  OLDS OL8..................92 B1
  OLDTF/WHR M16............141 G1
  PWCH M25..................86 B5
  ROCH OL11..................28 D5
  SALE M35...................154 A5
  SWIN M27..................98 D4
York CI CHD/CHDH SK8........170 D4
York Crs WILM/AE SK9........199 G3
Yorkdale Rd OLDE OL4..........76 C5
York Dr ALT WA14.............177 E3
  BRAM/HZG SK7.............185 G4
  MANAIR M90...............179 C5
  RAMS BL0..................16 B5
York PI AULW OL7.............119 F3
York Rd ALT WA14............177 F3
  CCHDY M21................141 F3
  CHAD OL9..................74 A4
  DROY M43.................117 G2
  DTN/ASHW M34.............132 C4
  HTNM SK4.................159 E1
  HYDE SK14................148 A3
  IRL M44..................150 C1
  SALE M33.................154 B1
York Rd East MDTN M24........89 F2
York Rd West MDTN M24........89 F2
Yorkshire Rd PART M31.......150 D4

Yorkshire St AULW OL7........119 C1
  CSLFD M3...................6 C3
  MILN OL16................10 D5
  OLD OL1...................9 H3
  WHIT OL12................11 F4
York St AULW OL7............118 D5
  BNG/LEV M19..............144 A3
  BURY BL9....................5 G4
  CHAD OL9....................8 E4
  CMANE M1...................7 F7
  CMANE M1.................128 B1
  CMANW M2...................6 E3
  DID/WITH M20.............157 G3
  EDGY/DAV SK3..............12 E5
  FWTH BL4..................66 B4
  HALE/TIMP WA15...........177 H1
  HEY OL10..................41 E4
  HULME M15................127 H1
  MILN OL16................26 D5
  RAD M26...................53 F4
  WHTF M45..................69 G4
York Ter SALE M33 *.........139 C5
Young St CSLFD M3.............6 C5
  FWTH BL4..................66 A5
  RAMS BL0..................16 C2
Yulan Dr SALE M33...........153 F2
Yule St EDGY/DAV SK3..........12 C5

Z

Zama St RAMS BL0 *...........16 B4
Zealand St OLDE OL4...........76 B4
Zedburgh WHIT OL12...........10 B4
Zeta St BKLY M9.............103 C3
Zetland Av BOLS/LL BL3........64 A2
Zetland Av North BOLS/LL BL3..64 A2
Zetland Rd CCHDY M21........141 F3
Zetland St DUK SK16.........119 H4
Zinnia Dr IRL M44...........136 A3
Zion Ter SALE M33..............3 C3
Zulu St BOLE BL2..............3 K4
Zurich Gdns BRAM/HZG SK7....183 H1
Zyburn Ct SLFD M6...........111 H2

Index – featured places

AA Office CHD/CHDH SK8 ....170 B3
Abbey College Manchester
  CMANW M2.....................6 E5
Abbey Hey Primary School
  GTN M18...................130 D3
Abbey Tutorial College
  CMANE M1....................7 F4
Abbotsford Preparatory
  School URM M41............138 A1
Abbott Primary School
  NEWH/MOS M40.............115 F2
Abingdon Primary School
  RDSH SK5..................145 F4
Abraham Moss High School
  CHH M8...................102 C2
Acacias CP School
  BNG/LEV M19..............143 H4
Acorn Business Park
  EDGY/DAV SK3...............12 D4
Acorns School MPL/ROM SK6 ...175 E4
Acre Hall Primary School
  URM M41..................137 F1
Adlow Industrial Park
  WGTN/LGST M12............115 F5
Adswood Clinic
  EDGY/DAV SK3.............171 H4
Adswood Industrial Estate
  EDGY/DAV SK3.............171 G4
Adswood Primary School
  EDGY/DAV SK3.............171 G4
Adult Learning Centre
  RUSH/FAL M14.............128 B4
Agecroft Crematorium
  SWIN M27..................100 C2
Air & Space Museum CSLFD M3 ..6 C6
Al-Afifah High School for
  Girls OLDTF/WHR M16......127 F4
Albany Trading Estate
  CCHDY M21................141 F2
Albert Close Trading Estate
  WHTF M45..................69 H4
Albion Drive Clinic DROY M43 ..117 H2
The Albion High School
  BRO M7...................101 C5
Albion Road Industrial Estate
  ROCH OL11.................29 G5
Albion Trading Estate
  AUL OL6..................120 A2
  CCHDY M21................141 F2
Alder Community High
  School HYDE SK14.........149 F1
Alderley Edge CC
  WILM/AE SK9..............201 G4
Alderley Edge Golf Club
  WILM/AE SK9..............200 B2
Alderley Edge Hotel
  WILM/AE SK9..............201 E5
Alderley Edge Primary School
  WILM/AE SK9..............200 D3
Alderley Edge School for Girls
  WILM/AE SK9..............200 D3

Alderman Kay Special School
  MDTN M24..................72 D1
Alder Park CP School
  ECC M30..................110 C1
Aldwyn CP School
  DTN/ASHW M34.............118 B4
Alexandra Business Centre
  UPML OL3...................79 E5
The Alexandra Hospital
  CHD/CHDH SK8.............170 A3
Alexandra Industrial Estate
  DTN/ASHW M34.............132 D4
Alexandra Park Junior School
  EDGY/DAV SK3.............171 F2
Alexandra Retail Park OLDE OL4 ..9 H5
Alice Ingham RC Primary
  School MILN OL16............30 D1
al-jamiyah-islamiyah-
  darul-Uloom Islamic College
  EDGW/EG BL7...............23 E7
Alkrington Clinic Centre
  MDTN M24..................88 D2
Alkrington Moss Primary
  School MDTN M24...........89 E2
Alkrington Primary School
  MDTN M24..................88 D1
All Hallows RC High School
  ORD M5...................112 C2
Alliance Francaise CMANE M1 ...7 F7
All Saints Catholic College
  DUK SK16.................133 G1
All Saints CE Primary School
  FWTH BL4..................66 A3
  HTNM SK4.................159 G2
  MPL/ROM SK6..............175 H4
  NEWH/MOS M40............104 B5
  WHIT OL12.................10 E1
  WHTF M45..................69 H2
All Saints Primary School
  GTN M18..................130 A2
All Souls CE Primary School
  HEY OL10...................41 G3
All Souls RC Primary School
  ORD M5...................112 C4
Alma Industrial Estate
  WHIT OL12.................10 E3
Alma Lodge Hotel OFTN SK2 ...172 B3
Alma Park Primary School
  BNG/LEV M19..............144 A3
Alpha Court Industrial Estate
  DTN/ASHW M34.............131 H5
Alt Primary School OLDS OL8 ...92 C4
Altrincham CE Primary School
  ALT WA14.................164 A1
Altrincham College of Arts
  HALE/TIMP WA15...........166 B5
Altrincham Crematorium
  ALT WA14.................164 A1

Altrincham General Hospital
  ALT WA14.................165 F5
Altrincham Golf Club
  HALE/TIMP WA15...........166 A4
Altrincham Grammar School
  for Boys ALT WA14........177 G2
Altrincham Grammar School
  for Girls ALT WA14........177 F1
Altrincham Ice Rink ALT WA14 ..165 G3
Altrincham Industrial Centre
  ALT WA14.................164 D3
Altrincham (Kersal) RFC
  HALE/TIMP WA15...........166 D2
Altrincham Leisure Centre
  HALE/TIMP WA15...........165 H4
Altrincham Preparatory
  School ALT WA14..........177 G2
Altrincham Priory Hospital
  HALE/TIMP WA15...........178 B4
Altrincham Retail Park
  ALT WA14.................165 F2
Alvanley Industrial Estate
  EDGY/DAV SK3.............161 G2
Amalgamated Sports Club
  POY/DIS SK12.............197 G1
Ambiehurst Hotel SALE M33 ...154 B2
AMC Cinema CSLFD M5...........6 D7
Ancoats Hospital ANC M4 ......7 G1
Angel Trading Estate ANC M4 ..7 G1
Angoulme Way Retail Park
  BURY BL9....................5 F5
Ann Street Health Centre
  DTN/ASHW M34.............132 B5
Anson Medical Centre
  RUSH/FAL M14.............129 E4
Apollo Theatre
  WGTN/LGST M12...........128 D1
Aquinas College OFTN SK2 ....172 C3
Arcades Shopping Centre
  AUL OL6..................119 G2
Arcadia Sports Centre
  BNG/LEV M19..............144 A2
Arden Business Centre
  MPL/ROM SK6.............146 C5
Arden Primary School
  MPL/ROM SK6.............161 E3
Aries Printshop STLY SK15 ....108 B5
Armitage CE Primary School
  WGTN/LGST M12...........129 F2
Arndale Shopping Centre
  STRET M32................140 A2
Arrow Trading Estate
  DTN/ASHW M34.............132 A3
Arts & Craft College BURY BL9 ..4 D5
Arundale Primary School
  HYDE SK14................135 G5
Ashbury Meadow Primary
  School OP/CLY M11........116 A5

Ashdene Independant Pre
  School WILM/AE SK9.......198 C5
Ashfield Valley Primary School
  ROCH OL11..................42 D2
Ashgate Specialist Primary
  Support School
  WYTH/NTH M22............169 E5
Ash Lea School ECC M30.......111 F2
Ashton on Mersey School
  SALE M33.................154 A2
Ashton Retail Park AUL OL6 ...119 G2
Ashton Swimming Pool
  AUL OL6..................119 G2
Ashton-under-Lyne Golf Club
  AUL OL6..................107 H5
Ashton-under-Lyne RFC
  AUL OL6..................107 E5
Ashton-under-Lyne Sixth
  Form College AUL OL6......120 A1
Ashton United FC AUL OL6 ....107 G4
Ashton upon Mersey Cricket
  & Tennis Club SALE M33....139 E4
Ashton upon Mersey
  Golf Club
  SALE M33..................88 B2
Aspinal Primary School
  GTN M18..................130 D5
Astley Bridge CC BOL BL1 .....33 G2
Astra Business Park
  TRPK M17.................111 G5
Astra Industrial Centre
  ROCH OL11..................42 B3
Atlantic Business Centre
  ALT WA14.................165 F2
Atlas Trading Estate
  RDSH SK5.................145 E4
Audenshaw Primary School
  DTN/ASHW M34.............131 H1
Audenshaw School
  DTN/ASHW M34.............131 E3
Austerlands CC OLDE OL4 .....77 F4
Avenue Medical Centre
  SWIN M27..................88 B2
Aviation Viewing Park
  HALE/TIMP WA15...........189 H2
Avicenna Grammar School
  DID/WITH M20.............157 G2
Avondale Health Centre
  BOL BL1...................33 F5
Avondale High School
  EDGY/DAV SK3..............12 A7
Avondale Industrial Estate
  EDGY/DAV SK3.............171 E1
Avondale Recreation Centre
  EDGY/DAV SK3.............171 E2
Baguley Hall Primary School
  NTHM/RTH M23............167 H3
Baillie Street Health Centre
  HYDE SK14................135 G5
Balderstone Technology
  College ROCH OL11..........43 F3

Bamford Business Park
  RDSH SK5.................159 H1
Bamford Primary School
  ROCH OL11..................28 B5
Band on the Wall ANC M4 ......7 G2
Bankfield Trading Estate
  HTNM SK4.................159 H2
Bank Meadow Primary School
  WGTN/LGST M12...........115 G5
Banks Lane Infant School
  STKP SK1.................172 C1
Bare Trees J & I School
  CHAD OL9..................74 C4
Baring Street Industrial Estate
  CMANE M1....................7 K7
Barlow Hall Primary School
  DID/WITH M20.............156 B1
Barlow Medical Centre
  DID/WITH M20.............157 F3
The Barlow RC High School
  DID/WITH M20.............157 H4
Barrack Hill Primary School
  MPL/ROM SK6..............161 H4
Barrington Medical Centre
  ALT WA14.................165 G3
Barton Business Park
  ECC M30..................110 D4
Barton Clough Primary
  School
  STRET M32................125 E4
Barton Moss Community
  Primary School ECC M30 ...110 A4
Bayley Industrial Estate
  STLY SK15................120 C4
BBC North CMANE M1.........128 B1
Bealey Community Hospital
  RAD M26...................53 E5
Bealey Industrial Estate
  RAD M26...................53 E4
Beal Vale Primary School
  ROY/SHW OL2...............60 A2
Beaumont Hospital
  HOR/BR BL6................46 C1
Beaumont Primary School
  BOLS/LL BL3...............47 F4
Beaver Road Primary School
  DID/WITH M20.............157 G3
Beech House School
  ROCH OL11..................42 D1
Beech Street Primary School
  ECC M30..................110 C4
Beetham Tower CSLFD M3 ....6 E6
Beever Primary School OLD OL1 ..9 J4
The Beis Yaakov Jewish High
  School BRO M7............101 F2
Belfield Community Primary
  School MILN OL16...........11 J4
Belfield Trading Estate
  MILN OL16.................31 E2

Belford College *OLDS* OL8 .... 90 D3
Belfry House Hotel
WILM/AE SK9 .... 192 A1
Belle Vue Regional Hockey
Centre *WGTN/LGST* M12 .... 129 H4
Benchill Primary School
WYTH/NTH M22 .... 168 B3
Bentinck Street Industrial
Estate *HULME* M15 .... 127 C1
Best Western Cresta Court
Hotel *ALT* WA14 .... 165 C4
Best Western Hotel Smokies
Park *OLDS* OL8 .... 106 C2
Birches Health Centre
PWCH M25 .... 86 B1
Birchfields Primary School
RUSH/FAL M14 .... 143 C2
Birch Industrial Estate
HEY OL10 .... 55 F3
Birchinley Manor Showground
MILN OL16 .... 31 C3
Birtenshaw Hall School
EDGW/EG BL7 .... 23 C5
Birtle View Special School
HEY OL10 .... 40 C4
Bishop Bilsborrow Memorial
RC Primary School
OLDTF/WHR M16 .... 142 B1
Bishop Bridgeman CE Primary
School *BOLS/LL* BL3 .... 48 D5
B & J Leisure Centre
WILM/AE SK9 .... 198 D3
Blackbrook Trading Estate
BNG/LEV M19 .... 144 B3
Blackley Cemetery *BKLY* M9 .... 87 F3
Blackley Crematorium
BKLY M9 .... 87 F3
Blackley Golf Club *BKLY* M9 .... 89 E3
Blackshaw Lane CP School
OLD OL4 .... 59 H5
Blackshaw Primary School
BOLE BL2 .... 50 D3
Blessed Thomas Holford RC
College *HALE/TIMP* WA15 .... 165 H5
Blue Chip Business Park
ALT WA14 .... 165 E2
Blue Coat CE Primary School
OLD OL1 .... 9 H2
Bnos Yisroel Schools
BRO M7 .... 101 H3
Boarshaw Industrial Estate
MDTN M24 .... 73 E4
Boarshurst Business Park
UPML OL3 .... 95 E1
Bodmin Road Clinic
SALE M33 .... 153 C1
B of the Bang *OP/CLY* M11 ... 116 A4
Boggart Hole Clough Track
BKLY M9 .... 88 C5
Bolholt Country Park Hotel
TOT/BURYW BL8 .... 37 F2
Bollin CP School *ALT* WA14 .... 177 E3
Bolshaw Primary School
CHD/CHDH SK8 .... 181 G5
Bolton Business Centre
BOLE BL2 .... 3 G6
Bolton CC *BOLS/LL* BL3 .... 65 F2
Bolton Community College
BOLE BL2 .... 3 H6
Bolton Gates Retail Park
BOL BL1 .... 3 F2
Bolton Institute
HOR/BR BL6 .... 46 B1
Bolton Institute
BOLS/LL BL3 .... 2 C7
Bolton Little Theatre
BOL BL1 .... 2 C5
Bolton Muslim Girls School
BOLS/LL BL3 .... 48 D5
Bolton Old Links Golf Club
BOL BL1 .... 32 A3
Bolton Open Golf Club
BOLE BL2 .... 35 E3
Bolton Parish CE
Primary School *BOLE* BL2 .... 3 J4
Bolton Road Industrial Estate
WHTN BL5 .... 62 A3
Bolton Rugby Union FC
BOL BL1 .... 2 A2
Bolton School (Beech House,
Junior Department)
BOL BL1 .... 48 A2
Bolton School Girls Division
BOL BL1 .... 48 A2
Bolton School
(Junior Boys Division)
BOL BL1 .... 48 B2
Bolton School
(Senior Boys Division)
BOL BL1 .... 48 B2
Bolton Sixth Form College
North Campus *BOL* BL1 ...... 33 E2
Bond Street Industrial Estate
WGTN/LGST M12 .... 7 K7
Bonholt Industrial Estate
TOT/BURYW BL8 .... 37 F2
Booth Hall Hospital School
BKLY M9 .... 88 C4
Booth House Trading Estate
CHAD OL9 .... 8 B5
Boothstown Methodist
Primary School *WALK* M28 .... 96 A4
The Borchardt Medical Centre
DID/WITH M20 .... 142 B5
Bornmore Industrial Centre
TOT/BURYW BL8 .... 37 F2
Boundary Industrial Estate
BOLE BL2 .... 50 D2
Boundary Trading Estate
IRL M44 .... 122 D4
Bowdon CE Primary School
ALT WA14 .... 177 F3
Bowdon CC *ALT* WA14 .... 177 F5
Bowdon Preparatory School
for Girls *ALT* WA14 .... 177 F2
Bowdon RUFC
HALE/TIMP WA15 .... 166 C5
Bowdon Vale CP School
ALT WA14 .... 177 F4
Bowker Bank Industrial Park
CHH M8 .... 87 G5

Bowker Vale Primary School
CHH M8 .... 87 E3
Bowness Primary School
BOLS/LL BL3 .... 66 C1
Brabyns Recreation Centre
MPL/ROM SK6 .... 175 F2
Brabyns School
MPL/ROM SK6 .... 175 F2
Brackley Municipal Golf Club
LHULT M38 .... 80 D1
Bradley Fold Trading Estate
BOLE BL2 .... 51 F3
Bradley Green Primary School
HYDE SK14 .... 134 A2
Bradshaw CC *BOLE* BL2 .... 34 D1
Bradshaw Hall J & I School
CHD/CHDH SK8 .... 182 B3
Bradshaw Trading Estate
MDTN M24 .... 89 G2
Bramall Hall & Park
BRAM/HZG SK7 .... 183 H5
Bramall Park Golf Club
CHD/CHDH SK8 .... 183 F3
Bramall Park Lawn Tennis
Club *BRAM/HZG* SK7 .... 183 G2
Bramall Park Tennis Club
BRAM/HZG SK7 .... 183 G4
Bramhall Golf Club
BRAM/HZG SK7 .... 194 A1
Bramhall Health Centre
BRAM/HZG SK7 .... 193 H1
Bramhall High School
BRAM/HZG SK7 .... 184 A4
Bramhall Moor Industrial
Estate *BRAM/HZG* SK7 ...... 184 C2
Bramhall Park Medical Centre
BRAM/HZG SK7 .... 183 H2
Bramhall Village Shopping
Centre *BRAM/HZG* SK7 ...... 193 G1
Branwood Primary School
BOLS/LL BL3 .... 48 B5
Branwood Preparatory
School *ECC* M30 .... 111 F2
Bredbury Clinic
MPL/ROM SK6 .... 161 G2
Bredbury Green Primary
School *MPL/ROM* SK6 .... 161 G5
Bredbury Hall Hotel & Country
Club *MPL/ROM* SK6 .... 161 E4
Breeze Hill Comprehensive
School *OLDE* OL4 .... 92 C2
Breightmet FC *BOLE* BL2 ...... 50 C2
Breightmet Golf Club
BOLE BL2 .... 35 H5
Breightmet Industrial Estate
BOLE BL2 .... 50 C2
Brentnall Primary School
BRO M7 .... 101 G3
Brentwood Special School
ALT WA14 .... 165 H2
Bridge College *OFTN* SK2 .... 173 E1
Bridge Hall Primary School
EDGY/DAV SK3 .... 171 C3
Bridge House Medical Centre
BOLS/LL BL3 .... 183 E1
Bridge Mills Business Park
SLFD M6 .... 100 C5
Bridgeside Business Centre
MPL/ROM SK6 .... 146 B5
Bridge Trading Estate
TOT/BURYW BL8 .... 4 A4
Bridgewater Concert Hall
CMANE M1 .... 6 E7
Bridgewater Preparatory
School *LHULT* M38 .... 81 H3
Bridgewater School
WALK M28 .... 97 H4
Brighton Road Industrial
Estate *HTNM* SK4 .... 159 E5
Brimrod Primary School
ROCH OL11 .... 42 C1
Brindale Primary School
RDSH SK5 .... 160 D2
Brindle Heath Industrial
Estate *SLFD* M6 .... 113 E1
Brindle House Community
Mental Health Centre
HYDE SK14 .... 147 H1
Brinksway Trading Estate
HTNM SK4 .... 12 B5
Brinnington Health Centre
RDSH SK5 .... 160 D1
Briscoe Lane Primary School
NEWH/MOS M40 .... 104 A5
Britannia Business Park
BURY BL9 .... 34 C4
Britannia Mill Industrial Estate
HEY OL10 .... 40 C4
Broadbent Fold Primary
School *DUK* SK16 .... 134 B1
Broadbottom Primary School
HYDE SK14 .... 149 H3
Broadfield Industrial Estate
HEY OL10 .... 40 C5
Broadfield Primary School
MILN OL16 .... 10 C7
Broadford CC *OLDS* OL8 .... 91 G3
Broadheath Primary School
ALT WA14 .... 165 F1
Broadhurst Primary School
NEWH/MOS M40 .... 104 B3
Broadoak Business Park
TRPK M17 .... 125 E1
Broadoak High School
PART M31 .... 150 D4
Broadoak Primary School
AUL OL6 .... 107 F4
SWIN M27 .... 98 B4
Broad Oak Primary School
DID/WITH M20 .... 169 G1
Broadoak Sports Centre
AUL OL6 .... 107 F4
Broadstone Hall Primary
School *HTNM* SK4 .... 144 D5
Broadwalk Primary School
SLFD M6 .... 113 F2
Broadway Business Park
CHAD OL9 .... 89 G3
Broadway Industrial Estate
HYDE SK14 .... 133 E3

ORD M5 .... 113 F5
Brookburn Primary School
CCHDY M21 .... 141 E4
Brookdale Golf Club *FAIL* M35 .. 105 G5
Brookfield Industrial Estate
CHD/CHDH SK8 .... 170 C4
Brookhead Junior School
CHD/CHDH SK8 .... 170 C4
Brooklands Primary School
SALE M33 .... 154 B4
Brooks Bar Medical Centre
OLDTF/WHR M16 .... 6 E2
Brookside Business Park
MDTN M24 .... 89 G1
Brookside Primary School
MPL/ROM SK6 .... 196 D1
Brookway High School &
Sports College
NTHM/RTH M23 .... 167 F1
Broomwood CP School
HALE/TIMP WA15 .... 167 E4
Broughton CC *BRO* M7 .... 101 G4
Broughton CE *BRO* M7 .... 101 F4
Broughton Jewish Cassel-Fox
Primary School *BRO* M7 ..... 101 G2
Brownhill Countryside Centre
UPML OL3 .... 78 D3
Brownhill Special School
WHIT OL12 .... 10 B3
Brownlow Business Centre
BOL BL1 .... 33 G5
Brownlow Fold Community
Learning Centre *BOL* BL1 .... 33 G5
Brownlow Fold Primary
School *BOL* BL1 .... 33 G5
Brunswick Health Centre
BRUN/LGST M13 .... 128 C2
Bruntwood Primary School
CHD/CHDH SK8 .... 182 B2
Buckley Road Industrial
Estate *WHIT* OL12 .... 30 C1
Buckstones Primary School
ROY/SHW OL2 .... 60 C1
Buckton Vale Primary School
STLY SK15 .... 109 G3
Buile Hill High School
SLFD M6 .... 112 C1
Bullough Moor Primary
School *HEY* OL10 .... 40 B4
Burgess Primary School
BKLY M9 .... 103 F3
Burnage High School
For Boys *BNG/LEV* M19 ...... 158 C1
Burnage Rugby Club
HTNM SK4 .... 158 B5
Burnden Industrial Estate
BOLS/LL BL3 .... 49 G5
Burnley Brow Community
School *CHAD* OL9 .... 74 D3
Burrs Country Park
TOT/BURYW BL9 .... 27 E5
Bury Athenaeum *BURY* BL9 .... 4 D3
Bury Business Centre *BURY* BL9 .. 5 H1
Bury Catholic Preparatory
School *BURY* BL9 .... 53 F1
Bury CE High School *BURY* BL9 .. 53 F1
Bury Cemetery *BURY* BL9 ...... 53 G2
Bury College *BURY* BL9 .... 4 D6
Bury County Court *BURY* BL9 .. 4 B5
Bury FC (Gigg Lane) *BURY* BL9 .. 53 G2
Bury Grammar School (Boys)
BURY BL9 .... 4 B5
Bury Industrial Estate
BOLE BL2 .... 50 C1
Bury Market *BURY* BL9 .... 4 E5
Bury Sports Club *BURY* BL9 ... 53 F1
Bury & Whitefield Jewish
Primary School *BURY* BL9 ... 70 A1
Business & Arts Centre
PWCH M25 .... 85 H5
Button Lane School
NTHM/RTH M23 .... 155 G4
Byron Street Infant
Community School
ROY/SHW OL2 .... 59 F5
Cadishead Recreation Centre
IRL M44 .... 150 C1
Caius House School
WHIT OL12 .... 28 C2
Caldershaw Primary School
EDGY/DAV SK3 .... 171 H2
Camberwell Park School
BKLY M9 .... 87 H3
Cambrian Business Park
BOLS/LL BL3 .... 48 C4
Cambridge Industrial Estate
BRO M7 .... 114 B1
Campanile Hotel *ORD* M5 .... 113 H5
Cams Lane Primary School
RAD M26 .... 68 A1
Canalside Industrial Estate
MILN OL16 .... 43 G1
Canon Burrows CE Primary
School *AULW* OL7 .... 106 C5
Canon Johnson CE Primary
School *AULW* OL7 .... 119 G1
Canon Slade School *BOLE* BL2 .. 34 C2
Capital Business Centre
BRAM/HZG SK7 .... 193 G1
Cardinal Langley RC High
School *MDTN* M24 .... 57 F5
Cariocca Business Park
NEWH/MOS M40 .... 115 H2
WGTN/LGST M12 .... 129 E2
Carlton Industrial Centre
BOLE BL2 .... 3 G6
Carrbrook Industrial Estate
STLY SK15 .... 109 H4
Carrington Business Park
PART M31 .... 137 G5
Castlebrook High School
BURY BL9 .... 70 B1
Castlefield Gallery *CNLD* M3 .... 6 C7
Castle Hawk Golf Club
ROCH OL11 .... 41 H5

Castle Hill Primary School
BOLE BL2 .... 34 C4
Cas... Hill School *RDSH* SK5 .. 146 A5
Castle Leisure Centre
BURY BL9 .... 4 C4
Castle Park Industrial Estate
OLD OL1 .... 76 A5
Castleton Swimming Pool
ROCH OL11 .... 42 C4
Cathedral Gardens *ANC* M4 ...... 6 E2
Cavendish Industrial Estate
AUL OL6 .... 119 F2
Cavendish Road Primary
School *DID/WITH* M20 .... 157 F1
Central Art Gallery
AUL OL6 .... 119 G3
Central Industrial Estate
BOLS/LL BL3 .... 49 E4
MDTN M24 .... 72 D4
Central Leisure Centre
MILN OL16 .... 10 E6
Central Primary School
DTN/ASHW M34 .... 132 B5
Central Retail Park *ANC* M4 ...... 7 G2
Century Mill Industrial Estate
FWTH BL4 .... 65 G4
Chadderton AFC *CHAD* OL9 ..... 74 C4
Chadderton Cemetery
CHAD OL9 .... 74 B2
Chadderton Hall Junior School
CHAD OL9 .... 74 B2
Chadderton Industrial Estate
MDTN M24 .... 89 F2
Chadderton Shopping
Precinct *CHAD* OL9 .... 74 C4
Chadderton Sports Centre &
Public Baths *CHAD* OL9 ...... 74 C5
Chadderton Town Health
Centre *CHAD* OL9 .... 74 C5
Chadkirk Industrial Estate
MPL/ROM SK6 .... 174 A1
Chantlers Primary School
TOT/BURYW BL8 .... 37 F4
Chapelfield Primary School
RAD M26 .... 68 D5
Chapel Medical Centre
IRL M44 .... 136 C1
Chapel Street Primary School
BNG/LEV M19 .... 144 B2
Charlestown Industrial Estate
AULW OL7 .... 119 G1
Charlestown Health Centre
BKLY M9 .... 88 D5
Charlestown Primary School
BKLY M9 .... 89 E4
SLFD M6 .... 113 G1
Cheadle Catholic Primary
School *CHD/CHDH* SK8 ...... 182 B2
Cheadle CC *CHD/CHDH* SK8 .. 169 H4
Cheadle Golf Club
CHD/CHDH SK8 .... 170 B5
Cheadle Heath Clinic
EDGY/DAV SK3 .... 170 D1
Cheadle Heath Primary School
EDGY/DAV SK3 .... 170 D1
Cheadle Heath Sports Centre
CHD/CHDH SK8 .... 170 D3
Cheadle Hulme High School
CHD/CHDH SK8 .... 183 E5
Cheadle Hulme Recreation
Centre *CHD/CHDH* SK8 ...... 183 E5
Cheadle Hulme School
CHD/CHDH SK8 .... 182 D5
Cheadle & Marple Sixth Form
College *CHD/CHDH* SK8 ..... 182 B1
Cheadle Primary School
CHD/CHDH SK8 .... 170 A3
Cheadle Royal Business Park
CHD/CHDH SK8 .... 181 H1
Cheadle Royal Hospital
CHD/CHDH SK8 .... 181 H2
Cheadle Royal Shopping
Centre *CHD/CHDH* SK8 ...... 182 A2
Cheadle Swimming &
Recreation Centre
CHD/CHDH SK8 .... 170 B5
Cheadle Town FC
CHD/CHDH SK8 .... 170 B4
Cheetham CE Community
School *BRO* M7 .... 102 A3
Cheetham Hill CC *CHH* M8 .... 101 H1
Cheetwood Community &
Sports Centre *BRO* M7 ...... 102 A4
Cheetwood Primary School
CHH M8 .... 114 B1
Cherry Manor Primary School
SALE M33 .... 153 F4
Cherry Tree Hospital
OFTN SK2 .... 172 D4
Cherry Tree Primary School
FWTH BL4 .... 64 D4
Chesham Industrial Estate
BURY BL9 .... 38 D2
Chesham Primary School
BURY BL9 .... 27 G1
Chester Court Hotel
STRET M32 .... 126 C4
Chethams Library & Music
School *CSLFD* M3 .... 6 E2
Chichester Business Centre
MILN OL16 .... 11 F7
Child Health Clinic *MDTN* M24 .. 72 C3
Chinese Medical Centre
CSLFD M3 .... 6 C6
Chorlton CE Primary School
CCHDY M21 .... 141 E3
Chorlton-cum-Hardy CC
CCHDY M21 .... 141 F5
Chorlton-cum-Hardy Golf Club
CCHDY M21 .... 156 B1
Chorlton High School
CCHDY M21 .... 141 F2
Chorlton Leisure Centre
CCHDY M21 .... 141 F2

Chorlton Park Primary
School *CCHDY* M21 .... 141 G4
Chorlton Shopping Centre
CCHDY M21 .... 141 G2
Chorlton Water Park
CCHDY M21 .... 156 B2
Christchurch Ainsworth CE
Primary School *BOLE* BL2 .... 36 B5
Christ Church CE Primary
School *ECC* M30 .... 90 B1
Christchurch CE Primary
School *ECC* M30 .... 110 D3
TOT/BURYW BL8 .... 37 F2
Christie Hospital &
Holt Radium Institute
DID/WITH M20 .... 142 D5
Christie Street Industrial
Estate *STKP* SK1 .... 13 J7
Christs Church CE Primary
School *BOLE* BL2 .... 35 G4
Christ the King RC Primary
School *NEWH/MOS* M40 ...... 104 B5
WALK M28 .... 82 B5
Christ the King School
SALE M33 .... 154 A3
Church Road Primary School
BOL BL1 .... 32 D4
Church Street Industrial Estate
MDTN M24 .... 72 D2
Cineworld *BOL* BL1 .... 34 B3
DID/WITH M20 .... 158 A5
STKP SK1 .... 13 H2
City Centre Campus *CSLFD* M3 .. 6 B4
City College Manchester
CHH M8 .... 102 C2
DID/WITH M20 .... 157 E2
NTHM/RTH M23 .... 156 B5
NTHM/RTH M23 .... 167 E1
NTHM/RTH M23 .... 167 G1
City Course Trading Estate
OP/CLY M11 .... 129 H1
City Court Trading Estate
ANC M4 .... 7 K2
City Park Business Village
OLDTF/WHR M16 .... 127 E3
Claremont Primary School
RUSH/FAL M14 .... 128 B5
Clarendon Cottage School
ECC M30 .... 111 G2
Clarendon CP School
BOLS/LL BL3 .... 48 D4
Clarendon Fields Primary
School *DUK* SK16 .... 119 G5
Clarendon Industrial Estate
HYDE SK14 .... 133 H5
Clarendon Road Primary
School *ECC* M30 .... 111 G2
Clarendon Square Shopping
Centre *HYDE* SK14 .... 147 H1
Clarke Industrial Estate
STRET M32 .... 125 F4
Clarksfield Primary School
OLDE OL4 .... 92 B1
Clayton Health Centre
OP/CLY M11 .... 116 C3
Clayton Industrial Estate
OP/CLY M11 .... 130 C1
Cleavley Athletics Track
ECC M30 .... 110 B2
Cleggs Lane Industrial Site
LHULT M38 .... 81 G1
Clevelands Preparatory School
BOL BL1 .... 47 H2
Clifton Country Park
SWIN M27 .... 83 H2
Clifton Industrial Estate
SWIN M27 .... 84 D4
Clifton Primary School
SWIN M27 .... 84 D4
Cloughside School *PWCH* M25 .. 85 G2
Cloverlea Primary School
HALE/TIMP WA15 .... 166 C4
The Club Theatre *ALT* WA14 .. 177 C1
Cobden Mill Industrial Estate
FWTH BL4 .... 65 G3
Coldhurst Community Centre
OLD OL1 .... 8 E1
Coldhurst Industrial Estate
OLD OL1 .... 9 F1
Coliseum Theatre *OLD* OL1 .... 9 J3
Collegiate Medical Centre
CHH M8 .... 102 B3
Comfort Inn *WGTN/LGST* M12 .. 128 B4
Commonwealth House
MANAIR M90 .... 180 A4
Community Hall *STLY* SK15 ... 120 D3
Concord Business Centre
WYTH/NTH M22 .... 180 D3
Constellation Trading Estate
RAD M26 .... 52 A3
Co-operative College *ANC* M4 .. 7 F3
Co-operative Museum
WHIT OL12 .... 10 B5
Copley High School *STLY* SK15 .. 121 G3
Copper Beeches School
SALE M33 .... 154 A2
Coppice Industrial Estate
OLDS OL8 .... 8 C6
Coppice J & I School
OLDS OL8 .... 91 F3
Copthorne Hotel *SALQ* M50 .. 126 D2
Cornbrook School
HULME M15 .... 127 G1
Cornerhouse Cinema
CMANE M1 .... 7 F7
Cornishway Industrial Estate
WYTH/NTH M22 .... 180 C4
Cornwall Street Industrial
Estate *OP/CLY* M11 .... 130 C1
Corpus Christi RC Primary
School *CHAD* OL9 .... 74 C5
Corpus Christi with St Anne RC
Primary School *ANC* M4 ..... 115 G4
Corrie Primary School
DTN/ASHW M34 .... 146 D2
Counthill School *OLDE* OL4 .... 76 C2
County End Business Centre
OLDE OL4 .... 77 E5
Covenant Christian School
HTNM SK4 .... 159 G2

Crab Lane Primary School
BKLY M9 .... 87 G3
Cravenwood Primary School
CHH M8 .... 102 A2
Crescent Community High
School For Girls
RUSH/FAL M14 .... 129 E5
Croft Industrial Estate
BKLY M9 .... 53 H4
Cromer Industrial Estate
MDTN M24 .... 73 E3
Cromford Business Park
OLD OL1 .... 76 A4
Crompton CC ROY/SHW OL2 .... 60 A1
Crompton Fold Primary
School BOLE BL2 .... 50 B2
Crompton Health Centre
ROY/SHW OL2 .... 60 A3
Crompton House CE School
ROY/SHW OL2 .... 59 G2
Crompton Place Shopping
Centre BOL BL1 .... 2 E5
Crompton Primary School
ROY/SHW OL2 .... 60 A3
Crompton & Royton Golf Club
ROY/SHW OL2 .... 59 G4
Crompton Swimming Pool
ROY/SHW OL2 .... 60 A3
Cromwell High School
DUK SK16 .... 133 H2
Cromwell House Community
Mental Health Centre
ECC M30 .... 111 E3
Cromwell Special School
RDSH SK5 .... 145 F1
Crosland Industrial Estate
MPL/ROM SK6 .... 161 F2
Crossacres Primary School
WYTH/NTH M22 .... 169 E5
Crossgates Primary School
MILN OL16 .... 31 H4
Crossley Primary School
BKLY M9 .... 88 D3
Crowcroft Park Primary
School WGTN/LGST M12 .... 129 H5
Crown Business Centre
FAIL M35 .... 105 E2
Crown Industrial Estate
ALT WA14 .... 165 H2
ANC M4 .... 7 K2
Crown Royal Industrial Park
STKP SK1 .... 13 H5
Crumpsall Lane Primary
School CHH M8 .... 102 B1
Culcheth Hall School
ALT WA14 .... 177 F1
Curzon Ashton FC
AULW OL7 .... 119 E3
Curzon Cinema URM M41 .... 124 A4
Cutgate Shopping Precinct
WHIT OL12 .... 29 E2
Dagenham Road Industrial
Estate RUSH/FAL M14 .... 128 D5
Daisy Nook Country Park
OLDS OL8 .... 106 B3
Dale Grove Primary School
(Bankside) HYDE SK14 .... 148 B2
Dale Grove Special School
AULW OL7 .... 6 A4
The Dale Primary School
MPL/ROM SK6 .... 174 C2
Dale Street Industrial Estate
RAD M26 .... 68 B2
Dancehouse Theatre &
Northern Ballet School
CMANE M1 .... 128 B1
Dane Bank Primary School
RDSH SK5 .... 145 G1
Dane Road Industrial Estate
SALE M33 .... 154 D1
Darnhill CP School HEY OL10 ...... 40 A5
Darul Uloom Al Arabiya Al
Islamia TOT/BURYW BL8 .... 16 B4
Davaar Medical Centre
DUK SK16 .... 119 H5
Davenport Golf Club
POY/DIS SK12 .... 196 A3
David Cuthbert Business
Centre OP/CLY M11 .... 130 B1
David Lloyd Fitness Centre
BOL BL1 .... 2 B4
David Medical Centre
CCHDY M21 .... 141 G5
Davyhulme J & I School
URM M41 .... 124 C5
Davyhulme Park Golf Club
URM M41 .... 123 G4
Deakins Business Park
EDGW/EG BL7 .... 22 C1
Deane Golf Club BOLS/LL BL3 ..... 47 H4
Deane Leisure Centre
BOLS/LL BL3 .... 47 G5
Dean Lane Medical Centre
NEWH/MOS M40 .... 185 E4
Dean Row Community Junior
School WILM/AE SK9 .... 199 H1
The Deans CP School
SWIN M27 .... 98 C2
Deans Road Industrial Estate
SWIN M27 .... 98 C2
Deanway Trading Estate
WILM/AE SK9 .... 192 A4
Deeplish Primary School
ROCH OL11 .... 43 F1
Delamere School URM M41 .... 137 F1
Delta Business Park
DTN/ASHW M34 .... 132 B1
Denton Cemetery
DTN/ASHW M34 .... 146 D3
Denton Cricket & Sports Club
DTN/ASHW M34 .... 132 B3
Denton Golf Club
DTN/ASHW M34 .... 131 G4
Denton St Lawrence CC
DTN/ASHW M34 .... 146 D1
Denton West End Primary
School DTN/ASHW M34 .... 131 F5
Department of Clinical
Psychology ROY/SHW OL2 .... 75 F2
Derby High School BURY BL9 ...... 53 E1

Derby Shopping Centre
BOLS/LL BL3 .... 48 C4
Derwent Street Trading
Estate ORD M5 .... 127 F1
The Designer Outlet
SALO M50 .... 126 C1
Devonshire Road Primary
School BOL BL1 .... 47 H1
Devonshire Street Industrial
Estate WGTN/LGST M12 .... 129 E2
Dial Park Primary School
OFTN SK2 .... 173 F5
Diamond Lodge GTN M18 .... 130 A3
Didsbury CC
DID/WITH M20 .... 157 H5
Didsbury CE Primary School
DID/WITH M20 .... 157 G3
Didsbury Golf Club
WYTH/NTH M22 .... 157 E5
Didsbury Medical Centre
DID/WITH M20 .... 157 F2
Didsbury Road Primary
School HTNM SK4 .... 158 C4
Didsbury School
DID/WITH M20 .... 157 G2
Disley Golf Club
POY/DIS SK12 .... 187 H5
Disley Primary School
POY/DIS SK12 .... 187 F5
Doffcocker Lodge Nature
Reserve BOL BL1 .... 32 B5
Downing Street Industrial
Estate WGTN/LGST M12 .... 128 C1
Dowry Park Industrial Estate
OLDE OL4 .... 76 D5
Dowson Primary School
DUK SK16 .... 148 A3
Droylsden AFC DROY M43 .... 117 H4
Droylsden High School for
Girls DROY M43 .... 117 F3
Droylsden Sports Centre
DROY M43 .... 117 F3
Droylsden Swimming Pool
DROY M43 .... 117 H5
Ducie Athletics Ground
Running Track
WGTN/LGST M12 .... 130 A4
Ducie High School
RUSH/FAL M14 .... 128 B4
Ducie Sports Centre
HULME M15 .... 128 C4
Dukesgate Primary School
LHULT M38 .... 81 F2
Dukinfield Crematorium
DUK SK16 .... 120 A4
Dukinfield Golf Club
DUK SK16 .... 134 B1
Dukinfield Joint Cemetery
DUK SK16 .... 120 A4
Dunham Forest Golf &
Country Club ALT WA14 .... 164 C5
Dunham Massey (NT)
ALT WA14 .... 176 A1
Dunscar Golf Club
EDGW/EG BL7 .... 22 C3
Dunscar Industrial Estate
EDGW/EG BL7 .... 22 D4
Durnford Medical Centre
MDTN M24 .... 72 C3
Durn Street Industrial Estate
LIT OL15 .... 21 F2
Eagley Infant School
EDGW/EG BL7 .... 23 F5
Eagley Junior School
EDGW/EG BL7 .... 23 G5
East Crompton St Georges CE
Primary School
ROY/SHW OL2 .... 60 B2
East Crompton St James CE
Primary School
ROY/SHW OL2 .... 60 A2
East Lancashire Railway
BURY BL9 .... 5 H7
BURY BL9 .... 27 E3
BURY BL9 .... 54 D1
RAMS BL0 .... 16 D3
East Ward Primary School
BURY BL9 .... 5 K4
Eaton Place Business Centre
SALE M33 .... 154 B2
Eccles Crematorium ECC M30 ... 110 A5
Eccles Health Centre
ECC M30 .... 111 G3
Eccles Recreation Centre
ECC M30 .... 111 G4
Eccles Town Hall ECC M30 .... 111 G3
Edge Fold Industrial Estate
FWTH BL4 .... 64 B3
Egerton & Dunscar Health
Centre EDGW/EG BL7 .... 23 E3
Egerton High School
URM M41 .... 124 D4
Egerton House Hotel
EDGW/EG BL7 .... 22 D1
Egerton Park Arts College
DTN/ASHW M34 .... 132 B3
Egerton Park Community High
School WILM/AE SK9 .... 199 H1
Elk Mill Central Retail Park
OLD OL1 .... 74 C1
Ellenbrook Primary School
WALK M28 .... 96 C3
Ellesmere Bowling & Tennis
Club WALK M28 .... 97 E2
Ellesmere Golf Club
WALK M28 .... 97 G1
Ellesmere Retail Park
WALK M28 .... 81 H4
Ellesmere Shopping Centre
LHULT M38 .... 81 H4
Elmridge Primary School
HALE/TIMP WA15 .... 178 D4
Elms Bank Community High
School WHTF M45 .... 69 G1
Elms Medical Centre
BURY BL9 .... 69 F3
Elm Wood Primary School
WHTF M45 .... 75 F4
Elsinore Business Centre
OLDTF/WHR M16 .... 126 D4
The Elton Primary School
TOT/BURYW BL8 .... 37 F3

Elton Primary School
TOT/BURYW BL8 .... 37 H3
Emmanuel Christian School
WHIT OL12 .... 10 A2
Emmanuel Holcombe Primary
School TOT/BURYW BL8 .... 16 B2
Empress Business Centre
OLDTF/WHR M16 .... 127 F2
English Martyrs RC Primary
School URM M41 .... 138 C1
Enterprise Trading Centre
GTN M18 .... 130 D2
TRPK M17 .... 111 H5
Esplanade Arts & Heritage
Centre ROCH OL11 .... 10 B7
Estcourt Preparatory School
OLDS OL8 .... 91 E3
Etchells Primary School
CHD/CHDH SK8 .... 181 H3
Eton Hill Industrial Estate
RAD M26 .... 52 D4
Etrop Grange Hotel
MANAIR M90 .... 180 A3
Etz Chaim School
CHH M8 .... 86 D5
Europa Business Park
EDGY/DAV SK3 .... 171 F5
Europa Trading Estate
RAD M26 .... 67 E5
Ewing School DID/WITH M20 .. 157 F1
Express by Holiday Inn
SALO M50 .... 126 C1
Express Trading Estate
FWTH BL4 .... 82 A1
The Eye Clinic CMANW M2 .... 6 E5
Fahay Industrial Estate
NEWH/MOS M40 .... 115 H3
Failsworth Health Centre
FAIL M35 .... 104 D3
Failsworth Industrial Estate
FAIL M35 .... 104 B4
Failsworth Shopping Centre
FAIL M35 .... 105 E2
Fairfield Community Primary
School BURY BL9 .... 39 G3
Fairfield General Hospital
BURY BL9 .... 39 H2
Fairfield Golf & Sailing Club
DTN/ASHW M34 .... 131 G1
Fairfield High School for Girls
DROY M43 .... 117 G5
Fairfield Road Primary School
DROY M43 .... 117 G5
Fairhill Industrial Estate
IRL M44 .... 136 B4
Fairview Medical Centre
URM M41 .... 138 D1
Fairway Primary School
OFTN SK2 .... 173 F2
Fairways Lodge PWCH M25 .... 101 E1
Falinge Park High School
WHIT OL12 .... 29 G2
Fallowfield Medical Centre
RUSH/FAL M14 .... 143 F3
Fallowfield Shopping Centre
RUSH/FAL M14 .... 143 G2
Farjo Medical Centre
CMANE M1 .... 7 G5
Farnworth Cemetery
FWTH BL4 .... 66 B3
Farnworth Leisure Centre
FWTH BL4 .... 66 A4
Farnworth Little Theatre
FWTH BL4 .... 66 A4
Farnworth Park Industrial
Estate FWTH BL4 .... 66 A3
Farnworth Social Circle CC
FWTH BL4 .... 65 H5
Farrowdale House School
ROY/SHW OL2 .... 60 A3
Fiddlers Lane Primary School
IRL M44 .... 122 C5
Fieldhouse School ROCH OL11 ... 28 B5
Fieldhouse Industrial Estate
WHIT OL12 .... 10 D1
Firbank Primary School
ROY/SHW OL2 .... 59 E2
Firgrove Business Park
MILN OL16 .... 31 E3
Firs CP School SALE M33 .... 153 G2
Fir Tree Primary School
RDSH SK5 .... 145 E1
Firwood Industrial Estate
BOLE BL2 .... 34 A4
Firwood Manor Preparatory
School CHAD OL9 .... 74 C3
Firwood Special School
BOLE BL2 .... 34 D4
Fishbrook Industrial Estate
FWTH BL4 .... 66 C5
Fishpool Infant School
BURY BL9 .... 53 G1
Fishwick Hill Shopping Centre
OLDS OL8 .... 91 G4
Five Fold Industrial Park
CHAD OL9 .... 8 D4
Flixton CC URM M41 .... 137 E5
Flixton FC URM M41 .... 123 E5
Flixton Girls High School
URM M41 .... 138 A1
Flixton Golf Club URM M41 ...... 138 A3
Flixton Health Clinic
URM M41 .... 137 F1
Flixton J & I School
URM M41 .... 137 H1
Flowery Field Primary School
HYDE SK14 .... 133 G4
Forest Gate Community
Primary School PART M31 .... 150 C3
Forest Park School SALE M33 ... 154 B2
Forest School
HALE/TIMP WA15 .... 166 A3
Forge Industrial Estate
OLDE OL4 .... 76 A5
Forum Leisure Centre
WYTH/NTH M22 .... 180 B1
Fourways Trading Estate
TRPK M17 .... 125 F2
Freehold Community Primary
School CHAD OL9 .... 8 A6

Freetown Business Park
BURY BL9 .... 5 G1
The Friars Primary School
CSLFD M3 .... 6 A1
Friezland Primary School
OLDE OL4 .... 94 B2
Fulshaw CE Primary School
WILM/AE SK9 .... 198 C4
Furrow Community School
MDTN M24 .... 71 H1
Galleon Leisure Centre
DID/WITH M20 .... 169 H1
Gallery of Costume
RUSH/FAL M14 .... 143 E1
Gallery Oldham, Library &
Lifelong Learning Centre
OLDE OL1 .... 9 H4
Garrick Playhouse ALT WA14 .. 165 G3
Garrick Theatre
EDGY/DAV SK3 .... 13 F4
Gaskell Primary School BOL BL1 .. 2 B2
The Gates Primary School
WHTN BL5 .... 62 A2
The Gates Shopping Centre
BOL BL1 .... 2 E4
Gateway Industrial Estate
CMANE M1 .... 7 J5
Gatley Golf Club
CHD/CHDH SK8 .... 181 G1
Gatley Health Centre
CHD/CHDH SK8 .... 169 F3
Gatley Primary School
CHD/CHDH SK8 .... 169 F4
Gee Cross Holy Trinity CE
Primary School HYDE SK14 ...... 148 B3
Gee Cross Social & Sports
Club HYDE SK14 .... 148 A3
George H Carnall Leisure
Centre URM M41 .... 124 D4
George Tomlinson School
FWTH BL4 .... 82 B1
Georgian Health Centre
OLD OL1 .... 9 H3
Gilnow Mill Industrial Estate
BOL BL1 .... 48 B3
Gilnow Primary School
BOL BL1 .... 48 B2
Glebe House School
ALT WA14 .... 29 H5
Glen Trading Estate OLDE OL4 .. 92 C1
Globe Industrial Estate
RAD M26 .... 66 D4
Globe Lane Industrial Estate
DUK SK16 .... 133 E1
Globe Lane Primary School
DUK SK16 .... 133 E2
Glodwick Health Centre
OLDE OL4 .... 92 A1
Glodwick Infant School
OLDE OL4 .... 92 A2
Gloucester House Medical
Centre WGTN/LGST M12 .... 129 H2
GMB National College
OLDTF/WHR M16 .... 141 G1
Godfrey Ermen Memorial CE
Primary School ECC M30 .... 110 D5
Godley CP School
HYDE SK14 .... 134 A5
Golden Tulip Hotel TRPK M17 .. 124 A5
Gorells Industrial Estate
ROCH OL11 .... 42 D3
Gorsefield Primary School
RAD M26 .... 52 B5
Gorse Hall Primary School
STLY SK15 .... 120 C4
Gorse Hill Health Centre
STRET M32 .... 126 B5
Gorse Hill Primary School
STRET M32 .... 126 B5
Gorsey Bank Primary School
WILM/AE SK9 .... 198 C5
Gorton Brook First School
WGTN/LGST M12 .... 129 H2
Gorton Industrial Estate
GTN M18 .... 130 B2
Gorton Medical Centre
GTN M18 .... 130 C3
Gorton Mount Primary
School GTN M18 .... 130 A5
Gorton Retail Market
MPL/ROM SK6 .... 161 H4
Goshen Sports Centre
BURY BL9 .... 53 H3
Grafton House Preparatory
School AUL OL6 .... 119 G3
Granada Studios CSLFD M3 .... 6 A6
Grange Primary School
WILM/AE SK9 .... 191 H3
Grange School CHAD OL9 .... 8 A2
RUSH/FAL M14 .... 129 E5
Grasscroft Independent
School OLDE OL4 .... 93 H2
Great Moor Infant School
OFTN SK2 .... 172 C4
Greater Manchester Police
Headquarters
OLDTF/WHR M16 .... 141 H1
Great Moor Infant OFTN SK2 .. 172 D4
Great Moor Infant School
OFTN SK2 .... 172 C4
Great Northern Shopping &
Leisure Centre CSLFD M3 .... 6 D6
Greave Primary School
MPL/ROM SK6 .... 162 B2
Greenacres Primary School
OLDE OL4 .... 77 E4
Greenbank Primary School
CHD/CHDH SK8 .... 182 C5
Greenbrow Infant School
NTHM/RTH M23 .... 179 G1
Greencourts Business Park
WYTH/NTH M22 .... 181 F5
Green End Junior School
BNG/LEV M19 .... 158 B1
Greenfield CC UPML OL3 .... 95 E2
Greenfield Primary School
UPML OL3 .... 95 E1

Green Fold Special School
FWTH BL4 .... 65 E4
Greengate Industrial Estate
MDTN M24 .... 89 F2
Greenheys Business Centre
HULME M15 .... 128 B3
Greenhill Primary School
OLDE OL4 .... 9 H6
TOT/BURYW BL8 .... 37 E5
Green Lane Industrial Estate
HTNM SK4 .... 12 B2
Greenmount CC
TOT/BURYW BL8 .... 26 A2
Greenmount Primary School
TOT/BURYW BL8 .... 25 H1
Green Room Theatre
CMANE M1 .... 6 E7
Greenside Primary School
DROY M43 .... 117 G3
Greenside Trading Centre
DROY M43 .... 117 H4
Greenwood Business Centre
ORD M5 .... 113 F4
Greenwood Primary School
ECC M30 .... 111 F1
Creswell Primary School
DTN/ASHW M34 .... 146 C1
Greyhound & Speedway
Stadium GTN M18 .... 130 A3
Greyland Medical Centre
PWCH M25 .... 86 A1
Griffin Business Centre
SLFD M6 .... 101 F5
Grosvenor Business Park
MPL/ROM SK6 .... 146 D5
Grosvenor Industrial Estate
AULW OL7 .... 119 F4
Grosvenor Road Primary
School SWIN M27 .... 99 G4
Guardian Angels RC Primary
School TOT/BURYW BL8 .... 37 G3
Guide Bridge Industrial Estate
AULW OL7 .... 118 D5
Guide Bridge Theatre
DTN/ASHW M34 .... 118 C5
Guide Bridge Trading Estate
DTN/ASHW M34 .... 118 C5
Guinness Road Trading Estate
TRPK M17 .... 111 G5
Hale Barns CC
HALE/TIMP WA15 .... 179 F4
Hale Golf Club
HALE/TIMP WA15 .... 178 B5
Hale Preparatory School
HALE/TIMP WA15 .... 177 H1
Halfpenny Bridge Industrial
Estate MILN OL16 .... 30 B5
Hall i' th' Wood Museum
BOL BL1 .... 33 J1
Halliwell Industrial Estate
BOL BL1 .... 33 G3
Hamer CP School MILN OL16 ...... 11 H1
Hampson Street Trading
Estate ORD M5 .... 114 A4
Handforth Dean Shopping
Centre WILM/AE SK9 .... 192 B3
Handforth Health Centre
WILM/AE SK9 .... 192 A4
Hanover Business Park
ALT WA14 .... 165 E2
Harcourt Industrial Centre
WALK M28 .... 82 A2
Hardman Fold Special School
FAIL M35 .... 104 C3
Hardy Mill Primary School
BOLE BL2 .... 35 G2
Harper Green School
FWTH BL4 .... 65 G5
Harp Industrial Estate
ROCH OL11 .... 42 C4
Harp Trading Estate
TRPK M17 .... 111 H5
Harpurhey Business Centre
BKLY M9 .... 103 E1
Harpurhey Health Centre
BKLY M9 .... 103 E2
Harpur Mount Primary School
BKLY M9 .... 103 E2
Harrop Fold School WALK M28 .. 81 G4
Harrytown Catholic High
School CHAD OL9 .... 8 B5
Hartshead High School
AUL OL6 .... 107 H3
Harwood Golf Club (Bolton)
BOLE BL2 .... 35 H2
Harwood Health Centre
BOLE BL2 .... 35 G2
Harwood Meadows Primary
School BOLE BL2 .... 35 G3
Harwood Park Primary School
HEY OL10 .... 41 E5
Haslam Park Primary School
BOLS/LL BL3 .... 48 A4
Hathershaw Technology
College OLDS OL8 .... 91 G5
Hattersley Health Clinic
HYDE SK14 .... 149 G1
Hattersley Industrial Estate
HYDE SK14 .... 149 G2
Hat Works Museum
EDGY/DAV SK3 .... 13 F3
Haveley Hey Primary School
WYTH/NTH M22 .... 168 B5
Hawkins Clinic MILN OL16 .... 10 D7
Hawksley Industrial Estate
OLDS OL8 .... 90 D4
Hawthorns Special School
DTN/ASHW M34 .... 132 A3
Hayward School
BOLS/LL BL3 .... 64 B2
Hayward Sports Centre
BOLS/LL BL3 .... 64 B2
Hazeldene Medical Centre
NEWH/MOS M40 .... 104 D1
Hazel Grove Clinic
BRAM/HZG SK7 .... 185 F1
Hazel Grove Golf Club
BRAM/HZG SK7 .... 186 A3

Hazel Grove High School
BRAM/HZG SK7 .....184 D3
Hazel Grove Pools & Fitness
Centre BRAM/HZG SK7 .....184 B3
Hazel Grove Primary School
BRAM/HZG 185 F1
Hazel Grove Recreation
Centre BRAM/HZG SK7 .....184 D4
Hazlehurst Community
Primary School RAMS BL0 .....16 B4
Heald Green Medical Centre
CHD/CHDH SK8 .....181 G4
Heald Place Primary School
RUSH/FAL M14 .....128 C5
Healey Dell Nature Reserve
WHIT OL12 .....18 A4
Healey Primary School
WHIT OL12 .....18 D5
Heap Bridge Primary School
BURY BL9 .....39 G5
Heathfield Primary School
BOLS/LL BL3 .....63 H2
Heaton CC BOL BL1 .....32 D4
Heaton Cemetery BOL BL1 .....48 A3
Heaton Medical Centre
BOL BL1 .....32 C5
Heaton Moor Golf Club 158 D1
Heaton Moor Medical Centre
HTNM SK4 .....159 E1
Heaton Moor RUFC
HTNM SK4 .....159 E1
Heaton Norris Health Centre
HTNM SK4 .....159 G3
Heaton Park PWCH M25 .....86 D2
Heaton Park Golf Centre
PWCH M25 .....86 D1
Heaton Park Primary School
WHTF M45 .....86 A1
Heaton Special School
HTNM SK4 .....159 E1
Helen O'Grady Drama
Academy
ALT WA14 .....165 F5
Hempshaw Business Centre
STKP SK1 .....172 C2
Henshaw Society for the
Blind OLDTF/WHR M16 .....126 D4
Hertford Industrial Estate
AULW OL7 .....119 F4
Heybrook Primary School
WHIT OL12 .....11 F3
Heyes Lane Infant School
HALE/TIMP WA15 .....166 C1
The Heys Primary School
AUL OL6 .....120 A2
Hey-with-Zion Primary School
OLDE OL4 .....76 D5
Heywood Cemetery
ROCH OL11 .....41 G2
Heywood Community High
School BURY BL9 .....39 H5
Heywood Industrial Park
HEY OL10 .....40 A5
Heywood Sports Complex
HEY OL10 .....40 C3
Higginshaw Sports Club
.....9 J1
Highbank Trading Estate
OP/CLY M11 .....130 C1
Highbarn Junior School
ROY/SHW OL2 .....59 F4
High Birch Special School
ROCH OL11 .....42 A1
Higher Broughton Health
Centre BRO M7 .....101 H4
Higher Failsworth Primary
School FAIL M35 .....105 F2
Higher Lane Primary School
WHTF M45 .....69 F4
Higher Openshaw
Community School
OP/CLY M11 .....117 G5
Highfield Cemetery
MPL/ROM SK6 .....161 G4
Highfield Hospital ROCH OL11 .....42 C1
Highfield Primary School
FWTH BL4 .....65 F4
URM M41 .....139 F1
High Lane Medical Centre
MPL/ROM SK6 .....186 D5
High Lane Primary School
MPL/ROM SK6 .....186 D4
High Lawn Primary School
BOL BL1 .....22 D5
Highlea Secondary School
WALK M28 .....96 A2
Hillcrest Grammar School
EDGY/DAV SK3 .....172 A3
Hillgate Business Centre
STKP SK1 .....13 H6
Hill Top Community Primary
School ROCH OL11 .....43 F5
Hill Top Community Special
School OLDE OL4 .....61 F5
Hilton Lane Primary School
WALK M28 .....81 F4
HM Prison CHH M8 .....114 C1
Hodge Clough Infant School
OLD OL1 .....76 C1
Hodge Clough Junior School
OLD OL1 .....76 C1
Holcombe Brook Primary
School RAMS BL0 .....26 B1
Holcombe Brook Sports Club
RAMS BL0 .....16 B5
Holden Clough Primary School
AUL OL6 .....107 G5
Holiday Inn BOL BL1 .....2 E3
NEWH/MOS M40 .....103 G5
WILM/AE SK9 .....190 A5
Hollingworth High School
MILN OL16 .....31 H5
Hollingworth Lake Activity
Centre LIT OL15 .....31 H1
Hollin Primary School
MDTN M24 .....72 D1
Hollins Grundy Primary School
BURY BL9 .....53 H4

Hollinwood Business Centre
FAIL M35 .....105 G2
Hollinwood Cemetery
OLDS OL8 .....105 H1
Hollinwood CC OLDS OL8 .....105 H2
Holly Bank Industrial Estate
RAD M26 .....68 A1
Holly Mount RC Primary
School TOT/BURYW BL8 .....25 G2
Hollywood Bowl
NEWH/MOS M40 .....104 C1
Holt Town Industrial Estate
NEWH/MOS M40 .....115 H3
Holy Cross & All Saints RC
Primary School ECC M30 .....111 E3
Holy Cross College BURY BL9 .....53 F1
Holy Family Catholic Primary
School SALE M33 .....155 F2
Holy Family RC Primary
School OLDS OL8 .....106 A2
Holy Family VA RC Primary
School BOL BL1 .....43 F4
Holy Infant RC Primary School
BOL BL1 .....33 H2
Holy Name RC Primary School
HULME M15 .....128 B3
Holy Rosary RC Primary
School OLDS OL8 .....91 G5
Holy Trinity CE Dobcross
School UPML OL3 .....78 C2
Holy Trinity CE Primary School
AUL OL6 .....119 F2
BKLY M9 .....105 F2
BURY BL9 .....4 E6
LIT OL15 .....21 F2
Hong Sing Chinese Medical
Centre
BRAM/HZG SK7 .....185 F1
Hooley Bridge Industrial
Estate HEY OL10 .....40 D2
Hope High School SLFD M6 .....112 B1
Hope Hospital SLFD M6 .....112 A3
Hopwood Hall College
MDTN M24 .....57 E4
WHIT OL12 .....10 B6
Hopwood Medical Centre
HEY OL10 .....41 F5
Hopwood Primary School
HEY OL10 .....56 B1
Hotel Ibis CMANE M1 .....7 F6
CMANE M1 .....128 B1
Hotel Rossetti CMANE M1 .....7 H5
Houldsworth Golf Club
RDSH SK5 .....145 E3
Houldsworth Medical Centre
RDSH SK5 .....145 F4
Hoyle Street Industrial Estate
WGTN/LGST M12 .....128 D1
Hubert House Jewish Boys
School BRO M7 .....101 G2
Hulme Adult Education
Centre HULME M15 .....127 H2
Hulme Arch HULME M15 .....128 A2
The Hulme Court Preparatory
School OLDS OL8 .....91 E3
The Hulme Grammar School
for Boys OLDS OL8 .....91 E3
Hulme Hall Grammar School
CHD/CHDH SK8 .....182 A5
Hulton Hospital BOLS/LL BL3 .....63 H1
Hurstfield Industrial Estate
RDSH SK5 .....145 E5
Hursthead Junior School
CHD/CHDH SK8 .....182 A5
Hurst Knoll CE Primary School
AUL OL6 .....119 H1
Hyde Clarendon Sixth Form
College HYDE SK14 .....133 G4
Hyde CC HYDE SK14 .....133 H4
Hyde Leisure Pool HYDE SK14 .....148 A1
Hyde Technology School
HYDE SK14 .....133 F4
Hyde United FC HYDE SK14 .....148 B1
IKEA Store Manchester
AUL OL6 .....119 F2
IMAX Cinema ANC M4 .....7 F3
IMEX Business Park
BRUN/LGST M13 .....129 G5
Imperial War Museum North
TRPK M17 .....126 B1
Indoor Tennis Centre
OP/CLY M11 .....116 A3
Inland Revenue Office
CSLFD M3 .....6 C4
Innes Special School
WHIT OL12 .....29 F2
Innkeeper's Lodge HTNM SK4 .....159 F2
OLD OL1 .....74 C7
WILM/AE SK9 .....200 D2
Inscape House School
WALK M28 .....97 F1
Inscape House Special School
WALK M28 .....97 F1
The Instructor College
STKP SK1 .....13 G4
International Convention
Centre CSLFD M3 .....6 D6
Iranian School of Manchester
WGTN/LGST M12 .....130 A5
Irlam & Cadishead Community
High School IRL M44 .....136 A4
Irlam CP School IRL M44 .....136 B2
Irlam Endowed Primary
School IRL M44 .....136 C1
Irlam Industrial Estate
IRL M44 .....136 A4
Irlam Swimming Pool
IRL M44 .....136 C2
James Brindley Primary
School WALK M28 .....96 D1
The Jeff Joseph Sale Moor
Technology College
SALE M33 .....155 E4
Jewish Museum CHH M8 .....114 D1
Jewish Senior Boys School
BRO M7 .....101 G3
John Rylands Library
CSLFD M3 .....6 D5
Johnson Fold Community
Primary School BOL BL1 .....32 C3

Joseph Adamson Industrial
Estate HYDE SK14 .....147 G1
Joseph Rayner Independent
School OLDS OL8 .....106 D2
Jumbles Country Park
BOLE BL2 .....24 A2
Jurys Inn CMANE M1 .....6 D7
Kaskenmoor School
OLDS OL8 .....105 G1
Kassim Darwish Grammar
School for Boys
OLDTF/WHR M16 .....142 A2
Kayley Industrial Estate
AULW OL7 .....119 E2
Kearsley West Primary School
FWTH BL4 .....66 B5
Kenmore Medical Centre
WILM/AE SK9 .....198 D4
Kentmere Primary School
WHIT OL12 .....19 C5
Kenyon Business Park
BOL/LL BL3 .....48 D4
Kiely Business Park BURY BL9 .....5 G1
Kingfisher Community Special
School CHAD OL9 .....90 A2
The King of Kings School
ANC M4 .....7 G1
Kings Road Primary School
OLDTF/WHR M16 .....126 D5
King Street Remedial Clinic
DUK SK16 .....119 G4
Kingsway CP School
URM M41 .....124 D4
Kingsway Retail Park
MILN OL16 .....31 E4
Kingsway School
CHD/CHDH SK8 .....169 H5
Kingsway Secondary School
CHD/CHDH SK8 .....169 H4
Knoll Street Industrial Park
BRO M7 .....101 G3
Knowsley Junior School
OLDE OL4 .....77 F5
Kratos Industrial Estate
URM M41 .....125 E3
Lacey Green Primary School
WILM/AE SK9 .....198 D1
Lady Barn House School
CHD/CHDH SK8 .....182 A1
Ladybarn Primary School
DID/WITH M20 .....143 F5
Ladybridge High School
BOLS/LL BL3 .....47 G5
Ladybridge Primary School
BOLS/LL BL3 .....47 G4
CHD/CHDH SK8 .....171 E4
Ladybrook Primary School
BRAM/HZG SK7 .....184 A5
Ladysmith Shopping Centre
AUL OL6 .....119 G2
Ladywell Hospital Lodge
SALQ M50 .....111 F5
Ladywood School BOLS/LL BL3 .....51 E5
Lancashire CCC (Old Trafford)
STRET M32 .....126 C5
Lancasterian School
DID/WITH M20 .....156 D1
Lance Burn Health Centre
SLFD M6 .....113 F3
Lane End Primary School
CHD/CHDH SK8 .....183 F2
Langley Primary School
MDTN M24 .....72 B1
Langworthy Clinic SLFD M6 .....113 E3
Langworthy Road Primary
School SLFD M6 .....113 E2
Lark Hill Primary School
EDGY/DAV SK3 .....12 B5
CHD/CHDH SK8 .....183 E3
Last Drop Village Hotel
EDGW/EG BL7 .....23 F2
The Last Drop Village
EDGW/EG BL7 .....23 F2
Lavenham Business Centre
BURY BL9 .....8 B5
Lawn Cemetery ALT WA14 .....164 D4
Lawnhurst Trading Estate
CHD/CHDH SK8 .....171 E4
Leigh Infant & Primary School
HYDE SK14 .....148 A1
Leigh Street Primary School
HYDE SK14 .....148 B1
Lemon Park Industrial Estate
SLFD M6 .....41 F5
Levenshulme Baths
BNG/LEV M19 .....144 B2
Levenshulme Health Centre
BNG/LEV M19 .....144 B2
Levenshulme High School
BNG/LEV M19 .....144 A4
Levenshulme Trading Estate
BNG/LEV M19 .....144 C1
Lever Edge Primary School
BOLS/LL BL3 .....64 C2
Leverhulme Park Athletics
Stadium BOLS/LL BL3 .....50 A3
Light Oaks Junior School
SLFD M6 .....112 A1
Lily Lane J & I School
NEWH/MOS M40 .....103 H2
Limelurst Primary School
OLDS OL8 .....106 A2
Limeside Primary School
OLDS OL8 .....105 H1
The Limes School AULW OL7 .....119 F1
Lime Tree Primary School
SALE M33 .....155 F3
Linden Road Primary School
DTN/ASHW M34 .....132 D5
Lindow Primary School
WILM/AE SK9 .....200 A2
Linguard Business Park
MILN OL16 .....10 E7
Linkway Industrial Estate
MDTN M24 .....73 E1
Linnyshaw Industrial Estate
FWTH BL4 .....82 B1
Littleborough CC LIT OL15 .....21 F1

Littleborough Primary School
LIT OL15 .....21 E1
Little Heaton VC CE Primary
School MDTN M24 .....71 H5
Little Hulton Skills Centre
WALK M28 .....81 F3
Little Lever School Specialist
Language College
BOLS/LL BL3 .....66 B1
Littlemoor Primary School
OLDE OL4 .....76 B4
Littlemoss Business Park
DROY M43 .....118 B2
Littlemoss High School
DROY M43 .....118 B1
Livingstone Primary School
MOSL OL5 .....108 C2
L & M Business Park
ALT OL15 .....165 E5
Lobden Golf Club WHIT OL12 .....18 D1
Local Studies Library OLD OL1 .....9 H4
Lockside Medical Centre
STLY SK15 .....121 E3
Longdendale Recreation
Centre HYDE SK14 .....135 G5
Longford Park Special School
STRET M32 .....140 D1
Longford Trading Estate
STRET M32 .....142 B1
Longsight CC
WGTN/LGST M12 .....129 H5
Longsight Health Centre
WGTN/LGST M12 .....129 G4
Longsight Industrial Estate
WGTN/LGST M12 .....129 G4
Lords College BOLE BL2 .....3 G7
Loreto Grammar School
ALT WA14 .....165 F4
Lostock College STRET M32 .....125 F5
Lostock Hall Primary School
CHD/CHDH SK8 .....194 C4
Lostock Primary School
HOR/BR BL6 .....46 D3
Lower Broughton Health
Centre BRO M7 .....114 A1
Lowercroft Primary School
TOT/BURYW BL8 .....36 D4
Lower Kersal Primary School
BRO M7 .....100 B1
Lower Park Primary School
POY/DIS SK12 .....194 D3
Lowerplace Primary School
MILN OL16 .....43 G2
Lowes Park Golf Club
BURY BL9 .....27 H5
The Lowry Hotel CSLFD M3 .....6 C3
The Lowry TRPK M17 .....126 B1
Ludworth Primary School
MPL/ROM SK6 .....175 F1
Lum Head Primary School
CHD/CHDH SK8 .....181 G1
The Lyceum Musical Theatre
OLD OL1 .....9 G4
Lyme Park Country Park
POY/DIS SK12 .....197 G5
Lyndhurst Primary School
DUK SK16 .....119 H4
OLDS OL8 .....91 E4
Lyntown Trading Estate
ECC M30 .....111 E3
Lyon Industrial Estate
ALT WA14 .....165 E2
Lyon Road Industrial Estate
FWTH BL4 .....82 B2
Macdonald Norton Grange
Hotel ROCH OL11 .....57 F2
Macdonald Road Medical
Centre IRL M44 .....136 A3
Mackenzie Industrial Estate
CHD/CHDH SK8 .....171 E3
Magda House Medical Centre
CHD/CHDH SK8 .....173 G5
Malbern Industrial Estate
DTN/ASHW M34 .....131 H4
The Mall Shopping Centre
ECC M30 .....111 C3
Malmaison Hotel CMANE M1 .....7 F5
Mancentral Trading Estate
ORD M5 .....6 A4
Manchester Academy
RUSH/FAL M14 .....128 B4
Manchester Airport Hotel
MANAIR M90 .....180 B5
Manchester Airport World
Freight Terminal
MANAIR M90 .....189 H1
Manchester Aquatics Centre
BRUN/LGST M13 .....128 E1
Manchester Arndale Shopping
Centre CMANE M1 .....7 F5
Manchester Art Gallery
CMANE M1 .....7 F5
Manchester (Barton) Airfield
ECC M30 .....123 F1
Manchester Business Park
MANAIR M90 .....180 B2
Manchester Business Park
HULME M15 .....128 B2
Manchester Cathedral
CSLFD M3 .....6 E2
Manchester Cathedral Visitor
Centre CSLFD M3 .....6 E3
Manchester Central CSLFD M3 .....6 D7
Manchester Central Library
CMANW M2 .....6 E6
Manchester Centre for the
Deaf BRUN/LGST M13 .....128 C2
Manchester Centre for Vision
CSLFD M3 .....6 E3
Manchester City FC (City of
Manchester Stadium)
OP/CLY M11 .....116 A4
Manchester City Museum &
Tour OP/CLY M11 .....116 A3
Manchester College of Arts &
Technology CMANE M1 .....7 H4
CSLFD M3 .....6 B5
WGTN/LGST M12 .....129 G1
Manchester Conference Centre
& Hotel CMANE M1 .....7 H7

The Manchester Crematorium
CCHDY M21 .....141 G5
Manchester Golf Club
MDTN M24 .....57 F3
Manchester Grammar School
BRUN/LGST M13 .....143 G5
Manchester High School
for Girls RUSH/FAL M14 .....143 E5
Manchester Industrial Centre
CSLFD M5 .....6 A6
Manchester International
Airport MANAIR M90 .....190 A2
Manchester Islamic High
School for Girls
CCHDY M21 .....141 E3
Manchester Junior Girls
School BRO M7 .....101 G1
Manchester Mesivta High
School PWCH M25 .....86 A4
Manchester Mesivta High
School PWCH M25 .....86 A4
Manchester Metropolitan
University BRUN/LGST M13 .....128 D4
CMANE M1 .....7 G6
CMANE M1 .....128 E1
DID/WITH M20 .....157 E3
DID/WITH M20 .....157 G4
OLDTF/WHR M16 .....142 B1
RUSH/FAL M14 .....128 D5
Manchester Metropolitan
University Institute of
Education Didsbury
DID/WITH M20 .....157 G4
Manchester Museum
BRUN/LGST M13 .....128 C2
Manchester Road Primary
School DROY M43 .....117 F4
Manchester Royal Infirmary
BRUN/LGST M13 .....128 C3
Manchester RUFC
CHD/CHDH SK8 .....192 D1
Manchester School of
Management
BRUN/LGST M13 .....128 B2
Manchester Southern
Cemetery CCHDY M21 .....141 H5
Manchester United FC
(Old Trafford)
OLDTF/WHR M16 .....126 C5
Manchester United Museum
& Tour Centre TRPK M17 .....126 B3
Manchester University
BRUN/LGST M13 .....128 C3
Manchester Victoria & Albert
Hotel CSLFD M3 .....6 A5
Manchester Youth Theatre
HULME M15 .....128 A3
Mandelay Health Centre
BOL BL1 .....22 D5
Manley Park Junior School
OLDTF/WHR M16 .....141 G1
Manley Park Primary School
OLDTF/WHR M16 .....141 G1
Manor Golf Club FWTH BL4 .....83 E3
Manor Green Primary School
DTN/ASHW M34 .....147 E3
Manor High School
SALE M33 .....153 F1
Manway Business Park
ALT WA14 .....165 H2
The Maples Medical Centre
NTHM/RTH M23 .....167 G5
Marcliffe Industrial Estate
BRAM/HZG SK7 .....185 G3
Marjory Lees Health Centre
OLD OL1 .....9 H2
Market Place Shopping Centre
BURY BL9 .....4 E7
Market Street Athletics Track
BURY BL9 .....4 E7
Markland Hill Primary School
BOL BL1 .....47 G1
Marland Hill Primary School
ROCH OL11 .....42 B1
Marland Park Golf Club
ROCH OL11 .....41 H1
Marlborough Road Primary
School BRO M7 .....102 A4
Marple Clinic MPL/ROM SK6 .....175 E3
Marple Golf Club
MPL/ROM SK6 .....186 D1
Marple Hall School
MPL/ROM SK6 .....174 B2
Marriott Hotel
HALE/TIMP WA15 .....179 F5
Marriott Worsley Park Hotel &
Country Club WALK M28 .....97 E3
Marsland Street Industrial
Centre BRAM/HZG SK7 .....185 E2
Masefield Primary School
BOLS/LL BL3 .....51 E5
Mather Street Primary School
FAIL M35 .....104 C2
Matthew Moss High School
HEY OL10 .....41 H2
Mauldeth Medical Centre
DID/WITH M20 .....143 F4
Mauldeth Road Primary
School RUSH/FAL M14 .....143 G4
Mayfield Industrial Park
HYDE SK14 .....122 D5
Mayfield Primary School
OLD OL1 .....76 A4
Maypole Farm Estate
PART M31 .....137 F5
Meade Hill School CHH M8 .....87 E3
Meadowbank Primary School
CHD/CHDH SK8 .....170 C4
Meadow Industrial Estate
FAIL M35 .....104 C4
STKP SK1 .....160 A3
The Meadows School
BKLY M9 .....88 C3
Meadway Health Centre
SALE M33 .....153 H4
Meanwood Primary School
WHIT OL12 .....29 F2
Mechinoh School BRO M7 .....101 H1
Medlock Infant School
BRUN/LGST M13 .....128 C1

Medlock Leisure Centre
DROY M43 .... 118 A2
Medlock Primary School
BRUN/LGST M13 .... 128 D1
Medlock Valley Community
School *OLDS* OL8 .... 91 H4
Megabowl *BURY* BL9 .... 54 A3
OLDTF/WHR M16 .... 126 D5
Meiland High School
GTN M18 .... 144 D1
MEN Arena *CSLFD* M3 .... 6 E1
Mental Health Centre
BOLE BL2 .... 35 G5
Mereside Educational Trust
SALE M33 .... 155 E3
Meridian Clinic
BURY BL9 .... 4 C5
Mersey Drive Primary School
BURY BL9 .... 70 B2
Mersey Road Industrial Estate
FAIL M35 .... 105 G1
Mersey Trading Estate
HTNM SK4 .... 158 C5
Mersey Vale Primary School
HTNM SK4 .... 158 D5
Merseyway Centre *STKP* SK1 ... 13 F3
Mesne Lea Primary School
WALK M28 .... 97 F1
Methodist Cemetery
BOLE BL2 .... 35 F2
Metro Cinema *AUL* OL6 .... 119 G3
Micklehurst All Saints Primary
School *MOSL* OL5 .... 109 F1
Micklehurst CC *MOSL* OL5 ...... 109 F1
Middleton Cemetery
MDTN M24 .... 73 F2
Middleton Crematorium
MDTN M24 .... 73 F2
Middleton CC *MDTN* M24 .... 72 C2
Middleton Parish Church
School *MDTN* M24 .... 72 C2
Middleton Public Baths
MDTN M24 .... 72 D4
Middleton Shopping Centre
MDTN M24 .... 72 C4
Middleton Technology School
MDTN M24 .... 73 E4
Midland Hotel *CMANW* M2 ...... 6 E6
Miles Platting Pool
NEWH/MOS M40 .... 115 G2
Milking Green Industrial
Estate
OLDE OL4 .... 92 D2
Mill 5 Belgrave Industrial
Estate *OLDS* OL8 .... 91 H4
Millbrook Business Centre
NTHM/RTH M23 .... 167 F3
Millbrook Industrial Estate
NTHM/RTH M23 .... 167 F3
Millbrook Primary School
STLY SK15 .... 109 F5
Mill Gate Shopping Centre
BURY BL9 .... 4 E5
Mills Hill Primary School
CHAD OL9 .... 73 H4
Mill Street Industrial Estate
BOL BL1 .... 3 G4
Millwood Primary Special
School *BURY* BL9 .... 53 G3
Milnrow CC *MILN* OL16 .... 44 C1
Milnrow CE Aided Primary
School *MILN* OL16 .... 31 G5
Milnrow Health Centre
MILN OL16 .... 44 C1
Milo Industrial Park
DROY M43 .... 118 A3
Milton St Johns CE Primary
School *MOSL* OL5 .... 93 H5
Minden Medical Centre
BURY BL9 .... 5 F4
Moat House School
HTNM SK4 .... 159 H3
Monde Trading Estate
TRPK M17 .... 125 F2
Montague Business Park
OLDTF/WHR M16 .... 126 D4
Monton Bowling Club
ECC M30 .... 111 F1
Monton CC *ECC* M30 .... 111 F1
Monton Green Primary School
ECC M30 .... 111 F1
Monton House Hotel
ECC M30 .... 111 E2
Monton Medical Centre
ECC M30 .... 110 D1
Moor Allerton School
DID/WITH M20 .... 157 E2
Moorfield Community
Primary School *IRL* M44 ... 122 B5
Moorfield Primary School
BRAM/HZG SK7 .... 184 D3
Moorgate Primary School
BOLE BL2 .... 3 K2
Moorgate Retail Park
BURY BL9 .... 5 F3
Moorhouse Primary School
MILN OL16 .... 31 F5
Moorlands Junior School
SALE M33 .... 155 F1
Moorside High School
SWIN M27 .... 98 C3
Moorside Leisure Centre
SWIN M27 .... 98 C3
Moorside Primary School
DROY M43 .... 118 A4
SWIN M27 .... 98 C3
Moravian College *DROY* M43 ... 117 H5
Morris Green Business Park
BOLS/LL BL3 .... 48 B5
Moses Gate Country Park
FWTH BL4 .... 66 B2
Moses Park Country Park
BOLS/LL BL3 .... 50 A5
Moss Field Community
Primary School *HEY* OL10 ... 40 D3
Mossfield CP School *SWIN* M27 ... 99 E1
Moss Hey Primary School
BRAM/HZG SK7 .... 193 F2
Moss Industrial Estate
MILN OL16 .... 43 G1

Moss Lane Industrial Estate
ROY/SHW OL2 .... 75 H1
Mossley AFC *MOSL* OL5 .... 108 D1
Mossley Health Centre
MOSL OL5 .... 108 D1
Mossley Hollins High School
MOSL OL5 .... 109 F1
Moss Park Junior & Infant
School *STRET* M32 .... 139 H1
Moss Side Health Centre
RUSH/FAL M14 .... 128 B4
Moss Side Leisure Centre
HULME M15 .... 128 A3
Moss View Primary School
PART M31 .... 151 F3
Moston Fields Primary School
NEWH/MOS M40 .... 103 H1
Moston Indoor Market
NEWH/MOS M40 .... 103 G2
Moston Lane Primary School
BKLY M9 .... 103 F2
Mottram CE Primary School
HYDE SK14 .... 135 H5
Mount Carmel RC Junior
School *BKLY* M9 .... 88 A5
Mount Carmel RC Primary
School *BKLY* M9 .... 103 E1
Mountheath Industrial Park
PWCH M25 .... 101 E1
Mount Pleasant Business
Centre *OLDE* OL4 .... 76 A5
Mount St Joseph Business &
Enterprise College
BOLS/LL BL3 .... 65 E2
The Museum of Science &
Industry in Manchester
CSLFD M3 .... 6 A6
Museum of the Manchester
Regiment *AUL* OL6 .... 119 G2
Museum of Trade Union
History *CMANE* M1 .... 7 F6
Museum of Transport
CHH M8 .... 102 B4, 102 B2
The Music School *CHH* M8 ...... 102 D2
Mytham Primary School
BOLS/LL BL3 .... 67 E1
Nasmyth Business Centre
ECC M30 .... 110 D3
National Cycling Centre
(Velodrome) *OP/CLY* M11 ... 116 B3
National Industrial Estate
AULW OL7 .... 119 F3
National Squash Centre
OP/CLY M11 .... 116 A3
National Trading Estate
BRAM/HZG SK7 .... 184 D1
Natural History Museum
CHAD OL9 .... 8 B7
Navigation Primary School
ALT WA14 .... 165 G3
Navigation Trading Estate
NEWH/MOS M40 .... 103 H5
Nelson Business Centre
DTN/ASHW M34 .... 132 C4
Nevill Road Infant School
BRAM/HZG SK7 .... 183 H2
Newall Green High School
NTHM/RTH M23 .... 167 G5
Newall Green Primary School
NTHM/RTH M23 .... 168 A5
New Ardwick Sports Centre
WGTN/LGST M12 .... 129 E2
New Bridge School
OLDS OL8 .... 105 G2
Newbridge Special School
OLDS OL8 .... 92 A5
Newbrook School
DID/WITH M20 .... 156 D1
Newby Road Industrial Estate
BRAM/HZG SK7 .... 185 E2
New Croft Community High
School *SLFD* M6 .... 113 E2
New Harvest Learning Centre
CSLFD M3 .... 6 A3
Newhaven Business Park
OFTN SK2 .... 111 F4
Newhey Community Primary
School *MILN* OL16 .... 44 D2
New Kingsway Health Centre
BNG/LEV M19 .... 158 A2
Newlands Medical Centre
BOL BL1 .... 47 H2
New Moston Primary School
NEWH/MOS M40 .... 89 H5
New North Manchester Golf
Club *MDTN* M24 .... 72 A4
Newton Business Park
HYDE SK14 .... 134 B3
Newton Moor Industrial
Estate *HYDE* SK14 .... 133 H3
Newton Street Police Museum
CMANE M1 .... 7 H4
Nicholas Varley Community
School *NEWH/MOS* M40 ... 115 H1
Nicholls Sixth Form Centre
WGTN/LGST M12 .... 129 E2
Norbury Hall Primary School
BRAM/HZG SK7 .... 185 F3
Norden Community Primary
School *WHIT* OL12 .... 28 C1
Norden CC *WHIT* OL12 .... 28 B1
Norris Bank Medical Centre
HTNM SK4 .... 12 A3
Norris Bank Primary School
HTNM SK4 .... 159 E3
Nortex Business Centre
BOL BL1 .... 48 B1
Northbank Industrial Park
IRL M44 .... 136 A5
North Cestrian Grammar
School *ALT* WA14 .... 165 F4
North Chadderton School
CHAD OL9 .... 74 B2
North Cheshire Jewish
Primary School
CHD/CHDH SK8 .... 181 G2

Northenden Golf Club
WYTH/NTH M22 .... 156 D4
Northenden Primary School
WYTH/NTH M22 .... 156 C5
Northern A & O Medical Centre
BURY BL9 .... 4 E4
Northern Cemetery
SWIN M27 .... 100 C3
Northern Moor Clinic
NTHM/RTH M23 .... 155 G5
North Grecian Street Primary
School *BRO* M7 .... 101 F4
North Heaton Primary School
HTNM SK4 .... 144 C5
North Manchester General
Hospital *CHH* M8 .... 102 D1
North Manchester High School
for Boys *BKLY* M9 .... 89 E4
North Manchester High School
for Girls *NEWH/MOS* M40 ... 88 D5
North Quays Business Park
ALT WA14 .... 153 H5
North Reddish Health Centre
RDSH SK5 .... 145 F2
North Reddish J & I School
RDSH SK5 .... 145 F2
North Trafford College
STRET M32 .... 126 C4
North Walkden Primary School
WALK M28 .... 81 H2
Novotel *CMANE* M1 .... 7 F6
WALK M28 .... 97 F5
Oakdale Special School
DUK SK16 .... 133 G2
Oakenclough Primary School
WILM/AE SK9 .... 199 G1
Oakfield Primary School
HYDE SK14 .... 133 H3
Oakfield Trading Estate
HALE/TIMP WA15 .... 165 H4
Oakgrove School
CHD/CHDH SK8 .... 181 H5
Oakhill Trading Estate
WALK M28 .... 81 G2
Oaklands Infant School
WILM/AE SK9 .... 199 H1
Oakleigh Medical Centre
CHH M8 .... 102 C1
The Oaks Business Park
NTHM/RTH M23 .... 167 E2
The Oaks Primary School
BOL BL1 .... 23 E5
Oakwood High School
CCHDY M21 .... 141 H4
SLFD M6 .... 99 H5
Octagon Theatre
BOL BL1 .... 2 E5
Odeon Cinema
ROCH OL11 .... 42 D2
Offerton Green Clinic
OFTN SK2 .... 173 G4
Offerton Health Centre
OFTN SK2 .... 172 C1
Offerton High School
OFTN SK2 .... 173 F2
Offerton Industrial Estate
STKP SK1 .... 172 C2
Oldfield Brow Primary School
ALT WA14 .... 164 C4
Old Hall Clinic *CHD/CHDH* SK8 ... 169 G3
Old Hall Drive Primary School
GTN M18 .... 130 C4
Old Hall Primary School
TOT/BURYW BL8 .... 26 C4
Oldham Athletic FC
(Boundary Park)
ROY/SHW OL2 .... 75 E2
Oldham Broadway Business
Park *CHAD* OL9 .... 73 H4
Oldham Business Centre
OLD OL1 .... 9 F5
Oldham Central Industrial Park
OLD OL1 .... 9 K1
Oldham College *OLD* OL9 .... 8 D3
Oldham County Court *OLD* OL1 ... 8 E2
Oldham Crematorium
OLDS OL8 .... 105 H1
Oldham CC *OLD* OL1 .... 76 B3
Oldham Golf Club *OLDE* OL4 ... 93 E5
Oldham RUFC *OLDE* OL4 .... 106 C2
Oldham Sixth Form College
OLDS OL8 .... 8 E5
Oldham Sports Centre *OLD* OL1 ... 9 J3
Oldham Theatre Workshop
ROY/SHW OL2 .... 59 E5
Oldham West Business Centre
CHAD OL9 .... 74 C5
Old Mill Hotel *RAMS* BL0 .... 16 C1
Old Moat J & I School
DID/WITH M20 .... 142 C4
Old Rectory Hotel
DTN/ASHW M34 .... 147 E4
Old Trafford Community
WYTH/NTH M22 .... 127 F2
Oldwood Primary School
WYTH/NTH M22 .... 168 C4
Olympia Trading Estate
HULME M15 .... 127 H1
Olympic House *MANAIR* M90 ... 180 B5
Open University *CCHDY* M21 ... 141 F2
Opera House *CSLFD* M3 .... 6 C5
The Operating Theatre
STRET M32 .... 126 B5
Orchard House Day Hospital
ROY/SHW OL2 .... 59 F5
Orchard Industrial Estate
SLFD M6 .... 113 F1
Orchard Trading Estate
SLFD M6 .... 100 C5
Ordsall Hall Museum
ORD M5 .... 127 G2
Ordsall Health Centre
ORD M5 .... 113 G5
Ordsall Recreation Centre
ORD M5 .... 126 D1
Oriel Bank High School
OFTN SK2 .... 172 A4
Oriental Arch *CMANE* M1 .... 7 F5
Orion Business Park
EDGY/DAV SK3 .... 171 F4

Orion Trading Estate
TRPK M17 .... 111 H5
Orrishmere Primary School
CHD/CHDH SK8 .... 182 D1
Osborne Trading Estate
CHAD OL9 .... 8 B1
Oswald Road Primary School
CCHDY M21 .... 141 E2
Oulder Hill Community School
Language College
ROCH OL11 .... 29 E4
Our Lady of Grace RC Primary
School *PWCH* M25 .... 85 H1
Our Lady of Lourdes Catholic
Primary School *PART* M31 ... 150 D3
Our Lady of Lourdes RC
Primary School *FWTH* BL4 ... 65 F4
TOT/BURYW BL8 .... 26 D5
Our Lady of Mount Carmel RC
Primary School *AUL* OL6 ... 120 A1
Our Lady of the Rosary RC
Primary School *URM* M41 ... 124 B4
Our Lady & St Anselms RC
Primary School *HEY* OL10 ... 39 H4
Our Lady & St Pauls RC
Primary School *HEY* OL10 ... 39 H4
Our Ladys Catholic Primary
School *EDGY/DAV* SK3 .... 12 E6
Our Lady's RC High School
BKLY M9 .... 88 A1
Our Ladys RC High School
ROY/SHW OL2 .... 75 E1
Our Ladys RC Primary School
OLDE OL4 .... 76 D1
OLDTF/WHR M16 .... 127 G5
Our Lady & the Lancashire
Martyrs RC Primary School
WALK M28 .... 81 F4
Outwood Primary School
CHD/CHDH SK8 .... 181 H5
Overdale Crematorium
BOL BL1 .... 47 H3
Overdale School
MPL/ROM SK6 .... 161 G5
Owl Business Centre *OLDE* OL4 ... 92 C1
Oxford Grove Primary School
BOL BL1 .... 33 F5
OYY Lubavitch Girls School
BRO M7 .... 101 G1
Palace Cinema *STLY* SK15 .... 120 D3
The Palace Hotel *CMANE* M1 ...... 7 F7
Palace Theatre *CMANE* M1 .... 7 F7
Palm Business Centre
CHAD OL9 .... 8 E1
Paragon Industrial Estate
LIT OL15 .... 20 C5
Parish Church CE Junior School
OLD OL1 .... 9 G1
Parker International Estate
DUK SK16 .... 133 E1
Parkfield Industrial Estate
MDTN M24 .... 72 B4
Parkfield Primary School
MDTN M24 .... 72 B4
Parklands High School
WYTH/NTH M22 .... 180 B1
Park Mill Industrial Estate
MOSL OL5 .... 94 A3
Park Parade Industrial Estate
AUL OL6 .... 119 F3
Park Road CP School
SALE M33 .... 139 G5
Park Road Primary School
ALT WA14 .... 165 E1
Parkside Industrial Estate
ROY/SHW OL2 .... 59 F5
Parkview Centre *OLDS* OL8 .... 9 H6
Parkway Business Centre
OLDTF/WHR M16 .... 142 B2
Parkway Four Industrial
Estate *TRPK* M17 .... 125 F1
Parkway Trading Estate
STRET M32 .... 125 H1
Parochial CE Primary School
AUL OL6 .... 119 H2
Parrenthorn High School
PWCH M25 .... 86 B1
Parrs Wood Technology
College *DID/WITH* M20 ... 158 A5
Partington CP School
PART M31 .... 151 E2
Partington Health Centre
PART M31 .... 151 E3
Partington Shopping Centre
PART M31 .... 151 E2
Partington Sports Centre
PART M31 .... 151 E4
Peacefield Primary School
MPL/ROM SK6 .... 174 D4
Peacock CP School *GTN* M18 ... 130 D2
Pear New Mill Industrial
Estate *MPL/ROM* SK6 .... 160 D4
Peel Brow Primary School
RAMS BL0 .... 17 E2
Peel Hall CP School *LHULT* M38 ... 81 E4
Peel Hall Primary School
WYTH/NTH M22 .... 181 E1
Peel Health Centre *BURY* BL9 ... 4 E4
Peel Moat Recreation Centre
HTNM SK4 .... 159 E1
Peerglow Industrial Estate
ALT WA14 .... 165 G5
Pendleton College *SLFD* M6 ... 112 B2
Pendleton Medical Centre
SLFD M6 .... 113 F3
Pennant Industrial Estate
OLD OL1 .... 76 A4
Pennine Business Park
HEY OL10 .... 30 C5
Peterloo Medical Centre
MDTN M24 .... 72 B4
Philips High School *WHTF* M45 ... 69 F4
Phoenix Industrial Estate
FAIL M35 .... 105 F2
Phoenix Medical Centre
STKP SK1 .... 13 H5
Phoenix Park Industrial Estate
HEY OL10 .... 56 C1

Piccadilly Trading Estate
CMANE M1 .... 115 F5
Pictor Special School
SALE M33 .... 154 A2
Pike Fold Primary School
BKLY M9 .... 87 H4
Pikes Lane Primary School
BOLS/LL BL3 .... 2 A7
Pilot Industrial Estate
BOLS/LL BL3 .... 49 G5
Pilsworth Industrial Estate
BURY BL9 .... 54 A3
Pinfold J & I School
HTNM SK4 .... 149 G2
Pinnacle Business Centre
HTNM SK4 .... 159 H3
Piper Hill School
NTHM/RTH M23 .... 156 A4
Plantation Industrial Estate
AUL OL6 .... 119 H3
Plant Hill High School *BKLY* M9 ... 87 H3
Plasman Industrial Estate
BNG/LEV M19 .... 144 A2
BNG/LEV M19 .... 144 D2
Playhouse Theatre *ORD* M5 ... 113 F3
Plodder Lane Primary School
FWTH BL4 .... 65 G3
Plymouth Court Business
Centre *BRUN/LGST* M13 ... 128 D3
Plymouth Grove Primary
School *BRUN/LGST* M13 ... 129 F3
The Point Retail Park
MILN OL16 .... 10 E6
Poland Industrial Estate
ANC M4 .... 7 K2
Portland Basin Museum
AULW OL7 .... 119 F4
Portland Industrial Estate
BURY BL9 .... 38 D2
Portwood Trading Estate
STKP SK1 .... 13 K1
Potters House School
BURY BL9 .... 27 G5
Pownall Green Primary
School *BRAM/HZG* SK7 ... 183 H5
Pownall Hall School
WILM/AE SK9 .... 198 C2
Poynton Clinic *POY/DIS* SK12 ... 195 F3
Poynton High School &
Performing Arts College
POY/DIS SK12 .... 195 F5
Poynton Leisure Centre
POY/DIS SK12 .... 195 G5
Poynton Sports Club
POY/DIS SK12 .... 195 F3
Premier Travel Inn *ALT* WA14 ... 153 H5
ALT WA14 .... 165 G3
CCHDY M21 .... 156 C1
CHAD OL9 .... 8 B5
CHD/CHDH SK8 .... 181 H2
CHH M8 .... 87 E3
CMANW M2 .... 6 E6
DTN/ASHW M34 .... 131 H5
HOR/BR BL6 .... 46 A1
HULME M15 .... 128 A1
MDTN M24 .... 71 G5
MILN OL16 .... 44 D2
OFTN SK2 .... 172 B3
PWCH M25 .... 85 H2
SALE M33 .... 138 C5
SALQ M50 .... 126 D1
STKP SK1 .... 13 H5
SWIN M27 .... 98 D4
SWIN M27 .... 99 H3
TRPK M17 .... 124 C2
WILM/AE SK9 .... 192 A4
WILM/AE SK9 .... 198 B5
WILM/AE SK9 .... 200 D5
WYTH/NTH M22 .... 181 F4
Premier Travel Inn
(Manchester Trafford
Centre) *URM* M41 .... 124 C1
Prestolee Primary School
RAD M26 .... 67 E4
Prestwich Arts College
PWCH M25 .... 86 A2
Prestwich Golf Club
PWCH M25 .... 100 D1
Prestwich Health Centre
PWCH M25 .... 85 H2
Prestwich Hospital
PWCH M25 .... 85 G1
Prestwich Preparatory School
PWCH M25 .... 86 B2
Priesthall School *HTNM* SK4 ... 158 C3
Prince of Wales Business Park
OLD OL1 .... 76 B4
Princess on Portland
CMANE M1 .... 7 F6
The Printworks Leisure
Complex *ANC* M4 .... 7 F2
Priorslegh Medical Centre
POY/DIS SK12 .... 195 F3
Propps Hall Primary School
FAIL M35 .... 104 D4
Prospect Vale Primary School
CHD/CHDH SK8 .... 181 G3
Pump House People's History
Museum *CSLFD* M3 .... 6 B4
Python Industrial Estate
LIT OL15 .... 21 F2
Quality Hotel (Altrincham)
ALT WA14 .... 177 G2
Quarry Bank Mill & Styal
Estate (NT) *WILM/AE* SK9 ... 199 G4
Queen Elizabeth Hall *OLD* OL1 ... 9 F3
Queen Elizabeths School
MDTN M24 .... 56 C5
Queensbridge Primary School
FWTH BL4 .... 65 H4
Queensgate Primary School
BRAM/HZG SK7 .... 193 H5
Queens Road Primary School
CHD/CHDH SK8 .... 182 D1
Rack House Primary School
NTHM/RTH M23 .... 155 H5
Radcliffe Borough AFC
RAD M26 .... 51 H5
Radcliffe CC *RAD* M26 .... 51 H5

Radcliffe Hall CE Methodist Primary School *RAD* M26 .....52 D5
Radcliffe Hall CE Primary School *RAD* M26 .....51 H5
Radcliffe Riverside School *RAD* M26 .....68 A1
Radcliffe Tower (Remains of) *RAD* M26 .....69 E1
Radclyffe Athletics Centre *ORD* M5 .....74 A5
Radclyffe Primary School *ORD* M5 .....126 D1
The Radclyffe School (Lower) *CHAD* OL9 .....90 A1
The Radclyffe School (Upper) *CHAD* OL9 .....74 A5
Radisson SAS Hotel *MANAIR* M90 .....180 A5
Raikes Lane Industrial Estate *BOLS/LL* BL3 .....49 G5
Railway Street Industrial Estate *GTN* M18 .....130 B2
Ralph Williams Clinic *WHIT* OL12 .....19 H5
Ramillies Hall School *CHD/CHDH* SK8 .....183 F2
Ramsbottom Cemetery *RAMS* BL0 .....16 B4
Ramsbottom Cottage Hospital *RAMS* BL0 .....16 D3
Ramsbottom Health Centre *RAMS* BL0 .....16 C2
Ramsbottom Swimming Pool *RAMS* BL0 .....16 D1
Rassbottom Industrial Estate *STLY* SK15 .....120 C3
Ravensbury Community School *OP/CLY* M11 .....116 B3
Ravensfield Industrial Estate *DUK* SK16 .....119 F4
Ravenside Retail Park *BOLE* BL2 .....3 F7
Reddish Vale Golf Club *RDSH* SK5 .....145 G4
Reddish Vale Technology College *RDSH* SK5 .....145 F4
Red Lane Community School *BOLE* BL2 .....35 G5
Red Rose Retail Centre *ORD* M5 .....113 G4
Regal Industrial Estate *WGTN/LGST* M12 .....129 G1
Regent Cinema *MPL/ROM* SK6 .....175 E3
Regent Park Golf Course *HOR/BR* BL6 .....46 C2
Regent Trading Estate *ORD* M5 .....114 A4
The Regimental Museum of the Lancashire Fusiliers *TOT/BURYW* BL8 .....37 G5
Reliance Trading Estate *NEWH/MOS* M40 .....104 B3
Renaissance Hotel *CSLFD* M3 .....6 D3
Ribble Drive Primary School *WHTF* M45 .....69 H3
Richmond Medical Centre *AUL* OL6 .....119 H2
Richmond Park Athletics Stadium *AUL* OL7 .....118 D1
Richmond Park School *WGTN/LGST* M12 .....129 F5
Richmond Primary School *CHAD* OL9 .....8 D4
The Ridge College *MPL/ROM* SK6 .....174 D4
Ridge Danyers College *CHD/CHDH* SK8 .....182 B1
Ringway Golf Club *HALE/TIMP* WA15 .....178 D3
Ringway Primary School *WYTH/NTH* M22 .....180 C4
Ringway Trading Estate *WYTH/NTH* M22 .....180 D4
River Meadow Dyeworks *STLY* SK15 .....121 F2
Riverside Business Park *WILM/AE* SK9 .....199 E3
Roaches Industrial Estate *MOSL* OL5 .....94 B3
Rochdale AFC (Spotland Stadium) *ROCH* OL11 .....29 F3
Rochdale Cemetery *ROCH* OL11 .....29 E4
Rochdale Crematorium *ROCH* OL11 .....29 E4
Rochdale Cricket, Lacrosse & Squash Club *ROCH* OL11 .....29 F4
Rochdale Curtain Theatre *ROCH* OL11 .....29 E4
Rochdale Golf Club *ROCH* OL11 .....28 D5
Rochdale Healthcare *WHIT* OL12 .....20 A3
Rochdale Industrial Centre *ROCH* OL11 .....29 E4
Rochdale Infirmary *WHIT* OL12 .....10 C3
Rodney House School *BNG/LEV* M19 .....143 H3
Roe Cross Industrial Park *HYDE* SK14 .....135 H3
Roker Industrial Estate *OLD* OL1 .....76 A4
Rolls Crescent Primary School *HULME* M15 .....127 H5
Roman Fort *CSLFD* M3 .....6 B7
Romiley Golf Club *MPL/ROM* SK6 .....162 C3
Romiley Health Centre *MPL/ROM* SK6 .....162 B4
Romiley Primary School *MPL/ROM* SK6 .....162 C4
Roscow Fold Primary School *BOLE* BL2 .....50 B1
Rosedale Shopping Centre *NEWH/MOS* M40 .....104 B5
Rosehill Methodist Community Primary School *AUL* OL6 .....108 A4
Rosehill Methodist Community School *AUL* OL6 .....108 A5

Rose Hill Primary School *MPL/ROM* SK6 .....174 D3
Rossendale School *RAMS* BL0 .....17 G1
Roundthorn Industrial Estate *NTHM/RTH* M23 .....167 F3
Roundthorn Industrial Estate *OLDE* OL4 .....92 B2
Roundwood School *RAMS* BL0 .....168 B2
Roxy Cinema *OLDS* OL8 .....105 F1
Royal Bolton Hospital *FWTH* BL4 .....65 E3
Royal Exchange Clinic *CMANW* M2 .....6 E4
Royal Exchange Shopping Centre *CMANE* M1 .....6 E3
.....*MILN* OL16 .....10 B6
Royal Exchange Theatre *CSLFD* M3 .....6 E4
Royal Manchester Childrens Hospital *SWIN* M27 .....99 G3
Royal Northern College of Music *HULME* M15 .....128 B2
Royal Oak Industrial Estate *STKP* SK1 .....13 H6
Royal Oak Primary School *NTHM/RTH* M23 .....167 H2
Royal Oldham Hospital *OLD* OL1 .....75 E3
Royal Pennine Trading Estate *ROCH* OL11 .....42 B3
Royce Trading Estate *TRPK* M17 .....125 E1
Royle Pennine Trading Estate *ROCH* OL11 .....42 B3
Royton & Crompton School *ROY/SHW* OL2 .....59 H5
Royton Medical Centre *ROY/SHW* OL2 .....59 G5
Royton Public Baths *ROY/SHW* OL2 .....59 G5
Rugby Road Industrial Estate *WHIT* OL12 .....10 E3
Rumworth School *BOLS/LL* BL3 .....47 G4
Rushcroft Primary School *ROY/SHW* OL2 .....60 A1
Russell Scott Primary School *DTN/ASHW* M34 .....132 B4
Rycroft Park Sports Club *CHD/CHDH* SK8 .....182 C3
Rydings Special School *WHIT* OL12 .....19 G4
Ryecroft Business Park *WILM/AE* SK9 .....119 E4
The Ryleys School *WILM/AE* SK9 .....200 C3
Sacred Heart RC Infant School *GTN* M18 .....130 B4
Sacred Heart RC Junior School *GTN* M18 .....130 B4
Sacred Heart RC Primary School *MILN* OL16 .....30 D5
.....*NTHM/RTH* M23 .....167 G3
.....*OLD* OL1 .....76 B2
.....*WHTN* BL5 .....62 A3
Saddleworth Golf Club *UPML* OL3 .....78 D4
Saddleworth Museum & Art Gallery *UPML* OL3 .....78 D4
Saddleworth Preparatory School *OLDE* OL4 .....77 H4
Saddleworth School *UPML* OL3 .....79 E3
Saddleworth Swimming Pool *UPML* OL3 .....79 E5
St Agnes CE Primary School *BRUN/LGST* M13 .....129 G5
.....*OLDE* OL4 .....93 F2
St Aidan & Oswalds RC Primary School *ROY/SHW* OL2 .....75 E1
St Aidans Catholic Primary School *NTHM/RTH* M23 .....156 A5
St Alphonsus RC Primary School *OLDTF/WHR* M16 .....127 F3
St Ambrose Barlow RC High School & Salford College *SWIN* M27 .....99 E3
St Ambrose College *HALE/TIMP* WA15 .....178 C3
St Ambrose RC Primary School *CCHDY* M21 .....156 C2
.....*EDGY/DAV* SK3 .....171 G4
St Andrews CE Primary School *BNG/LEV* M19 .....144 B3
.....*RAD* M26 .....51 H5
.....*RAMS* BL0 .....16 C3
.....*WALK* M28 .....96 B5
St Andrew's CE Primary School *WHIT* OL12 .....20 B4
St Andrews CE Primary School *WHTN* BL5 .....63 H4
St Andrews CE School *ECC* M30 .....111 F4
St Andrews Medical Centre *ECC* M30 .....111 F3
St Andrews Methodist Primary School *WALK* M28 .....81 G4
St Annes CE Lydgate Primary School *OLDE* OL4 .....93 H1
St Annes CE Primary School *ROY/SHW* OL2 .....75 F1
.....*SALE* M33 .....154 D2
St Annes Bar Nose & Throat Hospital *ALT* WA14 .....177 F1
St Annes Primary School *DTN/ASHW* M34 .....132 D4
St Annes RC High School *HTNM* SK4 .....159 G2
St Annes RC Primary School *CHH* M8 .....102 B2
.....*DTN/ASHW* M34 .....131 F1
.....*STRET* M32 .....140 B1
St Anns RC Primary School *STRET* M32 .....140 B1
St Anthonys RC Primary School *WYTH/NTH* M22 .....180 C3
St Antonys Catholic College *STRET* M32 .....139 F1

St Augustine of Canterbury RC School *OLDS* OL8 .....91 E4
St Augustines CE Primary School *NEWH/MOS* M40 .....103 F5
.....*SWIN* M27 .....99 G2
St Barnabas CE Primary School *OP/CLY* M11 .....116 C5
St Bartholomews CE Primary School *WHIT* OL12 .....14 B5
St Bede CE Primary School *BOLS/LL* BL3 .....64 B2
St Bede's Preparatory School *OLDTF/WHR* M16 .....127 H5
St Benedict's Catholic Primary School *WILM/AE* SK9 .....192 B4
St Bernadettes RC Primary School *RDSH* SK5 .....160 C2
.....*WHTF* M45 .....69 G2
St Bernard RC Primary School *BOLS/LL* BL3 .....47 F4
St Bernard's RC Primary School *BNG/LEV* M19 .....143 H5
St Boniface RC Primary School *BRO* M7 .....101 F4
St Brendan RC Primary School *BOLE* BL2 .....35 F1
St Brigids RC Primary School *OP/CLY* M11 .....116 B4
St Catherines Preparatory School *MPL/ROM* SK6 .....175 G2
St Catherines RC Primary School *DID/WITH* M20 .....157 H3
St Chads CE Primary School *UPML* OL3 .....79 F3
St Chads RC Primary School *CHH* M8 .....102 B5
St Charles RC Primary School *SWIN* M27 .....98 C2
St Christophers RC Primary School *AUL* OL6 .....107 H4
St Chrysostoms CE Primary School *BRUN/LGST* M13 .....128 D3
St Clares RC Primary School *BKLY* M9 .....87 H2
St Clement (Egerton) CE Primary School *ORD* M5 .....113 G5
St Clement's CE Primary School *OP/CLY* M11 .....130 D1
St Columbas RC Primary School *BOLE* BL2 .....34 D2
St Cuthberts CE Primary School *MILN* OL16 .....43 G5
St Cuthberts RC Primary School *OLDTF/WHR* M20 .....157 H1
St Damians RC High School *AUL* OL6 .....107 H3
St Dunstans RC Primary School *NEWH/MOS* M40 .....103 H2
St Edmunds RC Primary School *LHULT* M38 .....81 G3
.....*NEWH/MOS* M40 .....103 F4
St Edwards CE Primary School *ROCH* OL11 .....42 A4
St Edwards RC Primary School *OLDE* OL4 .....76 D5
.....*RUSH/FAL* M14 .....142 D1
St Elisabeths CE Primary School *RDSH* SK5 .....145 E3
St Elizabeth RC Primary School *WYTH/NTH* M22 .....180 D2
St Ethelbert RC Primary School *BOLS/LL* BL3 .....48 A4
St Gabriels CE Primary School *MDTN* M24 .....73 F5
St Gabriels Medical Centre *PWCH* M25 .....86 C5
St Gabriels RC High School *ROCH* OL11 .....42 C5
St Georges CE Primary School *HYDE* SK14 .....147 H2
.....*MOSL* OL5 .....108 C1
.....*OFTN* SK2 .....172 A3
.....*SLFD* M6 .....100 D5
St Georges Craft Centre *BOL* BL1 .....2 E3
St Georges RC Primary School *WALK* M28 .....81 H5
St Gilberts RC Primary School *ECC* M30 .....110 B3
St Gregory RC Primary School *FWTH* BL4 .....66 B4
St Helens CE Primary School *GOL/RIS/CUL* WA3 .....150 A4
St Herberts RC Primary School *CHAD* OL9 .....74 B5
St Hilarys School *WILM/AE* SK9 .....200 D4
St Hildas CE Primary School *OLD* OL1 .....8 E1
.....*PWCH* M25 .....86 B3
St Hugh of Lincoln RC Primary School *STRET* M32 .....125 E5
St Hughs Catholic Primary School *HALE/TIMP* WA15 .....166 A2
St Hughs CE Primary School *OLDE* OL4 .....92 C4
St James Catholic High School *CHD/CHDH* SK8 .....182 C5
St James Catholic Primary School *HYDE* SK14 .....149 F1
.....*AUL* OL6 .....119 H2
.....*FWTH* BL4 .....65 G5
.....*GTN* M18 .....130 C2
.....*RUSH/FAL* M14 .....143 F1
.....*WHIT* OL12 .....19 H2
St James CE Secondary School *FWTH* BL4 .....65 F4
St James's RC School *SLFD* M6 .....99 H3
St James's RC Primary School *RAD* M26 .....52 B5
St John Bosco RC Primary School *BKLY* M9 .....88 C3

St John CE Primary School *FWTH* BL4 .....66 B4
St John Fisher RC Primary School *MDTN* M24 .....147 F2
.....*MDTN* M24 .....73 E1
St John Fisher & St Thomas More RC Primary School *WYTH/NTH* M22 .....168 C5
St Johns CE Primary School *ROCH* OL11 .....30 A5
St Johns Cathedral *CSLFD* M3 .....114 A3
St Johns CE Infant School *FAIL* M35 .....105 E2
St Johns CE Junior School *FAIL* M35 .....105 E2
St Johns CE Primary School *BRUN/LGST* M13 .....129 F4
.....*HTNM* SK4 .....158 B4
.....*MDTN* M24 .....57 H5
.....*RAD* M26 .....68 B3
.....*STLY* SK15 .....120 B5
St Johns Industrial Estate *OLDE* OL4 .....92 D1
St Johns Medical Centre *ALT* WA14 .....177 F1
St Johns Mosley Common CE Primary School *WALK* M28 .....96 A2
St Johns RC Primary School *CCHDY* M21 .....141 E2
St John the Evangelist RC Primary School *EDGW/EG* BL7 .....23 E4
St John Vianney School *HTNM* SK4 .....158 C2
St John Vianney Upper School *OLDTF/WHR* M16 .....141 F1
St Josephs & St Bedes RC Primary School *BURY* BL9 .....39 E2
St Josephs RC High School *HEY* OL10 .....55 H1
St Josephs RC Infant School *RDSH* SK5 .....145 E3
St Josephs RC Junior School *RDSH* SK5 .....145 E3
St Josephs RC Primary School *BOL* BL1 .....33 F4
.....*BRUN/LGST* M13 .....129 H4
.....*HEY* OL10 .....40 D5
.....*LHULT* M38 .....81 F2
.....*MOSL* OL5 .....108 D1
.....*ORD* M5 .....113 G5
.....*RAMS* BL0 .....16 C2
.....*ROY/SHW* OL2 .....59 H4
.....*SALE* M33 .....154 C2
.....*STKP* SK1 .....13 G3
St Josephs the Worker RC Primary School *IRL* M44 .....122 B5
St Judes CE Primary School *ANC* M4 .....7 K3
St Kentigerns RC Primary School *RUSH/FAL* M14 .....142 C1
St Lukes CE Primary School *WGTN/LGST* M13 .....129 F5
.....*BURY* BL9 .....53 G1
.....*CHAD* OL9 .....74 B5
.....*HEY* OL10 .....41 E5
St Lukes with All Saints CE Primary School *ORD* M5 .....112 C4
St Malachys RC Primary School *NEWH/MOS* M40 .....102 D5
St Margaret Marys RC Primary School *NEWH/MOS* M40 .....89 G4
St Margarets CE Primary School *HEY* OL10 .....40 B5
.....*OLDS* OL8 .....90 D5
.....*OLDTF/WHR* M16 .....141 H1
.....*PWCH* M25 .....85 E3
St Margaret Ward RC Primary School *SALE* M33 .....153 F4
St Maries RC Primary School *BURY* BL9 .....4 E6
St Marks CE Primary School *MPL/ROM* SK6 .....161 H2
.....*NEWH/MOS* M40 .....115 G2
.....*WALK* M28 .....97 G4
St Marks RC Primary School *SWIN* M27 .....84 B5
St Martins CE Primary School *OLDS* OL8 .....90 D5
St Martins School *SALE* M33 .....153 H1
St Mary CE Primary School *BOLS/LL* BL3 .....47 G5
St Mary's Catholic Cemetery *WALK* M28 .....98 A2
St Marys CE Primary School *DROY* M43 .....117 H4
.....*NEWH/MOS* M40 .....103 H4
.....*OLDTF/WHR* M16 .....127 H4
.....*PWCH* M25 .....85 (?)
.....*RDSH* SK5 .....145 C5
.....*ROCH* OL11 .....43 F2
.....*ROY/SHW* OL2 .....59 C1
St Mary's CE Primary School *IRL* M44 .....150 B1
.....*SALE* M33 .....154 A2
St Marys CE Primary School *TOT/BURYW* BL8 .....25 E1
.....*URM* M41 .....124 A4
St Mary's Hospital *BRUN/LGST* M13 .....128 C3
St Marys Medical Centre 9 H3
St Marys RC Primary School *BNG/LEV* M19 .....144 A3
.....*DTN/ASHW* M34 .....132 B5
.....*DUK* SK16 .....133 H2
.....*FAIL* M35 .....104 D4
.....*HTNM* SK4 .....12 E1
.....*MDTN* M24 .....72 C1
.....*MPL/ROM* SK6 .....161 H2
.....*RAD* M26 .....52 B5
.....*SWIN* M27 .....99 E2

St Mary's RC Primary School *ECC* M30 .....111 F4
.....*LIT* OL15 .....20 D2
St Matthew CE Primary School *BOL* BL1 .....
.....*BOLS/LL* BL3 .....66 D1
St Matthews CE Primary School *OLD* OL1 .....74 A2
St Matthews CE Primary School *EDDY/DAV* SK3 .....12 E6
.....*STRET* M32 .....140 A3
St Matthews RC High School *NEWH/MOS* M40 .....89 F5
St Maxentius CE School *BOLE* BL2 .....35 E1
St Michael CE Primary School *BOLS/LL* BL3 .....65 G1
St Michaels CE Aided Primary School *URM* M41 .....137 H2
St Michaels CE Primary School *HEY* OL10 .....40 D2
.....*MDTN* M24 .....88 D2
St Michaels RC High School *WHTF* M45 .....70 A3
St Monicas RC High School *PWCH* M25 .....86 B4
St Monicas RC Primary School *URM* M41 .....137 G2
St Osmunds & St Andrews Primary School *BOLE* BL2 .....50 A2
St Patrick's Catholic High School *ECC* M30 .....110 C3
St Patricks RC Primary School *ANC* M4 .....115 F2
.....*CHAD* OL9 .....8 D5
St Patricks VA RC Primary School *WHIT* OL12 .....10 E2
St Paul CE Primary School *BOL* BL1 .....34 A3
St Pauls Catholic High School *NTHM/RTH* M23 .....168 A5
St Pauls Catholic Primary School *POY/DIS* SK12 .....195 F5
St Paul's Cemetery *BOL* BL1 .....33 F4
St Pauls CE Primary School *BRO* M7 .....101 E2
.....*BURY* BL9 .....5 J1
.....*DID/WITH* M20 .....142 D5
.....*OLD* OL1 .....113 G4
.....*RDSH* SK5 .....160 C2
.....*ROY/SHW* OL2 .....74 D1
.....*STLY* SK15 .....121 F3
.....*WALK* M28 .....82 B4
St Pauls Peel CE Primary School *LHULT* M38 .....81 E2
St Pauls Trading Estate *HYDE* SK14 .....134 A4
St Pauls Trading Estate *STLY* SK15 .....121 F3
St Peter CE Primary School *HEY* OL10 .....66 A5
St Peter & St John Primary School *CSLFD* M3 .....6 A2
St Peter & St Paul RC Primary School *BOLS/LL* BL3 .....48 D4
St Peters Catholic Primary School *BRAM/HZG* SK7 .....185 E5
.....*NTHM/RTH* M23 .....179 H1
.....*STLY* SK15 .....121 E4
St Peters CE Primary School *AULW* OL7 .....119 F4
.....*BURY* BL9 .....53 F3
.....*SWIN* M27 .....98 D2
St Peters RC High School Upper School *DROY* M43 .....117 F5
St Peter's RC Primary School *NEWH/MOS* M40 .....72 D5
St Peters Smithills Dean CE Primary School *BOL* BL1 .....33 E2
St Peters VC CE Primary School *MILN* OL16 .....43 G1
St Philips Catholic Primary School *OFTN* SK2 .....173 F3
St Philips CE Primary School *HULME* M15 .....128 A2
St Philips RC Primary School *PWCH* M25 .....101 F1
St Phillips *CSLFD* M3 .....114 A4
St Raphaels Catholic Primary School *STLY* SK15 .....109 F5
St Richards RC Primary School *WGTN/LGST* M12 .....130 A5
St Saviour Primary School Ringley *RAD* M26 .....67 F5
St Sebastians RC Primary School *SLFD* M6 .....100 D5
St Simons Catholic Primary School *BRAM/HZG* SK7 .....185 F1
St Stephen & All Martyrs CE Primary School *BOLE* BL2 .....49 H4
St Stephens & All Martyrs Infant School *OLD* OL1 .....9 H1
St Stephens CE Primary School *DTN/ASHW* M34 .....118 D5
.....*FWTH* BL4 .....82 D1
.....*OFTN* SK2 .....173 G5
.....*TOT/BURYW* BL8 .....37 G5
St Stephens RC School *DROY* M43 .....117 H3
St Teresa RC Primary School *BOLS/LL* BL3 .....66 D1
St Teresas RC Primary School *IRL* M44 .....136 A3
.....*OLDTF/WHR* M16 .....126 D5
St Thomas Aquinas RC High School *CCHDY* M21 .....141 G4
St Thomas CE Primary School *BOL* BL1 .....33 C4
.....*BURY* BL9 .....5 J6
.....*HTNM* SK4 .....144 C5
.....*MILN* OL16 .....45 E2
.....*OLDS* OL8 .....8 E6
.....*STLY* SK15 .....13 H5
.....*WHTN* BL5 .....62 C3
St Thomas Leesfield CE Primary School *OLDE* OL4 .....92 D2
St Thomas Moorside CE (VA) Primary School *OLD* OL1 .....60 D5

St Thomas More RC College DTN/ASHW M34 ....146 D1
St Thomas More RC Primary School MDTN M24 .....88 D2
St Thomas of Canterbury RC Primary School BOL BL1 ....47 H1
BRO M7 ....101 H4
St Thomas Primary School CHH M8 .....8 D2
St Thomas's Hospital EDGY/DAV SK3 ....13 F7
St Vincent RC Infant School HALE/TIMP WA15 ....165 H4
St Vincents RC Primary School WHIT OL12 .....28 D2
St Wilfrids CE Primary School NEWH/MOS M40 ....104 C5
WYTH/NTH M22 ....168 D1
St Wilfrids RC Primary School HULME M15 ....127 H2
St William RC Primary School BOLS/LL BL3 .....64 D1
St Willibrords RC Primary School OP/CLY M11 ....116 D2
St Winifreds RC Primary School HTNM SK4 ....158 D4
SS Simon & Jude CE Primary School BOLS/LL BL3 ....65 E1
Sale CC SALE M33 ....155 H3
Sale Golf Club SALE M33 ....155 G1
Sale Grammar School SALE M33 ....154 D3
Sale Leisure Centre SALE M33 ....154 D1
Sale Water Park SALE M33 ....140 C5
Salford City Academy ECC M30 ....110 A4
Salford City Reds RLFC (the Willows) ORD M5 ....112 C3
Salford College ECC M30 ....110 D1
SALQ M50 ....126 D1
SWIN M27 .....85 F5
WALK M28 .....97 E1
Salford County Court ORD M5 ....113 F4
Salford Medical Centre ORD M5 ....112 D2
Salford Museum & Art Gallery ORD M5 ....113 H3
Salford Shopping City ORD M5 ....113 F2
Salford University Business Park SLFD M6 ....113 G1
Samuel Laycock Special School AUL OL6 ....120 C1
Sandbrook Community Primary School ROCH OL11 ....42 D3
Sandilands Primary School NTHM/RTH M23 ....166 D1
Saviour CE Primary School NEWH/MOS M40 ....102 D5
Savoy Cinema HTNM SK4 ....158 D3
Saxon Hall Leisure Centre MILN OL16 .....11 J5
School Street Industrial Estate BRAM/HZG SK7 ....185 F2
Seaford Industrial Estate SLFD M6 ....113 G1
Sedgley Park Community Primary School PWCH M25 ....86 B5
Sedgley Park RUFC WHTF M45 ....85 E1
Sedgley Park Trading Estate PWCH M25 ....101 E1
Seedley Primary School SLFD M6 ....112 D3
Severnside Trading Estate TRPK M17 ....125 G3
Seymour Park Primary School OLDTF/WHR M16 ....127 E4
Seymour Road Primary School OP/CLY M11 ....117 E4
Shandon Clinic (Europe) HULME M15 ....128 B3
Sharples Primary School BOL BL1 .....34 B1
Shawclough Community Primary School WHIT OL12 ....18 D5
Shawclough Trading Estate WHIT OL12 .....18 C5
Shawgrove School DID/WITH M20 ....142 B5
Shaw Heath Health Centre EDGY/DAV SK3 ....13 F7
Shay Lane Health Centre HALE/TIMP WA15 ....178 D3
Shepherd Cross Industrial Estate BOL BL1 .....33 F4
Shepley North Industrial Estate DTN/ASHW M34 ....132 D1
Shepley South Industrial Estate DTN/ASHW M34 ....132 D2
Sherborne Trading Estate CHH M8 ....102 A5
Sherwood Business Park ROCH OL11 .....42 C4
Shiv Lodge Medical Centre BRUN/LGST M13 ....129 C5
Showcase Cinemas Belle Vue GTN M18 ....130 A3
Siddal Moor Sports College HEY OL10 .....56 A2
Skylink Walkway MANAIR M90 ....179 H5
Slough Industrial Estate ORD M5 ....113 H5
Smallbridge Health Centre WHIT OL12 .....19 H5
Smallbridge Industrial Park MILN OL16 .....11 J1
Smedleylane Junior School CHH M8 ....102 C4
Smithills Hall Museum BOL BL1 ...33 E2
Smithills School BOL BL1 .....33 E3
Smithy Bridge Primary School LIT OL15 .....20 C5
Snipe Retail Park AULW OL7 ....118 C5
South Chadderton School CHAD OL9 .....90 A5
Southern Cross School CCHDY M21 ....156 B1

South Failsworth Primary School FAIL M35 ....104 D5
Southfield Industrial Estate TRPK M17 ....125 H3
Southgate Industrial Estate HEY OL10 .....41 C5
Southlink Business Park OLDE OL4 ......9 K4
South Manchester High School WYTH/NTH M22 ....180 C1
Southmoor Business Park NTHM/RTH M23 ....167 F2
Southmoor Industrial Estate NTHM/RTH M23 ....167 F2
South Oldham Business Park CHAD OL9 .....74 D4
South Reddish Medical Centre RDSH SK5 ....160 A2
South Trafford College ALT WA14 ....165 G1
South West Manchester CC CHDY M21 ....141 G2
Spa Road Industrial Estate BOL BL1 ......2 B5
Spindle Point Primary School FWTH BL4 .....83 E2
The Spindles Shopping Centre OLD OL1 ......9 F4
Sport City OP/CLY M11 ....116 A3
Sports Injury Centre MDTN M24 .....72 D5
Spotland Bridge Industrial Centre ROCH OL11 .....29 F3
Spotland Primary School WHIT OL12 .....29 G2
Spring Brook School CHAD OL9 .....74 A1
Springfield Business Centre CSLFD M3 ......6 D1
Springfield Hotel MPL/ROM SK6 ....175 E2
Springfield House Medical Centre OLD OL1 .....76 B4
Springfield Industrial Estate FAIL M35 ....104 D2
Springfield Primary School SALQ M50 ....154 C2
Springhead Community Infant & First School OLDE OL4 ....93 E1
Springhill High School MILN OL16 .....43 H1
Springside CP School BURY BL9 .....27 F4
Springwood Primary School MPL/ROM SK6 ....162 D3
SWIN M27 .....99 F3
Spurley Hey High School BNG/LEV M19 ....144 B1
Stag Industrial Estate ALT WA14 ....165 G3
Stakehill Industrial Estate MDTN M24 .....57 G5
Stalybridge Celtic AFC STLY SK15 ....121 F5
Stalybridge CC DUK SK16 ....120 B5
Stalybridge Millbrook CC STLY SK15 ....121 G1
Stalybridge St Pauls CC DUK SK16 ....134 A1
Stalyhill Infant School STLY SK15 ....135 F1
Stalyhill Junior School STLY SK15 ....135 F1
Staly Industrial Estate STLY SK15 ....121 G4
Stamford Golf Club STLY SK15 ....109 F3
Stamford High School AUL OL6 ....120 B1
Stamford Park Junior School HALE/TIMP WA15 ....177 H1
Stanley Green Industrial Estate CHD/CHDH SK8 ....192 B1
WILM/AE SK9 ....192 B3
Stanley Green Retail Park CHD/CHDH SK8 ....192 C1
Stanley Grove Primary School WGTN/LGST M12 ....129 G4
Stanley Road Primary School CHAD OL9 .....90 C3
Stanneylands Hotel WILM/AE SK9 ....191 G5
Star Industrial Estate OLDS OL8 ......8 A2
Station Approach Business Centre ALT WA14 .....30 A5
Staveleigh Medical Centre STLY SK15 ....120 D3
Stella Maris School HTNM SK4 ....158 B4
Stepping Hill Hospital BRAM/HZG SK7 ....172 C5
Stockport Air Raid Shelter STKP SK1 .....13 F3
Stockport Art Gallery EDGY/DAV SK3 .....13 F5
Stockport Bus Station STKP SK1 .....13 E4
Stockport CC EDGY/DAV SK3 ....172 A3
Stockport College HTNM SK4 ....144 B5
Stockport College of Further & Higher Education EDGY/DAV SK3 .....13 F6
Stockport County Court STKP SK1 .....13 F4
Stockport County FC & Sale Sharks RUFC (Edgeley Park) EDGY/DAV SK3 ....171 G2
Stockport Crematorium STKP SK1 ....172 D5
Stockport Golf Club OFTN SK2 ....174 A4
Stockport Grammar School OFTN SK2 ....172 C4
Stockport Mega Bowl STKP SK1 .....13 F5
Stockport RUFC BRAM/HZG SK7 ....184 A4
Stockport Trading Estate OFTN SK2 ....172 C4
Stockport Trading Estate STKP SK1 ....171 E1
Stone Hill Industrial Estate FWTH BL4 .....65 H5
Stoneleigh Primary School OLD OL1 .....76 A2

The Strand Medical Centre ROCH OL11 .....43 E4
Stretford Grammar School STRET M32 ....140 C2
Stretford High School Community Language College STRET M32 ....126 B4
Stretford Leisure Centre STRET M32 ....126 C4
Stretford Memorial Hospital OLDTF/WHR M16 ....127 E5
Student Union Building CMANE M1 ....128 B1
Styal Country Park (NT) WILM/AE SK9 ....190 D4
Styal Golf Club WILM/AE SK9 ....191 F2
Styal Primary School WILM/AE SK9 ....190 D3
Sudden Health Centre ROCH OL11 .....42 B2
Sudell Street Trading Estate ANC M4 ......7 J1
Sugden Sports Centre CMANE M1 ....128 B1
Summerseat Methodist Primary School BURY BL9 .....27 E1
Summerville Primary School SLFD M6 ....100 A5
Sunning Hill Primary School BOLS/LL BL3 .....48 C5
Sunnybank Clinic BURY BL9 .....69 H1
Sunny Bank Primary School BURY BL9 .....69 H1
Sunset Business Centre FWTH BL4 .....82 C2
Swinton Cemetery SWIN M27 .....83 H5
The Swinton County High School SWIN M27 .....98 D1
Swinton Industrial Estate SWIN M27 .....99 F2
Swinton Leisure Centre SWIN M27 .....99 E2
Swinton Park Golf Club SWIN M27 .....99 F4
Talmud Torah Chinuch Norim School BRO M7 ....101 G3
Tameside Business Development Centre DTN/ASHW M34 ....132 A5
Tameside Business Park DUK SK16 ....133 E1
Tameside College AUL OL6 ....120 A2
HYDE SK14 ....147 H4
Tameside County Court AUL OL6 ....119 H3
Tameside General Hospital RDSH SK5 ....146 A4
Tandle Hill Country Park ROY/SHW OL2 .....58 B3
Tashbar School BRO M7 ....101 H1
Tavistock Industrial Estate OP/CLY M11 ....130 C2
Taylors Sports Club ECC M30 ....111 F4
Temple Primary School CHH M8 ....102 C4
Ten Acres Sports Complex NEWH/MOS M40 ....103 H5
Thames Industrial Estate WGTN/LGST M12 ....129 E1
Thames Trading Centre IRL M44 ....136 B4
Thistle Hotel CMANE M1 ......7 G5
WILM/AE SK9 ....192 A2
Thomasson Memorial Special School BOL BL1 .....48 A2
Thorn Grove Primary School CHD/CHDH SK8 ....182 D1
Thornham CC MDTN M24 .....57 G2
Thornham St James CE Primary School ROY/SHW OL2 .....59 E1
Thorniege Salesian College BOL BL1 .....33 G2
Thorp Primary School ROY/SHW OL2 .....58 D4
Times Retail Park HEY OL10 .....40 D4
Timperley Health Centre HALE/TIMP WA15 ....166 B2
Tithe Barn Primary School HTNM SK4 ....158 D3
Tonacliffe Primary School WHIT OL12 .....18 B2
Tonge Bridge Industrial Estate BOLE BL2 ......3 J3
Tonge CC BOLE BL2 .....34 D3
Tonge Fold Health Centre BOLE BL2 .....49 H2
Tonge Moor Health Centre BOLE BL2 .....34 D5
Tonge Moor Primary School BOLE BL2 ......3 K1
Tootal Drive CP School ORD M5 ....112 B3
Top o' th' Brow Primary School BOLE BL2 .....35 F4
Torkington Primary School BRAM/HZG SK7 ....185 H2
Tottington Health Centre TOT/BURYW BL8 .....37 E1
Tottington High School TOT/BURYW BL8 .....26 A5
Tottington Primary School TOT/BURYW BL8 .....37 E1
Towers Business Park DID/WITH M20 ....157 G5
Townfield Industrial Estate OLDE OL4 .....76 A5
Towngate Business Centre LHULT M38 .....80 D2
Town Hall & Albert Halls BOL BL1 ......2 E4
Town Square Shopping Centre OLD OL1 ......9 G3
Trafalgar Business Park CHH M8 ....114 B1
Trafford Athletics Track CCHDY M21 ....140 D2
Trafford Centre TRPK M17 ....124 C2

Trafford Centre Leisure Complex TRPK M17 ....124 A2
Trafford FC URM M41 ....138 A2
Trafford General Hospital URM M41 ....123 H5
Trafford Healthcare SALE M33 ....155 E3
Trafford Retail Park URM M41 ....124 B3
Trafford Water Sports Centre SALE M33 ....140 C5
Trans Pennine Trading Estate ROCH OL11 .....42 C3
Travelodge ANC M4 ......7 H3
BURY BL9 .....69 H3
CHAD OL9 .....89 H3
CSLFD M3 ......6 B2
DID/WITH M20 ....158 A5
HEY OL10 .....55 C5
Trent Industrial Estate ROY/SHW OL2 .....60 A1
The Triangle ANC M4 ......7 G3
Trinity CE High School HULME M15 ....128 B2
Trinity Retail Park BOLE BL2 ......3 H7
BOLE BL2 .....49 F4
Trinity School STLY SK15 ....122 A4
Tudor Industrial Estate DUK SK16 ....132 D2
Tulip Inn Hotel URM M41 ....124 B2
Tulketh Street Industrial Estate BKLY M9 ....103 G2
Turton Golf Club EDGW/EG BL7 .....23 F1
Turton High School EDGW/EG BL7 .....23 G4
Turton Leisure Centre EDGW/EG BL7 .....23 F1
Two Trees High School DTN/ASHW M34 ....147 F2
Tyntesfield CP School STLY SK15 ....153 H5
UCI Cinema TRPK M17 ....124 C2
Union Mill Industrial Estate MOSL OL5 .....94 A4
United Trading Estate OLDTF/WHR M16 ....126 C3
Urbis CSLFD M3 ......6 E2
Urmston Grammar School URM M41 ....124 B5
Urmston J & I School URM M41 ....138 B1
Urmston Leisure Centre URM M41 ....138 B1
Urmston Town FC URM M41 ....137 H2
Vaishali Medical Centre CCHDY M21 ....141 F2
Vale Park Industrial Estate URM M41 ....102 D3
The Valley Community School BOL BL1 .....34 B3
The Valley Leisure Centre BOL BL1 .....34 B3
Valley Special School BRAM/HZG SK7 ....193 F2
Varley Street Clinic NEWH/MOS M40 ....115 G1
Varna Street Primary School OP/CLY M11 ....130 C2
Vaughan Street Industrial Estate WGTN/LGST M12 ....129 G1
Vauxhall Industrial Estate RDSH SK5 ....145 E5
RDSH SK5 ....160 A2
Vernon Industrial Estate STKP SK1 .....13 H2
The Vernon Infant School POY/DIS SK12 ....195 F4
The Vernon Junior School STKP SK1 .....13 H2
Vernon Park Museum STKP SK1 .....13 J3
Vernon Peak Road Medical Centre TOT/BURYW BL8 .....26 B2
Victoria Avenue Primary School BKLY M9 .....88 A2
Victoria Industrial Estate ANC M4 ....115 G4
Victoria Medical Centre CMANE M1 ....138 D1
Victoria Park Infant School STRET M32 ....140 B5
Victoria Park Junior School STRET M32 ....140 B5
Victoria Trading Estate CHAD OL9 .....90 C4
Victory Trading Estate BOLS/LL BL3 .....49 F4
The Village Hotel & Leisure Club HYDE SK14 ....133 F2
Village Medical Centre LIT OL15 .....21 E3

VIP Centre Industrial Estate OLD OL1 .....76 B3
Vue Cinema BURY BL9 .....54 A3
SALQ M50 ....126 C1
Wadsworth Industrial Park BOLS/LL BL3 .....48 D5
Walkden High School WALK M28 .....82 B5
Walmsley CE Primary School EDGW/EG BL7 .....22 D2
Walshaw Sports Club TOT/BURYW BL8 .....37 E1
Walton Park Leisure Centre SALE M33 ....154 B4
Wardle High School WHIT OL12 .....20 A3
Wardley CE Primary School SWIN M27 .....83 H5
Wardley Industrial Estate WALK M28 .....98 B1
Warren Wood Primary School OFTN SK2 ....173 H4
Wasacre Primary School BURY BL9 .....52 D2
Washway Road Medical Centre SALE M33 ....154 B2
Waterfold Business Park BURY BL9 ......5 K6
The Watergate Clinic MILN OL16 .....10 D6
Waterloo Industrial Park BOL BL1 ......3 C2
Waterloo Primary School AULW OL7 ....106 C5
The Water Place BOL BL1 ......2 E6
Waters Edge Business Park ORD M5 ....127 E2
Watersheddings Primary School OLD OL1 .....76 B3
The Waterside Hotel CHD/CHDH SK8 ....170 A5
Waterside Industrial Park BOLS/LL BL3 .....65 H1
Watersports Centre SALQ M50 ....126 C1
Waybridge Business Centre SALQ M50 ....112 C5
Weaste Trading Estate ORD M5 ....112 C3
Welfare Clinic MDTN M24 .....72 A2
Welkin Road Industrial Estate STKP SK1 ....160 C5
Wellacre Technology College URM M41 ....137 F1
Wellfield Infant School SALE M33 ....139 F5
Wellfield Junior School SALE M33 ....139 F5
Wellfield Medical Centre CHH M8 ....102 A2
Well Green Primary School HALE/TIMP WA15 ....178 C2
Wellington Road Industrial Estate ECC M30 ....119 F2
Wellington School HALE/TIMP WA15 ....166 A3
Wentworth High School ECC M30 ....111 G1
Werneth Cricket Bowling & Tennis Club OLDS OL8 ......8 E7
Werneth Golf Club OLDS OL8 ....106 B1
Werneth J & I School OLDS OL8 .....91 E3
Werneth Low Country Park HYDE SK14 ....148 D4
Werneth Low Golf Club HYDE SK14 ....148 D5
Werneth School MPL/ROM SK6 ....161 G4
Wesley Methodist Primary School RAD M26 .....51 H4
Westbrook Trading Estate TRPK M17 ....126 A1
Westbury Street Industrial Estate HYDE SK14 ....133 F3
West Croft Industrial Estate MDTN M24 .....71 H5
West End Medical Centre AULW OL7 ....119 E4
West End Primary School AULW OL7 ....119 E3
West End Trading Estate SWIN M27 .....99 E1
Westerniea Clinic DTN/ASHW M34 ....132 B3
West Gorton Medical Centre WGTN/LGST M12 ....129 G2
West Hill School STLY SK15 ....120 C3
Westhoughton High School & Specialist Technology College WHTN BL5 .....62 A3
Westhoughton Primary School WHTN BL5 .....62 A4
Westinghouse Industrial Estate TRPK M17 ....126 A3
Westmorland Primary School RDSH SK5 ....146 A5
West One Retail Park SALQ M50 ....111 H4
Westpoint Medical Centre BNG/LEV M19 ....143 H2
Westwood Business Centre CHAD OL9 ......8 C3
Westwood Industrial Estate CHAD OL9 ......8 C3
Westwood Park Primary School ECC M30 ....110 C2
Westwood Trading Estate CHAD OL9 ......8 C3
Westwood Trading Estate MPL/ROM SK6 ....174 C4
Whalley Range FC CCHDY M21 ....141 H2
Whalley Range High School OLDTF/WHR M16 ....142 B3
Wharfside Business Centre TRPK M17 ....126 C2

Wharton Primary School
LHULT M38 .... 80 D1
Wheatfield Industrial Estate
ROY/SHW OL2 .... 75 E1
Wheatsheaf Industrial Estate
SWIN M27 .... 99 G1
Wheatsheaf Shopping Centre
MILN OL16 .... 10 D5
White City Retail Park
OLDTF/WHR M16 .... 126 D3
Whitefield Community
Primary School WHTF M45 .... 69 H4
Whitefield Golf Club
WHTF M45 .... 69 F5
Whitefield Medical Centre
WHTF M45 .... 69 F4
Whitegate End Primary School
CHAD OL9 .... 89 H4
Whitehill Industrial Estate
HTNM SK4 .... 159 H1
Whitehill Primary School
HTNM SK4 .... 159 H2
White Swan Industrial Estate
OLD OL1 .... 76 B4
Whitley Road Medical Centre
NEWH/MOS M40 .... 115 F1
Whittaker Golf Club LIT OL15 ...... 21 G4
Whittaker Moss Primary
School ROCH OL11 .... 28 A2
The Whitworth Art Gallery
HULME M15 .... 128 C4
Whitworth Community High
School WHIT OL12 .... 14 B5

Whitworth Football & CC
WHIT OL12 .... 14 B4
Whitworth Park School
RUSH/FAL M14 .... 128 B4
Whitworth Swimming Pool
WHIT OL12 .... 14 C3
Wilbraham Primary School
RUSH/FAL M14 .... 142 C2
Wild Bank Community School
STLY SK15 .... 121 G3
Willan Industrial Estate
ORD M5 .... 113 E4
William Andrews Swimming
Baths DUK SK16 .... 133 G1
William Hulmes
Preparatory School
OLDTF/WHR M16 .... 142 B2
William Wroe Municipal Golf
Course URM M41 .... 138 A1
Willow Bank Hotel
RUSH/FAL M14 .... 143 E3
Willow Grove Cemetery
RDSH SK5 .... 160 B1
The Willows Primary School
HALE/TIMP WA15 .... 166 A3
WYTH/NTH M22 .... 180 B2
Wilmslow Albion FC
WILM/AE SK9 .... 191 F4
Wilmslow Grange Community
Primary School
WILM/AE SK9 .... 192 A2
Wilmslow Health Centre
WILM/AE SK9 .... 198 D4

Wilmslow High School
WILM/AE SK9 .... 199 E4
Wilmslow Leisure Centre
WILM/AE SK9 .... 199 E4
Wilmslow Preparatory School
WILM/AE SK9 .... 199 E3
Wilmslow RFC
WILM/AE SK9 .... 198 C1
Wilmslow Road Medical
Centre RUSH/FAL M14 .... 128 D5
WILM/AE SK9 .... 192 A3
Windlehurst School
MPL/ROM SK6 .... 187 E2
Windmill Lane Industrial
Estate DTN/ASHW M34 .... 146 A1
Withington Bowling Club
RUSH/FAL M14 .... 143 E4
Withington Girls School
RUSH/FAL M14 .... 142 D3
Withington Golf Club
DID/WITH M20 .... 157 E4
Withington Hospital
DID/WITH M20 .... 142 B5
Withington Swimming Baths
DID/WITH M20 .... 142 D5
Withins High School BOLE BL2 ...35 F4
Wolfenden Primary School
BOL BL1 .... 33 H4
Woodbank CC TOT/BURYW BL8 ..38 A2
Woodbank Park Athletics
Track OFTN SK2 .... 160 D5
Woodbank Primary School
TOT/BURYW BL8 .... 38 A2

Woodend Mills Industrial
Estate OLDE OL4 .... 93 E2
Woodfields Retail Park
BURY BL9 .... 4 D3
Woodford CC
BRAM/HZG SK7 .... 193 H5
Woodhey High School
RAMS BL0 .... 16 B5
Woodheys Primary School
SALE M33 .... 153 H4
Woodhouse Primary School
URM M41 .... 123 H4
Woodhouses Voluntary
Controlled Primary School
FAIL M35 .... 105 H4
Woodlands Hospital
WALK M28 .... 81 E3
Woodley Health Centre
MPL/ROM SK6 .... 161 H1
Woodley Primary School
MPL/ROM SK6 .... 162 A1
Woodley Sports Centre
MPL/ROM SK6 .... 147 E5
Woodsend Primary School
URM M41 .... 122 D5
Woolfold Industrial Estate
TOT/BURYW BL8 .... 37 G2
Woolworths Sports Club
ROCH OL11 .... 42 B3
Worsley Business Park
TYLD M29 .... 96 A2
Worsley Golf Club
ECC M30 .... 110 D1

Worsley Road Industrial
Estate OLDE OL4 .... 93 E2
Worsley Trading Estate
LHULT M38 .... 80 D2
Worthington Primary School
SALE M33 .... 155 G2
Worth Primary School
POY/DIS SK12 .... 195 G4
Wright Robinson Sports
College GTN M18 .... 131 E2
The Wycliffe Hotel
EDGY/DAV SK3 .... 12 A7
Wythenshawe Hall Country
Park NTHM/RTH M23 ...... 168 A1
Wythenshawe Hospital
NTHM/RTH M23 .... 167 G5
Wythenshawe Park Track
NTHM/RTH M23 .... 167 H1
Xaverian Sixth Form College
RUSH/FAL M14 .... 128 D5
Yeargate Industrial Estate
BURY BL9 .... 39 G4
Yeshivah Ohr Torah School
BRO M7 .... 101 G2
Yesoiday Hatorah School
PRES M25 .... 86 A5
Yew Tree Community School
CHAD OL9 .... 90 A3
Yew Tree Primary Community
School DUK SK16 .... 133 G1
YMCA Leisure Centre
CSLFD M5 .... 6 B6

Acknowledgements

Schools address data provided by Education Direct

Petrol station information supplied by Johnsons

Manchester transport information provided by GMPTE © 2007

Garden centre information provided by:

Garden Centre Association   Britains best garden centres

Wyevale Garden Centres

The statement on the front cover of this atlas is sourced, selected and quoted
from a reader comment and feedback form received in 2004

How do I find the perfect place?

AA Lifestyle Guides
Britain's largest travel publisher
order online at www.theAA.com/travel